A LIBRARY OF LITERARY CRITICISM

A Library
of Literary Criticism

MODERN IRISH LITERATURE

Compiled and edited by

**Denis Lane
and
Carol McCrory Lane**

Ungar • New York

1988
The Ungar Publishing Company
370 Lexington Avenue
New York, NY 10017

Printed in the United States of America

Library of Congress Cataloging-in-Publication Data

Lane, Denis.
  Modern Irish literature.

  Bibliography: p.
  Includes index.
  1. English literature—Irish authors—History and
criticism. 2. English literature—20th century—History
and criticism. 3. Ireland in literature. I. Lane,
Carol McCrory. II. Title.
PR8753.L36   1988   820'.9'9415   87-5090
ISBN 0-8044-3144-2

CONTENTS

INTRODUCTION

Like its companion volumes in the Library of Literary Criticism, this book provides a comprehensive view of a major national literature by bringing together selections of criticism on the individual writers whose works constitute that literature.

Our subject here is Irish writing of modern times. In this collection of more than seven hundred items the reader will find not only a composite picture of the literary history of Ireland in the twentieth century, but also a series of portraits of this century's outstanding Irish authors—poets, dramatists, novelists, short-story writers, essayists—as seen through the eyes and minds of their most thoughtful reviewers and critics. Collectively, the entries on a particular author, arranged chronologically, give an impression of that writer's growth, status, or special qualities; or they may trace new avenues of interest in his work taken by successive generations of readers; or, if he or she is a younger writer, they may indicate those features of the work that have attracted early recognition.

Modern Irish Literature covers 87 authors, both of the north and the south, all of whom may be termed Irish by virtue of birth, parentage, and domicile, or by the fact that their work consistently makes use of the "matter of Ireland": its culture and history, its topography and iconography. The inclusion of each author was determined by one additional criterion: the degree to which each has provoked significant and sustained interest among various commentators. That so small a country as Ireland should have produced in so brief a period of time as many writers of standing as we are able to represent here is evidence of the astonishing creativity and vigor of Irish writing and of the preeminence of the Irish writer in the development of modern literature in the English language. The chief figures in this development—the giant figures of W. B. Yeats, Sean O'Casey, James Joyce, Samuel Beckett—have, of course, achieved monumental recognition, but there are others—among them Patrick Kavanagh, Flann O'Brien, Austin Clarke, Seamus Heaney—who are also on their way to achieving paramount status. All are well represented here, together with others of established reputation, and together also with many who are perhaps less widely known outside Ireland.

The earliest selections in this volume date from around the turn of the century. The reader will find that then, as now, it was often the literary artist himself who was the first judge of the efforts of his fellows, and for that reason there is value to be gained in reading, for example, Yeats's 1894 opinion of Russell's *Homeward: Songs by the Way*, or Russell's own reception of Colum's 1907 collection *Wild Earth*. Even when the author-critic had been joined by the literary journalist and the academic critic, his voice still remained a vital one in the assessment of modern Irish letters, an involvement illustrated by a number of selections, particularly those by Denis Johnston on Flann O'Brien, Kiely on Stuart, Fallon on Kavanagh, O'Faolain on Lavin, and Seamus Heaney on Richard Murphy.

In compiling this volume we have attempted to use as wide a range of sources as possible. Much emphasis has been placed on the use of periodicals, especially since in the first quarter of the century they provided a primary forum for literary evaluation, particularly for the author as critic. [For this reason there is cause to regret the present absence of a comprehensive index to twentieth-century Irish periodical literature.] By the 1930s, however, Irish literature had become an international possession, its reception falling firmly within the preserve of critics American, British, and European as often as Irish.

Another aim in selecting the items of criticism for this volume has been to illustrate the different elements from which modern Irish literature has been formed. We recognize, for instance, the central influence of Gaelic culture, as embodied in the traditions of folk drama, the oral peasant poetry, and early Irish myth. In a land fraught with political and religious contradictions this same literature was both a witness to, and an instrument of, the urge toward cultural and political synthesis. Equally, the Irish writer has absorbed cultural and literary perspectives from Europe and America with the result that he, or she, has become not only the practitioner, but also, on occasion, the fount of an international modernist style. Given these various components (each in itself the product of many parts), it is not surprising, therefore, to find in modern Irish literature works that range from the pastoral to the apocalyptic, or (to use the words of two early commentators, David Morton and George Russell respectively), from "the literature of lamentation" to "the sun of realism." It is the reception accorded that literature over a period of almost ninety years that is chronicled in these pages.

A list of authors included and a list of periodicals used with an explanation of abbreviations appear after this introduction. Bibliographies of each author covered are provided at the back of the book.

The editors are grateful to the many copyright holders who have granted permission to reproduce the selections in this book. Specific acknowledgements are provided in the section beginning on page 711. (Only in a very few instances have we been unable to use an excerpt because a copyright holder either denied permission or requested an unreasonable fee.)

Finally, we wish to record our appreciation to the following institutions and individuals whose generous services, great or small, assisted in the completion of this work: the reference librarians at New York University, Columbia University, and the New York Public Library; The Center for Research Libraries, Chicago; the reference librarians of John Jay College, City University of New York, especially Robert Grappone, Jane Gurney, and Anthony Simpson: the librarians of the Hawthorne-Longfellow Library, Bowdoin College; Joyce Kordyban, Main Library, University of Detroit; the Hoover Library, Stanford University; A. Fred Sochatoff, Emeritus Professor of English, Carnegie-Mellon University; Prof. Mary M. Fitzgerald, University of New Orleans; colleagues Tom Dardis, Carl Wiedemann, and Sherwood Smith; and particularly Rita Stein, our editor at The Ungar Publishing Company, whose acumen and counsel proved indispensable.

D.L.

C.M.L.

NOTE: Further selections on many of the authors in this volume may be found in *Modern British Literature*, Vols. 1–3, ed. Ruth Z. Temple and Martin Tucker, 1966; Vol. 4, ed. Martin Tucker and Rita Stein, 1975; and Vol. 5, ed. Denis Lane and Rita Stein, 1985; and in *Major Modern Dramatists*, Vol. 1, ed. Rita Stein et al., 1984, all in the Library of Literary Criticism series.

AUTHORS INCLUDED

Banville, John
Beckett, Samuel
Behan, Brendan
Bowen, Elizabeth
Boyle, Patrick
Boyle, William
Bullock, Shan F.
Campbell, Joseph
Carroll, Paul Vincent
Clarke, Austin
Colum, Padraic
Corkery, Daniel
Cousins, James H.
Devlin, Denis
Dunsany, Lord
    (Edward John Moreton Drax
    Plunkett)
Ervine, St. John
Fallon, Padraic
Fitzmaurice, George
Friel, Brian
Gogarty, Oliver St. John
Gregory, Lady
    (Isabella Augusta Persse)
Heaney, Seamus
Hewitt, John
Higgins, Aidan
Higgins, F. R.
Hyde, Douglas
Johnston, Denis
Johnston, Jennifer
Joyce, James
Kavanagh, Patrick
Keane, John B.
Keane, Molly
    (a.k.a. M. J. Farrell and
    Mary Lesta Skrine)
Kiely, Benedict
Kinsella, Thomas

Lavin, Mary
Ledwidge, Francis
Leonard, Hugh
    (pseud. of John Keyes Byrne)
Longley, Michael
MacDonagh, Thomas
Macken, Walter
MacLaverty, Bernard
MacManus, Francis
MacNamara, Brinsley
    (pseud. of John Weldon)
MacNeice, Louis
Mahon, Derek
Martyn, Edward
McGahern, John
McLaverty, Michael
Molloy, Michael J.
Montague, John
Moore, Brian
Moore, George
Muldoon, Paul
Murdoch, Iris
Murphy, Richard
Murray, T. C.
O'Brien, Conor Cruise
O'Brien, Edna
O'Brien, Flann
    (pseud. of Brian O'Nolan)
O'Brien, Kate
O'Casey, Sean
Ó Conaire, Pádraic
O'Connor, Frank
    (pseud. of Michael O'Donovan)
O'Donnell, Peadar
O'Duffy, Eimar
O'Faolain, Julia
O'Faolain, Sean
O'Flaherty, Liam
O'Kelly, Seamas

PERIODICALS USED

Listed below are their titles, their abbreviations, if any, and place of publication.

AmS	The American Scholar (Washington, DC)
AWR	Anglo-Welsh Review (Caerleon, Wales)
ArQ	Arizona Quarterly (Tucson, AZ)
At	The Atlantic (Boston)
	The Bell (Dublin)
	Best Sellers (Scranton, PA)
BkmL	The Bookman (London)
	Books Ireland (Goshigstown, Ireland)
CambQ	Cambridge Quarterly (Cambridge, England)
CJIS	Canadian Journal of Irish Studies (Vancouver, BC)
	Catholic World (Ramsey, NJ)
	Chicago Daily Tribune (Chicago)
CSM	Christian Science Monitor (Boston)
Cmty	Commentary (New York)
Com	Commonweal (New York)
CP	Concerning Poetry (Bellingham, WA)
ConnR	Connecticut Review (Storrs, CT)
ContempR	Contemporary Review (London)
	The Critic (Chicago)
	The Criterion (London)
Crit	Critique (Atlanta, GA)
	The Dial (New York)
DM	Dublin Magazine (Dublin)
	Éire-Ireland (St. Paul, MN)
Enc	Encounter (London)
	English (London)
EJ	The English Journal (Chicago, Ill.)
ES	English Studies (Lisse, The Netherlands)
EIC	Essays in Criticism (Oxford)
	Genre (Norman, OK)
HC	The Hollins Critic (Hollins, VA)
	The Honest Ulsterman (Belfast)
Hor	Horizon (London)
HudR	Hudson Review (New York)
	The Irish Book (Dublin)

	The Irish Book Lover (Dublin)
	The Irish Citizen (Dublin)
ILS	Irish Literary Supplement (Selden, NY)
	The Irish Monthly (Dublin)
	The Irish Press (Dublin)
	Irish Review (Dublin)
	Irish Times (Dublin)
IUR	Irish University Review (Dublin)
	Irish Writing (Cork, Ireland)
	Journal of Beckett Studies (London)
JIL	Journal of Irish Literature (Newark, DE)
JNT	Journal of Narrative Technique (Ypsilanti, MI)
KR	Kansas Review (Manhattan, KS)
LL	Life and Letters (London)
List	The Listener (London)
LondonMag	London Magazine (London)
LM	The London Mercury (London)
LRB	London Review of Books (London)
	Malahat Review (Victoria, BC)
MR	Massachusetts Review (Amherst, Mass.)
MD	Modern Drama (Toronto)
MFS	Modern Fiction Studies (West Lafayette, IN)
	Mosaic (Winnepeg, Manitoba)
NewR	The New Review (London)
NR	The New Republic (Washington, DC)
NS	New Statesman (London)
NSN	New Statesman and Nation (London)
	The New Yorker (New York)
NYHT	New York Herald Tribune: Book Week (New York)
	Outlook (London)
NYTAL	New York Times Arts and Leisure Section (New York)
NYTBR	New York Times Book Review (New York)
NYTd	New York Times, daily (New York)
	Outlook (London)
	Parnassus (New York)
PR	Partisan Review (Boston)
	Poetry (Chicago)
	Poetry Ireland (Cork, Ireland)
PoetryR	Poetry Review (London)
	Punch (London)
	The Quarterly Review (London)
	Renascence (Milwaukee, WI)
RCF	Review of Contemporary Fiction (Elmwood Park, IL)
REL	A Review of English Literature (Calgary, Alberta)
Sat	Saturday Review (New York)
SwR	Sewanee Review (Sewanee, Tenn.)
SCB	South Central Bulletin (Houston, Texas)

SoR	Southern Review (Baton Rouge, LA)
Spec	The Spectator (London)
	Stand (Newcastle on Tyne)
	Studies: An Irish Quarterly Review (Dublin)
TSLL	Texas Studies in Language and Literature (Austin, Tex.)
	Threshold (Belfast)
TT	Time and Tide (New York)
UR	University Review (Dublin)
WSJ	Wall Street Journal (New York)
YR	The Yale Review (New Haven, CT)

BANVILLE, JOHN (1946–   )

John Banville has so far produced three books: *Long Lankin* (1970), *Nightspawn* (1971), and the prizewinning *Birchwood* (1973). In each one of them he shows himself to be very conscious of the fact that he is writing fiction, and this lends to his work both a literary and an introverted humour which relieves him from the accusations of monotony, plagiarism and preciousness which could otherwise be justifiably levelled against him. He is a *litterateur* who has a horror of producing "literature." This horror is equalled only by his amusement at the notion that literature might (by accident or innate capacity) reproduce life. He rejects mimetic realism by practising it in the avowed consciousness of its incompetence. Various authors betray their influence on his writings—Nabokov, Henry Green, Hermann Hesse—and, in addition, he makes his relationship to the reader as quizzically autocratic as does John Barth, Borges or even Richard Brautigan. He favours his sensibility as something so electrically endowed that it can only be glimpsed in its movements with the help of modern, high-speed, novelistic lenses. Like some of those authors mentioned, he joyfully commits technical narcissism over and over again, photographing every mutation of the self in the act of mutation, reproducing in words a wordless process, recording for ever a fugitive experience:

> Only here, in these sinister pages, can time be vanquished. These little keys on which I dance transfix eternity with every tap.

The three books are all interlocked in their sets of characters and preoccupations. Each is an odyssey of a writer for whom the act of writing is itself the only Ithaca and the only Penelope his Muse or his memory. (The fact that *Nightspawn* and *Birchwood* are both told in the first person and in the past tense is a trite but important one. The pastness of that which is written about is the source of much of the writing's grief.) There is a good deal of Gothic glare and glamour—exotic parties and exotic parts, revolutions, Greek and Irish, famine, circus, arcane relationships, codes, puns and riddles—but, basically, Mr. Banville writes about writing and the relation of the thing written to the thing written about. Like many modern novelists, he is a scholastic, one of the *cymini sectores*, splitting atom-sized distinctions, watching the flight and disappearance of neutron sensations in the quantum world of the self and yet always aware of the fact that the self and its sensations are always determined by the very act of watching. Consciousness is, for his heroes, a burden and it

1

creates other burdens which are in direct proportion to its own mass. The plot of his fictions is Sisyphean, repetitive. Their structure, which in its inner parts is largely a matter of consequential images, is outwardly (and sometimes pretentiously), that of a myth. . . .

[E]ven *Birchwood*, for all its manifest achievement, still appears as if it were no more than a preparation for something other, something more exclusively Banvillean to come. One can be more assured that he is inventing as we see his heavily dislocated fictions move in their typical constellations of event—incest, murder, inconsequence, breakdown—around their inner subjects of time, memory, freedom, and death, converting these stiff concepts more and more surely and profoundly into the substance of our consciousness. No other Irish novelist seeks the effect of timelessness more hungrily than this one.

Seamus Deane. In Patrick Rafroidi and
Maurice Harmon, eds., *The Irish Novel in Our Time*
(Lille, Publications de L'Université de Lille, 1975),
pp. 329–30, 338

John Banville's novel [*Doctor Copernicus*] has the qualities—earnestness, ambition, and stern historicity—which appeal to the judges of glittery literary prizes, and the defects—clotted prose and humourlessness—which deter readers. It reminds one of Johnson's comment on Congreve's *Incognita*, that he would rather praise it than read it. Nor has Mr. Banville exactly picked one of the more gripping greats: [Arthur] Koestler describes Copernicus as "perhaps the most colourless figure among those who, by merit or circumstance, shaped mankind's destiny." Mr. Banville naturally plays up the man-for-our-time side: the astronomer is sceptical, detached, secretive out of disgust at the world's pretences, and half certain that the whole set-up is absurd. He inhabits a world in political and religious chaos, full of arbitrary suffering, vain scholarship and joyless whoring.

Mr. Banville presents this background with some informed vigour, especially the sense of cosmic claustrophobia which agonised Copernicus into the idea of the heliocentric universe. But as for his prose, the best that can be said is that it is, in all its awkward sincerity, at least his own. He favours those inelegant nominal marriages (nerveknot, cloudshadow, dogmerd) which claim vainly to add up to more than their partssum. The attempt to describe mental processes drives him to empty, hulking metaphors. Copernicus has a head "packed with granite blocks of knowledge"; on the next page he "ventures out in the frail bark of his thoughts" (a wonder he doesn't capsize); and when he makes his famous break-through, the solution arrives "like a magnificent great slow golden bird alighting in his head with a thrumming of vast wings." At such vital moments it would be profitable to switch to Koestler, both for the astronomy (*The Sleepwalkers*) and for the intellectual processes (*The Act of Creation*).

Julian Barnes. *NS*. Nov. 26, 1976, p. 21

It is not surprising in a conscientious artist such as John Banville, who pays meticulous attention to form, that [in *Nightspawn*] he should try and reflect the theme of his fiction in its compositional design. Among other narrative strategies, the futility of representing reality through fiction is expressed by means of a circular narrative movement. The circularity of texture is evoked in the very first section; it is sustained throughout the account and fully brought into its own at the end. The evocation is effected by a slightly modified quotation from Eliot's "The Love Song of J. Alfred Prufrock": "How should I begin?" Banville's Prufrockian protagonist wonders. "Should I say that the end is inherent in every beginning?" (p. 7). The end of the story Ben White recounts is indeed inherent in its beginning, or reversely, the beginning inherent in its ending, as at the start of his efforts to transfix his experiences, he is as far from his goal as at the close, where he is compelled to confess his failure. "One more effort" (p. 224), he urges himself on, and he starts anew: "Chapter one. My story begins at—" (p. 224). This fresh attempt, however, will be as feckless as his first one.

Ben's efforts are unconventional indeed. Advancing from the conviction that "art is, after all, only mimicry" (p. 217), he places his principal interest in demonstrating how this mimicry is accomplished. The metafictional elements can roughly be classed into two groups. Whereas the laying bare of the general narrative conventions is brought about through explicit commentary on the descriptive procedure, the turning inside out of the conventions pertaining to the thriller or novel of suspense is worked out by means of parodic treatment. The concept dominating the metafictional activities is that of the novelist as magician or Aristophanic sorcerer who opens a box of tricks and conjures up a self-sufficient world.

By far the most telling example of the kind of game the narrator in *Nightspawn* plays with the reader concerns the thematic, stylistic as well as compositional, elements of outstanding excellence with which Ben claims to have invested his story. "There are," he maintains, "pearls here strewn among this sty of words. Time enough to rend and tear, time enough" (p. 36). Probably only the most inattentive of readers would not jump at the suggestion and be sent off on a quest for these pearls; and there are, indeed, enough to discover. There are those pearls which reflect the artistic skill of the fictionist Banville: descriptive passages of great beauty and evocative power, or the ramification of plot. Contrary to customary practice, where such constitutive elements of a fiction are pulled into polyphonic relations by the dynamics of the aesthetic purpose connected with the story, in *Nightspawn* they are employed for their own sake, to demonstrate how a successful description is effected, how a complex plot is worked out; the aesthetic end they strive towards is not the story itself, but how a story is *made*. And there are those pearls which, once the secret springs of fiction have been revealed, serve to bring home to the reader what impact they have on him in conditioning his creative participation in the communicative act between text and reader through which a literary work of art is brought into being.

Rüdiger Imhof. *IUR*. Spring, 1981, pp. 59–61

Kepler, John Banville's fifth book, is the second in his quartet of historical novels that deals with the scientific mind and artistic creation. An Irishman whose work is little known in America, Mr. Banville is a prose stylist of extraordinary merit, and his novels have already garnered him several prestigious awards in Europe. *Kepler* itself comes to these shores having won the Guardian Award for fiction.

Like its excellent predecessor *Doctor Copernicus, Kepler* is a portrait of a man and his age. The man, Johannes Kepler, was born in 1571 in the town of Weilderstadt in southern Germany. One of the world's foremost astronomers and mathematicians, Kepler discovered three laws of planetary motion which later formed an indispensable part of the foundation of Isaac Newton's discovery of universal gravitation. Kepler, a graduate of the University of Tubingen, was a Copernican. Rather than undergo compulsory conversion to Roman Catholicism he left his post as a teacher of mathematics in Graz, and became an assistant to Tycho Brahe, the greatest astronomical observer before the introduction of the telescope. After Brahe's death, Rudolph II, the Holy Roman Emperor, appointed Kepler to the position of Imperial Mathematician. Striving for several years to find an orbit to fit all of Brahe's observations of the planet Mars, Kepler made his most significant discovery. He suddenly realized that Mars' orbit could not be circular but elliptical. The ellipse worked, and Kepler destroyed a belief that was 2000 years old. He died, still struggling to unlock the mysteries of the Cosmos, in 1630.

So much for the bones of the story. These events Banville skillfully records. He brilliantly recreates the 17th-century world and brings the reader into intimate contact with the chaotic atmosphere of Kepler's age. Here are the plagues, furies, agues, witchcraft, bawdiness, and uncertain politics of Church and State. And through it all comes the picture of the fevered, struggling, oft-humiliated and angered figure of Kepler. Perpetually at the center of things, his portrait is extraordinarily rendered. Banville manages to capture the private, domestic Kepler, husband and father, a fretting, dishevelled man with complaining wife always at his shoulder, and also the public "Imperial Mathematician and Court Astronomer" whose life is dedicated to discovering a cosmic harmony. Both sides of the man are beautifully balanced and blended. Whether painting the tensions and minor dramas of Kepler's family life (witness the vivid scenes with his jeering wife, churlish father-in-law, and mad mother) or the grand intensity of the astronomer's inspiration, Banville is marvellously at home.

Kepler, then, is a tour-de-force of historical fiction and a worthy successor to the prize-winning *Doctor Copernicus*. It enhances Mr. Banville's growing reputation as an artist of supreme craft, and confirms him as one of the major writers of prose fiction to have emerged from Ireland in many years. With the next volume in the quartet, *The Newton Letter*, due out later this year, it is to be hoped that his work will finally achieve the recognition he deserves on both sides of the Atlantic.

Niall Williams. *ILS*. Fall, 1983, p. 29

In *The Newton Letter*, Banville does not try to tell a story. He interrogates the very nature of story-telling in the double sense of the narrative form of the writing and the imaginative powers of the writer. The narrator is an historian who attempts to make sense of the nervous collapse suffered by another "scientific" mind, Isaac Newton, in another point in history, 1693. The only "factual" evidence he has to go on is an enigmatic letter sent to the philosopher, John Locke, in which Newton intimates his crisis of faith in the ability of the mind to explain the "true" workings of the external universe. Scientific facts, Newton seems to suggest, are themselves fiction. The task of the contemporary historian-narrator in the novel is to establish and interpret the "facts" behind this decisive "interlude" in Newton's career. Not an auspicious project by all accounts. . . .

This historian, not surprisingly, begins his narrative by conceding his own failure of imaginative nerve: "Words fail me . . . I have abandoned my book . . . I don't really understand it myself . . . I've lost faith in the primacy of text." The beginning of the novel thus bespeaks the ending; and the entire intervening narrative is written retrospectively in the past tense; that is, in the form of a reminiscence which would explain the narrator's own failed quest for narrative understanding or coherence. In this respect, Banville's novel is no less circular and fated a narrative form than [Bernard] MacLaverty's [*Cal*]. But the circle moves in opposite directions. Whereas *Cal* showed the mind unable to escape from the insular circularity of history, in *The Newton Letter* the mind is its own prison and history the one possibility of salvation (what its narrator calls the possibility of "the innocence of things, their non-complicity in our affairs"). In short, while MacLaverty's hero struggles to be delivered *from* the historical past, Banville's seeks to be delivered *into* it.

But can the fiction-spinning mind ever dispense with its own interpretations? Can it ever hope to suspend its adulterating interference with the "innocence of things?" Banville's narrator brings guidebooks on trees and birds with him to Ferns only to discover that the "illustrations would not match up with the real specimens." In similar fashion, the human specimens of Fern

House, and indeed the elusive Newton himself, stubbornly defy the historian's code of decipherment. Just as the ultimate and enigmatic truths of the universe defied Newton's scientific blueprints. History thus repeats itself in a timeless pattern of recurrence. . . .

Like Newton before him, whose "interlude" represented a crisis of belief in the mind's ability to reach truth, the historian determines to abandon his writings in order to commit himself to silence. (A decision which recalls Banville's Wittgensteinian conclusion to an earlier novel, *Under Birchwood*—"Whereof I cannot speak thereof I will be silent.") The narrator explains his move by alluding to a *second* letter to Locke in which Newton avowed his preference for a wordless communion with the common mortals of this world—"the sellers and makers of things"—a non-fictional language "in which commonplace things speak to me." . . .

What then of Banville's narration—the novel itself? What of the author's own narrative "interlude" on his narrator's "interlude" on Newton's "interlude?" In an editorial note at the end of the novel, Banville informs us that the second Newton letter to Locke is in fact a fiction! And it requires no great leap of the imagination to realize that the narrator's own final letter is equally fictional. (A realization confirmed by the tell-tale fact that the narrator speaks of the future's resonance "for me," that his own feeling of pregnancy is itself metaphorical and that the reference to "supernumerous existence" is a direct literary quote from Rilke's *Duino Elegies*.) The attempt to abandon fiction is thus exposed as fiction. Where Banville goes from here, his story of interlude, is, presumably, another story.

Richard Kearney. *ILS*. Fall, 1983, pp. 24–25

BECKETT, SAMUEL (1906–   )

There are novels which are likely to be interesting to the many, and novels which are certain to be only of interest to the few. On some such rough and ready principle of selection publishers presumably select the wares they have to offer. On the other hand it is, of course, not nearly as easy as that; and one of the catches is that through the prevalent disease of intellectual snobbery books which seem only interesting to the few become stamped on that account with a value of their own. And when I turn to Mr. Beckett's book [*More Pricks Than Kicks*], I do not mean to imply that here are stories which are of no intrinsic value, but that here are stories which while certainly not likely to achieve any wide circulation are calculated to seduce any publisher who refuses to call himself a Philistine. He would feel that they should be published because their extreme cleverness is so unblushingly highbrow as to overawe all but the very plain man. The very plain man, of course, turning up some such sentence as: —

> "Open upon her concave breast as on a lectern lies Portigliotti's *Penombre Claustrali*, bound in tawed caul. In her talons earnestly she grasps Sade's *Hundred Days* and the *Anterotica* of Aliosha G. Brignole-Sale, unopened, bound in shagreened caul. A septic pudding hoodwinks her, a stodgy turban of pain it laps her horse face. The eyehole is clogged with the bulbus, the round pale globe goggles exposed . . ."

will close the book promptly, suspecting acute cleverness. And he will, needless to say, be right. Mr. Beckett is an extremely clever young man, and he knows his *Ulysses* as a Scotch Presbyterian knows his Bible.

The ten stories are episodes centring round a Dubliner, Belacqua, more akin to Bloom than to Dedalus, but, unlike Bloom, completely stuffed and upholstered in self-consciousness. The best episode, since it is informed by some faintly human appetite, is the account of Belacqua's search for the perfect piece of cheese, to match the toast he has made for himself and the lobster which has been ordered. Here certainly is something of the meticulous intensity in personal ordinances of the introvert, Bloom. And Mr. Beckett has also a gift for the strange and arresting phrase. A book that glitters and will make holiday for the highbrows. Those who are not highbrows must also admire that glitter even if they should also remember a certain proverb. . . .

DM. July, 1934, pp. 84–85

Murphy, at least for this humble examiner, sweeps all before him. Rarely, indeed, have I been so entertained by a book, so tempted to superlatives and perhaps hyperboles of praise. It truly is magnificent and a treasure—if you like it. Quite useless to you, quite idiotic, if you don't. It is a sweeping, bold record of an adventure in the soul; it is erudite, allusive, brilliant, impudent and rude. Rabelais, Sterne and Joyce—the last above all—stir in its echoes, but Mr. Beckett, though moved again and again to a bright, clear lyricism— as for the kite-flying of Mr. Kelly in the park, or always for Celia, lovely, classic figure—is not like Joyce evocative of tragedy or of hell. He is a magnificently learned sceptic, a joker overloaded with the scholarship of great jokes. There are two ways for the man in the street to read him—the one, which has been mine at first reading, is to sweep along, acknowledging points lost by lack of reference in oneself, but seeing even in darkness the skirts of his tantalising innuendo, and taking the whole contentedly, as a great draught of brilliant, idiosyncratic commentary, a most witty, wild and individualistic refreshment. If he takes it so, with modesty and without a fuss, the sympathetic reader will be amply rewarded by the gusts of his own laughter, by the rich peace of his response to Murphy's flight from the macrocosm into the microcosm of himself and his own truth, and by the glorious fun of his world's pursuit of him—Neary, Wylie, Miss Counihan—never has there been a more amusing presentation in fiction than Miss Counihan—and the sweet, classic Celia. There is no plot, as novel-readers mean plot, but there is a glorious, wild story, and it is starred all over with a milky way of sceptic truths. And read once simply and sportingly as it flies, this book is then to be read again, very slowly, with as many pauses as may be to pursue the allusions and decorations which may have had to be guessed at in first flight. There is no more to be said. One can only hope—being eager for the gladdening, quickening and general toning up of readers' wits—that a very great number of people will have the luck and the wit to fall upon *Murphy* and digest it. For the right readers it is a book in a hundred thousand. My own great pleasure in it is not least in the certainty that I shall read it again and again before I die.

Kate O'Brien. *Spec.* March 25, 1938, p. 546

In *Molloy*, a powerful vision of humanity *in extremis* has had its effect on the structure of the book. Beckett, once a professional *littérateur*, is here preparing himself to abandon literary writing, and in matters of technique and structure the world he is abandoning is no less in evidence than the one he is striving to attain. It is a dual narrative, a self-sufficient book that had its finishing touch and glitters everywhere. While the later books go further, there can be no talk of finishing touches; they end with a gasp, a cry interrupted, an expiry of breath. Yet the usual machinery of structure has become superfluous, replaced by the natural rhythms an artist may develop with command of his medium. Compared with the work of James Joyce, for example, *Molloy* is a revelation of the power which may reside in simplicity.

The first narrative is of Molloy himself, in quest of his mother. The second [*Malone Dies*] is of Moran, a kind of agent or detective, in quest of Molloy. Both narratives are of great power and beauty, including thought and memory with a series of wayside observations, all intermingled in a continuous internal monologue. Both Molloy and Moran speak in more or less classical language, about the familiar public world, "our own." The *décor* is distinctive, but unstartling; Molloy has a mother, Moran a son, and both move through the world, even if in the end on crutches. There are towns, or a town. There are forests, or a forest. It is not clear whether the forest and town through which both pass are the same; in the human comedy, purgatory is purgatory wherever it takes place. There is a sea, and a beach.

Already behind the grotesquerie and the sardonically balanced phrasing, the anguish of the later books begins; the condition and utterance of Molloy announces it, the end of Moran is a presage. But speech in the usual sense, controlled and orderly, that is still possible; both Molloy and Moran go so far as to crack their endless self-annihilating jokes, and then even to laugh at them. But first, in the nostalgia of desire, and the fear of decay, the stage of Beckett's world is prepared, for the time when it will cease to be a stage, with actors and characters playing their parts, and behind them an omnipotent author, helping them on, watching them wistfully away. The actors have begun dismantling the stage, there is still an author, but one is not aware of him as of a man of letters, he is close to his creations, they speak as it were from his image.

Patrick Bowles. List. June 19, 1958, p. 1011

The passage just cited (it is from *Malone Dies*) was first written and published in French. Art chose for its battleground the French language, into which, by the time *Murphy* was being written, [Beckett's] endemic morbidity had transferred itself. The strange instinct that, about 1937, divided the two halves of his temperament, the gentle comedian and the morbid solipsist, between two languages, was obeying a psychic principle not difficult to reconstruct. Between a native language and a language of adoption is a difference not merely of tools but of selves. The words in which I carry on that unending dialogue that accompanies my conscious existence, these words cluster, ramify, and so color the unique person that I am as to precipitate within it what introspection knows as a *self*. ("It's a question of words, of voices," thinks the Unnamable; "the words are everywhere, inside me, outside me . . . I'm in words, made of words.") New words then will seek to precipitate a modified self, though the person is the same. And a system of new words learned later in life with the assistance of the disciplined understanding will attract, if they are allowed to invest the consciousness, whatever potential selfhood floats closest to the ratiocinative. (And we may note in passing how Beckett's French keeps recalling the systematic drill of the classrooms in which it was learned: "Elles n'ont pas germé. . . . Si elles devaient germer elles auraient germé. Elles ne germeront jamais.") It is perhaps not impertinent to speculate that a precocious morbidity in our author did not mature or assimilate but hung in the pit of his psyche, indigestible; that so long as he was a monolingual writer it infected his words with frenzy; that he was freed to pursue in English the gentle career of Murphy when this clot of despairs had begun speaking French; and that in writing the trilogy in French a decade later he was facing it down on what had become its home ground, as Moran in the first division of the trilogy hunts down Molloy.

Molloy and Moran are more or less the author's Irish and French selves respectively. The former, wild and erratic, moves on "the island" in the vicinity of Bally, a town whose name is half Irish cliché, half English obscenity. The latter, prim and constrained, with his chickens and his parish priest, hails from a Turdy which suggests not only a second Anglo-Saxon obscenity but the Tour Eiffel. The hunt ruins Moran forever (there are to be no more books like *Murphy* and *Watt*), but the writer has thenceforward the freedom, in whatever he does, of his whole personality.

Hugh Kenner. *Samuel Beckett: A Critical Study*
(New York, Grove, 1961), pp. 56–57

The convention of total illusion, and of man's inability to communicate, seems . . . merely the most recent and most bourgeois of platitudes. But when this is so, we are in danger of missing those few works which go beyond the formulas and create the experience in depth.

The most remarkable example, in this kind, is Beckett's *Waiting for Godot*. . . . It presents a total condition of man, and this belongs within the familiar structure of feeling. . . . Yet the dramatic method is in fact unlike that of Chekhov and Pirandello, where the movement is normally a single action showing how the characters fit in with each other, sharing comparable illusions. The method of *Waiting for Godot* is older. The play is built around an unusually explicit set of contrasts: between the tramps, Vladimir and Estragon, and the travellers, Pozzo and Lucky; and the further contrasts within each pair.

This polar opposition of characters was used in early expressionism to present the conflicts of a single mind. But now the method has been developed to present the conflicts within a total human condition. It is an almost wholly static world, with very narrow limits set to any significant human action. Yet the struggles for significance, of each of the pairs, are sharply contrasted. The movement of the play is the action of waiting. . . .

The compassion which was always present in Chekhov had virtually disappeared by the time of Pirandello and his successors. Their exposure of illusion (as indeed in Beckett's own other work) carried a mocking harshness which could not go beyond itself. The world and life had been "seen through," and that was that. In the Pozzo-Lucky sequences, Beckett continues this tone, but he combines it with what had seemed to be lost: the possibility of human recognition, and of love, within a total condition still meaningless. Strangely, this answering life, at a point beyond the recognition of stalemate, is convincing and moving.

Raymond Williams, *Modern Tragedy*
(Stanford, Cal., Stanford Univ. Pr., 1966),
pp. 153–55

[Beckett's] art cannot be judged irresponsible or idiosyncratic because it does not apparently concern itself with the social or political circumstance of its time. It is precisely because the destructive forces of the twentieth century have given the lie to progress, reason, stability, perfectability and simplicity that Beckett subscribes to none of them and his writing is as it is. Beckett does not write of the hydrogen bomb or of Dachau but he does portray in a unique poetry, and with an even more unique truthfulness of the cruelty, suffering and helplessness which is the human climate of a world in which the bomb exists and such events take place. . . .

The one fundamental behind all of Beckett's work is the ancient tragic knowledge which has been revived by the absurd, of man's solitude, imprisonment and pain in an intolerable universe that is indifferent to his suffering. Beckett is, if in these conditions the word retains a meaning, a pessimist, which is to say he writes what he considers to be true and not what he knows is diverting. This is not a criticism of a right or wrong approach: only a test of where one places the value in life. The world in which Beckett begins to write is without unity, clarity, rationality or hope, and where man, absurdly conscious that he is conscious and bound to die, feels himself alone and a stranger in a place which itself will one day cease to exist. From this confrontation between the unreasonable silence of the universe and the human need to be and to be known, there arises that futile revolt against existence; the anguished rebellion of the spirit against Apollinaris's three necessities, the abject necessity of being born, the hard necessity of living and the sharp necessity of dying, which is constant throughout his work.

Michael Robinson. *The Long Sonata of the
Dead: A Study of Samuel Beckett*
(London, Hart-Davis, 1969), pp. 299–300

Although the episodes in *Murphy* are located, with Joycean precision, in London and Beckett's early environment near Dublin, where *Watt* also begins and ends, the scenes of the succeeding novels become progressively vague. Hill, swamp, shore, sea, forest, open country, city are eventually reduced to a single flat stretch of mud. This too, however, is related to medieval metaphysics: the universe of concentric zones, the symbolism of the circle and the center, of the elements and seasons, of light and movement. Beckett's man, like medieval man, is "molded from all the kingdoms." "There somewhere man is too," Moran solemnly remarks as he reflects on his mission to find Molloy, a "vast conglomerate of all of nature's kingdoms, as lonely and as bound" (*Molloy*, 151). When Beckett's characters refer to birth, wombs, expulsion, copulation, excrements—Beckett seems particularly obsessed with fecal matter and urine—in short, to human existence, the situations and images have Freudian overtones. But, after *Watt*, Beckett's characters evolve in a setting which is, on the whole, more in the tradition of Dante or of Milton; we sense a familiar metaphysical vision beyond the imaginary structure.

This world, with its primeval slime, its expulsions, falls, and painful progressions, its halts and temporary refuges, its play of light and shade, its creatures sinking into or emerging from the mud, is now and then strikingly reminiscent of Dante's *Divine Comedy*—particularly, perhaps, as seen through Gustave Doré's illustrations. "Nights without Night" and "Days with-

out Day," to borrow Michel Leiris's title—everything unfolds in the "imperfect shade" and "doubtful light" of an engraving, each character evolving in
what Malone calls "my personal light," or else in that indirect lunar light in
which this dim world is sometimes rather gently bathed.

Dante, to be sure, as many critics have pointed out, made a deep impression on Beckett's imagination. The lazy Belacqua, whom Dante places in the
indecisive zone of Antepurgatory, is one of his special favorites, as also,
though to a lesser extent, Sordello, his companion—the poet who at first is silent. And Beckett, as he constructs his "mental country," occasionally alludes
to Dante. The narrator of *The Unnamable*, "stuck like a sheaf of flowers in a
deep jar, its neck flush with my mouth" (55), his head held up by an iron col-
lar; the narrator of *How It Is*, crawling on his stomach with his face in the
mud; the crippled Moran, painfully proceeding through a forest during an
entire winter; Macmann, lying under the open sky during a violent rain
storm—how Dante-like these situations and places are! They recall the gla-
cial rain in the third circle of the inferno; the forest of suicides in the seventh;
and, persistently, the memory of Malebolge's domain, the eighth circle,
where the perjurors, or falsifiers in words, drag themselves through the mud
throughout eternity.

Germaine Brée. In Melvin J. Friedman, ed., *Samuel
Beckett Now: Critical Approaches to his Novels,
Poetry, and Plays* (Chicago, Univ. of Chicago Pr.,
1970), pp. 77–79

Beckett's poetry turned out to be less "self-contained" than is some poetry. It
has its aesthetic dimension and its antiaesthetic dimension. It points both to itself as art and to its maker as man, existing in the outer world of time and
space and the inner world of the "Nothing, than which . . . naught is more
real." The poems are difficult, if not hermetic, primarily because they are
filled with allusions to worlds beyond the world of poetry—to literature and
philosophy, to Ireland and France and especially the Dublin and Paris that
Beckett knew as a young man, to events in the life of the poet. . . . This complex was the habitat of the young Beckett, the universe of his loves and antip-
athies. Perhaps there is something more deeply human than idle curiosity that
leads us to look beyond even privileged works of art to the human realities
from which they spring. In any case, there is no easy breaking point between
the best of Beckett's poems and their existential ground. . . .

As we move through the collected poetry an evolution becomes apparent, an evolution in thought, attitude, and style that transcends the poetry. The
last two poems Beckett wrote, published in the Addenda to *Watt*, are at once
the clearest expression of the reality he reached at the terminus of his poetic
evolution and the manifesto of the prose and drama to come, which he envi-

sioned as explorations and *approfondissements* of this essential reality. These two little poems form, as it were, the ideal bridge between the early Beckett and the mature artist possessed of and by his vision and fully in command of his artistic means. . . .

His later prose and dramatic writing are densely poetic in the sense that narration and dialogue expand at every moment beyond storytelling and communication to produce the distance of aesthetic contemplation through images that in the context become emblematic of man's condition and destiny. When he writes in a reflexive mode—as critic and theorist—about the novel, drama, poetry, painting, and criticism and theory themselves, we become aware that the practitioner of poetry was not long in developing a consistent view of art as making that can apply not only to poetry, not only to the various literary genres, but to all the arts.

Lawrence E. Harvey, *Samuel Beckett: Poet &
Critic* (Princeton, N.J., Princeton Univ. Pr.,
1970), pp. ix–xi

Beckett's people are not so unlike the rest of us as to fail to look for solaces of various kinds in art, love and nature. What these solaces may be, and to what extent they sustain the mind, to what extent deepen its suffering, are subjects upon which Beckett is intent. His world is an extraordinary one, but not so remote from other human worlds as to lack these sources of sustenance. Art, love and nature are sources of meaning, and sources of pleasure, though meanings and pleasures are frail, transient, scarred, scotched and annihilated in Beckett's fiction. Even though and even as they disappear or are discredited, these so-called solaces give his strange world a familiar density.

There are a few of Beckett's stories where love has virtually diminished to the vanishing-point of dream or remote memory. There are some where the habitable universe has given way to an invented construction, as in *Imagination Dead Imagine, Ping*, or *The Lost Ones*. But art is always present, a subject as well as a medium. Beckett's art is an unflaggingly self-reflective activity, and the arts he is chiefly concerned with are theatrical and literary. His plays dramatise and discuss dramatic action, like dialogue, entertainment, scenes, continuous action, performance, exposition, and final curtains. Just as *Waiting for Godot* strangled such theatrical conventions as continuity and conclusion, so some of the novels and stories attack the narrative convention of autonomy, completeness, and steady action. His fiction is concerned with its own genre, of narrative. It illustrates and inspects the need and nature of story-telling, in many forms and guises, as well as the bare possibility of doing and going without. Both plays and stories push their genre as far as possible in the direction of self-destruction, of silence and inactivity, partly, one supposes, out of sheer imaginative zeal and curiosity, partly in admissions of defeat, partly as preparations for dying. They also take a close look not only at forms and conventions, but at language.

Barbara Hardy. In Katharine Worth, ed., *Beckett the Shape Changer* (London, Routledge & Kegan Paul, 1975), p. 107

The language in Beckett's most recent prose has, however, sought more and more to attain consonance between what it is and what it says. *Enough*, a very fine short work from 1966, is written in a resigned style of great simplicity, which is constantly redefining what it is saying. *The Lost Ones* proceeds on a different level, in the unengaged manner of *Imagination Dead Imagine* ("Hold a mirror to their lips, it mists"), but more ethereal: "Floor and wall are of solid rubber or suchlike. Dash against them foot or fist or head and the sound is scarcely heard. Imagine then the silence of the steps." Along with this goes a resuscitation of the tendency towards notation found in Malone's final pages, as if the recording consciousness were weary of the effort of writing carefully cadenced sentences: "Inside a cylinder fifty metres round and eighteen high for the sake of harmony or a total surface of roughly twelve hundred square metres of which eight hundred mural. Not counting the niches and tunnels." Both *Ping* (a reduction of material from the drafts of *The Lost Ones*) and *Lessness*, the most recent texts of all, take this notational technique to its logical conclusion. Whereas in *The Lost Ones* the sentence could contain material fully explored (even though the lack of subsidiary punctuation tends to test the reader's powers of involvement to the full), the sentence now becomes full of material only half-expressed. Whereas in *The Lost Ones* each subsequent sentence tends to amplify the preceding one (as do the sections), in *Ping* they tend towards uniformity. The sentence "traces blurs signs no meaning light grey almost white" appears three times, and many of the others are very similar without being exactly the same. At a casual reading, as a result of the repetition, the piece is completely mesmeric. *Lessness* represents only a minimal advance on this, consisting of 120 sentences, the second sixty repeating the first sixty but in a different order. Such extreme simplicity, which may seem crude, is not, of course, adopted without good reason. In *Lessness* it is as if an area is staked out, an area to which (though other experience may have been arbitrarily omitted) some kind of assent is going to be given. But the narrator discovers that even with a severely circumscribed amount of material, problems of order and arrangement are not, and never can be, solved: the possible order of the sentences is so much more infinite than that of Murphy with his six biscuits or Molloy with his sixteen stones. However, this desperate realization has its compensations. By repeating the same material again (as happens also in *Play*) one suggests to the reader (or audience) that this limited amount of material is all that can be said, repeated verbatim (or almost verbatim) *ad infinitum* through time. There is, that is to say, an inbuilt feeling of eternity in the device, which helps to convey Beckett's feeling that we live in a continuum, where past, present and future mix indistinguishably.

John Pilling. *Samuel Beckett* (London, Routledge & Kegan Paul, 1976), pp. 50–51

Samuel Beckett, like Edward Bond, writes about pain. His break with the homogeneous "culture"-talk of the past has been more decisive: he is not merely a modern writer, he is a difficult modernist. The break with the past has a direct bearing on the subject-matter he has chosen, and the manner of his break, the adoption of a modernist style, reflects the subtlety as well as the seriousness of his artistic practice. Like Bond, he disowns the past, but not in its entirety—Dante and Swift are recurrent points of reference for him. He rejects it as it has been assimilated to the world of talk about literature. The great writers survive despite, not because of, that talk, and in the days when Beckett himself talked about literature it was in a fashion defiantly his own and apart from the stream of "culture"-talk. His "difficulty," his modernism, entails an attempt to ward off that sort of talk, to permit us to encounter his art without preconceptions. He is not concerned to destroy "culture" in the cause of some even larger abstraction. The self-protective skin which Bond would like to break figures for Beckett as something which needs, instead, to be sloughed off. A new sensitivity to pain in his reader, in his audience, is for him a criterion of success: it shows that the film of custom which is "culture"-talk has been cast off. The earth may one day like a snake renew her winter weeds outworn. When that happens we are, or shall be, returned to the old masters in a new way. We shall experience their work, like Beckett's own, on our very pulses.

The kind of sensitivity to pain that this work encourages certainly is not Shelleyan (how could it be? Shelley's sense of pain is almost exclusively self-referring) and the facile optimism of Shelley's conclusion to *Hellas* is never a possibility for Beckett. Yet he also is an apocalyptic writer. His visions of an ending world demand that we should affirm, if we can, and in despite of all suffering, that the world, capable of change, does not deserve to end in destruction. His recent plays for the theatre, *Not I* and *That Time*, brought together with *Footfalls* and six other pieces for stage, radio and television in *Ends and Odds*, make this demand with greater authority and more persuasive economy of means than almost anything else in his *oeuvre*. The volume in which they are now printed, since it contains work written more than fifteen years previously, allows us to see what Beckett had to get through in order to achieve this authority. It enables us to contrast one kind of exposure to pain with another, and so to understand better why it is that the experience of suffering in the latest plays is, against all the odds, benign.

Martin Dodsworth. *English*. Spring, 1977,
pp. 83–84

It is impossible—for me at least—to find the same philosophic unity in *Watt* as there is in *Murphy*, nor is Watt's way of life the product of a conscious choice, as Murphy's at least *seems* to be. Watt is predestined to go to Mr. Knott's house, to stay there, and to leave it again. His experiences result in a profound disorientation, so that his account of them, given to Sam in the third chapter while they are both confined in a psychiatric institution, is, in Hesla's words, "a tale told by a psychotic to a psychotic." Sam attempts in this chapter to give some idea of the form as well as the content of Watt's communications, which distort language in ways akin to those used by schizophrenics. (Whereas Murphy vainly envied the schizophrenics he nursed, Watt has had the good fortune to be able to join them.) In spite, however, of the many distracting themes—mathematical, psychiatric, linguistic, logical, semantic, ethical—I find two dominant philosophic patterns in *Watt*: one ontological, the other epistemological. Watt at Mr. Knott's house experiences, however dimly, both the difference between being and non-being and the difference between knowing and not-knowing. It seems *a priori* impossible that such negative experience should be communicated, but Beckett's narrator knows exactly how these things are managed in practice—by the philosophic equivalent of sleight of hand or rule of thumb. . . .

The point to remember about poor Watt is that, far from being an aggressive Pyrrhonist, he is not even a conscious skeptic. He wants to believe in whatever he has been taught, whatever is in front of his nose. If an event occurs without a self-evident cause, he doggedly searches for an explanation. The wild humor of many passages in *Watt* depends upon the way in which things, people and ideas—words even—elude the simple demands made on them by Watt. Even a pot, in a passage much quoted by commentators, ceases to be a pot for Watt. Eventually, the narrator and the reader find themselves participating in this intellectual equivalent of the clown's stepping on the missing rung of the ladder. . . . Perhaps if the narrator had never attempted to solve it, if Watt had been contented with his pot that was no pot, we should not have been tempted to laugh; but earnest bewilderment in search of the unattainable—the man in the bath with his eyes full of soap trying to find the towel that he has left in the bedroom—is one of the saddest, funniest sights known to man or God. The philosopher's quest for "truth"—a word most contemporary philosophers would not dare to use—or for something theoretically easier to find, such as an agreed terminology, is the comic image that underlies many pages of *Watt* and gives the book whatever unity it possesses.

Vivian Mercier. *Beckett/Beckett* (New York, Oxford
Univ. Pr., 1977), pp. 166–68

Many lines of the European imagination meet in Beckett, but as playwright he is above all the heir of Yeats and the Irish/French drama. . . . He strides from Dublin into France like the modern man of Synge's imagining whose role it would be to "take Ireland into Europe." In himself he seems the epitome of that union. With almost uncanny appropriateness he takes his place among those Irish predecessors who felt so strongly the lure of France, sometimes even to the extent of turning themselves into Frenchmen; Wilde writing *Salomé* in French, bilingual Synge, one foot in Aran, the other in Paris, Yeats so receptive to the flow of experience and ideas from European art and drama. Beckett seems to sum all this up: an Irishman who lives in France, writes with equal facility in French and English, regularly translates himself from one to the other and always keeps in his English an Irish lilt, whether his characters are called Rooney and grope their way down a road near Dublin or Estragon and Vladimir who might be travelling on any road in Europe.

Modernism arrives in the popular theatre with Beckett. "Popular" may seem an unlikely word, but must be the appropriate one for plays which, for all their strangeness, have become known all over the world, and are continually being revived by the professional as well as the amateur theatre: it was hardly fortuitous that the repertoire of the National Theatre for its opening season in its new South Bank home should include *Happy Days*: Beckett now occupies a position in the English theatre where it is natural to turn to his plays for such great occasions; they have become our "modern classics." And yet he has drawn these international audiences for a theatre which is intensely inward, the complete fulfilment of Yeats's idea of a drama of "most interior being." Such a drama was confined to corners of Dublin and of London in Yeats's day; it is a measure of Beckett's virtuoso skill and also of his humaneness that he has been able to give it this great extension into the public domain and in doing so change the course of modern theatre, for nothing has been the same since *Waiting for Godot*.

Katharine Worth. *The Irish Drama of Europe from
Yeats to Beckett* (Atlantic Highlands, N.J.,
Humanities Press, 1978), p. 241

Murphy's sessions in his rocking-chair represent an attempt to achieve not only the temporary freedom afforded by imagination, but ultimately, the permanent freedom he believes to flow from the complete transcendence of worldly desire. Though various critics have shown that his faith in the rewards of self-transcendence derives partly from Geulincx, the way in which Beckett draws Spinoza and Schopenhauer, too, into his satire has not been discussed. Guelincx and Spinoza agree that complete self-transcendence is a supreme good; for once an individual has renounced the world, they argue, he is able to discover the will and thought of God and make his volitions conform to divine reason. What the individual achieves, in Geulincx's terms, is "the unique love of right reason," the equivalent, as S. V. Keeling tells us, of Spinoza's "intellectual love of God." In both Spinoza and Geulincx love of God is clearly distinguished from self-love, which is held to be the root of all moral evil. Murphy, however, is either unaware of this, or has dismissed it from mind on the basis that God does not exist. For, as Beckett's parody of Spinoza in the epigraph to chapter six indicates, Murphy's behaviour is based not on the intellectual love of God, but on the love of himself. . . .

Murphy eventually experiences "Nothing." But in a careful selection of "filmic" scenes, Beckett demonstrates first, that the path he follows in pursuit of freedom is one of imperfect aceticism; and second, that his assumption that freedom *from* will is equivalent to freedom *of* will is mistaken. Early in the novel, Murphy is revealed as too weak to undertake voluntary chastity: though his will-less self wants to deny Celia, his willing self craves for her, and it is in answer to this craving that he agrees to abandon his search for freedom temporarily in order to find work. His failure to cultivate indifference to worldly objects is clear from his attempt to defraud a tea-shop by paying for one cup of tea, but consuming "1.83 cups approximately" (p. 84). His inability to welcome insult and suffering is *divine comedy*, where the usual physical laws are overturned. Because Murphy never meets him, Cooper is not a part of his "actual" experience; because he never imagines him, or even a character like him, Cooper is not a part of his "virtual" experience either. Through Cooper, Beckett reaffirms both that Murphy's experience is too narrow for the "actual" and "virtual" of his mind to mirror the world accurately; and that our impression that *Murphy* is a straightforwardly realistic novel is a complacent simplification.

James Acheson. Journal of Beckett Studies. Autumn,
1979, pp. 16–18

All of Beckett's work previous to *Watt* depended in varying degrees on ironic references to a wealth of Irish literature and on burlesques of Irish literary precedents, notably those set by Yeats and Joyce, for its meaning. This literary self-consciousness was clearly apparent in *More Pricks Than Kicks*, for example, because of the manner in which Beckett dwelled on the literary landmarks of inner Dublin made familiar by Joyce despite the fact that his own home environment was suburban—Foxrock, Leopardstown, and the southern area of County Dublin. The setting of Watt is a significant innovation in the series of Beckett's *oeuvre* because, in addition to anticipating qualities of his later work, it is a suburban environment, one which marks the emergence in Beckett's fiction of his own home environment, a development which eliminated some of the most obviously derivative features of his earlier work. The deliberately vague treatment of setting in *Watt* has often been explained through reference to Beckett's statement in a tribute to Jack B. Yeats, painter, writer, and brother to the poet, that the true artist "*est de nulle part.*" That statement was made in 1954, however, a year after the publication of *Watt* but a decade after its completion, by which time Beckett had already written his trilogy of novels and *Waiting for Godot* as well. A more accurate description of Beckett's method in *Watt* appeared in his 1936 review of Jack B. Yeats' *The Amaranthers*, which Beckett praised because in that novel "The Island is not throttled into Ireland, nor the City into Dublin." The point, then, is not so much that the true artist "comes from nowhere," but that true artistry is a product of original treatment of one's home environment, a thought which Beckett reiterated in a third essay on "the national aspects" of Yeats' work published in Dublin in 1945. These statements about Jack B. Yeats and the national aspects of any artist's work are indicative of the extent to which Beckett developed his own aesthetic in Irish contexts and formed his distinctively original prose style through innovative presentation of Irish elements in fiction.

These processes are best observable in *Watt*, the last novel Beckett wrote in English and the work which immediately preceded "the siege in the room" during the late 1940s and early 1950s when his French trilogy was composed. The events described in *Watt* are not presented in chronological order, but in the order in which Watt related them to the narrator of the novel, whose name is Sam. One of the effects of this chronological discontinuity is that the first and last parts of the novel, dealing with Watt's arrival and departure from Knott's house, are set in recognizable Irish surroundings while the middle chapters, describing Watt's experiences within Knott's estate, and more vaguely suggestive of Ireland, are not "throttled" into it. The first and last chapters of *Watt* are filled with derisive and satirical references to Irish literary and social stereotypes which relate them to Beckett's earlier fiction as surely as the vaguer and more abstruse middle two chapters of the novel are related to his later fiction. As this structure suggests, *Watt* marks a particularly important transition in Beckett's work, and the correspondences created between the recognizably Irish world outside Knott's estate and the vaguer, more confusing world within it document the manner in which Beckett developed his mature prose style out of Irish contexts rather than independent of them.

John P. Harrington. *JNT*. Winter, 1981, pp. 2–3

Beckett is often considered . . . the artist of fragmentation. Whereas T. S. Eliot created from the broken segments about him a bulwark against uncertainty and fluidity, Beckett rigorously and unflinchingly explodes even those segments. His works progressively break down and strip away the tatters of conventional associations. The fragmentation is the result of Beckett's unremitting efforts to find a shape for the possibility that no relationships exist between or among the artist, his art, and an external world. Once his earliest fictions had mocked traditional relationships and once *Murphy* had exploded them by following them to their logical ends, Beckett sought to create a nonrelational art by breaking apart whatever pieces of identity, time, space, and language remained. Like the emergence of the first person narrator and the switch to composition in French, fragmentation is one of the identifying characteristics of Beckett's most prolific period (1944–50). *Watt* splits once and for all the logic of language from the world of events. The chapter summaries of *Mercier and Camier* sever the illusions of plot and narrative time. The trilogy is a masterpiece of negation, contradiction, and disruption. As a glance at the list of works written and translated between 1944 and 1950 reveals, the period is astounding in its quantity, quality, diversity, and disintegration. . . .

As disintegrated as these pieces apparently are, they are nonetheless still works of literature. It is inadequate to describe them in terms of fragmentation only. Beckett does take conventional literary shapes and structures and break them apart, but his works are intelligible only if the reader assumes partial responsibility for them and accepts the task of reconstructing the disruptive and broken forms. Although Beckett may not provide T. S. Eliot's cultural synthesis, he does demand that his reader be involved in the reconstruction of a discourse. Although his works may never proffer completed conventional structures, his pieces depend on the reader's perceptions of the disparity between the recognizable fragments he is given and the traditions they deliberately do not fulfill. The "failures" of Mercier and Camier's trip or of Moran's report are evident only in contrast to our unsatisfied expectations about the nature of the quest or detective report. Like the reader, the narrator of Beckett's fictions devotes much of his energy to shaping and reshaping the fragments available to him. Watt obsessively explores all possible explanations of the appearance of two piano tuners. Malone keeps rearranging his possessions and stories. The Unnamable orders and reorders the images and words that might constitute his pensum. They are all, as the narrator of *Enough* suggests of himself, cursed by the "art of combining."

J. E. Dearlove. *Accommodating the Chaos: Samuel Beckett's Nonrelational Art* (Durham, N.C., Duke Univ. Pr., 1982), pp. 39–40

Despite the multiplicity of solutions to the problems of creation, fundamental patterns are evident in Beckett's creative process. At least some sense of a field of aesthetics emerges. The most discernible pattern is the intentional undoing of a text's origins. It is a tendency toward abstraction, which is finally, as it was in Picasso's late work, essentialist, toward what Husserl might call a "phenomenological reduction." One invariably finds in Beckett's undoing a movement toward simplicity, toward the essential, toward the universal, and with such universalizing Beckett achieves much of the antiemotional quality Brecht achieved with his Alienation effect and historicizing. Such an artistic preoccupation in Beckett's texts might be anticipated given the sparse, often minimalist nature of the drama and late prose especially, given Beckett's tendency to lay bare his means of production, as did Brecht. What is surprising, however, is how rooted and dependent that work is on its more traditional and realistic sources. Often the early drafts of Beckett's work are more realistic, the action more traditionally motivated, the world more familiar and recognizable, the work as a whole more conventional than the final. Revision is often toward a patterned disconnection, as motifs are organized not by causality but by some form or recurrence and (near) symmetry. This process often entails the conscious destruction of logical relations, the fracturing of consistent narrative, the abandonment of linear argument, and the substitution of more abstract patterns of numbers, music, and so forth, to shape a work. It is finally a consciously literary process, which results in what the Russian formalists might call "defamiliarization," or what Brecht, in *A Short Organum for the Theater*, termed "estrangement."

The work's evolution is finally almost a devolution, the doing an undoing, the movement toward higher and higher levels of abstraction, not so much to obscure (although one suspects some of this given the Unnamable's adage, "The discourse must go on. So one invents obscurities" [p. 294]), as to de-empathize—not so much to disguise autobiography as to displace and discount it. Such a tropological thrust is particularly evident in both stage image and discourse of *Not I*, a play whose very title denies at least the autobiographical impulse, if not ego psychology itself. The result is almost paradoxical, at least dialectical. We see in both Mouth and Beckett an autobiographical ambivalence as they struggle not to reveal, not to talk about self (or mind, or self-consciousness) and thereby reassert self's centrality. The creative struggle is to undo the realistic sources of the text, to undo the coherence of character and to undo the author's presence. Exposing Beckett's creative process reveals an image of the artist caught in a web of cultural intertextuality, struggling to create with erasure.

S. E. Gontarski. *The Intent of Undoing in Samuel Beckett's Dramatic Texts* (Bloomington, Indiana Univ. Pr., 1985), pp. 3–4

Some of Beckett's most provocative allusions to religious thought are to be found in his plays. *Godot*, as its title suggests, is at once a comic and compassionate portrayal of man's search for God as he "pines and wastes . . . towards the great dark" of death. The clowns of *Godot* share the same quest for absolute meaning as the intellectuals of *Murphy*. (Beckett admitted to Colin Duckworth: "If you want to find the origins of *En Attendant Godot* look at *Murphy*.") The essential difference between the novel of the 1940s [*sic*] and the play of the 1960s [*sic*] is that Beckett's focus has turned from a metaphysical to a theological perspective. (The Cartesian rationalisations of divine being are hilariously derided in Lucky's "think" about "God quaquaquaqua with white beard quaquaquaqua outside time without extension" etc.) *Godot* is, amongst other things, a play about the Judeo-Christian hope for an eschatological God, the waiting for the coming, or second coming, of a Messiah. Several commentators have suggested that Estragon and Vladimir represent Judaism and Christianity respectively; and while remembering Beckett's warning against the "neat identifications" of the analogymongers it is perhaps unwise to completely dismiss the innumerable theological suggestions to this effect in the play.

Beckett has stated that his use of St. Augustine's interpretation of the two crucified thieves in *Godot* epitomises the drama of choice. But if the choices of the Judaic Estragon and the Christian Vladimir are as mutually exclusive as those of the two thieves, the *unknown* nature of Godot's identity (Jehovah or Christ or simply an absurd joke?) means that both share the same human condition of hoping against hope. Their shared agnosticism is a shared paralysis: they cannot hang each other and yet cannot justify their existence; they cannot communicate and yet cannot go silent; they cannot stay together and yet cannot separate. Their relationship is sustained by the fact that they *both* need Godot: "In this immense confusion one thing alone is clear. We are waiting for Godot to come—or for night to fall. We are not saints, but we have kept our appointment."

"Christianity is a mythology with which I am perfectly familiar." Beckett once confessed to Jack McGowran, "and so I used it." *Endgame* is probably Beckett's most concentrated exploration of "Christian mystology" and certainly his most uncompromising attempt to demythologise some of its more dogmatic interpretations. Now of course *Endgame* operates at numerous levels of meaning, none of which is privileged; and we must take Beckett's comment on the play seriously: "no symbols where none intended." Nonetheless, it is undeniable that even the title of the play refers not only to a technical chess position (where play comes to a halt because of diminished forces which cannot culminate in checkmate) but also to the Christian apocalyptic theme of the "ending of the world." The play is mined with scriptural allusions—especially to the *Book of Revelation*—suggesting that Beckett intended a parallel with the eschatological drama between Christ and mankind. Already in *Murphy* Beckett had played with possibilities for such a parallel (the novel is replete with quasi-quotations from *Revelation* and Murphy himself is cheekily attributed with qualities of the apocalyptic Christ), but it was not until *Godot* and more particularly *Endgame* that these possibilities materialised into a sustained parody.

Richard Kearney. In Richard Kearney, ed., *The Irish Mind: Exploring Intellectual Traditions* (Dublin, Wolfhound, 1985), pp. 280–81

BEHAN, BRENDAN (1922–1964)

In *The Quare Fellow* Behan confronted a theme of daunting difficulty. An exclusively 'male cast, a principal character who is never seen, a setting of unrelieved gloom. From these unpromising materials (or, of course, being the artist he is, because of them) Behan has made a drama that is funny, humane, and a profound affirmation of the life that everything in the prison is trying to destroy.

The play opens with a song (and closes with a variant of it). . . . Behan has been criticized for his addiction to incidental songs in his plays—in my view quite mistakenly. . . . I cannot account for this objection (or rather, don't want to bother to try to) if only because all theatre is in one sense illusion, and everything depends on the conviction with which the artist uses any theatrical device. In *The Quare Fellow* Behan introduces song sparingly, with great tact and dramatic effect. From the outset, the very fact that an invisible prisoner is singing, and that the first character we see, a warder, stops him, establishes at once his central theme which is the conflict of life and joy with cruelty and death, and the triumph of life despite judicial murder. . . .

As we meet the prisoners and warders we are made aware that the forthcoming execution of the "quare fellow" is a shared obsession: the warders, the active party in the matter, being far more disturbed by it than the inmates. Snobberies, resentments and frustrations of the prisoners are conveyed with comic irony, reminding us that a jail population differs from that outside in no essential respect whatever. The first Act ends with an attempted suicide by a reprieved prisoner; and the dramatic effect of this, by bringing us so close to death so early, and by contrasting its "voluntary" nature in this instance with the irrevocable killing that must come, reinforces the gathering sensation of impending horror.

The central "character" of the second Act is the grave the prisoners are digging for tomorrow's victim: a riveting theatrical device, since the condemned man, though still unseen, becomes even more visible to the audience's imagination; and a device saved from the merely macabre by the intensity of feeling with which Behan invests this gruesome emblem, and by the speed and point of the sardonic dialogue he gives to the prisoners and warders who surround it. As time passes (by now we too are counting the hours till the execution) we meet in later Acts, and in increasing order of seniority, the heirarchy who are going to destroy this human life (and, by implication, meet the invisible judges, ministers and the society who have willed the deed). The warders at first seemed omnipotent, but now we see their Chief, their Governor and the Hangman: an imported Englishman (since the "violent" Irish do not care, apparently, for this task) and, without doubt, one of the most revolting personages yet to be created by an English-writing dramatist. The one character we are drawn to is the young Gaelic-speaking warder Crimmin, who is as yet an innocent. It was a bold and characteristic device of Behan's to put the only really likeable man in the play among the oppressors, and he brings this off without a trace of sentiment or artifice. As the hour approaches, there are detailed physical descriptions by the prisoners of exactly what will happen to the quare fellow, so clinical as to be unbearable. . . . As the clock sounds the hour, the prison is bedlam: warders and prisoners, locked in the same disaster, become indistinguishable, and the bars melt in the heat. The play ends with a brief and calculated dying fall . . . a life has been snatched, but life will go on forever.

Considered as a drama that soars from initial apparent *grand guignol* to authentic lyric tragedy, the play is beyond praise. Viewed as a demonstration that any alternative to judicial murder must be better—and, as forcefully, that prisons defeat their own supposed ends of humiliation or redemption—it will carry conviction to anyone capable of being convinced. Yet so fine is it as a play that, just as Greek tragedy haunts us still despite the moral mainsprings of the drama being quite different from our own, so I am sure *The Quare Fellow*, in whatever kind of social order that may replace our own, will never lose its human relevance.

Colin McInnes. LondonMag. August, 1962, pp.
58–60

He was . . . always glad and grateful that London Town gave him his first and best welcome as a playwright and that once when on the way through England from Ireland to France he was arrested under a deportation order the British authorities deported him not back to Ireland but onwards to France, paying his fare – a humorous and decent people.

For all previous sharp statements about the neighbours [the English] he made amends [in *The Hostage*] in the character of Leslie Williams, the hostage, also a voice from a prison, an ordinary young English boy caught fatally and wonderingly in a situation he cannot hope to understand. Teresa, that sweet young country girl, so lovably played by Celia Salkeld, an orphan as the hostage is, tells him that Monsewer, the old mad owner of the house in which he is held, is an English nobleman: "he went to college with your king."

SOLDIER (i.e. Leslie): We ain't got one.

TERESA: Maybe he's dead now, but you had one one time, didn't you?

SOLDIER: We got a duke now. He plays tiddly winks.

TERESA: Anyway, he (i.e. Monsewer) left your lot and came over here and fought for Ireland.

SOLDIER: Why, was somebody doing something to Ireland?

TERESA: Wasn't England, for hundreds of years?

SOLDIER: That was donkey's years ago. Everybody was doing something to someone in those days.

Caitlin Ni Houlihan and John Bull have never spoken so simply, so comically nor so wisely to each other as in that passage. And mad Monsewer was, indeed, English, the son of a bishop, and had gone to "all the biggest colleges in England and slept in one room with the King of England's son" until one day because his mother was Irish he discovered he was an Irishman, or an Anglo-Irishman, which in Behan's misleading definition was "a Protestant with a horse." Anglo-Irishmen only work at "riding horses, drinking whiskey and reading double-meaning books in Irish at Trinity College." To become Irish, Monsewer took it "easy at first, wore a kilt, played Gaelic football on Blackheath . . . took a correspondence course in the Irish language. And when the Rising took place he acted like a true Irish hero." But when he lays down his bagpipes and raises his voice in song, as all Behan's people, including himself, were forever ready to do, his father's blood proves living and strong.

Monsewer has a dual, lunatic significance: the house he owns and in which the young hostage is held and accidentally killed by his rescuers is, as Pat the caretaker says, a "noble old house that had housed so many heroes" and is, in the end, "turned into a knocking shop." It is also romantic, idealistic Ireland fallen on sordid, materialistic days, and that a madman of that most romantic people, the English, should in his imagination, lead the last Irish Rebellion, playing the pipes and making heroines out of dacent whores, would seem to be a fair chapter of our national story. But the house is more than heroic Ireland down in the dumps; it is the world in a mess and God gone off his rocker: the very first stage direction says: "the real owner isn't right in the head." Monsewer, in fact, is one of Behan's visions of God, and as he parades, salutes, plays the pipes and sings of tea and toast and muffin rings, the old ladies with stern faces and the captains and the kings, he falls into line with images of the Divinity that appear elsewhere in the plays and prose.

The ministers of religion, because of Brendan's experience with prison chaplains who had to tell him that as a member of the I.R.A. he was excommunicated, seldom come well out of his story.

Benedict Kiely. In Sean McCann, ed., *The World of Brendan Behan* (New York, Twayne, 1966), pp. 105–7

Everybody says Brendan Behan loved life. If he did he did not dominate it; it dominated him. He loved it so much that it slew him. He gave himself no time to tame it or to write it. He did not write his last book [*Confessions of an Irish Rebel*]; it was recorded on tape, transcribed and edited by Rae Jeffs, a proper English lady whom he enchanted into nonconformity; "once-proper" is her own word today. I am not sure that it is right even to call this record a book, if that word conveys at least a beginning, middle and end—temporalities that no more existed in Brendan's being than they do in eternity.

Who recorded it anyway? Brendan, or Life pouring over him and out of him in song, verse, drink, passion, guff, rude jokes and flat statements (such as that Lord Carson's real name was Carsoni, or that London is named after a Celtic god), blasphemy (he says he always liked it and most Catholics do— who else *can* blaspheme?), cursing, praise of the Lord, lots of F-words, S-words, and other such explosives, but all too rarely that priceless stuff that ends up as unforgettable print. How lamentably the good Lord distributes talent! I could name offhand 10 Irish writers with 10 times Brendan's talents who would give their eyeteeth for a hundredth part of his amazing vitality and combustibility, and a thousandth part of his experience.

What a man! And then one pauses, and asks the chilling question: What kind of a writer? Did he really and truly ever want to be a writer at all? Or did he belong to that type of writer, something on the order of Thomas Wolfe, who acts as if he believes that if you live hard enough, and emotionally enough, literature will follow as a matter of course—the eye in a fine frenzy rolling? I do not know if Brendan ever read Thomas Mann's "Tonio Kröger," with its dismaying if salutary description of how an artist really works, moving from primal, hot excitement into coldly deliberate creation. It could hardly have been Brendan's cup of tea, or glass of malt.

Rae Jeffs, in her highly percipient Foreword, sees the fundamental truth about him: childlike in his frankness and candor, full of innocence, tenderness and sensitivity behind all his outward ferocity, the prisoner and victim of a fatal persona or role, a man who did not want to die, only to stop living the self-destructive life that he had concocted for himself. All this is made perfectly clear in these *Confessions*, where his reactions to life are sometimes deep but mostly very simple, and utterly spontaneous—always provided one agrees that every Irishman is conditioned from birth by the immemorial and inescapable Irish myth and tradition.

Sean O'Faolain. *NYTBR*. June 26, 1966, p. 7

Behan can not be ranked among the great writers, for he did not produce a sufficient volume of work, and even what he did produce is not without flaw. . . . Nevertheless, Behan was much more than a gifted leprechaun. He was a conscious artist, and the charge that his work is slapdash is not altogether justified. He took the same liberties with traditional notions of language, plot construction, and character development as have many other contemporary writers. He realized, with such writers as Beckett, Ionesco, Osborne, and Pinter, that nineteenth-century standards would not serve twentieth-century artists. Unfortunately, a good many critics who admire the unorthodox structure of the plays of Beckett or those of Pinter decry the same structure in Behan's plays. . . .

Behan possessed a marvelous comic talent. That he wasted a good deal of it cannot diminish his solid achievements. He wrote two of the best plays of the contemporary theater, and one of the best autobiographies of this century. He wrote with an exuberance and a humanity which will remain unexcelled. To a confused and self-destructive world, Behan gave a simple and cogent reminder: human existence, though painful, is worthwhile. Or, as Behan stated it in *The Quare Fellow*, life is "a bloody sight better than death any day of the week."

Ted E. Boyle. *Brendan Behan* (New York, Twayne, 1969), p. 134

Brendan, at his eloquent best, was the equivalent of a one-man show—except that he had no script and the run was unlimited. Unlike a stage act when his performance is over, Brendan's obligation to his art did not cease when he stopped talking. It was then he should have settled down to serious writing. But in his public performance he had syphoned off so much energy that he was often too exhausted to lift a pen. This was to be his great dilemma. If he indulged the extrovert side of his character, he lessened his chances of doing the only thing in life that really mattered to him—writing. . . .

After Christmas in 1960 Brendan began the first of the books that he was to produce by tape recorder. He had been commissioned by Hutchinson some time before, to do a book on Ireland with drawings by Paul Hogarth, the English artist. Hogarth had gone to Ireland and finished his part of the job, and was understandably anxious to see his illustrations in print, and accompanied by a text. . . .

Brendan Behan's Island was to receive wide acclaim two years later when it appeared. "One immediately likes Behan," writes Cyril Connolly in the *Sunday Times* in October, 1962, referring to the book. "He has more than charm, he has instinctive kindness and charity. A verbal grace, an unforced assertion of his strong personality that may even have a touch of greatness, a demonic energy that notoriety has not entirely dimmed." . . .

Compared with *Borstal Boy* or *The Quare Fellow*, Brendan's "talk" books are not of great value, but they do preserve a record of the range and variety of his conversation. On one page the reader can be taken through history, poetry, politics, or sport, all told in the special form of anecdote and humorous comment which was the keystone of his conversational technique. . . .

Brendan was a popular writer in the sense that no literary personality of his time had been. Thousands who had never read his book felt they knew him intimately from his appearances on television and the reports of his escapades in the newspapers.

With his death, the legend grew. He was to become a symbol for many too young even to have known his name when he was alive.

He has remained in the public mind as an iconoclast who defied convention, a precursor of the permissive society. Of those who manned the barricades in Paris, who sat-in at Berkeley or loved-in in Central Park, there are not a few to whom Brendan has been a father-figure.

Had he chosen it, his role might have been a different one. At the back of his mind lurked the image of the eighteenth-century Gaelic poet who had beguiled his boyhood; mocking, picaresque figures who brought high culture to the hearth, indifferent how they used their bodies in drink, lust, or rage if they caught for a moment in verse, the fine frenzy that overflowed their imagination.

Ulick O'Connor. Brendan Behan (London, Hamish
Hamilton, 1970), pp. 225, 235–37, 319

The most striking feature of *An Giall* is the contrast between the innocent romance of Teresa and Leslie and the brutal world in which it takes place. The setting may be a bawdy house, but their behaviour is remarkably chaste. For a while they manage to transform the brothel room into a haven of innocence and beauty, but the audience is not allowed to forget the menace outside. Whenever Teresa enters and leaves, she does not open and close the door herself; it is done for her by the I.R.A. guards lurking outside. There is far less emphasis on the romance in *The Hostage* and its tone is altered. Leslie and Teresa are alone on the stage for about three quarters of act two of *An Giall*; this is reduced to about one third in *The Hostage*. They are both eighteen years of age in *An Giall*, and Leslie, who is an innocent from Lancashire, is about seven months older than Teresa. In *The Hostage* they are older, tougher and obviously more experienced sexually: both are nineteen, but now Teresa is about seven months older than Leslie, who is a tough Cockney. In *An Giall* Teresa is described as being "neat" and "pretty" (p. 8); in *The Hostage* she is "a strong hefty country girl" (p. 27), and she shows little hesitation in hopping into bed in response to Leslie's blunt invitation.

The reasons for the differences between the two versions of the play are fairly obvious. A serious play about the age-old "Irish Question" stood little chance of notice in England in the late fifties, particularly in view of the fact that it contains no drinking except tea, no wild Irish jigs, no anti-English rebel songs and no mob scenes. By the random addition of such ingredients, *The Hostage* panders to popular conceptions of the Irish. *An Giall* contains many allusions to Irish figures, organizations and places which would probably be lost on English audiences. This problem is handled in *The Hostage* by substituting English allusions for many of the Irish ones, but the effects are frequently incongruous. The appeal of *The Hostage* is widened by making it bawdy and peppering it with allusions to most of the popular issues of the day, ranging from the Wolfenden Report to nuclear disarmament, none of which appear in the original.

The principal effects of the changes are the destruction of the integrity of the original play, a drastic alteration of its tone, and a reduction of the impact of its most striking feature: the tender romance between Teresa, the Irish orphan girl, and Leslie, the English orphan boy, in a brutal world that will not permit their simple, unconscious and human solution to the eight centuries of hatred and bloodshed which have divided their people.

Richard Wall. *MD*. June, 1975, pp. 170–71

[*The Quare Fellow*] has been criticised as "a rather shallow bit of propaganda directed largely towards the evils of capital punishment." To deny this is not to deny that Behan was opposed to capital punishment or to underestimate the assistance the London production got from a contemporary campaign against hanging, but the play itself is not essentially propagandist. Regan is the only character who offers anything like explicit criticism of the system and even he fails to offer any active resistance. The prisoners, because they are aware of its crudeness, criticise it on physical grounds but accept it as an aspect of a social order which they find inherently hostile. The Governor and his staff know that they are merely carrying out the instructions of society. Thus there is nothing of the tract in the play and it retains its impact even where capital punishment has been suspended. Its effect should be felt wherever there is an imperfect society which, in its desire to organise itself for the good of the majority, makes imperfect laws which alienate the exceptions, the unusual, the 'quare' fellows. (It is not necessary to believe in the burial rites of ancient Greece in order to be moved by Sophocles' *Antigone*.) Though the play is an occasion of laughter it is by no means shallow, for the laughter springs from the darkest depths of our consciousness and registers the rebellious vitality of man against the forces of oppression, dehumanisation and death.

To its credit, the play lacks the simplicity of propaganda. There is no sentimental utopianism and no attempt to show man as greater or less than we know him to be. The audience laughs at the Governor not because his comfortably small mind is alien to us but because it recognises the Governor in itself, and this holds for the other characters, including the hangman.

The play is structurally sound and is, perhaps, the only work by Behan of which this may be said. Nothing is superfluous: those elements which are not immediately concerned with the central action—for example, Dunlavin's methylated spirits and the prisoners' admiration of the females in the laundry yard—not only serve to establish the penal atmosphere but also show the efforts of the prisoners to preserve some semblance of normal life. The anticlimax which follows the hanging underlines other aspects of the horror by showing the lack of respect for the victim even in death: staff and prisoners are eager to forget what has happened and to get on with the business of life. Once again, the relationship between the characters and the audience is hinted at: the audience will soon leave the theatre and go back to their normal lives. Both audience and characters have attended a play, an imaginative version of what actually happens, although neither has seen it. The dramatist controls the reactions of the characters in order to direct the reactions of the audience. Far from being thematically unsubtle or structurally unsound, it is dramatically extremely effective and a deeply moving play. The persistence of the theme in Behan's mind and the strange structure of the play — the unnamed victim, the imagined agony, the drunken camaraderie of Death the Entertainer and the hysterical climax — suggest that the dramatist was attempting to exorcise some horrible recurring nightmare of his own, the twisting of another rope, another neck.

Colbert Kearney. *The Writings of Brendan Behan*
(New York, St. Martin's Press, 1977), pp. 79–80

We are still too close to Behan to measure his full worth, but *Borstal Boy* and *The Quare Fellow* are among the best things in modern Irish writing. His other books are, as they say, of interest. The celebrated *Hostage*, however, gets carried away in its Theatre Workshop version by the music-hall elements which swamp the delicate love story of the soldier and the girl.

The plot of *The Hostage* was derived directly from the kidnapping of a young British soldier in Northern Ireland who was brought down to Dublin and kept prisoner in a Nelson Street brothel. This incident from the same campaign in the fifties in which Sean South and Fergal O'Hanlon were killed, provided the immediate idea. But in Behan's imagination it fused with a story he had been told about from the Troubles. An old IRA man had once described to him how he had waited in ambush for a British troop train. The train came around a bend with the soldiers, some scarcely more than boys, singing happily. The next moment the shooting started. Behan could never forget that image of happy song obliterated by machine-gun fire.

His politics — the politics of machine-gun fire — clashed with his writing, his kind of happy song. He was intensely loyal to the family tradition of Republicanism — he often boasted how his father had snubbed de Valera at his uncle's funeral. But the artist had seen enough of life in jail and out to know that human beings were difficult characters, good enough in themselves, but often led by duty to awful deeds. If *The Quare Fellow* unleashes its jovial scorn on capital punishment, *The Hostage* is equally hard on the Organisation and its pietistic career rebels. Yet in the end it is the mad pride in

the IRA—almost the pride of a St Cyr officer, Sean O'Faolain once observed
—that comes through.

Peter Costello. *The Irish Revolution in Literature*
(Totowa, N.J., Rowman & Littlefield, 1978), p. 295

BOWEN, ELIZABETH (1899–1973)

Miss Bowen certainly does not let *her* inability to describe the passage of time
dictate the theme. Her latest novel, *The House in Paris*, covers a period from
before the birth of an illegitimate child until he has reached the age of nine.
The popular novelist would have described every one of those years, however
dull to the reader the accumulation of trivialities. Miss Bowen has simply left
them out with the merest glance backward; we may believe that she has been
forced to omit, but she has made of her omissions a completely individual
method, she has dramatized ignorance. How with so little known of the
"backward and abysm" can she convey her characters with any clearness? It is
impossible, but her consciousness of that impossibility proves her great value
as a novelist. She makes it the virtue of her characters that they are three parts
mystery; the darkness which hides their past makes the cerebration which we
are allowed to follow the more vivid, as vivid as the exchanges of people
overheard talking on a platform before a train goes out. It is an exquisite
sleight of hand: the egg was in the hat, now it is being removed from the tip of
a robust woman's nose. We must fill in for ourselves what happened between;
the burden of that problem is passed to the reader. To the author remains the
task of making the characters understand each other without our losing the
sense of mystery: they must be able to tell all from a gesture, a whisper,
a written sentence: they have to be endowed with an inhuman intuition as
James's characters were endowed with an inhuman intelligence, and no writer
since James has proved capable of a more cunning evasion. Unable to convey
the passage of time, she has made capital out of the gap in the records; how
can we doubt the existence of a past which these characters can so easily convey to each other?

Graham Greene. *LM*. Oct., 1935, pp. 563–64

Just as Miss [Ivy] Compton-Burnett is essentially an *ear*, Miss Bowen, despite the unquestionably real quality of her dialogue, is above all an *eye*. Her
business is with the complexities of the heart, light with perceptive wonder, or
heavy with some burden of unwelcome knowledge. But always the visual accompaniment of emotion is what gives to that emotion its force and colour,

and so fixes it in our minds. The scene, however fleeting, is always *set*, the characters may not give voice to their thoughts, but a sudden sunbeam, a shape of cloud, a sly look, a door ajar, a smouldering cigarette—these speak for them.

Like Miss Compton-Burnett, then, Elizabeth Bowen exhausts her material, but in pursuit of a very different theme. This—to put it roughly—is the conflict between Innocence and Guilt (using those words in the Christian sense). It is the same theme which fascinated Henry James in so many stories, from *The American* to *The Wings of the Dove* and *The Golden Bowl*. I say "conflict," but "attraction" better describes this most poignant of all situations; and it is in the corruption of guileless persons by those who simultaneously love and hate them that Miss Bowen finds her clue. Innocence is not the prerogative of girls, but although she has portrayed at least two innocent males (Colonel Bent in *The House in Paris*, Major Brutt in *The Death of the Heart*), it is natural that women should be her main target. Intense feeling— perhaps the most intense *personal* feeling he ever knew—kept Henry James at a respectful distance from Daisy Miller, from Milly Theale and Maggie Verver. Miss Bowen takes the analysis a step further, into the dead centre of the personality, exploring that distressful limbo which rings with the faint cries of those whose trust has been betrayed. She is adept at conveying to us the fateful calm in which, at the outset of her novels, the heroine waits for something to happen. And it is always the worst that happens—the humiliation that injures the soul so much more direly than physical rape. Portia (*The Death of the Heart*), Emmeline (*To the North*), Lois (*The Last September*), Karen (*The House in Paris*): these fine-grained creatures—*jeunes filles en fleur* trembling on the brink of "life"—are the descendants of Mignon, but for them fate is less foreseen. They all experience the heartbreak which is not (save in one instance) irreparable, either through the insouciance of philanderers (Portia, Emmeline, Karen), or through the selfish conventionality of their immediate surroundings (Lois). Evil, as a motive, has not in these novels the impersonal, terrifying power, working *from outside*, that it acquires in the work of François Mauriac or Graham Greene; but its precipitation in the alembic set a-boil by a chance encounter is the measure of Miss Bowen's seriousness as a critic of life, and of her importance in the history of English fiction.

Edward Sackville-West. Hor. June, 1946,
pp. 378–80

Miss Bowen inspires confidence: the popular novelist, recently elected a Companion of the British Empire, with a London home in Regent's Park and a family house in County Cork, a sensitive, careful writer whose fineness of feeling is neatly ruffled with wit and laced with snobbery. E. Sackville-West speaks of her cleverness, her fresh and startling style; V. S. Pritchett thinks of her as a poet.

To go on from there is much more difficult. First, there is the well-bred woman of sensibility, moderately elegant, sensitive to differences in class, moralistic about taste, courtesy and fidelity; but there is another Elizabeth Bowen, a sturdy, determined writer, a romantic feminist who serves up a perennial dish: the tragedy of the Fine Girl and the Impossible Man. These are obviously women's books. The surface is urbane and complex, but unusually evasive, as though it were in some kind of secret struggle with the franker soul which has devised these stories of an innocent woman's maltreatment by the reprobate, the mysterious man, the weak or unfaithful lover. This theme, this bold heart throb, perhaps contributes to the popularity of her novels, and no doubt the decorative writing, the slow, oblique presentation of character are peculiarly necessary—without the latter adornments the sophisticated reader might reasonably question the whole matter. The style—Henry James, Virginia Woolf and Katherine Mansfield—is extraordinarily fluent and diverting; one hardly notices, under its spell, the bias of the content, the oppressive tidiness of the values. In these novels, love's prerogatives are real; ambivalence is wicked, a moral and also a social failure, for the conflicts are somehow a part of the class struggle and the author appears to be a conservative of nostalgic temperament.

The opinion, or sentiment, that occurs again and again in Elizabeth Bowen's fiction and which seems to have commanded the labors on her ancestral chronicle, *Bowen's Court*, is that to know *who* you are, to be close to your past, to feel the pride and obligations of family and place, are, if not the most exquisite and difficult attainments, a great source of personal and national virtue. These warm, sustaining emotions are found most frequently in the gentry and upper class; the disloyal, the insincere and unreliable are the homeless, the shapeless nobodys, the complacent, vapid middle class, the mysterious foreigner, the restless, self-loving *arriviste*. . . .

As a sort of subhead to hereditary class, there occurs the abstract notion of Home, representing familiarities, allegiances, duties and affections; under Home there is a particularity, the actual house in which the character lives. From the Home or lack of it, one's house, enriching or blighting the senses and manners, Elizabeth Bowen creates a fantastic environmental psychology, as implacable, materialistic and mortifying as the verdict of a property assessor. For those who pass the test, and it is character that is at stake, the images are loving and generous.

Elizabeth Hardwick. *PR*. Nov., 1949, pp. 1114–16

Miss Bowen has admitted that many of her novels and stories had their genesis in the vision of a particular place—a compelling, insistent vision which seemed, as she says (I am quoting again from the broadcast already referred to), to "draw one into itself." Only at a much later stage would the characters and their actions emerge, as it were, from the middle-distance into the foreground—and note that I say "emerge," for there is no question, with Elizabeth Bowen, of grafting a story arbitrarily upon an imagined scene; the *dramatis personæ*—and the drama itself—are already there, implicit in the landscape of which indeed they form an essential part, though they have yet to be picked out, as it were, by the camera-eye of the novelist's vision. . . .

It is interesting, in this connexion, to learn that Miss Bowen did, in her early youth, intend to be a painter. Another possible source for this pictorial quality in her work—and especially for her sensitivity to light—is the fact that Miss Bowen has spent much of her life in Ireland, where light is an extremely important factor in the landscape, and can, as Miss Bowen herself has said, "determine one's mood, one's day, and one's entire sense of the world." Each of her novels and stories seems, in retrospect, to be lit by its own particular radiance—one remembers, for instance, the ripe, late-summer sunlight of *The Last September*, the bleak, wintry afternoons on the south coast in *The Death of the Heart*, the blanched London moonlight of *Mysterious Kôr*.

This preoccupation with the visible world suggests a further comparison—not with painting, in this case, but with the work of another distinguished woman-novelist of a slightly earlier generation than Miss Bowen's: I mean Virginia Woolf. In Mrs. Woolf's novels one finds the same acute awareness of outside things, the same almost pictorial intensity of vision; yet Mrs. Woolf tended, I think, to become preoccupied with the thing seen *for its own sake*, whereas, in the case of Miss Bowen, the landscape—however important—is never allowed to swamp the figures who inhabit it. . . .

In 1929 appeared Miss Bowen's second novel, *The Last September*, and with it she emerges for the first time as a mature and entirely original novelist. Many of her admirers consider it her best novel, and I am almost inclined to agree; Miss Bowen herself has a particular affection for it, and this is understandable, for *The Last September*, more than any of her other books, seems to have been written from the heart. It has, indeed, a quality which can only be called lyrical: the descriptions of the "Great House" and its demesne linger in the memory with an extraordinary persistence, so that in retrospect the story seems to belong to some far-distant, half-forgotten phase of one's own life.

Jocelyn Brooke. *Elizabeth Bowen* (London, BC/
Longmans, 1952), pp. 5–7, 13

Elizabeth Bowen's fiction at its best is conscious, intelligent, even austere. One can say relatively little about the relationship of her art to that of her contemporaries, for her debts to them are either explicit and self-evident, or so oblique as to be nonexistent. She has always read widely in literature (poetry as well as prose) of all periods, and is fully aware of the debts she owes to past and present for the body of literary experience on which her own art draws. It is pointless to draw attention to the concerns her fiction does *not* dramatize, in domestic and professional life, in social classes other than her own. The world one could construct from all her novels and stories would seem "narrow" indeed, compared with that of almost any other major novelist. As [Sean] O'Faolain notes, for instance, anything "elemental" is usually circumscribed—not for the sake of "elegance" (as he implies) or prudery—but simply because she has always been cognizant of what any writer's language cannot do, and of the limits of her own powers.

It is certainly a measure of Elizabeth Bowen's stature as a novelist that these powers are used unremittingly in the dramatization of events that are important, in giving a unique form of life to propositions that are essential. What is at stake in her fiction one must call, for lack of less pompous terms, a sense of reality: in any world, the intelligent, imaginative person cannot make things of people and survive with integrity, cannot crudely substitute art for life and live with sanity. Yet one must in some way (her novels consider many) make art of life in order to live, for to deny the risk of imagination, inherent in its ability to expose the sensibility, is to abandon one's self to imagination's revenge as chaos and fantasy. This moral proposition her art repeatedly sets; but because these terms, like those of a parable, are extensive, her fiction is rarely repetitious.

To speak of any writer's success "within limits" usually implies denigration, even if one adds that the limits are "deep if not wide." Spatial metaphors used for evaluation too often introduce irrelevant nonsense. What a reader *can* say of Miss Bowen's achievement in the art of the novel can only be said of the greatest: that she has kept going a worthwhile continuity without submitting to nostalgia; that she has attempted honestly to assign importance to the elements of the world she and her readers share, without resorting to clichés of material or attitude; that she has given to her age and to her culture an image of art within which life can go on with relative fullness and sanity. Because she accepts and comprehends the work of those who have preceded her, thus giving her own art a role in a tradition, and because she has adapted what has gone before to a contemporary world, Elizabeth Bowen's novels, at their best, have the quality she herself has called (in a different sense) the most difficult to achieve: relevance.

William Heath. *Elizabeth Bowen: An Introduction to Her Novels* (Madison, Univ. of Wisconsin Pr., 1961), pp. 158–59

This, essentially, is what we find in Elizabeth Bowen's novels: a sense of good and evil blunted by the fact that the two qualities are really aspects of the same thing. We find, also, that the innocent, good person is very often the cause of the evil and guilt that is manifest in his antagonist. Frequently, the good person is drawn to the evil one, for good and evil in this scheme lie within the framework of what are considered "normal" human relationships; and humiliation becomes the sole vehicle of evil action.

This view of human nature places Miss Bowen much closer to the feminine tradition in English literature than it does to the masculine. Like her early nineteenth-century predecessor, she believes in clarity of detail, precision of phrase, and irony of expression, in exploiting the humorous while eliminating the sentimental, in destroying the hypocritical and the vain, in maintaining the traditions of the past against the incursions of the present. Yet she cannot be certain of what is right, as was Jane Austen, and when her doubts do appear, she finds herself close to the assumptions of the twentieth-century novelist: unsure of what success entails, doubtful of what love is, afraid that romance can be easily maimed or destroyed, aware that relationships hang precariously on unknown threads whose clues are mysterious. In brief, she finds herself in the world of Virginia Woolf and Katherine Mansfield.

Nevertheless, Elizabeth Bowen's novels are more a measure of the past than of the present, more a mirror of a still sharply remembered childhood than of a problematical and uncertain adulthood. What she focuses upon in her most brilliant novel, *The Death of the Heart*, she has repeated in her major fiction before and after: the loneliness of the teen-ager; the isolation of the child amid adults who seem to lack feeling, hope, or illusions (one thinks of James's *What Maisie Knew*); the need to reach out and find love, even while one realizes that he cannot successfully "connect," to use E. M. Forster's sense of the word; the impossibility of depending upon anyone except oneself, the necessity of cultivating one's own resources. Obviously, Miss Bowen is an intensely feminine novelist, showing allegiance to authors as different as Fanny Burney, Jane Austen, George Eliot, Virginia Woolf, and Katherine Mansfield, with more than passing reference to Henry James, perhaps the most feline of male writers. Since, therefore, she is concerned with the intangibles of the human personality, she is often inadequately described as a novelist of sensibility.

In *Notes on Writing a Novel*, Miss Bowen defined the object of a novel as the "non-poetic statement of a poetic truth," further qualifying that the "essence of a poetic truth is that no statement of it can be final." By poetic truth, she undoubtedly means those elements within as well as outside people which remain undefinable except in the kind of approximation which language allows the novelist. Thus, in talking about love, human relationships, and "connections" between people, she tries to indicate emotions that lie beneath language; the poetic truth of these feelings must, however, be caught by "non-poetic statements." These are the limitations within which every novelist must work. At her most successful, Miss Bowen has created women who represent the filminess of existence, who convey the daily pains involved in the act of living under conditions which stifle what one really feels. In one way, all of Miss Bowen's novels are concerned with "the death of the heart," which is for her the chief "poetic truth."

Frederick Karl. *The Contemporary English Novel*
(New York, Farrar, Straus and Cudahy, 1962),
pp. 108–9

[Bowen's] heroines want a "modern" sense of living without sacrificing the continuity or stability won by those who consolidated the values of a landed aristocracy with success in commerce. Where novelists of the twenties often disdain the past and industrial society, she sees no future in flights to the Alps or islands off the coast of Africa and little sustenance in elite London coteries of fellow-intensives. Miss Bowen's most thorough critic, William Heath, sees society as a rude limiter of the sensitive will, but her adults actually love-and-hate commercial civilization. She speaks for those adaptable aristocrats who moved the old furniture into the town house and got rich in the advertising business. And she knows what made them leave the farm. Over and over she shows the purposelessness, ineffectiveness, eccentricity, and insanity remaining in the less adaptable. Her heroines want to maintain or even construct continuity, but they do not foresee giving up London for a return to agriculture. (The author's part-time return to Ireland in later life may say something different.) Miss Bowen's best novels show imaginative energy so confined as to express only a small part of itself and ask, is this enough? They show, too, a resentment at situation so great as to make looking for new worlds—or old ones—impossible. But the sensitive will operates in contemporary circumstances *by choice*. To eliminate the taste for Regent's Park or even the rented flat would be to eliminate reality. Miss Bowen's heroines want to stay and complain.

The force behind this scene of an enlarged continuity comes from superimposing upon it a revolutionary scene—the twentieth-century shift in women's aspirations. Two of Miss Bowen's best novels express dissatisfaction with the role of wife and mother; her heroines find themselves inadequate to it and it inadequate to them. Her third important novel tests the possibility of free woman, man's comrade but not dependent. The books are not *about* this problem; they use it as a given condition for restlessness. And Miss Bowen pictures society's part in the conflict not as rules, but as feelings bred in by people whom the heroine respects, likes, and wants to please. Inner and outer merge—and have merged since birth. Women are expected to be sensitive and warm; they are also expected to make correct choices in marriage. Only a woman novelist realized fully the discrepancy in these prescriptions and put so directly the question that gives Miss Bowen a great part of her historical importance: is sensibility practical?

James Hall. *The Lunatic Giant in the Drawing*
Room: The British and American Novel Since 1930
(Bloomington, Indiana Univ. Pr., 1968), pp. 18–19

Perhaps it is wrong to attempt to place authors too carefully—wrong . . . to try to sort them into first, second, third and fourth divisions. But even if wrong it is a natural desire, and I can think of few novelists who more arouse the desire and more successfully frustrate it than Elizabeth Bowen. What, after all, is she up to? Is she merely the highly elegant, dazzlingly intelligent star of the psychological thriller class, or is she a serious contender for a place in the great tradition? And what, anyway, would be the distinctions—of genre, of talent, of purpose?

Her new novel, *Eva Trout*, is certainly a most impressive book. It creates a world so engrossing, so fully imagined in its own terms, that when interrupted while in the middle of reading it I would look up, vaguely, no longer quite sure where I was. This kind of creation is in itself a rare gift: one shared by Iris Murdoch, who also shares some of Miss Bowen's other eccentricities. Their worlds, in fact, are not dissimilar: the background of *Eva Trout* is one of Gothic castles, vicarage gardens, expensive hotels and restaurants, feminine institutions, suicidal homosexual passions. . . .

The theme—corruption, wealth and innocence—is worthy of Henry James, whose name is indeed invoked by the writer herself. . . . As well as the theme, as an additional benefit, there are those marvelous passages of description, for which Elizabeth Bowen is so justly famous: the prose, always elegant even when—or perhaps most when—tortuous, achieves a number of effects that are breathtaking. . . . She is also witty: several of her puns are really most satisfying. . . .

With all these qualities, it would seem grudging to complain. And yet finally one must, because there is something about the book that cheats the very seriousness with which the reader wishes to take it. The ending is symptomatic. It is crude, melodramatic, improbable—despite the careful plotting of the revolver and the constant premonitions of violent death—and it is at once facile and contrived. Worst of all, it makes one look back through the book at things which had seemed solid, and question their substance. . . .

Also, it is a pity that some of the characters should be so insubstantial. . . . Miss Bowen is magnificent when she writes about conspiracy, duplicity and ambiguity, and her achievement—despite her final cutting of the Gordian knot—is extremely impressive. But with the simple, with the world of common sense, she does not cope. Though perhaps in that (for good or for ill, see it as one may) she is merely the closer to Henry James.

Margaret Drabble. *List.* Feb. 13, 1969,
pp. 214, 216

If it is true that every author has only one story to tell and seeks repeatedly for its ideal form, then Miss Bowen's essential narrative begins with the destruction or delimiting of a woman's ideal desires, with her expulsion from a self-defined Eden. She is then confronted with, in Robert Frost's phrase, "what to make of a diminished thing." What she evolves is a mode of living which provides sufficient drama, or occasion to involve and satisfy her lunatic feelings, but which runs no risk of emotional involvement at a level which might entail further disappointment and frustration. This creative activity, which is not engaged in, of course, simply by the protagonist, Miss Bowen terms "art."

A considerable portion of the archetypal Bowen novel is devoted to examining variant forms of this protective artistry. In being defensive and in involving "playing about" to a considerable measure, these created roles remain essentially selfish. In seeking to give an idealistic girl some insight into the whole practice, an older man in *The Death of the Heart* tells her: "What makes you think us wicked is simply our little way of keeping ourselves going. We must live, though you may not see the necessity. In the long run, we may not work out well. We attempt, however, to be more civil and kindly than we feel"(303–4). . . .

A danger to which most of these life-denying art forms are susceptible is the condition of stasis, or to what may be termed "the comfort principle." Once acclimatized to a relatively undemanding role, an individual is content to perpetuate it. Life may not be truly satisfactory, but it is adequate and that suffices. Unlike many fictional protagonists of the last twenty years, Miss Bowen's are not incapacitated by aimlessness; they have a sense of the game they must play in order to survive—and most of them, within its limitations, play it quite well. But their expertise is part of the trouble: it calls for too little effort from them. Several Bowen novels actually commence with their protagonists emotionally more dead than alive.

The Bowen novel begins by attacking youthful emotional ignorance or extravagance, but it concentrates its full force against the twilight security of the pleasure principle. And in this assault Miss Bowen turns the century's mutability to an advantage. Conditions refuse to stay settled for her characters, and sooner or later the unexpected ambushes them. Most of her novels and stories culminate with a moment of shock, a disclosure, or an experience which is sufficiently disturbing to the heroine's emotional being that her formalized role is cracked, increasing the likelihood of a richer, more responsible comportment with life. Miss Bowen stops short of showing the better life, for the achievement of enlarged comprehension and of honest assessments suggests the inevitability of an improved existence—and she will guarantee nothing more.

A. E. Austin. *Elizabeth Bowen*
(New York, Twayne, 1971), pp. 21–22

Elizabeth Bowen is the adult author-narrator in her novels, and she is also still the Anglo-Irish only child, for one grows up but one does not after all outgrow being an only child. Sometimes one senses in her attitudes about her art the feeling that the world of her writing is a new demesne where she can be again, as her ancestors had been, a rather detached, preoccupied Anglo-Irish landlord, where she can make patterns of her adolescent crises for her lonely characters. To go back even further, it is a return to that Eden where fact and fiction are the same, perfect and clear as a bubble. . . .

Miss Bowen seems to have dealt with, if not resolved, her identity confusion by remaining between being Anglo and Irish, only child and grown-up in a form of accommodation achieved in her role as writer. Elizabeth Bowen the novelist was the only adult Elizabeth the only child could trust. As an adult she knew she was lying, and as a child she knew she was being lied to, but the needs of both were fulfilled in the fiction, as before she and her parents had accepted the fictions of their future while her mother was dying of cancer and they all knew it, and as the Anglo-Irish landlords accepted the fiction of the eternality of their country-house world while it was being threatened from all sides. If, especially after the experience of World War II, the death of her husband at Bowen's Court in 1952, and the loss and final destruction of Bowen's Court itself in 1960–63, life came to mean—as it does for one of her child characters—"waiting for something awful to happen and trying to think of something else"; and if her life as a writer was all a lie, a precarious bubble world for a lonely child sick midway between Holyhead and Kingstown, it was a life and a lie that allowed her to say with characteristic toughness and candor, "it is not only our fate but our business to lose innocence, and once we have lost that it is futile to attempt a picnic in Eden." Her limitations were her strengths; she could and did act as though she believed in her own illusions because she had to, but she also knew and accepted them for exactly what they were. This was the achievement of her life and art.

Edwin J. Kenney, Jr. *Elizabeth Bowen*
(Lewisburg, Pa., Bucknell Univ. Pr.,
1975), pp. 37–39

At this close remove, [Elizabeth Bowen's] position is a little obscured by the established reputations of writers who preceded her and by the impact of contemporary writing. But she is a major writer; her name should appear in any responsible list of the ten most important fiction writers in English on this side of the Atlantic in this century. She is to be spoken of in the same breath as Virginia Woolf, on whom much more breath has been expended. She shares much of Virginia Woolf's perception and sensibility: but Elizabeth Bowen's perception and sensibility are more incisive, less confined, more at home in the world as well as in worlds elsewhere.

Her best-known and most widely read novels are probably *The Death of the Heart* (1938) and *The Heat of the Day* (1949); these, for different reasons, have a universal appeal. But if I were to pick the novels essential to illustrate both the quality of her writing and its development, they would be *The Last September* (1929), *The House in Paris* (1935), *A World of Love* (1955), and her last novel, *Eva Trout* (1968). Elizabeth Bowen had an active writing life of half a century. She is what happened after Bloomsbury; she is the link that connects Virginia Woolf with Iris Murdoch and Muriel Spark. She changed with the century in approach and technique without losing her original inimitable voice.

She made the short story particularly her own. In the stories—which were, she said, "a matter of vision rather than of feeling"—she achieved a mastery that gives the best of them a perfection and a unity that the sustained narrative and shifting emphases of a novel do not attempt. It may be that posterity will judge the best of her stories over the novels: and the best Bowen stories, for me, are "The Disinherited," "Summer Night," "Mysterious Kôr," "The Happy Autumn Fields," "Ivy Gripped the Steps," "A Day in the Dark."

She can be compared with Colette in her evocation of colour, texture, flowers, landscape, neighbourhoods, rooms, furniture; but her style, her characteristic and essential rhythms, are utterly her own, as is her evocation of light, space, mood, shifts in time. She suggests—and suggests only, never describes—the fantasies, fears, and manipulations that underlie social behaviour. Her writing is full of tension even when her plots are tenuous. She was herself both a romantic and a woman of the world, and she wrote on, and of, the tightrope between innocence and disillusion. As Spencer Curtis Brown has written, "What she saw was an Eden in the seconds after the apple has been eaten, when Evil was known, immanent and unavoidable but while there was still awareness of what Innocence had been."

Victoria Glendinning. *Elizabeth Bowen*
(New York, Alfred A. Knopf, 1978), pp. xv–xvi

The Last September was the only one of Elizabeth Bowen's works, fiction or non-fiction, written prior to World War II that extensively drew on or reflected the life Bowen had known in Ireland. The preface in which she relates the importance of that life to her as a person and as a writer, however, was not written until 1952. Why is it then that after World War II Bowen felt the need to make explicit her claims to that life, claims that are reiterated in her autobiographical reminiscences—*Bowen's Court* (1942), *Seven Winters* (1942), *The Shelbourne* (1951), and *Afterthoughts* (1962)? *The Heat of the Day*, her first post-war novel, is significantly not only a picture of life in England during the war but a novel divided in its setting between England and Ireland. As reflected in both autobiographical statements and in fictive constructions, it was Bowen's experience of the Second World War that led to her questioning of what was lacking in the culture and life of those persons who were both its victims and its perpetrators. Bowen now struggled with the questions that Yeats and T. S. Eliot had struggled with earlier: how in an age without belief or tradition can the individual live with purpose? how can the individual be kept from a solipsistic working of his selfish will upon the rest of mankind? where is to be found a standard for value judgment other than the pure numbers of the mob? since man's reason does not curb his cruelties, how foster his sympathetic identification with his fellow man?

The similarity in the landscapes which Bowen makes explicit in her autobiographical writings seems to have suggested the importance of the life she had known and loved as a child. The landscape which Bowen emphasizes for that heredity—the ruins surrounding the homes of the Anglo-Irish ascendancy—prefigures the landscape of Bowen's environment, the crumbling world of Europe after two world wars. Thus she began her self-conscious immersion in that world through extensive reading in Ireland's histories and imaginative writings. As if aware of the tenuousness of her claims to that world (Bowen lived in Ireland only as a sojourner after the age of eight), she carefully supports them: she repeatedly cites Proust on the importance and vividness of early memories in determining the art and life of the individual. Such extensive explorations and explicit apologies can be understood only if that life has assumed the larger significance of a symbolic value, and we can understand that symbolic value only by examining the context of the Irish landscape which Bowen saw as making her experience of import for her contemporaries.

> Barbara Brothers. *Mosaic*, special issue on "The
> Irish Tradition in Literature." Spring, 1979,
> pp. 129–30

Elizabeth Bowen has not written a short story as totally impressive as Lawrence's "Odour of Chrysanthemums" or Joyce's "The Dead," but she has produced the most consistent and extensive body of work in this form by any author writing in English. Unlike Joyce's and Lawrence's, her stories are not over-shadowed by her novels. "The Demon Lover" at least rivals *The Heat of the Day* in its imaginative response to war-time London. Yet she has never been fully assimilated to the canon of modern English literature, and this failure of judgment on the critics' part is intimately connected with her mastery of the short story form.

The ultimate and lasting impression which this entirely welcome collection [*The Collected Stories of Elizabeth Bowen*] will create is of Elizabeth Bowen's supremacy in responding to the civilian dimension of the second world war. In contrast to *The Heat of the Day* such wartime stories as "The Happy Autumn Fields" are faultless embodiments of concentrated perception and intelligence. The novels after 1946 fall away, and it is strikingly evident from this present collection how little Miss Bowen wrote in the short story form after that date. The war provided her with the circumstances and symbols in which her art flourished: there was little thereafter to be said.

This centrality of the war in her career reminds us paradoxically of her Irishness; Louis MacNeice and Samuel Beckett (so different in every way) similarly found the war to identify a chasm in their own experience. For Elizabeth Bowen was not Irish in Joyce's sense; she was Anglo-Irish, her identity revolving round a hyphen, a linking minus. Meaning for such a writer involved the acknowledgment of two frequently hostile realities. "Mysterious Kor," one of her finest stories, sets up the remote and deserted city as antithesis to spectral London. This kind of fiction, closer, at times to a self-effacing allegory than to the classic mimetic novel, is illuminated more successfully by reference to Yeatsian masks than to the practice of the Greenes or the Murdochs. . . .

It seems pointless then to insist on Elizabeth Bowen as one who "brilliantly portrayed classically English, reticent, emotionally secretive characters." Her real strength as a writer of fiction lay in the external perspective in which she presented character and the emotional grammar with which she deployed character.

These stories trace the growth of a remarkable writer who transformed uncertainties of origin, and limitations of convention and form, into a body of work uniquely (because tangentially) English. Fiction of the 1920s and 1930s, so often reduced to the *illuminati* of Bloomsbury and Eastwood, or inflated into a tired continuum of Huxleys and Greenes, might be very astutely approached by way of a reassessment of Elizabeth Bowen. This collection provides the very best starting point.

W. J. McCormack. *NS*.
Feb. 13, 1981, pp. 19–20

If there ever was a writer of genius, or near-genius—time will decide—who was heart-cloven and split-minded it is Elizabeth Bowen. Romantic-realist, yearning-sceptic, emotional-intellectual, poetic-pragmatist, objective-subjective, gregarious-detached (though everybody who resides in a typewriter has to be a bit of that), tragi-humorous, consistently declaring herself born and reared Irish, residing mostly in England, writing in the full European tradition: no wonder all her serious work steams with the clash of battle between aspects of life more easy for us to feel than to define. It is evident from the complex weave of her novels that it can have been no more easy for her to intuit the central implication of any one of those conflicts—she never trod an obvious line; nor easy for her to express those intuitions in that felicitous language which, more than any other writer of her generation, she seemed to command as if verbally inspired. But that suggestion of inspiration lifts a warning finger of memory. Once, when one of her guests at Bowen's Court, I inadvertently interrupted her when she was, as I at first thought, tapping away fluently at her desk. She turned to me a forehead spotted with beads of perspiration.

And yet these thematic conflicts in her novels can sometimes seem quite clear in the first couple of pages. It is only a seeming: the sinuosities are waiting in ambush. See, for example, the later of her two masterpieces, *The Death of the Heart*. (The other, and for some readers the even finer novel, was *The Last September*.) If we again open it and read its first two pages to peer through the first wisps of its smoke of battle in search of the central theme, it is there as plain as an opened diary. The "catch" is, as old lovers of this poignant, funny, passionate story will at once remember, that this first open declaration carries with it a complexity of themes and subthemes: among others, Innocence versus Worldliness, Youth versus Maturity, Romantic dreams versus cruel Actuality, Love's illusions and delusions, the frailty of Ideals, the clash of the Generations, Society versus the Individual, and, this above all (it is a constant Bowen theme-song), the lust to do the heroically honest thing when one does not know what the hell the heroically honest thing to do is in a socially "edited" world. On that terrible adjective we may pause for a long time. It throws the clearest and coldest beam of its presiding author's mind, and perhaps her final capital judgment on those cool conventions, those prophylactic artifices, with which, with the best of intentions, every organised society devitalises the instincts of the "unedited" heart. It was very much a theme of the Twenties and Thirties. . . .

How on earth did Elizabeth Bowen succeed in conveying so many emotional variations in so large a cast of characters held together by one consistent discipline—that is, by her personal *manière de voir*, her rational view of life? The answer is too obvious to have any meaning—by her technique. . . .

Hermione Lee, in her indispensable, scholarly, penetrating and sympathetic study of Bowen's work, puts her finger on the tap-root of her author's powers when she says that her "best work was done in the 'subjective,' 'personal' novels and stories of the 1929–1945 period, and not in the more cryptic 'distanced' last work. It is as a subjective writer that she is either praised or denigrated." So, if we airily say that she "does it" by her technique, what we are really saying is that she has some cryptographic, occult way of her own of using images, words, grammar, even punctuation, to communicate in her own personal style her own personal reaction to life. But is there, actually, a recognisable Bowen style, as there is, say, a recognisable Jamesian style? One single style for so complicated, so protean a personality? She has to employ half a dozen styles to suit her varying responses to her various occasions. There are the familiar Domestic Style that we all use, the Hectic Style that uses all of us when we get over-excited, the Sibylline which we whisper over a coffee, glancing about lest the victim overhear, the Impressionist style that is only for the most delicate artist to employ, the Waggish which only a few command, the Moody Style with which we address ourselves when alone and overcome, the Social which requires a great deal of cold, or amused, observed experience, the Grand Duchess which can also be disrespectfully called the Fortnum-and-Mason, or the Bond Street, or the Ritzy Style, unless those places have all been taken over by Lord Forte within the last couple of weeks, or, of all her styles that one which I feel she held most close to her heart, and which, again disrespectfully, I call the Bowen 707 or the Take-Off Style, which lifts her into the skies of her poet's imagination. For her essential nature is not, as has been so often asserted, that of the social critic, but of the visionary [idealist].

Sean O'Faolain. LRB. March 4, 1982, pp. 15–16

Although all Elizabeth Bowen's fiction has a sense of place, an appropriateness of background detail, her short stories differ from her novels in that geographical setting is not always specific. Her characters speak and behave for the most part as one might expect upper-class English or Anglo-Irish characters to speak and behave (exceptions are the young woman on the park bench in "Tears, Idle Tears" and the distraught source of the monologue of "Oh, Madame"), but the reader is not always told whether their dining rooms, sitting rooms, and bedrooms are in England or in Ireland. Even when the setting is specifically English, so alike are the speech and behavior patterns of the Anglo-Irish educated in England and the native upper-class English, and so often do the Anglo-Irish move back and forth between Ireland and England, that the exact background of specific characters may not be determined. Nor does it really matter. In fact, the very sense that on the surface these well-behaved people maintain their composure and relate to one another in the predictable ways prescribed by social class, the very sameness of their manners and chitchat, heightens the contrast between what they appear to be and what they are. It is in this contrast that the power of Elizabeth Bowen's short fiction may be found.

In eight stories, however, published in *Elizabeth Bowen's Irish Stories* (1978), setting is clearly and identifiably Irish. A ninth, "The Happy Autumn Fields," is also included in this volume, despite the fact that its Irish setting is not identified, because (as Victoria Glendinning explains in her brief introduction) the author herself had written in her preface to *The Demon Lover and Other Stories* that it was, for her, "unshakeably County Cork." Given this flimsy basis for selection, a tenth title could have been included: the story-within-story of "The Back Drawing-Room" also has an Irish setting. In these ten tales, Elizabeth Bowen's descriptive passages are more vividly rendered, more painterly in style, more nostalgic in mood, than those usually found in her short fiction. None of the so-called Irish stories, however, is useful in analyzing Elizabeth Bowen's impressions of or attitudes toward Ireland. For these the reader must turn to other sources: her only Irish novel, *The Last September*; her two histories, *Bowen's Court* (1942) and *The Shelbourne: A Centre of Dublin Life for More Than a Century* (1951); her essays, reviews, and autobiographical writings.

Janet Egleson Dunleavy. In James F. Kilroy, ed.,
The Irish Short Story: A Critical History (Boston,
Twayne, 1984), p. 157

BOYLE, PATRICK (1905–1982)

To come upon a sex novel laid in Ireland, which has passed through Irish censorship on its way from London (where it was originally published), is to wonder if the bishops are getting careless—and if an unsuppressed novel has a chance. Why should Patrick Boyle be denied, in this respect, the advantages once accorded Joyce? Then, reading on—and *Like Any Other Man* is very much a book that drives the reader right through to the end—one realizes that other matters must be taken into account. This is a retelling, in a modern idiom, of the Samson and Delilah story; by taking a pagan theme that fits nicely into biblical sanction, the author has been able to smuggle an outrageously funny, frank, and terrifying book into his own country. Patrick Boyle is the best thing that has happened to literary Ireland in a long time.

Because he relates the modern obsession with sex to a vanishing sense of guilt, he is also something of an out-of-season Jansenist, a man who can make sin still seem Original. This is a disturbing novel, dealing with the shattering calamity of a man who is destroyed by his own strength, and by implication it challenges much of the new theology, with its emphasis on secular redemption. I don't mean to suggest that the author is grinding an axe for religion. There is not a priest in the book, and if anything Boyle sees the church as having lost its hold on the individual sinner. He is dealing here with what might properly be called the Masculine Mystique, the prideful obtuseness by which some modern Celts (Behan? Dylan Thomas?) fulfill their natures, and shatter their careers, through alcohol, sex and—in the protagonist at hand—the lifting of heavy weights.

This, at least, would seem to be the case with James Simpson (Samson), the branch manager of a small-town bank in western Ireland, and playboy extraordinary. Given to drink and carnality, Simpson meets Delia (Delilah) Clifden, a local barmaid who is more than willing to share her couch with him. Simpson's vulnerability is lust and, knowing this, Delia urges him on to self-destruction. At one point, while he sleeps off a drunken orgy, she snips a lock of his hair. When he suffers a series of retinal hemorrhages and is advised by his doctor to "go easy," she dares him to make love to her.

Boyle is obviously not updating the biblical tale solely as a literary exercise. Yet, what else he may be trying to do is not readily apparent. Is this modern Samson revolting against an outdated society, typified here by the archaic workings of the Irish banking system? Does his wild, randy nature symbolize the paganism that lies beneath the surface of Irish life, as it once antedated Christian Ireland? Is Simpson's failure the failure of a church that is no longer relevant to personal sin? He talks repeatedly of going to confession, but instead he trots from doctor to doctor getting pumped full of calcium as he seeks a physical cure for a spiritual disease. Simpson is doomed because he cannot act on the truth of his condition without a belief in something greater than himself. In this sense he is "like any other man."

David Dempsey. *Sat.* July 20, 1968, p. 25

Whereas [Benedict] Kiely has been writing and publishing steadily since the late 1940s, Patrick Boyle ceased writing at one stage and did not, by his own account, take up the pen for seventeen years. His precipitous success in the mid-1960s, aided immensely by the interest Grove Press in the United States has shown in his work, has been recognised as something of a literary phenomenon. On the strength (and I use the word advisedly) of one novel, *Like Any Other Man* (1966), and two volumes of stories, *At Night All Cats Are Grey* (1966) and *All Looks Yellow to the Jaundiced Eye* (1969), Boyle has been acknowledged as a brash and original talent by readers whose resolve has already been stiffened by such writers as J. P. Donleavy, Joseph Heller and Philip Roth. In his work the naturalistic theme of blight has been neatly wedded to a black comedy that has found a ready American audience. . . .

Boyle is fascinated by the absurd foibles of the countrymen and country townsmen of Donegal, Derry and beyond, and these he transcribes with a perfect ear for colloquialisms and with a surface realism that both borders on caricature and tickles the reader with the shock of recognition. His portrayal of dodgers, malingerers and grafters is made even funnier because the narrator of the story is very often one of the boys himself whose perceptions have the ringing truthfulness of the insider. . . .

It ought to be clear just how conventional a moralist Patrick Boyle is in his stories. But I think the ostensible moral issues are a pretext and that something more subversive and perhaps only half-conscious is going on in his fiction. To begin with, Boyle's originality lies in the way he intensifies foibles into crime and sin, and regret and guilt into penance. On occasions sin and crime even generate a kind of mock-apocalypse which can be very funny. "Suburban Idyll," for example, in setting up Mr. Hunter's death, has concealed references to the apocalyptic cargo-cults of dark Melanesia. Hunter teases his wife with baroque tales of people jettisoning their worldly goods in preparation for Doomsday, a recurring motif in cargo-cults. Unbeknown to either, Mr. Hunter is himself about to savour the fruits of Apocalypse. Even in such a trivial story as "Home Again, Home Again, Jiggety-Jig," Boyle can make the sight of a drunk father enmeshed in the bedclothes conjure up an apocalyptic vision. In more serious stories, however, the mock-apocalyptic inclination has the more dubious result of blurring Boyle's moral intent. There is, in such a story as "Meles Vulgaris," a mock-apocalyptic approach difficult to distinguish from parody, though nothing else in the story suggests that parody is intended.

Just as sin and crime are intensified into mock-apocalypse, so punishment and penance are intensified into mock-purgatory. Again, "Meles Vulgaris" is a useful example, for the husband's tortured re-enactment of the apocalyptic badger-baiting is a kind of purgatory. The question arises here too as to what is being achieved by parodic hyperbole and supercharged realism when they accompany emotional imprecision. Boyle's serious stories, while often large achievements, tend unintentionally to mock and thereby devalue the heroism from which Boyle means his chief characters unwisely to depart. This is one sense in which we might call his fiction mock-heroic. In the darkly comic stories he intentionally mocks the mean and lowly who absurdly aspire to a warped and bar-room sense of heroism. This is the other more conscious and successful sense in which his work is mock-heroic. Heroics of the second kind lie in ample readiness for the satirist in Ireland's pub life and rampant anecdotage and have been tapped by fiction writers from Carleton through Lynn Doyle to Kiely and in fact, as Vivian Mercier has shown, by all kinds of Irish writers for as long as there has been Irish literature.

John Wilson Foster. *Forces and Themes in Ulster Fiction* (Dublin, Gill & Macmillan, 1974), pp. 100–1, 106–7

Sometimes—in moments of bleakness—it seems as though the main teams of modern fiction writers are the Moralists and the Amoralists. If this is so, then Patrick Boyle is a solid and creditable full-back for the first team. Beyond its humour and its sophisticated representationalism, *A View from Calvary* aims to lay bare the movements of the will; and, especially, that fatal lethargy, born so often from the self-imposed constraint of fear of social opinion, which leads to moral failure and human pain.

This is, of course, the traditional business of fiction: still a large and pleasant field to till. And Mr. Boyle is an impressively competent husbandman. In those stories where he spreads himself, the narrative posture demanded of moral fiction—a more or less explicit authorial judgment—is never simplistic: it aims for, and sometimes reaches, that tough acceptance of ambivalence which passes from moral fiction to enter upon the moral life itself. The smaller squibs, really only elaborate jokes, are supported by this broader vision in much the same way that popular jokes are supported by the strength of popular culture.

This said, it must be added that Mr. Boyle has a lot of growing still to do as a writer. He is saddled with that peculiar temptation which goes along with being an Irishman. Irishism is by no means a played-out literary vein; and though, to everyone's relief, he largely escapes this comfortable vocation, he does have a weakness for Irish Humour.

Mr. Boyle's biggest difficulty is the technical problem of writing moral fiction about people who are not morally articulate. Indeed, this can be seen as very much the problem which created *Ulysses* and the whole modernist movement in fiction: to step outside the enclave of the self-conscious bourgeoisie, one must find new non-representational modes to represent those states which "characters" cannot plausibly articulate in well-rounded phrases. Every time one of Mr. Boyle's characters faces the camera, as it were, the living, energetic dialogue which is his strongest asset performs a belly-flop.

Nick Totton. *Spec.* Aug. 21, 1976, p. 23

Patrick Boyle might appropriately be considered the last of the Old Guard, for his stories only began to appear as late as 1965 when the author was sixty years old. Nevertheless, the stories really look back to O'Faolain and particularly to O'Connor in their range of tone, in their variety of subject, and in their thoroughly dramatized and distanced control.

Born in 1905 in County Antrim, Boyle was more a contemporary of O'Flaherty, O'Connor, and O'Faolain than of White, Trevor, or Plunkett. However, most of his adult life he was not a writer. He worked for forty-five years in the Ulster Bank, and it was only after his retirement that he seriously and vigorously turned to writing. In 1965 he submitted pseudonymously fourteen stories to a contest sponsored by the *Irish Times*, and de Vere White later wrote, "When I came to look at the entries I found an extraordinary thing. The first, second, fourth, fifth had all been written by the one man, Patrick Boyle." As the judges of the contest were White, Mary Lavin, and Frank O'Connor, Boyle may certainly be said to have been launched with the approbation of the Old Guard.

In 1966 Boyle published a novel and followed it by three collections of stories: *At Night All Cats Are Grey*, also in 1966; *All Looks Yellow to the Jaundiced Eye* in 1969; and *A View from Calvary* in 1976. These three collections are remarkable for their mature accomplishment and their generally consistent excellence. Indeed, it is difficult to single out Boyle's best work, but such an attempt does bring a rather startled awareness of Boyle's diversity. One finds satiric farce in "Pastorale" or "In Adversity Be Ye Steadfast." Or something that borders on eccentric fantasy in "Dialogue." Or blackish comedy in "Interlude" and "Shaybo." Or rueful stories of childhood in "Age, I Do Abhor Thee"; of adolescence in "Sally"; of middle age in "The Rule of Three." The writing is ever fluent and sometimes admirable—see the comic description of singing in "Interlude" or the long, serious description of piano playing in "A View from Calvary." There is a gallery of quickly caught, memorable character types and stereotypes.

Boyle, of course, had his failures and his faults. The novella, "A View from Calvary," is too leisurely and too long; and "All Looks Yellow to the Jaundiced Eye" is too silly. But he has so many successes and so many excellences that he needed only to have started earlier to loom as large in importance as his most distinguished contemporaries.

Robert Hogan. In James F. Kilroy, ed., *The Irish Short Story: A Critical History* (Boston, Twayne, 1984), pp. 188–89

BOYLE, WILLIAM (1853–1922)

One wonders if justice has been done Mr. William Boyle. If it has not it is because he is a playwright of one play, *The Building Fund* (1905). He has written three other plays that count, *The Eloquent Dempsey* (1906), *The Mineral*

Workers (1906), and *Family Failings* (1912), but *The Building Fund* is of a higher power than any of these. *Family Failings*, produced in the spring of 1912, I have not read, but according to all accounts it does not mark any advance upon *The Mineral Workers* or *The Eloquent Dempsey*. *The Mineral Workers*, essentially a propagandist play, and *The Eloquent Dempsey*, essentially a satire, are hardly, even in intention, of the first order of seriousness in art. There are characters in these two plays faithful to human nature, and faithful to the ways of eastern Galway, where the scenes of all of the plays of Mr. Boyle are laid. But there are so many other characters in them that are either caricatures or "stock" that, funny as the plays seem upon the stage, they do not impress the deliberate judgment as real. The many characters of *The Mineral Workers* and its several motives are too much for Mr. Boyle; he loses his grip and the play falls to pieces. *The Eloquent Dempsey* suffers from the caricaturing of its characters, and its action degenerates into unbelievable farce almost on the curtain-rise. *The Building Fund*, however, is serious and true, and at the same time just as full of wit and just as biting in satire and just as effective on the stage as *The Eloquent Dempsey*. Its characterization is recognized as distinctive and authentic even on reading. Revealed through the almost perfect work of the players trusted with its presentation by the Abbey Theatre on their American tour of 1911–12, it seemed even more than distinctive and authentic, it seemed inspired by profound insight.

The play is not any more complimentary to Catholic Galway than *The Drone* of Mr. [Rutherford] Mayne is complimentary to Protestant Down, but it is seldom that comedy is complimentary to human nature, and *The Building Fund* is comedy. That is, it is comedy as Ibsen sees drama, or character farce as Coleridge defines it. It is, in the Greek sense, perhaps even tragedy; certainly, it is tragedy from the standpoint of Shan and Sheila, for circumstances certainly get the better of them. From Mrs. Grogan's standpoint it is comedy, for she, through her will, even though she is now dead, has got the better of circumstances as represented by the plotting of her son and granddaughter. If we look at *The Building Fund* from the standpoint of Shan and Sheila, but without sympathy for them, it is only character farce, for although circumstances get the better of them, we do not then care for them, and a play in which characters are overwhelmed by fate, but in which our sympathy is not with them, is, if we follow Coleridge, really farce. Whatever *The Building Fund* is, its characterization is admirable. Some might say its men and women approximate to types, that Mrs. Grogan is the avaricious old woman, Shan the sanctimonious miser, Sheila the sly minx, Michael the benevolent old man, and Dan the gay blade. Types or not, you will find all of them in Ireland, and all of them wherever human nature is human nature.

Cornelius Weygandt. *Irish Plays and Playwrights*
(Boston and New York, Houghton Mifflin, 1913),
pp. 208–11

The Building Fund is the only work [of William Boyle] which calls for more than passing comment. It was written out of that knowledge of the Louth peasantry which was evident in the author long before he was attracted to the theatre by the first London visit of the Irish Players. While *The Eloquent Dempsey* and *Family Failing* are commonplace caricature, farcical to an extreme only found in a few of Lady Gregory's latest comedies, *The Building Fund* is a sincere picture of rural manners. It relates how Mrs. Grogan, a grasping old woman, succeeds in defeating her equally selfish son and grand-daughter, on the pretext of performing an act of charity. When two farmers call to ask for her contribution to the building fund of the new church, she and her son drive them away empty-handed. But she has conceived a plan whereby the greedy calculations of Shan and Sheila will come to nought, even when her much-wished-for death takes place. When the farmers return on another occasion, she contributes to their collection by making a will leaving her money to the church. The plot is of the slightest, yet, so excellent is the characterization of the various types, and so skillfully is the dialogue woven, that the play holds the audience and the reader alike.

Technically the later plays are perhaps more perfect in their conformity to the accepted conventions of the "well-written" comedy. Surprises and stage effects are plentiful in the comedy of Jeremiah Dempsey, the opportunist politician whose eloquence betrays him, and in *The Mineral Workers*, with its account of the difficulties experienced by an Irish-American when he tries to arouse the energies and enterprise of a community whose soil is rich in mineral qualities. Yet neither can be compared to that first play through which one feels the throb of real life, and hears the voices of authentic human beings. The variety of characters and motives is beyond the dramatist's control in *The Mineral Workers*, while the absence of every dramatic element renders *Family Failing* as tiresome as its artificiality is incredible. The degradation of a powerful theme was never more striking than in this dull farce, which might have been a great comedy. In the hands of a writer who could exploit the dramatic quality of the theme, — the demoralizing effect of laziness and improvidence upon all who are subjected to their influence, — a fine play would have resulted. As it is we must conclude that William Boyle had given his best when the early enthusiasm of the Fay's organization stirred him to write *The Building Fund*.

Ernest A. Boyd. *The Contemporary Drama of Ireland* (Boston, Little, Brown, 1917), pp. 139–40

The failure of William Boyle as a dramatist is remarkable when all the advantages at his disposal are taken into consideration. He had shown that he could write short stories of Irish life with grace and some artistic accomplishment; his plays prove him to be a dramatic technician without superior in the range of Irish dramatists; and he had the great advantage of living for long periods in different parts of the country in his capacity of Government official. He seemed, however, to be unable to blend all these when he came to write a play. The stage tricks are all used, but the characters are never quite life-like enough to be convincing, and nowhere does the dialogue reach above the mediocre. Perhaps it is that Boyle had known too many places to become thoroughly impregnated with the spirit and the speech of any one of them, and perhaps, also, his work as a Revenue Officer tended to make him suspect to the people so that they never expanded in his presence. He was not a young man when he came to write plays, being considerably older than any other of the earlier Irish dramatists, with the possible exception of the four founders of the Literary Theatre. He was, therefore, of an earlier tradition, which had accepted Boucicault, and his familiarity with the English theatre of the eighteen-nineties is obvious in all his plays. It was probably his patriotic leanings, in addition to his knowledge of the stage, which prompted him to write plays for the Irish rather than the English Theatre. Whatever be his shortcomings he certainly fulfilled the early requirements of the Abbey Theatre by providing it with those vehicles of amusement which taxed nothing more than the power of laughter.

Andrew E. Malone. *The Irish Drama* (London,
Constable, 1929), pp. 234–35

If [Lennox] Robinson too easily forgives all his characters for their innocent follies, William Boyle, the civil servant and part-time writer who was one of the earliest playwrights for the Abbey Theatre, wrote several popular comedies in which the central character carries one dominating trait to excess, for which comic transgression he is ridiculed and corrected. In his first and most promising work, *The Eloquent Dempsey* (1906), Boyle began with a colorful hero who is a potential comic rogue, but then he proceeded to sentimentalize and reform him. Jeremiah Dempsey is an ambitious publican, grocer, and county councillor whose "eloquence" is his dissembling habit of telling people what he thinks they want to hear in his attempt to sell more whiskey and get reelected to public office. As a result he is invariably on the verge of making everyone very happy or very furious. Although there are many comical possibilities in this situation, they are only partially fulfilled. And once more it is a wise and good woman who diverts the direction of the play from comedy to common sense. It is Dempsey's devoted wife who sees through his trickery and even plots to expose him in order to save him, and it is she who reveals the soft spot that takes the bite out of the laughter, especially in one of her explicit speeches that assures us once again that life is worth living. . . . [Her] deadly touch of tenderness gives the comic game away and the rascal proves to be so harmless that a barbarous possibility is shifted to a benign reality. There is no room for a Pelagian heresy in this promise of a compensating heaven for the wayward Dempsey. Virtue must triumph when, as a result of his wife's well-intentioned scheming, Dempsey is defeated in the election and retires from public life to live quietly and happily on a farm with his dear wife. Like Robinson, Boyle couldn't resist softening and oversimplifying his comic figures. His play is a type of transparent and tractable comedy that illustrates a mild form of Bergsonian automatism that is too readily curable. Above all, Boyle lacked an ironic and sustaining point of view, perhaps something that approximated the comic irony of an O'Casey in his ambivalent attitude toward the rascally "Captain" Boyle and Joxer Daly who are at the same time seen as irrepressible and reprehensible, or heretically comic and therefore beyond any hope of tender reformation.

Another indication of Boyle's limitations can be illustrated in his *Family Failing* (1912), in which the single flaw of family laziness becomes the main source of comic frailty and redemption. Dominic and Joe, the slothful or "Donothing Donnellys," have allowed their farm to fall into heavy debt and near ruin, until their Uncle Robert returns from America with the hint that he might bail them out with his reputed great wealth. The moralizing Robert is actually penniless, but his sermons on the glory of the work ethic, plus his pretended promise of money, suddenly inspire Dominic to work hard for the first time in his life and save the farm as well as himself in yet another benign transformation, and thus the "family failing" is conquered. It is of course a manufactured ending, and a gross oversimplification of life and comedy.

David Krause. *The Profane Book of Irish Comedy*
(Ithaca, N.Y., Cornell Univ. Pr., 1982), pp. 202–3

BULLOCK, SHAN F. (1865–1935)

We have received for review a copy of a new novel, *Hetty*, by the most sincere of Irish novelists, Shan Bullock. No Irish story-teller is so free from personal bias, exaggeration, party or political feeling. He is in love with Irish life and character, seeing all its weakness and defects, but unable to love any people better. The liking he has he communicates. Most story-tellers choose exceptional people, and exceptional incidents to excite attention, keying life up for popularity purposes as the musician tunes up his instruments to concert pitch, or the artist squeezes out the raw colours from his tubes onto the canvas when he tries to paint what is called the "Picture of the Year." We were much struck lately in reading *The Old Wives Tale*, by Arnold Bennett, one of the most distinguished of English novelists, to find how much there was to like and love in the story of most common-place people in the most common-place surroundings doing the most common-place things. When the life history of any person is told faithfully and minutely and sincerely it wants no tragic events, no Titanic passions, no heroic circumstance to make it as moving as tragedy, as exciting as passion, as enthralling as romance. This faculty of following patiently and affectionately the lives of ordinary people and of communicating his own interest Shan Bullock has in full measure. He knows his Ulster well. His characters are distinguished clearly from each other, and are yet all recognisably human, which means that the reader recognises they are all part of his own being. There is really only one human being in the world of whom we individuals manifest in ourselves little portions, fractions, flashes, and hints. That great human being implicit in every one of us is the life breathed into man by God, and we none of us recognise how great and manifold it is, what a being of multitudinous desires and affections it is. The storytellers of the world, by the varied characters they unfold, open to us some vistas of our own being, the heights we may attain, the depths we may sink to, and the sweetness there is in the normal life. We can only say of Shan Bullock's story that we felt his Hetty, his Maurice, his Mark, and his Rhona as part of our own being, and it made the thought of the life on an Ulster farm more real to us. It is a good story, one of Shan Bullock's best, and how good that is readers of *Dan the Dollar* know. The publishers are T. Werner Laurie, Clifford's Inn, London. The sole credit for such a book otherwise attaches to Ireland. [Aug. 19, 1911]

George William Russell (A.E.). *Selections from the Contributions to "The Irish Homestead,"* Vol. II, Henry Summerfield, ed. (Atlantic Highlands, N.J., Humanities Press, 1978), pp. 866–67

In a long series of novels, [Shan F. Bullock] studied various phases of the countryside in which he was brought up: the region whose centre is Enniskillen and which lies about the maze of land and lake-water that is called Upper Lough Erne. This Ulster is remote in every way from the industrial area centring in Belfast; its life is as purely agricultural as that of any region in the Free State; and what Shan Bullock describes is the existence of strong farmers, of their sons, of the men who come back changed from the United States to their old homes. He has no passion for the land, and seems conscious more of the hardships than the pleasures in a farmer's life; he realizes the permanent estrangement between the two camps—for in Fermanagh Protestant and the Catholic are equal in numbers—yet has no zeal of partisanship. His whole work is sombre in tone, a blackavised view of the life, and more specially of the climate; but the writing has a sinewy strength and a fine sincerity, and everywhere in it is conveyed the strong attachment of a man to his home and his people that he sprang from, and an admiration for their rough-hewn endurance. One story of schoolboy life, *The Cubs*, deserves to be compared with the several studies of Catholic schooldays presented to us by Joyce, by Conal O'Riordan (in *Adam of Dublin*), by Eimar O'Duffy in *The Wasted Island*, and others. But perhaps Shan Bullock's best work is in *The Loughsiders*, in which he skilfully enhances the quality of the people who had never stirred from their parish, by settling down among them a much travelled man. None of his novels had wide popularity, but in the close of his life he received the recognition of being chosen by the most distinguished of his fellow-workers to a seat in the Irish Academy.

Stephen Gwynn. Irish Literature and Drama in the English Language: A Short History (Thomas Nelson & Sons, 1936), p. 203

Shan F. Bullock the Fermanagh novelist was separated both by temperament and background from the last echoes of the land struggle heard in [Seamus O'Kelly's] *Wet Clay*, and from the fierce pride of possession going before a fall that Francis MacManus has mirrored in *This House Was Mine*. . . . His life and his work with the exception of one novel published when he was almost sixty years of age belong to the period before the First World War. But since that novel *The Loughsiders* is one of the best novels that rural Ireland has inspired or provoked no comment on the relation of the land to the novel in modern Ireland would be satisfactory if it did not take Bullock into account.

William Carleton belonged to the cabins, and the people of his best books are the ancestors of the poor Catholics who were shut out by the wall of Protestant ascendancy from any intimate part in Bullock's childhood. The Fermanagh novelist belonged to the solid world of the fairly prosperous Protestant farmer, and here and there through the twenty-two books that he wrote he saw that world as radiantly distinct as an Orange lily in a green garden. His book *By Thrasna River*, published in 1895, was one of those vivid records of normal life on a farm that have been written about rural England but very seldom about rural Ireland. The closest parallel in contemporary writing would be in Adrian Bell's trilogy: *The Cherry Tree, Silver Ley,* and *Corduroy*. In the novel *Dan the Dollar* he was the first and possibly the only Irish writer to realise for Ireland and for Europe the social significance of what the people of the Irish countryside called the "returned American."

For Sir Horace Plunkett, Bullock's writings were important primarily because of their carefully objective description of men and women living on the land, because of the equally objective account given in an autobiographical volume *After Sixty Years* of the way in which within the lifetime of Bullock and Plunkett the power had drained out of the landlord's big house. That was what Bullock had seen. He described equally well what he felt in his own soul: love for the land, for the locality, for the people and their quiet lives and, at the same time, the haunting desire to cross the mountain into a bigger and busier world. He left the Crom country against the wishes of his father and found himself a job as a clerk in London. . . .

Bullock's case was not, though, the ordinary case of flight from the land, for even if he left the land by Thrasna River to work in an office in London, he had, deep down in his soul, the desire to write something about the people and places he loved. Again and again in his early work he syllables the enchanted names, changing them and altering as a loving parent might do with the name of a child, drawing in the soul the map of his own hallowed locality. . . .

In spite of this nostalgia and the genuine love that it indicated, his last and his best novel, and the only one of his novels that directly concerns us here, is a hard book about a dying world, about a countryside and a mentality where youth is resented. The hardness may have been meant by Bullock as a reproach to his own Protestant people, for he had always a charitable weakness for attributing to the Catholic peasant a detachment from material things that other Irish writers who dealt exclusively with the Catholic peasant have been unable to discover. In the character of Richard Jebb in *The Loughsiders* he may have been giving flesh to all the accusations of barren and unfruitful hardness that could be levelled against the Ulster Protestant. . . .

The Loughsiders is Bullock's best novel because he was the sort of artist who never stopped learning and never allowed the practice of his art to degenerate into the repetition of a few tricks. The people in the novel move distinctly against their background but never melt into it as they do in some of his earlier novels. He sees deeper than ever before into the souls of his characters.

Benedict Kiely. *Modern Irish Fiction: A Critique*
(Dublin, Golden Eagle Books, 1950), pp. 29–31

[T]hough he lived most of his adult life in England, [Shan F. Bullock] was rooted emotionally to the countryside of his boyhood and youth. He is, in effect, the regional writer *par excellence*; all his deepest work is inspired by his own people. Though he lived the life of a London civil servant, his imagination remained focused on his native province. He produced novel after novel, none of them shoddy and most of them more than competent, and nobody seemed to regard his writing as of any significance. . . .

The result was that until *Dan the Dollar* (1906) appeared his novels were almost entirely ignored by the Irish Press (and *Dan the Dollar* sold only 150 copies in Ireland). But Bullock continued to write about his native people till the day he died, remaining scrupulously faithful to his conception of life; he was completely neglected for his efforts, and it is only now that his work is receiving any recognition at all.

In face of the treatment he received during his lifetime, it is tempting to overvalue Bullock's achievement now by way of compensation. There is no doubt that he is an attractive writer, a writer who took his art seriously: indeed, he perhaps took it too seriously. But it cannot justly be claimed that he was a writer of genius. Certainly he had talent and taste and a gift for writing good descriptive prose and lively dialogue. But his mind does not seem to have been particularly interesting or vigorous; at any rate, the autobiography he wrote at the end of his life, *After Sixty Years*, is disappointingly impersonal and dull.

In its opening sentence, however, it does, I think, reveal the source of Bullock's strength as a novelist. "It is surely a great thing to be born in an island: great in actual fact, in effects of many kinds, and chiefest in a long and crowded memory." His memory was certainly long and crowded, and he relied on it from the time he published *The Awkward Squads*, in 1893, till the appearance of his last novel, *The Loughsiders*, in 1924. His first book, *The Awkward Squads*, consists of four stories, each of them dealing with the political and social tensions of life in Cavan and Fermanagh, tensions which Bullock observes with a tolerant and humorous eye. Behind the tolerance and the humour, however, there is a streak of bitterness: indeed, lacking this streak, the four tales would have been negligible as art. And they are not negligible. The shortest and best of them, "A State Official," which concerns the fate of a village cobbler whose sense of kindliness makes him a traitor to "the cause," resembles Tchekov in conception and mood.

Bullock's best novels are probably *The Squireen* (1903), *Dan the Dollar* (1906), and *The Loughsiders* (1924). *The Loughsiders* exemplifies his mature work. It is the story of a grasping and stiff-necked farmer, Richard Jebb, and his interferences in the affairs of his neighbours, the Nixons, a family whose head is a tippler and the mother a kleptomaniac. An unpleasant story about rather unpleasant people, Bullock in it never appears to be fully aware of just how unpleasant his characters really are. He appears to be overready to forgive them, merely because they are victims of an unfavourable environment; and he suggests that the Jebbs and the Nixons are bound to be dull, unperceptive people because their normal existence would not allow them to be otherwise. Their chief escape from dreariness is by means of talk—talk which Bullock faithfully reproduces, and obviously delights in. . . .

To read Bullock is to be reminded of Hardy, particularly the earlier Hardy; for both novelists have the same lyrical touch, the same delight in a homely phrase; but Bullock's novels are thin and lumpy compared with Hardy's, lacking in both vigour and colour; they give the impression of being written by a man who had no firm grasp on life, who was unsure not only of himself but of his art. He was a genuine writer, but his art lacks character and compulsion.

John Boyd. In Sam Hanna Bell, ed., *The Arts In Ulster: A Symposium* (London, Harrap, 1951), pp. 106–9

Shan F. Bullock set his work in the Erne country in Co. Fermanagh, a landscape variable enough to afford him imagery both of fertility and of barren failure. Though he recollected this world when he was "in city pent," office-bound in London like Lamb before him, his novels are not particularly nostalgic or sentimental, partly because of their curious edge of irony, partly because his characters are not, as John Boyd has rightly remarked, especially likeable. In company with the other rural naturalists, he packs his narratives with documentary information about local customs. These customs belong to the last century, but Bullock's canon bridges the nineteenth and the twentieth centuries; *The Loughsiders* (1924), for example, his last novel, introduces modern mechanisation into the landscape but at the same time features the Big House. According to Benedict Kiely, "Bullock was the last Irish writer to see the Big House functioning efficiently."

Bullock's primary theme, as it is developed in three novels—*The Squireen* (1903), *Dan the Dollar* (1906) and *The Loughsiders* (1924), the last generally accounted his best—has the appearance of tragedy, but the novels are really a combination of romantic melodrama and local naturalism. The theme can be simply stated. The chief character, through arrogance, insentience and a penchant for intrigue, manages to alienate the spirit of the land and the people around him. Against the current of what we sense is his hidden, better self, he is guilty of hubris and at the novel's end must be punished for it. The careers of the eponymous heroes of *The Squireen* and *Dan the Dollar* describe therefore a tragic curve, beginning in modesty or difficulty, reaching a high point of good fortune before plummeting to ruin or death. For Bullock, hubris is a tendency in the Protestant character whereas its opposite—idleness and passive endurance—is a Catholic vice; both result in the land's spiritual or material bounty being lost or perverted. However, because Bullock's characters do not rise much above caricature, his work falls far short of tragedy and is at best naturalistic folk allegory. . . .

It is difficult to gauge Bullock's own attitude towards the hubristic characters, for there is a vein of mockery and irony running through his work. In the case of Richard Jebb, for example, it is hard to know whether emotion (even loneliness) or avarice is his chief motive in asking Rachel for her hand; and are we to find offensive his toadying behaviour with the Master of the Big House? Are Bullock's sympathies with the squireen? And does he realise that Dan Ruddy is the most likeable character in *Dan the Dollar*? Perhaps such confusions reflect Bullock's own kind of "hubris," for like his hubristic characters he became separated from the land and saw his loughsiders through the eyes of an outsider. But perhaps they are the price local naturalists pay for faithfully creating an allegorical world in which they cannot totally participate and which is not in any case a particularly lovely or pleasant world. The truth is that none of the local naturalists create wholly sympathetic characters, though Bullock's are probably the least likeable.

John Wilson Foster. *Forces and Themes in Ulster
Fiction* (Dublin, Gill & Macmillan, 1974),
pp. 29–30, 36

CAMPBELL, JOSEPH (1879–1944)

Another dramatist from the North and of promise is Mr. Joseph Campbell. His *Judgment* is of the northwest, however, the whole breadth of Ulster between its Donegal mountains and the Belfast of [St. John Ervine's] *Mixed Marriage*; and it is of the country, not of the city; and of an Ireland wholly Catholic, not of an Ireland of Protestant and Catholic at war over religion. There are moments of real drama in *Judgment*, but no such inevitable rise to climax as in *Mixed Marriage*. Its undoubted power is in the feeling underlying it, in its characterization, and in its style. Mr. Campbell was already known when his play was put on at the Abbey Theatre, April 15, 1912, as the author of *The Mountainy Singer* (1909), a volume of freshly felt and singing verse; and of *Mearing Stones* (1911), little prose records of things seen and of moods felt in a corner of Donegal. Many a striking phrase of *Judgment*, indeed, is already written down in the paragraphs of *Mearing Stones* as actual talk heard in the roads, and several of the situations of the plays are workings-up of situations of which its author found himself a spectator on the streets of Andara or on the highway between Slieve a-Tooey and the sea. . . .

It is not antiquity, however, that Mr. Campbell has chosen for his play. Indeed, he rejects antiquity, deliberately "using peasants as . . . protagonists instead of kings—who, like Pharaoh, are 'but a cry in Egypt,' outworn figures in these days with no beauty and no significance." *Judgment* is made out of the story of the countryside concerning "a tinker's woman," Peg Straw, and we may well believe Mr. Campbell has changed it but little, as he says, for the purposes of his play. It had been a better play, perhaps, had he changed more the facts of the story. As it stands, the first act of the play is adequate dramatically, and beautiful with that sort of wild and outworld beauty Synge brought into English literature in Ireland; and the second act beautiful with that beauty, and inadequate dramatically. . . .

All the characters in *Judgment* are "created." The personality of each colors his words and puts him before you distinct from every other. Owen Ban the weaver, who takes in Peg when his wife Nabla, heavy with her first child, and nervous because of her condition and fearful of the birth, would keep out the outcast; old Parry Cam; John Gilla Carr; Colum Johnston and Father John; Nabla herself; and Kate Kinsella the midwife—each is himself or herself, each remains as distinct in your mind as the unforgettable scenes of the play. Somehow or other, too, the country is suggested; you are aware that you are on a wild hillside above a glen,—you are aware of this not because the author tells us at the outset that the scene of the play is in the mountains of western Donegal, south of Lochros Beg Bay, but through the dialogue of the play itself. Both scenes of the play are indoors, and on dark nights of midwinter, but so instinct with many phases of the life of the people is it that its background of landscape rises before you only less distinctly than the visualization of its characters. Atmosphere the play has, and quality, both sprung of the sincerity of its feeling and imagination. So true are these, and so keen the author's reading of human nature, and so sure his character drawing, that for all his weakness of construction we may speak of his play alongside of the best Irish plays. The future promises finer things: meanwhile we are thankful for what is, for *Judgment*,—especially for its far-offness, its desolateness as of the world's end and the wind crying.

Cornelius Weygandt. Irish Plays and Playwrights
(Boston and New York, Houghton Mifflin, 1913),
pp. 246–50

The work of Joseph Campbell I encountered . . . after [Seumas] O'Sullivan's: his *Irishry* was my next purchase. It came as a strong contrast. Here were no long waving lines, no sensitive broodings on the past, but short, athletic, hard-hitting portraits of men and women. The one characteristic shared by the two poets was a liking for the thing half said, a power of conveying a world of meaning in a hint or a brief, apparently casual phrase. Campbell's masterly portrait of the unfrocked priest, one of the finest short biographies I ever hope to read, derives its power from these hints, and from the accumulation of small touches, the books he wrote, the one occasion when the narrator saw him—"he bled at the nose"—which combine into a picture upon which the mind broods long. Campbell's verses are far rougher than O'Sullivan's; almost shockingly rough they seemed to me in those far-off days, used as I was only to the more obvious classics; and their themes are not those to which I had been accustomed.

> "Drunk and battered she, with a little eye,
> She hitches up her tins and totters by."

But it is a tonic power, and, at the end of his book, there is that small masterpiece for all to admire, the poem by which he is best known, "The Old Woman." . . .

The man who could so consummately use his muscular verse could do no wrong, I decided. Later, I picked from a barrow in Bayswater his earlier book, *The Gilly of Christ*, and liked it nearly as well. Joseph Campbell has not written a great deal, but he is a fine poet, and his place in the history of his movement is secure.

L. A. G. Strong. Com. June 7, 1935, p. 155

Most accomplished of the poets associated with the Ulster literary movement prior to 1914 was Joseph Campbell (1879–1944). If he chose to restrict his utterance to shorter lyrical forms the loss in power and scope was more than made up for by the fastidious economy of language and the classical restraint of feeling of which he had command. His first publication was *Songs of Uladh* (1904), a work of collaboration in which Campbell's share was to match with appropriate words the traditional Ulster melodies collected and arranged by Herbert Hughes.

Like another undoubted poet of the next generation, Lyle Donaghy, Campbell wrote best of the things with which he had grown up—the leafy suburbs of his native city, Belfast, the Lagan Valley, the blue hills of Antrim, quiet places, simple people. Any trace of exoticism, any element of alien thought or tradition, is absent from his poetry. His religion, too, which flowered so beautifully in such lyrics as "I Am the Gilly of Christ" and "I Met a Walking Man," had a childlike innocence. *Sancta simplicitas* was what for him gave beauty its holiness and holiness its beauty.

> I am the mountainy singer—
>> The voice of the peasant's dream,
> The cry of the wind on the wooded hill
>> The leap of the trout in the stream.

The book of verse which took its title from this lyric contained his best work up to 1909. In *Irishry* (1914) he revealed another facet of his genius. These poems are described as a "pageant of types," each one of which is delineated with the incisiveness of an etching. The fiddler, the mill-girl, the turf-man, the silenced priest, the Orangeman are invested with an aura of realism that renders them archetypal rather than merely typical. Thus, of the old-age pensioner he writes:

> He sits over the glimmering coal
> With ancient face and folded hands:
> His eye glasses his quiet soul,
> He blinks and nods and understands.
> In dew wetted, in tempest blown,
> A Lear at last come into his own.

Earth of Cualaan (1917) marks an advance on all that went before, for each of the twenty-one poems is a distillation of pure poetry, each lyric, pared to the bone, disclosing a rare perception in structure:

> On the stones
> The shadows of fern-stalks
> Write secretly in Ogham.

On the stones
The ferns, with moveless strokes
Write the saga of time.

Like Gray, Joseph Campbell never spoke out: his was the still, small voice. His reticence, however, did not hide anything trivial or weak. The fineness of his work is deceptive, like the fineness of tempered steel, tensile and resilient. His range may not have been great, but by refusing to venture beyond it he achieved a measure of perfection denied to many poets who would have been cramped within such narrow bounds.

> J. N. Browne. In Sam Hanna Bell, ed., *The Arts In
> Ulster: A Symposium* (London, Harrap, 1951),
> pp. 137–39

Joseph Campbell (1879–1944) was the one poet from the North of Ireland who made of the national mode a vehicle to express a coherent personal vision. Both his subject-matter and his manner are conventional; his rhythms derive from Gaelic poetry as realised into English, while his landscapes and descriptive passages are familiar. . . . Yet he manages rhythmic subtlety, employs verbal music with skill, and his sense of Irish peasant life moves beyond realism or simple romanticism to establish an individual interpretation of Irish experience.

For Campbell Irish peasant life is a spiritual estate. His sense of it is grounded in an almost animistic apprehension of life quickening in the seed, in the womb, in the bread and wine on the altar. His verse has something of the blend of pagan nature-worship and mystical piety associated with medieval carols, as Christ is born in Ireland. . . . His vision is pantheistic, mediated in terms of Catholic ritual and imagery, reminding one of the early Irish hymns:

O Mother of the Word,
O Myrtle Leaf,
O Scented Hazel of the Seven Hills. . .

("O Beauty of the World")

His seasons are springtime and harvest and his peasantry move through a landscape that Christ himself has blessed by his mystical presence:

Then Christ dreamed awhile in silence,
And wandered into the night:
And his feet were a running river,
And his head a star of light.

("The Women Bore Their Children")

The peasantry, in their craft-culture and husbandry, live close to the source of this presence. The properties of his poems of peasant life are therefore the emblems of a spiritual ritualising condition rather than the items of realism. Cradles, currachs, pots, straw crosses, crofts, trades, spells and rural magic, trout dreaming in the rivers, "the fire on the open hearth," corn ripening, babies in the womb, are the substantial manifestations of his visionary sense of Irish life that show he learnt symbolist techniques from Blake:

> I am the mountainy singer—
> The voice of the peasant's dream.

It is on behalf of this rural Holy Land that Campbell writes his poems, producing at times nationalist effusions that are as bloodthirsty as any of Alice Milligan's or Ethna Carbery's. His ideal Ireland is one that knows little even of mercantilism, let alone industry or the city.

Terence Brown. *Northern Voices: Poets From Ulster*
(Totowa, N.J., Rowman & Littlefield, 1975),
pp. 73–75

[Joseph Campbell's poem "The Dancer"] is a description, but is it the description of a particular dance and dancer or of a type of dance? The poem has been quoted [by F. R. Higgins and W. B. Yeats] to illustrate the traditional Gaelic dance, "no expression no movement above the waist," but we cannot, at the same time, avoid seeing individual tragedy in the figure of the dancer.

I think the strength of this poem, and it is very effective indeed, comes not only from the marvelous handling of the rhythm, but also from the way in which the individual and the type are fused. This fusion would be impossible if the dance were one which demanded animation of the dancer's face and of his entire body. . . .

We are left with a fairly objective picture. His face *is* a mask. We know nothing of what goes on inside. We know only that this is a performance of a traditional dance, a superlative performance in which the effect created is like that of a man who dances "as if his kin were dead."

The poem is told in the third person and from the point of view of an observer who is objective, yet sensitive and perceptive. The same point of view regards "The old fiddler fiddling" and the people sitting and standing round the dark walls. The observer confines himself to objectively noted details and to "As if" (the dancer dances "As if his kin were dead), and this is as far as the observer will go in interpretation. He does not know what goes on behind the mask any more than we.

Does the speaker of the poem see more than does the old fiddler or than do the people standing and sitting around the walls? Do they see that the dancer's face is white as death and that he dances as if his kin were dead? Such a scene, even if one knew that it were only an effect of the dance, would hardly produce the reaction of the fiddler, his laughing eye and lip. But we can't judge by him because he's the music, and some of the dancer's effect (in the poem, that is, not in the actual dance form) depends on the contrast with the merry old fiddler. His softly beating foot and merry fiddle go inevitably on with the tune to which the tall doom-faced man dances.

The people praise the art of the dancer. Does the art include looking as if his kin were dead, and if so do they notice that look? One cannot say for sure.

In short is it impossible to know whether the very strong impression that the dancer is wrapped up in thoughts of the grave and is utterly oblivious of his audience as he performs so magnificently is *the truth about the dancer* or *the appropriate effect of the dance*. We can't help feeling that the personal tragedy of the dancer is the subject. But perhaps that is the poet's way of involving us in the scene too. If we knew whether the dancer really did or did not have reason to dance as if his kin were dead, we would cease to be witnesses of the dance alone; our interest would shift to biography. As it is we are in the dark with the other spectators, watching the light on that still face and those lightning-like feet and left free to imagine whatever we will.

David R. Clark. *Éire-Ireland*.
Autumn, 1969, pp. 82–83, 85–86

The poetry of Joseph Campbell differs in several important respects from the work of other Irish poets who began writing at the opening of the present century. Like [Padraic] Colum and others, he was inspired directly by folklore and folk song. But alone among these writers he drew inspiration, as I have noted before, not only from Irish sources but from the Gaelic tradition of the Highlands. No doubt this was due to his northern ancestry. Certainly his awareness of legends and beliefs existing not only in Ulster but in the Hebrides gave an imaginative spaciousness and range to his early lyrics. We feel that such a legendary figure as the Gilly of Christ belongs to the entire Gaelic world. We feel that this mysterious messenger might appear one day in Cantyre or Skye and the next in Glen Columcille. Campbell drew his early inspiration from folk song but he is not in the ordinary sense of the word a folk poet. He is essentially a lyric poet whose power of expressing a memorable simplicity is the result not only of inspiration but of subtle art. He himself wrote:

> I am the mountainy singer—
> The voice of the peasant's dream,
> The cry of the wind on the wooded hill,
> The leap of the trout in the stream.

And it is this dream, this inner spirit of the folk itself which he makes articulate for us. With great skill he tinges his lyrics at times with dialect phrases and at times he uses a Gaelic word to sustain atmosphere. I want to stress this point as much as possible because it marks a very great difference in our Irish literary revival between its poetry and its prose. Poets, such as Campbell and Colum, express directly and in clear simple English the traditional spirit of Irish life. By this restraint as well as by their imaginative intuition, I think they came closer to its secret than the later prose writers. . . . In four lines Campbell can express the religious folk imagination of the centuries, the loneliness of the inner life, the communal livelihood:

I am the gilly of Christ,
The mate of Mary's son;
I run the roads at seeding-time,
And when the harvest's done.

Campbell was the first to explore this religious folk lore. Later [Padraic] Pearse in "Iosagan" and other works followed his method. But Pearse, I think, fused the tradition with a modern sentiment. Campbell's work is the voice of legend itself purified by the centuries, aloof and, though gentle, without an alloy of external sentiment.

Campbell, I would suggest, learned his art from Herrick and from him gained that mastery of a subtle and simple art which is suddenly apparent in his second book, *The Rushlight*. But a strong sense of the elemental forces of nature, of the seasons upon which man depends for his bread, gives an underlying strength to all his work. In a poem on the Grasslands of Meath he sums up an entire economic system in a phrase:

The silence of unlaboured fields
Lies like a judgment on the air. . . .

In his later work Joseph Campbell abandoned even the decoration of rhyme. He was the first Irish poet to use free verse effectively and *Earth of Cualann* is, I think, his greatest achievement. Here he used not human types but heroic symbols to express the spirit of the land and of his own philosophy. For those unacquainted with Gaelic mythology this book, in its terse symbolism, offers difficulties. It was inspired by that northeastern corner of Wicklow where the poet lived for so many years. In a note the poet describes it in this way: "Wild and unspoilt, a country of cairn-crowned hills and dark watered valleys, it bears even to this day something of the freshness of the heroic dawn." And the book captures this quality. *Earth of Cualann* has been neglected because it pays no concession to popular taste or to that English public whom some of our poets always keep in mind. But it has deeply influenced many of us and when the time comes it will be remembered again.

Austin Clarke. *JIL*. Sept., 1979, pp. 23–25

CARROLL, PAUL VINCENT (1900–1968)

Shadow and Substance can hold its own as a play dealing with profound matter and exhibiting an unusual degree of boldness in the sheer use of culture itself—for in any production these days the mere implication of culture, or "choice," or cerebral rigor, implies a certain amount of either courage or of reckless vision. It is no little matter for a play to succeed in making one side of its dramatic struggle the force of the classical and austere Church, felt as acting through a man of distinction, choiceness, and human frailty.

The other element involved in this dramatic struggle, while quite as difficult to create, is, when it comes off, more immediately perceived. It would lie in the direction of humility, warmth, expressive humanity, and the power of rapture and self-forgetfulness; and it may be found in a person, simple, total, plain and luminous like the Irish maid Mr. Carrol has written so well. . . .

Stark Young. *NR*. May 4, 1938, p. 396

To synopsize Mr. Carroll's new play [*The White Steed*] is to make a script, at once simple and effective, sound like the fuzziest of fuzzy allegories. It is to lose sight of the gaiety underlying its overtones; to ignore the pungency of its dialogue; to fail to indicate the compassion with which its meaning is pointed; and to overlook unfairly some of the characters Mr. Carroll has drawn with genuine skill.

Above all, it is to forget Mr. Carroll's wisdom as a dramatist. He is a propagandist, attacking egotism, persecution, and cruelty, who knows and avoids the dangers of "raving" and "raging." By his own confession, he is well aware of what he has described as man's "love of this battered imperfect thing called life." In the presence of a serious subject he does not forget the curative and persuasive powers of laughter. No wonder that in last Sunday's *Times* he could write with affection of the Aristophanes who is "still laughing," of Boccaccio and Rabelais still dancing, of Voltaire's "grand guffaw that still blows up the Seine and over the tops of Paris," and of Chaucer who "still goes roaring down to Canterbury." Mr. Carroll is himself a merry sage. His laughter, like his humanity, is a proof of his sagacity, even as *The White Steed* is a proof of how much he has grown in authority as a dramatist since he wrote so good a play as *Shadow and Substance*.

If he still has difficulty in establishing his young lovers, if he cannot quite make us believe in their affection for one another, or if once in a while his machinery creaks, if some of his village snoopers remain no more than broad types, Mr. Carroll, nonetheless, shows he is a man who can write from his heart and set ideas spinning in dramatic form. His dialogue is rich with all the music and wit of his race. Moreover, when it comes to his drawing of Canon Matt Lavelle and Father Shaughnessy he works with a master's skill.

John Mason Brown. *Broadway in Review*
(New York, W. W. Norton, 1940), pp. 207–8

On May 14th I reviewed here another play, *The Old Foolishness*, also by Paul Vincent Carroll, but *Shadow and Substance* is a far finer and more successful piece. Indeed, it is of quite exceptional merit, and it says much for American taste that it should have been a success in New York. Mr. Carroll, who looks like being a worthy succcessor of the great line of Irish dramatists, has chosen an ambitious theme, namely, the contrast between the attitude of an official Church, represented by Canon Skerritt, the Roman Catholic vicar of a small town in Ireland, and his two curates (admirably played by Harry Hutchinson and Edward Byrne) and that of his young servant girl, Brigid, to the saint of the Church, St. Brigid, on whose day the servant girl happened to be born. Like Joan of Arc, the girl Brigid has visions, and sees and speaks with her namesake the saint, but the Canon, naturally, treats all this as illusion, the hysteria of an unbalanced and overwrought young girl. The relationship between the priest and his servant is beautifully worked out, and makes the human core of the play which otherwise might have been nothing more than a theological discussion, or a mainly verbal dramatisation of two opposing points of view—as in Shaw's *St. Joan* or Dostoievsky's "Grand Inquisitor" chapter in *The Brothers Karamazov*. The Canon is brilliantly drawn as an educated man of fine taste and scholarship, a personality marked out by mental gifts and knowledge of the world for high office in any church, who suffers agony from the superstition and ignorance with which he is surrounded.

James Redfern. *Spec*. June 4, 1943, p. 523

In just about every play that Paul Vincent Carroll has written, he seems to have a twofold critical purpose: to hold up to reprobation certain very unpleasant habits of thought and conduct in Irish Catholic life—or any Catholic life—and to provide a corrective in the character of one or two admirable persons in each play, excepting *Things That Are Caesar's*, which is unrelievedly bleak. Carroll's plays, however, are not solely caviling; they are also a plea for the restoration of those virtues which infused and vitalized the spiritual life of an older Ireland, particularly the virtues emanating from the monastic spirit on which Irish spirituality was formed long ago and which writers like Carroll seem to believe have become obfuscated by laziness, unworthy ambition, materialism and mediocrity, which have overgrown the soil of Irish life.

Although Paul Vincent Carroll has castigated the clergy and the merchant class for waxing rich or powerful, or both, on the outcome of civil war and national independence; although he has written a stinging exposé of Catholic Ireland's school system; although he has created a portentous picture of religious hypocrisy, fanaticism, bigotry and the mob spirit they can let loose, in no sense can Carroll be said to be either anticlerical or anti-Catholic. His most lovable priests are eminently worthy priests, and they usually carry the weight of the play's meaning. And if in some of Carroll's plays there is the shadow of gloom, there is finally the substance of Christian hope.

Nevertheless, there is an abundance of fine satire in Carroll's plays (as well as wit and mysticism, with which George Jean Nathan credited him), and it is generally directed against pietism in which there is neither innocence nor enthusiasm, but cunning and self-interest. At the heart of some Catholic Family life Carroll sees and attacks all the bleak pharisaical bitterness and jealousies; he sees and deplores spiritual pride born of a narrow concept of religion, vindictiveness hidden under the show of duty, a combination of vulgarity and insincerity, and a mad pursuit of material prosperity in which every standard is thrown aside except success.

We could use another play or two in the better Paul Vincent Carroll tradition.

Anne Gertrude Coleman. *Catholic World.*
Nov., 1960, p. 93

Those who remember his two big Broadway successes tend sometimes to classify Carroll as primarily a satirist of the Irish clergy and bigoted peasantry. This is not correct. Actually, Carroll has not always continued to deal even with the Irish scene. Much of his work has been concerned with the area near the border of North Ireland that he knew as a boy. But *Green Cars Go East* and *The Strings, My Lord, Are False* are laid around Glasgow, and in these plays Carroll portrays various types of Scots and captures effectively their speech, utilizing it—within the Synge tradition—for its color and rhythm.

He has also attempted various types of plays, various not only in subject matter but in mood and desired effect. After *The White Steed* he abandoned clerical satire for all-out sentiment and attempted to create a mood of romantic nostalgia for the old Irish spirit, untrammelled and dreaming, in the peasant play, *The Old Foolishness*. Then he turned to a series of grim proletarian dramas in the realistic tradition. The first of these, *The Strings, My Lord, Are False*, deals with the blitz of the Clydeside industrial area during World War II, and the heroism of the slum-dwellers headed by an Irish priest during two especially bad nights of bombing. Carroll, himself, had recently served as a member of the Auxiliary Fire Squads, and the play, while some of its lines seem "literary," catches the scene with the feel of authenticity; it is at times quite moving, and conveys Carroll's great anger at war and inhumanity. *Green Cars Go East* is laid in the east-Glasgow slums, where Carroll taught English and mathematics for many years. While it takes a dimmer view of the character of slum-dwellers, it is an earnest picture of the struggle of at least one girl, a schoolteacher, to raise herself and her family out of the gutter. In its brooding quality, its capturing of the small-talk of lower-class family life, it may remind a modern reader of Wesker's work. In *The Wise Have Not Spoken* Carroll returned to the area of northern Louth, Ireland, but his tone is again "realistic" as he shows the struggle of a farm family to resist eviction and disintegration.

After a lapse of over a decade, Carroll then tried something entirely different. *The Wayward Saint* is a fantasy, full of magical effects, dealing with the battle of the devil for the soul of an Irish rural canon with St. Francis-like qualities. This innocent lover of nature is almost trapped by a representative of hell in the form of a debonair nobleman who plays upon his vanity, but he is saved at the crucial moment by the prayers of an innocent girl and the entry of a friendly lion. When Carroll, as here, is relying heavily on Irish whimsy, or when elsewhere he goes in for bare-faced romanticism, the success of his play, of course, depends on a person's taste—a taste that possibly is of limited extent in this country. But his plays almost always show his sense of the theatrically effective, and his love of language and wit.

Drew B. Pallette. MD. Feb., 1965, pp. 376–77

The best known of Carroll's recent plays is *The Wayward Saint* of 1955. In it, he returns to the Mourne Mountains and the Paul Vincent Carroll stock company. His Canon Daniel McCooey is a simple, gullible priest who like St. Francis talks to birds and animals, and who is a kind of male counterpart to Brigid of *Shadow and Substance*. However, the girl's part was played straight, whereas the Canon's is permeated by a charmingly humanizing faultiness. The devil, in the form of Baron Nicholas de Balbus, is able to play on the Canon's pride and to give him a droll self-importance about being a saint—a fact which suggests the influence of D'Alton's *The Devil a Saint Would Be*. Also, the Canon's saintliness is humanized by his willingness to trick his bishop, his housekeeper, and his grocer in ways not far distant from outright lies.

The play is nicely of a piece, and its pleasant humor never deserts it. Its main fault lies in the quality of Carroll's inventiveness. The Canon's miracles—stopping clocks, making lights blink, raising chairs—are pleasant theatrical devices, but not particularly fresh or striking. The play, even when compared with O'Casey's *Cock-a-Doodle Dandy*, seems imaginative, but the imagination does not seem first-rate. The piece is mildly charming, but never quite delightful, and Carrol's own wild mind seems muted in it. . . .

Despite his "rebel heart," Carroll has always been brought up short by authority. His strictures on the Catholic Church have always been blunted by his ultimate belief in the Church, and his irritation with realism has always been foiled by his debt to it. Just as he always follows a criticism of the

Church by a eulogy of it, so technically does he follow up a tentative diversion into experiment by an example of total realism. The upshot is that his great artistic promise has never been completely realized. He has not developed as a thinker, but wavered between two conflicting impulses. He has not developed as an experimental playwright, but only tried furtive forays away from realism. He is a rebel who has never truly rebelled.

That seems to me an enormous waste, for, make no mistake about it, Carroll has a talent rivaling O'Casey's. O'Casey's genius was strong enough to hammer out an inimitable style because he was not afraid to be the conscience of his race. Carroll could never quite do that.

Still, he has made a rare contribution to Irish drama, and a larger one than he has so far been credited with. He must be remembered not only for the superb realism of *Shadow and Substance* and *The White Steed*, but also for the equally fine realism of *Green Cars Go East*, and for the beautiful lyricism of *The Old Foolishness*, and for the wild hilarity of *The Devil Came from Dublin*. In these plays, he was writing at the top of his form, and that top was very high indeed.

Robert Hogan. *After the Irish Renaissance*
(Minneapolis, Univ. of Minnesota Pr., 1967),
pp. 62–63

With all his accomplishments and abilities, it is distressing that Carroll did not, particularly in the 1940s, achieve his potential. Curiously enough, his career in one basic respect parallels O'Casey's. They both successfully started with a gripping realistic play—*Things That Are Caesar's* and *The Shadow of a Gunman*; then they experienced two hit dramas, and then a decline from their two most important works. Unlike O'Casey, however, Carroll did not possess the lyrical and poetic qualities that would have given his secondary work more distinction. But, like O'Casey, he became caught up and waylaid by the siren call of symbolism and allegory and also, like O'Casey, he became too message-and-thesis conscious so that with the advent of *Kindred*, instead of the themes emerging subtly from the play, they too often seem to be the principal reason for the play's existence.

If Carroll is not so great a dramatist as he should have been, these are the reasons why. He came to allow his heart to rule his head, to preach almost unceasingly the nobleness of, and need for, love, dignity, tolerance, and understanding at the expense of retaining consistent dramatic control, clearness, and firmness. To say this, however, is not to ignore the fact that as long as the modern English theatre exists, Carroll's best dramas will be played, and these works, and the characters existing therein, are sufficient reason indeed for placing him in the pantheon of significant modern playwrights.

Paul A. Doyle. *Paul Vincent Carroll*
(Lewisburg, Pa., Bucknell Univ. Pr., 1971), p. 110

Although Carroll's strength as a dramatist is generally associated with his life-like portrayals of the Irish clergy, his rebels are well drawn and, perhaps, more interesting from an autobiographical standpoint. Dermot O'Flingsley is one such rebel. His function in *Shadow and Substance* . . . is to provide opposition to the Canon. As the Canon's schoolmaster, or more appropriately chattel, he believes the Irish school system a whited sepulchre and under the pseudonym "Eugene Gibney" writes an exposé of it and the Irish clergy entitled *I Am Sir Oracle*. If left to its own merits, the work would have aroused little attention. With the assistance of Canon Skerritt's curates, however, it so inflames the provincial gentry, most of whom would ban the book without having read it, that they envision a moral crusade in which *I Am Sir Oracle* is burned publicly in every village in the republic. Canon Skerritt, in his official position, prohibits such a spectacle. . . .

It is evident from Carroll's own pen that the raw material for dramatic rebels such as O'Flingsley was provided early in life. He writes: "Refusing to teach, as my father had done, under an unbearable clerical yoke, in Ireland, I sailed out of Dublin on a cattle boat and landed in Glasgow. . . ." Since Carroll's formal education was exclusively parochial, and since his own father was the local schoolmaster and the boy's teacher until Paul Carroll was thirteen, he no doubt learned early as a child the servile and underpaid status of a teacher in a school system whose ultimate authority was the parish priest. Nothing in his experience from St. Mary's College, Dundalk, to St. Patrick's Training College, Dublin, served to change that early impression.

In his plays, as in his life, Carroll directed what bitterness he possessed against ignorance, intolerance, bigotry, and sham in whatever form. He was, as he testifies, capable of distinguishing between doctrine and administrators. "In religion, I cling by conviction to Catholicism, but God save me from its administrators! Thank Heaven I have always managed to separate the one from the other." It is apparent from Carroll's own observations that his formal schooling in Ireland provided him with much of the richest material of his dramas. . . .

The achievement of *Shadow and Substance* might best be put in perspective by noting the direction of the modern theatre at the time that Carroll enjoyed his first New York success. In 1938 Luigi Pirandello and Bertolt Brecht were perhaps the most powerful forces in the modern theatre. Their work made possible what followed by Genet, Ionesco, Beckett, Pinter, and others associated with the theatre of the absurd. The trend of the modern theatre was moving relentlessly in the direction of cynicism, despair, and nihilism. Regardless of what perspective one believes most valid for the modern condition, it is apparent that both in 1938 and later Carroll found himself at variance with the direction of the modern theatre. . . . What merits emphasizing in Carroll's position is the fact that his disagreement with the modern theatre is nearly total. In matters of both content and form he is at the opposite end of the dramatic spectrum from such contemporaries as Pirandello and Brecht. *Six Characters in Search of an Author* and *Shadow and Substance* might conceivably have been written in different centuries instead of within two decades of each other. Pirandello's revolt against the well-made play is so complete that he literally turns the theatre inside out in attempting to achieve dramatic effect. His plays are deliberately inconsistent in their development: they advance with jerks and surprises. Because of Pirandello's considerable influence in the modern theatre, especially among those playwrights associated with the theatre of the absurd, one can appreciate the full extent of Carroll's variance.

This is not to suggest that Carroll has attained the stature of a Pirandello or a Brecht in the modern theatre. Such an assertion would be sheer folly, but it is not excessive to suggest that when he is most effective Carroll proves himself a worthy descendant of Yeats, Synge, and the early O'Casey. He employs no gimmicks. He tells a simple story of the people and sustains it by a dramatic idiom at once beautiful and eloquent. Carroll's plays are not written in verse as the vast majority of Yeats' are, but throughout *Shadow and Substance* is visible the hand of the poet.

John D. Conway. *ConnR*. April, 1973, pp. 63–65

During the fifteen or so years prior to the Abbey fire and the temporary exile of the company to the Queen's Theatre in Dublin, the two outstanding Irish plays were Carroll's *Shadow and Substance* (1937) and Molloy's *The King Of Friday's Men* (1948). Paul Vincent Carroll was born in Co. Louth and spent most of his adult life in Glasgow where, with James Bridie, he helped found the Citizen's Theatre in 1943, writing several plays for it and for the BBC. His first Abbey play of note was *Things That Are Caesar's* (1932); in it he introduces the figure of the overbearing priest which was to feature in several of his plays and of which he was to make a superb character study in *Shadow and Substance*.

Carroll was naturally accused of anti-clericalism, but in fact his real target is the abuse of clerical power and responsibility, and the tyranny of misused authority. Canon Skerritt finds himself opposed to the village schoolteacher O'Flingsley, who has published a controversial book which the canon finds subversive enough to warrant dismissing the teacher from his post. The servant girl at the presbytery confides to O'Flingsley that she has seen a vision of her namesake, St. Brigid. O'Flingsley advises her to consult the canon, who refuses to take her simple belief seriously. When local feeling against the teacher's book erupts, Brigid is accidentally killed in a local brawl, and both priest and teacher realize that they are mutually responsible for her death.

Carroll very subtly allows the audience to sympathize with the canon in his downfacing of certain hypocritical parishioners; he also presents the teacher as something of a hothead, so there is no obviously black-and-white conflict. *Shadow and Substance* won the New York Drama Critics Award for the best foreign play of its year – as did Carroll's next work, *The White Steed*, in which the leading character, Canon Matt Lavelle, an easy-going elderly priest, confined to a wheelchair, finds himself having to oppose the narrow morality of his young curate.

Paul Vincent Carroll was inadvertently involved in a curious theatrical venture in Dublin during the war years. Press censorship was so rigid in Ireland, and the public was so cut off from external events, that when the actress and director Shelah Richards presented Carroll's play of Glasgow life, *The Strings, My Lord, Are False*, at the Olympia Theatre, Dublin, during the German bombing, the queues of people hoping to catch a glimpse of the reality of life and death in a participating country, stretched for several city-blocks. There is no official theatre-censorship in Ireland—in any case, it would have been difficult to find a convincing reason for banning this touching play—and so Shelah Richards was able to mount several productions of plays which would have been considered too "controversial" for the Abbey during the period euphemistically known in neutral Ireland as "the Emergency."

Christopher Fitz-Simon. The Irish Theatre (London,
Thames and Hudson, 1983), pp. 164–65

CLARKE, AUSTIN (1896–1974)

We read *The Vengeance of Fionn* with the deepest interest, for in the work of this young Irish poet, Austin Clarke, we think we see the promise of greatness. If a young man of twenty can write a poem so sustained and so imaginative what may he not do when he has come to the fulness of power. Every young man of literary talent has a volume or two of poetry in him, for youth is itself poetry, but we can see in most that the flight will be short, and the literary career will, however distinguished, be along the path of prose. There are some minds of whom we can feel sure that poetry is their birthright, and that they will be poets and nothing else. We could tell that in reading the early poetry of Shelley, or in *The Island of Statues* of our own Yeats, when he was little more than a boy, and in so far as it is possible for us to prophesy from reading *The Vengeance of Fionn* we would say that Austin Clarke is a born poet, and if he takes his gift with the high seriousness which it deserves he should become a great name in Irish literature. *The Vengence of Fionn* is the most sustained poetical narrative by an Irish writer since Mr. Yeats enchanted us with *The Wanderings of Usheen*. Mr. Yeats by that time had come to the fulness of his powers, and was, if we recollect rightly, a few years older than Mr. Clarke. But those who had read Mr. Yeats' earlier *Island of Statues* foresaw the poet's greatness. *The Vengeance of Fionn* may sustain a comparison with Mr. Yeats' early work, and excites in us hopes that another magician of the beautiful is going to enchant us. *The Vengeance of Fionn* is a series of episodes imagined around the story of Diarmuid and Grainne. Here and there we have the imperfect taste or technique of youth, but very soon we are carried along by the imagination and beauty of the writing. It is undoubtedly the vision of a poet. [January 5, 1918]

George William Russell (A.E.). *Selections from the Contributions to "The Irish Homestead,"* Vol. II, Henry Summerfield, ed., (Atlantic Highlands, N.J., Humanities Press, 1978), p. 921

[W]hen Austin Clarke writes a play, *The Flame*, about the reaction of a community of Irish nuns to a supposed miracle, and sets it in the Middle Ages, do not be misled. Another similar play of his, about a supposed miracle among a community of nuns, *Sister Eucharia*, is set in or near present-day Dublin. To point the similarity, one choral passage from the first play is repeated *verbatim* in the second.

Modern or medieval, the Catholic mind would appear at first glance to have little relevance for a twentieth-century audience which should happen to consist neither of Catholics nor—quite probably—of believers in any religion whatsoever. But, in fact, what Clarke has to say is often of supreme importance to our time. Most of his plays can be discussed in political terms, as struggles between authoritarianism and individual liberty. Shaw, in *Saint Joan*, used the Middle Ages as a background for one such struggle. This play raises the whole problem of how to facilitate the mutation of the species without which evolution is impossible. If society is not to stand still and finally to regress, normal people must learn to make room for the deviation from the norm—genius or saint—who is to lead the way to a higher type of society.

But while Shaw discusses this whole problem at the temperature of a debating society, Clarke feels himself personally involved it it, and his plays carry a tremendous emotional charge because of this. For the greater part of his life Clarke—like Joyce before him—has been at war with his environment. I mean by "environment" not only the Catholic Church and his Jesuit schoolmasters, but almost the whole of Irish society as at present constituted. . . .

Over and over again, therefore, Clarke dramatizes the persecution by the group of the individual who will not conform, whether it be a novice nun who refuses to have her hair cut off (*The Flame*), or a King who rebels against the clergy by taking a mistress (*The Plot Is Ready*). But the most insidious form of persecution is that which comes from within the individual himself. A little servant girl sees the compulsions of society as bogey-men (*The Viscount of Blarney*), and vows to be chaste after her vision of the night-hag or "Foster-mother," who carries the victims of infanticide to Limbo. More sophisticated people are haunted by conscience and the sense of guilt—devices which society has developed for its own protection, but which the individual himself is powerless to control.

Since society always defeats the individual in real life, Clarke can only attain his wish-fulfilment by supernatural intervention. The individual triumphs by miraculous means—and the medieval background makes such miracles acceptable, at least till the play is over. But society still wins, for its representative—usually an Abbot or a Mother Superior—can supply another interpretation of the "miracle," by which society's aims are upheld and even furthered.

Hence it is that Clarke, in his plays dealing with conventual life, cares little about the vows of poverty and chastity which his monks and nuns have made. It is the third vow, that of obedience, which matters. The insistence upon obedience to one's spiritual superiors humbles the intellect as nothing else can. As in a totalitarian state, the individualist detests, not the power assumed over his body, but that assumed over his mind.

Vivian Mercier, *LL*. April, 1947, pp. 10–12

One must not be deceived by Mr. Harry Kernoff's admirable cover-design into a false impression of Mr. Austin Clarke's novel [*The Singing Men at Cashel*]. For the cover-design, excellent piece of work though it is, is untrue to the book. The design suggests satire; the book is pure poetry. It almost seems, indeed, that Mr. Clarke intended originally to write a satire in the rare and deadly vein of his earlier novel, *The Bright Temptation*, but that, quarter of the task accomplished, he succumbed to the piteousness of his own theme, fell in love with the loveliness of his own creation, and thereafter, consciously or unconsciously, converted his work of satire into a rich, sympathetic story of womanhood stifling in a close atmosphere, where either body or soul must be dominant, but never both.

The scene of *The Singing Men at Cashel* is laid in mediæval Ireland —the ninth or tenth century, as it appears—at a time when the export of saints and scholars had ceased, and Ireland, virtually having lost contact with the exterior world, was thrown in upon herself. The theme, a legendary one, is the progress of Gormlai, daughter of Flann, the Ard Ri of Ireland, to realisation of the full functions of her womanhood. Three marriages constitute her progress. One is with Cormac, scholar, ascetic, priest-king of Cashel —and, as far as Gormlai is concerned, more priest than king. Carrol of Leinster is her second husband, a warrior and barbarian, who radically alters Gormlai's conception of the wedded state. In her third marriage, with Nial, the companion of her childhood, she finds happiness.

This is a theme of an eminently modern type, and the marvel is that Mr. Clarke has contrived to harmonise it so admirably into an ancient setting. If he had tried, as so many reconstructors of historical romance have tried, to employ the language of modern psychology, the result would have been continuously jarring. But the poet's taste prevails, and its outcome is a book of real beauty. There are faults, it is true. Gormlai's soul-searchings here and there are too long drawn out, and might be tedious if they were not redeemed by the sustained loveliness of the language. The loosely intertwined escapades of Anier, a wandering bard, having furnished an overture to the tale of Gormlai, are then forgotten for a hundred pages, when he is reintroduced in a pleasantly Chaucerian episode, and are forgotten once more until the very end.

But these are small matters which weigh little against the fineness of Mr. Clarke's achievement. He has delved into a period that no other author has penetrated—a period of learning and barbaric splendour, of colour and alternate drabness, of mingled enlightenment and narrowness, of monasticism at once ennobling and depressing, of clashing cultures, of piety and of savagery. He has probed the soul of a tenth-century woman, to show her common humanity with the woman of to-day. And he has clothed his creation in the language of the poet.

Irish Times. April 4, 1936, p. 7

With a scholarly knowledge of the past, to which neither [William Butler] Yeats nor [James] Stephens could lay claim, as the foundation for his work, Mr. Clarke is to-day the greatest living Irish poet and one of the few writers living in Ireland who could be described as a beneficent encouraging influence. The path which the wanderers stumbled on by dark earthing in a lightless wood has brought this poet back to a place where sharply-defined values are perpetually threatened by ancient shadows, where man in the darkness makes definitions with edges as hard as the verses of the old poets who also worked in seclusion and darkness. . . .

The long prose romance *The Singing Men at Cashel* . . . , after his poems and his verse plays, is Mr. Clarke's most important work. As a fly-leaf inscription for that book he wrote down Saint Patrick's words to Caoilte in the *Acallamh na Seanorach*: Gabhlanach an rud an scealuidheacht—Storytelling is a complicated affair; and certainly this poet who can fashion in assonantal verse what Mr. Jack B. Yeats might call a shape that is just swan has encountered difficulties in the business of telling a tale in lowly prose. Dreams and visions, the adventures of Anier the poet, the loves of Gormlai, the ascetic life and violent death of Cormac, are all tumbled together in one book as blocks of priceless marble might lie in heaped confusion in a rich quarry. But it is only when the poet inserts into the story a fragment of verse that the style takes shape—as if in that disorderly quarry a searcher had found among the valuable confusion a Greek statue. Austin Clarke telling a story in prose is never as completely at home with the medium as James Stephens is; but his knowledge of the period in which his mind lives, his ability in showing that lost world to his readers will, I think, be a permanent source of inspiration to fiction writers reaching back into the past for the materials of romance or satire. Even if *The Singing Men at Cashel* were to be regarded as nothing more than the notebook of a poet—and it is much more than a notebook—it would still be very important in the whole scheme of Irish prose literature. A poet who knows and loves a period in the past and who has used that period to great account, here writes down in prose, marred by a crawling story and amateurish dialogue but ornamented by knowledge and love, the richness that the past as he sees it can bequeath to the imagination.

Benedict Kiely. *Modern Irish Fiction: A Critique* (Dublin, Golden Eagle Books, 1950), pp. 67–68

[Clarke] soon left behind the flaccid romanticism of his youthful verse and by 1929, with the publication of *Pilgrimage*, he was producing a harsher, much more potent kind of poetry. Clarke's poem, "The Young Woman of Beare" —the Old Woman of Beare, a well-known figure in folk stories, was reputed to have had seven periods of youth before age came upon her—may well have served as a prototype for Yeats' Crazy Jane poems. The peasant woman upon whom Clarke based his characterization resembles in some ways the old woman of Gort who, Yeats tells us, served as a model for Crazy Jane. In a note to his poem, Clarke comments: "In Glendalough, that holy place, a man told me of a poor old crone who had lived in the ruined settlement below the abandoned mines. She refused even the consolations of religion, for she remembered with great anger her own times of merriment and the strong mortals she had held" (*Poems*, p. 312). In certain of his ideas and images, too, Clarke seems to anticipate Yeats. In one stanza the woman says:

> I am the dark temptation
> Men know—and shining orders
> Of clergy have condemned me.

In another she tells of the pleasures she has known with men who "gallop to my house":

> Half in a dream I lie there
> Until bad thoughts have bloomed
> In flushes of desire.
> Drowsy with indulgence,
> I please a secret eye
> That opens at the Judgment.

Clarke's "The Young Woman of Beare" is long and lacks the masterful control which Yeats gave to his sequence of poems about Crazy Jane. Yet

Clarke's poem was published in *Pilgrimage* in 1929, a year before the first of Yeats' Crazy Jane poems were printed in *The New Republic* and *The London Mercury*. The elder poet never befriended or encouraged Clarke, as he did [F. R.] Higgins; yet surely he read Clarke's verse.

After 1930 Clarke turned his talents in new directions. His *Collected Poems* were published in 1936 and in 1938 he produced a small volume of new verse, *Night and Morning*. But during the same period he tried his hand at prose, publishing in 1932 a "romance," *The Bright Temptation*, and in 1936 another, *The Singing Men at Cashel*, both of them satiric attacks against the puritanism of the Irish Catholic Church, medieval and modern, and both banned in Ireland to this day. More important in his development as a poet, he began to experiment with verse drama. This experience of writing for the theater benefited Clarke in much the same way that it had Yeats decades earlier: it gave him a sharper, more precise diction and a new sense of dramatic conflict, both of which were to serve him well when he returned to the writing of poetry. He also discovered in himself—something which Yeats never really found—a remarkable capacity for comic irony.

> Richard J. Loftus. *Nationalism in Modern Anglo-Irish Poetry* (Madison, Univ. of Wisconsin Pr., 1964) pp. 261–62

In his introductory note to *Too Great a Vine*, Clarke comments, "As I have few personal interests left, I have concentrated on local notions and concerns which are of more importance than we are, keep us employed and last long." This statement goes far to explain why from *Ancient Lights* onward the poet has focused upon certain themes, but it does not tell the whole story. Although Clarke may have few personal interests left, whatever does interest him he views through the myopic lens of his tragic personal history. And the dominating factors in his vision are disillusionment and rejection. The illusions of faith and romance which vitalized his youth have been brutally destroyed by his mature experience. He finds in his mature world, however fervently the clergy may proclaim the contrary, no personal God, no sin; only the elementary forces of power and desire exist. No saints and heroes walk among us; only prelates and politicians. But without God and sin, without saints and heroes, the conflicts between flesh and spirit, faith and reason sink into nothingness. What is left to the poet is a sterile, pragmatic society whose tastes and values he must of necessity reject. In angry despair he probes deeply into his own personal history and that of his race to secure evidence of the truth of the illusions which had once given his joy and suffering meaning. The evidence, however, is not forthcoming. The best that he can find, in the streams that flow past Rathfarnham and the noble Irish horses, are symbolic representations of ages past which cherished those illusions he has lost, symbols made all the dearer to him by the fact that both horse and stream have been barbarously treated by his contemporaries. But the symbols do not have sufficient force to satisfy Clarke's quest. To the questions the poet asks there are no final answers, a fact which he ultimately concedes in his final anguished query,

> What dare we call
> Our thought, Marcus Aurelius,
> Unwanted void or really us?

. . . Each of us has made his private pilgrimage into the past in the hope of resuscitating those beloved illusions of our youth. Clarke searches for a way to live with human dignity, at peace with himself in a world that has apparently lost the traditional values that had sustained it for centuries. Specifically he seeks a faith. Insofar as his search involves an almost total rejection of the society of which he is a part and which, as he acknowledges, he has done his own bit to create, we may demur at following him. But to the extent that he points up the longings of the human spirit, man's need for faith in someone or something, we must respond empathetically to his words. In spite of his obscurity, or perhaps because of it, Clarke has succeeded in drawing a portrait of contemporary man, lonely in his isolation, confused and frightened by the horrible gap he discovers between reality as he experiences it and reality as he had imagined it.

William John Roscelli. In Ray B. Browne, William
John Roscelli, and Richard Loftus, eds., *The Celtic
Cross: Studies in Irish Culture and Literature*
(Lafayette, Ind., Purdue Univ. Studies, 1964),
pp. 66, 68

Clarke lead[s] a parade of poets who find ways of being at once deeply traditional, in his sense, and authoritatively modern.

One of the most interesting aspects of his modern side is that Clarke's most recent book, a single narrative poem called *Mnemosyne Lay in Dust* (1966), approaches the spirit of confessional poetry as closely as any work that has yet appeared in the British Isles. Though written in the third person, this book has an autobiographical ring to it. It has to do with the hysterical breakdown and amnesia, hospitalization, and recovery of one "Maurice Devane," Clarke's relatively youthful protagonist. Formally, it represents a culmination of Clarke's entire development. After his early period of romantic work, he has for years cultivated an astringently compressed style employing certain rhyming and alliterative devices that appear eccentric in English but that are precisely that "influence of Irish versification" to which [John] Montague refers. The remarkable turn, achieved in old age, that *Mnemosyne Lay in Dust* represents is clearly the result of a fusion of resolutions, artistic and psychological. . . .

Though Clarke began his career under the influence of the Celtic renaissance, he always combined romanticism with harsh wit and realism. His major books between the *Collected Poems* of 1935, now long out of print, and *Mnemosyne Lay in Dust* are, like the latter, the work of his old age. *Later Poems* (1961) and *Flight to Africa* (1963) contain a good deal of satire of an unusual sort. It is the self-flagellant satire of a man of strong and compassionate feeling, and this is the root of Clarke's late confessional tendency. His identification with Ireland is as complete and unself-conscious as with his own family, and the criticisms he directs against her have the domestic authenticity, so to speak, of a man complaining of a wife or mother.

M. L. Rosenthal. The New Poets (New York,
Oxford Univ. Pr., 1967), pp. 268–71

"I have endured," Clarke writes, "the enmity of my own mind that feared/ No argument," and when asked by Robert Frost what kind of verse he wrote, Clarke answered, thinking of a London strong-man and escapologist he had seen. "I load myself with chains and try to get out of them." *These* manacles are Irish and self-imposed, and they do not hold back to meaning because, along with the attempt to shake them off, they *are* Clarke's meaning. Clarke's verse is the eloquent record of a long bafflement—sexual, religious, political—and if the reasons for his distress rarely seem properly focused, that too, that blur of the wavering mind, is part of the condition that is being evoked. Clarke sees the Church, for example, as Ireland's glory and Ireland's misery —glory in the past, source of much misery in the present—but this contradiction doesn't yield paradoxes or battles so much as a lightly querulous wobbling. . . . Because he feels strongly and sees no better than the rest of us, Clarke makes an excellent witness to the world he lives in. But all too frequently he is only a second-rate poet, unable to shape his poems into a commanding clarity, unable even to let Ireland's contradictions stand clear. . . .

Clarke stands very much in the shadow of Yeats. From his early work based on Celtic legend and equipped with appropriately Northern landscapes . . . to his jaunty, randy, late verse, looking back to Ovid and the variegated sex life of Tiresias and others. Clarke is caught in an echo, never more than a modulation away from the master. So that Clarke's distinction, perhaps, lies less in his freeing himself from the influence of Yeats than in his turning himself into a reputable member of Yeats' poetic family—not a poor relative, but not the principal heir either. In a poem like *Forget-Me-Not* (1962), for example, Yeats' voice, even Yeats' evoked presence, mingle with Clarke's own compassion and concern as Irish horses, literal victims to be slaughtered for meat and exported to England, call up a crumbling mythology and enact Ireland's disgrace. . . .

Mnemosyne Lay in Dust (1966), Clarke's finest work, gathers these voices, borrowed and half-emancipated, into a long poem where rambling is not a fault, not even a venial Irish fault, but a fine virtue, the means by which Clarke revisits a lost year of his life, recalls without falsification or enhancement his ragged days spent in a mental hospital. There are unforgettable lines here, and it doesn't really matter whether they sound like Yeats or not. . . . What does matter is that this elegantly produced volume should save all its most graceless printing errors for this moving poem, so that the beautiful *loony-go-round*, for example, becomes *loomy-go-round*, and Clarke, in his grave, is cruelly visited by what too many myths have long seen as cheerful Irish carelessness.

Michael Wood. *Parnassus*. Fall/Winter, 1975,
pp. 42–45

The body of Clarke's poetry constitutes one of the notable modern poetic careers. A view of modern poetry which does not take it seriously into account is not adequate. One must ask, therefore, why so little attention has been paid to it.

There are reasons. To begin with, Clarke's work is uneven. He was capable, at any stage of his career, of writing poorly. Even whole books can, on the whole, disappoint. *Old-Fashioned Pilgrimage*, published in 1967, is a worrying book, though the book that preceded it, and the book that followed, contain some of his best work. Given this unevenness, the reading of his poetry demands patience and discrimination to an unusual degree; it is a constant test of one's powers of judgment. At the same time, it does little to satisfy the casual appetite for large or "interesting" subject matter; it strikes no glamorous or tragic or rhetorical poses.

In addition, the range of Clarke's interests is narrow. His poems, with few exceptions, are content to be parochial (bearing in mind Patrick Kavanagh's valuable distinction between the parochial and the provincial). They reflect only the immediate milieu. In its narrowness of reference, in fact, much of his work raises the whole question of legitimate obscurity in poetry. Some poems are virtually private, or so particular in their comments that it would be helpful to have the relevant newspaper handy. There are poems of such economical means, like "Usufruct" in *Too Great a Vine*, that they require us, if we are to understand them at all, to extract the essential facts—the facts on whose basis the poem's statement communicates—with Holmesian care. But the facts *can* be extracted. And a reading of "Miss Marnell," coming two pages later in the book after "Usufruct," acts as a confirming footnote. The poems accumulate, particularly the later ones. They illuminate each other and establish relationships among themselves so that a microcosm of the human scene is formed, small in scope but complete. Raising the question of obscurity, these poems, by their authority and integrity, lay the question to rest.

There is also the matter of verbal idiosyncrasy. With one of his strongest books, *Night and Morning*, published in 1938, Clarke abandoned the derivative richness of his previous work and plunged into linguistic darkness. The diction is compacted and constricted, full of puns. The elements of grammar and syntax transfer and contort. The mature style of his later work is easier; it absorbs these complexities. But it does not simplify them. The diction of his last poems, as in *Tiresias*, is a great achievement. It is a vivid, particular voice, rich and supple, alert to every dart and twist of the imagination; nothing is unsayable. But it is no "natural" voice. Its ease is achieved in the face of rupture, truncation, displacement, fusion and confusion under pressure. . . .

Clarke's positive achievement, extricated from all these negative coils, is clear. He has dealt with certain fundamental human matters, manhandling his spirit from the shallows into the depths and then upward into a serene light. He has done so directly and completely, in a unique language of flexibility and power.

Thomas Kinsella. Introduction to Austin Clarke,
Selected Poems (Dublin, Dolmen, 1976), pp. ix–xi

It is not altogether surprising that there should exist in modern Irish poetry, both north and south of the border, a tradition of public verse that takes as its concern the historical, social, and political condition of the island.

The poet whose work initiates and most completely embodies this tradition is Austin Clarke, a writer who was, for most of his life, without honor in his native land. Apparently because of their sexual explicitness several of his early books were banned by the Irish censors, and his career as a university teacher was abruptly terminated when he married outside the Church. Clarke saw in the medieval monastic Irish culture of saints and scholars a political, religious, and artistic integrity conspicuously lacking in modern Ireland. . . .

With the publication of *Ancient Lights* in 1955, Clarke began to confront directly the modern world and assume his role as satirical conscience of Ireland, as player of the bad morality and crippled hearts and minds of the Irish establishment. In many of his poems since the mid-fifties he has eloquently and often savagely inveighed against clerical domination in the state. (Clarke has, though, perceived that other countries have been afflicted, on occasion at least, with the same sort of complicity of Church and state, as in "Dirge," a poem inspired by Cardinal Spellman's sanction of the Vietnam War.) Clarke's satirical attacks on Irish society are clearly motivated by an outraged compassion for its victims: he sympathizes with the thwarted, guilt-ridden young in a puritanical society (in "The Envy of Poor Lovers") and he attacks the cold comfort enunciated by a Catholic bishop on the death by fire of sixty children in their firetrap orphanage (in "Three Poems About Children"). To read "Martha Blake at Fifty-One" is to be made to feel dismay and pain. We are made to care about the ignominious suffering and death of a pious spinster, and to feel anger at the failure of her society and her religion to provide her (and many thousands like her) with the simplest consolation. Clarke's satire attains its emotional intensity in large part by his compassionate identification with other victims of his society. It is as though he realized that his own maiming at the hands of society—the sexual guilt deeply injected into his life, the proscription of his work, the punitive attitude of society toward him because of his marriage, the lifelong searching for spiritual values frustrated by clericalism—gives him common cause with those victims of society whose lot is so much worse than his. Unlike Yeats's satiric poems, then, Clarke's speak for the disenfranchised and from their viewpoint, rather than from identification with an aristocratic Anglo-Irish culture. It is this humble and deeply felt identification with those damaged by an unjust society that lends to Clarke's excoriation of modern Ireland so much of its moral force and intensity of emotion.

Anthony Bradley. Introduction to Anthony Bradley,
ed., <i>Contemporary Irish Poetry</i> (Berkeley,
Univ. of California Pr., 1980), pp. 4–5

The medieval period provided the source of several of Clarke's most successful poems, and he returned to it occasionally in works after *Pilgrimage*—in isolated poems and in the prose romances *The Bright Temptation* (1932) and *The Singing Men at Cashel* (1936). The *Pilgrimage* volume contains also some of his best experiments on using internal assonance in place of rhyme and shows off his fine craftsmanship with words; the individual poem "Pilgrimage," for instance, contains the description of a monastery which is "a barren isle,/Where Paradise is praised," and on whose chapel windows "in stained glass the holy day/Was sainted."

But just as he had finally given up the mythological past for the middle ages, so Clarke was to give up the middle ages for the modern world. He had brought forward intact his image of frustrated love from the early epic verse into the lyrics on the medieval period, but its impact was still not strong enough on his audience. He felt a need and a pressure to write poems more openly critical of the church and its stifling effect on Ireland. Accordingly, his volumes after the 1930s—*Night and Morning* in 1938, *Ancient Lights* in 1955, *Too Great a Vine* in 1957, *The Horse Eaters* in 1960, and *Flight to Africa and Other Poems* in 1963—deal directly and scathingly with social issues. His wit is sharp and precise, but never petty. As Thomas Kinsella observes, in these later poems "Small clear evils magnify into Evil,/Pity and mockery reflect a humane Good" and Denis Donoghue echoes much the same sentiment: "there is a strange and wonderful synecdoche in these late poems, so that little things implicate big things, the Irish part stands for the human All."

Speaking in a late prose work, the autobiographical *Twice Round the Black Church*, Clarke reports on what led him to open distrust of the church, both wryly—"The Jesuit Fathers accepted the Victorian belief that the problems of puberty could be solved by the playing of British games, such as cricket or rugby," and more seriously—"There is no doubt that a country in which an ever-increasing number of celibate orders continually exert influence must suffer from a hidden uneasiness." Thus the poet-scholar who speaks in "The Straying Student," the first poem in *Night and Morning*, has the right to be afraid of

> . . . this land, where every woman's son
> Must carry his own coffin and believe,
> In dread, all that the clergy teach the young.

Throughout these later poems, sharp images of sexuality and love, scorned, thwarted, and even brutally used by the Church, come into agonized focus.

Beth Timson. In Dennis Jackson, ed.,
Irish Renaissance Annual III (Newark,
Univ. of Delaware Pr., 1982), pp. 64–65

[T]o dismiss Clarke as a writer of purely provincial interest is to do him a great disservice. Clarke's work deserves to be appreciated, because it succeeds, to an extent that the work of no other modern Irish writer succeeds, in expressing accurately the Catholic and Gaelic dimensions of the Irish sensibility and in describing the political, social, and religious realities of life in modern Ireland. But Clarke's poetry does much more than this, and it is in ignoring the universal dimensions of his work and his vision that the label of provincialism does him the greatest injustice. . . .

No other Irish poet of this century was more convinced of the "social and artistic validity of the parish" than was Clarke. Moreover, beneath the sometimes forbidding surface of Clarke's persistently Irish point of view is a poet motivated by a broad humanistic vision, a poet profoundly concerned with "the fundamentals" of human existence. The experience of being Catholic in modern Ireland is, assuredly, "of the parish"; but in coming to terms with this specific experience, and with the legacy of guilt bequeathed by a vision of man as essentially fallen, Clarke's poetry stands as an impressive affirmation of an uncompromisingly humanistic vision, a vision that celebrates man's inherent worth and insists on his right to moral, intellectual, and spiritual freedom. The political, social, and religious realities of twentieth-century Ireland—the subject matter of most of Clarke's public poetry—are, again, matters decidedly of the parish; but Clarke's satirical attacks on Irish politicians and clergymen also express a broad concern for social justice and individual freedom and, in the face of the increasing homage that the twentieth century pays to a calculating materialism, a concern for the importance of distinctively human and nonmaterialistic values, especially human love. Finally, the most obvious manifestation of Clarke's belief in the "artistic validity of the parish" is his lifelong commitment to Ireland's Gaelic culture; yet Clarke's celebration of that culture calls attention not just to its uniqueness but also to the value that it placed on human dignity and freedom.

Gregory A. Schirmer. *The Poetry of Austin Clarke*
(Notre Dame, Ind., Univ. of Notre Dame Pr., 1983),
pp. 5–6

COLUM, PADRAIC (1881–1972)

Padraic Colum is the first Irish poet who has chosen to write of the common life [*Wild Earth*]. He has not gone, like W. B. Yeats, to fairyland for his inspiration, nor taken any obscure light of the soul to mean the light of the world. He has not looked down on his people like Mr. Synge and the writers of his school, to whom life is only a subject for art. He has not looked up to them, unwisely idealising his characters, like so many sentimentalists, who write as if every Irish peasant was only a little lower than the angels. Padraic Colum is in love with the normal. He feels with truth that there is the substance of more noble poetry in the divine average than in the exceptions. He walks among his people, accepting them for what they are, in the same way as Whitman, Burns, and the great masters of everyday life. He writes of his people with love, the rarest of all sentiments in literature. You feel he could trudge along for hours with his drover, quite happy because he is walking beside a living human being. He could sit by the hearth for hours with any old woman, and be happy listening to her gossip and memories. He watches motherhood with tenderness and reverence, and at rarer moments he attains to a grandeur of conception, as in the magnificent close to the "Plougher," where the night falls and man and beast are silhouetted against the sunset. . . .

Surely a poet for the countryman to read. Here he can see his life again freshly, and think of it with more acceptance and with less of bitter protest against his fate. We hope the work of this young poet will be in every country house in Ireland. If he fulfils the promise of those early verses, he may end by being the most familiar and best-loved name in our literature. [1907]

George William Russell (A.E.). *Selections from the
Contributions to "The Irish Homestead,"* Vol. II,
Henry Summerfield, ed. (Atlantic Highlands, N.J.,
Humanities Press, 1978), p. 861

There is in this book [*My Irish Year*] a peculiarly personal note. I am always quite certain when I am being made intimate with Michael or Thady Gilsenan,

Bartley Mulstay, and a host of others, for with these we are instantly placed on speaking terms, I am equally certain when the author himself takes his turn in the ceilidh, for this is not so much a book as a ceilidh. Neither the author nor any of the people he writes of ever merge their individuality, and yet, strangely, the distance between Mr. Colum, when speaking in his own person, and that of Michael Heffernan is scarcely perceptible. The temptation to exploit country people in a literary way has not been resisted by others whose books attempted to do what Mr. Colum has now finely done. Seldom does the literary artist emerge from these pages, and yet, as many a beautifully balanced and vivid passage can testify, he is never absent from them, but even this beauty and colour are lined unobtrusively and quietly. I am quite satisfied that the country folk whom we meet here, with their wives and daughters and cronies, speak with the honest homeliness which is their proper speech. The chance remark heard on a road, the chatter of three or four people in a house, what the priest said to the schoolmaster, or what an old stroller said to whoever chanced along—these are the things which gave me most pleasure, and in these unsophisticated exchanges we often get lightness, grace and beauty.

Somehow the impression remains with me as of a quiet, wise people who can afford to overlook many immediate, shifting necessities, regarding these with a slightly cynical perturbation. The extreme quietude of Mr. Colum's writing may be the cause of this. Mr. Colum has a remarkable eye: he sees with the steady sharpness of a camera, and his pictures have an unwavering, wiry outline which is quite peculiar to himself. This, it seemed to me, sometimes reacted on his writing, so that the effect at first was unpleasantly mechanical, but afterwards I came to look for and like it. . . .

I think this is the finest book that has ever been written about Irish humanity. It is inclusive. Many types are here, the playboy, the clodhopper, decent, quiet men and women and those others, stubborn and reckless, to whom God and man are a jape—they are all here, but the unity which underlies all diversity is here also, and it is that which makes the book truly representative of Ireland.

James Stephens. Irish Review.
Sept., 1912, pp. 384, 387

It is not . . . difficult to see how it came about that Mr. Colum, who began to write so young, came to write so much about youth and the rebellion of youth, and to write about those other themes of his, themes all of them made more intense by the youth that is concerned with them—the land that obsesses the life of the man of the house all Ireland over, and through him obsesses the lives of his family; and love of woman.

Mr. Colum does not intrude his own personality into his plays, but it is felt, as it should be felt, in every one of his lyrics. Reading them one has a sense of a youth like the youth of some characters in his plays; a youth more

manly than Cornelius's, less restless than Ellen's; a youth serious and troubled with thought; a youth in revolt against much in the old order, but tolerant
of the passing generation that fears it "knocking at the door." It is a youth impassioned rather than passionate, more pronouncedly a youth of mind than a
youth of heart. When I say youth of mind, I mean not immaturity of mind, but
the outlook of the young mind; not radicalism, but a fixed determination to
think things out afresh and not to accept them because of any convention.

Eloquence one always looks for in the writing of an Irishman, and humor
and power over dialogue, but Mr. Colum is too serious with youth to care
much for humor, and, like Mr. [Edward] Martyn, though not to the same extent, he has trouble with his dialogue. The feeling for the situation, the understanding of what is in the characters' minds, is in Mr. Colum, but the dialogue does not always accommodate itself to situation and thought. What Mr.
Colum makes his characters say has in it the thought and the sentiment of
what they would say, but the words as often lack life as have it. It is this difficulty with dialogue that has prevented Mr. Colum, in his plays, true and
finely planned as they are, from reaching great achievement. As dramatist he
is still more full of promise than of achievement, and to be a dramatist of
promise after ten years of playwriting is to be at a standstill. In lyric poetry it
is otherwise with Mr. Colum. There he has attained. You will find his real
value in *Wild Earth*, slight though the book may seem. Here is reading of life,
here is imagination, here is lyric cry. Read these little poems once and they
will be your familiars forever.

Cornelius Weygandt. *Irish Plays and Playwrights*
(Boston and New York, Houghton Mifflin, 1913),
pp. 206–8

Some writers pay special attention to the relation between form and subject in
their works. They strive that matter and substance shall be harmonious, or
bear that definite relation to each other that satisfies the instincts of the reader.
Others throw form to the winds and treat big and little subjects alike, just as
the impulse of the moment demands, and without regard to the whole of
which they are a part. It is to this latter class that *Castle Conquer* belongs. It is
a book full of wonderful writing, of sympathetic insight, of varied characters
dramatically drawn, and all steeped in an atmosphere of half-lights and shadows which few others besides Padraic Colum could achieve. But it is composite in its compilation and lacks the enduring impressiveness that can only be
obtained by cumulative effort of mood on thought. It is part story, part idyll,
but owing to its discursiveness it does not wholly satisfy as either, while
partaking of the nature of both. The author's original intention evidently was
to secure a sense of unity by a succession of impressionistic sketches. These
are admirably done, though at times somewhat vague, and occasionally the
drift of the plot through them becomes momentarily obscure. And towards the

end of the book, when the force of the narrative becomes more direct, this method is frankly abandoned altogether.

Running through it all there is the love motive, which is chiefly cast in the idyllic mode. It is delicately and beautifully wrought, and, if isolated, could easily be made into an almost perfect thing. The story part deals mainly with the hero's excursions into the troubled agrarian agitations of his day, terminating with his arrest and trial on a charge of murder. But the author is not at his best when dealing with plain matters of fact like this. He loses his delicacy of touch and is inclined to become prosy. Witness the soliloquy of John Fitzsimons, the junior counsel. And in any case this part of the book contains little that is fresh about such affairs.

As well as these two main motives *Castle Conquer* is crowded with a variety of secondary and subsidiary themes, each one bringing its own appropriate list of characters. These interludes are full of life and vigour, and many are cast in a terse dramatic dialogue reminiscent of the plays in which Mr. Colum first distinguished himself. Some stand out very vividly in the memory. For instance, Chapter VII, that embodies the story of Michael Philabeen, the weaver—which, by the way, illustrates my remark about the discursiveness of the book, as this character appears nowhere else, and is introduced here in quite an irrelevant manner. Then in Chapter X we have Maelshaughlinn's account of his adventures at the fair—a really remarkable piece of writing, quite a *tour de force* of dexterous word manipulation done with extraordinary skill and eminently effective. But, perhaps, the best of these scenes is Chapter XX, called Saint Brighid. It is not strictly a detached item like the others just mentioned, as it deals with the main texture of the book. But it is complete in itself, as it could be read and understood without reference to the rest. The manner in which it is related is a triumph of literary craftmanship. It is a story told, as it were, aslant. It is the whispered comment of two people inside a house, recalling a tragic story, and overheard through the open window by a girl outside who is churning. But what a touching story, and how its pathos is heightened by the method of telling! It is a tale of external law and inward affection at war, and human feeling triumphant at the end.

In *Castle Conquer* Padraic Colum has given us a book full of defiance of conventional methods. And he has clothed his conceptions in a druid mist of beauty which bewitches mundane criticism.

DM. Nov., 1923, pp. 344–45

Thomas Muskerry was first staged at the Abbey Theatre on 12th May, 1910. . . . It is a study in the Ibsen manner of a man being brought to ruin by the pressure of his family. From being the Master of the Workhouse Muskerry is brought by stages to his death in a pauper's bed in the institution over which he ruled. It is the blind piper Myles Gorman who gives the play its significance, and when the skirl of the pipes is heard on the road in joyous celebration of Gorman's freedom one feels that Thomas Muskerry, too, has only been set free to live the life that he would have chosen. The play is true to life in rural Ireland, sparing nothing of the drab existence in an Irish country town. As a picture of the "*petty bourgeois*" of Ireland the play is memorable.

Of his outlook and his method Colum himself has said all there need be said in the Preface of *Thomas Muskerry*. "Life, in terms of Catholic philosophy, is means to the individualization of the spirit . . . the dramatist is unable to conceive of one life being less significant than another. . . . We are in a studio and painted canvasses are lying about. The artist puts a frame before one of the canvasses and at once the picture is a mark for our attention. . . . The dramatist is concerned not primarily with the creation of character, but with the creation of situations." Thus is Colum divided from Synge and brought close to the position held by Lady Gregory.

In the speech which he uses in his plays Colum is far removed from either. It is without the rhythm of the Western peasant, but it is a poet's selection of the more pedestrian speech of the Irish Midlands. In point of fact the speech used by Colum is a very close approximation to the actual speech of the greater part of Ireland. His dialogue seldom suggests the poet, and it is his characterisation rather than his speech that indicates the poet behind the play. The speech and the situations given to the stage by Colum led to the flood of ready-made "peasant" plays which every one in Ireland seemed capable of writing.

"Some years ago I thought of a grandiose task, the writing of the comedy of Irish life through all the social stages. I had thought of this work (perhaps after discovering Balzac) as a piece of social history." In these words Colum brings himself into the Ibsen circle, and therein he discovers his master. That grandiose task was soon given up, much to the regret of his admirers who saw in him the potential master-dramatist of Ireland. It must be regretted by everyone who knows his work that Colum so quickly tired of that task which was as necessary as it certainly was grandiose, as it is to be regretted also that he ceased to write plays at a time when his best work was confidently expected.

Andrew E. Malone. The Irish Drama
(London, Constable, 1929), pp. 168–69

In form and manner [the] verses of [Padraic Colum] were perhaps midway between [those of Joseph Campbell and Seamas O'Sullivan]; less harsh than Campbell's, simpler than O'Sullivan's. Indeed, their simplicity was the outstanding fact about them. Not till long afterward did I hear that those verses were learned by heart by cottagers and farmers and simple people, who spoke them at the fireside in the same way that they might sing a song or play a tune on the concertina. Almost alone among modern poets, Padraic Colum had an unlettered as well as a lettered audience. And it is easy to see why. Though there is nothing about him of the boy-who-wouldn't-grow-up, that sickly English abstraction which goes with the worship of games and an indigenous form of sentimentality, Colum has brought to mature manhood a curious innocence of vision, a power of seeing familiar things as if he had only just come across them. His verse has wisdom, but it seems to be intuitive wisdom, not the wisdom of experience. It is untouched by the stain of the world. This innocence of outlook, somewhat akin to Blake's, but more untroubled, more essentially pagan, Colum has kept to the present day. It has survived his years in America, his visits to the South Seas, and the work a poet must do to get his living. The peasants who delighted in the songs from *Wild Earth* would find nothing alien to them in any of the volumes which come afterward, for this poet's skill is nowhere harder to analyze than in his faculty for instantly comprehending a complex situation and reducing it to simple and apparently inevitable expression.

L. A. G. Strong. Com. June 7, 1935, p. 155

A broad plain, frequently accented by little hills, would certainly form an appropriate metaphor to describe the effect of Padraic Colum's new novel [*The Flying Swans*]—his second in a lifetime of writing. The leisurely sweep of its narrative includes many vivid incidents—fights, deathbeds, loves, betrayals—but all of them in the end leave the characters unchanged; even the chameleon-like Robert O'Rehill, the hero's absconding father, retains an odd consistency through all his evasions of reality. The mountains of tragedy loom always on the horizon, but the upheavals they symbolize never come to pass.

Padraic Colum, who heard folk tales before he could read and has spent much of his life retelling the folklore and epics of the world—Irish, Greek, Hawaiian—has woven into his book many of the archetypal characters and themes beloved by the shanachie and the epic poet: the Lost Father, the Wronged Wife, the Hunchback, the Witch, the Wicked Uncle, the Counselor, Expulsion, Fosterage, Youthful Exploits (*Macgnímartha* in Gaelic), and Return. The last four of these are among the titles given to sections of *The Flying Swans*; the title of the book itself reminds us of the wronged Children of Lir, who were changed into swans in the famous Irish tale.

I would not recommend this contemplative book to the kind of reader who expects a novel to give him a roller-coaster ride, on which, once pinned down by the safety bar, he is swept breathless up dizzy heights and hurtled screaming down dizzier depths, until the vehicle deposits him, retching and staggering, on firm ground once more. This is rather the kind of book that one lays aside from time to time in order to daydream over one's own youth. Yet Ulick O'Rehill, the future sculptor, finally chooses reality and responsibility in preference to the daydreaming fecklessness of his father and thus rejects the man who has rejected his mother, his younger brother and himself.

In the long run, when this novel's characters and incidents have faded from the reader's mind, one abiding influence will remain with him—its style. Perhaps it would be more correct to call it a language rather than a style, that collective language of the first generation of the Irish literary revival. The most recent generation of Irish writers seem to have lost it completely. To them Gaelic is Gaelic, English is Oxford or Hollywood, and Irish English is a bastard dialect never spoken off the stage of the Abbey Theatre. As a result, their novels and plays are unreadable, their poems readable but not speakable.

But here, with scarce-diminished vigor, that sinewy style rides once more, giving—in narrative as well as dialogue—the old sense of a language reborn, of an English grafted on Gaelic, almost every phrase of which has been formed, not by pen or typewriter, but on the living lips of men. "Oisín in the wake of the Fianna" says the Gaelic proverb for survivors of a great generation. But Padraic Colum is an Oisín not yet fallen from his horse, an Oisín who still miraculously retains his youth and strength.

Vivian Mercier. Com. July 19, 1957, pp. 404–5

Padraic Colum champions the cause of peasant Ireland. The nationalism which informs his verse bears little resemblance to the nationalism given expression by Yeats, A.E., or the Rising poets. He is concerned neither with creating a national mythology from which his countrymen may draw spiritual strength nor with justifying Ireland's sacred cause of rebellion against the Gall. Ultimately, Colum's nationalism derives from the stuff of everyday existence, from the simple people and the homely properties of the Irish country scene. To be sure, until his departure for America in 1914, Colum participated in a more militant kind of nationalism and had his hand in the curious mixture of cultural and political agitations that constituted Irish public affairs. . . . The names mentioned in dedications to his numerous books comprise a kind of litany of Irish patriots—Pearse, MacDonagh, Griffith, Michael Collins. In his *Collected Poems* one finds a number of poems that are specifically topical: an elegiac panegyric on Arthur Griffith's death, another on the execution of Roger Casement. . . . Colum's lines have the same bitter ring one notes in Yeats' Casement poems; like most Irish poets, Colum has been moved to respond to the stimuli of contemporary events. Yet significantly, his topical poems are omitted from *The Poet's Circuits*—which Colum describes as his "collected poems of Ireland"—for they are only incidental to the central statement of his nationalism. . . .

The Poet's Circuits includes several previously unpublished selections, the most significant of which is "Fore-Piece," a discursive and autobiographical poem in which Colum attempts to define for the reader the underlying inspiration for his work and by implication its purpose. Significantly, the speaker of the poem finds his way to the hearth of the country cottage, the meeting place for various elements of the popular peasant tradition. . . . The men and women who lived on the land, the birds and the beasts, the fields and the bogs: these are the images of the countryside; and with these images Colum identifies himself and his work. . . .

Colum's poetry, like much of his early drama, represents an attempt to achieve "expression of the national character" as he perceived it in the people of the countryside (*Poems*, p. v). His verse is crowded with what [L. A. G.] Strong terms the "common furniture" of life, or, more specifically, the common furniture of Irish peasant life—the quaint (one cannot avoid the word) characters, the homely proprieties of hearth and pasture. But his art embodies more than realistic detail, for Colum, more than any modern Irish poet writing in English, with the possible exception of Joseph Campbell, captures in his verse the underlying spiritual naïveté of the peasantry. In this respect, his portrayal of the Irish peasant is more accurate, more true to life, than either Yeats' portrayal or that of Padraic Pearse. Yeats employed folk materials to give substance to his occult vision and Pearse used them to support his own peculiar belief in mystical nationalism. Colum, on the other hand, is innocent of any extrinsic design; the attitudes and beliefs of the peasantry are presented in his verse for their own sake and are recorded in the form in which he found them among the people. Mary Sturgeon perceived this quality in the early work of both Colum and Campbell: "they are innocent of ulterior purpose and free from the least chill of philosophical questioning into origin or ends."

Richard J. Loftus. *Nationalism in Modern Anglo-Irish Poetry* (Madison, Univ. of Wisconsin Pr., 1964), pp. 164–66, 169–71

Colum thinks of himself as one of the few authentic national poets of Ireland because his upbringing is rural and Catholic, as opposed to the Protestant ascendancy backgrounds of poets like Yeats, AE and Lady Gregory, whose links with the peasant people are at best studied and vicarious. Much of Colum's poetry retains its roots in the Catholic peasantry of the Irish Republic, dealing occasionally with the joys and aspirations of the people but far more with their sorrows, hopelessnesses and disintegration. Always, however, his people are uncomplicated and readily understandable and his language sparse and accurate.

Colum cannot be considered typical of any particular modern tradition. Hailed as a poet of the Irish Renaissance, his poems lacked the nationalistic didacticism which plagued other Irish poets. . . . During the years following World War I, a period of realism, surrealism, Dadaism, and naturalism, each with its own limitations on subject matter and emphasis on a particular variety of experiment, his poems bordered on the sentimental, and were more often about the beautiful, the remote and the wondrous than the ugly, the despairing and the hopeless. . . .

Any overall assessment of Colum as a dramatist would be less than candid if it did not admit that his chief contributions to the stage were historical rather than literary. While his importance to the Irish theatre cannot be overstated, his contributions were noteworthy because they were precedents rather than because they were destined some day to be recognized masterpieces of drama. Many of Colum's plays had merit, but none, in the final analysis, could be called great, as can a number of his poems. On the other hand, it has already been shown that his poetry has depended in large measure on his dramatic background and techniques, and to the extent that his poetry enters into his last plays it has improved them. It is difficult to imagine Colum not writing for the theatre. Without the influence and experience of his playwriting, we would have had a poet and storyteller of a vastly different and less important kind.

Most students of Irish literature know Padraic Colum as a poet, a dramatist and perhaps even a writer of children's stories. It may come as a surprise that he has written a considerable number of short stories, two novels, two biographies and four books of essays, as well as contributions and prefaces for fifty-one books and pieces of various sorts for more than sixty newspapers and periodicals. . . . [W]hen Colum's fiction and nonfiction prose are considered as a whole, certain patterns begin to manifest themselves; altogether these patterns comprise a style as distinctive as that of any writer of the twentieth century. . . .

Almost all of Colum's fiction grows out of its Irish milieu, and similarly most of his nonfiction is an elaboration on the country, its people and its customs. There have been excursions to Hawaii, France and America but the bulk of his work concerns his home. Because of this preoccupation he has become for many Americans the window on the Irish scene, the chronicler of its folklore and customs, a sort of literary tourist bureau. Though this role had its inception in his early poetry and plays, he has striven to maintain it through his novels, biographies and essays.

Just as his subject matter is predominantly Irish, his style can also be generally described as familiar and colloquial. His most characteristic stylistic trait is his abundant use of the present tense narration in fiction as well as nonfiction. This together with a first person narrator places him in the role of a storyteller sitting by a turf fire spinning out tales of things familiar to him and wondrous to his audience. This posture that Colum tries to maintain in his work is one he is well suited to. The particular criteria of excellence in evaluating Colum's work are not the normal currency of contemporary literary critics, because few other serious writers attempt what he is doing, and our appreciation of it has fallen into disrepair through disuse.

Zack Bowen. *Padraic Colum: A Biographical-
Critical Introduction* (Carbondale, Southern Illinois
Univ. Pr., 1970), pp. 25–26, 89–91

In the first decade of the century, the most promising new Irish writers were two brilliant young men, John Synge and Padraic Colum. Synge died in 1909, after a short turbulent career that produced two masterpieces for the repertoire of the world and a week of rioting that carried his name and that of the Abbey Theatre around the world. Padraic Colum is still alive today, writing as clearly, as charmingly, and as vitally as ever he has at any time in the last seventy years.

In those years he has produced an immense and varied body of work that includes plays, poems, novels, memoirs, travel books, children's books, and a legion of fugitive articles, reviews, and letters to the press. Most of his serious work in the drama, however, appeared in this early period, and his later pieces have been the occasional efforts of a busy man of letters who is at his ease in many genres. In the first ten years of the century, though, he devoted himself to the drama with a serious consistency. His first plays were one-acts, and at best are only talented apprentice work. They include *The Children of Lir*, a poetic Yeats-like tragedy (1901); *The Foleys*, an uncomfortable mélange of Irish patriotism and Ibsenism (1902); *The Kingdom of the Young*, a peasant drama foreshadowing his later fine play *The Land; The Miracle of the Corn*, a peasant miracle play which perhaps owes something to Yeats' *The Countess Cathleen; Eoghan's Wife*, a short lyrical monologue; and *The Saxon Shillin'*, which was first produced in 1903, by the Daughters of Erin's children's dramatic class, after having been strongly considered by the Irish National Theatre Society. Colum's later full-length work showed an astonishing growth in power, and includes *Broken Sail* (later revised as *The Fiddler's House*) of 1903; *The Land* of 1905; and his masterpiece *Thomas Muskerry* of 1910. In later years, he was to make some interesting experiments, including *The Desert* (later revised as *Mogu of the Desert*) which is somewhat reminiscent of Lord Dunsany; the mildly expressionistic *Balloon*; and the Yeatsian Noh-drama *Moytura*; but he was never again to equal the passion and the pathos of *Thomas Muskerry*.

The Saxon Shillin', like Maud Gonne's *Dawn*, is an example of the many patriotic dramas which fervent young Irishmen were turning out. However, its plot has both a simplicity and an irony that lift it above many similar dramas of its time. It has also a definite historical importance in its ability to dramatize for us the temper of the Irish audience in 1903.

Robert Hogan and James Kilroy. Introduction to
Robert Hogan and James Kilroy, eds.,
Lost Plays of the Irish Renaissance
(Newark, Del., Proscenium Pr., 1970), pp. 14–15

At bottom . . . Colum's romanticism is no less than a conscious affirmation and celebration of the origins and growth of the traditional rural Irish folk ethic. It is the childhood motif that can be found in such romantic, or at least romantically inclined, poets as Thomas Traherne and William Wordsworth. For all three, the truest apprehension of the world comes in infancy—whether of a nation or an individual. Undoubtedly, Colum's success as a writer and translator of children's stories is evidence of this sensibility to infancy.

What critics have recognized as the romantic quality of Colum's poetry can now be seen as the expression of a sensibility to the infancy of a nation, or a rural Irish folk ethic. The three main characteristics of his celebration of the value or authority of the world view in this folk ethic are succinctly summarized in the memoirs of his private notebooks in a description of early Ireland, "There poetry is recited, scholarship imbibed, stories told." A look at each of these three characteristics also helps to distinguish his poetry from peasant verse.

Significantly, the poems were "recited" and the stories "told" in early Ireland. Colum feels that the characteristics of this oral literature should be kept and applied in the techniques of written poetry. One of these characteristics is rhythm. In a 1965 mimeographed essay, Colum writes, "Poetry is what the early people know it for—not a statement, but an incantation—the chant makes for enchantment." Secondly, his interest in the rhyme of oral poetry is made explicit in an essay on poetry for children. . . .

Yet it is a mistake to call his poetry simple or childish because he tries to make it child-like through such devices as heavy use of rhythm and rhyme. While Colum feels, for example, that rhythm is one of the qualities that distinguishes poetry from prose, his understanding of rhythm is not childish, but very complex. . . . Clearly, Colum's emphasis upon rhythm and rhyme is an attempt to recover in his sophisticated poetry of infancy the sensibilities of a child's more direct and romantic apprehension of the world.

In addition to the recitation of poetry, another value of infancy which Colum notes is that scholarship is imbibed. What he means by imbibing is a natural wonder at and love of the world. He feels that this outlook is found most perfectly in a child since the child has a sort of intrinsic poetic soul. . . .

Unlike his contemporaries, Colum's sense of modern man's alienation from his own world results in an emphasis upon those values that have enabled men in the past to feel an intimate tie to the universe. While his little people such as the farmer in "Reminiscence" and the basket maker are not important in themselves, they are filled with significance in his poetry as the expression of a healthy, vital, and positive style of life that has enabled them to deal effectively with the vicissitudes of life. The affirmation of the value of a basket that has so many uses for a housewife is a microcosmic example of his celebration of the macrocosm of an at least partly successful rural Irish folk ethic. Certainly, one of the most important reasons for reading Colum's poetry is that in it one can find reassurances that the values, authority, and world views of the past are not entirely without relevance to modern man.

Douglas S. Campbell, *Éire-Ireland*.
Autumn, 1974, pp. 62–63, 68

For Padraic Colum's centenary Liam Miller has reprinted *The Poet's Circuits* (1960) and has given back the "emotional history" or saga of "succession" that Colum drew from his Irish verse in the late 1950s. While his poems date from earlier in the century, Colum's design does not. Its Modernist ambitions, resembling those of [John] Montague's *The Rough Field* (1972), should renew interest in Colum's talents, as should Benedict Kiely's lively preface. Colum quilts together the lyrics, soliloquies, narratives and ballads of his eight "circuits" with the voice of an observant persona tutored by a Yeatsian countryman named Owen Paralon: "I made poems out of glimpses I was given/Of days and nights of women and men." After this plain beginning Colum picks up remembered patches of Irish tradition—from the Fenian "Cétemain" through Jacobite aislingí to echoes of Yeats in the dialogue "The Hearthstone and the Loom," in the lyric "Black tassels, black tassels." Kiely rightly praises "The Market Place" and "Honey Seller," but I note them for their Wordsworthian elements, for echoes of *The Prelude*. And, if we refrain from reading Colum with a late 19th-century tongue, then "Dreamer of the New Hearth" and "Man Who Gains a Charm"—*Uisge cloiche gan irraidh* —display Colum's mastery of elemental language, resonant spareness, while "Branding Foals" and "Crows" glisten with dramatic tone, verbal color. For artistry, Colum takes instruction from his anonymous scribe bent over a leaf of the Book of Kells: "make a letter like a monument," then "on a ground of gold/Compose a circuit . . . a strict pattern."

Colum's generosity, however, fills his circuits so full of lore observed, tradition translated that the "poet" fades from focus—his character muted in the diction of other voices. Except in the "After-pieces," Colum's persona becomes in the later circuits a looker-on.

Thomas Dillon Redshaw. *ILS*. Spring, 1983, p. 28

Padraic Colum was a Catholic writer and thus different from the many Protestant Irish writers who did much to create the literary revival of modern Ireland. The discipline of his verse, his love of classicism, his concentration, his surety, and his unquestioning, unequivocating acceptance of the presence of God and the sanctity of the Church are all products of his background and a tribute to his faith. If Colum's God is imprecisely drawn and his belief implied but not stated, it is because he no more questioned the Deity or his institution on earth than he would ask about the air he breathed. In his delicate depictions of the landscape he loved, Colum included a priori his belief that God's hand had made the model for his images.

Colum was thus a poet of the senses, not an intellectual writer. He strove to reconstitute by his writing the sight and sound experiences of his youth. Psychological problems and metaphysical debates caused him little anxiety. It was enough to call life as he saw it and felt it. There was no Tennysonian crisis in Padraic Colum's life. He never doubted the existence of God, the reality of an afterlife, the coming independence of Ireland, and the greatness of Gaelic culture.

Colum loved, admired, and respected the peasant. In their long-suffering relationship with alien landlords, in their age-old struggle with the soil, in their deep-rooted love for the land, in their pride and their dignity, in their generosity and hospitality, in their courtesy and gentleness, and in their courage and stoicism, Colum saw the true nobility of humankind. "Colum's view of life is in essence that of the peasant as a noble savage endowed with the secrets of life and death. This valuable but somehow simple viewpoint is projected in poetry where not alone sowers and reapers but honey-sellers, drovers, blacksmiths, ballad-singers, bird-catchers, and tin whistle-players move in delightful but somehow silent mime."

The poetry and fiction of Padraic Colum are a cultural bridge. They bring together the images and values of a people grown remote with time and the modern world of Ireland. Colum's adaptation of Gaelic speech rhythms and patterns into English verse and prose helps to unite the older Irish culture with the mainstream of English letters. Thus his work, including much of his children's literature, also serves as cultural history. In his rendering of the myths and folklore of Ireland specifically, and the myths and folklore of Europe generally, Colum was able to present and pass on in popular reading form the elemental building blocks of the literature and psychology shared by most of what is called the Western World.

Colum conceptionalized the modern Irish poet as a peasant bard, a preserver of the oral tradition, a storyteller with dramatic skill, a codifier of mores, and a conveyer of cultural values. In this concept he again identified conservatively with the past. The living poet, not the poem, is the personal link with ancient times. Today Colum's lyric poems are read and memorized by thousands of Irish schoolchildren yearly. Most often they do not learn or do not remember the author's name. They only know the poem is poetry from "older times," beautiful poems that tell them of and teach them about the past. Thus Padraic Colum has become both a national poet and an anonymous bard. It is exactly as he would have wished.

Sanford Sternlicht. Padraic Colum
(Boston, Twayne, 1985), pp. 146–47

CORKERY, DANIEL (1878–1964)

It might have been anticipated that the great strike in Dublin in 1913, when the figure of James Larkin loomed menacingly upon the Irish mentality for the first time, would have been the occasion for some contributions to drama. And if there were any such anticipations they were more than realised during the following half-dozen years. . . . *Blight* [written under the pseudonym "A & O"] is undoubtedly the best play yet produced by an Irish dramatist dealing with a specifically Irish social problem. But it is to Daniel Corkery's fine play, *The Labour Leader*, that attention must be directed if it would be seen how that social problem may be exploited with greatest dramatic effect. *The Labour Leader* was staged at the Abbey Theatre for the first time on 30th September, 1919, but it would seem to have been written some years earlier. Immediately it suggests that it is a study of "Jim" Larkin in his heyday, as in the person of David Lombard, the secretary of the Quaymen's Union, there is portrayed all the egoism and all the arrogance of that stormy petrel of Irish Labour. But it is a study marked by all the sympathetic insight that made *The Threshold of Quiet* the most attractive Irish novel of recent years, in which the characterisation is meticulous, the dialogue is pleasing as it is effective, and the sincerity obvious. It is the work of a man who is at the same time a connoisseur of words and a stage craftsman of considerable ability. Unfortunately *The Labour Leader* is the only full-length play he has yet had produced, but he has produced a few short plays, one of which was staged at the Abbey Theatre. Nowadays he would seem to have deserted the theatre and devotes his time to novels, short stories, poems, and the painting of pictures. Altogether a versatile man is Daniel Corkery, and withal he is one of the most distinguished figures in the Irish literary movement. Nowhere, however, does his work seem to have anything like the appreciation that its excellence deserves. Much may be expected from him in the future, but it may be doubted whether he will ever again be lured into the theatre.

Andrew E. Malone. *The Irish Drama*
(London, Constable, 1929), pp. 274–75

Now for the general theory [of Corkery's *Synge and Anglo-Irish Literature*]. It is, in a nutshell, that only an Irish Catholic Nationalist can write Irish literature. Others possess "certain inherited prejudices as well as an inherent lack of spiritual delicacy." But Mr. Corkery goes even further. Even an Irish Catholic Nationalist can only write Irish literature under certain conditions, he must write out of certain material—otherwise he is, in effect, an "Ascendancy" writer. Mr. Corkery thus defines for us the material out of which, and out of which only, Irish literature can be written:—"The three great forces which, working for long in the Irish national being, have made it so different from the English national being, are: (1) The Religious Consciousness of the People; (2) Irish Nationalism; and (3) The Land."

On this basis he examines and rejects everything before Synge—Griffin, Banim, Carleton, Lever, Lefanu, everybody down to Sean O'Casey who, we are gravely told is "an ascendancy writer." Kickham is damned with faint praise. Of Synge he writes: "Greatly moved on one occasion, he achieved the shedding of these prejudices, and wrote his masterpiece: *Riders to the Sea*. It is the unique example where an Ascendancy writer entered with any effective intimacy into the life of the Catholic Gaelic people."

Need I say more on this than that this theory of Mr. Corkery's is wrong-headed and damnable. It is carrying bigotry and intolerance into literature. It is a denial of the Irish Nation. It is prejudiced and, in the real sense, ignorant. Mr. Corkery specifies *Irish Nationalism* without having the faintest understanding of what it is. He quotes with approval Turgenev's "Russia can do without us, but we none of us can do without Russia" and he forgets a saying by a great Irishman "Ireland cannot afford to do without a single Orangeman." The principles of Irish Nationalism have been often stated. They were stated by Swift, by Tone, by Grattan, by Mitchel, by Parnell, by Griffith, by Pearse. They have never been seriously challenged. The Irish Nation includes all the people of this Island, Catholic and non-Catholic, Gael and Sean-ghall, native and "ascendancy." An Irish national literature must include all of them, and an Irish "cosmos"—word beloved by Mr. Corkery—must include all of them.

Mr. Corkery appears to be under the impression that people write for the purpose of expressing their race-consciousness or their religious consciousness, or to serve their people, or something else like that. They don't. They write to express themselves, and the value of their expression is not measured by their material but by their workmanship. The difference between *Riders to the Sea* and *The Racing Lug* is the difference between a great artist and a minor one—the material is the same. The same thing may be observed if one compares Ibsen with Edward Martyn, or any good Abbey play with its imitations. Further, the artist is selective and creative. He selects such of his material as suits him, and he shapes and alters it to suit him. He creates something out of raw material. Take, for instance, Mr. Corkery's own novel *The Threshold of Quiet*. The people in it have the accents and the lineaments of Cork people, but there are no people in Cork so grey, supine, dejected, and spineless as these people are. Yet the novel is a fine novel. What Mr. Corkery did was to take a small piece of raw material, which is at his door, re-shape and remould it, and out of his own artistry and a silly phrase of Thoreau's make a thing of beauty. Every artist does that. The greatest literature does not come out of any of Mr. Corkery's three essentials, or out of all of them, but out of the artist's own consciousness. If you go to the trouble of examining great literature, you will find that the greatest of it deals with individuals, and not with causes, types, sociologies,—isms, or any of the things which in other countries correspond to Mr. Corkery's three essentials for this country. . . .

I think this book is a bad book and a mischievous book. There is hardly a critical opinion expressed about Synge with which one can agree for Mr. Corkery's reasons. There is hardly a critical opinion expressed about anyone else which is not superficial or flippant or unsound. The book, in fact is not a book of criticism but a book of propaganda. Some time ago Mr. Corkery made the statement in public that "What Ireland needs is Catholic Literature," made it to an audience which, as he was well aware, not alone was not interested in literature but actually disliked and was suspicious of literature, an audience which meant by Catholic Literature a pietistic formalism which is neither Catholic nor Literature. The present book is written in the same mood.

P. S. O'Hegarty. *DM*. Jan.–March, 1932,
pp. 53–54, 56

[After attempting dramas of Irish life], Corkery turned to the writing of a novel [*The Threshold of Quiet*] and a volume of short stories. The stories, ineptly called after Yeats's *A Celtic Twilight—A Munster Twilight* appeared first: the novel was published the year after. These stories have little about them that is likely to suggest the delicacy and fantasy of Yeats's lovely verse: they are cast in a different key and came out of a more direct approach to life. Here and there, as in the opening story, "The Ploughing of Leaca Bán," the too-literary quality still asserts itself, but in the city stories, often, nearly always indeed, of the poor-folk in the slums of the city, the note is much more like that of a folk-tale. At the end of the book, grouped under the title of "The Cobbler's Den," we get stories that could with a little more shaping be called pure city-folklore.

This is an entirely original note in Anglo-Irish literature for though a novel like James Stephens' *Mary Mary* may antedate *A Munster Twilight*, there is a self-conscious fantastical note of the more practised literary man in Stephens' little masterpiece of frolic, and the compact, intimate, "folksy" quality of life that is revealed, as typical of Cork city, in Corkery's stories could not, in fact, have been evoked in a metropolis. Not that Corkery has not his own whimsical humour; it is the charm of his personality; but it is not whimsy because it is the laughter of a kindly delight in reality, and no doubt nothing would so please its author as to be told that in the grotesquerie of these little yarns there is a distinct echo of the medieval note in literature.

The novel, delicate, brooding, sensitive, tragic, not without a grotesque note—as in the character of Stevie Galvin—fulfilled absolutely the promise of the stories. It is, without question, a lovely novel, and for many even a perfect novel. Almost aggressively regionalist, it admits no view of life but the local, Irish view: a glimpse of other worlds serving only to support the sense of the inevitability of that view, and to sear the heart with a sense of the delimitation of life within a code, humbly accepted, loyally unquestioned, despairingly followed to tragedy in the one case, to renunciation in the other. It is a somewhat gloomy book, and the emphasis of the motto that introduces it makes it almost unbearable to recall—Thoreau's chance statement that "the mass of men lead lives of quiet desperation." Yet there is a balsam to soothe as one reads, a tenderness, almost too-sweet, for the girl Lily Bresnan and her young brother Finbarr, both secretly contemplating the renunciation of life in religion when, in despair, the other brother Frank has abandoned an unequal struggle by suicide. This feminine note in Corkery has to be noticed—it seems to vanish almost completely in his later work: it could scarcely, indeed, survive a widening of interest, an acknowledgment of the validity of other worlds. . . .

There is no need to comment [upon his description of Lily Bresnan]: the words convey the lyrical quality of the mind that so pictured life—mellow; flushed foliage; lingered; dappled; gentle; homely; sweet; very faint. If one had any criticism to make it would be that life so gently imaged, and in a plot of such humble and effortless evasion, could hardly offer many themes, little action, little drama, and must end by reducing almost to inarticulateness so quietly lyrical an observer. The characters of such a world, so will-less, so quiescent, so passionless, may—and here did to perfection—offer matter for a lyric in prose: or might, if conceived with more masculinity, offer matter for a Greek tragedy: but as for the novelist they out-Chekov Chekov [sic] who wrote, also, many lovely lyrics, and with a wider experience of life, and an acceptance of a greater variety of valid worlds, many stories that were more than lyrics; but, he also, no series of novels.

Sean O'Faolain. DM. April–June, 1936, pp. 50–51

Corkery's attitude . . . is primarily contemplative and his writing has always been happier in dealing not with the aggravations of controversy but with the cloistral, candle-lit places of the soul. . . .

A storyteller, even if he has a lot to be content about, has also a lot to be complicated about, particularly if he is an Irish storyteller reacting violently against the Irish storytellers who saw the common people of Ireland, very simply, as comic relief. Daniel Corkery has reacted in that way against Somerville and Ross, against Lever and Lover and George Birmingham, and, I fear, even against Seán O'Casey and Liam O'Flaherty. How far that reaction is justified every reader must judge for himself. Certainly Corkery's conclusion is justified: that moral responsibility does not belong to a people playing the part of comic relief and that the writers who say the Irish people in that light had to paint them "as if they were incapable of ever going beyond the teaching of mother wit." The people in his own stories, whether they are hard people from the mountains, or tattered people from the lanes, or young rebels, or chaste and clerkly men, or women like nuns, always go a long distance beyond the counsels of mother wit, beyond the remotest possibility of being confused with Handy Andy or taken for comic relief, into places where the shadows of moral responsibility are as bewildering and terrifying as the mists on the stony mountains.

Turning from the writing of a novel like *The Threshold of Quiet* to the writing of a book of stories of armed revolution like *The Hounds of Banba*, Corkery showed how completely he had accepted his own people, how he felt with them and hoped with them. But inevitably the men with the guns who moved through those stories borrowed something from the contemplative turn of mind of the storyteller—like a singing procession of fighting men silent for a few moments as they march in the shadow of a convent wall. . . .

Other European countries have become pitiably familiar with that atmosphere and balanced against their experiences the Irish ordeal is only a very tiny sound in the echoing horror-chamber of modern Europe. But within the modest limits of the material at his disposal Corkery has accurately registered the atmosphere, carefully sketched the incidents, truly interpreted the spirit of a people in revolution.

Benedict Kiely. *Modern Irish Fiction: A Critique*.
(Dublin, Golden Eagle Books, 1950), pp. 2–5

In Corkery's stories there is little or no sense of the supernatural; strangeness comes from men's minds or the effect of landscape upon them. Like the earlier story called "The Stones," this is particularly strong in "Death of a Runner," in which a man is haunted by a horse he has killed. When he is found drowned the mood is early morning, with a heavy dew everywhere on ground that has dried in summer heat and "the river flowed on, very gently yet alive, saying its say quietly, as it has been doing the live-long night."

It is not often that Corkery moves out of Cork or Kerry but in "Strange Honey Dew"—not a very good title—he has described that area round the Liffey from Kingsbridge to O'Connell Street, decaying, nostalgic, certain only of its past. The old man who tells strangers of the businesses he has owned, only in imagination perhaps, is so much a part of it. I cannot go by without mentioning the priest in this story, so beautifully is he suggested in a line or two . . . "a very humble looking, moody looking old priest." "He has a large and almost empty parish in the midlands, I thought." Later he crossed the roadway and "let his head hang, and fell at once into patient plodding, himself and his umbrella, as if miles and miles of bogland road lay before him."

Maybe the mind is rather like a ciné-camera at work all the time whether we know it or not, memory being the developing and printing of its exposures. Corkery is often like the man who as he processes and then projects the film, is often surprised at what he finds there. The image of that "patient plodding" is not a conscious observation so much as the reliving of an instant of time. In the earlier story he writes of the toss of defiance given by young men in court. "I had never observed it until then, as I say, and I was quite unaware that it could be observed by me in my ordinary moments." . . .

I have perhaps made little reference to Corkery's power of conveying states of mind. In "Her Thank-offering" we are told of the young wife living near Howth, whose husband is seriously ill, and how she inhibited her memories of happiness "with all her might" so that she might have courage to face the present. Very skilfully he builds up tension and then at the right moment, when our interest is completely caught by the atmosphere, he can gently leave it slacken and we share in a sense of warmth and gratefulness—one of those occasions, as he said in another context, "when we see into the life of things."

The little I have read of Daniel Corkery's poetry has meant nothing to me, all has gone into the prose; the plays, *The Yellow Bittern, The Labour Leader* and *Resurrection* are very simply and effectively constructed. "Each was a thing in itself, occupying the whole of my mind while I was making it," Corkery wrote in one of the prefaces. The poet dying, rejected by the hardness of the people, the king and hermit who symbolise perhaps the world and detachment from it, are figures and voices we do not forget. . . .

I am not concerned here with Corkery's part in the revival of the Irish language but the literature which has come from his concentration on the material around him. For many years a professor, he has not lived by writing so much as through it, nor has he attempted to reach the wider labour market which welcomes the "wild gesse of the pen." "Unless a writer sink himself in the heart of his own people," he wrote, "he will never, let his own gifts be as they may, accomplish work of such a nature as permanently satisfies the human spirit."

At the same time, Daniel Corkery's work has prepared the way for certain writers to live in Ireland and carry on a considerable export trade. Their stories and novels show that many of the day and night dreams of his period have taken on the hard and sometimes disagreeable shapes of reality. Father Reen, were he still alive, would see an Irish government and middle class, a people greatly improved in self-confidence and well-being, the once powerful families finally descended, where they are represented at all, to the same problems of earning a living as everyone else, while other groups consolidate themselves.

It was an important day for Irish writing when sometime before the first World War, Corkery stood with twenty thousand others to watch a hurling match at Thurles. "It was while I looked around on the great crowd I first became acutely aware that as a nation we were without self-expression in literature." The question he asked—if the possibilities suggested by Synge were to be followed or writing to remain "colonial" or expatriate—had in that moment of dedication been answered. This is not to claim that Corkery has reflected more than certain aspects of Irish life, but his stories came at a time when comfort and a little praise for the best side was needed by people trembling after war.

Patricia Hutchins. *Irish Writing.*
Dec., 1953, pp. 47–49

Corkery, like too many of his fellows, was extremely miscellaneous in his publications, and only chauvinists will persuade themselves that uniform excellence marks the entire corpus. Other readers will be more apt to judge him a competent playwright, a readable versifier whose appeal is suggestive of that of Padraic Colum and Seumas O'Kelly, a biased and verbose scholar, a tedious novelist, a competent but religiously prejudiced reviewer, a strongly opinionated propagandist, and a writer of short stories which are in numerous instances so superior as to argue him one of Ireland's most distinguished practitioners. His significance lies in the sporadic quality, by no means the quantity, of his work—work which has a pervasively rock-grey tone. And perhaps it is not unkind to reiterate, as in any case one must, that for all his to-do about Irish as a language ("No native vernacular, no nation": *The Fortunes of the Irish Language*), almost all his work, and certainly all that is likely to count, is in English. In other words, his achievement clearly contradicts his critical stance.

Repondering the critical, historical, and didactic work, one inevitably endorses what Benedict Kiely has said in "Chronicle by Rushlight," one of the very few judicious essays on Corkery: "It is hard to know how to meet the illogicality of a man who writes well in English about Ireland and is then, apparently, prepared to maintain that only writing in Irish can properly express the soul of the Irish people." Fortunately, what is bound to persist in the end is the best of the purely creative work—a little set of plays and at least two volumes of short stories fine enough to stand in the front rank of their category. It was in these that Corkery *really* honored Ireland and his heritage.

George Brandon Saul. *Daniel Corkery* (Lewisburg, Pa., Bucknell Univ. Pr., 1973), pp. 64–65

[Corkery] himself would probably have been pleased to be associated with the more extreme, exclusive, "pure," anti-English cultural positions which he expressed with such force and conviction, but, in so far as these distract us from, or even prejudice us against his prose fiction and his more detailed criticism, they are a nuisance.

At his best, rooted in the same obsessions that nourished his prejudices, there was in him a knowledge and love of his own place and people which made him a powerful writer, and a critic in whom intuition and intelligence held a fine and exciting balance. . . .

It seems that it is fashionable to think that, as a short story writer, Corkery was left far behind by his sometime disciples, Seán O'Faoláin and Frank O'Connor. To anyone who has really read Corkery this must seem muddleheaded. The first real observation is that Corkery is very different to either of the younger men; the second is that he is more *uneven* and that his worst stories like some of those in *The Hounds of Banba* (propagandist parables rather than stories) are far worse than the worst work of the other two; the third is, that, at his best, his stories, like his novel *The Threshold of Quiet*, have a deeper tone, a more impressive *gravitas* than we almost ever find in the work of the younger men. . . .

We might express the difference between Corkery and the younger men simply by saying that he was a countryman, or that he understood the country while they were essentially "townies." This statement must be carefully qualified, for O'Faoláin has a rich gift for describing landscape and weather, and O'Connor has some brilliant stories of country life and attitudes. Yet they are always, to some extent, strangers in the countryside, always, somehow, outside observers, and often patronising or ill-at-ease.

Corkery on the other hand shows that identification, that sense of belonging which, in all its moods from desolation to a sense of glory, marks him truly as *in* and *of* the landscape. . . .

The essential difference, then, between the attitudes of the two younger writers and that of Corkery is that, whatever the rich range of emotions they may feel about the country, and particularly the wild country of West Cork, it remains for them, as it always is for the true townsman, somewhere "out there," almost as though the only real, human, dry land was the town and all the rest was an uncharted and shifting ocean.

Corkery, it is true, was a country boy by adoption rather than by origin, for he too was born and bred in the city of Cork, and indeed only came to the Irish language and to Irish Nationalism as an adult. Yet he knows and thinks about the countryside as one who belongs there. And he brings the artist's eye, for he was also a painter, to the places he visits in his words. Landscape for him is a matter, not just of physical feature, but always of light and weather; and this must be so for an Irish writer or painter because there is probably no other country on earth that changes mood and character so often and so strongly as Ireland under the shifting skies of the Atlantic. There is hardly a story by Corkery for which one could not write a fairly detailed weather report; and this weather moves over specific, vividly conjured-up landscapes which have a real geography, and have names which, even when invented, are based on the names of a thousand places like them. . . .

For Corkery the people and the land are inseparable, different dimensions of the same reality. His eye is exact and fierce, but never patronising. His style matches it: being at its best, spare, vivid and energetic. He is a master of the physical detail that will give you both the person and the situation; and, particularly in gesture, he shows a precise eye for the mannerisms of the particular area in which his people live. They are both individuals and also representative of types and attitudes which are accurate local examples of universal country types. . . .

Sean Lucy. In Patrick Rafroidi and Terence Brown, eds., *The Irish Short Story* (Lille, Publications de l'Université de Lille, 1979), pp. 160–61, 163–65

COUSINS, JAMES H. (1873–1956)

I believe one poet of Ireland has succeeded in the task of rendering in purest poetry the best thoughts and sympathetic strivings of the modern mind. I speak of Mr. J. H. Cousins and his recently published volume, *Etain*. In this little epic of heroic Ireland the expression is felt to be equally in harmony with the ancient, and with the best in the modern, world. I venture the suggestion that the probable reason is that the poet has fulfilled the Aristotelian canon by making his art universal. Alike in the perfection of his technique and in the pure beauty of his characterisation and setting, he has succeeded in lifting his work clear of the temporary imperfections and débris of Nature's handiwork, which is superficially, though painfully, apparent in every generation. His golden verse moves along the ways of that common human love and effort which is inspired by an intuitive perception of high ethical and spiritual verities, which the poet seeks to make real to the reader in the only way possible, not by the dogmatic insistence of legal or moralist pedantry, but by a representation of their operation in the actual tissue of human passion and character. Touches are not absent of that intense sympathy with every kind of human failure and misery which is becoming so prominent a feature of the best modern thought. Nor does he compel his art to cloud its beacon brightness by actual contact with an external hideousness: a magic phrase imparts the spirit and atmosphere of compassionate understanding for which the reformer pleads, when he

> crowds the ways, where human sorrow pleads
> With generations of exalted deeds.

The spirit of a thousand reiterated demonstrations of the human claims of Labour breathes, sweetly without bitterness, in the little poem of intense Celtic feeling, entitled "Laborare Est Orare." . . . Potent, too, in depth of comprehension and in fidelity to the tradition of Ireland is the poet's sympathetic recognition of woman as spiritually co-equal with man, and of her, not as struggling to retrieve her position of equal freedom against those who would keep her in dishonour, but craved as his needed complement in the joint human task of social government. Nowhere can I remember to have read so noble and imaginative a presentation of the universal fact of sex, so true to the modern findings of science and psychology, as in those stanzas, where the feminist gospel rings out clear in a single line—"Diverse in gift, in essence one and whole." . . .

Matthew Arnold spoke of the Magic of Celtic descriptions of natural objects. That power, consisting in a kind of spiritual surrender of the temporary personal ego to receive the illumined consciousness of intimate union with

Nature's moods, has been noted as a feature alike of ancient Irish poetry and of poetry in English by Irish poets and writers of Irish extraction. Mr. Cousins is appreciated by many admirers chiefly on the score of his already published poems, like "The Corncrake," which reveal this sympathetic quality in a marked degree, and the present volume contains some striking examples, like "The Starling and the Robin," which should endear him to the rising generation.

Irish Review. July, 1912, pp. 276–78

On Thursday, 29 May, the complimentary performance of two of Mr. Cousin's plays took place in the Hardwicke Street Theatre, which was crowded with friends and admirers of Mr. and Mrs. Cousins, desirous of paying them a final tribute of regard before they left Ireland [for India]. The two plays, representing widely different aspects of Mr. Cousins's genius, were enthusiastically received. *The Racin' Lug* is a study of the life of fisher-folk in a north of Ireland sea-coast village—a piece of real life, sympathetically interpreted. *The Sleep of the King* is a poetic allegory, an interpretation of Celtic story in terms of esoteric philosophy. In both, the special feature of the acting was the appearance of Miss Máire Nic Shiubhlaigh in the roles which she created on the first performance of the plays. Miss Honor Lavelle, Mr. Jack Morrow, Mr. Crawford Neil, and Mr. Mac Shiubhlaigh appeared in the other chief parts, while the scenery and staging were looked after by Mr. Jack Morrow and Mrs. Roberts. . . .

Mr. Padraic Colum said that Mr. and Mrs. Cousins had made comrades by scores in every field; and it was the experience of those comrades that the Cousins were always loyal to their ideals and to their friends. He desired to speak more particularly of Mr. Cousins as a poet and dramatist. His powers in this field had been exemplified by the two plays produced that night. *The Sleep of the King* had been produced with great dignity and beauty. *The Racin' Lug* was one of the plays dealing with the north of Ireland, of which they had too few, as compared with those dealing with other parts of Ireland. It was one of Mr. Cousins's distinctions that he had introduced to them in the south the humanity of the north; and on the other hand, to the north he had introduced Ireland's "inextinguishable dream." He was difficult to place among Irish writers. He had studied the philosophy behind the Irish myths; and he (the speaker) regarded him as having affinities less with Celtic poets than with the Celtic philosophers—with those philosophers of the ninth century whose interests were in all that was difficult, rare, and esoteric. Mr. Cousins carried on the tradition of Johns Scotus Erigena. Writing before Mr. Cousins had published any of his poems, Mr. Stopford Brooke had defined the task of Irish poetry in words that might fittingly be applied to Mr. Cousins's work. More than any other man, he had deliberately undertaken to show the powers which spiritually moved under the visible surface of human life. His wonderfully clear handling of difficult themes, his technical excellence, and his observation of nature, earned the admiration of all. Moreover, he was distinguished for those qualities without which the poet becomes a mere dilettante—for his hatred of injustice and his genuine patriotism. His wish to Mr. and Mrs. Cousins would be that they reach the highest achievement that belonged to their own spirit. . . .

The Irish Citizen. June 7, 1913, pp. 20–21.
Reprinted in Robert Hogan, Richard Burnham,
and Daniel P. Poteet, *The Modern Drama:*
The Rise of the Realists, 1910–1915
(Dublin, Dolmen, 1979), pp. 306–7

Strictly speaking [James H. Cousins] should not be counted amongst the poets of the younger generation, as his first book, *Ben Madighan and Other Poems,* was contemporaneous with [A.E.'s] *Homeward: Songs by the Way* [1894]. But that volume and its immediate successors, in the purely imitative, eighteenth-century manner, did not bring the author the success he now enjoys, which dates approximately from the same period as saw the arrival of his younger contemporaries. He was engaged in the initial enterprise which led to the creation of the Irish National Theatre, and owes his reputation to the work he has written under the inspiration of Irish legend. It is noteworthy that the book which inaugurated his later and more successful phase, *The Quest,* was published in 1906, after the Dramatic Movement had fully expanded. The most interesting pages are those containing the poetic drama, *The Sleep of the King,* whose production in 1902 was the point of departure of the National Theatre Society. Since 1906 James H. Cousins has maintained a good level of workmanship, without either serious retrogression or remarkable progress. He uses the sonnet form with skill, and in his latest work, *Straight and Crooked* (1915), he has preferred the short lyric to those lengthy narratives of legend like *The Marriage of Lir and Niav, The Going Forth of Dana* and *Etain the Beloved,* which constitute the bulk of his work. Whatever be his subject, he writes with a certain carefulness and absence of subtlety, which reveal him as following largely the pre-Revival tradition of Anglo-Irish poetry. Moore, Aubrey de Vere (and even Byron), are the names which friendly critics mention when instituting comparisons. It is curious that the interest in mysticism betrayed by his prose writing has not appreciably determined the character of his verse.

Ernest A. Boyd. *Ireland's Literary Renaissance*
(New York, John Lane, 1916), pp. 283–84

There are over a hundred poems in this collection [*A Wandering Harp*], selected by the poet to represent forty years of poetical aspirations. Written under the skies to eastward and westward of the land of his birth, in atmospheres as far apart in all respects as are the Himalayas and New York City, they wrap the reader around with many-coloured veils of thought.

Twenty years ago Seumas was with us in Dublin, and his essays and poems were food and flame in the National movement, and he sang of the gods and heroes of the Gael. In this collection we have some of these songs, including *The Sleep of the King,* a play in verse. This was the first play performed by the Irish National Theatre, as far back as 1902. Since then we are carried to share the thoughts of the poet on the seas and mountains of the wide earth. He has drunk deep of wells that are from ancient days open to the skies of the East, wells flowing in the days of the Aryan westward tide that brought the Gael on his long journeying to the outside edge of Europe. The poet's year in Japan is represented by nature poems, but it is India and Ireland that his songs most constantly reveal to us. All his work is rich with colour, and there is much that one would like to quote did space permit. . . .

Mr. Cousins has added notably and richly to the store of poetry given to the world by the Irish brotherhood of singers, who for the last quarter of a century have lit up the dawn-sky of the new-old Ireland.

DM. July, 1933, pp. 89–90

James Cousins interpreted the imaginative realm to multitudes. In Ireland and England, words, literary myths, and drama were the prism he used. In India and Japan the visual, pictorial and plastic arts increasingly absorbed his attention, but did not exclude his vital awareness of literature, music and the natural sciences. He perceived the unique artistic excellence of many Oriental artists in early youth; he encouraged, patronised, and extolled their work in lectures and published essays. . . . Young poets too he served well with technical advice, and essays introducing their published poems. And all these endeavours were focussed on an awareness of the significance which art may, and should have in the life of the community. . . .

Words written or spoken by James Cousins or his wife Margaret Cousins were published widespread over three continents and at least eight countries, for almost sixty years. If at all, they are remembered now only in India, which was their domicile from 1915. Although their words seem to have been largely forgotten their influence has endured over the generations with whom they were associated. Emotionally stabilised in each other, they attracted friendship, had access, and were accessible to people of all races, nations, ideologies, creeds, cultures, and temperaments. Colour, caste, status, condition seemed to them wholly irrelevant artificial barricades against understanding and reciprocal appreciation. Sincerity was their sole arbiter. . . .

Dr. and Mrs. Cousins's collaborative autobiography *We Two Together* (1950) is an absorbingly interesting book for open-minded sympathetic readers, although its enormous length was perhaps self-defeating. This defect is paradoxical because their earlier publications were conspicuous for aphoristic vigour, reverberant brevity. *The Play of Brahma* (1921), *Work and Worship* (1922), and *The Path to Peace* (1928), for example, perfectly exemplify James Cousins's powers as "a congenital teacher" (the phrase is his wife's). . . .

There are perhaps fifty poems by James Cousins which will endure. Much of his verse is in one key, and palls if read often. The unflattering (and offensive) gibes levelled at him in the W. B. Yeats and James Joyce canon deserve to be weighed against one important fact. Neither Yeats nor Joyce appear to have had any "knowledge of Cousins" books written after 1915. Whilst they lived out their lives in service to their own self-centred ideals James Cousins devoted his best energies and his subtlest intellectual powers to the education of the young and the welfare of the poor and oppressed. . . . James Cousins believed education through the emotions could prove to be a source of life-affirming, life-enhancing activity. It may prove to be one panacea for the ills which mankind has cultivated domestically and collectively; but perhaps there is not a *general* panacea, only the dream of it? His trust was evolved from a life-time's selfless effort. His efforts, his example, and the example set by Margaret Cousins remain an inspiring guide to their friends in India and elsewhere.

> Alan Denson. *James H. Cousins and Margaret E.*
> *Cousins: A Bio-Bibliographical Survey* (Kendal,
> England, Denson, 1967), pp. 14–17

For Cousins an important aspect of his regard and enthusiasm for Celtic mythology was that it proved to his satisfaction that the early Celts were practitioners of the same kind of pagan religion he himself felt drawn to, and that it was a local manifestation in mythic form of the fundamental truths of the universe. Even more than AE, Cousins felt a vigorous repugnance for the tenets of orthodox Christianity. He espoused pagan religious doctrines with a scornful denigration of the sectarianism of the Christian churches. Where [Samuel] Ferguson had been almost unconsciously sympathetic to non-Christian elements in his source material, Cousins was frankly progagandist, sharing Yeats's preference for Oisin over Patrick. . . . Cousins's vision of Celtic paganism remains, however, an intellectual and spiritual one. None of Ferguson's zest for brutal energy and heroic physical exploit sullies his diaphanous, silken re-creations of mythological matter. He wrote of his long poem "Etain the Beloved" that it is "an attempt at transfiguration, by seeking to 'unfold into light' the spiritual vision that was the inspiration, and is the secret of the persistence and resilience, of the Celt.". . .

Much of Cousins's poetry attempts to treat Celtic material in this religio-mythic manner. He produced ornate, tapestry-like verse that clothed his subjects with a sheen of glamour. His effects are often over-literary, reminding one at moments of the weakest passages in Matthew Arnold's foray into the misty regions of Nordic myth, "Balder Dead." There is the same heavy dependence on rather overworked Miltonic similes, and a similar static, adjectival quality to the verse. Cousins, for all his elevated intentions, really only achieves a picturesque glamorous Edwardianism. He is an Irish Alfred Noyes whose occasional attraction is a pleasing painterly exoticism, mediated in rhythms of mellifluous banality.

Terence Brown. *Northern Voices: Poets From Ulster*
(Totowa, N.J., Rowman & Littlefield, 1975),
pp. 65–67

While his drama is of value in literary history, the verse, which spanned the years in Ireland and in India, is more central to Cousins' talent, and of more inherent literary worth. There are lyrics and narratives in a variety of complex forms, rhythms, and meters, displaying careful workmanship and discipline in poetic craft. The better short poems, such as "Slieve Cullen" and the sonnet, "Vision," show a responsiveness to nature, an idealism, and a love of country. The verse of value reveals a sensitivity and delicacy of description, invested with supernatural meaning in a cosmic perspective. It is here that Cousins' major value and significance lie, as a poet giving lyrical voice to the Theosophical point of view, a view that reveals itself throughout some of the major literary work of the Irish Literary Renaissance, a view that is a part of the broader Celtic vision of an existence made up of the natural and the supernatural. Cousins' own expanding personal spiritual consciousness brought him to investigate and interpret the Celtic myths in his own way, and while he never penetrated or presented the national consciousness in works, as Yeats and Synge may be said to have done, he evolved his own harmonizing vision of being, his own set of beliefs through the Celtic myths as a form of spiritual symbolism bridging the ages. The mythological narrative, notably "Etain the Beloved," is best suited to Cousins' talent and interest. There, he can and does present his personal Theosophical view of the cosmos and man's place therein in verse of delicate and otherworldly lyricism, telling events that suggest a philosophy which unites all men, West and East, and all things, real and spiritual. The verse, like the drama, has significance in literary history, but it also has an artistic quality that qualifies it as significant and revealing poetry coming from the Literary Renaissance in Ireland, and, in a broader view, testifying again to the idealistic aspirations of humanity as it continues to attempt to assure itself of a supernatural mission in a spiritual universe.

The failure of Cousins to become a major author is at least in part the result of his self-satisfied narrowness of view. It is strange to conclude that of a man whose philosophy was so unconfined, but he clung so tenaciously to the comfortable beliefs he discovered in his earlier years that everthing was funneled into his preconceived framework. Cousins' critical insight into the poetry of George Russell—that it had the "peculiar feature as of a preconcerted movement in one direction, as though its trees were bending always westward before a wind which blows ever from the East"—could justifiably apply to Cousins' writings. As a result, his writing is static. Nothing really *happens*. There is merely the narration of events, the illustration of points, the explication of a point of view. There is never tension or discovery; there is no passion; there is no challenge. There is, however, order, skill, control, lyric delicacy, and sporadically expanding loveliness.

William A. Dumbleton. *James Cousins* (Boston, Twayne, 1980), pp. 128–29

Although Cousins wrote no more for the Irish National Theatre [after 1902], he remains an interesting figure because of *The Racing Lug*. In Cousin's notes on that play, he crosses out a passage which, however, can still be read, stating that the play was "in some ways a precursor of *Riders to the Sea*." While Synge's play featured the life of the Catholic Aran Islanders, Cousins looked at the tragedy brought to a Northern Protestant fishing island at the end of the last century. A minister enters the quiet, domestic cottage of Johnny and his wife Nancy. He warns the fisherman that the young men are planning to take the racing lug out in the bad weather, and Johnny hurries off to prevent the men from this action. One of the young men is Rob, the boyfriend of Johnny's young daughter, Bell. The second scene leaves the two women, like Maurya and her daughters in *Riders to the Sea,* to worry over what is happening outside the cottage. There is disaster as the the boat capsizes, and Johnny, who has gone out with the young men, drowns. On hearing the news, Nancy also dies, leaving behind their daughter Bell who will probably marry Rob, the young fisherman. The same tragic pattern of the islander's life will be repeated. Colum wrote that when Cousins left the theatre "Synge's somber *Riders to the Sea* became the great sea-piece, and *The Racing Lug* was staged [there] no more."

Perhaps that is the clue to Yeats's great dislike of Cousins. Yeats was anxious to launch Synge's career, and wanted *The Racing Lug* out of the theatre repertoire. He managed to get rid of Cousins at the same time. Cousins worked for a while with the Theatre of Ireland, the seeming depository for all of Yeats's rejects, but he wrote no more plays. In 1913 he went first to England and then on to India, Japan, and finally to New York as an educator, journalist, and professor of poetry.

The Racing Lug never came near the greatness of Synge's *Riders to the Sea*, perhaps because of Cousins's lack of dramatic experience. Also Cousins, in his zeal to get the play to the company, was never allowed to rewrite or perfect his work. [He wrote:] "I suppose I had no business constructing cloud castles on a piece which I knocked off in a sitting at white heat and never cleaned up, but handed straight to the stage manager."

Cousins' plays are never revived in modern repertory. *The Racing Lug,* though it lacked finish, was, according to the reviews, "a fine acting piece" in the hands of the Abbey company. . . . Though James Cousins never achieved greatness as a playwright, Lennox Robinson wrote: *The Racing Lug . . .* may be regarded as one of the earliest of the Abbey Theatre 'school.' These dramatists and the Fay brothers were laying the foundations of the Abbey Theatre."

Brenna Katz Clarke. *The Emergence of the Irish Peasant Play at the Abbey Theatre* (Ann Arbor, Mich., UMI Research Press, 1982), pp. 104–5

DEVLIN, DENIS (1908–1959)

Mr. Devlin, inheritor of the Irish poetic tradition, brings to his work its feeling for rhythm and cadence, Celtic mother wit and rich religious background. But he adds modern youth's re-examination of the past and awareness of the significant part that science now plays in man's universal orientation. Using greater economy of language than most of his Celtic forebears, he attains a strength of structure sometimes lacking in even the greatest of them. The bone structure of a philosophy is here more clearly defined than in other Irish poets, beneath that metaphorical process which is the flesh of all poetry.

"Lough Derg," the poem from which the book takes its title, is the story of an Irish abbey, ancient and famous as a place of religious pilgrimage. The reference to Dante in it is not merely metaphorical but historical: tradition has it that Dante once stayed in retreat there. "Est Prodest," one of the loveliest poems in the book, is full of the deeply religious background and demonstrates the view of modern occultists that praise is more efficacious than prayer. The poem "Annapolis" shows Devlin's keen observation of the American scene. In "Diplomat" and "Memo from a Millionaire," the poet becomes the social critic with a light touch. "The Victory of Samothrace" and "Venus of the Salty Shell" are effective poems on subjects that because of their triteness are difficult to handle, but which in this case are handled exceedingly well.

Inez Boulton. Poetry. Dec., 1946, p. 169

Denis Devlin's first volume of *Poems* (in collaboration with Brian Coffey) appeared in Dublin in 1932. Since then, residence abroad, the vissitudes of publication and his undoubted quality as a poet have combined to earn him a reputation which stands much higher elsewhere than in his own country. The present issue of *Poetry Ireland,* containing his new, long poem, *The Heavenly Foreigner,* and a selection from his earlier work, should do something to redress the balance.

Up to the present Devlin's reputation has rested mainly on two volumes of poems—*Intercessions* (London, 1937) and *Lough Derg and Other Poems* (New York, 1946). But it has been much enhanced by his splendid translations of the important French poet, St.-John Perse, whose work had not previously been introduced to the English-reading public. These translations appeared in America under the titles, *Rains* (1945), *Snows* (1945) and *Exile and Other Poems* (1949).

His latest poem, *The Heavenly Foreigner,* has already appeared in the Italian review, *Inventario* (March, 1950), with a facing translation by Tommaso Giglio. It is due for American publication in the *Sewanee Review* (Winter, 1950).

The Heavenly Foreigner is unquestionably Devlin's most considerable poetic achievement to date. It is a complex poem, making what may seem unusual demands upon the reader. But they are the legitimate demands of a poet, and the reader who concedes them will find himself well rewarded. On a careful reading, superficial obscurities vanish, new imaginative horizons open in "the casual unwilled depths of the poem," complexities of thought and feeling fuse into a glowing lyricism. Indeed, certain sections of this long poem, taken out of context, have the smooth charm of anthology-pieces.

On one level *The Heavenly Foreigner* communicates as a love-poem, rich in poignant and tender moods. But sexual love is the incidental and minor theme, as it was in the Catharist songs of the Troubadours. The deeper preoccupation is with the problems of Time and human destiny, the anguished alliance of flesh and spirit. What God had joined Descartes has put asunder, and the wound still festers. . . .

Devlin's poetry is the product of a cultured and flexible mind, and in handling these fundamental themes he shows a rare power of stating abstract ideas and philosophical concepts in terms of poetry. Bergson can tell us: "Duration is the continuous progress of the past which gnaws into the future and which swells as it advances. The piling up of the past upon the past goes on without relaxation . . . In its entirety, probably, it follows us at every instant . . . Doubtless, we think with only a small part of our past, but it is with our entire past . . . that we desire, will and act."

The poetic statement is equally valid:

> In memory, years interweave: they do not follow one another
> Like jealous ambassadors in the Mayor's procession.
> All years flow from a hundred streets
> Intemperately towards the mansion
> Last year no less than this
> For her mercurial year threads through them all since;

And only the poetic imagination strives to arrest the flux, to crystallise past, present and future in

> . . . an instant precognising eternity
> Borne between our open eyes
> With no perceptible bank of land between
> Nor oblique eyesight deciding other objects were there.

The word "oblique" occurs more than once in the poem and it suggests an important element in Devlin's approach to his material. This is his faculty of observing from the corner of the mind's eye, which has the effect of adding another dimension to his vision. . . . It is this faculty, too, which makes much of his imagery at once surprising and satisfying, as in the line

Rodents in the corn like the black gas in the heart of the sun. . . .

In the varying moods of the poem Devlin displays great technical virtuosity — in his skillful use of internal assonance and half-rhymes, Biblical cadences, traditional modes and passages of straight prose. His handling of cliché is particularly effective, and I doubt whether any contemporary poet can load the banal, colloquial phrase with such overtones of pathos and irony.

I feel that certain passages are marred by technical weaknesses and unresolved difficulties of syntax, but these are minor flaws in a work which proves Denis Devlin to be a real force in the development of modern poetry. The extent of his achievement in *The Heavenly Foreigner* depends finally on whether this long poem makes, on its own esthetic terms, an intellectual and emotional synthesis.

I believe that it does. And I am glad that *Poetry Ireland* has given its readers the opportunity of seeing this new and very stimulating work by an Irish poet.

Niall Sheridan. *Poetry Ireland*. July, 1950, pp. 3–5

Like most Irishmen of his generation, Devlin had closer ties with France than with England, and his education in modern poetry was mostly French. The influence of Valéry is pervasive; and there is a little of Yeats. His originality is not spectacular; it is subtle and subdued, consisting in a slight modification of the language and conventions of his immediate elders. He wrote a few bad poems, many good poems, and perhaps three great poems. These are "The Passion of Christ," "From Government Buildings," and, above all, "Lough Derg," a poem that may rank with Stevens' "Sunday Morning," Eliot's "Gerontion," and Crane's "The Broken Tower." In all these poems, the poets are exploring the difficult region where doubt and faith have been conducting an inconclusive dialectic since the middle of the last century.

"Lough Derg" takes its title from that part of Donegal where annually Irish pilgrims gather to pray. The poem is composed of nineteen six-line stanzas, rhymed *ababcc,* a modification of rhyme royal, or perhaps an adaptation of the stanza, *aabccb,* of *"Le cimetière marin."* In other ways the poem suggests a derivation from, but in no sense an imitation of, Valéry. Like *"Le cimetière marin,"* it poses a universal religious conflict which, in Valéry, Mr. Yvor Winters has described as a sense of the "flaw in creation"; in "Lough Derg" the conflict moves within a definitely Christian orbit: a civilized Irishman of the Catholic faith mediates on the difference between the scepticism of faith and the simple, fanatical faith of the Irish peasant—with whom he partly identifies himself—praying at Lough Derg. It is a sufficiently commonplace subject, yet one that still seems to give rise to great poetry.

Allen Tate and Robert Penn Warren. Preface to
Denis Devlin, *Selected Poems* (New York, Holt,
Rinehart and Winston, 1963), p. 13

Denis Devlin, who died in 1959 while he was Irish Ambassador to Italy, published widely and won the approval of several important tastemakers. . . . However, he has received scant critical attention for a poet so well introduced [by Tate and Warren]. He is, nevertheless, one of the most impressive poets to come out of modern Ireland. What may have kept Devlin from wider approval is what irritated Austin Clarke about his poetry: his similarity to intellectual poets of the Continent. Devlin has translated St.-John Perse, and his own progression has been from a surrealistic portrayal of disgust to a mythic celebration of love. In his presentation of a psychological reality, metaphor becomes reality. He searched for ontological relationships which could raise him above the enforced fears and the miserable squabbles of opportunists. . . .

Understandably, Devlin did not become one of the people he wrote of in "Lough Derg" for whom "all is simple and symbol in their world,/The incomprehended rendered fabulous." He was a civilized European who came to see the history of Ireland and the soul of man without the guilt-inspired fear and reticence so prevalent in his early poems. Yet he did achieve a complex and, I believe, more fabulous world than those who did not share his struggle. Though Devlin's inquiry and his desire for joy took him to beliefs that would be strange to many of his countrymen, he discovered the living divine within himself and those he loved. He does not seem to have abandoned Christianity. Like Charles Williams, whose magical writings about love resemble Devlin's, he sought in various cultures a belief founded on the permanence of the divine in the temporary body of humanity.

Frank L. Kersnowski. *SwR*. Winter, 1973,
pp. 113, 122

In his *Connoisseurs of Chaos,* Denis Donoghue describes the kind of poet whose consciousness is historical:

For these, tradition is a great drama of people and institutions, conflicts of values in their full temporal idiom.

Denis Devlin is this kind of poet. *Lough Derg* (published 1946), midway in the second and most significant phase in his poetic development which begins in the early 1930s, is such a poem, built around that most acute of modern dilemmas, the loss of God and the seeming bankruptcy of efforts at replacement. Devlin, sensitive believer that he became, approaches his theme from the traditional standpoints of humanism ancient and modern, the theocratic symbolism of European Christianity and the emotional piety which he found in the Ireland of his time. *Lough Derg* belongs with Wallace Stevens's "Sunday Morning," if for the latter's "complacencies of the peignoir" we read "rosary rounds." It is unsparing in its analysis of self and self's actions, that analysis which we find in almost all of Devlin's work, and which produced *The Heavenly Foreigner,* his greatest poem, surpassed in orchestration only by Eliot's *Four Quartets.* Devlin makes unsparing demands on us as readers. Obscure he is if we understand that poetic obscurity is imaginative whereas ambiguity is grammatical. Obscurity is positive when the poem succeeds in holding itself down to an emotional unity. . . . The emotional unity of *Lough Derg* compels our attention to the relevance of its concerns. [A study of the poem can] underline Devlin's justification as our great poet, with Kavanagh and Clarke, to come after Yeats.

Lough Derg puts three central questions before the reader: How can we know God and how can this knowledge change our lives? What forms has this quest for God taken in history and how have different religious traditions responded to its implications? Can these traditions serve the needs of modern man? Devlin locates this drama of traditions and institutions confronted with Western man's anguish against the background of an Irish pilgrimage site known to Europe throughout the centuries and celebrated by Dante. He argues out this drama in four movements which are linked and unified by the presence of the poet-pilgrim. The first movement (1–36) traces out the main elements which have gone to the making of European Christianity, Greece and Judah, and their influences combining in the totalitarian spirituality of the Gothic style. The second movement (37–67) explains the construction of Irish tradition from druid to Catholic peasantry. The third movement (68–84) articulates modern man's search for meaning, a search which is agonized because his consciousness is split between fact and value, matter and spirit and he cannot be sure of reality beyond the world of appearances. The fourth and final movement (85–114) asserts the values of mysticism in this search for meaning. Irish belief, insular and over-emotional, is found wanting. In the twelfth stanza Devlin asserts that he is no better nor no worse than those spiritual leaders who have robbed the Irish race of the living adventure of their Christian heritage.

> No better nor worse than I who, in my books
> Have angered at the stake with Bruno
>
> (68–69)

Chaucer-like, his "books" his authority, his ironic compassion, his flexible instrument in stating abstract ideas and handling philosophical and psychological concepts, he manages to awaken us to the importance of persons.

Mary Salmon. Studies. Spring, 1973, pp. 75–76

I do not feel one should go further and call Devlin a religious poet because, in these interesting times of variegated confusion, dissension and dissent—times indeed ready for Roland Knox's lethal *Creed for All*—it has become difficult to use the label of religious poet in any unambiguous sense. . . . But we can follow the development of a religious theme through the entire span of Devlin's poetry.

Leaving aside the as-yet-unpublished religious verse of his schooldays—verse which reflects the habitual thoughts of a serious and pious boy—the poems most obviously concerned with religious thoughts and attitudes can be placed in a group of three poems which display a progress and a deepening of religious understanding, namely the "Est Prodest" of 1933, the "Lough Derg" of 1946 and "The Passion of Christ" of 1958. Apart from these poems, there stands alone the poem called "The Heavenly Foreigner" which we know, from the evidence of the manuscript, to have preoccupied Devlin from very early in the thirties until its publication in 1950—following which event, Devlin continued to work over the text until his death in 1959.

"The Heavenly Foreigner" enverbs the struggle of a person who is both lover and poet with very different loves and the beloved subjects of these loves, in each of whom he sights a paradise, and for each of whom he suffers agonies of sensibility. He undergoes, often in painful and sorrowful circumstances, the labour of an independent grasping at the source of his being, a striving which is not dependent on a principle of private judgement, but is a learning the lesson of pain without the telling of lies to self—while the poet despairs of a physical body weakening towards death. . . .

Devlin had a great love for the verses of John of the Cross: nevertheless it would be a mistake, I believe, to see or try to see in "The Heavenly Foreigner" a report of mystical experience. . . . Devlin's poem remains, I judge, in the antechamber of conflicting loves and in the end resolves into something like that curiosity which Leon Bloy said consumed him at the approach of death.

Brian Coffey. In Andrew Carpenter, ed., Place,
Personality, and the Irish Writer (New York,
Barnes & Noble, 1977), pp. 152–53

In Devlin we frequently find the anguished or tormented persona, an "I" figure, intensely involved with and the victim of experience, usually of love or of religion. The intensity is conveyed through the language which is sometimes surrealistic and at all times elegant, even dandyistic, and concerned with the manner of its saying. In love with language, using it like a virtuoso, his inner stress of feeling puts strain on the syntax; as in "Farewell and Good," where the harsh, blunt language conveys the drama of the individual situation.

"The Colours of Love" also reveals Devlin's delight in language. One of its interesting aspects, significant as an example of his attempt to marry the local and the remote, is the way in which the landscape and social reality of the west of Ireland is transformed within the poem. The actual is given little autonomy. Where Synge or O'Flaherty respected what they recorded from the outside, Devlin subordinates it to his own creative purposes. The descriptive details shift into emblem and allegory.

That process of absorption and transformation may also be observed in "Jansenist Journey" where the personal and familial become part of a pilgrim's progress in which the actual is made emblematical. When the process is not achieved, the result is an uncertainty of grasp, as in "Lough Derg," which is a meditation on the nature of the Irish way of penitence and of Christianity. The poem joins the Irish and the European in a many-sided and compact manner.

That Devlin is a poet of great power is apparent in "The Passion of Christ," a sequence of vivid, epigrammatic poems, each of which is a gloss on the Biblical account. Devlin's intellectual passion may be seen in the compressed and paradoxical poems which challenge the sense and the intelligence, defining and asserting significant, homilectic interpretations. The whole sequence, which is rich in memorable lines and phrases, and dramatic in its vividness of image and definition, is an exploration of Christ's passion and triumph over death to discover and declare their meaning. Throughout is the feeling of moving with conviction towards its final celebration of Christ's ascension and transfiguration, an accomplishment similar to Devlin's own need for a poetry that transforms feeling and events by an act of linguistic transfiguration. The serenity of tone in the poem's conclusion reveals a radiance and confidence found nowhere else in his work.

Maurice Harmon. Introduction to Maurice Harmon,
ed., Irish Poetry after Yeats (Dublin, Wolfhound,
1979), p. 20

DUNSANY, LORD (EDWARD JOHN MORETON DRAX PLUNKETT, 1878–1957)

I think that Lord Dunsany is one of the best poets that Ireland has yet produced—he and Mr. Yeats are enough to justify that distressing humbug of a country of its existence. . . . But I rather doubt whether Lord Dunsany has much idea of the greatness of his particular conjuring trick—or else he is as great a humbug as the rest of his countrymen. And that I do doubt. I fancy that he has the national gift of prestidigitation without really thinking that he is doing any more than eating potatoes with a fork. For, as I understand it, in the considerable Irish group that now exists—in the group that more or less contains himself and Mr. Yeats and the Abbey Theatre people and Mr. Moore and the gentlemen that Mr. Maunsel publishes—in that group Lord Dunsany imagines himself to represent the revolt against realism.

He does nothing of the sort, of course, since he is one of the chief realists of them all. He is so much of a realist that he produces an effect of mysticism; just as his countryman who is thinking of filling the old pig with buckshot. This is not paradox; it is part of the whole scheme of art and of the way art works. . . . For this, more or less, is the way Lord Dunsany sets about it. Says he: "I am sick of this world, and the Land Purchase Act, and the defectively sanitated cabins in Connemara. I will build up a world that shall be the unreal world of before the fall of Babylon. I am sick of the hogarths and their way; I will build seven thrones for seven gods of green jade." And so he goes and does it—with all the arts of the inspired realist! One is tired of the knocking on the door of Macbeth as an instance, but it is still the best instance in the world of how horror is heightened—of how horror is produced—by the projection of, not the writing about, purely material things. And Lord Dunsany is doing the knocking-on-the-door stunt all the way through four at least of his five plays [*Gods of the Mountain, Golden Doom, Unknown Warrior, Glittering Gate*]. And all the effects of these . . . plays too are got by the methods of the sheerest realism.

Ford Madox Hueffer. Outlook. April 11, 1914,
p. 491

After he had written *The Gods of Pegana*, Lord Dunsany discovered a figure that was more significant than any of the Gods—the figure of Time. "Suddenly the swart figure of Time stood up before the Gods, with both hands dripping with blood and a red sword dangling idly from his fingers." Time had overthrown Sardathrion, the City they had built for their solace, and when the oldest of the Gods questioned him, "Time looked him in the face and edged towards him fingering with his dripping fingers the hilt of his nimble sword." Over and over again he tells about the cities that were wonderful before Time prevailed against them—Sardathrion, with its onyx lions looming limb by limb from the dusk; Babbulkund, that was called by those who loved her "The City of Marvel," and by those who hated her "The City of the Dog," where, over the roofs of her palace chambers, "winged lions flit like bats, the size of every one is the size of the lions of God, and the wings are larger than any wing created." Bethmoora, where window after window pours into the dusk "its lion-frightening light." Those fair and unbelieving cities with the heathen kings who rule over them were found in the Bible, and the language in which they are written of never shames themes that have so grand a source. One might read Lord Dunsany's characteristic work and believe that he had read no book since the Prophets filled his mind. Sometimes it has the form of Biblical poetry, as in [his] meditation upon the Sphinx at Gizeh, on whose face the paint still remains. . . .

The people in Lord Dunsany's plays are like the people in his stories— as simple as his gods. It is not they but the things that happen to them that are extraordinary. In *King Argimenes and the Unknown Warrior* (printed in the *Irish Review* and produced in the Abbey Theatre, Dublin), an enslaved King finds a sword, and by its aid makes himself King again; and in *The Gods of the Mountain* (printed in the *Irish Review* and produced in the Haymarket in 1911) certain beggars impersonate the gods and sit in state receiving the gifts and homage of the people until the gods tramp down from their seats on the Mountain and turn the imposters into stone. The theatre of to-day has need of the qualities Lord Dunsany can bring into it—the glamour that comes from an unusual imagination moving through strange places, and a rich and rhythmical speech.

Padraic Colum. Irish Review.
June, 1914, pp. 218–20

It has been remarked that most of the plays would fit well into the form of stories, and it is quite as true, on the other hand, that many of the stories would do well as plays. Some of them could not be dramatised, they are too light, too fragile, and too lacking in action; but others would be splendid material. The tale of the magic window and of the war in the other world, the story of the quest of the Queen's tears, the dreadful adventure that befell three literary men, would all make plays and there are many more that would go with them. Yet were they put in dramatic form there would be so much that would have to be lost from them that the change would be of questionable wisdom. For in these tales Dunsany has permitted the bridle rein to droop upon the neck of Pegasus, and the steed has wandered to and fro among the hills and meadows, he has sniffed the woods and has paused to drink from the stream that runs through the pasture, and all life has known a golden and glorious awakening. So there are some things which are too delicate to be transmitted to a play, but though this be so the tales themselves would never have risen to their present importance had it not been that some of their kind were embodied in dramatic form. There is a force, a directness, a concentration, not only of attention, but of energy, which gives a carrying power to the play which the tale can never attain. Nor is such attainment intended. . . .

Edward Hale Bierstadt. Dunsany the Dramatist
(Boston, Little, Brown, 1920), pp. 131–32

Since by birth and by calling Lord Dunsany combines what is admirable to Irishmen, it is natural to ask if his work shows racial characteristics. All his readers know that he has invented a country of his own, wherein he has laid the scene of most of his stories and plays. He has given this country a mythology set forth in his first book, *The Gods of Pegana,* and elaborated in later volumes. Country and gods recall the East of long ago; about them clings the strange charm of Persia, of Babylon. The nomenclature of the gods, and of the cities, the mountains, the rivers, of this imaginary land, suggests sometimes classical literature, particularly Greek; sometimes characteristics of the deities of places named; and sometimes both. Thus Skarl is the god who beats a drum; Slid, the god of the sea; Wohoon, the Lord of Noises in the Night; Alderon, a valley; Eidis, a river. Story after story deals with these fabulous dominions, their gods and men. The sustained imagination with which the author has presented the various aspects of his dream land, the fantasy he manifests, are qualities long associated with the Irish mind. In early Gaelic literature there are, for example, the various islands visited by Bran in his voyaging, the extraordinary transformations of gods and men.

As is the vigor of his imagination, so is the type of his plots an indication of Lord Dunsany's nationality. The Celt has ever been conscious of the laws of Nature which he cannot control; Change and Death fascinate and terrify him. In many cases, this feeling, which lends a wistfulness to Celtic music and to Celtic poetry, rises to fatalism. "They went forth to battle, but they always fell," is the motto chosen by Matthew Arnold for his famous essay, "On the Study of Celtic Literature." The queens left behind by Cuchulain when he goes to his last fight set up a cry of lamentation; before the birth of Deirdre, a druid declares that evil deeds will be done because of her. In no other modern writer of English is the consciousness of an inexorable universe more strong than in Lord Dunsany. This is suggested by the title of his second book, *Time and the Gods,* and is clearly enunciated in that well-sustained tale, "In the Land of Time," as well as in many other instances. . . .

Lord Dunsany is concerned with the simplicities of life, with what is common to men wherever they may live, and in whatever age. This preoccupation is a Celtic characteristic, but it is also the charm with which the writer touches those beyond the boundaries of his native land, and becomes universal.

> Norreys Jephson O'Conor. *Changing Ireland:*
> *Literary Backgrounds of the Irish Free State,*
> *1889–1922* (Cambridge, Mass., Harvard Univ.
> Pr. 1924), pp. 149–50, 152

Lord Dunsany did not turn to the rich mine of Irish mythology and rural folklore to find the basis or the colour for his work; instead he created a very hierarchy of gods whom he enshrouded in glowing colours of the fabulous East and permitted in complete freedom to control the destinies of their fantastic cosmos. If the gods of Pegana have never themselves appeared upon any stage they have certainly given their benediction to many of Lord Dunsany's later plays. There was nothing of Pegana in *The Glittering Gate,* it was not one of the pleasant jokes of the beneficial deities, rather was it a grim satire on the eternal Hope that is the very basis of human life. *The Glittering Gate* dismissed Hope as a fraud, or, as Dean Inge has said, "Hope was regarded as a gift of dubious value, an illusion which helps us to endure life, and a potent spur to action; but in the last resort an *ignis fatuus*" (*The Idea of Progress*). It is evident in this early play, and more marked in the plays that have succeeded it in time, that Lord Dunsany regards humanity as altogether fatuous, and that human effort is doomed to eternal frustration. . . .

King Argimenes and the Unknown Warrior, which was staged for the first time in January 1911, is another illustration of Lord Dunsany's characteristic attitude of aristocratic detachment. In this two-act play he again demonstrates his technical equipment, and from the rise of the curtain the attention of an audience is gripped. In this play will be found the beginning of the line of plays of Eastern glamour and Eastern cruelty which have made the name of their author so well known to audiences in two continents. The theme of *King Argimenes* is not without its touch of arrogant snobbery; a king will be a king, and will act as a king, be recognised as a king, even when he is actually a captive and a slave. The assertion of aristocratic superiority in blood could hardly be more explicit, and it is, perhaps, to be counted to Lord Dunsany for excellence that the assertion has given no offence, even in the "sweet land of liberty" itself where it is very popular. . . . In technique and in dialogue, in characterisation and in setting, the play is excellent; its theme is too sharp for any Irish audience which is itself essentially snobbily aristocratic, and with its quota of the impoverished and enslaved descendants of kings.

Andrew E. Malone. The Irish Drama (London,
Constable, 1929), pp. 249–51

Of the ten short plays in this book [*Plays for Earth and Air*] four were written for the stage and the rest for wireless broadcasting. But all plays, with the exception of *The Use of Man,* are suitable for the stage. To read Lord Dunsany's dialogue alone is to realise the wealth of his dramatic gift. Character is conveyed immediately by dialogue alone, and in almost gradual conversation, often in the briefest of sentences, the momentum of the drama increases. Thus, in *Mr. Sliggin's Hour,* the Dark Stranger makes a bargain with the Vicar that he will help him write a sermon, moving his parishioners to tears, on condition that one hour later they will deride it. We see them in tears, and then in a couple of moments' conversation they deride. The transition is typical of Lord Dunsany's work, and its perfection lies in a masterly control of direct dialogue. Several of the plays are built out of allegory and fantasy. *Golden Dragon City* is the tale of Bill, who bought a strange window from a foreign-looking man with a dark beard, and of the adventures that befell him when he set it up to look through it. In *The Seventh Symphony* the playwright brings Beethoven, Cervantes, Milton, Shelley and Herrick to the bedside of a sick musician, and in *The Use of Man* a sportsman has to face a jury of animals in defence of his species.

All these plays are up to the level of Lord Dunsany's best work. They make excellent reading, particularly to those interested in the technique of plays for broadcasting.

Irish Book Lover. July–Dec., 1937, p. 111

If Dunsany's spirit survived the routine and discipline of an army school [Sandhurst], it endured because of influences earlier still — the breath of the woods and skies about Dunsany Castle and the aloofness, rather than the loneliness, they provided. These were part of his heredity. In his childhood he was protected from slipshod and ignoble reading. He had access to nothing but language of the Bible and of romances such as those that had set Don Quixote's spear in rest. These, acting on a mind of extraordinary sensitiveness and discrimination, have given us some of the purest and most distinguished English of today.

Where did he get those names of thrones and dominations and principalities from some astral hierarchy all his own which he uses so effectively: Perdondaris, Erl, Ziroonderel, Thek, Yann, Lirazel, Alveric, Tharrabas? Names that never were on sea or land, astronomic and skyey names, yet with an echo of the Gospel in the last. I cannot tell; but I remember one afternoon, while walking in the woods of Dunsany, I spoke of Coleridge and his name for the Sacred River in his *Kubla Khan*.

"Where did he get it?" I asked.

"From the first word in the Greek alphabet obviously," Dunsany answered, and that came as a revelation to me.

When I mention beautiful prose, I think of a comparison: Dunsany's prose is as pure, fabulous, and as rare as the unicorn of which he writes so familiarly. . . .

There were other causes at work to keep his lips more eloquent than words of army command required—causes that have been the making of many a poet; and these were the sounds of the wind in the trees and the light on the fields and bogs around his Irish home. This love of nature is seen clearly and simply, because it is not as idealized as in *The King of Elfland's Daughter*, when he writes of the Ireland that he knows as no one else knows it who can transmit it so well. *My Ireland* is the best book about the Irish countryside that has been written. His sympathy with wild nature glows through it, and that wry humor of his enlightens its every page. The quest he sets for himself which is never achieved is an example. He pretends that he is writing about the one thing that anyone will want to hear (as if all were not sick of it), Irish politics.

Oliver St. John Gogarty. *At*. March, 1955, p. 68

A Dreamer's Tales suggests Dunsany's apogee as a writer of wonder tales, though the bronze warmth of its pages sometimes lays a drowse on the spirit as the "old and holy figure" of Romance, "cloaked even to the face, comes down out of hilly woodlands . . . and brings a hush . . . over the grey lands," a hush out of which "rises faintly on far-off hills the voice of a lute." The pulse of its King James rhythms is essentially the pulse of tragedy; and perhaps not words, but the echoes of words — not deeds, but the shadows of deeds — may be the most memorable element here. Inevitably, the tales are variable in imaginative strength and compulsive enticement: in one or two cases, thoroughly trivial; but one can forgive a good deal while listening to "the sea that the moon led up the shore, dragging the months away over the pebbles and shingles and piling them up with the years where the worn-out centuries lay." One can be glad of eyes that were fixed on ships as old as those of Flecker's imaging or strained toward amorphous gods withdrawn into the haze on dim mountains. And one can find a joy to return to in the tales of "Poor Old Bill," sitting in a tavern ageless and undying since the soul of the captain he had marooned went " 'cursing over the sea' "; of strange Andelsprutz, that city "quite dead, and her soul gone hence"; of Hilnaric, whom Athelvok dreamt to be more lovely than the sea, yet to whom he never returned after he had heard the sea singing "a dirge at sunset for all the harm that he had done in anger," and afterward, his "prayer-like blessings." — Dunsany was never to create anything more beautiful than this latter tale, "Poltarnees, Beholder of Ocean"; he was never within its kind to surpass *A Dreamer's Tales,* which to date has fortunately, with the rest of his work, escaped the clawing of the hounds of symbol.

George Brandon Saul. *ArQ*.
Autumn, 1963, p. 200

In June 1933 Beatrice [Lady Dunsany] could record: "E. wrote his Irish novel in 3½ breathless months; bits of it have been in his mind for years and I never let it be forgotten for too long and then it came suddenly." The book, *The Curse of the Wise Woman,* was immediately successful, and is now the best-known and loved of all his work. The reviews were excellent but Dunsany was labelled and many of the opinions seem to have been trundled out rather than felt. This was particularly unfair for there is more direct feeling than he had ever conveyed before; if *The Blessing of Pan* had sung his love for Kent, then *The Wise Woman* did the same for Meath, adding his feelings about his lonely childhood. The story — of a boy spending his holidays from

Eton in Ireland shooting snipe and geese on the bogs with the keeper, his mother dead, his father soon to disappear, is the most autobiographical of his books. The narrator is an old man (seventy whereas Dunsany was fifty-five at the time of writing it) looking sadly back from exile and occasionally the description of shooting and scenery slow the plot to a standstill; this concerns the Troubles, shifted to about 1890, and the Wise Woman who is successfully cursing the English who are going to drain the bog and "compress the turf by machinery and sell it as coal." So a boy's adventure story blends with magic and a feeling for the country and country people to make a book which appeals particularly to unbookish people, perhaps because few who appreciate shooting and weather so simply can write evocatively about them. It appealed sufficiently to bookish people as well to receive £100 and the Harmsworth Award as "the best work of imaginative prose by an Irish author," selected from three books sent by the dreaded Irish Academy to John Masefield. So it was a score off them as well as a gratifying success all round.

The light it throws on Dunsany's feelings shows him in benign mood. Uncle Horace [Horace Plunkett] appears but is scarcely criticised, de Valera is rather a romantic figure dressed always in black and the Anglo-Irish hero, far from condemning Irish murderers, almost becomes one of them in face of the coal-threat: "It was then that my Irish heart sorrowfully regretted what my English education had taught me, to interfere with my friend who would have killed these men." Similarly the keeper who tells him not to fire at some snipe because, "There is no man living could hit them walking up wind," is not called a liar; on the contrary "It was his old way of worshipping the golden idol of Tact before the Goddess of Truth if they got in each other's way." But under the excitement and affection there is a pervasive sadness, more appropriate to the nostalgia of an old man, than to one in his mid-fifties.

Mark Amory. *Lord Dunsany: A Biography* (London,
Collins, 1972), pp. 232–33

ERVINE, ST. JOHN (1883–1971)

One of the most masterly of all realistic studies of Irish character has just been published by Messrs. Maunsel. It is *Mrs. Martin's Man*, by Mr. St. John Ervine, better known hitherto as an Irish playwright than as a story teller. Here an Ulster Irishman, dealing with the folk of the towns, brings to their portraiture the same high seriousness Mr. Shan Bullock brought to the portraiture of the Ulster country folk. To the southern Irishman, the first feeling he will have in reading *Mrs. Martin's Man* is what a hideous, what a hateful life, is depicted here. But let him read on and he will find the core of fine character underneath this unbeautiful surface. He will lay down the book with the feeling that he would be proud if a woman like Mrs. Martin was mother, wife, or sister of his. She excites in us the same real feeling of affection as the old mother in Mr. Ervine's play, *Mixed Marriage*. It is a true portraiture of an Ulsterwoman. But it is indeed much more than that, for there is in her a bravery, a kindness, a pity, a humour, an understanding and sympathy which are the most loveable things in womanhood anywhere. Mr. Ervine's power of depicting women is really remarkable. His men are good enough, but they are to some extent foils to set off his women. We do not feel a soul in his men as we do in his women. His men are characters, and do not convey the same sense of a wisdom of the spirit behind their words and actions. That may not be because Mr. Ervine is incapable of seeing in men what he sees in women, but arises in this book probably because he fell in love with his principal character, and people in love are proverbially blind to the merits of more than one person. If he had not been in love with Mrs. Martin, he would not have made her man so detestable. Mr. Ervine would probably have discovered some good points in Mr. Martin if he had been forced to write his biography. Books like this are good for Ulster. Mirrors so generally faithful as this are good to look at even if the people who behold their image squirm a little. It should prove absorbingly interesting as a tale to people of almost any nationality, because local colour, although it is laid on unflinchingly, is only a setting for universal human character. With books like this and Mr. James Stephens' *Charwoman's Daughter* and Mr. Shan Bullock's *Dan the Dollar*, we have passed a long way from the old idealistic pictures of the finest peasantry in the world, the patriotic Irishman and his faithful colleen. The sun of realism has arisen and revealed many things that the moonlight of sentiment concealed. We will say this, that Irish daylight, with all the disagreeable things it reveals, does not make us lose faith in Irish character. Mrs. Martin is as loveable as any colleen the most idealistic of Irish writers ever adored in verse. We congratulate Mr. Ervine upon a real achievement in Irish story telling. [Jan. 9, 1915]

George William Russell (A.E.). *Selections from the Contributions to "The Irish Homestead,"* Vol. II, Henry Summerfield, ed. (Atlantic Highlands, N.J., Humanities Press, 1978), pp. 890–91

John Ferguson is a play deeply felt and sincere, and in the character of John Ferguson Ervine created a man which the stage had not previously known. His faith did not brace him to meet the facts of life, nor did it comfort him when action was useless, but it was all he had to use merely as a drug to deaden his sorrow. For his wife it lacked even that. Fate plays with these little lives as Hardy made it play with Tess or Jude, and there is as much of Hardy in the play as there is of Ulster. Nevertheless *John Ferguson* is a great play despite the minor blemishes in its construction. Like T.C. Murray Ervine is apt to strain accidental happenings, and in this play there are two upon which the entire action is made to turn. The seduction of Hannah by Witherow is not made at all probable or convincing, there was nothing to indicate that Hannah was attracted by Witherow. Then there is the loss of the mail by John's brother in America when a day would have avoided all the sorrow and destruction. However, it is John himself who makes the play great, he stands like Lear against the buffets of fate, and at the end his "head is bloody, but unbowed." His body may be broken, his life-work ruined, but nothing can break his "unconquerable soul." These Fergusons are little people, but they can show life great, life tragic, as well as the kings and the aristocrats. Their stoicism is ennobling to the audience, even if they wear no crowns and work with their hands. They do not speak a language that rises to poetry, their emotions are all subdued; but they do present the Northern Irish peasant as he had never before been presented to the world. His very defects come from his qualities, his dourness, his staccato speech, his religious fanaticism, his contempt for his more soft-spoken compatriots in Ireland's other provinces. John Ferguson would have enjoyed his creator's gesture when farewell was bidden to Ireland in *The Island of Saints, and the Way to Get Out of It*. This little play was staged in 1920, and is as unworthy of its author as of the Theatre in which it was produced. *John Ferguson* is Ervine's gift to Ireland, and it is his greatest play.

Andrew E. Malone. *The Irish Drama* (London, Constable, 1929), pp. 204–5

John Ervine, Helen Waddell, and Joyce Cary are three examples of our older writers who have transplanted themselves, and all of them are writers of great vitality and adaptability. To wonder what creative work they would have done if they had remained in Northern Ireland is hardly a useful pursuit. Better accept the fact that a certain number of writers—as of other people—successfully transplant themselves, and their work is done in two or more contexts.

Of these three writers St. John Ervine is the one who is certainly the most closely tied to his native province by his work—plays, novels, short stories, biographies, criticism. He is primarily a dramatist, and his dramatic work is considered elsewhere in this volume. Born in the Ballymacarrett district of Belfast in 1883, he left Northern Ireland before he was twenty for London; and there he made a name for himself as a dramatic critic. But throughout his career Ervine has repeatedly turned to Ulster for the setting of his work. His best-known novels are *The Foolish Lovers* (1920), *Mrs. Martin's Man* (1914), *The Wayward Man* (1927). His greatest achievement is probably the heroine of *Mrs. Martin's Man*—Martha Martin. She is a more convincing person than Robert Dunwoody or John McDermott, the chief characters in the other two novels. Ervine is the opposite to Forrest Reid in portrayal of character: Ervine's young men are less convincing than Reid's; but Reid was incapable of portraying a woman like Martha Martin. Commenting on Arnold Bennett in *Some Impressions of My Elders* (1923), Ervine summarized the type of novelist he himself is: "He fights the battles of the romantic with the weapons of the realist." Indeed, Bennett and Ervine are novelists with many qualities in common: both are profoundly interested in normal human beings, and both write with great gusto and with an Edwardian sweep. For, although *The Wayward Man* was published in 1927, and his latest novel, *Sophia*, in 1941, Ervine's work is built like the work of the great Edwardian novelists—Bennett, Galsworthy, and Wells. Like these novelists, he is interested in telling a story for its own sake, and is blessed with a sense of humour. If he has affinities with any other Ulster novelist it is with William Carleton. He has Carleton's forthrightness, and he never flinches from telling the truth as he sees it. He has never minced his words, and indeed has been guilty of overstatement and provocativeness. Like Shaw (who has obviously influenced his polemical prose), he stings his reader into thought. He is, in many ways, a man of the eighteenth century, with something of the robustness and dogmatism of Dr. Johnson, something of the sentimentality of Goldsmith, and something of the fierce indignation of Swift. Like Swift, too, Ervine hates mankind in the mass, but loves individuals. The proof of this is that he has created many more sympathetic than unsympathetic characters. A man of intense love and hate, he has no time for the niceties of psychological analysis; his mind is remarkable for strength rather than for subtlety. Essentially a man of prose—being an essayist, novelist, biographer, and dramatist—St. John Ervine belongs to a tradition of Anglo-Irish literature that has endured for at least two centuries and seems likely to endure much longer.

John Boyd. In Sam Hanna Bell, ed.,
The Arts in Ulster: A Symposium
(London, Harrap, 1951), pp. 117–19

As a vigorous and controversy-loving dramatic critic in the nineteen-twenties, St. John Ervine did much useful service for the theatre. Like Lennox Robinson, he was for a time manager of the Abbey Theatre, and his two Irish domestic tragedies, *Mixed Marriage* (1911) and *John Ferguson* (1915), had fair success, particularly in America. Both these plays, powerful and moving, contain excellent examples of character-drawing, though a strain of hopelessness runs through their picture of the invincible and devastating stubbornness of men in the grip of religious and political "convictions." St. John Ervine afterwards had a notable run of success in the commercial theatres of London and elsewhere with such competent and agreeable comedies as *The First Mrs. Fraser* (1929), *Anthony and Anna* (1925), and *Robert's Wife* (1937). He was then an exponent of the settled views of middle age, opposing its stable standards of conduct to the raw enthusiasm and predatory instincts of the young. The clash was always entertaining and the issue gratifying to middle age; it might have carried more conviction if it had been made clearer that Youth, even when most self-seeking, has a point of view that should in fairness be ably and fully expressed in any play in which Youth is a chief protagonist.

A. C. Ward. *Twentieth-Century English Literature: 1901–1960* (London, Methuen, 1964), p. 115

St. John Ervine, in a long and illustrious career in drama and fiction, produced several fine novels set either in the Ballymacarrett area of East Belfast (where he was born) or on the Newtownards-Donaghadee shoulder of the Ards peninsula. His is a world of small shopkeepers, often vain and ambitious, among whom a few black sheep come down with wandering fever and sail the seven seas in clippers and schooners during the time of Ervine's own boyhood in the 1890s. In his three Ulster novels, *Mrs. Martin's Man* (1914), *The Foolish Lovers* (1920) and *The Wayward Man* (1927), wanderlust not only propels the narrative but is a lifestyle that threatens the stay-at-home shopkeepers. These shopkeepers are Protestant and Scots-Irish and their names have a resilient Ulster cast that suggests an ancient family residence in the area—Clegg, Mawhinney, McDermott, Greer, Mahaffy, Magrath, Dunwoody. This sense of place is especially important in Ervine's fiction because of the wanderlust it opposes, and is both a good (suggesting security and ancestral pride) and an evil (suggesting staid provincialism and unadventurousness).

Like the rural writers who came after him, Ervine makes use of the motif of bad blood, particularly in *Mrs. Martin's Man* in which family quarrels play a big part and metaphorise the sectarian feuds in Belfast at the beginning of the anti-Home Rule agitation in the 1880s and 1890s. Like these writers, too, and in a manner occasionally recalling Carleton, Ervine captures with realism the mores of the country town and working-class Belfast. However, Ervine's naturalistic elements belong to a different literary school from that of the writers we have so far discussed, and his sweeping narratives, as John Boyd has said, are of the same Edwardian tradition in which Galsworthy, Wells, Bennett and the early Maugham participated. Ervine's interest is not in social forces which preclude moral choice (as in local naturalism) but in moral choice within rather practical contexts. Adolescence in Ervine is a pre-Joycean concept in which the young hero seeks an appropriate lifestyle instead of truth or vision. The basic choice facing his young men as they approach manhood is between travel and sedentariness, independence and commercial ties. Because wanderlust is one of the choices, Ervine's novels are romantic in a vulgar sense, for they recount adventures that take the young heroes to Belfast, London and America. There is a second, equally vulgar sense, in which his work is romantic. "Frequently the choices facing the hero are embodied in women among whom he has to choose not merely a wife but a lifestyle. Frustrations in love are major stumbling-blocks for Ervine's protagonists as they flounder indecisively among prostitutes, demure hearth-lovers and hard-bitten business-women. This is how sex, like other relationships, is presented in Ervine's novels, as symbolic of a lifestyle or a value-system rather than in terms of pleasure or beauty. Ervine is not really a romantic writer despite the romantic trappings. His strength as a novelist lies in the fluency of his storytelling and in the realism of occasional and powerfully atmospheric episodes. His weakness lies in the basic moral simplicity of his fictional universe and the running to type of his characters.

John Wilson Foster. *Forces and Themes in Ulster Fiction* (Dublin, Gill & Macmillan, 1974), pp. 130–32

FALLON, PADRAIC (1905-1974)

It would be quite a spectacle to see anybody taking Mr. Fallon in hand. He knows his own mind. The Ariel part of him—and there's much Ariel—can be quickly suppressed for the part of an intransigent Falstaff who has gone off the sack. The Wise Old Owl who has hooted at being collected can become as argumentative as a woodful of jackdaws. And the man who can deceive by appearing at one moment as a harmless bucolic character can, after a conversation or an argument or a reading of his work, leave a room full of echoes of Lorca, [Anthony] Raftery, Rilke, Higgins, Clarke, Yeats, Synge, the wind in *The Golden Bough*, the gossip of old sailors and, of course, Mr. Padriac Fallon. He is himself, and he is a Shape Changer. He seems in his writing to take on the colour and form of the physical or spiritual world into which he projects himself. One recalls that a fellow writer—in a fit of exasperation—said sharply of his capacity for being influenced by other men's work that "Fallon takes the whitewash off every wall he leans against." It would be easy to remember nothing of him except the taking of the whitewash. It would be easy to forget that there is a solid independent Mr. Fallon who builds and whitewashes his own walls.

He has written verse, short stories, a few essays, and many scripts for radio among which is his longest, most ambitious and successful work, *Diarmuid and Grainne*, a perfect ballet of sound. Excepting this script, the bulk of his published work is not large. By hunting and questing and perhaps omitting nothing, one could get together a respectable volume of short stories. By more hunting and questing in magazines and anthologies, one could assemble a slim volume of his verse. (One anthology which proffers the work of thirty-seven Irish poets honours him with the note: "Many consider him Ireland's best living poet.") The quest, though exasperating, would be worthwhile, for anything that this man has written is marked with the qualities of his original, forceful, somewhat confused and not completely articulate genius. They are the qualities of an imagination that delights rapturously in the shape and texture of things, in folk-taled landscapes, and in people whose trades or occupations have given them character or link them with ancient, traditional modes of life. Yet, his genius is not content merely to repose in delight. His mind tries to plumb the depths below the sparkle of the surface and to explore the mysterious tugging currents. One perceives in the verse as in the stories a curious movement, a stirring, like the wind on a summer morning before it decides which way to breathe or blow. Beneath the richness of Mr. Fallon's evocation of things, beneath the images that are often nearly as palpable as the things they symbolize or represent, there is a stirring for direction, a hither-and-thither of the water waiting for the strong salt tide. There was the strength and flow and fresh saltiness of a tide in *Diarmuid and Grainne* in which Mr. Fallon, in the way Frenchmen have taken Greek and Roman classical themes, took an Irish legend and made it his own.

Francis MacManus. The Bell. Feb., 1951, pp. 20–21

Finally a word must be said for at least the two—and I use the word deliberately—greatest plays of Padraic Fallon. Neither *Diarmuid and Grainne* nor *The Vision of Mac Conglinne* could be staged, and, in fact, neither was meant to be. Both are plays for radio, originally produced by Micheál Ó hAodha for Radio Éireann. The quality of imagination in both is so superb that I approach them with considerably greater feelings of inadequacy than usual. There is just too much in these sprawling, funny, beautiful plays for a page or two of summary to do justice to.

Unlike most modern versions of myth and legend, they preserve the wonder and magic at the same time that they infuse the story with meaning. Most modernizations fall into one of two categories: they either become dramatic by reducing the legendary characters to realistic human stature, as in the Synge and MacDonagh versions of the Deirdre story, or they preserve something of the heroic stature but become formalized, lifeless, and undramatic, as in some of Yeats's plays. On the one hand, we have the way of Mark Twain and T. H. White; on the other, the way of Tennyson and Charles Williams. Perhaps halfway between we get such rare works as those of Tolkien the novelist or of Fallon. . . .

It is difficult to suggest the quality of such creatively legendary scenes [in *Diarmuid and Grainne*] as the battle with the Green Planet or the great concluding battle with the boar of Ben Bulben or the curious and fascinating scenes in the sacred wood of Dubhros with the giant of the Quickentree. Really Fallon is doing much more with the legend than anyone else who has ever handled it. It is as if, by making Diarmuid and Grainne larger than nature—magical—by even making them blend into the elements of nature, he intends a parable illustrating fully and finally certain aspects of man's nature. Into his mixture he has poured a strange blend, perhaps consisting of bits of Jung and Freud and anthropology as well as legend. . . .

[In *The Vision of Mac Conglinne*,] the characters, as in the previous play, take on such a legendary size, and the actions are of such a free-wheeling, expansively imaginative nature, that one fumbles among such huge adjectives as "immense, titanic, gargantuan" to describe it. I think, however, that basically the play is a paradoxical paean to and a mournful analysis of the lamentable effects of woman on man. The action seems to show that woman fills man with a sense of glory, romance, security, passion, and is also the source of man's greatest agony and humiliation. . . . The wit and humor in the play are as fantastic as anything in *Diarmuid and Grainne*, although the earlier play is, by the necessity of its story, the more moving; it has also the more beautiful lyrics. However, this comic play is so much more inventive in incident, stirring in language, and meaningful in theme, that one is finally convinced: despite all of the contrary evidence of sapless poetic drama, from Tennyson to MacLeish, poetry really can bring fullness and glory to the modern drama.

Robert Hogan. *After the Irish Renaissance*
(Minneapolis, Univ. of Minnesota Pr., 1967),
pp. 159, 161–63

Diarmuid and Gráinne, produced by Radio Éireann in 1950, is based on the best known of all the Fianna sagas. It had already been treated in dramatic form by Yeats and George Moore in an unhappy collaboration, by Lady Gregory, and by Micheál MacLiammóir in his play in Irish. Fallon's work is neither an adaptation of redaction for radio of the saga material nor a good theatre craftsman's compression of a great tragic love story into three-act form. It is a work of intricate complexity which reveals several patterns of meaning. It has the morning freshness of the folk-tale of a beautiful young princess who, being forced to marry an old king, elopes with a young prince. But Fallon does not confine himself to a folk-treatment with strange wonders rooted in the commonplace. Combining the archaic and the colloquial, blending primeval simplicity with psychological interpretation, he fashions his material in an individualistic mould. When Diarmuid and Gráinne hide in the giant's quicken-tree in the wood of Dubhros we are imaginatively transplanted to the Garden of the Hesperides, or, if one prefers it, to the Garden of Eden itself. When Diarmuid fights the great boar of Ben Bulben, he not only shares the fate of the Greek Adonis, the Egyptian Osiris and the Cretan Zeus, but he shows a surprising Freudian insight into his unconscious. When Diarmuid plays chess with a vegetation God, the Greek Planet—an incident not to be found in the saga, they play with the signs of the Zodiac and the game ends in geological eruptions.

These three examples are sufficient to illustrate that neither the physical nor mental action of the play can be fixed in place or time; it is not set in pre-Christian Ireland nor in an Irish other-world of pagan belief but in a mythopoeic universe where Orpheus, Jung, Sir James Frazer, Adonis, Robert Graves, Demeter, Freud and Dionysus can wander at will.

Micheál Ó hAodha. *Theatre in Ireland* (Oxford,
Basil Blackwell, 1974), pp. 102–3

His poetry, however, at times does move in the other direction, towards the nether-gut, and of this group "Boyne Valley" and "The Head" are of particular interest. One reason for this is their mythological nature; they belong in part, even without the "intrusion" of the poet, to mythology. His "western" poems preferred the actual, invoking a heraldry of nature's plenitude— "Boyne Valley" is ultimately tethered to the visible world of the "swaying sunheaded reed," the "crow daubed on the ripple of/A black poplar," the details of place in which "Esquires" and "Jaguars" depart from the meet. But these notations of the here and the now are placed against a background of mythical associations. History is declared to go on slowly as usual, "somewhere." . . .

His finest achievement is this attention to the world beyond the visible, within the self; in this poem the effect is of something obscurely seen, yet offering perceptions that are distinctive, there in the historical imagination. . . .

There are poems too, . . . in which Fallon's childhood world is rendered in terms evocative of personal myth, poems that give testimony to the lasting pull of that world: his town, the people, the ways of life. The distinction is drawn between towns that are complete in themselves, whose essences are projected in buildings, in developing histories, in full personalities and his "ideogram of a town," "almost intact" but essentially destroyed: "The wooden horse in the square." Like so many Irish writers, Fallon makes poetry through and despite a sense of diminishment and incompleteness, and in his case we have to add the pervasive feeling of alienation and fragmentation, of a "wound" at the heart of things. . . .

Fallon's sense of the past, of the minor gentry, the faction fights, the violence of the land struggle, the devil-may-care Irishman is strong, accounting for a strain of extravagance in some of his poetry. "If I wrote ebulliently," he once explained, "it was only to cope with it, for in it was the earlier century alive and kicking!" For him the past was contemporaneous with his own youth, not something created out of books and not just a congenial region of the imagination. For him the eighteenth century died with 1916, as far as Galway was concerned, and with 1922 for the rest of Ireland. His natural affinities were with that century, with its assonantal poetry, and particularly with Raftery. "I got a lot out of Raftery, a lot more from an Irish-speaking workman we had, who had all the local gossip of the poet and his work." Because of this personal contact with rural Ireland, it may be argued that his poetry of the Galway countryside is more successful that his poetry of the western seaboard. When he deals with Synge's islanders and seacoast dwellers, his romantic temperament creates a subjective, idealistic picture, but when he attends to the realities of Athenry and the surrounding countryside, he unites his myth-making with the dimensions of a visible world in which people live and die.

Maurice Harmon. *Studies.*
Autumn, 1975, pp. 271–74

Behind many of Padraic Fallon's best poems lies an impulse to evaluate, do justice to, estimate and esteem the objects of his attention. More than a rage for order, his work manifests a passion for equity. Marked by a judicious affection, free of sentimentality, speaking their own authentic speech, the poems can bring us a revived consciousness of phenomena we may have taken for granted. While this judgement seems to hold true for a great deal of the work, it may be most clearly observed in a number of poems which claim myth or the mythopoeic as their object. Such poems, I would argue, form a coherent centre to the work, a point from which the rest of it may be better appreciated. These poems may be divided into three major areas: his treatment of existing myths; his revelation in ordinary phenomena of a mythic, ritual essence; his reflection on the notion of myth itself and the absence or presence of the mythic dimension in actual experience. While these three areas do not contain all the best or most important of Fallon's poems, they do provide a summary of Fallon's imaginative life, the lyrical embodiment of what I call his critical intelligence. . . .

In poems dealing with the myths of Odysseus and of the Virgin Mary, Fallon grants the stories fresh life in the present moment. This he does by means of the intensely domesticated nature of his language, the muscularly matter-of-fact tones of the poems' speakers. In bringing the big stories down to earth he reveals an instinct that is one of his most telling poetic gifts, and part of his imaginative being from boyhood. As he says in the late autobiographical poem, "Lost Man," his youthful need was for "a local God" who was at home in "The weather or the weekday sod . . . amenable to ewes/And quiet moonbodies like fat turnips." By grounding his treatments in ordinary phenomena that challenge the abstractions of conventional piety, Fallon deepens our sympathetic awareness of the tangible human substance of his chosen myths.

Eamon Grennan. *IUR*. Autumn, 1982, pp. 174–75

FITZMAURICE, GEORGE (1877–1963)

When *The Country Dressmaker* was revived in 1912, the author had faded almost completely from the memory of all but the few who recognized the promise of the young dramatist when that play introduced him in 1907. In 1908 George Fitzmaurice followed up his first contribution with a second of slighter texture, *The Pie-dish*. This curious little piece in one act, which failed to secure the sympathies of an audience already in search of digestive amusement, was soon forgotten on the accession of the new régime of imitative peasant playwrights. It is not surprising, therefore, that he should have waited for seven years before publishing his first play. Meanwhile, in spite of discouragement, Fitzmaurice had not been idle. In 1914 *The Country Dressmaker* had scarcely appeared, when it was supplemented by a volume entitled *Five Plays*, containing *The Moonlighter, The Magic Glasses*, and *The Dandy Dolls*, as well as the two plays already mentioned.

As is the case in the best of our folk drama, *The Country Dressmaker* is contrived out of the simplest elements. . . . The play is packed with observation, and is brilliantly written, in an idiom rich with quaint terms and delectable words, which, nevertheless, differs fundamentally from the stereotyped "Kiltartanese" and its variants, to which so many writers have abandoned themselves. Here and there one is shocked by gross caricature, whose defects are emphasized by the faithful characterization of most of the figures in this perfect comedy of rural manners. Seldom has a first play shown such qualities of style and dramatic technique as *The Country Dressmaker*. The great development of the author's talent during the seven years which followed it did not surprise those who read *Five Plays* with a precise impression of Fitzmaurice's début. . . .

Some of the typical violence of the new conventional peasant melodrama mars *The Moonlighter*, but Fitzmaurice is too good a craftsman to succumb to mere formulæ. He has made a penetrating study of the conditions which breed violence in peasant Ireland, and he depicts the knaves and braggarts with the same care as the patriotic idealists. Peter Guerin is a remarkable characterization, and though he necessarily has all the sympathy of an Irish audience, he must be recognized as a fine psychological portrait, equaled, perhaps, by Eugene. The play shows a distinct advance upon *The Country Dressmaker* in the contrivance and the manifestations of incident. In spite of its greater length, the interest is sustained to a moving climax.

Together with an increasing technical skill, Fitzmaurice shows an ever greater command of picturesque and forcible idiom, which finds its maximum expression in *The Magic Glasses* and *The Dandy Dolls*. These two plays are in one act, and have neither the style nor the substance which would repay an attempt to summarize them. The former piece is a realistic fantasy, which relates to the world in which we live, but the latter is an exercise of pure fancy, situated beyond the limitations of human experience. . . .

In the domain of pure fantasy George Fitzmaurice has only one rival, Lord Dunsany, while in the vigor and exuberance of his peasant speech he is surpassed by Synge, but unequaled by any other of the Irish dramatists. There is none of the poetry of Synge's language in Fitzmaurice's plays, but there is the same wealth of virile and vivid phrasing, in which every speech is "as fully flavoured as a nut or apple," to quote the preface to *The Playboy*. The "joyless and pallid words," which Synge condemned, find no place in what Fitzmaurice has written, though he never uses an expression traceable to any of his predecessors. The Anglo-Irish idiom as he employs it offers no analogies either with Hyde and Synge or Lady Gregory, beyond the fact of their common source in Gaelic. He has made of peasant speech an original creation which, if not the potent instrument of Synge, is measurably finer than the monotonous "Kiltartanese" and its minor variants, in vogue with the later playwrights. George Fitzmaurice has, therefore, imagination and style of a sufficiently personal quality to give him rank as the greatest folk-dramatist since the death of J. M. Synge, and the practical withdrawal of [Padraic] Colum's plays from the current repertory of the Abbey Theatre.

Ernest A., Boyd. *The Contemporary Drama of Ireland* (Boston, Little, Brown, 1917), pp. 143–45, 147–49

Both *The Magic Glasses* and *The Dandy Dolls* may have, in some ways, anticipated too rashly the experimental drama of to-day. But how Lady Gregory, Yeats and their associates could have failed to have been excited by their energy, vehement rhythm and imaginative originality is almost incredible. George Fitzmaurice published his volume of collected plays in the unfortunate year of 1914 and he made a mistake which is fatal to the experimentalist. Unlike other Irish writers of the time, he did not explain even in a brief prefatory note his aims and intentions.

To appreciate the experiments of George Fitzmaurice it is necessary to realise that he was writing at a time when the delight in folk idiom and traditional language was both genuine and formative. Since then the influence of Synge has become a habit rather than a provocation and both playwrights and novelists have turned the excitement of idiom into the horrors of brogue. Synge enriched his idiom with the metaphors and images which he found in *The Love Songs of Connaught*. Fitzmaurice helter-skeltered a rhythmic extravagance of words, and it seems to catch its pace from those fantastically long place-names which one finds in Kerry. The hardy language of Fitzmaurice should survive the turn of fashion for it is his own but I feel that it would be improved for us if some of the strained grammar and idiom of the period were discreetly excised. *The Magic Glasses*, which is a one-act play, begins at once by interpreting the common aches, ailments and wretched infirmities of humankind in the folk terms of wonder and hope. Even before the long-striding Mr. Quill comes to the cottage to cure Jaymony Shanahan of melancholia, we are swept into that marvellous world of half-miracle in which boils, pimples, ulcers, abscesses, wind, fire in the veins and rot in the bones can disappear at a touch, a mutter ot the uncorking of a bottle. The half-crazy Mr. Quill, a cynical rogue and yet a wonder-maker, who has come to believe in his own wonders is half real and half a figure of the folk mind. When Mr. Quill lures Jaymony from the loft and inveigles him into telling him what he sees in the magic glasses he has bought at a fair, the three brown glasses, the three red glasses and the three blue glasses, both knave and natural are caught into the same fanciful world of riches and sight-seeing. The little scene reminds us obviously of Peer Gynt and his mother in that marvellous and pathetic sleigh ride into childhood. But one notes that in the Irish scene the underlying tragedy of poverty and ignorance is not really felt. This is due perhaps to the fact that the catastrophic ending of the play is in the nature of a thunderbolt which buries everything even deeper in a world of fantasy. . . .

George Fitzmaurice discovered what Yeats, Lady Gregory and others were looking for and, as I have said, it is almost incredible that the interest of his experiments should not have been seen at the time. There are signs that our folk lore may quicken an Irish ballet and, since we must assume that Irish drama will continue to develop, it is possible that dramatists will interpret our folk lore before it is too late. It that is so, the precarious difficult art-form in which Fitzmaurice experimented at the expense of immediate recognition will be its real starting point.

Austin Clarke. DM. Jan., 1940, pp. 10–11, 14

Very few modern Irish dramatists have accomplished so large a body of interesting and varied work as George Fitzmaurice. As a folk dramatist he stands alone; as a realistic dramatist he may be classed with that small group among the poetic-prose writers who have employed a heightened common speech with true dramatic effectiveness. Fitzmaurice uses rich country speech as Synge did when he sought for an effect of extravagant imagination firmly wedded to reality. Where Synge's people at other times launch out into splendid imaginative flights, Fitzmaurice places these fanciful images upon the stage before us and weaves them into the dramatic fabric of his plays. Christy Mahon's verbal flights are beautiful and effective, but The Hag's abduction of Roger Carmody before our very eyes is, in all its noise, colour and flurry equally poetic, incredible and convincing. Few of us would maintain that drama consists of words alone, and until someone defines the dramatic phenomenon we may continue to allow colour, movement, rhythm and song to have their place in the more-than-literary art of the drama.

Fitzmaurice is concerned with idealism and aspiration as they stand opposite reality and human limitation. I am not sure that the plays attempt to show the two extremes in actual conflict, but in presenting dream and reality side by side he has revealed each in a more just and honest light than many artists have been able to do. And in showing the final and rather lonely superiority of the real, he pays tribute to the unreal, and to the whole of life. I believe that he emerges as an artist of stature, and that in recording his vision with such good-natured fidelity he has become Ireland's most adventurous and successful experimental dramatist. Though scarcely a part of the historical movement of his time, he has succeeded in fulfilling an important part of its aim.

J. D. Riley. DM. Jan., 1955, pp. 18–19

[*The Magic Glasses*] is a beautifully shaped little play, rooted equally in everyday life and in the laws of fantasy, and combining the two in an expansive idiom which can accommodate black superstititions and death within a comic framework. It is also one of those works which remind one of how foreign Ireland is to the rest of Europe (a version of the play by Kan Kikuchi, retitled *The Madman on the Roof*, was published a few years ago as a representative specimen of modern Japanese drama).

In *The Green Stone*, Fitzmaurice produced another variation on the same theme, this time telling the story of a boy with a magic stone which allows him to see into the future; as in the other plays he is surrounded by obtuse parents and neighbours who are enraged by his possession and seek to destroy it. Compared with its predecessors, it is a flimsy piece: partly because of a slackening in the writing's vitality, and partly because of the symbol itself. A prophetic stone is obviously a valuable object; even the thick-headed family could be expected to see that. The whole point of the previous symbols—the dolls [*The Dandy Dolls*], the pie-dish [*The Pie-dish*], and the glasses [*The Magic Glasses*]—is that they, like art itself, are absurd and useless, indefensible to anyone who does not already apprehend their value. And, true to his Irish inheritance, Fitzmaurice is half on the side of the enemy. His men of imagination are not lonely heroes upholding a noble cause; they are fools and their sacrifice is worthless. There may be conflict, but there is no hope for either side: all share the plight of the peasant farmer in one of his early pieces who tried to clear his land of crows by taking a gun into the field and waiting for it to go off. "A tendency to upbraid fate," he writes primly, "to brood over misfortunes rather than immediately to seek by what means they can be palliated or overcome, seems to be generally characteristic of the Celt." So it does; and his own writings are deeply rooted in that tendency. At the same time, he never takes refuge in the artificial escapes practised by other writers of "the most distressful country." Like other early Abbey dramatists, he built his one-act plays around miracles and revelations—but, unlike them, he never offered these as spiritual consolation. The figure of the Yank saviour, wherever he appears, is a buffoon or a crook (one of his later plays, *The Coming of Ewn Andzale*—an anagram on New Zealand—deals specifically with the wish-fulfilment fantasy of the emigrant relative returning laden with money bags). And neither his comic nor his lyrical writing are what other Irish writers so often provide—a verbal substitute for alcohol.

It was presumably the stimulus of the Literary Revival that first attracted Fitzmaurice to the theatre; but almost from the first he was an odd man out. After *The Country Dressmaker*—which, no matter what Yeats says about it, is a charmingly innocuous study of village wooing—he was out of step with the times; producing sombre works when audiences wanted comedy, bizarre fantasies when realism came into fashion, and anticipating O'Casey in tragi-comedy by nearly twenty years. He did write one full-length realist play on a national theme: this was *The Moonlighter*, an ambitious drama of the Land War contrasting the characters of a reformed Fenian and his fiery patriotic son against a background of the secret revolutionary organizations of the time. (Inexplicably rejected by the Abbey in 1910, it was not performed until 1948.) But, with this one exception, he did not write "timely" plays.

In spite of his connections with the Dublin movement, it seems to have meant far less to him than Kerry: and in some ways he seems to belong less among the founders of a modern tradition than among the inheritors of a very old one.

Irving Wardle. LondonMag. Feb., 1965, pp. 72–73

When George Fitzmaurice died in 1963, he was given only a couple of short paragraphs in the *Irish Times*, which remembered him mainly as the author of *The Country Dressmaker* and a few one-acts performed early in the century by the Abbey Theatre. Despite this scant notice, a few perceptive poets, such as Padriac Colum and Seamas O'Sullivan and Austin Clarke, had always regarded Fitzmaurice as a master dramatist. That regard was based upon the volume *Five Plays* which appeared in 1913 and upon the handful of plays which O'Sullivan brought out over the years in the *Dublin Magazine*. These magazine publications and about a half a dozen amateur productions were the only attention that Fitzmaurice's work received in the last forty years of his life. He was ignored as few writers of the first rank have ever been, but he was a rare and original genius. . . .

It is hard to sum Fitzmaurice up without sounding extravagant. He has written a body of plays nearly as large as O'Casey's and three times as large as Synge's. He has as unmistakably individual a voice as either, and his wry resignation is as fresh as his exuberant imagination. His plays are a fantastic, a brilliant, and an alternately joyous and grim body of work. There is no one like him in the modern drama.

Why, then, was he so long ignored? Why did the Abbey Theatre not encourage him? Perhaps it was partly a matter of luck; perhaps it was partly, as Austin Clarke thinks, the jealousy of Yeats. But, whatever the reason, it is clear that he was one of the masters; the theatre of Ireland and of the world can continue to ignore him only to its own impoverishment.

Robert Hogan. After the Irish Renaissance
(Minneapolis, Univ. of Minnesota Pr., 1967),
pp. 164, 175

There are many parallels between the symbolism of *The Pie-dish* and the life of George Fitzmaurice. Both Leum Donoghue and his creator strove for perfection. Both artists spent over fifty years in the attempt. Leum in the play and George in life were largely misunderstood. Neither hankered after recognition and acclaim. Both had a gift and they followed their own stars. They were essentially secretive men, labouring away at their pie-dishes in dark and gloomy rooms. They were not men of their time but "pagans suckled in a creed outworn." . . .

[Fitzmaurice] lived in the twilight world of fantasy and of the folk-imagination. He retreated into that world. Apart from his plays, we know little about him. And if anyone turns to books for information about him, he is in for some surprises. The first surprise is that his name figures in Burke's *Landed Gentry*. . . . But genealogy apart, it is important to realize that George Fitzmaurice created his own legend. Many playwrights have fashioned wild and extravagant folk-tales into well-constructed conventional plays. *In the Shadow of the Glen, The Pot of Broth* and many of Lady Gregory's plays are based on folklore. But Fitzmaurice did not go to Patrick Kennedy's *Legendary Fictions of the Irish Celts*, or to [Jeremiah] Curtin or [Douglas] Hyde for plots. As a result, Fitzmaurice's characters leap on to the stage with an exuberance and wild abandon, as if they had suddenly broken loose from the mind of their creator. Jaymony Shanahan and his magic glasses, Roger Carmody and his dolls, the King of the Barna Men and his blue ointment are original figments of Fitzmaurice's imagination. There is nothing quite like them in modern drama except perhaps the Trolls in Ibsen's *Peer Gynt*. One can no more analyse or paraphrase the plots of these pieces than one could describe exactly a haunting dream or a violent nightmare. On one level the plots are as nonsensical as *Alice's Adventures in Wonderland* or *Snow White and the Seven Dwarfs* but we are left with a similar impression of wild tomfoolery hiding a share of common sense. Again one notes the sub-stratum of pagan belief beneath the top-soil of conventional Christianity. The Priest in *The Dandy Dolls* in search of "his goose with the cuck on her" is every bit as much a witch doctor as the quack, Morgan Quill from Beenahorna, in *The Magic Glasses*. Modern critics will resort to a Freudian interpretation of what are essentially dream plays. They will search for sex symbols. But there is little of guilt or sin of any kind. His characters are, in the main, pure pagans. But many playgoers will baulk at such implications, and prefer to accept the fantasy plays as a glorious free-for-all where the imagination runs riot in a swirl of colour and a welter of words.

Fitzmaurice had a mastery of Kerry idiom. His dialogue owes little to Synge or other folk-dramatists. Like everything he fashioned, his language, like the 'figarios' on the pie-dish, was essentially his own. He is not equally successful in his longer plays; his realistic tragedy *The Moonlighter* and his comedy *The Country Dressmaker* show more promise than achievement. He is really a miniaturist. Fitzmaurice could carve a leprechaun on a cherry stone; he could not hew a life-size statue out of a rock.

Micheál Ó hAodha. *Theatre in Ireland*
(Oxford, Basil Blackwell, 1974),
pp. 68–69

The Coming of Ewn Andzale is a puzzling play which one is tempted to call a failure. One recent critic, J. D. Riley, who has no hesitancy about putting Fitzmaurice at his best on a level with O'Casey and Synge, calls this play "the only real failure among Fitzmaurice's plays." It is certainly a different sort of Fitzmaurice play. Dialect is gone completely and what Robert Hogan calls a language of "polite formality" has replaced it. The play is not set in Kerry, but in Monkstown, a suburb of Dublin. Fitzmaurice tells us we are in the drawing room of the Davenport family which, to judge from the furnishings, is comfortably middle-class. The play deals with the return of the native, a plot Fitzmaurice has used before, most successfully in *The Country Dressmaker*. And the play's characters are a dull lot, without a Luke Quilter or a Morgan Quille among them. All of this adds up to a pretty mediocre effort, certainly not vintage Fitzmaurice.

Why would Fitzmaurice write such a play? He knew perfectly well that a Fitzmaurice play without dialect and without Kerry characters was risky. No doubt he had to work over the drawing-room conversations in *The Coming of Ewn Andzale* much more than he did his native Kerry speech or even the Dublin dialect which seems to flow so naturally in *One Evening Gleam*. And the result was still such a stiff and self-conscious speech that he was probably never satisfied with it himself. And yet he had the play published.

I think Fitzmaurice was trying to accomplish something in *The Coming of Ewn Andzale* which required him to forsake dialect and the country, and concentrate on the experience of an educated, middle-class, urban, probably Protestant, Anglo-Saxon family. His most moving earlier plays—*The Magic Glasses, The Linnaun Shee, The Dandy Dolls, The Green Stone*—suggest a certain kind of Irish consciousness, spontaneous, close to nature, in touch with supernatural powers. No one, not even the priest in the community, doubts the presence of the fairies, which indeed manifests itself violently in each of the plays.

In *The Coming of Ewn Andzale*, however, another kind of Irish consciousness appears, one which is removed from the land, one in which orthodox education has replaced natural lore, and faith in the fairies has become faith in reason and empiricism. And yet events in the play belie this "modern" consciousness and suggest that mysterious powers are still at work in human life, even though no one in the play has more than a glimmer of awareness. . . .

The Coming of Ewn Andzale was George Fitzmaurice's last play, begun in 1950 and published in 1954. How appropriate and sad that it should deal with an attenuation of the Irish folk consciousness so complete that not even one evening gleam from the other world manages to come through.

Arthur E. McGuinness. *George Fitzmaurice*
(Lewisburg, Pa., Bucknell Univ. Pr., 1975),
pp. 75–76, 81

Fitzmaurice wrote folk plays which, when successful, dramatized the living folk imagination of Kerry in their fusion of peasant superstition with everyday farm life. Fitzmaurice's legendary figures are always conceived of in a small-town context. His dramatic techniques in staging his folk vignettes are unique in that he has tried to preserve the folktale as nearly as possible in its distinctive narrative form, and yet mold that form into drama. Moreover, Fitzmaurice presented his audiences with dark and somber plays when they were led to expect comedy—this resulting from his habit of inserting considerable harshness into a comic framework. He often dramatized symbols which focused the spectators' attention on the plays' central themes, even though the symbols themselves are often open to differing interpretations. He consistently mingled realism with fantasy. And finally, the characters of Fitzmaurice's fantasies are no longer realistically motivated but are manipulated to demonstrate the author's case. George Fitzmaurice was writing at a time when delight in folklore and folk idiom was both genuine and formative, and his experimental dramaturgy is a curious outgrowth of this activity. . . .

The dramatization of folktales recreated in their distinctive narrative form, as well as the staging of a part of the living folk imagination is probably what Austin Clarke meant when he wrote that Fitzmaurice experimented with a difficult, precarious art form. The very nature of the dramatic form is opposed to the heavily descriptive narrative which forms a major part of most of Fitzmaurice's folk plays. His occasional success in this curious mode, in plays like *The Magic Glasses* and *The Dandy Dolls*, is remarkable. The very form of the folktale is dependent upon the fact that it belongs to an oral tradition; a long expository section followed by a short climatic action is essential to the storyteller's art. Not only did Fitzmaurice dramatize the "form" of the folktale, but he staged the "living folk imagination" in the way in which his legendary figures are envisioned: the small-town context for the hags and mermaids, the mixing of shees with butter churns, the witch as real as the priest, the magic stone as solid as the hearth. This combination of the real and the fantastic is native to the Irish folk imagination. The fantastic we understand: fairies, fairy forts, and the like are not part of the real world, but why did Fitzmaurice not employ total fantasy? Yeats explained why he thought fantasy must mingle with the real. "No conscious invention can take the place of tradition, for he who would write a folk tale, and thereby bring new life into it, must have the fatigue of the spade in his hands and the stupors of the field in his heart." Because the folktale belongs to the group rather than to the individual, and because it was handed down by word of mouth, seems almost to guarantee it will always come trailing mystery and fantasy, but as Yeats has said, without a thorough grounding in the Irish earth as well as in Irish mist, the tale will not represent the real peasant.

Ireland is one of the last homes of the oral traditions of prehistoric and medieval Europe. Fitzmaurice has dramatized fragments of this tradition in the way he mirrors rural life always from the point of view of the folk, and in the way he sets up the deeds of his half legendary figures, again, always from the perspective of the peasant.

If there is any generalization possible, it is that folktales are often success stories, success achieved not through merit but by luck or cunning. Perhaps this explains their appeal to hard-pressed and luckless peasants. In this respect Fitzmaurice departs from the folk-tale norm, at least in most cases, for success is an inappropriate resolution for a man writing about life's compromised ideals. His folk characters are not successful, nor are they full bodied as are the realistic characters of *The Country Dressmaker* and *The Moonlighter*.

Carol W. Gelderman. *George Fitzmaurice*
(Boston, Twayne, 1979), pp. 79, 94–95

Because Fitzmaurice's subject is the very elusiveness of imagination and belief, the reader in search of "meaning" finds himself inside a world in which such moonstruck dialogue and manic business lead straight into subjectivity and solipsism. Sometimes Fitzmaurice's sing-song yellow brick roads go nowhere.

The escape from this enigma depends at least in part on placing this playwright within a context. George Fitzmaurice (1877–1963) gained his artistic identity as a popular Abbey dramatist, contemporary with Yeats, Synge, and Colum. But these playwrights share more than the coincidence of talent and nationality: many of their plays reflect a concern for art and the artist in Irish society. Inevitably their themes encompass a treatment of the role of the artist, the function of art, and the nature of the artists' audience. To readers of Colum's *The Fiddler's House*, Synge's *The Playboy of the Western World*, and Yeat's *The King's Threshold*, this information is of course not new. But interpreters of Fitzmaurice, though they often tag Roger, Leum, and Jaymony as artists, fail to employ this conventional theme to illuminate his plays satisfactorily. This theme, I think, may allow us to enjoy the seductive flamboyance of these plays and appreciate Fitzmaurice's compelling treatment of a major theme in modern Irish drama. . . .

Though Fitzmaurice and his contemporaries share the same theme—the separation of the artist from Irish society—their points of attack are essentially and significantly different. Yeats, Synge, and Colum question those social values which force the artist into exile; their concern is essentially social. Fitzmaurice attacks this problem at the level of imagination itself. He is not directly concerned with the quality of society, but with the quality and function of imagination in a world which cannot accept its artists: society and artist each hide behind impenetrable masks—one of reactionary belief, the other of impotence and solipsistic fantasy.

Though Fitzmaurice's works are delightful exhibitions of truly original genius, a morbid distrust of this playwright's greatest asset—his imagination— lurks beneath every exorbitant line. This distrust gradually became a theme in Fitzmaurice's life as well as his art. Though his early play, *The Country Dressmaker* (1907), was a regular in the Abbey repertory for many years, and *The Pie-dish* found a small following on a London tour, *The Magic Glasses* was condemned as "the silliest production ever attempted on the Abbey stage," and *The Dandy Dolls*, probably Fitzmaurice's most extraordinarily theatrical play, did not grace the Abbey boards until 1969, six years after the playwright's death. With few exceptions, his other plays suffered similar neglect. . . .

At their center, *The Pie-dish, The Magic Glasses*, and *The Dandy Dolls* evade and confound us as readily as the artworks contained in them. Further, Fitzmaurice's world, when stripped of its enchanting language and dream-like surrealism, harbors no communication, justice, or love. Those apocalyptic resolutions deny us any belief that what came before them is worth any more than the lackluster company left behind. Fitzmaurice's plays—like the artists and artworks within them—seem created to self-destruct; they leave us charmed but empty-handed and uninspired. But these feelings should not diminish our estimation of this playwright and his contribution to Irish dramatic literature. In seeing the victim of the separation of artist and society to be not one or the other, but the imaginative and creative capacities of both, Fitzmaurice gives us a remarkably original and compelling vision of Irish life.

John Cooke. In Zack Bowen, ed., *Irish Renaissance Annual I* (Newark, Univ. of Delaware Pr., 1980), pp. 33, 51–53

The principal feature . . . which distinguishes Fitzmaurice's tragedy of 1909 [*The Moonlighter*] and places it right next to O'Casey's work of 1926 is a shift of focus effected by his new plot structure. As the plot outline of *The Moonlighter* shows, the focus is not on the downfall of a single tragic hero; it is rather on the passion, highly noble in the abstract, which conventionally motivates the tragic hero: in this case on patriotism. Fitzmaurice achieves this shift of perspective by injecting the noble passion into the complex personal motivations of a group of realistically conceived characters. Thus each character, potentially a tragic hero, becomes a case study of the workings of his individual set of motive forces under the impact of the noble passion.

Given Fitzmaurice's harsh manner of characterization, it is a foregone conclusion that none of these case studies results in a very noble or heroic image. Thus the "Boys of Meenanaar," i.e. the Moonlighters, are united by much national feeling and more common hatred of the landlords, no doubt, but their unity is shown to be riddled with rivalry, jealousy, personal rancour and vendettas, cowardice and superstition. Tom Driscoll goes to his death with the courage of despair, for there is no choice left between life and death but only between the gun and the rope. Peter Guerin's heroic and useless gesture of solidarity with Tom is an act of suicide; we are left wondering whether it is based on personal motives (viz. Luke's refusal, Eugene's return), or on idealistic ones (viz. the pass the Fenian cause has come to). But the most devastating portrait of the "national man" is Eugene's. His conversion or his "regrettably sensible decision," as [J. D.] Riley describes it, is more than a patriotic audience in 1909 could have been expected to bear. Eugene points beyond *The Plough and the Stars* to such "patriots" of O'Casey's later plays as the Binningtons and McGilligans in *The Drums of Father Ned*. Those are treated with irony, it is true, but they are resented by Irish audiences and critics to this day. . . .

It would seem that apart from the subject, the Land War, this tragedy was out of step with, or rather, ahead of the times as much as Fitzmaurice's other early plays: that is what kept it off the Abbey stage. It anticipated O'Casey not only in tragi-comedy, in the use of melodrama, in increased authenticity of dialogue and characterization but, most importantly, in the manner of treatment of a "timely" theme. . . .

Like *The Plough and the Stars* in O'Casey's work, *The Moonlighter* marks among Fitzmaurice's plays the utmost limit of innovation that Abbey directors and Dublin audiences could be taxed with at the time.

Wolfgang R. Sänger. In Heinz Kosok, ed.,
Studies in Anglo-Irish Literature
(Bonn, Bouvier, 1982), pp. 178–80

FRIEL, BRIAN (1929–   )

One reason Brian Friel's new Irish play, *Philadelphia, Here I Come!*, is so likable may be that it so honestly assesses two unsatisfactory civilizations: inhibited and materially impoverished Ireland and its opposite, America. The playwright's view seems to be that Ireland's tragedy is the constant emigration of its best young people, and that the Irish emigrant's tragedy is that his achievement elsewhere is rootless and disconnected. For the play's entire action is its protagonist's sometimes humorous, sometimes sad, search for any reason to stay where his roots are.

To make this search more dramatic, Mr. Friel has employed the device of having one actor . . . deliver young Gareth's outward behavior, and another . . . portray the same character's private self. The latter argues and provokes, hopes and laments, underlines and comments, but surprisingly enough emerges as almost more real than the actual Gareth. . . .

While the author doesn't demonstrate a capacity for writing dialogue comparable to that of an O'Casey or a Behan ("You wait, says she, till the rosary's over and the kettle's on" is about as lyrical as he gets), his powers of observation permit him to recreate characters with telling accuracy. . . .

Furthermore, like *The Glass Menagerie*, this play expresses a tender awareness of how memory distills events, with the evening's nicest irony being that the uncommunicative father remembers his son through one past incident, while the lonely young man remembers his father through a different one. But the tragic fact is that neither can recall the other's incident.

Because it is such an honest piece of work the play ends inconclusively, and one feels that the playwright may have missed an opportunity to allow the private Gareth to stir us with a more passionate and poetic summing up. Nevertheless, *Philadelphia, Here I Come!* achieves great poignancy without pretension and deserves to be widely appreciated.

Henry Hewes. Sat. March 5, 1966, p. 54

Brian Friel's stories are usually set in MacGill country, among the hard, empty hills and obscure villages of Donegal and Derry, and demonstrate vividly the connection between social deprivation and sentimental fantasy. As starvation of the body leads to hallucinations of the mind, so Friel's characters are inveterate fantasists, and the cheapest, most poignant fantasies are those that colour the harshest landscape. In "Mr. Sing My Heart's Delight" the narrator's grandmother, whose husband is wintering in Scotland earning enough money to tide them over the rest of the year, moons deliriously over the vulgar coloured wares of the travelling Indian salesman and, there in a remote Donegal cottage, listens to his equally cheap chatter about the Garden of Eden in the distant Punjab. Having chosen such fantasies as his subject-matter, the author has to walk a thin line if he is to record them without exposing too ruthlessly their cheapness and thereby have his stories collapse into mere sentimentality.

In solving this problem, Benedict Kiely . . . takes the bull by the horns by plunging into mock-heroics, but Friel, on the other hand, relies somewhat dangerously on the pathetic irony of such fantasies taking place at all among brooding western hills and stony fields. Many of his stories concern a character's initiation into the reality behind illusion. Illusion might take the form of a belief in a golden tomorrow (e.g., "The God in the Sea"), the memory of a golden yesterday ("Among the Ruins") or the daydreams of exotic places ("Mr. Sing My Heart's Delight" and "Straight from His Colonial Success"). The author pierces such hopes and memories with humour and compassion but allows his characters to retain an altered illusion to make life bearable for them. The whole process is rather formulaic. Initial information which also establishes the story's tone (exposition) is followed by the setting up of an illusion (complication), followed by disillusionment (climax) and ending with the reinstatement of a modified illusion (coda). This formula is imposed on a naturalistic background of poverty and hardship. The question that comes to mind when we read story after story is whether Friel (primarily a dramatist) is on a busman's holiday in his short stories, whether he is doing much more than playing deftly with an emotional and structural formula learned from Frank O'Connor, Sean O'Faolain, Michael McLaverty and Kiely. This is not to say that Friel's two volumes of short stories—*The Saucer of Larks* (1962) and *The Gold in the Sea* (1966)—do not in their unevenness (despite the levelling influence of constant publication in *The New Yorker*) throw up some very fine stories which almost manage to transcend their formulism and which stand on the brink of real and liberating insight.

> John Wilson Foster. *Forces and Themes in Ulster*
> *Fiction* (Dublin, Gill & Macmillan, 1974),
> pp. 64–65

Brian Friel, also well known for his short stories, is best known as a playwright for works written after *The Enemy Within*, which has been preceded into print by his most discussed play, *Philadelphia, Here I Come!*, and five others more recently written. *The Enemy Within*, while interesting, is recognized by Friel himself as an early and not altogether successful effort. Its plot concerns the forces which lead St. Columba at age sixty-six to renounce the strong secular bonds of family and ancestral Irish homeland that to this point in his life have deflected his energies from his spiritual mission as Abbot of Iona, Friel sees Columba as one who combines monastic virtues with a herculean constitution and disposition, but his character falls short of being convincing as either a saint or a hero. Columba's abundant physical energy inclines him to respond with ingenuous enthusiasm to the call from kinsmen to provide spiritual leadership in their military escapades. To curb this natural energy which tends to blur his judgment, Columba subjects himself to severe ascetic practices which, ironically, prove more a tonic than a restraint to his vitality. His uncanny life force charismatically attracts others to his austere monastic colony at the same time that it stimulates his yearning for his Irish family and homeland. Irish place names like Tirconaill, Errigal, Gartaan Lough, Leinster, and Conall enchant Columba with their very sound and make the self-imposed exile on Iona a greater sacrifice for him than for other monks like the holy scribe Caornan for whom Iona, not elsewhere, is home.

The story has the seeds of effective drama, but Friel fails to convey feelingly in Columba's language and actions the greatness which everywhere is accorded him. We are told of his extraordinary asceticism and we see the unqualified joy and devotion he excites in those around him, but the inner turmoil he experiences over denying his disreputable brother's request for aid in one of a string of family-tribal disputes creates more the impression of a romantic than of a spiritual leader. Moreover, the inner conflict is superficially resolved in the play's climax where Columba's decision to choose Iona over kin comes not as the result of his developing self-knowledge but by the chance entry of the senile monk Dochonna, whose search for his dead comrade Caornan reminds Columba of his monastic responsibility.

Despite its shortcomings, *The Enemy Within* captures with some power an archetypal pattern in human experience. Columba's wavering allegiance between Iona (his castle of perseverance) and Ireland (the world) manifests a prodigal son morality pattern which the clean, spare lines of the play accentuate memorably.

Robert B. Bennett. JIL. Sept., 1976, pp. 148–49

Translations is set in a Donegal hedge school and the time is August, 1833. It is written in the English language, yet seven of the ten characters speak in their native tongue, which is Irish. The suggestion of a paradox here does not intrude: there is no linguistic confusion on the part of the audience, for Mr. Friel is a very excellent craftsman and there is no difficulty in accepting that the language spoken is, where necessary, Irish. There are two important points in the play's construction. One is that a new system of national education introduced by the English will make the hedge school redundant and wean Irish speakers away from their native tongue. Another is that the first Ordnance Survey map of Ireland is being prepared under the control of the military, and old and untranslatable Irish placenames are being Anglicized. A culture is in a state of transition, in the process of being absorbed, and traditional values are being disturbed creating an identification dilemma. The conflict postulated by Mr. Friel still exists, unresolved. The scene, set in a Donegal townland close to 150 years ago, has a peculiar relevance to community divisions that exist today. The point was not missed by Derry audiences.

The play has historical, social, and cultural connotations, but it is also human, and, in one scene, beautifully and delicately so. A young English army officer on Ordnance Survey duty falls in love with the quiet, dreamy countryside, and also with a young peasant girl. Mr. Friel involves them in a love scene which is remarkable. He can talk only in English, which she does not understand, and she can speak in Irish, and haltingly in Latin, both of which are meaningless to him. But they articulate through the universal language of eyes and heart. It is a jewel of a scene, and significant threads lead to and from it. The girl has expressed a desire to learn English, because she hopes to emigrate to America. The boy later disappears, murdered perhaps by a jealous rival, and his commanding officer promises brutal reprisals if he is not found. Some of Mr. Friel's interweaving elements are there: an ancient tongue in decay, an imposed and resented authority, violence. The brief idyll of innocent love stands out.

Desmond Rushe. Éire-Ireland. Winter, 1980,
pp. 127–28

If a story takes its form from the author's desire, it also gives form to the desire of its reader. The reader of this selection of Brian Friel's stories will find his desire moulded into form by the pressure of that local, intimate detail which emerges out of the author's knowledge of his society's moral code. Each story is social in its setting, moral in its implication. Time and again we have the impression that the small-town or village society, no matter how sharply it may be observed in its conformity to the powers of Church or class, has a moral code that belongs elsewhere. The narrowness of the social life is bitter, but the complexity of the moral life within is generous. Yet Brian Friel does not counterpose the two for the sake of contrast. Instead, he illustrates their interdependence, eliciting from us the recognition that the formal structures of social life are what we live by, not what we live for. Yet what we live for is clarified only by the insufficiency of what we live by. This may be no more than glimpsed in these stories; it receives a more sustained and indeed harsher treatment in the author's plays. But the co-existence of two realms, one clearly etched and social, the other amorphous and imaginative, which constitute together the one and the only world is insistently asserted. The separation of these realms, often threatened by sudden disaster, farce or illumination, is never permitted in the stories. In the plays, especially the more recent, it is enforced. But here, the author's insistence on the actuality of event and on the reality of imagination is quite impartial. His linguistic diplomacy is directed towards gaining recognition for both sides. This must be conceded by the reader when it is achieved by the writer.

The concession can only be willingly made when the language has a suasion that disguises its coercive aim, when the modesty of tone and approach is such that we feel persuaded we have discovered what we have just been shown. The syntax and vocabulary of these stories present no apparent problems. Brian Friel is, technically speaking, a traditional writer. The dislocations and the nuanced egoism of many modern texts are sternly avoided, even rejected, here. Yet each paragraph has the tension of writing that demands unremitting care from the reader. Nothing wilful, nothing willed, the workaday words, only slightly coloured by figure or weighted by pronounced rhythm, manage to be so informative, so quickly and easily blended into a narrative medium that we are at first aware only of the story, not the teller. [1979]

Seamus Deane. Introduction to Brian Friel,
The Diviner (Dublin, O'Brien Press, 1983),
pp. 9–10

In most of Friel's plays time is a great healer. In *The Freedom of the City* (1973) the author seems to be less detached, more concerned with the particularities of contemporary affairs in Northern Ireland, or, indeed, in Derry itself. The waste of human energy and creativity occasioned by the local conflict, and its brutalizing effect on the attitude and daily habits of the citizens, are presented with unusual pessimism, for Friel is normally the observer who discerns good in the midst of evil. Another play with a topical application is *Volunteers* (1975), a metaphorical comment on the Irish propensity for self-destruction.

Brian Friel is a conventional dramatist in that he generally employs a linear plot. He does, however, make some startling experiments with that form: the physically split personality of Gar O'Donnell, which affects the structure of *Philadelphia, Here I Come!* is a case in point. Such effects surprise the audience into a different kind of awareness, and cause its members to listen more closely. In *Translations* (1980), a play with a completely conventional structure, he introduces a linguistic contrivance which affects the play on all levels: the complete dialogue is written in English, but a convention is established whereby the "Irish-speaking" characters cannot be understood by the English-speaking characters. Without this highly original device the play succeeds in various ways—as an observation on one of the causes for the decline of the Gaelic cultural tradition, as a tale of Donegal in the era of the hedge-schools, or as a love story of social and racial opposites; but it is really about language—about the destruction of a language by that of a superior colonial power, about the basic notion of language as a means of conveying thought, and about the nature of words.

An earlier play, *Faith Healer* (1976), is also concerned with language, though in a different way. In this instance, Friel abandons the linear plan. The story is narrated by three players, each giving a diverging interpretation of certain shared incidents which took place in the past; the Faith Healer returns in a fourth monologue to give the final *coup-de-grâce*. There is virtually no dramatic action, except the drama of the recounted occurrences. Yet *Faith Healer* is intensely dramatic in another sense—possibly in the way it unites the art of the *seanchai* with the craft of the stage. A great deal is demanded of the audience, especially as the text is exceptionally compact. Much depends upon the quality of the production and the casting; the play's comparative failure in New York may be attributed to failure in these departments. When produced four years later at the Abbey by Joe Dowling, it emerged triumphantly.

When forming a company of players to produce *Translations* in Derry in 1980 Brian Friel spoke of the need for "a brave and violent theatre that in some way expresses the country." In fact, he had already created a brave and violent theatre through his own writing.

Christopher Fitz-Simon. *The Irish Theatre*
(London, Thames and Hudson, 1983), pp. 194–95

Friel has always been absorbed in the figments of memory: in *Philadelphia, Here I Come!* a day in a rowing boat, a song, remembered differently by father and son. In *Crystal and Fox*, Fox, the proprietor of a travelling show, methodically destroys his present situation because of its incongruity with the past of his recollection. In *Aristocrats*, Casimir's fables of the patrician dignity of the Catholic Big House of his childhood break into the ruin of its decline confirmed. The characters persuade us to accept their views of what may have been or happened. Its actuality is perhaps irreclaimable, a re-creation of fond memory, which may comfort, or equally, destroy. *Faith Healer* is similarly concerned with the apparitions of memory, now shifted to different outlines.

"But that's another story," says Frank Hardy, faith healer, early in the play. It is made up of stories and other stories, a riddling account of the lives of its three characters—the faith healer himself, his wife (or mistress) Grace, and Teddy, Frank's manager and warm-up man. In structure it consists of four monologues: by Frank, who we gradually learn is dead, at the beginning and end; by Grace, also now dead, and Teddy in between—a boldly demanding form. Inconsistently, the monologues reconstruct the itinerary of Frank's career through Welsh and Scottish villages until his killing (never directly so named) outside an Irish pub by the four drunken friends of a cripple whom, we infer, he has failed to heal. That is the major tale that is told, or partly told. From what it tells us we may compose answers for its riddles, or leave them as perfectly articulated questions. Some of them tease us with matters of plain fact. What is the "truth" of the episode at Kinlochbervie? All three speakers evoke it in solid and often brutal physical detail, converting it, however, each into his own version of an event. Is the reality the cruel birth of Grace's stillborn child, or that Frank heard there of his mother's death; the idyllic weather in Teddy's mind, "all blue and white and golden," or Grace's "heavy wet mist"? Or have the memories a validity of their own? . . .

The meaning proposed by *Faith Healer* is a harsh one, but gestured by language into an elevation of feeling. Both the comic and the sombre spirits are observers. Friel has never written more splendidly comic prose than in Teddy's monologue, modulating with total assurance into grief and loss. We move from the grotesquely funny account of Rob Roy the Piping Dog as Dedicated Artist—"Morning, noon and night he'd sit there blowing the bloody thing and working them bellows with his back leg"—to Kinlochbervie and Grace's child, "that little wet thing with the black face and the black body, a tiny little thing, no size at all—a boy it was." Comic or tragic, memory tries to come to terms with the past. Reality, both malleable and stubborn, as of the three of them Frank Harvey most clearly and consciously sees, is the material with which faith and imagination live, remembering and re-creating, and, if they work, changing. Frank is an image of the artist, the mystery of his enhancing powers and their capricious release.

As a parable of the artist, Frank Harvey makes explicit that particular expression of the allure of make-believe. Throughout Friel's plays the characters are interpreting the reality of their situation by imagining it into other possibilities, or supplying alternatives to it. What might be, or might have been, is being asked to put its pressure on, and perhaps alter, actuality; or at least to relieve, to displace, facts which have become intolerable. That exercise too, conscious fantasy or illusion, is in its way a creative act.

These metaphors of the imaginative operations which lead to art are recurrent in Friel's plays. They do not, however, at all make the plays a dramatised discourse on aesthetics. The characters and their predicaments are urgent with entirely human distresses and desires. Frank Harvey is latently a symbol of the artist. Primarily he is Frank Harvey, faith healer, in the suffering of choice, indecision, self-indulgence.

D. E. S. Maxwell. *A Critical History of Modern Irish Drama, 1891–1980* (Cambridge, England, Cambridge Univ. Pr., 1984), pp. 201, 203

GOGARTY, OLIVER ST. JOHN (1878–1957)

A modern philosopher has said that a poet, degenerated, becomes a wit. What he meant was that the poet, having lost his fine frenzy and clarity of vision, might still be able to play more skilfully than anyone else with the counters of expression we call words. This book of Dr. Gogarty's [*An Offering of Swans, and Other Verses*] would lead one to believe that the converse of the proposition might also be true: that one who was naturally gifted with a very nimble mentality might find himself borne by some favouring breeze into the regions of poetry, even though his stay might not be long.

These verses have varying degrees of quality; they range from what seem to be mere *jeux d'esprit* to half a dozen lyrics that are, in our view, worthy to be set beside the best in modern English verse. "Begone, Sweet Ghost," "Non Dolet, "Good Luck" have a brightness and strength of expression that make them good to remember and repeat. "The Ship," "The Old Goose" and "Please Drive Slowly Through Little Waltham" are fine efforts of the romantic imagination.

There are minor blemishes: such as an impatience to bring off epigrammatical effects at the expense of the general design, and a desire to pour the full heart "in the mould of rhyme" a little too soon. But these are the faults of what Bacon would call "a full man."

We find it hard to agree with Dr. Yeats when he suggests that these poems came out of English country houses and English lyric tradition. We fancy rather that an antique Roman is singing the praise of Life and the scorn of Death. . . .

DM. Nov., 1924, p. 281

A luncheon party, casually and briefly introduced in a chapter dealing at some length with other matters, provides a clue to the description of this unusual and very delightful book [*As I Was Going Down Sackville Street*]. An American publisher, on the track of Dr. Gogarty's memoirs, suggested a formal volume which should "include an historical perspective from the inside" of the eventful period through which Dr. Gogarty had lived; he baited this proposal with a vision of posthumous utility, pointing out that such a book "would be a valuable contribution when the history of the time comes to be written." This was not the way to catch an individualist whose mind is so much above the gratitude of unborn research students as Dr. Gogarty's, who at once replied that, on the contrary, "the only way to treat this town is the way the Chinese treat their pictures: eschew perspective. . . . If you make Dublin the hero of a book and let it portray itself as it is every day, you may get an effect such as the wisest of Masters, the Chinese artists, achieved." That is what Dr. Gogarty has done. He knows Dublin and Dubliners as few men else, and in his own person are united many of the most characteristic types (the wit, the poet, the classicist, the doctor, the unconventional politician) which gave in the past its peculiar flavour to Dublin society. Linked to his own extraordinary varied experiences, almost every element in Dublin life is drawn together into a coherent picture. The chronology and the sequence of events may, while one reads, seem arbitrary; Dr. Gogarty moves without explanation or apology from Dublin in 1910 to Dublin after the Treaty, from a dinner party, where everyone is either witty, elegant or amusingly eccentric, to a public-house on the quays, where there is squalor instead of elegance and where the humour is of a more desperate kind; but Dublin is still in many ways an eighteenth-century town, and these contrasts give as much point to one another now as they would have done before the Union; on looking back, one cannot see how the themes and episodes of the book could have been more effectively arranged. . . .

It can be enjoyed for the shrewdness of Dr. Gogarty's comments on anything from politics to poetry on which he chooses to touch. And above all it can be enjoyed for the episodes in everyday Dublin life which Dr. Gogarty describes so well. Only those who are inclined to stand on other people's dignity will regret that Dr. Gogarty has not written his memoirs in a more formal and documentary manner. The essence of a vanishing way of life has never been better caught in print.

Derek Verschoyle. Spec. April 9, 1937, pp. 673–74

The "entertainment value" of Dr. Gogarty's phantasmagoria of fact and fancy [*As I Was Going Down Sackville Street*] is so high that many who glance at the initial quotation from Berkeley may easily overlook the ironic significance. So accustomed are we to the polite memoirs in which late Victorians and Edwardians apologize for the vigour of their past that the vitality and unabashed gusto of this book should administer a salutary shock. In a crowded, tumultous, and at times lyrical prose—a prose which is often good and often indifferent—Dr. Gogarty knocks the heads of the present and past together in order to convince us that the heyday is all. He unseals the hidden springs of Dublin song, discloses (though with discretion) the subterranean regions of gross parody, and translates us into the heaven world of inspired gossip. . . .

For all the metaphysical wit and ingenuity, there is no fundamental grasp when we come to the political and social problems of present-day Ireland.

Austin Clarke. LM. May 1937, pp. 80–81

Admirers of *As I Was Going Down Sackville Street* will find that after seventeen years [in *It Isn't This Time of Year At All!*] Dr. Gogarty is still offering the same prescription, "the mixture as before." He even adopts the same time scheme, writing about the past as if it was all simultaneously present—hence the book's title—and skillfully mixing his past and present tenses. In effect, under the guise of an autobiography, he is retelling all the old scandals and all the old witticisms of a Dublin that was small enough for everyone to know everyone else's vices and big enough for each man to practice his own. The scandals all sound pretty funny so long as you think of the people involved as characters in fiction; if you don't come from Dublin and never knew any of them, they might as well be. In a disarming note to the earlier autobiography Gogarty wrote: "The names in this book are real, the characters fictitious." The witticisms, on the other hand, must be authentic—I've heard them so often before. They are as much as a part of Dublin—or of Trinity College, Dublin—as its stones and mortar.

The only thing that a lucky man should never do is complain. True, self-styled Republicans burned down Gogarty's country home, probably in settlement of a private grudge or in the hope of dividing up the land that went with the house. True, other Republicans took Gogarty himself as a hostage and probably intended to shoot him. But he escaped, didn't he? And he received compensation for the house, unlike a Catholic friend of mine, whose family's bakery was burned down in a Belfast pogrom. Yet Gogarty's bitterness against De Valera, as Republican No. 1, has to be read to be believed; what he has written about Joyce pales beside it. Perhaps he understands De Valera's hair-splitting kind of integrity no better than he did Joyce's.

For me, the bubbling gaiety of three-fourths of this book was spoiled by the unnecessary bitterness of the remainder. Autobiography, no matter how fictional in intent, always betrays its author into sincerity at the wrong moment. It is sad that Gogarty should have to appear once again in this bear-garden where he himself is both the aging bear and the snarling dogs. I say in all sincerity that I believe him to be one of the greatest of living poets—as Yeats did, too—though his Horatian style is now temporarily out of fashion. The pathos of Gogarty is that he cannot earn a living by his poetry and conversation, and therefore must stoop to prose—a medium in which he has little faith or interest.

Vivian Mercier. *Com.* Feb. 12, 1954, pp. 479–80

As a man of action Gogarty was a practitioner of poetry rather than a theorist, and just as in his surgical practice his preoccupation with research was short-lived, the task of the moment a sufficient problem and one to be rapidly completed, so in the practice of poetry the revisals and emendations of more patient craftsmen were uncongenial to his temperament. For him, as Professor Carens has pointed out, poetry was a social act. It need not, of course, be an exclusive occupation—life is too many-sided for that. But in the company of men of like minds it was what mattered most to him. Poetry was a major topic of his correspondence with Joyce and Bell, and apart from such well-known figures as AE, Yeats, and Seumas O'Sullivan, the Bailey coterie George Redding, George Bonass, Tom Kettle, Joseph Boyd Barrett regarded it as an indispensable topic of conversation. When James Stephens joined them he heard for the first time, as he recalled later, "Poetry spoken of with the assured carelessness with which a carpenter talks of his planks and of the chairs and tables and oddments he will make of them."

By his early twenties Oliver Gogarty was already a competent poet and well-read in poetry, taking as his models the Greek and Latin classics and the English Elizabethans. James Stephens has singled him out as Ireland's only classical poet; F. R. Higgins wrote in a personal letter: "Poetry has many tablelands; yours are peaks scarred with gold—rhythm's mountain ranges illuminated by fastidious craft." Austin Clarke, a dissident voice, has said that he "took every care to avoid the difficult, scarcely-known ways of Irish tradition," and faulted him, perhaps unfairly, for ignorance of Gaelic literature, which makes one feel that Clarke was really complaining because Gogarty's Muse did not link arms with his own. But Gogarty, despite his classical leanings, is very much a national poet though in no narrow sense; and more than any other, he has succeeded in marrying the ancient Mediterranean myths with those of ancient Ireland; his eclecticism reestablishes old links between Irish and European cultures.

> J. B. Lyons. *Oliver St. John Gogarty* (Lewisburg,
> Pa., Bucknell Univ. Pr., 1976), pp. 39–40

Crudely interpreted, Yeats claimed a place for Gogarty among the major poets of the first part of the century. Understood, he sought to bring Gogarty's work to the attention of a larger audience and claimed a place for Gogarty's poetry "among the greatest lyric poetry of our time." It may be that Yeats's definition of the lyrical—which led him to deny the applicability of the term to Eliot—was too special to be acceptable; and it may be argued also that the connotations of his words of praise for his friend were excessively honorific. But the context in which Oliver Gogarty is found in Larkin's anthology [*The Oxford Book of Twentieth Century English Verse*] is surely not the place for him. In the whole body of Gogarty's poetry, published and unpublished, there are perhaps a hundred poems by which he will live. Of these, at the very least, some two dozen shorter lyrics and a dozen longer poems are exceptional enough to hold their own in the diverse body of modern poetry. Uneven at times and sometimes careless, as Yeats noted, Gogarty could also carry off whole poems flawlessly and achieve effects of unequalled lightness, delicacy, and wit. Never departing from conventional forms, rhythms, and rhymes, Gogarty was indifferent to the romantic impulse constantly to devise new modes of expression, to re-invent, as it were, poetic language and forms. So to the *avant-garde*, whether real or imagined, he is not apt to appeal. Moreover, one of the ironies of his poetic and his practice (as of Yeats's) was that he wrote a poetry that will never have a wide popular appeal. But just as, over the decades, readers have turned from, say, Donne to Herrick or from Wordsworth to Landor to find pleasure in a very different kind and intensity of expression, one can hazard the opinion that, in the future, readers will turn from Yeats to Gogarty and understand what Yeats found to admire in him— and other pleasures too in poems Yeats did not quote or anthologise. . . .

Considered from a historical point of view, two of Gogarty's works, the play *Blight* and the memoir *Sackville Street*, must survive as documents, for the first played a role in the development of the Abbey Theatre, the second records first-hand impressions of a great cultural epoch in Irish history. But if my efforts to explore the interior of Gogarty's works have been in any way successful they should have demonstrated that, like the best of the poetry, *Sackville Street* is something considerably more than a piece of historical source material, that both it and *Tumbling in the Hay* are among the most impressive books to have been inspired by the Irish Literary Renaissance. Copious, highly individual as literary forms though belonging to a unique tradition of the fictive, thematically and imaginatively complex, these two works in themselves, had not Gogarty also been a poet or produced three lesser but also memorable prose works—*I Follow Saint Patrick, Rolling Down the Lea*, and *It Isn't This Time of Year at All!*—would ensure him his proper place in the history of modern Irish literature and modern literature in English.

James F. Carens. *Surpassing Wit: Oliver St. John Gogarty, His Poetry and His Prose* (New York, Columbia Univ. Pr., 1979), pp. 237–39

Gogarty knew his Dublin slums, wrote plays, *Blight* (1917), *A Serious Thing* (1919) and *The Enchanted Trousers* (1919) that denounced the conditions under which people lived in them; he knew and loved the countryside; he joined Sinn Fein though he neither believed in nor practised violence; and he became a senator in the Irish Free State. His house at Renvyle was burnt down in the Troubles; he himself narrowly escaped being murdered by gunmen; and he had to practise—very successfully—in London for nearly a year. He attended Senate meetings regularly and returned to Dublin in 1924.

His life in Dublin was the subject of *As I Was Going Down Sackville Street* (1937), a book that led to a libel action. This is a volume in the tradition of Moore's *Hail and Farewell*, and it conveys with brio the atmosphere of a more troubled Dublin than the one Moore knew. It was followed by *I Follow St. Patrick* (1939) and *Tumbling in the Hay* (1939), which are probably his best prose works. He left for America in 1939 and wrote novels there, *Going Native* (1940), *Mad Grandeur* (1941) and *Mr. Petunia* (1945), as well as another piece of autobiography *It Isn't That Time of Year at All!* (1954). These lack the freshness and vitality of his earlier prose, as Gogarty himself seemed to lack the stimulating background of Dublin's talk and competitive malice. He should be read for his poetry, which appeared in *An Offering of Swans* (1923)—the title poem celebrating his famous escape from the gunmen who kidnapped him as a hostage in the Civil War in January 1923 and from whom he escaped by swimming the flooded Liffey—*Wild Apples* (1929), *Selected Poems* (1923) and *Collected Poems* (1950). Here is a rich profusion, poems celebrating the beauty of places in Ireland and digging into their history, as in the poems exploring the surroundings of Dublin and its heritage, "Just One Glimpse" or "Liffey Bridge," "Fog Horns," "High Tide at Malahide," "Glenasmole" or elsewhere in "New Bridge"; poems too, exploiting himself as a Horatian poet in poems to women; and poems expressing his own personality freely once he had balanced his knowledge of classical poetry with the romantic in his own make-up. His friendship with Yeats led, in the twenties and thirties, to a free exchange of ideas, even an echoing of words and phrases in poems, notably those linked with the myth of Leda. . . . He could capture the poignant moment in a poem such as "Golden Stockings," written about his daughter playing in a field. To him poetry was ultimately a gesture; seriousness was to be worn lightly; his cavalier manner demanded that he should write with ease, even when summing up the worst of death as the loss of friends. "Death may be very gentle" rises above classical cliché, but the achievements of simplicity in all his poems on death comes from the classical mastery of form, of architectonic control, varied metrics and cadences. Gogarty's wit is discursive, and blended with genuine sentiment.

A. Norman Jeffares. *Anglo-Irish Literature*
(New York, Schocken, 1982), pp. 180–81

GREGORY, LADY (ISABELLA AUGUSTA PERSSE, 1859–1932)

It was Mr. Bernard Shaw who, in commenting on the rowdy reception of the Irish players in some American theatres, spoke of Lady Gregory as "the greatest living Irishwoman." She is certainly a remarkable enough writer to put a generous critic a little off his balance. Equal mistress in comedy and tragedy, essayist, gatherer of the humours of folk-lore, imaginative translator of heroic literature, venturesome translator of Molière, she has contributed a greater variety of grotesque and beautiful things to Anglo-Irish literature than any of her contemporaries. . . .

She is one of the discoverers of Ireland. Her genius, like Synge's, opened its eyes one day and saw spread below it the immense sea of Irish common speech, with its colour, its laughter, and its music. It is a sort of second birth which many Irish men and women of the last generation or so have experienced. The beggar on the road, the piper at the door, the old people in the workhouse, are henceforth accepted as a sort of aristocracy in exile.

Lady Gregory obviously sought out their company as the heirs to a great inheritance—an inheritance of imaginative and humorous speech. . . . Her sentences are steeped and dyed in life, even when her situations are as mad as hatters.

Some one has said that every great writer invents a new language. Lady Gregory, whom it would be unfair to praise as a great writer, has at least qualified as one by inventing a new language out of her knowledge of Irish peasant speech. This, perhaps, is her chief literary peril. Having discovered the beautiful dialect of the Kiltartan peasantry, she was not content to leave it a peasant dialect—as we find in her best dramatic work, *Seven Short Plays*; but she set about transforming it into a tongue into which all literature and emotion might apparently be translated. Thus, she gave us Molière in Kiltartan—a ridiculously successful piece of work—and she gave us Finn and Cuchulain in modified Kiltartan, and this, too, was successful, sometimes beautifully so. Here, however, she had masterpieces to begin with. In *Irish Folk History Plays*, on the other hand, we find her embarking, not upon translation, but upon original heroic drama, in the Kiltartan language. The result is unreality as unreal as if Meredith had made a farm labourer talk like Diana of the Crossways. . . . It is because the characters in the comic plays in the book are nearer the peasantry in stature and in outlook that she is so much more successful with them than with the heroes and heroines of the tragedies.

Robert Lynd. Old and New Masters
(London, T. Fisher Unwin, 1919), pp. 178–81

Lady Gregory has written thirty-one original plays, of which all but two have been produced at the Abbey Theatre. She has been writing plays for twenty-five years, in addition to her splendid work as a Director of the Theatre, a biographer, historian, and folk-lorist. Her industry and enthusiasm are amazing, resembling somewhat those Spanish dramatists at whose versatility Northern Europe stands aghast. Most of her work can be studied on the printed page as it has nearly all been published. Her first volume of plays, *Seven Short Plays*, 1909, contains her most popular and much of her typical work. Some of these plays have been referred to already, they are farcical comedies with a strong undercurrent of satire. In *The Workhouse Ward*, 1908, is satirised that tendency to quarrel about nothing which is marked in (though not peculiar to) Irish people. It is possible that a political satire was intended, and perhaps the play says more about Irish politics than the politicians have yet learned. The political interest is stronger in *The Rising of the Moon*, 1907, in which those

who appear to be against the Irish struggle for political liberty are shown not
to be so in fact. A conflict between sympathy and duty rages about the police
sergeant who is the central figure in the play. The sergeant's choice is difficult, and the artistry by which Lady Gregory enables the ballad-singer to
arouse his latent patriotism is a masterpiece of dramatic technique. Another of
these short plays, *The Gaol Gate*, 1906, has all the tragic intensity of *Riders
to the Sea*, reaching a climax in the triumphant *caoin* of grief and joy with
which the mother greets the news of her son's fidelity till death. All the
elements of doubt and uncertainty, pity and helplessness, are combined in
this little play to make it one of the great tragic experiences of the modern theatre. . . .

Grania is Lady Gregory's highest achievement in historical tragedy, and
here she is superior to the Ibsen of *The Vikings at Helgeland*, the Strindberg of
Gustavus Vasa, or the Hauptmann of *Florian Geyer*. In emotional content and
poetic intensity *Grania* can bear the comparison with Synge's *Deirdre* to
which it has been subjected. Deirdre has had her admirers in plenty, almost
every Irish poet is included in the number, but Grania has had, if the result of
the Moore-Yeats collaboration be ignored, only Lady Gregory. . . . "I think,"
says Lady Gregory, "I turned to Grania because so many have written about
sad, lovely Deirdre, who when overtaken by sorrow made no good battle to
the last. Grania had more power of will, and for good or evil twice took the
shaping of her life into her own hands." In this three-act tragedy of love and
jealousy there are only three persons, but in falling under the spell and "fascination of things difficult," Lady Gregory achieved her masterpiece in tragedy.
It is generally considered that she is at her best in the one-act play, and it is
true that she has failed more often in her long than in her short pieces, but the
success of this three-act play in characterisation, dialogue, and construction is
a standing refutation of the statement.

Andrew E. Malone. The Irish Drama
(London, Constable, 1929), pp. 158–61

She started to write comedy because the Abbey was short of comedies,
and she was craftsman enough to shape what she had to the theatre's needs.
Spreading the News came to her as an idea with possibly tragic connotations:
she "kept seeing" an image of a girl going to market, "gay and fearless," but
coming home in the evening with her head hanging and avoided by the crowd
because of a story that had arisen from a chance word. It might have made a
serious play, but comedy was needed at that time for the Abbey, and Lady
Gregory made it her quickest comedy. Quickness and spareness are her as-
sets. Her tragedy has them too. If she had only a limited range of things to
say, at least she knew better than to say more. Yeats regarded himself as a
sparer, quicker, conciser developer of stage situations, yet whereas he and
Moore had made a *Grania* traffic-blocked with characters, she astonished him

by making a *Grania* out of three characters and with those three eliciting from the traditional story the Irish father-son problem and her private problem of the appeal of a strong woman.

It is both a limitation and an excellence of her theatre that the allusions depend on her intimacy with the audience. Think of her as a writer thinking of her audience, and you see that she chooses every word with warmth and purpose. In her first draft for a play, *Colman and Guaire*, she conceived herself as providing material for Kiltartan schoolchildren to play to Kiltartan people. Later, even in the most ambitious work, the conception was similar. She hoped that her histories would be played in the schools of Ireland to inform and inspire Irish children. The texts crackle with topical allusion, with instruction and exhortation. . . . Lady Gregory works entirely on the basis of that consent between author and audience to discuss—even if to quarrel—Ireland and Irish issues: actually, she herself never challenges a quarrel; she never gives less than a whole-hearted treatment of the issues, she never is unorthodox on them, she never goes outside them to use the enriching terms of other interests and other literatures.

Herbert Howarth. The Irish Writers: 1880–1940
(New York, Hill & Wang, 1958), pp. 100–101

The base to Lady Gregory's personal theatre was the little community of Kiltartan, where through restricted dialect and characterization she managed to express her universal comic vision. Closer examination reveals two basic themes which are both universal and persistent: the idealist and his shattered dream. As all who knew her attest, and as can readily be observed from her writings, Lady Gregory had a deep sympathy with the "image maker," the rebel who must stand alone, apart from his community and yet bound to it by his dream. "To think like a wise man, but to express oneself like the common people" was her favourite quotation from Aristotle; perhaps she too felt the inevitable loneliness of the leader who must take his own way. For as Yeats has said, "always her wise man was heroic man."

It is not surprising to discover in her first folk-histories, therefore, an emphasis far more personal than historical in her examination of three "strong people of the world": the tragic heroines of Irish history, Gormleith, Dervorgilla, and Grania. . . .

It is perhaps inevitable that the celebration of the rebellious individual should appear under the mantle of tragedy, for in Lady Gregory's universe, as in Yeats's, such is the fate of those who take destiny into their own hands. But as one observes in Yeats's heroic fool, clearly the struggle is worth it, for only in controversy against inevitable Fate or overwhelming odds does he realize his full strength. This is the message of Grania, Gormleith, the penitent Dervorgilla; it is the message of Ireland's history. And when we turn from the tragic "tragi-comedies" to the "pure" tragedies, *MacDonough's Wife* and *The Gaol Gate*, we find the same stirring call to inner strength and the independent spirit.

The world in which Lady Gregory's plays have reality is very much a people world, inhabited by characters who are all gifted with loquacity and infinite capacity to believe, their individuality a result of fertile imagination. Consequently she rarely scales the heights of heroic tragedy, for as Yeats pointed out, the spirit of laughter is a great deflater, and once Lady Gregory allows her little people to take on their wayward personalities, she is no longer in control. . . .

Ann Saddlemyer. *In Defence of Lady Gregory,*
Playwright (Dublin, Dolmen, 1966), pp. 63, 72

Lady Gregory's use of character in her comedies is far from romantic; it is classical. She would subscribe to the Aristotelian view that character is present for the purpose of the action. In some ultimate sense, however, for her the action is there to present the static image of a world. One imagines that with the conclusion of one of her actions and with, say, the next morning's opening of the shops in Cloon Square, all things and all people will be at the places appointed them in the original stage directions. This is obvious in such shorter plays as *The Workhouse Ward* and *Coats*, least obvious but equally true in *Spreading the News*, where at the play's end certain things remain to be cleared up among the characters before the original situation is restored.

The Workhouse Ward (1908) has the quality of a tableau that is for a little while interrupted by a minor crisis resolved ironically. It invites a brief meditation on its scene—two old paupers endlessly wrangling in their separate beds. It is not surprising that Lady Gregory herself meditated upon the scene and observed, "I sometimes think the two scolding paupers are a symbol of ourselves in Ireland—'It is better to be quarrelling than to be lonesome.' " *Coats* (1910) offers the picture of two rival newspaper editors lunching at the Royal Hotel, Cloonmore. The action of the play is a confused argument between them over their respective obituary notices. It breaks the quiet of their lives, but is resolved. One imagines them sitting there again at the next noon, the next argument on another subject, but again resolved.

Lady Gregory's plays are very Irish, but they arise out of a conception that life is everywhere fundamentally the same and that the fundamentals do not change from age to age. This is the attitude of the folklorist and of one who is conscious of a tradition and seeking to preserve or restore it. Finally, it is one of an artist observing a society that has been conservative, isolated, and jealous of its privacy, suspicious of the invader.

Hazard Adams. *Lady Gregory* (Lewisburg, Pa.,
Bucknell Univ. Pr., 1973), pp. 73–74

The false image of Lady Gregory's personality and capacities painted by Joyce, Gogarty, and Moore has survived almost to the present day; for even her recent critics have tended to ignore the extent to which her plays, translations, and organized powers were respected in the early years of the twentieth century. Moreover, what these three satirists left unscathed, the august presence of Yeats tended to obscure. Lady Gregory throughout her lifetime, however, was as much a rebel as any one of her detractors. Her muted but dedicated refusal to accept the status quo began in her desire to break away from the repressive surroundings of Roxborough. . . .

A few years later her rebelliousness and her objectivity were evinced by her abandonment of a short-sighted and restrictive Nationalism in favor of a consideration of the individual. Her synthesizing ability resulted in her perception of the magic behind everyday country experiences, in her eye for the key anecdote that reveals the human being behind the political mask, in her surprise with and fulfillment in the resuscitating Gaelic movement, and in her power of remaining distant from the more esoteric philosophizing of Yeats. On a few occasions, Lady Gregory's exuberance led her to judge falsely; but these instances occur primarily in her "wonder works," the magic and fantastic collections which, by implication, she finds equal in importance to the eloquent and noble *Cuchulain of Muirthemne*. In the totality of her work in Irish myth, however, she succeeded in sending Irish culture abroad, even though she paid little attention to historicity. . . .

In her final years, Lady Gregory emphasized a strain of mystical thinking that had been present from the start in her works. Its two embodiments, fantasy and spirituality, were objectified by the political horrors of the years after 1916, by her disappointment over the theft of Hugh Lane's pictures, by the growing importance of Realism in the theater, and by the necessity, after so many years, of capitulating to a governmental censor. The fantasies, such as *The Dragon* and *Aristotle's Bellows*, are notable for their blend of burlesque and pathos. The mystical works, especially *Dave*, have their share of literary permanence.

In short, Lady Gregory's career was a rich and full one. She participated in all the central movements of an interesting and vital age, and she shaped the energies of the principals and added her own blend of humor and magic to the more dour moments of Irish Renaissance literary polemics and politics. With a personality that was a combination of deep-rooted tradition and lofty idealism, Lady Gregory seemed to know always just what was needed and how to go about accomplishing her design. At all times, her great wish was to create what was worthwhile and artistically truthful, in spite of nationalistic and religious pressures, and to provide a forum for others capable and willing to add dignity to Ireland.

Edward A. Kopper, Jr., *Lady Isabella Persse Gregory* (Boston, Twayne, 1976), pp. 138, 140–41

[*Cuchulain of Muirthemne*, 1902] and *Gods and Fighting Men* (1904), a re-telling of Irish mythology and the stories of the Fianna, became basic source books of Irish legend for many writers who could not read the tales in their Gaelic originals. Both books, and others which followed, showed that Lady Gregory was very skillful in adapting the work of scholars to the style, point of view, and idiom of native storytelling; she was, in fact, the best popularizer of legend and folklore the Irish Renaissance produced. . . .

She was a very productive writer during a career which began when she was almost fifty and only ended with her death at eighty, producing several books of legend and folklore, more than twenty original plays plus almost as many collaborations and translations, books on the Irish theater, and auto-biographies. All this was the product of constant hard work, hard work which also attended to years of day-to-day management at the Abbey, an enormous correspondence, the upkeep and supervision of Coole, and constant attention to her family and to younger writers. Those who knew her often describe her strength and purposefulness, and she must have been a rather daunting figure at times. Yet there is a controlled twinkle in the eye in her best photographs; control of herself and amusement at the world's foibles were two of the se-crets of her career. A third secret was her passionate love for Ireland, the Ireland of Coole with its beautiful house and deep woods, but love also for the Ireland of dull little Gort, the Ireland of urgent nationalism, and the Ireland which the Abbey embodied. She was a persistent and courageous woman, fearless in defending her friends, the theater company she nurtured and sus-tained, and the ideals she came to believe in. One night during the Anglo-Irish War, when she was in her late sixties, she was waiting for a tram with the sec-retary of the Abbey after the night's performance. Shots rattled in the street, and she was begged to lie down on the pavement. "Never!" she answered as she shouted out encouragement to the rebels. That courage carried her through "the troubles" in Ireland, the death of her son in World War I, and the even-tual sale of Coole. She was herself a great rebel against her background and her class, a fighter determined to do all she could for Ireland and Irish drama, a rebel who knew that every cause worth fighting for has its funny side. Only a person of great courage and great humanity could write as she did toward the end of her life, "Loneliness made me rich—'full' as Bacon says."

Richard Fallis. *The Irish Renaissance* (Syracuse,
N.Y., Syracuse Univ. Pr., 1977), pp. 99–101

Lady Gregory published in 1912 two volumes of what she called *Irish Folk History Plays—First Series* and *Second Series*. The *First Series*, "concern-ing strong people of the world," as she says in her dedication to Theodore Roosevelt, "one of the world's strong men," is labelled "Tragedies," the *Sec-ond Series*, "Tragic-Comedies." While she unabashedly places her play *Grania* as the first of the "tragedies," however, critics have since been reluctant to see it as a real tragedy. That is, they concede tragic elements within the play, but imply that the real tragedy is associated with external personal matters that generated the play to begin with. . . .

There is no question . . . about Grania's strength. But we [see] a very real reluctance to confer upon her story the distinction of tragedy. While she does not physically die in the end, however, we cannot say that she goes off to marry the king and live happily ever after. Dying, in fact, might have been the easier course, and it is only her extraordinary strength that allows her to reject it. But in a sense Grania does die in the last act, because through the process of selection and emphasis in her work with the myth, Lady Gregory has defined Grania's character and her very being as that of the lover, even to the extent of having her love endowed by fatalistic powers beyond the realm of human intercourse: the exposure of Diarmuid's love spot corresponds to Juliet's crossed star, to Iseult's love potion, and to the prophecy about Deirdre and the sons of Usna, and so is removed from an ordinary human love that is kept impure by life's other motives and instincts. The Grania who is this lover is certainly dead at the end of the play, killed by a tragic vision brought about through the sequence of events that close in upon her. Her last gesture may be to open the door and with a look of fierce nobility put a sudden stop to the derisive laughter, but that look itself has behind it the bitterness of a terrible cynicism, as revealed in her final line, when she says that "there is not since an hour ago any sound would matter at all, or be more to me than the squeaking of bats in the rafters, or the screaming of wild geese overhead!" Finn's new queen cannot participate in human affairs even as do other queens, because she has really lost her humanity with her love in playing out her tragic role. This is Lady Gregory's embellishment, or contribution to the myth—to answer the "riddle" that Grania's behavior "asks us through the ages." The ambivalence that many critics have found in Grania's role as a tragic lover does exist in the myth; it does not exist in Lady Gregory's play.

Finally, as to the other two characters in the drama. Finn is more or less enlightened in the end, but enlightenment instead of inspiring him to heroic action, subdues him, and the man who was once a giant and hero is led off by his new queen a broken old man—one could say timid and doddering, even, if it weren't for the bit of strength with which Grania infuses him, and which allows him to face the crowd at the very end with his arm around her. He is a figure, certainly, of pathos rather than tragedy. Both Finn and Diarmuid had been treated more generously by Yeats and George Moore, who had, while making some departures, generally kept more closely to the myth that Lady Gregory had prepared for them. Motives are considerably muddled in the 1901 *Diarmuid and Grania*, but Grania is more aggressive in luring Diarmuid into the woods (the love spot is not mentioned), Diarmuid generally carries more of his own weight in the love affair afterwards, and Grania's love for Diarmuid is compromised by an ambivalent attraction she feels for the great

Finn after the seven years in the country. In the end Diarmuid, consistent with the myth, is killed by the wild boar as had been foretold, and the play closes with eulogies of him by Grania, her father King Cormac, Finn, and other members of the Fianna. Only in the last lines does the usually troublesome Conan the Bald say that "Grania makes great mourning for Diarmuid, but her welcome to Finn shall be greater." The implication here is that Grania is simply the fickle lover, which, indeed, is consistent with her reputation as it has come down through the ages in the myths. In Lady Gregory's version Diarmuid, after rushing out like a raging beast to kill the King of Foreign, dies in a delirium, mocking his lover and proclaiming an endless loyalty to his lord. But this occurs several pages before the end of the play, the final pages devoted to the ultimate development of Grania's tragic stature. This play's title, after all, bears only Grania's name.

Joseph Ronsley. CJIS. Spring, 1977, pp. 41, 55–57

The circumstances of her childhood, the teaching of family, church, and class all told her that her role as a female was to serve others. She believed it; duty was the lifeline from which she hung all her actions and achievements. Her life is dazzlingly instructive in the utility of those drab virtues within command of the will: self-restraint, tenacity, hard work, devotion. But she also had fairy gifts: a great, long-term vitality, a soldier's courage, and a detachment that—taking away from love—brought laughter. . . .

First she served her brothers as junior nursemaid and later as housekeeper. She served the poor on her family's estate far in the west of Ireland. There was not much future in it. Then when she was twenty-seven she captured the catch of the Irish marriage market, sixty-three-year-old Sir William Gregory, master of neighboring Coole Park, a former colonial governor of Ceylon, a delightful and cultured gentleman who moved in the highest social circles in Ireland and England. She was, she wrote, "happy in the thought of being with him, of serving him." At his death when she was forty, she put on mourning and continued to wear it, long after her sorrow was gone, for the remaining forty years of her life. It was the appropriate costume for her role as a dutiful woman. She edited several books about her husband's family, she collected folklore for Ireland, and she again captured the one man in Ireland who could do her the most good, the thirty-one-year-old poet William Butler Yeats, poor, overworked, and ready for all the good she could do him.

She looked after him at Coole Park, she loaned him money, bought furniture for his flat in London, sympathized with his hopeless love for Maud Gonne, collected folklore for his collections, wrote pleasant dialogue for his plays, founded the Irish theater with him. . . . Their relationship, as complex, rewarding, and limiting as a marriage, was the masterstroke of her life—and immensely important to his. As he wrote, "I doubt I should have done much with my life but for her firmness and care." And, as she wrote him on her deathbed, "I have had a full life & except for grief of parting with those who have gone, a happy one. I do think I have been of use to the country. & for that in great part I thank you." Serving him, founding the Abbey Theatre with him, she found at last the broadest, most congenial and rewarding objects of service: Ireland and literature.

But there was a break in the continuity of her service. When she was fifty, in the middle of a renaissance, when she was busier and happier than she had ever been, in the service of Yeats, the Irish theater, Ireland, and literature, she set out to write plays. Unlike Yeats, who was continually making the night sea-journey through his soul, she was suddenly dunked into her subconscious—and discovered her creativity. She came up gasping, "*Sinn fein*, 'we ourselves'—is well enough for the day's bread, but is not *Mise Fein*—'I myself'—the last word in Art?"

Her short comedies are explosions of laughter. Her patriotic plays touch immediately a deep tribal identification with the Irish people united against an oppressor. All her plays provide a satisfying, touching demonstration of the power of the psyche to balance itself, to supply in one form the love and freedom denied in another. Many of her plays were very popular. She never stood centerstage at the Abbey, spread her arms, and exulted, "I made it!" But she did smile and bow.

Mary Lou Kohfeldt. *Lady Gregory: The Woman Behind the Irish Renaissance* (New York, Atheneum, 1985), pp. 5–7

HEANEY, SEAMUS (1939–)

Seamus Heaney's *Death of a Naturalist* is a first book of verse and, as such, many of its poems are explorations of the poet's roots, attempts to define the rural life of Ulster he was once part of. The title of the book indirectly refers to this earlier rootedness in a way of life grimly dependent on making the best of the soil; but it also defines an autobiographical difference with which several of the poems are concerned. A "naturalist" is one who studies nature by observation, and not one who labours with it to exact from it a subsistence. Thus Heaney's father and grandfather cut peat and dug potatoes; and although to see and to smell what is dug reminds him of what was once a common way of life, its damp, truculent activity now divides him from them. . . . Their activity defines for the poet the difference between them and him. Unlike them, the poet's concern with nature, although vivid, and alert, is a naturalist's, one whose connection with it is not intimate any more since not dependent on it. . . .

The last two lines of the title poem, with their clinching rhyme, instance a different aspect of Heaney's language—a desire for incisiveness, which tends towards an over-neat epigrammatizing quality. This is already familiar to us through some of the poems in the first of the *New Lines* anthologies, and through the rather precocious *dicta* that surrounded its appearance in 1956. Yet although this incisiveness does not express the sharpness of feeling that one supposes Heaney wants to convey in his love poems, its bitter, reprimanding quality is the very instrument for the poem concerning The Great Hunger.

Jon Silkin. Stand. No. 4, 1967, p. 69

It was not until he began to teach that Seamus Heaney discovered contemporary Irish literature, and with it, the possibility of exploring his own background—a small farming community in Northern Ireland. He said in his interview with Peter Orr that he found in the work of Patrick Kavanagh "what I took to be archaic subject-matter . . . treated in a modern way, in a way that made it universal and tragic, especially in this poem 'The Great Hunger,' which I think is a great poem." He turned also to Clare, Edward Thomas, Hardy, and Robert Graves—poets who stand in opposition to, or at least outside, the tradition of Anglo-American modernism that dominated English verse during the first half of this century. . . . He acknowledges the effect on his diction of Ted Hughes's work. . . . The curt, abrupt, elliptical movement of the verse unmistakably derives from Hughes. . . .

It is in the poems based on an anecdote, or grounded in a moral observation, that Heaney's strongly individual voice is heard. The tone of these poems is often Wordsworthian: Heaney shares Wordsworth's recognition that suffering and fear may play a valuable part in chastening and subduing the human spirit, and that a child is nurtured by terror as well as by beauty. But he faces the fact (and here he differs from Wordsworth) that, judged by human standards, Nature is sometimes malign and disgusting.

John Press. *SoR*. Summer 1969, pp. 681–82

[Heaney] talks about the cloud of unknowing, about what Patrick Kavanagh, an older Irish poet who died a few years ago, called the fog, "the fecund fog of unconsciousness." Kavanagh said that we have to shut our eyes to see our way to heaven. "What is faith, indeed, but a trust in the fog; who is God but the King of the Dark?"

What is acceptable in aesthetics may be a little off-putting in theology, if, that is, one at all desires a theology, and Heaney here may be a conscious victim of an Irish obsession which he can describe so well. For his childhood and adolescence, the equivalent of the dark Gallarus was the confessional, the Irish Catholic sense of sin, "a negative dark that presides in the Irish Christian consciousness," and, "the gloom, the constriction, the sense of guilt, the self-abasement." Every creed has its own creepy methods and for Irish writers, as witness O'Connor and O'Faolain, the confessional, for facetious and other purposes, has, so to speak, paid its way. "Penance," says Heaney, "indeed was a sacrament that rinsed and renewed—you came out light-footed and alert as those monks—but although it did give a momentary release from guilt, it kept this sense of sin as inseparable from one's life as one's shadow."

Waking or sleeping that King of the Dark would be just as uneasy a companion, or a master, as the capricious Something that Alexander Kuprin sensed at work, a spirit neither of good nor of evil, just an irresponsible and sometimes nasty Sense of Humour, writing at its worst moments Newman's scroll of lamentation. In a poem, "Against Blinking" (not yet collected) Heaney meditates on the folk-belief that an ill-disposed person could, merely by looking at it, "blink" a cow so that its milk would yield no butter. Is God the Blinker, Kuprin's law of logical absurdity?

Of all this, as I've indicated, Heaney is perfectly aware with the strong, balanced, humorous mind that he displays in poetry, in talk and in comment.

Benedict Kiely. *HC*. Oct., 1970, pp. 10–11

In three volumes of poems to date Heaney's contribution to the current renaissance has been outstanding, but his importance outweighs his role in that ongoing event. He is a special instance of a poet who has transcended the limitations of the provincial by being inordinately true to the material of his locality. It is not that his method has remained insulated from those "broad perspectives" from England (or America) but that his central impulses have derived from the "more intimate" Northern Irish tradition. In his introduction to *Causeway* [Michael] Longley quotes Patrick Kavanagh on the distinction between the provincial and the parochial: a provincial, with "no mind of his own," trusts only "what the metropolis . . . has to say on the subject"; on the other hand, "parochialism is universal; it deals with fundamentals." In this sense Heaney is a parochial poet. With his own sensibility and mind he has dug into the fundamentals of his conscious and unconscious experience, into the mythos of place, the traces of racial memory, the dark human and natural forces, the archetypal patterns, and done so with such urgency that he breaks through the bonds of provincialism. His poems should give pause to those who automatically reject poetry that has its roots in the regional and traditional.

In technique Heaney's poetry would appear to be traditional; and for this reason it is also rejected by some. Outwardly, the forms are traditional; the poet does usually compose in stanzaic patterns, often (though less and less frequently in the three volumes) with set rhyme-schemes. But what goes on within those patterns is very innovative, it seems to me: art and locality relate in a style that is inimitably Heaney's. In "Traditions" (*Wintering Out*) he complains, "Our gutteral muse/was bulled long ago/ by the alliterative tradition,/ her uvula grows/vestigial," but we notice that the verbal energy of the complaint is hardly vestigial. If Mallarmé is the poet for whom language attenuates into the condition of music. Heaney is one poet for whom language coalesces into living texture and movement. His poetry is worth serious study for this reason alone.

Robert Buttell. *Seamus Heaney* (Lewisburg, Pa.,
Bucknell Univ. Pr., 1975), pp. 14–15

"Kinship" and "Funeral Rites," two poems in Seamus Heaney's latest volume, *North*, suggest a theme that recurs in many of his poems, namely, the importance of connection in human experience, the personal and social value of a cultural matrix within which behavior can have intelligibility. . . .

Heaney's first two volumes, *Death of a Naturalist* (1966) and *Door into the Dark* (1969), are almost totally concerned with farming and domestic life in the rural area of Northern Ireland where he grew up. Profoundly aware of the traditions that once gave meaning to rural Irish life—the land, the rhythms of farming and fishing, family customs, the mysteries of nature and love—he is equally aware that rural Ireland has nearly lost its customary life. Many of the poems in *Death of a Naturalist* and *Door into the Dark* look back longingly to the old ways. Heaney's more recent volumes, *Wintering Out* (1972) and *North* (1975) both broaden and deepen his subjects. Aware of the need to develop his own imagination on the one hand and conscious of being part of a violent and ungovernable society on the other, he looks for answers in the bogland, in the goddess-mother whose "wet centre is bottomless" ("Bogland"). His imagination is stimulated by traces of the ancient Irish language he finds embedded in bogland placenames that have survived the imposition of English. These words may enable one to make contact with an ancient Irish spirit. For a present-day Northern Ireland, which has lost its cultural roots, he finds "antecedents" in the traditions of prehistoric societies recently discovered buried in Danish and Irish bogland. . . .

Provided that it has not degenerated into platitude and habit, ritual can still give order to life. Digging into the "bog" of his imagination as well as into the archaeological lore of the real bog has convinced Heaney that, even in these desperate times, one might hope to connect with life-enhancing elemental powers and, through the discipline of language, to give these connections shape.

Arthur E. McGuinness. *Éire-Ireland*. Summer, 1978, pp. 71–72, 92

[Heaney's] work [in *Wintering Out* and *North*] leads away from the personal and narrower confines of the poet's own past and towards the wider, public inheritance of the country's history. It is felt by Heaney to be an inheritance that is deep and sometimes violent. Certainly in poems written after 1970 there is an increasing recognition of the political troubles of Northern Ireland (although some of the most political poems have not yet been collected into book form). Yet it is not simply the acknowledgement of the facts of social division nor the terror of the Troubles that makes *North* important. It is important because in this volume, as in parts of the previous one, Heaney relates past and present, his personal past and the country's history, in order to get beneath the dangerously oversimplified political perspectives on Ireland and its people. He maintains the poet's traditional role of guardian of the word-hoard, that deep repository of a people's reality and their dreams. Through this commitment to a continuity of past and present explored in the language of people and place, Heaney begins to discover an identity for himself that acknowledges his own part in a strife-torn land but which does not take the easy way of identifying himself with that side of history to which his birth would align him. The ground (literally in the poems about the soil of Ireland) on which he has chosen to stand is beyond, or rather beneath, the normal divisions and inevitably exposes him to the ridicule and hatred of those on any side who believe salvation lies in being partisan. It leaves him to appear as either enemy or deserter. It is not an easy stance but he draws his courage from the fact that ultimately it is the only stance that can include the whole of Ireland—the only possibility for resolution.

The strain of this lonely task is seen in *Wintering Out*, where many poems, although not overtly political in subject, are about the estrangement and isolation that the poet feels ("Servant Boy," "The Last Mummer," "The Wool Trade," "Shore Woman" and "Bye-Child"). In them the poet identifies with various conditions of alienation in others, and they seem to reflect a suggestion that he is circling round some deep centre in himself which he has not yet clearly traced, touched or understood.

P. R. King. *Nine Contemporary Poets*
(London, Methuen, 1979), pp. 209–10

In almost every essay [in *Preoccupations*] Heaney discusses this dialectic between "intellectual baggage" and "instinctual ballast." And over the years he has enormously increased the range of his own "technical" resources. The character of his first two collections derives in large part from their craftsmanship—for all their subtle sensuality, they tend to treat straightforwardly a clearly perceived set of subjects. But since *Wintering Out* he has been more readily prepared to admit what cannot easily be articulated. In many respects, the change recalls the distinction that Conrad makes in *Heart of Darkness* between tales in which the "whole meaning" lies within "the shell of a cracked nut," and others in which the meanings are "not inside like a kernel but outside, enveloping the tale which [brings] it out only as a glow brings out a haze." This isn't to imply imprecision in Heaney's recent poems, but to admit their element of mystery. Significantly, one of the things he admires in Yeats is the narrowing of "the gap which etymology has forced between mystery and mastery."

This enlarging of imaginative resonance and association—what Wordsworth calls "wise passiveness"—has a complex political dimension. Just as experience and remembered innocence strove to achieve their mature relationship, so he has had to maintain "a notion of [himself] as Irish in a province that insists it is British." The first "literary language" he encountered was "the classic canon of English poetry," but its resented dominance was quickly challenged as he investigated his own native culture. The result was not usurpation but interinanimation (Heaney approvingly uses Donne's word himself.) "If you like," he says, "I began as a poet when my roots were crossed on my reading. I think of the personal and Irish pieties as vowels, and the literary awareness nourished on English as consonants." The poem "Anorish" [*Selected Poems, 1965–1975*] confirms this:

Anahorish, soft gradient
of consonant, vowel-meadow
after-image of lamps
swung through the yards
on winter evenings.

Since the Troubles began, this process has taken a new turn. As well as continuing to construct "the satisfactory verbal icon," he has undertaken a search for "images and symbols adequate to [his] predicament." The "Bog Poems" are one outstanding result—and their reconciliations of Irish and English locutions, and past and present histories, allow him to maintain a profound commitment without becoming narrowly partisan.

Andrew Motion. *NS*. Nov. 14, 1980, p. 24

A poet often writes prose to articulate an investigative technique or explanatory procedure, by which his intended discovery, probably initially intuited, may be claimed and justified. An exhibition of need and will, it's also an act of self-declaration. The essays in *Preoccupations* demonstrate Heaney's aspirations, his awareness of his own position in the larger poetic tradition, and an account of those patterns of exploration which comprise the nervous system of his verse. Heaney is almost obsessively concerned with what we might call the natural history of language, its origins, morphologies, homologies. Whatever the occasion—childhood, farm life, politics and culture in Northern Ireland, other poets past and present—Heaney strikes time and again at the taproot of language, examining its genetic structures, trying to discover how it has served, in all its changes, as a culture bearer, a world to contain imaginations, at once a rhetorical weapon and nutriment of spirit. He writes of these matters with rare discrimination and resourcefulness, and a winning impatience with the received wisdom. In his essay on Hopkins, for example, he describes and analyzes one kind of poetics which regards the emergence of poetry as a feminine action, "Almost parthenogenetic," a seeping forth of language that "tends to brood and creep, crop and cluster, with a texture of echo and implication, trawling the pool of the ear with a net of associations." In another essay, Wordsworth's "hiding places of my power" provide an occasion for Heaney to announce his own view of poetry: "poetry as divination, poetry as revelation of the self to the self, as restoration of the culture to itself; poems as elements of continuity, with the aura and authenticity of archaeological finds . . . poetry as a dig."

Heaney's essays are studded with reiterated phrases and notions, but such repetition is less a sign of indolence than of a coherent and strong-willed intellect testing, tuning, and revising its themes. We hear more than once of Eliot's "auditory imagination" and "dark embryo," of Yeats's "bundle of accident and incoherence," of Shakespeare's "Our Poesy is as a gum which oozes / From whence tis nourished." And to these Heaney contributes his own passionate, conspiratorial language— of poems "earthed" in provincial recognitions, of words "as bearers of history and mystery." The very selectivity of quotation, its rather narrow range, indicates Heaney's predilections. I believe a poet reveals the vision he has of his career in part by revealing those predecessors he chooses to ignore as much as by those he claims as occasions for statements about his own work. Without faulting Heaney's choices, one would at the same time very much like to hear him on Browning (Heaney's own dramatic monologues are very fine), and on the rural Hardy of the "feel of old terrestrial stress" and "Earth's old glooms and pains," and on W. S. Graham.

At every point, Heaney shows himself a discriminating and intense diagnostician of the poetic tradition. He brilliantly explains the way in which poetry issues from the roughly shaped, vaguely stirring beginnings in intuition and compulsion. He draws firm distinctions between his predecessors, clarifying that diversity (and divisiveness) which gives such quarrelsome vitality to poetic tradition.

W. S. Di Piero. AmS. Autumn, 1981, pp. 560–61

What anyone reading Heaney's early work for the first time today would immediately be struck by is the tendency they share with certain works of the modern spirit (not least Beckett's plays) to weigh inarticulacy against articulation, to acknowledge the claims of silence as well as those of speech. And what such a reader would secondly be struck by is that, like certain writers who have earned the tag "post-modernist" (Borges and Ashbery, for example), Heaney devotes much of his energy to producing a literature that is about itself. His first book begins with an image of him holding a pen (in "Digging") and ends with him gazing like some "big-eyed Narcissus" into a well: "I rhyme / To see myself, to set the darkness echoing" he tells us ("Personal Helicon"); and such narcissistic self-consciousness about the business of writing is indeed a major theme of his work. In this company of minimalists, absurdists and termination theorists, Heaney cuts an unlikely figure, and it must be said that he comes at the themes of silence and solipsism from his own special angle. None the less it is impossible now to read Death of a Naturalist and Door into the Dark without noticing these two preoccupations.

The preoccupations arise from the same source: Heaney's sense of belonging to a silent ancestry, an ancestry with which he, as someone who went away to boarding school on a scholarship at the age of eleven (he was an early beneficiary of the 1947 Education Act, which gave Northern Catholics greater educational opportunities) and who has become a writer, has embarrassed relations. What links the various traders, labourers and craftsmen who fill his first two books is that, unlike him, they are lacking in speech. His water-diviner works "without a word." His Lough Neagh fishermen, whether out in a boat or eel-catching in the fields, carefully avoid noise ("better not clatter now"), allowing themselves only terse epigrams and prophecies—"We'll be the quicker going down," "The lough will claim a victim every year," "Once the season's in." The haymakers in "A Wife's Tale" are seen "smoking and saying nothing." On a "Dawn Shoot" the narrator and his companion remain "mostly silent." A thatcher, though "bespoke for weeks" (a nice word-play in the context), goes wordlessly about his business, leaving his clients "gaping." The blacksmith, returning to his forge from the half-door he has been leaning on, merely "grunts." A docker sits "strong and blunt as a Celtic cross, / Clearly used to silence" (*Death of a Naturalist,* p. 41): he demands "quiet" of his family and practises tight-lipped extremity himself—"Speech is clamped in the lips' vice." That final image is one that might stand as an epigraph for Heaney's early work, and its obsession with silence.

Blake Morrison. *Seamus Heaney*
(London, Methuen, 1982), pp. 19–20

I see *Field Work* as building directly on the four previous volumes, and in this Heaney sets the model of Yeats before himself[:] . . . to "deal with public crisis" by developing imagery out of his "own terrain." His poetry is now clearly committed to dealing with the violent situation in Ireland. Whilst acknowledging and defining his Catholic background, Heaney's poetry does take its base on non-sectarian, humanitarian principles. The imagery in this book engages the problems of Ireland as directly as anyone writing there during the Troubles. There is, of course, a danger implicit in Heaney's comments. By "making your own imagery and your own terrain take the colour of it, take the impressions of it," you are open to the danger of posturing as a public figure. However, I think Heaney unlikely to strike the senatorial stance of Yeats. He has, to this point, refused to wear "the great fur coat of attitude," though that could be a temptation, for the media picked up on the new book *Field Work* with alacrity; there have, over the last few years, been calls for writing that deals more fully, directly, with the Troubles. But Heaney himself has said, "to forge a poem is one thing, to forge the 'uncreated conscience of the race,' as Stephen Dedalus put it, is quite another and places daunting pressures and responsibilities on anyone who would risk the name of poet."

Field Work matches the hour in this respect, but on Heaney's own terms. The Troubles in Ireland, the involvement of the British Army again, the breakdown of democratic rule, these are highly charged subjects in the British Isles. Seamus Heaney's new book constructs an Irish landscape at once politically-charged, shared and relevant. At the same time it carries the considerable weight of personal emotion, grief and anger.

Writing of Yeats, Heaney wishes that the *Collected Poems* had ended with "a kinder poem" than the "too male" "Under Ben Bulben." He would have preferred to see "Cuchulain Comforted" as the final statement:

> "Your life can grow much sweeter if you will
> Obey our ancient rule and make a shroud;

There is evidence in *Field Work* that Seamus Heaney has the poetic intelligence to bring to bear on the situation that in which history has placed him.

He celebrates this "rite whose meaning is subsumed into song, into the otherness of art."

Tony Curtis. In Tony Curtis, ed., *The Art of Seamus Heaney* (Bridgend, Wales, Poetry Wales Press, 1982), pp. 125–26

Personal questions of Heaney's disposition toward oppression in the North and his need for independence as an artist are raised in the central part of the volume, "Station Island," not lyrically here but in dialogues with and evocations of the past. In direct references to Dante, the subject of pilgrimage, sporadic use of terza rima, dialogues with the notable dead, and the placement of the individual artist against a tumultuous political background, "Station Island" summons up the spirit of Dante, particularly of the *Purgatorio*. The poem also returns to a setting—the site of the ancient pilgrimages, mentioned by Dante, to Lough Derg on the border between Donegal and Tyrone—already explored in long poems by Devlin and Kavanagh and a prose sketch by William Carleton. Only the latter two writers figure overtly in the dialogues of "Station Island."

Carleton greets the poet with "O holy Jesus Christ, does nothing change?," adapting a Tyrone voice to iambs but not to the "I am" of Heaney's characteristic diction. Kavanagh upbraids his understudy: "Sure I might have known / once I had made the pad, you'd be after me / sooner or later. Forty-two years on / And you've got no farther!" Neither Kavanagh's nor Heaney's best lines, this credible japing demonstrates Heaney's willingness to suspend his timbre to serve his dramatic purpose.

The dead pilgrims who waylay the poet have visited the stations of the poet's mind and uncovered his most troubling anxieties. For example, the poet first encounters Simon Sweeney, a figure from his childhood who, as a notorious Sabbath-breaker, haunted the child's dreams. The significantly named Sweeney recalls these dreams to the poet and establishes the volume's keynote with the warning: "Beware of the empty forms." Other characters needle the poet concerning his tendencies to conform, his overinvolvement with the Irish dialect, and the remoteness of his art from life. Yet, in recounting these revenants' deaths, the poem depicts the horror of political murders more starkly than in any previous Heaney poem excepting his translation of the Ugolino passage from the *Inferno*.

The strongest rebuke is delivered by Colum McCartney, a murdered cousin Heaney commemorated in a *Field Work* elegy "The Strand At Lough Beg." Just as Virgil daubs Dante's eyes with dew and plaits into his belt the reeds of humility to prepare him for Purgatory, so in his elegy Heaney asperges and adorns his murdered cousin. In "Station Island" the cousin reproaches the poet for translating his gory death into art. . . . Later, the poem suggests the necessity of art translating life, as a familiar kitchen mug was borrowed for a local play and thereby "dipped and glamoured from this translation."

The speaker's principal literary advisors are William Carleton and James Joyce. Joyce admonishes him to abandon poems about Irish and English dialects: "The subject people stuff is a cad's game." For both his elders, writing is natural functioning, not self-expression so much as self-maintenance. Carleton says, "We are earthworms of the earth, and all that / has gone through us is what will be our trace."

Joyce, however, provides the last speech in the closing canto, advising the "dolphin's way". . . . Abandoning a monumental literature, Heaney's advisors espouse an art that is sinuous and ephemeral. Even with echoes of "A Lough Neagh Sequence," Joyce's imperative characterizes the author of *Finnegans Wake* more than that of "Station Island." Heaney, however, has taken on the courage of Joyce, and of Yeats, in his willingness to swim out beyond the shallows, Although he has written poetry of extraordinary accomplishment, the innovativeness of *Field Work* and *Station Island* promises even further development of his talent.

Dillon Johnston. Irish Poetry after Joyce (Notre
Dame, Ind., Univ. of Notre Dame Pr., 1985),
pp. 163–65

HEWITT, JOHN (1907–   )

Poets are self-revelatory in different degrees and John Hewitt occupies an extreme position on the scale — the position of those who constantly dilate upon, to use an American term, "what makes them tick," and whose poetry consists almost without exception of a personally-conducted tour of the whole "ticking apparatus." But because Nature is Hewitt's compelling theme and because his treatment of this [in *No Rebel Word*] is so vital, we do not immediately realise that we are learning as much about the poet as we are about his Antrim countryside. He is more than a mere observer, more even than a nature-lover, he is the *genius loci*. The balance is struck — and struck unfailingly — between the poet revealing himself through his theme and the theme being amplified by its sifting through the poet's sensibility.

> If life's to mean full fist and riper wisdom
> these things must turn to blood, to blood and muscle.
> till lash of eye is April rain transmuted
> and lift of knee the sun on Antrim cliffs.

Everything else — the outer world, personal relationships, Europe, — is muted background music to this large tune. Even John Hewitt's technique is moulden into a seemingly passionless, (though not impersonalised) almost by-the-way, thing, varying unobtrusively. He has described it aptly himself in one poem when he calls it "quiet verse deliberately wrought."

No Rebel Word is the work of one firmly rooted in time and place and richly gifted in the tools of his craft.

David Marcus. *Poetry Ireland*. Jan., 1949,
pp.26–27.

John Hewitt eschews the spiritual knight-errantry which has led Louis Mac-Neice to make symbolical figures out of Columbus and Child Rowland, and he lacks the verbal exuberance of W. R. Rodgers. He believes in the value of tradition and in the importance of a sense of continuity. He likes to walk in the country of his kindred, where something of the timelessness of the Golden Age still broods and amid the trees and stook-lined fields. There, even in a world at war, life goes on much as it always did:

> . . . The boys I met
> munching their windfalls, coming late from school
> are like that boy a hundred years ago,
> the same bare kibes, the same drab heirloom rags,
> but they must take another road in time.

Hewitt's verse has the wholesome, nourishing grain that makes us think, somehow, of wheaten bread. Plainness and the lack of obvious ornament designed to catch the eye or the ear of the reader does not convey anything stark or dour. On the contrary, his poetry has at its heart a warmth, a friendliness, an innocence which comes not from folly or ignorance, but from understanding. If comparisons are in order, the work of Robert Frost comes to mind, for, like him, John Hewitt has mastered the art of quiet, leisurely utterance, following, often, the rhythms of natural speech. This is an utterance, which, cumulative in its effect, reaches the recesses of the mind and soul and finds an echo there.

J. N. Browne. In Sam Hanna Bell, ed.,
The Arts in Ulster: A Symposium
(London, Harrap, 1951), pp. 144–45

If one was asked who best, in twentieth-century Ulster, continued the sceptical, broadminded tradition of William Drennan and William Allingham, one could do no better than to point to work of John Hewitt. His essays and his poems are the work of a humane, serious man seeking to fulfil what he conceived as his duty as he attempted to embody and blend the best of Ulster tradition in his own writing. . . . Hewitt's poetry attempted . . . a task of social comprehension and cultural amelioration. That its success was minimal is all too evident in the divisive excesses that characterise contemporary Ulster and render it a focus of widespread, often uncomprehending, attention. Yet it would be churlish to blame this failure on any deficiency in Hewitt's effort. The fault surely lies with the province, which, by its frequent rejection of any possibility of integration in the political, cultural and religious spheres, must surely also reject the poet who encourages cultural synthesis.

If such encouragement, such social effort, were the whole of Hewitt's achievement, he would indeed seem to have failed as an artist, and to be merely one more victim of "the savage complications of our past" and of our present. But it is not the whole, for Hewitt's regionalist experiment was by no means only a matter of solemn duty and community service. The social role was not inimical to the natural inclinations and cast of the poet's mind. It allowed him to explore themes and subjects which he would naturally have turned to, and it enabled him to give free expression to his own distinctive vision of the world. This is an important point, for had Hewitt's poetry been all duty and regional commitment, it would surely have been dull, if worthy, stuff. Yet this reader does not find it so. Let me suggest how Hewitt transcends his merely local role and becomes a poet with a personal vision, a vision which commands interest and respect.

His fundamental interest is not, as it would seem, Ulster, but the relation of man to his environment, the shaping and controlling of consciousness by locale, climate and topography. The region provides a ready-formed laboratory for observing these processes at work. Hewitt is a materialist poet who accepts that "a tree is truer for its being bare" ("Frost") and is content to

> lose
> mortality's despair,
> having so much to choose
> out of the teeming air.

("Lyric")

He observes and celebrates man's relationship with the earth believing that

> talk of weather is also talk of life,
> and life is man and place and these have names.

("Landscape")

Yet Hewitt also senses the dislocation that city life has effected in man's psyche; and the description of the Ulster scene with its remarkable blend of urban and rural, its bizarre juxtaposition of technological development and rustic antiquity, allows the poet to deal with that widespread contemporary experience, alienation. Many of Hewitt's most characteristic poems are ironic pastorals in which we observe the rhythms of country life through the urbanite's perplexed eyes. He seeks acceptance but is more aware of alienation from beast, landscape and peasant, knowing that "we are no part of your world, your way, / as a field or a tree is, or a spring well."

Terence Brown. *Northern Voices:*
Poets From Ulster (Totowa, N.J.,
Rowman & Littlefield, 1975), pp. 91–93

There seems an aspect of Hewitt's poems that calls promptly for recognition. At least he is one of a very sparse number of Unionists who was aware of those outside his state and tradition. He wanted to raise the consciousness of his fellows. . . . [Seamus] Heaney has been generous to Hewitt in his criticism, perhaps because of this movement towards his side of the racial division. It is not as easy a tribute as it looks: "A stubborn determination to belong to the Irishy and yet tenaciously aware of a different origin and cast of mind." Hewitt has been at an unusual and solitary crossroads most of his life, but I cannot go along with Terence Brown who suggests that his career has been a failure. Standing alone in a literary situation, conscious of an inner righteousness, does not imply an artistic defeat—quite the contrary. Hewitt has stood in the middle of the Ulster impasse, keeping his counsel, maintaining his connections to Planter and Gael. He is not disowned by extremist takeover, his patience seems all the more necessary. John Montague, who was born a Northern Catholic but has written as a Southern poet for most of his working life, possesses more lucidity than Brown: "To be Irish was bad enough, but to insist on being Ulster as well seemed to drag literature to the level of a football march. But, as we shall see, Hewitt's instinct was right. . . ." Hewitt's instinct was not a gamble, it was the discovery and retention of a subject matter that was embedded in every stratum of the social psyche. One cannot agree with Montague that Hewitt is ". . . that oddity in our literature, a poet of sustained political thought." He is rather a poet of political response, limited to one dimension. Though his sense of nationality has been thus fruitfully insecure all his life he has, in spite of it, become a spokesman for the moderates among the Unionist majority. The Irish leader, Jack Lynch, recognized this when speaking in commemoration of the 1916 heroes in the Garden of Remembrance, Dublin, in July, 1971: "Perhaps the national majority need to examine their consciences in relation to the national minority. Have our political concepts been sufficiently wide to include them? Have we been considerate enough about the things they believe in as passionate as we might believe otherwise? Do we agree that as John Hewitt writes, 'they have rights drawn from the soil and sky' which are as good as any title held by any previous migration into Ireland?" This is to remark that Hewitt is in fact an Irish nationalist, a more realistic one than Yeats.

James Liddy. *Éire-Ireland*. Summer, 1979,
pp. 124–25

Although [Hewitt] preferred the country to the city, his poetry is by no means confined to country themes. It ranges widely over different times and places, wherever personal reminiscences and reflections lead him. He responds quickly to the life around him, and when the present "troubles" began in Ulster his mind and spirit were drawn into them, although he was then living and working in Coventry, as Art Director of the Herbert Art Gallery and Museum. He published privately a small volume of poems in 1971 which he called *An Ulster Reckoning*. In the foreword he writes: "To one living outside Ireland the impact of the terrible days of August, 1969, was heartbreaking. As I could not readily walk among the barricades with my white flag, I found release for my sense of frustration in verse." The second poem in the collection is entitled "A Dilemma" and it states his position with an honest anguish. Neither a Unionist nor a Republican, he cannot readily take sides. "So, since this ruptured country is my home,/it long has been my bitter luck to be/caught in the cross-fire of their false campaign."

In spite of a sense of helplessness to influence the course of events in Ulster, Hewitt wrote some telling poems at this time. "The Coasters" is an effective satire on those who go easily with the tide and so assist the drift to disaster and violence." "Conversations in Hungary" reveals vividly the difficulty of explaining sectarian riots in Ulster to foreigners. But perhaps Hewitt's most characteristic response to the troubles in Ulster is to be found in a later poem from *Out of My Time*. "Neither an Elegy nor a Manifesto" is addressed to "the people of my province and the Rest of Ireland.". . . Hewitt's poem insists, perhaps over-insists, on a plain low-profiled approach to the violence in Ulster, but it seems to me an honest and moving poem.

His poetry has considerable range and variety. He can write long discursive meditative poems in heroic couplets, like "Conacre" and "A Country Walk in May," that recall the Augustan mode of Goldsmith and Crabbe, and he can write brief unrhymed pensées, such as he offers in *Scissors for a One-Armed Tailor*. Here, for example, he catches deftly the mood of a grey day on the Ulster coast in a poem shorter by one syllable than a haiku.

Grey sea, grey sky,
two things are bright;
the gull-white foam,
the gull, foam-white.

He can move from a lyrical sensuous mode, as in the last two lines of "A Green Shoot" (*Collected Poems*): "I am the green shoot asking for the flower / soft as the feathers of the snow's cold swans," to the deliberately bare, plain statement of "Neither an Elegy nor a Manifesto." He can use most of the traditional verse forms with skill and flexibility. In recent work he has shown a partiality for the sonnet. *Kites in Spring,* his most recent collection, consists entirely of sonnets, moulded to his own personal and unobtrusive tone.

His preference is for plain, unrhetorical statement, but he can exert a quiet force that compels our attention. By the careful choice of an adjective or a metaphor he brings a mood or scene sharply into focus. . . .

Seamus Heaney referred to "a typical Hewitt area, halfway between statement and evocation." When he describes a scene or an incident, or recalls a memory, he often does it in a way that evokes resonances, ripples of thought and feeling that spread when the poem has ended. "The Distances," from *Out of My Time,* has this effect. He recalls a very simple, ordinary scene, in language that is only distinguished from prose by delicate pause and rhythm, and yet the distances of loneliness are hauntingly suggested.

Alan Warner. In Heinz Kosok, ed., *Studies in Anglo-Irish Literature* (Bonn, Bouvier, 1982), pp. 371–73

John Hewitt has, over the years, become a venerable figure in Belfast, and all sorts of honors are now raining down on his head. He was accorded the honor of being the first writer-in-residence at Queen's University a few years back, and was granted the freedom of the city of Belfast last year (a privilege he confessed that he had been enjoying for some time previously). These accolades come at a time when he is more prolific than ever.

This volume's title [*Loose Ends*] suggests a collection of occasional pieces: There are memories and reflections, poems on childhood, aging and dying, places, work, politics, a Big House, and so on. Hewitt's poetry resists resonance in favor of nuance, music in favor of speech, the showy in favor of the plain. Seeking modest epiphanies in the commonplace, Hewitt's poems sometimes conclude on a note of enigmatic irony. An explicit sense of his priorities in technique and composition comes through in the poem "On the preservation of work sheets":

> It should not matter how I shaped my lines,
> hit on a cadence; shuffled adjectives,
> replaced a showy word with one that gives
> a truer texture, or, precise, defines
> a signal smudged by clumsy countersigns,
> or altered phrase to mark a change of gear
> when word proposing word at once combines
> to make some level of intention clear.

In addition to Hewitt's quiet craft, a number of things tie the loose ends of this collection together. There is his sense of human solidarity, which is bedrock in all his work. And in this volume a number of poems celebrate the

creative faculty of indomitable artists whose "husbandry is going well" despite the winter of their old age. I find "Calling on Peadar O'Donnell at
Dungloe" particularly effective and moving—the author is lost as storm and
darkness descend but perseveres eventually to find his friend "still working in
the garden." When he shouted, O'Donnell "straightened up to answer, and in
the gloom his fine head glimmered white." The last poem in the collection,
"St. Stephen's Day," is also on this theme of the creative impulse heroically
conquering the adversity of winter and mortality:

> The old men bundled in their coats
> creep out to greet the peeping sun,
> as if, like jewel-headed toads,
> they'd splintered winter's flinty stone.

Anthony Bradley. ILS. Spring, 1984, p. 30

HIGGINS, AIDAN (1927–   )

There were outcrops of huge talent in his first book, *Killachter Meadow*
[American title of *Felo de Se*]. In those dark stories lone individuals, often bizarre or grotesque or gigantic, are seen at large in settings cramped or limitless, working out dooms whose causes Higgins all but ignores. These people
are fixed not so much in their ominous Irish, German, English, or South African landscapes as in the process of their fates. One remembers them almost as
impersonations of nonpersonal lines of force. But Higgins' rather heavy craft
and erratic tones indicate that at that stage he had yet to accommodate various
techniques he wanted to use. Except for the long story "Asylum" (refuge,
tomb) with its uncanny coupling of diurnal document and a Dinesen-like sub-
patterning of occult vectors, *Killachter Meadow* is most promising in the mel-
ancholically sluggish, doom-dark pieces that grope for an indefinite ground
between mood and action.

In Higgins' novel, *Langrishe, Go Down,* that promise is patiently fulfilled. If in ten years this book is seen to have been a genuinely new work,
perhaps the reason will be that by subtle differences in seemingly stock materials and an economy of balances Higgins makes a whole mysteriously unlike
its parts. . . .

In his style, phenomena are held as if between the subject's response and
some existence independent of an observer—perhaps in that perceptual silence Beckett says it is the function of objects to restore.

The Beckett influence is strong. . . . But despite the entropic mono-focus
of *Langrishe, Go Down,* Higgins is much less mannered than Beckett. And
despite the conscious linguistic variety . . . Higgins has nothing of the exhibi-

tionist self-indulgence to be seen occasionally in Nabokov or Grass. Time will tell whether the comparison that makes most sense is with James Joyce.

Joseph McElroy, *NL*. Sept. 25, 1967, pp. 18, 20

The Balcony of Europe is a bar overlooking the Straits of Gibraltar in Nerka, a community of 10,000 (the population of Guernica before the bombing) with one church and 50 tavernas. Overhead bombers from the US airbase at Morón de la Frontera maintain an hourly air patrol, while *extranjeros* of a different sort, mostly would-be writers and artists, patrol the plaza in front of the bar in between drinking bouts of absurdly cheap (it is the early Sixties) brandy and *vino tinto*. These exiles include Bob Bayless, an American academic working on Shelley, and his Polish-Jewish wife, Charlotte; and Dan Ruttle, an Irish painter who is the narrator of the book [*Balcony of Europe*] and married to Olivia. Dan, middle-aged, moderately successful, has an impassioned and hardly concealed affair with Charlotte, young enough to be his daughter, which ends with her pregnant but not knowing by whom.

This love affair occupies the central three sections of Aidan Higgins's new novel with a section on either side. The first is a finely written account of Dan Ruttle's childhood in Sligo at a house called Nullamore, its subsequent sale and the move to Dun Laoghaire when he was about 15, and his mother's death some two decades later. This section reminds one very much of the Joyce of *Portrait of the Artist* and the earlier part of *Ulysses;* deliberately, it would seem, since Joyce is mentioned and quoted as Higgins brings off "a fadograph of a yestern scene" which will certainly stand comparison.

The last section describes a return to Dublin, declines anti-climatically into a series of over-trivial letters from the cuckolded Bob, and closes with Dan and Olivia on the Aran islands. This stops the book rather than ends it. Higgins himself seems aware of its shortcoming when at the end of the final chapter he asks: "Are you asleep? Answer me."

Stand by for my reply. It is difficult to believe in Dan Ruttle as a painter. There is no painterly detail, he is too concerned with psychological detail; not concerned with how things look, but with how people think. Dan is far more like a writer, in fact; but the incidental characters certainly live, read as though taken from life. There is the homosexual, jewel-thieving person-of-restricted growth Eddy Finch, for instance, and the Finn who drinks five or six litres of wine a day and claims to have been not only a member of the Hitler Youth but one of those inspected by the Führer himself just before the end and who is still aware that he swore an oath to kill the enemies of the Reich wherever they were to be found.

No, I was not asleep, Mr. Higgins, your writing, page to page is too good: particularly your sensual descriptions of women, so accurate, so moving. But I was certainly feeling the strain, for this novel is 463 large pages long. At a time when more than ever the only honest response to life seems to be to laugh, harshly and briefly, there is clearly a case to be made out for the novel being funny, brutalist, and short. . . . But *Balcony of Europe* deserves to be widely read for its example of a very fine writer trapped in this dilemma, and not yet free to write the outstanding novel of which he is capable.

B. S. Johnson. *NS*. Sept. 29, 1972, p. 442

One reviewer of *Felo de Se* detected "muted echoes of James Joyce." He was, I think, both right and wrong—wrong in that the whole thrust of these early stories is towards a most un-Joycean end—and right in that Higgins, like Joyce, was providing himself with the first of a series of books which relate intimately to one another, each of which reveals a deepening of intention and a development of stylistic methods. Joyce's progress was like Higgins' only inasmuch as both reveal a movement towards an overview which offers us human life as a unity combining present with past, conscious with unconscious, and man with myth. Joyce brought his work to a conclusion (or so we must believe) with *Finnegans Wake*. Higgins is still moving towards that final vision.

That Higgins is one of those who are searching for "the Total Book" can hardly be doubted by anyone who has read his three works of fiction. The shape that "Total Book" will take is something we cannot as yet guess at with any safety, but the "rejected epigraphs" to the third work, *Balcony of Europe*, do give us a hint. There we read a passage from Edmund Husserl, who, we must remember, was once the teacher of Otto Beck, the central priapan figure of *Langrishe, Go Down*. . . . If we attempt to translate the phenomenology of Husserl, its emphasis upon the way in which the mirror within us distorts (by intention as well as by accident) the phenomena we say we perceive, we are faced with a problem of showing these distortions without suggesting that they are invalid, for who is to say what image is correct? We are faced, perhaps, with presenting a subjective viewpoint whose inconsistencies are clear, but whose coherence is never seriously in question. Higgins does this in his two novels by giving us changing perspectives upon the central characters. He offers us detailed descriptions of persons and scenes, and then further and further descriptions, each one implying a different perception. He moves us back in time, and then forward. He allows third parties to comment for our benefit. We see Helen Langrishe's view of the Otto Beck affair as well as the changing views of Imogen herself, and these last are never quite in the order in which they developed. Longing, nostalgia, and regret may provide a bright and positive vision immediately following a dark and savage one. This shift in perspective in both novels, and to a lesser degree in the short stories, gives all Higgins' work its ironic cast, and yet irony is not what he is truly after, at least in the narrow point-making sense of the word. Irony can, after all, only be absolutely effective if there is a standard of truth, and in Higgins there is none. His is a fluid, fluent universe, a movement of tides ebbing and flowing, a series of withdrawals and returns that are only surprising to those who see life, as some of Higgins' characters attempt to see it, as a progress, a Roman road driving straight to a destination foreplanned and foreordained.

Robin Skelton. *Mosaic*. Fall, 1976, pp. 28–29

Aidan Higgins's latest novel [*Scenes from a Receding Past*] has as its narrator and protagonist Dan Ruttle, who also served those functions in *Balcony of Europe*, yet the two books are quite different. Indeed, no two of Higgins's works are alike. As each one has appeared, it has marked new departures: *Langrishe, Go Down* from *Felo de Se, Images of Africa* from *Langrishe*, and *Balcony of Europe* from *Images*—while *Scenes from a Receding Past* has echoes of all of them and is not really like any of them, except insofar as it is the work of a man obsessed with words and language and who cares about how they are used.

At first, to be sure, the diligent care behind this novel is not fully evident, and no doubt the book will strike some readers as needlessly self-indulgent. Higgins does not impose form on the "scenes" he evokes, warning us of that immediately by quoting as an epigraph to Chapter I Richard Brautigan: "I've been examining half-scraps of my childhood. They are pieces of distant life that have no form or meaning." . . . Yet Higgins is after all a disciplined artist, and this is a crafted work. In contrast to *Balcony of Europe,* its mode is one of omission and concision; to adapt the terms of the dispute between F. Scott Fitzgerald and Thomas Wolfe, if *Balcony of Europe* seemed like the work of a "putter-inner," *Scenes from a Receding Past* seems the book of a "leaver-outer": it quickly and effectively evokes scenes, incidents, and characters—and then moves on to the next ones. Often, the method seems cinematic, with Dan Ruttle serving for Higgins the role that Antoine Doinel serves for François Truffaut.

Certainly Ruttle's function as an autobiographical figure is never hidden. For some reason, nevertheless, Higgins pretends to disguise the actual places of his own childhood in Kildare (Ruttle's childhood is in Sligo)—but only after having supplied a key in the Author's Note specifying that for Sligo Town we may read Celbridge, for Lissadell House we may read Killadoon House, and so on. Perhaps Higgins had simply trapped himself into the fictional locations in *Balcony* and now feels that he must be consistent. Or perhaps he wishes to encourage a sense of separation and distancing (the title of the first chapter is "Distant Figures") even while undercutting it. This is in fact a book neither of nostalgic sentimentality, although nostalgia and sentiment are important in it, nor of sordid unpleasantness and easy condemnations of "rustic ignorance" (the words Ruttle applies to himself as a child). The major achievement of the novel may well be the balance of tone, especially in the first half concentrating on Ruttle's early years. . . . But that is not to say Higgins's only successful characterization is Ruttle himself; actually, perhaps the most moving scenes out of the receding past are those dealing with his brother Wally, who is secretive and uncommunicative—"distant," again. Wally has a complex and cruel relationship with their mother; both of them suffer "nervous breakdowns," the mother's "a nervous disease that would keep her with Wally."

In numerous ways the material in this novel illuminated and looks "forward" to the earlier *Balcony of Europe,* but it stands on its own as well. It is a moving and brave book, a short novel that presents a great deal, none of which is ever simplified.

Morris Beja. IUR. Autumn, 1978, pp. 252–53

Aidan Higgins' 1972 novel *Balcony of Europe* is a stab at establishing a major work, on which the basis of a canon may grow. Thus it is self-consciously in harrying pursuit of Irish times past (also pastimes, if you understand the tribe). Two of the commonest criticisms fielded against Higgins have been his derivations in style and personal narrator mannerisms from Joyce and Proust; he has been regarded, justly in his early work, as a neo-Joycean, and in *Balcony of Europe* he has been accused of the airs and graces—to use native slang—of a "spoiled Proust." This novel attempts to create a structure, and aesthetic content, by ignoring such comments and by concentrating on the traditional concept of exile in a new form. The novel begins and ends with faded slices of internal emigration in Ireland, and between is sandwiched the expatriate slum of the Spanish coast in the sixties: the dreadful mass elitism of golden beaches whose comic vulgarities Higgins rips apart with Celtic thoroughness. Here the narrator-painter preens himself, observes various rootless types, and takes in prose and alcohol in rhythmic patterns. The faults of an alien exile society are faultlessly bestowed in the eye of the beholder. . . .

This novel is both major and minor, both over-written and underfelt—both blemishes are, however, solid in the context. A vanity fair could not be put together without these qualities. It is, for example, too long—a pig of a book, to use another nativism—it might be a journal translated into a novel; a European fiction form in itself. Boorish with words yet planted with lovely prose poems of landscapes. Garish with jewelry yet hungry for more life than can be sustained; a tribute to the fed and the dead. And definitely a take-or-leave-it piece.

The style, so pure, cold, and long-suffering, needs a word of explanation. To veer away from the masters, Joyce and Proust, Higgins takes stylistic rides into the territory of lesser yet immortal folk. Flashes of *Nightwood* occur both in dramatic monologue and in character. Both the Baron (even to title) and the English angel of "How strange is the homo-fire!" are recreated from Djuna Barnes's work. For surface, he parades titbits from Durrell's *Alexandria Quartet,* down to a name for the narrator's wife Olivia and to back pages of work notes in the form of rejected epigraphs. If a major theme is the stealing of slices of other couples' wedding cakes, Higgins ices them perfectly. In the background of his rhythms, digressions, and monstrous flashbacks I hear the cloying echo of the garrulity of the most minor of Irish masters, George Moore. The feeling in Higgins is that there is nothing that an extended anecdote can't do to improve a book. Do as Moore did when stuck with dictating to his secretary: pile on the memory and fish out a story from the sea of narcissistic reflections. In *Balcony of Europe,* though, this habit is as revealing as irritating. The book matches the restlessness of the reader, in a way *Hail and Farewell* cannot. . . .

The material is largely familiar to Irish readers. The early sketches of the old age and decay of the father and mother are parallel in location and type, even to a detail like anti-Semitism, with the situation in Hugh Leonard's *Da.* The difference is stylistic and in terms of social class. The fall of man, the fall of the narrator's house, parodies the fall of Ireland, both Celtic and Anglo-Irish, to the seediness of itself in a peasant state, to the contemporary country with an upstart Tiberius ruling on an island. Like all good literature out of this super-bog, the result is a new tour of the nuances of Irish history.

James Liddy. *RCF*. Spring, 1983, pp. 180–82

The acceptance of the document as the art form he relishes is as yet only a threat, but is one he has been considering these past few years; yet in the new novel, *Bornholm Night-Ferry,* which contains letters between the author himself and a poetess from Denmark, Higgins must have taken note that if the old characters that sustained his early work are gone, and autobiographically rounded off in this book, new fictional figures are already appearing, cities, dreams, sunlight, more earthy if desultory observation of a competing world. The figures are no less an act of imagination just because they exist and can be named. The figure of Higgins that emerges at one period of the book is actually more reminiscent of the figures in *Asylum.* We have come the full turn. Inspiration means starting a new story. *Bornholm* is a fitting end to the old. At last Higgins has succeeded in giving himself the fictional life he was always seeking, one where the author/narrator can only own up to half of what is told and where his every word is interpreted, criticized, evaluated by another.

The reader, too, has at last also found a doppelgänger in the poetess. If Higgins had failed to find this corrective to himself, he would have considered himself dishonest. This is what I think he feels mainstream fiction fails to do, to keep a reasonable, biting dialogue going between different intelligent people. Entering the world of theatre (as he will surely do now) will allow his recordings of people to gain an extra dimension—the actor's voice, thereby eliminating certain descriptions he found burdensome. *Bornholm* has an equal voice at odds with his own, ringing out the opposition with polite conviction. The male and female in direct confrontation. In *Bornholm* he has thrown himself wide open before a woman who when she bites, bites deep, and leaves—

what is now a particularly Irish consciousness—wilting. She takes him to task over his cynical or guarded attitude to his former work. His discourses about love are held up to ridicule. His self-hate, she points out, is just as deafening as self-pity.

Yet, where all former interiors were guarded by humorous barricades, a breach is made here.

For in *Bornholm* Higgins is brought beyond his obsessions about the correct order of things into the tight barbs of survival, and this is what makes the novel one of the most truthful and sensual love stories to emerge in many a day. He is self-pitying for a change, defends himself with decent shows of bad temper, goes up and down the scale of the humiliated, shows a stubborn unfeeling streak, and we can see clearly the self-hate and the negative effects this can have on—never mind the writing—the human personality. This is memory enacted in the present, without any doubtful selections from time past. He continually expects the ogre and then is surprised to find himself still intact at the end of the day. No sham female psyche here. This is a full-blooded woman of a strong purpose. We are ecstatic under the toughness of her reprimands and the sensual threats. It is Higgins the writer, not some fictionalized company director from Hamburg, who must bear the brunt of these truths, and the ending of the book, as in all of Higgins' books, is how the writer/narrator will act upon all the sensitive knowledge gained, of being only one of many that he has listened in upon, and of the story going beyond the moment when he called a halt. It should mark the end of the I-person in his work (as coequal to himself), for by now he has written himself as a character out of the series. The reader or listener has other claims on his talents. In *Bornholm* the conflict between the European and the Irish parts of himself has been successfully resolved. Another pinnacle has been reached. *Bornholm* is both document and fiction in one.

Dermot Healy, *RCF*. Spring, 1983, pp. 186–87

HIGGINS, F. R. (1896–1941)

A.E. in his preface says, "I find myself murmuring lines of his as I walk about the streets." It will be the fate of any who read *Island Blood*; for F. R. Higgins has a great power of seeing things which we all might see and of recording them unforgettably. . . . *Island Blood* is full of lines and couplets and quatrains that one does not want ever to forget.

Mr. Higgins finds his most perfect expression in the simpler of his poems. He can be sensuous, almost tropically luxuriant, oversweet. He can spoil the beauty of his image with the richness of words; several of his verses bear this defect. To read him in these is like breathing the heavy, still air of an oriental garden. But the freshness and beauty of his less ornate lyrics is worth it all. . . . It is hard to say which of the poems pleased me most, but I find myself saying over the lines of "The Broken Tryst" very often. . . . "After Harvest," "The Roving Lover," "June," "Connemara," "Ruins," and many others have the same deep, simple charm of a bird's song together with a power of picturization which makes *Island Blood* a great book. . . .

Mr. Higgins can sing of passion and death and loneliness as well as of nature and love and sunshine. His "Cleopatra," despite its over-ornamentation, is very powerful and there is gauntness in his "Death in the Mountains." I like his "Cattle Boats," too, with its protest against the grazers: "Their kerchiefs were full of red money;/Our green hills were bare without herds."

Clearly, Mr. Higgins has it in him to be worthy of a high place among our poets. If he frees his feet from the snare of luscious words, if he learns that his voice is rich enough to be spoiled by trilling, who knows how high he may not go? Now that he has started for the summit I would call after him: "Above all, sing naturally."

Cecil O'Hanlon. *DM*. May, 1925, pp. 683–85

Mr. Austin Clarke and Mr. F. R. Higgins are definitely products of the [Irish literary] movement. Mr. Clarke, who began in 1918, chose his first subject from Gaelic mythology. . . . But in the main Mr. Clarke seems derivative from Yeats, and Gaelic rather by the matter of his work than by the spirit of it. A new and fresher voice comes in with Mr. F. R. Higgins, whose whole thought and expression seem to be coloured by Gaelic, as if it were to him a living language, habitually used. Sometimes, indeed, he writes with deliberate suggestion of the ballads written by Irish schoolmasters who were just beginning to write in English, though to the quality of their "come-all-ye's," he adds a very different quality. . . .

Sometimes, again, his aim is to suggest through English such a poem as one of the seventeenth century poets, who preserved the tradition of their bardic schools, might have written in Irish. . . .

Either of these [approaches] it will be agreed, has charm; yet in each the poet relies for his effect on the use of an artificial idiom. But here is the natural utterance of Mr. Higgins in a powerful piece of evocation; and it will be noted that though rhyme is very sparing, his verse is bound together, Gaelic-wise, by internal assonance of the broad vowels, and by alliteration of consonants carried all through:

> With these bawneen men I'm one
> In the grey dusk-fall,
> Watching the Galway land
> Sink down in distress—

With dark men, talking of grass,·
    By a loose stone wall,
In murmurs drifting and drifting
    To loneliness.

Stephen Gwynn. *Irish Literature and Drama*
(London, Thomas Nelson & Sons, 1936),
pp. 219–21

In his later years "Fred" Higgins was Yeats's closest friend; there was even sufficient physical resemblance to make somebody say, after meeting them walking side by side in O'Connell Street, "They are like father and son." They were bound by natural affinities. It is probable that Yeats found in his young friend a bridge across the generations: an assuagement of the feeling that "we were the last romantics;" found in him an Ireland more sweet than that pictured by Joyce and O'Casey and O'Flaherty, the critical generation. At any rate, Higgins does form that bridge between the obstinate anti-romanticism of our time and the lofty and fantastic imagination of pre-revolution poetry, with its pliable subjects, all ready to hand, caparisoned by mythology and traditional awe. ("We . . . chose for theme," Yeats wrote, "traditional sanctity and loveliness.") For Higgins also loved the traditional subject, loved to see at all times behind the lore of the people, and folk-tunes and ways, and in the aerial, almost tenuous beauty of nature, the classically lyric face of life. . . .

His death cannot fail to tell sorely against the development of a native tradition in verse, for he was a most careful craftsman; his influence was growing every day. As for his own contribution to that tradition, it was remarkable, since it was a double achievement when he captured a native vigour and pungency hitherto considered suitable only for novels and plays and then held it in a net of the most iridescent verse written in Ireland since *The Wanderings of Usheen*. That must not suggest to us that his death unfortunately breaks the Yeatsian continuity: on the contrary, he would have had to disrupt that tradition *had he lived* and done it, thereby, a noble service. For unless a tradition is continually interrupted and re-directed it dies. *Dans la littérature il faut toujours tuer son père*; one does it because, almost in Wilde's phrase, one loves deeply. Literature moves like that—obliquely as the knight in chess cornering the king for a new game. From disciple Higgins would have become apostle, and perhaps begun a new canon. But a pawn has taken the knight, and the king has escaped again.

Frank O'Connor. *The Bell*. Feb., 1941, pp. 53, 55

His being a countryman made him at home in the fields; but the fields were at home in his work through his personal gift. It is this, the personal gift, which defies definition; I cannot so much as show—in small space anyhow—exactly what it did; cannot give enough examples of Higgins's at-homeness. In default I must only *suggest* illustration; while as to explanation, the vaguest phrases must do: that with Higgins, so to speak, our poetry moved nearer to the centre of the Irish ethos.

I begin my suggestion with a general impression. When I think of his second volume, which he called *The Dark Breed*, I immediately experience an atmosphere. Submitting to that atmosphere in memory, I recollect particular words and species of images, with the sorts of gaits his rhythms have, and a general feeling of ancientness. The particular words are *Spain, island* and *Mass, bawneen, poteen, stone-walls*; the rhythms have in them the pacing of clay-caked boots; the images are plentifully drawn, I remember, from waters; and the feeling of ancientness comes in part from the themes, in part besides from sudden flarings of memory. Superadded to these remembrances, I think how physical all seems in him, even when his theme is old eremitical religion. The body's hungers, and its violence in games and labour, are often sung; and the senses of the poet are forever fiercely in action, his sounds and imaginings full of the ear and the eye, and his nerves and his bloodstream seconding the thoughts of his mind. Summoning back these things from the *Dark Breed* poems, a masterful sense of the region they treat of returns to me.

There, perhaps, speaking of this poet's senses and sensuous vocabulary, I have lit on the secret of his power. Higgins is notably sensuous. He can fail in form; he can muddy his total effect; he can hide his sentences' meaning in a nest of boxes; but failing to be sensuous is rarely a fault of his. Rarely does a poem of Higgins's appear to be contrived; he may fail to make, but he does not often make-up. He was, if I do not mistake him, too slothful at once and too lacking in common cleverness, ever to have started a poem which was not self-starting. The poem which he muffs is somewhere about, though not on his page.

The sensuous with him was primarily, though not entirely, a business of images; of visual images first and tactile secondly. More than think things or hear them, he saw them and touched them; pictures and feelings composed the mass of his world.

Robert Farren. The Course of Irish Verse in English
(New York, Sheed & Ward, 1947), pp. 137–39

In *Salt Air, Island Blood,* and *The Dark Breed*, and in his miscellaneous prose writings, Higgins dedicates himself to the celebration of the popular romantic image of the Irish people and nation that O'Casey saw fit to ignore. He sings the glory of the Fenian heroes, of the Gaelic resistance to foreign rule, and, most significantly, of the noble peasant, his traditions and customs, and the countryside in which he lives. In many respects, Higgins' vision of Ireland is similar to Colum's. Both try to adapt Gaelic poetic technique to their verse in English; both develop the same basic themes; and both attempt to depict modern Ireland as a kind of latter-day Arcadia, a survival of the Golden Age. Higgins' verse, however, lacks the artistic discipline of Colum's; his imagery is often exorbitant, his sentiment too often unrestrained. The ideal nation in which his "dark men" and "bare-limbed girls" gather their eels is "a gold and honey land"; to such a land Higgins meant to ride his "winged horse." . . . More often than not, Higgins' honeyed language and opulent rhythms serve only to make his verse heavy, lethargic, and unexciting. In any event, they are merely decorative. Beneath the ornamentation one finds only the stereotyped ideals of the popular nationalist movement. The passion of Cathleen Ní Houlihan has been tamed by conventional morality. Ireland's wine has been watered down with sentimentality. What are truly lacking in Higgins' vision of the ideal nation are intellectual originality and emotional energy.

In a poem entitled "Repentance," published in *Arable Holdings* in 1933, Higgins passes judgment upon his own earlier poetry and rejects what he terms the "frailties of a bardic will." His repentance does not involve a rejection of Ireland; he does not mean to divorce his art from his nationality, as James Stephens had done. . . . Ireland will remain Higgins' subject; but his aesthetic attitude toward that subject will be radically changed. . . . What his new attitude will be is fairly clear. He has left behind the "withered towns" where "Thoughts housed too long grow pale"; in other words, he has rejected the sentimental conventions of the popular traditions, those worn, effete conventions that permit the poet only a "trickster's mental albegra / Of nods and winks." He renounces also his soft, voluptuous imagery, which now seems to him like "moss and rheumy candlelight." In a subsequent stanza he again observes that he has turned away from the "twilight pools" of romanticism and then adds that he has done so in order to achieve in his verse "pure commerce with the sun," and he promises to "climb above the night, / That preys on mounds of holy stone." The tokens of his new aesthetic are "sun" and "wind and rain" and "fierce hail"; they point toward a harsher and more piercing quality in the thought and technique of Higgins' verse, and, in consequence, toward a new, more violent, and perhaps angry vision of Ireland.

Richard J. Loftus. *Nationalism in Modern Anglo-
Irish Poetry* (Madison, Univ. of Wisconsin Pr.,
1964), pp. 248–51

. . Like Yeats, Hyde, and AE of the earlier generation, Higgins was born a Protestant but worked hard to identify himself with Catholic, Celtic Ireland. A poem of Padraic Colum's and Douglas Hyde's *Love-Songs of Connacht* inspired him to write verse. Three volumes appeared in the twenties, *Salt Air* (1924), *Island Blood* (1925), and *The Dark Breed* (1927). The poems showed a remarkable talent, undisciplined perhaps and given to an uncritical glorification of the peasantry, but genuine. The man could put words together as no other Irish poet of his time except Yeats. Higgins' problem, in fact, was his fluency; the phrases were memorable and the verbal music gorgeous, but sometimes the overall form was uncontrolled. Like his friend at the time, Austin Clarke, Higgins was fascinated by the techniques of assonance in Gaelic poetry, and he used these to create poems of lush sensuality, beautiful often in the way that the poetry of the Celtic Twilight was beautiful, but more intense, specific, and passionate.

By the early 1930s Higgins' obsession with the peasantry and his native Mayo led him to move to a cottage near Loch Conn, not far from his birthplace at Foxford. What was to have been a year there stretched out to three, and it was 1935 before Higgins and his wife returned to Dublin. *Arable Holdings* (1933), an important book of poems, was published during this period, and it showed a real change in Higgins' work. He was slowly excising sentimentality and with it some of his voluptuous imagery. *Arable Holdings* drew some excellent reviews, and after Higgins returned to Dublin, Yeats began to take an active interest in his career. Together they prepared a series of broadside ballads which the Cuala Press printed, and each began to influence the other. Yeats taught Higgins something about disciplining his art, while Higgins helped Yeats catch something of the authentic voice of folksong in his later poetry. . . .

His last volume, *The Gap of Brightness* (1940), had some valuable work in it, but the influence of the later Yeats was almost too strong, and, as Richard Loftus observes, the volume fails because, unlike Yeats, Higgins never developed a coherent aesthetic. He died in 1941. He was as prodigal with his imagery as Dylan Thomas, and his poems are always striking for their musicality. Yet all that talent seems to add up to a good deal less than the sum of its parts, and the reasons seem clear enough: a lack of intellectual grasp in his early work and too much imitation of Yeats's mannerisms in his later. Even so, some of his poems, "Repentance," "Father and Son," "Changeling," "A Tinker's Woman," are remarkable achievements, and his elegy for his friend Padraic Ó Conaire, the Gaelic short-story writer, begins and ends with two of the great stanzas in Irish poetry.

Richard Fallis. *The Irish Renaissance* (Syracuse,
N.Y., Syracuse Univ. Pr., 1977), pp. 236–38

HYDE, DOUGLAS (1860–1949)

In the notes at the end of *Beside the Fire* Dr. Hyde contrasts with certain tales of Indian jugglery an old Gaelic account of a magician who threw a rope-ladder into the air and then sent climbing up it all manner of men and beasts. It reads like an allegory to explain the charms of folk- and fairy-tales: a parable to show how man mounts to the infinite by the ladder of the impossible. When our narrow rooms, our short lives, our soon-ended passions and emotions, put us out of conceit with sooty and finite reality, we have only to read some story like Dr. Hyde's "Paudeen O'Kelly and the Weasel," and listen to the witch complaining to the robber, "Why did you bring away my gold that I was for five hundred years gathering through the hills and hollows of the world?" Here at last is a universe where all is large and intense enough to almost satisfy the emotions of man. Certainly such stories are not a criticism of life but rather an extension, thereby much more closely resembling Homer than that last phase of "the improving book," a social drama by Henrik Ibsen. They are an existence and not a thought, and make our world of tea-tables seem but a shabby penumbra.

It is perhaps, therefore, by no means strange that the age of "realism" should be also the harvest-time of folk-lore. We grow tired of tuning our fiddles to the clank of this our heavy chain, and lay them down to listen gladly to one who tells us of men hundreds of years old and endlessly mirthful. Our new-wakened interest in the impossible has been of the greatest service to Irish folk-literature . . . and now appears Dr. Hyde's incomparable little book. There has been published in three years as much Irish folk-lore as in the foregoing fifty. Its quality, too, is higher. Dr. Hyde's volume is the best written of any. He has caught and faithfully reproduced the peasant idiom and phrase. In becoming scientifically accurate, he has not ceased to be a man of letters. His fifteen translations from traditional Gaelic originals are models of what such translations should be. Unlike Campbell of Islay [John Francis Campbell, folklorist], he has not been content merely to turn the Gaelic into English; but where the idiom is radically different he has searched out colloquial equivalents from among the English-speaking peasants. The Gaelic is printed side by side with the English, so that the substantial accuracy of his versions can always be tested. The result is many pages in which you can hear in imagination the very voice of the sennachie, and almost smell the smoke of his turf fire.

Now and then Dr. Hyde has collected stories which he was compelled to write out in his own Irish through the impossibility, he tells us, of taking them down word for word at the time. He has only printed a half of one story of this kind on the present occasion. One wishes he had not been so rigorous in the matter, especially as it is for this reason, I conclude, that *Teig O'Kane*, still the weirdest of Irish folk-tales, has been omitted. He has printed it elsewhere, but one would gladly have had all his stories under one cover. He is so completely a Gael, alike in thought and literary idiom, that I do not think he could falsify a folk-tale if he tried. [1891]

W. B. Yeats. *Uncollected Prose of W. B. Yeats*,
Vol. 1, John P. Frayne, ed. (New York,
Columbia Univ. Pr., 1970), pp. 186–88

The name of Douglas Hyde has naturally been more prominently associated with the Gaelic Movement than with the Literary Revival. As a Gaelic writer he has attained a distinction which considerably enhances the force and value of his propaganda. The Revival, however, must always count him a powerful influence. It has derived strength and support from the collateral effect of Hyde's labours for the restoration of Gaelic, and to his direct collaboration it owes in part, if not entirely, some of its most fortunate achievements. The fundamental importance of the *Songs of Connacht* in the evolution of our contemporary literature has been insufficiently understood by the general public. Once Hyde had set the example, the possibilities of Gaelic-English were realised by the other writers, and greater credit has fallen to the better-known work of his successors. Lady Gregory, notably, employed his method in *Cuchulain of Muirthemne* and *The Book of Saints and Wonders*, with such effect that it is frequently forgotten how [Standish] O'Grady preceded her by a quarter of a century, in the field of legend, and Hyde by ten years, in the use of Anglo-Irish idiom. . . .

If peasant speech has now become an accepted convention of the Irish theatre, it is because the younger dramatists have confined themselves almost exclusively to the writing of peasant plays, both these mutually dependent facts being due to the prestige conferred upon the *genre* by Synge. His plays removed this speech from all the associations of low comedy and buffoonery which clung to it, and established the dignity and beauty of Anglo-Irish. While he consummated the rehabilitation of the idiom, the process had been definitely inaugurated by Douglas Hyde. *The Love Songs of Connacht* were the constant study of the author of *The Playboy*, whose plays testify, more than those of any other writer, to the influence of Hyde's prose. In thus stimulating the dramatist who was to leave so deep a mark upon the form of the Irish Theatre, Douglas Hyde must be counted an important force in the evolution of our national drama. Without injustice to the labours of W. B. Yeats, it may be said that the success of his efforts would not have been complete but for Synge. Had it not been for Hyde, the latter's most striking achievements might never have been known.

Ernest A. Boyd. Ireland's Literary Renaissance
(New York, John Lane, 1916), pp. 77–79

The lamentations attributed to Oisin, son of Finn, who lived in the fourth century and enjoyed a prolonged existence of some hundreds of years, are more or less of a piece . . . in the bemoaning of splendors irrevocably lost. The extravagant melancholy of the family bards of the seventeenth and eighteenth centuries sounds a similar note, and, in these latter, particularly, our minds fall away from the dirge, with a feeling that there is more duty than grief in some of the pieces.

We are apt to find more moving the melancholy songs of the country-side, composed by peasants and schoolmasters in the back-country of Ireland, after the disappearance of the professional bard, early in the eighteenth century. The love songs collected and translated by Dr. Douglas Hyde in the countryside of Connaught are, plainly, what he calls them—songs of the people, and not the work of professional poets. The dates of composition, naturally, are uncertain, since in many instances the songs have lived until now only on the lip, but one would hazard the guess that they belong to the eighteenth and nineteenth centuries. Dr. Hyde, in translating the poems, has sought to reproduce the exact meters and vowel rhymes of the originals. Many of these poems were sung to Irish country airs reputed to be of a marvelous beauty, and in reading the verses one must allow for the absence of that aid to appreciation. It would be difficult, I fancy, to find a slender body of literature anywhere that is so consistently sad, or a record of anonymous singers whose lives were so filled with the misery of poverty and broken hopes and unhappy love. The rescue of these songs serves to enrich enormously Ireland's already elaborate literature of lamentation.

David Morton. *The Renaissance of Irish Poetry: 1880–1930* (New York, Ives Washburn, 1929), pp. 192–93

Considering that the greater part of Hyde's energy was given up to propaganda, it is remarkable that no trace of this is to be found in his Literary History [*Literary History of Ireland*, 1899] which at once impresses the reader as being the work of a scholarly mind. In the early chapters this is shown in a careful analysis of the earliest writing from the point of view of historical accuracy. Hyde does not take anything for granted, but works carefully from step to step in his enquiry as to how far it is possible to rely on the early authorities and as to how much of the legendary history of Ireland is founded on fact. His critical attitude towards Irish literature is maintained all through; in places he seems to be unduly cautious, and to reject as unproved, episodes which if they were related in the history of any other land would be readily accepted as true. All this is interesting in the light it throws on Hyde's character. The leader of a popular movement seldom shows moderation and restraint in his writings on subjects akin to his movement. . . .

It appears that the Irish literary movement owed much to Hyde's work for its basic ideas. It also owed much to him in that his movement for educating Irishmen in a knowledge of their own country prepared an audience for Irish writers. When this has been said, how far is Hyde identified with the Irish writers of the early twentieth century?

On the whole, the answer seems to be that Hyde is not to be regarded as one of them. He stands quite apart. He does not base his reputation on his writings or his literary work; he was associated by environment and friendship with many of the literary men, but he did not seem to belong to them. His writings are all more scholarly than literary. This does not mean that he is a dry, pedantic writer; his writing is living and virile and shows that had he chosen to devote himself to writing he would have been among the leaders of the literary men. Yeats has expressed his indebtedness to Hyde's clear and simple style. But Hyde has not written a single book of pure literature. All his writings are associated with the Gaelic Revival. He has published folk tales, but not as did [Standish] O'Grady in *Finn and His Companions* or Yeats in *Irish Fairy Tales*. These are clearly the writings of men who hear a fine story and feel impelled to tell it in a beautiful form. Hyde's publications are as clearly those of a man whose first object is to record the tale in its traditional form. If there are two or three renderings, he compares them from the point of view of their antiquity or style. If he writes a translation, the translation is intended to show the spirit and, as far as possible, the form of the original story. The fact that Hyde is a fine writer enables him to do this with singular success, but this is accidental to the main object.

> Diarmid Coffey. *Douglas Hyde: President of Ireland*
> (Dublin, Talbot, 1938), pp. 133, 136–37

It was [an especial] kind of help that Yeats sought and received from Hyde when the twenty-three-year-old Yeats was eking out an existence by editing and selecting *Fairy and Folk Tales of the Irish Peasantry*, in 1888. Hyde supplied Yeats not only with many of the notes at the back of the book, and, within these, numerous translations and etymologies of Irish words important to the stories, but also three stories which he had translated from the Irish. One of these stories, "Teig O'Kane and the Corpse," Yeats called "the best told folk-tale in our literature." In letters Yeats told Ernest Rhys that it was the "finest thing in the book," and he noted to John O'Leary that "William Morris praises much Hyde's stories in Folklore book."

"Teig O'Kane," which serves so well to illustrate Hyde's superb story-telling art, is an incredibly weird story of the encounter of a mortal with fairy folk and people of the other world. Like many of the stories that fascinated Yeats, and of which he wrote a goodly number himself not unlike this one of Hyde's, the story requires not so much a suspension of disbelief as an attitude. This attitude is best described in the account of a great lady who was asked if, indeed, she could possibly believe in fairy folk, in the little people. She drew herself up grandly and replied, "Of course not! But they're there just the same." . . .

There is a brilliant simplicity in the story-telling, that seemingly artless art that doesn't seem a moment's thought. In this story, in more serious stories, in stories in the oral tradition surrounding the great mythological heroes of Ireland and the holy men, Hyde is an impressive artist and has left his imprint upon many of the great short story writers that have followed him. There are echoes of him in Yeats's *The Celtic Twilight* and particularly in the Red Hanrahan stories. But the impress is discernible in many others, in Padraic Colum, James Joyce, Frank O'Connor, and Mary Lavin, to mention a few. All these and more are in a direct line of a tradition in short story writing which, if not begun by Hyde—there were others before him, William Carleton, Patrick Kennedy, Crofton Croker, Standish O'Grady—nevertheless was a tradition made most vital by him at just the right moment in the course of a new movement in the literature of Ireland.

Lester Connor. In Raymond J. Porter and
James D. Brophy, eds., *Modern Irish Literature*
(New York, Iona College Pr./Twayne, 1972),
pp. 98–101

I have little time left in which to illustrate the skill of many another translator, or writer, "after the Irish" or "from the Irish"—such as Whitley Stokes, John Todhunter, Stopford Brooke, and above all, Douglas Hyde, to whom justice has by no means yet been done. His *Love Songs of Connaught* seems to me a crucial book from an historical point of view, but it is more than that. It was ostensibly translation, but was really poetry in its own right, written with perfect self-confidence and in a language understandable as English but with the allure of a foreign tongue, with a freshness as of spring water and a piercing simplicity. I think it is not unjust to say that Hyde's *Love Songs of Connaught*, published in 1893, contains some of the best poems of the second half of the century: for lyric intensity there is little to equal them. There seems to be no doubt that his translation into an idiom recognizably Anglo-Irish, but quite different from the Lover-Graves tradition, gave to the writers of the Irish Renaissance what we might almost call a distinct language, fresh and malleable, unset, unlike standard English, and without which they could hardly have done what they did.

I suggest also that the translation of the old Irish tales into English developed a feeling for narrative poetry, which in turn prepared the way for the dramatic work, and that all this translation from Irish into English verse of a high quality must have confirmed the sense of self-possession of Irish poets and further demonstrated to the world that there did exist an Anglo-Irish "poetic literature" quite distinct from the English poetry.

Lorna Reynolds. In Séan Lucy, ed., *Irish Poets in
English* (Cork, Mercier, 1972), p. 102

. . . A fact not hitherto sufficiently noted is the extent to which Hyde, as an author, was influenced by the work of Scottish Highland writers. It is a significant fact that of his original collection of Gaelic books, one quarter is made up of Scottish works, and these are mainly collections of folk literature. The similarity between these publications and Hyde's own is striking. . . . It can hardly be doubted that the example of men like John Mackenzie inspired Hyde to do for his corner of Ireland what they had done for the Highlands of Scotland. His growing interest in the work of the Scottish folklorists is proved by the fact that whereas the first five or six books in Scottish Gaelic that occur in his list were acquired by chance (at the auction of John O'Daly's library), the remaining twenty or so volumes were ordered expressly from Scotland, and these, acquired between August 1879 and July 1880, when he was about twenty years of age, made up almost the whole of the final quarter of his basic Gaelic library. It is surely more than a coincidence that it was around the same time that he began seriously to devote himself to rescuing from oblivion the songs and stories of the native Irish speakers around his corner of Connaught.

Next to guaranteeing the authenticity of his Gaelic originals, Hyde's main concern was to find the form of language best suited to their presentation in English. Here we come to one of the most important aspects of Hyde's work, the fact that he pioneered a manner of speech that was to become the vernacular, so to speak, of the Anglo-Irish literary movement, the model for Lady Gregory's "Kiltartanese," Synge's plays and indeed the standard speech of the early Abbey Theatre.

The first thing to be said in this regard is that nothing could have been further from Hyde's conscious mind that the evolution of a distinct idiom for Irish poets and playwrights who worked in English. First and last, Hyde's aim was to convey, as far as any translator could, to those who could not experience it in the original Gaelic, the genuine essence and flavour of the people's songs and stories. He was in no way satisfied with "the various garbs in which the sophisticated minds of the ladies and gentlemen who trifled in such matters, clothed the dry bones" of the traditional tales. In his estimation, "When the skeletons were thus padded round and clad, although built upon folklore, they were no longer folklore themselves."

Dominic Daly. *The Young Douglas Hyde* (Totowa, N.J., Rowman & Littlefield, 1974), pp. 106–7

An Ascendancy child who early rejected the Ascendancy attitudes ticked off by Daniel Corkery—insolence, recklessness, cynicism, hardness—Hyde also rejected the Ascendancy role assigned him—that of a Protestant clergyman—as his unpublished allegory of 1883 reveals. But historians allude to him today as "the gentle Hyde" angry at not a living soul; a man of gentle demeanor, derived, they claim from his upbringing in an Irish-Anglican rectory. It is hard to find Hyde the poteen-drinker, snuff-user, crowd-mover. Rather is he depicted as the genteel idealist who thought that Ireland's twin traditions of poverty and spirituality should be made to find new expression in a fast-fading language for some ill-defined purpose.

There is no such ambiguity surrounding the literary Hyde. In his most important books, *Beside the Fire* (1890), *Love Songs of Connacht* (1893), and

Religious Songs of Connacht (1906), he showed himself to be the most serious collector and translator of Gaelic verse. Yeats called the *Love Songs of Connacht* "one of those rare books in which art and life are one . . . completely blended." What had happened was that Hyde, the Ascendancy man, himself sprung free of that class's worst attributes, had created an Anglo-Irish speech that was a new literary idiom—a source for the rise of a new national drama in the hands of Synge and Lady Gregory. Its power and flexibility would also improve Hyde's own verse in Irish. With the ear and technical skill of a poet he would reproduce internal rimes and assonances and even the stresses of his Gaelic original. Ironically, his connection with the Ascendancy helped give prestige to the peasant dialect he had first uncovered as a folklorist and then revived as translator and poet.

Gareth W. Dunleavy, *Douglas Hyde* (Lewisburg,
Pa., Bucknell Univ. Pr., 1974), pp. 88–89

JOHNSTON, DENIS (1901–1985)

. . . Denis Johnston comes before us as a satiric dramatist with *The Moon in the Yellow River* and *The Old Lady Says 'No!'*

My judgment is subject to revision when I see the plays performed; but in the meantime I am not satisfied with *The Old Lady*. Mr. Con. Curran who saw the plays and contributes a Foreword, hails *The Old Lady Says 'No!'* "a play brilliantly witty, an Ithuriel spear at work, stabbing and revealing." I hail a brilliant stage-piece, but I reserve the title of drama. In *The Old Lady Says 'No!'* the mechanical technique is good, the "thematic pastiche" admirable, the satire rare, passages exhibit a power of dramatic characterisation, as in the dialogue between the Flapper and the Medical Student, others again are perfunctorily artistic as in the Speaker's speech to Sally (p. 242), the one including a line from "Dark Rosaleen." (It would be impossible to show the quality of these speeches as excerpts).

If this is a play in the creative dramatic sense, if it is capable of striking ultimately with a simple dramatic effect, it is as the play of a city where the Blind man walks seeing (tragically) "no City of the Living: but of the Dark and the Dead!" That is the keynote of the play in so far as it has for me real dramatic being. It may be that all its complexity of situation, its brilliance of dialogue and satire, of intellect, sub-serve through this idea, a dramatic purpose. My opinion formed from reading it, is that the dramatic principle in it has succumbed to the destructive method.

The Moon in the Yellow River is a play, partly, also, expressionist in form; it dips into the region of Strindbergian psychology, but, unlike Strindberg, without being morbid. Perhaps in the satirical commentary it is too careful to give always both sides, between Republic and Free State, spirit and machine—though a few things stand out luminously in the debate, for example, the revolutionary Blake's motive—"to keep one corner of the world safe for humanity"—but *The Moon in the Yellow River* is a play—a curiously inverted tragedy, in which, with a flash of genius, Mr. Johnston has perceived the drama of the industrialist Fausch to be the drama of Octavius—

"DOBELLE. Your World! your memories! Brutus is avenged, O, Octavius."

But although these works are accidentally blown up, in the third act—the play is still a tragedy, the tragic drama of nothing learned and nothing done, as Dobelle sees "There's no end and there's no solution."

No more remarkable first work was ever written surely than *The Old Woman Says 'No!'*; no second play more distinctly an original dramatic achievement than *The Moon in the Yellow River*.

DM. Jan., 1934, pp. 80–81

Mr. Denis Johnston is the most important new force in Irish drama since Mr. Sean O'Casey, but his two latest plays are a little disappointing. The more important of the two is *A Bride for the Unicorn*, a satiric fantasy, whose style reminds one of *The Old Lady Says 'No!'* and whose construction is even more daring. It has been re-written since it was first produced at the Gate Theatre, but the alterations, while they make the plot a good deal easier to grasp, do not take away the impression that the author has attempted to cover too much ground. All the major follies of life—those of war, finance, politics, the law and marriage—cannot be treated together in a single play with much hope of success, and this modern quest for the Golden Fleece explores so many byways that it tends to lose itself.

Storm Song contrasts in the strongest possible manner with the intricacies of *A Bride for the Unicorn*. It is a perfectly straightforward drama, with few subtleties either of thought or expression, and its subject was evidently suggested by the making of the film *Man of Aran*. Mr. Johnston has provided an interesting study of the producer, Szilard, and the minor characters are drawn with skill.

Irish Times. June 1, 1935, p. 7

Denis has passion, his life and his work give proof of it. And in his work one may glimpse the poet and the mystic. There are passages of rare beauty. Here the phrase is not just cliché, but an exact assessment. Moments of inspired penetration, and moments of deep sentiment. But always these are followed by that scuttling back up the mountain. It is never a retreat to a hole in the ground: there is nothing furtive about Denis, nothing mean; but there is a littleness that is all the more evident for his moments of greatness. He seems to require the bleak West British mountain to give him stature.

The things that we like or that influence us are the best guides to ourselves. Denis has proved himself a Ulysses. It is no accident that in his early work he was as much influenced by Joyce as the later O'Casey seems to have been influenced by Denis Johnston.

For his first play *The Old Lady Says No!*, I have nothing but admiration and gratitude. It is the finest Irish work that has been written for the theatre since I came to this country years ago. It is marred a little by obscurity. This is the hall-mark of its period. In the twenties we credited our audiences with the kind of intelligence that a few among them claimed. This was a mistake. Our mistake, not the audiences'. But the play has genuine greatness, real power to move, and leaves a lasting impression; more it has humour. We have not mentioned Denis's humour, but it is there in abundance. Of course it is a wicked and malicious humour. How could it be otherwise in a man reared among the cave-boys and girls of Dublin's intelligentsia? Their motto is "Don't look; smite with your laughter, and back to the cave lest you are trapped into admiration or respect." Therefore, Denis must scoff a little at everything, particularly at his own feelings, and at what he most admires. *The Old Lady Says No!* is fine because, in spite of this, all that was pent up in him from birth to the moment of writing came surging out—his genuine loves, his less genuine hates. It is a triumph over himself, and here I think is part of his secret revealed.

But there was still something left; enough to fill the sails of the argosy that carried the *Bride for the Unicorn* out to a sea on which she has never quite found a port. Here again is the Ulysses theme; *The Old Lady Says No!*, possibly unconsciously, was given a Greek structure, the shape and form of Greek drama; Protagonist, The Speaker, Robert Emmet; Deutoragonist, Sara Curran, The Old Lady; Tritagonist, Grattan; and then the Chorus. Now, in *A Bride for the Unicorn*, the perfection of structure is shattered. It becomes cumbersome and overcomplex, and in its place the Ulysses theme merely inspires a Greek feeling expressed through constant analogy. Yet the form of the play is as unGreek as the Gothicism of Notre Dame . . . relying for its efficient performance upon mechanical appliance, rostra, steps and swift scenic changes, and even requiring for complete representation a revolving stage.

It is an interesting and inevitable development of the author's stage technique, answering to the call of the theatre fashion of its period. But, like other plays in this method, it is a step in the wrong direction. The author has started to produce his play on paper. But it is only half-produced. *The Old Lady Says No!* was as unproduced as a Shakespeare play.

Hilton Edwards. The Bell. Oct., 1946, pp. 10–12

Denis Johnston had just turned forty when he was sent out to the British Eighth Army as a war reporter for the BBC. He reached the front at the time Rommel had the British on the run; he worked in the desert, then in the long uphill campaign through Italy, and finally with the Americans in Germany; and out of his experiences has come a powerfully written book, *Nine Rivers from Jordan*. One cannot classify it, for it is autobiography, adventure, parody, mysticism, and farce.

This is the realistic and spiritual odyssey of one man in war. It is a moving and personal document charged with the frustrations, the comedy, the gallantry, and the revulsion of the conflict. The narrative begins in Egypt as we follow the retreat and ultimate victory at El Alamein. We see the author at a formal dinner with the Arabs and in a forward command post with a hot-tempered South African general who is blasting the RAF for having bombed his trucks. We feel Johnston's exasperation as a war correspondent not knowing whether his recorded discs have reached London, and his humiliation when he hears his stale records being played on the desert air for the jeering troops. We have his vivid portraits of Montgomery and Churchill and Alexander, and his more intimate thumbnail sketches of those against whom he competed in his search for news that would pass the censor.

The author describes the three periods of his war experiences this way: Egypt and the Arabs were his Homeric period; the British and the Italians his middle period; the Americans and the Germans his final, New World period. And this categorical development marks a moral development in his own life. He observes that the first steps being taken in our post-war policy toward the Germans will be harsh, and he strenuously objects. His sympathy and concern are still with the Germans. He finds himself in Eckartsberga, where the German girl lived who wrote the letters he had come upon in Egypt. She is nowhere to be found, but he is directed to a concentration camp at the outskirts of town. It is there that be beholds the full horror of war, and its impact is devastating.

Denis Johnston is a fine reporter, a romantic Irishman, and a sensitive, searching, conscientious human being who is interested in all manner of men and has a wonderful time talking to himself about religion, about his divorced wife, about his young son whom he misses, about his love of poetry, and about anything else that catches the attention of his warm-blooded Irish imagination. He writes with a zest, a power, and a sense of mystery which T. E. Lawrence would have respected.

Edward Weeks. At. Sept., 1955, p. 78

Johnston's plays have not had the popular impact of O'Casey's or Carroll's or Behan's, for none of them has a simple theatrical theme as even the best plays of O'Casey do. His plays are not obscure in the way that Beckett's are, for Johnston is not, I think, an ambiguous writer. He does use the drama as an intelligent rather than as a simple-minded art. To that extent, he is at war with his form; this conflict makes him both interesting and somewhat unproduced.

Perhaps the best way to make sense out of his diversity of styles is to note how in succeeding plays he seems to be searching for a compromise between significant statement and theatrical necessity. His first play *The Old Lady Says "No!"*, is his most unbendingly intellectual. It is perhaps a young man's play, because of its brilliance, its brittle ironies, its dazzling reliance upon allusions and its uncompromising demand for an amount of information no audience has ever collectively had. As Johnston became more a man of the theatre—came to know more about audiences, acting, directing, set design, theatre construction, the college and the commercial theatre—he became less willing to settle for excellence *in vacuo*. A play in the theatre must touch its audience constantly, and his later plays attempt to do just that. However, they attempt to touch the audience not merely emotionally, as O'Casey and Behan do, but more fully—both emotionally and intellectually. This poses a knotty problem and is probably the reason Johnston once remarked, "The variety of style that the plays disclose is simply a reflection of my search for an adequate means of communication." He has certainly not reached the end of his search; but in an ideal theatre in an ideal civilization, with an audience composed of Shavian He-Ancients, Johnston might appear a better playwright than either O'Casey or Behan who, despite their excellences, used the stage as a primitive and naive art.

Johnston's first play, *The Old Lady Says "No!"*, is one of the few plays to use allusion as thickly as does modern poetry. Its strong theatrical merits can hardly be fully appreciated unless one has studied the playscript closely, chased down many unfamiliar allusions, and understood their historical context. That seems an unusual demand for a play to make, but modern poets like Eliot and Pound have made even more burdensome demands. One may laboriously disentangle the wealth of allusions in *The Waste Land* or *The Pisan Cantos* without being able to bring either work into intellectual focus. Not so of *The Old Lady*. When one has the information, the play has the clarity that the theatre demands.

I have no space to write a gloss of the play, but I can appropriately theorize about Johnston's technique and intention. His intention is to criticize Ireland by creating provocative ironic contrasts between ideals and practice. Mainly, he contrasts a romantic patriotism of the past with a modern sentimentalizing of that ideal and with an even more modern emptiness of spirit. The effect is sardonic negation: the ideal has been punctured, the sentimental has been made to appear spurious, and the tawdry emptiness has triumphed.

Robert Hogan. *After the Irish Renaissance*
(Minneapolis, Univ. of Minnesota Pr., 1967),
pp. 134–35

Denis Johnston is alive but he won't lie down. Or so it would appear, for according to the jacket of the first volume of *Dramatic Works* the second volume is to contain a pageant called *The Tain*, a dramatisation of *Nine Rivers from Jordan*, as well as reprints of four other plays. Johnston was from the first an experimentalist, at the very fore-front of the newly-founded Dublin Gate Theatre Studio. Subsequently he wrote for the Abbey Theatre and for the Gate with dizzying variation—now an obscure allegory using all the technical resources of the theatre, as in *A Bride for the Unicorn*, now a seemingly conventional piece of realism, as in *Strange Occurrence on Ireland's Eye*. A certain amount of restlessness is evident in all this oscillation, and perhaps a certain amount of uncertainty also. In the Preface to the *Collected Plays*, published in 1960, Johnston himself adverted to the variety of his output and the difficulty of finding any unifying principle in it, and he concluded:

"Whether or not there is any common denominator, I should perhaps say that the variety of style that the plays disclose is simply a reflection of my search for an adequate means of communication." It is perhaps this very restlessness, this steering clear of any movement or programme, that gives to Johnston's work its unique place in the history of modern Irish drama.

"Search" is, indeed, the predominant motif of the plays in general. In his most famous, though hardly his best, play Johnston sets Robert Emmet in search of Sarah Curran, the impossible ideal. In the later plays the search is often for an exit from the nightmare imposed by history or by circumstances. As one character in *Strange Occurrence* puts it, they are "in search of a miasma that they're pleased to call the truth." In every case, even in his play about 1916, *The Scythe and the Sunset*, the search is individualistic, concerned less with social than with existential ends. His heroes are all Holy Fools, absurdly out of phase with the society they inhabit. Yet they are capable of self-realisation, as Emmet is, through resolute adherence to the individual dream. The cost of pursuit, Johnson admits, is often violence and even death, but he is sufficiently romantic—for all his Shavian qualities—to promote the quest no matter what the price. A' neglected play in this context is *Storm Song*, here reprinted. It tells of a fanatic director who prefers to die in filming a real storm at sea rather than to fake it in a studio. Johnston here uses the stage and the imagery of cinematography to explore the ambiguities of authenticity. As the film being made is clearly based on *Man of Aran* the style of the play is in the main naturalistic, as it were Syngean; but repeatedly there are breaks away from the unit set, and one gets this kind of direction: "*We are back in the living-room at Tigh na Beith, except that on this occasion we view the room from another angle.*" The last phrase sums up how Johnston unites theme and technique. The meaning of the search is conveyed by the variety of angles from which experience is viewed. Johnston's plays are explorations of the knowable, always in terms of the theatre itself, the area of necessary illusion.

Christopher Murray. IUR. Autumn, 1977,
pp. 288–89

By the time he was thirty-five, Johnston had four plays behind him, two of which—*The Moon in the Yellow River* and *The Old Lady Says "No!"*—seem destined to represent substantial and lasting contributions to Anglo-Irish drama of the first half of the twentieth century. Curtis Canfield, his first serious American critic, wrote in Johnston's thirty-fifth year that he was "the spearhead of the new Irish Drama," in whom, "more than in any other Irish playwright of the present time, the hope of the literary drama lies." There have been those who feel that promise was not fulfilled. Some, like Hilton Edwards, the masterly director of his first play, thought he had simply tried to do too much to be able to realize his potential as a dramatist.

Certainly Johnston's work is uneven. After beginning his career with two striking plays which were highly praised, in the Thirties and early Forties he went on to do five more which were interesting but would hardly comprise the cornerstone of a major reputation. In the 1950s, he wrote a serious courtroom drama as well as an extremely fine Irish history play, which have temporarily concluded his career. Of his nine full-length plays, then, three are superb. In addition, there is also an excellent historical study of Swift and an unusually fascinating, multi-leveled report of the war years. These would seem to be the basis of Johnston's reputation at present, and it is a substantial foundation. There seems no reason to question the assessment that outside Synge and O'Casey (Beckett constituting a special case), Johnston is probably the only other Irish dramatist "who might stand up to serious critical examination in the context of world drama. . . ." Robert Hogan goes further and insists that Johnston has more than lived up to his promise. "The promise that has not been fulfilled is that of the theatre itself." To cavil about Johnston's *oeuvre* is really, in Hilton Edwards' words, to pay him "the compliment of expecting more from him, knowing . . . his potentiality." . . .

Owing practically nothing to the poetic folk drama or the realistic peasant plays of the early years of the renaissance, he is really in the mainstream of experimental world drama of the 1920s. Johnston's work will indeed stand up to critical examination in comparison with the best of modern drama.

Gene A. Barnett. *Denis Johnston* (Boston, Twayne, 1978), pp. 154–55

Denis Johnston's best work is characterized by compassionate detachment, by fairness and a long view. Interestingly, with one exception his work is grounded in fact, in events that have really happened. His writing is pervaded by objectivity, decency, integrity and a steady impulse towards clarity. One feels safe in the worlds of his best plays, trustful that he will wrest from his interpretations of history a balanced, humane view without sacrificing artistic or factual complexity. Johnston writes to understand more, not to purge his private nightmares or his personal demons. He is a reflective writer. I felt, as I worked in his home and sometimes talked with him about his grandchildren or his daughter's budding career as a novelist, that he didn't write to survive, but to make sense. It's a quality in his work that I admire and enjoy; it helps us all hold on to the essential sanity of life beyond the tragedy and irony of history.

One thing that continues to intrigue me is Johnston's habit of not considering his work as finished—of not treating it as complete for eternity. Much to the scholar's consternation, Johnston periodically changes his plays, and particularly the endings ("finalities" he calls them). If he sees differently over time, he simply makes changes to accord with his new vision. His autobiography, *Nine Rivers from Jordan*, has two different endings; *The Moon in the Yellow River* has several conclusions; *A Bride for the Unicorn* is still, according to Johnston, a play he's working on nearly half a century after its pre-mière; and he just recently revised the ending of *The Scythe and the Sunset* eighteen years after its first production. It's possible, though, instead of con-sidering these changes as evidence of uncertainty (as several commentators have), that we can see them as representing, very simply, a free attitude to-wards art. Nothing is so perfect or so sacred that it must exist for all time in unaltered form.

Actually, this iconoclastic view is in accord with one of Johnston's im-portant philosophical tenets. He is fascinated by the nature of time and pos-its multiple time dimensions. We live in a linear past, present, future time scheme. He asks: How could we even perceive this linearity if we weren't outside it or beyond it in some way? Thus, only in linear time, which is a very limited and incomplete approach to the nature of time, does an event have a fixed beginning, a conclusive end or an unalterable meaning. However, Johnston's philosophy of time does not completely explain his organic and open view of the artistic process. I see the alterations and revisions of his work as expressions of his own deepening understanding of life. It's wonder-ful that as Johnston sees more deeply and truly, he feels the freedom to alter his work and not to view it as finished and inviolable.

> Harold Ferrar. In Joseph Ronsley, ed.,
> *Denis Johnston: A Retrospective* (Gerrards Cross,
> England, Colin Smythe, 1981), pp. 190–91

The dismal dialectics Dobelle sees at work everywhere [in *The Moon in the Yellow River*] develop into Johnston's philosophy of history in *The Scythe and the Sunset*, his reply to O'Casey's *Plough*. Contrary to O'Casey, Johnston concentrates on the motives of both the rebels and the British and not so much on the effect the Rising has on the Dublin population. . . . In his preface Johnston mentions the "passing of an imperial civilization" and the "conflict of the man with the idea against the man of action" and not the bitter fate of helpless individuals in a world of chaos as the play's universal themes.

Johnston's approach to the 1916 rebellion is deductive. The mental pa-tient Endymion fulfils a choric function voicing in verse Johnston's convic-tions that the Easter Rising meant the beginning of the decline of the British Empire and that historical progress is not simply the result of one conflicting party's victory over the other, but rather of a subtle dialectic in which the side wins that can best abstain from self-destruction by playing "the other fellow's game." . . .

The manner in which Johnston tries to vindicate the men of 1916 and to explain the events they were involved in is less [than] convincing. The Blakean dialectics of the rulers engineering their own downfall and of the reb-els turning martyrdom into redemption do not figure as what they are, the con-struction Johnston puts upon the rebellion in retrospect, but as the universal law of history which necessarily manifests itself in the Easter Rising too. The rebels' loss of their innocence, their realization that wars can only be won if military conventions are disregarded, appears as a late confirmation of Dobelle's sinister belief that historical progress is brought about by evil men only. Tetley's readiness to sacrifice himself is presented as his strategy to provoke severe reactions by the British which will turn the rebels' military defeat into a psychological victory. Whatever may have induced the men in the Post Office to see themselves as martyrs defending a holy cause and to act accordingly, it can hardly have been the prescience of Sir John Maxwell's harsh and politically foolish retaliatory measures. Johnston imputes that the results of his retrospective analysis of the Rising underlay the insurgents' actions as conscious motives. This method of presenting retrospection as foresight makes Tetley's martyrdom appear as forced as Palliser's suicide.

The real problem with the philosophical superstructure Johnston imposes on the Easter Rising in *The Scythe* is not that it cannot be integrated into the play in a psychologically convincing manner, but rather that it tends to make a singular event in history look like a model of historical change as such. In *The Old Lady* Johnston reveals and criticizes the cycle of destruction that seems to determine Irish politics and in *The Moon* he tries to show that there are humar ways to get the better of it. But in *The Scythe* he seems to reinstate the vicious circle of rebellion and ruin as the inevitable pattern of history.

Jochem Achilles. In Heinz Kosok, ed., *Studies in Anglo-Irish Literature* (Bonn, Bouvier, 1982), pp. 275–77

JOHNSTON, JENNIFER (1930–   )

The most balanced view of [the Big Houses] is to be found, not surprisingly, in fiction rather than in history books, and though it is not, I presume, the author's direct intention, the novels of Jennifer Johnston can act, if not as defence counsel, then as mitigation pleader, in chronicling the latter days of the unceltic twilight. Somerville and Ross had recorded seismographically early tremors, especially in *The Real Charlotte*, but they could not bring themselves to face the end of their world directly. Miss Johnston, with the knowledge that their ideals while not specifically concerned with the good of an independent Ireland were real (and, as it turned out, helpful to the raw self-conscious country), can present their case without special pleading and do it skillfully so that even the most rabid Nationalist is left with a sense of compassion at their eclipse and relief that some of their achievements survived. . . .

[Miss Johnston's] most recent novel, *How Many Miles to Babylon?*, deals with the last full-bloom of the Big House rose. It is the personal narrative of Alexander Moore, whose career as an officer on the Western Front is about to be ended rather unusually with his execution for the murder of a private soldier. "Because I am an officer and a gentleman they have not taken away my bootlaces or my pen. . . ." His memories range over his childhood —the largest part of his short life—and we recognise it as the childhood of MacMahon and Prendergast: private education in a gracious house in a landscaped demesne, a mother happily trapped in upper-class aspic, and a father, wise, gentle and weak. Also, the solitary son of the Big House makes his only friend in Jerry Crowe the stable boy and there is some nice comedy as each influences the other; Jerry's peasant coarseness is smoothed down while Alec learns of Granuaile and the Sean-Bhean Bhoct. In spite of rancorous opposition from the mother the friendship continues until each is driven to enlist. Alec by his mother's insistent need for sacrifice and Jerry so that he may learn to be a soldier for Ireland in the coming struggle.

It is here that Miss Johnston's writing takes a great leap forward. Her description of the recruits' leavetaking, the botched suicide attempts, the ultimate madness of the trenches is a miraculous piece of imaginative reconstruction. Her writing about the war is as good as Graves' and Remarque's though in a quite different way. One set-piece which, without being obtrusive is screaming to be anthologised, is an hilarious account of a fox-hunt in Flanders with Jerry, Alec and another expendable youngster, Lt. Bennett. Jerry leaves the line to find his missing father, establishes that he has been killed (necessary this for his mother's pension) and on his return is sentenced as a deserter. Alec in a last act of friendship shoots him while in his mind dance the words of "The Croppy Boy," surely the most haunting of the '98 ballads and one that he originally learned from Jerry. At least one Anglo-Irishman did something to even the score and in death was not divided. The novel reads like the tying-up of the last threads of a tapestry. It is a statement of reconciliation— the closing of an account besides being an expression of fine anger at gross wastage.

It is likely that Miss Johnston will fare further now; she never staked out a claim on the Anglo-Irish territory. Her technical ability, her handling of dialogue, her tact when writing about youth and age, her detachment, her humour, her quality of imagination, above all, her economy—the longest of her books is only 117 pages—all mark her out as a writer who may someday become great. She is perhaps lucky that it is in their gothic decay that the Big Houses are most attractive. . . . She has helped to define the past they played in the Ireland of their time and their effects now. . . . I will be surprised if Miss Johnston continues to work this theme, but if she does, since harking back is *le vice Irlandaise*, her work will still have relevance and of course delight.

Sean McMahon. *Irish Press*. Feb. 22, 1975, p. 32

Jennifer Johnston's third novel [*Shadows on Our Skin*] is a sophisticated account of a family in Northern Ireland during the present troubles. Seen through the eyes of a schoolboy, the novel focuses primarily on his relationship with his family: a cranky, ex-Republican father, a fussy, protective mother, an elder brother home from England with the confused and dangerous notion that he will carry on in the "Movement" and emulate his father's "heroic" past. The boy is also drawn to a girl teacher from Wicklow whose own loneliness in Derry causes her to befriend him and then, to his dismay, to have a brief relationship with his brother, ending for her in a beating by his "friends." In the background of these relationships lie the troubles of Derry: gunfire, soldiers in the street, ambushes, house searches and arrests. It is one of the book's achievements, and an indication of its skill, that public distress and private stress impinge on each other, the one an extension and a definition of the other.

The novel's taut narrative portrays the world of self and family, conflict within and without in a compelling manner. Jennifer Johnston has a good eye for detail, for the accurate depiction of concrete reality that gives grit to the novel and gives the reader confidence in her work. There are several moments of fine realised writing capturing, for example, the tensions of the boy's home or the warm delicacy of his feelings for the schoolteacher, and there is the release and powerful evocative picnic to the old fort of Grianan that lifts mythically above the whole surrounding landscape of Derry and from which they look down at the fortified city.

Projecting her vision of things through the consciousness of the boy, the novelist accepts the limitations that follow as the story reveals his progress through innocence into experience; events grind at his innocence, even as he deals bravely with them and tries to capture some of the experience in words. This novel of adolescence is mercifully free from the familiar traumas of Irish Catholic youth. In a quite brilliant and contemporary way Jennifer Johnston frees herself and her characters from intrusive social, religious and political contexts, from the nightmare of history, although they too belong to the shadows that are present.

Maurice Harmon. *IUR*. Autumn, 1977, pp. 298–99

[In *The Old Jest*] Jennifer Johnston treads easily and gracefully through the Ireland of the 1920 "troubles," avoiding all pitfalls of Irish caricature and period charm. Nancy is just 18, an orphan living with her Aunt Mary and her grandfather, old General Dwyer, on the coast about half an hour's train-ride south from Dublin. Although in love with 26-year-old Harry, she is intelligent enough and realistic enough to know that he is unsuitable and in any case is in love with someone else. She teases Harry unmercifully—about his job as a stockbroker, about his conventional clothes, about his lack of experience with girls. When she goads him into admitting his virginity, he calls her "a dreadful little brat" and she retorts. "I'll tell you one thing. I'll have done it by the time I'm twenty-six." Nevertheless, she remains potty about him, wishing she could "see how his body looks when he is naked, coming stark out of the sea, shining with wetness."

Nancy's unsatisfied romantic longings are focused on a mysterious stranger whom she meets one day on a lonely stretch of beach. She wonders if he could be her father, who perhaps had not died in India after all. After several meetings, during which she learns that he is an active revolutionary, a republican idealist who believes that it is necessary to kill for the cause, she falls under his spell and agrees to deliver a message for him in Dublin. Unwittingly, she has a hand in the murder of some British soldiers at the Curragh—and in her hero's death when a party of British soldiers finds the two of them together on the beach.

The Old Jest is a quite delightful novel about growing up. While the old General sits in his wheelchair scanning the railway line with his binoculars and singing snatches of hymns like "Swift to its close ebbs out life's little day," Nancy experiences unrequited love and witnesses violent death. Aunt Mary, who comes back from a race meeting one evening "gaily intoxicated by several wins, several drinks and the undemanding good humour of her friends," talks seriously for once to Nancy: "I've been happy, calm and useless most of the time. The great thing to remember is that there is nothing to be afraid of. You learn that as you get older. We live in a state of perpetual fear. All the horrible things we do to each other, all our misunderstandings, are because of fear." What Nancy learns, as she grows older during the events of August 1920, seeing her admired revolutionary shot and killed after he'd thrown down his own weapon, hearing that her "beautiful" Harry is going to get engaged to the tiresome girl whose father is going to "develop" the village, is that "you can always choose, and then . . . you've no one to blame but yourself." The strength of *The Old Jest* lies in its delicacy, in its restraint, untypically Irish qualities which make Jennifer Johnston's books so satisfying: no lip-service here to "My Dark Rosaleen."

John Mellors. LondonMag. Dec., 1979, pp. 131–32

"Profoundly moving," "magnificent," "totally absorbing," "marvelous," "noble"—I read these quotes from British reviews of *The Christmas Tree* and I thought well, perhaps it won't be so bad. And I was right. Jennifer Johnston is a polished and talented writer, but in her latest novel she hasn't shown us a surprise, a quirk, a style all her own, a moment that sticks in the mind, or anything else that deserves those encomiums.

Constance Keating leaves Ireland when she is about 20 years old to go to London and try to be a novelist. After producing three novels, she is told by an editor that though she has some talent she doesn't want or need or love writing enough to produce a good book. She believes him, although she is a virgin in her 40's who has given up everything else in order to write.

On a holiday in Italy she meets Jacob Weinberg, a Polish Jew who has had his fingers broken by the Nazis so that he could not play the piano like his father. As Jacob puts it, he plays the typewriter instead. He writes funny books—a funny occupation for a man with his history.

Except for the fact that he calls Constance "Irish woman" and inclines toward what someone described as "cafe weltschmerz," Jacob is all right. I like him for saying to Constance after their first night together: "We won't set the world on fire. For a little while we will struggle to be a little content."

Mostly, people in *The Christmas Tree* say the expected things. Constance's mother says of her father, "He gave me everything I wanted and left me alone." She says that he was one of those men who "need women, but don't like them." Constance's father is, of course, remote, abstract in utterance, a bit bored and a bit at a loss in the role. Are there any other kinds of fathers in novels now?

Without Jacob's knowledge, Constance gets herself pregnant—an idea that is no better in a novel than in life. But no sooner does she deliver the baby, at the age of 44, than she discovers that she is dying of leukemia.

Now Miss Johnston's troubles start. While it is impossible to write about death without sentimentality—it is the one inevitable moment of sentimentality in our lives—this sentimentality must have weight, be drastic. Whatever originality there may be in a character who is dying in a novel, the author has to find it. It is depressing to write routinely about death: it puts everything in doubt if even *this* can't stir up something strong. To make death new might be said to be one of the obligations of fiction. . . .

Though we can't expect everyone in real life to die with powerful imagery, we do expect it in a novel. Death is the strongest image we've got, even stronger than love or hate, and if an author can't conjure with it, she ought to leave it alone. Please do not litter death.

Constance says she would like to "see the pattern" of her life, or in life. She makes quite a fuss about a Christmas tree with blue lights. Well, as Hemingway said, death might come on a bicycle, so I suppose it can come on a Christmas tree with blue lights too. It is one of those images, though, like the fog coming on little cat feet, that is too diminutive, too endearing.

Anatole Broyard. *NYTd*. March 31, 1982, p. 21

The self-contained world that Johnston's fiction describes, the sealed spaces where the storyteller plots his fictions and maps his battle plans, is a world that bears significant resemblance to the separate, isolated, enclosed spaces that have so meticulously been described by women novelists writing about women: a similar atmosphere of exclusion and seclusion has been portrayed with clinical precision by Doris Lessing, Margaret Drabble, Susan Hill, Edna O'Brien, Barbara Pym, Jean Rhys and Elizabeth Bowen. The "woman's novel" predicates itself on the notion that social separateness is an *a priori* condition of the woman in contemporary society. Johnston's work seems to

suggest that such exclusive status is not necessarily peculiar to women: the title of this essay ["The Masculine World of Jennifer Johnston"], then, is entirely inappropriate to her subject as I have described it: this world is not masculine, not open, access.ble, social, a world of action, but rather specifically
feminine: closed, suffocated, lonely, and inward-turning. The apparent suggestion of these novels is that the *male* world is secret, sealed off, plotted by
means of battle lines and codes, cut off by arbitrary divisions, checkpoints,
military demarcations, that life is perceived to be a series of strategies and di-
versionary tactics to keep the enemy at bay and that privacy is a retreat to the
"comparative safety of the trenches," while the more social, open stance sub-
mits the ego to constant scrutiny and observation. The metaphorical terms
delineating this world are certainly masculine, but the world itself—and the
condition of those who inhabit it—shares more with Virginia Woolf than with
Anthony Powell. While the component elements of her world are certainly
drawn from the little-boy games of playing war, which turn out to be the
grown-up games of making war, it is not at all clear that the essential subject
of this fiction has anything to do with masculinity or maleness. The metaphor
of trench warfare, of warfare under conditions where one's loyalties are un-
clear and one's ultimate goal is held in question, of tracking the enemy
through field glasses down the railway line, seems to hold as a kind of statement about the survival of human beings in general and of the literary artist in
particular. Against the myth of Irish storytellers, the ebullient, social beings,
at home amidst the hard-drinking and long-talking pub patrons, Johnston pos-
its another kind of Irish voice—one that is not clearly even Irish but rather
transplanted and misplaced, one that is neither male nor female (there is little
difference in tone or style, even in subject matter, between Minnie Mac-
Mahon and Nancy Gulliver's tales and Alexander Moore's or between Joe
Logan's poetry and Diarmid's battle plans), one that is distinctly separate
from and aligned against its origins and impetus. In short, these do not seem
to be stories that are told "naturally," that arise from shared assumptions
between speaker and audience as to the efficacy of or the motivations for
storytelling; rather, they seem to be bred in spite of the impetus to stop them,
against the tactics of the enemy (the larger social intrusion) which would force
these to be stories of another kind, to be tales of community rather than the
lonely individual, stories of success rather than of stalemate, stories that are
shared rather than kept secret. Instead, these narratives are told outside the
time frame they delineate, are told from the perspective of an isolation that
has been enforced (*How Many Miles to Babylon?* and *Shadows on Our Skin*)
or by one that has been violated (*The Captains and the Kings, The Gates, The
Old Jest*). They exist on a plotted space between the entrenched encampments
of the enemy, in a figurative no man's land to which the reader has gained access by being an accomplice to the intrusion these stories resist, but to which
they bear testament. That the common denominator of these fictions should be

the activity of war suggests that they serve to explicate the furthest reaches of artistic alienation.

Shari Benstock. In Thomas F. Staley, ed.,
Twentieth-Century Women Novelists
(Totowa, N.J., Barnes & Noble, 1982), pp. 215–17

JOYCE, JAMES (1882–1941)

Mr. Joyce's merit, I will not say his chief merit but his most engaging merit, is that he carefully avoids telling you a lot that you don't want to know. He presents his people swiftly and vividly, he does not sentimentalize over them, he does not weave convolutions. He is a realist. He does not believe "life" would be all right if we stopped vivisection or if we instituted a new sort of "economics." He gives the thing as it is. He is not bound by the tiresome convention that any part of life, to be interesting, must be shaped into the conventional form of a "story." Since De Maupassant we have had so many people trying to write "stories" and so few people presenting life. Life for the most part does not happen in neat little diagrams and nothing is more tiresome than the continual pretence that it does.

Mr. Joyce's *Araby*, for instance, is much better than a "story," it is a vivid waiting.

It is surprising that Mr. Joyce is Irish. One is so tired of the Irish or "Celtic" imagination (or "phantasy" as I think they now call it) flopping about. Mr. Joyce does not flop about. He defines. He is not an institution for the promotion of Irish peasant industries. He accepts an international standard of prose writing and lives up to it.

He gives us Dublin as it presumably is. He does not descend to farce. He does not rely on Dickensian caricature. He gives us things as they are, not only for Dublin, but for every city. Erase the local names and a few specifically local allusions, and a few historic events of the past, and substitute a few different local names, allusions and events, and these stories could be retold of any town.

That is to say, the author is quite capable of dealing with things about him, and dealing directly, yet these details do not engross him, he is capable of getting at the universal element beneath them.

The main situations of *Madame Bovary* or of *Doña Perfecta* do not depend on local colour or upon local detail, that is their strength. Good writing, good presentation can be specifically local, but it must not depend on locality. Mr. Joyce does not present "types" but individuals. I mean he deals with common emotions which run through all races. He does not bank on "Irish character." Roughly speaking, Irish literature has gone through three phases in our time, the shamrock period, the dove-grey period, and the Kiltartan period. I think there is a new phase of the works of Mr. Joyce. He writes as a contemporary of continental writers. I do not mean that he writes as a faddist, mad for the last note, he does not imitate Strindberg, for instance, or Bang. He is not ploughing the underworld for horror. He is not presenting a macabre subjectivity. He is classic in that he deals with normal things and with normal people. [1914]

Ezra Pound. The Literary Essays of Ezra Pound, ed.
T. S. Eliot (London, Faber and Faber, 1954),
pp. 400–401

But the cultivated reader whom I have postulated will . . . analyse *Ulysses* as he reads. And this is what will certainly be the result of his analysis after a first reading. He will say: This is still the society of *Dubliners*, and the eighteen parts of *Ulysses* can provisionally be considered as eighteen tales with different aspects of the life of the Irish capital as their subjects. Nevertheless each of these eighteen parts differs from any of the fifteen tales of *Dubliners* on many points, and particularly by its scope, by its form, and by the distinction of the characters. Thus, the characters who take the principal rôles in the tales of *Dubliners* would be in *Ulysses* only supers, minor characters, or—it comes to the same thing—people seen by the author from the outside. In *Ulysses* the protagonists are all (in a literary sense) princes, characters who emerge from the depths of the author's inner life, constructed with his experience and his sensibility, and endowed by him with his own emotion, his own intelligence, and his own lyricism. Here, the conversations are something more than typical of individuals of such and such social classes; some of them are genuine essays in philosophy, theology, literary criticism, political satire, history. Scientific theories are expounded or debated. These pieces, which we might treat as digressions, or rather as appendices, essays composed outside of the book and artificially interpolated into all of the "tales," are so exquisitely adapted to the plot, the movement, and the atmosphere of the different parts in which they appear that we are obliged to admit that they belong to the book, by the same rights as the characters in whose mouths or whose minds they are put. But already we can no longer consider these eighteen parts as detached tales: Bloom, Stephen, and a few other characters remain, sometimes together and sometimes apart, the principal figures; and the story, the drama, and the comedy of their day are enacted through them. It must be acknowledged that, although each of these eighteen parts differs from all of the others in form and language, the whole forms none the less an organism, a book.

As we arrive at this conclusion, all sorts of coincidences, analogies, and correspondences between these different parts come to light; just as, in looking fixedly at the sky at night, we find that the number of stars appears to increase. We begin to discover and to anticipate symbols, a design, a plan, in what appeared to us at first a brilliant but confused mass of notations, phrases, data, profound thoughts, fantasticalities, splendid images, absurdities, comic or dramatic situations; and we realise that we are before a much more complicated book than we had supposed, that everything which appeared arbitrary and sometimes extravagant is really deliberate and premeditated; in short, that we are before a book which has a key.

Where then is the key? It is, I venture to say, in the door, or rather on the cover. It is the title: *Ulysses*.

Valery Larbaud. Criterion. Oct., 1922, pp. 96–97

I hold this book [*Ulysses*] to be the most important expression which the present age has found; it is a book to which we are all indebted, and from which none of us can escape. These are postulates for anything that I have to say about it, and I have no wish to waste the reader's time by elaborating my eulogies; it has given me all the surprise, delight, and terror that I can require, and I will leave it at that. . . .

The question, then, about Mr. Joyce, is: how much living material does he deal with, and how does he deal with it: deal with, not as a legislator or exhorter, but as an artist?

It is here that Mr. Joyce's parallel use of the *Odyssey* has a great importance. It has the importance of a scientific discovery. No one else has built a novel upon such a foundation before: it has never before been necessary. I am not begging the question in calling *Ulysses* a "novel"; and if you call it an epic it will not matter. If it is not a novel, that is simply because the novel is a form which will no longer serve; it is because the novel, instead of being a form, was simply the expression of an age which had not sufficiently lost all form to feel the need of something stricter. Mr. Joyce has written one novel—the *Portrait*; Mr. Wyndham Lewis has written one novel—*Tarr*. I do not suppose that either of them will ever write another "novel." The novel ended with Flaubert and with James. It is, I think, because Mr. Joyce and Mr. Lewis, being "in advance" of their time, felt a conscious or probably unconscious dissatisfaction with the form, that their novels are more formless than those of a dozen clever writers who are unaware of its obsolescence.

In using the myth, in manipulating a continuous parallel between contemporaneity and antiquity, Mr. Joyce is pursuing a method which others must pursue after him. They will not be imitators, any more than the scientist who uses the discoveries of an Einstein in pursuing his own, independent, further investigations. It is simply a way of controlling, of ordering, of giving a shape and a significance to the immense panorama of futility and anarchy which is contemporary history. It is a method already adumbrated by Mr. Yeats, and of the need for which I believe Mr. Yeats to have been the first contemporary to be conscious. It is a method for which the horoscope is auspicious. Psychology (such as it is, and whether our reaction to it be comic or serious) ethnology, and *The Golden Bough* have concurred to make possible what was impossible even a few years ago. Instead of narrative method, we may now use the mythical method. It is, I seriously believe, a step toward making the modern world possible for art. . . . And only those who have won their own discipline in secret and without aid, in a world which offers very little assistance to that end, can be of any use in furthering this advance.

T. S. Eliot. *The Dial*. Nov., 1923, pp. 480, 482–83

Ulysses is wonderful, not because it is obscure, but because so much of its obscurity is imaginative. *Ulysses* is wonderful, not because it is blasphemous, but because so much of its blaspheming is imaginative. *Ulysses* is wonderful, not because it is disgusting, but because so much of its disgustingness is imaginative. And imagination is not just invention or fancy. It is an impassioned intellectual energy, which half-reveals and half-creates a certain essential aspect of the universe. *Ulysses* is not a Saturnian Bible because "it gives us such an interesting picture of life in Dublin twenty years ago." It is not an Epic of Four Dimensions because "it contains a new experiment in psychoanalytical novel-writing." It is not the Horn-pipe of Chaos because, if you hunt long enough, and consult enough mythology you "can find in it a modern transcript of the tale of Odysseus." . . .

Persons opening *Ulysses* at random are easily scarecrowed away by the first shock of [its] queer mixture of vulgar slang and metaphysical obscurity. His trick, for instance, of playing so jocosely upon the words "Bloom" and "Leopold" is alone enough to worry the fastidious and tease the refined! But there is much more in all this than appears at first sight. Joyce realizes, as few writers before him have done, what enormous imaginative possibilities there are, what evocations of obscure half-physical responses, in mere verbal assonance; while his audacious habit of dovetailing separate words is a quite legitimate experiment in philological psychology.

Personally I regret the parody upon pseudo-mediaevalism into which he falls in the Holles House scene; but then I have always myself disliked the famous mock-heroic chapter in *Tom Jones*. This is what I call Knave of Spades writing. The root of it is in a savage play-instinct.

It is no easy task to make a rich planetary Pie, worthy of the palates of Olympians, out of the maudlin onion-peel and bob-tail messes of parlour sentiment and tavern backchat. But the success of *Ulysses* lies exactly in the idiosyncratic pestle and mortar, wherewith these unsavoury oddments are slapped and pounded into good pastry, the mixture well yeasted with scholastic erudition, well salted with cosmosbaiting blasphemy!

James Joyce has indeed the power of playing the devil's own tattoo upon the swollen bellies of pregnant words. [1923]

John Cowper Powys. *James Joyce's Ulysses—An Appreciation* (London, Village Press, 1975), pp. 4, 9

The verse in *Chamber Music* has not the finality of single intention. Its deficiencies have been ascribed to the fact that, where it does not reflect the vaporous mysticism of the early Yeats, Æ, and the other Irish revivalists, it is a patent imitation of the Elizabethan song-books. Examination reveals in these poems little more than a superficial verbal similarity to the poetry of the Celtic twilight whose obvious accents appear only in *XXXVI*, "Oh, it was out by Donnycarney." Whatever Joyce retained from the bardic songs (or their modern translations) in the way of simplified expression and elegiac motives, was overlaid with the formal decorum, yet enlivened by the lucid sensibility, of Jonson and Herrick, or of those poems by Byrd, Dowland, and Campion which he knew from boyhood. To read *Chamber Music* with its familiar refrains is to revive sensations first gained from the *Book of Airs* or *A Paradise of Dainty Devices*. Yet the overlay of artificial elegance never conceals wholly a nerve of sharp lyric refinement. Little more than elegance is present in *VI*. . . . Adjusted to the courtly tone of Suckling and the Cavaliers, it reappears in *XII*. . . .

It is clear that in such poems one has, instead of direct and unequivocal poetic compulsion, a deliberate archaism and a kind of fawning studiousness which attempt to disguise the absence of profounder elements. Yet the archaism which exists at its extreme level in *X* and *XI*, or, phrased as *vers de société*, in *VII*, was converted into Joyce's own material in two or three lyrics which, for spiritual suavity and logic, approach the minor work of Crashaw, or at least of Crashaw's descendants in the nineteenth century, Thompson and Lionel Johnson. . . .

It has been remarked before, by Edmund Wilson, that Joyce was closer to continental literature during his apprenticeship than to current English and Irish. In a writer so intentionally derivative, affiliations are natural. They can probably be traced here to the kind of lyric impressionism that grew, by a curious process of inversion, out of Dehmel and Liliencron toward the broken accent of expressionism as one finds it in Werfel, Joyce's closest ally among the figures of later German poetry. Through his lively contemporaneity and his curious sympathy with modern French art, Joyce was undoubtedly attracted by the inferential subtlety of the Symbolists. But his lyricism, like Dowson's or Rilke's, betrays too much diffusion to enable him to approach Mallarmé's faultless penetration or Rimbaud's intense discipline. It was more readily susceptible to the colors and moods of Verlaine's songs.

Morton D. Zabel. *Poetry*. July, 1930, pp. 208–10

[In] Mrs. Bloom's soliloquy. . . . inner narration [is] brought to its logical use, not as mere assistant of proper narration, but as creation of a new form. There is no frame work of outer narration at all in the soliloquy. The only outer narration is *our own supposition*, such as that Mrs. Bloom's musings take place while she is lying in bed on the morning with which she began the book. But she may be standing, or kneeling, or sitting down. We are told nothing of that, and it is all absolutely unimportant. And although the soliloquy, the sequence of thoughts concatenated not according to a logical factual development, but by Mrs. Bloom's own associations, goes on for 42 pages, we never feel loss of verisimilitude, because the only verisimilitude is that proceeding at the moment from concatenated thoughts. Where no initial starting point of outer narration is given, no loss of it can arise. The tables of narration are completely overturned. Insight into thoughts of a character originally appeared as a kind of excrescence on normal outer narration. But as the conditions determining the devices of art change, so was it inevitable for the economic causes of interest turning to our inner workings, to result in the climacteric of Mrs. Bloom's soliloquy, the first great piece of pure inner narration in English.

We have now come to a *result* of *Ulysses* which may prove, not at all because of any bulk or thrillingness, or even notoriety, but because of its special merits, to be a landmark. Joyce, in *Ulysses*, brought inner narration to such a point that by it destruction of normal, or outer, narration was finally completed. But out of the ruins come two things: an awareness of the dangerously corroding action of inner narration, which may make a healthy normal narration possible, and the possibility of a special new form, the prime purpose of which is not to narrate. In short, Joyce has shown that inner narration is not narration at all, but either an adjunct to proper narration or a new thing.

It is curious, indeed, that this culmination of the first age of the novel, in the triumph of inner narration, came just at the point where the main interest of mankind is no longer in individual matters, but social matters. But it is curious only on first thoughts, for on closer examination we see how characteristic of the development of a form this is. We may throw further light on the significance of *Ulysses* as a landmark, for we may note, in conclusion, that in this final destruction of the novel which contained the canker of inner narration we have merely the final throes of individualistic narrative art. It is necessary to destroy in order to rebuild; Joyce helps destroy the bourgeois novel; it remains for others to rebuild.

Alec Brown. *DM*. Jan.–March, 1934, pp. 48–49

I have spoken of *Finnegans Wake* as a universe. We can now see that in describing the external universe through the veil of Earwicker's dream, it also describes the internal universe of the unconscious. The internal universe, too, captures the whole of time; it preserves, with that "prodigious conservatism" of which Jung spoke, the record of history. As Joyce says, "the world, mind, is, was and will be writing its wrunes for ever, man, on all matters that fall under the ban of our infrarational senses." Earwicker is all men: that is why he is called "Here Comes Everybody"; that is why he is "magnificently well worthy of any and all . . . universalization", and that is why we discover in the dream of Earwicker a whole archeology of experience, "a jetsam litterage of convolvuli of times lost or strayed, of lands derelict and of tongues laggin too." Indeed, Earwicker descends below the human level of evolution. He is an animal, a fish, an insect, a compound known as H_2CE_3; he is an atom, in a nascent universe in which there is nothing but "atoms and ifs."

This opposition of the external and the internal universes leads us back to the life-and-death cycle which runs through *Finnegans Wake*. For in psychological terms the life-and-death cycle is the path of the mystic, the path back into the unconscious and the re-emergence of the mind with new vigor and new faith. A great many twentieth-century men of letters, having lost faith in rational thought, have become convinced that truth and goodness can be found in mysticism. Toynbee, to give one example, regards the mystic experience as the crucial one in human destiny.

Joyce too has his moments of mysticism. The rhythm of his book is the rhythm of his mind passing back and forth from the conscious and the civilized to the unconscious and the primitive. The mind of Earwicker rises and falls through the range of unconsciousness. The cries of his children, "Hide! Seek! Hide! Seek!" become "High! Sink! High! Sink! Highohigh! Sinkasink!" in time with the movements of his mind. This rhythm, embodied in the death-and-resurrection myths of all times and societies, is the main theme of *Finnegans Wake*.

It ought to be pointed out, however, that Joyce is not temperamentally a mystic; while one of the functions of *Finnegans Wake* is to record the apocalyptic mysticism and fertility worship of our time, another is to poke endless fun at them. . . .

There are, of course, various valid criticisms of Joyce's novel; each reader will find his own. What I have tried to suggest here is that the book cannot be put easily aside on the ground that it is irresponsibly unorthodox or of only special interest. If this is an oecumenical period of history, *Finnegans Wake* is our oecumenical novel. And far more striking than its exoticism is its appalling orthodoxy.

Richard Chase. AmS. Autumn, 1944, pp. 425–26

In *Finnegans Wake* Joyce begs the indulgence of the "ideal reader suffering from an ideal insomnia"; and, indeed, that work requires an encyclopedic knowledge of philology, folklore, history, and metaphysics. No such extensive demands are made by *Ulysses*. The work can be understood by the literate reader. It requires patience and intelligence—above all, sympathy and insight. The elucidation of minor points, tracing of literary echoes, and other methods of scholastic exegesis bid fair to discourage the public who should read *Ulysses*. Just as Shakespeare has often been ruined for schoolboys, so Joyce's brilliant insights into the dilemmas of modern civilization are too often smothered under a moraine of footnotes.

It is unfortunate, too, that Joyce is chiefly known as a technician, a bewildering experimentalist. This kind of fame is sterile; it creates of one of the most vital and provocative of novels a preserve for graduate courses in literature. It makes *Ulysses* a monument of art for art's sake. The fascination of seeing a genuinely original and creative mind at work upon the factors of our culture is lost. Joyce is prophetic, as all great writers have been prophetic. His is the clearest and most incisive voice of our age, and we should do well to heed him.

For *Ulysses* is a world book. The "Divine Comedy" of our age, it brings an uncompromising intelligence to bear upon the moral failures of modern civilization. The dislocations of society, as well as the diseases of the soul, are dissected with searing brilliance by one who was in a rare position to observe them, who possessed rare skill in analyzing them and rare courage in revealing them. Not for nothing were Joyce's heroes Swift and Ibsen. Like them he had the intelligence to see and the intrepidity to utter what he saw. The words of the young Joyce, in *Stephen Hero*, are pertinent: "Civilisation may be said indeed to be the creation of its outlaws." As Swift mercilessly demolished the eighteenth-century idols of the tribe and Ibsen those of the nineteenth century, so Joyce has done for our day. We are all in his debt.

Nor is *Ulysses* as grim as this introduction might seem to make it. Joyce's humor is infectious, his gusto irrepressible. He has much of the "joyicity" of the grasshopper of *Finnegans Wake*. Moralists who point to his "message" and moralists who lament his apparent lack of a "message" both fall into one misinterpretation. They forget that Joyce is a satirist, and a satirist without a sense of humor is as much an anomaly as a Dublin without pubs. *Ulysses* is fun to read.

Richard M. Kain. *Fabulous Voyager: James Joyce's
Ulysses* (Chicago, Univ. of Chicago Pr., 1947),
pp. 2–3

Like Rabelais, Joyce made grotesque catalogues of words. Like Nashe and Shakespeare, enamored of words in the age of discovery, he delighted in abundance. He called Shakespeare, whom he admired less as playwright than as poet, a "lord of language," richer than Dante and better to have on a desert island. Detesting "vague words for a vague emotion," he admired the precision of Flaubert. The Male Brutes who appear before unmanned Mr. Bloom in the brothel have only one thing to say. "Good!" they say. That is the *mot juste*. When the printers objected to the word "bloody" in the manuscript of *Dubliners*, Joyce replied that bloody is the one word in the language that can create the effect he wanted.

As he admired the words of other artists, so he exulted in his own command of what he considered the greatest of powers. To Eugene Jolas he announced: "I can do anything with language." His study of archaic language and his notes on living language in street or pub had made him master of all verbal effects from the divine speech of thunder to "lowquacity." The words "Sechseläuten" and "lebensquatsch," which occur throughout *Finnegans Wake*, are examples of both kinds. Sechseläuten is the spring festival of Zürich, and lebensquatsch or life's muddle is the interpretation by a Zürich waitress of Joyce's demand for lemon squash. He once told Frank Budgen that he had been working all day at two sentences of Ulysses: "Perfume of embraces all him assailed. With hungered flesh obscurely, he mutely craved to adore." When asked if he was seeking the *mot juste*, Joyce replied that he had the words already. What he wanted was a suitable order.

He composed a novel as great poets compose their poems. Under his hand all the resources of word, rhythm, and tone conspired to create intricate beauty. His novels are more like poems or symphonies or statues than like ordinary novels. Maybe they are not novels at all but works of their own kind like *Tristram Shandy* or *Gargantua*, which we call novels for want of a word for them. We must approach Joyce's greater works as we would a poem or a symphony. That reader who reads *Ulysses* as if it were a common thing would be disappointed.

William York Tindall. *James Joyce* (New York,
Charles Scribner's Sons, 1950), pp. 95–96

Pattern: that was what Joyce most needed [in *Finnegans Wake*]. The world of dream is as vast and formless as the chaos out of which Vico's cycles rise and into which they finally collapse. The framework of the *Odyssey*, spiritually appropriate, if arbitrary, held together the swarming content of *Ulysses* and enabled each part and episode to be pigeonholed in its appropriate place. The far looser framework offered by Vico, an idea instead of a story, its nexus not episode but free association under three broad headings, enabled Joyce to organise Earwicker's dream experiences into something approaching order. It is possible that his success in fitting Dublin into the framework of the *Odyssey* tempted him, in retrospect, to look on *Ulysses* and the *Odyssey* as corresponding cycles of experience. He may have been inclined to forget that he had made one correspond to the other, and regarded the correspondence as inherent in the Dublin material, a view which would make Vico's theory all the more attractive to him. In any case, there is no doubt that he had the solution pat to his hand. The Liffey, personified as *Anna Livia*, was not only all rivers at all times, but the water of the unconscious mind, the water from which all life emerged in the creation, the water of the womb, the woman principle, the stream of time on its way to the formless timeless ocean, yet never for an instant losing its local precise identity as the Liffey flowing into Dublin Bay. "Them four old codgers" with their Dublin names, could be the four apostles, the four green fields (provinces) of Ireland, the Four Courts of Dublin, the Four Waves of Irish mythology, Blake's Four Zoas, Jung's four types, four trees on the Liffey bank, commenting on her goings-on—and, when she is in Earwicker's dream, sniggering in senile glee over his goings-on; four points of the compass, four bed-posts: Earwicker himself could out-range his own narrow boundaries, be anyone whom his personal unconscious chose, then escape into the collective unconscious and inherit the whole range of human experience through all ages. What is more, the language which was to record these spreading concentric rings upon the water—the moving water of the stream, that would not let them be static circles, but made the watery graph a spiral and so gave to history the moral significance which Joyce needed, the significance he could not find in the history books—this language had a like freedom. If the unconscious is to range up and down time, the language that records its journeyings must not be anchored to one place or time, but must be free to discover and build from its own associations, must have all the riches which the extended mind of its creator can give to it: his mind which, as [one commentator] pointed out, never lets anything go: his mind which, a fading coal, can be at all places in his life at once: the associations of this mind make "the prism of a language manycoloured and richly storied" in which we shall see not only the local label, but the timeless essence of the thing itself. From this reservoir, into which every writer, speaker, and singer he had ever encountered had poured his contribution, Joyce, attended by the ghosts of Shakespeare, Swift, and Blake, with Freud and Jung standing by, dipped his bucket for sixteen working years, secure in a magic that made each bucketful a type of the whole, that made Dublin lingo associate with every language he could reach, a starting point from which the unconscious mind could travel everywhere and make a speech that is not only new, but a new Myth.

L. A. G. Strong. *The Sacred River: An Approach to James Joyce* (New York, Pellegrini & Cudahy, 1951), pp. 103–5

One of the qualities which delighted me in *Exiles* was that evidently nothing would induce Mr. Joyce to make his characters less complex and interesting than he saw them to be. He would rather obscure his theme than do that, and though a fault, it is a fault on the right side—on the interesting side. The second respect in which he has learnt from the master [Ibsen] is his practice of intensifying our interest in the present by dialogue which implies a past. . . .

The merits of this play make it hard to tell its story. Summarized, that story would not distinguish it from many a play in which the love relations of two men and a woman wove the plot. Its distinction lies in the relations of the three points in that familiar triangle being complex and intense. Art is usually so superficial, life so profound. I admire Mr. Joyce for having tried to deepen our conventional simplification of such relations and bring them nearer to nature. Now and then I lost my way in his characters as in a wood, but that did not make me think they were not true; rather the contrary. When I put my fin-

ger on his spinning rainbow top, I do not see the coloured rings which produced that iridescence so definitely as in the case of Ibsen. The theme of *Exiles* is not so clear to me. I conjecture that I get nearest to it in saying that the
play is a study in the emotional life of an artist. (I am sure, at any rate, that I
am giving the reader a useful tip in bidding him keep one eye *always* upon
Richard Rowan, whatever else may be interesting him besides.) And when I
say that the play is a study in an artist's life, I mean that its theme is the complication which that endowment adds to emotional crises which are common
to all men. It makes sincerity more difficult and at the same time more vitally
important. Imagination opens the door to a hundred new subtleties and possibilities of action; it brings a man so near the feelings of others that he has
never the excuse of blindness, and keeps him at a distance, so that at moments
he can hardly believe he cares for anything but his own mind.

When he acts spontaneously, he knows he is acting spontaneously—if
not at the moment, the moment after—much as some people, thought modest, have hardly a right to be considered so, because they invariably know
when they are. *Exiles* is a play in which two men are struggling to preserve
each his own essential integrity in a confusing situation where rules of thumb
seem clumsy guides; and between them is a bewildered, passionate woman—
generous, angry, tender, and lonely. . . .

If you ask how Richard Rowan and Robert Hand stood towards each
other, the answer is they were friends. There was a touch of the disciple in
Robert. Richard was the intenser, more creative, and also the more difficult
nature. He was an exile in this world; Robert was at home in it.

Desmond MacCarthy. *Humanities* (London,
MacGibbon & Kee, 1953), pp. 90–92

Critics are sharply divided on Joyce's relationship to Ireland. In this matter it
is not possible to accept their judgments at face value. . . .

Not even Joyce's words themselves, treasured and preserved and later
recorded by his awed interviewers, may be accepted without question. It was
a subject so close to the raw edges of the exile's nerves that he was often
forced to hide his true feelings behind a conventional oath, a snarl, a bitter
paradox, or a dignified understatement. If the words of Francini-Bruni, who
gave up his friendship with Joyce to discredit him in public lectures, may be
believed, the Irish exile thought poorly of his birthplace. He quotes Joyce as
saying that "the Emerald isle is a field of thorns . . . hunger, syphilis, superstition, alcoholism. Puritans, Jesuits and bigots have sprouted from it. . . .
The Dubliner is of the mountebank race the most useless and inconsistent.
. . . However, Ireland is still the brain of the United Kingdom." Perhaps to
Djuna Barnes he came closest to a matter-of-fact statement, though it covers
only a small part of the relationship: "The Irish are people who will never
have leaders, for at the great moment they always desert them. They have pro-

duced one skeleton—Parnell—never a man." Alfred Kerr describes vividly Joyce's reaction, during an interview, to the mention of the Irish. The author dropped his calm aspect and became sharp. The Norwegians expelled Ibsen, he recalled, and the Irish had never forgiven Joyce for painting certain types of his countrymen and the city of Dublin. Revenge was the spur.

There was no reason, indeed, why Joyce should have remembered the Ireland he left behind with any pleasure. Even those who should have understood his feelings—the literary elite of Dublin—gave him no encouragement. If we may believe Stanislaus Joyce, the poet A. E. (George Russell) told him that his brother was a worthless cad and that starvation on the Continent would do him good. In fact, says Stanislaus, when Joyce reported from Europe that he had found a job as teacher in the Berlitz schools, Stanislaus woke the poet after midnight to taunt him. When Joyce worked at the library in Dublin, the staff did little more than tolerate him. The professors at the university regarded him with suspicion for his unorthodox behavior and his dangerous reading of authors like Maeterlinck and Ibsen. Religious authorities warned his favorite aunt, Josephine Murray, not to let her children fraternize with their strange cousin. And the "greats" of Ireland, George Moore and William Butler Yeats, though they may have recognized the genius in the youth, were puzzled and repelled by his attitude and behavior. This is not to say that Joyce was blameless or that he tried in any substantial way to alleviate the rapidly deteriorating situation. There is much biographical truth in the portrait of Stephen Dedalus in *Ulysses*, wandering from place to place in Dublin, seemingly doing his best to antagonize even those who are trying to be on his side. But his youthful arrogance does not change the fact that his memory of this period in his life was sad and bitter.

Marvin Magalaner. In Marvin Magalaner and
Richard M. Kain, eds., *Joyce: The Man, the Work,
the Reputation* (New York, New York Univ. Pr.,
1956), pp. 20–21

Joyce was the cool, proud, fanatical artist, who despite his scornful and youthful desire to go for everything in life when he broke with Ireland, in fact never left family life. Without invention as a writer, he plunged into the known not the unknown, worked continually the same ground. He was the artist of the lowest common domestic denominator which he transposed so that it became myth. His imagination began with the word and met the thing later and returned to the word again. In words he was enclosed. He saw life as an illuminated pun. He was ready to believe at the beginning of the last war, for example, that there was some mystic connection between the resistance of Finland against Russia and the apotheosis of Finn in *Finnegans Wake*. Such fantasies kept at bay the boredom to which perhaps his isolation had exposed him; just as well to make no distinction between language and life. One has seen the same thing in other Irish writers—Beckett with his cries of "What tedium!"—whose gift of language knocks the intolerable minutes on the head. But when Jung said that Joyce was a classic case of the schizophrenic who successfully translated his obsessions into literature and saved his reason, and added that, as a psycho-analyst, he had learned a great deal from him, Joyce was pleased by the flattery, but laughed at Jung for making such heavy weather out of comic writing. Psycho-analysis was blackmail, he said, on many occasions. There was not a single serious line in *Ulysses!* What he meant was made clearer when he spoke of the attempt of the psychiatrists to cure his daughter's madness. What was the point of being cured when normality meant seeing the "battered cabman's face" of the world? Better madness! Better words!

V. S. Pritchett. *Enc.* July, 1960, p. 80

Any moral work, *Dubliners* included ("a chapter in the moral history of my country"), seeks a modus vivendi for man, an interim pattern or set of goals tolerably acceptable while the ultimate quest is in progress. The moral pattern in *Dubliners* cannot lead to salvation, whatever the ultimate quest may uncover. With no worthy ends of their own to work toward, the inhabitants of that world are entrepreneurs at best: Lenehan, Mr. Duffy, Farrington and Mr. Alleyne, Maria's Alf, Mr. Tierney, Mrs. Mooney and her son Jack, Mrs. Kearney, Tom Kernan, even Gabriel Conroy. Their modus vivendi reveals itself as a cracked sort of one-upmanship, success at which brands the entrepreneur on the treadmills of self-promotion as damned, as exploiter, as selfish cad. The comedy of a story such as "Grace" is sardonic and sordid indeed. What is sordid in the naturalistic slice of life is that its characters are frozen in wrong-headedness, in mistaken motives. Joyce's characters are egotistically grubbing on a small scale at the expense of other values, stated or implied. They are afflicted by a diseased and unrewarding paralysis in habitual gestures which can bring no respectable reward. Put the entrepreneur on the psychiatrist's couch, and you can only cure him of his nervousness by getting him to give up the game, getting him to stop caring whether he is one up or not. This is the lesson Gabriel learns, at least momentarily: throw away certain values in your present life the pursuit of which cuts you off from other and more essential values. Michael Furey, never one up, turns out to have been one up on Gabriel. Dead, he has the last laugh. He had the love of a woman whose love Gabriel had not questioned, and had hardly missed.

Of the four chief works of fiction Joyce wrote, *Dubliners* is the most negative. The "cracked looking-glass" of these stories reflects the miasma only, not the way out, and what comedy the book contains is painful and unconstructive.

Helmut Bonheim. *Joyce's Benefictions* (Berkeley
and Los Angeles, Univ. of California Pr., 1964),
pp. 136–37

Joyce cannot resist the lure of parody in his later work, and in yielding to this he is forging much more than the "uncreated conscience" of his race. His use of the misspelling, "hesitency," throughout the work—the classic error of a forger through which Parnell triumphed over Piggott—is a continual warning that he is up to his tricks in this respect.

But what then is he parodying in presenting us with this odd amalgam of false clues? The answer may lie in the other element that I have yet to mention—Joyce's return to religion in this, his final work [*Finnegans Wake*]. While the first half of his life is devoted to denial and doubt, there is every indication in the Wake that the Joyce of later middle age was not only a Gracehoper but was profoundly concerned, maybe not with a heavenly life-hereafter, but with the eternity of this life. Hence the significance to him of the river as an image or model of a working Viconian cycle—a phenomenon that is being born in the hills, that flows and grows, and is finally lost in the sea, from whence it returns once more to the hills. And here's the point—there is no mutual exclusiveness in all of these phases. They are all happening "Now." Finn again and again and again. What a hell for the damned, as Sartre has since pointed out. But Joyce is not damned, for all his *Non Serviams*. He has got the mysterious gift of Grace, as even Clongowes will agree nowadays. . . .

In spite of the fact that it is one of the dirtiest books in public circulation, Joyce shows a far greater sense of religious purpose in the *Wake* than in anything else that he has written. Why he has to be so secretive about this fact is one of the charms and peculiarities of the man. Why he feels bound to conceal the message of his newly-born Penelope in the pidgin English of page 611 is perhaps an expression of his arrogance, or maybe it is a feature of his Irish love of a secret, or indeed of his Irish fear of a nasty laugh wafting out of Davy Byrne's. [1964]

Denis Johnston. In Robin Skelton and David R.
Clark, eds., *Irish Renaissance: A Gathering
of Essays, Memoirs and Letters from the
"Massachusetts Review"* (Dublin, Dolmen,
1965), pp. 126–27

As a native of Ireland, Joyce has often been accused of being a middle-class author whose work is a denial of history and attempts to make itself a mediaeval *summa* rather than a realistic portrayal of his times. It is true that Joyce wrote no historical novel, and it is true that *Finnegans Wake* is an encyclopedia of mythology; but Joyce is profoundly an Irishman and his work is truly the product of his own inner Ireland. Joyce's Ireland is not that of Yeats and perhaps even less that of Eamon de Valera.

What he retains from it is less its legendary past or its political future, than its present, that of the beginning of the twentieth century; from a reading of *Dubliners* and *Ulysses* one can discover all urban Ireland and Dublin society. As a social document it still retains its value today. But that is only the framework for the story of a developing consciousness, that of the artist, and, in *Ulysses*, that of an ordinary Dubliner—and by extension that of Dublin itself. There will always be a realistic basis to this spiritual or intellectual history, but neither is it presented objectively, nor does it distort the real; in the center of the work Joyce places individuals, and around the individuals, the three circles of family, homeland and Church are interpreted by those whom they surround and who at the same time serve to define them.

The family, the economic and social problems, are thus both concrete elements of surrounding reality—an end in itself, but limited—and the means by which the artist's mind is sharpened. In this, any realism is at once overtaken and assimilated, to become the surface of a symbolism which is made less and less publicly significant as it is more and more charged with personal meaning, until, with *Finnegans Wake*, it becomes a Joycean form of occultism, initiation to which is achieved by a progress *through* Joyce enabling one to reach reality.

How far and to what degree can one speak of "realism" in Joyce's art?

When Joyce writes *A Portrait*, he already possesses that "double consciousness of one watching himself live" (J. J. Mayoux, *Joyce*, p. 44), which enables him to reconstitute by memory a time which is experienced and now past. This retrospective glance at his own history reveals both the *image* he has of himself (not himself), and the exterior forces which have caused him to develop in opposition to them; what he sees is the social alienation of his family and of Ireland to which he has responded by withdrawing, by declaring his *difference*, while still, in the tones of the romantic and idealistic *fin-de-siècle* artist, claiming the role of moral reformer within this very society that he rejects. [1968]

Hélène Cixous. *The Exile of James Joyce*
(New York, David Lewis, 1972), pp. ix–x

Eugene Jolas, who knew Joyce well from 1927 on, once characterized him as "never an ebullient man. His moments of silence and introspection frequently weighed . . . on his immediate surroundings. Then a profound pessimism, that seemed to hold him prisoner within himself, made him quite inaccessible to outsiders. Usually, however, among his intimates, there finally came a festive pause, when he would begin to dance and sing, or engage in barbed thrusts of wit; when he would show flashes of gaiety and humor that could, on occasion, approach a kind of delirium."

It is almost as though Mr. Jolas were describing Joyce's books along with their author. That "profound pessimism" manifests itself first in those studies of Irish moral paralysis, the *Dubliners* stories, written in a spare, almost reticent prose, which Joyce himself termed a style of "scrupulous meanness." When the snow begins to fall upon all Ireland at the close of "The Dead," falling, "like the descent of their last end, upon all the living and the dead," an icy Joycean pessimism descends simultaneously upon us, and as we look back over the sorry lot of Dubliners just encountered—the paralyzed and perverse alike—we may be tempted to reflect upon the bleakness of the moralist who created them. In the *Portrait* that same pessimism, expressed this time in a different style, lurks beneath the many passages of soaring, silvery romanticism. . . .

But just as in Mr. Jolas' characterization, "there finally came a festive pause." Enter Bloom, and with him Joyce's barbed wit, humor, and sometimes delirious comic satire. Enter Molly Bloom as well, and later Earwicker and Anna Livia and certainly "the twins that tick *Homo Vulgaris*," Shem and Shaun.

Joyce's pessimism, of course, is never banished: but it requires redefinition, revaluation. It dresses now in cap and bells, covering a sad heart with a gay costume, even as a Shakespearean Fool. It is resigned to the doubleness or duplicity of life, recognizing the common reality co-existing with every vision of beauty, but choosing to laugh rather than to rail at life's irreducible antinomies. Adopting this ironic stance, Joyce directed his comic satire against a wide range of human follies, some truly reprehensible and others merely amusing.

Darcy O'Brien. *The Conscience of James Joyce*
(Princeton, N.J., Princeton Univ. Pr., 1968),
pp. 240–41

Joyce as an artist was confronting basic issues throughout the time of his apprenticeship, and only the incredible skill of *Dubliners* and *A Portrait* might make us forget that they were written by a very young man. Within a decade Joyce had to make vital decisions about his life and his art. The process by which he made them and the decisions themselves unfold before the reader of the early works (and are re-examined and relentlessly dissected before the reader of *Ulysses* and *Finnegans Wake*). Joyce is the one author who must be read sequentially; whereas Yeats desperately hoped that all of his writings were one work, Joyce was convinced that his entire canon was a single progression. As he arrived at the concepts that would contain him completely, he felt the power of language become magically his own, from the opening triad of key words on the first page of *Dubliners* (paralysis, simony, gnomon) to the final "the" of the *Wake*.

To many of us in the second half of the twentieth century James Joyce is a paradigm of the literary movement of the first half. He personified experimentation in technique, concern with form and structure and texture, and a culmination of the belief in the supremacy of the artist and the demand for absolute artistic integrity. He did not arrive at these positions without anguish and regrets. During those formative years Joyce tenaciously swam against the current: at a time when a young Irish writer could finally feel himself part of an indigenous literary movement, join Yeats and Moore and AE and others in a proud reaffirmation of Celtic inspiration, Joyce found himself an Irishman alone. He could not allow himself to accept a literary tradition that he considered primitive—even barbaric—merely out of chauvinism. As much as he might secretly have longed to be included in AE's anthology of young poets and invited into Moore's salon on Thursday evenings (and *Ulysses* records the pain of those rejections), he remained uncompromising. To be a great writer meant to be alone in his generation, and it meant total commitment to the full development of a world literary tradition.

> Bernard Benstock. *James Joyce: The Undiscover'd*
> *Country* (New York, Barnes & Noble, 1977),
> pp. xiii–xiv

Joyce saw no reason why first-person narration should be the sole code for signalling some limitation of awareness, and "Eveline" (1904), his second published story, is his first not altogether reluctant deception. He must have been both resignedly and cheerfully aware that numerous readers would share Eveline's fantasy, would suppose that a sailor who has "fallen on his feet in Buenos Ayres" is credible, one who has bought a house there and is spending a holiday in a rented room in Ireland; who proposes moreover to take her back as his bride to that South American house, though for some reason not gone into they can't get married till they've gotten there. Eveline believes all this because "Frank"—what a perfect name!—has skilfully shaped his yarn by the penny romances from which she derives her sense of the plausible. Penny romances are the liturgy of the innocent. The reader believes such stuff—most readers seem to—by accepting as fact what seems to be the narrative base of the story and is really no more than a careful statement of what naive Eveline has accepted.

Part of the narrative skill has gone into shaping the story's perceived world in such a way as to communicate Eveline's pathos. Another part is occupied in bestowing commas and minutiae of diction—"He had fallen on his feet in Buenos Ayres [comma] he said [comma]"—with a legalistic precision that shall cast slight but erosive doubt on certain aspects of Eveline's sense of the real. This has required the most steely control of style, one part of the writer's mind checking on the activities of the other, and exemplifies—so early!—something characteristic of Joyce, something he did in a variety of modes including the mode of pastiche. Pastiche and parody, these are modes which test the limits of someone else's system of perception. Any "style" is a system of limits; pastiche ascribes the system to another person, and invites us to attend to its recirculating habits and its exclusions. That is why Joyce, the student of Dublin limits, turned to stylistic imitation so frequently. There is nothing in his work more remarkable than the poem in memory of Charles Stewart Parnell the recitation of which climaxes "Ivy Day in the Committee Room": the pathos genuine, the rhetoric frigid and ludicrous, falsity exposed in the very grief it expresses.

> In palace, cabin or in cot
>   The Irish heart where'er it be
> Is bowed with woe—for he is gone
>   Who would have wrought her destiny.

And "Mr Crofton said that it was a very fine piece of writing." Joyce knew there would be readers who would believe that.

> Hugh Kenner. *Joyce's Voices* (Berkeley, Univ. of
> California Pr., 1978), pp. 80–82

Up to a point, Joyce's moral theology [in *Ulysses*] is unerringly orthodox. The good man is like the Good Samaritan coming to the aid of one with whom he has no apparent kinship. Bloom, who has been so comical and pathetic in his various costumes, is not at all absurd when [near the conclusion of the Nighttown episode] he takes up Stephen's stick and stands guard over his inert form. In the literal sense, he protects Stephen's identity, his belongings, and helps him to breathe. But as he does these things, he also creates Stephen in his imagination. He names him and fashions Stephen's half-conscious mutterings from Yeats into a poem of his own. . . .

It does not matter that Bloom has mistaken the Fergus of Yeats's poem for a girl named Ferguson or that he has summoned up fragments of the Freemason's oath of secrecy in his promise not to reveal Stephen's unguarded confessions. Nor does it matter that he cannot reveal his "art or arts," since Joyce does that for him. Bloom's errors in detail, typically, convey truths beyond detail. By leaving his post at the reader's side as fellow observer, he participates in the scene in a way that demonstrates how we, like him, are reader-authors, putting together a bit of this, a bit of that, a rhyme here, a verse there, and fashioning from them a portrait—surely not an objective one, but more than merely our own reflections. In Bloom, we see ourselves in a responsive, creative relation to lives outside our own.

Bloom's sympathetic and imaginative act momentarily makes Stephen his son. The truthfulness of this newly created relationship cannot be tested by plot as in a Dickens novel, in which Stephen would leap to his feet, embrace Bloom, and go home to live with him as an adopted child. The point is not that it leads to a story about family life, but that it is an instantaneous, indelible, universally familiar realization of human relationship. Bloom is not rewarded with an adopted son. But in a recurrence of the kind of dramatic projection employed throughout the episode, his action toward Stephen produces a vision of his dead son Rudy. In the intersection of the dramatic and the narrative, the paradigmatic gesture and the syntagmatic act, Bloom recovers the past in the present, the dead in the living. In short, he reconciles what for all but God and the artist is irreconcilable.

Robert Kiely. *Beyond Egotism: The Fiction of James
Joyce, Virginia Woolf, and D. H. Lawrence*
(Cambridge, Mass., Harvard Univ. Pr., 1980),
pp. 207–8

Whether we know it or not, Joyce's court is, like Dante's or Tolstoy's, always in session. The initial and determining act of judgment in his work is the justification of the commonplace. Other writers had labored tediously to portray it, but no one knew what the commonplace really was until Joyce had written. There is nothing like Joyce's commonplace in Tolstoy, where the characters, however humble, live dramatically and instill wisdom or tragedy in each other. Joyce was the first to endow an urban man of no importance with heroic consequence. For a long time his intention was misunderstood: it was assumed he must be writing satire. How else justify so passionate an interest in the lower middle class? Marxist critics leaped to attack him, and Joyce said gently to his friend Eugene Jolas, "I don't know why they attack me. Nobody in any of my books is worth more than a thousand pounds." To look into the flotsam of a city was common enough after Zola, but to find Ulysses there was reckless and imprudent. It was an idea quite alien, too, to Irish writers of the time. Yeats was aristocratic and demanded distinctions between men; Joyce was all for removing them. Shaw was willing to accept any man so long as he was eloquent, but Joyce took for his central hero a man not outwardly eloquent, thinking in fits and starts, without Shaw's desire to be emphatic or convincing. Joyce deals in his books with the theme of Tristram and Iseult that his fellow-Dubliners were freshening up, paradoxically, with the more ancient Irish names of Naisi and Deirdre, but the love story interests him hardly at all, his interest is in the commonplace husband. Unimpressive as Bloom may seem in so many ways, unworthy to catch marlin or countesses with Hemingway's characters, or to sop up guilt with Faulkner's, or to sit on committees with C. P. Snow's, Bloom is a humble vessel elected to bear and transmit unimpeached the best qualities of the mind. Joyce's discovery, so humanistic that he would have been embarrassed to disclose it out of context, was that the ordinary is the extraordinary.

To come to this conclusion Joyce had to see joined what others had held separate: the point of view that life is unspeakable and to be exposed, and the point of view that it is ineffable and to be distilled. Nature may be a horrible document, or a secret revelation; all may be resolvable into brute body, or into mind and mental components. Joyce lived between the antipodes and above them: his brutes show a marvelous capacity for brooding, his pure minds find bodies remorselessly stuck to them. To read Joyce is to see reality rendered without the simplifications of conventional divisions.

Richard Ellman. *James Joyce*, new and rev. ed.
(New York, Oxford Univ. Pr., 1982), p. 5

Ulysses is an unruly book in its design, its surface, its architectures, its details, and its interweavings, quite apart from the constant allurement away from the tangible referents to the words themselves—signifiers, if you want—and their capricious linguistic discharges. Symptoms are numerous and, some, well-known. In order therefore to indicate, provisionally, and to help us observe some of the energetic, restive, and defiant animus of *Ulysses* in all its diversified manifestations I suggest a term that should be reasonably precise, so as to retain some denotative edge, and yet implicatively loose enough to accommodate multifarious features. *Dislocution* has the advantage of not being predefined. It suggests a spatial metaphor for all manner of metamorphoses, switches, transfers, displacements, but also acknowledges the overall significance of speech and writing, and insinuates that the use of language can be less than orthodox. The prefix should alert us to a persistent principle of *Ulysses*, evinced in a certain waywardness, in deviations, in heretical turns, but also in multiple errors and miscommunications. In a merely negative meaning, the term might even serve as a convenient blanket for all subgroups of transmission errors in the book's chancy progress from one stage to the next, due to understandable clerical inadvertence.

Some methodical typology of *dislocution* would be a natural next step, but even if it were feasible, the gains of systematic neatness would not make up for the intrinsic falsification. For dislocutions are not so much isolable qualities as they are entangled processes that defy administrative classification. Even so, the following representative samples will hint, though vaguely, at some elementary differentiation.

At one extreme of the scale, on the surface level, there are obvious instances of transformations in space, as in Bloom's experience of "the alterations effected in the disposition of the articles of furniture," when he reenters his drawing room. A sofa has been "translocated," a table been "placed opposite the door," a sideboard "moved from its position." This experience is concrete and, as we know, painful; the redisposition of furniture suggests an actual domestic change. But it is analogous to various rearrangements within the whole book. The Wandering Rocks chapter could be cited as a further example: it disrupts the pretense of linear chronology by offering a collocation of disparate scenes, but it also tries to dovetail the heterotopical actions by fragments of dislocated narrative. In its transversal interlockings the chapter has left the tracks of the previous nine, which, for all their diversity, were still basically sequential. The Cyclops chapter also has unmistakable displacements, interpolated passages, which, in tone, style, attitude, and angle of vision, contrast markedly with the personal narration that they interrupt. It is the conspicuous dislocutions that set off the later chapters from those of the first half (which are *relatively* uniform): we experience these later chapters as jarring deviations from what looked like reliable narrative practices. [1983]

Fritz Senn. *Joyce's Dislocutions*, ed. by John Paul
Riquelme (Baltimore, Johns Hopkins Univ. Pr.,
1984), pp. 202–3

As the number of his stories [that constitute *Dubliners*] grew, Joyce arranged them in a design. He explained to the publisher Grant Richards that the stories were grouped to reveal life in Dublin "under four of its aspects: childhood, adolescence, maturity and public life." (For those who are puzzled that the protagonists of stories like "Two Gallants" and "The Boarding House" are adolescents, though they are over thirty, it helps to know that Joyce derived his categories from those of Greece and Rome, which were very different from those of this century.) Characteristically, Joyce grouped the stories in sets of three, four, four, and three to achieve a formal balance. He then added the last item in the collection, "The Dead," as an afterthought. If it upset the established sequence of triads and quartets and Joyce's intention to begin and end with a story featuring a priest, "The Dead" did not violate the pattern of a life's progression, adding indeed, the kingdom of death.

Just as George Moore insisted upon the unity of *The Untilled Field* so Joyce, when he wrote of *Dubliners* as "a chapter of the moral history of his country," was implying the unity of his work. In providing an arrangement based upon the stages in the development of human life, in emphasizing the theme of individual and social paralysis, in depicting throughout the stories the condition of entrapment, in concentrating, for the most part, on the lower middle class of Dublin, in emphasizing certain harmonies of tone and color and imagery in the stories, Joyce went much further than had Moore to achieve unity.

Far more extensive claims have been made for the underlying unity of *Dubliners*, however, and these claims have tended to suggest that the stories are based upon an extensive network of correspondences, motifs, allusions, parallels, and symbolic significances no less intricate than those in *Ulysses* and *Finnegans Wake*. Critics and scholars have argued for the manifest presence of an extensive series of correspondences to Homer's *Odyssey*, to the three graces (or theological virtues), to the four cardinal virtues, to the seven deadly sins, to the episodes of Dante's *Inferno*, to Ibsen's *When We Dead Awaken*, to a pattern of eastward and westward movement. If, indeed, at this point in his career, Joyce was able to contain within his imagination all these patterns and associations—as he would in fact have been able to do later in his career—he was an even more extraordinary young artist than has usually been thought. The problem with many of these interpretations is that they depend upon the universal archetypes of Roman Catholic symbology or earlier myth; while they discern ways in which Joyce's imagination was shaped by his religion and make convincing cases for particular allusions or parallels, they so insist upon the consistency of their insights that they turn Joyce's suggestiveness into crude allegory. Furthermore, much of the criticism devoted to the explication of the "unity" of *Dubliners* had been so extremely moralistic that it seems bent upon flailing the pathetic creatures of Dublin's petit-bourgeoisie with a zeal eclipsing Joyce's own desire "to betray the soul of that hemiplegia or paralysis which many consider a city."

James F. Carens. In James F. Kilroy, ed.,
The Irish Short Story: A Critical History
(Boston, Twayne, 1984), pp. 77–78

There is no doubt that Joyce was superbly equipped with all the endowments of more traditional writers—an absolute ear for dialogue, a sharpshooter's eye for visual detail, and an extraordinary feeling for the voice and tone of narrative. In his early works he plays a definite author—the celebrant in *Chamber Music*, the observer in *Dubliners*, the participant in *Portrait*.

But if Joyce early became different authors, he never became one author, the single familiar voice of the kind we find throughout Fielding, Austen, Dickens, Thackeray, Hardy, and even in such contemporaries as James, Conrad, D. H. Lawrence, Virginia Woolf, and E. M. Forster. To some extent such writers formed a bond with the reader by agreeing to render the unfamiliar familiar. To a large extent Joyce deliberately reversed the process, taking the familiar and making it unfamiliar. To read Joyce properly one should read all that he wrote, yet the experience of reading any one book by Joyce is certainly no preparation for what to expect in any other book from his pen.

The notion of making the familiar seem strange, complex, or obscure was hardly original with Joyce; indeed it was inherent in the naturalistic renderings of perception and other mental processes that was essential to impressionism. It can be found playfully in Richard Strauss's *Domestic Symphony* (1903), shockingly in Picasso's *Demoiselles d'Avignon* (1907), analyti ally in Gertrude Stein's *Three Lives* (1908), and hauntingly in Boccioni's triptych, *States of Mind* (1911–12).

Yet each of these works is accompanied by a sense that there is some coherent code to be discovered which will unlock all its secrets. The reader of *Ulysses* and *Finnegans Wake* has no such assurance. The familiar "author" in early Joyce—celebrant, observer, participant—is different from the sublime "author" in middle and late Joyce—the entity who can tell a story eighteen ways in *Ulysses* or dream while reinventing language in *Finnegans Wake*.

The absence of the author as guide may be the reason why a visual reading of Joyce on the page often seems incomplete, just as an auditory reading of Joyce in performance or recording also seems inadequate—until the separate readings of eye and ear are brought together in glorious union. Thus it may be helpful to think of Joyce not as a painter or musician imposing spatial design or temporal variations on his material, but rather as a painter and musician doing both such things simultaneously.

Heyward Erlich. In Heyward Erlich, ed., *Light Rays:*
James Joyce and Modernism (New York,
New Horizon, 1984), p. 17

KAVANAGH, PATRICK (1904–1967)

Intimate contact with any people is likely to persuade one that the theories of the anthropologists are a sort of inflated currency, and that there is an unfathomable difference between scientific and psychic content, and between the conventions that arrange life and life as it is actually lived. In *The Green Fool* Mr. Patrick Kavanagh, a young poet well known to contributors of the *Dublin Magazine*, tells of his life in a county of little hills somewhere between Carrickmacross and Dundalk, and the patterns of country life which he unfolds, while they may have little anthropological interest, have a human value which is measurable only in terms of actual living. His book is not fine literature, if one sights it through a literary lens, but out of it there drifts, literally, the sights and sounds of the Monaghan farmlands, and a people whose very bloodbeat seems to come out of the soil.

Mr. Kavanagh, one of a large family, was born in Mucker, a townland in the vicinity of Carrickmacross. His father was a shoemaker, his mother a careful, wise woman who would impose on her poet son the bread-and-butter ideology of her farming blood. Farmers, however, are born, not made; and Mr. Kavanagh, though he was unaware of his function for many years after leaving school, was born, definitely, a poet. Poetry is one way of adjusting the psychic scales in one's favour. In a community where values are hardheaded but not intellectual, hearty but not of the heart, our poet was not the shining light he would have been in a more urbane section of society; and while he entered fully into the life of the neighbourhood—it would have been impossible, indeed, to escape it—he was, even to his own thinking, not exactly of his environment. It was just that difference between himself and his neighbours which enables him, now, to keep things at imaginative distance, and to tell of them with an unprejudiced objectivity which is humourous, likeable and charmingly lyrical.

Luckily, however, he had plenty of time to take part in the life about him before he awakened to his poetic gift. The scenes and the people he describes for us are part of an experience that does not suffer from any literary self-consciousness whatsoever. They are juice of life. . . .

Mr. Kavanagh, . . . though he is entitled to the poet's dispensation, rules out religion as a topic. Actually his earliest poems are, in time, somewhere B.C. Ploughing a field, lazing on a hillside while his horses crop the headland, he is involved in that outbreathing of Deity which the ancients called Pan . . .

I find a star-lovely art
In a dark sod;
Joy that is timeless! Oh heart,
That knows God.

Only in verse does he transcend his rural Ireland. In prose he is of the people, realistic and hardheaded, a man with two eyes in his head, and a faculty for fine generous, lively conversation. A delightful book.

Padraic Fallon. *DM*. Oct., 1938, pp. 68–69

In Patrick Kavanagh peasant Ireland has a poet. But "peasant Ireland" needs an explanation. . . . The older poets took their matter from a folk; today's poets take theirs from the individual peasant.

Patrick Kavanagh writes under this new dispensation. His verse has no longer a traditional lilt with the overtones of folk-poetry: again and again we catch a rhythm that recalls *The Waste Land*. But *A Soul for Sale* is of the Irish countryside, and its figures are recognizable as the farmers and priests, the boys and girls of a parish. . . .

Perhaps it is because he belongs to a transition period that this poet is so unequal: Patrick Kavanagh has not made up his mind whether he should celebrate or satirize. In *The Great Hunger* he attempts to give monumental treatment to the peasant. But he also wants to satirize the joylessness of the countryside: to do this he has to give his Pat Maguire an extra raw deal by giving him a vinegary sister as well as a dominating mother. When Patrick Kavanagh is wholehearted he writes poems that have the tang of sloes pulled off the bushes.

Padraic Colum. *Sat*. Sept. 20, 1947, p. 24

When Mr. Kavanagh published his poem *The Great Hunger* in 1942, it was confiscated by the police and he was threatened with prosecution. I have not seen it; but this novel of his, obviously autobiographical in part, makes me feel that it must have been good enough to warrant the attention it provoked with its picture of a small-farming Irish community. *Tarry Flynn* is not entirely successful as a work of art. There is a certain clash between the objective satirical approach, scathing and yet warm with a good love of life, and the personal note which seeks to define a poet's youth in the peasant world. I feel that Tarry the cautious country-lad is not always quite coincident with Tarry the earth-loving poet. But having made this slight criticism, I can go on to express my simple admiration of the book. There is vitality, a sharp edge of scorn and yet an intense delightedness. The effect is perfect when Mr. Kavanagh is solely concerned with Tarry the amorous dead-scared lad who knows that the moment he falls into the open lap of one of the girls he is trapped for life. His evasions and anguishes are finely rendered. I can think only of A. E. Coppard's *The Higgler* as giving just this aspect of the shrewd peasant, and Mr. Kavanagh comes out well from the comparison.

In Mrs. Flynn there is no confusion of motive, and she emerges as a vivid fullsize character of the sort that any self-respecting novelist would sell his boots to create. The persistence in her of something reckless, wholly on the side of life, despite the deep and twisting fears of the peasant, the mingled acceptance and defiance of the world: all this is beautifully expressed. By his direct lyric gift, allied to a hearty sense of character, Mr. Kavanagh has brought something new to a theme which has been well worked over, that of the priest-ridden Irish village with its crushing boredoms and frustrations. His book is as fresh as a daisy, an unusual event in our grey literary soil. It aptly reminds us that after all, in art as in life, an ounce of clear merriment is worth several tons of indecisive gloom.

Jack Lindsay. LL. April, 1949, pp. 80–82

As a poet with a small but valuable output, as the author of a book of prose sketches *The Green Fool*, and as a Dublin character, Patrick Kavanagh has built up for himself a celebrity without which life in Ireland would be the poorer. The white light of the innocence of a remembered childhood shines out from his poetry and may ultimately be of more importance than the lines in his poem *The Great Hunger* or the paragraphs in his novel *Tarry Flynn* where he writes of the cold hand of the clay falling down to stifle the life of the spirit. The thwarted unmarried mother-dominated peasant in *The Great Hunger* and the thwarted moments in the life of innocent mother-dominated Tarry have a dismal correspondence with Franz Kafka finding relief in the writing of his diaries or J. Alfred Prufrock, conscious of incipient baldness, retreating down interminable stairs. Tarry Flynn is, in fact, a neurotic. But when Kavanagh either in prose or in verse turns to the poetry of white wet stones or tall green nettles or dry earth on a July headland he never fails to be a fine writer.

In *Tarry Flynn*, too, he displays a wonderful talent for caricature that can be comic without being spiteful, that extends but never distorts the truth. His peasants hiding the teacups at the sound of approaching footsteps so as to avoid the obligations of hospitality, his peasants invariably wishing each other ill, his Redemptorist preachers thundering about the dangers of young blood to pews filled with withered virgins and bachelors, are all caricatures; but who can honestly say that he has not put out a strong fist, browned with clay and dung, and innocently struck rural Ireland where it hurts.

Benedict Kiely. Modern Irish Fiction: A Critique
(Dublin, Golden Eagle Books, 1950), pp. 40–41

The career of Patrick Kavanagh presents extraordinary features completely outside the usual literary framework. His *Collected Poems* reveals an astonishing talent—according to some enthusiasts, the finest not only in Ireland but in all English-speaking areas—that has kept on renewing itself not so much by a process of orderly growth as by a continual breaching of boundaries. Judging by his recent poetic practice as well as his comment on that practice, it is clear that Kavanagh now stands free of all obligations except the deepest and most demanding claims of the open imagination.

The early work of this poet, born in 1904 in the Irish countryside, reflects a life close to the pieties and rude circumstances of the agricultural laborer. His disillusions with the lot of the Irish countryman came into being only after he had described that lot—in *The Great Hunger* (1942)—with mixed affection and loathing. His subsequent descriptions of Dublin literary life and politics were again filled with the blackest disillusion. Kavanagh's chief object of detestation has come to be the coat-trailing, charming, Irish semi-clown—a tragicomic caricature designed, according to the poet, for the foreign trade. Behind Kavanagh's intransigence stands a thorough understanding of modern traps laid on all sides for the bafflement of human dignity, as well as an unfaltering sense of some human innocence, marred but indestructible.

His satire, cutting close to the bone, spares neither cause, nor institution, nor individual. He names person and place, and he can be as scathing in a sonnet as in a piece of parody or a stretch of doggerel. Since, as he frankly states in his introductory author's note, written in London in 1964, he now dislikes much of his early verse, the selection of the poems in the new volume, of nearly two hundred pages, was left to his friend Martin Green, who has carried out his task admirably. To come upon Kavanagh's spontaneity is delightful, and one understands the sober reasons that have kept him from being listed among the more official and solemn post-Yeatsians. Far from officialdom of any kind, Kavanagh survives and flourishes in that invigorating region where, without respectable let or hindrance, the wild rivers run and the wild timber grows.

Louise Bogan. New Yorker, April 10, 1965,
pp. 194–96

"I have never been much considered by the English critics"—in the first sentence of Kavanagh's "Author's Note" to the *Collected Poems* it is hard to separate the bitterness from the boldness of "not caring." It was written towards the end of his career when he was sure, as I am, that he had contributed originally and significantly to the Irish literary tradition, not only in his poetry and his novel, *Tarry Flynn*, but also in his attempts to redefine the idea of that tradition.

Matters of audience and tradition are important in discussing Kavanagh. How do we "place" him? . . . Kavanagh's proper idiom is free from the intonations typical of the Revival poets. His imagination has not been tutored to "sweeten Ireland's wrong," his ear has not been programmed to retrieve in English the lost music of verse in Irish. The "matter of Ireland," mythic, historical or literary, forms no significant part of his material. There are a few Yeatsian noises—"why should I lament the wind"—in *Plowman* (1936), but in general the uncertain voice of that first book and the authoritative voice of *The Great Hunger* (1942) cannot be derived from the conventional notes of previous modern Irish poetry. What we have is something new, authentic and liberating. There is what I would call an artesian quality about his best work because for the first time since Brian Merriman's poetry in Irish at the end of the eighteenth century and William Carleton's novels in the nineteenth, a hard buried life that subsisted beyond the feel of middle-class novelists and romantic nationalist poets, a life denuded of "folk" and picturesque elements, found its expression. And in expressing that life in *The Great Hunger* and in *Tarry Flynn* (1948) Kavanagh forged not so much a conscience as a consciousness for the great majority of his countrymen, crossing the pieties of a rural Catholic sensibility with the *non serviam* of his original personality, raising the inhibited energies of a subculture to the power of a cultural resource.

Much of his authority and oddity derives from the fact that he wrested his idiom bare-handed out of a literary nowhere. [1975]

Seamus Heaney. *Preoccupations: Selected Prose, 1968–1978* (New York, Farrar, Straus & Giroux, 1980), pp. 115–16

All the younger poets, and by that I mean poets ranging in age from the mid-forties down to the twenties, seem to find it necessary to declare whether and if so how much they have been influenced by Kavanagh. All would agree, I think, that he did away with what was left of the Literary Renaissance and the idea of Ireland as a vague spiritual entity. Some, however, believe that he substituted a boastful, proud ignorance of the past for the romantic and nationalistic view of the past that characterized the Renaissance. Some are unwilling to junk the Irish language and its historical associations as Kavanagh did: he was opposed to the requiring of Irish in the schools, and he felt that if misguided people wished to study the language, they should be free to do so, but it was their own problem. Some have stopped at midpoint, as it were, to worry: they reject romantic nationalism, but they ponder the meaning of Ireland and the talismanic nuances of the names of important men and places. . . .

But Kavanagh's example has freed many younger Irish poets to find their own subjects and means of expression untrammeled by any tradition. In the case of the most talented of the younger poets, Seamus Heaney, who is thirty-five at the present writing, Kavanagh's influence has been fundamental. Heaney acknowledges that reading Kavanagh made him think that he might have something to write about himself. . . .

What has not as yet been passed on to a succeeding generation is Kavanagh's willingness, like Yeats's before him, to involve himself actively if individually in political and social issues. Several poets have written occasional verses in reaction to the situation in Northern Ireland, but aesthetically these works have been inferior, and they suggest the degree to which the rhetoric of romantic nationalism blights Irish poetry and politics have never been separate. They are not often separate elsewhere either, but the Irish, like all dominated people, have for centuries represented an especially dramatic example of the interpenetration of politics and poetry, life and art, so much so that it becomes impossible to speak of either realm without including the other. In designating *Kavanagh's Weekly* not a journal of the arts but *A Journal of Literature and Politics*, Kavanagh gave formal recognition to this truth, that when a nation's literature is confused about its national identity, it reflects confusion in the nation as a whole.

Darcy O'Brien. Patrick Kavanagh (Lewisburg, Pa.,
Bucknell Univ. Pr., 1975), pp. 66–69

Patrick Kavanagh repudiated his early and best known book *The Green Fool* as "Stage-Irish autobiography," and in one sense his so-called "autobiographical novel" *By Night Unstarred* looks like an attempt to reclaim Irish rural life from the lush romanticism and sometimes strained folksiness that marred the earlier venture. *Tarry Flynn*, Kavanagh's only other major fictional work, also has its roots in his formative years and like *The Green Fool* concerns itself with the growth of the poet against the background of the Irish countryside. Although Kavanagh was much more pleased with *Tarry Flynn*—modestly finding it "uproariously funny"—both it and *The Green Fool* are damaged by Kavanagh's semi-mystical love of nature and a certain platitudinous idealism that occurs whenever the subject of the poet's privileged insight and depth of feeling is raised.

By Night Unstarred* on the whole avoids these pitfalls; largely, I suspect, because the main portion of it has nothing to do with poets or poetry. Although claiming to be a "novel," the book really consists of an unfinished short novel and a short story that would have been far better left unjoined. Peter Kavanagh, the author's brother and the editor, has sought to produce a unified work of fiction by labelling the two disparate stories parts 1 and 2.

Part 1 is far and away the most successful of the two, and, not surprisingly, the least autobiographical. Set in the parish of Ballyrush near Dundalk at the beginning of the century it charts the remorseless rise to prosperity of a weasely Irish peasant called Peter Devine. Initially an impoverished farm labourer, he impregnates the local half-wit Rosie and has to flee the wrath of her family and the censure of the parish. He returns seven years later an obsessed and oddly motivated man. Maniacally set on becoming the richest man in the county, he courts the bulky daughter of the wealthiest farm-owner in the district and enlists the help of various colourful local characters to this end.

By sly manipulation and unscrupulous use of the village gossips a myth grows up about his eligibility and fairly soon he is accepted as a suitor. Devine's sole interest is in wealth and his romantic yearnings are wholly subservient to this drive ("When he noticed her wobbling breasts beneath the loose blouse he dreamt of the field before the door with the deep hollow in the middle"). Ultimately his dedication proves highly successful, and in material terms Peter Devine triumphs in everything he does from siring children to planting potatoes. The end of part 1 sees him poised on the edge of bourgeois prosperity—a rich mill owner and county councillor—with his financial horizons beginning to broaden: "The priest had smoked three cigarettes since coming into the room: a bit of money in a cigarette factory would be no dead loss, he thought."

The strength and vigour of Kavanagh's portrayal of the villagers of Ballyrush are due to the constancy of his ironic gaze; a steadfastness of viewpoint that *The Green Fool* and *Tarry Flynn* sadly lacked. Kavanagh sees all too clearly that country people are as pusillanimous, bitchy and determinedly mercenary as the rest of us, if not more so: "The misfortune of a neighbour provided nearly all the best delights of that part of the country." And Peter Devine, who dominates part 1, is explicitly alluded to as a personification of "the slime-stuck peasant unconscious of cities, of cultures, of everything but the power of money." There is a sharp Flaubertian cynicism in evidence, free from any romanticism or fond simplicity, which makes Ballyrush as mordant a picture of a rural community as Yonville in *Madame Bovary*.

William Boyd. *NewR*. Feb., 1978, p. 52

There is . . . a good deal to John Montague's celebrated remark that Kavanagh liberated Montague's generation, but into ignorance. Certainly Kavanagh was vulgarly disrespectful towards greater artists; in a 1963 radio discussion, Yeats is pronounced "all right," Synge a phoney and O'Casey "overrated." Certainly a sense of history is conspicuously absent from Kavanagh's poetry, something that would have enriched *The Great Hunger* as it enriched Montague's more ambitious long poem of the rural Catholic Irishry, *The Rough Field* (1972), though Montague has generously called Kavanagh's one of the four best long Irish poems since the eighteenth-century. And certainly Kavanagh was foolhardy in ignoring a Gaelic heritage that belonged more rightfully to him than to Yeats who inherited only his own fanciful version of that heritage. Devoid of history and cultural mythology, Kavanagh's parish (the lean parish of his art, to adapt Montague) could not provide him with sufficient fodder and we often have to settle in his poetry for mere gestures towards universality, repetitive discussions of possible topics, endless warming-up with very little energy left for the competitive leap. It got worse towards the end, as "the wish without will" caused him to flail around. . . .

But in earlier years, when the leap was made, it was done so with an illusion of effortlessness, as though he were some country champion who had never heard of training, with a lightness that the heavy responsibility of an historical awareness might indeed have prevented.

It is hard not to see Kavanagh as a somewhat comic scapegoat, bearing in his figure that vulgarity, ignorance, sense of inferiority, disrespectfulness and country cuteness that had to be purged before the culturally dispossessed Catholic rural writer could come into his own. This was Kavanagh's liberating legacy to the generation of [Seamus] Heaney and [Seamus] Deane. Kavanagh was conscious of his role of scapegoat, of "the undone/god-gifted man," as he described himself in "Love in a Meadow," but not of its poetic implications. A stable identity and consistent voice, lyrically expressed, might seem to have been Kavanagh's supreme and tragically wasteful sacrifice, yet it ironically enabled him to become a pivotal figure in twentieth-century Irish poetry, as significant for his influence as for the score of lovely and entangled lyrics and *The Great Hunger* that were his more immediate achievement. But perhaps Kavanagh should have been even more faithful than he was to his thwarted dramatic and mythopoeic drives, thwarted because he believed himself at bottom a lyricist. The impulse was there. Critics such as [Alan] Warner and Deane who see Kavanagh as always himself, "a bare-faced poet" who has "no masks," would do better to see him as never himself. For which is the truest poetry—the allegorical filigree, the lyrical remembrance, the social indictment, the scathing doggerel, the alleged repose? Kavanagh knew himself cannily, but the self he knew was always his previous role into which he believed himself seduced, and never the current role from the point of view of which the previous role was repudiated.

John Wilson Foster. *Mosaic*. Spring, 1979,
pp. 151–52

Not surprisingly of all the poems he wrote the one that has received the highest praise and that will ensure his reputation as a man of great talent is also the one that has been the most influential. Despite his remarks to the contrary, Kavanagh sensed the importance of *The Great Hunger* before he died. In a letter to his brother Peter in which he complained about the critics' lack of enthusiasm for his work, he called himself a "literary diamond mine which has been till now viciously ignored by American 'critics' and neglected by English ones," and predicted that "within a few months or a year the critics are about to awaken to realize the enormous influence I have had on such poets as, for instance, R. S. Thomas." Though the great awakening that he predicted has yet to occur, he was not at all wrong about the influence of his poetry on younger writers. His choice of R. S. Thomas as evidence of his influence was not only quite apt, but was also an indication of the impact he believed *The Great Hunger* had made on other poets. Even the most casual reading of Thomas's long poem *The Minister* (1953) indicates the debt it owes to *The Great Hunger*.

The Great Hunger's influence is even more apparent in the work being produced by some of Ireland's better younger writers. Instead of merely imitating Kavanagh, these poets work the poetic ground broken by *The Great Hunger*. To them, the importance of Kavanagh's poem lies in the fact that it has opened the way and provided a model for writing about universal themes without losing the texture of the Irish scene. Examples of this are Richard Murphy's *Sailing to an Island* and John Montague's *Poisoned Lands*. While these poets treat different materials, and while they employ form and language in different ways, they are representative of those younger writers who follow Kavanagh's practice of treating human problems in an Irish setting without reverting to the trite divisions of squire and peasant. One of the ironies of Kavanagh's life is that in not being overly concerned with literary traditions he should be praised for starting one.

However one chooses to view Kavanagh, the vitality that he brought to Irish poetry, the lyrically articulated vision of the self that emerges from his writing, and the final affirmation of life and its possibilities combine to ensure his continued reputation as one of Ireland's great literary artists.

John Nemo. *Patrick Kavanagh* (Boston, Twayne, 1979), pp. 146–47

Kavanagh is at once more local and more cosmopolitan than the nationalists. His work insists on the poet's partial relation to the nation. He sees Irish life, and life in general, through his small parish in Inniskeen, County Monaghan, Republic of Ireland, and later, through Baggot Street, near the Grand Canal, Dublin, Ireland. But while his subjects are personal, immediate, and local, his standards are universal. If an Irish poem had value, he argued, it would have the same value for a Chinaman as for an Irishman. . . .

From the point of view of literary nationalism, Kavanagh's position offered enviable possibilities for a poet: from his little farm he enjoyed a permanent view of mists, heather, swans, and the other paraphernalia of Celtic poetry. In the cabin kitchen, the parish church, and the village pub, he could drink deep from the springs of folk wisdom and poetical speech . . . he might even get to know a beautiful Irish virgin who could serve as a symbol for the spirit of Ireland! But in "Inniskeen Road: July Evening," Kavanagh insists on his disappointment with his region as a place to live in or write about. . . .

Lionel Trilling, writing about Wordsworth in *Sincerity and Authenticity*, observes that "authenticity is implicitly a polemical concept, fulfilling its nature by dealing aggressively with received and habitual opinion." Kavanagh's presentation of an ordinary evening in Inniskeen is intended to be offensive in this way. It attacks, both implicitly and explicitly, the habitual opinions of

Irish nationalists and literary sophisticates on country quaintness, traditionalism, and solitude. Few other Irish poets would have transported peasants by
any other means than the quaint donkey-cart, or forgone the opportunity to introduce the traditional ballad-singing, match-making, and jig-dancing into the
festivities of Billy Brennan's barn. But the details of Kavanagh's poem are
negative instances which challenge the nationalist opinion that quaint old
Gaelic ways survived in rural Irish society. Not donkey carts, but bicycles.
No expression of social instincts through ancient courtship rituals; those instincts have been repressed into furtive and ridiculous channels. Instead of
ballads, there is half-talk; and instead of dancing, there is winking and el-
bowing. One can guess that this dance will be a bunch of men lined up along
the barn walls nudging each other as they ogle the shufflings of the few couples with nerve enough to dance. Although Kavanagh does not make the point
as explicitly here as in later poems (such as "The Great Hunger"), he implies
that "the ancient spirit of Ireland," in Inniskeen at any rate, is weak, old, and
well on its way to death. The nationalist poets looked to rural Irish society
for presences of the past, but Kavanagh finds in his parish only palpable
absences.

Adrian Frazier. *MalahatR*. Jan., 1980,
pp. 112, 114–15

Patrick Kavanagh often described his work and his life in the image of a journey: "All we learn from experience is the way from simplicity back to simplicity." It is a traditional image, at root that of an Eden lost and a journey
through the infernal places of the world to a recovered innocence, a paradise
regained which is like and unlike the original, its innocence more aware, radical, profound, its simplicity "the ultimate sophistication." Although, therefore, he bemoaned the lack of a sustaining myth ("A myth is necessary, for a
myth is a sort of self-contained world in which one can live," *Pruse*, 268), his
own poetic identity is a product, casual as well as deliberate, of the most accessible of Western myths, that of the pastoral. The early poems represent an
experience of pastoral innocence; the later reflect upon this and repossess it in
a new mode. To look at Kavanagh's poetry through the pastoral lens permits
the design of that work to emerge in a rich, consistent light. . . .

   In summary . . . the pastoral convention with a number of its traditional
variants supplies a coherent frame for the poetic identity Kavanagh's work
composes. It does not, of course, account for the poetry, but its does provide
a way of organizing it critically. It offers a way into the poetry in terms of the
poetry itself, rendering it in certain ways independent of its time and place. At
the same time it allows us to see that the value of this myth, this conventional
design, consists in the particular life Kavanagh gave to it, filling the traditional literary outline with the matter of his own time and place, his own self.
In this way he extends the form, substantiating in an unlikely context the en-

during validity of this particular mode. He proves, I would argue, that the genre is not merely a literary imposition designed for the convenience of critics, but is a fundamental shaping mode through which the material of a poet's identity comes to coherence, even when on the surface that material seems as inchoate as that often provided by Kavanagh. The pastoral impulse and design, therefore, reveal a human response solidified into a literary form, and enable us to look at Kavanagh's work with a fresh eye.

Eamon Grennan. Renascence. Autumn, 1981,
pp. 3, 15

The Editorial of the final issue of *Kavanagh's Weekly* refers to "the very useful lesson" which the editor [Patrick Kavanagh] had learned. For one thing he was, perhaps, shown the need to be an "insider" if one were to make a success of a weekly of that kind. No "journal of literature and politics," as its masthead claimed it to be, could be wholly successful without access to the kind of privileged, behind-the-scenes information which the correspondents, say, of the *New Statesman* and the *Spectator* enjoy. By the very nature of its policies and its producers, *Kavanagh's Weekly* had to remain in this sense an "outsider." . . .

[T]he cultural criticism in the *Weekly* and elsewhere may be seen as covert autobiography, in the sense that by defining the enemies of his poetic vision Kavanagh was aided in the process of self-realization. Insofar as his cultural criticism reveals Kavanagh's personal poetic vision as, essentially, the apotheosis of the everyday, one may be reminded, strangely, of Yeats's early resolve to show that the ordinary, everyday feelings of a lifetime were enough for poetry and of his observation near the end of his life that only a relatively small part of the total personality can be given substance in poetry. It may be argued that, in Kavanagh's case, that part of his personality which could not be brought fully to expression in his poetry found its expression through his cultural criticism, visionary, humorous and satirical. This paper has also tried to trace the emergence, from Kavanagh's days as the poet-isolate of Mucker to his days as *Envoy* critic and editor of *Kavanagh's Weekly*, of a belief that he could bring to bear through his cultural criticism the socially-redemptive influence of "the poetic spirit"; a quasi-messianic conviction that his role both as poet and critic was to galvanize a society virtually moribund. The importance of *Kavanagh's Weekly* in his overall development is that as well as providing him with an opportunity to advance that concept, it also killed it. Just as it may have been necessary for his poetry to pass through a period of satire to achieve a condition of convalescence if not regeneration, so it may have been necessary for his critical aesthetic to pass through the annealing fire of the failure of *Kavanagh's Weekly*.

Certainly, his later cultural criticism, while addressing itself to the same targets and conveying the same message—that the Ireland of the 1950's and

1960's was not the social and cultural community it ought to be—was marked by an absence of arrogance, a gentler humour and a mellower tone. Certainly, too, it seemed that through his cultural criticism he was able to aspire nearer to a Keatsian condition of "negative capability"; and his sense of that progress is summed up in the closing verses appended to the final Editorial of *Kavanagh's Weekly:*

> We must be nothing,
> Nothing that God may make us something.

> G. H. M. Brian Baird. In Heinz Kosok, ed., *Studies*
> *in Anglo-Irish Literature* (Bonn, Bouvier, 1982),
> p. 366

KEANE, JOHN B. (1928–   )

The popularity of *Sive* seems at first difficult to explain. The play is not original in its situation, theme, or realistic manner. The problem of a young girl forced into a marraige with an older farmer by her grasping relatives has been used and reused in Irish plays. Carroll's *Things That Are Caesar's* is basically the same situation, and D'Alton's *Lovers Meeting* is even closer. . . . All of the curtains, save the last, dribble away; and much of the last act depends upon the ancient device of the undelivered letter. There is, in other words, nothing in the plot that other authors could not have done more felicitously.

Some of these flaws, however, loom larger in retrospect than they do in the playing. In a really good production, the charge of melodrama seems an academic quibble, for the piece hovers close to tragedy in its grip upon the audience. . . . The reasons for the play's theatrical strength seem to me the meticulously faithful realism, the firm character-drawing, the brutally observed theme, and the emotionally effective songs of the two wandering tinkers.

Shiels, D'Alton, Murray, Robinson, and MacNamara were all excellent realistic playwrights, but their realism hardly ever caught an audience up with a shock of recognition. Keane, however, has focused his vision with a harder clarity upon the minutiae of everyday life. Superficially, this clarity can be seen in his diction. Words like "Bogdeal, doodeen, bocock, muller, lurgadawn, tathaire" appear frequently enough to suggest that these characters are not far removed from a time when Irish was spoken. The diction is only one of several qualities which suggest a whole culture and complex of ideas. . . .

In many realistic plays, the minor characters at the edge of the picture fade off vaguely. They are only stereotypes, there for the purpose of the plot. The edges of Keane's photograph are never fuzzy. Sean Dota, the obscene and senile old farmer who hopes to marry Sive, is a small part, and so is Liam Scuab the boy who loves her, and so is Carthalawn the simpleton poet son of the tinker—yet each is defined with a convincing individuality. If there is any deficiency in the character-drawing, it is in Sive herself, for she does not really hold her own with Mena or the matchmaker or the tinkers.

The strongest quality of the play is the cold accuracy with which Keane paints the lust for money. This is the basic theme of innumerable Irish plays, but it has rarely been put with such cold clarity since William Boyle's most venomous play *The Building Fund* or since Carroll's *Things That Are Caesar's*. Keane's characters have a Jonsonian rapacity. Sive's Aunt Mena and the matchmaker Thomasheen Sean Rua are almost monsters of greed, but yet never unbelievable. . . .

One of the most deadening qualities of realism is its lack of the theatrical elements of song, spectacle, color, dance, and music. Keane avoids this pitfall by means of the traveling tinkers, Pats Bocock and Carthalawn. These characters emerge naturally from his landscape, but in the play they function in about the same way that the Greek chorus did—that is, they help arouse emotion by theatrical rather than literary means. Carthalawn's songs are stinging commentaries upon the action and immensely effective. The song at the end of the play, for instance, does not have great effect as a poem on a page, but when sung to Keane's tune it creates a conclusion of haunting intensity.

Robert Hogan. *After the Irish Renaissance.*
(Minneapolis, Univ. of Minnesota Pr., 1967),
pp. 210–13

One of Mr. Keane's problems is that he shows a noted disregard for the disciplines of stage craft. Another is that the characters he creates tend to be too locally rooted in idioms and attitudes. They may be perfectly true to type in relation to their immediate natural environment, which is largely Mr. Keane's native county of Kerry, but in a wider context, they tend to be quaint.

Many of them have quaint names, like Thomasheen Sean Rua, Dora MacMoo, Mickey Molly, Pats Bo Bwee, Tom Shawn and Daheen Timineen Din. They are quaint in their manner of speaking and they are quaint in their behavior. Their language is often colorfully and authentically rich, for Mr. Keane has a keen ear and a way with words, but like some excellent local wines, they do not travel well.

The latest Keane play is titled *The Chastitute*, and it has been performed at the Olympia Theatre. The principal character is a 53-year-old farmer who explains that a "chastitute"—in this case himself—is the opposite of a prostitute. He has been terrified into a state of chronic sexual repression by a fire-and-brimstone sermon he heard a dour missionary preach when he was a youth, and nothing can release him from his trap of involuntary celibacy. A knowing parish priest eggs him on to break loose, but to no avail, and a number of assignations arranged by acquaintances end ludicrously and disastrously. There is nothing left for the farmer but either to shoot himself, which he decides against, or to take a bottle of whiskey as spouse and live out what remains of his barren existence consoled by alcohol. He is determined to follow the latter course as the curtain falls. In one respect, Mr. Keane is ploughing a furrow beloved of Sean O'Casey. He proclaims that life should be lived fully, uninhibitedly, and joyously, and that love should be exalted and encouraged. He also condemns Jansenistic aspects of Irish Catholicism. In this he is wasting his time, because the type of hell-fire missionary he portrays is as irrelevant to life in Ireland today as is last year's snow.

Desmond Rushe. *Éire-Ireland*. Fall, 1980, pp. 114–15

An independent theatre company which has survived from the late 1950s is Gemini Productions, founded by the actress and producer Phyllis Ryan and the actor Norman Rodway.

Gemini presented the first productions of many of John B. Keane's best plays, among them *The Highest House on the Mountain* (1960), *The Field* (1965), *Big Maggie* (1968) and *The Chastitute* (1980). John B. Keane (b. 1928) may not have been influenced by the work of George Fitzmaurice, but the language of his early plays shares the North Kerry quirkiness of the older writer. *Sive* (1959) was rejected by the Abbey but presented by the amateur drama group in Listowel and subsequently on Radio Eireann. It is no exaggeration to say that it caused a sensation—the rediscovery by the urbanized Ireland of the rural background from whence it had sprung was quite traumatic in the age which saw the establishment of Shannon New Town, the first jumbo jets carrying the Irish insignia, the inauguration of the television service, and the first Programme for Economic Expansion. *Sive* is a bleak and cruel story of rural poverty, in which a young girl is forced to make a match with an older man. The story was not a new one, but its treatment was new, and Keane did not feel compelled to exclude crudities of language which earlier writers of folk plays could not have used.

In Keane's *Sharon's Grave* (1960) the two grotesque brothers Jack and Dinzie Conlee have the appearance of a two-headed monster, for Dinzie is a cripple and is carried around on Jack's shoulders; instantly one is reminded of the blind and lame beggars in Yeats' *The Cat and the Moon*—with the difference that the strong, even violent, sexuality of Keane's characters introduce a force hitherto strangely muted in Irish drama.

Sharon's Grave was first produced by the Southern Theatre Group in Cork, under James N. Healy's direction. Keane's canon of plays gradually moves from the remote rural setting to the county town. He is at his best when ridiculing inhibition and hypocrisy. Many of his plays have benefited from work in production, especially by the director Barry Cassin, for Keane, once a script has been accepted for performance, seems reluctant to prune and revise.

Christopher Fitz-Simon. *The Irish Theatre* (London, Thames and Hudson, 1983), pp. 190–91

Keane was born in 1928, son of a local teacher in Listowel, Co. Kerry, where he now owns a pub. Apart from a couple of years as a labourer in England, from where he returned in 1953, he has spent his life there. He is a prolific writer: journalism, essays, fiction, and over a dozen plays. Of the last, produced mostly by the Southern Theatre Company, the most notable are *Sive* (1959), *Many Young Men of Twenty* (1961), *Hut 42* (Abbey, 1962), *The Man from Clare* (1962), *The Year of the Hiker* (1963), *The Field* (1966), *Big Maggie* (1970). Geographically but not imaginatively, their locale is George Fitzmaurice's countryside, no longer so evocative of demonic dolls.

Like M. J. Molloy, Keane writes in the main line of Irish peasant drama. Unlike Molloy, he has not turned to historical subjects, though his plays never come wholly to terms with contemporary Irish life and the erosion, if not the loss, of old customs. During a crucial scene in *The Field* a jet plane is heard flying by, perhaps to contrast with the community, or enclave, beneath it, where the feuding land hunger of the nineteenth century persists. The play certainly has nothing to do with jet planes, nor with the myriad psychological implications they might represent. In it, an outsider who has bought a field over the rival claims of a local farmer is murdered. Though known, the murderer is never charged, a bullying victory in which he is subtly aware of a defeat. The play is an authentic enough portrayal of the speech, the close-mouthed privacies and parochial defensiveness of "a small village in the southwest of Ireland." The central character, "Bull" McCabe, emanates a brooding physical menace, but the play never brings him, its story, and the telling of its story, into "The Present." The aircraft, the electricity and television, the talk of women as 'birds' remain trappings.

In *Hut 42*, set on a building site in the north of England, much of the chat of the characters—essentially the joke trio, an Englishman, an Irishman and a Welshman—is easy listening. They do their "turns" while—the simple plot unrolls—a bad Irishman disgraces his nation and is put down. Though *Hut 42* sentimentalises the exile, his drunken heart of gold and "love of a small home in Ireland," it has a promise which Keane's writing since his plays returned to Irish settings has not realised. He takes up urgent themes whose Irish forms, fully expressed, are comprehensible beyond their locality: exile, loss of faith, dead or dying folkways and their often garish replacements. Keane's Kerry is an indecisive fiction which falls short of wider identifications.

D. E. S. Maxwell. *A Critical History of Modern Irish Drama* (Cambridge, England, Cambridge Univ. Pr., 1984), pp. 168–69

KEANE, MOLLY (also known as M. J. FARRELL and MARY LESTA SKRINE, 1905?–)

[*Mad Puppetstown*] follows a more or less familiar pattern, but it is written with so much beauty and freshness that it seems, while one is reading it, to be alone of its kind. It is primarily a novel of locale, and nothing in it is so important as the feeling of a particular place that it conveys—the atmosphere, the color and activity, the sights and sounds of an Irish home. The considerations of plot and character are secondary—though the plot, what there is of it, is quite adequate, and the characters are ably and unmistakeably drawn. Puppetstown, the seat of the Chevingtons, dominates the book.

In those mellow and prosperous years before the war and before the turbulent outbreak of the Irish rebellion, Puppetstown had been the centre of life for the Chevingtons—a beautiful old house, with its parks and paddocks and bridle paths, with its flower gardens, where Aunt Dicksie was perpetually occupied with shears and trowel, with its ponds and trout streams where the children played, with its brooding guardian mountains, Mandoran, Mooncoln, and the Black Stair. It was a place of easy and gracious hospitality, with its stables filled with good horses and its cellars with fine wines, with sporting prints on its walls and a fire of ash or laurel on its broad hearth. Above all, Puppetstown was Irish to the core—there was something that set it apart from a similar country place in England, a hint of savagery or romantic wildness that responded perfectly to the romantic wildness in the blood of the Irish Chevingtons.

M. J. Farrell succeeds admirably in evoking this characteristic atmosphere as it grew into the consciousness of three children—Easter Chevington and her two cousins, Basil and Evelyn—who were bred with the spirit of Puppetstown and the love of racing and hunting in their blood. Then comes a break in their lives. Easter's father is killed in the war and the children are removed to relatives in England because the countryside round Puppetstown is being ravaged by the Sinn Feiners. In the leaner years that followed the great war and the little, bitter forgotten war in Ireland, there remained to them only a few golden memories of Puppetstown, where Aunt Dicksie stayed on, growing madder and more miserly with the passing years. Then Easter attains her majority and the ownership of Puppetstown passes to her. Basil and Evelyn have finished at Oxford and Evelyn engages himself to a girl of adequate fortune and irreproachable antecedents and succumbs to English respectability. But in Basil and Easter there is a lingering homesickness, a sense of being strangers in a strange land. "England," said Basil, "she's too crowded. We want a littler, wilder sort of place. We're half English, both of us, Easter, but we haven't got the settled, stable drop of blood that goes down with the English."

So Basil and Easter return to Puppetstown—but to a Puppetstown that is changed, to a house fallen into decay from neglect and disuse under the jealous and miserly care of Aunt Dicksie. There is a double tragedy in the conflict of their homecoming—tragedy on the part of the young people who find the place spiritually closed against them and on the part of Aunt Dicksie, who sees it about to be taken from her. . . .

To reveal the fashion of the tragedy's resolving would do as much injustice to the beauty of Miss Farrell's writing, as to the tact and appropriateness of her conception. Suffice it to say that *Mad Puppetstown* is a novel superb in its kind, and that there will be few who can read it unsympathetically.

NYTBR. June 19, 1932, p. 7

The title of this new novel [*The Rising Tide*] by Miss Farrell covers the mystery of one more "Big House." In Garonlea the rule of Lady Charlotte McGrath brought not only gloom but rebellion. The revolt of the children against the rule of parents is now too hackneyed to be interesting; but Miss Farrell brings a novel type of rebel into her story. As in *The Silver Cord*, [Sidney] Howard's play, it is a daughter-in-law who starts the whole business.

The Victorian atmosphere, which had survived the death of the Queen, was dispelled, although the seeds of revolt remain. They sprout anew in the offspring of Cynthia, bringing about a rebellion against the tyranny of the mother who would have her children live the kind of life she had chosen for herself and them. When her husband is killed in the Great War Cynthia pursues the gay life with even greater avidity, plunging from the open-air sporting world into a boisterous whirl of love and alcohol. She is the "Merry Widow" in a new guise, and when she goes down against the rising tide she leaves behind her a trail of sympathy and admiration. The characters are all drawn with Miss Farrell's customary skill, and the novel will be found thoroughly entertaining.

Irish Times. Oct. 25, 1937, p. 7

M. J. Farrell is feminine and Irish and fanciful, but she does not belong to the peaty school. The plot of *The Enchanting Witch* is a gay exaggeration of how people in love behave. The setting is precisely right for what is to come—an "absurd" Victorian Gothic dwelling on the south coast of Ireland, perched on a cliff overlooking an inlet of the Atlantic. With its flying bastions, preposterously mullioned windows and elegant but cluttered interior, it suited its poised and willful, willowy châtelaine—a beautiful widow of forty-seven who "held her chin so high against the flying years that it gave her a silly look sometimes." Her son and daughter called her Angel, and so did Oliver, who managed the estate admirably and courted her lightly, being the only person in her orbit who saw through her. The rest of the ménage comprised shy Tiddley, a niece who adored Angel and received cast-off finery and crumbs of thanks for her devotion; Miss Birdie, the cook, who saw love in the cards, and Finn Barr, a young ex-poacher who helped in the kitchen and the garden.

All the troubles in this household have one origin: Angel rushes in and fears to tread on no one's life. Masked as affection and superior wisdom, her motives are selfish in every instance. Birdie has missed out on a husband, more than once, thanks to Angel who enjoys the intoxication of power—and wants to hang on to a good cook.

When the curtain rises—*The Enchanting Witch* has the tight construction of a play, with most of the action within a twenty-four-hour span—Angel is up to her uptilted chin in two projects. She is strewing misunderstanding between her daughter, Slaney, and a neighbor boy madly in love with her and a good match besides. And she has everything in readiness to welcome her son after three years in the war. What the adoring mother does not know is that Julian is bringing home from the Tyrol an American divorcee who helped him through shock and has promised to marry him. Sally Wood has been an actress and knocked about considerably; she knows the Angels of the world and quickly takes the measure of this one. The antagonists are well matched, however, and they purr before they scratch.

The witches' brew has some added ingredients that are quite delicious. Sally has a worshipful manservant, her ex-husband's valet, who can whip up a toque, a drink or an omelet with equal speed and skill. He is the answer to Miss Birdie's dream and the cards. Poor Tiddley, as you probably surmise, has always been secretly in love with Julian, and Oliver, the farseeing overseer, happens to be an old flame of Julian's fiancée. The issue is joined at the tea table, in the pantry, in the flower garden and up in Angel's room.

The Enchanting Witch is by no means a romantic soufflé: it has scenes as sharp as vinegar. The climax is comedy—a well-kept secret we shall not unguard here.

Lisle Bell. *NYHT*. Oct. 14, 1951, p. 21

The story behind *Good Behaviour* has been widely publicised, as part of a promotion campaign for the book. As "M.J. Farrell," the author was a successful novelist and dramatist who ceased writing fiction in the 1950s and plays in the early 1960s. The reason given is that sudden widowhood "broke the springs of her creative energy." In 1980, Farrell was, in literary terms, dead. None of her books were in print; encyclopedias like *Contemporary Novelists* did not mention her. At midsummer 1981, *Good Behaviour* was published *in propria persona* and became a best-seller in America and Ireland. In early autumn the novel was published in Britain, and Molly Keane joined six others on this year's somewhat extended list of Booker Prize candidates.

One might suspect hype in reports of this extraordinary come-back story. But in fact *Good Behaviour* is as successful a novel as Deutsch's hand-outs claim it to be. It opens with a scene which cunningly draws the reader into false sympathy. A spinster daughter forces rabbit on a bedridden mother for whom the meat is revolting. The mother chokes and dies, and the daughter is upbraided by a faithful servant for her sadistic bullying: "We're all killed from you and it's a pity it's not yourself lying there and your toes cocked for the grave and not a word more about you, God damn you!" As if to challenge this, the remainder of the novel flashes back to an earlier generation, and the daughter's victimisation by her mother, then a woman well-bred to the pitch of domestic monstrosity: "She had had us and she longed to forget the horror of it once and for all. She engaged nannie after nannie with excellent references, and if they could not be trusted to look after us, she was even less able to compete. She didn't really like children; she didn't like dogs either, and she had no enjoyment of food, for she ate almost nothing."

The setting is Irish, and the novel exploits an Irish comic situation which goes back at least as far as Thackeray: gentility's struggle to preserve itself against invading shabbiness. The St. Charles family is first discovered living a pre-war, prosperous "leisured life." 1914 brings catastrophe and gradual decline. The heroine's dashing father loses a leg in the Great War and survives a whisky-sodden philanderer. The family's only son is killed in a motoring accident. Debts accumulate. The father has a stroke and dies leaving the two St. Charles women destitute, except for the house, Temple Alice. To everyone's surprise, this is left to the fat, unwanted pathetic daughter; she has no marriage chances, but she can devote the rest of her life to a filial revenge of the violence of which she is clearly unaware. Hence the distasteful rabbit of the first scene.

The charm of *Good Behaviour* is in its telling. Aroon's narrative (it may be a journal, or interior monologue—we're not told) is marked by total recall, habitual impercipience and odd flashes of eloquence. "Good behaviour" is shown to be her guiding principle, and it preserves her in the various crises of her life. When her brother's friend comes to her bed (in fact, he is using her as a decoy, to hide a homosexual involvement with the brother) it is good behaviour that keeps her virginity and her consoling romantic illusions intact. When the scheming lawyer makes advances to her (he knows the terms of the will), it is not penetration of his motives but the instinct of good behaviour that saves her: "One of Mummie's phrases came to me and I spoke it, in her voice: 'You must be out of your mind,' I said, and I knocked his hand away. In spite of my heartbreak and tears, I was, after all, Aroon St. Charles."

I hope *Good Behaviour* wins its prize. But it will have to combat the fact that its author's literary resurrection happened in America, and caught on here.

John Sutherland. *LRB*. Oct. 15, 1981, p. 16

In *Time After Time* . . . Molly Keane has written a novel of locked lives, of four people imprisoned in age and habit. Living together in a decaying Irish mansion, Jasper Swift and his three sisters suffer from what Ronald Blythe in *The View in Winter*, his study of old people, called "the destruction of progressive movement."

Jasper, a bachelor who is 74 years old, lives for his cooking and his garden. April, the eldest of the three sisters, is widowed and deaf. She lives for her elegant clothes and the remnants of her beauty. May, who never married because of a deformed hand, devotes herself to handicrafts in order to forestall the world's pity. June, the baby sister at age 64, is a barely literate dyslexic, an upperclass peasant who cares only about the farm attached to the house.

As if they had triangulated the major possibilities of personality, the three sisters dislike one another. Jasper, the inspired cook, despises the poverty of their ingredients. He laughs at them as he laughs at the absurd recipes of the woman's page in the newspaper. While their lives are hollow dramas, his is a thin comedy.

So they might have remained, if Leda, their cousin, had not returned to Durraghglass, as the house is called, for a visit. She is Jasper's age and he had loved her when he was 7 years old and she lived with them. Leda left the house in her teens, surrounded by scandal and suggestions of an affair with their father. After more than 50 years, Jasper and his sisters had assumed that she was dead.

Leda is blind, as if Miss Keane had set herself the task of exploring every kind of disablement. "Since she could not see Durraghglass in its cold decay, or her cousins in their proper ages, timeless grace was given to them in her assumption that they looked as though all the years between were empty myths," Miss Keane writes. "Because they knew themselves so imagined, their youth was present to them, a mirage trembling in her flattery as air trembles close on the surface of summer roads." . . .

Blindness, Leda says, is "an adventure" for her. It shields her, she believes, from the vulgarity of the visual. She maintains that she gets to know people better, that she approaches them through the superior channels of the spirit. The sisters, who all have dogs instead of friends, respond to Leda as if she were the only surviving human being in their world. . . .

As Montaigne said, "We are always beginning again to live," and this is the underlying theme of *Time After Time*. When Yeats asked, "Why should not old men be mad?" he might have spoken for women as well. In Miss Keane's novel, madness is only the beginning of sanity for her characters. She's a drastic woman, Miss Keane is, which is just what a novelist should be. She, too, went through an interesting rebirth. After establishing herself in the 1930's as one of Ireland's most interesting novelists, she fell silent for several decades. In 1981, in her 70's, she reappeared with a novel called *Good Behavior*, which seems to have delighted everyone who reviewed it. Now, with *Time After Time*, Miss Keane continues her "progressive movement."

Anatole Broyard. *NYTd*. Jan. 11, 1984, p. C22

Through writers as various as Aldous Huxley, Evelyn Waugh, D. H. Lawrence, Elizabeth Bowen, Dorothy Sayers, we have been exposed to a group of people who responded to the disintegration of the First World War with a brittle determination to cut themselves off from the world that had been too real for them. The novels and plays about these people would lead us to believe that there had been no General Strike in 1926, and that the poor existed to be invisible and perfect servants and a source of Cockney jokes. One wouldn't have thought the same thing was going on across the sea in Ireland, but two early novels by M. J. Farrell assure us that it was. *Devoted Ladies* was first published in 1934 and *The Rising Tide* followed three years later. They are now made available by Penguin Books, which has taken on distribution in this country of the splendid books of the British Virago Press, which is reissuing works by 19th- and 20th-century women that we otherwise would not have known.

M. J. Farrell's novels are brilliant evocations of a world that strained to combine, to its peril, the old way of life that centered on hunting and the foreign modern influences of cocktails, homosexuality, adultery and inappropriate fur coats. We are pulled up short remembering that the Ireland M. J. Farrell (the pseudonym used by Molly Keane in her early books) is describing had just been torn by a murderous and suicidal civil war; politics has no corner in these rich people's world. There are hardly even any Catholics.

What strange and vivid books they are, these two, their timbre female in some sexually stinging way: unloving mothers hiding and demanding in the background and cruel beauties exacting obeisance from the unfortunate, the plain, the merely lovesick. Miss Farrell is Anglo-Irish, but she shares the native Irish female tendency to assume that real life is lived by women; the men in these two books are handsome, stupid, amiable, ineffectual and balked. These are the heterosexuals; the homosexual men are as vicious and rapacious as the women, and their vision is as comprehending and as sure. . . .

Miss Farrell's genius lies in her remorselessness. Cruelty, she suggests, is the dominant feature of any human landscape the eye can fall upon. One chooses merely one's mode, which differs with the age. The Victorians and Edwardians were smothering and dishonest; moderns are heedless and anonymous. The poison is the same; only the vessels change. . . . She has in all her work taken her countryman W. B. Yeats's advice to "cast a cold eye," and we are chastened and refreshed by her singular vision.

Mary Gordon. *NYTBR*. Sept. 29, 1985, p. 43

KIELY, BENEDICT (1919–   )

As a schoolboy of eighteen I stood within a few yards of Carson (short for Carsoni) at the great review of Ulster Volunteers at Balmoral. I had got there by a trick, and contact at a distance of a few yards with demagogy in action did nothing to dispel the loathing I felt for the man and his works. When I got home again after the review to a house with its attic packed with Carson rifles, I was asked what I thought. I said, "Any fool can do that sort of thing, but it will take a man to put it together again!" For that slight exaggeration I was nearly put out on the street minus even the proverbial shilling!

That was my first impression of Carsoni the Illusionist, the man who tried to persuade himself and history that he had successfully sawn Kathleen Ni Houlihan in two. Now, more than thirty years later, comes Mr. Benedict Kiely with *Counties of Contention*, a fresh account of the whole operation. The first piece of Mr. Kiely's writing I ever read gave me a sensation of smoothness and power. Here is an Ulsterman, from Tyrone, that Ulster island in the heart of Ulster, a man whose writing has the qualities of the rock whence he was hewn. I don't know whether Mr. Kiely is a native Gaelic speaker or not, but he writes English in a way that reminds me of Peadar O'Donnell, and that is the highest praise I know how to bestow. Some of the purest writing in English that I know has come from Gaelic-speaking Ulstermen: there is a gaiety and a sparkle, a serene, pellucid flowing through which you gaze downwards at the depths below. . . .

Here, at any rate, is a young Ulsterman from Tyrone who has written a history of Partition in such a mood of serenity and justice that not even a rabid Orangeman should see red on reading it. But serene as the mood of *Counties of Contention* may be, the language is vivid and forceful. . . . It has a dark, Swiftian mastery. . . .

[Mr. Kiely] has managed to compress a literary-historical account of the background to Partition into the compass of 186 pages. Carson, John Redmond, the decline and fall of the Irish Parliamentary Party, the climax to all that "delirium of the brave" in 1916, Lord Randolph Churchill play-acting for Belfast business men in the Ulster Hall—here is the whole shooting-gallery set against the panorama of our times in Ulster.

Politically-minded young men reading from the extreme "left" probably will not approve; they would probably prefer more of Connolly and more of Carson as a kind of stalking-horse for the industrial bosses of the north-east. But for the middle-aged, who lived through the times, and for all those who believe that the ending of Partition must precede any really sensible solution of the problem of our relations with the outside world, this story of Partition, written by a young Ulsterman of rare literary and imaginative power who never allows himself to misuse facts, is like a lens, collecting and concentrating light from an extraordinarily wide variety of original sources. Mr. Kiely has dug deep into the history of Partition, and in digging has unearthed some gems.

Denis Ireland. The Bell. Aug., 1945, pp. 450–52

Benedict Kiely is remarkable primarily in that among contemporaries who write often badly and generally seldom he has published five novels of some importance, two critical studies, and a political work while yet on the right side of thirty-five. That is not to suggest that his is mainly a quantitative achievement—quite the contrary. If there is any sense at all in talking of "the European novel" the best of Kiely belongs in that category beside Gide's and Mauriac's and Green's and Koestler's and Soldati's. His world [in *The Cards of the Gambler*] is essentially a beleagured one, in which the integrity of the individual is threatened both from within and without; less concrete a threat perhaps than that which shadows say Koestler's people, and far more dangerous. A man might survive the press of prison walls and be crumbled by the pressure of suburbia, a peculiarly Irish suburbia of course, where a fur-coated woman is good because her uncle has a parish in Limerick, and the children of her neighbour must not be played with because their father doesn't belong to the confraternity, and was once seen drunk in Santry. The threat within is often quite as deadly—more often than not a sense of guilt uneasy on the brain as a tumour, with God as a sort of Bogey Doctor forever looking over one's shoulder. Brian Flood's unsuccessful seduction is due as much to his guilt-consciousness as to the virtue of his lady. The Doctor's joy in ruining himself is vitiated by a sickly remorse that is strong enough to make him uneasy and too weak to reform him. The pleasures of misery are never fairly weighed against the miseries of lawful pleasure and the choice intelligently made. Sometimes one feels that when Kiely himself reconnoitres fully around the territory on either side of the paradox that teases his characters he will be the better novelist.

However one can still be grateful for him as he is. Nobody else has set so well the contemporary scene, or has had so often the careful facades of his prose split wide open by life itself. . . . Compare, too, *The Cards of the Gambler* with any novel say of William Sansom's (his exact English contemporary) and one sees at once the measure of Kiely's achievement, the admittedly not quite flawless creation of a character bounded by his own place and time of birth yet touching constantly a universal plane where such boundaries have no meaning.

Val Mulkerns. Irish Writing. Sept., 1953, p. 52

A year ago I reviewed the American edition of this book [*Honey Seems Bitter*] in these pages. Re-read now, it was as readable as ever. But I can now see more clearly why I made mental reservations about this literary murder-story.

The book is *too* literary. Kiely himself is one of the most formidably well-read men I ever met, expert apparently in all the bypaths of literature as well as the main road of the classics which we are all supposed to have read (but usually haven't). In *Honey Seems Bitter* he has chosen for his narrator a man for whom literature is the real and only thing. For Donagh Hartigan, the Civil Servant recovering from a breakdown, Malory, Marcus Aurelius, Eustache Deschamps, these and the other inhabitants of his "four shelves of books" are the real people, and the living are seen through a veil of literature. We admire them, we are interested in them, but we cannot touch them, nor can they touch us. It is a tribute to the vitality of the living, and the quality of the writing, that even at third-hand they can interest us so strongly.

From its viewpoint the book is entirely consistent. I only wish that it had been written from the viewpoint of Jim Walsh, the "spoiled priest" with the one shaky lung, who is hanged for a murder he did not commit, just because nobody cared enough about him to tell the truth—least of all himself. That would have been life, at first hand, in the raw. But it would have also been quite another book (though perhaps greater), and we should be thankful enough for what we have.

Maurice Kennedy. Irish Writing. March, 1954, p. 67

A tangle of themes and a gamut of moods, *Dogs Enjoy the Morning* is an Irish jig, robust and gamey for the most part, but melancholy, atrabilious even, at times, and like most Irish jigs, however frisky, suffers from not knowing when to stop. Kiely invites us to consider Cosmona, a village not far from a Dublin bus route, where priests are tough and crack down on error, but where for all that the sound of copulatory bedspring creakings can often drown the mutter of novenas.

The atmosphere is farmyard-comfortless: "In a peaceful corner of the long meadow by the canal lock and beyond Charles Roe's house the Cawley boys were amusing themselves by scything the head off a duck." If you like sentences like that then this is the novel for you. Idiot girls, criminal boys, soldiers returning from Far-east prison camps to die from a grand alliance of disgusting tropical diseases, drunken journalists from Dublin—including Larry, the doyen, who "had five women shot from under him at the battle of Balaclava"—these are only some of the ingredients. The book is exhausting in spite of its fizz.

David Williams. Punch. July 17, 1968, p. 102

There are those who would argue that it is his short fiction that really matters. . . . But it is in the novel that Benedict Kiely excels and in the novel that he will be best remembered. The early novels move through the lush, green Ulster landscape and against the starkness of the Donegal seascape and inevitably gravitate to the metropolitan sprawl of Dublin. They offer plots that are more than acceptable, characters that are credible, and wonderful lyrical runs that lend a sense of wonderment to the scene. As works in the formative years, *Land without Stars, In a Harbour Green*, and *Call for a Miracle* might be excused for their failings, but each is a finished novel and each is enviable in its own right.

The later novels further develop the existentialism of *Call for a Miracle*, each offering a fascinating narrative variation. Donagh Hartigan's perversity is studied in the unraveling of a murder in *Honey Seems Bitter*, and the doctor challenges death, reenacting the plot of the Gaelic folktale in *Cards*. An eighteenth-century house in the Irish Midlands spurs faith and hope, while the house of the bewhiskered Captain at Bingen has a rank infectious air. In every case there is rejection of the positive good; there is loneliness, despair, intellectual barrenness, and the threat of annihilation. Kiely joins company with Hawthorne and Poe, Gorki and Dostoevsky, with Sartre, Kafka, and Greene. It is, however, in *Dogs Enjoy the Morning* that he introduces an element of comedy and achieves the proper cosmic balance. The novels are all commendable, but *Dogs* ranks as one of the outstanding contemporary English-language novels.

Writing of the Irish, Heinrich Böll said, "It is not good for an author to write on a subject which he likes too well." The novelist from Tyrone draws his fiction from a Northern town whose Gothic church has hopalo spires, from "an unbewildering city of a few bridges," from the experiences of an infirm seminarian and a successful journalist, and from Joyce, Yeats, Stephens, Carleton, and O'Casey, and from a myriad of sources that he loves all too well. Mr. Böll has obviously not read enough Kiely, but, then, we might all make the same claim. There are the eight novels and the thirty-eight stories, but there are many more to come.

Daniel J. Casey. *Benedict Kiely* (Lewisburg, Pa.,
Bucknell Univ. Pr., 1974), pp. 102–4

Kiely's literary career up to this point—as distinct from his life as a professional journalist, an untidy trade at best—is a model of order and organization, worth looking into for that reason alone. For, as if moved by an instinct that was some part of itself, Kiely's talent began early to test the possibilities on all sides of his native ground, assessing those possibilities, classifying them, discarding some, setting others aside for future use, but always, whether instinctively or deliberately, this was a talent that from the beginning was preparing a way in the world of usable experience for its own realization. . . .

In [his] early novels Kiely is, so to speak, a coat-and-tie realist, everything tucked in and buttoned down, as one might expect from a resident in a traditional house of fiction. Once, it is true, he goes off—in *The Cards of the Gambler*—to a masquerade party apparelled in allegorical robes signifying Life and Death and a number of things in between, but mostly he is the proper, and properly detached, observer of his environment and its inhabitants, speaking "in the voice of his people."

But when it appears in 1960, *The Captain with the Whiskers*, like its single successor to date, *Dogs Enjoy The Morning* (1968), is Kiely the realist with his coat off and his tie undone, a new tone in his voice and with less patience than ever.

God in the shape of square or triangle is a more reasonable presence than the monstrous captain who, in life and death, dominates the landscape (with figures) in the first of these novels. But having rendered divinity irrelevant in earlier work, Kiely is left here with a world whose moral structure is the result not of providential design but of the sinister interplay or elemental, abstract, Manichean forces never, to the human eye, adequately distinct in their uneven distribution of yielding light and overwhelming darkness. In the cruel and creepy mind of Captain Conway Chesney, the mystery of the universe is reduced to a diabolic conundrum: "Is it better to be born and damned than not to be born at all?" The question, which becomes the theme of the novel, mocks itself in parodic echo of "It is better to have loved and lost etc. . . ." There is no love possible in this romantically inverted society; sex perhaps, but even sex is soured and tends either to self-disgust or, *in extremis*, to suicide. The novel grows into a great black joke, formidable in its humour, fascinating in gothic detail, lively in its deadliness, and ingenious in its attempt at the disambiguation of appearances which collapse in upon themselves to a kind of horror that we laugh at when we waken, if we ever do awaken, from the nightmare of an unredeemable world. It is the kind of world that Buck Mulligan, for example, had he a smidgin of Kiely's talent, might have created, for as literature this is self-mocking romance in the guise of realism that poses and then eludes, through a Manichean hatch, the problem that Job on his dunghill and Faust in metaphysical loneliness had pondered to quite contrary conclusions.

Kevin Sullivan. In Patrick Rafroidi and Maurice
Harmon, eds., <i>The Irish Novel in Our Time</i> (Lille,
France, Publications de l'Université de Lille, 1975),
pp. 199, 205–6

Kiely's art begins with a profound sense of place, of both physical and human geography, and of the integuments by which people and landscape are bound together. It would be entirely wrong, however, to "place" him as a regional writer, for the strong center of his craft, in his novels no less than his short stories, is the shaping voice of the narrator. This voice may seem at first to be that of the *seanachie*, the traditional Irish storyteller, but in fact it is a far more complex and sophisticated instrument. Kiely moves very close indeed to the people of whom he writes—farmers, tradesmen, mechanics, journalists, doctors, priests, publicans—but the voice can complicate itself suddenly, distancing the speaker and reminding us that Kiely is a man of wide literary culture, with a deep, unyielding tolerance for almost every range and variety of human experience. It is this shaping voice within the stories that, I suspect, has fallen strangely upon the ears of a generation schooled to expect from art only a stern, ironical impersonality. But fashions have changed once more, and allow us now to see in his work a sensibility and an intelligence engaged in an exchange both with his readers and with his created world.

Benedict Kiely was born, in 1919, in County Tyrone in what now is Northern Ireland, and grew up in Omagh, its county town, built where the Drumragh and the Camowen rivers join to form the Strule. . . .

There are resemblances between Kiely's Omagh and Faulkner's Yoknapatawpha. Within each of the two created worlds an imagination that is at once conservative and radically wayward is brought to bear upon a society shaped by history and wedded to traditional modes of feeling and action. Nowhere, however, is the resemblance more clear than in the presence, within each world, of a grave and deep evil, which rises at last to challenge both the society and the artist. The rich soil of Yoknapatawpha sustains black and white alike, and the two races respond to each other by complex silences and ambiguous pacts that, in day-to-day matters, involve a mutual respect. But slavery, and those tribal loyalties to race and caste that are its historical legacy, is a destructive evil buried beneath the soil, cancerous and dehumanizing. So too, in Kiely's Omagh, the seeming innocence, indeed the childishness, of sectarian badges and slogans issue at last into the moral and physical corrosion of the society. And these are truths that the two writers, the Southern American and the Northern Irishman, confront with reluctance, for they challenge and mock those versions of the pastoral to which each has been committed. For this reason, the response of each has been impassioned and unmodulated.

"Proxopera" is Kiely's *Intruder in the Dust*, an indictment of those people, passions, and malignant principles by which the culture that claims his deepest loyalties has been savaged.

> Thomas Flanagan. Introduction to Benedict Kiely,
> *The State of Ireland* (Boston, David R. Godine,
> 1980), pp. 3–4, 12

[Kiely] may find his literary ancestry as much in Samuel Lover and Charles Lever as in the nowadays more respectable, viewed artistically, William Carleton. Kiely had published seven novels before his first collection of stories, *A Journey to the Seven Streams* (1963). A second collection was *A Ball of Malt and Madame Butterfly* (1973) and a third, *A Cow in the House* (1978). A year before the last-named he published *Proxopera*, described as a novel, but two years later, in an American collection, as a *novella*. It might have been included as a very long "short story" in the *Cow in the House* volume. It must be considered in a short story context for it is evidence of how far Kiely can extend the form, as well as for its uncharacteristically elegant shape and its acerbity of feeling. Written "In Memory of the Innocent Dead" its indictment of mindless terrorism cuts across the usually genial, even complaisant, Kiely of the other shorter fictions. Formerly it belongs with Brian Moore from Belfast and his *Catholics* (1972) and *The Newton Letter* (1982) of John Banville from Dublin. The three fictions provide models for Irish short story writers, who lack the material or the stamina for the novel.

As indicated above, Benedict Kiely is in the *seanachaí* tradition, complete with digressions and diversions. At their best, these exercises in sheer story-telling, with their heavy stress on nostalgia and the transience of youth and physical beauty, and the chasm of the tomb, bring us into an extraordinary peopled world. It is also a world where the strands of Irish Catholicism and Irish paganism, of Irish piety and Irish superstition, are inextricably intermingled. The folk element may be seen uppermost in stories like "The Dogs in the Great Glen" and "God's Own Country" from the first and second collections respectively. In the last-named, a dyspeptic hack journalist is transmuted into a healthy and confident professional man by a trip to a western island. Significantly, his rehabilitation is brought about quite as much by an act of generosity to a tormenting colleague as by a half-tumbler of a bishop's whiskey, as much by benevolence as by barley. The folk element in Kiely is accentuated by his acute sense of place and the associations, historical-pastoral-comical, of the remotest nooks in, if not the whole island, his own county and province. Anecdotage, topography and pawky humour are the makings of the title story in *A Journey*. The special Kiely earthiness can be heavy-handed as in the title story of *A Ball of Malt* but redeemed by sad lyricism and a sense of the burden of time as in "The Green Lanes" from the same volume. I have mentioned Carleton, Lover and Lever in connection with Kiely. It might be more apposite to invoke the Somerville and Ross of *The Irish R. M.* crossed with the *Sportsman's Sketches* of Turgenev.

John Jordan. The Genius of Irish Prose (Dublin and
Cork, Mercier, 1985), pp. 133–34

Mr. Kiely's novel [*Nothing Happens in Carmincross*] is linked in subject matter to his book of short stories *The State of Ireland*, published here in 1980. Most particularly, it is linked to the novella in that collection, *Proxopera*, which is a small masterpiece about a bombing in a provincial town. But whereas *Proxopera* was constructed with great attention to plot and suspense, *Carmincross* is written as if plot and continuity were as inimical to the author as are the depredations of the British Army, and the murders by the Roman Catholic and Protestant fanatics of the North's political war.

He depicts Mervyn Kavanagh as a fat, bald, middle-aged storyteller incapable of not interrupting himself. Kavanagh, "a reading man cursed with a plastic memory, who also goes to the movies, and watches television," has a mind that "is a jumble sale, a lumber-room, a noisy carnival. . . ." Add the fact that Kiely-Kavanagh is a man of great and curious erudition in literature, history, myth, song and barroom folklore, and what you end with is an incorrigible archivist, a manic associationalist. . . .

[The book's] style is the novelistic stream of consciousness writ large; the work of a man with a godlike view of history, and the didactic urge of an angry man for whom the tidiness of art (like *Proxopera*) is not enough. The man needs to sprawl cosmically, for how else can one tell the story of a heavenly garden decomposing into a backyard of hell? How else can the reader be made to see not only consequences but causes?

Mr. Kiely has succeeded so often as an artist that he needs no further consecration, but I sense that this work will be viewed as something of a tract, a political argument in which the politics are not only implicit but also imposed. The thin plot is Kavanagh's odyssey to the North from New York City, onto an airplane bound for Shannon, then to a nearby hotel where he is reunited with an old mistress and a childhood pal, and where he also meets people with whom he will eventually rendezvous at Carmincross.

But the people—with the exceptions of a priest and a garrulous Fenian "hero," who exist only to be satirized for their solipsistic immersion in Irish irreality, and the former mistress, who is Kavanagh's partner in sex and bedroom banter on their way to Carmincross—are chiefly complements, or contraries, of the Kavanagh point of view. When the book is not an argument, it is a monologue, or a collage of actual, violent news stories, or a tissue of legendary or mythic tragedy, remembered in that plastic mind.

John Montague, one of Ireland's major poets and an old friend of Mr. Kiely's, has described him as one of the most beloved of Irish writers, who is "almost overcome by the variety of life." This book is testimony to the truth of that observation. . . .

Benedict Kiely loves the North, but despite his great wit and exuberance of language, he must surely be one of the saddest men in Ireland because of what is going, and gone. No man not weighted with loss could summon the anger that is behind this book. He gives us the natural world, the evolutionary history and the society that is in shreds within them.

William Kennedy. *NYTBR*. Oct. 27, 1985, p. 7

KINSELLA, THOMAS (1928–   )

Mr. Kinsella writes two kinds of poem. One kind is reflective and personal, his response to a specific occasion or situation; the other kind is hardly to be found in Irish poetry outside W. B. Yeats, a sort of impersonal *poésie pure*, each poem creating its own small universe of images not derived from any occasion nor tied to any particular situation. It's in this second kind of poem that

Mr. Kinsella is most original and apparently most at home. Of the other, the occasional sort, the only example here [in *Poems*] is "Dusk Music," a careful longish poem about visiting a patient in a hospital or sanatorium. What the others are about it is often hard to say, beyond remarking (what doesn't really get us far) that most of them are in some sense love-poems, and others are about the poet's experiences in the making of poems. This is not to call them obscure: for in this kind of poem, which goes back to the French Symbolist movement, the ostensible themes hardly matter.

Take for example "Ulysses." The theme suggested by the title is certainly in the poem, but it is neither less nor more important than others, particularly (what is most apparent in the poem as we first read it) the movement from summer through autumn into winter, and also, arising from the homecoming of Odysseus to Penelope, the nature of love between man and woman. The truth is that none of these is the chief concern of the poem, which is rather the tracing of their inter-relations. These flash out at us by fits and starts; at each fresh reading we are startled by fresh connections we had missed. . . .

In a case like this, the most outstanding thing is the structure of the poem as a whole, the way the poet keeps the threads going all at once, interlacing them, shifting from one to another, as a juggler keeps three balls in the air. All the same, the poem ultimately stands or falls on the conduct of the language; for the themes are interwoven in the whole, only as words are interwoven in the stanza and the line. And at this level too there are many fine touches: "aftermath" has been noted already; another very fine and daring expression is the image for Ulysses' final landfall—"the stroke/And collapse of sails." On the other hand "daring" is certainly the word: Mr. Kinsella uses his words like a dandy, with an insolent fastidiousness—and this is exciting; but sometimes the dandy becomes a fop, and falls into effeminate preciosity—as in "Fifth Sunday after Easter":

April's sweet hand in the margins betrayed
Her character in late cursive daffodils:
A gauche mark, but beautiful: a maid

Another danger for him is the colloquial: the language can afford to be florid, even a little precious, so long as the whole poem is in that key: but when in "Ulysses" Penelope is permitted to say, "And I am being tampered with," it is as if the dandy had begun to giggle. Occasionally, as in the tour-de-force "Soft to Your Places" (stanzas out of Auden, refrains out of Yeats), Mr. Kinsella can risk the colloquial and get away with it, because he stays close to the idiom of his masters. But of course he cannot afford to stay as close as that (which is why "Soft to Your Places" is a tour-de-force and no more); and in fact, in "Ulysses," in the very beautiful "An Ancient Ballet," and the strange and difficult poem "Who is my proper art," he has got far past the stage where his language is a whispering gallery for his masters. In these poems, he has his own style and his own vocabulary, and all credit to him. . . . Let it be said in conclusion that this is an Irish poet who has learned his trade; we have to go further back than Mr. [Valentin] Iremonger, further even than Mr. Kavanagh, to find an Irish poet who on his first appearance was—whatever else may be said—so accomplished.

Donald Davie. *Irish Writing*. Autumn, 1957, pp. 47–49

I think [*Nightwalker*] is Kinsella's most accomplished book, and that is saying a good deal. Kinsella had to convince himself that he could do what the poets he admired did. He set himself to learn how to handle the metaphysical conceit, how to combine the familiar and exotic, how to use myth while ironically questioning it. He worked at putting the old themes of song into strict patterns of rhyme and meter. Among the masters he schooled himself in are Donne and Herbert and Marvell, Keats and Wordsworth and Arnold, Yeats and Eliot and Auden. And his debt to the old ballads and carols, and to the wisdom and folk poetry of Ireland is obvious. But I am not competent to judge the effect on his work of his Gaelic heritage. At least on the evidence of his own poetry, he has not much interest in the techniques of association or the theories of correspondence developed by the French symbolists or in the free-flowing inclusiveness of Whitman and his latter-day followers. He likes a poem to focus its meanings, even when these are logically inconclusive or emotionally unsettled, with force and lucidity. His quest for form in poetry mirrors, or parallels, his quest for order in life. If his earlier poetry could be said to choose its occasions for their adaptability to styles of traditional lyric, the later poetry, by contrast, may be said to seize its occasions from whatever is more pressing in the poet's life as though confident that, however grim the subject, the words could be relied on to perform their poetic duty.

This diagrammatic contrast is of course false if taken too literally, but it is indicative of what I have in mind in speaking of Kinsella's accomplishment. His art has come to seem unpremeditated, and this at the very time when the life his poetry so frequently describes seems threatened with collapse. One feels more pressure on the poetry to justify itself in human terms, and this perhaps accounts for the special attention given to the theme of art and life, not a new subject for Kinsella but one never so fully developed in his earlier work.

John Rees Moore. *HC*. Oct. 1968, pp. 11–12

It may be that we have to accept all Kinsella's œuvre . . . as being good in parts: brilliant passages robbed of their resonance and context by over-anxious manipulation, by a lack of instinct for what makes a poem, by uncertainty where to start or when to stop. Kinsella's poetry cries out for an Ezra Pound to differentiate between what belongs in the wasteland and what in the wastepaper basket.

Paradoxically then, with all his superior qualifications for feeling at home in Ireland and the world, Kinsella, to a more radical extent than [Richard] Murphy, writes the displaced poetry of a displaced person. His consciousness of "a gapped, discontinuous, polyglot tradition" results in "gapped, discontinuous, polyglot" poems confused as to their true focus, form and tongue. Harmon's observation that "the typical movement" in the work of poets of this generation "was an initial outward trend and then the return to Ireland" does not apply literally to Kinsella—he has lived in America but has never adopted either the exile stance or noticeably un-Irish subject-matter—yet can be metaphorically adjusted to his apparent feeling that Ireland has left him. In "A Country Walk" and "Nightwalker," and with glancing references in other poems, he reaches out from his solitude to the nation, as he does to the universe, only to retreat dissatisfied into his shell.

The recent signs of a more lasting return or commitment are not all good. In taking on the "legendary duty" of translating from the Gaelic the Ulster epic, *The Tain*, Kinsella must have fertilized his own poetic roots as well as putting Ireland and Irish literature deeply in his debt. But *Butcher's Dozen*, his response to the events of Bloody Sunday, constitutes a more dubious arousal of the heroic passions of the past. Into the mouths of rather gruesomely evoked phantoms of the dead victims he puts a fascist hysteria unqualified by any words of his own. . . .

A pamphlet called *Kinsella's Oversight*, issued by the British and Irish Communist Organization, has supplied a political corrective to the attitudes of the poem, but it is alarming that Kinsella's search for meaning and an inspiring cause in contemporary Ireland should find expression in a backward- rather than forward-looking emotion, in language on every level so uncontrolled. Lacking all along John Montague's enthusiasm for "swimming/Against a slackening tide," he seems readier to be swept off course by the resurgence of old currents.

Edna Longley. In Douglas Dunn, ed., *Two Decades of Irish Writing* (Chester Springs, Pa., Dufour, 1975), pp. 136–37

The long *Nightwalker* poem (1967) has a significant place in Kinsella's work, marking a decisive shift to poetry that is private and inward in direction. Like *The Waste Land* it is made up of a series of states of feeling within one figure. Its fluid narrative manner is similar to the technique found in parts of *Ulysses*, in which there are also apparently random associations of an individual consciousness. In its material and setting it acknowledges Kinsella's appreciation of Joyce's acceptance of the here and the now as subject-matter.

The poem is specifically Irish in its immediate contexts, as well as being personal and autobiographical in some respects, but its connecting theme is the violence inherent in modern life. This is projected through the walker who responds to his immediate surroundings in the Sandycove area of Dublin, close to Joyce's martello tower, and to the memories and associations that rise to the surface of his mind. In contexts that are generally apathetic, his consciousness is the active force. He accepts all that he encounters in the belief that through such patient and honest perception and apprehension he discovers meaning. The walker's anguish is intensified between the deceiving simplicities of education and his own actual experience, between Government pretensions and actual policies, between pseudo-nationalism and actual cultural loss. He suffers from a feeling of violence and betrayal done to himself and to his generation. To portray this sense of the gulf between appearance and reality the poem relies on a configuration of contrasting and related elements; a seemingly random assembly of incidents produces a meaningful pattern. And when the focus shifts to the lunar landscape, the reality is only marginally different from what has been seen on earth: sterility and evil there reflect in a radical and unambiguous fashion what the walker has experienced here.

Maurice Harmon. Introduction to Maurice Harmon,
ed., *Irish Poetry after Yeats: Seven Poets*
(Portmarnock, Ireland, Wolfhound, 1979),
pp. 23–24

And Kinsella: "Dr. Kinsella," a friend insists: the poems of Dr. Kinsella. A proper treatment—not an Introduction meant to predispose readers—would note how the purified diction, the found voice, is accompanied by a withdrawal into intense, intensely private speech. "In the Ringwood," an early poem, offers a reader gestures of hospitality—familiar Victorian diction, "red lips," "the green hill-side," and a six-line stanza thrice rhymed. But these are conventions, a reader soon senses, not meant to be trusted; for though the year is 1958 the stanza and diction pertain to "The Blessed Damozel." . . . [It is] a language impossible to believe in, which is just the point: not accommodation to a reader, not living ceremony, but a husk of ceremony, due to wither before our eyes. . . .

So as early as that we have the Kinsella Effect: an irruption of darkness and of violent enigmatic language. As early as that, too, the reader is placed as in a Piranesi dungeon, where surfaces are illusory. . . .

Insofar as "The Clearing," or almost any late Kinsella poem, treats a reader at all, it treats him as an element in the poem's strategy: not someone addressed, but someone to be deceived, by various devices of rhetoric and typography, into expecting what will not be provided. For that is how it is in the world of these poems: nothing we might expect will be provided. . . .

Rejecting any more communality than that, rejecting everything save the license to tell private nightmares, these poems take the important risk of rejecting the grounds of poetry itself: poetry as it was defined for Ireland by Yeats ("Irish poets, learn your trade"). A "trade" is objective, that for which standards and criteria exist. Kinsella's poetry is definable as that which *he* does. Therein lies both its interest and its risk. Therein too lies the seed of much anxiety among his well-wishers, for the question, how you judge his poetry, converts readily into the question, what do you think of Tom?

Hugh Kenner. *Genre*. Winter, 1979, pp. 596–98

Kinsella's affirmations are always hardly earned, for he sees life, as Yeats saw it, as tragic in ineluctably involving a conflict of opposites, a recognition of human limitations, an unbridgeable gap between the dream and the reality.

From his earliest work Kinsella has dreamed of finding a rational order in the universe, but as early as *Another September* (1958) he makes clear his suspicion that reason is not useful in moral issues; in the title poem of that volume nature only half tolerates human consciousness and "Justice, Truth, such figures" move, as the poem says, like women: that is, are knowable not by ratiocination but by intuition. Throughout Kinsella's poetry the feminine is the bearer of visionary as opposed to rational or intellectual wisdom.

A major and persistent theme records Kinsella's difficult acceptance of the validity of irrational knowledge. Tracing the theme through *Poems 1956–1973*, a reader would find it imaged in many ways. The poet who in the earliest volumes sees reality in the mathematical order of the stars or of music comes to accept, through the agency of his wife and other women, a different kind of order: organic, pulsing, cyclical. And the forms that his poems take reflect his changing notions, moving from the traditional rhyme and stanzaic form of the earlier volumes to the freer shapes and imagery of his most recent works.

As he puts it in "Downstream," Kinsella is "searching the darkness for a landing place." In "Phoenix Park" the search finds its conclusion in a realization of the paradox that order is, in our life, only in flux, not in a starry precision, and that meaning comes through live, difficult as that is of achievement; he realizes

The flesh is finite, so in love we persist;
That love is to clasp simply, question fiercely;
That getting life we eat pain in each other.

"Phoenix Park" bridges earlier poems and those in *New Poems 1973*, in which Kinsella relaxes the tight rational control of the first volumes and allows the emotions he is expressing to find their own rhythms, forms, images. It is, as the first poem of the book says, a demanding task. . . . We are seeing the continuation of the quest adumbrated in the first of the "Night Songs," . . . The honest record of a man's painful battle to find himself as artist and human being in his relationship with others.

Kinsella is largely a poet of relationships. To read through [his] books is to be struck by the multiplicity of his connections: with family, with friends, with the peopled past. Contemporary poetry is so frequently concerned with more inner notions than these: the question of reality, the search for identity, the investigation of the role of the imagination and the role of the poet. Kinsella is also concerned with such questions, but he grounds them in concrete human relationships, defining the self, for example, in its relationship to others, past, present, and future.

Peggy F. Broder. *CP*. 14, 2, 1981, pp. 133–34

Who touches this book [*Peppercanister Poems 1972–1978*] touches a man. Reading these poems, I kept doubling back to Whitman's romantic brag, even though Thomas Kinsella is as far from romantic as they come. We don't just overhear Kinsella; we watch him ritualize a process of radical understanding and remaking. I can think of no other poet today—ecstatic primitivists like Galway Kinnell included—who has so seriously and consciously taken the myth of the self as his domain. But Kinsella rules it at some artistic peril. One problem among several here is that he writes long sequences that build on his earlier poems much as a person builds on a remembered past. Unless you have followed Kinsella closely, on your first glance at this new book you may feel like you arrived late at the wrong party: they seem to know each other and you don't get the jokes. Don't despair. Though it takes some getting used to, Kinsella's eccentric world is expansive enough to welcome you. Creation, growth, and survival are the stuff of us all. . . .

Kinsella is at home now in darkness, the secret shadows where we create and were created. If he invites us into a world that at times proves too elaborately personal, if he tries to do too much with his poems, these are generous blunders. They shouldn't obscure the fact that Kinsella is a serious poet of invention and honesty. In the States, he started to get some of the attention he deserves a decade ago, but still it has come slowly. All poets face hurdles mean and numerous, but the Irish face a particularly frustrating one, a certain Olympian shadow, stilts and all. Almost unwittingly, one looks to Yeats as a gauge or, worse, simply assumes that the Irish vessel ran dry in 1939. This situation is changing slowly. In America you hear Heaney's name about frequently, and occasionally even those of John Montague, Derek Mahon, and young Paul Muldoon. With Kinsella's newest and another released simultaneously by Wake Forest, *Poems 1956–73*, a virtual "collected" for those years, American readers will have another reason to take recent Irish poetry seriously. It's time they do. For too long they haven't seen a rich forest for the great-rooted blossomer.

John D. Engle. *Parnassus*. Spring, 1981,
pp. 187, 198

Rather than pinning his hopes on the star of the sublime, and trying to substitute his personal phantasmagoria for the larger communal forms of the imagination that have gone by the boards—religious myths and rituals, moral values, shared political attitudes—Kinsella, like [Robert] Lowell, rejects heroic posturing and chooses instead to rely on the minimal general things we all do still share: the coils of the family romance. He builds his mature poetry on this admittedly meager if inescapable basis, tracing in the long sequence of poems inaugurated by "Phoenix Park" the growth of an individual consciousness. Consequently, critics, like [Hugh] Kenner, who go to the poetry expecting the sublime in its modernist variant are in for a shock. In fact, as John Montague recently suggests, Kinsella's real achievement, the finest and strongest of "post-Yeatsian Irish poetry," stems from his progressive shedding of the high modernist manner, that "thickness of language and old-fashioned technique," that balancing of tensions and carving out of poetic wholes, that "willed rhetoric," which affected Kinsella's poetry up to the *Nightwalker* (1968) volume. As Montague also suggests, the "subterranean psychic explorer" of *Notes* and after has been able to develop and to deploy tactfully a remarkable "corrective variety of tones" to wean himself away from a certain "heaviness of diction" and a once apparently unappeasable "appetite for horror."

What Kinsella recognizes, and such critics as Hugh Kenner ignore, is that whether the country is Ireland or America, England or France, Western culture generally no longer possesses a credible public realm. There is no space of rationality and concern in which we can discuss our differences, criticize our poems, and reaffirm our values. Instead, as Kinsella powerfully asserts in "The Irish Writer" (1966), among even the most creative people, we find only "a scattering of incoherent lives . . . a few madmen and hermits, and nothing more." There are simply no commonly shared standards of any kind. Even the model of the life lived that Kinsella claims good poetry offers to the careful reader is nontransferable. Each individual must work out such a model of creative response for him or her self.

Kinsella has worked out his model by wrestling with the influence of Yeats, the inescapable modern poetic father. He has done so by mediating or handling his influence, first, by imitating Auden's ironic manner and self-deprecating stance. Next, he turned away from Yeats's selective Ascendency ideal erected above the filthy modern tide, and turned to Joyce's comprehensive vision of Irish reality, filth and all. Then, finally, since *Notes*, Kinsella has been adapting the open American voice of William Carlos Williams and the ideogrammatic method of Ezra Pound to his autobiographical project as the heart of which stands a quest-myth of the contemporary poetic imagination.

Daniel O'Hara. In James D. Brophy and Raymond J.
Porter, eds., *Contemporary Irish Writing* (Boston,
Iona College Pr./Twayne, 1983), pp. 70–71

. . . In miniature *The Messenger* [1978] answers Kinsella's own appeal, fifteen years ago, for "an exploration into the interior to find what may guide us in the future." Such Jungian introspection entails a regressive method, beginning with the present and stepping both backward and inward. *The Messenger*'s transitions support this: "It is outside . . . ," "Inside . . . ," "Deeper . . ." mark three stages of regression. If it is out of ourselves that history came, then also we contain within ourselves the pattern of the past.

To represent this relation of self to world, Kinsella employs hinged images that suddenly open the partition between the present and past, as I have shown, and between the subject and the object, such as the dragonfly that witnesses the parents' coition at the moment of the poet's conception. As the seed enters the womb, "a gossamer ghost" floats overhead, his "body, a glass worm, is pulsing." Like the egg-seed, this dragonfly contains at this moment the code of its past existences, as larva, cocoon, and imago. The poem's advance through the stages of the poet's recovery—from nightmare of the body's putrescence and vulnerability to the resplendent image of fresh beginnings—has its analogue in the dragonfly's rise from slime into "insect-shimmering" beauty.

Such intricate matching of part to whole—here, the microscopic image to the macroscopic process of the volume—extends to the relation of the volume to the sequence, although the complexity and inclusiveness of the sequence requires our faith on this point. The pleasure in reading Kinsella arises from the resonance among parts of his work, between a part and the whole process of repossession, and among parts of Kinsella's and related works. In attention to sequence, he seems, on occasion, to lose coherence, becoming too fragmentary, as in the conclusion of "Survivor" which Calvin Bedient criticized. However, when we recognize the dramatic nature of his poetry and learn to identify which poetic self is speaking—the anima-muse, the redactor, the order-seeking poet—or which character, then even fragmentary patches often seem appropriate. Furthermore, one can argue that Kinsella has drawn the fragmentary and inchoate into art, reminding the critic that such aspects of real discourse as muttered words, broken syntax, and fragmentary sentences have their legitimatizing classical tags: parataxis, anacoluthon, and aposiopesis, if you will. Although Kinsella has written as lyrically as any Irish poet in poems such as "The Shoals Returning," he can relinquish graceful phrasing to manifest the truth of the turbulent world and its shadow psyche.

Dillon Johnston. *Irish Poetry after Joyce*
(Notre Dame, Ind., Notre Dame Univ. Pr., 1985),
pp. 118–20

LAVIN, MARY (1912–   )

To me [Mary Lavin] seems reminiscent of the Russians more than of any other school of writers and, with the exception of the gigantic Tolstoy, her searching insight into the human heart and vivid appreciation of the beauty of the fields are worthy in my opinion to be mentioned beside their work. Often, as I read one of her tales, I find myself using superlatives, and then wondering if such praise must not necessarily be mistaken, when applied to the work of a young and quite unknown writer. And yet are not such doubts as these utterly wrong-minded? For if there is no intrinsic thing in any art whatever, irrespective of its date or the name or age of the writer, how then can there be anything in good work at all? How, if we cannot recognize great work when we come across it unexpectedly, have we any right to say that even Shelley or Keats wrote well? Should we not rather say in that case: "I have been told that they wrote well"? I know people who can never tell a beautiful piece of silverwork or furniture until they have first found out the date of it. If it is over a hundred years old they think it is bound to be good, and if it is made in this century they think it is bound to be bad. Often they are right in both cases, but they have no judgment whatever and, though they are quick to find out the date of a Chippendale chair or the hallmark on a piece of old silver, and will praise their beauty immediately after doing so, nevertheless the emotions that should respond to beauty can only be awakened in them by the aid of a catalogue. That is a very sorry state to be in.

Let us therefore always praise intrinsic beauty whenever we see it, without concerning ourselves with irrelevancies, such as the age or name of Mary Lavin or how on earth she came by her astonishing insight.

Lord Dunsany. Preface to Mary Lavin, *Tales from Bective Bridge* (Boston, Little, Brown, 1942), pp. ix–x

Miss Lavin's novel [*The House in Clewe Street*] was partially published in serial form in America as *Gabriel Galloway*.. the change of title points to the weakness of the book. If the central subject is the boy his fortunes do not really begin to unfold until about a third of the way through—on page 149 he is not yet quite seven: if the theme is the fortunes of the house then that drops out of the picture not much under a third from the end. This frailty in forming the central concept, the "What-is-this-I-am-at-exactly?" also affects our pleasure in Miss Lavin's stories which equally charm us by their delicacy and puzzle by their dissipation.

This may be purely a matter of a technique that is not as yet quite sure-footed, and the timing all through *The House in Clewe Street* is possibly mainly responsible for it. Thus the death of the child's father is given a slow treatment, although Miss Lavin agrees that the boy will hear of this past only in gossip about lives before his own "that will not provide any depository of experience from which he can supplement his own inexperience": whereas the death of the grandfather occurs in a flash, although of the boy's consideration on death *that* night she says: "Leaf by leaf, petal by petal, our impressions are laid down": and just before that he has had a slowly-told day in the fields with a poor neighbour's children—ending, it is true, in a graphically-pictured mimicry about what dead people look like, but, surely, taking a disproportionate time to get to that point, if that is the point?

The pleasure of the book, as by corollary, is that it contains a great many separate delights; whether she is describing a girl letting out the tucks of her dress; or swans on the river—"one had to glance at the banks along which they passed in order to perceive that they were in motion; nothing about their compact, calm demeanour suggested the furious activity of webbed feet that propelled them forward".. or a girl opening her umbrella—"such gestures at once familiar and unfamiliar pierce the heart like a shaft."

She is, however, herself alone responsible for our impatience with her faults, natural in a first novel. Here is a quality that demands to be judged by the highest standards: she is, obviously, the most promising young Irish writer of our time.

Sean O'Faolain. *The Bell*. April, 1946, pp. 81–82

Miss Lavin's novel [*Mary O'Grady*] is the story of Mary O'Grady, the country girl from Tullamore, who loves and marries a Dublin tram driver: it is the simple life of a woman whose love dictates her days, love for her husband and for the children that are soon born to them—and for the first thirty pages or so it is exquisite. Truly and surely, with that gift which Miss Lavin has for understanding what life means to the simple, that gift of illumining the commonplace and making touching the ordinary, she moves over Mary's married life in Dublin, with its babies coming like the seasons, and the young woman's instinct for beauty fastening itself upon the grass of a vacant building lot. Miss Lavin's rich and poetic powers of writing are well seen in what she makes of that grass.

But this enchanting prelude, at once momentarily satisfying us and sending our expectation questing ahead for its development, is not followed by a body of work equal to it. I do not mean to suggest that the level of the writing does not rise through the book to the standard of the opening. All through there are passages of great beauty and grace—it would hardly be Miss Lavin's, if this could not be said of it. But the development of the theme does not equal as a whole the opening; still less does it swell out from it, and the reader ends baffled and disappointed.

What happens is that into the closed, warm and loving world of Mary O'Grady, whose only weapon against Fate itself is unquestioning affection, disaster on disaster crowds. Death, madness, illness, estrangement stalk in, as in an Elizabethan play. Tragedy supplants idyll and lyric, or rather, what should be tragedy, but remains only inexplicable calamity, supplants early happiness. . . .

Mary O'Grady, therefore, full of evidence as it is of the writer's talent, is yet a disappointing book. It is disappointing because this extraordinary talent, which no one doubts, has as yet not found its appropriate outlet in the novel. It is a talent highly poetic, sensitive and subtle in many directions, which to use Coleridge's words of Wordsworth has the power to throw the colouring of the ideal world over the ordinary things of life, and yet which has not refined itself of much dross, which still lies fitful and gleaming, embedded in a mass of the arbitrary, the ludicrous and the inexplicable. If Miss Lavin could cut away these needs, there would shine a jewel indeed.

Lorna Reynolds. *DM*. April, 1951, pp. 58–59

Miss Lavin is much more of a novelist in her stories than O'Flaherty, O'Faolain, or Joyce, and her technique verges—sometimes dangerously—on the novelist's technique. That has its advantages of course. In her later stories there is an authenticity and solidity that makes the work of most Irish writers seem shadowy; not the life of the mind interrupted by occasional yells from the kitchen, but the life of the kitchen suddenly shattered by mental images of extraordinary vividness which the author tries frantically to capture before the yells begin again. The only story in which she deliberately eschews the physical world is the fable of "The Becker Wives," which she sets in a capital city that might be either Dublin or London, and among merchants whose names might be Irish or English, and, for all its brilliance and lucidity it seems to me only the ghost of a story, a Henry James fable without the excuse of James' sexual peculiarities. She has the novelist's preoccupation with logic, the logic of Time past and Time future, not so much the real short-story teller's obsession with Time present—the height from which past and present are presumed to be equally visible. Sometimes she begins her stories too far back, sometimes she carries them too far forward, rarely by more than a page or two, but already in that space the light begins to fade into the calm gray even light of the novelist.

She fascinates me more than any other of the Irish writers of my generation because more than any of them her work reveals the fact that she has not said all she has to say.

Frank O'Connor. *The Lonely Voice* (Cleveland,
World, 1963), pp. 211–12

It is a truth not universally acknowledged, that the short story is so subtle an art form, and at the same time so independent of its surroundings, that a reviewer does violence to any collection if he reads it straight through, as he would a novel. Only frail, meagerly developed stories profit from such an approach; the accumulative momentum, then, provides assurance from story to story that the author has really constructed a world for us. The richer and more demanding the story, the more it forces us to participate in its imaginative drama; to read too swiftly a number of stories that require us to think and feel—like Mary Lavin's superbly artistic stories—would result in exhaustion that might wrongly be attributed to the stories.

A Memory is Mary Lavin's fifteenth book, and her thirteenth collection of short stories. She has long been recognized as one of the finest of living short-story writers. Uninterested in formal experimentation, she has concentrated her genius upon certain archetypal or transpersonal experiences as they touch—sometimes with violence—fairly ordinary people. The five stories in this collection emphasize the universality of certain experiences—love, self-sacrifice, the need to relinquish the world to those who follow us—but never at the expense of the particular. Mary Lavin's ability to transcribe the physical world, especially the green damp world of rural Ireland where many of her stories are set, is as remarkable as ever. She rarely strains for metaphors, yet her prose is "poetic" in the best sense of that word; if her people talk perhaps more beautifully than might seem credible, that is what art is all about.

Joyce Carol Oates. NYTBR. Nov. 25, 1973, p. 7

[The Becker Wives] embraces the normal narrative point of view for Lavin, selective omniscience. This narrative pattern is most obvious in Lavin's character vignettes. Many of her stories seek solely to present a character trait or portrait through an action which will enhance its development. In doing so Lavin has created a remarkable catalogue of characters such as Miss Holland, the Inspector's Wife, the Nun's Mother, the butlers of "A Joy Ride," the young nun of "Chamois Gloves," Pidgie, and the widow of "In a Café." In all of these cases the narrative point of view reflects the mind of the protagonist and in several stories approaches stream of consciousness.

Deviations from a third-person narrative pattern are comparatively few, and often these are stories which are so obviously autobiographical that Lavin drops the third person distancing for a more natural first-person narrative. "Tom," a story which recounts a little girl's relations to her parents, particularly her father, is a prime example. There is still the element of fiction even in those stories which seem purely autobiographical, but the emotions, if not the facts, have their counterpart in the author's life. "Story with a Pattern," to be discussed later, and "Say Could That Lad Be I?" are further examples of Lavin's involvement in her own stories: first, because they concern the nature of her art; and second, because the narrative point of view differs so remarkably from her normal perspective. The latter, "Say Could That Lad Be I?" is a first-person narration by the author remembering the voice of her father, who in turn recollects his boyish adventures with his dog. There is about the story the amorality of elders' tales of youthful derring-do, not the kind that Lavin herself would normally write. It is a father's story, and, as such, presumably holds a place in the author's heart sufficient to publish it along with her own more sophisticated fiction. . . .

There are few experiments in structure in the Lavin canon. Many of her stories are character vignettes in which the action is a mere vehicle for character revelation. Others, in which plot plays a more paramount role, often begin in *medias res*, with the ultimate details of the action informing the meaning of the characters who participate as well as the plot itself. An example of this is one of the most popular of Lavin's stories, "The Great Wave." The exciting details of the tragedy appear in a flashback in the mind of a bishop revisiting the island on which he and another youngster were the only survivors of the great wave. The story carries with it, because of this distancing of time, the attitude that the disaster may have been the work of divine providence. The realistic details of the frame and the disclosure of the identity of the bishop at the end lend both a sense of reality and a perspective of distance at the same time, putting the disaster in an historical context but preserving its immediacy.

Zack Bowen. *Mary Lavin* (Lewisburg, Pa., Bucknell
Univ. Pr., 1975), pp. 54–56

Each of Mary Lavin's stories appears linear in structure, supporting the first impression of simplicity. Between beginning and end, however, stretch particles of life, held by forces that both repel and attract, vibrating with unseen energy like the famous line that Marcel Duchamps perceived and tried to paint. Applied to the fiction of Mary Lavin, such metaphor and analogy are appropriate, because they introduce ideas that affect her work: as an artist conscious of and curious about the creative process, she is intrigued by all concepts and perceptions that challenge the human mind. Techniques and theories of other forms of art are, to her, applicable to literary art: she herself tries consciously to see with the eyes of a painter or sculptor, to hear with the ears of a composer or musician. But she is intensely interested also in those developments in the social and natural sciences that affect human understanding of the world in which she, we, and her characters live. The observations and speculations about the nature of the human species that these offer are refracted for her by the prism of human personality in respose to questions that, attempting to understand these observations and speculations, she asks herself.. What kind of person would think or feel that way? Under what circumstances would that kind of person think or feel that way? What kind of person never would think or feel that way? How would that kind of person think or feel under those same circumstances?

Such probing of personality, sometimes painful and relentless in its intensity, invites comparison with the work of Virginia Woolf. At the same time, the author's awareness of the self-protective limitations to human understanding seems similar to that of Henry James. And her evolution of a range of personality types, particularized in different roles and different situations, with different identities and different social and intellectual backgrounds, is not unlike Gertrude Stein's attempts to present "bottom nature." But this focus on character is never separate from consideration of milieu. Accidents of birth and environment are presented by Mary Lavin as forces that play on universal sensibility. Thus she exhibits also, for those seeking her literary antecedents, if not the English, something of the French naturalists.

Janet Egleson Dunleavy. *IUR*. Autumn, 1977,
pp. 222–23

The key narrative event in Lavin's "A Cup of Tea" is deliberately and deceptively simple and insignificant—a mother and daughter fall into a heated argument over whether or not boiled milk spoils the taste of tea. The truth of "A Cup of Tea" exists in the emotional undercurrents in the family which briefly come to the surface during the incident of the boiled milk. The unspoken antagonism between Sophy and her mother, because of the mother's empty life with her husband and Sophy's desire to escape the emotional circle of her mother's failure, flares out into the open for a brief moment in spite of their efforts to avoid a confrontation. The fact that the daughter has been away at the university and has just returned home for a visit aggravates and intensifies the emotional conflict and sets the stage for any minor incident, even boiled milk, to provoke an outburst of pent-up emotions.

"A Cup of Tea" is told from the third person limited perspective of the mother and shifts to Sophy's perspective only in the last moments of the story. The narrative, then, focuses on the mother's desperate and futile efforts to keep her feelings of frustration and loneliness under control, while she tries to enjoy her daughter's visit. Her need for her daughter's affection and approval, however, is so strong that it is only a matter of the time it takes the milk to boil until mother and daughter release their mutual resentment and hostility. When Sophy is finally alone, she comes up with a simple solution to her family's emotional problems that, unfortunately, reveals only her own inexperience and her fragile hope that she will escape the mistakes of her father and mother: "People would all have to become alike. They would have to look alike and speak alike and feel and talk and think alike. It was so simple. It was so clear! She was surprised that no one had thought of it before."

One of Mary Lavin's finest stories, "A Cup of Tea" also has the basic characteristics of her fiction, the eternal conflict between individuals with naturally opposed interests and sensibilities and the brief revelation of one individual's lonely and bitter life when faced with a disturbing confrontation with its opposite self. Other early stories like "At Sallygap" and "A Happy Death," are carefully designed studies of the breakdown of the emotional relationship between husband and wife. In each story, Lavin skillfully uses a shifting perspective to expose the secret loneliness and buried hostility and frustration that have been festering over the years. Later in her career, after her brief and temporary interest in the story with a pattern, she converted her basic theme, primarily because of the tragic loss of her first husband, William Walsh, into the widow's painful and frightening search for self-identity. "In the Middle of the Fields," "In a Café," and "The Cuckoo-spit" are not only symbolic of her recovery from her own grief and despair; they also signal a return to the form of her early stories after a phase in which she gave her critics what they wanted. Each of her widow stories, narrated from the perspective of the widow, marks a phase in a long and difficult struggle to understand the relationship between past memories and the emotional pain of the present in finding a new life and identity.

Richard Peterson. *MFS*. Autumn, 1978, pp. 392–93

"The Great Wave," from the author's 1961 collection, most completely renders, in a single story, Miss Lavin's most extreme vision of the relation of the forces of the extended dimension to conscious life and feeling; more directly and explicitly than any other story, it posits realistically, as the early "The Green Grave and the Black Grave" posits poetically, the fully independent reality of a sensate cosmos apprehended by, and influencing, the individual imagination. "The Great Wave" makes clear that this cosmos is in purposeful motion related to man, but its motions are antipathetic to man's consciousness.

Significantly, the great wave which overwhelms all but two of the islanders in the story is not a plane of reality known only through imagination, as are the planes of reality apprehended by the characters in "In a Café," "The Cuckoo-Spit," and "In the Middle of the Fields"; the wave is an objective phenomenon, a tangible and dreadful intrusion into the normal world. . . .

Thus, in "The Great Wave" as, indeed, throughout Miss Lavin's work, the fragility of the necessary partnership of imagination and consciousness is at its roots inescapable: to evade involvement with the ambiguous forces of the larger cosmos is to evade vital human life; to become involved with these forces is to risk being overwhelmed directly by them, drawn from the meaning and order of conscious life into a formless inhuman chaos. The human being of vital imagination exists, then, with an aware allegiance to conscious life in its fullness as his only bulwark; and that bulwark, "The Great Wave" implies, is arbitrarily subject to an unequal encounter with the ambiguous forces of a supra-human cosmos linked to his imagination. Miss Lavin's awareness of the power and indifference—even malignity—of this supra-human and influential cosmos would seem to be the foundation of her ironic vision, its existence casting into question the strength and pride of conscious human choice; her recognition of the courage of the men and women of vital imagination who live at risk in the face of it is her testament to human beauty and value.

Catherine A. Murphy. *Mosaic.*
Spring, 1979, pp. 77, 79

It is evident from the didactic strain present in Mary Lavin's early stories such as "Brigid," "Magenta," "Sarah," "Brother Boniface," and others that moral idealism is one of her artistic motivating forces. Some of her earlier work makes its message obvious by the over-explicit use of symbolic imagery such as the sheep-raddle in "Sarah." Among early stories those in which ironic implication is pronounced, such as "The Becker Wives," "A Happy Death," "At Sallygap," but which keep the message in the background and subordinate the didactic to the dramatic, emerge as artistically superior.

In contemporary Anglo-Irish literature Mary Lavin stands apart in her deliberate restraint, her decision to concentrate on the inner play of feeling to the exclusion of political documentation. A recent reviewer called her "The Vermeer of the Irish short story." She is nearest to Joyce in her attempts to enlarge areas of consciousness, but at once more ironic and less allusive, more compassionate and less sardonic; more inhibited and less explicit than he, and her aesthetic base is intuitive rather than philosophical. Her fastidiousness is partly social choice but also perhaps an inability to face up to the depths of her own nature, and to the confusions of modern society with its strong strain of nihilism. She believes that the shape and matter of the short story is determined by the writer's own character and that "both are one," yet there are further depths which have not as yet been plumbed. It is here, researching into her own inhibitions, that Mary Lavin will continue to contribute to literature.

Apart from the fact that she is still writing, Mary Lavin's contribution to the short story genre will not receive its full acknowledgement until she is more generally understood and appreciated, as a writer. Her reserved, oblique, sometimes ambiguous implications are demanding. Her work reflects the customary Irish tendency to present multiple and opposing points of view. There are often two ways of interpreting events, and the Irish—they are not alone in this—have always been masters of half-meanings. Is this one reason why Ireland is today producing a high number of competent writers and poets? For this is an age in which the half-meaning is the nearest anyone can get to being categoric.

As Mary Lavin is a writer who stresses the importance of the intuitive, mystical and non-verbal areas of human understanding, I believe the survival values of her work will depend upon a more general appreciation of these aspects. Is it because she comes from a linguistically gifted race with a long tradition of oral literature that the plasticity of an earlier dimension of consciousness, wider and more subtle than that which now pertains in western society, and impossible to produce in words, yet adheres to Mary Lavin's writing? There is in all her work a sense of meaning present to the mind as an unexpressed essence, a distillation of feeling, which demands more than eye-reading. As time goes on one hopes that more and more readers will grasp the significance of this, whether she be read for her social revelation of a particular milieu in Ireland, or for her humane enlargement of reality giving greater scope for mutual human communication.

A.A. Kelly. *Mary Lavin: Quiet Rebel* (New York, Barnes & Noble, 1980), pp. 176–77

LEDWIDGE, FRANCIS (1887–1917)

Of pure poetry there are two kinds, that which mirrors the beauty of the world in which our bodies are, and that which builds the more mysterious kingdoms where geography ends and fairyland begins, with gods and heroes at war, and the sirens singing still, and Alph going down to the darkness from Xanadu. Mr. Ledwidge gives us the first kind. When they have read through the profounder poets, and seen the problem plays, and studied all the perplexities that puzzle man in the cities, the small circle of readers that I predict for him will turn to Ledwidge as to a mirror reflecting beautiful fields, as to a very still lake rather on a very cloudless evening.

There is scarcely a smile of Spring or a sign of Autumn that is not reflected here, scarcely a phase of the large benedictions of Summer; even of Winter he gives us clear glimpses sometimes, albeit mournfully, remembering Spring. . . .

Let us not call him the Burns of Ireland, you who may like this book, nor even the Irish John Clare, though he is more like him, for poets are all incomparable (it is only the versifiers that resemble the great ones), but let us know him by his own individual song: he is the poet of the blackbird.

I hope that not too many will be attracted to this book on account of the author being a peasant, lest he come to be praised by the how-interesting! school; for know that neither in any class, nor in any country, nor in any age, shall you predict the footfall of Pegasus, who touches the earth where he pleaseth and is bridled by whom he will. [1914]

Lord Dunsany. Introduction to *The Complete Poems of Francis Ledwidge* (London, Herbert Jenkins, 1919), pp. 9, 11–12

For some two or three years past scraps of poetry by one Francis Ledwidge have been passed round Dublin in manuscript, or quoted from memory by lovers of verse, and now and then a lyric would appear in print, all of which like the growing brightness in the east before sunrise, gave the impression that a new poetic light would soon appear above our horizon. *Songs of the Fields* has just been published, and it is a volume of extraordinary promise. Rarely has a very young poet such an art in the precise and felicitous use of words which recreate to our imagination the poet's vision of beautiful, natural objects. In this our new Irish writer reminds us of Keats, who, for a kind of magical fitness of phrase, is supreme in English poetry. Keats never failed to get the exact word. . . . There have been lords of language who revealed greater things than Keats, but none surpassed him in that word picturing which is so precise and which yet makes a dream out of the object described. Now, with our new Irish poet words are wonderfully mobile, and, as with Keats, recreate in sound what is a vision of light to the eye, and do this with a felicity hardly any living poet could equal. That, so far as one can judge from this first book, is Francis Ledwidge's great and almost only gift, but it is a great gift. There is little thought in the book. It is a mirror held up to nature more than to the human heart, but it reflects nature exquisitely. . . .

We do not know whether behind this tranquil eye there are in the imagination mightier images gathering than the physical eye could see. Sometimes we suspect there are, and we pray with Lord Dunsany for our last poet, who is now in the trenches, that the gods may not be the only listeners when he next begins to sing. An exquisite artist is seen unfolding his talent in this book. Just as the dazzling wings of a dragon fly half struggle out of the chrysalis, so at least one dazzling wing is here clear, and rarely is it touched by the clay of commonplace. Let us hope that in the next volume both wings will be free and the poet show us as lovely things in the heavens as he now shows us in the world. [Oct. 30, 1915]

George William Russell (A.E.). *Selections from the Contributions to "The Irish Homestead,"* Vol. II, Henry Summerfield, ed., (Atlantic Highlands, N.J., Humanities Press, 1978), pp. 894–95

One would despair, I should suppose, of finding anywhere in modern poetry a more tender and intimate—and withal poetic—outlook on the natural world than one encounters in ["A Song of April"] by Francis Ledwidge, a poet who died young in the World War, and in his first flush of fame.

The personalizing of the season—because it is an old convention—and the use of diminutives—because they make for sentimentality—are two practices alien to the urbane and sophisticated modern poet. They are sufficient, perhaps, to remove this poem from his favorable consideration. Yet the poem survives, and comes among the stale airs of self-conscious modernism like a refreshing wind.

Not many poets of our day, in Ireland or out of it, looked out on the world of nature with the intimacy of feeling and the minuteness of observation that are everywhere present in Ledwidge's verse. Belonging to a race of poets noted for these qualities, he stands out as one possessing them in an even more marked degree than his fellows.

David Morton. *The Renaissance of Irish Poetry:*
1880–1930 (New York, Ives Washburn, 1929),
pp. 64–65

I happened to be at Dunsany Castle when a letter with some specimens of poetry was delivered. [Lord] Dunsany read them aloud. They were the first poems of Francis Ledwidge. I remember how unsophisticated they were, crude and ungrammatical, but fresh with the freshness of morning mist. Dunsany was full of understanding and sympathy. He said that he would point out the lapses when he saw Ledwidge and that it would be all right.

How long the tuition then begun lasted, I do not know. I do know that Dunsany's teaching was effective. How effective it was may be seen in the improvement from Ledwidge's faltering to assured writing. This was a feat of instruction which proves that Dunsany could transmit learning by sympathy; there was no time to teach in the schoolmasters' way. Somebody encouraged a poet in Francis Ledwidge, and filled him with the joy of elevated thought. That man was Dunsany. And, seeing that poetry in a way is courage, Dunsany's encouragement of Ledwidge was a vitalizing and indispensable force.

Not only did he teach Ledwidge English, but he settled a sum of money on him (frequently augmented many times over) which made him independent of earning his living as an overseer of road work.

Ledwidge went with his master to the war and served through many campaigns, to fall, after a return home on sick leave, behind the lines in Flanders where he was building a road.

Oliver St. John Gogarty. *At.* March, 1955, p. 70

What emerges from the gloom produced by reading every line Ledwidge ever wrote—which on seeing the new edition [of *The Complete Poems*] I undertook to do—is that he achieved a semblance of mind and strength only in three or four poems about characters and situations of Celtic saga (especially Findebar's dilemma). His talents for pure song and Keatsian image appear more strongly in the earlier work, and weren't, after all, quite Burns or Keats. Whether he'd have done more if born in a wild place like Mayo than he managed as a son of Meath is not relevant: what he got from his native county, which on a summer day can be the loveliest in Ireland, was its lushness, not its exhilaration. [F. R.] Higgins, once or twice got exhilaration.

In three poems Ledwidge used the phrase "the world's great lie," and in a fourth "the world's untruths." But each time incidentally, there is no single poem to probe the lie, and all that welter of catkins. He begins a final stanza promisingly:

> I often think my soul is an old lie
> In sackcloth, it repents so much of birth.

One thinks: "Now truth is rushing in." But hope is dashed, he tells himself another old lie:

> But I will build it yet a cloister home:
> Near the peace of lakes when I have ceased to roam.

War didn't make a poet of him, as it did of Sassoon. Or, more exactly, it couldn't save the true poet who was dying slowly, imprisoned in ignorance.

Pearse Hutchinson. *Irish Writing*.
Autumn, 1955, pp. 59–60

Ledwidge's reading may be clearly traced in his poems and is confirmed by allusions in his letters: the Bible, Dante's *Divine Comedy*, Homer's *Odyssey*, the *Mabinogion* (Welsh medieval romances) and the Celtic Sagas. All these books were the common font of his fellow poets of the Anglo-Irish Renaissance. The vast canvas of the Old Testament particularly appealed to Ledwidge and his verses contain many allusions to Biblical personages. He was in the current fashion, too, in his continuous flow of classical references. He shared the contemporary enthusiasm for the Celtic Sagas, popularized through the verse translations of Samuel Ferguson and the later work of Standish O'Grady and Lady Gregory. Thus Ledwidge uses place names like Dun Dealgan and Emain Macha. Also Ailill, Maeve, Findebar, Cuchullain, Sualtem, Ferdia, King Connor, Deirdre, Cathbad, Leag, Emer, Conall, Caoilte, Oscar, Finn, Conan, Fand and many others come thronging from the native pantheon into his verse.

Ledwidge's poetry is of the Romantic School, which enjoyed great prestige in the Victorian era, but was rapidly losing favour in the second decade of the twentieth century. . . . The influence of the Celtic Twilight, too, is on Ledwidge's poetry in its dreamy moods and dim landscapes.

Among the poets of the past on whom Ledwidge modelled his early work, Keats came first as is well known and has been too often said. The conformities in their lives attracted too the sympathy of the Irish poet: both had to fight against poverty and mockery in their youth; the shadow of tuberculosis (Keats died of this disease and also his mother and brother) lay on both families.

The influence of Yeats's early poetry is also evident on Ledwidge's work: dwelling on unrequited love, repining for a lost Arcadia, recalling the heroic personages of the Celtic Sagas, being comforted by fairy visitants. But Ledwidge very soon learned to dominate the echoes of his contemporary and develop his own mature and distinctive mode of expression.

The best feature of his style is simplicity, not achieved without immense effort and for that reason deceptive to the uninitiated. People like Lady Dunsany and Joseph Ledwidge, who had the opportunity of observing him at work, told me that he slaved at perfecting his verse. "You know how I love short words," he wrote in a letter to Dunsany. He preferred not only short words, but short lines, too, and short poems. This passion for terseness and economy sometimes led him into awkward constructions and flawed lines, but on the other hand its effect when completely successful was a dewy freshness, a delicate airy lightness as in that near perfect lyric "A Little Boy in the Morning."

He pursued intensity of expression not only in his choice of words and in the calculated length of lines and poems, but in his metre. Most of his first fifty poems are in lines of two-syllable feet, usually four or five iambs, varied with the trochee. But if the ground beat of his verse is simple, his rhyme patterns are attractively original. In his later period, Ledwidge becomes more adventurous, embarking on two long poems, "A Dream of Artemis" and "The Lanawn Shee," and using a greater variety of two-syllable metre. But he never resorts to novel experimental verse merely to convey effect.

The notable development of his personal poetic genius was when he made his own of the Gaelic verse form of internal rhyme and assonance. The deep satisfaction of communicating with the past then thrilled through his poems. Notice the new assurance in the metre of his laments for Easter Week: "The Blackbirds," "Thro' Bogac Ban," "The Dead Kings." If the poet was snuffed out of life in his springtime, his genius had reached maturity in more than one enchanting lyric. . . .

Alice Curtayne. *Francis Ledwidge: A Life of the Poet*
(London, Martin Brian & O'Keeffe, 1972),
pp. 192–94

"Your harper," as Gogarty described Francis Ledwidge in a letter to Lord Dunsany, was born at Slane in County Meath in 1887. A labourer from the age of twelve, he was warmly encouraged by Dunsany, to whom he sent some of his verses in 1912. He had been contributing poems to the *Drogheda Independent* and his friendship with Dunsany meant that he had access to the library at Dunsany Castle, and much helpful criticism. Dunsany introduced him to literary life in Dublin, remarking in a paper that "He knows nothing about technique and far less about grammar, but he has the great ideas and conceptions of the poet, and sees the vast figures, the giant forces, and elemental powers, striving amongst the hills." He selected fifty of Ledwidge's poems for *Songs of the Fields* (1915).

In the summer of 1913 Ellie Vaughey, with whom he was deeply in love, told him that their meetings must cease: her family owned land, he was merely a road-ganger. Like Yeats writing defeatist love poems to Maud Gonne such as "The Cloths of Heaven" with its wish for the heavens' embroidered cloths to lay under her feet and its realisation that he can only offer her his dreams—"Tread softly because you tread on my dreams"—Ledwidge had only his songs to offer Ellie Vaughey. "A Song" records the frustrating melancholy enforced on him by poverty, itself a spur to poetry. . . .

Hoping to improve his financial position, Ledwidge took a temporary post as secretary to a Labour Union, was founder of the Slane corps of the Irish Volunteers, and aimed to become a journalist. Then he enlisted in October 1914 in the Royal Inniskilling Fusiliers because, he said, the British army "stood between Ireland and an enemy common to our civilisation." Dunsany, who had joined the regiment in August, was annoyed, having hoped that Ledwidge would develop his poetry at home. Ellie Vaughey had married, but died suddenly in Manchester in 1915 and Ledwidge continued to mourn the death of their love in his poems. He survived Gallipoli, returned to Ireland after the 1916 Rising, writing a poem on the executed leader Thomas Mac-Donagh, which shows the influence of the Irish poetry he had begun to read in translation, which included MacDonagh's translation of "The Yellow Bittern." . . .

Ledwidge continued to mourn the death of his former comrades in the volunteers. "The Dead Kings" is a good example, with its Irish internal rhyming. . . . He himself was killed instantly by a shell in the third battle of Ypres on 31 July 1917. *Songs of Peace* was published posthumously and followed by Dunsany's selection of his *Last Songs* (1918). Ledwidge's *Collected Poems* (1974) have been edited by Alice Curtayne, whose excellent biography of the poet was published in 1972. The last poems show Ledwidge, always psychic, turning to religious meditations, to an interest in Irish literary and historical material: but he remains at his best in his short-lined fluid lyrics with their short words, their limpidity; like John Clare, he observed his local countryside with deep love of its detailed beauties.

A. Norman Jeffares. *Anglo-Irish Literature*
(New York, Schocken, 1982), pp. 183–85

LEONARD, HUGH (1926–   )

Stephen D . . . is one of the most impressive plays to appear in Dublin since the war. . . . From the Catholic point of view, there is some justice to the charge that the play is blasphemous and immoral, for the theme of Joyce's novels [*A Portrait of the Artist as a Young Man* and *Stephen Hero*, of which *Stephen D* is an adaptation] and Leonard's play is the revolt of the artist—a revolt which in Irish terms means a repudiation of what Leonard calls "the four great 'F's' of Ireland: faith, fatherland, family and friendship." The "F" most stressed in the play is faith, and this most exacerbates the feelings of devout Catholics. . . .

The compression of the novels' details and the heightening of their dramatic effect is firm evidence of Leonard's craftsmanship. He presents salient dramatic scenes bearing on the theme and all linked by the narrator Stephen, who remembers them as he leaves Ireland for exile. The play would require imagination and skill from a director, for Leonard incorporates no stage directions in the text. The modern stage has been long aware, however, that it possesses a fluidity nearly as great as the film's. . . . In *Stephen D* Leonard handles this free realism consummately.

Robert Hogan. *After the Irish Renaissance*
(Minneapolis, Univ. of Minnesota Pr., 1967),
pp. 187–88

I was working in Manchester when the idea for *Stephen D* came to me. I was lunching in Dermot McDowell's flat in London when he played me Cyril Cusack's recording of extracts from *A Portrait of the Artist as a Young Man*—the Christmas dinner scene and a couple of other passages. I thought of what a marvellous one-man play it would make. Cyril was the wrong age for the part of the young Joyce, but I thought of writing a one-man play for Norman Rodway. He liked the idea and I wrote ten pages. When I showed them to him he went white and said he didn't feel he could do it. I then suggested writing a fullscale play and from that the idea grew.

I spent only three to four weeks in writing it; and when you spend such a short time on a play you feel very cold about it. One may feel professionally proud of a play without having any great liking for it. I could not understand why Phyllis Ryan was so enthusiastic about it. Jim Fitzgerald made a splendid producer and the play became a great success. But I could never understand why. I admire the content of *Stephen D*, but I have never really liked it because it wasn't my own. To me it was always Joyce and it was more of an arranging job than anything else; not only an arranging job but a matter of instinct, a knowledge of what would work on the stage even though one did not know how to stage it. I knew whether certain things were possible and whether they worked dramatically; and that, I think, was my only contribution to *Stephen D*. . . .

The Irish writer is alone in the world in the sense that in every other country the existence of God is doubted and a serious play becomes a search for a god, not God, a search for a purpose and a meaning. The Irish writer is different in that he accepts God and so do his characters. That is his starting and his finishing point, and it is inclined to put him out of step with the rest of the world's writers. Basically I think this is the reason why Irish plays are not always acceptable in Britain and America. At the beginning of every Irish play there is the presumption, which audiences cannot readily accept, that God exists. In nearly every European country among the *literati* who attend the theatre, and I am speaking of theatre in a serious sense, there is a belief that God is dead and that we must carve our own meaning out of life. This is a premise to which Irish writers cannot subscribe, and it creates an interesting problem. I suppose it would be easier to write if the problem was not there. I think any man who believes in God is a saint. The rest of us hope there is a God. As a character in a Spanish play said, we should always behave as if there is a God in Heaven, although we can never be sure until the last moment whether there is.

Hugh Leonard. In Des Hickey and Gus Smith, eds.,
Flight from the Celtic Twilight (Indianapolis and
New York, Bobbs-Merrill, 1973), pp. 194, 198–99

In Hugh Leonard's *Da*, Charlie, the protagonist, . . . is a subtle but unheroic intellectual. An adopted son and a playwright by profession, Charlie has returned to Ireland from England to bury his foster father, who has died in a psychiatric hospital at age eighty. Centering upon Da's influence on Charlie, the play probes the paradox that kindness which places one in another's debt can be cruelly discomforting. Charlie's early musing, "The man who will deliberately not cause pain to his mother must be something of a sadist," whimsically states the play's theme although it is Charlie who is the victim of his foster father's generosity. Charlie's mother's self-righteousness over adopting him relieves him of any sense of unpaid obligation, but the rough natural virtue of Da subjects Charlie to a life debt he cannot repay; and Da wills to Charlie a haunting image of goodness he both envies and detests. Da, we learn, is a poor, uneducated gardener who, by conventional standards, is oppressed by a nagging wife, a stingy employer and an arrogant son. But Da overwhelms those dehumanizing pressures with an earthy, unprepossessing spirit that survives unwarped and dominant. The remembrance of Da torments Charlie because it makes his own intellectual cynicism and wit seem by contrast protective covers for a mean spirit.

Leonard sets the play in a kitchen following the burial where Da enters to haunt Charlie. The terse, combative conversation between Charlie and Da leads Charlie into memories of the past which help explain Charlie's presently plagued conscience. Because Charlie cannot rid his mind of Da, one has to feel that beneath Charlie's cynicism there is a persistent humanity; but Leonard's theatrical method of a self and ghost in a flyting match communicates the strong paternal-filial bond without sentimentalizing it. In the character of Charlie, Leonard portrays just those hard-surfaced impulses of independence and self-justification that resist the intrustive humanity of Da. The total person, Charlie, must necessarily include the character of Da, who now is his enemy within. Leonard has the memory sequences freely interplay with the present in such a way that Charlie, in his naturally detached manner, never gets wholly lost in thought. Charlie will, at times, coach his remembered self, "Young Charlie," on what to say and how to respond. Such alienating techniques keep our perspective on Charlie's problem a clinical one. *Da* is not a play of grandeur or memorable passion; rather it impresses with its polished sensibility, inventiveness, and theatrical craftsmanship.

Robert B. Bennett. *JIL*. Sept., 1976, pp. 149–50

Home before Night ventures into the territory of author/playwright Hugh Leonard's recent Broadway success *Da*, giving us a wider view of his Irish homeland and compatriots than did the play.

Not only do we find Leonard's wry and silly Da here, but also his grandmother, mother, neighbors, friends, and employers.

He guides us through his childhood in Dalkey, a village just south of Dublin, during the economically depressed 1930's, through maturity in the war years, to his decision to leave Ireland in the late 1950's after 14 years in the civil service. Much of the memoir recalls the Joycean archetype—the young artist struggling to escape family, religion, and social mores—to escape Ireland itself in order to survive.

Some of Leonard's passages make one laugh aloud. His social comedy arises from a number of dissociations. Perhaps the most obvious and pleasing lies in the elaborate texture of his formal prose, which slides incongruously into the colorful "begobs" and "bollixes" of working-class Dublin slang. In addition he has a remarkable gift for extravagant comic simile ("trying not to offend him was like crossing a minefield on crutches"). And throughout most of the memoir Leonard refers to himself in the third person, a distancing device that separates the childhood of John Keyes Byrne (an adopted child, like Joyce) from his later life as a professional writer with the pen name of Hugh Leonard.

Despite the comedy, a good deal of pain seeps into all these fissures, and Leonard doesn't disguise it. In large measure, Irish comedy is the comedy of pain. Seven centuries ago Ireland lost her equilibrium in the Norman Invasions and has been fighting to regain it ever since. Any recovery of national language, custom, or identity will be partial: only territory can be fully reclaimed. The rest is lost to tragedy.

The preponderance of the book has tragic overtones: recollections through a child's eyes of the mortifying public displays of a drunken mother, the savagery of priests in the classroom and confessional, the twisted lives of relatives, neighbors, and friends, and the broken genius of Mr. Drumm, Leonard's civil service mentor and the subject of his new play, *A Life*. As Leonard observes, "The Irish love failure."

But despite its pained moments, this story is not a tragedy. In 1970

Leonard settled with his wife and daughter back in Dalkey, no longer a blighted town, but a fashionable suburb. The Ireland of a failed generation is gone, and with it the tragic world of parochial hates, infantile morality, and appalling poverty. What once threatened the very existence of Leonard's genius (and he has considerable genius) now nourishes it. You can go home again, he finds.

This is a tragicomedy, then, of the survival and recovery of an adopted son who, unlike Joyce, did return home, a celebrated artist in his own country, in his own time. And this may be the rarest of all Irish comedies, a comedy of forgiveness.

Parkman Howe. *CSM*. June 4, 1980, p. 17

. . . Virtually everything [Leonard] has ever written has been about Ireland or the Irish. And while he says he is an agnostic, and has on occasion, like Joyce and Behan, taken swipes at the Church, remnants of his Catholic upbringing continually surface in his work. It is a sense of ritual, of tradition, a way of perceiving the world. Drumm, the central figure in *A Life*, for instance, is described as a man with "lips, as thin as Lent," a man with "a face on him like mortal sin." . . .

As for Mr. Leonard, he says, "I'm very interested in the nature of time, the sense that the past is coexistent with the present." In his case, though, it is not a past taken from history or myths, but a nearer and more personal past, one represented by his own parents. His attitudes toward Ireland and how it has changed, in fact, are very mixed up with his own familial feelings of love and guilt. As in Synge's *The Playboy of the Western World* and O'Casey's *Juno and the Paycock*, the family and its generational conflicts become, in his work, a kind of epiphany for society at large.

With his last three plays—*Da, Summer* and *A Life*—Mr. Leonard has turned increasingly towards autobiographical material. Like Eugene O'Neill, he has come to terms with personal history through his work, though by a different route. People "kept seeing parallels between *Da* and *Long Day's Journey into Night*," he says. "They're both about fathers and sons, but we set out to do different things. O'Neill set out to blame and incriminate his family and finally to extend an absolution. *Da* set out to be a monument to my father."

"I wrote the play to pay off a debt to my father," he goes on. "But the play made me successful as a writer and since I couldn't have written it without my father, the debt's now greater than ever." *Da* helped him realize, the playwright says, that "for all the indecent haste to bury my childhood like a dead cat, there was an ache of loss."

And throughout his plays, there is an echo of that loss. In *Summer*, a group of friends revisit the site where six years earlier they had met on a summer's eve. What they find there, however, is not their youth, but intimations of mortality. The ghosts in *Da* are more real. The stage in that play, after all, is not occupied by a family, but by one man, surrounded by his memories. And in *A Life*, a man named Drumm learns that he is dying of cancer, and as the evening proceeds, he searches his past to find meaning in what is passing and to come.

Michiko Kakutani. *NYTAL*. Nov. 2, 1980, p. 4

The [critics'] suspicion of facility [in Leonard's work] is neither unfounded nor wholly fair. Two plays, highly acclaimed in Ireland and the United States, which Leonard wrote after his return to Ireland in 1970 are the test cases: *Da* (1973) and *A Life* (1976). "Stop it," says Charlie to his dead foster-father in *Da*, "it's not then any more, it's now." Now a successful writer, Charlie has come back to Dalkey to clear up his father's few relics. Unwillingly, he conjures up *revenants*: Da at various ages, Mother, Young Charlie, the cynical Mr. Drumm, who found him his first, menial job. Moving around a stage in whose space lighting isolates scenes from his past, its "womb" the kitchen at home, they re-enact the growth of their relationships.

The earliest "then" is Charlie's childhood—"Da, I love you"—its "now" Charlie's sardonic, "When I was seven. You were an Einstein in those days." Young Charlie too, gauche, resentful of his circumstances, is both derided by his alter ego—"that little prick"—and re-possessed. "I listened, faint with shame," Charlie takes over from him in one episode. The scorn he cultivates wilts under Da's placid acquiescence, his stock jokes, his proverbial opiates, his total incomprehension of Charlie's doing well by him. . . . At the end, Da will not be banished, irreducibly a part of Charlie, following him as he exits with a song that recalls his blundering on Young Charlie's first inept effort at seduction.

A Life picks Mr. Drumm out of *Da* and places his desiccated married life against his self-conscious adolescence. Here, the two adult couples are unaware, apart from two intrusions by Drumm, of their past being recapitulated around them. The doubling of times and parts achieves some moving effects. It does little more, however, than corroborate our knowledge of the grown selves, much as they were, and their quite faithful reminiscences. Our sight of the past requires no adjustment of our focus on the present, though it seems to hint at a disturbance of the single view. In the present action the centre is an autocratic attempt by Drumm, who has been told he is fatally ill, at reconciliation with his wife and oldest friends. Perhaps he moves towards it. "Make a start," is his curtain line. He is telling his wife to set off for home, but may mean more than that. That, however, is another story, and again, time remembered does not significantly comment on it.

Though the transitions of time in *A Life* are cunningly stitched, by Act II one is aware more of the stitching than of a garment taking shape. The device is a trick that ends up by drawing attention to itself. Without it the drama of Drumm's acrid defensiveness, crumbling in his mature years and station, would have been better served. *Da*, a superior piece of work, is made coherent by Charlie, who is the reason for the form it takes, a subject of the play and its medium, where times and feelings intersect. Both plays are set in the location that may inspire in Leonard the work that would finally still the reservations.

D. E. S. Maxwell. *A Critical History of Modern Irish Drama, 1891–1980* (Cambridge, England, Cambridge Univ. Pr., 1984), pp. 176–77

LONGLEY, MICHAEL (1939–   )

There's a tight-lipped quality about Michael Longley's verse which could lead one to think of it as protestant, not just in the sense in which all art may have to be, but in a narrower and more restrictive sense as well. Of the contemporary Northern Irish poets Longley is probably the one who finds it hardest—or is least willing—to give himself over to expansive gestures or rhythmic fluency. His first book dealt with personal subjects through mainly natural settings and in an unreconstructedly metrical way, and its air of sleeves rolled up and of a job of work being done made an agreeable enough impression. His second book was formally rather freer, and although one was allowed to hear the guns and bombs going off on the periphery of the poet's experience its underlying concerns seemed to be just as personal. His latest collection, *Man Lying on a Wall*, gives itself over to private subjects almost unreservedly—there are poems on all kinds of domestic matters and none that reach for anything pretentiously public—but the overall impression it leaves is of an only marginally greater degree of relaxation. Rhythmically, Longley still feels boxed in: even though he has now largely abandoned traditional metres and stanza-forms the lines of any of his poems tend to be of unvaried length and to back up in a rather mechanical way the always guarded and understated tone of what is being said. A good many of the poems here are love poems, and they have a responsibility and thoughtfulness which one might find appropriate to that kind of subject—except that their emotions nearly always feel as though they have been processed on some slightly too conscious level of the poet's mind before they came to be worked out into poems on the page. The avoidance of overt emotionalism which seems to be a cardinal condition of Longley's being in business as a poet at all tends to get in the way of anything that one might think of as ease or naturalness of response. His lack of a singing line (Empson's phrase) could be why on a line-by-line basis his verse tends not to be memorable. The poetry in it often comes through best when he stays closest to straightforward description and can (perhaps) avoid having to think of himself as facing up to an emotional problem—as for ex-

ample in a poem called "The Goose." . . . One of Longley's attractive qualities is a wry humour which one feels might some day work its way through the
general texture of his poetry and loosen it up all over. In the meantime it gets
an airing in two or three poems towards the end of *Man Lying on a Wall* which
provide some lighter touches for those who may feel they need them.

Colin Falck. NewR. July, 1976, pp. 55–56

Michael Longley is one of about half-a-dozen younger poets that I really look
forward to reading. His new collection *The Echo Gate* is less domestic and
somehow less vulnerable than his last. The tough-mindedness has returned
and, after a period of more intimate and personal poetry, he's out in the streets
again. It must take real creative courage to face up to the daily horrors of life
in Northern Ireland, and to act as witness to the human suffering going on
there. Longley knows what he values in his own life and his sense of enjoyment in wife, family, and community is always there as a sounding board to
the mindless bloodletting going on around him:

> He was preparing an Ulster fry for breakfast
> When someone walked into the kitchen and shot him:
> A bullet entered his mouth and pierced his skull,
> The books he had read, the music he could play.

Or these lines about a murdered grocer:

> Astrologers or three wise men
> Who may shortly be setting out
> For a small house up the Shankill
> Or the Falls, should pause on their way
> To buy gifts at Jim Gibson's shop,
> Dates and chestnuts and tangerines.

In an atmosphere of terrible abstractions these poems remind us again and
again what human loss is all about. The sheer "ordinariness" of the imagery
shines out against the banality of TV reportage and government statistics. The
poetry really is in the pity, and the analogies with the First World War are further heightened when Longley looks back at his own family history:

> My father's mother had the second sight.
> Flanders began at the kitchen window—
> The mangle rusting in No-Man's Land, gas
> Turning the antimacasers yellow.

Of course not every poem's a winner. There's a touch of the crank handle about poems like "Botany," "Entomology," "Architecture." Longley's
imagery working itself out through set-pieces can be a bit of a bore, but when-

ever the imagination is in direct sympathy with human observations then the poems come wonderfully alive. "Household Hints" is Longley at his domestic best. Some of the rural backward glances and more folksy stuff is saved by the sheer directness of his recollections. He has a way of suddenly tightening up the endings of otherwise slack poems. Poems such as "Arrest" show an increasing interest with telling a story. All in all I know of few other poets now writing in English who can combine a mature imagery with such direct compassion.

Peter Bland. LondonMag. June, 1980, p. 75

Selected Poems 1963–1980, Longley's introduction to an American audience, contains three new poems as well as selections from four previous volumes. Collected here is a rich sampling of the poet's measured, poignant verse, which touches on political and historical as well as domestic and artistic concerns. Although these poems span nearly two decades, the volume exhibits a structural and thematic unity which testifies to Longley's close attention to form, his preoccupation with the act of shaping a poem or a text. *Selected Poems* has a circular shape: the poet sets out to find an authentic communal and individual voice, a cyclical quest which leads him on a poetic exploration of degeneration, death, and rejuvenation. Linked in an intricately rounded pattern, these forty-three lyrics comprise what in "Leaving Inishmore" the poet calls "quiet variations on an urgent theme."

"Leaving Inishmore," in fact, sets the tone for the entire volume, revealing both the quietness and the urgency which inform Longley's work. . . . From [its] epiphanal "point of no return" Longley embarks upon a series of finely crafted, private meditations. An exuberant declaration of love for "this new dimension, my last girl" is found in "No Continuing City": a hauntingly lovely dirge for the poet's father in "In Memoriam":

> My father, let no similes eclipse
> Where crosses like some forest simplified
> Sink roots into my mind. . . .

Hovering around the edges of such lyrics, however, is an ominous aura of chaos which the poet cannot fully escape. Such confusion often surfaces as a crisis of artistic identity, as in "Journey out of Essex," which Longley once called his "provisional farewell to poetry":

> I am lying with my head
> Over the edge of the world,
> Unpicking my whereabouts
> Like the asylum's name
> That they stitch on the sheet.

This fear of creative stasis and its corollary, the need to affirm a strong poetic stance, emerge as central concerns in Longley's verse-letters to Derek Mahon and Seamus Heaney. Characterized by a long line and looser rhythm, these lyrics reveal the poet's confusion as he experiences the fragmented, violent world of Belfast. As "two poetic conservatives/In the city of guns and long knives," Longley tells Mahon, the poets must confront "the failures of our trade"—failures, one assumes, to come to terms poetically with the forces of conflict that rack Ulster. This merging of public and private themes appears also in the "Letter to Seamus Heaney," as Longley seeks spiritual and poetic renewal through Ireland's natural landscapes yet realizes that he must not take refuge in nature. The poet cannot remain detached from the violence about him, Longley suggests; he owes it to himself and to his audience to become what Wallace Stevens called a "connoisseur of chaos."

Hence the poet images himself as one who detonates ("I explode their myths before it is too late,/Their promises I detonate"); dissolves ("I dissolve in a puddle/My biographies of birds/And the names of flowers"); dismantles ("In the meantime we dismantled it limb by limb"); disinters (For her sake once again I disinter/Imagination like a brittle skull"). Rather than contributing to the chaos, however, such dissections effectively counter confusion by invoking a new vision of society and self, by rediscovering the mystical circularity which connects human and natural worlds. The poet dismembers, then, not to destroy but to transform, to "remember" an old order and so construct a new.

In recent poems, therefore, Longley emphasizes the poet's role as a healer of wounds, a reintegrating force. A favorite image, the field of wheat, suggests the poet's efforts to replenish wasted soil, to serve as an emissary of peace.

Mary DeShazer. *CP*. Fall, 1981, pp. 126–28

[Seamus] Heaney, [Michael] Longley, and [Derek] Mahon have been described as "the tight-assed trio," the implication being that they are bound up by words, forms and formalities; that life, vigour, and earthiness are buried under aesthetics. A critic observed in Longley's last collection, *An Exploded View*, a "lack of commitment to the subject itself." As to commitment, one might fairly say that all it will lead to is poems which politicians will quote when they need them. And as to aesthetics, it is true that Longley has a remarkable technical command, as in his hold over stanza/sentence relationships. He gives a certain primacy to the act of composition, the poetic shaping which is, so to speak, its own experience. But his consideration of what art may contrive from life implicates life itself, the Northern violence included.

"We are trying," says the epigraph to *An Exploded View*, "to make ourselves heard." One subject that gets a hearing is Ireland and its renascent discontents. In "Skara Brae" an excavation gives "an exploded view/Through middens, through lives" to expose strata of the past beneath the present, a mosaic of revelations. So Longley's contemplation of his native country and province enters violence as one of the co-ordinates, one stratum, of the world he maps. It is often a disquieting world, its parts fragmenting. Words like "splintered," "fractured," "detonates," "splintering," "lesions," "dispersals," "elisions," "scatter," most obviously state the motif. They run through not only the poems about the violence, though that is their home base.

There is a touch of Grand Guignol in the grotesques of "The Adulterer," "Confessions of an Irish Ether-Drinker," "Nightmare." In "The Fairground," various monsters spirit "the solitary spectator" into their company. "Caravan" projects reality into uneasy, menacing possibilities. A gypsy caravan suggests a family companionship, which in the poet's mind becomes his own. Watched ("tiny, barely in focus") by—his wife?—he imagines riding off through a blizzard to buy food. . . .

Episodes like these are disquieting, but not depressing, partly because they have contrary aspects. There are poems of union, of a solacing perfection caught in some balance of objects. . . . More important, however, whatever afflictions he observes, the poet keeps his head, not aloof but composed. The poems addressed "To Three Irish Poets" reflect within "The stereophonic nightmare/Of the Shankill and the Falls," on personal friendships, on memories of places and people which assemble to

> Claim this country mine, though today
> *Timor mortis conturbat me. . . .*

In *An Exploded View* Longley moves about a world more apparently "serious" than that of his first collection. "Wounds," for example, movingly associates memories of the poet's father in the first world war with the manifold atrocities of Belfast. Delicate, brutal, it memorializes a legion of the dead. . . .

The political violence is a form of terror with its counterparts in private risks and insecurities. The poems are constantly making such connections. The poet's commitment is to the words and structures which will shape these diversities into his imagined world:

> The accommodation of different weathers,
> Whirlwind tours around the scattered islands,
> Telephone calls from the guilty suburbs,
> From the back of the mind, a simple question
> Of being in two places at the one time.

"Being in two"—or more—"places at the one time" is the very heart of the problem. Being in reality, and being in the world of art, and establishing a contour between the two. And within that secondary world to authenticate its happenings as events which occur only there. They will not persuade us because something exactly the same happened yesterday. These problems are at their most acute with political matter, for then ideology, dogma, is most favourably placed to subvert the allegiance to language. . . .

The language of poetry is not demonstrative, declarative, litigious. As Yeats said of Synge, its intent is to add "to our being, not to our knowledge," and what it adds is itself. It was Yeats, too, who recommended a proper tone of poetic discourse: "Only that which does not teach, which does not cry out, which does not condescend, which does not explain, is irresistible."

D.E.S. Maxwell. In Peter Connolly, ed., *Literature and the Changing Ireland* (Gerrards Cross, England, Colin Smythe, 1982), pp. 171–74

MACDONAGH, THOMAS (1878–1916)

Among the modern Irish poets MacDonagh strikes one, perhaps, as the most Irish in his character and the least so in his mentality. In the man, one finds the courage and warm-heartedness (the best of friends, as Stephens calls him), the fierce patriotism and gentle simplicity, which one has come to associate with the name of Irishman; in the poet, we find a tendency to pure speculation, to abstract philosophy, to mere intellectualism, which are qualities more common as a rule in Göttingen than in Dublin. We have to lift those wrappings from his work to find the warm fevour, the spiritual passion, the other world atmosphere, which are characteristic of Irish character and Irish thought.

There is altogether a strange dualism in Thomas MacDonagh. The professor who lectured daily on English literature as if he had no other thought in the world, and the patriot who was one of the most active organisers in the political movement—what had these two in common? The poet, rhetorical, learned, over-charged with ideas, and the poet who, occasionally lifting the veil from his inner soul, gives us a glimpse of intense feeling in words brief and simple—how are these two to be reconciled? Much of his poetry might be taken as subjective, the "Songs of Myself" might be taken as wholly so; yet they seldom reveal anything of this inner soul. With true artistic instinct he saved his poetry by this intended or unintended duplicity; his own nature was too passionate to attain to the aloofness necessary to poetic subjectivity. To live a poem, and to write one, are very different things, and art demands that the living be kept very much in subjection to the writing. . . .

It is possible that most of MacDonagh's poetry is influenced by his early religious life and by the acquired habit of religious meditation, and that, what makes it difficult to understand is that the unity of outlook, proper to the true mystic, is lacking. His visions are intellectual visions, not such as are awarded to simple faith, or are the result of a love that sees itself and all things mirrored in the love divine. To the vision of the saint faith can always give us a key, but to the vision of the intellectual poet there can be no key but that of a kindred intelligence. For this reason probably not many of Thomas MacDonagh's poems will appeal to a general public; but a few, such as the "Ballad of John John," "Of a Poet Patriot," and some others are bound to make a universal appeal.

In "John John," the simple human note, the unerring psychology—the typical woman who desires sympathy, even pity for herself but scorns such pity for the man she loves—strike a chord that must go straight to every heart. Add to this the swinging metre, the slight air of mystery, the quaint humour, and we have all the elements of not only a true, but a popular ballad.

In "Of a Poet Patriot," which in the light of after events reads like Mac-Donagh's own epitaph, we find the intenser vein of feeling, the white fire of subdued passion expressing itself in simplest words, which is the truer expression of the man, if not of the poet, the man, whose deed must echo down the ages, even if a time may come when his songs have lost their power to thrill.

A. Raybould. *Irish Monthly*. Sept., 1919, pp. 476–79

I had a good deal of correspondence with Thomas MacDonagh long before he came to Dublin, or was known in literary or political circles. He was teaching in the Diocesan Seminary, Fermoy, when he wrote me, under date of 28th March, 1906, recalling the fact that he had written to me three years before regarding his first volume of poems, *Through the Ivory Gate*. . . .

The last letter of his I received was also from Fermoy, on the 30th of the same month [October, 1907], and is of much interest, as it conveys his own views regarding his play, *When the Dawn Is Come*: "I have been very busy of late with a play which I have written and which I am offering to the Abbey. Those who have seen it think it wonderfully good; it breaks new ground, being a play of Ireland fifty years hence in time of insurrection, in the main, a study of a subtle Hamlet-like character. I have used a kind of noble, rhythmic prose, the best version, I think, of what may be a noble Gaelic idiom of that time. One friend of mine, who is a fine dramatic critic, in one way, too, an Abbey critic, says it will be an unique success, and adds, in utilitarian mood, that it will make also the success of *The Golden Joy*. What a long confidence has grown out of my apology for not writing. . . . You had an impression that the Belfast notices of the 'G.J.' were good: one said the book was a puzzle; another made jokes about 'halfpenny dips' and 'Ireland was Ireland when England was a pup,' certainly a witty commentary on one of my pieces; the third counted the poems, and gave the number with two quotations, but no opinion on the worth of the volume." As is known, the play was produced at the Abbey Theatre, and published in book form, but in neither case with marked success, much to his disappointment.

When MacDonagh was appointed lecturer on English literature at University College, Dublin, our friendship ripened. Scarcely a day passed without his coming into the library and discussing books and authors, old and new. His mind was stored with information, and he, being one of the greatest conversationalists I ever listened to—with the possible exception of Tom Kettle—had a peculiar power of imparting that information; hence his success as a teacher. He had read deeply in the classics and English literature, but less deeply in Gaelic. Of quiet, unassuming manners, no one could have dreamt that under his calm, scholarly exterior lay the stuff that heroes and martyrs are made of. I knew, of course, that he was an enthusiastic officer of Volunteers, but it was the surprise of my life to learn, when on a short holiday with William Boyle, the Abbey dramatist, at Dromiskin, Co. Louth, that he was a prominent leader of the insurrectionary movement of Easter Week. Yet, looking back and recalling odd fragments of conversation little heeded at the time, and re-reading his play and poems, one is led to believe that he gladly trod the rough road of duty, and perhaps, after all, found the death he would have chosen.

D. J. O'Donoghue. *Irish Book Lover.*
Feb., 1922, pp. 134–35

[MacDonagh's] earliest work shows a strong influence of Yeats' poetry; it is romantic and vaguely mystical, and invokes the spirit of ancient Ireland to help regenerate the soul of the Irish race. But MacDonagh soon rejected Yeats' occult "unearthiness" and chose instead for his model William Wordsworth. In *Literature in Ireland* MacDonagh suggests that Anglo-Irish poetry should be "the record of speech of the people, the living word—sometimes, no doubt, heightened to use the old phrase, but of a directness that Wordsworth would have adored. Indeed, it would seem that the desire of Wordsworth for a literature written only in the common language of the people is best fulfilled in the work produced in Ireland." MacDonagh proposed to carry to fulfillment the revolution against poetic diction which Wordsworth proclaimed in his preface to the *Lyrical Ballads* in 1798. But although he avoids luxuriant imagery in his verse, he rarely achieves the effect of "common language"; for in rejecting one form of affectation, he thrives on another.

The essential weakness of his poetic technique is evident in the rambling poem, "A Season of Repose." . . . The passage begins in language that is colloquial enough, and the omission of the indefinite article in the initial phrase, if an affectation, provides a kind of rhetorical power. But after the first two lines MacDonagh moves steadily away from the world of commonplace reality into that of artifice. The metaphor of grape and wine is effective, although hardly the stuff of everyday conversation. Even in this first stanza, however, MacDonagh is guilty of that same stylistic sin, poetic diction, that he condemns in his criticism. . . . MacDonagh occasionally achieves a lyric charm, such as one finds in his simple song, "The Coming-in of Summer," inspired by a thirteenth-century lyric:

Corncrake's ancient sorrow
    Pains the evening hush,
But the dawn to-morrow
    Gladdens with the thrush—
And summer is a-coming in.

He is at his best when he attempts, as he does here, to recapture the simplicity of another age in unaffected songs and in translations of simple Gaelic poems. But these are the exception rather than the rule in his work; his favorite vehicle is that of "A Season of Repose," the philosophical epistle, and his language in the genre suggests not the utterings of an unspoiled child of nature but the jargon of a logician.

Richard J. Loftus. *Nationalism in Modern Anglo-Irish Poetry* (Milwaukee, Univ. of Wisconsin Pr., 1964), pp. 128–29

Soon after his execution, The Talbot Press issued *The Poetical Works of Thomas MacDonagh*, with an introduction by James Stephens that praises the man but is rather noncommittal about the poet: "It is yet too early for anything in the nature of literary criticism . . . if, outside of rebellion and violence, you wish to know what his thoughts were like, you will find all his thoughts here." The book had practically no editorial supervision. *Songs of Myself and Lyrical Poems* were reprinted from the original plates, without any change in the pagination; even obvious typographical errors (enternal for eternal) were left uncorrected. A third section, Miscellaneous Poems, was added, with the pagination of *Lyrical Poems* continued; this was a selection (perhaps made by Stephens) from his early and his uncollected poems. Of the new work, the best is easily "Barbara;" of the early work, the sonnet "To James Clarence Mangan." There are translations from the Irish and from Catullus and some pleasant verses of his own, but little except the poem to his daughter that adds to his literary stature.

Like an Elizabethan wit, MacDonagh occasionally made one word serve a double purpose. In the poem "Barbara," the rose is primarily a symbol of an independent Irish nation, but there are suggestions of a Catholicism which he desired, but did not find in the Irish Church.

> When the life of the cities of Europe goes
>   The way of Memphis and Babylon,
> In Ireland still the mystic rose
>   Will shine as it of old has shone.
>
> O rose of Grace! O rare wild flower,
>   Whose seeds are sent on the wings of Light!
> O secret rose, our doom, our dower,
>   Black with the passion of our night.

It seems a mistake to read too much of religious feeling into these stanzas; something there is, of course, and the Biblical phraseology justifies the interpretation. But MacDonagh is essentially using the grandeur of ancient Irish-

Catholic scholarship to justify the emergence of an independent nation: the "passion of our night" has practically nothing to do with any persecution of the church, and in fact everything to do with what he regarded as the enslavement by the English of the Irish people.

Yet it is on this book that MacDonagh's poetic reputation now rests. In the main it is a good book. A stricter selection would more immediately reveal his very real ability, but all the poems worth preservation are included. The author of "John-John," "Of a Poet-Patriot," "The Yellow Bittern," and other equally good poems has earned a secure place in Irish Literature.

> Edd Winfield Parks and Aileen Wells Parks. *Thomas*
> *MacDonagh: The Man, the Patriot, the Writer*
> (Athens, Univ. of Georgia Pr., 1967), pp. 98–99

The motives of the thousand-odd men who mobilized on Easter Monday were extremely varied; many thought that they would win, others thought that they were on route march, and certainly many simply never weighed the consequences of what they were doing. To say that MacDonagh knew implicitly that he was going out to die, and that this was the culmination of idealistic dreaming, is not proved, especially if such a statement is based on his works or his speeches. The theme of early death in a heroic cause was present in MacDonagh's works from the very first, and he brought that theme to the Irish Volunteers; it infused the rhetoric he used in his speeches for the movement. But death was always with MacDonagh a convention, a metaphor that he constantly relied on, just as he did the dream-reality organizational technique. Literature was for him a divine art and therefore was about elemental matters—death had to be a part, an integral part, of that conception.

Thomas MacDonagh's place in the literary revival will always be a minor one; as a poet he never developed beyond the point of showing promise, and only a few of his later poems are anthologized. Yeats's final assessment [in "Easter, 1916"] was accurate:

> This other his helper and friend
> Was coming into his force;
> He might have won fame in the end,
> So sensitive his nature seemed,
> So daring and sweet his thought

MacDonagh's plays are ignored (and very likely will always be so) by the theater movement, and *Literature in Ireland* continues as a required or recommended text on academic syllabi, though not as a work that is much more important than for its statement of the "Irish Mode." There is some evidence of a general move toward reassessing MacDonagh's work, but this move has not gone much further than oblique statements in journals to the effect that such reassessment is needed. Donagh MacDonagh's view of his father—with Pearse and Plunkett—as one of the "young revolutionary writers of the time" will probably for long remain the standard view of Thomas MacDonagh's work.

Johann A. Norstedt. *Thomas MacDonagh: A Critical Biography* (Charlottesville, Univ. Pr. of Virginia, 1980), pp. 142–43

Three principal Deirdre plays precede MacDonagh's and might be called *synoptic* as they each examine the Deirdre myth with the disposition to view Deirdre as an heroic woman of positive, though differing, tragic values. AE's (George Russell), John Synge's and W. B. Yeats's *Deirdres* made up the synoptic triad. . . .

Then comes MacDonagh's *Lady Spider* taking a radical posture to the earlier three. He sticks closely to the most ancient versions of the tale and is anxious to reject all that it has accumulated in the meantime, flatly rejecting the heroic and tragic definitions that have conventionally marked later recensions of the story. All becomes *modern*.

In *Lady Spider* the feeling for time itself is modern. It opens on a hurry-up sense of rush into the past, directly opposed to the way time used "in the olden times" to pass slowly, if it passed at all. Deirdre is eager for love, though she knows of her inauspicious origins and the prophesy of the Druid that she is to trouble all Ireland. She knows about literature *per se* and how she may be of use to the poets, but she declares herself for life and the future, not for poetry. She craves and is ready for sensual experience. . . .

In the play's most audacious stroke, she declares that the poets may place her where they like in the various recessions of her legend, but that *she will not have been there*—not in those conventionally tragic spaces. . . . She side-steps that grave, side-steps the Romantic Tradition, side-steps her complex role as inspiration, support and soul's companion to Irish heroes. Denying her archetypal role in literature, she opts for what *power* she can get in a deeply flawed world. She rejects prophesy now and a well-ordered place in a well-defined and synoptic "Deirdre" scheme. None of it is worth her death when power is waiting to be picked up at Connor's feet—or in his stale bed where she will accomplish his impotence. She is now fully the Lady Spider. . . .

There is no victory of souls for the future as in AE, no transformation into the lineaments of the art-object as in Yeats, no declaration of the splendor and intensity of the wild, free life in nature and the final justification of honor and right roles as in Synge. Here is a low-mimetic design of heroic material, analytical and literary. It is, in fact, a play made out of literature, not life. A good part of its pleasure is derived from its complex yet systematic modern literary consciousness and mode, its specific resistance to tragedy. MacDonagh's stance to his material replicates that of Deirdre's stance to her material within the play. As Deirdre is aware of the dimensions of her situation, almost the details of other Deirdre tellings, so MacDonagh writes in full consciousness of all the Deirdres who have gone before his. He wants to be held accountable for them all and paradoxically—as with Deirdre herself—for none of them. He is eager to account for himself among the poets of Ireland, his final special task being to end all the "Deirdre nonsense" once and for all.

Gordon M. Wickstrom. *JIL*. Sept., 1980, pp. 4, 6–8

MACKEN, WALTER (1915–1967)

Beautifully written in its lyrically Irish way is *Rain on the Wind* by Walter Macken, an actor, playwright and novelist. This is a rarely lovely book, a fine combination of narrative skill and tender affection for people. Doesn't it take an Irishman, anyway, to be tender in print without being sentimental? You can find laughter and drama in *Rain on the Wind*, and that is all to the good; but you can also find the true wisdom of the heart, and that is not to be come by every day in life or in literature.

Rain on the Wind is only the story of a poor Galway fisherman. It is simple, unpretentious and as clear as spring water. It is very good indeed.

Its hero is Mico Mór, who "never wanted anything but to be a fisherman and to be at peace and to have a quiet life." But Mico was cursed with a disfiguring birthmark, and "a blind cod could see that he hadn't a brain in his head." It was Mico's brother, Tommy, who was the clever one, and handsome, too.

Mico Mór is one of the most appealing characters in recent fiction. His lack of brains was a matter of the intellect alone. His basic intelligence, his ability to face life and to judge between practical or moral issues, was great. Mico's kindness, loyalty, affection for his friends and courage were all unusual. Everyone liked Mico, "the big eejit," and everyone knew that he would never be anything except a poor fisherman.

Rain on the Wind is written in a series of dramatic episodes which provide a rich and fascinating picture of life in Galway. Local ways of speech, habits of thought and traditional customs fall neatly and naturally into place. Mr. Macken hasn't just written an immensely entertaining story about a likable hero. He has delved deeply into one corner of Ireland and done much to deepen his readers' sympathies. Any sensitive reader of *Rain on the Wind* will never again be so hasty to judge unfavorably an outwardly stupid person.

Maybe, if one only knew him better, as well as Mr. Macken makes Mico Mór known to us, he would turn out to be as fine a person. [1952]

Orville Prescott. *In My Opinion: An Inquiry into the
Contemporary Novel* (Indianapolis and New York,
Bobbs-Merrill, 1962), pp. 233–34

Boola, a little village behind and beyond Connemara, was a dangerous spot to live in while Bart O'Breen was around. Look what he did to might-have-been Breeda, and to Joseph his half brother for instance: threw them both off a cliff and blinded one and, it was thought, stupified the other so much that he couldn't become a priest after all. *Sunset on the Window-Panes* is Walter Macken's most violent tale to date. Having accidentally blinded one girl Bart goes on to ditch another, and wanders off, leaving her with her shame, to wander the world in an attempt to find his soul.

But Bart hasn't got one, nor has he a conscience, and, to tell the truth, never, to this reader anyway, becomes a believable character at any point in the book. But all the others are there in the round: wise, quiet John Willie, his nagging, careful wife, and too-late-married Martha worried that Luke might not get the farm after all. Stock characters, perhaps, but Mr. Macken brings them to full life. And his story is a quick and moving one, simple and exciting, except, perhaps, when Bart writes home in near-O'Casey to tell of his travels.

One of the most refreshing aspects of Mr. Macken's clear writing is his lack of affinity to all those who tilled the same rocky ground before: there's no hint of Synge in this Connemara, no O'Flaherty. Walter Macken has seen it all for himself, and no literature comes between what he sees and what he writes.

The story ends in riot: weak, sad Joseph sees a vision on a turf-bank, and he is told that he will see the vision again on the May-day at the same time when the sun is gone beyond the peak. Joseph sees no vision when he visits the turf bank again, and the crowds stone him as he stumbles back to the village.

But in his room he sees the vision—or was it just the sunset on the windowpanes? The question isn't answered, Joseph dies, and Bart, by this time the owner of a travelling shop, runs off wildly through the crowd, running, running, leaving Breeda for ever, Sheila for ever, and young Bart, the son she bore him.

Sunset on the Window Panes is a strong and exciting novel.

Jim Edwards. *Irish Writing*. Dec., 1954, pp. 67–68

Mr. Walter Macken is another contemporary Irish dramatist whose plays have been produced and have pleased audiences. Now we have from him a volume of short stories [*The Green Hills*], which add up to a socio-economic fantasy—people and ways which never were except in the private dreams of third-generation Irish-Americans. Later I shall have some qualifications to make.

Where is the Walter Macken of *Quench the Moon* and *I Am Alone?* Those were most promising early works. They were perceptive, stark and austere—qualities which Mr. Macken has of late replaced with physical violence and sentimentality. In *Home Is the Hero* Mr. Macken went so far as to try to carry dramatic climaxes on violence alone.

In *The Green Hills* there are twenty-one short stories, mostly of peasant life. The style which Mr. Macken affects in them (I am too assured of his talent not to believe that the style *is* affected) is a peculiar amalgam of compressive O'Flaherty ("The doctor heard the clock striking midnight as he finished his last entry for Monday in the diary"), colloquial O'Connor ("So what did he do? He went back into the pub and he got rotten stinking drunk. That's what he did."), and Kitty the Hare (". . . most of the lassies in the pictures were more than half-naked and were showing more of their bumps to the world than a rawhide cow, bless the mark."). Only—*fiat justitia*—weaker than O'Flaherty, less skilled than O'Connor and stronger than Kitty the Hare.

Occasionally these stories, for an Irish reader, are almost embarrassing with their sentimental idealized content, ingratiating narration, and their aren't-we-Irish-the-terrible-divils acceptance of feyness and the unexpected as normal. But then the stories are obviously not written for the Irish reader; among other evidence, one story contains a detailed description of the rules and procedure of the game of hurling.

Now for my qualifications. The stories are most vigorous and entertaining. They are neatly plotted (but Mr. Macken's forte is not plot at all—a qualification of a qualification, bless the mark!) and he most dexterously makes no demands whatsoever on the reader.

Laurence Ryan. *Irish Writing*. Summer, 1956,
pp. 125–26

Walter Macken is one of the most successful modern Irish writers, and one of the best. His plays are little known outside Ireland, but his fiction has found a fairly wide, Book-of-the-Month Club, upper-middle-brow audience. His critical reputation lies about halfway between that of a Frank O'Connor and that of a Maurice Walsh. Still, even though his stories lack the qualities likely to get them discussed in the *Hudson Review* or *Modern Fiction Studies*, they are fine work, and no less fine for being both traditional and easily readable. . . .

His first play in English was *Mungo's Mansion*, which was performed at the Abbey on February 11, 1946. His other published English plays are *Vacant Possession*, which has been produced so far only by amateurs, *Home Is the Hero*, in which he played both on Broadway and in the film, and *Twilight of a Warrior*, which is possibly his best. . . .

Macken's early plays, with their broad characterization and heightened speech, suggest the early O'Casey. *Mungo's Mansion* is both a strong evocation of slum life and a strong condemnation of it. . . .

The O'Caseyan reminiscences are still evident in Macken's best known play, *Home Is the Hero*, though the characterization has become more restrained and truer to life than to the theatre. The play is set in a County Council house in Galway, its story a variation of a favorite Irish theme, the revelation that the hero is really a villain. The O'Reilly family, like the Boyle family in *Juno*, is composed of a false-hero father, a long-suffering mother, a son, and a daughter. The daughter is as headstrong as Mary Boyle, the son Willie maimed like Johnny Boyle. It is Willie, however, who holds the family together, rather than the mother Daylia, who likes her drop. Paddo, the father, is a brute of a man who five years earlier had killed a neighbor and is now returning home from prison. His cronies plan a great welcome, but his son and daughter greet him less enthusiastically. And before the evening is over, Paddo has beaten Josie, terrified Daylia, and knocked Dovetail downstairs. Then, faced with his children's revolt, he leaves home, and the play ends with the family happy as they were before.

This résumé makes Paddo appear a great brute, which apparently is what Macken wants. Yet there is an ambivalence about the character. Paddo has paid for his murder and suffered remorse, yet Macken seems to squelch sympathy for him. When Paddo apologizes to the wife of the murdered man, Macken presents the apology as wrong. Paddo is horrified at Willie's wanting to marry the daughter of the murdered man, at Rosie's flashy beau, at Daylia's drinking. In other words, the facts make a case for him, but Macken never allows the audience to feel as much sympathy as the facts would allow. The result is a curiously cold, almost ill-tempered play, although technically it is an adroit example of the best Abbey realism. It is tightly structured, and its characters, with the exception of the Joxerish Dovetail, are drawn with believable restraint.

Robert Hogan. *After the Irish Renaissance*
(Minneapolis, Univ. of Minnesota Pr., 1967),
pp. 65, 66, 68

Each of Macken's historical novels is introduced by a "Historical Note" that is both expository and didactic, both informing readers of key historical facts and preparing them for an Irish nationalist interpretation of the facts. . . . In 1959, Macken no longer needed to write an apologia for Irish nationalism, as the Banims had done in the 1820s. His is an all-out attack on the British historical repression of the Irish, concerning which he could assume that his average British reader might be as critical as he was.

While changing its tone, Macken shares the Banims' [John and Michael Banim] expository didacticism; he also adopts a romantic approach similar to theirs. Like their heroes, his are larger than life. In the development of his protagonists, Macken is part realist and part romancer. His heroes struggle with realistic, historical problems, but at the same time they have some of the virtual anonymity of the old knights. Dominic in *The Scorching Wind*, for example, is never assigned a surname; his namesake in *Seek the Fair Land* has a surname, but it is never clear what he did for a living before the holocaust at Drogheda. The point seems to be that either Dominic might be *any* Dominic in Ireland during these particular periods of history. Furthermore, Macken's endings are romantic. Like the Banims' protagonists, Macken's heroes escape from the nightmare of history at the end. In *Seek the Fair Land*, at the end of the Cromwellian war, Dominick goes home to live in peace with his daughter and son-in-law, recalling the ending of Banim's *The Last Baron of Crana*; similarly, at the end of *The Silent People*, Dualta, in spite of the Famine, walks the road home with his wife and child ("We will survive"); and even at the end of *The Scorching Wind*, although Dominic has just found his brother dead in the Civil War, he finally gets the girl.

Consistently, Macken's historical heroes are reluctant rebels on the run. Each is forced into a rebellious, fugitive posture. . . . [But] while [his] protagonists are forced into rebelliousness, there is at the same time a countermotive in the novels, a higher lesson: the peace beyond tragedy. . . .

The pacifist theme of Macken's novels sets him sharply apart from O'Flaherty, who ridiculed pacifism and disdained Daniel O'Connell. Macken is less willing than O'Flaherty to glorify violence. It might be said that O'Flaherty is the better writer and Macken the better moralist. While O'Flaherty's central historical protagonist is the animal-man turned rebel, Macken's pivotal figure is more often the schoolteacher: Dominick MacMahon in *Seek the Fair Land*, who is never called a schoolteacher but who is introspective and left shelves full of books behind in Drogheda; Dualta's crafty, resigned Uncle Marcus in *The Silent People*, who sends him on his way out of trouble to Clare; and Dominic's and Dualta's father in *The Scorching Wind*, who is arrested because he taught Irish nationalism for years in the schoolhouse and who dies of pneumonia contracted in jail. And the priest and the pacifist politician educate Macken's rebels. In these respects Macken is much closer to [Francis] MacManus than to O'Flaherty.

James M. Cahalan. *Great Hatred, Little Room: The Irish Historical Novel* (Syracuse, N.Y., Syracuse Univ. Pr., 1983), pp. 160–62

MACLAVERTY, BERNARD (1945–   )

With brilliantly purposeful prose and observation, Bernard MacLaverty explores [in *Lamb*] the dilemma of a young priest, Brother Sebastian (Michael Lamb in civilian life) who finds himself increasingly uneasy in his role of school-master at a reformatory-cum-boarding establishment in Northern Ireland. Moreover, Brother Sebastian has succumbed to the temptation which haunts all teachers and social workers—emotional involvement with a particular individual; in this case, Owen, the epileptic, maladjusted son of cruel, neglectful parents, who has slipped early into a career of wrong-doing. Lamb decides that Owen's only hope of salvation lies in removal from the school and the dour, repressive attitude of the head administrator, and so sets out to elope with the boy to England, there to begin life afresh on a modest £800, drawn from a legacy.

Once in London the futility of the scheme is quickly revealed. Lamb is an inadequate and sentimental father figure, incapable of reconstructing the life-style of his bed-wetting, chain-smoking protégé. Educational sight-seeing soon takes second place to amusement arcades, and even the important daily dosage of anti-epileptic medicine becomes dangerously erratic. And of course, once appeals are being made over the radio for the absconding pair, the situation rapidly deteriorates. After a disastrous "squat" in a homosexual nest, Lamb settles for a return to Ireland—not, as might have been anticipated, to obtain better conditions for Owen in a more sympathetic environment but to save him from "the future" by killing him—and in a particularly callous and unpleasant manner. First, he substitutes aspirin for the epilepsy tablets and then entices the boy on to lonely beach for a swim. Conveniently for the bizarre plan, immersion in the chilly water soon brings on a fit. Throughout the seizure, Lamb keeps the boy submerged. What is likely to happen after the premeditated crime is not made clear. Presumably, Lamb will be convicted of murder as well as abduction, with the worst possible moral inference placed on his actions. The final impression is one of incredulity that a man of God, even though "lapsed," could so arrogantly disregard the limitless possibilities and advantages of simply being alive!

Rosalind Wade. *ContempR*. Nov., 1980, p. 58

The tales [in Bernard MacLaverty's collection *Secrets, and Other Stories,*] are recognizably Irish for setting and wit—here with the bite of a Belfast accent—and usually display that ease of language peculiar to the Irish writer and exasperating to the American or British. MacLaverty has obvious talent and discipline, but he often lacks the consciousness of the tradition and techniques with which he is working to achieve successfully the modern voice within anecdotal structures.

The opening story, "The Exercise," is endearing, the sort that usually promises a good collection. A young boy thinks his father, a publican, can do no wrong; he gets the man's help on a Latin lesson; next day, the boy is chosen to read his answers in class, and all of them are wrong; the priest is stern, punishes the boy for relying on his father, but after class gives reassurance. At the end we realize that it makes little difference to the boy—the nice touch of the story. There are no traumatic re-evaluations, no tarnishing of the world. He still loves his father very much, but now with a bit more wisdom from the lesson he has learned. Were the volume to continue in such a vein, it would be enjoyable and commendable. The second story, "A Rat and Some Renovations," shows MacLaverty's ability in a different mode: farce. It is a terse and very amusing anecdote, the kind of reminiscence a friend might tell over a drink. . . .

"St. Paul Could Hit the Nail on the Head" does not begin with the warmth of childhood memory or the bite of wit. Its more sombre tone, even pace, and strain of silence between the characters—a housewife and a distant cousin she hardly knows, a priest on his yearly visit en route to stay with a friend—all alert in the reader that appetite ignorant of the anecdote. . . . Seemingly, it is a deeply felt story, even deeply written, but what has really been offered, what given? We receive another anecdote, this time pathetic rather than amusing. All that is said is that it is hard to make new friends in old age. Most details are wasted—her being married to a Protestant whose job is wrecking buildings, the emphasis on an epistle of St. Paul. There are certainly the beginnings of characterization, but they are all invested, or dissipated, in the anticlimactic ending, in the anecdote. The characters have little flesh, little pulse.

There is nothing wrong with that in itself. The problem lies in what is offered. The author's tone and craft are harmonized for intimacy with the reader, for insight of some degree, but the materials on which he goes to work are unsuitable. The story suffers from the author's not being fully aware of, or decisive about, his purpose and his tools. It suffers especially, from anecdote. This is not to say that the remainder of *Secrets* is given over to such failures. There are several well-conceived stories executed with control. . . .

Such is the case with the title story. A young boy begins a stamp collection with only mild interest. His great aunt Mary, an old single woman who lives with his family, offers him the stamps from some faded postcards, telling him never to touch the bundle of letters in her desk. He describes the stamps offhandedly: "Spanish, with a bald man, French with a rooster. German with funny jerk print, some Italian with what looked like a chimney-sweep's bundle and a hatchet." The forbidden bundle of letters fascinates him. Once when the old woman is at devotions, he sneaks into her room and reads them. They are from one man, the same Brother Benignus whose enigmatic postcards had aroused the boy's interest. In the letters, the man professes quite beautifully his love for Mary, his horror at the carnage, and at last his decision to make recompense for the senseless horrors by entering the religious life. The boy is discovered by his aunt, who vows never to forgive him. He little understands what he has glimpsed: an old woman's ruined hopes, the deep pain of those two lives, a continent's turmoil just decades before. Thankfully, MacLaverty is controlled, even reserved in handling the war subject, always referring it back—through the innocent boy's eyes—to the woman. In the beginning of the story she is dying, and at the end the boy quietly cries at her death, wishing for her forgiveness.

This story must carry the volume, and it is indeed a strain. Though some of the other stories are good, and all are at least tolerable, the failures and the awkward mixture detract from such a fine story as "Secrets." . . . Yet, MacLaverty is not to be dismissed. The trial-and-error search for a voice, the uncertainty and unevenness of *Secrets* do not obscure MacLaverty's talent.

Thomas Kelly. *Éire-Ireland*. Spring, 1981,
pp. 156–58

MacLaverty's quintessential talent is for the short story, as he so cogently demonstrated in his first book, *Secrets*. And it is arguable that his second book, *Lamb*, proved less successful as a novelette than as an extended moral tale. (Indeed, it was originally intended to be a short story.) One of the problems with *Cal* is that it tries to stretch the modest fabric of the short story formula to cover the broad shoulders of a "national novel" of almost classical-epic proportions. The seams of credibility rip under the pressure and we are left, at times, with a naked and rather ungainly caricature.

The novel opens with two premonitory episodes—innocent beasts of burden being led to slaughter in an abattoir; and a preacher proclaiming the evangelical message that "the wages of sin is death." The abattoir appears to be some kind of symbol for "sacrificial" Catholicism (Cal's father works there and also his IRA schoolmate, Crilly, who initiates him into the republican faith of bloodletting and revenge.) The preacher, by contrast, is unmistakably Protestant and his censorious admonition preordains the fatalistic rift between Cal and Marcella. The novel ends with Cal's arrest by the Royal Ulster Constabulary on Christmas Eve, with Cal feeling "grateful at last that someone was going to beat him to within an inch of his life."

In between the preacher's opening prophecy and its final fulfillment, we have 200 pages of predictable (because predestined) narrative. The overriding sense of ineluctable doom ensures that the characters are deployed as quasi-mechanical props in the author's tragic scenario. Even Oedipus, one feels, had more room for maneuver, more odds on his side to outwit the Sphinx and outflank fate. The plague of Thebes, it would seem, was less incurable than the plague of Ulster. . . .

MacLaverty has cast Cal as the victim of his historical circumstances. No matter how hard he tries, he cannot forget the past which sired him. His repeated attempts to immunize his passion for Marcella against the epidemic of historical memory—by isolating her in a shutter-image of timeless consciousness—are invariably frustrated. Cal's guilt keeps resurfacing and shattering the fragile peace of the present like an epileptic fit. This condemnation to historical conditioning is perhaps most vividly, if rather contritely expressed, in a scene where Cal spies on Marcella through a border of bookshelves in the library where she works. "From the very outside of the Irish History Section he could see her from between the shelves. . . . He touched the spine of the books and went so far as to take one out and flick through it . . . there was a picture of Patrick Pearse in profile. . . . Cal read on the opposite page what Pearse had said, that the heart of Ireland would be refreshed by the red wine of battlefields, that Ireland needed its bloody sacrifice." Cal bears the sign of Cain, the hallmark of his fratricide "like a brand in the middle of his forehead." History has condemned him to love the one woman whom history has forbidden him to love. There is no exit. Only Marcella D'Agostino, the author suggests, has some possibility of freedom, for her Italian parentage affords her a measure of distance from the pincer-jaws of "two opposing ideals [Orange and republican] trying to grind each other out of existence." Ulster's heritage is portrayed as some kind of congenitally inherited "original sin." Which makes it appropriate and inevitable that the ultimate moral of the novel should be pronounced by the non-Irish Marcella: "Ireland. It's like a child. It's only concerned with the past and the present. The future has ceased to exist."

MacLaverty's repudiation of history as a fatal and malignant growth finds its nearest ideological equivalent in the ahistorical messianism of the Peace Movement. Cal's final conversion to the purgative cure of repentance and chastisment epitomizes this creed. This work of an Ulster novelist brought up in the Catholic republican faith is less an *apologia* than an apology for his tribal heritage. And one is left with the slight suspicion that if the crime is perhaps too Catholic, the punishment is just that little bit too Protestant.

But while MacLaverty's use of dialogue or authorial commentary tends to slip, on occasion, into the molds of didactic conventionalism, his writing comes brilliantly alive whenever he abandons his "message" for the sake of unencumbered visual description. Time and time again, the author displays his ability to home in unerringly on concrete phenomenal details which liberate the prose from professional intrusion. . . . Such *descriptions* preclude the need for awkward moralizing *explanations*. They speak for themselves.

Richard Kearney. *ILS*. Fall, 1983, p. 24

A Time to Dance collects Bernard MacLaverty's short stories since *Secrets* (1979), and the earlier title suggests a theme that pervades this book as well. MacLaverty is fascinated by the inarticulate and the reticent, often in the triply-repressive atmosphere of the Catholic working class in Northern Ireland. He is equally fascinated by the possibility that any of his characters might for a moment find the words to describe or define a feeling, an event. "You're agog," shouts the wife in "Language, Truth and Lockjaw" when her husband, a philosophy don with a "pernickety approach to language," cannot close his jaws. "Agog describes you perfectly . . . you're the perfection of agogness." Two past-it whores in "Phonefun Limited" grow rich by describing for clients over the telephone the activities they can no longer provide in person. A retired schoolmaster on the borders of senility delivers a speech— but it is the wrong speech. MacLaverty's characters are defined by their sense of the limits of language, and his spare narrative precisely portrays their straightened lives in a way that transcends them, that makes them matter.

Robert Tracy. *ILS*. Spring, 1984, p. 44

MACMANUS, FRANCIS (1909–1966)

When a story keeps one up, crouching over a fire that has turned to cold ashes, it must be an unusually well-told tale, and that can be said of Francis MacManus's latest novel. *This House Was Mine* is a story without complications. It tells simply of a family in County Kilkenny which is so proud of itself and its possessions that the wives of its men are merely chattels to add to the lands with their dowries, to slave in the service of the house, and to produce sons to carry on the tradition of progress. A son rebels against the choosing of a wife for him, and in the struggle to bend his will the family is humbled and the house reduced to ruins. There are many farmers in Ireland like those in the story, which has the ring of real probability. Mr. MacManus writes in the simple language that is common to the people of the country, and without any strained effects he is able to build up the stuff of drama. He has drawn a great picture of the grandfather, whose intense pride and autocratic will really are the cause of the fall of this house, and, notwithstanding the tragedy of the tale, he has contrived to produce a natural happy ending.

Irish Times. Nov. 27, 1937, p. 7

Many will read this story [*Watergate*] for its own sake without realising that its sparse style, deliberate restraint, and firm technique represent an advance in contemporary Irish novel writing. They may wonder why the novel falls short of the customary length and so fail to appreciate this writer's revolt against the arithmetic of publishing. In turning to the *conte*, Mr. MacManus has gained in strength and concentration. His dialogue has the tension and dramatic forwardness which one finds in a good play. It has been clear for some time that the methods used by some of our younger realists both in the novel and the short story are doubtful and involve a new kind of pathetic fallacy. Violent colloquial speech against a background of literary descriptiveness may eventually be regarded as an unfortunate contradiction. Even the Russian influence has outstayed its welcome, and it is refreshing to find a novelist who has learned a lot from modern French technique.

It is a hopeful sign, also, when a young Irish novelist can deal, so to speak, with our own household problems without thinking in terms of an English or American public. Dirt, slovenliness and inertness—these are some of our peculiar qualities which might lend themselves to sensational treatment by our realists. But Mr. MacManus gets down to his task with all the joy of scrubbing brush, bucket and elbow grease. The action is outwardly direct and simple; inwardly complicated and tense. Alice Lennon comes back from America after an unhappy marriage to settle down with her relatives at home. She bustles into her brother-in-law's dilapidated farmhouse, only to find that her sister is a nervous wreck, and that everything is left in the hands of a slattern of tinker blood, Ruby Butts. Mr. MacManus does not spare our feelings in the complicated combat which ensues between the Woman from the States and the Woman from the Roads.

DM. April, 1943, p. 74

Mr. MacManus' only important book to be published in this country is *The Fire in the Dust*, an expert and quietly moving novel written with pungent power and disciplined restraint. He uses words with precise skill, creating effects without straining for them. And he writes with pity and objective understanding about matters which might well lure him into bitter fury.

The Fire in the Dust is a terrible picture of the twisted puritanism of modern Ireland. Everyone in the small town of Kilkenny twenty-five years ago seemed to be cursed with a ferocious prudery not far from prurience. The schoolboys alternated between shamefaced propriety and foul obscenities. Brother Brutt, the schoolmaster, was hysterically determined to find evil and sin where there was none. And Miss Dreelin, the old maid who kept the shop where rosaries, statues and holy pictures were sold, in her private crusade for holiness spread vicious scandal all over the town.

All of Mr. MacManus' characters are well portrayed, always in scenes of revealing action and dialogue. The first-person narrator, remembering what happened in his youth, is a subtler storyteller than he realizes. He tells what he saw and felt at the time and doesn't try to analyze character with greater understanding than he possessed as a boy. But he supplies the evidence on which the reader can go on to extensive ruminations of his own about the cussedness of human nature. And many of these are sure to be provoked by Miss Dreelin.

Although Miss Dreelin is one of the most dreadful human beings I have encountered in many years of close association with horrible people in fiction, she is neither a caricature nor a villainess. She is malicious, sanctimonious, hypocritical, mean and evil-minded. The scenes in which she holds the center of the stage are so painfully real and unpleasant that they leave a queasy feeling in the stomach. One wants to forget that Miss Dreelin is a pitiful psychopath and hate her as if she were Simon Legree. But Mr. MacManus never allows you to do any such thing. He insists that you should pity and understand as well as despise. And he doesn't moralize about it. He just shows that the gruesome Miss Dreelin is an unhappy human being driven by her private furies well along the road to madness.

Francis MacManus is severe in his implied criticisms of prudery, gossip and bigotry, but he is not bitter or even angry. This is the way some people are in a small Irish town, he seems to say. They are not deliberately cruel. Most of them are kind and decent folk. Their prejudices are reflections of the only life they have known, the exaggerated responses of an emotional people to their cultural environment. [1952]

> Orville Prescott. *In My Opinion: An Inquiry into the*
> *Contemporary Novel* (Indianapolis and New York,
> Bobbs-Merrill, 1963), pp. 229–31

Seal ag Rodaiocht [On the Road for a Time] is Mr. MacManus's account, in journal-form, of a three-month's tour of the United States. He begins at Cork (where, in a most moody passage, he describes emigrants weeping, drinking and singing): on board ship we enjoy with him the urbane company of Thornton Wilder: and from New York he travels by rail to St. Louis, Santa Fe, Peoria, and back to New York.

Mr. MacManus's attitude to his subject is that of the historian, the novelist, and the European Christian humanist—with irritatingly often a visitation of Irish self-righteousness. By way of fair-play, however, Mr. MacManus takes an occasional salutary side-slap at the Irish-Americans, for their concept of Ireland, and at the native Irish for their philistinism.

The novelist in Mr. MacManus is patent: all along the way he skilfully presents the reader with a series of human cameos. They are all humanistically significant but I feel rather doubtful about the validity of sociological and moral pronouncements based on such particular, selected and eccentric evidence.

Mr. MacManus is, however, interesting and pleasant in his local descriptions, which he enriches with his sense of history.

> Laurence Ryan. *Irish Writing*. Autumn, 1955, p. 61

Regularly I return to read a novel of [Francis MacManus] because he was a good writer and a careful craftsman and also, let me admit it, because he was a friend of mine. But mostly I'd reread *The Fire in the Dust*, generally accepted as his best novel; or *The Wild Garden* or *Flow On Lovely River*, for both of which I have a particular regard; or *The Greatest of These*; but never until quite recently *Watergate*, which, when I first read it, I regarded as defective because of reservations and the pulling of punches.

Was the shambling farmer a quiet man with moments of violence, or was he not, bedding down with the gypsy woman, who had practically taken over his rich but unkempt farmhouse by the river Nore? Twenty-eight years ago I thought with impatience that MacManus should have told us, and in some detail—or have allowed some of the people in the novel to tell us. Now, having, I hope, grown a little more mature, I realize that one of the qualities that places the novel among the best he wrote is the restraint, the suggestion, the half-hint that was typical of MacManus. He was a Prosper Mérimée man.

The novel is about a returned American, a description that with the coming of the jet age and the crossing of the Atlantic in a few hours and by installment payments, will soon come to mean little or nothing. Generations will grow up for whom the old heartrending songs of exile will have no significance. Before 1939 in the Irish countryside a distinction was made between a "returned" American, an Irish-born person who had lived and worked in the States and come back to settle down in Ireland, and a "born" American, who would normally only be in Ireland to see the relatives of a father or mother, or a homestead or a townland that a parent had mentioned. Born Americans weren't all that plentiful. Hitler changed all that. . . .

At a time when a bloody war was crowding the roads of the world with displaced persons, he wrote this novel about homelessness and loneliness, about, in fact, displaced persons: two very different women who are to fight like savages over a home, a place to live in. One of them fears to return with her imbecile child to the homeless roads of Ireland. The other fears to return, childless as she is, to the great American cities. . . .

The victory is to be with the American woman. But in the end, we, and perhaps she, are left to wonder who was the real destroyer. Afterwards, she never speaks again of the days of squabbling and the night of violence that brought her to victory and a home to live in. "She put it from her," the favorite nephew says, "like some of her time in America." For the gypsy may only have been, as I have said, seemingly sinister. I must confess that when I first read the novel I got it wrong, and thought that MacManus meant us to think that the victory of the goodhearted, bleached, efficient woman, and the defeat and the driving back to the homeless roads of the dark woman and her child, was a good thing. Now I feel that he meant something else—and a lot more. A little dirt and slovenliness and laziness never really threatened to destroy the world. But here and now in the 1970s it appears that efficiency may very well manage that destruction. *Watergate* remains the most enigmatic of his novels, and I wish he were alive today so that I could argue the matter with him.

Benedict Kiely. In David Madden, ed.,
Rediscoveries (New York, Crown, 1971),
pp. 272–73, 278

MacManus' fiction is unashamedly Catholic. But it is not propaganda. Mac-Manus can sound the propagandist in his essays, but in his fiction he always sought, like Joyce this time, to serve Art, not Church. Catholicism colors but does not dictate his fiction. He felt that Catholicism could "place a novelist on a centre-point of understanding" but that it "may not help a novelist to write technically well." In "The Artist for Nobody's Sake," he rejects the artist as moral propagandist: "His actions in relation to the work to be made can be neither moral nor immoral. His actions are not concerned with his last end and getting into heaven. They are concerned simply and solely with making something well. If he fails, he is not an immoral wretch. If he succeed, he is not a saint. He is either a good or a bad artist." MacManus' Catholicism was like his nationalism: generous and conscientious. . . .

Though MacManus generously admired Ó Faoláin's *A Nest of Simple Folk,* he was inspired to write his trilogy about the Gaelic poet and school-teacher Donnacha Ruadh MacConmara [*Stand and Give Challenge*] by two other books: Sigrid Undset's trilogy *Kristin Lavransdatter* (1920–22) and Daniel Corkery's *The Hidden Ireland* (1925). The latter gave him his material and the former provided him with his method. . . .

MacManus' trilogy, like Undset's, is unified by its focus upon a single protagonist: Donnacha Ruadh MacConmara, one of the many Gaelic poets about whom MacManus learned in Daniel Corkery's *The Hidden Ireland.* In similarity to [William] Carleton's Redmond O'Hanlon and [Standish] O'Grady's Red Hugh O'Donnell, MacConmara was a real historical personage, but as with these other characters "we catch only haphazard glimpses," as Corkery notes, "of that long life." Like O'Hanlon and O'Donnell, Mac-Conmara was relatively obscure, almost semilegendary. The difference is that MacManus avoids the extremes represented by Carleton's disregard of fact and O'Grady's enslavement to it, creating a MacConmara who is historically grounded yet a full-fledged fictional character in his own right. Corkery provided only the bare bones, merely suggesting the course MacManus' imagination would take. . . .

In his trilogy MacManus develops the various Donnachas sketched by Corkery, adding a number of allusive features to his protagonist. In his own way, he follows Joyce's "mythical method." There are three major archetypal frames developed: Donnacha is progressively Odysseus, Job, and Lear. MacManus' allusions, however, are direct and earnest, not subtle and ironic, as in Joyce. There seem to be three Donnachas, one for each book. In *Stand and Give Challenge* he is the courageous, arrogant young rebel, compared most frequently to Odysseus, or often thinking about Odysseus himself; he is, after all, a classically trained schoolteacher. The Odysseus motif continues in *Candle for the Proud,* but more often Donnacha is Job, the poor, oppressed, long-suffering sinner. In *Men Withering* he becomes Lear, the old man, the raging, tragic seer, feeling shirked by his offspring and forgotten by the world. The setting shifts, too, but always within County Waterford: first Donnacha returns from the Continent to be a schoolteacher in Slieve Gua; then he lives with his daughter in Kilmacthomas and serves as Reverend Grimshaw's sexton; finally, having reconverted, he joins his son in Knockanee before spending his last days at his daughter's. The Donnacha who emerges from the whole trilogy is, like Ó Faoláin's Leo Donnel, the rebel as failure, but a rebel who recognizes his shortcomings, repents his sins, and dies in peace.

James M. Cahalan. *Great Hatred, Little Room: The*
Irish Historical Novel (Syracuse, N.Y., Syracuse
Univ. Pr., 1983), pp. 124, 126–27

MACNAMARA, BRINSLEY (1890–1963)

We feel that Mr. MacNamara writes about life in the little country town [in *The Clanking of Chains*] in almost an ecstasy of hatred, and we are a little dubious about his rank as a thinker because of his hatreds. He can see nothing good. We rather suspect he has a contempt for his hero. It is not poured on him in the book, but we fancy if Mr. MacNamara met his hero in real life he would characterise him as an ignorant fool. But Mr. MacNamara is a writer of real power. We must not hate him because we hate his characters. There are backwaters and pools of human life in Ireland unstirred by any angel, and as Blake says, "standing water breeds reptiles." These human swamps have to be reclaimed, and that is the work of the satirists and the realists, like Mr. MacNamara. It is not pleasant work cleansing a pool green with slime and excrement of cattle and pigs before one's house, but it is necessary for health. It is not pleasant to study the psychology of the population of Ballycullen depicted with unrelenting realism by Mr. MacNamara; but as it is necessary that the light of day be let in upon the breeding-place of noxious germs, so is it necessary that the light of the mind be turned on these stunted, vulgar, violent or ignorant characters which grew up in certain communities isolated from the highways of human life. A great many people may read Mr. MacNamara's book; many may praise it and pass it on to others, saying this is Ireland, but those who praise its truth will not like it. Yet we are not sure that there is not all through the book the anguish of an idealist who simply could not breathe in the society he was born in, and Mr. MacNamara may be much more of an idealist in his heart than those who portray more lovable people. [Dec. 13, 1919]

George William Russell (A.E.). *Selections from the*
Contributions to "The Irish Homestead," Vol. II,
Henry Summerfield, ed., (Atlantic Highlands, N.J.,
Humanities Press, 1978), p. 953

Mr. Brinsley MacNamara always makes us sup deep of horrors, and his latest novel [*The Mirror in the Dark*] is also compounded of tragedy. In it he traces the lives of four people, whom we meet as children gathering sour fruit. The teeth of all of them are set on edge before we part. The problem he sets himself to discuss is that of the loveless marriage, but on this well-worn theme he brings a light to bear that is pitiless in its searching brightness. The inevitable climax dawns in adultery, murder, and the madhouse, while the survivors eat out their hearts in loneliness. These are themes unpleasant enough, but it would be doing the author an injustice to style this book morbid, for it seems to me that he has described these abnormal and stunted souls as a warning to men and women not to exchange their love and ideals for all the wealth of Damer. It is a pity that the little interludes he has introduced of true lovers should be merely interludes, and not part of the main plot; but this is a mere personal opinion, and no doubt the author has his reasons for not mixing some livelier hues with his blacks and sepias. As a piece of writing it is much in advance of anything Mr. MacNamara has done yet, or "Oliver Blyth" [his pseudonym] for that matter.

Irish Book Lover. Dec., 1921, p. 89

The Master, Brinsley MacNamara's latest play and his best to date, was produced for the first time at the Abbey Theatre on 6th March, 1928. To some extent it is indebted to his first play, *The Rebellion in Ballycullen*, inasmuch as its theme is concerned with the effects of revolution in Irish politics after the General Election of 1918. The central character is the schoolmaster, James Clinton, but the theme of the play is really the power of the priest and the public-house owner to control political effort in Irish villages. In the midst of the Anti-Conscription agitation of 1917–1918 the schoolmaster is dismissed his school on a trivial pretext, and he blames the parish priest for his dismissal. Never had James Clinton been popular with his neighbours in the village of Clunnen; he had been domineering and, they said, cruel. His own opinion was that "the mob is always wrong," and upon that opinion he based his conduct. So no one mourned when he was dismissed. His chance to achieve popularity presented itself, and he undertook to lead the armed revolt in the village. From this vantage-point he would dictate his terms to priest and traders alike. . . .

As played in the Abbey Theatre on its first production the theme of the play was rather obscured, and the bumptious behaviour of the schoolmaster tended to alienate the sympathy of the audience. But a little consideration will make clear that *The Master* is another portrayal of the disillusionment which has overtaken young Ireland since the establishment of the Irish Free State in 1921. Brinsley MacNamara shows in his characters, particularly his young men, something of the idealism which fortified Ireland during the troubled years from 1918 to 1921, and he shows no less clearly the selfishness and the desire for power actuating the older people. In the end it is the ideas of the older people which predominate, and the grand dreams of those who fought, and died, for an idealised Ireland are shattered by the realities of rural life. "The more things change the more they are the same" might be the motto for *The Master*, as it shows the New Ireland settling down to become as like the Old Ireland as possible. In his presentation of this New Ireland Brinsley MacNamara approaches the view-point of Sean O'Casey, but in no other point is there any similarity between the two playwrights. MacNamara's play is more closely woven than anything O'Casey has yet done, and his dialogue is modelled upon the speech of the Irish Midlands. There is no rollicking humour in MacNamara's play, as there is in O'Casey's, as there is no attempt made to introduce that "comic relief" which seems to be so much desired, and admired, by the controllers of the commercial theatre. This play definitely ranks Brinsley MacNamara as one of the most promising playwrights upon which the Irish Theatre must rely in the immediate future, as it ranks him also as one of the most uncompromising realists. He has, so far, made no attempt to break with the realist tradition and method; he carries the banner of Ibsen as well as any in the range of Irish dramatists.

Andrew E. Malone. *The Irish Drama* (London,
Constable, 1929), pp. 207–9

I am almost certain that Brinsley MacNamara's experiments in fantasy are more important than the savage realism attributed to him quite falsely when he wrote *The Valley of the Squinting Windows*. Reviewers of that novel went out of their way to force comparisons with George Douglas's novel *The House with the Green Shutters* probably because both novels had names six words in length. Andrew E. Malone in *The Bookman* wrote of MacNamara as an Irish realist, as if an Irish realist was a greater rarity than an English leprechaun. And of the decade that saw both the publication of *A Portrait of the Arist as a Young Man* and *The Threshold of Quiet* Malone wrote unwisely that MacNamara's book was "undoubtedly the most realistic novel of Irish life published in the present decade." All this sprang from the fatal error of supposing that because a novel dealt uncharitably with uncharity and savagely with parochialism, and because it touched on two seductions, and ended with a bloody murder, it was a realistic novel. But "realism" is a method of using material, not a description of the material used, and a murder or a seduction or a satire on a village postmistress can be as genuinely matter for fantasy as a man changing into a donkey or a pooka with a good fairy in his pocket. MacNamara in the bitterest moment of *The Valley of the Squinting Windows* is always walking a few paces to the fantastic side of realistic observation. His decided hatred of parochialism means that he sees his Midland village through a sort of Midland mist. Even his very style, slow and elaborate and mannered like the gesture of an actor or a classical orator, is against his doing for

Garradrimna what [Michael] McLaverty has done for Belfast or Peadar O'Donnell for Donegal or Frank O'Connor for Cork. It is greatly to his credit that when he wrote *The Various Lives of Marcus Igoe* he was not misled by foolish praise of his supposed realism to attempt to play Zola to the life of an Irish cobbler. He followed the natural twist of his genius and wrote his best book.

On the title-page of that book he wrote a sentence borrowed from Montaigne: "We are never present with, but always beyond ourselves," and in the very first paragraph he is remembering Garradrimna and the squinting windows: "A man! But, upon examination, perhaps only the semblance of a man, with little, if any, suggestion of immortal quality in his lineaments or gesture. He did not suddenly strike the onlooker as a man who had ever done anything in the past, or as one who might ever rise to action in the future. He was as one fixed immutably in the uneventful present, in his way, a perfect specimen of that type, for had he not lived for what were already a great many years behind a little squinting window in the very middle of Garradrimna." Marcus Igoe's window is the ugliest of all the ugly squinting winows, yet it possesses a magic power to crack the world into fragments for the benefit of the person who looks out through it. And the mind of Marcus Igoe the villager goes out after the glance of his eye to fasten on and identify itself with this and that life: a hunting lady-killing buck, a man of business, a frequenter of literary pubs in the city of Dublin. His lives illuminate much of Ireland past and present, and in the haze of dream that drifts across each page of the book MacNamara learns to love and laugh in his own Midland mist, and to triumph over his own youthful hates.

Benedict Kiely. *Modern Irish Fiction: A Critique*
(Dublin, Golden Eagle Books, 1950), pp. 93–95

[MacNamara] was a moody, perhaps egotistic figure, but a playwright of craft and strength. His plays are about evenly divided between fluent, lightweight comedies and stark, grim tragedies. Though the comedies are smoothly good-natured without being exactly witty, the tragedies seem written in moods of unrelieved depression. His comedies of domestic intrigue were popular and no worse than John McCann's later sagas of the Kelly family, but they probably accelerated the deterioration of the Abbey standard of realism.

Margaret Gillan, however, is a strange, strong play about domestic intrigue, marriage, and money. What distinguishes it from many similar plays is the superb title character and the intensity of tone. Margaret is a full and demanding role that would require a virtuoso performance to overcome the pervasively overwrought tone of the whole. The play is packed with fiercely angry confrontations, and if power and vehemence were enough to make a tragedy, MacNamara would have written a resounding one. There is no rest, however, no pause, and perhaps even no wisdom in the play. Everything is turmoil, passion, and violence; it would take accomplished playing to keep the play from slipping over into screaming melodrama. Probably the piece is more embarrassing than cathartic. The fault, though, is not a matter of technical control; if anything, the play's structure is overcontrolled. The real flaw is the unnatural vehemence, the mad exacerbation, the raw attack upon the human state in Ireland, and the lack of any humanizing alleviation. Nevertheless, it is a remarkable play that reminds one of the frenetic blood tragedies of the Jacobeans—powerful, savage, and unhealthy.

Robert Hogan. *After the Irish Renaissance*
(Minneapolis, Univ. of Minnesota Pr., 1967), p. 33

The Valley of the Squinting Windows is very much a novel of its time and, in its florid strength and slightly unctuous treatment of sex, full cousin to the best sellers of the day. Though the castigation of the hypocrisy, the malevolence and the narrowness of the valley people is perfectly proper, it is done in such loving detail that the moral attitude of the author becomes questionable. The work lacks detachment and, in spite of an apparent sympathy, mercy. To see how dubious [MacNamara's] standpoint really is, one has only to compare *The Valley of the Squinting Windows* with, say, [Hawthorne's] *The Scarlet Letter,* a much superior book, written seventy years before but containing certain similar situations. The New England novel is cool, compassionate and, considering the literary conventions of the time, spare. . . . Hester Prynne, subject to the public humiliation of a Puritan township, in which she was guilty not only of sin but of felony, has a dignity invested in her by the author without condonation, while the girl [Rebecca Kerr] in the Irish story is insulted in such a sickening way that one almost feels that the author is joining in the scourging. . . .

Again, the book is full of stock characters and situations, "stock" not only in the Q. D. Leavis sense but also in the sense of the traveling stock companies. . . . It was Benedict Kiely who pointed out how close the tone of the novel is to the idiom of the stage: "The style of his novels can often be the slow, mannered speech—with appropriate gestures—of the old-time touring actor, or the names of his characters, including his own pen-name, can belong as much to the stage as to the green quietudes of the Irish Midlands."

The characters indeed have theatrical names: Padna-Padna, Marse Prendergast, Shamesy Golliher, Bartle Donohue, but their dialogue has an authentic ring about it, forecasting that MacNamara's real talent lay in the theatre and especially in rural comedy. . . . It is unfortunate that he is best known as a prose writer by the first—and inferior—novel.

His picture of the valley and the village is blacker than black. The three million of us who do not live in Dublin, Belfast or Cork know that the average Irish small town is no Cranford. There is spite, viciousness and hate. . . . But there is love and joy in these places too. And MacNamara will not admit it.

All one remembers [of *The Valley of the Squinting Windows*] is the black valley with its complete, seamless hopelessness. Even the children have no future but brutalization and spiritual dehydration—the "lucky" ones emigrate. The darkness of his vision is almost Bunyanesque: perhaps some homiletic exaggeration is permissible in this kind of writing. Perhaps, too, some of the importance of the book lies in its truth (however overstated): we all have felt the stare of the eyes behind the windows; we all, too, have stood behind them looking out. But I feel that its greatest importance is that it opened the way for better writers to write about Ireland with the scales dropped from their eyes.

Sean McMahon. *Éire-Ireland*. Spring, 1968,
pp. 113–17

MACNEICE, LOUIS (1907–1963)

[In *Poems*] Mr. MacNeice's music is strong and rough and exact; it can express minute and subtle thought with perfect clarity. Perhaps the rhymes are, from time to time, a trifle too clever. But it is not a simple age, and he is quite modern, of course. He cannot be imagined as a popular poet; for he needs the reader's whole mind. He gives of his riches generously, and cannot be shallowly received. Not that he cannot be simple. A child could enjoy this gay image:

> The mayfly flirting and posturing over the water
> Goes up and down in the lift so many times for fun.

It would seem that the poet, like the lover, must give himself entirely to be of any worth, and in these poems we have the entire man; his dreams, his realities, deep thought and sincere emotion.

His canvas is a large one. He paints for us the "peasants with long lips and the whiskey drinker's cough"; the individualist who escapes with his dog from those "who scale off masks and smash the purple lights"—on the far side of the fair, or the "town-dweller like a rabbit in the greengrocer's who was innocent and integral once." He says truly of himself:

> I give you the incidental things which pass
> Outwards through space exactly as each was.

Mr. MacNeice is a very young man. Perhaps the only danger that could be feared for his development is his abundant intellect; the thoughts, so many, so strong, and on so deep roots. It would be a pity if they should ever in the future choke the qualities of gentler growth.

He is a poet one wants to be quoting all the time, for his book is uniformly enchanting.

Irish Times. Feb. 22, 1936, p. 7

Now that the disturbance caused by the much-advertised impact of Auden, Spender, and Day Lewis has somewhat abated, it would appear that the most mature and in many ways the most interesting poet of this group is Louis MacNeice. As the publishers say of his last book, *The Earth Compels* (1938), now that he has arrived he needs no advertisement. MacNeice has quietly profited by the experiments of the other three without allowing himself to be taken in by any of their more facile enthusiasms. He is not concerned with their problems of growing-up because he is grown-up already. We may see in his example the much-talked-of ideal of the poet integrating himself with society. MacNeice is very much awake to everything going on around him, but he has sufficient strength and integrity to go his own way as well. His great value for us is that he is not ashamed to lead his own life, nor does he pretend to be something other than he is. He does not strike heroic attitudes or adopt a platform manner of address. He is not difficult or obscure, because he knows what he feels and thinks and is not afraid to say it out. You can feel at ease with him because he is not concerned with telling you what you ought to feel and think. These qualities are rare in modern poetry.

Philip Henderson. *The Poet and Society* (London,
Secker and Warburg, 1939), pp. 226–27

If Louis MacNeice had not been public-schooled in Dorset and Oxford-universalised he would have been an Ulsterman—an Ulsterman with a drop of dark Connaught-Spanish blood. Yet MacNeice cannot be considered an uprooted man, save in the sense that we are all uprooted in a world of debased values, in a general society that has nothing but the lash and the gag for that non-conformist, the artist.

The poem "Carrickfergus" gives us an early piece of autobiography:

I was born in Belfast between the mountain and the gantries
To the hooting of lost sirens and the clang of trams. . . .

MacNeice realises that he is not quite English. Behind his sophistication, his *littorae humaniores*, there exists a directness that may be best described as "peasant." That patient solidity constitutes one of the principal Ulster qualities in his work; even in his less successful poems one finds fundamentalness, sparingness. He does not throw away the potato peelings. And it may have been that relative nearness to the peasant mind which prevented him taking a definite Left-wing stand in such movements as the struggle towards a Popular Front in the near-Red Decade of the Thirties. There and elsewhere he has revealed the reservations of "the jutlipped farmer gazing over the humpbacked wall." . . .

Someone may protest that MacNeice is joyless, all ashes, "acid drop and a bandage," all disillusionment and soured hope. Such a critic would be forgetting, willingly or not, that the core of his poetry is an essential lyricism. He knows, too, "the laughter of the Galway sea," "the vivid chequer of the Antrim hills," "the brass belt of serene sun upon the lough."

What then distinguishes MacNeice's Ulster-ness—and remember it is only one of his facets—from the Irish-ness of most Southern poets? It is said that F. R. Higgins asked him—"Does your kind of poet never sing?" MacNeice retorted—"Does your kind of poet never think?" There you have it. MacNeice is the cerebral poet *par excellence*, crammed but not suffocated by theories and ideologies. But he will not accept the readymade in thought; he observes and duly incorporates into his verse the fifty-shilling-tailor lives of others, but he himself shops in more fastidious stores. He prefers occasional dryness of phrase to the rich and somewhat empty boom of organ music whether in Gothic or cinema style.

So far as Ireland is concerned, ideologists of every camp might learn from his work something of that tolerance which is one of the true marks of civilised men. His later development as radio dramatist may help to widen the audience for sensitive work, prose and verse, in dramatic form. MacNeice will, one hopes, not deflect too much vital energy from the composition of verse as such to the more complicated demands of the broadcast play. Whatever his future as a writer it seems unlikely that Ulster, and Ireland generally, will be ousted from that definite but uneasy niche in his mind, reserved for wayward but frequently lovable children.

Robert Greacen. *Poetry Ireland*. Jan., 1950,
pp. 15, 17–18

Telling what music, piping what truth he can, [in *Autumn Sequel: A Rhetorical Poem*] Louis MacNeice has added a long and honest poem to his count. It makes a wiry book of more than 160 pages and is not easily left aside.

There is little of the quality of sequel about it although the *Autumn Journal* of 1938 is used as a point of departure and is subjected at times to a certain stringent commentary. The new concern is narrower, and deeper, than the great anxiety which upset London's pubs and covered Primrose Hill with gun-emplacements in those distant, drab MacSpaundays. There is no more clique. The nostrums they peddled have long evaporated. Mr. MacNeice is giving the lie to them all. . . .

Through these cantos the poet conducts his choir of friends. . . . The trivial threads they drop, more durable than steel, are picked up and reveal what the years teach—the need for everydayness: Wimbush who chiselled his vision in a midland shed chip upon chip, undaunted and unknown; Gavin, innocent in his lust, who met his death by water, far from all dust and women; Boyce twinkling Greek wisdom in his potting shed; and above all, Gwilym, jester and bard, triumphantly at bay, drowning his enemies in drink. These are the doors Mr. MacNiece is glad to have opened, the portraits that occupy his mind. And, as with the young man who went to the back of the picture because he saw a Shape there, he has found primal man in a busy darkness, battering down the walls for Light.

The constant theme, lightly and craftily handled, is the "passing" of personal time, "thirtieth inst., too soon the thirtieth ult.," attended with the minimum of nostalgia. Mr. MacNiece has learned to regard his past with suspicion. Oxford revisited proves to be irrelevant; London is no longer littered with remembered kisses. It is in things present and at hand,—"particular dayness," better even than everydayness, that hope lies. . . . This poet has found that, if anything is to be gained, problems must be lived through, not solved, and so his pen homes constantly on the place where the heart is. And it travels over pleasant country.

The world of his imagery is, as one experts, wide and well-lit. It has reached a high state of order. The diction is of a tough, lively temper, sustained for the most part at a mildly passionate level. There is occasionally a sense of strain in the more self-conscious flights of viruosity, but these scarcely affect the main virtue—a scattered beauty which runs steadily on from page to page, rising easily to its maximum pitch, as in the Lament for the Maker, Gwilym. This is ironic and moving.

It is difficult to point the precise quality which transmutes these reminiscences into poetry. Perhaps it is honesty, the determination not to be trumpeted off into ghostly battles, not to wave any banners. It is at any rate a quality in the poet's own personality, which comes through clearly enough. This is straight talk rather than rhetoric, despite the sub-title.

Autumn Sequel is a considerable poem, the work of an old master who has achieved great ease and style, and who takes the world personally, as one may who is satisfied of his own stature. He offers no judgments; merely observes his daily round with accuracy and a sober brand of sympathy and strikes a minor chord of hope that all will be well, if it is left alone. He is impatient at times with his fellow men and can be goaded by them into a harmless kind of fury when he is in the proper mood, but it passes quickly, for who has the right to complain? It is better to view through the window the continuing mildness of December and be happy that there are men somewhere who have climbed a large mountain merely because it is there.

Thomas Kinsella. Irish Writing. Dec., 1954,
pp. 65–67

Louis MacNeice, like most poets, was a good critic, and his criticism seems to me to have been unjustly neglected. His early book *Modern Poetry: A Per-*

sonal Essay is unobtainable, while many far more dated and trivial books are re-issued in paperback; his *The Poetry of W. B. Yeats* (1941) is also unreprinted at a time when inert academic books on that poet are distributed by the hundredweight. And when his *Varieties of Parable* appeared last autumn, reviewers—the ones I saw, at any rate—seemed curiously unwilling to take it seriously, as the considered and wide-ranging utterance of an important English poet. It came out at the same time as the posthumous autobiography, *The Strings Are False*, and the reviews concentrated on the autobiography and bundled *Varieties of Parable* into a perfunctory last paragraph. I have even heard it dismissed as "just reprinted lectures," as if some of the most important English criticism, from Coleridge through Arnold to Eliot, were not reprinted lectures.

Perhaps MacNeice's modesty of tone is against him; many reviewers think that a critic who hasn't a portentous tone must have nothing to say, and Cambridge, where *Varieties of Parable* was given as the Clark Lectures, is the home of a certain critical cant, a tone at once bullying and pious, from which again MacNeice is entirely free. . . .

Tolerance, decency, acuteness, the honest facing of difficulties: these are the marks of MacNeice's criticism, and when they are added to his initial advantages—a good education (particularly a first-hand acquaintance with Greek and Latin) and the imagination of a practitioner—the result is criticism which has few equals in our time. One other quality should be added: the courage to tackle a large general subject. The theme of *Varieties of Parable* is nothing less than the basic question, "How does literature make its statements? Why are they not the same as the statements of science or history?" By discussing a line of writers who either ignore surface realism or, as in Bunyan, employ surface realism but wed it to a subject-matter avowedly emblematic, MacNeice was evidently concerned to open the reader's mind to the great things that are possible to a literary art which has cast off "realism" in the old hampering sense. Indeed, a recurring fault in the book is that "realism" is used too exclusively as a term of disapprobation. . . .

The Strings Are False, though beautifully written, is minor MacNeice; most of it is anticipated either in the poems or in the interesting "Case-Book" chapters of *Modern Poetry*. It is *Varieties of Parable* we should read carefully; for all its modesty it makes many important observations, some of which had waited twenty years to get on to paper, and good criticism is not so common that we can leave it to gather dust.

John Wain. Enc. Nov., 1966, pp. 49, 54, 55

The collected poems of Louis MacNeice form a thick volume of 575 pages, running from a section of "Juvenilia, 1925–29" to poems written shortly before his death in 1963 at the age of fifty-six. His poems thus span the central creative era of twentieth-century poetry, the great age that emerges emphatically with Eliot's *Waste Land* in 1922 and closes with Eliot's own death in 1965. Whether it comes to be called the Age of Eliot or the Age of Pound, it is an era that surely achieved the beginning of the Renaissance that Pound prophesied in 1914. MacNeice's work shows everywhere the liberating influence of those early masters who made it possible for the poets of MacNeice's generation to break with the Victorians and the Georgians, to bring into their poetry the modern colloquial idiom and the imagery of the daily world, urban and industrial. . . .

Pound and Eliot could write in the eclectic manner of exiles; they could override the English tradition with French and Italian and Chinese examples. But a poet like MacNeice had the idiom of Wordsworth and Hardy indelibly in his mind. We can see the situation more clearly in MacNeice than in Auden, for Auden's technical brilliance and his removal to America, Ischia, and Austria have veiled and in the end, I think, have broken his allegiance to the English scene. But with MacNeice (though he was born in Belfast) the English tradition moves on into the modern age with unbroken power. . . .

MacNeice seems to be outlasting the vogue of Auden, and we can now read him for what he always offered: an acute sense of the changes that England has been reluctantly enduring under the impact of the various forces that, both in war and in peace, have undermined the sovereignty of her ancient ways.

Louis L. Martz, *YR*. Summer, 1967, pp. 593–95

For this apparent falling off in [MacNeice's] powers it was fashionable to blame his long years of work as a feature-writer at the B.B.C. Well, he had his living to earn, and he found the work and the company congenial, more congenial, I am pretty sure, than the obvious alternative, which was university teaching. And the work he wrote for the B.B.C. was a completely legitimate extension of the function of poetry as he understood it. He took to writing for radio and to production too—he was a very brilliant producer—like a duck to water. One looks back to perhaps the first half of his years in radio as to the high peak of sound broadcasting, when the radio feature became an art, an ephemeral art admittedly but still an art. MacNeice, of course, was not alone in making radio an art; he was one among many; but he did give it an elegance, a sense of style, a vividness, and a verbal distinction that was his own and essentially that of his poems.

In any event, it is a rash act to write off any poet, or novelist for that matter, so long as he is still alive; and in MacNeice's case there was in the last years of his life a new outburst of creative energy that produced poems certainly as fine as any he had written before. This is particularly true of the poems in the collection *The Burning Perch*, which appeared within a matter of weeks after his unexpected death in September 1963. Posthumous volumes, especially when they appear so quickly after a poet's death, are an open invitation of sentimentality: it is almost impossible not to read them differently from the way in which we read the work of the man while alive; and it would be easy to read into the poems of *The Burning Perch* premonitions of the poet's death. MacNeice himself said that he had been "taken aback," while preparing the volume for the press, "by the high proportion of sombre pieces, ranging from bleak observations to thumbnail nightmares." He had, of course, always been aware of the dark underside of things, of the terror of life, and mortality; they are there in his work from the beginning. He was, I think, an unillusioned, stoic humanist very much in the tradition of E. M. Forster; and like Forster's Mrs. Moore, he had heard the "oum-boum" of the echo in the Marabar Caves. And certainly *The Burning Perch* is the most sombre of his collections: "bleak observations," "thumbnail nightmares"—the descriptions are accurate. All the same, the sombreness is lit up by the energy of the wit and a grim, sardonic, almost contemptuous gaiety. They are the poems, I feel, of a man who knows the worst and is not intimidated, the poetic equivalents of the smile, almost the snarl of derision, one had sometimes seen on Louis's face in life.

Walter Allen. In *Essays by Divers Hands*, Vol. 35
(London, Oxford Univ. Pr., 1969), pp. 15–16

Louis MacNiece is the only Irish poet to form a natural part of the English literary scene; after Auden he was the most gifted poet of the Thirties. Their collaboration in *Letters from Iceland* is an example of poetry confronting the problems of a period as they arise. The precedent of Byron is capital for both of them (MacNiece pays homage to him in "Cock of the North) with his wide ranging, almost novelistic gift. But Byron was much more of a European phenomenon than MacNiece, or even Auden, ever succeeded in being, and those who present him as a corrective example to more locally based Irish poets tend to forget this. So far as I know, Louis MacNiece has rarely been translated into another language, and even in America, his reputation has never been high.

I am not denying his sensibility, nor the obsession with transience and death which is his most moving central theme. I am just saying that his work is very much in the nonexperimental tradition of English modern poetry, and, as such, nearly unexportable. Paradoxically though, the one aspect of his influence which seems to me particularly healthy is his diversity of landscape: the ease with which Northern poets, like Seamus Heaney and Derek Mahon, seem to move in the outside world may well derive from MacNiece's restless photographic eye. Few American poets, for instance, could equal his description of New York in "Refugees" where the skyscrapers

> . . . heave up in steel and concrete
> Powerful but delicate as a swan's neck

and the trains (it was before the destruction of Penn Station) leave "from stations haughty as cathedrals."

To sightsee, though, is not necessarily to accept the influence of another culture: for MacNeice Spain, Greece, India are backgrounds against which he defines his personal problems.

John Montague. In Sean Lucy, ed., *Irish Poets in English* (Cork, Mercier, 1972), pp. 147–48

MacNeice remained the prisoner of his childhood. He could never escape the nostalgic chains this placed upon him either as lover or thinker. That his love for his mother rested, not unusually, on so profound a sexual base that her early death was permanently crippling emotionally, he half realized, as we see from the story of the twig that he tells in *The Strings Are False.* . . .

In *Experiences with Images* he comments in a note:

> Almost the most disastrous experience of my childhood is for ever associated in my mind with a doubled-up poplar twig—but I have never yet used this image as a symbol of evil. Were I to do so, I should certainly elucidate the reference.

The importance of this lies in the last phrase. He never brought himself to "elucidate the reference." His ambivalent attitude to this story, so that he must tell it, shows that he realized that it contained a significance which it was difficult to face. His inability to use it in his poetry constituted in a major degree a moral failure in one for whom self was a major source of interest and inspiration. A parallel and not dissociated failure lay in his inability to make the intellectual effort either to achieve faith, to deny all belief, or to systematize his agnosticism.

This ethical and intellectual weakness led to a certain sentimentality in his approach to social criticism and equally made any firm political attitude impossible. So MacNeice could find neither spiritual faith, political belief, or personal love and understanding to form the basis of his poetry, but relied instead on the conflicts of indecision. In so far as it lacks a passionate attempt to cope with the conflicts that arise from doubt and indecision, the poetry of MacNeice sometimes falls short of greatness. The tragedy is that he could not escape from within himself to wider exploration.

D.B. Moore. *The Poetry of Louis MacNeice* (Leicester, Leicester Univ. Pr., 1972), pp. 248–49

There have been several attempts, notably by W. T. McKinnon in *Apollo's Blended Dream*, to upgrade MacNeice from minor poet to major. He was, says McKinnon, a philosophical poet of unsuspected depth, one who struggled through life to reach a higher synthesis of sense and spirit. The argument is persuasive and often illuminating, but the conventional estimate of his achievement is probably here to stay. Ian Hamilton, in his *Poetry Chronicle*, warns us not to be too solemn about a poet "who loved the surface but lacked the core." But Hamilton misses the point, I think. For MacNeice, as for Wallace Stevens, the surface *was* the core. Like Horace, he was *profoundly* superficial.

The poems that made his name in the 1930's are the ones where the love of surface is most in evidence, culminating in *Autumn Journal*, which provides the most extraordinary visual and tactile sense of the period outside the early novels of Graham Greene. If Dublin could be reconstructed from the pages of *Ulysses*, as Joyce claimed, the pre-war urban England of rainy tram-lines, Corner Houses, Bisto Kids and Guinness Is Good For You could probably be roughly simulated from a reading of Greene and MacNeice. . . . Was he the first English poet to make habitual use of brand names? It seems likely. At a time when the British documentary cinema was at its most accomplished, in the days of John Grierson and Alexander Korda, when Auden scripted *Night Mail* and Isherwood *I Am a Camera*, and Greene wrote film criticism for *The Spectator*, there was nothing bizarre in the notion of poetry-as-documentary; and this is where MacNeice excelled. He might even be said to have invented the genre. So far as the British reading public is concerned, it's probably what he will be remembered for. The Irish reading public will be looking for other things.

Derek Mahon. In Terence Brown and Alec Reid,
eds., *Time Was Away: The World of Louis MacNeice*
(Dublin, Dolmen, 1974), pp. 114–16

MacNeice is a technical virtuoso. He is a professional poet. The variety of poetic forms that he employed, frequently with an assured mastery, is amazing. He is the poet of leisurely, rambling, loose verse, and of taut, elliptical, gnomic utterance. He wrote ballads and nursery-rhyme and light, sparkling verse. He was also capable of maintaining the difficult *terza rima* verse form through the twenty-four cantos of "Autumn Sequel," which, although it is a very uneven work, has passages of great beauty. Faced with such fecundity the critic can only point to particular examples of the poet's writing in a certain form, as representative of the total work in that form. In the ballad we have such rollicking pieces as "The Streets of Laredo" (which uses the rhythms and stanza of a cowboy song) and "Bagpipe Music." In these, the verse form and the context work together to produce a scarifying violence, a fantasia of almost surrealistic effects. . . . This is to use the traditional ballad form to brilliant effect. These two poems (and a number of others) suggest the horrifying violence which is so close to the surface of modern life, where cities can be laid waste and the crime of violence is a commonplace.

"The Streets of Laredo" is fierce with moral indignation at wreckage and destruction. The note of indignation is created partly by the ironic discord between the subject matter and the rollicking rhythms, but also by description of the two prophet-like, denunciatory figures of Bunyan and Blake. . . . "Bagpipe Music" has a nihilistic cruelty in its pointless violence, while both poems move from event to event with electrifying speed. The poems rush to their conclusions with a rapidity suggestive of the violence of the world, to which they record their horrified reactions.

Terence Brown. *Louis MacNeice: Skeptical Vision*
(New York, Barnes & Noble, 1975), pp. 151–52

The most celebrated poem in *Poems* is perhaps "Snow," and it epitomises MacNeice's orientation towards the world and the stylistic consequences of that orientation. . . . It is a poem in which "things" exist in their own right, a poem that is reflective, yet derives its strength from the tact and integrity with which the poet refuses to extend that reflection beyond the limits that the experience allows. The experience itself is a personal one and is highly individuated in terms of the outside world. Some years after the poem was written, MacNeice remarked: ". . . it means exactly what it says; the images here are not voices off, they are bang centre stage, for this is the direct record of a direct experience, the realisation of a very obvious fact, that one thing is different from another—a fact which everyone knows but few people perhaps have had it brought home to them in this particular way, i.e. through the sudden violent perception of snow and roses juxtaposed." In spite of this directness, there is nevertheless a subtlety of detail in the construction of the poem that is closely attuned to the purpose of the poem as a whole. The diction may seem in places flashily intellectual: "Soundlessly collateral and incompatible . . ."; and this may seem to clash with the simplicity of other phrases. Similarly, the poem may seem to lurch rather suddenly from the abstract to the sensuous, or from the conversational to the conceptual. All this is true, but it does not constitute a criticism of the poem. The shifts of tone and diction and imagery mirror "The drunkenness of things being various," which is the subject of the poem. . . .

The diction and the images are, like good furniture, functional; but, again like good furniture, they are also expressive of the person who has selected them. A reading of *Poems*, or of MacNeice's poetry as a whole, will leave the reader not merely with the feeling that the poet has a very definite and personal style, but that a great deal of what the poems say resides in the style. This comes close, of course, to being a critical commonplace. However, in the case of MacNeice, we can go so far as to say that some of the poems—particularly in his early volumes—give the impression that they exist largely for the purpose of creating that style. Style for MacNeice, as for Yeats, is an attainment—at once an attainment and a projection of the qualities of being that the author values.

A. T. Tolley. *The Poetry of the Thirties* (London,
Victor Gollancz, 1975), pp. 178–80

MacNeice visited many different countries, taught for some months in America at the outbreak of war and spent a year in Athens in the early '50s, and there is a sense in which he was a visitor everywhere, the man from no part. For the English reader he appears to be Irish, while for certain Irish readers he doesn't really belong to Ireland. . . . The Irish sense of place is very exacting and intransigent, and many people can never forgive the man who goes, in that tantalising phrase, "across the water."

MacNeice is always crossing the water, and the feeling of unease and displacement, of moving between different cultures and nationalisms, which he paradoxically returns to in his poetry, means that his imagination is essentially fluid, maritime and elusively free. . . . [I]t is a shore and a seascape crossed by a journey which is at the centre of MacNeice's imaginative vision. From his first mature poem, "Belfast," to his last poem, the stoic "Thalassa," his imagination is caught by ships and "the salt carrion water." . . .

[I]n the *Collected Poems* there is a short and little-known poem called "House on a Cliff" which is one of MacNeice's finest achievements. . . . The hard boxed circling rhythms build a terrible stoic isolation. The voice is variously and tautly cadenced in a cross between stress and quantitative metre—that word "cross" stretches bitterly in so many directions—and there is a mysterious openness within or beyond the poem's mirror-like reflections of a dead closed universe. If this is one man facing his lonely mortality on the far extremity of an unnamed place, the "ancestral-curse-cum-blessing," the cross purposes and the broken sleep, suggest that the house is Ireland. Again, the silent moon and the garrulous tides obliquely suggest a Yeatsian reference to cold fanatic ideals and mob action. As in "Death of an Old Lady," Mac-Neice recapitulates some of his favourite symbols—sirens, sea, wind, clock—in a manner that is almost playful. Although the demand for "meaning" will discover and insist that "the blind clock" is the pulse of an indifferent and mechanical universe—the earth's compulsion—the poem is best appreciated in terms of voice, atmosphere and a pure symbolism. It is a bitter and tragic poem with a freedom in its intensity that transcends its unflinching sense of cosmic indifference, malignity or mischief—the "winking signal" of the lighthouse and MacNeice's favouritely ambiguous "the siren" simultaneously warn and lure. If this poem fits that baffled and contradictory term "Irish," it also has an asocial, even a derelict, quality which makes it difficult to place. It subverts any comfortable notion of belonging and this is true of all MacNeice's poetry. The anguished sense of displacement that is so fundamental to his imagination means that many readers glance at him and then hurry on. Instead he needs to be read and cherished. There are many places that should be proud to lay claim to him.

Tom Paulin. *PoetryR*. March, 1980, pp. 52–56

Unlike Yeats, MacNeice had a stance in a formal political theory—Marxism. MacNeice was not a communist, nor even a communist sympathiser. He detested the monolithic Stalinist orthodoxy of the thirties, the stratagems, the expedients, the dishonesties which a Communist Party, he said, "allows and even encourages." Yet he did respond to classic Marxist theory. Particularly, it seemed to him to admit the human actor as the essential agent in historical change. When systems failed, they failed not because of blind determinism, but because the human beings in charge of them had ceased to appreciate their dynamism—the emergence in them of new ideas, new groups, new coalitions.

Two Marxist axioms, widely cited in the thirties, summarize forcefully what was in fact the very complex argument which drew MacNeice to Marxism: "Freedom is the appreciation of necessity"; "History is nothing but the activity of men in pursuit of their ends." Writing about marxism in *The Strings Are False*, MacNeice had this to say: "while it attacked human individualism, it simultaneously made the cosmos once more anthropocentric; it—asserted purpose in the world. Because the world was *ours*." Elsewhere in the same book, he offers a translation of "Freedom is the appreciation of Necessity" into Aristotelian terms: "*energia* can only be achieved by the canalisation and continued control of *kinesis*."

It is impossible, reading through MacNeice's poems, to deny in them a kind of translation from his personal experience of these ideas. . . .

The world of the senses was liable always to sideslip into sinister territories of the mind. And that is very much a part of his Irish inheritance, public and private. His reservations about his country of birth were not only the political ones already suggested. But even the political disaffection enters into a region of secret childhood terrors, among goblins and evil fairies, over the boundary between familiar day and disturbing night: "And I remember, when I was little, the fear/Bandied among the servants/That Casement would land at the pier." Any one part of his world is an ante-chamber to the rest.

MacNeice was disposed to people his childhood world, which he recalls as a lonely one, with demons, whether from the violence of reality or the badlands of the mind. *The Strings Are False* is full of memories of macabre dreams and waking nightmares. So is his poem, "Autobiography," which begins with auguries of innocence, fated to betrayal:

> When I was five the black dreams came;
> Nothing after was quite the same.
>
> Come back early or never come.

Generally, though not exclusively, it is from Ireland that these sombre images come to MacNeice. He has contrasted the English wood, domesticated, "reprieved from the neolithic night/By gamekeepers or by Herrick's girls at play" with "the wilds of Mayo"; and concluded—"These woods are not the

Forest." It might stand as a metaphor of the two countries as they appear in MacNeice's secondary world.

Ultimately, it is in the presence of the forest, the outpost of region or of character, that MacNeice, in Yeats's words, "names and numbers the passions and motives of men," and finds "images of his own secret thoughts." Recognising these images diversely in his experience, he was able to convene them within a single perception. He absorbed political abstractions into places and feelings—and the words for places and feelings—which encounter other emissaries from his engagement with the mutable world of sensible life.

D. E. S. Maxwell. In Peter Connolly, ed., Literature
and the Changing Ireland (Gerrards Cross, England,
Colin Smythe, 1982), pp. 164–65, 167–68

[MacNeice's] last pre-war exploration of childhood and Ireland occurs in *The Earth Compels* (1938). "Carrickfergus" is direct autobiography and signals that taut style of the volume as a whole. The brisk movement of the verse matches its observations of external factors, there is nothing introspective or speculative. Objects are catalogued with adult detachment, yet they possess that solidity they have for a child, who sees them in juxtaposition without distinguishing them in terms of value: the terrier's yapping and the soldiers' singing make an equal impact on the consciousness. This picture of Carrickfergus is dominated by the War, an incomprehensible event. MacNeice recalled, because "all foreigners were foreigners to me and at first I could not distinguish between the English and the Germans." It was also the period of his mother's departure and death (1914) and his own dispatch to Sherborne (1917). None of the emotional turmoil is recorded. . . . Except for an identifying sentence in the fifth stanza, "Carrickfergus" is a public poem, while it escapes the charge of journalism sometimes levelled against MacNeice.

The almost jaunty rhythm of its quatrains conveys none of the brooding, subdued fury of "Belfast"; no item is dwelt upon, no scene intensified by adjectives in the manner of the earlier poem's "melancholy lough / Against the lurid sky over the stained water." The vocabulary, too, is spare, so that the one note of flamboyance has resonance: "Under the peacock aura of a drowning moon."

> I was the rector's son, born to the anglican order,
> > Banned for ever from the candles of the Irish poor;
> The Chichesters knelt in marble at the end of a transept
> > With ruffs about their necks, their portion sure.

It is an economical notation of alienation: the candles carry a hint of liveliness and warmth as well as poverty, set against the arrogance of the Elizabethan monument in his father's church, confident of gaining heaven, and secure in their earthly glory founded on their exploitation of precisely the Irish poor. Following "sure" with "The war came" in the next stanza, and the springing up of a military camp, at least partially undercuts any sense of order.

There is perhaps no other poem that touches on World War I from this perspective. The difference war makes to the appearance of familiar, civilian territory is the only way it might be expected to impinge on a child. . . . The great accumulation of heroic myth, in the shadow of which MacNeice's generation grew up, is entirely excluded from the poem. The isolation he experiences is both that of a Protestant rector's son, and that common to children sent away to school, whose world become completely separate from that of their family and town: "the world of parents / Contracted into a puppet world of sons." With the transition from smoky Carrickfergus to Dorset the sense of division is confirmed; henceforth the poems about Ireland and childhood betray a suspicion that paradise had been on the margins of both, irrecoverable by art.

Robyn Marsack. *The Cave of Making: The Poetry of Louis MacNeice* (Oxford, Clarendon Press, 1982), pp. 13–15

MAHON, DEREK (1941–   )

In Derek Mahon's poetry it is possible to see what can be made of the Irish urban and suburban experience. . . . Mahon, born in 1941 and educated in Belfast and at Trinity College, Dublin, has produced a small body of remarkable verse, developing out of a sense of the complex, aesthetically uninspiring tensions of Northern Protestant middle-class identity. Mahon has spoken of the difficulties of writing out of such a background, from a "suburban situation which has no mythology or symbolism built into it." . . .

This is, of course, a note we have heard before, implicitly in the work of Louis MacNeice, explicitly in the manifestos issued by [Roy] McFadden and [Robert] Greacen in the early 1940s. And indeed, Mahon is taking up problems which exercised those poets, coping with them, I would suggest, through writing poems so tensely controlled as to recall MacNeice's own work. Mahon's poetry is a force-field of unresolved tensions and ironies explored in a verse of elegant, exact eloquence.

In "Glengormley" and "As It Should Be" Mahon considers the implications of suburban existence in a country whose past has been heroic, dramatic, mythological. "Glengormley" recognises the new heroism of suburban survival, contrasting it, a little too predictably, with Ulster's prehistoric titanism.

. . . For Mahon is no eulogist of suburban possibilities nor of industrial society's blessing. He cannot even rise to MacNeice's excited response to its bright surfaces, sensing rather a new barbarism beneath a façade of materialist disregard for ideology, social hierarchy and commitment. . . .

An antipathetic reaction to the conditions of advanced capitalism is, of course, a fairly commonplace response in modern poetry. Often the poet who responds in this fashion turns to a local tradition in quest of roots, identity, fragments that he may shore against what he feels is the contemporary ruin. Mahon rejects such a strategy, such imaginative Jacobinism, since the local tradition he knows in his bones is not one with which he feels much ready sympathy. Mahon's "hidden Ulster" is no Gaelic pastoral-aristocratic idyll, but the Protestant planter's historical myth of conquest, and careful, puritan self-dependence frozen to a vicious, stupid bigotry which constricts personal identity, crippling the possibility of change, growth and excellence. . . .

Terence Brown. *Northern Voices: Poets from Ulster*
(Totowa, N.J., Rowman & Littlefield, 1975),
pp. 192–95

Despite the Northern Poets tag, [Seamus] Heaney and Mahon have very little in common as poets. Behind Heaney, one senses Gerard Manley Hopkins, Ted Hughes, Patrick Kavanagh, perhaps Keats; behind Mahon, Louis MacNeice, Beckett, Cavafy and early Auden. In fact, MacNeice's poems like "Valediction" and Section XVI of *Autumn Journal*, although they do not wear well as poetry, are important as statements of a kind of rejection-in-acceptance of Ireland which is typical of the Northern Protestant mind in one of its subtler manifestations. Mahon belongs here, although with more verve and point, as in a poem like "Beyond Howth Head." The ambition of many of his poems seems to be astringency; their achievement is more often wryness or irony, but an irony that carries within it a note of lamentation, a grief that almost always becomes exquisite just as it is on the point of becoming profound. . . . Mahon is evasive, not because he avoids feelings, but because he passes through them quickly. However saturated he may be in them, he is careful that whatever tear is squeezed out in a poem will have an ironic, deprecatory highlight glistening within it. He goes into dangerous areas, but in a fast car, not on foot. He visits his origins but never finds them satisfactory and seems to wish he had spent time so used out in the world instead—and then regrets having had that wish. For him, Belfast is a dark country, an archaeological site, bleak monuments of men, hard flints of feeling. But Dublin never counterposes as the alternative modern capital. It is, after all, like Belfast, wanting perhaps in the dignity of that ruin, and being merely a consumers' dump instead. Mahon is a poet who cannot conceive of history as anything other than something from which he should escape. It is remarkable how often the figure in his poems is that of a spectator; or in the love poems as a man brought in from the outside to share a basic warmth. His escape is into Marxism, socialism, perhaps—there are faint attitudinal hints of this—but is into himself and his poems more surely and more finally. If Ireland is his fate, the meaning of it is to be gained outside Ireland. Stylish, fluent and then staccato, Mahon is our true exile—the man who belongs but does not wish to believe so, or disbelieves that he must always. His country is his art, and his fear of being tied that of the cosmopolitan who is always walking in the shadow of his provincial self. . . .

Mahon in fact exercises a very severe form of restraint in his poems. His is a poetry of manoeuvrability, each poem having the appearance of an artefact originally conceived to hold more feeling than in fact it does. He seems to want a deeper source of feeling than any he has yet probed; he refuses to will it out, but when it comes it has an ancestral ring to it. . . . Yet Mahon suspects both ancestry and its absence. It is not enough either of or in itself; so, on that score, he remains at an oblique angle to the present troubles, wishing there were some other way to take them than the only way in which they offer themselves—so far, at least. He is an Irish writer whose Protestantism survives in his uncertainty about Ireland—whether he wishes to belong to it, or whether he would be allowed to belong if he so wished. In a marvellously elegant manner, with his young Belfast mandarin hesitation and ease, he encapsulates a whole phase of Irish and Protestant feeling; and then, of course, as poets do, he uses this in other forms of development and exploration which are peculiarly his own.

Seamus Deane. In Douglas Dunn, ed., *Two Decades of Irish Writing* (Chester Springs, Pa., Dufour, 1975), pp. 11–13

Of the younger Irish poets Derek Mahon is probably the one who has taken the greatest interest in civilisation and the modern world, but he has also tended to unload his thoughts on these matters rather undiscriminatingly into his verse. In his latest book *The Snow Party* he has them under better control but still gives himself over to the occasional pretentious abstraction. . . .

If Mahon knows what he's talking about here he certainly doesn't make it easy for his readers to. And yet it's possible, even so, that some kind of admixture of conscious reasoning may be necessary to his poetic processes: as a straightforward lyricist he lacks precision, perhaps from an unwillingness to let his images or rhythms find their own shape without being intellectually interfered with, and the best pieces in *The Snow Party* are the more dramatic (including some nicely understated versions from Cavafy) and more reflective ones. The best poem of all—duly placed at the end—is "A Disused Shed in Co. Wexford," which starts off with Marianne Mooreish obliquity but then focuses in to contemplate a once-cultivated but now long-neglected shedful of mushrooms, which it gradually and impressively anthropomorphises into the "Lost people of Treblinka and Pompeii." There's real power in this fantasy (it's far and away Mahon's best poem to date), but one could also remark that it gets two-and-a-bit pages to work itself out in where (say) Sylvia Plath might have managed the imaginative gist of it in two-and-a-bit lines. One of the things Mahon should devote some of his thinking to is how he wants his thinking to relate to the more primitive imaginative levels which his best poems are in touch with. "A Disused Shed in Co. Wexford" has star-quality, but it's not the kind of thing you can hope to go for every time.

Colin Falck. NewR. May, 1976, p. 59

With three published volumes of poetry behind him—*Night-Crossing* (1968), *Lives* (1972), *The Snow Party* (1975)—Derek Mahon has now clearly emerged as one of the most talented of the present generation of Northern Ireland poets. Indeed, in the wider context of English poetry of the last ten years, his work has retained qualities that looked increasingly likely to disappear with Auden's death—qualities of wit and wry humour in poems that reveal a lively and quirky intelligence. He has early shown a technical mastery in poems where humour and a lightness of touch often combine to achieve an unexpected seriousness. Taken as a whole, one can discern in his work a preoccupation with man's spiritual loneliness and isolation which is reflected in the large number of poems that deal with individuals or groups forced by temperament or circumstances to live outside the normal social framework. At its most sombre, Mahon's verse reveals an acute awareness of the brevity of all human life and the futility and pathos of man's existence as a finite being. It is these central themes in his work that I propose to explore as well as the imaginative richness and wealth of formal skills that Mahon has brought to his task.

As a northern Irishman Mahon has, on several occasions, dealt with the state of the Six Counties in his poetry. These handfuls of poems are, in their way, as valid and moving as many of the more historically conscious probings of Seamus Heaney and John Montague, poets who have made the evolution of the province their chief concern as artists. These poems are, moreover, part of Mahon's preoccupation with the individual's sense of isolation, for in them the speaker is usually looking at events in his native place from the outside, at a safe, if uncomfortable, vantage point. In "Glengormley" (*Night-Crossing*), a poem written before the present unrest began, Mahon celebrated the then unheroic quality of life in a Belfast suburb. The tone and humour of the opening lines recalls to mind much of MacNeice's verse: "Wonders are many and none is more wonderful than man/Who has tamed the terrier, trimmed the hedge/And grasped the principle of the watering can." Ulster's mythic and violent history is alluded to in the same mock-heroic vein: "Now we are safe from monsters, and the giants/Who tore up sods twelve miles by six/And hurled them out to sea to become islands/Can worry us no more." Admitting that much was lost with the passing of the more perilous ages in the country's history, he concludes:

> . . . I should rather praise
> A worldly time under this worldly sky—
> The terrier-taming, garden-watering days
> Those heroes pictured as they struggled through
> The quick noose of their finite being. By
> Necessity, if not choice, I live here too.

Viewed in retrospect, few utterances by Ulstermen can have proven so ironic given the course of events in the province over the past six years.

Brian Donnelly. ES. Feb., 1979, pp. 23–24

Mahon's compelling independence of voice and vision; the elegant mastery of craft that marks everything he writes; a range of imaginative commitments that link him not only to major Irish poets of the preceding generation like Louis MacNeice and Patrick Kavanagh but also with Auden, with Robert Lowell, with Matthew Arnold of "Dover Beach," and the Wallace Stevens of "The Idea of Order at Key West"—all these and other excellences have made him indispensable to any comprehensive understanding of Irish poetry at the present time. . . .

The strongest impression made on me when I read any poem by Derek Mahon is the sense that I have been spoken to: that the poem has established its presence in the world as a kind of speech. In addition, I am aware that its status as speech is an important value in itself, carrying and confirming those other, more explicit values which the poem endorses as part of its overt "meaning." What I hear in these poems is a firm commitment to speech itself, to the act of civil communication enlivened, in this case, by poetic craft. Listen, for example, to a few lines of the elegy for MacNeice, "In Carrowdore Churchyard":

> Maguire, I believe, suggested a blackbird
> And over your grave a phrase from Euripides.
> Which suits you down to the ground, like this churchyard
> With its play of shadow, its humane perspective.

The mannerly plainness of this makes the speech itself a tribute to MacNeice as well as a revelation of Mahon's chosen way as a poet of being in the world. Here is wit in the delicate, inventive animation of the cliché, modesty in those self-effacing hesitations. Intimate and polite, such speech is a gesture of admiration and reconciliation, its perfect pitch and balance denying the excesses of feeling and form which would jeopardize the whole enterprise:

All we may ask of you we have. The rest
Is not for publication, will not be heard.

I hear in this speech (some of the qualities of which are probably derived from
the influential practice of MacNeice himself) a tenacious commitment to what
is private in experience. Intimacy is the desired end of such poetry — with the
dead poet (an intimacy of shared idiom, gratiude for the gift of speech) and
with the reader—but such an intimacy as permits the experience to have a
"public" expression without losing its essentially private nature. This kind of
skater's balance, this decency of deportment, locates Mahon's deepest instinct for form, an instinct which makes its presence felt in the actual body
and pressure of his poetic speech.

Mahon's belief in speech as value and as an epitome of identity is extremely clear in those poems in which he invents another speaker. In "Van
Gogh in the Borinage," "Bruce Ismay's Soliloquy," and "The Forger," he
gives each of these outsiders a voice of his own: in speech, he seems to be
saying, human identity finds itself. These poems act out of and act out the
pressing need to be articulate in difficult straits. By converting distress into a
distinct clarity of utterance, each speaker raises his speech to a value in itself,
a civil declaration of independence against the forces of disastrous circumstance. . . .

For Mahon, then, poetry is speech, an act—perhaps the fundamental
act—of true communication between one human being and another. . . .

Eamon Grennan. In James D. Brophy and Raymond
J. Porter, eds., Contemporary Irish Writing (Boston,
Iona College Pr./Twayne, 1983), pp. 15–17

The poems of Derek Mahon are the writings of an ambivalent cavalier. Forced
to live among roundheads he has always shared an opposite political desire: to
turn the world upside down. As things stand now, he is a young writer.
I am sure he does not guess how many young readers estimate him to be the
Marvell of his age. The styles of his poems have become, through half a
dozen slim volumes, moderately varied. These varied styles remain anxious
not to appear too composed nor to be at ease with each other. Yet Mahon's
composition is exquisite and ease comes easily to him. The strength of
his poems continues to impress; not by their gravity but by their resistance.
Mahon travels light and his poetics are the habits of a traveller: wariness, curiosity, trim. . . .

In [his] most recent volumes [*Poems: 1962–78, Courtyards in Delft*, and
The Hunt by Night] Mahon has continued a detachment which is most often
the curious gaze of the spectator. Mahon is in love with what is to be seen: the
numerous poems to painters, to Munch, Botticelli, Magritte, Uccello; the recurrent image of windows; the emphases on colors and geometrics. Whatever

distance is given to objects by picture- and window-frames imposes on them a kind of exile in which they can more easily be imagined to become restless. They are restless for the sea, for otherness, and that is why "the bird forsakes the bird." And that is why Mahon forsakes Mahon, catching himself as a spectator/*flâneur*/voyeur seen at the window, a Narcissus uneasy with his own reflections: "Sometimes—a deliberate exercise—/I study the tide-warp in the glass."

The journey away from history is an impossible one, although too much Irish poetry has attempted by means of pastoral to conceal that fact. Mahon's poems, however, are a time-traveller's return ticket, passwords to the way out and to the way back.

Kevin Barry. ILS. Fall, 1983, p. 37

MARTYN, EDWARD (1859–1923)

The hero of *The Heather Field*, Carden Tyrrell, is the first appearance of humanity in the English prose drama of to-day—of the eternal instinctive humanities and not the ephemeral differences which divide the grocer from the baronet. It were surely impossible to point to a scene in the English prose drama of the present century so essentially human as the scene in which Carden Tyrrell speaks to his brother Miles of the days when they sailed their skiff to Lorlie, and Carden, who is the elder brother, tells Miles, who was then a boy, the legends of the Rhine. This scene is certainly a beautiful and pathetic expression of that passionate wistfulness which rises up in the heart and brain when we look back on the days of our early youth, those days fresh and fugitive as the days of early spring, when the buds are breaking into tiny leaf and the daffodils star the grass. In a moment we are in the midst of the emotion which Mr. Martyn has expressed in this scene, an emotion known to all over thirty, to the hind as well as the king. Expression of it has hitherto been sought by bringing together an elderly spinster and an elderly bachelor who did not marry, and who fear that it is now too late, the assumption being that if they had married they would have been happy. But Mr. Martyn probes deeper than the ephemeral griefs which circumstances create, and in the scene between Carden Tyrrell and Miles Tyrrell we are face to face with that primal melancholy which is at the root of human existence, we look into its eyes, infinite as the sky, and are absorbed in pity for all things that live, and we feel in our soul the truth that man was not intended to be happy.

George Moore. Introduction to Edward Martyn, The
Heather Field and Maeve (London, Duckworth,
1899), pp. xxii–xxiv

The characters in *The Heather Field* are less rigid than those in the later plays, but even in this play you feel about them, as you feel so often about the characters of Hawthorne, that they are characters chosen to interpret an idea rather than children of the imagination or portraits done from observation of life.

As one recalls the motive and situations and background and symbolism of *The Heather Field*, not having read the play for some time, it seems far finer than when one returns to it. Fine, too, it must seem to any one reading a scenario of it and not offended, as one reading it constantly is, by the inability of its dialogue to represent more of the person speaking than his point of view. The dialogue of Mr. Martyn is almost never true dramatic speech, and not only not true dramatic speech, but despite the very clear differentiation of the characters, with little of their personality or temperament in it.

Maeve has always seemed to me a lesser play than *The Heather Field*, and it now leaves me even colder than of old. Nor, though I can see how fine in conception was the character of Mrs. Font in *The Enchanted Sea*, does that one character seem to me, now, to redeem the undeveloped possibilities of the situations of the play, the incomplete characters of Guy and Mask and the failure of the dialogue assigned to the characters to approach true dramatic speech. *Maeve* is the better play of the two. With all its shortcomings it has about it an unearthliness of atmosphere, a quiet coldness of beauty that has come of the thought Mr. Martyn had, as he wrote it, of the moonlight on the Burren Hills in his home country. In this one respect Mr. Martyn has done what he would, for he holds that "the greatest beauty like the old Greek sculptures is always cold."

Cornelius Weygandt. *Irish Plays and Playwrights*
(Boston and New York, Houghton Mifflin, 1913),
pp. 82–83

Naturally, Edward Martyn was subjected to the Norwegian influence, and so far as the latter has colored modern dramatic technique, he is truly a product of the period. He seems, nevertheless, to have given a more personal imprint to his rendering of the lesson learned by his contemporaries from Ibsen. Instead of merely seizing upon the facilities for propaganda afforded by the abolition of worn-out conventions, he applied Ibsen's method to the portrayal of national character and the interpretation of Irish life. Consequently, his plays resemble those of his master much more than does anything written by the author of *The Quintessence of Ibsenism*, who has been so instrumental in obscuring the true purpose of the dramatist. While Shaw has read into Ibsen a most interesting commentary upon contemporary social problems, he has caused us to lose sight of the original spirit in which that commentary was presented. There have been innumerable minor variations upon such themes as *The Doll's House*, but none of the later English playwrights has approached a local theme in the Ibsen manner. In Martyn we get the essence of Ibsenism, rather than that quintessence extracted by Bernard Shaw. He does not concentrate upon one aspect of Ibsen's genius, but envelops his subject in an atmosphere which we recognize as akin to that of *Hedda Gabler* or *The Lady from the Sea*. . . .

The faulty characterization and a certain amateurishness, noticeable in the earlier plays, are almost wholly absent from *Grangecolman*, which shows that the intervening years have left their experience of the stage upon Edward Martyn. The mystic, symbolic Ibsenism of *Maeve* and *The Heather Field* has made way for a cold realism, which holds the spectator by the intensity of its reflection of reality. The characteristic touch of Scandinavian melodrama is not wanting, but the author is able to carry it off as successfully as did Ibsen before him. When one sees how Martyn has triumphed over his natural tendency towards an over-formal dialogue, one cannot but regret that his talent should have lain almost quiescent for want of an occasion for its exercise.

Ernest A. Boyd. *The Contemporary Drama of Ireland* (Boston, Little, Brown, 1917), pp. 18–19, 29

Edward Martyn is a hard man to understand, perhaps impossible to an Englishman. He inherited on the one side the tradition of the West of Ireland gentry and peasant and on the other "the grand aesthetic distinction of Catholicism" and the citizenship of Europe. As man or as artist he leaves an impression strong beyond all proportion to any one achievement, and those who have written of him have made penetrating interpretations—which differ fundamentally. His attachments and his capacities were strong and incompatible; the result less an organism than a state in conflict, bound together by a mastering will. Nature-mystic and satirist, devout pietist and ambitious dramatist, affectionate in friendship and a hater of women, ascetic in habit of life and cosmopolitan in culture, a Greek scholar, a lover of Palestrina and an acrimonious politician—no sooner do we settle upon one quality than its opposite comes to confound it. Various in interests and parochial in mood, a subtle and acute critic of Ibsen and as naïve as a child in his own estimates of men, it is easy to draw a series of portraits, but hard, to the verge of impossibility, to see the man.

[George] Moore has left picture after picture, unforgettably vivid, revealing through the medium of habits, clothes and mannerisms, the obfuscation of intellect and the immovable massivity of soul. "One comes very often to the end of a mind that thinks clearly, but one never comes to the end of Edward." . . .

He was one of those men whose minds have been divided deeply and early by strong influences in conflict with each other and with the proper nature of the man, and whose lives, by consequence, are not a growth but a succession of actions, who survive rather by the sum than by the height of their achievements and whose vast energy passes into the stream of events without making for itself any one memorial commensurate with its force.

And the artist was like the man, a mass of conflicting tendencies and of inconsistent levels of thought. To study his eight plays is a baffling and in some ways a thankless task, for not many of them have great intrinsic merit and nearly all of them are contorted and spoiled by unevenness of intention and execution. Yet, hard to understand, he is also hard to turn away from, for his success and his failure alike lead directly to some major problems of dramatic aesthetics. Moreover the mind, and its record of deep and incoherent suffering, becomes dear to us. "There is always the original pain," a pain which Martyn, by reason of his tradition and discipline, never falsified nor weakly condoned. [1939]

Una Ellis-Fermor. The Irish Dramatic Movement
(London, Methuen, 1964), pp. 117–18

The plays of the Scandinavian dramatists were a point of departure for Martyn. His own temperament entered into his work, positively in the character of Tyrrell, negatively in his avoidance of potentially scandalous topics. Uncommonly scrupulous in the practice of his Catholic faith, Martyn burned a manuscript poem because it did not glorify God and the church, cancelled a subscription to a periodical whose contents offended his moral sensibility, and even requested formal permission to read works on the Index of Prohibited Books. As noted earlier, he thought of withdrawing from the Literary Theatre when the morality of *The Countess Cathleen* was challenged. A man so tender of conscience would not write of murky secrets lying below the surface of respectability. Ibsen by contrast endured a demoralizing family environment in his boyhood and at the age of eighteen fathered an illegitimate child. He would not be deterred by the limitations Martyn imposed on himself. Martyn's admiration of a writer whose work upset some proper Victorians may seem paradoxical, but in an essay reproduced in Denis Gwynn's biography he insists on a distinction between Ibsen the craftsman, for whom his respect is unqualified, and Ibsen the teacher, with whom he often disagrees.

Ibsen's plays contain sociological overtones which are not to be found in *The Heather Field*. The Norwegian portrays venal journalists, bogus liberals as well as narrow conservatives, urbanely unscrupulous businessmen, persons who consciously or unconsciously uphold false social values. Martyn's focus is predominantly psychological. Only the vacillating doctors and perhaps Lady Shrule would be at home in a hypocrisy-ridden community such as that in Ibsen's *An Enemy of the People*. Tyrrell's contention that a landowner betrays his class by reducing rents is an editorial comment by Martyn; but Tyrrell's relationship with his tenants is of peripheral importance in the play. The really significant conflict takes place in the mind of Carden Tyrrell.

By steering away from sociological issues, Martyn deprives *The Heather Field* of the irritant effect that vitalizes Ibsen's plays even though the issues themselves no longer are pertinent. In what he has chosen as his province, the dramatizing of internal struggle, Martyn has been only moderately successful. Ideas are not theatrically viable unless the audience takes an emotional interest in the characters who embody the ideas. Martyn's characters are understandable, articulate, drawn in sharp outline; yet except for Tyrrell they are voices rather than persons, unable to evoke more than an intellectual response from an audience.

William J. Feeney. Introduction to Edward Martyn,
The Heather Field (Chicago, De Paul Univ. Pr.,
1966), pp. 11–12

As a pivotal work in Martyn's career, *An Enchanted Sea* points forward to his later rejection of unworldly aestheticism but also backward to the essence of the Irish Renaissance and his two major plays. Lord Mask, a scholar and connoisseur of art, imagines himself the spokesman of an Irish spiritual awakening. His young friend Guy Font brings to Mask's intellect a childlike, visionary quality, one directly in touch with the elemental spiritual forces of Ireland and its mythology. With Guy's imagination to sustain him, Mask can endure the "shadows," the mundane external world he finds so repressive, but finally follows Guy into "a vision of eternal art in the antique glory of the sea!" Mask once imagined that in the depths of the ocean he saw the young boys in the court of Mananaan, the Irish god of the sea. After Guy's death by drowning, therefore, vision in the appearance of Guy beneath the waves beckons Mask to his own death. The final words of the play, a marriage proposal offered by a practical naval commander who knows the sensible way to deal with oceans, lead back to the world of society and the living. Yet Martyn has put more conviction behind Mask's speeches and his wistful adoration of the dead.

Martyn's later work clearly repudiates much of the aesthete's role. In terming this development a "progression towards realism," however, [Marie-Therese] Courtney tends to obscure its negative side. Martyn's final memoirs, bitter and satiric in tone, returned to the style of *Morgante the Lesser* in describing the Literary Revival. Martyn borrowed a phrase from the novelist Samuel Lover, "Handy Andyism," which he repeatedly used for all the bumbling, narrow-minded, bureaucratic, materialistic forces in Ireland. Yet in this self-serving chronicle, entitled "Paragraphs for the Perverse," even Yeats and Lady Gregory received only ironic praise. In turning away from aestheticism, the flailing irony of the memoirs, as in his play *The Dream Physician* (1914), progresses not so much toward realism as toward bitterness and disappointment. During the last decade before his death in 1923, arthritis and general poor health kept Martyn confined to his tower study, frequently in pain, never able to put the records of his career into publishable form.

Wayne E. Hall. *Shadowy Heroes: Irish Literature of the 1890s* (Syracuse, N.Y., Syracuse Univ. Pr., 1980), p. 125

MCGAHERN, JOHN (1934–   )

Mr. McGahern [in *The Barracks*] is . . . concerned with characters in an institutional setting who fear that life is slipping away from them, its joys untasted. Reegan is a sergeant in the Irish police, stationed in the West, a volunteer in the early days of the Irish Free State whose hopes and ambitions have been dissipated by the mediocrity of modern Ireland, and whose energies are increasingly drained by a bitter feud with his superintendent. His wife Elizabeth, whose thoughts occupy most of the book, balances the small satisfactions of her provincial life against the keener joys and sorrows of her past in London, and the uncertainty of death forced upon her by the knowledge that she has cancer.

These themes are elaborated against the rhythms of domestic and barrack life, the details of which are evoked with a scrupulous yet enchanting accuracy that reminds one of the young Joyce. Where Joyce would have concentrated the experience of *The Barracks* into a short story, Mr. McGahern has extended it over the length of a novel whose structure is too frail to support the weight of detail. But for a young man of twenty-seven, he is astonishingly successful in penetrating the mind of a mature woman confronted with pain and death. Mr. McGahern is the real thing, and his development will be well worth watching.

David Lodge. *Spec*. March 8, 1963, p. 300

[A] father-son relationship lies at the heart of *The Dark*. This is a second novel, now some months old, by the talented Irish author, John McGahern. His first, *The Barracks*, was a careful and understanding study of an unhappy stepmother: an excerpt from it won the AE Memorial Award for 1962. The new book seems to have got Mr. McGahern into typically Irish hot water: exception is taken, it appears, to his treatment of homosexuality and the Church. To an English reader, his offence seems mild indeed. Although a priest is shown as unduly tender to the boys in his care, their relations are only on the borderline of sentiment, and there's enough ambivalence and ambiguity to make them true to the complex realities that most people have to face at some time in their childhood.

What's more, the real subject of the book is the slow evolution of the narrator's feelings about his father, moving from fear and disgust at his embraces to a shared pride in his own school achievements, followed by renewed embarrassment when the father publicly celebrates his winning a scholarship. In the end, the boy renounces it, returning to the safe rut his father had once recommended: it may be wisdom, but it smells of defeat. The skill of the book lies in its persuading us that all this was inevitable, given the proud, timid nature that the boy's upbringing encouraged. It seems tough on the author to hound him for this—unless it was for printing F-U-C-K (like that, hyphenated) on the first page.

Richard Mayne. *NS*. March 18, 1966, p. 390

A short but penetrating comment by Michael Foley on the novels of John McGahern (in the September, 1968 issue of *The Honest Ulsterman*) is, clearly, the response of one who has warmed to this writer's sterling qualities of tenderness and compassion. Mr. Foley has sympathetically indicated the sombre nature of the writer's vision, the dark conditions of his fictional universe. He prompts me to take the matter a little further and to enquire into the degree of the writer's success, in novelistic terms, in the realization of that vision. It seems to me that McGahern's first novel, *The Barracks*, a remarkable *tour de force* for a young writer, perfectly achieved his purpose but that *The Dark*, which attempts to present a similar universe in confessional form is, though often interesting and compelling, ultimately much less successful. I do not suggest that Elizabeth Reegan's view of the nature of life is argued more convincingly than young Mahoney's, rather that McGahern makes her predicament vividly credible but fails to repeat this effect in the second novel. The success and the failure depend, I think, on form.

The form of *The Barracks* perfectly suits the writer's purpose. Elizabeth Reegan is thirty-nine years old and soon to die. This life has been lived and its imaginative reality is vividly created for us in a series of capably controlled flashbacks. The boy in *The Dark* is embarking on life—flashbacks are impossible here, the experience must be created chronologically. The second book is, thus, denied one of the earlier work's most powerful ingredients, the moving current of nostalgic regret which rolls through the novel like a dark tide. The middle-aged woman, dying of cancer, trapped in a marriage which has tenderness but no real sympathy in it, is the perfect vehicle for McGahern's purposeful pessimism. Elizabeth Reegan's life is made up of long periods of gallant, dogged silence and occasional moments of visionary joy which blaze like meteors in the darkness of her ordinary existence.

John Cronin. *Studies*. Winter, 1969, p. 427

[*Nightlines*] is an extremely good book of short stories, and one which quite plainly reveals a talent in the process of striding development. The stories in the earlier part, though true and spare, don't always free themselves from the two conventional categories into which short stories are apt to fall: the inexplicit slice-of-novel category and the moment-of-revelation category, often of childhood or adolescence. Apart from some occasional (and successful) oddnesses of syntax, Mr. McGahern is a traditional writer: he employs no gimmicks to relieve him from the grave obligation of giving us a fresh view of human beings and human relations, of landscapes, thoughts and dialogues. . . . One must add, too, that even at his most conventional Mr. McGahern rarely fails to present us with the moral questions whose presence is the hallmark of a considerable writer, and though he is helped in this by the Irish society that forms the basis of most of the stories, the thing is also carried into the long piece with a Spanish setting, "Peaches," which is one of the most remarkable in the book.

In "Peaches" Mr. McGahern moves into dangerous fictional seas—the creative artist "abroad," with a writer's block and a matrimonial problem—but comes through them triumphantly unbattered. There is a rather poker-faced emotionalism, a committed concern with food and other apparatus of day-to-day life, and even a political delineation harking back to the Spanish Civil War. These Hemingwayesque properties, however, the author makes entirely his own: and we don't feel, as so often with Hemingway himself, any sentimentality beneath the mask, or mere literary contrivance in the described sensuous aspects of existence, or oversimplification in the questions raised of courage, the ability to love, and so forth. Possibly we may judge that Mr. McGahern is in safer waters when he returns in the fine last story to the Ireland of primitive schools and religious bigotry that is also the setting of his two novels, but we are grateful for the indisputable evidence of ambition and the continuing absorption of experience (also shown in another strong story about a London building site).

Reviewers confronted suddenly by an author of this quality are apt to make wild and perhaps unhelpful comparisons, but it is worth saying that for me the present book constantly recalled *Dubliners*. Joyce's collection, in the publishing convention of its time, was bulkier and therefore constituted somewhat more solid grounds for optimism about the author's future; but *Nightlines*, too, has an exciting blend of penetrating realism and sad lyricism, and a sympathy with and understanding of great stretches of human life extraordinary in a young writer.

Roy Fuller. List. Nov. 26, 1970, pp. 752, 755

The Leavetaking is indeed a novel rich in imagery. . . . The images add to the richness and complexity of the prose, a prose frequently with rhythms and texture of poetry. Critics concur in their praise of McGahern's style in this novel: "at his best McGahern writes so beautifully that he leaves one in no doubt of his equality with Joyce." McGahern has also succeeded with the form of this novel. As in *The Barracks* his use of flashbacks for the revelation of the past of the central character is appropriate for the explication of the central theme: that a man can successfully resolve to cut the ties of family, country, and heritage—and set his life on a new course.

Some critics have noted similarities between John McGahern and James Joyce, one drawing a parallel between Patrick Moran at the end of *The Leave-taking* making a mature and responsible decision to seek a new life outside Ireland and Stephen Dedalus at the end of *A Portrait of the Artist as a Young Man* arriving at a similar decision. McGahern's vision, however, has not always encompassed the possibility of happiness outside Ireland. Elizabeth Reegan had lived in London, and young Mahoney knew that for a "fiver" any fool could go to England—their lives were no happier for such experience or knowledge. The malaise in Irish society of the first two novels is intimately linked to McGahern's deep and almost bitter pessimism—he will not countenance any escape for his protagonists. A lifting of the gloom, however, has occurred in the latest novel. McGahern, like Joyce, may continue to look to his native land or, like his character Patrick Moran, seek for inspiration elsewhere.

F. C. Molloy. *Crit*. April, 1977, p. 26

McGahern's short-stories are most interesting when . . . the processes of his prose combine an unsentimental apprehension of the physical world with symbolist resonance and where he manages to generate the symbolic charge of his tales without dependence on the dynamism of a traditional religious or cultural symbol system. In his novels the rituals of the Church provided that charge; in *Nightlines* McGahern turns to imagery of wheel, river, sea. The wheels of the first tale are the wheels of a train bearing a man back through his past across the Shannon and also the "ritual wheel," the repetition of a life in the shape of a story that had as much reason to go on as stop. And the collection ends with a character, who has recognised that life "is all a wheel," contemplating the Shannon as it flows to the sea. Roger Garfitt has suggested that "McGahern sometimes seems more Buddhist than Catholic" and sees the imagery of the Wheel as possibly owing something to that tradition. But, if this is so it functions in a much less obtrusive way than does the Catholic imagery of the novels.

It is in the detailed interrelationship of the facts of McGahern's stories, the blend of event, physical milieu and meaning that McGahern's symbolism is least obtrusive and, I think, most effective. Each story employs one or two central images which, as Henri D. Paratte remarks, "offer a symbolic frame to his vision of reality." That vision is austerely metaphysical but reductively so as the human world of desire and meaning is set against images which suggest iron physical law, machine-like inevitability, cruelty, decay, the ritual wheel which breaks all backs as it turns. The world of these stories is a world of chainsaws, hooks, chains, ice, flame, shovels, metal, shot, coffin-wood, bait, mallets, chisels, rusting tools, iron-bolts, whips with metal tips, glass inseminating plungers, knives, pumps, concrete lavatories, ticking clocks.

The framing images of each McGahern story contain within them accumulations of detail and fact which further serve to symbolize the writer's ambiguous, metaphysically bleak vision of reality, though they do so without any suggestion of overt symbolist technique. It is only on a close examination of these works that a reader realizes how far he is here from the direct, unselfconscious discourse of the traditional tale-teller, how much he is in the hands of a skilled, very self-conscious imagist. For in McGahern the moments of traditional tone distract from the modernist techniques.

Terence Brown. In Patrick Rafroidi and Terence
Brown, eds., *The Irish Short Story* (Lille, France,
Publications de l'Université de Lille, 1979),
pp. 296–97

Although *The Dark* has some apparent similarities with Joyce's *Portrait of the Artist as a Young Man*, the comparison should not be pressed. Like Stephen Dedalus, the boy in *The Dark* has overpowering sexual drives and considers a vocation to the priesthood. Young Mahoney is highly intelligent and excels in his studies, but he has none of the intellectual arrogance and psychic certainty with which Stephen Dedalus leaves Ireland to "encounter for the millionth time the reality of experience." Unlike Stephen, the boy does not desire to be a creator of mortal beauty nor does he reject his faith. Instead, young Mahoney fumblingly works out his life, walking hesitantly toward freedom. It is significant that in scenes at Father Gerald's house where he weighs the decision to become a priest, he picks up the one volume that seemed livelier than the rest, Tolstoy's *Resurrection*. By choosing not to become a priest, the boy is beginning the resurrection of his own life; but it will move by fits and starts—no one choice is clear-cut before him. McGahern, through his protagonist, seems to be indicating that human decisions are fraught with uncertainty but that to achieve some happiness, freedom must be won daily. Stephen Dedalus is an urban hero who can leave Ireland boldly: but young Mahoney is a farmboy whose sights are set no higher than the city.

The Dark, with its sexually explicit scenes, caused a *succès de scandale* for McGahern, a teacher in a Dublin Catholic boys' school. Following the banning of the book for indecency or obscenity by the Irish Censorship Board and McGahern's marriage outside the Church, the author was forced out of his teaching position. Perhaps, for these reasons, McGahern makes the flight to freedom even more explicit in his third novel, *The Leavetaking*, where he draws heavily upon his personal experiences. That book portrays a single day in the life of the protagonist, Patrick Moran; and the decisive event of that day is linked to his whole biography through stylistic devices like reverie, association, and recurring imagery. These techniques emphasize one of the thematic concerns of the novel, the long shadow time past casts on time present.

Eileen Kennedy. In James D. Brophy and Raymond J. Porter, eds., *Contemporary Irish Writing* (Boston, Twayne/Iona College Pr., 1983), pp. 120–21

MCLAVERTY, MICHAEL (1907–   )

Among [Northern] prose writers, Michael McLaverty is undoubtedly pre-eminent. He has now published three novels and one volume of short stories, all remarkable for a fresh and delicate prose, shrewd observation and a gentle lyricism. His latest novel has been eagerly awaited.

On closing *In This Thy Day*, one is tempted to ask what William Blake would have thought of it; for here we have a delighted observation of the vegetable universe and an exciting revelation of detail, so that one laughs aloud with pleasure at exact descriptions and genuine idiomatic phrases: and when one leaves the book and walks through a field or along a road, one notices with sharpened vision the mark of a hoof in damp soil, a triangle of paper thorned in a hedge, the wicked glitter of glass from a distant farmhouse; and one hears the language of a county anew with a quick realisation of its subtlety and power. McLaverty has done what no other northern writer has succeeded in doing: from local speech which abounds with material for the novelist but which remains raw and crude until an artist by selection and arrangement effects the necessary transformation, he has made literature. Where so many have throttled the idiom in an orthographical hell, McLaverty has preserved it in sensitive and tactful prose.

Blake might have classed McLaverty with Wordsworth as an atheist; but he could not have failed to be impressed by the author's devotion to minute particulars, for, like Blake, McLaverty sees a world in a grain of sand. The accumulation of details, microcosms important in their own right, remind one of Blake's *Everything that lives is holy*. A leaf, a bluebottle booming behind glass, an arrow of sun flaming in a tree: these, the author seems to say, are important, not as symbols, but as themselves, for they live.

McLaverty is probably unique in modern fiction as a non-intellectual writer, a novelist unconcerned with ideas, who remains surprisingly free from the disintegrating forces of his age. He is important for his wholeness. He does not argue; he does not even comment: instead, he presents his readers with words as firm as unbroken apples. He is not a reformer: he is a healer.

This novel strengthens one's belief that the Irish are perhaps the only innocent people remaining in Europe. . . .

Technically he has learned something from Chekhov and something from Synge, but his innocence, and his determination (in his own words) to "expose and not exploit the people and their language—using the local speech with a delicate sense of selection and now by a massacring of that speech by an insistence on verisimilitude," are his own. Within an Irish context at least he is an important writer, and his work alone justifies hope in the future of Irish letters—that strangely animated corpse.

Roy McFadden. *DM*. Oct., 1945, pp. 60–61

It is a considerable distance from the rampageous spirit of *Lanty Hanlon* to the quiet attention that Michael McLaverty has given to the portions of rural Ulster within reach of the city of Belfast. His observation of the lives of the contented poor is so acute that it ceases to be mere observation and becomes a sympathetic sharing of those lives. His novels, *Call My Brother Back, Lost Fields* and *In This Thy Day*, show country people torn up from their roots in the countryside and drifting to the black streets of industrial Belfast, taking with them bright and detailed memories of the fields: "The days were fiercely hot and the blue skies were grained with twirls of cloud. Heat shimmered over the bean fields and wriggled like flame-shadow above the rocks. Cows crushed into the thin shade of the hedges and swished the clegs madly with their tails." . . .

The face of rural Ireland is studied there as a lover might study the face of the beloved. There is no suspicion that the soul behind the lovely face might be rotten as there is in Brinsley MacNamara's *The Valley of the Squinting Windows* or *Return to Ebontheever*; there isn't even a suspicion that the heart might be hard as it is in [Francis MacManus's] *This House Was Mine* and [Shan F. Bullock's] *The Loughsiders*. McLaverty, simply, poetically, without any reservation, loves the life of rural Ireland for its own sake. It is not for him as it is for Liam O'Flaherty in *The Black Soul* a place of healing refuge from the things that war and the world can do to the spirit of man; it is the great reality that has been and is and will be, without relation to any other mode of life in any other place, and even when his uprooted people find themselves in the streets of Belfast they bring with them, through poverty and pogrom, the innocence of children examining flowers or speculating on the mysterious flight of birds.

Benedict Kiely. *Modern Irish Fiction: A Critique*
(Dublin, Golden Eagle Books, 1950),
pp. 39–40

McLaverty, like Bullock before him, is a writer whose entire work appears to have its impulse in love of *patria*: in this sense and in others, both are good examples of the regional novelist. Bullock had of course to rely on his memory—he saw Fermanagh from afar: McLaverty, on the other hand, relies on his eye and ear. A schoolmaster by profession, he has an intimate knowledge of the life and speech of the Province. He portrays Ulster life as he sees it and Ulster speech as he hears it; he neither heightens the life in the interest of so-called "dramatic" action nor vulgarizes the dialect in the interest of "local colour." He began his career as a short-story writer, and some of his best work is in this form. His short stories are conveniently collected in the volume *The Game Cock, and Other Stories* (1949). McLaverty now prefers the novel, and has published four—*Call My Brother Back* (1939), *Lost Fields* (1942), *In This Thy Day* (1945), and *The Three Brothers* (1948). He is a quiet writer whose virtues are unobtrusive. He has, for instance, an excellent style; he writes simply and clearly, and when he uses an image it is fresh and appropriate; and he is a beautiful descriptive writer. But none of his novels is completely satisfying: *Call My Brother Back*, which is probably the most moving, is too episodic, and *The Three Brothers*, which is certainly the most complex, is too carefully fabricated. *The Three Brothers* is a novel of "character," in which the lives of three Ulstermen are compared and contrasted. They are the three brothers Caffrey: John, a good husband and father, properly ambitious for his family; Bob, a rather "near" country shopkeeper; and D. J., a ne'er-do-well. Each of these brothers is well drawn, Bob in particular; but, though the brothers are closely observed characters, they are not particularly interesting people: each of them runs to type, and the three types give the impression of being contrived to illustrate his thesis. McLaverty is a novelist whose moral purpose, though hidden, is never very far from the surface; in *The Three Brothers* he makes sure that Bob suffers and dies because his spirit is a mean spirit, and that D.J. survives because he is blessed with a generous spirit. The moral pattern of the story I find conventional and slightly unreal; the three main characters seem to be cut too neatly to have an interest of their own; they fail to have an independence outside the pattern of the story. It is not surprising that the minor characters in the novel have a certain charm which the three brothers Caffrey lack.

John Boyd. In Sam Hanna Bell, ed., *The Arts in Ulster: A Symposium* (London, Harrap, 1951), pp. 121–22

In these twelve tales [*The Game Cock, and Other Stories*] Mr. McLaverty always maintains the quiet mood of one thoughtfully recalling the past without idealizing it or indulging in nostalgic sentiment. His use of exact observation is as authoritative as that of the most heavy-handed realist. But Mr. McLaverty is selective. When he describes the dreary life of a Belfast street he achieves his effects with a few significant details and forgoes the pleasure of the useless cataloguing. When he describes the routine of life on a lonely seaside farm he conveys both its unceasing labor and seasonal fluctuations without describing every forkful of manure in the manner of many "epics of the soil."

There are no neatly dramatic plots in these stories of the wonder of childhood, the stale misery of age and the sour smell of poverty. But out of each small fragment of experience to which he turns Mr. McLaverty distills a satisfying emotion, a feeling of being allowed to share his complete understanding of his universally human characters.

It is this sense of artistically rewarding satisfaction which is the chief pleasure to be found in *The Game Cock, and Other Stories*. Gentle, restrained, and told in a beautiful but austerely simple prose, all these stories are too cool and quiet to please undiscriminating tastes. They are not funny, angry, exciting, brutal or clever. They are only true and touching and exceedingly well done.

Many of them are about children. Without the precious attitudinizing which so often serves for a child's point of view in fiction some of them reveal more about the adults in the child's world than about the child himself. In other stories about lonely old age, about the selfish cruelty of youth and about the bitter frustration of poverty and pride and the conflicting demands of love and duty, Mr. McLaverty is equally expert. . . .

Michael McLaverty is not always so impressive as a novelist as he is as a writer of short stories. . . . But in his latest novel, *Truth in the Night*, he achieves a memorable full-length characterization of an utterly obnoxious woman which is a triumph of objective understanding and cool pity. With all his customary technical skill and Irish artistry with words, Mr. McLaverty tells an intensely dramatic story, captures all the atmosphere of a small island off the Irish coast and lays bare the malignant soul of a bitterly unhappy woman. *Truth in the Night* is a profoundly moral novel written to dramatize its author's firm convictions about character and conduct. The truth about herself and selfishness which Mr. McLaverty's heroine learned in the night is one of the most important truths known to men. Mr. McLaverty makes it plain without spoiling his story by crude didacticism. *Truth in the Night* is too grim and harsh to achieve great popularity; but it is good. [1952]

Orville Prescott. *In My Opinion: An Inquiry Into the Contemporary Novel* (Indianapolis and New York, Bobbs-Merrill, 1963), pp. 225–27

It is sad to reflect that for two decades most of [McLaverty's] exemplary work was unavailable, but heartening to find audiences in the seventies responding so strongly to *Call My Brother Back* when it was reissued by Riverrun, and to Poolbeg's selection of the stories, *The Road to the Shore*, published in 1976. The purity of the art, the sureness of touch and truth of vision, all grow clearer as the mastery in his voice is discerned behind the modesty of its pitch.

Michael McLaverty has been called a realist, and we can assent to that description. The precision with which he recreates the life of Belfast streets or Rathlin shores or Co. Down fields and the authenticity of the speech he hears in all those places—this affords us much pleasure. But realism is finally an unsatisfactory word when it is applied to a body of work as poetic as these stories. There is, of course, a regional basis to McLaverty's world and a documentary solidity to his observation, yet the region is contemplated with a gaze more loving and more lingering than any fieldworker or folklorist could ever manage. Those streets and shores and fields have been weathered in his affections and patient understanding until the contours of each landscape have become a moulded language, a prospect of the mind.

What McLaverty said of a wordy contemporary could never be said of his own stories: "Exciting at first blush, but not durable." His language is temperate, eager only in its exactitude. His love of Gerard Manley Hopkins is reflected in a love of the inscape of things, the freshness that lives deep down in them, and in a comprehension of the central place of suffering and sacrifice in the life of the spirit—never in that merely verbal effulgence that Hopkins can equally inspire. His tact and pacing, in the individual sentence and the overall story, are beautiful: in his best work, the elegiac is bodied forth in perfectly pondered images and rhythms, the pathetic is handled as carefully as brain tissue.

A contemporary of Patrick Kavanagh and, like him, a Monaghan man by birth, sharing the poet's conviction that God is to be found in "bits and pieces of everyday", that "naming these things is the love-act and its pledge", but averse to the violence of Kavanagh's invective and satire, McLaverty's place in our literature is secure. It is time that it was vaunted.

Seamus Heaney. Introduction to Michael
McLaverty, *Collected Short Stories* (Dublin,
Poolbeg, 1978), pp. 8–9

The name of Turgenev is sometimes mentioned in connection with McLaverty, but though the Irishman shares the Russian's deceptive simplicity and has a similar eye for rural detail, he does not have Turgenev's spaciousness nor the dominating awareness maintained by Turgenev's sportsman. To mention Frank O'Connor, Liam O'Flaherty and *Dubliners* is to illuminate portions of McLaverty's canon of stories, but one feels uneasy about imposing public influences upon what seems to have been a rather private, even lonely movement towards an odd breed of excellence. If McLaverty is parochial in form as well as theme, it is in the praiseworthy sense championed by Patrick Kavanagh. The public issues of Irish life are sometimes there in the stories, but are so mutely, obliquely, even ironically. The universality of war is far more important in "Uprooted" than the specific war intended—is it World War One or World War Two?—and the universal pain of having one's local roots destroyed far more important than the universality of war. In "Father Christmas," urban unemployment is but a shadowy though necessary presence. Indeed, in McLaverty's best stories, for example "Pigeons" and "The Game Cock," McLaverty will ironically reverse or undermine an initial illusion or fantasy that is too publicly Irish for such a private visionary as the writer to accept. The governing irony in "Pigeons" is the disparity between the public abstraction "Ireland" for which Johnny dies and Frankie's mundane but life-enhancing concern for the safety of the pigeons he has inherited from his dead brother. "The Game Cock" registers the uncle's vengeful satisfaction that the cruel Ascendancy fell, but in the chanting of an essentially private repetition of his satisfaction by his homebound nephew (*"They took the land from the people"*) is hinted a great emptiness of spirit, a sense of opportunity tragically squandered by the boy's own people, perhaps even the notion of a lost paradise.

This is not to say that McLaverty abandons the Northern Catholics, especially the poor countrymen and slum-dwellers, who seem to constitute for him a hidden Ireland beneath the public surface (always offstage) of Protestant Ulster, a leaderless and submerged population cut off from their southern compatriots who have now, one feels, grown foreign to them: often we overhear McLaverty's children being taught, like the devout in penal times being reminded by the fugitive priest of their faith, chants and sayings about Ireland which seems so distant a country as to be imaginary. Yet—perhaps because of this indeed—stories like "Pigeons" and "The Game Cock" arguably install a myth of the beauty and freedom of the Irishry less vulnerable and more poetic than the more public myths of manifest Irish destiny and inevitable Irish unity which McLaverty silently abandons. If he seems a diffident champion of his Ulster Catholic heritage, it is because his priority is the human heart whose corners are inaccessible to the affairs of kings and state, for even when such affairs cause grief, as they do in "Pigeons" and "Uprooted," it is the exclusive privacy of grief, the heart's self-nourishing, that begs McLaverty's attention.

John Wilson Foster. In Patrick Rafroidi and Terence
Brown, eds., *The Irish Short Story* (Lille, France,
Publications de l'Université de Lille, 1979),
pp. 256–58

MOLLOY, MICHAEL J. (1917–   )

Mr. Molloy's latest one-act play is most interesting, both in its own right and as containing most of the elements which constitute what is not too early to term the "mystique" of his dramatic work.

The Paddy Pedlar is set in the year 1840, among a peasant-community on the Galway-Mayo border.

Thus Mr. Molloy provides himself, as he has done before, with the universe of a rather loose, almost anarchic, polity which allows uninhibited development and expression of his theme.

The play has six characters, two of whom—Ooshla Clancy and the Paddy Pedlar—reduce the others to dwarfishness and near-passivity.

The central figure of Ooshla, an egregious rogue who lives by his wits, on poteen, and in the conscience-salving conviction that he is by Divine appointment a gentleman—though God, "overlooked the riches some way or other."

Ooshla is, in fact, another King of Friday's man: there is no place for him within the constraints of responsible, conventional society.

A solution comes when Ooshla, touched and impressed by the filial devotion, earnestness and goodness of the Paddy Pedlar, decides to accompany him and "live in the wind."

Those two were very skilful, clearly-etched creations. Indeed, so impressive is Ooshla he seems rather too large to be contained by a one-act play, and one is tempted to wonder if he is not a guest-artiste—or escapee—from a full-length conception.

As regards structure, control and dramatic economy, *The Paddy Pedlar* pleases. It has rather more incident, more turns of plot, more wordiness (in no derogatory sense) than the usual one-act play, yet loses nothing in impact or tautness. Mr. Molloy knows his stage.

And he knows his audience: wit, near-melodrama, pathos and occasional real beauty of language are combined in a play that should have a very wide appeal.

Laurence Ryan. *Irish Writing*. Dec., 1954, p. 68

When Michael J. Molloy's *The King of Friday's Men* was staged at the Abbey Theatre in October, 1948, many Irish critics hailed him as a second Synge. Their enthusiasm has since cooled, for Molloy is a slow writer, and the memories of journalistic critics are short. Still, the comparison was not inaccurate, for Molloy is the most Syngean of all Irish dramatists—Synge included.

Or, perhaps more accurately, Molloy might be called a more authentic Synge. . . .

Though *The Old Road*, produced at the Abbey on April 26, 1943, is Molloy's first play, it shows his continuing characteristics. The language is richer than that of other realistic playwrights. George Shiels's language, for instance, is basically, save for an occasional locution, General English. Synge's language, especially in its heavy rhythm and the great lengths of its sentences, is more of an artistic translation than a literal transcription. Molloy's language stands midway between Shiels's thinning of the language and

Synge's thickening of it. Shiels's dialogue adds little to the literary merit of his plays; Synge's dialogue is one of his chief literary excellences. On the other hand, Synge's dialogue is a problem even for accomplished actors, whereas Shiels's is easy and unobtrusive on the stage. Molloy's dialogue welds the literary richness of Synge to the theatrical fluency of Shiels, and the result is remarkably fine.

Like all of Molloy's plays, the piece is set in the West of Ireland and portrays farmers and laborers. Its theme is almost the basic one of the Irish drama—land and money versus love and life. Or, as Molloy put it, "The OLD ROAD of the title refers both to the old road of emigration and to the still older road of romance." The old people have the desire for land and money and the young people the desire for love and life; the young only win by running away from Ireland.

The theme grows neatly from the characterization and adequately from a rather messy plot. Most of the characters exemplify reactions to the traditional Irish feeling that people should marry for practicality rather than for romance. The most memorable is the crazed old farmer Patrick Walsh, nicknamed the Lord or the Lordeen. Aften a long bachelorhood, he is now roaming the countryside, semi-senile, in a frantic search for a wife. The plight of Brigid and Myles, the impoverished young lovers, suggests how impossible it is to marry for love in the West of Ireland. This plot is well handled until the last act, when there is too much decision and indecision about whether they will emigrate and marry or stay home and be single. At one moment they are going, at another they are not, at another they are, and this back-and-forth is neither strong nor suspenseful. Molloy often takes two years to write a play; this slowness helps to enrich his dialogue, but it also tends to overcomplicate his plots.

Still, in his strong character-drawing, in his rich dialogue, and in his occasional violent theatricality, Molloy is more interesting, even in *The Old Road*, than many of his contemporaries. That theatricality is especially present in this play in the fine fight between Myles and the Lord in Act I. One of Molloy's continuing excellences is this willingness to be violent; after a long succession of low-keyed realistic comedies it is indeed refreshing.

Robert Hogan. *After the Irish Renaissance*
(Minneapolis, Univ. of Minnesota Pr., 1967),
pp. 86–88

Molloy's second play, *The Visiting House*, was staged at the Abbey on 18th October, 1946. It is "mainly a realistic comedy about the rural Irish 'Visiting House' as it is called, really the story-telling house," where the neighbours go for news and gossip, story-telling, songs, and general entertainment. This is a very different kind of play from the earlier one [*The Old Road*], and is not apparently realistic in its plot or handling. The dramatist wants to get away from the hackneyed Abbey themes and is out to find unexplored avenues of realism. Judged from a different angle, it is all realistic, for in Ireland there are such houses where the existence of spirits and fairies is discussed, where playacting, dancing, and gossip are freely indulged in. The basis in not unrealistic, but the content is apparently more romantic than realistic. It is an atmosphere far removed from the daily humdrum reality of life. It does take us away from the narrow confines of mortality, as a romantic play does, but the figures are all realistic, though they appear glamorous because, in a way, they are all acting. In the midst of the highly romantic content, there are flashes of grim reality. There is once again a pointedly realistic reference to the Land Commission. The old people are disgruntled at the reforms enunciated by the Commission. Since the Land Commission shifted some people to new holdings in Kilduff, Mickle is discontented with Ireland, although his land is now better than what he had. The old men feel that the Land Commission villages are too widely scattered and lonesome. Broc says, "Whether the village is dying or not, the Land Commission'll scatter us at last, for scattering villages is their way of living. 'Tis in their minds to leave no village standing in Ireland." He is of the view that the rising generation is interested only in sports, dances, cards and company-keeping and so fears that the Visiting House will have no future.

Interpositions like the statement of Tim that "they reckon the two worst things for a man are a nagging wife and a dripping roof " have the force of taking us immediately back to our earthly reality from such strange otherworldly speeches as, "One that seized a cow had to go through the world evermore with a small stick, hitting every piece of cow-dung on the way," or "the Voice is not allowed into any house unless a living person directs him and can appear only one week in fifty years in his true image, but in the image of a black dog on any dark night."

Molloy has extended his scope wonderfully without breaking away from realistic bounds. Whereas in the first play, he was imitative of more than one dramatist, in this play he is almost wholly original. The subject is one that has been treated by no other Irish dramatist. The play is a clear indication that Molloy is no more going to imitate the oft-repeated Abbey themes, and that he must plough his own furrow.

N. Sahal. Sixty Years of Realistic Irish Drama
(Bombay, Macmillan, 1971), pp. 178–79

In the 1940s and 1950s the name of M. J. Molloy was one of the most respected on the Irish theatrical scene. From a small farm near Tuam, Co. Galway, Molloy supplied the Abbey stage with several notable works: *The Old Road, The Visiting House, A Will and a Way, The Wood of the Whispering* and, the finest of them all, *The King of Friday's Men*. He wrote in a folk idiom of much richness and there were those who considered his dialogue equal to Synge's and perhaps more authentic.

The King of Friday's Men was a particularly good play and it gave to the Irish stage a character of exceptional appeal in Bartley Dowd, the hero of the piece, a rugged shillelagh fighter with a face battered by blows received in many battles invariably won. Bartley's arrival prevents a comely young girl from being pressganged into tallywoman service with a local landlord. The play teems with flowing language, conflict, comedy and innocence. The drama is set in 18th-century Ireland, when shillelagh fighting was common and when it was customary for a landlord to summon peasant girls to pleasure his Big House bed, turning them out with a purse of sovereigns when a younger and more delectable creature came into view. The maiden who refused could be pressed into service by the overlord's ruffians, or her family could be evicted. Feminine beauty had its hazards, and life was harsh for the have-nots. Molloy captures the mood excellently. Bartley Dowd is inveigled into saving the lovely Una Brehony from the degradation of being tallywoman to Caesar French. It remains a golden piece of period theatre.

The Visiting House has a West of Ireland setting in the early 1940s. The play mourns the passing of the "rambling house," that felicitous rural Irish institution which allowed people of a district to gather together for singing, dancing, and storytelling. *The Wood of the Whispering* is also a folksy social document. This time the theme is the ruinous effects of emigration: the wood which once whispered with the words of young courting couples is now silent and there are poetry and comedy in Mr. Molloy's lovely lament. In the remarkable short play, *The Paddy Pedlar*, the travelling pedlar carries the corpse of his mother in a sack so that he can lay her to rest in the spot she desired. Here again, the writing is superlatively, hauntingly rich. While the theme might sound a trifle incredible, it has the stamp of authenticity. There is, perhaps, a small grain of truth in an old joke about the Irishman's aversion to coming directly to the point, especially in affairs of the heart: the boy proposes to the girl by asking: "How would you like to be buried with my people?"

For many years now, M. J. Molloy has been in a state of almost total eclipse at the Abbey Theatre. New plays have been rejected and old ones revived infrequently and indifferently. One Abbey reject, *Daughter from Over the Water*, was seen in a successful amateur production by Siobhan McKenna, at the Gaiety Theatre in Dublin. But there is at least one Molloy work which has never been performed. Like the "rambling house," the time of fine, Synge-like writing and of rural themes rooted in history and folklore has, apparently, disappeared. W. B. Yeats and Lady Gregory may be weeping in their graves.

Desmond Rushe. *Éire-Ireland.*
Fall, 1979, pp. 126–27

MONTAGUE, JOHN (1929–)

Montague's ear for folk-speech and ability to combine the stuff of fantasy and legendry with a kind of flat factuality are seen . . . in "The Sean Bhean Vocht" (the poor old woman—"one of the traditional symbols for Ireland, most familiar in the eighteenth-century patriotic song of that name"). Most of this poem describes an actual old woman whom the poet knew in his childhood and who rather frightened him with her ragged ugliness, her smell ("her clothes stank like summer flax"), and her talk of battles between the fairies of Ireland and the fairies of Scotland and other magical events. Her speech, "heavy with local history," had the quality of prophecy and wisdom literature in its rhythm as in its idiom. . . .

This is the unconscious sort of incantation that suffuses ordinary speech when uttered by someone who sees supernatural force at work in the plainest events. The poet, in the final stanza, speaks of striding "through golden light" among the local hills and fields "in high summer." Though it had been logical to point out a few lines earlier that "age is neither knowledge nor authority," he cannot help wondering "what illusive queen lay dust" in the grounds where the old woman now lies buried. The balance of elements in this poem is like that of "Poisoned Lands," but Montague's love of the sound of Irish speech and his deep engagement with Irish tradition come through more beautifully and genially. In *Poisoned Lands* as a whole, indeed, that sense of involvement with the whole of Irish reality, at once nostalgic and critical, appreciative and uncompromising, is what gives the work its authority. One feels it even in a poem as modestly unsensational as "Irish Street Scene, with Lovers," an impressionist composition that gets the precise ambience of a "rainy quiet evening" in Dublin when lovers walk "linked under the black arch of an umbrella" through "this marine light." The restraint and confidence of "Irish Street Scene, with Lovers" are as true to that urban ambience as the released whimsy and fantasy of some of the other poems are to their motives in legendry and folk-tradition.

M. L. Rosenthal. *The New Poets: American and British Poetry since World War II* (New York, Oxford Univ. Pr., 1967), pp. 300–301

Someone is always rediscovering Thomas Hardy *as a poet*. I suspect John Montague will be rediscovered in the same way. He doesn't raise his voice to summon a contemporary audience. Nobly [in *A Chosen Light*], he tells tales, explores a place-and-a-life with extraordinary simplicity (not really) without trying to jolt his reader into a sentiment more vivid than reverence. Before you know it, his poem is over; he has put the world in your lap, a small montage of pain or waste, "The sober structure of a land where/ Decay retains its ritual," or another kind of land where cattle "between shelving ditches of whitethorn . . . sway their burdensome/ Bodies, tempted at each turn/ By hollows of sweet grass. . . ." In "The True Song" he sings himself a warning of the temptations that assail the poet: to "descend into beauty," to become "a detached god" or to be overwhelmed by "the body brought in from the street." An open-air man, a loving man—"There is no hawk among my friends," he writes (apostrophizing Roethke)—Montague makes songs from half-door cottages, hillside byres and forges, from self-division and the divorce of true minds, from the short terrible life of an Irish "whure." To say that he writes of Ireland, Brooklyn and France is only to say that most of his poems take *place*; yet something other than landscape will imprint his verse in your memory.

Vernon Young. HudR. Winter, 1970, pp. 743–44

Montague's best and most characteristic work, in my judgement, describes the evanescent kept fresh by memory in terms of stone, or the permanent, as in "Like Dolmens." After all here is the real work of the artist: to choose to honor—or make enduring—what is actually permanent is less of an accomplishment. In "Dolmens" Montague describes a number of old, eccentric people like Jamie MacCrystal and the Nialls (who are also described in "The Road's End"), all of whom die. . . . But their death, we note, gives them in Montague's pantheon a truth of longevity—they are significantly "cast in the mould of death," where "mould" suggests both decay and permanence. The poet emphatically denies ("Ancient Ireland, indeed!") that the past is not present, that his old neighbors,

Gaunt figures of fear and of friendliness

steeped in

The rune and the chant, evil eye and averted head,
Formorian fierceness of family and local feud

are different from the ancients. At any rate, he concludes that

. . . once, in a standing circle of stones,
I felt their shadows pass

Into that dark permanence of ancient forms.

But why "dark"? If recovery and a resulting kind of permanence are the goals of Montague's art, why here do we have a rather antipathetic qualification? Because the image the poet is using is one of unmodifiable physical state, of monolithic monument. Such relics are fascinating to Montague as are the Monks' cells of "Monasticism." But as in that poem where the monks prayed among "darkening rocks," the ultimate, higher goal is someting closer to life, like "purifying waters." In "Dolmens" the village eccentrics "trespassed on [his] dreams" until they passed "into that dark permanence of ancient forms." There is definitely a sense of relief and honor in this statement, but there is also some diminution of the figures who are the subject of the poem. A *brighter* permanence would be to keep them still amidst his dreams, part of the ever-present material for his "restive sally-switch." The main effort of Montague's poetry, which is to restore or recover, is not to create a "dark permanence" but something nearer to a permanent light where "permanent" has the sense of "continuous" or "active." A poem like "Dolmens," in which the ultimate metaphor is of stone, is a poem of some sadness. His later companion piece to this poem, "The Road's End," is much different in tone and does, in fact, establish the old people in a "bright" permanence with its concluding symbol of the "yellow cartwheel" propped against the old door. In that poem, rather than in "Dolmens," we find the symbolic continuity with which Montague can brilliantly invest memory. There is his "living source, half-imagined and half-real"; there, the "pulses in the fictive water" to feel.

James D. Brophy. In Raymond J. Porter and James
D. Brophy, eds., *Modern Irish Literature: Essays in
Honor of William York Tindall* (New York, Iona Col-
lege Pr./Twayne, 1972), pp. 162–64

John Montague has been known to his contemporaries as a lyric poet concerned with love. A poem such as "All Legendary Obstacles" gives credence to the view. . . . Implicit, and sometimes explicit, in this praise is the suggestion that Montague can only write one kind of poetry. And that one is distinctly non-political. Valentin Iremonger and M. L. Rosenthal, two of his most perceptive reviewers, realize that Montague has based his poetry on an understanding of humanity rather than on an understanding of literature. To be only a lyric poet writing of love would limit him to being the student of a genre. Ignored, though, is Montague's long and continuing political poetry and the change in it as Ireland becomes what I must regard as a violently stagnant culture.

As is generally true of Irish poetry in the 1950's, Montague's early verse fought a father-son battle with the precedent of Yeats and Co. To free the self from the Anglo-Irish personage that strode across literature dressed in bowler and spats, often thought of as helmets and greaves, then became a dominating theme, even an obsession. . . . With the sound of Joyce to encourage them, Montague and many of his contemporaries continued to write of an Ireland peopled by human beings flawed by character and circumstance, graced by love and kindness. . . .

Freedom from the past came as Montague accepted the strength of his belief in the people of Ireland, citizens of a new age, and no longer tilted on the plain of the past. Many poems in *A Chosen Light*, the second collection, speak of the new understanding that has come to the poets and to the "plain people of Ireland" as Myles naGopaleen called them. "Vigil" recalls the bombing of the North in World War II. . . . As the third and last part of "Waiting," "Vigil" stresses remembrance of destruction and relief that such danger has not gathered itself into form again. Nowhere does certain calm present itself, not even in Ireland stuck by its neutrality on the backshelf of Europe. Changes in the world have come and are to be seen even at a festival of traditional music. . . . Though describing sexual and social attitudes among the young, the poem announces a revolution. It should be remembered that such festivals as these were created by Hyde's Gaelic League, an organization that provided the structure and impetus for the 1916 Uprising.

Probably no revolution is singularly political or cultural; for politics describes the ideal life that within a culture becomes modified, compromised by locale, time, and power. Montague's concern, almost without exception, has been the human, the cultural, the non-idealized part of the revolution. From his enjoyment and love of all peoples, Montague has built poems that show the humanity of all men, even Irishmen.

Frank L. Kersnowski. SCB. Winter, 1972,
pp. 224–25

The Rough Field allows a reader many moods, provides moments of subtle feeling and refined sensitivities, takes us through moving experiences. But these are the limits of the work, with which we would not quibble did not the later movements indicate, with a certain portentousness, the poet's feeling that something of larger significance is being offered.

So I would read the poem's epilogue, "Driving South," as an escapist journey, not a voyage into that new experience which the poet might have revealed in the ways by which poets can show us the future, through entirely original imagining.

This criticism of *The Rough Field* should not be allowed to detract from its considerable merits. A sturdy realism of detail throughout the work allows us to discover a world in its physical distinctiveness. *The Rough Field* has something of a novel's density of texture as the poet realises the life of a small region. The flowers, birds, beasts, trees, agricultural implements, houses and hills of the poem are not simply conventional counters in a pastoral idyll (as to the revival writers they so often were) but the closely observed particularities that determine the "felt life" of Garvaghey. Before they achieve any status in the work as symbols of a self-contained, threatened order of life, they serve to establish the exact physical constituents of that very order. Furthermore, the work has something of the sweep and energy of conception of epic. The canvas is crowded with men, women, animals, birds and artefacts. Ideologies and historical events are constantly in mind. The poet's attention shifts from an isolated townland in Co. Tyrone to many cities—Belfast, Dublin, Derry, Paris, New York, Chicago, Berlin—while the work is rich in mood and emotion. Satire, anger, humour, tenderness, despair, anguish, sympathy characterise its emotional colouring. It is a work prepared to risk the foolishness of personal expression, declining to disguise feeling in ironic self-protection or aesthetic formalism. An engaging openness of tone is one of its most attractive qualities.

Yet the work lacks the organising authorial intelligence we expect from a novel that purports to deal with social and cultural themes. Works such as *Middlemarch* or *Nostromo* (and *The Rough Field*'s reception in Ireland was of a kind that would suggest that it was of an equivalent significance) which consider the effects of historical change on particular regions are each governed by a much greater cultural and social intelligence than Montague can bring to his examination of a similar process. The work also lacks that compelling vision of the nature of order, its actual structures, that we expect from epic. The work as I have argued, derives from an essentially lyric sensibility. John Montague has recently suggested: "An Irish poet seems to me in a richly ambiguous position, with the pressure of an incompletely discovered past behind him, and the whole modern world around. . . A tradition, however, should not be an anachronistic defence against experience." I am not sure that in *The Rough Field* Montague has avoided this danger, despite his claim that Ireland can be understood as a microcosm of modern experience. A lyric poignant regret for lost possibilities, when Ireland might have resolved her problems in a rural setting, is the work's central emotional response to the ambiguity of the contemporary poet's (and Ireland's) position which has concerned Montague since the early 1950s.

Terence Brown. *Northern Voices: Poets From Ulster*
(Totowa, N.J., Rowman & Littlefield, 1975),
pp. 168–70

Montague's more complete sense of Ireland, his conflicting Northern and Southern, regional and national, urban and rural perspectives, must also have helped him to become a more complex poet. . . . Despite its relatively high concentration on Irish subject-matter, *Poisoned Lands* is a more varied collection than either *Another September* or *Sailing to an Island*. It includes, for instance, poems more particularly engaged with childhood experience in the countryside—poems which anticipate, and may have influenced Seamus Heaney's more consistent use of this approach in *Death of a Naturalist*. "The Water Carrier" may ultimately symbolize the poet's relation to his larger subject (one bucket for "rust-tinged," the other for "spring water"), but the immediate texture of the experience is primary: "Inhaling the musty smell of unpicked berries, / That heavy greenness fostered by water." Subsequently, however, the poem moves into less Heaneyish areas:

> Recovering the scene I had hoped to stylize it,
> Like the portrait of an Egyptian water-carrier:
> Yet halt, entranced by slight but memoried life.

All this a Heaney poem takes for granted. Although both poets often draw water from the same source, Montague tends to remind us of the presence of the buckets, to make explicit in a poem the attitude from which he writes it. Similarly, "The Mummer Speaks," strikingly similar in imagery and implication to Heaney's "The Last Mummer," includes this distancing or detachment: "A scene in farmhouse darkness, / Two wearing decades ago." This need not be a qualitative distinction, but rather emphasizes a contrast in stance which could be referred to the ten-year generation gap. Looking for a pattern underlying the variety of *Poisoned Lands*, and picking up Montague's hint that "the decisive influence was Auden," we notice that the influence in his case goes beyond verbal and rhythmical echoes, though it includes them: "Now the extraordinary hour of calm / And day of limitation," "At times on this island," "At times, we turn in most ordinary weakness," "The city had lost interest and / Even his chosen friends" ("The Quest").

Montague's concern with line, outline and all kinds of architecture, noticeable chiselling of word and image, and the willingness to generalize implied by a vocabulary which contains "Ireland," "mythology," "legend," "history" and "memory" as well as more local abstraction can all be paralleled in Auden, and suggest in particular that he is adopting Auden's 1930s role of cultural diagnostician, analyst and therapist. A compulsion to "stylize" and schematize experience, to set the "scene," appears at its most universal in "Musée Imaginaire" which begins "Consider here the various ways of man" and proceeds to consider them in terms of "conflicting [artistic] modes," just as in other poems he lays out for our inspection rooms in the museum of Irish history. It seems to me that Montague makes a much better job of being Ireland's Auden than Kinsella does of being Ireland's Eliot.

Edna Longley. In Douglas Dunn, ed., *Two Decades
Of Irish Writing* (Chester Springs, Pa., Dufour,
1975), pp. 138–39

John Montague prefaces *The Great Cloak* with these words:

> These poems should not only be read separately. A married man seeks comfort
> elsewhere, as his marriage breaks down. But he discovers that libertinism does
> not relieve his solitude. So the first section of the books ends with a slight affair

which turns serious, the second with the despairing voices of a disintegrating marriage, the third with a new and growing relationship to which he pledges himself.

. . . The intellect, which in previous volumes had been as self-consciously withdrawn from the love poems as it had been overasserted in the political ones, finds play in the disposition of the individual units of emotional intensity, without which disposition the volume would lack most of its (barely narrative) coherence. The obtrusive metaphors of *Tides* give way to a plainer imagery which frees the individual to suffer and to hope.

The first section of *The Great Cloak* plots the movement from careless promiscuity—"A slight girl and easily got rid of "—towards a sense of (reluctant) commitment and identity. This section ends with a contrast between the "joy" and "ease, not raw desire" of "Talisman" and the methodical and frustrating promiscuity of "Don Juan's Farewell." . . . The "ease" and "developing dream" of the first section give way in the second to a darkness "where animals move stealth-/ily, coupling and killing," while the waking hours are punctuated by the monotonous rising and falling of the hooves of horses "parading side by side" in an ironic parallel to Don Juan's insomnia. The private suffering, the fish "tugging/against the stream" with "the golden/marriage hook/tearing its throat," intense though it is, gives precedence to the turmoil of the still-existing, yet betrayed, marriage. . . .

The "new and growing relationship to which (the poet) pledges himself" in the third section is characterized by a rejection of the earlier dream imagery. The animal violence and harnessed monotony give way to scenes of pastoral fruition and contentment. . . . [Yet] the poet's pain reaches out in an ambiguous symbol of guidance to assert distinctions amidst the confusion of "Rocks jagged in the morning mist." . . . The final poem, "Edge," celebrates this state

where we rest, beneath
the clarity of a lighthouse

balancing the risk taken by those who "attempt the dream," who "cast off," against the "true luck" of those who find "between this harbour's arms/ a sheltering home." The poem's, and the volume's, concluding lines re-emphasize the terms of the success:

So fate relents.
Hushed and calm,
safe and secret,
on the edge is best.

The Great Cloak is a substantial achievement, and together with *A Chosen Light* and *Tides* marks John Montague out as a formidable poet indeed. To trace the line of development in his poetry is to see how much the Irish matter with which it is natural that the poet should be concerned has in fact endangered the maturing of his art. It is perhaps a sign of the distance he has now come that the Catullan introduction to *The Great Cloak* can make use of that subject-matter without diminishment either of poetic force or of his feelings for the day-to-day horrors so fleetingly alluded to.

Tom Wharton. *English.* Summer, 1979,
pp. 190, 193–95

Montague reminds of [Pasternak's] Zhivago because he is haunted by the long travelling shapes of his country; he cannot move away from the silhouettes of its history. Life and nationality are cradle and grave. When the Lord gives this he cannot take it away. Montague's poetry tells the story of Ireland as surely as Kiely's prose; their visions are sorties from the fortress of Ulster-memory. So many of Montague's poems express the sensuous facets of Irish experience—to the alert reader, walking here the delicious folk minefield, bombs of reference and recognitions will detonate all the time. This *Selected Poems* is issued from the womb of Celtic time and is not for the simplified soul. Not for the trans-Atlantic romantic for green fields nor for the middle-class acquirer of elves.

The first poem represented is the 1952 "Irish Street Scene, With Lovers" a lovely canvas of town life to begin with. Splashed with rain and colour it preserves carefully the required ambiguous zone. Montague exudes confidence in seizing the third party objective elan: the local capacity for seeing through surfaces into loneliness and pride. The theme of the poem is not accidental; there remain large deposits of *amour courtois* in the informed Irish consciousness. But Montague writes better when he is looking at love and its thorny pains than when he sees it as directly relating to himself. He is not a lively love poet, though he picks up when coiled inside his divorce. In his amorous descants I nearly inevitably encounter strain and embarrassment; Eros is a pretty god who must be courted more toughly, and with more candor. This failing sometimes operates with the only other weakness I can find in Montague's work: stretches sometimes of tired writing where one is conscious of model-replication; it is relatively easy here to identify patches of Auden and Williams (I exempt Yeats-dependence; all Irish poets must suffer this mutilation—Willie the bad fairy standing at all the cradles). For all this Montague seems superb as storyteller, folklorist, historian, speaker of anecdotal reminiscence, translator, and elegist. For example, "O'Riada's Farewell" glistens as a tight marker of the crossroads between art and death. . . .

Particularly masterful are the poems from *The Dead Kingdom* yet to be published in book form; they transcend the painterly eye, the visual glance, of Montague's earlier evocations of Irish importance. There is yielded an authentic power of discourse at the highest level of poetry. In "The Well Dreams" I am thinking of the changes that flow through the "recomposition" of the activities at the holy well. The breathing delicate description of the performing essence of water, earth, and people recall the magnificence of *At the Hawk's Well*—the difference is that Yeats is forgotten in the language Montague employs.

James Liddy. *ILS*. Fall, 1982, p. 16

John Montague's *Selected Poems* reinforce the impression left by his individual volumes: that of a great talent growing increasingly apprehensive at the conditions in which it must be exercised. Since 1958, when his first volume *Forms of Exile* appeared, he has been renowned for a certain elegance and formality of phrasing, and for a nervous delicacy of rhythm: these bestowing upon his poems an air of fragility which has to survive the often desperate occasions which initiate them. This discontinuity between the form of the poems and their environment can be partially understood as a product of modern Irish conditions. There are two main versions of contemporary Ireland in his work. The first is that of the dilapidated Republic of the Fifties and Sixties, first clerical, then commercial; the second is that of the broken North of the last two decades, violent and bitter, but touched by the promise that crisis can bring. Beyond these are other, vanished Irelands which nevertheless retain a considerable force in his imagination: the Ireland of Yeats and the Revival, the Ireland of his childhood in the North, the old Gaelic Ireland of Tyrone. All of them are finally disappointing. They encumber his art, although he struggles to make them liberate it. The problem is deepened by the fact that these territories do give release to many of the contemporaries whose presence in these domains shadows his own—Kinsella in the South, Heaney, Mahon, Longley and others in the North. A pathfinder who discovers that the territories he broke into have been settled by others, he is left to forage where others feed.

Yet this may have been Montague's good fortune. From the beginning his poetry has been concentrated around images which determine its procedures. . . . In "O'Riada's Farewell," the image of fire is tested against a series of other images and references—ice, music, light, desire, race, death—in a ballet of dainty interchanges for which the narrative provides a stage. The language is purged of its customary aids—punctuation, capitalisation of the initial letters in the line. The line itself is reduced at times to a single stress. The voice becomes disembodied, then is relocated again in the "I" of the narrator. The whole poem, and many others like it, refuses the restful incarnation in the actual which is characteristic of Seamus Heaney. It harnesses energy but does not convert it into something else, its force remains pure, does not become weight. In that respect it is closer to modern French poetry (like that of Bonnefoy or Supervielle or Frenaud) than to poetry in English.

It is this phosphorescence of the image and the accompanying ghostliness of syntax which distinguish Montague from his contemporaries and allow one to say that it is his good fortune to have been left to forage rather than to feed. He seeks to endorse his loneliness by imagining a community in which it would be healed. Culturally, the home ground is Gaelic Ireland; politically, it is Irish Republicanism; privately and personally, it is marriage. All of these, save marriage, are residual communities. . . .

The failure of his ideal communities is not the cause of the failure in the poetry itself. More truly, Montague's work reminds us of the force of John Crowe Ransom's precept that the object of a proper society is "to instruct its members how to transform instinctive experience into aesthetic experience." In that light, John Montague is, in the Irish tradition, powerfully instructive.

Seamus Deane. LRB. Dec. 30, 1982, p. 9

Montague's newest sequence, *The Dead Kingdom* (1984), deliberately combines the theme of the region with that of the feminine principle, in this case invested most fully in the character of the poet's mother. . . . Finally quite different in effect from *The Rough Field, The Dead Kingdom* is at the same time more intimate and more universal than the earlier sequence concerning Ulster.

The book retains its title-page connotation of death and morbidity, which we might assume from the beginning pertains to Ulster. Ironically, Munster, the province from which the poet departs at the beginning of the book to attend his mother's funeral in Ulster, retains ancient legendary right to that morbid title. The landing-place of the first invaders, the province of female deities and supernatural hags, such as the Hag of Beare, and the corner of Ireland associated with the dead, Munster was called "the dead kingdom." As the sequence traces the poet from his home in the South to the midlands of Ireland and the North, the grim connotations of the title are extended to all of Ireland. . . .

The title also forewarns us, as in the *nekyia*, the hero's descent into the underworld, that the poet will encounter the spirits in the manner of Odysseus's questioning his mother among the shades. The encounter occurs in the last two of five sections in *The Dead Kingdom*, after the poet has explored his childhood memories in Goldsmith's county, Longford. There he visited his cousin, crossed the border with its chilling associations, and reached his childhood home in Tyrone. The ulcerous fact, which the poet must mitigate, is the other's rejection of the son, emotionally from birth and overtly when he was four, as mentioned earlier in this chapter: "All roads wind backwards to it./An unwanted child, a primal hurt" ("Flowering Absence"). In 1933 she sent her three sons back to Ireland from Brooklyn and separated John by placing him with his paternal aunts. When she herself returned, she did not bring her youngest into the family circle. . . . At great risk, Montague dips into the pathos of this relationship without altogether escaping a note of self-pity. . . .

The success of *The Dead Kingdom* may depend on how each reader judges the sequence's climax, "The Locket," which offers balm for the "primal hurt." The poem's final revelation, that his mother always bore his picture in a locket, can seem only pathetic if it is not amplified beyond this individual, but hardly unique, case of maternal rejection. The amplifying apparatus in this volume is the richly evocative epigraphs to each section, a round-about of related images, the echo of countless popular songs, and the italicized "universal" poems which end each section. Of the relation of these terminal poems to the volume Montague has said, "Another, less autobiographical, urge kept adding distancing poems (how many mothers have died? countries been sick?) to enlarge the framework. . . . It is not especially Irish, but invokes many archetypes; mythical and maternal."

Dillon Johnston. *Irish Poetry after Joyce*
(Notre Dame, Ind., Notre Dame Univ. Pr., 1985),
pp. 197–99

MOORE, BRIAN (1921–   )

Modern "tragedy" has moved far from the majesty of Oedipus and King Lear. Its most somber dramas are played out in essentially mediocre spirits: in the death of a salesman we feel our own death and, recently, we queued up in New York to join two tramps in a hopeless wait for Godot. *The Lonely Passion of Judith Hearne*, too, is the tragedy of a third-rate soul, and in its pathetic history we are moved to pity and fear.

In this, his first novel, Brian Moore has done his native Belfast somewhat in the same service James Joyce did his native Dublin: he has taken an Irish city and laid bare its most secret soul through a character who could not have been born elsewhere. Stephen Dedalus, at the end of *A Portrait of the Artist as a Young Man*, goes forth from Dublin to seek freedom, but we know that Dublin's mark will be forever upon him. At the end of Mr. Moore's novel, Judith Hearne has lost everything—her pride, her friends, her faith—but she has lost them on Belfast's terms and we know that it is on Belfast's terms alone she will continue, however wretchedly, to live. The city is not a place; it is a colossus that creates, shapes, and then devours its children. . . .

In resume, Mr. Moore's novel may seem merely maudlin. But it is not. In its relentless pursuit of this woman's sorrow, in its refusal to sentimentalize or easily alleviate her plight, the book achieves a kind of vision, and it is a tragic vision. As she accepts, finally, the end of all her hopes, Judith Hearne attains, as the publishers claim, a certain grandeur. There is something awful in the death of even the meanest thing, and Judith Hearne, for all her delusions and mediocrity, had dreamed of those minimal things that all of us feel we have some right to expect from life—love, kindness, truth. Her defeat is the defeat, in a way, of all mankind, so relentless, final, and universal has Brian Moore made it. . . .

William Clancy. Com. Aug. 3, 1956, p. 448

The singular strength of Brian Moore's novels is manifest in their abolishing brow-distinction. Their way of doing so is not by what is essentially a high-brow strategy: the offering of different "levels," with its implicit condescensions (they read it for the story, we read it for the symbols and themes). Mr. Moore's new novel [*The Emperor of Ice-Cream*], like its predecessors, makes itself accessible to everyone, not by offering different things to different men, but by concentrating simply, directly and bravely on the primary sufferings and passions that everybody feels. Of all our present novelists he is for me ("for me," not because of any hesitation, but because of the nature of the praise) the one whose books most immediately evoke and touch my private feelings and fears, memories of what it was, when one was like that in the past—dismay at what it will be, when one is like that in the future. Kingsley Amis, not a lachrymose man, once paid R. S. Thomas's poems a tribute such as few reviewers feel it quite proper to pay: "It is enough to say he often moves to tears." The best moments in these novels have such a power—you have to pull yourself together. Agreed, it is a power than can often be felt strongly enough in bad films, but few good novels can do any such thing.

Sentimentality, some will say. But a novel such as Mr. Moore's first, *The Lonely Passion of Judith Hearne*, does not move us by any kind of illicit manipulation. Humphry House spoke of sentimentality as "the imposition of feeling as an afterthought upon literalness." But that wouldn't apply to *Judith Hearne*, where the emotion is intrinsic to the description, itself a matter of sharp delineation. It is natural that it should have been a literary critic of the Victorians who found so good a definition, and Mr. Moore's novels belong without any embarrassment in the tradition that the Victorians magnificently established. He is, if you like, a "conventional" novelist, quite without experimentalisms and gimmicks. In none of the novels is anything concealed except the art by which they transmute "an ordinary sorrow of man's life" into something we care about.

Christopher Ricks. NS. Feb. 18, 1966, p. 227

One of Moore's problems has been how to invest his characters with sufficient stature to draw the interest of the reader to them, for with the exception of Brendan Tierney and Mary Dunne, all of his characters are marginal, both in achievement and in the status that society accords them. A major premise of Moore's fiction is that society is basically composed of insignificant, lonely, and frustrated individuals, much like Arthur Miller's Willy Loman, to whom "attention must be paid" for the simple and convincing reason that they are human beings to whom "something terrible is happening," and it is to such people that Moore devotes most of his attention. "A good writer," he said on one occasion, "must feel sympathetic with even the least of his characters, and it is only the second-rate writer who will make out of his flat characters mere caricatures." To this aesthetic principle Moore has remained constant, and one of his genuine accomplishments has been the recreation of the Irish stereotype into a believable figure who elicits our compassion rather than our laughter. As human being and as artist, Moore displays a sensitive sympathy for life's losers, and his fiction abounds in grotesques and misfits of all sorts, but he effectively distances himself from these characters to ensure their humanness and credibility; as a result of this perspective and his technique, his fiction is remarkably clear of both moralizing and sentimentality.

It is just this skilful exploitation of the constituents of failure that represents one of Moore's major contributions to contemporary fiction. It is his individuality, his apparent unconcern for critical assessment, his faithfulness to the materials of his fiction, that strike one as indices of his integrity and his stature, and which have rendered his vision a dynamic and cumulative one. And though his characters are at times victimized by society just as remorselessly as those in the most naturalistic of novels, he rarely allows sociological observations or theories to challenge the priority of character. One does not, for example, experience a sense of anger or hostility towards Belfast as a society, but only a feeling of compassion for the Judith Hearnes or Diarmuid Devines who are defeated within that society. In Moore's view, no sociological or ideological imposition can essentially alter the major facts of existence: that the individual is confronted by a complex and unpredictable set of circumstances, and that somehow he must respond to this situation. He may or may not come to terms with what he finds, in the sense of gaining a compromise or a triumph, but the confrontation does take place and it is its nature and outcome which constitute the substance of Moore's fiction.

Hallvard Dahlie. *Brian Moore* (Toronto,
Copp Clark, 1969), pp. 10–11

In *Catholics* (New York, 1973) Moore restores the hierarchically ordered objective world which he attacked in the first phase of his career and disintegrated in the second. In this most recent of his books, he approaches a structured and divinely sanctioned world from the viewpoint of the order-giving father, rather than that of the rebellious child. It is true that he presents that world at the moment of its disappearance, but the fiction is ordered to show that the disappearance is the ultimate proof of that world's validity. *Catholics* is quite literally an apocalyptic book, and apocalypse as Moore conceives it depends on the existence of God and of the Roman Catholic Church. The book is set in the 1990s; the ominous year 2,000 hovers just beyond its range. The Roman Catholic Church, committed to ecumenism and social change, is about to absorb yet one more world religion—Buddhism. (As every Catholic school child used to know, just before the last day, there will be one fold and one shepherd.) Images and lines from Yeats's "The Second Coming" flash through the book, and a helicopter out of Bergman's apocalyptic *Through a Glass Darkly* violates Muck Island with its inhuman menace.

Once again, Moore brings together a conservative Ireland and an authoritarian Rome, but this time the previous meanings of the configuration are altered. Rome has renounced the old mysteries and rituals, to involve itself in the world of daily actuality. Muck Island, off the west coast of Ireland, clings to the Latin Mass, to all the old ways. Rome in the interests of uniformity and obedience sends James Kinsella, a young priest who does not believe in God and who sees the church as an instrument of social change, to bring into line Tomás O'Malley, the sixty-nine-year-old Abbot of the monastery on the island. Rome intrudes because television, that associate of destroyed moral value for Moore, has interested itself in the Irish religious ceremonies. . . .

In this book, Moore returns to the old view of the world as objective and ruled by God through a human network of fathers, and to Ireland for setting. The media paradigms for experience, as used in *Fergus* and *The Revolution Script*, have vanished, their only trace the Bergman helicopter. This book is intensely literary; in it Moore seems at pains to join himself to the great Irish writers who opened the century which his book implies is the last one. Moore's Abbot is a hawklike man, a man like the old artificer whom Stephen Dedalus recognized as his father. Yeats's "Second Coming" is closely woven into the language of the book, and Synge's journal of life on the Aran Islands is woven into both its content and its language. Moore at fifty-two seems at peace, for the moment, with all fathers. Like the Abbot, he seems to be now in the world of the father, which is a complex and mysterious new one, waiting to be explored.

Jeanne Flood. Brian Moore (Lewisburg, Pa.,
Bucknell Univ. Pr., 1974), pp. 93–96

Moore's early novels are about failure, his later ones about displacement. His canon therefore spans that entire scenario that takes us from the ritualised land to the provincial town and then to the depersonalised cities of the New World. With his latest work, *Catholics*, he even returns us to the ritual and rural beginnings of modern Ireland to make the scenario, in time and space, circular.

Moore's Belfast is somewhere between the two extremes of primitive rural society and dehumanised cosmopolis. The city is still heavily ritualised but its ritual and ceremony are impersonal and the weaker individuals have to fall back on their own ritual resources. Moore's fictional approach in his Belfast novels reflects this ambivalence of setting. If the mental stress caused by loneliness is a feature of life in the big city, then the extent to which Moore in his early novels explores mental decline (Judith Hearne, for example, ends her novel in premature senility) re-creates a Belfast on the way to becoming a cosmopolis. But while Miss Hearne and Diarmuid Devine could remain unnoticed in a really large city, they cannot escape detection in Moore's Belfast. Detection means victimisation. Moore's ritual portrayal of their victimisation balances his psychological portrayal of their mental distress. In the Belfast novels, then, Moore's style is midway between psychologism and ritual naturalism. In *Judith Hearne* this ambivalence of style is very obvious. In the sixth chapter Moore suddenly depicts events from the successive viewpoints of several characters, using a rudimentary stream-of-consciousness technique. This chapter is a kind of psychological intermezzo framed by conventional, third-person, naturalistic narrative.

The failure can be described as a primitive outsider. Moore's later novels, set in North America, might on first impression be seen as novels about existential outsiders, but it is important to understand how the consciousness which informs these novels has developed out of an originally rural and particularly Irish situation.

> John Wilson Foster. *Forces and Themes in Ulster
> Fiction* (Dublin, Gill & Macmillan, 1974), p. 153

In *Fergus* (1971), a rich hoard of Irish literary allusion serves as backcloth to the hero's anxious probing of psyche and belief. A passage from Wallace Stevens's "The Auroras of Autumn" prefaces the novel. This poem celebrates an unsurprised acceptance of conventionally "outlandish" events, just as Fergus, fairly calmly, comes to accept the paranormal scenarios he finds himself entering. But the importance of a specifically Irish literary tradition, both to Fergus and to Moore, is as evident here as in the case of Stephen Dedalus and James Joyce. The hero's very name should recall Yeats's poem "Who Goes with Fergus?"—itself abundantly quoted in the opening pages of *Ulysses*. There is no denying, however, that as it is used in *Ulysses* and as it is reflected in Moore's novel, this poem is problematic. And underlying these, as a piece of idiosyncratically interpreted Irish mythology, the Fergus story proves problematic too. The poem suggests that Fergus is an elemental leader, unshackled by cares and reflections, a man of action, of seductive physical power in control of all the disparate elements of nature. In Lady Gregory's version of the legend, however, Fergus becomes a proud king who gives up his throne to Conchubar in order to learn, by dreaming and meditating, the bitter wisdom of the poet and philosopher. Here, Fergus seems precisely the sort of *penseroso* who would "brood / Upon love's bitter mystery."

As for Joycean associations, we may see *Fergus* as a dramatized essay on what, on several of the early pages of *Ulysses*, Stephen terms "the ineluctable modality of the visible." In such overlapping of interests with those of Yeats and Joyce we can see the true "Irishness" of Moore. In a much more direct echoing, Fergus celebrates the sonorous syllables of the Greek word for "sea"—*Thalassa*—at the novel's opening, just as Buck Mulligan, at the opening of *Ulysses*, invokes "*Thalatta*," our great mother, the sea. Fergus, like Stephen an artist facing a crisis in his life, is similarly stimulated by a polyvalent sea whose shores he inhabits. Further parallels with *Ulysses* proliferate: the shared 24-hour time scheme; Fergus's attempt to understand his parents, mirroring Stephen's parallel attempt. Fergus's mock trial, echoing Bloom's; and so on. It would be inaccurate to suggest that *Fergus* "uses" *Ulysses* for the rich mythic purposes that Joyce had used the Greek legend: rather, *Ulysses* figures as the work and expression of the paradigmatic modern Irish literary artist.

Michael J. Toolan. Éire-Ireland. Fall, 1980,
pp. 102–3

Graham Greene is quoted as saying that Brian Moore is his favourite living novelist, and one can see why. All those Pelagian notions anathema to Mr. Greene—that man might save himself by his own efforts, or improve his arrangements for living in the world—are silently dismissed in Brian Moore's fiction. Not that anything dismissive is said, or even openly suggested. These grimmish anecdotes, in great variety (it is also true, as Graham Greene says, that Moore never repeats himself), are ideologically taciturn and severely self-contained. They rely on absolute authenticity and solidity of specification. His characters draw nothing from the common stock of the Novelist's Supply Stores. And if the stories have more vivacity than this account would suggest, it is because the detail, the handling of small events and settings, is so skilful and well-informed.

The Temptation of Eileen Hughes, like *The Doctor's Wife* five years earlier, is about a failed sexual adventure. But here Eileen Hughes, the ingenuous unsentimental employee, is herself never really tempted at all. The accent falls on Bernard McAuley, wealthy, confident—the commonplace boss seducer, as it appears at first. But the story is not the expected one: it is not a case of the randy businessman having a bit on the side. It is a fatal passion; and McAuley's wife realises this from the start. And as she needs at all costs to preserve her marriage, she colludes, condones, becomes Eileen's patron and protector, acquiesces in her accompanying them on the lavish holiday in London that turns into a nightmare. The action mostly takes place in a hotel near Victoria, with backward glances towards the small Ulster town from which they all come. The drawing is brilliant; depths and perspectives of character and background are suggested with the greatest economy. What are we to think of it all? Well, you are not supposed to ask: judgment is neither offered nor invited. But this is not the programmatically-assumed objectivity of the nouveau roman: more like a touch of Maupassant.

Graham Hough. *LRB*. Oct. 1, 1981, p. 13

The title of Brian Moore's latest novel, *Black Robe*, is somberly suggestive of magisterial power and occult menace, but such fanciful images hardly survive the Author's Note which comes between us and the fiction proper. Here we learn that Blackrobe (one word) was the term used by North American Indians of the 17th century to identify Jesuit missionaries. Sounded like this, it seems almost a tribal name, like Blackfeet or Cheyenne, and it is appropriate to the novel's disorientating perspective that "cannibals and Christians" should be confused in this way.

A Jesuit priest, Father LaForgue, and a young European volunteer, make a hazardous journey upriver from Quebec to rescue a beleaguered mission in remote Ihonatiria. They are accompanied by a party of Algonquin Indians, referred to by Europeans as "the savages." This simple, fluent narrative is presented from several, carefully balanced viewpoints, so that the reader can identify with radically different individual perspectives more or less at the same time. In the long run, however, although suspense is generated by reader-identification with particular characters, the overall effect is to dilute our sense of the importance of individual life. This impression is accentuated by the fact that we are handcuffed to a protagonist who is dedicated to the idea of his own martyrdom.

Moore's technique of the variable viewpoint justifies itself in the dramatic skill with which the Christian world is presented from the "Savages'" perspective. . . . In his efforts to create a realistic picture of part of precolonial Canada, Moore is careful not to idealize the Indian or caricature the Blackrobe, but he is not always successful in this aim. His flexible narrative style generates a vivid and varied sense of separate racial worldviews. But the Indian ethic is used in an all too familiar way to point up the deficiencies of Christian practice. . . .

In spite of this conventional idealization, the novelist shows himself to be resourceful at finding ways to present the Indian way of life in all its brutal actuality. It is a vividly sensuous world, realized with an overwhelmingly physical intensity: the ascetic Jesuit watches his volunteer missionary copulate with an Indian girl, himself enacting a solitary ritual of frustrated desire; later, his acutely roused physical sensibilities are racked beyond endurance by scenes of gruesome torture.

The reader is not given, therefore, a historical guided tour, as the author's note might seem to suggest, but an imaginative initiation into the Indian world. Like many "historical" novels, *Black Robe* is a fable for our world, insistently contemporary in its exploration of the conflict between religious faiths, or rival sorceries, as they must always seem to each other. In such a world the Christian faith takes its place as one of many sophistries devised by humanity to interpret or appease what is memorably called "that mystery which is the silence of God."

William Kelly. ILS. Fall, 1985, p. 45

MOORE, GEORGE (1852–1933)

The short stories and the novels . . . more than any writing of his, reveal his inherent dramatic power. By dramatic power I mean not his power of situation and evolution of dramatic technique, but his power to change his point of view with the character he is creating. A sensual exquisite himself whose predominant thought is of woman, and of woman from a standpoint closely akin to an epicure's toward an ideal meal, Mr. Moore can identify himself with people in whom there is none of himself but the essential humanity common to mankind. . . .

It is this power of Mr. Moore that makes him the great novelist that he is, this power of identifying himself with the personality and this looking out on life from the viewpoint of Esther Waters or Lewis Seymour, or Edward Dempsey or Rose Leicester, of Kate Lennox or Mr. Innes. Such a power is akin to one of the greatest powers of the Gael, his quick sympathy with what appeals to him in others, his momentary absorption in their interests, and his passing possession by their purpose. . . .

Mr. Moore is, then, Ireland's greatest novelist because he has in greatest measure—in full measure—this greatest gift of the Gael, the gift of dramatic impersonation of all manner of men in all their changing moods. A personality as intense as was that of Meredith, as is that of Mr. Hardy, Mr. Moore has not always one attitude, as have both Welshman and Saxon of the Saxons, however completely they write from the standpoint of each character they create. . . . He almost never plays chorus to his characters, either through a commenting character or by direct interposition in the manner of Thackeray, though, of course, the characters again and again express his views.

Cornelius Weygandt. Irish Plays and Playwrights
(Boston and New York, Houghton Mifflin, 1913),
pp. 99–101

While we are engaged in reading Mr. George Moore's novels he is "there," but once they are put back on the shelves he has softly and silently vanished away until he is heard of again.

The publication of a new edition of *Esther Waters* provides an opportunity for seeking to understand this curious small problem. It is generally agreed that this novel is the best he has written, and the author himself has expressed his delight in it—"the book that among all other books I should have cared most to write, and to have written it so much better than I ever dreamed it could be written." *Esther Waters* is, on the face of it, a model novel. Having read it carefully and slowly—we defy anyone to race along or skip—from cover to cover, we are left feeling that there is not a page, paragraph, sentence, word, that is not right, the only possible page, paragraph, sentence, word. The more we look into it, the more minute our examination, the deeper grows our amazement at the amount of sheer labour that has gone to its execution. Nothing from: "She stood on the platform watching the receding train," until the last pale sentence, the last quiet closing chord is taken for granted. How is it possible for Mr. George Moore to have gained such precise knowledge of the servants' life in Esther's first place unless he disguised himself as a kitchen-maid and plunged his hands into the cauliflower water? There is not a detail of the kitchen and pantry life at Woodview that escapes his observation; the description of the bedroom shared by Esther and the housemaid Margaret is as complete as though the author were preparing us for some sordid crime to be committed there. And this intensely scrupulous method, this dispassionate examination is continued without a break in the even flow of the narrative. . . . Could all this be more faithfully described than the author has described it? Could it possibly be more complete, more probable? The technique is so even, it is as though a violinist were to play the whole concerto in one stroke of the bow.

And yet we would say without hesitation that *Esther Waters* is not a great novel, and never could be a great novel, because it has not, from first to last, the faintest stirring of the breath of life. It is as dry as the remainder biscuit after a voyage. In a word it has no emotion. . . . Without emotion writing is dead; it becomes a record instead of a revelation, for the sense of revelation comes from that emotional reaction which the artist felt and was compelled to communicate. To contemplate the object, to let it make its own impression—which is Mr. Moore's way in *Esther Waters*—is not enough. [Aug. 6, 1920]

Katherine Mansfield. *Novels & Novelists*, ed. by J.
Middleton Murry (New York, Alfred A. Knopf,
1930), pp. 243–45

In the continuous and deliberate calm of . . . all his mature work, there is something spell-bound and trancelike. His detractors call it monotonous, frozen, dead. To me it is a calm enforced; I am aware in every line of the exercise of a rigid discipline; but it is a discipline which, though it touches me sometimes with unease, for I cannot escape knowledge of the struggle that produced it, fills me also with admiration and excitement. Here, plainly, at whatever cost to Moore himself, is something new in English literature that will have a lasting influence precisely because it is not new in the sense of being without roots. It will have a future because it has a past. Three great influences are perceptible in it: the majestic austerity of Landor; the translucence of Turgeniev, whose stories are shaded by none of the mists that trouble other men; and Pater's doctrine that sensation is the touchstone of value, a doctrine which Moore, having less moral prejudice than the author of *Marius*, was able to accept more fully than Pater himself. Moore made no greater secret of these influences than he did of the earlier influence of Flaubert. His claim was that he had assimilated them, and the claim is just. Landor and Pater were not, in essence, novelists; Turgeniev was not an English novelist; and Moore had evolved a style through which all three were made contributors to the English novel. He called them in as allies against Amico Moorini, and *Héloïse and Abélard* was the result. "There are only two prose epics in the English language", Moore would say. "One is *The Brook Kerith*."

"And what is the other?" you were expected to ask.

"The other", he would reply, "is *Héloïse and Abélard*."

Charles Morgan, *Epitaph on George Moore*
(London, Macmillan, 1935), pp. 36–39

Hail and Farewell, which many critics hold to be its author's greatest work, seems likely to retain a permanent interest which will outlive the interest of its subject-matter—has indeed already partly outlived it: even at the time of its appearance all but the greatest figures of the Irish literary renaissance must have been obscure to English readers, and with every year they grow more obscure. Such changes seem to leave the stature of the book undiminished: *Hail and Farewell* is one of the world's great autobiographies, though it is unlike any other. Three long volumes of this unique blend of novel and reminiscence, with no more unity of theme than lay in the personality of the narrator and in the singleminded aim (how differently fulfilled!) of all the conspirators who planned to rescue the Irish Cinderella from her rags, contain scarcely a flaw or an irrelevancy. An enormous mass of disparate material went to their making: memories of childhood in Mayo, of France, of Sussex, a visit to Bayreuth, intimate conversations with women, arguments about the Boer War with artists in London, with everybody about everything in Ireland—all these are mingled with those early struggles of the Irish movement which appear to be the theme of the book. How could unity be imposed on such material, generally presented not in recollection, but vividly, at first hand? It might have seemed impossible, but the sense of form was now so strong in Moore that the shape of the whole work came to him, he says, in a week of inspiration: the rough outline from which he never strayed, beginning in the Temple and ending with the visit to Moore Hall. The outline is of a singular perfection; but it may not be until a second or third reading that we perceive it, so vivid and so brilliant is the detail. A great deal of the art of *Hail and Farewell* is the art of transition: never were joins more ingeniously made, and John Eglinton acutely likens the work to a series of galleries opening on one another. Such smoothness is more than a technical triumph, it is proof of the writer's perfect grasp of his subject.

Desmond Shawe-Taylor. Afterword in Joseph Hone,
The Life of George Moore (New York, Macmillan,
1936), pp. 471–72

Mr. Moore is completely lacking in dramatic power. On the face of it, *Esther Waters* has all the appearance of a great novel; it has sincerity, shapeliness, style; it has surpassing seriousness and integrity; but because Mr. Moore has not the strength to project Esther from herself its virtues collapse and fall about it like a tent with a broken pole. There it lies, this novel without a heroine, and what remains of it is George Moore himself, a ruin of lovely language, and some exquisite descriptions of the Sussex downs. For the novelist who has no dramatic power, no fire of conviction within, leans upon nature for support; she lifts him up and enhances his mood without destroying it.

But the defects of a novelist may well be the glories of his brother the autobiographer, and we find, to our delight, that the very qualities which weaken Mr. Moore's novels are the making of his memoirs. . . . He has brought a new mind into the world; he has given us a new way of feeling and seeing; he has devised—very painfully, for he is above all things painstaking, eking out a delicate gift laboriously—a means of liquidating the capricious and volatile essence of himself and decanting it in these memoirs; and that, whatever the degree, is triumph, achievement, immortality. [1942]

Virginia Woolf. *The Death of the Moth* (London,
Penguin Bks., 1961 [orig. pub. Hogarth Press,
1942]), pp. 136, 138

To call *Hail and Farewell* a "sacred book" is a high claim, which is justified. A sacred book need not be directly "inspirational." It may be castigational. Ireland had inspirers. It was good then, and is good still, since a literature is effective and continuously relevant long after the hour when it is written, that she also had a castigator in Moore. To Ireland then and to us who read him now it is obvious what Moore did not and could not see. He did not appreciate the strength of the forces mustering under the surface of the nationalism of 1900–10. Repeatedly he gibed at the patriotic school that the Irishman's dreams are always in conflict with reality, a gibe true but trivial, since the Irish insisted—in the manner of T. E. Lawrence (who participated, by emotional displacement, in a nationalist movement not his own)—on compelling reality to take the shape of their dreams. Moore could not follow the dreamers. If he had, he might have been compelled to make peace with his family, with his antecedents, and that was a decisive impossibility: his brother's image is imposed on Ireland: "my mind reverted to the Colonel, and he stood up in my mind, Ireland in essence, the refined melancholy of her mountains and lakes, and her old castles crumbling among the last echoes of a dying language. In his face, so refined and melancholy, I could trace a constant conflict between dreams and reality. . . ." The future and reconciliation being closed to his view, he sees correspondingly more clearly into the past. As in the 'eighties when he wrote *A Drama in Muslin* he is the recorder of the old Ireland, and now with the keenest sensibility, detecting and recording everything with which there should be no reconciliation. *Ruins and Weed* is the thought in his mind at the beginning of *Ave* when he remembers his childhood and speculates on a title for his book. Implicated in the ruins and weed, he could not take adequate part in the life of revolutionary Ireland. But the ruins and weed had a hold on the land and on the Irish mind. It was important that they should be seen, and it is important that they should be seen now where they still ramify in the body social of Ireland under the welcome changes. They can only be dealt with when recognised, and can best be recognised through the work of the writers, and especially Moore who knew them thoroughly because exclusively, and who described them most realistically and most elegiacally. That is the fundamental sense in which *Hail and Farewell* is a prophet's book, that, though with so much subtlety, with dancing shifts of tone outside the range of the Old Testament, it diagnoses an evil.

Herbert Howarth. *The Irish Writers* (New York, Hill
& Wang, 1958), pp. 69–70

It is a commonplace of literary history that Moore held the decisive point in the line of attack against the tyranny of antiquated Victorian ways in art and literature. If Victorian prudery and evangelical priggishness were a dragon to be slain, Moore, as much as any literary figure, deserves to be remembered as the Siegfried who did the deed. As Ruth Zabriskie Temple has shown, he was not only the most knowing critic of living French and continental culture in late-Victorian England but also its most influential publicist, broader and more generous than his illustrious predecessor, Swinburne, and more authoritative and perceptive than his dedicated contemporary and friend, Arthur Symons. He discovered Laforgue before Ezra Pound was born; and a generation before T. S. Eliot made Bloomsbury familiar with Gérard de Nerval's unhappy Prince of Aquitane of the fallen tower, Moore was quoting with glittering eye the sestet of the same sonnet:

J'ai rêvé dans la grotte où nage la sirène.

How many readers owe their discovery of Balzac, Flaubert, Zola, Turgenev, Huysmans, Verlaine, Manet, Degas, and even Wagner to the infectiousness of Moore's enthusiasm?

Moore's allegiances were both fanatical and mercurial. He was totally devoid of loyalty to yesterday's absolute and ruthless in casting off ideas and emotions, not to say friends, when they no longer served him. The variety of his aesthetic adventures was unparalleled. Every important literary and artistic circle of late-Victorian and Edwardian times saw him arrive—and depart. At one time or another he considered himself to be a pre-Raphaelite, a "decadent," a symbolist, a naturalist, an Ibsenite, a Wagnerian, a Gaelic Leaguer, an imagist, an impressionist, and at last the creator and sole practitioner of his own late literary manner. He embraced no fewer than seven distinct literary styles and manners. This was the peculiarity that occasioned Oscar Wilde's famous jibe, "Moore conducts his education in public," and that led other contemporaries to mutter angrily about his opportunism and meretriciousness. "He stands for nothing," said his estranged brother Maurice somewhat oversimply. The same trait was applauded by his friends as a "passion for self-renewal." He was the most adventurous of the important artistic figures of his time, and his career was an incomparable aesthetic journey, ranging more widely than the careers of Shaw, or Bennett, or Wells, or even Joyce and Yeats, though he did not always return from his expeditions as enriched as they.

Malcolm Brown. *George Moore: A Reconsideration*
(Seattle, Univ. of Washington Pr., 1955),
pp. xii–xiii

By his critical commentary and the example of his early work, Moore helped to inject new vigor and potential into the ailing late Victorian novel. He had studied under Balzac, Flaubert, and Zola who, writing in the realist-naturalist tradition, taught him what he could never have learned about the art of narrative from the Victorians, and thus his novels appeared radically different from the contemporary British novel in technique and purpose as well as theme. The French realists had instilled in him a concern for formal considerations and style in narrative, a concern largely lacking in nineteenth-century English fiction. . . .

Without undue sensation, Moore was one of the first British novelists to deal with the omnipresent power of sexuality in a wholly straightforward, unromantic manner. From *A Modern Lover* to *Héloïse and Abélard* eroticism bulks large in Moore's work. It should be noted that Moore, though a member of the Irish gentry and reputedly a descendant of Sir Thomas More, appeared on the literary scene in 1880 in revolt against the myth of bourgeois propriety and morality.

In contrast to the Victorians, Flaubert and Zola taught him to eschew contrived, improbable plots and to concentrate on a natural, organic unfolding of events. Art, said Flaubert, is not made to paint the exceptions, and therefore the novelist should create and examine ordinary rather than unusual characters. . . . Not only was Moore the first British novelist to embrace the French conception of characterization, he likewise departed from the Victorian custom of manipulating characters for social or moral ends. George Eliot, Meredith, and other Victorian novelists, Walter Myers observed in his study of characterization in the English novel, "were not intent upon the utter truth about individuals or even about types; in the long run they valued actuality, both objective and subjective, as a means of discussing with art and clarity topics of practical social value." Moore, an early partisan of the notion of art for art's sake, was singularly "intent upon the utter truth about individuals," and like most twentieth-century British novelists, his characterizations and works in general in no way buttressed middle-class social values. Like many modern novelists, he believed that the writer is more artificer than interpreter of life, more a creator of meaningful forms than a moral guardian for society.

Douglas A. Hughes. In Douglas A. Hughes, ed., *The Man of Wax: Critical Essays on George Moore* (New York, New York Univ. Pr., 1971), pp. viii–x

Perhaps it was Moore's fascination with oral narration during the last twenty years of his life that increased his interest in writing for the stage. In any case, the period is marked by publication of a number of plays: *Esther Waters* (1913), a skillful dramatization of his most successful novel; *Elizabeth Cooper* (1913), a clever little comedy that makes use once again of a character so unsure of himself that he must borrow the identity of another; *The Coming of Gabrielle* (1920), a revision of *Elizabeth Cooper; The Apostle* (1923), a dramatization of a portion of *The Brook Kerith* (not to be confused with *The Apostle* of 1911, which was little more than a scenario); *The Making of an Immortal* (1927), a humorous tale of an unscrupulous Shakespeare who steals all credit for plays actually written by Bacon and others; *The Passing of the Essenes* (1930), a revision of *The Apostle* as it appeared in 1923. Although never a successful dramatist, Moore was by no means a failure: many of his plays were quite well received, and critics noted particularly his gift for clever dialogue. To what degree the dialogue was his is a matter that invites scholarly investigation. It was no secret that Moore openly sought help in constructing his plays, although the equal responsibility of collaboration usually was too much for him to allow to another.

Moore's interest in oral narration is evident during the last period of his life not only in his last prose style and in the plays of the period but also in the structure of his autobiographical works. Instead of writing reminiscences in the privacy of his library, he preferred to dictate recollections of conversations—real or imaginary—to a secretary. *Conversations of Ebury Street* (1924) was, as a result, more personal than his earlier autobiographies; in it

Moore seems to be facing his readers directly rather than allowing them to look in through the window of his mind.

Janet Egleson Dunleavy. *George Moore: The Artist's Vision, The Storyteller's Art* (Lewisburg, Pa., Bucknell Univ. Pr., 1973), pp. 142–43

In the *Confessions of a Young Man*, the first of several autobiographical works, Moore turned even more directly to the theme of himself as the artist in the process of trying to consolidate his talent. Within a constantly shifting maze of insecurity and doubt obscured by outrageous verbal bluffs, of giddy success plunging to dispossession and pessimism, he charts his early stages as an artist, particularly the French influences. For only in Paris, Moore suggests, can the artist find the combination of atmosphere and companionship necessary to stimulate greatness. Elsewhere, uniformity and democracy soon condemn genius to exhaust itself within the limits of a too common humanity. . . . Despite his ironic distance, Moore enjoys playing the pagan and the snob. Throughout the work, however, shrill declarations of superiority echo off his own doubts about his ability to succeed as an artist.

In his attempts to resolve such uncertainty once and for all, Moore begins in the *Confessions* the mental process that, by the early years of the twentieth century, had firmly enshrined art as his supreme value. If society condemns its members to follow predetermined patterns, the artist can create and command his own, patterns more beautiful and enjoyable than those around him. The inviolate idea of art insulates him against a world of mechanistic formulas and industrial utilitarianism. He was later to explain to Geraint Goodwin: "I have sought and found and taken refuge in art." And in the same conversation: "Art to me is sacred. It is my religion." Without the sanctity of an ideal to sustain him, the artist might lose his creative vision or find himself at the mercy of the crowd's indifference and coarse tastes, forced to earn his survival by slaving over his work like any ordinary factory hand. Industrialization had already swept away traditions and values, even transformed the production of books. Who knew where it might lead? The *Confessions* suggest that "The world is dying of machinery; that is the great disease, that is the plague that will sweep away and destroy civilisation." Such thoughts haunted him most in his early career, when it seemed that civilization might perhaps endure, but not his own standing as an artist.

Wayne E. Hall. *Shadowy Heroes: Irish Literature of the 1890s* (Syracuse, N.Y., Syracuse Univ. Pr., 1980), pp. 88–89

Reverie is the narrative mode of Moore's work, and in it he tries to capture and present, as Monet did, the evanescent past and present, not by reading but in thinking, by *interrupting* reading with thinking. Reading passively follows the past, what has come before, while thinking, more active than reading, joins and engages the present and the past. Thus Moore's "thinking" attempts to achieve a state of conversation rather than the logic of plot: as Moore told his disciple, Charles Morgan, he attempts to capture "the virtue of oral narrative" in which the "passing from plane to plane" of narrative—especially from the "objective" plane of exposition to the "subjective" plane of dialogue—can be achieved in "a disciplined fluency that belongs to a new voice in literature." Moore took pride, Morgan says, "in inventing anecdotes which should sustain the narrative beneath the burden of . . . philosophy," and his anecdotes allow him both the illusion of a "living voice" and the "plan" of a reading; they allow him forgetfulness and remembrance. This is why, I suspect, *Hail and Farewell* culminates in the great revelation of Moore's sexual impotence, why the central event of his personal life in Dublin is what he is unable to do: digression and its forgetfulness, like the never-ending conversations and reveries the trilogy presents, are impotent, seemingly unrelated to what comes next. Impotence is the fact of the self-contradiction of autobiography, the lack at its center. Autobiography can have no "individual" end, but only the illusion of closure that embodies its final forgetting: the "individual death" that transforms Nature into Art is beyond the power, the potency, of autobiography, even while it is its goal. And in this exaggerated contradiction autobiography marks the duplicity at the heart of narrative altogether.

Ronald Schleifer. In Ronald Schleifer, ed., *The Genres of the Irish Literary Revival* (Norman, Okla., Pilgrim Books, 1980), pp. 66–67

If some writers are born, and others are made; then George Moore was both. Few writers of comparable stature have ever allowed themselves to be so governed by studied theories and acquired principles as he was in the composition of the early novels; and yet, once he had mastered other people's ways of doing it and found his own, it is impossible to imagine this voluble, egotistical, eccentric and unpredictable man as other than a writer of highly individual books.

The contrasts are extreme. Whatever the results—and the results are, in at least three instances, quite considerable—there was something more than a little comic in the way he set about applying his French-learned principles and forcing an entrance into English literature, after shrinking rent-rolls and the realisation that he was not destined to be a painter forced this natural *boulevardier* and *bon vivant* back to London in 1880. Everything he did was justified by Zolaesque theory; a lot of what he did would have killed off anybody else's creative impulse straightaway; and he did nothing by halves.

A natural aesthete, he sought out the ugliest and least promising subjects. An impressionist to the core and a lover of all that was fleeting, light and airy, he bent himself nightly to the blue books and the police court reports. In search of material for *A Mummer's Wife* he endured not only a sojourn in Hanley, the ugliest of all the pottery towns, but a stint with a tenth-rate touring company playing French operetta in the dreary Midlands. Everybody knows how he spent hours listening to the maid of all work in the Strand and the laundress in the Temple. Eliza Aria has recorded how he investigated hospital conditions; and Havelock Ellis has told of his interest in the statistics about unmarried mothers.

Yet when George Moore finally achieved his masterpiece he wrote a book which clarified and obeyed his own deepest and most fundamental instincts as a literary artist; was breathtakingly original in form; and, so far from owing much to any contemporary model, anticipated in one way or another most of the masterpieces of the next half-century. And if, moreover, the subject of *Esther Waters*—misfortunate servant girl, or *A Mummer's Wife*—Madame Bovary with tawdry theatrical ambitions, and even of *Evelyn Innes*—rich people with aesthetic pretensions, are too easily defined and too obviously chosen with cold-blooded care, the subject of *Hail and Farewell* is still almost impossible to define or describe. It is certainly not, as Richard Cave seems to think, a history of the Irish Literary Renaissance, for apart from anything else, if it were it would be as dead as mutton. It is certainly not either, as critics with a penchant for cliché have assumed, a record of Dublin doings and gossip. . . .

Nor is it, in any ordinary sense, an autobiography. Moore was an egotistical man who in the early novels had gone far towards suppressing his own ego entirely and performing not only the feat—rare enough for a male novelist—of entering into a woman's psychology; but that of entering into the life of classes and types known to him only from observation as well. By contrast, of course, and in plain subsidiary intention, *Hail and Farewell* is autobiographical, much of it revealing and confessional to a degree not only rare then, but rare at any time when combined with Moore's insights and interest in the world through which his ego-figure moves. . . . He had done what no Irishman had ever done before—and, with the exception of the two ladies [Somerville and Ross] whose masterpiece, *The Real Charlotte*, had appeared the year after *Esther Waters*—what no Irish person has done since. He had written a first-class, straightforward novel which bears comparison with the masterpieces of other literatures. To do this, however, he had had to suppress a great deal of himself; and he had had, to a degree, to turn English and French: adult and responsible. [1982]

Anthony Cronin. *Heritage Now: Irish Literature in the English Language* (New York, St. Martin's Pr., 1983 [first pub. Dingle, Ireland, Brandon, 1982]), pp. 69–71

Although, astonishingly, Celtic tradition is *terra incognita* to many medievalists and modernists, in it certain well-known twentieth-century poets and dreamers have found inspiration for some of their most significant work. The evidence that Moore was among those who borrowed, reworked, and "remoulded" (his word) material from medieval sources, both continental and insular, is strongest in three of his later works.

In the short stories of *A Story-Teller's Holiday* (1918), George Moore drew heavily on the anthology of Old Irish monastic and secular poetry and the lives and legends of Irish saints that had become available to readers of English in the nineteenth century. In *Héloïse and Abélard* (1921) he turned to France for his story of the conflicts of "the cathedral of the thousand arches," the courts of love, and the cult of permissive adultery celebrated in troubadour lyrics. In *Ulick and Soracha* (1926) he grafted the remnants of the fast-fading continental world of castles, crusades, and courtly love on to fourteenth-century Ireland, deep in the throes of the Bruce invasion and savage civil factionalism. Amid this murderous strife Moore returned Ulick de Burgo, *émigré* Irish trouvère and bastard son of the great Red Earl, Richard de Burgo, to Ireland, ostensibly to help his father repulse Edward Bruce, but actually to snatch from her nunnery a compliant Irish princess, daughter of his father's ally.

Moore's preparation for the writing of his three major "medieval" books was thorough and wide-ranging: he drew from his own reading, from extensive travel, and from carefully cultivated associations with historians, philologists, philosophers, and friends who were enthusiastic students of the medieval scene. In the rearrangement and remoulding of his material, Moore telescoped chronology, cut and spliced eras and events, expanded or invented both imaginatively and mischievously on the basis of a clue or suggestion in his sources. For Moore, the thrill of the hunt lay not in recording the killing of kings but in tracking the unicorn of artistic truth. The effect on readers familiar with his medieval sources at first may be disconcerting, somewhat like trying to collate the Irish *Annals of the Four Masters*, held in one hand, with the Duc de Berri's *Book of Hours* held in the other. Moore, however, may have brought off the near impossible merger or integration, not of the facts of "objective history" lying in disparate and remote cells in twelfth-century France and eighth- through fourteenth-century Ireland, but of three artistic themes, popular in medieval literature and selected by him because of their special significance for twentieth-century Ireland. What Moore created, in other words, was not the *speculum* or mirror of medieval iconography but the triptych. In its three panels are presented, first, "The Ruin of Ireland" (an elegy with apocalyptic undertones); second, the antithetical medieval imagery of "Friendly Forest" and "Fearsome Wood" (the former, a nearly pastoral romantic refuge or liberating landscape, the latter, a savage, predatory, alien place); third, another antithesis, the ascetic, self-denying, spiritual love of the monastery cell and the erotic, self-indulgent, profane love of the castle bedchamber.

Gareth W. Dunleavy. In Janet Egleson Dunleavy,
ed., *George Moore in Perspective* (Gerrards Cross,
England, Colin Smythe, 1983), pp. 84–85

MULDOON, PAUL (1951–   )

Paul Muldoon's *Mules* is an interesting and satisfying new collection expressing the poet's often subtle and complex ideas in a taut, concise style. One of Muldoon's basic themes is the conflict in everyone between the "darkness" in our characters, our primeval passions, our sensuousness, and the intellectual detachment emphasized in modern society. In particular, religion is implicated, as the poet reveals our longing for the deep-rooted earth-worship of old, rather than the ethereal sanctity of conventional religion. In the poem "Mules" this sense of division is clearly evoked. . . . Usually Muldoon's description of this primitive pulsing of emotion deep within us is created in a powerful, yet precise and delicate style which is one of his most exciting gifts. . . .

Counteracting our need for immersion in a purely sensuous life, however, the poet finds that the fear of decay and death drives us to philosophical escape, as in the aching poignancy of "At Master McGrath's Grave." The complexities of sexual relationships are also explored by Muldoon, and in this he displays a characteristic economy and skilful accuracy. The poet often feels repelled by the falseness of modern youth, and their rejection of the mystery and promise of their physical natures, so that it is a rare woman who is like "a dappled orchard/That's scarcely been touched by frost" ("De Secretis Mulierum").

Although some of the poems are obscure and difficult, one often finds that they will explode softly into meaning after a few readings, and this discovery is far more rewarding to the reader than the lucidity of a more simple poem. The poet's frequent use of word-play and punning is another impressive facet of his work: in "The Girls in the Poolroom," both the loneliness and the promiscuity of the girls is captured in the image "out on their own limbs," and in "Cider," a beautifully precise phrase crystallizes exactly the drunkard's self-deception: "Now that the glass had taken my other hand."

This collection is certainly a richly rewarding experience for the reader, in both the stimulating boldness of the poet's ideas, and the stark, pared beauty of his style. Although in some of the lesser poems Muldoon may be inclined to ambiguity and obscure references, at his best he is deeply memorable.

Karen Worthy. *AWR*. No. 62, 1978, pp. 146–47

Paul Muldoon's third book, *Why Brownlee Left*, stresses the searching or questing for sources and origins, particularly the question of identity, a theme which has dominated poetry in Northern Ireland from Kavanagh and MacNiece to the present. Mystery is at the center of the book, both in subject matter and in the manner in which individual poems release their meanings, slowly, begrudgingly, waiting for other poems to illuminate them, building toward a unified thematic whole. The book moves by association, as the poet-narrator who appears so often in the poems tries to place parts into a whole with the reader looking over his shoulder. The pattern is reminiscent of the one followed by another seeker after the mystery of identity, Tristram Shandy, who appropriately is echoed in the book's second poem "October 1950," which explores the arbitrary and confusing nature of origins. . . . The attempt to discover whatever it is and to illuminate that dark guide the direction of the book although the search takes us backward in digressions more than we go forward. As if to underscore the theme of searching Muldoon features questers a-plenty; besides Tristram, Ulysses is here, as well as a modern comic version of the Irish wanderer Immram, and the puzzling Brownlee, whose poem gives the book its title.

> Why Brownlee left, and where he went,
> Is a mystery even now.

Questing and searching for meaning and origins reach a high point in the books' final and longest poem "Immram," a modernist version of the Irish saga *Immram Mael Duin*. Here in a 30 stanza rendition combining Byron's *Don Juan* and *Childe Harolde's Pilgrimage*, Muldoon pursues the questing theme—the search for the father—while showing a great talent for comedy and a deftness for language, particularly rhyme in the Byronic style. The story involves a free-wheeling journey in the fast lane through the seedier side of American life as Raymond Chandler might describe it. . . . The plot is thin, "But I wanted to know more about my father./So I drove west to Paradise," and, like *Don Juan*, is pursued only when the poet is tired of digressions. In the process of its unravelling we learn that the poet-narrator finally meets his father, a dilapidated ex-drug smuggler, but only for a brief moment, and ends back at his beginning at Foster's pool hall.

Identity is probed elsewhere in the book with different effects. "The Boundary Commission" poses the ubiquitous Ulster dilemma, "He stood there, for ages,/To wonder which side, if any, he should be on," and "Come

Into My Parlour" describes the final resting place, a "bumpy half-acre of common," where all settle in eventually. . . .

Muldoon's poetry shows a great and growing talent, particularly in his use of language and his sense of form. In this, his latest book, he demonstrates the kind of poetry that drew praises from those who reviewed his earlier book *Mules*, calling him a fresh talent, unusually gifted with a sense of rhythm and a natural vocabulary; he also gives promise of richness and talent yet to come.

Robert F. Garratt. *ILS*. Fall, 1982, p. 15

Paul Muldoon . . . has closed down [the] relationship [between the poet and the City] and revels instead in the enigmatic, the half-said thing, the gesture that suggests it all. For instance, the fragile image of his poem, when cast against its title, illustrates the basic form of Muldoon's poetry:

> The Volkswagen parked in the gap
> But gently ticking over.
> You wonder if it's lovers
> And not men hurrying back
> Across the fields and a river.

The five lines are called "Ireland."

In "The Centaurs" we have a much more substantial example of the process whereby Muldoon takes a mundane, everyday event or image and transforms it. The metamorphosis in "The Centaurs" is one of Muldoon's most accomplished. . . . [Its] clichéd standard image of King Billy, the gable wall mural, becomes, as in the mind of its painter, a great blazing symbol of power and the sumptuousness of The Past, with all its Biblical undertones. What I find so impressive about "The Centaurs" is Muldoon's care: there is no parody, no playing to the literary gods. He is in sympathy with the folklore. Elsewhere this sympathy can seem rather patronising or colloquially self-exclusive but Muldoon's poetry shows an often stunning ability to lift the insignificant detail and the hackneyed clause out of their customary common place and make them new. This invigoration is the hallmark of Muldoon's poetry.

Gerald Dawe. In Maurice Harmon, ed., *The Irish
Writer and the City* (Gerrards Cross, England, Colin
Smythe, 1984), pp. 190–91

As Hermetic poetry, Muldoon's *Quoof* [1983] may violently yoke together comparisons, but it more often trips off a chain reaction of nominatives, a series of re-namings that necessarily include the dark side of the creature named. If a comparison between love and a cultivated garden seemed truthful for the Apollonian Renaissance poet, then Muldoon's bizarre horticultural comparison, between a bomb-blast victim's dismembered foot and "a severely pruned-back shrub" seems an equally truthful description of this Hermetic poet's dark world. Furthermore, the hermetic shape-changer seems intent on showing us that the benign face of the world is a disguise, so that in Muldoon's poetry our habitual and comfortable disposition toward the domestic and everyday is continually violated.

In fact, this poetic shape-changing and re-naming depend on the reader's familiarity with the stable form and standard names that Muldoon's poems transform. For example, the last short lyric of the volume before "The More a Man Has . . . ," entitled "Aisling," should bring to mind the political vision poems of Aogán Ó Rathaille and Eoghan Rua Ó Súilleabháin in which a beautiful, disguised personification of Ireland mourns her captivity and appeals for ransom. . . .

The squeamish reader of Muldoon's poetry must trade the pleasure of noble sentiments for the pleasure of truth: for example, that the Irish aisling wears many disguises and pseudonyms and that she can swallow up the unwitting, or allow them a narrow escape. Muldoon's best reader, however, will prefer the Protean experiences of his poems, often unpleasant, to the tired shibboleths and false truths they replace. The readers who wrestle with these experiences in *Quoof* and derive a truth confirm, to various degrees, Muldoon's version of the Irish tradition, which complements rather than supplants the various versions of Kinsella, Montague, Heaney, and Mahon. However, the method of *Quoof* suggests a new way of addressing the issue of violence in the Irish tradition: by unmasking it and disclosing its various universal aliases rather than by giving it a purely Irish or regional character. As Muldoon adds a distinctive new tone to Irish poetry, he also confirms the strength of this variable tradition. Of the poets studied in this book, the tanist seems to have appeared and the succession to have been assured.

Dillon Johnston. Irish Poetry after Joyce (Notre Dame, Ind., Notre Dame Univ. Pr., 1985), pp. 270, 272

MURDOCH, IRIS (1919–   )

In *The Flight from the Enchanter*, Miss Murdoch seemed to have come to terms with the novel far enough to permit herself a more elaborate plot, and to choose an impersonal narrative form which allowed her to generalize about her characters (Rainborough, for instance) in a series of epigrammatic asides which Hugo could hardly have sanctioned. . . . When *The Sandcastle* appeared, many people welcomed it as a sign that Miss Murdoch's writing had become more "realistic." It would be truer to say that it had become more conventional. The world of *The Sandcastle* is not necessarily more everyday than that of the earlier novels—the gipsy-like man who appears announcing disaster is quite as fantastic as anything in them—but it is more neatly and recognizably an artifact. It is the coherence as well as the plausibility of the plot that reassured critics that Miss Murdoch had, as it were, settled down to her trade. . . . The basic moral issue of *The Bell* is that of fundamentalist or interpretative ethics, as reflected in James's and Michael's sermons. It raises the infinitely difficult question of how far one can be guided by rules as opposed to experience, how far it can be good to renounce the world without knowing it, how far one must know one's own limits before setting oneself any moral objectives at all. . . . It is in every way an astonishing book, and one of its most impressive features is the extreme ease with which so tightly disciplined a conception is carried out. Even the style is supremely confident. . . .

In the light (if it is a light) of this, what can one make of *A Severed Head*? Obviously, Miss Murdoch has become more formal still—perhaps following as large a change of course as was marked by the publication of *The Sandcastle*. In her two previous novels the figures move to some extent in a pattern; in *A Severed Head* they go through an elaborate minuet worthy of Mr. Henry Green, in which six partners try out every possible heterosexual combination except one (Honor Klein and Alexander). Indeed the novel contains, in a sense, nothing but form. . . . The characters' backgrounds and occupations seem merely designed, as in the most crudely romantic novel, to give them the money and the leisure to pursue an intricate scheme of personal relations; and their personalities vanish in the midst of their own involvements. . . . The imperfections of *The Sandcastle* were a small and (if the suggestions of this article are true) a necessary price to pay for the smooth perfection of *The Bell*; the sequel to *A Severed Head* may be equally remarkable.

Francis Hope. *LondonMag*. August, 1961,
pp. 84–87

Each of Iris Murdoch's first four novels has, as its title, an image of the kind of illusion its characters face. The first novel, *Under the Net* (1954), tells the story of Jake Donaghue's wanderings about Bohemian London and Paris as he attempts to find or construct a satisfactory way of life. But planned ways of life are nets, traps, no matter how carefully or rationally the net is woven, and Jake discovers that none of these narrow paths really works. The nets in the novel range from logical-positivist philosophy and left-wing politics through miming theatricals to film scripts and sophisticated blackmail. In the second novel, *The Flight from the Enchanter* (1956), Miss Murdoch deals with a different sort of illusion. All the characters are under spells, enchantments, held in a kind of emotional captivity by another person or force. The principal agent of enchantment, an ephemeral cosmopolite named Mischa Fox, exercises a spell over a number of the other characters in the novel; yet he feels no responsibility for the effects of the spells he exercises and the spells provide no real meaning or satisfaction for the characters caught in them. Emotional enchantment works no better than the weaving of conscious and rational nets, and the characters are eventually forced, by their own natures, to flee enchantment as they must unravel nets. The third novel is called *The Sandcastle* (1957). The title is emblematic of the love affair a married, fortyish schoolteacher tries to build with a young artist named Rain. But the affair cannot last; it is a castle of sand. As Rain explains, when talking about her Mediterranean background, she has known only dry, dirty sand, unsuitable for building castles of any shape or form. From the schoolteacher's point of view, Rain provides too much energy, too much vitality, for him to cope with in his circumscribed world, as a deluge of rain can wash away a sandcastle. And, significantly, there is a torrential rain on the day when the school teacher displays his inability to deal with all the complications of the affair. The elements of the affair—the grains of sand and moisture—exist, but the sand is either too dry or too wet. Human beings are unable to control the moisture, to build a lasting shape out of the illusory dream, and the castle either crumbles or is washed away.

In Miss Murdoch's fourth novel, *The Bell* (1958), a group of people in a lay religious community attempt to place a bell on the tower of a nearby abbey. The bell is a postulant, a means of entering the religious life for each of the people involved. But the bridge leading to the abbey has been tampered with and, in its journey, the bell topples into the lake. The bell itself, the effort of human beings to construct and particularize their own means of salvation, is undermined by human action, emotion, and behavior. At the same time the traditional bell, the bell that once actually pealed from the abbey tower, is recovered from the lake by two of the least devout characters and sent to the British Museum as a historical curiosity. The tradition of the past is meaningful only for antiquarians, is removed from the central issues of experience, while the contemporary bell is another illusion, the image of another unsuccessful human attempt.

James Gindin. *Postwar British Fiction: New Attitudes and Accents* (Berkeley, Univ. of California Pr., 1963), pp. 178–79

All Miss Murdoch's novels can in an important sense be seen as studies of the "degrees of freedom" available to individuals. . . . The kinds of freedom studied vary, and the style and matter of the novels also vary greatly, but there is, I would maintain, a surprisingly constant unity of theme underlying the ideas of all the seven novels we have so far. Between the first two novels, *Under the Net* and *The Flight from the Enchanter*, and the third, *The Sandcastle*, there is a break—not only a stylistic attempt to move from fantasy-myth to depiction of character, but a break in subject-matter. The first two books have a social dimension, an emphasis on the possibilities of man's freedom in society at large and mechanized, an interest in work, in the sense of jobs, which is not importantly present in the later novels, which are more concerned with freedom within personal relationships, with Jamesian studies of one person's power over, or modification of another person—although both ideas are of course present in most of the novels.

The Flight from the Enchanter is certainly concerned with one individual's power over another within relationships as well as socially, and the problem of freedom in work, or how work limits freedom, recurs both in the organization of the community in *The Bell*, and in Mor's struggles with his job and the Labour party, or even Rain Carter's painting, in *The Sandcastle*. And the problem which Jake Donaghue encounters from time to time in *Under the Net*, the problem of economic freedom, of whether he can accept large sums of dishonourably earned money in order to live free of economic necessity, also, in a different form, besets Randall in *An Unofficial Rose*, who buys a kind of freedom with the money obtained from the sale of his father's Tintoretto.

But the general idea with which I want to begin the study of the freedom of the characters in the novels is that this freedom is worked out, very broadly speaking, in terms of a constant—and, in the nature of things, incomplete and unresolved—interaction of their own attempts to act, or to order their experience (a process which constantly degenerates into "deforming" reality by fantasy) with the transcendent "reality."

A. S. Byatt. *Degrees of Freedom: The Novels of Irish Murdoch* (New York, Barnes & Noble, 1965), pp. 11–12

I feel obliged to clarify further my use of the term *philosophical novelist* as it applies to Iris Murdoch. Unlike L. H. Myers or Thomas Mann in *The Magic Mountain*, she does not openly discuss philosophical ideas in her fiction. When her characters consider problems in ethics and morals, the problems are never presented as abstract doctrine. Her philosophical interest is always social morality rather than a moral code or set of principles that the reader is invited to apply to action and plot. Blending moral action and narrative structure, her novels convey a great urgency. The theme of prose fiction since the eighteenth century has been man's life in society, and the prevailing narrative method has been empirical. By refusing to sacrifice the individual to a principle or a universal, Iris Murdoch has contributed to and possibly enlarged the great tradition. Her philosophical essays make clear that without theory there can be no morality; with Socrates, Buber, and Marcel, she believes that the clarification of thought must precede man's redemption. This theoretical bias gains expression in the novels in the form of closely observed character inter-action. The portrayals of Michael Meade in *The Bell*, Emma Sands in *An Unofficial Rose*, and Otto Narraway in *The Italian Girl* reveal that ethical sys-tems matter far less than personal conduct. The final test of any professed mo-rality is direct social experience. Life is not a thought system, and any attempt to reduce it to one involves a falsification. But by dramatizing concrete situa-tions, the novelist shows personal conduct fortifying and even creating moral value.

The priority of distinct, incarnate beings and the attendant belief that man is his own measure also rule out a political reading of the novels: Iris Murdoch's primary emphasis as a moralist is the free discovery of self and of other selves within the living tissue of human imperfection. Although she has stated an academic preference for Guild Socialism in one of her essays, I do not find the criticism of political institutions a major accent in her novels, with the possible exception of *The Flight from the Enchanter*. Like Amis, Wain, and Sillitoe in this aspect, she never uses such terms as *the proletariat* and *di-alectical materialism*. But, unlike these writers, she studies the individual as a conscious entity responsible for making decisions that acknowledge the same degree of consciousness and reality in others. In this respect her awareness of social life may be called philosophical, for she sees the concrete presence of other people as something to be thought as well as perceived through the senses. The emphasis in her work on immediate experience suggests the term *novels of social education* rather than *novels of ideas*, per se. And her philo-sophical attitude is permeated by her artistic method, which combines objec-tivity and closely observed social relations; in our contingent world, dynamic interpersonal relations furnish the only escape from materialism and abstrac-tion and the only likely approach to transcendent values.

Peter Wolfe. *The Disciplined Heart: Iris Murdoch
and Her Novels* (Columbia, Univ. of Missouri Pr.,
1966), pp. 23–24

It is not the matter of specific Irish writers which is finally of greatest impor-tance in trying to assess Murdoch's debt to her Irish connection; it is, rather, in the less definable and demonstrable matters of her use of setting, her sense of the value of individual difference in characters, and her tolerance for and use of eccentricity as a way of achieving individual difference in a world of reductively dreary sameness. It is only sensible to acknowledge at once that any one of these aspects of Murdoch's work could have come to her from other sources, and, perhaps, ultimately did, but there is the inescapable fact that these aspects are strong indeed in the work and attitudes of those writers from Swift to Yeats who formed the modern Irish consciousness.

Murdoch uses setting for effect more unabashedly than most modern writers, except perhaps American Southern writers (who have their affinities with Irish writers), and while it is certainly true that a nineteenth-century English writer like Scott, whom Murdoch cites with approval in another context, could have provided her with her model for settings, it could have come as well out of the Irish literary tradition. In her penchant for the extremes of pastoral sunshine and gothic mists, for example, the influence could easily have been the Synge of *In the Shadow of the Glen, The Well of the Saints*, or *Deirdre of the Sorrows*. The perhaps overcareful emphasis upon the rain in *The Red and the Green* and the setting of Gaze Castle in *The Unicorn* are two cases which can be set beside the pastoral moment of the sunlit meadow in *The Sandcastle*, a moment which, insofar as versions of pastoral cannot be sustained, is quickly undercut by the weight of a real world in which expensive motor cars slowly but inexorably overturn to settle on their tops in crystal-clear rivers.

Equally difficult to establish with absolute certainty but coincidental enough to bear consideration is the insistence by Murdoch on eccentricity, the exaggeration of character and gesture which is everywhere in the Irish literary tradition. Again, it is clear that Murdoch's model might be elsewhere in Dickens, perhaps, but in the use Murdoch makes of eccentricity for mounting an attack on the comfortable veneer of middle-class life the echoes are those of Synge or Yeats, O'Casey or Joyce. Yet there is in Murdoch none of the rage associated with such attacks in these writers. Although her mode is also comedy, an ironic detachment like that Murdoch so admires in certain nineteenth-century English writers is a fact that makes it difficult to push too hard an exclusive claim of Irish influence in the treatment of character. Murdoch's eclecticism makes it difficult to speak of her solely within the Irish context, and yet it virtually guarantees that the force of her Irish background is to be felt, if only indirectly.

Donna Gerstenberger. *Iris Murdoch* (Lewisburg,
Pa., Bucknell Univ. Pr., 1975), pp. 77–79

A patient study of Murdoch's work reveals how deceptive the bourgeois surface in fact is, and how ironic her deployment of its materials. Although she operates structurally from situation and character, the process of her best books involves a subtle peeling-off of layers of bourgeois complacency and prejudice. Her primary tools are a devastating accuracy in the detail of human character and an enormous allusive frame which pushes the reader toward a willingness to see how large her intentions are. When the allusions fail, as they tend to in early novels like *A Severed Head* and *The Italian Girl*, the result is overplotted, tricksy books where the profound laws of causality central to Murdoch's thought are lost in clever satire. When these allusions to mythology, art and religion are functioning at a high level of imaginative power, however, their syncretic force is such that they become images assisting the novel towards profound and unnerving ends. These ends are religious in impact, but the novels never succumb to the warm fuzziness of consoling or salvational piety. Great mystics are invoked, especially Julian of Norwich and occasionally St. John of the Cross, and Christ actually makes a personal appearance in one novel, but the real direction of the fiction works through the characters of the workaday world which realism has always used as its basis: as a character in *Nuns and Soldiers* describes the process, the problem for Murdoch is "to try, to invent, to work through our nature against our nature." The goal is spiritual discernment; the enemy, debasement of the religious task.

The fact that ultimate reality, even the cosmos itself, lies behind the drifting and often frenetic bourgeois surface is the vast secret of Murdoch's best fiction, and the sheer nerve and ambition required in the projection of such a stage on which to place traditional realism make her fictions risky in the extreme. There can be no doubt, for example, that it is correct to read *A Fairly Honourable Defeat* as an oblique commentary on the combat of good and evil and the defeat of the Christian Trinity, and yet its psychological verisimilitude deflects the allegorical loftiness of its conception. Similarly, Murdoch's often studied references to sainthood are seen in her serious work as an ironic chimera, a product of bourgeois optimism and atavistic memory of a golden age long since past. As she studies the realms of ethics and spirituality in novel after novel, it becomes clear that such conceptions as sainthood are too sadly far from the realist world of our present, and the mediocrity of our response to her hard, cool moral discriminations can keep us from pursuing them in their final implications.

Art itself at its highest can be seen as equally elusive and impossible, largely because of its commitment to trickery and magic, yet the infinite usefulness of great art provides the base of Murdoch's connotative artistic practice. In *The Nice and the Good*, she evokes a painting which can be read as a central reference against which her work can be placed: Bronzino's *Allegory* in the National Gallery in London, in which Venus and Cupid are frozen in an elegant eternal kiss while Time either reveals them by removing the blue veil or prepares to annihilate them by shrouding them from sight. This image of beauty, idleness, sexuality and *luxuria* is puzzlingly positive and negative as it uncovers and displays, yet threatens concealment. Certainly much of Murdoch's work can be seen as an exposure of *luxuria* and decadence, but the sense of its hidden beauty, the problems of eternality and transience, the statements of lack of quality and duration in human activity, love, or recognition of truth, are all part of the power of her endlessly complex accomplishment.

Elizabeth Dipple. Iris Murdoch: Work for the Spirit
(Chicago, Univ. of Chicago Pr., 1982), pp. 3–4

It is always dangerous to impute a character's views to an author: but in Iris Murdoch's case there is a special hazard. Just because she does seem to hold that what makes utterances true or false is not the same as what makes statements true or false, so that a true statement can be uttered as a falsehood (but not, I take it, vice versa), Iris Murdoch's characters sometimes appear, for the moment at least, to deprive Iris Murdoch's philosophical views of credibility by the way in which they utter them. So in *The Time of the Angels* as the two brothers, Marcus and Carel, move unerringly and unintentionally towards disaster, what Marcus utters to himself as false consolation are pieces of Iris Murdoch's own philosophy. Marcus is writing a book called "Morality in a World Without God" in which he attacks those who have tried to understand judgments about goodness as expressions of will or choice in just the way that Iris Murdoch has done in more than one essay. Carel, an Anglican priest who no longer believes in God, and according to whom no one has as yet understood in a sufficiently radical way the consequences of not believing, embodies a view of which Iris Murdoch has said that she "is often half persuaded," but which she finally rejects: the view that if God is not credible, then Good too is a superstition. Marcus after the disaster reflects: "Would he go on working on his book? Perhaps it was a book which only a genius could write, and he was not a genius. It might be that what he wanted to say about love and about humanity was true but simply could not be expressed as a theory."

What this suggests is not only that a truth may be uttered so that it is a lie, but that moral truth may be such as to evade *any* theoretical expression—perhaps with the consequence that all theoretical expression of it will be to some degree a lie. Iris Murdoch's novels are philosophy: but they are philosophy which casts doubts on all philosophy including her own. She is an author whose project involves an ironic distance not only from her characters but also from herself.

Alasdair MacIntyre. *LRB*. June 3, 1982, p. 15

The Red and the Green is clearly an Irish historical novel in terms of its subject matter as well as many of the conventions it adopts. The Irish literary influences apparent in Murdoch's work are fellow travelers among the Ascendancy: [Sheridan] Le Fanu, [Standish] O'Grady, and Yeats. Her novel *The Unicorn* (1963) was a Gothic novel influenced by the work of Le Fanu. In *The Red and the Green*, the antiquarian Christopher Bellman expresses opinions remarkably like those of O'Grady: "Ireland's real past *is* the ascendancy. Ireland should turn back to the eighteenth century." Arguing that Anglo-Irish leaders of the eighteenth century would have worked with English leaders to relieve the Great Famine, Bellman calls the romantic Pearse an "idiot" and echoes O'Grady's nostalgia for the Anglo-Irish "Patriot Parliament" of Grattan and Flood. Similarly, throughout the novel there are echoes of Yeats, especially at the end, where the tone and even the language of the 1938 "Epilogue" to the Rising are very close to Yeats's pronouncement that the leaders of 1916 have been transformed, that "a terrible beauty is born."

As in [Walter] Macken's novels, a new sense of distance from history is evident in *The Red and the Green*. Writing in the 1960s, Murdoch has the detachment necessary to explore her main theme: the conflicts between energy and order, rebellion and law, eros and impotence, among an Anglo-Irish family fifty years earlier. But in contrast to Macken's chronologically sprawling novels, *The Red and the Green* is focused upon just a few days before and during the Rising in April 1916. This permits an interesting comparison of the novel to O'Flaherty's similarly focused *Insurrection*—a comparison which yields, for the most part, contrast more than semblance. . . .

Much of the criticism on *The Red and the Green* quite rightly focuses upon character conflicts in the novel; character is always Murdoch's prime concern. Weldon Thornton, for example, points out that the novel's characters seek an elusive balance between energy and order, passion and control, always desiring the qualities in others which they feel to be lacking in themselves. Pat Dumay's cousin Andrew Chase-White is jealous of Pat's resoluteness and courage—qualities we discover to be deceptive. Christopher Bellman seems to possess British restraint and good sense, but then he perishes on his way to join the rebels in the General Post Office. Barney Drumm seeks courage by participating in the Rising and then shoots himself in the foot. Aunt Millie seeks true individuality and discovers merely roles, a facade. These character conflicts possess a broader political, historical significance. The most important conflict is that between Andrew Chase-White and Pat Dumay, for they are really the Red and the Green of the novel, and they never understand each other.

James M. Cahalan. *Great Hatred, Little Room: The
Irish Historical Novel* (Syracuse, N.Y., Syracuse
Univ. Pr., 1983), pp. 165–66, 168

MURPHY, RICHARD (1927–   )

It would not be fair to Richard Murphy to dub him a "Nature" poet; he is certainly not that, but he uses an imagery that is almost exclusively natural, and recognisably Irish. In one of his most successful poems he gives me the impression of speaking through Nature, that is to say that his feelings are transmitted to the elements. The result is clearly fine writing. . . .

Mr. Murphy—who has distinguished himself by winning the AE Memorial Award—cannot properly be termed an exile, for the very good reason that he now lives in Co. Galway, however I do insist that the time he *has* spent abroad, mainly in England, has heightened his poetic powers. His work is possibly more introspective (in a sense of the word modified by what I have said above) than that of Patrick Galvin, but it is not unhealthily so—indeed there is a clarity about his poetry which is admirable.

Richard Murphy's images are hard and crystalline, he uses words with an almost fastidious precision, which is certainly justified in the face of the present shoddy state of our terminology. His failures occur through over-wordiness—so infrequent a fault that it is strikingly apparent among his usual economic use of words. This economy is a great power in Mr. Murphy's hands.

Gordon Wharton. *Irish Writing*. Sept., 1953, p. 59

A volume from an Irish poet is a rarity in these desolate days. Richard Murphy's book would be a welcome one for that reason alone, apart from its own merits, as a sign that the pulse still beats. In fact it is a book which all who are interested in current Irish writing should read.

Mr. Murphy was the AE Memorial Award winner in 1951. *The Archaeology of Love* is thus, in a way a near relation of Patrick Kavanagh's *The Great Hunger* and Valentin Iremonger's *Reservations*, but it would be unfair to judge it in company with these, as the selection of poems is too small— they number eighteen—to represent Mr. Murphy's work fully.

It is clear at once that his verse is totally different from that of either of his predecessors. He is conscious of textures in language in a way that Mr. Kavanagh could not be and Mr. Iremonger would not care to be.

In lyrics set in Crete, and places nearer home, his use of the short line and staccato, breaking rhythms keeps the verse taut, and yet not spare, because of a choice in words which tends towards a sensuous density of sound:

"Poems are songs," the Master said
"Piped by finches of Mantegna
As barley foments to bread
And milk into curds is shaken
By a shepherd's earthen hand."

His poems have in general a . . . consistent strength. . . . *The Archaeology of Love* is the product either of careful and wise selection or of a very even talent. Which is not to say, of course, that some poems do not rise above nor fall below their general average.

A few of them, for instance "September on the Embankment," "Dépaysé" and "The Photographer," are perhaps a little confused, not in themselves, but by reason of a certain over-ripeness; the substance of language and imagery runs together in too close a poem.

But there are some very good poems. "Eclogue in the Louvre" (the first stanza is quoted above), "Samson's Secret," the title poem and, if I may say so without seeming arch, the dedicatory verse, have succeeded and made satisfying lyrics. . . . The opening stanzas of "In Thanks for a Flask of Wine" [are] possibly the best in this worthwhile little book.

Thomas Kinsella. Irish Writing. Winter, 1955–56,
pp. 62–63

Of the significant Irish poets to emerge since the last war, Richard Murphy is the least introspective or tempted toward confessional writing. He shows exceptional narrative and elegiac powers, and his poems are highly local, sentimentally so when they are not rescued by his talent for loading every rift with objective details—and quite deliberately not with Romantic ore, especially of the psychomined variety. Fundamentally, he is an old-fashioned, rather conventional poet. Reading his "The Cleggan Disaster" and "Sailing to an Island," both poems about stormy sailing off the Connemara coast, one wants to check back to poems like Masefield's neglected *Dauber* or even to the relevant passages in Hopkins's "The Wreck of the *Deutschland*" for comparison. Mr. Murphy knows sailing—it has almost become his trade—and these accounts are sparklingly concrete and exciting. They serve a timeless artistic purpose in the way they repossess a particular kind of experience and lifestyle. Nostalgia for a lost and (sayeth the poet) a nobler past, as seen from the viewpoint of the Ascendancy, is heavy in these pieces.

M. L. Rosenthal. The New Poets (New York, Oxford
Univ. Pr., 1967), pp. 306–7

Some may hold that a poem should contain its own clarifications, but Mr. Murphy [in *The Battle of Aughrim*], speaking in the present (in his opening section) can justly say, "The past is happening today." The Matter of Aughrim is remote only in its particulars. In the week in which I write this, the Ulster government of Captain O'Neil has barely survived riots and a bitter election brought on by the most recent exacerbation of the very issues left, alas, unsettled by Aughrim or by any subsequent battle: these painful divisions of English vs. Irish, Catholic vs. Protestant interests survive, the unhealed wounds of a country tragically divided.

Mr. Murphy is a proven adept of the long narrative poem, but he has eschewed the straightforward telling of "The Cleggan Disaster" in *Sailing to an Island* (1963). A modern poet writing of history cannot help but have in mind the example of *The Cantos*, and an Irish poet must, besides, come out of the long shadow cast by Yeats. Mr. Murphy sounds a different note, his own, by adopting strategies consonant with his rather Augustan sensibility. An inheritor of traditions of the Ascendancy, he takes an objective view of history. His crucial event is chosen from a period not preempted by Yeats—neither the mythopoesis of Bronze Age demigods, nor the Easter Rising. To be sure, there are some intentional Yeatsian echoes. . . .

The first of the poem's four sections is "Now," a series of lyrics, some personal, which clarify the legacy of the battle—the despair and hatreds it bequeathed—before we participate in the ironical design of the event. The three succeeding sections are set "Before," "During," and "After" the battle. Each contains from five to ten brief poems, some lyric, some dramatic, some narrative, in various forms and meters. One—St. Ruth's sanctimonious address to his troops—is in prose; another, a versified quotation from a contemporaneous English history. Thus the texture is continually varied, juxtaposing effectively to the foreign commander's hauteur, his distrust of the lowly people he was commissioned to defend; juxtaposing to the righteous rhetoric of apologists for either side, the barbarity of both armies toward civilians and to each other; juxtaposing, too, the self-serving treachery of Luttrell and lesser turncoats to the butchery of their defeated countrymen. As Murphy says of Sarsfield, "Nothing he will do, or has done/Can stop this happening."

The directness of diction reinforces the dramatic objectivity of vision, isolating significant action with the economy of an ancient ballad. Though the texture of the lines is simple, the movement of history in the poem is complex. *The Battle of Aughrim* is surely one of the most deeply felt and successfully rendered interpretations of history in modern Irish verse, and in poetry in English in our generation. Seeking an American analogue, only Lowell's *Benito Cereno* seems comparable in intention, scope, and achievement.

Daniel Hoffman.*Poetry*. Aug., 1969,
pp. 342–44

Murphy is the poet who has most obsessively engaged in a kind of ancestral accountancy, tackling the theme of "Ireland" in an even more head-on fashion than the equally involved John Montague. Murphy's obsessiveness, his concern with the external facts of history, may be explained by an anxiety not only to digest Ireland but that Ireland should digest him. . . .

In seeking a "truly Irish" identity Murphy also seeks absolution from Ascendancy guilts. His persona in *Sailing to an Island* suggests the ex-landlord whose isolation or Absentee-ism has now turned against himself, returning to his ruined and lost possessions, with their legacy of human ruin, to attempt expiation and a revitalizing contact with the natives. The title-poem dramatizes the difficulties of such a pilgrimage. . . . There are in fact two islands, two Irelands, in the poem. Clare Island, the "chosen" destination, "its crags purpled by legend" as they might have been by the early Yeats, proves as inaccessible as the "mirage" and "dreams" it evokes. And it has to be exchanged for the disenchanting actualities of contemporary Inishbofin towards which the tide runs more favourably, and where the poet eventually finds a "bed." Even this harbour, attained after he has exiled himself from the pub chatter, is shadowed by the ambiguity—"the moon stares/Cobwebbed through the window"—which has characterized the whole journey with its sense of obstacles to be overcome or screens to be penetrated. The heavy seas off the cliffs of Clare Island, the boat with its "rotten hull" "bucking" as if to throw off its passengers, symbolize the racial experience which divides the visitor from true sailors and islanders. Such experience may be mimetically recreated "in holiday fashion," or in a poem, but can it ever be truly "known" or shared? . . . The answer is almost certainly "yes," despite an apparently penitential episode on Inishbofin: "I slip outside, fall among stones and nettles." . . .

It is hard to fault "The Battle of Aughrim" on its many-faceted adjustment of history to poetry, on humane intention, historical conscience and emotional accuracy, on precision of detail and image. But something programmatic in its design and designs (the poem was commissioned by the B.B.C. Third Progamme) stands in the way of total subjection to the offered experience. . . . The determined confrontation of History (compare Geoffrey Hill's "Funeral Music" launched under similar auspices) must involve a certain exteriority, the jettisoning of concerns which lie outside or inside that part of the self defined in terms of race and family. Despite the concreteness and power of individual scenes Murphy rings the changes on a rather limited number of components: the tensions, ironies and paradoxes of history, present set against past, violence against landscape—all adumbrated in the very first poem. The sequence itself is drawn up in battle-lines. It could be argued that the sea-poems (not the house-poems) in *Sailing to an Island* exhibit the same exteriority, coupled with a more monotonously documentary approach—the boat-lore ceases to grip—and louder gear-changing into the symbolic. The fact that the poetry goes so much more than halfway to meet the critic who is himself questing for "Irishness" may arouse suspicion.

Edna Longley. In Douglas Dunn, ed., *Two Decades of Irish Writing* (Chester Springs, Pa., Dufour, 1975), pp. 127, 130

Murphy's stiffness . . . is that of a man moving in a constricted space. The elemental characters and incidents in his work are not frozen in a heraldic procession but are in motion behind the pane of the style, where they are observed not with votive attachment but with precise detachment. They represent neither an exemplary nor an alternative world but are rendered as aspects of the world we inhabit and, if the epic note is occasionally sounded above them, they maintain a documentary presence that almost shrugs off heroism. Whereas Mackay Brown offers his world as the emblem of a desirable culture to which he would be affiliated, Murphy conducts us into a bleak and beautiful environment toward which he is sympathetic but finally ambivalent. Murphy's fidelity to the world of boatmen and tinkers and natural beauties and disasters does not altogether constitute a faith in it because that world is inadequate to his social and cultural recognitions. It is valid in so far as the poet participates in it as boatman, as neighbour, as eavesdropper, as annalist, but it is unsatisfactory because this participation can never be total. Murphy will not surrender his sense of caste, his manners, his educated consciousness, his willed individuality to this essentially communal fatalistic and half-literate culture, however attractively that culture presents itself to his imagination. The constricted space he moves in and writes out of is a march between his Anglo-Irish Protestant background and his Irish Catholic surroundings, a space at once as neutral and torn as the battlefield at Aughrim, as problematic and personal as the house he builds for himself from ruined famine cottages, sometimes invaded by nostalgia for the imperial, patrician past, sometimes hospitable to deprivations and disasters which somehow rebuke that heritage.

The title poem of his first collection, *Sailing to an Island*, discovers that space in the shape of a narrow bed, a point of rest attained after some bruising of the social self. The poem is at once a direct narrative about a boat trip, full of the swing and threat of the sea, confident in its relish of sailing lingo, rich in evocation of atmospheres; and at the same time it is a parable of another journey between cultures, from the sure ground of a shared but disappearing Ascendancy world to the suspecting community of the native islanders.

Seamus Heaney. *IUR*. Spring, 1977, pp. 18–19

So Murphy resembles Irish poets of his generation in both his initial indifference to his identity as an Irish writer, and his return home and inward, to family life, history, and place to discover who he is. But it is not enough to define Murphy in the Anglo-Irish tradition alone. A year after submitting *Sailing to an Island* to Faber and Faber, Murphy spoke of his background on BBC radio. "The Pleasure Ground" is a prerequisite to any understanding of his early poetry and more particularly of his attraction to the sea. In it he describes his movement from the order and tranquility of his ancestral estate in Aughrim to the barrenness of Connemara. As a boy, he lived blissfully on his grandfather's demesne whose garden "was surrounded by an Anglo-Irish wall." With his brother and sister he helped his mother to restore order to the garden that had run wild. The joy which came from exploring and ordering the garden permeated his education. At this time one of the children's tutors changed his interest from music to Milton, Wordsworth, and Eliot. Young Richard Murphy also discovered Connemara—its sea, mountains, and people.

Murphy was captivated by the West. It was bold and full of the promise of order, especially the sea, which became for him "that greatest of pleasure grounds." He marvelled at the local children who "were truly Irish and that is what my brother and I wanted to be. . . . We wished we could talk like them." But Murphy was never to talk like them, for at the age of fourteen, he won a scholarship to an English school. Death and emigration soon left his grandmother alone in Aughrim and the garden fell back into anarchy and decay.

This is the crux then. Connemara, which had been Murphy's original "pleasure ground," became the focus of his full attention. By identifying with the place and its people, he grafted himself onto their heritage and bridged the two cultures. After Oxford, Murphy spent two years in the West, alone and poor, working among other things, as a night watchman on the Erriff River. To this place he returned after his English and Mediterranean travels. At last on his "chosen Island," Murphy is drawn to the truth of a place—its drama and history. His poems are embedded in locale simply because they are accurate recordings of actual events. He has, in Ted Hughes's words, "the gift of epic objectivity." His concern is the world of action, of building, fishing, and living, of storms and drownings. He strikes one as an observer in "The Poet on the Island," or as a voyeur in "Seals at High Island," or as a listener in "Pat Cloherty's Version of *The Maisie*." Sometimes he enters the poem as a character. In "The Last Galway Hooker," situating the boat in the locale and in history, he sees himself in a historical line. In buying the boat, Murphy "marries" himself to the region.

Mark Kilroy. Éire-Ireland. Fall, 1981, pp. 129–30

Aside from his purchase and care of High Island, one of Murphy's most interesting Irish concerns has been his generous and symbolic rehabilitation of a family of tinkers. In 1972 he learned of an itinerant family in which the parents were estranged and the seven children put into an industrial school and an orphanage. Working to get the family back together, Murphy accepted responsibility for them, and obtained a house for them in Cleggan. Endeavoring literally to domesticate them, he discovered that the children liked keeping goats, and he bought pasture land for that occupation on nearby Omey Island (assessible at low tide). When I met him at Bard College in 1974, he told me that he had brought the two boys of the family with him to America, so that when they returned to Ireland they would be looked up to for that distinction, and given a much-needed "leg-up" in their lives.

Murphy's poem "The Reading Lesson" conveys some of the problems of this rehabilitation of the tinkers, and most importantly, the reason for his work on their behalf. The problems include the tinker's own unregenerate attitude, resisting the difficult business of learning to read:

> He looks at a page as a mule balks at a gap
> From which a goat may hobble out and bleat. . . .

The boy complains, "I'll be the same man whatever I do," and protests, "I'll not read anymore." The poet asks "Should I give up?" and in this is confronted by another problem for the tinkers, the attitude of other Irish toward them: "A neighbor chuckles, 'You can never tame / The wild duck: when his wings grow, he'll fly off.'" But the poet perseveres, because he sees the tinker boy with "hands, longfingered as a Celtic scribe's," and he believes that the tinkers of modern Ireland are the descendants of the Celtic bards who were turned out of their positions by the British invaders to find their lives in the lanes and hedges. Thus, the tinkers are highly and importantly symbolic to Murphy; in helping them he is restoring a rightful Irish patrimony. Regardless of whether Murphy's hypothesis about the tinkers' origin is correct or not, what matters in his commitment to the Irish past and the sense of duty it generates. The arduous task of bringing two boys, one nine and one fourteen, to America for a year is not explained adequately by Heaney's [charge of] "nostalgia." It is more understandable as an action informed by a sincere sense of justice and duty, the qualities that define *pietas*.

James D. Brophy. In James D. Brophy and Raymond
J. Porter, eds., Contemporary Irish Writing (Boston,
Iona College Pr./Twayne, 1983), pp. 61–62

In each of these fifty poems in the sequence [*The Price of Stone*, 1984], the speaker is a building or site, often an intimate of some period in the poet's life and sometimes a monumental correlative of the disposition of the poet or that of his Anglo-Irish forebears. To an extent, *The Price of Stone* may be seen as a literal, and therefore parodic, poetic rendering of the "big house" novel, pathologies of the Anglo-Irish Ascendancy by such writers as Kevin Casey, Aidan Higgins, and Jennifer Johnston. For example, an Ascendancy extravaganza, a "Folly," remains epicene, useless, and "Bricked up against vandals"; an anachronistic Victorian "Lead Mine Chimney" can only "go on uttering, while I may, / In granite style, with not a word to say." Other structures address the poet about his poetry. Wellington College, in Berkshire, which Murphy attended between 1943 and 1945, is made to speak candidly about poetic reticence. . . .

The "you" accused or addressed by conversant structures is usually the poet but also, because of irreversible convention, the reader. Consequently, as the stones confess or insinuate aspects of the poet's life, we share an intimate address with the poet. This approach to tone works with remarkable subtlety throughout the sequence as the referents for the second- and first-person pronouns converge or separate. For example, a "Georgian Tenement" appeals to youthful protestors who would block its demolition. . . . By such appeals a poet has drawn his audience to his tradition, which elsewhere is portrayed as anachronistic or reactionary.

As the sequence advances, it subtly revises Murphy's tradition. Evolving from isolated Anglo-Irish obelisks through cryptic witnesses of youthful intimacies, the volume ends with derelict dwellings accounting for themselves. The theme of poetry plays lightly across the desecrated dead or outcasts from life, itinerant or illegitimate, with whom the poet sympathizes. A comparison of the sequence's concluding sonnets with the conclusion of the penultimate version of *The Price of Stone* reveals much of Murphy's intention. Earlier, the volume's final line, offered lightly and ironically by a skating rink—"Old scores ironed out, tomorrow a clean sheet"—could be understood as a sign of personal poetic renewal. In this revised ending, two final sonnets about birth also foretell renewal, but one in which the poet is midwife, perhaps the minis-tering angel in line eleven of "The Beehive Cell." This poem celebrates the heroic feminine role in that sea-going tradition whose masculine side Murphy portrayed in *Sailing to an Island*. . . . Replacing his vocal structures in the fi-nal sonnet, the poet comforts a mother and invites "to share our loneliness" a newborn "natural son," who has just left life's most complete abode. Through enlarged poetic sympathies in this volume, Murphy expresses the ephemeral-ity and value of our abiding places.

> Dillon Johnston. *Irish Poetry after Joyce* (Notre
> Dame, Ind., Univ. of Notre Dame Pr., 1985),
> pp. 257–59

Since *Sailing to an Island* in 1963, Richard Murphy's collections have ap-peared in a roughly lustral rhythm, although this was maintained in 1979 only by his *Selected Poems*, which did contain some new work as well as revised versions of earlier pieces. *The Price of Stone*, therefore, is the first substantial body of new poetry from him since *High Island* (1974), an important book in which Murphy moved into a new idiom and broadened his range of material. Nevertheless, that book's style of reticent allusiveness, while engaging, con-stantly gave the impression of something being left unsaid. Such, of course, is the price of reticence, but a search for unspoken communication has been a feature of Richard Murphy's work from the outset.

The Price of Stone is more forthcoming than *High Island*. The title se-quence consists of fifty sonnets (cast in the "Shakespearean" form) in which the very stones speak. In each poem Murphy gives a voice to some particular structure (monument, dwelling-place, his old school, etc.) which has im-pinged on his experience. They speak to him, questioningly, accusingly, or reflectively, about passages of his life. This device of giving mouths to oth-ers, and putting words into those mouths, suits Murphy; he can appear to speak frankly to and about himself, and yet remain silent. . . .

"The Price of Stone" (the title sequence) begins with erections; these are either follies or monuments to the dead. It ends with the birth of the poet's son, with life. It is in this last sonnet that Murphy finally speaks as himself, addressing his son not through any surrogate or interlocutory structure. And the final word of the sonnet, and of the sequence and book, escapes language to affirm an alternative form of communication: "touch." There really is noth-ing more to be said. . . .

Of the 21 poems which make up Part I of *The Price of Stone*, the cen-tral ones are those dealing with Murphy's friendship with Tony White and White's death in 1976. Death dominates in these introductory poems: the death of friends ("Mary Ure"), the death of love ("Displaced Person"), and death-in-life ("Elixir"). There are also some trial pieces for the later sonnets, and the graceful elegiacs of "Stone Mania" serve as a rueful link between *High Island* and *The Price of Stone*. But it is for Part II, the sonnets, that this book will be cherished. As a sequence, they not only embody an intrinsic worth but they also give a retrospective shape to Murphy's work as a whole so far. Those readers who, like myself, have been fascinated by the turns of Murphy's poetry, at once allusive and aloof, will recognize here the quizzical and detached qualities of his earlier poems, but now set in a new lucidity. The book provides not a story, but a history, and adds new lustre to all his earlier volumes.

Peter Denman. *ILS*. Fall, 1985, p. 15

MURRAY, T.C. (1873–1959)

Seventeen years have passed since *Birthright* was named by competent American critics as the "best new play presented in America during the season 1911–1912." Yet despite that praise, and the fact that nearly all books on the drama mention his name in commendation, the plays of T. C. Murray have achieved little beyond a local recognition in Ireland. It was not until *Autumn Fire* was recently presented both in London and New York that the playgoers of these cities had an opportunity of judging his quality. With critics he has fared little better, some have said that he is merely a writer of melodrama, and one, at least, has hailed him as one of the world's great dramatists. In truth both estimates are far from the fact, but T. C. Murray is certainly one of the most considerable of the Irish dramatists, and the outstanding Irish Catholic dramatist. Perhaps the greatest obstacle to the wider fame of Murray as a dramatist is his own incurable modesty. He is one of the shyest and most retiring of living writers, shunning publicity of every kind. He is now in middle-age, and all his life he has been teaching in primary schools. Born in County Cork he began his teaching and play-writing careers in that county, and only after his plays had attracted the favourable attention of critics was he appointed to a school in Dublin. . . .

In his technique Murray is a realist—he presents real people in real situations—but he is a realist who presents without thesis or comment. He is too fond of accidents for his technique to be entirely satisfactory; coincidence and accident may pass on the stage in moments of excitement but they become monotonous when used too frequently. The use of such devices damages the reputation of the artist by suggesting a deficiency in the inventive faculty. It is

in his dialogue that Murray is supreme; in that he is surpassed by no dramatist of his time. His characters, too, are all alive and all recognisably Irish,
even if they have a close family resemblance to each other. Murray is the dramatist of quiet desperation, one of the best of the Irish dramatists who is nevertheless closely akin to the best writers of the English Repertory School. He
has tenderness and pity, a deep love for frail humanity which is probably religious in its source, he does not sit in judgment, and it is probable that he owes
much to that English dramatist who is master of pity and realism—John
Galsworthy. Much fine work may still be expected from him in the future as
he is still in the prime of his writing career.

Andrew E. Malone. The Irish Drama (London,
Constable, 1929), pp 185, 194

To pass from Mr. O'Flaherty to Mr. T. C. Murray is to pass into a different
world: and yet a world that has some familiar prospects. *Spring Horizon* is the
story of a boy; it is also the story of a renewal of hope in a country and a
community. Two generations have passed since the Famine when Stephen
Mangan is born in a Munster town. His parents own a public-house, and are
of the first bi-lingual generation Ireland knew. Hope revives in Carberymore,
and young Stephen knows the beginnings of the agitation which has since
placed his people back on the "planted" lands by which he was surrounded.
Seldom has the adolescent boy been presented with greater insight and sympathy than in Mr. Murray's pages. He understands the shy, sensitive boy, who
prefers the introspective and solitary life to that of the groups in his shop,
school or home environment. As the first novel from one who has been a notable contributor to, and a formative influence in, Irish drama, this book is singularly undramatic. It is in his introspective moods and descriptive passages
that Mr. Murray is at his best.

As a sequel is promised to *Spring Horizon*, this novel might be judged a
preparation rather than an actual achievement. It has in it, however, that
quality of quietude which first came into contemporary Irish fiction with
Mr. Daniel Corkery's *Threshold of Quiet*. It is contemplative, reminiscent,
brooding, as if in some quiet corner a most earnest man was discoursing about
his glamorous boyhood. That Mr. Murray's Stephen Mangan retains that
glamour is an indication of the quality of this book. If Mr. O'Flaherty gives
the reader the "bad times," Mr. Murray brings the first rays of returning
sunlight.

Irish Times. Feb. 13, 1937, p. 7

"Thomas Murray, Playwright, Dies." Glancing at the *New York Times* head-
line (March 9, 1959) no one who knew the deceased would have suspected it
was the obituary of Ireland's most distinguished playwright. Throughout
Ireland and far beyond it he has always been affectionately and familiarly

known at "T. C." The day of his death was the feast day of his patron, St. Thomas Aquinas. On that day ended a career that saw the dawn of the Irish Literary Revival, watched its progress and lived to witness its decline.

. . . T. C.'s sympathy was consistently and always on the side of youth as is evident in such plays as *Birthright, Spring, Maurice Harte* and *Aftermath*. Youth to him was a clean and wholesome thing. But he was not unaware of its follies and weakness. More explicitly than in his plays, this view of youth is the theme of his only novel, *Spring Horizon*—a story of an Irish boy's adolescence told with more wisdom and understanding than is to be found in the welter of studies by contemporary educators and psychologists.

Illumination, T. C.'s last play, is the only one that has not been published. But thanks to his gracious giving there is a typed copy in the Boston College Library. When it was completed, he wrote: "It isn't a very good play, but I think it is of sufficient interest to warrant its production."

Not many of the audience would have agreed with him when the play was first produced at the Abbey Theatre in July, 1939. . . . In a letter of June 6, 1939, he wrote: "The theme, as the title suggests, is the sudden awakening of a young man—a country lawyer—to the claim of his Creator for his service in the Church. The first impulse comes through a chance reading of Thomas à Kempis and as the spiritual struggle goes on he feels himself not unlike that runaway in the 'Hound of Heaven.'" . . .

The late vocation in *Illumination* is not merely to the priesthood, but to the contemplative life of a Trappist. The life of a contemplative had a peculiar fascination for T. C. On the Feast of the Immaculate Conception, 1949, he wrote: "I've been reading with intense interest Thomas Merton's *Elected Silence*, as his autobiography has been entitled here. It has been for me not only the book of the year but of many years."

Realist that he was, T. C. was not unaware of the human side of a vocation, especially when the source of its inspiration is a fond mother or ambitious father, rather than the Holy Spirit. This is the theme of *Maurice Harte*, a play in which the leading character is a young seminarian. . . . It is a deeply moving play, ending like all T. C. tragedies with overwhelming disaster that engulfs all the characters and leaves their grim future to the audience's imagination. Treated by a playwright of less understanding and talent, *Maurice Harte* could easily have degenerated into satire. But from T. C.'s sympathetic treatment it emerges a stark, realistic tragedy, without cynicism or caricature or bitterness. As a distinguished dramatic critic has said, "one trembles to think what Seán O'Casey would have done with such a theme, had he deserted the slums along the Liffey, for the farms on the banks of the Shannon."

Terence L. Connolly. *Catholic World*. March, 1960,
pp. 364–67

In this "People's Theatre," [in Yeats's phrase] the realists headed by Robinson and Murray revealed the real Ireland and completely did away with the

Stage Irishman. For them drama was an image of life, neither contorted nor twisted. A new awakening was in the air and these young people looked within and without and found the themes of drama in their own immediate neighborhood.

In pursuance of the policy of the Abbey Theatre, Murray wrote plays with the object of expressing the deeper thoughts and emotions of Ireland and transcending not only the political barriers which divided Irishmen, but also the higher barriers of religious differences. Though he has not Galsworthy's technique of showing both the sides of a case impartially, he has his pity, tenderness, restraint and dignity. Whereas Galsworthy's subjects are more social than domestic, Murray's are more domestic than social. Galsworthy dealt with Capital and Labour, courts and prison and justice, but Murray's world is that of the family and the priest. His subjects are home, marriage, land, schools (not education), and religion (not any specified types of it). Unlike [Paul Vincent] Carroll, he steers clear of religious dogmas and does not believe in protruding his own theses. With marked accuracy, sympathy, and understanding, he has presented the southern farmer, peasant, and small-town man. He is not interested in the complexities of the sophisticated gentry. In the fashion of Synge, he has dealt with the elemental man in all his simplicity and unaffectedness. He does not have Shaw's glitter nor the dazzling flashes and witty ebullitions of Oscar Wilde, nor even the satire of his own compatriot Lennox Robinson. But he observes keenly and interprets truthfully. He is a sober, grave dramatist. His art has very little of humour, but it has catholicity, love, and understanding, rendered felicitously in a language that throbs between poetry and prose.

N. Sahal. Sixty Years of Realistic Irish Drama
(Bombay, Macmillan, 1971), p. 45

The well-known classical legend recounting the illicit passion of Phaedra for her step-son Hippolytus and the tragic consequences caused each of them as well as her husband Theseus underlies a number of dramas written over the centuries. . . . [Among these] are two plays produced within a two-year span in the mid-1920's, T. C. Murray's *Autumn Fire* (1924) and Eugene O'Neill's *Desire under the Elms* (1926). In different ways each has departed from the classical original. . . .

Although *Desire under the Elms* is a tragedy, a note of exaltation is evident at the end not only in the continued possession of the farm by the person who has stamped it with "the years o' my life," but also in the dominance of the love expressed by Abbie and Eben over their other desires. It is perhaps significant that the play comes to its conclusion at dawn. Murray's *Autumn Fire*, in contrast, ends at nightfall: a lifetime of darkness is in prospect for each of the principals. The fire, moreover, which has burned in each of them is reaching the point of extinction, the "autumn" of its duration.

The adjective *autumn* has another signification in the play: it refers to the kindling of the fire of love [for Nance Desmond] late in the life of Owen Keegan, the Theseus character of the play. [The announcement that their father and Nance are to be married causes fires to burn in each of the children Keegan has had by his first wife. The son Michael is taken aback and crushed. The daughter Ellen, a frustrated spinster, has recourse to ranting, accusations, and outbursts which cast a pall on the atmosphere that has previously been fresh and wholesome.] . . .

The fires of the flames in each of the Keegan children are given an opportunity to burn more vigorously by an accident befalling Owen, one caused by his riding a spirited horse in a manner inconsonant with his advanced years. Rendered almost bedfast, he is obliged to turn over to his young wife and son most of his responsibilities, thereby bringing the two together almost incessantly. The closer relations, innocent though they are, give rise to a "great fondness" which Nance recognizes "is drawing us to each other in spite of ourselves." It is this recognition that leads her to insist that Michael must leave the household. With reluctance he agrees to go, out of consideration for her position. The Hippolytus of Murray's play is impelled to depart from his home because of the urgings of his step-mother, not, as in Euripides, because of her machinations. . . .

The husband of *Autumn Fire*, who may be regarded as wronged even though his wife and son have not been guilty of illicit relations, consigns himself to a living hell. He drives Michael from the home and dooms Nance to remaining with him in a relationship that has been irretrievably strained and that can never be restored to its earlier orderliness. Nor does Ellen have opportunity to gloat, as Owen turns upon her with the accusation that she has broken him. Left alone with his praying beads, he mournfully intones, "They've broken me . . . son—wife—daughter. . . . I've no one now but the Son of God." That he will find the solace which he expects from religion is to be hoped for, but the prospect before him is not nearly so reassuring as that before Ephraim Cabot, who is left totally alone at the end of *Desire under the Elms* but who can turn to the farm which he has sustained and which, in turn, has sustained him for many years. Murray's *Autumn Fire* is similar to O'Neill's play in that it makes free with the Phaedra legend that underlies it and plays upon the meanings of a key word, but a different key word, *fire*. We see the fire burning in Ellen, in Michael, in Nance, in Owen, but at the end it is the burned out fire of Owen that remains in our minds most prominently.

A. Fred Sochatoff. In *In Honor of Austin Wright*
(Pittsburgh, Pa., Carnegie-Mellon University,
1972), pp. 80–83, 85–86

Looking through Murray's plays one curious fact emerges: that in the work of one who felt very keenly for the positive forces in life,—for youth, vigour, imagination, there are almost no victories. *The Pipe in the Fields* follows the same pattern as *Maurice Harte*, but this time the strange young boy's sanity and vision are saved by the intercession of Father Moore who acknowledges that Peter's "wild imaginings" may be in fact a gift beyond his own understanding and that of Peter's parents. Yet this play is exceptional. In general those who have romantic ideals whether they be creative or emotional are broken and destroyed by life. There is a deep, pessimistic fatalism in most of the plays. From *Birthright* through *Michaelmas Eve* to *Autumn Fire* and *The Green Branch* minor characters and ironic echoes are used to emphasize and expand the pattern of defeat. Ellen, Owen Keegan's plain daughter in *Autumn Fire*, is just one example of the author adding an extra dimension to the play by repeating the main theme in a minor figure. It comes as a most dramatic revelation when we find that this bitter, carping spinster is as she is because she herself was betrayed in love by a philanderer who stole both her money and her faith in human happiness. In *Michaelmas Eve* there is a powerful sense of correspondence between the young Hugh Kearns who chooses to marry for money instead of love and the returned Yank, Terry Donegan; it is almost as if one were a pre-figuration of what the other might become. In *A Spot in the Sun*, even within such a brief little one-act play, a sub-motif of pride endangering happiness and love is worked in to second the main theme which involves the ruin of a young, foolish businessman through excessive regard for the pride, and "notions," of his artistically inclined wife. In this way Murray extends his dramatic world and makes general the patterns evident in the lives of his main characters. . . .

It seems to me . . . that Murray's analytical insight into, and repeated exploration of, the forces that underlie the lives of people in rural, backward communities seem inadequately expressed by the term "realist" (just as the term "photograph" seems inadequate to describe an X-ray). That he is powerfully aware of the human spirit pushing towards growth, knowledge, achievement, emotional completion could equally suggest that he is, in some senses, a romantic. That he almost always sees that urge as something crushed by spiritual or economic poverty, by prejudice, by the conflicting demands of family and tribe, or simply by the random operation of ill-chance, makes him seem a pessimistic fatalist. There is a constant sense in the plays of the author's own vision and of the continuing ambivalence of his response to the ideals and the embittering actuality of his subjects. Often the plays show us a sharp image of Irish rural life at a particularly crucial point of change in Irish society. Often they show insight into the general qualities and forces of any peasant society which is undergoing change. Always there is a deep understanding of the importance in rural society of economic survival, of price, of the hard service and profound love of the land. In some of the plays, however, Murray achieves a fuller tragic vision of the ways in which humanity thwarts, wounds and destroys itself.

T. Gerald Fitzgibbon. *Studies*. Spring, 1975,
pp. 63–65

O'BRIEN, CONOR CRUISE (1917–   )

The subject approached by Donat O'Donnell [Conor Cruise O'Brien] in *Maria Cross: Imaginative Patterns in a Group of Catholic Writers* is a formidable one. This area has been in a sense roped-off, and although voices confident in disagreement have been heard from the clustering spectators, almost no one has ventured in to have a go at dismantling the large, foreign, ticking, fuming, distinctly dangerous-looking thing. Some of its parts seem recognizable to various expert onlookers, but as a whole it is something strange, and not enough is really known of the way the parts work on each other. Mr. O'Donnell has set about the dismantling with assurance, but with delicacy, always aware that his subject may blow up in his face.

In considering the work of eight writers who are Catholics, Mr. O'Donnell has attempted in each case to trace the central imaginative pattern of the work, as a provisional indication of the central emotional pattern of the writer. As he points out, "The relation this [imaginative] pattern bears to Catholicism is inevitably complex and variable; a concept may be ostensibly wholly Christian and yet reveal itself, on closer inspection, to be a technical term, the key to the whole pattern and containing much that is at least non-Christian—for example, [Charles] Péguy's 'hope' or the 'pity' of Graham Greene."

The first eight essays, an examination of Mauriac, Bloy, Claudel, Bernanos, Péguy, O'Faolain, Greene and Waugh are excellent critical researches, conducted with perception and fine intelligence, into the work of these men. It is in these that the critic is most illuminating. The eight appear to differ enormously, but Mr. O'Donnell believes that the differences may be superficial and proposes in his final unifying analysis that they are "members of the family in more than a religious sense." The only obvious link is the fact of their Catholicism—that theirs are imaginations permeated by Catholicism. He holds that all signs point to another, not obvious link, a community of *feeling*. His inquiry is, as he says, "several steps removed from direct inquiry into religious experience, and not less remote from the sort of direct inquiry that a psychologist conducts." The answer he believes is to be found in the work itself. Even if these men had not been Christians, they would, according to this theory, have revealed their common dilemma in the pattern of human suffering as it occurs in their writings. Because they are Christians, suffering is understood by them to be the Cross; the connecting link between them is to be found in the way in which the idea of the cross, of crucifixion, used "not as a pious external, but as an integral part of the pattern," is developed. . . .

But what is this cross? What is the design of love and pain that has emerged for all as the crux of human suffering? Mr. O'Donnell proposes that "the shadow that lies over all this work" is that of Maria Cross, the unifying figure of woman, seen through different eyes in Mauriac's *Desert of Love*. Loved by both a father and his son, she appears to the latter as all that is sexually desirable. In rebuffing him, she "becomes" his "mother" and this concept of her is reinforced in the youth when he learns that she is also loved by his father. Thenceforth she is the core of his suffering. Maria Cross, the figure through whom all these writers are related, in Mr. O'Donnell's analysis, looms up then as Jocasta, and the emotional pattern of these "exile" artists is basically related to the Oedipus theme. . . . It is this emotional conviction, in the critic's view, that has formed—or distorted—the concepts of Christianity held by these unconsciously unorthodox Catholic writers, of whom only Claudel remains close to the hard intellectual center of Catholicism.

Donat O'Donnell stands somewhere between the philosophical objectivity of Maritain, whose literary influence he deplores, not altogether consistently, and the "anti-rational" position he ascribes to these creative imaginations. His sympathy is with the artists, but he is able to draw critical distinctions which must be drawn. He has written a valuable book, and an important one, whether or not his final insight is wholly valid.

S. M. Fitzgerald. NR. May 12, 1952, pp. 26–27

[*Murderous Angels*] was not conceived as an artistic and dramatic presentation of actual events after the fashion of a pageant. Rather is it a play which deals with a real political conjuncture, and the state of mind of some real and some not so real characters involved in the ensuing dilemma. Again and again during the play, it becomes necessary to approach it as an entity; to dissociate ideas about the characters and the turn of events in history from ideas about them in the play.

This point is not as facile as it may seem. The author has run a real risk in using names and describing events which have a significance for us outside the sphere of his play. While it may be useful to evaluate ideas about some of the characters in history, it becomes less so when these ideas will clash with the dramatic presentation of the character. So, we shall proceed warily, using history when it is helpful in coming to terms with the play, and spurning it when it is at odds with an understanding of the play.

In his Preface, the author deals at length with the conflict between Peace and Freedom, a conflict whose very existence shocks those who tend to associate, in reverent parlance and thought, absolutes which seem to be intricately intertwined in those elevated spheres where Man ceases to be an animal and adopts the attributes of an angel. The exigencies of this conflict procure the downfall and death of both chief protagonists in the play. But, underlying this theme, which dominates the lives of Hammarskjöld and Lumumba, is another, no less important, which involves and implicates all the characters in the play to varying extents. Each, wittingly or unwittingly, occupies a position in the conflict which creates much of the tension in the play. The conflict is that between racial groups, in this case, simply black and white. Although not the major theme, it nevertheless divides and unites the characters. It is the underlying area of gravest uncertainty, which is exploited to a great extent by the vested interests in delaying, or denying, African rule in the Congo. It is the sustaining material for the friendship between Hammarskjöld and Diallo Dop, between Lumumba and Madame Rose Rose, the hatred between Polycarpe and Boniface, between Bonham and Diallo Dop. The degree to which it affects personal relationships, the thought patterns and the outcome in action of the play, is the ground explored in this article.

There can be no doubt as to the author's position on this problem. His presentation of both Hammarskjöld and Lumumba shows an equal bias toward both their lifestyles. A respect for Hammarskjöld's humane dedication to the problem of world peace and for his solemn, humorless, overtly religious approach to his work is counterbalanced by a belief in Lumumba's inexorable wish for African freedom for African people and an obvious joy in depicting his riotous, spontaneous and often bizarre behaviour even in the midst of the gigantic problems which beset him. The cultural validity of both is juxtaposed, but does not lead to conflict. The two are rather components which go to make up the quintessential nature of human conduct. . . .

[O'Brien states:] "The artistic truth of the novelist, dramatist and essayist has social and political implications and is a form of justice." With this deadly serious background, he has written a play infused with impetuous mirth and scathing wit.

Nigel Deacon. In Patrick Rafroidi, Raymonde Popot,
and William Parker, eds., *Aspects of the Irish
Theatre* (Lille, France, Publications de l'Université
de Lille, 1972), pp. 246–47

In a sense I have never really left Ireland. In all my fifty-one years I have never spent an entire year outside Ireland. During the last eight years I have spent most of my time away, but I have not come back as a stranger or in any way been greatly surprised at what I have found.

I went to the Congo in May, 1961, after the death of Patrice Lumumba. I naturally had occasion to think about the Congo a good deal and its connexions with more general issues: with the great problem of relations between races and specifically the relation between white and black. When I wrote my play, *Murderous Angels*, I thought of Lumumba partly in that connexion. Lumumba is a symbolic figure representing the aspirations for black power and the liberation of the black people.

There is no doubt that Hammarskjold could have saved Lumumba from his fate. This has been documented in *The Congo since Independence* by Catherine Hoskyns, published by the Royal Institute for International Relations. You will find there the official instructions when Lumumba left the protection which had been provided for him at his villa and started to travel across the Congo. The instruction given was that there was to be no interference between Lumumba and his official pursuers, as the term went. I did not become aware of the full extent of the involvement of the UN Secretariat in the events which precipitated Lumumba's downfall until I read Miss Hoskyns's book; nor was I aware at the time of the extent to which they took care not to intervene to save his life. I am not saying that they knew he was going to be murdered, still less, of course, that they desired his murder. But as the old saying goes, they did not strive officiously to keep him alive.

I think a part of one's life is spent in the process of shedding illusions, and it is true in a sense that I shed some illusions in the Congo. I did not become disillusioned, if by that one means bitter and cynical; but I became more and more interested in how international affairs work. I have never taken, and I know I never shall take, a stand against the United Nations. I think the UN provides a very imperfect set of safeguards; however bad the world is now it would be in an even more dangerous condition if there was no such meeting place. When I wrote *Murderous Angels* I tried to take *Markings*, which was Hammarskjold's spiritual diary, and the record of his actions in the Congo partly as I experienced them myself, but mainly as they appear from Miss Hoskyns's detached narrative, to produce a dramatic character who could credibly be the same man who wrote *Markings* and also acted in a distinctly Machiavellian way (and I'm not using Machiavellian in the purely curse-word sense). I certainly wasn't trying to be either hard or easy on him; I was trying to see just what this man was. Lumumba could only have lived if the international forces surrounding the situation had been different. But those international forces called for his disappearance as a political force, and if you disappear as a political force in the Congo it isn't safe to remain there. So his death was inscribed in the logic of the thing.

Murderous Angels is a political play and a controversial play because you cannot have a political play that is not controversial.

Conor Cruise O'Brien. In Des Hickey and Gus
Smith, eds., *Flight from the Celtic Twilight*
(Indianapolis and New York, Bobbs-Merrill, 1973),
pp. 229–31

Some commentators have felt that . . . O'Brien's play, *Murderous Angels*, took unpardonable liberties with the characters of real individuals. An anonymous review in the *Times Literary Supplement* accused him of producing "what amounts to a character assassination of Dag Hammarskjold," and also noted that the play would be "deeply offensive to people alive and dead [sic]," and doubted that "Its dramatic qualities are sufficient justification for its pub-lication." To us it seems that public figures are in the public domain and must be interpreted freely from all shades of opinion, and that, further, a good play is its own justification.

O'Brien's Hammarskjold makes incomplete dramatic sense, but is cer-tainly one of the most intellectually arresting figures in recent drama. He is not an obviously theatrical character, such as the Butleys, Bill Maitlands and Jimmy Porters of the postwar stage. His attitudes are original, complex and incapable of being flamboyantly externalized. His two most revealing speeches are quietly, gravely delivered, but have a restrained eloquence. . . .

However, in *Murderous Angels* O'Brien's material is basically intrac-table. The scene is panoramic, the events are complicated, the historical mo-tives are often obscure, and some of the real characters are simply inscrutable. Nevertheless, in the play, it is not only the material, but also the arrangement that confuses. The apparent conflict is between the "murderous angels" of Peace and Freedom as embodied respectively in Hammarskjold and Lu-mumba. The basic conflict, however, is between each of them and what O'Brien seems to regard as the murderous devil of capitalist imperialism rep-resented by Baron d'Auge. It is d'Auge finally who causes the deaths of Hammarskjold and Lumumba, but the play does not stress d'Auge's central-ity. Hammarskjold and Lumumba are not protagonist and antagonist, but dual protagonists defeated by d'Auge. So what is apparently a sub-plot is actually the main plot, although the play camouflages that fact.

A second confusion arises from characterization. Baron d'Auge is a well-drawn stereotype of ruthless power, and his motives are as perfectly clear as Richard III's. Hammarskjold and Lumumba are meant to embody two types of idealism, but, even though O'Brien tries to thicken their characters, they remain perfectly perplexing. Attributing homosexuality to Hammar-skjold and hedonism to Lumumba does not explain why they became pas-sionate partisans of peace and freedom. Their human characteristics do not explain their political motivations, and so Hammarskjold remains a tragic enigma and Lumumba a Stage African. Hence, if the Baron d'Auge plot is quite understated, the Hammarskjold-Lumumba plot is not quite understood.

Nevertheless, O'Brien has attempted a modern tragedy, and achieved at least an adult pre-occupation with ideas rarely seen in plays since the days of Shaw and Granville-Barker. *Murderous Angels* exists in the realm of fiction, and what emerges from its appropriately literary pattern is the most convinc-ing statement that O'Brien had so far made about the political world.

Elisabeth Young-Bruehl and Robert Hogan. *JIL*.
May, 1974, pp. 31–33

To Katanga and Back: A UN Case History (1962) is an angry, painfully hon-est book; it is also very funny—some of the scholarly footnotes are particularly so. And for all the anger, it is an important source book for what is still, according to Brian Urquhart, "a matter of controversy and some mystery," the Katanga action.

Writers and Politics (1965), a collection of essays, articles, reviews and lectures, is important for the personal statement, in the introduction, of O'Brien's view of the mission of a political writer. He has been accused of a pro-communist, anti-Western—especially anti-American—bias. One answer to the charge is that he has always been a social democrat, which makes him a dedicated enemy of totalitarianism, right or left. But the real point is his passionate belief that the exposure of falsehood is infinitely more effective if it comes from within a country or institution than from without.

The image he uses is that of "chipping away" at lies, and he agrees that in the book he chips away mainly, though not exclusively, "at the expense—or for the benefit—of Western cultural and political edifices." There were indeed mendacities in the communist world, but efforts to demolish these were "being vigorously made by many writers, and I have not felt any great need to add my amateur efforts to those of the numerous professional critics of communist practice," He went on: "From the other side we can hear a few writers, Poles, Russians, Hungarians, and others, busily chipping away. Our applause can neither encourage nor help them. What might help would be that, from our side also, should be heard the sound of chipping."

That passage, besides irony, illustrates another of his characteristic literary devices, deliberate understatement: he can be wrong-headed; he never shouts. But it also illustrates a serious weakness in his political thinking. By so adamantly keeping silent on communist excesses, he has done himself and his cause disservice. Nor, for that matter, is it true that western efforts cannot help the Russian dissenters. One message constantly coming from them is that publicizing their efforts does have an effect. What they fear above all else, and what the Kremlin wants—as did similar regimes, whether in Czechoslovakia or Greece or Portugal—is silence.

John Silverlight. *The Critic*. Jan., 1975, p. 27

States of Ireland [1972] may be read as essay, as autobiography, as journal, and at times as fiction; that such a mixed form should be the most congenial for O'Brien's Irish testament needs explanation. But that self-dramatisation and contemplation should be at the book's centre need not be surprising. O'Brien introduces *Writers and Politics* with a playful self-characterisation:

"Are you a socialist?" asked the African leader.
I said, yes.
He looked me in the eye. "People have been telling me," he said lightly, "that you are a liberal . . ."
The statement in its context invited a denial. I said nothing.

Such epithets are used frequently by O'Brien to point towards a recognisable set of beliefs, but, as usual, the context here functions to heighten the significance of the distinction in that particular situation, and also as an escape route by which the author can elude this definitive categorisation.

O'Brien has consistently drawn criticism from those who would categorize him, as for example, socialist, liberal, anti-American, anti-Republican, or anti-Catholic. Yet his greatest intellectual and literary skill has gone into defining his identity in irreducible terms which would transcend those aspects of language which limit his freedom to express independent judgements. In a politician this might be seen as evasive self-protection. In a writer of O'Brien's consistency and subtlety it can be seen as the quality on which his authority rests: the ability passionately to uphold and argue a point of view, yet, sceptically, to elude the rhetorical cliché and the dogmatic orthodoxy which would invalidate the human and provisional truth of his particular argument. For O'Brien's identity consists in extending into the public domain of politics and international diplomacy the truth which he derives through trying to understand his own position, socially, psychologically, historically, religiously, educationally. The truth for O'Brien is rooted in the experience of living individuals, and in autobiographical records, and his greatest effort is to uphold that truth and to make public and corporate actions responsive to it, at a time when, for many writers, the supremacy of individual consciousness leads towards disengagement and, perhaps, solipsism.

His major interest in writing is biographical, and those he has chosen to write about help him to define himself through a dramatic identification with his subjects. Continually we find a note in his writing which suggests that the penetration of his insights derives from this identification, or, sometimes, from a relation of confrontation. Continually his commentary becomes a testing out of directions in which his own life moves. The muted critique of his own actions, or, as it appears in his writing, of those who were stereotypes in the group with which he was associated, leads us to the core of his search for truth. In the writings which followed his return to Ireland in 1969, and the abandonment of his role in the American Left, O'Brien has repeatedly used Edmund Burke as a touchstone. . . . The major interest of O'Brien's writing for us is [its] pattern of self-scrutiny . . . , the constant posture of being on guard, of discovering through experience the truth of one's identity in relation to the "myth, metaphor and ritual forms" which our culture gives to us.

States of Ireland is his most important book because in it autobiography and the history of the two major groups whose relation has shaped a prominent part of the cultural life of Irishmen, including O'Brien himself, meet in an appropriate search for personal and national definition.

Denis Sampson. *CJIS*. Dec., 1976, pp. 18–20

Conor Cruise O'Brien . . . begins his massive study of Israel and Zionism, *The Siege*, by describing those elements in his national, religious, and family background that drew him to the subject. In the late 1950's that most un-philosophical principle called the alphabet conspired with destiny to situate O'Brien, as Ireland's UN representative, between Iraq and Israel, a revealing perspective for a shrewd observer. In 1961 he left Ireland's foreign service but subsequently went into politics at home, where he served four years in opposition and four years as a member of the Irish government.

O'Brien is a liberal, but it was not his liberalism that made him see the Return to Zion, which took place under "harsher necessities" than any ever imagined by liberals, as "the greatest story of modern times." As an Irish Catholic he had no trouble recognizing, at the heart of Zionism, a powerful bond between religion and nationality. As the child of a lapsed or "enlightened" Catholic father, whom he labels a *maskil* (Hebrew for "enlightened one"), O'Brien grew up sufficiently "alienated" from Catholic society to feel yet another link with Jews living as strangers in Exile. Finally, he was moved by the conviction that "Irish Catholics . . . have had a greater experience of persecution, oppression, and stigmatization than any other people in Western Europe *except* the Jews."

Throughout his book, O'Brien freely and candidly uses his experience as an Irishman and a diplomat to shed coruscating light on the story of the Zionist movement as well as on the play of forces around that movement. This means that in his view of the British Mandatory government that ruled Palestine from soon after the end of World War I until 1948, the British Anglo-Saxon constitutional system . . . sometimes appears to be just what Matthew Arnold called it: "A colossal machine for the manufacture of Philistines." O'Brien remarks that among such Philistines, "anti-Semitism is a light sleeper," and offers as an instance the use in British official circles, starting in 1941, of the epithet "Jewish Nazi state." . . .

O'Brien's saga of Israel and Zionism is in two parts. The first recounts the story of Zionism from the assassination of Czar Alexander II in 1881 through the expiration of the British Mandate in 1948 and includes detailed analyses of the whole spectrum of Zionist ideologies, portraits of such central actors as Herzl, Chaim Weizmann, David Ben-Gurion, and Jabotinsky, and accounts of the Dreyfus Affair, Eastern European pogroms, and British motives and actions in Palestine. The second, longer part tells the story of Israel from its bloody beginning through the completion of the withdrawal from Lebanon in summer 1985. It comprises lengthy chapters on the inner life of Israel as expressed in its literature, on Israel's Oriental Jewish population, on the Arabs of Israel and the administered territories, and on the complex relations between international diplomacy and Israel's wars. *The Siege* is the work of a writer of flexible intelligence and boundless curiosity. The book therefore has a kind of noble imperfection, like that of large Victorian novels lovingly called loose and baggy monsters.

Edward Alexander. *Cmty.* Feb., 1986, p. 29

O'BRIEN, EDNA (1932–   )

The Country Girls is a first novel of great charm by a natural writer. It is the story of two girls growing up in Ireland, first in a derelict village, then in a convent, then in Dublin. It is not a series of idylls nor a breathless account of hilarious adventures, though its tone is light and there are passages of comedy. In mood and manner Miss O'Brien's novel resembles *The Bachelor of Arts* by R. K. Narayan. Caithleen's mother dies shortly after the novel opens; her father is a drunkard who steadily impoverishes himself. Baba comes from a more ordered home, though her mother likes to spend the evenings on a high stool at the bar of the village hotel. Baba is adventurous and bullying, and where she leads Caithleen must follow. It is Baba who engineers their expulsion from the convent; and when they go to Dublin, it is Baba, innocently and pathetically rapacious, who takes Caithleen into hotel lounges to pick up elderly businessmen. Baba falls ill. Caithleen prepares to fly to Vienna with the elderly man with whom she is in love; but he does not turn up.

Neither of these events is explicitly tragic; both girls will recover. The true tragedy lies in the sense of time passing, of waste, decay, waiting, relationships that come to nothing. Yet Miss O'Brien never says so. She makes no comment, stages nothing, She simply offers her characters, and they come to us living. She does not appear to have to strive to establish anything; the novel, one feels, is so completely, so truly realised in the writer's mind that everything that comes out has a quality of life which no artifice could achieve. Mis O'Brien may write profounder books, but I doubt whether she will write another like *The Country Girls*, which is as fresh and lyrical and bursting with energy as only a first novel can be.

V. S. Naipaul. *NS*. July 16, 1960, p. 97

It is always hard to evaluate a literary work that provokes so many nonliterary judgments as this one by Edna O'Brien. But maybe literature only begins to matter when it carries us beyond the safe confines of literary criticism. D. H. Lawrence thought so, evidently Miss O'Brien does too.

Girls in Their Married Bliss is a sequel to *The Country Girls* and *The Lonely Girl* (filmed as *The Girl with Green Eyes*). Here again are those former convent schoolmates, Baba and Kate, less spirited now and more, to their horror, like their mothers. They are living in London, and have husbands, lovers, and plenty of trouble. Yet the novel is no bedroom or bedhopping farce. Each sexual skirmish in the girls' lives in both a calamity and a narrow escape from a worse one. Miss O'Brien's portrayal of the psychology of adulterous love is brilliant. She describes how lovers are more difficult than husbands; how, if marriage is boredom and compromise (but compromise with what?), then adultery is a cave of madness. The sensitive spot she probes is the knot of impulses that shape our basic needs and, therefore, our personalities.

The characters in *Girls in Their Married Bliss* are dreadfully alone. They are not interested in music, sports, or handicrafts; family, religion, and politics also exert small influence. Baba's and Kate's need to heal their broken, disconnected lives drives them to trade anything for a scrap of love. Here is where many readers will recoil. Do social institutions and ties matter as little as Miss O'Brien suggests? Are we so desperately detached from any living tradition or ideas? Conceding the difficulty of summoning moral principles in times of stress, do these stresses always take a sexual form?

If Miss O'Brien fails to answer these questions, she does examine them honestly and diligently. Her subject is sex, its dynamics and ethics, and she treats it as a many-sided problem. Where one character views a love affair as passionate, a second sees it as simply cheap, even boring. Either interpretation is as convincing as its opposite, and Miss O'Brien's narrative technique does not weight the scales.

This technique is the book's core. Miss O'Brien does not explain sex; she conveys its sensations—the excitements, the limits, the renewals. She wants us to react to her book as we would to a first-hand experience, and to achieve this purpose she alternates her narrative between voices, between dialogue and description, between epigram and summary. The suddenness of these changes jolts us; the off-key logic and rhythm communicate, probably better than conventional writing could do, the immediacy of the impact. . . . *Girls in Their Married Bliss* is a minor masterpiece. Though it lacks the range of major fiction, Miss O'Brien must be credited for inviting the comparison with it.

Peter Wolfe. Sat. Feb. 17, 1968, pp. 38–39

When Edna O'Brien ceased to be a country girl and turned her fancy to thoughts of sex, some people complained. The freshness and charm of her first two novels, we were told, had been routed by bitterness: all that was left were the unholy passions of flesh. In this first collection of her short stories [*The Love Object*] the two faces of Miss O'Brien are laid down side by side and it is at once apparent that between them the difference is slight. Solitude has always been her subject, and it remains so. The sex, in her later novels and in some of these stories, is a single aspect of it: her girls' final effort, often wrought of desperation, to belong and to communicate. . . .

Miss O'Brien's stories rattle with an honesty that is as compelling as the style that shapes her lively prose. Her girls are frankly presented, without romance. . . . If you read Miss O'Brien's first three novels, one after another as parts of a single whole, you will find a perfect balance of comedy and tragedy and a pattern that begins and ends with loneness. This brief collection, eight stories in all, more swiftly exposes that same breadth of talent. From the whiff of fair-day dung outside the Commercial Hotel to the rich after-dinner figs, symbol of sex in a London restaurant, there is a ring of reality in every movement. One or two of the pieces are slight, but none is false, and taken together they confirm my impression that rarely has an Irish woman protested as eloquently as Edna O'Brien. In sorrow and compassion she keens over the living. More obviously now, despair is her province.

William Trevor. *NS*. July 5, 1968, pp. 18–19

"When I was young," Edna O'Brien said in an interview for *Hibernia* (December 3, 1971), "I always wanted to be a writer and since then I have realised this dream. It's some sort of ache or dissatisfaction which makes me go on. It's something terribly intangible—almost like seeing something superb in the sky, in behaviour, or in the land, and seeing it is not enough. You have to somehow set it down for someone else to see, even though that sounds arrogant." What she sees, as her vision becomes apparent through her fiction, has remained consistent in regard to her commitments to Ireland, to the theme of love, and to writing as a dedication.

The style during these years has developed from the simple and barren naïveté of the young Caithleen with her revealing touches of ingenuousness ("I felt badly about being the cause of sending them solicitors' letters but Eugene said that it had to be") to the discursive ruminations of Mary Hooligan who reels off exhaustive lists like those of Samuel Beckett's *Watt* and converses with herself in a stream-of-consciousness-with-plot technique somewhat like that of Molly Bloom. Most of the fiction is written in the first person, which enhances both its verisimilitude and, one suspects, the critical tendency to treat it as autobiography. The best passages of the early novels are those scenes which reveal contrasting personalities—in *The Lonely Girl*, when Gaillard comes to tea with Joanna, when the deputation of virtuous god-fearing farmers call upon the agnostic Gaillard to retrieve Caithleen's honor, when the locals in the pub insult Gaillard and Caithleen—and these point to a successful career in drama. *Girls in Their Married Bliss*, the most discomforting of the novels, is blunt and direct in diction. The same attitudes on love, or the female condition, or religious friction may be phrased more subtly in the later works. The progression in style has permitted experimentation in technique, notably in *A Pagan Place*, which is written in the second person with the child-heroine identified only as "you," the father as "he," and the mother as "she." The two kinds of fiction—the Irish and the urbane—are produced from two life styles in Ireland and in England. Caithleen from County Clare is, in Baba's terms, a "right looking eejit" (a Clare expression), and a heroine may appear "streelish" in Ireland and "wanton" in England. The last novel, *Night*, marks a maturity not only in style and content but also in perception about the home land. Using real Irish names, Miss O'Brien has now created a territory as Faulkner did with Yoknapatawpha.

Grace Eckley. *Edna O'Brien* (Lewisburg, Pa.,
Bucknell Univ. Pr., 1974), pp. 77–78

This collection [*Mrs. Reinhardt, and Other Stories*] has twelve stories by Edna O'Brien, three of which are of novella length. The settings of the stories are variously London, Vermont, Cambridge, the Italian Mediterranean, Brittany and, inevitably, Ireland: The Irish seaside, and the Irish countryside of Edna O'Brien's heart, mind and sensibility. The scenery is sketched vividly and briefly but its atmosphere pervades and illuminates; Vermont is crisp, cold and clear and Jane, who lives there, is fresh, open and clear-sighted while Nell, her guest from Ireland, is alien in her introspection and self-doubts. Cambridge is evoked by contrast. We all know of its ambience but we imagine it the more by feeling Len's disappointment in "In The Hours of Darkness" when her night there is spent in an anonymous, contemporary hotel bedroom.

The subjects of the stories are women: the subject of the collection is Woman. Each story is a search for identity, a search which continues during sleep; dreams are frequently and revealingly recounted and much of the action of "Number Ten" takes place during "sleepwalking." Characters find themselves in their relationships with mothers, lovers, husbands and in their own loneliness. Many facets of personality are explored and there is often the sense that they are the facets of one personality (and that same personality has been explored in other books by Edna O'Brien.) It is surely no concidence that in two of the stories the women use one man to help erase the remembrance of another, that in three of the stories the women renounce the final comsummation to retain their illusions, that many of the women put disproportionate faith in talismans—a pebble, a necklace, as ties to a loved one—and, more trivially, that two women press wild flowers under the hall carpet.

The Irish stories seem to be further incidents from the life described in the novel, *A Pagan Place* and it is in these that the author reveals the heights of her talents for comic characteristation. "A Rose in the Heart," explores the fierce, tender, suffocating and ultimately destructive love between mother and daughter—the same mother and daughter from the earlier novel (the mother in each uses a particularly primitive method of contraception).

The men of Edna O'Brien's stories are shadows, but shadows that, paradoxically, illuminate the women: they have life only in juxtaposition to the women. Even the male first person narrator of "Clara" becomes human only as his friendship and love for the girl from the asylum develops and he, finally, seems to be absorbed into her identity. The eponymous Mrs. Reinhardt's love for her husband is real and vivid but the recipient of that love is a vague figure until he briefly lives for the reader in his infatuation for a young girl. The closest the author comes to presenting a fully drawn male is in the story "Baby Blue" but, although an endearing and tender lover, he descends to weakness and vacillation and finally leaves his lover and returns to his emasculating wife. Edna O'Brien recognises that men are necessary to women but she does not seem to admire them.

Alice Harrison. *AWR*. No. 63, 1978, pp. 170–71

The journey back to the state of being before knowledge, to reclaimed innocence, is one Edna O'Brien's heroines have tried to make in each of her eight novels. That the journey is a perilous one, . . . earlier pilgrims attest. . . . But Miss O'Brien's heroines, pursuing an even course in the early novels, appear to have lost their way.

Reviewing the early novels in the pages of *Éire-Ireland*, Seán McMahon noted that the first novel, *The Country Girls* (1960), established Miss O'Brien "as an important new Irish writer with a fresh, unselfconscious charm, an acute observation of life, and a fine, ribald sense of humor"; the second novel, *Girl with Green Eyes* (1962), affirmed this reputation; and the third, *Girls in Their Married Bliss* (1964), proved startlingly disappointing. The trilogy, it is true, carries a pair of innocents, Caithleen Brady and Baba Brennan, from their school days in County Clare to divorce and adultery in London. Because the note of ironic disillusion first sounded in *Girls in Their Married Bliss* grows more strident with each succeeding novel, the reader asks why the journey, the quest for good love, so regularly fails for Miss O'Brien's heroines. . . .

The quest for "radical innocence" has taken a tortuous route for Miss O'Brien's heroines. Caithleen and Baba of the early trilogy looked for and failed to discover it in marriage. Disillusioned with marriage, Ellen of *August Is a Wicked Month* sought it in a festival of sex and found only boredom and despair. In *Casualties of Peace*, Willa's efforts to overcome her dread of sex, marital and extramarital, resulted in her death. And Mary Hooligan of *Night*, divorcée and many times mistress? Surely the murderess Nora of *Johnny I Hardly Knew You* . . . dissipates the theory that, in Mary Hooligan, the O'Brien heroine attained to maturity. In undertaking the journey to earned innocence, Miss O'Brien's heroines select one route only: sex. They never consider the professions, social service, art and music, politics, travel. Willa, it is true, works in glass, but less as a craft or art than as a defense; and Nora, who restores paintings, does so only for a livelihood. A monomaniacal lot, these women reject all of life but sex. Indeed, in greedily defying an incest taboo, Nora rejects life. Unless a future heroine plots the journey afresh, she must continue to record not "that trenchant childhood route . . . to one's original place," but a tedious sojourn in decadence and despair.

Lotus Snow. Éire-Ireland. Spring, 1979,
pp. 75, 82–83

Edna O'Brien left Ireland for London in 1960, taking her two young children with her and leaving a failed marriage behind. Filled with anger and self pity, she left, she said, to separate herself from "family, religion, the land itself." But as her latest collection of stories, *Returning*, demonstrates, Ireland is still at the heart of her work. O'Brien has often gone public in her quarrel with her native land; in fiction, interviews, the autobiographical *Mother Ireland*, she has detailed the problems created by her personal and social history. With five novels banned in Ireland in the past, O'Brien has lashed out against the indoctrination of Irish Catholicism, claiming it produces sexual repression, guilt, terror and confusion. Although she once described herself as a gypsy, she also admits that "leaving is only conditional." Like the heroines in most of the stories in this collection, she keeps coming back.

Most of these stories were published in the *New Yorker* between 1979 and 1982 and are filled with landscapes and characters familiar since the Country Girls trilogy established O'Brien's reputation more than twenty years ago. Women seeking love and acceptance while challenging moral and sexual codes, young girls craving a mother's love or a nun's favor, men drunken and confused act out a tragic drama of the minute details of Irish village life. O'Brien's characters can be cruel, promiscuous, arrogant, naive, but they are all inevitably alone. The narrator of the lead story, "The Connor Girls," speaks for many of them when, explaining how her marriage to a non-Catholic has alienated her from her community, she concludes: "we gradually become exiles, until at last we are quite alone."

In the conflict between men and women, the most persistent and pervasive theme in O'Brien's fiction, females are often victims of male cruelty and indifference. That her own memories helped shape these stories is evident from O'Brien's comments about her childhood; she once told an interviewer that in Taumgraney, her home town, the men had a "cruelty and a crossness," the women were "tenderer and nicer." Such characteristics, appearing often in the stories in *Returning*, lead ultimately to suffering. Women are naive martyrs whose pursuit of unrealistic dreams pushes them into destructive action. Some are like Mabel in "Savages" who "died, as she had lived, a simpleton." Juxtaposed with such women are foolish males, like the three in "Tough Men" who negotiate a secret business deal only to be swindled by a con man cleverer than themselves. O'Brien's characters, though they try various methods of escape, never quite succeed. . . .

O'Brien has said in the past that she was not interested in literature "as such" but that she felt strongly about the "real expression of feeling." This is indeed her strong point; the feelings expressed by the female narrators of these stories range from anger to sadness, humor and confusion. The narrators return in memory or in actuality to their Irish village and try from a distance, with an enlightened perspective, to objectify their childhood experiences. Their inability to completely understand, however, creates a vulnerability and an ambiguity which is both realistic and appealing.

Patricia Boyle Haberstroh. *ILS*. Spring, 1983, p. 38

You see a country and a culture impressing itself deeply on this writer. The country is Ireland, and from the evidence available, she is more succubus than mother. The need to escape is visceral. There is a sense of protest in these stories [*A Fanatic Heart: Selected Stories of Edna O'Brien*], but it is often concealed or channeled into pain, perhaps because the author is a woman. The aggression takes the form of an arresting and unfaltering scream. When the background is rural—even barbaric—there is a rawness and earthiness in Edna O'Brien that some critics have compared with Colette. But she is not like Colette, because the stories are darker and full of conflict. In an essay about James Joyce, Frank Tuohy says that while Joyce, in *Dubliners* and *Portrait of the Artist*, was the first Irish Catholic to make his experience and surroundings recognizable, "the world of Nora Barnacle had to wait for the fiction of Edna O'Brien."

The stories set in the heartland of Ireland almost always depict women—with men, without men, on the make, on the loose, cracking up, women holding to reality by the skin of their teeth. Many are love stories, among them eerily intimate stories relating to sexual love, and these are what people chiefly associate with Edna O'Brien. But her range is wider than that and there is an acute, sometimes searing, social awareness. The worlds depicted are not just those of small farms full of lovelorn women and inebriate men, but also the larger world of cities, of resorts, of estrangement, the world of the very rich and careless. In a long story, a novella really, "Mrs. Reinhardt," there is an idyllic recapture of the countryside of Brittany that ends in disenchantment and havoc; in another story, "Paradise," the narrator says of the fashionable house guests, "All platinum . . . They have a canny sense of self-preservation; they know how much to eat, how much to drink . . . you would think they invented somebody like Shakespeare, so proprietary are they . . . You could easily get filleted. Friends do it to friends."

The sensibility is on two levels and shuttles back and forth, combining the innocence of childhood with the scars of maturity. It is what gives these stories their wounded vigor. The words themselves are chiseled. The welter of emotion is rendered so sparsely that the effect is merciless, like an autopsy.

> Philip Roth. Foreword to Edna O'Brien, *A Fanatic Heart: Selected Stories of Edna O'Brien* (New York, Farrar, Straus, & Giroux, 1984), n. p.

In this collection of old and new stories [*A Fanatic Heart: Selected Stories of Edna O'Brien*], Edna O'Brien adopts Yeats's diagnosis of the disease of the Irish spirit, but she does not share his view of its etiology. Her Ireland breeds a fanaticism of anguish and despair, and her characters, maimed by their unfulfilled longing, cry out, not in rage and hatred, but in pain and desperation. Though apt in its suggestion of emotional intensity, the Yeatsian allusion in the volume's title seems ill-suited to the passivity and victimization that characterize O'Brien's vision of Irish feminine sensibility.

Indeed, if *A Fanatic Heart* bears any relation to Irish masculine experience and expression, it is not to Yeats's poems but to Joyce's dispirited *Dub-*

liners. As an exile, looking back at the land that formed her, O'Brien traces female consciousness from the fragility of childhood, through the disquiet of maturity, to the loneliness of senescence. Although she does not pursue her portrait with Joyce's chronological exactitude, her stories convey the sense of unfulfilled movement and growth found in *Dubliners*.

Despite its evocation of Yeats and recollection of Joyce, *A Fanatic Heart* speaks with O'Brien's unmistakable voice, articulating her singular view of Ireland and Irish womanhood. This excellent selection of her short stories includes the whole of *Returning*, her most recent volume never published in the United States; the best work from her earlier collections, *The Love Object, A Scandalous Woman* and *A Rose in the Heart;* and four previously uncollected but interrelated pieces. In each of the volume's stories, the central character and narrator (in every case but one, a woman) is excruciatingly aware of the inadequacies of her existence. It is this awareness that typifies O'Brien's women. Clinging to the experience of pain and sorrow as a means of maintaining identity and preserving vitality, her characters never lose their searing self-knowledge. As the narrator in "The Love Object" explains, savoring the torment of her lost love, "If I let go of him now . . . all our happiness and my subsequent pain . . . will have been nothing and nothing is a dreadful thing to hold on to."

What makes many of these stories so wrenching and so distinctly O'Brien's is the double sense of loss they convey. Returning to the world of childhood, O'Brien explores its griefs in exquisite detail, yet she reveals how the loss of the troubled past is, in itself, a blow—another source of sorrow. Pursuing the pain of love, she portrays the agony when love's special torture is gone. As the stories move from childhood to maturity, and from Ireland to England and the continent, the vulnerability of the characters intensifies; their self-awareness heightens. New losses compound old anguish.

The fanaticism of O'Brien's heart is not Yeats's. One almost wishes that she had chosen for her title the other organ in Yeats's memorable lines.

Adele Dalsimer. *ILS*. Fall, 1985, p. 50.

O'BRIEN, FLANN [BRIAN O'NOLAN] [also known as MYLES NA GOPALEEN] (1911–1966)

This book [*At Swim-Two-Birds*] is mostly fantasy, with a basis of realism, which is also shot through with a curious freakish whimsy. Its construction is most unusual, apparently meaningless, almost chaotic and in the hands of a less deft writer would be dreadful. But Mr. O'Brien has the knack of inveighling even a stick with fantasy, and so it happens that the absurd struts and props of his literary construction help rather than hinder his mirage of the bizarre, and for all its incomprehensibility the thing runs free and easily and with a distinctive life of its own. There is nothing here for lovers of the conventional or classical. But for all who think and dream a little out of normal focus it holds a wealth of surprise and delight. For his flags of fancy fly cheerfully from beginning to end.

The title gives no indication or clue as to the author's intentions. He mentions it on page 95. It is "the church of Snamh-da-en (or Swim-Two-Birds) by the side of the Shannon." That is all—whether real or fictitious is not mentioned, and it is the only help we get from him.

There are episodes that flow with fluency and freedom, one of the best concerned with mad King Sweeney's wanderings through Erin, with its delicious and entirely unoffensive satire of Celtic folk tales—or what one of the characters in the book calls "the real old stuff of the native land." Some of his characters are elusive and impalpable, but others stand out with the vivid intensity of unmistakable magic. One of his most enchantingly capricious conceptions is the conventionally named "Good Fairy," who is a voice only, but a voice "sweeter by far than the tinkle and clap of a waterfall and brighter than the first shaft of day." But it is only the tone of the voice that is suave, for the contents of the conversation is startling, entertaining, malicious, and the personality vivid as lightning.

Though *At Swim-Two-Birds* is externally incoherent it is fundamentally held together in essence by a pervading atmosphere, and it is the accomplishment of this on the part of the author that makes it such a remarkable literary feat. For his charm is irresistible and makes itself felt even in places that seem somewhat silly, affected or offensive. And it may be in the reconcilement of the opposing factors of fantasy and realism in his own mind that the mystery of his writing finds its flight.

DM. July, 1939, pp. 102–3

This brilliant and wicked book [*At Swim-Two-Birds*] was first published in 1939, a bad year for originality and laughter. In spite of praise from James Joyce—who was parodied in it—and Mr. Graham Greene, and from the best critics, it reached only a small public. Let us hope the prospects are brighter now, for Mr. O'Brien's is one of the funniest "novels" to come out of Ireland. To describe it is difficult. One could say that the author designed to reduce the total Irish literary tradition to farce and to make hay of the modern novel, but his irreverence is not journalistic. The book is not a skit. It is scholarly, vigorous and creative. . . .

Mr. O'Brien's gifts are startling and heartless. He has the astounding Irish genius for describing the human animal, its shameless and dilapidated body, its touching and proliferating fancy, its terrible interest in useless conundrums. On top of this he has an extraordinary freedom of the English language, perhaps because he is a Gaelic scholar, perhaps because the Elizabethan tradition has survived in Ireland. His people are either seedy Dubliners or ludicrous giants, but their wits are alight; they live in language, in comic image, rather than in life. It looks as though his idea was to knock the regionalism out of Irish literature by magnifying it. Since Joyce, the nose-picking, truculent porter-and-Guinness-swilling Dublin student has been an established figure in Irish literature, predating our own post-war Jimmies and resembling, in their unemployable way, the over-educated rogues of the Elizabethan universites and the picaros of Salamanca.

The sloth of Mr. O'Brien's sulky, superior narrator who, despite his beatnik behaviour, triumphs with cynical ease in his examinations at the end, is an enjoyable quality. I became tired of the joke only when Mr. Trellis's characters started writing about him, simply because of the excess. This kind of fantasy is apt to be self-destructive. But I shall often return to Mr. O'Brien's diverting brainstorm and shall often brood about one of his deluded characters who feared to sit down because he imagined his bottom was made of glass.

V. S. Pritchett. NS. Aug. 20, 1960, pp. 250–51

Neither *The Hard Life* nor *The Dalkey Archive* has the authority and inclusiveness of *At Swim-Two-Birds*, nor the deep, concentrated power of *The Third Policeman*. Both the later books seem to toy with symbolic overtones rather than genuinely incorporate them. They pick their way round the edges of vitally important subjects rather than going hell-for-leather through the middle. And this realization gives us a vantage point to look back on *At Swim-Two-Birds*, noting clearly now its elegiac quality, its sense that the problems posed by time are not soluble; and also on the quietly agonized exploration of the damned state in *The Third Policeman*.

If, in his first book O'Nolan came close to Joyce, in his second he anticipated the best work of Beckett. In temperament, he stands somewhere between the two. He is more discouraged than Joyce, less of a Yea-sayer. Joyce's work is bleak, but it is not elegiac. It affirms the stature of man. The eighteen hours of Leopold Bloom's life which we follow in *Ulysses* are full of shabbiness, failure, and discouragement, but they are also Homeric. Joyce's purpose in elaborating his technique of literary *son et lumière* was to affirm that his wandering Jewish salesman was no less important than Odysseus. By contrast, O'Nolan's parallels between Trellis and Sweeney, between the bardic feast and the paralytic loquacity of the saloon bar, are parallels of hopelessness. On the other hand, he is not a connoisseur of hopelessness like Beckett, who seems to have cast himself in the role of a vulture, waiting on some dusty branch for the kicking human body to become a nice quiet corpse. The sense of doom, of the curse of meaninglessness laid on all that a man is and does, is brilliantly conveyed in *The Third Policeman*, but it is set within a religious framework and shown as the punishment for taking a man's life, cruelly, for gain. In Beckett's work, the capital crime is simply to be alive; *that* is the stupidity, the evil, the appalling metaphysical *gaffe* for which we are to be snubbed and punished for ever. O'Nolan does not talk in this strain; if he lacks the gigantic affirmative energy of Joyce, he nevertheless has some of Joyce's centrality and sanity.

When, early in 1966, the news came that O'Nolan had died, I felt both saddened and amazed. Saddened that a writer who so interested and engaged me would now write no more; amazed that he was only in his early fifties. He must have been so young when *At Swim-Two-Birds* came to him; it must have formed in his mind, shaking him with laughter and dismay, at a time when he was no older than the two of us who stared down at his book, knowing that a new chapter in our own history was beginning, that morning in the Eagle and Child. *Vale*. [1967]

John Wain. *A House for the Truth*
(London, Macmillan, 1972), pp. 103–4

I am not much taken with the "life is absurd" theory, because I'm tolerably sure life is, on the contrary, preposterous. This may well be an ancestral conviction on my part: for, now I think of it, some such proposition is the point of most Irish discourse and a good deal of Irish literature.

Certainly *The Dalkey Archive*, one of Irish literature's grand triumphs, asserts the preposterousness of life. In doing so, it redeploys much of the material of another Flann O'Brien novel, written earlier but only now—posthumously—published, *The Third Policeman*, which makes the same assertion about death. The book's "I," a murderer, learns in the last chapter that he's been dead for 16 years—since, to be exact, Chapter Two, where he is blown up by a mine planted by his co-criminal. His death and damnation consist of his trying to escape death—on, principally, the gallows of the local police. By the last page of the novel he's re-entering the police station and, unknowingly, starting the whole literally damned sequence again. That's death.

Of course, some of the minor characters in *The Dalkey Archive* are dead, too: Saint Augustine, for instance. But it's a great help to coherency that they *know* they are. It's also a help to credibility that the improbable events have to be swallowed or doubted by the two contrasted, third-person consciousnesses of Shaughnessy and Hackett, that pair of fine *ficelles* drawn out of Stephen Dedalus and Buck Mulligan. And the surrealisms themselves stand out hard-edged against the pebble dash and faded bathing towels of Dalkey.

The Third Policeman, by contrast, is confined by its very *donnée* to a single consciousness—and, unaware as it is of so cardinal a fact about itself, a befuddled one. The narrative goes into dream-like drifts; it's hard for the reader to feel enough suspense about the hero's suspension. If the Dalkey diction occasionally plunges into funny-column facetiousness, *The Third Policeman* shows less retrievable flaws in the imaginative material itself. Its unlocated, underpopulated Irish country-side is sometimes haunted as banally ("the light had some quality which was wrong, mysterious, alarming") as Versailles in those ladies' adventures.

For all that, the reader's attention is fiercely grappled to the book here and there along the line: by exquisite comic constructs, Nabokovian ingenuities and flights of Lodovico-Carolingian pseudo- or hyperlogic. Only the structure as a whole is less beautifully inventive than in *The Dalkey Archive*, whose trinitarian or leaf-of-shamrocks design is built of three interrelated yet cumulative preposterousnesses.

Brigid Brophy. List. Sept. 28, 1967, p. 403

Like several others at the time—like Eimar O'Duffy in *King Goshawk and the Birds* and Brinsley MacNamara in *The Various Lives of Marcus Igoe* a few years before, or like Mervyn Wall and Austin Clarke in their Celtic-Romanesque romances a few years afterwards, or Jack B. Yeats—Brian O'Nolan pursued a vein of fantasy, but in his own inimitable way and for his own private reasons. He was never a member of a significant group or conscious movement—he wrote for *The Bell* as well as for *Ireland Today*—and what views he shared with friends like Niall Sheridan and Niall Montgomery are less important than his almost necessary sense of separateness. The only source of inspiration he acknowledged without qualification—though he took care to define it in his own idiosyncratic way—was the native Irish tradition for which he had a genuine love, and typically on the grounds of its uselessness and total separation from modern concerns. His M.A. thesis on nature in Irish poetry was on a subject with clear and fundamental attraction for him, but, characteristically, from all reports it was impeccably academic.

As a writer whose roots lie in the Ireland of the 1930's, Brian O'Nolan is in the end his own man. The combination of sheer ordinariness and sheer unpredictable fantasy is a paradox protected by privacy. Each of his *personae* at different times allowed different scope to his genius, but the attraction of his writing is also founded on the sense of something withheld and quite separate. We are struck by an intrinsic fastidiousness or reticence which involves mingled pride and humility, and which has little in common with the self-indulgent blether and boisterous farce of some of his latter-day admirers. It is a quality that colours all aspects of his writing, large and small, from the characteristic form of his sentences to the way in which he manipulates plot, and that enables the writing to be at its best mocking and humane, austere and extravagant, committed and shy, compassionate and gay, all this and more at the very same time. It encourages affection as well as respect. What delights and persuades in Brian O'Nolan's writing is ultimately a range of human qualities, paradoxical as it may seem when what is best in it is most impersonal.

J. C. C. Mays. In Timothy O'Keeffe, ed., Myles:
Portraits of Brian O'Nolan (London, Martin Brian &
O'Keeffe, 1973), pp. 84–85

It is a just tribute to the Irish genius, in particular to Irish writers' powers of observation, expression and dramatisation that whole tracts of general human experience are acknowledged to be specifically Irish, the Irish having acquired squatters' rights in them.

It is in this sense that O'Nolan is to be acclaimed as the kind of thing that could only happen in Ireland. He is one of those who strenuously and successfully addressed himself to the understanding and mastery of those above-mentioned twin problems of the Irish writer. In him, the Irishness of Ireland, the extremes of Dublin's Dublinicity, become simultaneously unique and immense, bursting geographical limits. The pressures of the well-known cultural heritage provide simultaneously a frame and that essential "background urgency." The tight casing of the hand-grenade is essential to the force of its explosion.

In this connection it is of symbolic significance as well as great factual importance that he wrote Irish as well as he wrote English. A lot of Irish writers claim, truthfully enough; that they can write Irish, meaning that they can write more or less fluently, clearly and "correctly" in that language. Hundreds of English writers claim, with equal truth, that they can write English, meaning the same thing. But this sort of thing is not writing in the way O'Nolan understood and practised it. He had an understanding of these instruments, and a passionate love and care in his use of them which can be seen as both classical and Elizabethan. The words and the syntax, the *nuances* and sinuosities, the elusive allusiveness, the double and treble meaningfulness of phrases, the controlled flexibilities of structure, are for the writer of O'Nolan's quality indispensable matters for study and experiment. Derision, and a kind of astounded disgust were in him evoked by the products of candidates for the title of Writer who seemed to have treated such studies as Optional Subjects in their Course. He could be put forward as an argument for the theory that a writer for whom English is not his native language, or not his sole native language, is better placed than others to appreciate, genuinely master and most richly exploit the instrument.

Claud Cockburn. Introduction to Flann O'Brien,
Stories and Plays (London, Hart-Davis, MacGibbon,
1973), pp. 12–13

The importance of *The Third Policeman* lies in its presentation of a vision of hell which implies man's reliance on order, pattern and harmony. O'Brien believes that these things are inherent in man's world even if the sophistries of philosophy seek to convince him that they are not. The emotional stress of the book lies aways in the evocation of nature and in the belief that it is this kind of perception which defines what is best in man.

This vision of horror and this perception of tranquillity in nature is subsumed within an overriding comic apprehension which can allow for the terror of bewilderment and negation at the same time as it presents simple guessing games and strange stories. The embellishment of a sinister and nightmarish story with pleasant and amusing detail proves how near is the vision of comedy to chaos and unreason. . . . Queer but authentic incomprehensibility that makes you wonder if you are mad seems an adequate description of the ethos of *The Third Policeman.* . . .

Can we postulate, therefore, that the comic essence of *The Third Policeman* lies in its being the comedy of negation, nullity and abstraction? The comic *reductio* tends to lead to the world of the absurd, and this was a world in which O'Brien was unable to live for very long. The new world which he had created out of fragments of philosophy, ideas of the Celtic otherworld and the topsy-turveydom of Sterne, proved to be unbearable, and when he put *The Third Policeman* aside and rewrote it as *The Dalkey Archive* O'Brien moved from the horrors of illogical abstraction and turned to the promise of accepted mysteries.

Anne Clissmann. Flann O'Brien: A Critical
Introduction to His Writings (New York, Barnes &
Noble, 1975), pp. 180–81

The most common experience we have of consciousness-collapse is laughter.

As his first three novels show, O'Brien knew all this early in his writing career. These books seem so effortlessly written, and so acute and uncompromising in their perceptions, that they read like the work of a man possessed by acuity. But having done so much so quickly, he then (in the early 1940s) ran into difficulty, expressed in terms of problems of form. The experience of laughter gives us a sense of beyond, an intimation of the arbitrariness of form. O'Brien desired his work to be a similarly haphazard and subversive kind of event.

The seeds of that desire were present in those early novels. All three contain attacks on books and on being book-bound. Novel-writing is dismantled in *At Swim*, critical exegesis damned in *The Third Policeman*, the sentimental style used to present "account[s] of neolithic civilisation from the inside" acidically satirised in *The Poor Mouth*. His rejection of an accredited form, bookwriting, was undoubtedly a major decision, particularly since the form with which he replaced it, the newspaper column, offered him the advantages of succinctness, immediacy, and directness—characteristics he prized in Irish.

The column, taken as a complete work . . . , is everything a book is not—random, uneven, momentary, disposable, flexible: and yet it retains its singularity. An unedited saga. Also, and possibly fatally, it did something no book could do. It allowed O'Brien to be completely and totally himself. He could write about whatever he wanted. So, he denounced City Hall and the Abbey Theatre. He deliberated loud and long on the character and achievement of James Joyce. He lambasted the ideologues and sentimentalists who had made Irish their province. Presented with complete liberty to express himself, he indulged his capacity at the expense of his vision. Words overran thought. Anne Clissmann says that "he regarded words as a consolation and a defence of the mind against being possessed by thought." Simplicity was smothered by circumstance. Over the years his keen-wittedness dwindled into spleen, his power to scourge expressed itself too hastily as chagrin. He didn't know what to ignore.

Not surprisingly, doubts about citizenship and artisthood run through the two late novels. *The Hard Life*, subtitled "An Exegesis of Squalor" and dedicated to Graham Greene, is an essay of mistrust in the pretensions of public life. *The Dalkey Archive* shows, among other items, Joyce as a quiet poor soul of a barman who denies having written more than *Dubliners* and tracts for the Catholic Truth Society: the artist divested of pride.

Yet the decision to express himself in the form of a newspaper column seems only a logical one, confirming what for me is O'Brien's major fault, an excessive concern with deployment. The problem of realising that it's impossible to represent the supersession of consciousness, that it's only possible to *be* in whatever new state ensues, is tacitly acknowledged, but never faced or worked out. One result of this disinclination to think through is that shock tends to take the place of drama. . . .

Whatever idea we have of the true I think we want it to be incontrovertible, seamless, buoyant—properties of O'Brien's work at its best, examples of which will be found in all his books. No one book, in my opinion, conveys a whole vision, possibly because, in his drive to by-pass thought, he forgoes the chance of searching out the experience of arrival at a more immanent set of realisations than thought engenders. He finally seems to regard the intelligence as a scar—livid, perhaps, and certainly singular, but also curiously bloodless.

George O'Brien. CambQ. 7, 1, 1976, pp. 90–92

The Hard Life: An Exegesis of Squalor (1961) was dedicated to Graham Greene, and after a preliminary warning that none of the characters is fictitious even in part, it opens with a text from Pascal to the effect that all the troubles in the world can be traced to the fact that nobody knows how to stay quietly alone in his bedroom. It is more restrained in its impact than *At Swim-Two-Birds*, and is, on the whole, the least off-beat of Flann O'Brien's works. Much more striking is his third novel published in 1964 and entitled *The Dalkey Archive*, and dedicated this time to his Guardian Angel with a solemn appeal "to see to it that there is no misunderstanding when I go home." Dalkey, a seaside suburb of Dublin—this "vestibule of heavenly conspection" as he terms it—seems to inspire O'Brien to some of the rare moments of coloratura in his prose. . . . It might also be added that this one-time Borough that gives its name to the book had, until recently, one of those rare things—a restaurant that closes for lunch.

The recurrent theme in the novel is concerned with the elusive nature of time, while the plot propounds a theory that James Joyce did not die, as is supposed, in Switzerland, but is living today under an assumed name in this suburb, where he is writing pamphlets for the Catholic Truth Society in expiation for the sins of *Ulysses*, and has totally forgotten all about *Finnegans Wake*.

But to my mind the most illuminating of all his works of fiction is the last—*The Third Policeman*—which oddly enough was not the last to be written, and which I distinctly remember being passed around in manuscript in the Pearl Bar while the war was far from over. Yet it was never snapped up and published until 1967, when the elusive author was dead. Why this should be so I cannot imagine, unless it is because in earlier days some publisher's delinquent reader could not bring himself to study the typescript, owing to the number of pages that consist of enormous footnotes. This, of course, is one of the best spoofs embodied in the book. It looks like a ponderous and unreadable thesis by an aspiring Ph.D., but it reads like a crazy Chinese Box, where each receptacle contains a smaller one. In the course of this hopeless quest for finality the multiple structure of Time and the Universe is illuminated by comments from the characters, such as:

It's a quare contraption—very dangerous—a certain death-trap—Life.

What an Epitaph! Upon the truth of which only Myles na Gopaleen himself can pronounce, for he died before his book appeared in print, a loss to Irish Letters that occurred at almost the same time as the destruction of another familiar feature of Dublin life—Nelson's Pillar. We would have been better advised to spare our Pillar, and put Myles up there in place of the Onehandled Adulterer.

> Denis Johnston. In Joseph Ronsley, ed., *Myth and*
> *Reality in Irish Literature* (Waterloo, Ont., Wilfred
> Laurier Univ. Pr., 1977), pp. 302–3

[*The Hard Life*] was published in 1961, twenty years and more after the publication of *At Swim-Two-Birds* and the writing of *The Third Policeman*. Because of the fate of *The Third Policeman,* the special audience for the Irish *The Poor Mouth* and the play *Faustus Kelly,* the novel was greeted as O'Brien's second full-length work, and he was welcomed back after what the critics could only assume was a strangely long absence.

Just why did O'Brien write this "exegesis of squalor" after the two bright inventions of the earlier novels, and why did he write it at this interval? The reissue of *At Swim-Two-Birds* may account for some of the motivation to write another book, but the choice of subject would on the surface seem inexplicable. O'Brien, however, thought of the book as "very important and very funny" and warned its editor, Tim O'Keeffe, that it's "apparently pedestrian style is delusive." O'Brien fans will also see that many earlier and later interests emerge in this book, which seems most untypical of any of his longer works. The brother is not only a frequenter of *Cruiskeen Lawn*, but a minor-league de Selby. Mrs. Crotty is the basic Flann mother. Mr. Collopy is much like *At Swim's* uncle, and, as [Anne] Clissmann points out, the Uncle Andy of the late TV series *Th' Oul Lad of Kilsalaher*. The Gravid Water is an anticipation of *The Dalkey Archive's* lethal D.M.P., and so forth. Perhaps more important for him was not the recognition of the squalor level, which had always been in O'Brien's longer works, but the ability in this work to hang in there, reveling in the grayness without recourse to tempting flights. Gravid Water wins out over tightrope walking and theology.

To keep our feet sticking to the ground, O'Brien uses a point of view that holds us closer to conventional realism than does that of any of the preceding works. In spite of the scheming by the brother and Mr. Collopy, there is no threat that the narrative itself will rise up and do us in after the manner of *At Swim* or *The Third Policeman*. In this sense, the book represents a technical step backward. O'Brien had, of course, been warned that he "should become less fantastic." The book sold well enough to justify such advice, although much of its commercial appeal might have been due to its naughtiness.

Stephen Jones. Introduction to *The Hard Life*, in
Stephen Jones, ed., *A Flann O'Brien Reader* (New
York, Viking, 1978), pp. 115–16

In *At Swim-Two-Birds* Flann O'Brien searches for a governing structure that will support a necessarily diverse panoply, while constantly suggesting that all structures are artificial and doomed to destruction. In effect he began with the destructive element, attacking the monochromatic and linear plot progression characteristic of the traditional novel. "One beginning and one ending for a book was a thing I did not agree with," states O'Brien's tentative artist-as-a-young-man with syntactical simplicity and glittering ingenuity; "A good book may have three openings entirely dissimilar and interrelated only in the prescience of the author, or for that matter one hundred times as many endings." (That the goal of such experimentation is the ideal "good book" gets quietly buried among the audacities, but it must be eventually resurrected as central to O'Brien's scheme in *At Swim*.)

For the premise challenged (the single vein of plot line) two species are presented: a workable but presumably arbitrary set of *three*, and an exaggerative and presumably unworkable hundred—actually three hundred. The nature of the exaggeration for hyperbolic emphasis is exposed in the construction which allows for a hundred different endings for each of the three openings. The trinitarian structure is hardly accidental: we need no Saint Patrick waving a shamrock under our noses to accept the traditional values of a trinity that remains and characterizes an essential unity. The chaos conjured up by the threat of vague hundreds is calmed by the assurance of a familiar three, and life parallels art from the opening sentence to assure us that the pattern is an intended and fixed one ("Having placed in my mouth sufficient bread for three minutes' chewing. . . ." Casually and almost half-heartedly the three openings are advanced (the first on the Pooka, the second on John Furriskey, and the third on Finn MacCool), yet the neat compartmentalization is immediately discernible as a patent fraud: Flann O'Brien's novel had already begun prior to these three openings with a narrator chewing bread, and thereafter continues with his hurting a tooth on a "lump of the crust." Hard reality—in the shape of a crust of basic bread—intrudes into the trinitarian fantasy and persists throughout the book. As soon as the essential One is sub-divided into a tight triangle of three, a back door has been opened unto the fourth (akin to the Irish folk-Trinity of the Father and the Son and the Holy Ghost and the Banshee).

Accepting the fiction of the fiction, a young novelist lying in bed writing a book which has three openings because he is juggling a trio of characters (and their individual plot lines leading toward inter-relationship), we willingly suspend disbelief to allow for the squared triangle and naively assume that we have reached a finite stasis. What we have failed to allow for are two vastly disturbing elements: the erratic ineptness of the young novelist that makes his manuscript problematical, and the persistence of external forces at work on his physical being, so that despite his tenacious retreat to his bedroom, there is no guarantee of uninterrupted progress on the novel. O'Brien presents not only the creative product (in bits and pieces) but also a parody of the creative process.

Bernard Benstock. In Dennis Jackson, ed., *Irish Renaissance Annual III* (Newark, Univ. of Delaware Pr., 1982), pp. 16–18

O'BRIEN, KATE (1897–1974)

Miss O'Brien has confessed to being a sentimentalist; and she certainly appears in the three novels [*The Ante-Room, Mary Lavelle,* and *The Land of Spices*] as a sentimental romantic human being. Mary Lavelle in Spain loses her heart and her virginity, returns to Ireland with tears in her eyes and the first seeds of experience sown in her soul. The young man in *The Ante-Room* loves his wife's sister with a hopeless love and ends it romantically and sentimentally by thinking of his childhood and looking down the barrel of a gun.

. . . In *The Land of Spices* the memory of the fearful moment when her father's abnormality had been revealed to her could not black out in the nun's mind the many memories of a lovable civilised man savouring Trahearne and Herbert and Crashaw.

But in *That Lady* Miss O'Brien has deliberately sacrificed every human consolation, has seen her people and their sin against the background of the reality of God. Outside Mauriac I do not know of any modern novelist who has so carefully analysed the motives and the results of a sin; and it would be possible to draw out a lengthy comparison between Ana in her dungeon and Thérèse Desqueyroux in the prolonged penance imposed on her by Mauriac in *La Fin de la Nuit*. The difference is that Kate O'Brien—and God—are a little closer than François Mauriac to the meaning of mercy and never in *That Lady* as in *Les Chemins de la Mer* do you feel that the novelist has condemned her people, has seen above everything the existence of hell, and is relentlessly driving the creatures of her imagination to a judgment already irrevocably given. . . . Kate O'Brien follows her own path, sees the attractiveness and the pity of the doomed passion, the doubt of the sinner, the complexities of repentance, the shakiness of the ground on which the king stands when he contrives judgment and punishment. Ana de Mendoza, with her lover in her arms and fearful scruples in her mind, thinks: "Is my poor scruple greater than what I give this man and take from him? Am I to set my little private sense of sin above his claim on me and his unhappiness? Am I cheating because I want him, and have grown tired of the unimportant fuss of my immortal soul? Am I pretending to be generous simply to escape again into his power?"

Those questions leave little room for romantic illusions but they open the door to pity—not the destructive pity outlined by Graham Greene in *The Ministry of Fear* or *The Heart of the Matter* but a tired welcoming pity that could be a faint shadow of the mercy of God. And when, towards the end of the book, Ana and her friend Cardinal Quiroga talk about her troubles, the novelist removes the last illusion by showing that even the mercy of God may be presumed upon.

Benedict Kiely. *Modern Irish Fiction: A Critique*
(Dublin, Golden Eagle Books, 1950), pp. 139–41

Considering the success of *Without My Cloak,* the distinction of both *The Ante-Room* and *Mary Lavelle,* and the polemical force of *Pray for the Wanderer,* it seems correct to assess that the thirties were a time of fulfillment for Kate O'Brien. Outward triumph, the making of new and lasting friendships and financial security helped bring about a temporary truce between those fractures of ritual and rite, sense and spirit, sexuality and intellect—all of which had wounded her deeply.

But the fractures still existed and the truce was not a treaty. And so with infinite courage she turned to explore the very source of her weaknesses as an artist, to vanquish or be vanquished by them. In three books, *The Land of Spices,* published in 1940, *That Lady* and *Teresa of Avila,* published in 1951, she confronted the quandaries of spirit versus sense. That she had the courage to attempt it indicates how bold was her imagination. That she failed to accomplish it is a measure of her honor, for she must have been aware of the odds: for after *That Lady*—with the exception of *Teresa of Avila,* which was not a novel—she never wrote well again, but degenerated into the repetitions and sentimentalities of writing which she herself would have been the first to scald with dismissal.

It is almost a critical consensus that after *That Lady* in 1946, Kate O'Brien's work never again had the attack, the flair, the perception it possessed before. It is also a critical consensus that in the novel which preceded it she achieved the highest perception into her world and made it accessible to others. This was called *The Land of Spices,* published in 1941, which Mary Lavin, the distinguished short story writer has called "an incredibly intricate piece of work, brilliantly brought off." It is, in fact, a study of convent life, and of a nun who in one passage remembers as a child having seen her father—and I quote—"in the embrace of love" with another man. For those five words the book was banned in one of the most ruthless acts of vandal censorship in an era which indulged in many of them.

In 1943 she published *The Last of Summer* but was already working on *That Lady,* a novel set in the Spain of Philip II, which was hailed in 1946 as "one of the finest historical European novels." She herself, that October night, told us that the scheme for the novel—the story itself had haunted her for years—came to her like a gift, after an air raid, in London. She had been writing letters, and after the all-clear set out to post them. And that simple journey clarified her plot, her vision and she set to work. It was a given moment, but the years of research were wearing. And yet curiously, the last part of the book was also something of a gift. She began the epilogue to it—some 7,000 words—as midnight lightened into a summer dawn in her sister's house in Currafin beside a lake. In three or four hours of writing, she had completed it and broke down when she told her sister.

Never again was she to write so well.

Eavan Boland. *The Critic.* Winter, 1975, pp. 22–24

To say that [Kate O'Brien] produced work which was "a chronicle of her time" is perfectly true. The ambience and milieu created are authentic and accurate. These are brought to life and vitality by the women who people her stage and through Kate O'Brien's method of "interiorizing," or allowing herself the liberty of knowing their thoughts and feelings. The author concerns herself with the resources that these women can evoke in times of crisis, in order to transcend the bonds that bind them: "The strictures are those of manners and morality." Kate O'Brien has an unswerving faith in womankind, most of whom find themselves "imprisoned in a code of response, a minuet of programmed answers and expectations." Love is the pivot of their emotional lives. The author peels back the layers of their personalities in denying them that love; in placing it out of their reach in their particular situation, or she allows it to be snatched away by circumstances outside the self. This is the tragic situation of Kate O'Brien's female characters. . . .

While the women of *Without My Cloak* and *The Ante-Room* lived out their lives as mothers and spinsters, and while their social values were evident in their jewellery, their clothes, their snobbery, their chat, their musical events and games of whist, their horses, carriages and servants; these characteristics were not of a peculiarly Irish nature in the later part of the nineteenth century. The author's concern is with the interior world of the female mind. It is of these characters that the claim has been made: "Miss O'Brien is as fond of the case of conscience as any zealous Jesuit could be." However, in *Pray for the Wanderer* the heroines, Una and Nell, are very much of their time and context. Their dialogue speaks their reality, they are in tune with their world, and Kate O'Brien chooses to define their characters against the dynamism of Irish society of that day.

Una . . . can be considered as the stereotype wife and mother who runs the home with infinite patience, efficiency and love, living through others with no obvious impulses of her own. The author portrays her as a flawless woman, admired by her family, radiating happiness. However, there are a few gentle question marks inserted here and there in the course of Una's characterization, which make her more believable; less of a stereotype. Kate O'Brien, I believe, thoroughly approves of Una, approving through her of the traditional, domestic role of women, and Una's weaknesses are part of the predicament of human nature. . . .

Nell, Una's sister, is almost the antithesis of Una in all aspects of her existence. She is thirty-three years old and a spinster. . . . She shuns the personal and moral responsibility that comes with personal integrity. She must have law and order, guidelines and rules; without the values inherent in these, Nell knows that she is personally abandoned to chaos.

The moral code that Nell adheres to is not inherently Irish. In the post-Famine era in Ireland "the prudish values of Victorian middle class morality, which simultaneously idealized and repressed women," were superimposed on Catholicism in the European context. Prudery and morality became synonymous. Kate O'Brien has very deftly personified the attitudes of the time in Una and Nell, but she has also given them hearts. Love is the pivot on which Una's world revolves, and Nell, disappointed in love, having rejected Tom when she discovers that he has fathered a child out of wedlock, almost misses love altogether. Nell believes in emotion, as all Kate O'Brien's heroines do. . . .

Kate O'Brien leaves Una and Nell in . . . a land that she knew and interpreted at first hand and which she presents to us through the aesthetic integrity of the novel form. She does not moralize or comment, but the reader is actively involved in the predicament of these women whose characters are defined against such a social and religious climate. The following comment can, I feel, be the hallmark of Kate O'Brien's artistic integrity: "I offer here as nearly as I can my Ireland, in possession of which I am unique, as are you, and you, dear readers."

Joan Ryan. In Heinz Kosok, ed., *Studies in Anglo-Irish Literature* (Bonn, Bouvier, 1982), pp. 322–23, 325–26

Like many of O'Brien's other novels, such as *The Land of Spices* and *Mary Lavelle, The Ante-Room* is about the unworkability of love, the loneliness of people, and how, ultimately, the best we can hope for is "a quiet mind." In *The Ante-Room* she explores a series of love-relationships, more or less repugnant or hopeless. The relationships which she explores in depth are those which fall outside the realm of "unequal dependencies": the love of Agnes for Vincent, her brother-in-law; and the love of William Curran for Agnes. These are central to the book's preoccupation with failed love. William Curran thinks that he has the measure of love: "emotional attachments . . . were only added things," the inessentials; and he considers that marriage is merely "a social and religious contract." But love is something that steals up on him. . . .

But as fate and the author's humor would have it, Agnes, the focus of this mad passion, is in love with someone else, Vincent. While Vincent, and also William, love what they *cannot* have, Agnes loves what she *must* not have: It is a question, for her, of morality. (O'Brien's concern for moral values makes for sober reading. There is nothing in her of the sentimental agony-aunt!) As in her other novels, sexual love cannot thrive.

Sisterly affection fares best in this novel. The relationship between Agnes and her sister Marie-Rose runs like a bright thread through the narrative. It is a real and exacting love that withstands the demands made of it. Through it Agnes finds the link with her past self: She needs Marie-Rose to affirm a vision of herself.

If sexual love is not the answer to human happiness, neither is the spirituality of Catholicism a final answer. As Eavan Boland points out in her fine introduction to this new edition of the novel, "The cold fears and aloneness of the characters in this book are not really warmed" by the rituals of Catholicism, which forms one of its strongest elements. In spite of the prosperity and sophistication of the domestic scene in Mellick, Kate O'Brien's novel concentrates on the inner life of the characters and on their grim struggle for peace of mind.

Louise Barry. *ILS*. Spring, 1984, p. 45

O'CASEY, SEAN (1880-1964)

Mr. O'Casey's most recent play [*The Plough and the Stars*] takes place immediately before and during the Easter Rebellion instead of during the post-war disturbances in which *Juno and the Paycock* was set. Nevertheless, it would seem to be increasingly obvious that Mr. O'Casey's dramatic inspiration comes almost entirely from the misfortunes of his countrymen during the last decade. Apparently he sees the sequence of revolutionary episodes as one vast drama, and from it selects for his own purposes dramatic episodes which he places against a shrewdly observed background of Irish proletarian life. This would seem to explain the very real lack of structure to be noticed in both these plays, since he conceives the frame of them to be outside of both of them, and many other plays which he has written and, it is to be hoped, will write. He himself sees so clearly a beginning, an end, and a middle in recent Irish history, that he conceives it unnecessary to stress these dramatic props in the segments of that history which he chooses to dramatise.

The Plough and the Stars is a better play than *Juno,* because there are not three distinct strings of plot to unravel—more poignant in the characters selected from Dublin's underworld as mediums for alternate passages of humour and terror. No one of the characters, perhaps, suggests the potential greatness of Captain Boyle, but none of them cheat their promise as did he. . . .

It is my guess that, although Mr. O'Casey will never *construct* a play so as to attain the maximum effect out of its rhythm and movement, he will in his succeeding plays increasingly eliminate such devices and other breaches of dramatic taste, with the result that we shall have greater power with no less of the entertainment which he undoubtedly affords.

Milton Waldman. *LM*. July, 1926, p. 299

In *The Silver Tassie* Mr. O'Casey experimented with chanting, treating nearly a whole act in this manner, and providing music for the chants in the appendix. That he is still interested in the dramatic possibilities of chant is shown by his last play *Within the Gates*. For he has been ambitious enough to try and make what he calls "The Drumbeat and Chant of the Down and Outs," the principal motive of this work. To do this he has sacrificed ordinary dramatic methods of development, and instead of calling the four sections of his play "Acts," he calls them "scenes," thus plainly indicating what he intends. "The Drum beat and Chant of the Down and Outs," is doom, destiny, fate or necessity, always in the background of life, and appearing amidst human affairs, suddenly, uncalled for and capriciously, and in the four scenes of his play, laid in a London Park, Mr. O'Casey shows us the sorrowful and trivial thing that life is played out against the background of inscrutable terror. But the curious thing is that he has allowed Mr. Herbert Hughes to set this chant to the well known Irish air "The Foggy Dew," and Mr. Hughes for some reason has incorporated a few bars of the opening of Chopin's Funeral March in the piano accompaniment he has provided for the air. It seems to be a bit of an experiment, an Irish air and Chopin, to symbolize the old Greek idea of fate amidst the miscellaneous life of a London Park. But the whole play is worked out with terrific energy by Mr. O'Casey, and he has put a vast amount of intellectual work, of a very high order, into every detail of it. The detail is almost too elaborate, for in reading it tends to obscure the main idea of the play. Another difficulty in reading is to try and find out the effect the music is intended to have on the progress of the play. Three scenes open with what he calls a chorus, and by that he means a melody sung in unison to an instrumental accompaniment. There is no music at the beginning of the Fourth Scene, this effect being reserved for the end, where the Down and Outs Chant is given in full, only portions being heard previously. Scene 2 ends with the loud playing of a Band in the Park, rendering the Blue Danube Waltz, and there are also songs scattered through the work, and a ghostly dance tune in the last scene for the death scene. it would be really impossible for the reader to judge the play properly. A performance would be necessary. But it may be safely asserted that *Within the Gates* is a play that makes a very deep impression on the mind. There are many unlovely phrases that do not seem necessary in the dialogue, and there are discussions between various groups of men, usually personalized by their wearing apparel, in which the figures speak mechanically as though they were toys. But in spite of such things, it seems to me that there is a strength underlying this play which would carry it through the test of a stage presentation, and I have a sort of an instinct that the author's adroit facility in the jeering fantasy of realism, which sometimes intoxicates him, is really a lesser thing to him than his genuine feeling for the outcast and forlorn.

DM. April, 1934, pp. 75–76

Having read *I Knock at the Door* and *Pictures in the Hallway* most theatre lovers felt "now, if O'Casey would only use that same material for the theatre, then we would have a play." Well, he did, and here it is; and if *Red Roses for Me* is not as satisfying a work as his biography it is nevertheless a most stimulating and exciting one, and theatrical in the best as well as the worst sense of the word.

The plot centres round a young Dublin worker, Ayamonn Breydon, and his passion for his girl, his books and his fellow-workers. Unfortunately the third of these is so strong that it completely dwarfs the other two; we know from the beginning that there must be a strike and that Ayamonn will lead it, so there is no real struggle in his nature and he remains rather one-sided and wooden. But the real core of the play is Dublin herself, her streets, her houses and the people who live in them. Like all of Sean O'Casey's work it is full of

rich and gorgeous characters, the old melodeon player, the Protestant clergyman, Eeada the appler-seller, Mulecanny the Darwinist and a dozen more all
full of life and vigour. There is only one exception, and that of course is the
heroine, Sheila Moorneen. Sheila is the latest addition to that dreary procession of Mary Boyles and Norah Clitheroes and Iris Ryans, weak and
clinging, hugging security rather than her lover, with his dreams and aspirations, losing him to clammy death and realizing too late, etc. At least she isn't
"wronged"—we are spared that. Why is it that neither Sean O'Casey nor Paul
Vincent Carroll can draw a decent, sensible, full-blooded young woman?
There must be a few Pegeen Mikes still left in Ireland.

The dialogue is not naturalistic, but highly coloured and flavoured as
much by Shakespeare and the Authorised Version as it is by ordinary Dublin
speech. "What would a girl born in a wild Cork valley, among mountains,
brought up to sing the songs of her fathers, what would she choose but the
patched coat, shaky shoes and white hungry face of th' Irish rebel? But their
shabbiness was threaded with th' colours from th' garments of Finn Mac Cool
of th' golden hair, Goll Mac Morna of th' big blows, Caoilte of th' flyin' feet
an' Oscar of th' invincible spear." People don't talk like that, but neither do
they talk like Christy Mahon. Synge, however, disciplines his language and
never lets the flow of words impede his action; O'Casey does sometimes, particularly in the first act where highfalutin speech seems out of place in a quiet
homely scene between mother and son.

There are flaws in this as in almost every work, but the play has life and
strength and powerful moments and these virtues are all too rare in our anae-
mic modern stage. I look forward most eagerly to seeing it performed. It
needs a producer of genius, an inspired cast and a most courageous management. Which Dublin theatre can provide all three?

Sheila May. *DM*. April, 1943, pp. 73–74

Mr. O'Casey tells his part of the story in *Inishfallen Fare Thee Well* and *Rose
and Crown* (the fourth and fifth volumes of his autobiography). His three
plays of the mid-twenties made enemies but they made powerful and numerous friends. They gave O'Casey an identity; and this proved precisely to be
the problem when, a little later, he proceeded to write a little differently. . . .

Mr. O'Casey rightly implies that there is a sense in which even his early
plays are not realistic. Conversely there is a sense in which it was the realism
of the later plays that offended an influential section of the public. *The Silver Tassie* gave offence for not being *Journey's End*—that is, for exposing
wounds instead of filming them over with gentility. *Within the Gates* gave offence for giving a close-up of a bishop instead of hiding him in a cloud of in-
cense. *The Star Turns Red* gave offence for turning red—when the palette of
a Cecil Beaton or an Oliver Messel had so many other colors to offer. It was
opposed in England not for its brand of politics but for being political at all.

The point of view is familiar to readers of Mr. O'Casey's arch-antagonist, James Agate, who, for example, complaining of J. B. Priestley, not that he wrote badly, but that he wrote politically, had clearly no means of distinguishing the Yorkshireman's defects from the Irishman's qualities.

One cannot study this man's career without convicting the world around him of jealous meanness. First, they shelved his early works as "classics"; second, they took a stand which explained and dismissed his later works before they appeared. Between these two phases, there was one crucial and receptive moment, a moment when the O'Casey story, as Hollywood would call it, could have been given another turn, and by a single man. This was the moment when W. B. Yeats was reading *The Silver Tassie* for the Abbey Theatre. Not understanding the crucial nature of this moment, we are likely to misread large portions of the autobiography as megalomania. Actually, we should be less surprised at Mr. O'Casey's continual return to the crisis of *The Silver Tassie* than at the fact that his attitude to Yeats even after it was one of filial love. [Oct. 13, 1952]

Eric Bentley. *The Dramatic Event* (New York,
Horizon, 1954), pp. 43–44

What are the later plays? What are O'Casey's intentions? Briefly, his intentions would seem to be the destruction of dramatic realism. It is something of a paradox that the reigning convention of the modern theatre should be realism although the greatest modern dramatists in their greatest plays are not realists. Perhaps the subtle influence of the film is responsible, and perhaps it is easier to understand the Ibsen of *The Pillars of Society* than the Ibsen of *The Master Builder. . . .* Today's theatrical growth is from *Murder in the Cathedral* to *The Cocktail Party,* from poetry to prose. O'Casey, who has never attempted to come to terms with theatrical convention, has progressed from prose to poetry. . . .

O'Casey's work, however, has tended in the direction of freedom, of breaking down the forms and conventions of dramatic realism. He cries with Shaw that there are no rules, but this statement should be taken probably as one of narrow polemic against realism, rather than as a broad statement of dramatic theory. In his early plays O'Casey was thought to be a realist of erratic and primitive genius, a dramatist of great original talent who, if he learned to harness and control his structure, would produce quite overpowering plays. *The Silver Tassie* and the subsequent plays, however, indicated the dramatist was getting too big for his britches, was setting himself up as an intellectual and a member of the avant garde, was throwing discipline out the window, whimsically dissipating his meager power in the slough of Expressionism and perversely biting the pale and poetic hand that fed him from the door (back door probably) of the Abbey Theatre.

Actually the early plays, like the later ones of Chekhov, seemed slovenly in form and slipshod in structure only because they were not based on the four-point traditional structure of *Protasis, Epitasis, Catastasis,* and *Catastrophe* which, under various pseudonyms, have been chewed over by critics from Donatus to Scaliger to Dryden to the latest composer of a "How to Write a Play" textbook. The early plays are far from structureless, but have a structure akin to *Bartholomew Fair* and *The Alchemist.* From the beginning, then, O'Casey was straining against the confines of realism and by the poorly understood success of *The Plough and the Stars* reasserting the vitality of this second structure with its unique utilization of tragic irony and its broadness of scope that the conventional, four-point, single-action plays of his contemporaries denied.

Robert Hogan. *The Experiments of Sean O'Casey*
(New York, St. Martin's Press, 1960), pp. 10–11

O'Casey's world is chaotic and tragic but his vision of it is ironically comic. It is in this war-torn world of horrors and potential tragedy that he finds the rowdy humour which paradoxically satirizes and sustains his earthy characters: they are the victims of their foibles yet they revel in their voluble absurdities. And it is clear that O'Casey himself enjoys his people no less for their follies, as he intends his audience to enjoy them. There is a sharp tone of outrage in his Daumier-like portraits of life in the slums of a beleaguered city, and this tone becomes even stronger in his later plays, but he was not dramatizing case histories. His plays do not follow the documentary principles of Naturalism—of Hauptmann's *Weavers* or Galsworthy's *Strife.* Low comedy is not one of the handmaidens of Naturalism. Even when he is in a serious mood O'Casey is likely to be satiric not solemn, poignant not pathetic. And when the tragic events or consequences of war and poverty become most crucial he will open up the action and counterbalance the incipient tragedy with a music-hall turn or a randy ballad or a mock-battle. While everyone awaits a terrifying raid by the Black and Tans in *The Shadow of a Gunman* the well-oiled Dolphie Grigson parades into the house spouting songs and biblical rhetoric in drunken bravado. Just when Mrs. Tancred is on her way to bury her ambushed son in *Juno* the Boyles have launched their wild drinking and singing party. While the streets ring with patriotic speeches about heroic bloodshed in *The Plough [and the Stars]* the women of the tenements have a free-for-all fight about respectability in a Pub.

This pattern of ironic counterpoint is maintained as a tragicomic rhythm throughout the plays. For each tragic character there are comic foils who constantly bring the action round from the tragic to the comic mood. . . . It is this attitude which keeps his plays from becoming melancholy or pessimistic. His humour saves him and his characters from despair.

David Krause. *Sean O'Casey: The Man and His
Work* (New York, Macmillan, 1960), pp. 71–72

I cannot express my opinion on the problem of O'Casey's exile as firmly as some critics have done. But if forced, I would say, taking into consideration the question of his personal happiness, that O'Casey did well in exiling himself. England in a large measure compensated for what he lost by breaking away from Ireland. In his new home he freed himself from the bitterness, the cynicism and the horrible impact of poverty that underline his Abbey plays. If not a new force, at least a new strain came into his writings: he began to sing of joy, love, healthy sex and the basic sorrows and pleasures of ordinary living. From England he could freely express himself on matters religious, political and social without any fear of interference or oppression. In Ireland his Communism and anti-clericalism would not have been tolerated for long, and exile would have eventually been thrust upon him.

There is one aspect of O'Casey's exile which is fundamentally more important than the controversy over it. The Irish expatriate writers, except for a few like Shaw and Ervine who cut themselves off completely from Ireland, still find their material in Irish life, but their treatment of it is often affected by alien considerations. O'Casey also finds his matter in Irish life but he differs from the other expatriates in not subjecting his treatment to outside considerations. The majority of his exile plays, in spite of their wider symbolic application, are essentially localised in Ireland. His plays are Irish before they are anything else, and Ireland unfortunately has decided to decry them.

Richard Findlater writes somewhere that "The story of Mr. O'Casey's later evolution is the story of a dramatist in search of an audience." Very true, but the reasons for it are not O'Casey's exile or his failure to transplant himself fully to England. Neither in England nor in America are people very keen on Irish plays; and even when the play has a universal significance, they are not anxious to view the world through Irish eyes. Moreover, the average playgoer wants plays with a "tidy parcelled message" and is frightened of experimental and symbolic drama. . . . Besides these, there are other causes that have led to the neglect of O'Casey; the lack of first-class Irish actors outside Ireland, and O'Casey's espousal of Communism and his insistence on going his own way. Lastly, his constant criticism of other dramatists, and of producers and critics has turned the theatre entrepreneurs against him. But what does it matter? In his own lifetime he has heard some of the very eminent critics refer to him as the greatest living playwright. That suffices for the present, and as for the future—

AN IRISH CRITIC: The long view of posterity may turn out to be a poor one.
O'CASEY: So it may, indeed, but I won't be there to hear it.

But we need have no fear of that. Posterity will know its man if it has to choose from our generation.

Saros Cowasjee. *Sean O'Casey: The Man Behind the Plays* (Edinburgh and London, Oliver & Boyd, 1963), pp. 247–49

The O'Casey of the *Purple Dust* vein cast a cold eye on the paralysis of rural Ireland (abandoning the Dublin urban scene in which he had lived for 46 years for the small town, the village, and the farm community in which social change was even slower in making itself felt than in the capital city). Here he uncovered the dead hand of the parish priest, the self-aggrandizing grasp of the new Irish landowners, and the occasional defiant fist of a socially aware rebel. The landlords are still British in the 1940 "wayward comedy," but thereafter in *Cock-a-Doodle Dandy* (1949), *The Bishop's Bonfire* (1955), and *The Drums of Father Ned* (1958) they are Irish parvenus, graduated to councillors and mayors and elected as papal counts. Hand in glove with the bigoted clergy, they keep a tight grip on the politics, economy, mores, and morality of their petty fiefdoms, attempting to stem the natural tide of freedom, love, rebellion, and life itself. O'Casey's young people often demand the right to shape their own futures, for romantic love and passion, for song and dance and an open investigation of all closed issues, and when denied these rights by parent and priest they opt for emigration to England rather than atrophy in Ireland. In the rare event of victory over the forces of the dead past, they jauntily take command of their world, leaving the rulers of the old society to atrophy. O'Casey's technique in these late comedies parallels that of the Dublin plays in their blend of the tragic and the pathetic with the wildly comic, but with strong elements of fantasy for leavening. Supernatural birds, superhuman heroes, mysterious priests who stir the youth to rebellion—all embodiments of the Life Force—take command in the more optimistic of the plays (*Purple Dust, The Drums of Father Ned,* and the shorter "Figuro in the Night") and usher in the O'Caseyan future. But in the more somber dramas, despite the many flashes of hilarity and song, the mood of bitterness predominates, and the fallen angels retreat, refusing to serve the fierce god and tyrannical master, often leaving behind those of their fellows who cannot muster the courage to take a stand: *Cock-a-Doodle Dandy, The Bishop's Bonfire,* and O'Casey's last full-length play, *Behind the Green Curtains* (1961).

> Bernard Benstock. *Sean O'Casey* (Lewisburg, Pa.,
> Bucknell Univ. Pr., 1970), pp. 19–20

Most of the male characters [in *The Shadow of the Gunman*] are caught up in the rhetoric of dying for Ireland. They speak eloquently of patriotism, philosophy, religion, poetry, and history. But their quasi-learned allusions, bombastic words, and arrogant postures reveal an inner emptiness borne out by their inability, or unwillingness, to act when the moment calls for heroic action. The verbal idiosyncrasies of these characters are often very amusing to the audience, but their behavior is not. All of them—not only Davoren—are mere shadows of the men they pretend to be. Maguire actually does die in an ambush, but even he is irresponsible for having left the bombs in Seumas's room.

The female characters in the play have no, or few, pretensions about themselves; but it is they who take action when the crucial moment comes. With calm resolution, Minnie removes the bag of bombs during the raid. When she is arrested, only Mrs. Henderson tries to help her. Even Mrs. Grigson, who had been critical of the flamboyant girl earlier in the play, pities her tragic death. Minnie's flaw of character, if it can be described as that, is a romanticism that invests Davoren with qualities a more knowledgeable person would never attibute to a man so obviously a poseur.

There were, and are, critics who condemned *The Shadow of a Gunman* for what they considered its stereotypic characters — like Mrs. Henderson, who talks in "stage Irish" — and its melodramatic incidents, such as the bloodied piece of paper on the pathetic little Minnie's still breast. But what these critics may have missed was O'Casey's original contribution to the modern stage. He had juxtaposed stock comedy and serious ideas in a drama that bore a powerful and ironic message: the old romantic Ireland was gone. Kathleen ní Houlihan, who once played the harp and sang to her valiant warriors, had become a grim reaper thanks to the would-be patriots who conducted rebellion with brave songs and boastful phrases — a far cry, indeed, from Ireland's invincibles.

Doris daRin. *Sean O'Casey* (New York, Frederick Ungar, 1976), pp. 34–35

O'Casey was Yeats's first heir. He took over the idea of total theatre, carried it from Dublin to London and turned himself into the flying wasp whose task was to sting the English theatre into modernity. The history of his later drama is a history of his struggle to naturalise techniques derived from Yeats in the realism-bound theatre of his adopted country. He had continually to explain or defend his experimental methods to the uncomprehending critics of the day. When James Agate berated him for causing confusion by mixing fantasy and realism he replied: "I do so, Sir, because, first, a change is needed in the theatre, and, secondly, because life is like that — a blend of fantasy and realism." On another occasion he said still more militantly: "I am out to destroy the accepted naturalistic presentation of character; to get back to the poetic significance of drama."

He was the coloniser of the Yeatsian theatre and in a way the populariser too, for although his experimental drama did not achieve popularity in his own time, being too far ahead of it, he gave a massive demonstration in the thirties and forties of how the Yeatsian dance drama could be opened up into popular forms and serve many purposes, including social satire, without necessarily losing the "interior" dimension. He suffered from a sense of neglect and his later plays were not generally understood, often, no doubt, because they were badly performed. But he did, after all, break into the West End theatre with two audaciously innovative plays, *The Silver Tassie . . .* and *Within the Gates* . . . , and the other plays, even the most fantastic, did usually find some enterprising company like the People's Theatre, Newcastle, to perform them: his influence seeped into the English theatre in this way and helped to create the climate in which a whole crop of later plays in musical/balletic mode could flourish.

> Katharine Worth. *The Irish Drama of Europe from
> Yeats to Beckett* (Atlantic Highlands, N.J.,
> Humanities Press, 1978), p. 220

Saros Cowasjee wrote that "O'Casey differs from the average Communist." Indeed he did differ. O'Casey differed fundamentally from the average Communist in that he never joined the Communist Party. I have shown earlier that O'Casey had good reason to distrust his role in political parties. Though he was well aware of the need for a revolutionary party to act as a vanguard in the struggles (as the Irish Citizen Army had done), he believed that he best served the cause in a supportive role. . . .

O'Casey probably would have had a difficult time in the Communist Party, and he and they had sense enough to recognize it. He had had too much experience in the past with political criticism of his plays, including criticism from his own comrades. He would have been asking for trouble by joining the Party, for there were many areas of probable contention. For instance, he was a dramatist, first and foremost. Although he always drew his strength from the working class, he realised his dreams from his skills as a playwright. He was, he said, both drama maker and revolutionist, "one looking at life in the terms of individuals, the other part of the collective urge and forward thrust of man." He had a great sense of history and of man's date with destiny. He was confident that the innate goodness of people would dominate the future and that Time would put everything into perspective. He had no desire to be remembered as a great Communist, only as a drama maker. He wrote that, from the perspective of Time, "the dramatist is neither Tory nor Communist, but only a playwright, setting down his characters as he knew them, giving, if he can, an added depth, height, and lilt to the words he makes them speak." Moreover, O'Casey believed in a separation of drama and politics, though not in the conventional sense. Critics have not understood that a delicate balance of the two always existed in O'Casey's life and in his plays, a balance he set up and one which he maintained, though not always successfully, for though his drama and politics were separate they were also united. For example, O'Casey would hardly agree with Clifford Odets' dictum, "art must shoot bullets" (*must?*), yet he would be the first to maintain that art could be a deadly sword in the hands of a skilled craftsman. O'Casey was willing to use any political tool to further his drama, yet he always denied that his plays contained any political propaganda. He would never have called himself a Communist writer, yet he always insisted that he was both a Communist and a dramatist.

Finally, O'Casey's subject matter was always Ireland and that was an area in which British Communists were not particularly strong. There were, then, areas which he was not willing to submit to judgement by committee, Communist or not.

Robert G. Lowery. In David Krause and Robert G.
Lowery, eds., *Sean O'Casey: Centenary Essays*
(Gerrards Cross, England, Colin Smythe, 1980),
pp. 152–54

The *Autobiographies* of Sean O'Casey, published originally from 1939 to 1954, at intervals of about three years, comprise six volumes—nearly 1/2 million words, by far the bulk of the Irish playwright's literary production. Yet only the first four, the Irish Books (*I Knock at the Door, Pictures in the Hallway, Drums under the Windows* and *Inishfallen, Fare Thee Well*), exemplify autobiography as genre; the last two, the Books of Exile (*Rose and Crown* and *Sunset and Evening Star*), are not autobiography but blends of reminiscence and memoir differing in structure, point of view, and major theme from what precedes them. There are, moreover, signs in the fourth of the Irish Books which predict O'Casey's eventual abandonment of the genre.

O'Casey's autobiographical intention in the Irish Books is predominantly implied. He achieves aesthetic distance from his material through the use of a persona and third-person narration; and he avoids mentioning dates, geographical details, and other particulars in the surveys of his childhood, youth and early manhood. Nevertheless, he is present as a distinct personality throughout the Irish Books; though O'Casey writes about himself in the third person, he writes, as a rule, in the brogue of the North Dublin slums; and he conveys it with suitable orthography. This practice identifies the autobiographer, of course; but it serves also, as aural sign-symbol, to delineate other 'characters' in his book.

The persona of Johnny-Sean-Jack Casside, which is admittedly transparent, is the organising principle of the Irish Books; it helps to sustain their major theme, which involves O'Casey's succeeding, yet cumulative interests in traditional religion, Irish republicanism, and Irish trade unionism and socialism during the first forty-six years of his life. And the Irish Books end with Sean's self-exile from Ireland; phases of his trinitarian personality have coalesced in his commitment to the life of artist; indeed, he has had his beginning with his first successes as an Abbey playwright.

The Irish Books cover a full range of literary forms—lyric, epic and dramatic—which show O'Casey as craftsman and artist. Though the Irish Books emerge as a confederation of such forms, the idea of common ground persists, attesting to the essential unity and coherence of the first four books of the *Autobiographies*. O'Casey's public accomplishment, which alone can aspire to art, results from his selection, rejection and moulding of materials available to him through memory and imagination and the *prism* of language (Joyce's term), in response to his most recent vision or reaffirmation of values.

William J. Maroldo. In Robert G. Lowery, ed.,
Essays on Sean O'Casey's Autobiographies
(Totowa, N.J., Barnes & Noble, 1981), pp. 147–49

O'Casey's relationship to the Theatre of the Absurd, made apparent first of all by his use of such key structural images as the "state o' chassis" and man in a wheelchair, is also clearly evident in the particular way he uses language. The "irreparable dissociation" of mind and world that puzzles and amazes Boyle and terrifies Harry finds concrete expression, not only in disintegrating stage sets, in the splitting apart of families, in violent quarrels, in blind and crippled bodies, in sudden, gratuitous deaths, but also, above all, in the violent rending apart of language itself, a convulsion that can result, however, in a new world of meaning rising out of the old. Accordingly, by the end of *Red Roses for Me,* even Brennan's ridiculous cliché, "Money's the root of all evil" (p. 211), is forced to impart its own unexpected truth. And what is revealed is that to choose Brennan's viewing of life—or, worse still, the Inspector's—is to choose to live in a world of cliché and absurdity. Such an ironic use of the cliché is a characteristic device of O'Casey's from the early plays onward. In *Juno and the Paycock,* for example, the hackneyed slogan "a principle's a principle" (p. 8) echoes throughout the play, but before it is over the actions of the various characters have exposed, and rejected, the hollowness of a world which tries to function according to completely arbitrary and inhuman principles.

Similarly, in *The Bald Prima Donna* [*The Bald Soprano*], Ionesco uses cliché to record the pettiness, meanness, viciousness—and, finally, the absurdity—of the world his characters inhabit. But, again, the difference between the two theatres is one of degree. For Ionesco, unlike O'Casey, often makes his characters speak nothing but cliché, so that, in effect, a process of *reductio ad absurdum* is constantly at work. Is it any wonder, then, that Ionesco's plays evoked the charge that language is in the process of being broken down and stripped of meaning altogether? Yet Ionesco denied that he felt language had become meaningless: "The very fact of writing and presenting plays is surely incompatible with such a view. I simply hold that it is difficult to make onself understood, not absolutely impossible."

Ionesco's reply makes clear that the difficulty of communicating new ideas in a language which has become riddled with clichés, truisms, and the slogans of outworn ideologies is, of course, basically the same for any writer. But what links O'Casey ahead to Ionesco and the Absurdists, rather than back to Toller and the Expressionists, is the fact that O'Casey is not afraid to satirize verbal formulas—to disintegrate language along with the stage sets—since he knows that, in the explosion which follows, a lot of false beliefs and prejudices will be swept away. Thus, while the basic device which O'Casey uses to force language to communicate again is the old, traditional one of dramatic irony, he often pushes it to an extreme which creates a new context: one which can replace walls with the limitless perspective of the universe.

Carol Kleiman. *Sean O'Casey's Bridge of Vision*
(Toronto, Univ. of Toronto Pr., 1982), pp. 96–97

Though the scaffold has been Ireland's loftiest stage and no patriot would refuse its leading part, such fine evocations as O'Casey provides were not admired in 1926. A certain skepticism was detected. He was generally felt to have restaged patriotism's High Mass in the likes of a whorehouse and profaned rebellion's solemnities with clowning. One critic, though, thought that his intentions were high, had not shameless actors played for the laughs they could get from the simple folk the Abbey drew these days.

It is his solemn parts that jar now, especially when he saves them all for the end. The last set of *The Plough and the Stars* discloses a tenement loft with a cardgame in progress foreground, a coffin on kitchen chairs background, and visible through a bullet-pierced window Dublin's sky aflame afar. Minutes after the curtain goes up we shall learn in rapid succession about (1) the death of the tubercular girl (coffined), (2) the madness of Nora Clitheroe (bereft), (3) the loss of her baby (miscarried), (4) the fate of her husband (killed in street fighting), and while still digesting these tidings we shall also witness (5) the violent end of Bessie Burgess (shot by mistake for a sniper). To three acts of peerless dialogue for his cast of temporizers, fanatics and poltroons, O'Casey seems to have affixed the last act of a different play about the roof of the universe falling in.

Nor was this a novel failing; it was a habit, quite as visible in *Shadow of a Gunman* (1923) and *Juno and the Paycock* (1924). "Faulty Construction" is a rubber stamp critics reach for. They also discuss whether "tragicomedy" be possible, as though *Waiting for Godot* did not settle that. But what wrenches these plays asunder is not some failure of structural intuition. It is a disparity between what O'Casey believed he should be telling his audiences and the way his gifts led him naturally. Like a wit with an obligation to preach hellfire, he'd indulge his gifts till his conscience could rest no longer, which would be about twenty minutes before the last curtain.

His belief, approximately Marxist, was that the System generates ruin, in part because people do not pay it heed but sit around being comic while it pares its claws. His talent, though, was for writing comic dialogue. Sam Beckett, another Irish playwright with a Protestant conscience, saw a kind of play that could equilibrate this: one that honors "the principle of disintegration in even the most complacent solids, and activates it to their explosion." Here was "the principle of knockabout . . . on all its planes, from the furniture to the higher centres," and to Beckett it seemed Sean O'Casey's special daemon.

Hugh Kenner. *A Colder Eye: The Modern Irish Writers* (New York, Alfred A. Knopf, 1983), pp. 203–4

Like Dion Boucicault, whose work he admired and with which he was familiar from an early age, O'Casey wrote plays that are highly melodramatic and that are enlivened by music, song, and dance; he even stages a hooley (a party) in *Juno and the Paycock*. He makes brilliant and frequently satiric use of the pageantry, the oratory, the parade of fierce national events. Despite its poverty, O'Casey's world is charged with great physical exuberance, much of it precipitated by the clowns: shrews, eccentrics, boozers, parasites, a rag-tag assembly scraped from the very bottom of the refuse pits of Dublin. The most memorable are Fluther Good in *The Plough and the Stars* and Captain Jack Boyle in *Juno and the Paycock,* who cavort around the perimeters of the central drama, shrewdly resisting any effort to draw them into a major role.

As Dubliners they are less naive and more self-assured than the earlier rogues. As Boyle puts it: "We're Dublin men, an' not boyos that's only afther comin' up from the bog o'Allen." Far from having any respect for the "quality," they are abusive or indifferent toward the occasional bourgeois who appears in their midst. They have shed many of the values along with the language of their peasant ancestors. Though the tenement community has some cohesion, and there is still a marked respect for religion and the family, their lives have a rootless quality. Limited employment brings little renumeration or personal satisfaction, and alcohol is a chronic problem. Although Fluther is always gallant toward the ladies, emnity between the sexes is inevitable in a culture where men go off to the local pub to escape from domestic problems.

The suppressed energies, the hostility, the obsessions of the Dubliners characteristically explode in verbal combat. Their language bristles with aggressiveness; it has a needling, restless quality, intended to prick, to deflate, to keep the listener slightly off balance. The sheer love of invective is carried to far greater extremes by O'Casey than by any of the other modern writers we have examined. It is a distinctly Irish quality, prominent in Swift and in the satire of the bards, but scarcely to be heard in the Anglo-Irish literature of the nineteenth century. The lyric strain is subdued in O'Casey's best plays; the language tends to be epigrammatic in contrast to the sheer verbal extravagance of later plays such as *The Silver Tassie* and *Red Roses for Me*. Much of the dialogue has an eccentric, disjunctive quality, which suggests the speaker's obliviousness to anything outside of his or her own obsessions.

In *The Plough* anger is easily triggered and easily forgotten. Fluther is threatening the Covey with sudden death in one scene and playing cards with him in the next. Trapped in the static inferno of the tenements, like the damned souls in Sartre's *No Exit*, O'Casey's Dubliners can only turn on one another. Unlike the French bourgeoisie, however, they have immense resources of furious comic energy to keep them from despair.

Maureen Waters. The Comic Irishman (Albany,
State Univ. of New York Pr., 1984), pp. 150–51

The comedic characters in *The Plough and the Stars* are perhaps more salvageable than those in *Juno and the Paycock*. But the play is as much a depiction of chaos, of "chassis". Act II, set in a pub, perhaps gives us the fullest index to maelstrom. Wonderful and desperately human wrangling goes on while outside, a speaker gives us extracts from Pearse's oration at the grave of O'Donovan Rossa and also from an article he published in *Spark,* December 1915, called "Peace and the Gael." O'Casey culled from it the passage in which Pearse declares, "The old heart of the earth needed to be warmed with the red blood of the battle fields . . . Such august homage was never offered to God as this: the homage of millions of lives given gladly for love of country." That statement, since it explicitly equates death in war "for love of country" with "homage" to the Almighty, is perhaps more crucial to Act II's overall significance than the passages from the Rossa speech. The Speaker's rhetoric and the several mini-wars of words in the pub (including that between the half-baked Marxist, the Young Covey, and the old-style nationalist Uncle Peter) make for an ironic counterpoint: dialogue and situation constitute O'Casey's first major pacifist statement. With hindsight we can see that it was on the cards that O'Casey would write an out-and-out anti-war play: which he did with *The Silver Tassie* (1928). While some of the characters in *The Plough* exhibit a kind of flawed nobility under stress—Fluther Good, Bessie Burgess—there is no nobility evident in *The Tassie* where even maternal, let alone conjugal love, is unmasked in the fairy light of separation allowances. Part of the harsh sadness of the physical and consequent spiritual mutilation of the hero Harry Heegan arises from the fact that he has confronted the actuality of war and returned to a society "in which civilians, in whom the springs of imaginative imagination have long since dried, if ever they existed, are now cocooned in their private fantasies, locked in themselves, and so, by the ethic of O'Casey, humanly half-dead, less alive in fact than Harry; who is paralysed from the waist down." Although O'Casey in *The Silver Tassie* has broadened his expositional technique (by way, of the expressionistic Act II which employs chant, repetition of catch lines, and other devices of the period) he maintains the method of the earlier so-called "naturalistic plays," achieving his effects by the juxtaposition of the grave and the farcical, the clownish and the heroic. And in all four [of these plays] the message is clearly pacifist: war, of any kind, entails the destruction of the innocent and the possible corruption of the living, and as much moral poltroonery and spiritual meanness as it does occasional grandeur of conduct.

It is not until *The Star Turns Red* (1940) that we find O'Casey as explicitly a propagandist of Marxist revolution. This is one of the more difficult of the later plays since, inevitably, its reception will be coloured by the political orientations of audience, or reader. In it O'Casey strives to create a massive allegory which embraces his thinking on the Dublin strike of 1913, the 1917 Russian Revolution and the Spanish Civil War. While at times the play is cumbersome, even jejeune, its cumulative effect is powerful, leading up to the apocalypic climax when the star of Bethelehem turns, literally, red, and the revolution begins just as the fatuous lord mayor and his wife are preparing for a Christmas Eve reception for the local notabilities, while somewhere off stage the poor are being entertained to tea (dispensed from a giant watering can, with another such can "of beautiful boiling water . . . to stretch out the lovely tea"). Although *The Star Turns Red* is as close as any Irish dramatist ever came to an explicitly communist play, the very fact that it is set during the last hours of Christmas Eve has immense qualificatory significance. Clearly O'Casey has a vision, however muddled, of a synthesis between communism and Christianity. His position might be summed-up as follows: basically communism is more Christian than institutional Christianity and the message of pristine Christianity is revolutionary. The expansion of the International is the expansion of the kingdom of God on earth: a naive concept, perhaps, but so far as I know O'Casey is the only dramatist in the English-speaking theatre to explore its theatrical possibilities.

John Jordan. In Richard Kearney, ed., *The Irish
Mind: Exploring Intellectual Traditions* (Dublin,
Wolfhound, 1985), pp. 222–23

If O'Casey tends to reduce action as the dominant structural device [after *The Silver Tassie*], it is important to note what he puts in its place. It is certain that the reduction in plot does not mean a loss of artistic unity. The structure simply becomes more complicated and can only be satisfactorily described in terms of each individual play. The underlying principle is that of contrast: O'Casey juxtaposes scenes that differ in their *dramatis personae*, in mood and in theme in such a way that they serve as commentaries on each other and increase their mutual effectiveness. Other structural devices vary from work to work. In *Within the Gates*, the unrealistic tendency of the whole play permits an allegorical presentation of human life by simultaneously presenting the times of the day and the seasons of the year. In addition to such a "vertical" structure, it was shown above that the play has a "horizontal" structure of "world picture," "satire" and "religious quest." The principle of the quest for a true belief regulates the sequence of the individual scenes. *Purple Dust* possesses a similar "horizontal" structure of comedy, farce and satire which is responsible for the structuring of the scenes. Since the progression of events in this play is especially limited, O'Casey introduced towards the end an additional element in the form of the symbolic flood that enabled him to bring his action to a conclusion, as well as to deepen its meaning. The problem of dramatic structure in *Red Roses for Me* has been discussed above in some detail: the central character and a few central symbols here serve as structural elements that are responsible for the sequence of scenes. The plays of his fourth phase form the climax in O'Casey's creation of a unique dramatic structure. The grouping of the manifold scenes is here controlled by the central motif of a public celebration. O'Casey's introduction of fantastic and fairy-tale elements, however, enables him to dispense with a logical progression of events, and the most important device in controlling the variety of themes and stylistic levels is again the principle of contrast.

Heinz Kosok. *O'Casey the Dramatist* (Gerrards Cross, England, Colin Smythe, 1985), pp. 320–21

Ó CONAIRE, PÁDRAIC (1883–1928)

Pádraic Ó Conaire is a Connacht story-teller who owes his racy modern style to [Peter] O'Leary's example, although his diction is by no means so rich as that of the master. It is claimed for him that he ranks among the best short story writers of contemporary Europe. Certainly, his gift for drawing scenes and characters in a few strokes, his power of holding the reader, and the ingenuity of his stories—every one of them has in it something unique that makes it worth retelling—render him the most considerable and most original of the revival writers. No more virile spirit has appeared since the great men of the seventeenth century.

Sometimes Ó Conaire writes of droll fellows met in the tavern, or at the fair; sometimes he draws compassionately the men and women who vulgarly are called the peasantry; sometimes he draws the nervous, scholarly priest, the modern Columcille, and sometimes the patriot or the poet, the modern Amergin. He is equally at home with gentle and with simple. He can write of the stir in a bishop's soul when the fires of insurrection redden the distant sky, and he can give us, with a choking thrill, the scorn of the Irish officers for the grotesque King James. He can draw a romantic encounter with a maiden at a forest fire, that has all the intensity of an *aisling*, and stirs the pulses; and he can tell a sombre tale of life darkened by sin and in hourly peril of judgment. Innocence and shame he draws with equal power. Most of all he draws Irish womanhood with a wonderful vividness, in beauty, in mockery, in sorrow. His picture of the mother and lover of a youth fallen in the strife, who mutually conceal from each other their knowledge of his death, is one of the most potent things that ever an Irishman wrote. Ó Conaire has romance of place as well as of person, and can call up the mystery that sails into harbour with a

Western boat. Yet his chief interest is in men and women; and he has left us the most comprehensive gallery of Irish character that we possess. Chivalry tempers all his pages. [1929]

Aodh de Blácam. *Gaelic Literature Surveyed* (New York, Barnes & Noble, 1974), pp. 379–81

It was in London that the seed of Pádraic Ó Conaire's mind came to flower and to early fruit. There his friendships were with noble fellows, with rough men and with vagabond poets, who lived their poetry and rarely wrote it. Indeed, it was an occasion of necessity that first compelled Pádraic to put his pen to literary use; and then, as he often told me, it was to write a story of thrills in English—on the suggestion of his strange friend Thomas Boyd, that vigorous Irish poet, who came into Ó Conaire's life as mysteriously as he left it, and was never heard of again. In London, as in Dublin, Pádraic O Conaire had no sympathies with those who were suckling at literary pretence; but his vigorous mind, his humour and his realism did much to wean many from such skim milk. And, as a matter of fact, the buoyancy in his own career of tragedy was that terrible passion for Gaelic life and speech that made him one of the greatest writers creating solely in Gaelic—poorly paid Gaelic; that turned him into a most effective teacher in the London Gaelic League; and that saved him, incidentally, from the possibilities of financial success in English letters. But the burst of war created a new London for Pádraic O Conaire; values changed; racial stocktaking was necessary, and in the process Pádraic resigned. . . . After his return every place west of Dublin and east of Galway became his abode.

Outside the lure of friendships in Dublin, Connemara and its people held his strongest ties. A Connemara-man readily understands such ties and particularly an Ó Conaire. Pádraic was part of that country—with his soft voice, his cold grey eyes well set apart in a broad, tawny face that was clean carved and lean from the slim nose to the strong chin. Even his illuminating talk had got the West in it—every phrase delightfully tanged. It was kindly, exuberant, full of charm, moving through stories of his many experiences—reminiscences partly of fact and partly of imagination—all revealing a queer interest in incidents of strange human traits and the zeal of living. Reminiscences surely, frequently related to his friends and mostly recorded in his stories. These may be found in "Nora Mharcus Bhig" ["Nora, Daughter of Marcus Beag"], in "Deoraidheacht" ["Exile"], in "An Chead Chloch" ["The First Stone"], in "An Crann Geugach" ["The Squeaking Tree"] and in *Seacht mBudah an Eirighe Amach* [Stories of the Easter Rising]—indeed in any of his seven volumes of short stories, his two novels, and his play, *Bairbré Rua* [*Red Nora*].

Although he made no poetry in song, one thinks of our old poets and their lives when thinking of Pádraic O Conaire; not so much of [Anthony] Raftery, one links him rather with Cathal Buidhe, with the "Mangaire Súgach" ["The Tipsy Peddlar"], or with Flaithrí O Maoilconaire, that noted member of the western bardic family from whose seed Pádraic traced his descent. O Conaire was one in whom the proud art of the genealogist was a living faculty. One found in him a survival of the Gaelic attitude towards life: rather fatalistic, dramatic, most realistic, with its keen sense for beauty in beast and being—its wild delicacy, fugitive from some other world, a world mentioned just under the breath.

F. R. Higgins, Introduction to Pádraic Ó Conaire,
Field and Fair (Dublin, Talbot, 1929), pp. 12–14

O'Conaire wrote of ordinary people, living ordinary lives, of fishermen, domestics, married women and spinsters, country and small town types of all kinds, that is to say of the life he knew. He wrote largely of people whose lives were not very happy, who made mistakes, did the wrong thing at the crucial moment, that is to say he wrote of life realistically. But his realism is shot through with pity and tenderness, and he never takes sides or loads the dice. For him, there are no sinners, only unlucky ones and unfortunates. he has no axe to grind, is propagating nothing, simply telling stories. His language is simple, and his use of words is economical. He has the faculty of getting the right word in the right place and in the right order, and he never pens sentences for the sake of writing. Every sentence is essential to his story, and when he has told that story adequately, he stops. In his economy of words in his best stories, and in the austerity of his style, and his ruthless ending of the story when it has been adequately told, he has resemblances to Tchekov [*sic*], while his general background, a background in which sinners are simply unfortunate people, is not unlike that of another great Russian writer—Dostoievski.

It used to be said of him that he was influenced by de Maupassant, and this he denied firmly. He said to me once that he had never attempted to read but one book of de Maupassant's, and that he did not read very much of it, because a story in it so revolted him that he threw the book away and read no more. He described the story to me and I recognised it. It is the story entitled "Idylle" in the volume *Miss Harriet*. It is not a free or an indecent story at all, but it has a grossness about its central incident, and I remember that when I read it myself it had revolted me. A writer is of course in a way influenced by what he reads, so that in that sense there is no such thing as an original writer, but O'Conaire was following nobody and copying nobody. He was an original talent, with an original outlook upon life, and with a sympathetic understanding of his own people. He had that one great quality which a writer of short stories must have, impartiality as between his characters, but not the cold inhuman impartiality of Galsworthy; O'Conaire's impartiality was sympathetic and he never either praised or blamed.

P. S. O'Hegarty. *The Bell*. June, 1944, pp. 238–39

Whatever else Irish schoolchildren bring from their study of Irish, it will be an acquaintance with a certain whimsical Little Black Ass, the property of Pádraic Ó Conaire, the first major figure in the literature of the Irish Revival. Regrettably, they are unlikely to know very much more about Ó Conaire than that he was a "character" who liked watching the stars, sleeping in woods, making friends with birds and squirrels, and that he died a pauper. But by the time Ó Conaire began to publish his little essays and sketches about the open-air life, in the early twenties, his career as an artist had come to an end. The stories in *Siol Eabha* (1922) had been written, some of them, many years before, and the last important creative work he undertook were the stories written after 1916, and published in 1918 as *Seacht mBuaidh an Eirghe-Amach* [Stories of the Easter Rising]. He was then only thirty-six. The last ten years of his life were largely given over to the provision of "suitable" texts for schoolchildren. It is painful to think that his career as an artist should have ceased, so far as major achievement was concerned, as soon as Irish became the official language of the country. It is even more painful to know that all his best work has been allowed to go out of print (though as recently as 1952 I was able to obtain a copy of his novel *Deoraidheacht* [*Exile*]: the fact that I could have obtained one previously in 1948, suggests that readers of Irish have not been avid for Ó Conaire's work).

Dr. [Tomás] de Bhaldraithe is to be congratulated for undertaking a selection of "best stories" [*Scothscealta*] and his publishers for realizing the importance of Ó Conaire, not only as a writer of Irish, but as a literary artist. And he was an artist, for all his gross faults of sentimentality and contrivance, his lack of staying power, his sometimes patent eagerness to get the thing over and done with. (Even that powerful, sorrowing, book *Deoraidheacht* suffers from patches of underwriting, passages which read like notes from a draught.) Dr. de Bhalraithe's selection is taken from work published between 1906 and 1918. The first thing that strikes one about the seven (out of ten) stories written before 1914, is Ó Conaire's astounding boldness in the choice of subject-matter: lust, madness, pathological jealousy, the tragedies ensuing upon forced marriage and "incompatibility," prostitution in exile. I do not believe that Ó Conaire took his subject matter for sensationalist purposes. Rather was it that his personal faculty for compassion was stirred most by the grotesque extremes of human misery. He loved the maimed and the sick, whether in mind or in body. Before any other Irish writer, whether in English or Irish, he turned and embraced the area of human suffering which cannot be labelled "noble" or "heroic" or "inspiring." he had read the great nineteenth century Russians and French, and realised that *la misère* was the legitimate territory of the artist. And as soon as he moved out of that territory, as is shown by the three stories from *Seacht mBuaidh an Eirighe-Amach*, he became stilted, unsure, and, as in *Beirt Bhan Misniúil* ["Two Courageous Women"], close to maudlin.

John Jordan. *Irish Writing*.
Autumn, 1956, pp. 190–91

With his battered hat, shabby clothes, old topcoat and stout ashplant, Padraic O'Conaire looked like an outcast, a lasting symbol of the writer in Ireland, and many avoided him whenever they could. Once he and I were walking down Grafton Street at the fashionable hour and saw James Stephens a short distance from us. "A hamus! A hamus!" called O'Conaire, hurrying forward, waving his stick. Stephens had heard him for he quickened his pace. We tried to catch up with him, but when we turned the corner of Anne Street, he was gone. No doubt, he had sought refuge in one of the Art Shops.

Nevertheless, Padraic O'Conaire, like the Russian writers, had great respect for the short story. He shaped each of his by telling it casually to friends and strangers, as he roamed from bar to bar. Then, when he was ready to set it down in his neat handwriting, he washed, shaved, put on his secret Sunday suit and sat at his desk in a top room which was reserved for him in the headquarters of the Gaelic League at Parnell Square.

Some years ago, Sean J. White told me a remarkable story. Padraic O'Conaire called one night to the Offices of *The Connacht Tribune* in Galway to collect ten shillings due to him for an essay. The Editor gave him the half note and he handed it back to him in payment of a loan. They left the Office and went down the road to a public-house. On their way they met a Professor from the University College, a perfervid Gael. Padraic drew him aside and asked for the loan of ten bob to stand his friend a drink. The Professor, weary, no doubt, of being touched too often in the Irish language, said he had no change. When the sound of his footsteps faded away down the street Padraic turned to the Editor and said in a grave tone which was unlike him: "The day will come, when that man will unveil a statue to me." That day came.

Austin Clarke. *A Penny in the Clouds* (London,
Routledge & Kegan Paul, 1968), pp. 78–79

The problem of translation has long bedeviled Gaelic literature. In the 1930s, the Irish government's publishing agency, An Gúm, released a flood of translations, almost entirely from the English, and in the process embittered a whole generation of writers forced by economic necessity to produce Gaelic versions of books readily available to any Irish reader in the original. Translations from Irish to English have, on the other hand, come in an erratic trickle—most of Pearse, some Ó Conaire, the Blasket books, Myles na gCopaleen's *An Béal Bocht*, and a few other titles that caught the fancy of individual translators. It has been impossible for the reader without Irish to have any idea of the richness and diversity of Gaelic writing, which has thus been simply ignored by the vast majority of students of "Irish" literature. The appearance of these two small volumes [Pádraic Ó Conaire, *Fifteen Short Stories*, and Mairtín Ó Cadhain, *The Road to Brightcity*] should, however, open some eyes and minds.

The Ó Conaire book contains fifteen stories translated by fifteen writers, many of whom will be known to readers of Irish literature in English, and it justifiably claims to be the first representative collection in English of the work of the writer who brought Gaelic literature into the 20th century. For this very reason it is unfortunate that the editor, who is not named, has not chosen to include even a brief introduction to Ó Conaire's life and work.

While several of these stories appeared in English in two volumes published shortly after Ó Conaire's death and later re-issued by Mercier Press, this Poolbeg collection offers the reader without Irish his or her first look at two of Ó Conaire's stories with biblical or Eastern settings from *An Chéad Chloch* [*The First Stone*] (1910), and two of the stories from his book centered on the Easter Rising, *Seacht mBuaidh an Eirghe Amach* (1918). The collection also offers fine renderings of the Gaeltacht stories such as "Páidín Mháire" and "The Woman on Whom God Laid His Hand," for which Ó Conaire first gained recognition and which remain the most powerful depictions in Irish or English of life in Connemara. Further, the inclusion of stories such as "The Woman in Torment," "Nell," and "Nora, Daughter of Marcus Beag" will enable readers of English to understand the lively debate in Gaelic circles on whether or not Ó Conaire was a master of female psychology.

The translations are, on the whole, free of awkward or inaccurate renderings. . . . Certain translations are very successful. Eoghan Ó Tuairisc, for example, rescues "My Little Black Ass" from the limbo of classroom classics with a translation that perfectly captures the rollicking good nature of the original. Brian Mac Mahon also manages, at the expense of a few minor liberties with the text, to evoke the brooding and frustrated sexuality of "My Poet, Dark and Slender," and Domhnall Mac Amhlaigh catches with precision the formal distance of "Lead Us Not into Temptation." Incidentally, as these examples illustrate, Ó Conaire made use of several widely different styles, and thus the translation of his work by fifteen different hands does not, as it could have with some authors, present the reader with a distorted impression of his writing.

Philip O'Leary. ILS. Spring, 1984, p. 46

O'CONNOR, FRANK (pseud. of Michael O'Donovan) (1903–1966)

Guests of the Nation is a collection of short stories and sketches by a new writer. I say "and sketches," because if one were in search of something to find fault with one might perhaps complain of a certain inconclusiveness, a lack of shape. One or two of the stories do not so much end as fade out, and some have almost the air of being fragments of a larger work. Their vividness and power, however, make this criticism of small account. Mr. O'Connor has all the gifts of the storyteller: sympathy, humour, detachment, and a style so unobtrusively the servant of his purpose that one hardly pauses to admire it. He writes of what he knows, of what he has seen and heard, and if his work is in some degree personal reminiscence it is perhaps none the worse for that. Certainly it is impossible to tell where memory ends and invention begins, and there is never a hint of mere contrivance. Most of the stories concern the Irish civil war, but there are others, racy and unforgettable, in witness that this author is not a man of one theme. The title-piece, in which two English prisoners are shot (in reprisal) by their reluctant guard, is almost unbearable in its horror and poignancy. The last story in the book—of a boy and a night watchman and a prostitute—is a small perfect thing of another kind. Between these extremes are thirteen stories varying in length and mood and merit. The slightest are done with skill and spirit, and the best have a quality that suggests permanence.

Gerald Bullett. NSN. Oct. 17, 1931, p. 481

When Mr. Frank O'Connor's first collection of stories was published a few years ago a distinguished English critic found it worthy of Turgenev or Maupassant. In this new volume, *Bones of Contention*, there is perhaps more that will remind the reader of Maupassant than of Turgenev, but there is much more of the Irish *shanachie* than of either of these masters. At least half of the stories in the volume, which contains a dozen really masterly stories, would be most effective if told orally.

Of these *shanachie* tales, "Orpheus and His Lute" would keep an audience convulsed with laughter by its recital of the doings of the Irishtown Brass and Reed Band. The title-story, "Bones of Contention," would probably have the same effect. Other stories which would be heightened in their effect by oral recital are "Peasants," "Tears, Idle Tears," "The English Soldier," and "What's Wrong With the Country." It is not that all the author's artistry and literary craft are not to be found in these stories—they are present in every line and sentence—but that to these qualities there is the additional quality of drama. Those who heard the author read his story, "The Majesty of the Law," over the radio—and this story is included in the volume—will realise how dramatic Mr. O'Connor can be. Had he chosen either "Orpheus and His Lute" or "Bones of Contention," or even "The Man that Stopped," his success as a radio *shanachie* might have been much more readily recognised.

The longest story in the volume, "Lofty," is probably the least successful. It is not that one fails to become familiar with "Lofty" Flanagan in his triumphant progress through the kingdom of the plumbers, but that his abject failure in the political realm does not seem quite in character. One who could so successfully dominate his fellow-workers would surely have been successful in obtaining at least a seat in an urban council.

There are two stories, "Michael's Wife" and "In the Train," which will certainly be acclaimed as masterpieces, equal to the best short stories ever written by Russian or Frenchman or Englishman or American. In both stories art and craft are so exquisitely blended that neither could well be separated, and no one could have written them but Mr. Frank O'Connor. There is, therefore, nothing to be gained by comparing his work with that of other masters of the short story: he is a master among masters himself.

Irish Times. March 7, 1936, p. 7

Mr. O'Connor has long been an expert in the short story form, for which he has a marked and seductive talent; and he is by now so much at home in it that he is entering the dangerous phase of actually being too easy to read, so smooth and suave of accomplishment as almost at times to make no greater impression on us than a passing ripple of pleasure. He has always had a great eye for the makings of a story, and he can move into his theme and carry it along with a virile naturalness which, when he is in his best form, can truly be called magnificent. But technique, and also that wisdom which counsels a writer to work rigidly and solely within the bounds of what his whole spirit knows by heart, can conceivably become dangerous to their happiest possessor; and there is a point at which the concealment of art must threaten the vitality, the memorability of the work of art. Mr. O'Connor never chooses a bad or sentimental theme; we can see a living, individual truth in each of his ideas—but sometimes in this volume [*Crab Apple Jelly*] we have to look more closely for it than of old, for he is getting into a trick of surface-finish which blurs what lies below and in one or two cases imposes a really sticky sentimentality on matter which should have been allowed to hold decorously to itself. It is the expert's danger—of being too deft at forcing his ideas into his own easiest manner. And I suggest that in such stories as "Song without Words" and "The Grand Vizier's Daughters," in this collection, Mr. O'Connor has fallen badly into his own trap. In the long story which concludes the book, "The Mad Lomasneys," too, I feel a conflict between conception and execution, as of the latter seeking to escape the consequences of the former, and I am unable therefore to feel truth resolved in it, though I believe I see, far-off and blurred, the shape of the true idea. But it is impossible to read Mr.

O'Connor's dialogue without delight; he uses a local Anglo-Irish *patois* with close fidelity indeed, but he so infuses each phrase with the character of its speaker, and rifts it so deep with the lyricism and wild humour of his own mind that it becomes a very rich, poetic medium, charged with greatness. At least three of these stories are as good as any he has written—which is saying a great deal; "Bridal Night" is superb and deeply original; "The Star That Bids the Shepherd Fold" is a very delicate and shrewd piece of mockery, and "Old Fellows" is a wonderfully balanced passage of farce and pathos— perhaps the best thing in the book.

Kate O'Brien. *Spec.* May 26, 1944, p. 484

Most of the stories in this latest collection [*Domestic Relations*] of Frank O'Connor's appeared originally in the *New Yorker*, where they served to confound those who criticize that magazine's fiction as a monolithic agglomeration of memoirs of dull and surly childhoods ("*Maman* and I used to visit Aunt Christobel at Baden-Baden every summer . . ."). Mr. O'Connor, to be sure, is fond of recalling his own childhood, but he does it with enough verve and enough sense of "story" to make it palatable. In many ways Mr. O'Connor is a natural *New Yorker* writer. He is urbane and witty and he instinctively avoids those shrill and harsh notes that—well, that wouldn't go in a humorous magazine is probably the most honest way of putting it.

Mr. O 'Connor is so urbane, come to think of it, that one is hard put to explain why he is so splendid an artist. One is inclined to be a little suspicious of so much charm. And perhaps Mr. O'Connor does at times let his charm carry him a little further than his other talents would take him. But we cannot justly quarrel with what he chooses to use as a paddle so long as it gets him where he's going. All possible strictures aside, he remains a superlative story-teller.

The reasons for his excellence are most discreetly inconspicuous in his work. His stories are as unassuming and as effortless as across-the-bar or over-the-back-fence gossip. He admits to aiming consciously for this effect—of avoiding the "literary," the line that does not read aloud naturally and conversationally. This effort has resulted in a superbly clean and lean style, with none of the "poetic" passages, sentimental moralizing and melancholy posturing so dear to some Irish writers.

His stories move. When you grab hold of the first sentence you know you're going somewhere. It picks up and starts off with you. O'Connor is truly a writer "hard to put down." This is partly because of the easy simplicity of his style, but largely because Mr. O'Connor magically makes you want to know why it is Shelia Hennessey married a man twenty years older than herself and whether the marriage worked out all right. He is interested in people and in their motives. And although he does not analyze their behavior in any depth, what he does say of them rings true.

William James Smith. *Com.* Oct. 25, 1957, p. 101.

Frank O'Connor's kind of storytelling is not modish just now. He is recognized as a fine short story writer—anthologized under the aegis of Brooks and Warren—and until his recent death he undoubtedly occupied the position of being Ireland's foremost living short-story writer. Yet his standing as a writer is uncertain, since critical commentators have either neglected or taken for granted his talents, as the dearth of O'Connor criticism shows. American short story writers of comparable parts at least enjoy critical notice, but like his Irish contemporaries, O'Connor is seldom courted, a situation partly due, one supposes to the fact that he writes stories in the manner of the nineteenth-century realists, stories in which plot and action interest him more than symbol, sensitivity, and experimentation.

Since an acquaintance with any short story writer is usually made through a few anthologized pieces, it is difficult to see the thematic unity and development of ideas that make the entirety of his work greater than the sum of its parts. Exposure to only "The Drunkard," "My Oedipus Complex," "Guests of the Nation," "Judas," or "Uprooted" obstructs a clear view of O'Connor's creative virtues. The selections often exploit the more specious aspects of his talent. Consequently he has become tagged as a humorist. And he is—a fine one. But unnoticed elements give him stature: his curious view of priestliness among the Irish laity; his probing into the themes of human loneliness and communication; his success at infusing new energy into stories about juveniles by creating not precociously passive sensibilities but active boys who get themselves into predicaments which incur both guilt and maturation; and his restoration of the storyteller's voice. But most important is his persistent sifting in the value of impulsive indiscretion and moral fecklessness in order to domesticate irrationality. And only by considering a larger sample of his work and the development of his canon can one see with some accuracy the value of this preoccupation.

Gerry Brenner. *TSLL*. Fall, 1968, p. 457

When O'Connor writes of the short story, in *The Lonely Voice*, he is not so much doing what he professes to be doing—stating the nature of the form—as he is stating in general terms the characteristics of his own craft. His stories are plausible treatments of the plights of those he called "Little Men"—his capitalizations show he wasn't patronizing—written in an apt style, one both witty . . . and poetic. . . . His stories have no heroes, but memorialize "a submerged population group" as they group and regroup in variations of family patterns. His stories show "an intense awareness of human loneliness" and the tactics people use to relieve that loneliness. They follow no "essential form," but an "organic form"; this configurates aesthetic elements in infinitestimal variations which dictate vastly different implications (like the triangles and squares of color within a kaleidoscope).

Compared with Joyce, his craft might be narrow, but he sees more possibilities of fulfillment within the strictures and structure of the narrow world

Joyce might too quickly reject in *Dubliners*. O'Connor's range might not be vast, but his eyes are clear, his ear is sharp, his heart is big and his craft is sufficient to his needs. The stories in *A Set of Variations* might be short and narrow, but they are more than small favors that he did for us in writing them before he died. We should be more than grateful.

Shaun O'Connell. MR. Summer, 1969, pp. 612–13

Perhaps [O'Connor] was right in thinking that with *Crab Apple Jelly* (1944), and in such stories as "The Luceys" and "The Mad Lomasneys" he came most fully into possession of his manner and his subject. "They describe for the first time," he was to say, "the Irish middleclass Catholic way of life with its virtues and its faults without any of the picturesqueness of early Irish writing which concentrated on color and extravagance."

Ireland, middleclass and Catholic, is a formidable instance of the closed society. Anthropologists squander their time frivolously by concentrating on islands afloat on more exotic seas. And O'Connor, when he takes us into those mahogany parlors in Sunday's Well, persuades us with the finality of art that we are entering that world, with its unspoken alliances and feuds, its pieties and evasions, its cautious and caustic pronouncements. Some of the stories are harsh and some display a deliberately casual brutality as they unfold lives wasted within a society which is both nurturing and oppressive.

It is a substantial, dowdy and unbreakably provincial world of publicans, doctors, priests, small merchants, builders, chemists and solicitors. And its inhabitants live desperate but never quiet lives in which pubs, conversation and romantic illusion offer, in their various ways, unavailing solace. And their histories are set down with such humor and verve that the melancholy depths are not visible, so that the conclusions, though inevitable, come with a wrench. What is most remarkable (remarkable, that is, for our day) is that the stories are set down without a shade of condescension; the narrator always identifies himself as part of that society, even when he laughs at it or rebels against it. . . . The narrative voice comes from deep within the society, the amused, tolerant and sardonic voice of a man commenting on his neighbors and his world. The many re-writings and revisions were devoted to the creation of just that illusion. "Generations of skilful stylists," he has written, "from Chekhov to Katherine Mansfield and James Joyce had so fashioned the short story that it no longer rang with the tone of a man's voice, speaking." He may well have been wrong in supposing that the short story has been robbed of narrative impulse—his critical opinions were invariably sweeping—but entirely right in supposing that the narrator's voice was at the exact center of his own art. It was through the cultivation of that voice that he worked out his complicated relationship of his land and his fellow-countrymen.

Thomas Flanagan. In Maurice Sheehy, ed.,
Michael/Frank: Studies on Frank O'Connor
(Dublin, Gill & Macmillan, 1969), pp. 157–60

Now and then [O'Connor] shook the dust of Ireland off his feet for ever. Presently we would hear with joy, but no surprise, that he was back. He had love affairs with England and America and brief flirtations with the Continent, but to Ireland he was fatally and indissolubly married, deny it as he would.

He had various other illusions about himself, some delightfully comic. More than once he assured me that he had missed his vocation and ought to have been a priest. One often hears such things from Irishmen in their cups; but Michael was dead sober and so plainly in earnest that, even if the vision of him celibate and caged in ecclesiastical discipline had not struck me dumb, I should not have dared to argue.

Undoubtedly he had a sense of frustration in his middle years, due perhaps to his gifts being greater than the scope they found. A writer of his talent required something bigger and grander than republican Ireland. That he felt this he seemed to show by the constant rewriting of work done long before, by the withdrawal into Gaelic mists, the obsessions and wrangles and hobbyhorses. But towards the end he found a new and happy outlet in the lectures at Trinity College, into which, ill and tired as he often was, he put his whole heart.

That association with Trinity meant a great deal to him. I well remember the scene when he got his doctorate *honoris causa* there. Apparelled in hired formal dress and academic robes, walking in dignity up the aisle to the platform with the other luminaries, he looked strangely unlike his bohemian self. As he went by he gave me a broad wink and a sardonic grin, which didn't fool me for a moment. This was one of the good days of his life.

Honor Tracy. In Maurice Sheehy, ed.,
Michael/Frank: Studies on Frank O'Connor
(Dublin, Gill & Macmillan, 1969), p. 4.

[O'Connor] wrote and produced four plays for the Abbey: *In the Train* (1937), a dramatization of his short story of the same name; *The Invincibles* (1937), about the little group of Dublin terrorists who assassinated the British Chief Secretary in Ireland, Lord Frederick Cavendish, and the Irish Under-Secretary, Thomas Burke, in 1882, in Phoenix Park; *Moses' Rock* (1938), about the effects of the Parnellite split upon an imagined small town Irish family, the O'Learys, and their friends—both of these last were written in collaboration with Hugh Hunt; and *Time's Pocket* (1938). His fifth play, *The Statue's Daughter*, was produced, incidentally, not at the Abbey but at the Gate Theatre, in 1941. This last, a comedy, deals with the present and its involvements with the past. Set in a small Irish town in which a committee of citizens had set up a statue to honor the memory of Brian O'Rourke, a dead hero of the War of Independence, the "statue becomes a focal point for the interplay of two generations, their revaluation of attitudes toward each other and towards the problems of modern Ireland, and their search for a common ground between people of different faiths and traditions."

None of these plays is distinguished; nor do they enhance in any appreciable way O'Connor's reputation as a dramatist. However, they do show enough ability to suggest that had he continued in this genre, he might very well have established himself as a significant playwright. But his *métier*, after all, was storytelling, in which he excelled. To be sure, *In the Train* does capture the mood of the "submerged population" in his characterization of Helena Maguire of Farranchreensht, accused of poisoning her husband, and of her alienation from society. As Moll, another character, comments: "Helena on the train by herself and no one to talk to her! What sort of neighbors will she think we are? Where is she?" All the tragedy of life — its meeting and parting, here today, gone tomorrow — is depicted on this train ride. . . . To be sure, the frightening loneliness of the "submerged population," their utter hopelessness comes through, surely, in this mood piece, the best of the plays. But where, for example, is the evolution of character and incident with which O'Connor took the measure of Yeats? Surely not in this play.

Of a different, though not insignificant interest, is O'Connor's choice of historical subjects in *The Invincibles* and *Moses' Rock*. One can only conjecture that he was motivated to choose as he did by the "strong streak of national consciousness in him," as is abundantly clear in *The Big Fellow* and *A Short History of Irish Literature*. He may well have felt the need to provide through dramatic historical themes the autobiography of his race. Again, he assumes here the role of a teacher, anxious to portray to future as well as present generations a dramatic rendition of the past. . . . Whatever the motivations, these plays, though good in part, are not outstanding; but, in their own way, they added new interest in the Abbey repertory while winning "much praise for themselves, [for] having raised the dignity of Ireland."

Maurice Wohlgelernter. *Frank O'Connor:
An Introduction* (New York, Columbia Univ. Pr.,
1977), pp. 174–76

O'Connor was a dogged craftsman, a perfectionist, an indefatigable rewriter and self-second-guesser — all habits he shared with James Joyce, as he did a devotion to deep learning of diverse sorts. Yet O'Connor branded Joyce as "the first of the Ph.D. novelists." *Dubliners* was to him an example of how not to write short stories, for it preferred characterization over a quality that O'Connor thought prime: incident, which he called theme. Accordingly, a character named Joyce in O'Connor's story "What's Wrong with the Country?" is described as "a small, stocky obstinate fellow with a precise and cynical mind." The polite encomia for *Dubliners* in *The Lonely Voice* aside, O'Connor found Joyce's short story technique more trivial than quadrivial.

In contradistinction, O'Connor's work is characterized by a yearning to recapture something lost—primal order or an older decency that has been overridden by social duty or, perhaps, a childhood of ineffable simplicity and trust. Ultimately, like Seán O'Casey, O'Connor is an Oedipist who discerns a better world before the advent of striving and grief. His longing for order, decency and love suggests his intense moralism which, along with a tone of unshakable equanimity, gives his stories their principal trademark. O'Connor says in *An Only Child* that, while he did not believe in the immortality of his own soul, he did believe in that of some souls, doubtless his mother's, and so "perhaps it was the thought of these [souls] that turned me finally from poetry to story-telling, to the celebration of those who for me represented all I should ever know of God." But these very characteristics engender his worst faults—a lack of complexity, occasionally muddy and ill-conceived plots, and a cloying nostalgic cheerfulness, what Walter Allen has called O'Connor's persistent stance of "What an interesting little boy I once was!" Temperamentally, O'Connor's vision was directed backwards to the time, recounted in his autobiography, when he was Michael O'Donovan from Blarney Lane. "Look back to look forward," he writes in his dedication to *The Backward Look.* And since his tendency is Oedipal, the habitual frame of reference in his stories is the family.

Richard J. Thompson. *Éire-Ireland.* Winter, 1978,
pp. 65–66

Owing to a Yeatsean pronouncement on his early work, now dutifully turned into a slogan by his publishers, Frank O'Connor (1930–1966) has come to be known as the Irish Chekhov. This title, which is also claimed for O'Faolain, highlights his standing as one of Ireland's foremost mid-twentieth-century writers, but it obscures his originality. Whatever O'Connor has in common with Chekhov, his genius is very much his own, with its virtues and its fault. It is less reserved, heartier, more emotional than the Russian master's. It reflects the shifting moods of a personality at once diffident and flamboyant, as quick to anger as to joy or despair, opinionated, irreverent, rebellious, full of violent likes and dislikes. O'Connor himself felt it dangerous to try to follow Chekhov: "He is inimitable," he observed, "a person to read and admire and worship—but never, never, never to imitate."

And yet, judging by his criticism, he may well have drawn from the latter something of what seems to form the mainspring of his creativity: his haunting sense of man's isolation. Such a sense, he contended, lies at the root of the short story—a form best approached, to his mind, in a mood akin to that of Pascal's saying: *Le silence éternel de ces espaces infinis m'effraie.* His conception of it as "a lonely, personal art" is unsatisfactory as a theory, but it is not unfair to take it as a clue to his own vision and achievement. His was a very subjective mind, whose general views were coloured by his personal problems.

One of the "strayed revellers of the Irish literary revival," he found himself out of place in the pious parochialism of postrevolutionary Ireland. But there was in him a deeper sense of alienation, traceable to his earliest life, and which shaped his vision of man and the world. A professed agnostic till his last years, he keenly felt the collapse of traditional beliefs and values, hence his reference to Pascal. This reference is paradoxical, for the main feel of his work is of warm humorous humanity rather than tragic metaphysical anxiety; but even in his lighter fiction, one may discern the dread, manifest in his more sombre stories, of a world in which "there is no longer a society to absorb (the individual), and . . . he is compelled to exist as it were by his own inner light." The warmth of O'Connor's fiction may be understood as a counter to this dread. Bracing his imagination against despair, he clung to faith in the individual, however insignificant the latter appeared in the alien vastness of the modern world. His art sprang from a need to overcome his sense of what he referred to as "the desolation of reality."

Roger Chatalic. In Patrick Rafroidi and
Terence Brown, eds., *The Irish Short Story*
(Lille, France, Publications de l'Université de Lille,
1979), pp. 189–90

Collected Stories reprints 67 of O'Connor's stories in loosely chronological order. The volume includes five stories previously uncollected, in the U.S., the best of which is "There Is a Lone House"; and its scope goes far beyond any two or three of the previous O'Connor collections. Nearly any serious reader of fiction will crave this handsome and abundant book from Knopf, O'Connor's publisher since 1940.

"Guests of the Nation," one of O'Connor's best known and most remarkable fictions, was recently dramatized on PBS. That this early story achieves such definition, symmetry, and finish is astonishing, for it is deeply autobiographical, like much of O'Connor's writing, and it presents a highly volatile theme—conflicting loyalties toward England and Ireland and, more especially, toward duty and friendship. The author is irresistibly drawn to life at its fullest and most humane—to baffled, decent people doing their best (and their worst) in the face of adversity. He is finally indifferent to idea or ideal, to church or state, to authority public or domestic, however much these forces may wrench his characters.

"Guests of the Nation," "The Majesty of the Law," "First Confession," "Peasants," "The Drunkard," "The Man of the House," and "My Oedipus Complex," all published between 1931 and 1950, are often and justly anthologized. They easily bear the most acid test—rereading. In my latest encounter with "First Confession" I shook with laughter when Jackie owned up to the "crimes of a lifetime" to the sympathetic and droll priest.

The remaining stories, early and late, run from good to near perfect. Among my favorites are the stories that constitute chapters in the life of Father Fogarty—from "The Frying-Pan" (1947) to "An Act of Charity" (1967). Fogarty is a profoundly humble and endearing man with an abiding commitment to his fellow mortals and no concern for himself. In several stories we perceive his agonized reactions to death, while in "The Mass Island" we attend his funeral. This story, with its heartrending conclusion, recalls "The Long Road to Ummera" and "A Set of Variations on a Borrowed Theme," fictions that explore the intersection of life and death.

O'Connor's priests, like his nuns, teachers, publicans, doctors, lawyers, businessmen, soldiers, laborers, his fathers and sons, mothers and daughters, young lovers and ancient crones, are persons of every shade of temperament, of every degree of warmth and coldness. He always tells a story but never allows narrative or plot to violate character. His figures form a rich gallery of human conduct, of folly and foible, of hopeless whim and undefeatable expectation. . . .

O'Connor not only avoids the extravagant emotion naturally inherent in Irish subjects such as nationalism, religion, and local pride, but he shuns the extravagant techniques of modernists such as Joyce as he straightforwardly relates his stories in an idiom based on the speaking voice.

To this author the short story is an art form that embodies in fiction a report from the provinces. "A good short story must be news." These stories are news that stays news long after the teller completes his tale and the book is closed.

George Core. WSJ. Sept. 21, 1981, p. 34

The stories [in *Collected Stories*] stand on their own—constructs of an imagination constantly refreshed by old obsession, performances of a virtuoso displaying set upon set of variations on a borrowed theme: innocence (and its loss), love (and its failure), loneliness (and its desperations), death (and other little disappointments). The autobiographies [*An Only Child* and *My Father's Son*] are a portrait of that imagination, a reduction to visual image, as it were, of the voice whose tone and texture give to each of the stories its characteristic vibrancy. This is a humorous and humane voice and its theme, sounding in praise or sorrow, resounding tragically or joyously, was already old before Homer set his heroes to sail upon the wine-dark sea or Job shifted his miserable bones upon that dung-heap to tell his story.

One may observe that the Ireland of today is no longer the Ireland of O'Connor's stories. In O'Connor the Irish countryside still retains an almost pastoral quietude, the country town an almost medieval isolation, the people turned in upon themselves in amity or envy, indifferent for the most part to the world beyond their vision. If the atmosphere is close, it is also comforting, an enclosure of familiar things and people. If vision is limited, there is no lack of individual insight, and personality is prized the more because the common character of the people had been formed in the crucible of custom—many of these customs (religious, social, sexual) preserved like relics in the keeping of a watchful and ubiquitous Church. All that has since changed as it was bound to change with the intrusion into O'Connor's Ireland of the modern world. In some places a kind of vacuity has dislodged the quietude, in others the air of apparent, if deceptive, innocence has been lost in the crackle of electric voices, the flickering of unghostly images—these and other innovations of a sort that, even as they open new windows on the future, draw the curtain upon an Ireland of which these stories were once a faithful contemporary record. . . .

But of course the value of the stories, and the pleasure they continue to impart, are independent of time. . . . These stories bear the ineradicable imprint of what is engagingly, disturbingly human. They are true to life, true to the life that Frank O'Connor knew and that we know—a truth that literature rescues from the illusions and disarray of time and preserves intact against whatever changes are to come.

Kevin Sullivan. ILS. Spring, 1983, p. 37

Length is not, for O'Connor, a major criterion for the form of a short story; the story gains in appeal and liveliness only if the narrator captures the tones of an actual speaking voice. O'Connor had already discovered this when he published his first volume of stories, *Guests of the Nation*, which arose out of oddities of behaviour observed in the Irish Civil War of 1922. As a result of equivocal motives attributed to patriots on either side, he wrote an adulatory biography of Michael Collins, whose cause on behalf of the Free State he had opposed by force of arms. From the tragic tone of the opening tale "Guests of the Nation," from which the volume is named, it is safe to conclude that O'Connor never again made himself an instrument of warring factions.

O'Connor was as sceptical about the activities of the Church, and in many stories saw through the hypocrisy or unwisdom of its social procedures. He attributed these to the Jansenist narrowness of the priesthood trained by Maynooth College; he held it responsible for the rigid control exercised over Irish family life. He was less concerned with Maynooth's political implications, which angered Moore, Joyce and O'Flaherty. It is worth noting that O'Connor's attitude was not dogmatic, but often generous, perhaps in deference to his mother's piety. The fallible priest in "My First Confession," regarded as an opportunity for humour rather than spleen, is not to be compared with the ineffectual one in "News for the Church." One can see from the attitude of the father confessor in the latter story that O'Connor reacted to the introspective and fatalistic turn that Irish Catholicism had taken; he thought it largely responsible for mass emigration, long after the initial impetus of the Great Famine.

O'Connor did not adopt the role of the apostle of freedom; but he believed he understood the ethos of the Irish tradition, and made clear its racial pride, mysticism and superstition in *A Short History of Irish Literature* (1968), a series of lectures delivered at Trinity College, Dublin, shortly before his death. The short stories dwell on the pertinacity of these influences, but also on the conflict he experienced between his mother's faith and his own belief in human compassion. He could see the evil effects of the harsh discipline exacted by priests who meddled in secular affairs, even sport, as exemplified by Father Crowley in "Peasants," a story remarkable for the rusticity of its language. A priest wielding power as tyrannically as he does, had not the right to expect exemption from criticism from members of his own parish.

A. C. Partridge. *Language and Society in Anglo-Irish Literature* (Dublin, Gill & Macmillan, 1984), pp. 334–35

O'DONNELL, PEADAR (1893–   )

Here is a play [*Wrack*] of which the chief character is the sea which we are made to understand in its every mood through the eyes of the several very human men and women who figure in the development. These people are the hardy, hard-working folk, who, dwelling on an island off the coast of Donegal, are dependent upon the sea for their livelihood. The sea is their master, their friend and their enemy, but never their servant. Mr. O'Donnell gives us a glimpse into their lives and, in the short space of two hours, we get actually a panoramic view of life among fellow-creatures and fellow-countrymen whose very existence most of us ignore or reck not of.

The author has an extraordinary sense of the sea which probably only those who have lived near or on the ocean will fully understand. The attitude is neither one of fear or love. It is not capable perhaps of description. It must be felt to be realised. But Mr. O'Donnell has, through his play, brought convincingly into perspective his vision of the sea and that of the islanders which cannot possibly fail to interest.

There is no hero or heroine. All concerned are heroic in the fullest sense of the term. All are alike and equal, and all share in good time the favours and the burdens which the sea brings to them collectively and individually. The tragic ending of this vivid little work leaves us thoughtful. It may be the end of the play for the reader or the spectator. That, however, is not all. The closing of one chapter is for the island folk only the beginning of another, which will in all probability be in every way like its predecessor, save for a change of actors. And so it has always happened and will always happen while the sea is the sea—and island folk must live.

In *Wrack*, Mr. O'Donnell has given us a canvas of many colours and rich in detail. It is the first play of the sea since Synge wrote his famous little tragedy, *Riders to the Sea*. And it is strange to think that this is so because we are, as a race, an island people, and none of us are so far from the sea that we fail to be conscious of it and its existence. Synge's play contained a certain lurid quality which *Wrack* has not. But there is about the latter work a strength of reality and a solidity of facts which make it the more convincing and, consequently, more valuable as a picture taken from life. It is life through and through. Synge built on solid ground, but his structure is that of the poet imaginative. Comparison is hardly possible.

As to the theatre, *Wrack* belongs to the modern school of drama; but the author asks a great deal of the producer when he gives us a scene in which a boat at sea and caught in a storm has to be made convincing. It can, of course, be done—but not in the average theatre.

Irish Book Lover. March, 1934, pp. 47–48

It would be almost impossible that Peadar O'Donnell should write a bad book. He has a delightful style, vigorous and tender in turns, full of subtle word cadenzas, and rich with the tang of the salt sea, for which he has a highly sensitive feeling. His English has all the purity and simplicity of the Western seaboard. It is free from all affectation, direct, forceful and intense, and, although one wishes that he would not use that abomination, "availed of," nobody can read his prose without genuine enjoyment.

Yet, [in *Salud!*] he very nearly has written a bad book. Now and then his literary sincerity bursts through a somewhat involved narrative of his adventures—or lack of adventures—in Spain; and there is poetry in his talk of the sea. But, on the whole, the reader will not be impressed by Mr. O'Donnell's story: it is too diffuse. One gains the impression that the author in his efforts to make a case strains at his style. . . .

The best portion of it is not about Spain at all; it is about Dublin. There is a delicious ballad about General O'Duffy after "Off to Philadelphia in the Morning," and Mr. O'Donnell has some amusing things to say about his Irish critics. Before one reaches this chapter, however, one has to wade through some pretty dull stuff about peasant proprietors and the like, and the average reader will refuse to take much interest in most of Mr. O'Donnell's Spanish Communists. Somehow they do not seem to ring true. They are pink rather than honest to goodness "reds," and one would expect to find them in a Bloomsbury boarding house rather than manning the barricades in Barcelona.

Let there be no mistake, there is good material in *Salud!* Peadar O'Donnell has the eye that sees, and there is a measure of humanity about the man that never can be suppressed, however eager he may be in his chase of rainbows.

Irish Times. May 3, 1937, p. 7

There is an interval of twenty-one years between the publication of *On the Edge of the Stream*, the last of O'Donnell's early novels, and that of *The Big Windows*, which appeared in 1954. As with so much of his life and work, the seed from which this novel sprang was sown during the fighting of the troubled times. After he had been wounded by the British, but escaped capture, he lay convalescing on a bed of straw in a friendly farmhouse in a remote glen of Donegal. It was then that he noticed something unusual in the bond between the young woman of the house and her mother-in-law. Often in rural Ireland this relationship is distinguished by an almost cannibal rivalry, but these two could laugh together like older and younger sister. The seed ripened slowly over the years until *The Big Windows* became the most complex of all Peadar's books. Into it he put a lifetime's observation of country ways of feeling coupled with the mellow compassion that always distinguished him.

Superficially the book's theme is simple. Tom Manus, a vigorous small farmer from a backward glen in Donegal, marries an island woman and one evening brings her home. But this incident and its aftermath are the pretext for a portrayal in depth of life in this small, self-contained community. . . .

Gaiety, harshness, lively humor, and grim tragedy alternate in the book's course, like cloud shadows flitting across April fields — the obscene jeering of the neighbor women at Brigid's arrival in the village, the symbolic breaking out of the big windows in the mountain-dark cottage, the fisherman's net to keep the hens out of the oats, which is the wonder of the village, Ann the Hill's strangeness, the killing of the dog that was worrying sheep, the christening to mark Brigid's acceptance in the glen, the drunken home-coming after the first days out selling lime.

In the earlier books, as already noted, O'Donnell's style is plain and direct. Here it is an artefact, just as Synge's or Lady Gregory's was. It still draws its strength from a realistic vision of country life, but it has now a slow, reflective rhythm, particularly in the passages that point a moral, which perfectly suits the author's mature purpose. . . .

The Big Windows is O'Donnell's epitaph on a way of life whose actual character and whose social context he understood better than any writer of his generation. Yet he does not here bemoan its passing, as perhaps he did in *Adrigoole*. For him the Big Windows were always opening on a new world, different, but just as good as the old. The Ireland of the cloistered glen, which had its grandeurs and its miseries, has passed. The Big Windows are in, and we can look out at the world and the world can look in on us. What shall we make of each other?

Grattan Freyer. *Peadar O'Donnell* (Lewisburg, Pa., Bucknell Univ. Pr., 1973), pp. 120–24

Mr. O'Donnell's interest in the West almost automatically turns one's attention to his many books and novels. For they are almost all about the lives and problems of the people of the West, from Donegal to Cork. But he says of this: "I like to think that people don't really look on me as a writer but as a man who took part in the struggle of ordinary people against sharply frustrating limitations on their powers to live fully. I also like to think that every agitation that I took part in was in reality itself. In this I did not confine myself to Ireland but worked also in other countries." Here he is referring to his period as chairman of the European Farm Workers' Movement where he found that there was more unison between rural men in Europe and Irish farm workers than there was between the city man and the rural worker in Ireland.

Yet his words of fiction were always close to deeds. For instance of his story *Islanders* he says "it wrote itself in my mind during my period of solitary confinement in Donegal." This was a time when he was held as a hostage to be executed if any Free State Deputy was killed by the I.R.A. If Dr. Johnson is to be believed about concentration of the mind before execution O'Donnell must be unusual in that his mind could think of new writing in such circumstances. Yet *Islanders* is a tender, thoroughly beautiful and life inspiring story of Island folk doing the simple things needed for life. It is illustrative of the quite enormous capacity for selfless depths of affection that island folk have for their children and their neighbours. His *Adrigoole*, a County Cork family tragedy, contains the same quality of realism. None of his characters are angels but even the "devil" in the rural and island folk seems likeable. The real story is one of endurance in such a battle and the zest and love for life with all its pitfalls and tragedies. The novels do give town folk some idea that problems of living have similar heartaches in town or country. Social problems are universal.

It would seem that Peadar's politics are not far away even in his novels. Certainly that could be said for *On the Edge of the Stream*. Here there is roguery, courage, cowardice, lies, truth and mock piety all struggling and jostling vigorously in the line up of gombeen men and their social prey. Respectability gets a severe wallop through the owner of the village bull but who is all things to all men and whose services must be given neutrally and without politics—to all, and paid for! In his responsible post he cannot take sides—public or otherwise. *The Big Windows* as with other writings has its origin in the Tan War. Wounded some time in 1921 Peadar was sheltered in a house where the woman of the house and her daughter-in-law stayed up talking until they thought their guest was well asleep—an old custom. But he heard some of their conversation and was puzzled by the wide philosophy of the younger woman. Leaving the following day he noticed the house had unusually big windows. And he made an inquiry and found that the daughter-in-law was an island woman. The story is that of a lonely island girl, the "foreigner," among the folk of the mountains who cannot understand her. It was the love and understanding of her man for her that built those windows so that she should share the full beauty of those mountains, and perhaps glimpse the sea beyond, for to island folk the sea is all.

Michael McInerney. *Peadar O'Donnell: Irish Social Rebel* (Dublin, O'Brien Press, 1974), pp. 185–86

Peadar O'Donnell's *The Knife* originally appeared in 1930, and this reprint [Dufour, 1983] appears with the entirely commendable hope—as expressed in the introduction by Grattan Freyer—that it "will stimulate fresh interest in [the author's] life and work." Because *The Knife* is an uneven novel, inferior to O'Donnell's other work, its reprinting is not likely to do much for O'Donnell's literary reputation; but, just the same, we must be grateful because it at least draws our attention to a man who is himself a very fascinating, remarkable person, one who does not deserve the neglect accorded him today. . . .

What we seem to have [in *The Knife*] is a novel with a little bit of everything: a "national" novel, one that encapsulates the modern history of one area of Ireland; the Lagan valley, complete with religious, social, and personal problems; life on the farm, life in jail, with an interfaith love interest thrown in. It is clearly too much, and it doesn't blend together. By the time one is reading the jail-life section, it is almost as though one is reading somebody's jail journal (O'Donnell's?), not the novel which began with Catholics and Protestants fighting over land in rural Donegal.

But there are some truly superb scenes: men on the run hiding in a dugout, peasants gossiping in scenes reminiscent of *Spreading the News*, old people cleaning up the debris left after a raid, scenes which show just what a good writer O'Donnell can be. Perhaps the most dramatic scene in the book is when before a thronged chapel Father Burns asks his congregation for a Lord's Prayer and Hail Mary for "the divine blessing of freedom that has crowned our struggle"—i.e., the signing of the Treaty. What follows is gripping, indeed . . . more like vintage O'Donnell, the author of *Islanders* (1928), that gripping story of widow Mary Doogan's attempts to eke out a living for herself and her children on a barren island, and *The Gates Flew Open* (1932), a superb account of prison life.

But if *The Knife* only occasionally rises to the strengths of O'Donnell's other work, it is, in the final analysis still a striking book because in 1983, over 50 years after it was first published, it presents a remarkably even-tempered view of Orangemen; it is even optimistic about the possibility of cooperation between the religious factions. . . . *The Knife* is, thus, a refreshing and timely book, and one hopes that we *will* see renewed interest in Peadar O'Donnell because his is a view of life from which we can all profit.

Johann Norstedt. *ILS*. Fall, 1983, p. 20

O'DUFFY, EIMAR (1893–1935)

As I followed Miss Rudd's *affaires* [*Miss Rudd and Some Lovers*], I began to realise that she was not a lady likely easily to succumb to what is flippantly termed "heart-trouble." Her engagement, when it does happen, is not at all on the conventional lines adopted by respectable suburban society, but that is remedied in the working-out of the particular *affaire*.

She has a detached way of sizing up the aspirants to her hand, and some of her criticisms on the veneer worn by imperfectly developed gentlemen are frank, almost to the borders of the territory usually recognised as that of the perfect lady. (I am sorry to say she is inclined to be hard on Rathmines, while a pressman of her acquaintance is equally rough on Rathgar—what he says about Rathgar and its association with the drink menace almost made me blush, to think that I rather like to live in the abandoned district.)

Tea under the direction of Mrs. Buck, who keeps the boarding-house that is Miss Rudd's Dublin home, is an experience that would put years (as the saying is) on any young man she suspected of having a liking for the company of her daughter, Vi'let. Mrs. Buck is a clever characterisation, and her mannerisms and conversations most entertaining. What a landlady!

Mr. O'Duffy has considerably added to his reputation by this novel. All his characters are well sketched, some finished studies, and they move naturally in the familiar Dublin suburbs, herein held up to posterity. Miss Rudd is a quite interesting lady to know, and entertains us with humour. Her preferences in Art show that she is somewhat of a connoisseur, although her plaster casts caused some disturbance of Mrs. Buck's sense of propriety, so that she had to remark that they were "not quite nice, ye know." Mrs. Buck's artistic leanings, which had never before leaned lower than Buck photographs, and holy pictures whose printing was a coloured profanity, were jolted quite off their balance. Had Miss Rudd not swept away all traces of Mrs. Buck's family pride, as well as the visible traces of religion, we should, no doubt, have heard her appreciation of Miss Solomons' etchings, which adorned the walls in company with a sketch by Mr. Jack Yeats.

This is one of the best novels published in Ireland in the present day, and we shall look forward with pleasure to the sequel. *Au revoir*, Miss Rudd.

DM. Feb., 1924, pp. 672–73

The Spacious Adventures of the Man in the Street is a digression from [O'Duffy's] epic tale [*King Goshawk and the Birds*]. The grand manner is laid aside, and O'Kennedy, the Dublin grocer's assistant, tries to explain to the Manager what has happened to his soul while Cuchulain has been using his body. The first use Cuchulain made of the body was to hit the manager a woeful punch in the stomach, so that O'Kennedy will have to do plenty of explaining if he is ever to get his job back again.

Apparently, O'Kennedy's soul went straight off to the planet Rathé. (Just as "Erewhon" is an anagram of "Nowhere," so "Rathé" is an anagram of "Earth." The reader, given this hint, can play the rest of the anagram game for himself.) There it arrived just in time to enter the newly-dead body of one Ydenneko, an executed criminal. O'Kennedy-Ydenneko goes to the town of Bulnid, where he lives long enough to observe most of the customs of the Ratheans, which very often turn out to be the exact reverse of ours on Earth, just as Rathean proper names are often merely our own spelt back to front.

O'Duffy's Utopia owes a great deal to Samuel Butler and St. Thomas More, among others, but he plays the topsy-turvy game with a crazy logic that is often more breath-taking and more consistent than Butler's. Some examples of O'Duffy's witty paradox are well worth giving here.

The Ratheans' attitude to food is the same as ours to sex, and *vice versa*; they are monophagous, each person choosing, at an early age, one type of food, to which he is bound for the rest of his life. Tmesis, or change of food, is very rarely allowed. Eating is never done in public, no one ever admits he is hungry, and the polite word for "hunger" is "taste," just as we never speak of "sex" in polite society, but only of "love." On the other hand, they show absolutely no reticence about their sex-lives. . . .

Of all the unusual features of Rathean civilization, the one that really shocks O'Kennedy is the economic system, and his brain is soon at work on a grandiose scheme of conquest, with the imposition of an earthly economic system as its object. O'Kennedy, however, proves an incompetent general. The army which he has recruited from the "bad lands" of Rathé is defeated, he is captured, tried, executed, and after his soul has had interviews with several gods and with the Devil, it returns to his body on earth. . . . On earth it is funerals which inspire processions and pomp, whereas in Rathé it is the ceremonies associated with birth. O'Duffy presents in these terms the difference between an economy of plenty and one of scarcity.

Vivian Mercier. The Bell. July, 1946, pp. 330–32

King Goshawk and the Birds is O'Duffy's most important work and the most relevant to our present purpose, for it reaches back to touch with reverence the heroic ideal as Standish O'Grady saw it while at the same time it is filled with a virulent hatred for all the works and pomps of Big Business. That hatred was a very large part of O'Duffy's thought, and even when he unbent to write a whodunit in *The Secret Enemy* he kept remembering with bitterness how the evil spirit of King Goshawk who made a corner in singing birds had blasted the face of God's earth. . . .

[I]n the beginning of *King Goshawk and the Birds* the awful people of the Fomor have triumphed; the chief of the merchants who sell blades of grass has decided to buy for the delectation of his wife, Queen Guzzlelinda, all the world's singing birds; and the intellect of man, again symbolised by a philosopher, lives in a garret in a back lane in a city broken by war. In the pillow-chat of Goshawk and his queen there is a suggestion of parody on the talk between Queen Maeve and her king that ended in the Connachtmen marching to take from Ulster the Brown Bull of Cooley. Yet Eimar O'Duffy approaches the heroic idea with reverence, and it has been left to another, more detached contemporary to stand the heroes on their heads and to leave them comically kicking their heels in the air.

In his back-lane in Stoneybatter the Philosopher pays rent to a landlord. . . . From this landlord, from the politics of Coddo and O'Codd, and above all from the intolerable power of King Goshawk the Philosopher goes to the heavens for help. He finds it not with the spirit of Socrates, where Bernard Shaw might have under similar circumstances attempted to find it, for Socrates happy in heaven has no wish to leave the pursuit of truth and the contemplation of God to endure again the wickedness, ignorance and folly of the world; but with the hero and demigod Cuchulain whom he persuades to return to Ireland where he begets on the daughter of a capitalist a son Cuanduine who carries on a somewhat inconclusive battle against capitalism and its attendant evils.

When Standish O'Grady was breathing new life—a life that naturally had something in it of Standish O'Grady—into the heroes of the ancient Irish sagas he may not have foreseen the possibility of an ancient hero appearing actively as the enemy of the modern world. Certainly O'Grady who was also a social reformer saw the contrast between ancient ideals and much that was misshapen in his own time. Eimar O'Duffy's sympathies are all with the philosopher, with Cuchulain and the son of Cuchulain. He never, I repeat, sees the hero as a figure of fun, as Flann O'Brien does; but his Cuchulain is just far enough away from O'Grady's serious, statuesque heroes to show how much the author of *King Goshawk and the Birds* has been affected by the author of *Arms and the Man*.

Benedict Kiely. Modern Irish Fiction: A Critique
(Dublin, Golden Eagle Books, 1950), pp. 71–73

In 1919 there appeared *The Wasted Island*, his most important work, at least from an Irish point of view. It is a long autobiographical novel full of insights into the evolution of Irish affairs leading up to the rising of 1916. It shows at the same time a more intense human feeling than any of his slighter earlier work could have done. Readers with a close knowledge of the period have no difficulty in identifying many of the thinly-disguised characters who figure in it.

It is an aggressive book, its principal target being the schemers, as he presents them, who foisted an unwanted rebellion on the Irish Volunteers.

Their mystical poetry is harshly dealt with and some skilled attention is given to the famous document circulated by the Volunteers a week before the rising. From internal evidence O'Duffy shows that the alleged intercepted government orders must have been a forgery, and his conclusion has been reinforced by the findings of more recent students of the episode.

This book made him even more unpopular among republicans than his allegiance to the MacNeill cause had done, and indeed the case that he changed his ground on national issues could be maintained, in view of his earlier writings. When the threat of conscription recalled the volunteers into more active work again, O'Duffy was invited to deliver a lecture on hedge-fighting to a Dublin unit. (It was a subject on which he had written in the *Irish Volunteer*.) He prefaced his remarks with the statement that he had no intention of aiding the volunteers in overthrowing the British Empire, but he was hastily interrupted by one of the organising officers and told to proceed with the proper business of the meeting. A contributor to the *Centenary History of the Literary and Historical Society, University College, Dublin, 1855–1955*, records that O'Duffy was refused a hearing at an L&H meeting because of the hostility which *The Wasted Island* had aroused.

The picture of his father and his homelife generally as presented in *The Wasted Island* is unsympathetic in the extreme and the story is told that when his father died, in circumstances much reduced from the elegance to which he had accustomed himself, his house was found piled with copies of the offending work which he had bought up. Be that as it may, in 1929 O'Duffy published from Macmillan's a revised version in which the first chapter is extensively rewritten, and indeed improved from a literary viewpoint, by the exclusion of some of the offensive matter about the father of the hero. There is further rewriting throughout the book.

Alf MacLochlainn. *The Irish Book*. Winter,
1959–60, pp. 42–43

O'Duffy is difficult to sum up. The circumstances of his life were against him, and he had no opportunity, or perhaps inclination, to develop in a straight line. His penchant for light verse he did toy with for most of his career, and most of his books have a few limericks or a bit of doggerel somewhere in them. However, he was no W. S. Gilbert and not even an Ogden Nash, and among his own countrymen Susan L. Mitchell beats him hands down. His plays are more than competent, and the dramatic form which he also used for a chapter in *Printer's Errors* and a chapter in *King Goshawk* indicates that he could well have become a significant dramatist. Indeed, P. S. O'Hegarty seems to think of him primarily as a dramatist. His *Wasted Island*, for all of its occasional crudities of style, is an engrossing, ambitious, and impressive book. Had he continued to write in this vein of fictionalized intellectual history, Irish literature would have been significantly enriched, as would it also had he continued his historical fiction which he began so promisingly in *The Lion and the Fox*. In fact, had he continued even to write in the vein of light comic fiction, which he so successfully essayed in *Printer's Errors* and *Miss Rudd and Some Lovers*, he would ultimately, I feel certain, have created an audience. His thrillers are best forgotten, and probably so also is his book on economics which has its primary interest as an overt statement of the attitudes impelling the Cuanduine trilogy. That trilogy had he been able to conclude it in the same dazzling manner in which he had written the first two volumes would have been an unforgettably imposing masterpiece. However, worries and ill health intervened, and the final volume, despite flashes of brilliance, has its dreary longueurs.

Yet despite his hectic and diverse and spotty writing career, O'Duffy had his memorable accomplishments, and this tone of rather severe reservation really only implies a regret that his splendid accomplishments were not so great as his remarkable potentialities.

Robert Hogan. *Eimar O'Duffy* (Lewisburg, Pa.,
Bucknell Univ. Pr., 1972), pp. 80–81

O'Duffy's first novel, *The Wasted Island* (1919), occupies a unique place among his works, for it is the only one of his novels which has generated even the slightest critical controversy about its merit. . . . But the novel is also unique for its intrinsic characteristics as well as for its mixed critical reception. Neither potboiler nor satiric fantasy, *The Wasted Island* is the only one of O'Duffy's novels which treats historical themes with the realist's devotion to documentation. Partly autobiographical, the narrative covers the first 26 years in the life of Bernard Lascelles, from his birth in 1890 until his involvement in the Easter Rising. So in part, *The Wasted Island* is a *bildungsroman*. . . .

[A]s I see it, the central feature which distinguishes O'Duffy's novel from other coming-of-age novels is not only the emphasis on the political character of the hero's education, but also the hero's final condition. The climactic insanity of Bernard Lascelles after the Easter 1916 Rising is an astonishingly powerful reversal of perhaps the commonest convention of the *bildungsroman*: the reconciliation of the protagonist with the society which threatens to make him a pariah. This unexpected *dénouement* functions as a kind of peroration to the main argument of the novel, which is that Ireland is a "wasted island" because her most important political leaders perpetuate what one of Bernard's friends names "the Irish lie." Bernard is the most important of several examples of this waste in the novel, for in his mental collapse O'Duffy shows his audience the most insidious result of accepting that lie. Simultaneously, O'Duffy demonstrates in Stephen Ward's survival how one may transcend that lie and the destruction attending it. It is clear that while O'Duffy agonizes and sympathizes with Bernard, he nonetheless looks to

Stephen Ward's image of Ireland as the best hope for the future. It is in O'Duffy's detailed account of Bernard's maturing years—the *bildungsroman* part of the novel—that the reasons for the protagonist's insanity become evident.

Gary Caret. *Éire-Ireland*. Autumn, 1976, pp. 66–68

O'FAOLAIN, JULIA (1932–   )

If a significant proportion of the new Irish writing is concerned with the survival of human values under reductive economic pressure, Ireland also has, in Julia O'Faolain, an outstanding satirist of the affluent society. For a number of excellent reasons, her work is different in kind to that of other writers I have discussed in this essay. Born and brought up in Ireland, the daughter of Sean O'Faolain, she is married to an American Renaissance specialist, has lived in France and Italy, and now lives in the United States. Consequently, she is, along with Francis Stuart and Aidan Higgins, among the very few Irish writers who are truly international in range. Sean O'Faolain and Mary Lavin have both set stories in Italy: Julia O'Faolain has been able to write, as it were, from inside Italian life. Where she differs most sharply, however, from other Irish writers is in choosing to work from within the contemporary flux of modes and passions. Her characters generally have comparative economic freedom. Not being pinned down in one situation, they escape that terminal haunting that gives most Irish fiction its metaphysical unease. They do not escape, though, essentially the same challenges: only in their case the pressure comes from within, generally as a conflict between the direction of their own vitality and the assumptions of the way they have been brought up. Sally Tyndal, in *Godded and Codded*, is as much an explorer after the true nature of herself as McGahern's Elizabeth Reegan: only where Elizabeth, dying of cancer in her mid-forties, searches for meaning through reflection, Sally, in her twenties and hungry for experience, searches through action. To call Julia O'Faolain a satirist, as I did a few lines back, is to do her work only partial justice: it suggests the incisiveness of her talent—for wit and verbal devastation she has few equals among her contemporaries—but not the strength nor the subtlety of her concern. There is a power of mind behind her work, as well as an irreverently perceptive eye, that catches the intensity of human drives, the essential seriousness of the effort to live, without swallowing any of the trends in self-deception. She is an acute observer, who is involved at a level of concern deeper than the substance or sum of her observations.

Immediately striking in Julia O'Faolain's first collection of short stories, *We Might See Sights!* (Faber, 1968), is the use of surreal imagery, particularly of expressions: "the wrinkles in her face moved in the sun like the long-jointed legs of agonizing insects." Agonizing can have a transitive, as well as an intransitive use. Age, disappointment or lust, like medieval vices, become monsters that take over the flesh: "multimouthed animalities stirred beneath her skin." . . .

In her first novel, *Godded and Codded* (Faber, 1970) this verbal skill is employed to show the contradictions involved in being young, awake and Irish. The first contradiction is that in Ireland it is the old who seem young: they had enough excitement in the Troubles to give them a perpetual lien on romance, despite the decades of stolid respectability since. The young are up-staged, and yet still bereft of advice, for an unspoken double-standard operates.

Roger Garfitt. In Douglas Dunn, ed., *Two Decades
of Irish Writing* (Chester Springs, Pa., Dufour,
1975), pp. 239–40

Julia O'Faolain's distinguished novel [*No Country for Young Men*], with finely controlled time-shifts, involves three generations. Years ago, Judith had been shoved unwillingly into a convent, because she might have known too much about the death of an American fundraiser in dreadful 1922. She was later given electric shock treatment, in circumstances increasingly suspicious. The convent is now dispersed, Judith packed off to unwilling relatives bemused with their own troubles. Her memories, scattered, raddled, now committed to tape, may endanger a slice of heroic Republican history. Old muck conceals nasty matter. Too many reputations were ambiguously earned, a dead hero-patriot is vulnerable, likewise the murdered American. A scandal may emerge about lost party funds and the clandestine extremist associations of political respectables. . . .

The link with Yeats' ideal Byzantium observed in the novel's title is ironic. This Ireland more relates to the actual Byzantium, with its maimings, vendettas, hypocrisies, theological nonsense, and threatened dispensations. As with Imperial Rome, one senses a community with too little to do, a lack of the useful, with wounds left untreated, a coarsened imagination blocked by too much history, under-used strengths finding malice the easiest remedy for mediocrity. Now, the demagogic film will never be made, the escape from a hopeless marriage will fail, the young son will probably end in violence, shocked by the futility of his elders—the bottle, the maunderings over endlessly lost chances, the cowardly ambushes enlarged into heroic battles, the spells woven by the dead, the imaginary and the contrived.

There are seering domestic scenes. A hockey stick reminds Judith of the bayonets of 1922 and indeed worse, setting her off stabbing a cushion like a crazed mechanical soldier. But in essence the book concerns myth-making, fear of reality, equivocation. The unattractive exterior greyness is periodically lightened by instants of perception: a lively dog, whose "bronze coat flashed like a needle ruffling lace": a landscape, melancholy yet fresh and profound: private needs for love and fulfilment, the sad forbearances beneath a blatant cuckoldry. The author knows what V. S. Pritchett has noted about the great Russian novelists' signal response to people sitting alone, "to the isolation, inertia, the off-beat in the human character." As James, the American visitor, walks alone through Dublin: "The long passion of Irish history mystified him though he had opened himself to the local geography, responding to the city's moist appeal. Dublin struck him as cryptic. It was all smear and glare. Rain filtered light. Mist masked it. Water threw it slantwise with the sly trajectories of knives. . . ."

The imagery derives from observation rather than the overblown generalizations that infect so many of the people, seen here with unusual proportions of sympathy and detachment.

Peter Vansittart. *LondonMag.* July, 1980, pp. 91–92

The contemporary Irish story seems to be to offer a paradigm of the condition of Ireland herself, both as she exists within herself and in relation to the world outside, and in the stories of Julia O'Faolain, the brilliant daughter of Sean, we see traditionally Irish themes merging into the Jamesean International Subject, though opening out beyond the mutual involvement of Britain and the United States.

Her range is wide. There is the story "It's a Long Way to Tipperary," which deals with the problems of the Irishman forced, in some sense, into Englishness. Cuddahy enlists as a private in the British Army in 1914, rises to the rank of captain, and marries an English woman of better class than himself. He eventually comes back to Ireland a renegade twice over, a renegade Catholic through his wife's influence and a renegade Irishman.

"It's a Long Way to Tipperary" is at once funny almost to the point of farce, a hard-headed and moving story of a specifically Irish dilemma. Julia O'Faolain is a writer of great flexibility, reminiscent to some degree of Kipling in her diversity of scene. Thus, besides "It's a Long Way to Tipperary," *Man in the Cellar*, the volume in which it appears, contains two other brilliant stories in modes very different from it and from each other. One is "This Is My Body," which is set in a convent in sixth-century Gaul and is a dramatization of the impact of Christianity on people still pagan in feeling and impulse. The other is "Man in the Cellar" itself, and here the International Subject is subsumed in another subject, one we may call in rough shorthand Women's Lib. It is an index of the story's success that it will almost certainly recall Poe. The story is in the form of a long letter to her mother-in-law written by a young Englishwoman describing the revenge she has taken on her domineering and sadistic Italian husband. "Marriage," writes Miss O'Faolain in her last paragraph, "like topiary, distorts growth."

"Romantic Ireland's dead and gone." Certainly the Ireland of today is a different Ireland from Yeats's and Joyce's or even O'Connor's. But, as the short stories being written at the present time show, it is no less Ireland, for all that it has moved into the modern world. The Irish dimension in these stories of the Sixties and Seventies is as pronounced as it has been at any time in the history of Irish writing in English, and in this respect the contemporary Irish story may be held up as a model.

Walter Allen. The Short Story in English (Oxford,
Oxford Univ. Pr., 1981), pp. 393–94

Julia O'Faolain often creates sexual encounters that are also encounters between cultures: Algerian and Irish in her first novel, *Godded and Codded*; Italian and Irish in many of her short stories; Californian and Irish in her recent *No Country for Young Men*. In doing so, she inevitably distances her lovers from one another, to throw into high relief the whole issue of differences between sexual partners—differences ignored or flattened in more conventional love stories—and therefore to focus our attention on the woman's apparent need to abandon or re-fashion her identity.

The protagonist of *No Country for Young Men*, a researcher from Los Angeles, finds a unique excitement in an affair with a Dublin woman who still takes sex—and sin—seriously. *The Obedient Wife* partly reverses this situation, and partly toys with it. Carla Verdi, from Rome and Milan, who is serious about her responsibilities as wife and mother, finds herself among the temptations of Los Angeles. Her obedience is to her absent husband's advice—orders—which are to explore the sexual freedom around her, to have an affair, acquire experience. His motives are not entirely clear, but are hinted with subtle ambiguity. . . .

Carla's choice is a Catholic priest, who is initially attracted by her dedication to marriage, her stability, even by her good cooking. For her there is no sense of supernatural risk in the affair. She comes of an old anti-clerical family. Nor does the priest seem much troubled by sin (I am probably too ingenious in imagining that Carla's last name puns on Graham Greene, who treats this sort of affair more portentously). His easy slide into sex is perhaps a further reminder of the easy morality along the Santa Monica littoral, as is the book's recurrence of casual and temporary matings, of infidelity impossible to condemn because fidelity itself can hardly be imagined. . . .

"Her life had been structured by rules as easily tested as a recipe for sauce," Carla muses, as she tries to decide whether to let her old personality "dissolve . . . What did happen to a family when the mother gave these [rules] up? Surely it must collapse like an umbrella with a broken spine? Like a belly released from a corset or a stern old society robbed too suddenly of hierarchy and belief?" When she cooly appraises both her marriage and her affair, and recognizes her own commitment to "'keeping things together,'" she has convincingly liberated herself to make a choice on her own terms, in response to her own needs. That it is a convincing choice is due to the care with which Julia O'Faolain has slowly developed her character, and placed her in a network of memories, affections, and desires that define and support her without stifling her, that paradoxically allow her independence.

Robert Tracy. *ILS*. Fall, 1983, p. 29

O'FAOLAIN, SEAN (1900–1985)

Sean O'Faolain is the latest addition to the ranks of Irish storytellers. I think that time will prove him to be a considerable one.

The first impression one has of his book [*Midsummer Night Madness*] and the last is that he is all the time a writer with a profound respect for his craft. In reading the work of Peadar O'Donnell and Liam O'Flaherty one cannot avoid the impression that though they are good storytellers they are not artists, their prose is the prose of men who despise their medium; the tone is uniform throughout, good but a little lacking in variety. The sense of words that is so lacking in them is obvious in the very first lines of *Midsummer Night Madness*. This, one says, is a man who has read widely, felt deeply, and written and rewritten endlessly, to achieve his effects.

The rich texture of O'Faolain's prose is not unlike that of Bax's music. It has the same solidity, the same natural magic, the same romantic variousness.

O'Faolain excels in the description of action. He may, I feel, yet write a fine romantic novel. He is at his weakest when action flags, when he is tied down to the description of states of mind. His strength and weakness are clearly shown in the first story and that which he calls "The Small Lady." In the title story, incident does not flag because there is a unity of time and place, characters are of the simplest sort, and no fundamental issues are touched upon. It is, in fact, a typical romantic tale and a brilliant success. There is magic in it.

There is no magic in "The Small Lady" though it contains what is probably the best writing in the book. For in the story of a woman who is shot as a spy he is compelled to touch upon fundamental issues, and whenever he does so he displays a curious insensitiveness to them. The woman in this tale takes a lover the night before her execution; when a drunkard steals a bottle of whiskey she "sniggers"; the young man who has been her lover goes off promptly to get confession (this which Mr. Garnett praises seems to me monstrous psychology); even the men who take her off to her death behave like the chorus in an Italian opera and sing for her a ballad about her execution.

But this is O'Faolain's worst fault. I have read some of these stories several times with the same admiration for their splendid artistry, and there are certain scenes which I shall always remember: the Drunkard and the Guest-master in "The Small Lady"; Stevey and the Teacher in "The Death of Stevey Long."

And I know that it will be among the dozen or so books about Ireland which I read again and again.

Frank O'Connor. DM. April, 1932, pp. 86–87

Here [in *Bird Alone*] is the tragedy of Cornelius Crone, the man who "sets his mouth against Heaven," but drinks deep of the bitterness of earth. "It was not that I could not believe in men," he says; "but that I could not believe in what men believed." Again, looking around him at the worshippers in a Cork city church, during a Holy Week service, "in all of them, whether they stared at the naked altar or prayed on their beads with wandering eyes, there was a look of awe that welded them into a oneness, that (as I realized) only such as they can ever know." But Cornelius, like his grandfather, was a "Bird Alone." "Weak in the carnalities, and too proud—proud as Lucifer." It is this pride which makes the old Fenian "grander" (surely, one of the most amazing and vivid pictures of an old man that fiction has given us) and live for forty years without the comforts of religion, because he would not retract his Fenian oath. It is this pride, too, which leaves his grandson, in the closing pages of the book, a "Bird Alone," because he will not be "untrue to his sins."

Ideo tenuit cos superbia: Operti sunt iniquitate et impietate sua. So chanted the monks when Cornelius paid a last visit to his city church before leaving Cork. The words of the Holy Week psalm might well be quoted as being the theme of the book. But it is to give a wrong impression to speak of it as a book with a single theme. It is a vivid picture of reality and, like reality, has many themes, each with its own complicated unravelling.

The vividness and beauty of some of the descriptive passages, the magic half-light of the opening pages, in which the lone "Bird" describes his solitary walks round his native Cork, the consistency of the fine writing in this book—all these may be read by even "he who runs." It is the complexity of character and human nature, the evolution of event from character and of character from event, the building up stone upon human stone of a structure, perfect in its beauty, and moving in its tragedy, which gives us pause.

Irish Book Lover. June, 1936, p. 96

The Censorship Board have seen to it that Mr. O'Faolain is without honour in his own country, and it remains ultimately for posterity to decide whether he is indeed a prophet or no. *A Purse of Coppers* reveals him as a short story writer, capable of supreme artistry. He is essentially Irish, and has succeeded in purging from his works the most usual Irish faults; he has banished sentimentality, and is ruthless, though, at the same time, just, in his treatment of his characters. His prose-style is admirable; even, though not monotonous; simple, though not naive; economic, though not obscure. It is clear that Mr. O'Faolain knows much of men and the workings of their minds. He lays bare a character, not by a paragraph of analysis, but by its reaction to circumstance and by the apparently casual remark. His men and women are real men and women, but they are not self-consciously created realist puppets. He has the invaluable hunch, in common with many authors of the past whose works have survived, of creating a character that is alive, who makes a positive impression as though he were indeed of flesh and blood. This is an unusual and very satisfying book.

Irish Times. Dec. 11, 1937, p. 7

A woefully large share of any consideration of Seán O Faoláin runs the risk of being absorbed in controversial matters of varying importance, but not one of them as important as the facts that he has written a biography like *King of the Beggars*, a novel like *Bird Alone*, or that in the opinion of Mr. William Saroyan he is about the best man there is at the short story. It is not easy to find the exact description to fit O Faoláin's mastery of the short story, a mastery as undisputed as that of O'Flaherty or O'Connor—or Maupassant. There is smoothness and grace in the actual writing; there is the preference for the significant moment which is frequently a contemplative moment and is more important for O Faoláin—and for any wise man—than the platform called plot or the unreality called a central character. Life, he maintains, has no central characters; and life flows smoothly through these stories as it does through the stories of Maupassant, so smoothly and easily that it is possible pleasantly to lose sight of the art involved. Humour breaks like coloured bubbles on the smooth flow, a whirling twist of the water reminds that life can be cruel and terrible and heedless of the results of its own cruelty. There are moments filled with contemplation and consideration, silent like some lost valley in Muskerry but alive with the life of silent places. There are stories as crowded with jostling characters and words and ideas as any lane in the city of Cork. And, indeed, the city of Cork is very important in much of what Seán O Faoláin has written. Life began there, and exile begins where life begins. Neither in Corkery nor O'Connor for Cork, nor in O'Flaherty for the rocks of Aran, nor in McLaverty for Belfast, nor in MacManus for Kilkenny, is there the same feeling of intense nostalgia. Corkery, McLaverty and MacManus have never for a moment shown any signs of feeling separated from their own people; O'Connor and O'Flaherty, like Harriet handy with the lariat, seem all the time to be having too much fun to give a damn whether they are or are not in exile. But Seán O Faoláin is among the most nostalgic of Irish writers; and reading his stories you get the feeling that for him memory is neither a locked box nor a tidy room with objects on orderly shelves but a living body still growing and capable of intense pain. . . .

For my own personal taste Seán O Faoláin has never written anything better than *Bird Alone*, and the old age of Corney Crone, his old man's love for morning and evening, has a place among the classical stories of exile—the exile of a man from his people, of the soul in the world, the loneliness of the soul when it is doubtful of God.

Benedict Kiely. *Modern Irish Fiction: A Critique*
(Dublin, Golden Eagle Books, 1950), pp. 119–20

Teresa (1947), Mr. O'Faoláin's last book of stories, reflects very much the same world as *A Purse of Coppers* did ten years before. The clergy are still dominant, artists are still frustrated. The "fusing image" longed for in "A Broken World" has clearly not been found. It still is being sought, however, perhaps less hopefully, but in the same places. The longest story in the book, "The Silence of the Valley," concerns the death of an old cobbler in the Gaeltacht, and the revelation to a group of visitors that this story-telling cobbler and his wife represented not merely the old Gaelic world but a primitive source of virtue, the natural state of innocence before the Fall of man. This cobbler—the earthiness of whose stories we know to have brought on him the castigations of the clergy—is a necessary hero in the mythology of "Delphic Nationalism." He is in fact the incarnation of the "true" Ireland: an Ireland before the Fall and therefore before Christianity, an Ireland which is its own religion and does not contradict.

This idea of the "true" Ireland has ceased to be an inspiring myth and has become a source of confusion and irritation. When Mr. O'Faoláin was still writing out of the experience of his youth romantic Ireland was not dead. It was natural for him, whose own youth had coincided and mingled with his country's successful revolt, to fuse subjective and objective, identifying his own inner experience with the Irish revolution. This identification, extending back into the penumbra which had helped to produce it, established itself as a general association. Nationalism was the communion of youth; freedom was a word of one indivisible meaning; the Irish-speaking districts of West Cork were a pagan Arcadia. Within a limited historical field, a period ending in the early 1930's—during which a powerful revolutionary tradition ran not only against the Crown, but against the Church also—this association was coherent and a source of power. But revolution is little more permanent than youth. The Ireland in which Mr. O'Faoláin now lives and writes is, as everyone knows, the least romantic and the least revolutionary of countries. It is one in which Church and State exist in harmony, as inexpugnable bastions of the family. Here the parents of Corney or Denis could live secure, for there is no fissure at all in the wall of acceptance. Parnell's place has been taken by a line of pious and blameless patriots and rebellion has become a praiseworthy but concluded activity. Ireland is now a middle-aged country. Youth can take it or leave it; and often leaves it.

Mr. O'Faoláin will neither take it nor leave it. He sees, of course, and bitterly resents, Ireland's staid paternalism, symbolized for him principally by the literary Censorship Board which has banned three of his books (*Midsummer Night Madness*, *Bird Alone*, and *A Purse of Coppers*). In scores of articles and letters he has denounced this institution and the spirit behind it, the spirit of Corney's father and of the teaching Brother who slashed young Denis's essay. His stories, with their great and increasing emphasis on the frustrations and stagnations of Irish life, show his oppression by that spirit and his knowledge of its power. But in combating it, which he has done more fearlessly than any other writer living continuously in Ireland, he has relied emotionally on something that has lost its meaning in the new environment—the old anticlerical nationalism.

> Donat O'Donnell [Conor Cruise O'Brien].
> *Maria Cross: Imaginative Patterns in a Group of*
> *Modern Catholic Writers* (New York,
> Oxford Univ. Pr., 1952), pp. 110–11

"I shall be content," Mr. O'Faolain writes in his modest and revealing foreword [*The Finest Stories of Sean O'Faolain*] (surely he is not responsible for the title of this book), "if half a dozen, if even three or four of my stories that have taken thirty years to write are remembered fifty years hence." It would be easy to name three, to take no more, which should be remembered: "Sinners," "Teresa," and "The Man Who Invented Sin."

These three stories, pre-eminent in a very distinguished volume, have permanently valuable things to say about the coming together of the Irish national character and Catholicism. They show Mr. O'Faolain as historian and social critic, characteristics which distinguish him from Frank O'Connor and O'Flaherty. Only he of the great masters of the short story in Ireland has attempted to show the development of the people he writes about. The Irish in the other two are static; it is impossible to tell their early stories from their later ones; characters, attitudes, and settings do not change. When you have read one of Mr. O'Faolain's stories, on the other hand, you have by no means read them all. Artist and Ireland both change and develop the span of thirty years as one reads these stories. And that is the best of reasons for reading them again.

> Riley Hughes. *Catholic World*. Sept., 1957, p. 472

After *Constance Markievicz* [1934] he entered on the greatest phase of his career. In a period of about ten years he wrote his best novel, his two great historical biographies, most of his finest stories, and a host of intelligent commentaries on Irish life and letters. His development was intense and varied as he worked out his views on Irish society, sought for ways of handling it in novels and stories, and turned back to the whole range of Irish history in quest of continuity.

It was by any standards a man-sized job, and his reputation rests securely on what he wrote at this time. It is in the range and intensity of that work, its intellectual vigor and imaginative power, its passionate devotion to Irish life, its achieved control of form and manner, that he emerges as the most important writer of his generation. In its totality it is by far the most complex and valuable response to Irish life in the generation that lived through the revolution into the realities of independence. It was, as has been seen in studying its manifestations in the three main forms, and achieved success, a working toward detachment, a hard-won victory over the enemies of promise in himself and in his surroundings.

He began his journey toward that success, toward, for example, the controlled intensity of *The Great O'Neill* or the dispassionate intellection of some of the editorials in *The Bell* in a mood of depression. The landscape of *Bird Alone* and of the early stories in *A Purse of Coppers* was peopled with artist-rebels defeated by the lack of vitality in their surroundings. These spiritual heirs of Leo Donnell were stranded after the tides of revolution. *Bird Alone* and the disillusion of the post-Parnellite period as its temporal background; Corney's sexual and religious liberation came at the height of Parnell's defeat, and he identified personal calamity with national disaster. Implicit in that identification was the analagous political and social realities of O'Faolain's own life after the Civil War and after DeValera's failure to bring about social reforms. The new Ireland was tinged with the same pressures Corney encountered, and in between the passionate individualism of Philip Crone, the old Fenian, and the boy-hero growing up in daily association with him was the dull rectitude of the boy's pious, middle-class father. The middle generation thus represented corresponded to the new middle class of the thirties—pious, materialistic, unadventurous, out of sympathy with the dreams and needs of rebellious youth. But although past and present were joined in the old rebel and his young disciple, there was one major difference. After Parnell, as after independence, there was no longer any large cause to which a dissatisfied youth could attach himself in half-forgetful dedication. He and his lonely compatriots in *Purse of Coppers* were birds alone, sadly separated by pride and principle from the common humanity about them.

Corney's strongest loyalties were to the past, to the heritage so fiercely and so passionately felt in the older rebel. Old Philip was presented as a parasitic figure feeding on the boy's innocence, corrupting him intentionally, bringing him into his own condition of social and religious alienation. There is some obscurity and confusion in Corney's account of this conscious abuse, but he has an intense conviction that he was made in the image of his master, not through any natural and gradual process of normal growth, but prematurely and so totally that he was broken away from his own people in an irreparable displacement. As the compulsive narrator of the novel he experiences again the dark confusions of his growth and displays his barren freedom as a judgment on the society he cannot accept. He shares his loneliness with many characters in *Purse of Coppers* similarly affected by inadequacies within their environment. All seek in vain for imaginative richness, and until society changes they cannot even hope for contentment.

The two major historical biographies were powerful and successful strategies for examining conditions around these lonely figures. It was typical of the rhythm of O'Faolain's output that he moved back and forth between short story, novel, and biography to find adequate ways of dealing with Irish life. Faced with social insufficiency, he could best express his criticism of life within the framework of a previous time and through the persona of a historical figure whose creative energy and representative value were unmatched in the postrevolutionary period. In [Daniel] O'Connell and [Hugh] O'Neill he depicted the forceful reformer he so much wanted in his own time, men joined in a unity of being with their people, absorbed in projecting the deepest feeling of the country. The lessons and principles they embodied served as enduring and valuable parables for his own time. They satisfied his needs as a man and gave him as a writer the kind of full challenge he needed.

He moved in these ten years from an oppressive feeling about Irish life, from didacticism, from a too personal involvement, to detachment, a calm objectivity, a poetic gentleness. This progress, so evident in the stories, was apparent also in the contrast between the romantic gusto of the O'Connell work, its mythic glorification of the hero, its hard-hitting moral asides, and the realistic, factual, and disciplined portrayal of O'Neill and his more reasoned and even reluctant approach to the problems of his time. O'Faolain reached his maturity as a writer in these years of intense intellectual and imaginative effort.

Maurice Harmon. *Sean O'Faolain: A Critical Introduction* (Notre Dame, Ind., Notre Dame Univ. Pr., 1967), pp. 182–84

Following Chekhov's standards, O'Faolain gives us Realism combined with lyricism; a pervasive sense of mood; compassion; a deep awareness of the inherent mystery of existence, and detachment, combining sensibility and intelligence.

In handling style O'Faolain has also progressed from the exuberant lush Romanticism found in his first collection of short stories to a controlled prose—still rich and lyrical—but toned down so that it is in keeping with realistic subject matter. Horace Gregory has made the most perceptive observation about O'Faolain's post-Romantic style: "Nor has O'Faolain dropped into another common pitfall of lesser Irish writers—that of writing 'poetic prose'—he can be and is eloquent enough, yet the nearly 'styleless' style in the prose of his later writings is prose in the sense just as Yeats' later verse 'withered into truth.'"

One more issue remains. O'Faolain himself is worried over whether he is a Romantic or a Realist. Ostensibly, he is a Realist, but his subject matter must of necessity have some Romantic overtones. Talking of this problem in relation to writers in general, O'Faolain comments: "For any kind of realist to write about people with romantic souls is a most tricky and difficult business, even when he is a Stendhal gifted with a lovely irony, a Chekhov holding on firmly to the stern morality of the doctor, a Turgenev informed by an intelligent humanism, or an E. M. Forster blessed with a talent for quiet raillery. If one has not some such gift, the subject is an almost certain pitfall."

O'Faolain acknowledges that one could write angrily about such material—but, as we have seen, he has rejected this course, or one could turn to satire—as Frank O'Connor suggested. But O'Faolain informs us that he cannot be a satirist. Nevertheless, no writer, O'Faolain maintains, should remain the same; any serious author should keep evolving, changing in some manner, and seek new forms. The genuine artist should possess a willingness to experiment. This O'Faolain has continued to do. His study of various ramifications of time and memory in *I Remember! I Remember!* and the probing of love in *The Heat of the Sun* are recent manifestations of his own continuing evolution to new themes and subject matter.

O'Faolain's perplexity over Realism and Romanticism in his own case appears, therefore, to be idle speculation. O'Faolain is essentially a Realist—in his objectivity, in his conscious intellectual handling of material, in his use of irony, in his grasp of truth, and in his portrayal of life as it is. Yet, at the same time, his work contains lyrical and atmospheric qualities that are usually labelled "Romantic." Like Chekhov, O'Faolain is a realist who can blend truth with mood and poetry so that his portrayal of existence is enhanced by nuances and subtleties which give a deeper meaning to the writing and a closer look into contradictions, deceptions, and mysteries.

Paul A. Doyle. Sean O'Faolain (New York,
Twayne, 1968), pp. 127–28

Sean O'Faolain has constructed another Daedalean maze [in *The Talking Trees*], and we must now decide whether that elusive Minotaur, the chaotic conscience of the Irish race, has been caught within the entanglements of his prose. O'Faolain describes an Ireland where some of the younger priests read Simone de Beauvoir, where the leap from feudalism into modern industrial society is finally becoming an actuality, and where sex is no longer the unspeakable area of life that it was in the pre-Leopold Bloom days. It's all the more striking, therefore, to find a mood of "spiritual paralysis" hovering over *The Talking Trees*—the same kind of paralysis that James Joyce discerned in the Dublin of seventy years ago. . . .

O'Faolain descends from a long line of Irish satirists, and when things get too sticky for his satire—when passion or death enters the picture—he regresses into the giddy provincialism that can be heard any evening in the pubs of Dublin or in the bars on Third Avenue. O'Faolain shows the true nature of this provincialism in "Thieves," where a cruel anti-Semitism intrudes upon a quiet Easter Sunday morning in the city of Cork. It is certainly brave of the author to mention this unsavory aspect of a society that is supposed to be founded on the Semitic idea of loving one's neighbor. But the reader may wonder why the glee of the little girls who witness it is allowed to divert our attention from the ugly underside of Irish Catholicism that has just been exposed. Or is this childish glee just another manifestation of those hidden forces?

Sean O'Faolain has brought courage and skill to the making of these stories, but the resolution of such problems is beyond his imaginative grasp. One is forced to conclude that the Irish Minotaur—the old sow who devours her farrow in more ways than one—has, in this case, escaped from the Daedalean labyrinth.

John W. Hughes, *Sat.* Feb. 6, 1971, pp. 30–31

After his brief intoxication with Irish Ireland [O'Faoláin] quickly became deeply sceptical about the possibility of reviving anything of real worth from the Gaelic past. He believed certainly that "Gaelic, both the language and the literature, is like a well in whose dark silence one sees an image of that shadowy other-self which is our ancestral memory" and in the need to communicate "with those drops that are part of the whole stream that fed us," but he was persuaded that modern Ireland was an English-speaking nation formed by the struggles of the nineteenth century, shaped by the social experience of democratic Nationalist politics. He believed that Gaelic Ireland, aristocratic, hierarchic, anti-democratic, died in the eighteenth century and that it was pointless to try and breathe life into a corpse. Modern Ireland had been, his thesis explained, invented by Daniel O'Connell in the nineteenth century. It was in his biography of the Great Liberator, *King of the Beggars* (1938), that O'Faoláin proposed this thesis with greatest force (the thesis is the inspiration of many of his journal articles). What is clear in this masterful book is that O'Faoláin does not regret the passing of the old order for all his distaste for contemporary Ireland. Indeed, the biography is essentially a polemic against those features of the modern Irish society he accepts as his own, that he found oppressive, since he believed they originated in a false understanding of Irish history which a true reading of O'Connell's life and work would correct. The romantic nationalism that had fed the revolutionary movement and the Literary Revival alike has fostered in O'Faoláin's sense of things a view of Irish history that was idealistic to the point of fantasy. Despite all that had happened in the eighteenth and nineteenth centuries, that questionable creed asserted, Gaelic Ireland had remained intact and had been restored in acts of Republican violence. The Rising of 1916 was a restorative culmination, not a beginning. O'Faoláin thought such a view romantic claptrap, proposing by contrast a vision of Daniel O'Connell as King of the Beggars, a great utilitarian, English-speaking, anti-Gaelic, Irish leader who took a mob of disenfranchised helots whose civilization was in tatters and made of them a mass movement that bore fruit in the democratic achievements of the twentieth century. For O'Faoláin the real Ireland, the only Ireland, the only Ireland because it was the real Ireland, was the Catholic, English-speaking, democratic, petit-bourgeois world he saw about him, troubled and oppressed by fanaticism and obscurantist doctrines of various kinds, bred of a romantic version of Irish history. Ireland was not the restored Gaelic nation, where defects could be accounted for in terms of inadequate restoration, but a new nation fashioned out of the scatterings of an old, where there still remained a great deal of nation-building to be done. For such a nation, the practical, almost Benthamite figure of O'Connell was a truer model than any idealistic image of Cuchulain or the Red Branch heroes.

Terence Brown. In Ronald Schleifer, ed.,
The Genres of the Irish Literary Revival
(Norman, Okla., Pilgrim Books, 1980), pp. 159–60

In the Ireland to which Sean and [his wife] Eileen had returned in 1933, criteria for distinguishing fact from fantasy had been deliberately mislaid. . . . Faced with a society of mummers, a writer could reasonably feel that before starting to write fiction it would be well to establish some facts.

It was partly as a writer then that Sean felt the need to make sense of the Irish experience. But as editor of *The Bell*, he was also performing a social service when he tried to cut through the prevailing rhetoric to where, as he wrote in his first editorial: "Among the briars and the brambles there stands the reality which generations died to reach—not, you notice, the Ideal . . ." Readers were encouraged to turn writer and tell about whatever patch of Irish life they knew at first hand: ". . . if you look through the first number," the editor invited, "you will see several things whose merit is not chiefly Art but Truth. . ." *The Bell* was asking ordinary Irish people to help "stir ourselves to a vivid awareness of . . . what we are becoming, what we are."

Odd for a literary magazine to eschew ideals in that wartime era of agit-prop? Yes and no. After the long social struggle with its surfeit of hope, truth in the land of blarney was in noticeably short supply. Mistrust, not only of absolutes but of the objective world itself, shows up in the Irish writing of those years. Flann O'Brien and Beckett were already writing what critics now call "metafiction"—fictions about fiction—; Frank O'Connor's stories display the same bifocal vision as those Camus was to publish in 1957, during another civil war, and a perennial Irish tradition of romancing pointed to that preference for taking hold of experience with the tongs of metaphor which prevails where reality is untractable or hard to find.

Sean was moving counter to this trend when he gave up his daydreaming to tangle with the phenomena around him and with the values of the new oligarchs. . . . In 1945 he was a founding member and Vice President of Irish Civil Liberties and though he gave up the editorship of *The Bell* in 1946, he was always apt to return for a Parthian penpointing at some fresh impropriety, as when the bishops, in 1951, torpedoed a public health project by intriguing with cabinet members behind parliament's back. This, Sean pointed out, was an example of a non-elected power using its ghostly sanctions to manipulate an elected one. The citizen in Sean was at odds with the writer who preferred personal relationships, privacy and art. He has always been protean and, mark, I don't say "chameleon." A chameleon blends into its background. Sean stood out. On a greenish tartan, he glows pinkly. Faced with a red flag, his eye will suffuse with a tincture of true blue individualism.

What he achieved in *The Bell* was, I think, to clear the ground of myths so that people could start to think. Myths do prevent thought. Think of Dostoevesky's character who says "if God does not exist, then all is permitted" and kills himself in despair. Locked into a belief that only divine retribution stood between mankind and savagery, he could not conceive of a social conscience. Neither would the Irish Church allow for one in 1951. You need lay moralists to elaborate a social code and Sean—moved by the civic spirit absorbed from his boyhood reading of English schoolboy papers?—took up the challenge.

Julia O'Faolain. *LondonMag*. June, 1980,
pp. 21–23

The early stories [of Sean O'Faolain] have two problems, which often merge. There is the large, general problem of Romantic Ireland, not that it was dead and gone but that it wasn't. In the first years of the 20th century it was impossible for a young writer to see Ireland "as in itself it really was": he saw it only through a veil of associations, ancient pieties, sagas not entirely forgotten, Corkery's "hidden Ireland" had to be recalled, disclosed. Romantic Ireland called for heroic emotions or, in defeat, elegiac emotions: either way, styles extraordinarily high and grand. The particular version of this general problem, for O'Faolain as a short-story writer, was to imagine characters and situations large enough to contain not only the "object" but the halo, the aura, that already surrounded it, the words that were already poetry, if only bad poetry. His early stories rarely succeed in finding such characters, such situations. So the narrative style has to force the characters to feel more than they could really feel, consistent with the probability the stories claim: the result is that there is always a remainder of sentiment which has to be added, as if between the words, to satisfy the demands of a rhetoric greedy as if by nature. O'Faolain's patriots, young warriors, priests, all those mothers, all their sons, are well enough, but not quite good enough for the rhetorical work they have to do.

These problems may explain why so many of O'Faolain's stories show their characters caught in the coils of memory. Most of his characters, especially in the early stories, live on their memories while they die otherwise. *I remember! I remember!* is the best of his titles, though not the best of his books, and it is all the better, all the richer, when you remember the way the old poem goes: "I remember, I remember, the house where I was born, the little window where the sun came peeping in at morn." Morn, yes. Indeed, O'Faolain's flair for memory, and the flare of his memories, were so vivid that he must often have been tempted to proust his way through the Ireland of his childhood and keep his art to that pleasure. But he hasn't yielded, as some of his colleagues yielded. . . .

In these respects, O'Faolain has been strong where his colleagues have been timid. He has written well of the mandatory themes, childhood, mothers, first confession, priests, monks, young girls, but he has forced his art to pay attention to an Ireland which has often disappointed him as a citizen. The stories he has written since 1945 have cast an ironic but not a cold eye upon Dublin, its upper-middle-class life, its lawyers and doctors, the remnants of Ascendancy Ireland, their marriages, their mistresses. This is a Dublin that found its symbol not in a desperate revolt proclaimed from the statue of Cuchulain in the General Post Office but in a referendum that decided, by a huge majority, that Ireland would indeed join the EEC and grow fat with German money. . . .

O'Faolain's imagination has kept up with the European Ireland. . . .

There are no really evil, wicked people in his stories: some are vain, pretentious, silly, but O'Faolain doesn't find satisfaction in observing malice. So, while he is often ironic toward his characters, and agile in detecting their follies, evil is not his theme. He is not, in fact, a satirist. "I still have much too soft a corner for the old land," he confessed in the Penguin Preface. It is true. In the years after the War, he was much occupied with public issues, the question of censorship, for an irritating instance, and he showed that he could write wounding prose when his ire was up. But that was in polemical vein. In his fiction, he is always ready to see the other side of the situation, and to feel the hidden motives. I mention, as if evidence were necessary, such stories as "A Meeting," "The Confessional," "Unholy Living and Half Dying," "Shades of the Prison House," "The End of a Good Man," "Passion," "Childybawn," "Lovers of the Lake" and "Charlie's Greek."

Thirty? Yes, I could name them, or as many, though they might not tally at every point with O'Faolain's choice. The differences would be slight. To write 30 successful stories, in an extremely competitive art (look at V.S. Pritchett's recent *Oxford Book of Short Stories*, and think of all the stories he had to leave out), is a rare and exhilarating achievement. I salute a master.

Denis Donoghue. LRB. Feb. 4, 1982, pp. 18, 20

This enormous volume [*The Collected Stories of Sean O'Faolain*] includes everything that appeared in the eminent Irish writer's eight previously published collections, plus half a dozen "uncollected stories" dated 1982. Among these 90 "stories and tales" are several undeniable classics, and a few dozen effective entertainments. But, on balance, this is uneven work, unworthy of his publisher's claim that Sean O'Faolain is "one of the great story-tellers since the death of Chekhov."

What he is is a remarkably skillful and sophisticated technician who can render a small private world in such evocative, echoing detail that its universal relevance is instantly suggested; a chronicler of local conflicts who's adept at presenting two sides of a contretemps. He's one of the masters of realistic dialogue, and he can bring a character to life in a quick, vivid paragraph.

Why, then, do I not feel O'Faolain qualifies as a great writer? The answer lies partly in his very virtuosity (his ability to create someone or something fascinating, and his habit of shifting impatiently to focus elsewhere), and partly in the distance and distastefulness I infer from his many portrayals of Ireland at war with England and itself. O'Faolain was a republican fighter during the Civil War, but his subsequent writings are far from a glorification of his country's rebellious history.

He seems to connect Ireland's ardent separatist spirit with its people's material poverty and their virtual enslavement to obsolete political and religious ideas. It's as if Ireland is a ghost that haunts its own citizens, and Sean O'Faolain is so appalled by their superstitiousness and timidity he's unable to take them fully seriously. . . .

There are numerous criticisms of the persistence of revolutionary sentiment throughout people's later lives. The two elderly protagonists of "No Country for Old Men" react differently to their accidental involvement in latter-day "underground" violence: One embraces the danger eagerly; the other laments that they are only shadows of their former vigorous selves.

But the revolution is scarcely O'Faolain's only target. We see strong condemnations of Ireland's mindless puritanism in "The Old Master," about a village intellectual's dismay over his neighbors' contempt for a visiting Russian ballet troupe. ("They know nothing. The beauty of the world. The grace of the human body. All lost on them.") The same sentiment is handled far more artfully in the fine story "A Born Genius," which tells of a promising young tenor's failure to put aside his inherited prejudices and adapt to an of-fered "new life" in America. . . .

The stories from "The Talking Trees" (1970) and "Foreign Affairs" (1976) bring their hidebound locals out of Ireland, into other countries, and into erotic involvements, handled with an increasing sexual explicitness that's far from O'Faolain's best manner. His narrative skills have remained undi-minished, and he's never less than entertaining. But of the final two dozen or so stories in this collection, the only one I'd strongly recommend is "Hyme-neal," the portrayal of an elderly couple in retirement that builds toward its protagonist's surprised understanding of the kind of person ("an irate man full of cold principle") he has always been.

It will not do, as I've indicated, to compare Sean O'Faolain with the short-story masters—certainly not with James Joyce (whose Olympian view of Ireland's cultural paralysis he shares and imitates), or Henry James (with whom he seems to beg comparison). Still, his best work will be remembered and should be properly valued.

Bruce Allen. CSM. Oct. 12, 1983, pp. 21–22

Leo Donnel [the protagonist of *A Nest of Simple Folk*] is no carbon copy of one man or two men, but rather a representative of a general type: the rebel. In *The Irish: A Character Study*, Ó Faoláin discussed this type: "The Rebel prob-ably never cared. He was devoted to failure. He was a professional or voca-tional failure. . . . There was only one thing at which the Rebel wished to be a success and that was at rebelling. Death did not mean failure so long as the Spirit of Revolt lived." Leo Donnel is a study in this kind of "failure" and "success." He is no saint; he is a very long way indeed from the chivalric he-roes of the nineteenth-century Irish historical novel. He is, like Stendhal's Julien Sorel, a social misfit. His title is repeatedly "a desperate character." This carrier of the noble name O'Donnell uses women, squanders money and land, and generally acts the fool, albeit a proud fool. He is no Wolfe Tone, no rebel who "sees beyond the immediate thing," as Ó Faoláin puts it in *The Irish*, "to the larger implications." He is the other kind of rebel, the first stage outlined by Ó Faoláin: the one who "rebels against an immediate in-justice—peasant risings follow, peasant societies of revenge, workers' asso-ciations. He sees no further." . . .

Leo is a study in repression and rebellion: he is Stephen Dedalus with politics substituted for art, action substituted for intellect. Ó Faoláin would create a Joycean *Bildungsroman* in *Bird Alone* (1936). Here his initial inspira-tion was Turgenev, whose novel *A Nest of Gentlefolk* he admired. In his auto-biography Ó Faoláin notes that his novel "was to be called, in a gesture of ad-oration toward Turgenev—whose work it no more resembled in treatment than in quality—*A Nest of Simple Folk*." Turgenev was the favorite novelist of Daniel Corkery, O Faoláin's first mentor, who urged Frank O'Connor and him to study the Russian realists in order to see how to merge realism and lyricism in their writing. . . .

By Ó Faoláin's time, looking to the Russians was a common enthusiasm among Irish writers. In *An Untilled Field* (1904), George Moore had modelled himself on *A Sportsman's Notebook*. Irish writers increasingly felt a kinship with the Russians who wrote about peasant life and history. Writers such as Corkery, Ó Faoláin, and O'Connor wanted to do the same thing for Irish history and Irish peasant life. By now Irish writers realized that they could spark their imaginations by looking to the great European writers, at the same time remaining vitally Irish. As Ó Faoláin wrote, he would be inspired, but he would not imitate. In *A Nest of Simple Folk* he shares with Turgenev a realistic attention to the foibles of common people as well as a fondness for their ways, "always the same for mile after mile through the whole length and breadth of Ireland," for "in a little town like Rathkeale all the joy of life is in its changeless ritual" (197, 187). But while Turgenev examined a tightly structured, highly class-conscious society, focusing specifically upon the Russian intelligentsia, Ó Faoláin was looking at "A Broken World," in the words of the title of his best story. . . . Furthermore, Turgenev's *A Nest of Gentlefolk* was not a historical novel at all; published in 1859, it centers on a love story occurring in 1842. In short, Turgenev was for Ó Faoláin a general inspiration, not a specific model. The only specific borrowing from Turgenev contained in *A Nest of Simple Folk* is its title.

James M. Cahalan. *Great Hatred, Little Room: The Irish Historical Novel* (Syracuse, N.Y., Syracuse Univ. Pr., 1983), pp. 117–19

O'FLAHERTY, LIAM (1896–1984)

There is elemental life in this book [*The Black Soul*]. With a hyperborean vigour it forcibly snatches the reader from the paltry imprisonment of the city and flings him hustling into the exhilarating turmoil of nature. The moods of sea and land, and the relation of people, animals, and birds to those moods, are conveyed with strength, simplicity, and force. To open such a book anywhere within the murky town atmosphere is, one feels, to risk arrest for the importation of some contraband distillation of fierce sea or mountain air.

In dealing with humanity in the mass the writer is acute and instinctive, and has the unusual gift of sensing the deep significance of common things. His treatment of individual characters, however, is limited. He can only see human beings as long as they remain strictly within the bounds nature has set for all her other children. As soon as they overstep these bounds he loses sight of them. If he allowed them to escape unopposed all might be well. Not content to do this, he continues to discuss them resentfully after they have gone beyond his vision. Later he begins to shout at them to come back, and tries to tie them to the apron-strings of their old mother nature with all the other creatures that he so profoundly comprehends. He calls upon their irresponsible old parent to discourage their continual unruly wild-goose chases into the void. In fact, he does everything he can to round them up with the rest of creation. And as a result of this the human beings in his book do not flourish. Man and woman are harder to catch alive than the scariest of stampeding cattle. Nature knows better than to try and herd them with the rest of her droves. The serpent himself only snared them by affecting a charming zeal to increase their liberty. They are an intractable couple in literature as well as in life, and when a writer tries to pen them up by force they are apt to droop and pine away in captivity. So the characters in *The Black Soul* have not entire vitality. They struggle for breath, but never quite gain it. And at times the living splendour and ferocity of the elements round them make this struggle appear painful rather than tragic.

DM. Aug., 1924, pp. 71–72

Ireland has become a *terra incognita* to us of late, Dublin a town of mystery, and its inhabitants strangers. The Irish writers we know already wrote of a past era. And so Mr. O'Flaherty's story of the Dublin underworld to-day is, in all its grimness, so much of a revelation that for this alone it compels our interest. He never makes the common error, either, of falling into sentiment about Ireland or slipping out of the world of reality into that non-existent world of petulant, half-godlike and utterly fictitious Irishmen that other writers have created out of their false vision and saccharine fancy. *The Informer* is the terrible story of a revolutionary ex-policeman's betrayal of his bosom friend, a gunman wanted by the police. This hunted creature, half dead of consumption, had crept home to see his parents. Gypo Nolan the ex-policeman knew it. . . . The stuff of the book is Gypo's relation to the dead man, to his antagonist Gallagher, head of the revolutionary force to which he belongs and whose ruthless power he so much fears, and to the dead man's mother. . . .

Though his dark and confused soul is chiefly concerned for his own safety, the strange relation which always holds between murderer and victim affects the giant Gypo. And there is another bond—the link between pursuer and pursued, strong as any passion—between Gypo the brute man of muscle and his Chief, the intellectual revolutionary, Gallagher. In the conflict between them Gallagher wins. Gypo is convicted of his treachery and shot down by gunmen comrades. Gallagher stands by with his hands in his pocket, smiling. . . .

For all its ominous atmosphere and its horror, *The Informer* is singularly restrained and full of sanity. There is no attempt to make our blood curdle, only a wish to show us an aspect of truth. Its author, neither for nor against the revolutionaries, simply exhibits them to us as men of virtue and vice mingled in dangerous proportions, men of action gone mad in a chaotic and disordered time and place. Gypo, though a brute, cunning and malevolent as any hungry tiger, is truly a man and dies like a man, strong in his soul. The dark vision of him which Mr. O'Flaherty gives us is not disgusting, though very awful and agonizing. We look on the gross figure of a contemptible wretch, but we can see, as only a serious and salutary writer about crime makes us do, even in that bloodstained monster Gypo, a reflection of a part of ourselves and of all humanity which we choose to forget, and hope to banish by forgetting. But it is good sometimes that the Beelzebub in humanity should be made manifest; for he is anything but vanquished, and Mr. O'Flaherty's fierce picture of revolution does well to remind us of it, lest we grow too self-complacent and come to be taken unawares.

Spec. Oct. 3, 1925, p. 560

In the past Mr. Liam O'Flaherty has been noted for a certain violence in his work, which, although it carried the reader breathlessly from the beginning of a book to its end, ultimately weakened its effect. In such books as *The Informer*, or *The Martyr*, this dynamic and demoniac speed tended to defeat the artist's purpose, by leaving only a blurred impression of characters and incidents and a feeling of exhaustion. In his new book, *Famine*, there is none of this breathless speed, and the book gains enormously in consequence.

Famine is, in fact, the best long story that Mr. O'Flaherty has yet produced. It is mature, calm, finely balanced, and beautifully written. It is as if Mr. O'Flaherty had pondered his story for years, sifting and winnowing his materials, living with his people, until he knew all that there was to be known about character and circumstance. In a sense *Famine* is a folk-tale: does not almost every inch of Ireland hold still the grim story of those terrible years? The "hunger" lived in the memories of people until a little while ago, and they transmitted the memory to their living descendants. It is this tranquilised memory that Mr. O'Flaherty has now given to literature. There is still the burning indignation, without which Mr. O'Flaherty would not be himself; but there is also a deep brooding pity that is new. Accepted merely as an historical reconstruction of one of the turning-points in Irish history, *The Famine* is a great achievement; but it rises beyond that to be an interpretation and an experience.

The story is that of the western village of Crom in the famine years—from 1845 onwards—and the effects of those years upon an entire community. The hero of the story is old Brian Kilmartin, and it is his family that is most intimately and lovingly presented. As the blight spreads hunger and death about the community the figure of Mary Kilmartin throws a gleam of beauty through the miasma; and in the end it is her bright spirit that lingers in the memory. Faced with the malignity of nature humanity is helpless; so that stupidity and selfishness seem to matter little or nothing. This is new in Mr. O'Flaherty's work, and it is a quality that adds tremendously to his stature as a novelist. *Famine* is, indeed, a book that must be read; for Irish readers it will bring the middle of the nineteenth century more vividly to the mind than anything that has since happened. People like Skerrett and Gypo Nolan will flit through the mind; Brian and Mary Kilmartin will remain.

Irish Times. Feb. 13, 1937, p. 7

The most important aspect of O'Flaherty's very important work is not to be found, except in certain implications in *Mr. Gilhooley*, in those three novels [*The Informer, The Assassin,* and *Mr. Gilhooley*], or in connection either with Irish-Ireland ideals or the particular revolution that opened the period of Irish life, as revealed in Irish fiction, with which I am dealing. Nevertheless, a revolution in arms was meat and drink to a novelist who once, in an essay on Joseph Conrad, stated his personal preferences for battle and blood, for Genghiz and his herd of camels and hosts of horsemen and jewelled concubines, for the storming of Troy and the war for the bull of Cuailgne, for "all the terrible madnesses of men and women crashing their bodies and their minds against the boundary walls of human knowledge." Genghiz Khan has at first glance precious little in common with Gypo Nolan the imbecilic brute of an informer who betrays his friends and is later assassinated on the threshold of the house of a poor girl who has only one thing in common with the jewelled concubines; but in Gypo Nolan in *The Informer*, in the gunmen in *The Assassin*, in the sodden relics of fighting men that impinge on the tragedy of Mr. Gilhooley, Liam O'Flaherty finds the reckless violent gesture that unites them both with Genghiz Khan and with O'Flaherty's own romantic soul. Nowhere in those books or in short stories like "The Sniper," or "The Mountain Tavern," is O'Flaherty at all interested in the revolution except in the power it shares with love and hate and other romantic things to draw the great gesture even out of the most degraded men. Dignified by that gesture even the troglodytes of the Dublin slums, as O'Flaherty sees them, can for moments be worthy of the earth on which they move; and it is the understanding of the earth, of animals worthy and human beings not always worthy of the earth, that makes O'Flaherty's work important. He does not enjoy recollections of revolutionary Ireland as Frank O'Connor does; neither does he analyse the meaning of revolution and post-revolution as Seán O Faoláin does.

Benedict Kiely. *Modern Irish Fiction: A Critique*
(Dublin, Golden Eagle Books, 1950), pp. 17–18

If one wished to write a thesis to show that the novel was not an Irish form but that the short story was, one could do worse than take O'Flaherty for text. His subject is instinct, not judgment. "When O'Flaherty thinks, he's a goose, when he feels, he's a genius," is how George Russell, the poet, summed him up. His best stories deal with animals, and the nearer his characters approach to animals the happier he is in dealing with them. With his passion for polemic, Moore in "Home Sickness" could not ignore the fact that emigration is largely caused by the sheer boredom of an authoritarian religion. With his own natural innocence O'Flaherty in a story like "Going into Exile" could ignore everything except the nature of exile itself—a state of things like love and death that we must all endure.

And one can easily imagine the sort of mess that George Moore would have made of O'Flaherty's "Fairy Goose," one of the great Irish short stories. It is the story of a feeble little goose whom the superstition of her owner turns into the divinity of an Irish village. She makes the fortune and turns the head of her owner until the parish priest decides to break up the cult, and the village louts stone the poor little goose to death. In essence, it is the whole history of religion, and it screams for a George Moore, an Anatole France, or a Norman Douglas, but because he is feeling rather than thinking, O'Flaherty never permits the shadow of a sneer to disturb the gravity of the theme. We laugh, all right, much louder than Moore or France or Douglas ever made us laugh— but at the same time we are moved, and eventually the impression left on our minds is something like that left by Turgenev's "Byezhin Prairie"—"the eternal silence of those infinite spaces terrifies me."

Frank O'Connor. *The Lonely Voice: A Study of the Short Story* (New York, World, 1962), pp. 38–39

As usual in O'Flaherty, the writing [in *Two Lovely Beasts, and Other Stories*] is of a sort almost bare of merely literary ornament—sparse even in figures of speech: writing dependent for effectiveness primarily on sheer impact of material. Plot counts for little; but then, O'Flaherty has frequently got along with a minimum of plot in his short stories, as also occasionally in his novels. Nor is there much of the wildness common to the earlier work. Indeed, there is less emotion than emotion recollected in tranquillity—a circumstance which, despite the sainted Wordsworth, does not usually make for the keenest poetry.

Perhaps one's disappointment stems from the fact that O'Flaherty seems mainly interested in offering a group of characters without much special significance in themselves. They are largely oddities—but without great claim to interest except for that fact in itself. And their presentation is curiously casual, its narrative vehicle rarely carrying the reader to any point of particular significance.

On the other hand, the prose is a good lean prose—for a change, so nearly free of clichés that it is almost startling to come on "foam-laced" and "eyes . . . as blue as the sea." And luckily, this prose preserves hints of the O'Flaherty who remains sensitive to the pathos of fierce age (typically the

Celt herein), affectionately observant of beast as well as man, and capable of poetry in individual dry point in his response to nature. All of which is some compensation for apparent weakening in vitality.

Of the 1956 selective *Stories of Liam O'Flaherty*, it is perhaps enough to remark that here may be found an assortment of many of the author's best things and not a few of his more commonplace. Of the here-first-collected tales, only "The Blow"—a story of brutality, tenderness, and illumination which luckily escapes sentimentalization—seems classifiable with the finest earlier ones.

Challenged in the large, O'Flaherty is an author whose miscellaneous achievement is critically somewhat disturbing. The dark tides sweeping through his best novels and short stories—the tumult, sometimes the un-couthness—can be very exciting; and the O'Flaherty who counts is both grip-ping and panoramic: never a man to say nay to life. On the other hand, he gen-erally lacks any impressive degree of real divination; his apparent lyricism is sometimes suggestive of the bogus—is too often merely a rush, rather than a grace, of wings; he is frequently tautological; and his minute descriptions and psychological meanderings can become very tedious, as can his seeming ob-session with cruelty. Nor does he induce the unfaltering conviction that he is an artist who is never satisfied with anything but the precisely right word. Probably the London *Times Literary Supplement* (19 April 1934) was correct in suggesting that "it is not unreasonable to surmise that his powerful and primitive imagination has been forced too rapidly, and therefore thwarted, by the modern cult of literary violence and exaggeration." Yet he remains, in the weary phrase, a "force to be reckoned with."

George Brandon Saul. *Rushlight Heritage*
(Philadelphia, Walton Press, 1969), pp. 88–89

O'Flaherty's essential artistic vision derived from the intensity of his aware-ness of his own existence in a universe that gives no meaning for existence. His subject is man as he becomes aware of himself in a universe which his reason shows him is absurd. In this sense O'Flaherty can be considered an existentialist. His awareness of the absurdity of existence, however, was not a philosophical position but a condition of his being. It was a condition from which he constantly struggled to escape, not a way of seeing he wished to pro-mulgate. O'Flaherty is an artist, not a thinker. Man's existential plight was the subject of art, not of truth. When O'Flaherty sought truth and became a positive thinker as the last novels indicate, he ceased being an artist.

O'Flaherty's subject is existence because he is a modern writer who sees man not as a manifestation of culture, tradition, or civilization, but as a naked soul alien to the culture, tradition, and civilization that offer only deceptions to obscure from men the true and awful nature of their being. His view of the artist is that which Lionel Trilling considers the characteristically modern belief: "the man who goes down into that hell which is the historical beginning of the human soul, a beginning not outgrown but established in humanity as we know it now, preferring the reality of this hell to the bland lies of the civilization that has overlaid it."

When O'Flaherty moved out from the isolated world of the Aran Islands into the world of Western culture, the image of reality that he bore from those elemental storm-lashed rocks was not shattered, but confirmed. The Aran Islands were reality in microcosm, for the Aran Islands were to earth as earth was to universe; and individual man on the islands, confronted with awesome nature, isolated, constantly aware of life because of his proximity to death, screaming out in horror at his inevitable fate, was true man, not overlaid by a complex culture that deceived. And because O'Flaherty was a modern writer he could not be an Irish writer in the sense of belonging to Ireland, speaking for Ireland, expressing Ireland and Irish dreams. What made Ireland significant for the Irish literary revival was a distinctive culture and tradition to which the Irish writers felt they belonged. It did not deceive them but sustained them.

O'Flaherty could only look at Ireland and envy, but he could not belong; for he had seen, felt to the marrow of his being, the awful truth of his own existence. He could cry out like Kurtz, "The horror! The horror!" but he could not deny that truth when, as an artist, he forced himself again and again to peer over the brink of chaos.

John Zneimer. *The Literary Vision of Liam
O'Flaherty* (Syracuse, N.Y., Syracuse Univ. Pr.,
1970), pp. 192–93

Some comment is required about the general neglect of O'Flaherty by literary critics. O'Flaherty is one of the significant Irish writers—Sean O'Faolain, Frank O'Connor, Mary Lavin, and Paul Vincent Carroll are some others—who have been pushed into the background because of the Irish Big Four syndrome that afflicts critics. Synge, Yeats, O'Casey, and Joyce have drawn so much attention that other important Anglo-Irish authors have either been neglected or unduly denigrated.

O'Flaherty must share much of the blame for his own critical neglect since he has taken every opportunity to censure, discourage, and mislead literary critics who might otherwise have given him a more complete hearing and might have been less inclined to judge him on the basis of his weakest books and his oral denunciations. Enraged that his first two novels did not receive the favorable critical reception he deemed them worthy of, O'Flaherty turned on the critics when they enthusiastically received *The Informer*. He then attempted to show how the critics had been easily deceived and erroneous about a book that he claimed to have written primarily as a prank.

O'Flaherty's overemphasis on the money motif for writers—some of this attitude being a pose and some of it again being a sneer at critics—also caused loss of critical prestige. Furthermore, O'Flaherty has too frequently with active belligerence met critical generosity or fair-minded attempts to analyze his work. Much evidence exists to support the theory that an ingrown sense of contrariness is forever active in O'Flaherty's makeup—some of the Samuel Johnson quality of taking the opposite side of an issue just for the sake of an argument also is present. O'Flaherty seems to enjoy a martyrdom complex. When he calls himself the "most unpopular man in Ireland," he takes a certain pleasure in this claim.

> Paul A. Doyle. *Liam O'Flaherty* (New York,
> Twayne, 1971), p. 120

In his stories, O'Flaherty's approach is that of the storyteller consumed with his narrative; he has significant or amusing people and events to talk about; he seems driven to move forward rapidly. He weaves in the briefest description, characterization, or comment; he eschews a piling up of detail. He reveres the present; his characters do not look forward or backward, nor do they indulge in reverie. This omnipotent present demands all of the narrator's energies, and so, despite his Communistic leanings, O'Flaherty avoids propaganda, a lesson apparently derived from his early training from Edward Garnett. Even when the situation might tempt him, as in "The Tramp," one of his best stories, he stresses the opposition between educated men who cling to the wretched routine of the workhouse instead of accepting the invitation of a tramp to revel in the freedom of the roads. In this story the grimness of the workhouse stands out as a natural event, not as a result of capitalism.

O'Flaherty's accomplishment in the short story lies in the immediacy with which his lyric sketches and comprehensive fables present uncomplicated emotions and instincts. In these stories O'Flaherty forgoes the intricate craft of modern fiction as he searches for an elemental form to convey his experience. He searches, often with admirable success, for an accurate expression of these instincts and emotions. Only by attending passionately to raw experience can O'Flaherty produce a literary effect. By relying on an ancient and simple narrative form, O'Flaherty reveals again the adaptability of man's love for direst narrative.

> James H. O'Brien. *Liam O'Flaherty* (Lewisburg,
> Pa., Bucknell Univ. Pr., 1973), pp. 115–16

O'Flaherty is rarely an introspective writer. Either he distrusts too much introspection, or feels himself incompetent at reproducing it. In one of his letters to Edward Garnett he said: "I cannot write about characters, I can only talk about them or create them."

Even in his novels, where there is more room for introspective development, and which hold the keys to the understanding of his major themes, O'Flaherty often takes delight in exaggerating the thoughts of his characters to melodramatic or fantastic proportions, and what introspection is shown is seldom peaceful, but caused by the spirit of grief, revolt or disgust. Think of the characters in "Going into Exile" all of whom make determined efforts not to become introspective. In "The Child of God" Mrs. O'Toole is considered queer by the villagers "because she had a habit of looking out over the cliff tops at the sea . . . for an hour at a time." It is only in his later work, in stories such as "The Lament," "The Fanatic" or "The Eviction" that introspection appears in unattractive characters who may be sensitive about their own feelings but are not sufficiently sensitive about the feelings of others, and all of them feel persecuted.

What might be called the persecution complex of O'Flaherty's central character, whether he is threatened by forces from without, or from the aberrations of his own temperament, is first weakened in *Skerrett*, in which the eponymous hero is indeed vanquished physically but not morally. The effects of persecution are overcome in *Famine* whose central character-group show incredible moral endurance in the face of the most crushing circumstances which threaten not only their existence but their dignity as human beings.

In his novels O'Flaherty moved away from one central hero, or anti-hero, as his vision of society became more complex and less personal. The splitting of the earlier central figure is first found in *The Wilderness* where, though Lawless is the principal character, Stevens and Macanasa rank closely below him in importance.

The House of Gold is O'Flaherty's first novel written round a group of characters who react upon and victimise each other, each being fixed in the cocoon of his own personal selfishness. *The Return of the Brute* is also centred round a group, united victims of the persecuting circumstances of war, virtually prisoners to their situation.

The Martyr, Land and *Insurrection* also each has a trinity of central figures which represent abstract principles. But an attempt to line up each set of three figures as consistently representing the same principle in each book breaks down for the soldier/poet/monk trio who stand for power, beauty and immortality mentioned specifically in *Land* (London, 1946, p. 53) and who reappear in *Insurrection*, have developed from the peasant/scientist/mystic trio round which *The Wilderness* story is woven. The theses behind these figures are important, however, because they form the only indication we have of O'Flaherty's inconsistent but conscious attempt at answering the question "What is ideal man?" or "What is man for?" The composite answer he gives is an oblique one, but would appear to be that by taking his peasant/scientist/mystic figures of *The Wilderness* and making all three soldiers in *Insurrection* he is suggesting that the contradictory forces within man should not weaken themselves by strife but unite in the face of the common enemy which is defeat. The story of the Irish rising gives an ideal illustration of this theme.

A. A. Kelly. Liam O'Flaherty the Storyteller
(New York, Harper & Row, 1976), pp. 122–23

Famine has long been, and deservedly so, O'Flaherty's most popular novel. Its panoramic portrayal of the Great Famine combines the sharp pictorial clarity of his short stories with his best narrative skill. Alone of all his novels he accepts here a social pattern of norms and values against which to dramatize the lives and destinies of his characters—indeed, in this sense, *Famine* is his most realistic work. Characters are placed within a well defined and intelligible society and they are motivated by real human passions and concerns. It is interesting to note that a number of the multifarious characters of *Famine* appear in previous works by O'Flaherty but are seen here with a difference. In *Famine* they are shorn of their wildest excesses, rooted in a place and time which contains and defines them. Perhaps the most remarkable quality of this work is its feeling for the ordinary, everyday life of rural Ireland in the nineteenth century. The famine corrodes and finally destroys that life and the reader is left, not so much with a sense of the individual tragedies of the lives portrayed but with a feeling of loss for a whole society and a way of life. . . .

   Famine presents special difficulties in that it is the longest (about twice the length of the usual O'Flaherty novel) and most populous of his work.

   On the level of plot and action the novel falls into three major sections. The first section (Chapters I to XV) deals with the domestic life of the Kilmartins, a peasant family and their relatives. One generation––Martin Kilmartin and his young wife, Mary Gleeson—takes over the running of the house and farm from old Kilmartin. The domestic theme of the conflict of father and son is played out against the growing ravages of the potato blight. In Chapters XVI to XL the theme is a much more public one. The scene broadens to include the whole of Black Valley and its village, called "Crom." At the centre of the section is the evil genius of the novel, the local landlord's agent, Chadwick. Famine drives the starving people to commit, in the language of the day, "outrages." Chadwick is assassinated by, among others, Martin Kilmartin. Chapter XLI to the end focuses, in the main, on Mary Kilmartin. Her husband is "on the run" as a result of the assassination. In order to save herself and her child she plans to emigrate to America. The Famine is portrayed in all its horror in this section and it is against a background of death and pestilence that the young family makes good its escape to the New World. Vague talk of the Young Irelanders and coming revolution adds to the hopeful strain on which the book closes.

Patrick F. Sheeran. The Novels of Liam O'Flaherty:
A Study in Romantic Realism (Dublin, Wolfhound,
1976), pp. 216–17

[T]he most clear example of the provincial, the parochial, in the Irish story is Liam O'Flaherty. In his introduction to his anthology *Modern Irish Short Stories*, Frank O'Connor makes a comparison between Moore's "Home-Sickness" and O'Flaherty's "Going into Exile," in which he says: "O'Flaherty ignores everything but the nature of exile itself: a state of things like love and death that all men must in some way endure." This is true. Whatever else he may have been, Moore was not an Irish peasant, and in a sense "Home-Sickness" is a dramatization of a theory of Irish exile, which, examined objectively, scarcely stands up. Was clerical authoritarianism a serious cause of Irish exile? It may have been for Moore himself, if he is seen as an exile and not merely an absentee landlord. But, for the peasant it seems doubtful, whereas there can be no doubt about the effect of poverty and landlessness.

With O'Flaherty's story, the question does not arise at all: O'Flaherty simply describes a fact of life. Michael Feeney and his sister Mary are going into exile, going to the United States, and the eve of their departure is the occasion of a dance, a dance which could be thought of as a wake. . . .

"Going into Exile" is a moving story precisely for what it does not say. Michael scarcely knows the meaning of exile. For him, it is an exciting event, an initiation into manhood even though his blue serge suit is shabby and does not fit. . . . For the parents, it is different: they know they may never see their children again.

What O'Flaherty does is to dramatize the experience of the moment of departure into exile. There is no comment, either direct or implied. "Going into Exile" is a much more highly oroganized story than, say, O'Flaherty's "The Cow's Death" but, apart from this, there is little significant difference between his stories of animals and those of human beings. "The Cow's Death" describes, again without comment of any kind, how a cow that has delivered a dead calf, the body of which has been tossed over the cliff, plunges over it herself in pursuit of her offspring. O'Flaherty's animals are not anthropomorphized; rather, men and animals seem to exist in the same context of nature where differentiation is comparatively rudimentary. At times, O'Flaherty achieves stories of great lyrical intensity: one admires them individually but finds oneself in the end asking: Yes, but where is the interest, what the significance? Something is missing, the interpretive mind.

Walter Allen. *The Short Story in English* (Oxford,
Oxford Univ. Pr., 1981), pp. 211–13

Much has been made in the criticism of O'Flaherty's novels about his development of the character-types of soldier, saint, and poet: O'Dwyer, Father Kelly, and Raoul in *Land*; Madden, Kinsella, and Stapleton in *Insurrection*. The Fenian, renegade priest Father Kelly in *Land* seems to Raoul to encapsulate all three types: "The soldier, the poet and the monk represent what is finest in man. They represent man's will to power, to beauty and to immortality. They alone among men are capable of complete love, because they love the unattainable. Their love is never tarnished by possession. Before all three of them, I always bow low. When I bowed to you, I bowed to all three." John Zneimer views the characters of Kinsella and his friend Stapleton in *Insurrection* as an artificial imposition of the saint and poet types upon the novel, arguing that O'Flaherty was more interested in the abstract, ideal character-types than in the development of realistic characters. There is some truth to this; like Madden, Kinsella and Stapleton are not adequately developed as characters. Viewed through Madden's simple eyes, they both die for the cause after a theoretical discussion about the beauty of revolution. But Kinsella and Stapleton also have a realistic, historical basis: Kinsella, identified as a secondary-school teacher and a selfless leader who knows the rebel cause is doomed, is obviously a fictional version of Pearse; and Stapleton, a dreamy poet suffering from a terminal illness, is clearly meant to reflect Joseph Plunkett. As with Raoul in *Land*, who was "quite as dangerous as Parnell," O'Flaherty's strategy is the conventional one of the historical novelist: he leaves the big names of history in the background and develops fictional characters who are meant to reflect them.

O'Flaherty's basic approach in all three of his historical novels is to show how his protagonists react to major historical crises like trapped animals but are ennobled in their tragic devotion to the cause. His ethic here is very close to that of Theodore Dreiser (whom O'Flaherty admired) in his socialist phase: the naturalistic hero must die but the cause will live on; socialism is the solution. Disaster is always looming on the horizon in O'Flaherty's novels, and they open and close with a bang. But he is no nihilist; the cause is Savior.

O'Flaherty is the most partisan of Irish historical novelists. His is not the glorious "middle way" of Scott but the one true faith of Irish Republican socialism. His politics can alternately strengthen and damage his novels, and his writing is dramatic one moment and lumbering the next. At his best, in *Famine*, the intensity of his vision creates a historical novel that is, even with its faults, perhaps the best of the genre in Ireland. While his peasant predecessor William Carleton could only escape from history, O'Flaherty combined Carleton's intimate grasp of peasant life with a close knowledge of Irish history and a determination to capture the bitter tragedy of it.

James Cahalan. *Great Hatred, Little Room: The Irish Historical Novel* (Syracuse, N.Y., Syracuse Univ. Pr., 1983), pp. 152–53

O'KELLY, SEAMAS (c. 1875–1918)

O'Kelly was a realist; the cheap, the sentimental, the insincere, were utterly abhorrent to him. But he was not a materialist. He looked at life simply and directly, and there was nothing significant in life from which he turned away; nevertheless, his work is conceived always in the spirit of poetry. Even when he writes of what is ugly, a spiritual beauty creeps in through the manner of the presentment. Several of the stories in *The Golden Barque* might have been sordid enough. The actual details are sordid. But because they have passed through O'Kelly's imagination they stretch out roots and branches into a world far beyond the world of immediate perception. Nothing is glossed over, nothing withheld, yet the impression of beauty triumphs. What, for instance, is the subject of the longest of the short stories? The squabble of three doddering old men about the exact locality of a grave—the weaver's grave. O'Kelly treats it in the spirit of comedy: only, it is a comedy through which, from beginning to end, we hear the rattle of spades and coffins. Behind the cracked, high-pitched, ancient voices, the flickering movements and flickering senile passions; behind the lonely ruin of the disused burial-ground, we see a tall, white, waiting figure—standing in shadow, motionless, and with lifted scythe.

That O'Kelly had the objective imagination and rich inventiveness of the born story-teller is proved by the variety of his tales. The stories connected with the Golden Barque bear little resemblance to "The Weaver's Grave" or "The White Goat," and less to *The Lady of Deerpark*; while those in *The Leprechaun of Kilmeen* break up completely new ground. This Golden Barque, despite its romantic name, is a very ordinary and ungilded river barge, its crew as tough as may be, the chronicle of its voyages a chronicle of just such everyday incidents as must come into the lives of just such men. Yet, as we journey on those trips up and down the river, with Michael and Hike and Calcutta and the Boss, we somehow *are* in a world of romance. The introductory story, "Michael and Mary," is pure romance, pure poetry. And how slight the material out of which it has been fashioned! . . . How, we may ask, do such things become stories at all? That was O'Kelly's secret, as it was the secret of Tourguéneff when he wrote *A Sportsman's Sketches*. . . .

His genius remains. I use the word deliberately, for his best stories have a poetic substance, a beauty of light and of atmosphere, a beauty of tenderness and of understanding, that imply something more than talent. And there is always the lonely natural beauty, rising dream-like through them, of the most beautiful country upon earth. [Dec. 6, 1919]

Forrest Reid. *Retrospective Adventures* (London,
Faber and Faber, 1941), pp. 178–81

The name of [Seamas] O'Kelly is practically unknown outside of Ireland, and even in Ireland his work has never had a large or widespread appreciation. His work has been most highly appreciated by discerning critics wherever he has been read, and his death at an early age in 1918 removed one of the most considerable, and most potentially valuable, of Irish dramatists. . . .

The Shuiler's Child had made a great impression upon literary and artistic circles in Dublin when it was first produced in 1909, with the notable actress Maire NicShuibhlaigh playing the principal part, but is was not until the play was staged at the Abbey Theatre in November 1910 that it became known to the larger playgoing public. The "shuiler" is a familiar figure in Ireland; he is the wanderer, the tramp, the tinker, somewhat akin to the roving "gypsy" of England. *The Shuiler's Child* is a drama of renunciation; a social problem set forth in stark terms. . . . In the person of Moll Woods O'Kelly created a character that gripped the public, and in the development of her tragedy he proved himself very proficient in the technique of the stage. *The Shuiler's Child* is a play of great power and intensity, full of life and sympathy, which at the same time attracts attention to an important social problem. . . .

The Parnellite, produced in September 1917, presents in terms of stark realism the meanness, the treachery, the moral cowardice, and the tragic consequences attendant upon the downfall of Charles Stewart Parnell. There is something of the psychological basis of *The Playboy* in *The Parnellite*, but O'Kelly's play is more pedestrian in its stark presentation of the ugly facts, and more bitter because he was a partisan and very obviously upon the side of "the Parnellite" against the horde of cowards and knaves who opposed him. The play is effective rather than thrilling, but it is certainly much above the average Irish play.

O'Kelly also wrote at least four one-act comedies of which only one has been produced by the Abbey Theatre. . . . Indeed it may be said that in his comedies O'Kelly never reached either the technical or creative levels of his tragedies, but they are not in any way inferior to numbers of one-act comedies which have been staged by the Abbey Theatre, and their exclusion is somewhat difficult to explain. But essentially O'Kelly's mind was tragic, and it was the sombre aspects of life that attracted him. There is no doubt that he had studied Ibsen to some effect; his three major plays have all the impress of that master. In his three tragedies he depicted with great dramatic power phases of Irish life in his own time. His language has none of the rhythmic grandeur of Synge, nor the smooth poetry of T. C. Murray, but it is true to his people and often reaches poetic heights. In technique and dramatic power he is the equal of any English-writing dramatist of the contemporary theatre, but always he is the dramatist with a thesis. In method he is thoroughly realistic, his men and women are those amongst whom he lived and whom he knew intimately, without romantic glamour of any kind. He dramatised the problems of his time in terms of the people whom he knew, and none who would know Ireland can afford to ignore his plays.

Andrew E. Malone. The Irish Drama (London,
Constable, 1929), pp. 194–98

Art has an inherent honesty and when it is twisted into postures which are morally dishonest, for no matter what reasons, it repays with failure. The problem, which determines the course of much of O'Kelly's . . . career, was a common one in the Ireland of the early part of this century, where art and politics maintained an uneasy relationship punctuated at intervals by explosions of open hostility. . . . Given O'Kelly's dilemma, then, it is inevitable that his art should have selected its own proper form, a form which allowed him to retreat into a world of total privacy and to concentrate upon single human lives occupied with the simplest and so the most profound business of living in a landscape that is not cluttered with political abstractions. This form is, of course, the short story and it is in his devotion to it that the genuine artist in O'Kelly is liberated towards his proper achievement. A good example of what is meant here may be seen in the story called "The Rector." . . . The mode is epiphanal rather than expository, but at its end the reader is aware of the essence of a cultural situation with all its sociopolitical nuances and implications, much more than if he had been bombarded with nationalist propaganda. A principal element in this success is the sympathy the narrator evokes for the Rector himself and it is this kind of moral subtlety and compassion, so obviously absent from the dramas and novels, that gives the short stories their unique power.

In all of O'Kelly's best work two themes stand out: land and human loneliness. A harshly dramatic statement on the first of these leaps from the early pages of *Wet Clay*: "If you went down to hell and opened up the heart of the first Connacht man you met the word you would find written there would be 'land.'" A vision of the necessary community between man and land informs most of the stories and when this band is unnaturally broken disaster follows. O'Kelly can often symbolically employ natural images as his means of dramatizing this disaster, a mode he begins to experiment in, with varying degrees of competence, in the very earliest stories. Thus, in a story called "A Broken Bramble," the object of the title is seen as the relevant and proper symbol for the blighting of the young love of the protagonists. In "The Return of Thade Furey" from the same early volume, *By the Stream of Kilmeen*, nature is described in terms of an idyllic, pastoral educator, symbolic of the growth of innocent love. . . .

Emigration is, as it so often must be in Irish domestic tragedies, the villain of this piece. Thade goes to America and is inevitably corrupted. As a consequence Ellen goes mad and retreats into her fantasies, recreating there the "far away time of gentleness," sustaining the pastoral image as compensation for the destruction of this image by the corrupting energies of the modern world. It is, to stretch the symbolic point a little, a reversal of the roles in the Eden myth, with Ellen, in her madness, creating her own "Paradise within." . . .

[T]he story called "Michael and Mary" is a muted and transmuted restatement, without social overtones or melodrama, of the theme of the destruction of young love; Mary's movement from innocence to experience, from pastoral dream to lonely reality, is charted by O'Kelly with a lyrical economy which he rarely equalled. The fact that abandonment may be thus mutely accepted—there is no escape but neither is there any retreat—may be seen as a metaphor for the maturity of O'Kelly's own vision and style. The story is itself an emblem for his artistic commitment to the private world of his actors.

> Eamon Grennan. Introduction to Seamas O'Kelly,
> *The Land of Loneliness, and Other Stories*
> (Dublin, Gill & Macmillan, 1969), pp. 6–8

The memorable O'Kelly tales remain those collected in *Waysiders, Hillsiders*, and *The Golden Barque and the Weaver's Grave*; but the cumulation therein contained would be adequate memorial for any man, even if unbuttressed by *The Lady of Deerpark* (sadly in need of reprinting) and several splendid plays. Why Ireland remembers the author of these almost exclusively in disregardful association with *The Weaver's Grave* in isolation is one of the perplexing annoyances of literary history.

Forrest Reid, in his essay in *Retrospective Adventures*, has very justly remarked: "O'Kelly was a realist . . . But he was not a materialist. He looked at life simply and directly, and there was nothing significant in life from which he turned away; nevertheless, his work is conceived always in the spirit of poetry." And in a rare personal reference, in "The Apparitions of Oul' Darmody" (*Hillsiders*), O'Kelly himself confessed, "the shanachie took the people of Kilbeg as he found them, the good and the bad, and sometimes he liked the bad better than the good," though the classification is too modest: O'Kelly was not merely a "shanachie"; he was on occasion an accomplished artist who had absorbed into his gift the finest qualities of the wandering hearthside storyteller and heightened them by his faculty for dramatization. Few authors have been able to absorb and reproduce more convincingly than he the sense of a primitive countryside and its people (with Galway best known).

His fundamental qualities are, I think, pastoral-dramatic in kind; they can lead to intense concentrations—as in the almost-epic, though restrained, story "The Elks," with its description of a storm by the sea. Often these qualities operate through satire, obvious or semi-submerged, as in "The Shoemaker" (with its "intelligent as Corkmen": and why not, with men like Frank O'Connor, Robert Gibbings, Seán O'Faoláin, and Daniel Corkery in evidence!); but the satire is never offensive, being nourished less by wit than by a most lambent humor: that humor "almost a charity"—whether of statement (as in a reference to Moses' angrily breaking the tables of the Commandments as "the most tragic destruction of a first edition that the world has known") or of the affectionate *illumination* of character. For to O'Kelly the human breed was, however flawed, curiously lovable; his handling of people has a warmth of comprehension in its large-heartedness that whispers of a faculty possessed in fullness only by the artist who has chewed the same bone that Chaucer worried. And, like most of his fellows of the Irish Renaissance, he moves most nobly when he is handling the strands of tragedy, as—it will be recalled—[A. E.] Malone, who valued the "passively meditative charm" of his work, also sensed.

George Brandon Saul. Seamas O'Kelly (Lewisburg,
Pa., Bucknell Univ. Pr., 1971), pp. 76–78

O'Kelly's youth, spent in the vicinity of the Clanrickarde estate and the poor lands of East Galway, had given him an intense awareness of poverty, deprivation, and the evils of emigration and depopulation. His involvement with Sinn Féin had added another, historical and theoretical, dimension to that essentially emotional reaction and was to colour everything he wrote in the future. It is easy to see why critics should have been impatient or embarrassed with some of his writing. Nevertheless, it is difficult to agree with Eamonn Grennan when he argues that O'Kelly, aware of the conflict between art and politics, had "to retreat into a world of total privacy and to concentrate upon single human lives occupied with the simplest and so the most profound business of living in a landscape that is not cluttered with political abstractions." O'Kelly's best stories are intensely political. In his finest work he found a means of integrating the major concerns of his life. "The Weaver's Grave," a story of old men, is also a story of the desolation of the land, the destruction of an old and integrated way of life, the loneliness and despair of a people without identity. The tone of O'Kelly's last story is a refinement of the mood of one of his earliest tales.

The style of "A Land of Loneliness" may seem unduly ponderous but its concerns underlie the vision of many of the best stories which are, mercifully, free of its excessive didacticism. . . .

Yet, if O'Kelly was occasionally to succumb to this kind of writing, he was also capable of the humorous detachment of the story of Gobstown ("The Shoemaker"), a town which suffers the awful fate of having a good landlord, where guns can be used only to stir the tea, where everyone is content and so talent stifles for want of grievances to set it aflame. Humour is, indeed, one of O'Kelly's greatest qualities—a gentle humour quite unmarked by satire. He seems to have had a genuine regard for the people who populate his world and wrote about them with warmth and affection, an attitude he articulates in one of the stories of *Hillsiders*; "Blame not the shanachie, for the shanachie took the people of Kilbeg as he found them, the good and the bad, and sometimes he liked the bad better than the good." It is, of course, easy for that kind of warmth to become mere sentimentality and O'Kelly could degenerate into the cloying sweetness of for example, always referring to Fardy Lalor's mother as "the little mother." "But one night the little mother quietly slipped the moorings of her earthly barque, moved out calmly from the harbour of life, and set sail for a far sea where a lost voice was calling."

Other major characteristics of O'Kelly's work are his realism and the sense of tragedy which pervades his writing. Yet tragedy can become melodrama and does in the dreadful second section of "Both Sides of the Pond" which pictures the almost infernal horrors suffered by a young countryman forced to emigrate to the Bowery. Melodrama and sentimentality were certainly faults but are more than compensated for by the intensity of O'Kelly's imagination, the accuracy and lyricism of his evocation of the natural world and the importance of his position as the chronicler of a dying culture.

Anne Clune. In Patrick Rafroidi and Terence Brown,
eds., *The Irish Short Story* (Lille, Publications de
l'Université de Lille, 1979), pp. 144–46

If only for a single masterpiece, "The Weaver's Grave," Seumus O'Kelly deserves critical recognition. In his short life, he published five collections of short stories, only few of which are true examples of the form, most being folktales, anecdotes, and even tales of leprechauns. But his range and skill, evidenced in even such a few stories, are impressive. . . .

"The Weaver's Grave" (1919) is undoubtedly one of the best stories of [its] period. Through its slow description of the graveyard, Cloon na Morav, the Meadow of the Dead, an atmosphere of timeless mortality is built. The place is so fully described and assigned such importance that it becomes as potent a force as any of the characters who come to it seeking the proper place to bury the weaver; in fact its description constitutes the first of the story's five parts. The two old men who come to identify the site seem at first caricatures; Meehaul Lynskey, the nailer, and Cahir Bowes, the stone breaker, mimic the actions of their occupations, and come to represent the builder and the destroyer. They fail to find the right plot, despite many attempts; in their vicious quarreling and feebleness they come to seem proper inhabitants of Coon na Morav. The third part of the story establishes the present state of the weaver's widow, his fourth wife; she is a woman who never experienced much passion or love, but who now wants to give her dead husband the proper burial he deserves. Attempting to learn the location of her husband's grave site, she visits the cooper, Malachai Roohan, the only living person entitled to be buried in the revered graveyard, now that the weaver has died. The old, bedridden man speaks of hope and of life's illusions, yet in his anger he reveals his own terror at approaching death. The first sentence of the final section of the story reveals the widow's change, when she says, "The day is going on me." Now the graveyard, as she approaches it, seems monstrous, while the single star in the evening sky seems to be very young. The twin grave diggers emerge in her consciousness as individuals, and the renewed search for the grave site is successful. Her awakened senses make her respond to the advances of the handsome young grave digger; she speaks like a girl at the end, when she utters the comprehensive concluding statement, "I'm satisfied."

Like "The Dead," the story's theme is death and resurrection, and psychological death is as final as physical dying. The widow clearly chooses life, as offered to her by the young grave digger, in the very graveyard where she will now bury her husband. The story's strongest comments are implied by gesture, not provided by the author. The stylized repeated actions of the two old men, the old cooper raising himself in bed by pulling himself up by a rope, and, most suggestive of all, the young grave digger leaping over the black grave to embrace the young widow—such gestures acquire meanings that may not be fully articulated, but they all indicate grasping for life. The amplitude of the story's theme, the vitality it celebrates, made more precious by setting it in the place of death, and the masterful use of symbolism to extend meaning, make the story comparable to the masterpieces of this genre.

James F. Kilroy. In James F. Kilroy, ed., *The Irish Short Story: A Critical History* (Boston, Twayne, 1984), pp. 141–43

O'SULLIVAN, SEUMAS (1879–1958)

We read this book of Seumas O'Sullivan's [*Poems*] with intense feeling, with the pleasure that delicate and beautiful workmanship gives, and with a poignant emotion that brings us poem by poem to—

> Lords of the morning, since you set
> Within this ancient heart,
> The flames that burned my youth away
> And set my life apart:
> I bring you in this urn of truth
> The dust-white ashes of my youth.

We would not quote this poem, for it seems to us that those portions of a book where an author draws apart from his public, as it were, and addresses himself to his own soul, are too intimate for quotation—but that the poet himself carried us to it so inevitably that it sets the keynote of the book and seems necessary to its harmony. Seumas O'Sullivan is so cunning a poet that he had almost persuaded us that he had led us to an urn of ashes, and we were prepared to be grateful that at least a warm and wholesome human heart once beat in them, and that no raw-head-and-bloody-bones bogey would arise out of them to affright us, no gruesome murdered emotion, such as passes for poetry in these jaded days. We know, however, from the intense vitality in our memory of so much of Seumas O'Sullivan's verse that it is not of the dead but of the

living. The still breathing of deep sleep may simulate death, but is life withdrawn into itself in a passion of intensity. Seumas O'Sullivan's verse is often
a very still and very intense breathing, but its roots are in life, and it has the
ache of living in it. Poems like "A Fiddler," "Calvary," "Winter," "Out of the
strong, sweetness," "The Earth Lover," "From a verse epistle," will rise up in
the memory with extraordinary vitality. Much of Seumas O'Sullivan's verse
burns with a white heat of spiritual passion, and the delicacy of his work is often misleading, for although his force is never that of the bludgeon, it is none
the less effectual as force. No, Seumas, the time has not come for the urn, the
flame is burning whitely still. [June 15, 1912]

George William Russell (A.E.). *Selections from the*
Contributions to "The Irish Homestead," Vol. II,
Henry Summerfield, ed. (Atlantic Highlands, N.J.,
Humanities Press, 1978), p. 871

Seumas O'Sullivan was the first of the *débutants* in *New Songs* who ventured
to publish an independent book of verse. Taking the most beautiful of his contributions to that volume as a title-piece, he issued *The Twilight People* in
1905. This was followed three years later by *Verses Sacred and Profane*, a
smaller collection of like inspiration, the two being representative of the earlier manner of O'Sullivan. His very first poem gives the key in which this best
and most characteristic part of his book is set:

> It is a whisper among the hazel bushes;
> It is a long, low, whispering voice that fills
> With a sad music the bending and swaying rushes:
> It is a heart-beat deep in the quiet hills.

O'Sullivan's verse has been, for the most part, concerned with the gentle,
pensive emotions of the singer who celebrates the soft beauties of twilight.
The shadows of the poplars, the reeds and sedges of lonely moorlands sway in
a delicate rhythm which his ears have caught. He would "seek out all frail,
immortal things," the white gleam of "foam-frail" hands, the murmuring
leaves, the gleam of "light tresses, delicate, wind-blown" and of these he
makes his song in praise of beauty. He is unexcelled as a painter of soft-toned
pictures pervaded by the quiet of evening solitude. [1916]

Ernest A. Boyd. *Ireland's Literary Renaissance*
(New York, Alfred A. Knopf, 1922), pp. 256–57

It was Seumas O'Sullivan who described so aptly the unliterary vernacular—"the living speech" that W. B. Yeats was counselling all the poets to put
into currency—"words with a spit upon them," he said.

   In one of his so rarely published essays he speaks of one who had realized that "to exchange the imagination for the reality was a spendthrift policy." Seumas O'Sullivan has not made the exchange ("In Dublin only the old are prodigal"), and his poems are, in subject and music, far removed from the work-a-day world. I have conned them again to make out what reference to business they make. There are two poems dedicated to the same commercial transaction: to the business carried on between the rag-and-bone man who pushes his truck over the cobble-stones in the back streets of Dublin and the children who bring to him rags and bones in exchange for the gaudy wares that his truck displays. I can find no other reference to commercial transactions. And yet, in the Ireland of his day, there were many temptations to exchange the imagination for the reality. Does Seumas O'Sullivan succumb to one of them in those poems of his that have political significance? Hardly. In "At Parnell's Grave," "Collector's for a National Cause," "Dublin Castle," we have bitterness, but it is the bitterness of a voice calling out from an ivory tower. Once, however, we see the poet standing in the street to cry over a young man who has been slain: "They have slain you, Sean MacDiarmuid."

Seumas O'Sullivan has interpreted perfectly—it could not be done more perfectly—one mood of the Irish country: the mood that comes with the slow, haunted Irish twilight:

O Herdsman, driving your slow twilight flock,

he cries, and the very music of the lines makes an invocation that brings before us the shadowy herdsman of shadows. Yes, he alone of all the Irish poets really knows The Twilight People. . . .

A.E. said of Seumas O'Sullivan, after he had published his first book: "He is the literary successor of those old Gaelic poets who were fastidious in their verse, who loved little in this world but some chance light in it which reminded them of fairyland." That is indeed a revealing criticism. The places in Seumas O'Sullivan's poetry, the loved one to whom the poems are addressed, all are seen in that "chance light" that makes them seem like the places and like the beings of another world. And he has another quality—I think A.E. mentioned this one too—that gives him kinship with the Gaelic poets: he can possess himself of some unobtrusive gesture or feature in such a way that when he speaks of it a whole existence comes before us. "Thin, white hand like foam of the sea," a Gaelic poet cries, and the beauty of some evasive woman is made plain to us. And Seumas O'Sullivan speaks of a hand laid over a half-door, and of eyes strange and dark above a half-door, and a beauty is created that makes us walk for a while on the path of romance.

Padraic Colum. Introduction to *The Poems of*
Seumas O'Sullivan (Boston, B. J. Brimmer,
1923), pp. 14–17

. . . The Dowson quality, strongly marked in [O'Sullivan's] earlier work, is soon assimilated. Only its virtues survive, a personal simplicity of diction, a rare control over the long line or phrase, and a music which even the so-called invective verses never lose.

O'Sullivan is a poet of melancholy. The occasional short gay pieces which lighten up the anthologies are like bursts of Dublin sunlight on a wet day, which make the cloud that follows seem darker than ever. He looks back to the past, and mourns continually for the great days of Greece. . . . Elsewhere he says—at the end of an essay in *Mud and Purple*—"Perhaps I am the last of the Greeks." It is a strange delusion. Bless his heart, there is nothing Greek about him. He lacks altogether the fierce objective outlook of the Greek writers. Synge came far nearer to it. "They're all gone now, and there isn't anything more the sea can do to me," might almost be a free translation of the cry of the bereaved mother in the Greek play, "I have no one to feed me in my old age." But O'Sullivan, with his long lines of melody, wavering yet controlled, his gentle melancholy of lake and sedge and rath, his spasms of conscience and Christian imagery—"Three crosses crown our Calvary"—his complete refusal to be up and doing—nothing less Greek could be found in a long day's march. The Greeks were no backward lookers. Now and then, it is true, the Irishman takes hold upon himself and tries to rouse up from the native nostalgic mood immortalised by Moore, who lamented Tara and saw the round towers of other days in the wave beneath him shining. . . . But the ensuing injunction to be gay as a butterfly comes soft and unconvincing. The poet is happier under his gray skies; the hard Greek sunlight would not suit him. We admire what we are not, and covet what we do not possess, as Socrates demonstrated to Euthyphro.

Hardness is the one quality his verse wants. Even the invectives, while they show him to dislike a number of men and things, completely lack the ferocity of Yeats or Stephens or Synge.

> You could have made of any other air
> The little careful mouthfuls of your songs.

Even A.E. went further than that, in his open letter to Kipling. No; O'Sullivan must be judged by what he does best. He is, in his verse at least, not a good hater. He has a sudden, brief gaiety, which usually takes the streets for its scene. But, best of all, he is the poet of regret. He is most himself when, in a graceful music, and with phrases chosen with care and connoisseurship, over his wine he laments lost fire, lost beauty, lost courage.

L. A. G. Strong. Personal Remarks (New York,
Liveright, 1953), pp. 88–89

Seumas O'Sullivan was first of all a poet, and his prime endowments were those of a poet. He was sensitive, witty, moody and generous: he had a care for the gentle, the scorned, the poor: he loved the "unassuming things/That hold a silent station in this beauteous world"—the lamplighter, the ragman, the fiddler, beggarmen, swans on the Liffey, the golden cat who went to join Lesbia's sparrow. He knew other worlds—Tir na nOg, "Castles in Spain, sheepwalks in Arcady," "An apple-garden somewhere easterly," but he loved his own country, and had to live in its air and on its fields and streets. From it he made his poems, and out of that love he could say to another poet whom he felt to be without it: "You could have made of any other air/The little careful mouthfuls of your songs." He belonged to his age: he was part of that splendid outcrop of songs and play and heroic effort that marked, in our country, the first decades of this century. He saluted the brave—Séan Mac Dermott, Thomas Mac Donagh, Padraig Pearse. He was the friend and associate of Yeats, A.E., Joyce, Gogarty, Padraic Colum, of all who made a mark on the life and literature of Ireland.

But Seumas O'Sullivan was other things besides a poet. He was a scholar, a bibliophile, and an editor of international repute. He had immense learning but it was learning worn with a grace, green learning, never dry, and offered to you in the hope that it would strike a root in your soul and grow there. As an editor he was unique. The greatest of his countrymen appeared in the pages of *The Dublin Magazine*, which he founded as long ago as 1923. To read the contents lists of old numbers is to read a roll call of famous or familiar Irish names:—W. B. Yeats, T. C. Murray, Lennox Robinson, James Stephens, Michéal Mac Liammóir, John Eglinton, Teresa Deevey, Austin Clarke, Daniel Corkery, Frank O'Connor, F. R. Higgins, M. J. MacManus, Seán O Faoláin, J. M. Hone, Padraic Colum, Mary Lavin, Arland Ursher, Andrew F. Malone. But it is to do more: it is to be made aware of Europe as well as Ireland: it is to see great but foreign names as well as Irish—Gorki, Pirandello, Vielè-Griffin, R. L. Mégroz, Hilaire Belloc, Jeanne Raumay, to take but a few at random: it is to read translations from the French, the Italian, the Swedish, the Russian. *The Dublin Magazine* reminded us constantly that there is a "world without Verona's walls," brought Europe home to us, so that we did not need to emigrate to assure ourselves of her reality. But other editors—perhaps—have done so much. Seumas O'Sullivan combined this ability to attract the great with instant and repeated generosity to the young and the unknown. He was ready to make mistakes rather than prove unwelcoming to possible new talent, and many younger Irish writers owe their first appearance in print to that openness of heart and mind. We cannot hope to find his like soon or easily: we must all grieve for such a loss to Irish letters.

Lorna Reynolds. *UR*. 2, 2, 1955, pp. 65–66

While Joyce was meditating over his early realistic stories of Dublin, Seamus O'Sullivan had already discovered for himself the poetic aspect of the city. In subtle rhythms he suggested the lingering Georgian atmosphere of Dublin and evoked in memorable glimpses that eighteenth century to which Yeats was to return later. The aristocratic grandeur of the past, the shabbiness of present-day alley and side-street are contained in lyrics which are all too few in number. A crazy beggar woman sits eating her evening meal on the steps of a Merrion Square mansion, the organ-grinder plays in drab streets, and from the tenements, which were once great houses, the children run to frolic around the ragman or the piper. At dusk through the quiet streets the last lamplighter steals:

> Soundlessly touching one by one
> The waiting posts that stand to take
> The faint blue bubbles in his wake;
> And when the night begins to wane
> He comes to take them back again,
> Before the chilly dawn can blight
> The delicate frail buds of light.

O'Sullivan learnt something of his art from the modern French lyric of Samain and de Regnier, and his prose and verse have the same precision. [*The Earth Lover*, 1909, contains] lines, humorously tantalising in their evasive rhythm, in which the Phoenix Park in sunshine, the lighter history of the British occupation, the daring of the young and the regrets of the old, are all suggested with an unerring touch.

Austin Clarke. *Poetry in Modern Ireland* (Dublin,
Three Candles Press, 1961), pp. 30–31

PEARSE, PATRICK (or PADRAIC) (1879-1916)

"I have squandered the splendid years that the Lord God gave to my youth. In attempting impossible things, deeming them alone worth the toil. Was it folly or grace? Not men shall judge me, but God." "I have heard in my heart that a man shall scatter, not hoard, shall do the deed of today, nor take thought of tomorrow's teen, shall not bargain or huxter with God." So wrote Padraic Pearse in a poem in which perhaps he told the faith which was in him and the hopes he had more perhaps than in any other. "What if the dream comes true," he asks, "if the millions unborn shall dwell in the house I shaped in my heart, the noble house of my thought? Do not remember my failures, but remember this my faith." We read this book [*Collected Works of P. H. Pearse*] in which is gathered the stories, plays, and poems of the dead leader of the last Irish rebellion, and we found in it not a single thought which is ignoble. Probably no more selfless spirit ever broke itself against the might of the Iron Age than this man's spirit which was lit up by love of children and country, a dreamer with his heart in the Golden Age. This man, much more simple than Thomas MacDonagh or Joseph Plunkett, had a much greater and more original personality, and as we read this book we understand his pre-eminence among the revolutionaries. The fact was he had infinite faith, he was selfless, and therefore he was a moral rock to lean on. As we read this book, with its gentleness and its idealism and think of the storm he raised, we are reminded of the scriptural picture of a little child leading the lion, only in this case it was in no idyllic fields the child was, but it was hallooing the beast on to rend its enemies. Undoubtedly Padraic Pearse was a powerful and unique personality, and the publication of this volume in which is collected his best writing will give him the place in Irish literature which he is entitled to by merit, and which would be justly his quite apart from the place in Irish history he has gained by his astonishing enterprise. We like him better as a poet than as a writer of plays or a story teller. There is a strain of something like sentimentality in him which we believe always arises in the heart which desires love and yet is solitary, and so its affections turned back on themselves become a little over sweet. This strain does not appear so much out of place in the verse as in the plays. What would have been intolerable in another was made pleasing by the Irish clothing of the mood. The children in so many of Sir John Millais' pictures so obviously well fed, well clothed, and well looking, tire us by over sweetness, whereas the same little heads with wilder hair, more ragged clothes, and with more of the imp in them would have enchanted us. The Gaelic clothing gave a wild rusticity to imaginations which might otherwise have been over sweet in the case of Pearse, and they will have a permanent place in Irish literature, not merely because the writer led a forlorn hope and amazed the world, but because a true poetic talent was mainfested there, and a purity of spirit which is rare in any literature. [July 14, 1917]

George William Russell (A.E.). *Selections from the Contributions to "The Irish Homestead,"* Vol. II, Henry Summerfield, ed. (Atlantic Highlands, N.J., Humanities Press, 1978), pp. 911–12

I take first what is most difficult—the very heart of antagonism. Everyone who desires to understand Ireland to-day should read Patrick Pearse's posthumous book, called boldly *The Story of a Success*. It is the spiritual history of Pearse's career as a schoolmaster, edited and completed by his pupil, Desmond Ryan; and it is a book by which no one can be justly offended—a book instinct with nobility, chivalry and high courtesy, free from all touch of bitterness; a book, too, shot through and slashed with that tragic irony which the Greeks knew to be the finest thrill in literature—the word spoken, to which the foreknown event gives an echo of double meaning. Pearse was concerned with Ireland's yesterday; he desired to bring the present and the future into organic rotation with the past. But his yesterday was not Miss [Edith] Somerville's nor mine. The son of an English mechanic and a Galway woman, he was brought up in Connemara after the landlord power had ceased to exist. Ireland's past for him and Irish tradition were seen through the medium of an imagination in touch only with the peasant life, but inspired by books and literature, written and spoken. His yesterday was of no definite past, for he had been born in a revolution when the immediate past was obliterated. In his vision a thousand years were no more than the watch of some spellbound chivalry, waiting for the voice that should say, "It is the time." Cuchulain and Robert Emmet were his inspirations, but the champion of the legendary Red Branch cycle and the young revolutionary of Napoleon's days were near to him one as the other, in equally accessible communion. Going back easily to the heroic legends, on which, though blurred in their outline, his boyhood had been fostered by tellers of long-transmitted tales at a Connemara hearthside, he found the essential beauty and significance where more learned though less cultured readers have been bewildered by what seemed to them wild extravagances of barbarism. What he gathered from them did not lie inert, but quickened in him and in others, for he was the revolutionary as schoolmaster—the most drastic revolutionary of all. [1920]

Stephen Gwynn. *Irish Books and Irish People*. (Freeport, N.Y., Books for Libraries Press, 1969), pp. 113–15

The bulk of Pearse's work in Gaelic is small—filling only a book of 268 pages—but it contains vital passages in the message of a prophetic mind. If we consider first his poems, we find some fifteen little pieces—one of only four lines. They are written in syllabic and stressed metres, but do not fulfill the rules. Expression with Pearse never was fluent. His thought was captured from the heights with pain. Yet a terrific intensity informs these lines, and makes us forget all technical defects as the words tell of a deadly intent, or lament mortality. . . . That poem which tells of the closing of the eyes to beauty—the beauty of the world, seen in its naked and blinding reality—and the closing of the ears to all seductive appeals as the poet addresses himself to the path before him and his foreseen death, is perhaps, the most passionate poem in the modern language. . . .

Pearse also wrote tales. When he began writing Gaelic short stories with modern "explosive openings," he was attacked as an innovator, and defended himself with the argument that one must innovate to save. He had much in common with [Padraic] O Conaire in technique. He was not so dexterous a craftsman. Not all the tales would hold the reader if he were ignorant of their authorship, and thus of their adventitious interest as illuminating the environment which moulded so remarkable a mind. Some, however, are true masterpieces, depicting with fidelity the inmost passions of the race. We are shown the sweet old world in which the boy Pearse learnt to see Columcille and Cuchulain in living men. It is true that we must share his idealism to see his people and their cause as he saw them—heroic and apostolic. To the extent that he lays demands on his readers for co-operation is debarred from easy popularity. This is true also of all writing that is in a highly spiritual vein. Young people in Ireland for all ages will find in Pearse a source of exaltation. To enter into the kingdom of his imagination, we must become as little children. Yet there is no manlier, no more robust writer in all our literature. In so far as Pearse, born in the Pale, achieved so much when Irish was but his second language, he proves that Leinster can share to the full in the heritage of the more Gaelic provinces. It is worthy of remark, ere we leave him, that he edited Fenian romances with a rare appreciation, and that in his English writings he drew upon Gaelic literature for his examples with an extraordinary fruitfulness, so that his redactions and his English essays afford precious Gaelic criticism. [1929]

Aodh de Blácam. Gaelic Literature Surveyed (New
York, Barnes & Noble, 1974), pp. 382 –85

Any genuine recollection of P. H. Pearse, however slight, must have interest and value. [*The Home-life of Padraig Pearse*] is a short book, simple and modest, but it is a real contribution to the biography of Pearse and to Irish history.

Its first part is an unfinished autobiography, in which Pearse was to offer his "only defence." Unhappily, it breaks off abruptly at his very earliest schooldays. "Its object," he says, "as I plan it, is simply to record things done and thought; not to explain, or to apologise for, or to justify anything." As it stands it is an incomplete, but charming, memoir of the childhood of a sensitive, thoughtful gentle man, who to the end retained some of the gaiety of the boy.

The second part is made up of Miss M. B. Pearse's recollections of her brother in their home-life; and its third of personal memories recalled by a few of his friends.

Here is a revealing passage:—

> When my father and mother married there came together two very widely remote traditions—English and Gaelic. Freedom-loving both, and neither without its strain of poetry and its experience of spiritual and other adventures. And these two traditions worked in me, and, prised together by a fire proper to myself— but nursed by that fostering of which I have spoken—made me the strange thing I am.

It was this dual origin surely that enabled Pearse to appreciate Synge, and put him, and his fellows in their rightful place in Ireland and in Irish letters, and that made him, too, a fighter for intellectual and spiritual freedom, as well as for political and economic freedom. He was what, indeed, most Irish people are—the offspring of the mingling of races that have made Ireland their home; and, while there is nothing in this book to prove it, he must have recognised that Irish nationality is a very different thing from the narrow nationalism founded upon an illusory conception of a single and undiluted racial stock. . . .

There are quotable stories on nearly every page of three hundred and sixty, and most of them throw light upon the character and personality of the man who founded St. Enda's, wrote *Suantraidhe agus Goltraidhe*, [*Lullabies and Dirges*] and *An Mhathair agus Sgealta Eile*, [*The Mother, and Other Stories*], and led his countrymen into insurrection in Easter Week. Here are the childhood and boyhood of the man called Pearse.

Irish Times. Mar. 2, 1935, p. 7

Pearse's published works are the most extensive of the three Rising poets [the others being Thomas MacDonagh and Joseph Plunkett]. They include plays, stories, translations of Gaelic verse, lectures on literary subjects, political tracts, and fragments of an unfinished autobiography; his collected poems, however, number only twenty. In his verse Pearse attempts to recreate the naturalness and simplicity which he believed characterized the Irish-speaking peasantry of Connacht. He does, in fact, manage to convey in some poems a convincing image of peasant naïveté, at times even a sense of simple tragic dignity. The final stanza of "A Woman of the Mountain Keens Her Son," for example, has a quiet emotional power. . . . Pearse's handling of the keening motif is in keeping with the traditional Irish theme of womankind oppressed by suffering and sorrow. Over and over again, from the tenth-century Deirdre of the Ulster cycle of sages to Synge's Maurya in *Riders to the Sea,* the Irish woman, in poem, story, and play, keens her menfolk gone to the grave. For men, death can be a moment of stoic triumph; for women it represents torment extended in time. Pearse's treatment of the Woman of the Mountain's sorrow is characterized by restraint, even though there is more than a trace of effusiveness in the fourth stanza where he uses the diminutives "little" and "narrow" to describe the grave and substitutes the euphemistic "treasure" for corpse, evoking a morbid kind of sentiment. Nevertheless, the poem as a whole manages to express a genuine sense of pathos.

However, the sentimentalism becomes almost oppressive in "The Mother," an autobiographical poem in which the poet's own mother repeats his name and that of his brother, William, "to my own heart / In the long nights; / The little names that were familiar once / Round my dead hearth." Pearse's treatment of children is similarly strained. They are forever prancing with "bare feet upon the strand," or confessing their "fault truly," or "watching the wee ladybird fly away." Pearse professed a belief in the child's "inner life" from which adults are excluded—and he had read Wordsworth—but except perhaps in his plays, *The King* and *The Master,* where his austerity of language in dramatic dialogue limits the frequency of offending modifiers, the point is generally drowned in excessive sentiment.

Richard J. Loftus. *Nationalism in Modern Anglo-Irish Poetry* (Madison and Milwaukee, Univ. of Wisconsin Pr., 1964), pp. 126–28

The self-image of Padraic Pearse was Jesus Christ, for Pearse saw the role of the rebel as the perfect Imitation of Christ. Because these images are not newly created but taken from cultural contexts, they come with burdens of responsibility, for the image demands the one action that can express it. The mythical image of Pearse as savior demanded the reality of crucifixion. Because these burdens of responsibility are unpleasant, most people shirk them or try to muddle the issue, not seeing that one cannot be a good monk by playing the lover, or a good poet by playing the popular rhetorician. The greatness of Padraic Pearse is seen in his refusal to shirk the burden of responsibility that came with the image he had chosen. He wanted to be a savior to his people, and he moved remorselessly and uncomplainingly into myth; perhaps that is why he achieved the apotheosis he desired.

Before Pearse fired a shot, he rehearsed insurrection by writing a play about it. *The Singer* is his most characteristic and most important work, for in it all his literary and nationalistic ideas are fully realized. Here one sees quite clearly that for Pearse the rebel is the perfect imitation of Christ. The pattern of the hero with the thousand faces is sharply evident in the story of the singer MacDara. The patriotic songs of the hero force him into exile, into *separation* from his people of Connacht. Wandering as an alien through the cities of men, MacDara earns his bread as a teacher, until he is again cast out onto the roads. There in the loneliness of the ditch, the despondent hero casts out God and denies the path to crucifixion that has been ordained for him. At the nadir of his despair, MacDara experiences the anguish of Christ in the garden of Gethsemane, but out of this extreme despair comes a new faith, a new birth. After the *separation* comes the *initiation*. The hero in this descent into hell is initiated into a wisdom the common man can never know; he realizes that a gay folly is the highest knowledge, and that to be truly wise one must abandon what the world knows as wisdom to become foolish. Initiated into this gay science (a rather scandalous mixture of Nietzsche and Christianity), the hero *returns* to his people. The son returns to comfort his mother, who is, of course, "Mary mother of us all." MacDara's return to his people, like Christ's return to Jerusalem, is joyous and everywhere is met by crowds. Yet the singer knows he goes to his death. The *Sassenach* are on the march, and the word that is to start the revolution has not been given. The common people would hold back, in prudence and wisdom, but the singer will have no part of this prudence and wisdom which is, in reality, the false security of the terror-stricken. The drama ends with MacDara's exhortation:

> One man can free a people as one Man redeemed the world. I will take no pike, I will go into the battle with bare hands. I will stand up before the Gall as Christ hung naked before men on the tree.

One can see why the lawyer and historian J. J. Horgan has called the Easter Rising a mortal sin and Pearse a heretic. Pearse's devotion is extreme, and, like all extreme devotion, it is perilously close to blasphemy.

William Irwin Thompson. *The Imagination of an Insurrection: Dublin, Easter 1916* (New York, Oxford Univ. Pr., 1967), pp.118–19

In his reviews and articles on literary matters, Pearse urged those attempting to forge a new literature in the Gaelic language to free themselves from conventions of style and subject, to use modern forms and modern language, and to express themselves in a fresh, imaginative way. Not content to merely offer this advice, he put it into practice himself and produced a small number of stories, plays and poems which were significant contributions to the new literature. Although in general the stories are weak artistically, they helped to establish a prose style based on spoken Gaelic rather than on the archaic, literary Gaelic of previous centuries, and they provided examples of the modern short-story form in Irish. And three or four of the stories—particularly "The Dearg-Daol" ["The Red Beetle"]—are rather good and offer evidence that Pearse had a developing, though modest, talent for prose narrative. The plays are his least successful creative works. Although they contain a number of passages memorable for their poetic beauty and rhetorical power and although they provide some moments of dramatic intensity, the plays are not good art. Spiritual and heroic in theme, they are of interest today merely as by-products of the Irish cultural revival and as revelations of the ideals that motivated their author.

Pearse's poetry, on the other hand is his finest creative achievement. The eighteen poems in Gaelic, which constitute two-thirds of his total output, include his best work. Using elements of both the syllabic and accentual systems of Gaelic prosody, Pearse wrote lyrics characterized by simplicity and economy of diction, directness of statement, and careful structuring based on skillfully arranged patterns of word, phrase, sound, and image. With these poems, Pearse brought Gaelic poetry into the twentieth century, and he carved a recognized place for himself in the Irish poetic tradition.

In the first two decades of the twentieth century, Ireland experienced cultural and political movements which were to have a profound influence in shaping its future. Patrick Henry Pearse played a leading role in both those movements, and his achievements constitute a significant contribution to Ireland's political and cultural life.

Raymond J. Porter. P. H. Pearse (New York,
Twayne, 1973), p. 140

In January 1914, the *Irish Review* published in book form a collection of his poetry, *Suantraidhe agus Goltraidhe* (Songs of Sleep and Sorrow), a slim volume of twelve poems, seven of which had already appeared in various newspapers and journals. This collection marked the zenith of Pearse's achievement as a poet. His later verse, usually written in English, was so strongly coloured by political or sentimental considerations that little of it could compare with this earlier work. Six of the re-published poems have been discussed earlier. The seventh, "Cronan Mna Sleibhe" (Lullaby of a Woman of the Mountain) was a simple pastoral song of maternal love. The five new poems were the product of a very different inspiration. "Cad Chuige Dhibh Dom' Chiapadh?" (Why Do Ye Torture Me?) was redolent of Pearse's spiritual anguish. The strength of the poem lies in one protracted image—rather than pursuing his desires, the poet has seen a bizarre reversal in the chase: only in his grave will he escape the pack, which "is the greedier of the satisfaction it has got." By the stage of his life, those human desires in Pearse which had not shrivelled from neglect had been forcibly suppressed—with one exception.

He still longed for success, and that appetite had been whetted by the moderate recognition he had received in his various endeavours. Death would bring relief through oblivion and, perhaps, satisfy the hounds with his posthumous glory.

"A Chinn Aluinn" (O Lovely Head) was a lament. . . . This poem . . . has been taken by many as proof of Pearse's love for Eveleen Nicholls, but the arguments are unconvincing. It was apparently not written until nearly five years after her death, and Pearse, where his poetry dealt with specific episodes (for example, [his brother] Willie's absence in Paris), wrote during or immediately after the occasion concerned. The poem was an exercise in a common romantic convention, by which the death of the beloved provided a vehicle for morbid reflections. Pearse did not speak from personal experience of the kisses of a little boy being sweeter than the kisses of women, or the honey of their bodies; and no more can it be assumed that when he wrote of his love in the tomb he was thinking of a particular woman. (In the consumption-ridden Ireland of that period love frequently gave way to death: Willie's Mabel Gorman was dying during 1913 and 1914.) All that can with certainty be said of Pearse's poems was that they represented his current moods and preoccupations. And while he wrote these poems, his mood was black and his preoccupation was with death.

Ruth Dudley Edwards. Patrick Pearse: The Triumph
of Failure (London, Victor Gollancz, 1977),
pp. 199–200

For Pearse [as for Joyce, too,] the maternal theme is centrally associated with Ireland. In his literary writing he presents and glorifies the figure of the mother who sends her sons to die for Ireland. One of these heroic women speaks in a 1915 poem, which is called "The Mother." . . . As happens often when Pearse turns to aesthetic rather than polemical expression, the language of the poem is deadened, inadequate to the emotion of the situation. The one element in the poem that achieves more than minimal expressiveness is the echo in the last two lines quoted of the words the pregnant Mary spoke to Elizabeth in the Magnificat (Luke 1:46–55). Clearly one function of this biblical resonance is to identify as messianic the dead or dying sons. But the echo also associates the pregnancy of Mary with the desolate condition of the speaker of the poem. Thus Pearse collapses into one moment the pregnancy of the mother and her calm contemplation of the death of her sons in the sacred battle. They separate from her only to die in the fight for Ireland. Pearse and Joyce work with precisely the same set of associations to the maternal when they present Ireland as mother. They converge on the moment of birth, and for both of them, the destruction of the child is involved with his bond to the mother. Pearse sees as heroic that which horrifies Joyce. Pearse's *mater dolorosa* and Joyce's murderous sow are the antithetical variations on the same image of mother/Ireland/church.

Jeanne Flood, In P. J. Drudy, ed., *Irish Studies 1*
(London and New York, Cambridge Univ. Pr.,
1980), pp. 106–7

PLUNKETT, JAMES (1920–   )

It is a fashion in Dublin just now to tell anybody who writes a short story that he ought to be writing a novel and anybody who announces work in progress on a novel that it would be wiser to master fully the slighter and more difficult medium of the short story before spreading himself in a novel. Why, by the way, does nobody ever tell the baker that he ought to be delivering potatoes? Anyhow, I am fully aware of the triteness of remarking that when James Plunkett produces a novel, as he inevitably will, all the wealth one finds scattered in his short stories will have been properly invested. His is a talent which inspires me personally with the liveliest admiration, and he sets it playing, as it were, in one's own back yard. Dublin he seems to regard with the sort of impatient tenderness Frank O'Connor has lavished on Cork, and he knows it better, one fancies, than he knows any room in his own housing. Time after time in Plunkett's stories the old strumpet city looks one brazenly in the eyes, without make-up, stripped even at the accosting stage as she seems to have been also for James Joyce. . . .

Plunkett's characters too can keep nothing from him. The inarticulate bitter adolescent is as silently voluble before him as that old labourer in "Mercy." His cold imaginative sympathy seems boundless. And, perhaps most important of all, Plunkett has not failed any more than Kiely has in coming to grips with the known daylight, Erin without the green, where a dangerously near romantic past has fathered a present in which Movements have dwindled into party moves, heroes into veterans 'scuffling for pensions,' even perhaps an austere ancient Faith into a local religion in danger of strangulation by Sodality. Born of all this, one of the most courageous and disturbing Irish stories of the last decade was Plunkett's "The Wearin' of the Green," which indicated more clearly than any of his previous work the hard road he will most likely follow.

Val Mulkerns. *Irish Writing*. Sept., 1953, p. 53

It is a measure of Mr. Plunkett's success in his first book [*The Trusting and the Maimed, and Other Stories*] the contents of which will be familiar to readers of *The Bell* and *Irish Writing*, that already one thinks of him as a man with a vision of his own. He cannot, and one hopes never will, be mistaken for anyone else. For one thing, though he is no propagandist, he is moved to pity and indignation (well controlled) by the unnecessary additional misery which society inflicts on the individual. His characters accept passively and unquestioningly the standards of their fellows, and live accordingly, lives of quiet desperation. But obviously Mr. Plunkett does not accept those standards. This is not to say that his compassion is a mere compulsion from the mind, the kind of pity by theory which so often goes in hand with (curse the phrase) a social conscience. Again, he is the only living writer I know of, who has had sufficient courage and sensitivity to capture the authentic atmosphere of the Dublin lower middle-class in its present phase. How superbly in the first and last stories he distills the poignancy of an existence in which Hollywood and London and export Port-Royal all have deposits. He is adept at recording office-chat and pub-chat, and arranging his findings to achieve the maximum effect of seedy misery.

He is not of course, always convincing in his communication of what has moved him. "Mercy" fails grotesquely because of lapses, the last one fatal, into picturesque bravura writing, wholly out of character and tone. "The Web" fails because it all hangs on a clumsily used symbol. "Janey Mary" does not quite succeed because the magnificently audacious symbolism of the child's feet being crushed in a bread-queue requires greater preparation, and either a starker or more grandiose treatment. And "The Damned" is neither as horrible or as moving as it should be given the theme of childhood and hell and mutilation. "The Half-Crown" goes astray in its last paragraph, because of over-explicit writing, not because of unauthentic feeling. The remaining stories give Mr. Plunkett the right to be judged beside his quinquagenarian elders in the craft of the short story. If I especially care for "Weep for Our Pride," it is because reading it I lived again my old childhood. I am grateful to Mr. Plunkett for having documented part of it.

John Jordan. *Irish Writing*. Autumn, 1955,
pp. 56–57

I do not believe that it is possible to be controlled and objective about this book. Perhaps that is where the absolute magic of James Plunkett's *Strumpet City* lies—in its effortless way of totally overpowering the reader, leaving him defenseless and exhausted. It is usually less than difficult to throw up something of a critical rubric and around lesser fiction—the less useful the book, the easier it seems to write about it. Here, reviewing of any kind seems like taking a vacation on a map.

Strumpet City is, as Chesterton used to say, "a welcomed exercise in simplicity"—but what thunderous reverberations . . . remarkable and brilliant. The book jacket and the advances call it "a magnificent epic novel" (already a best seller in Europe). It is every bit of that. Mr. Plunkett selects as his canvas seven years of Dublin-Irish history, from 1907 to 1914. He places upon it an astonishing variety of people, problems, and paradox. The focus of the plot is actually the turbulence and misery caused by several violent years of labor disputes—strikes, lock outs, starvation, bloodshed. In 1907, at 3:15 A.M. the royal yacht *Victoria and Albert* arrived in Dublin for a state visit about the same time as did the voice of the social revolutionary, Jim Larkin. One of the most masterfully delineated characters of the decade, an old scavenger named Rashers Tierney, is selling commemorative ribbons. They are colored red, white, blue, and green. "The green ribbon is for Ireland," he explains to a customer. "It doesn't match up somehow," she observes. "It never did, ma'am," he said, "Isn't that what all the bloody commotion is about for the last seven hundred years?" It's the "bloody commotion" that Plunkett explodes in front of the reader.

There is a range and depth of character and incident reflected in the commotion that forces the reader to start mumbling "Dickensian" or "Chaucerian." A slum lord, effete and frightened. Father O'Connor, the priest who wants to dedicate his soul to the Third World and its poor but first learns that he must accept its smell. His superior, Father Giffley, the whiskey priest with not one illusion left outisde the bottle. The compellingly tragic reprobate Rashers Tierney who carrying sandwich boards cries to himself, "Take up your cross was right. Here I come, Jesus, one front and back."

Strumpet City is a murderously grim novel—about a city where in the unexpected sun the cripples, the old, and dying are left out to air and are taken back in again from the steps to signal end of day. It is a far from delicate portrait of destitution, anger, poverty, degradation, and squalor. . . . Ironically, with all the grimness of this marginal existence, those most in trouble manifest a terrible kind of hope, a power, a strength, and a sense of humor that is both real and profound. The climactic incident in the novel is an attempt of anti-strike forces to prevent those striking from sending their children to safety in heathen England. There is a great riot with nationalists, socialists, laborites, unionists, clerics, and anti-clerics divided into opposite armies at dockside—all battling over the children. There are shouts of "Hail, Glorious St. Patrick," clubs and fists and bottles. In the heat of the melee, where one cause becomes indistinguishable from the other, the only truth available is between the lowest of the low—Rashers and his friend Hennessey: "They looked at each other in silence." . . . Mr. James Plunkett has presented us with an unforgettable picture of a maimed and crucified world.

H. T. Anderson. *Best Sellers*. Oct. 15, 1969,
pp. 257–58

The epigraph to Part One of this noble book quotes [John] Montague on "the dark permanence of ancient forms." It is precisely that monumental quality that invests *Farewell Companions*. It spans the period from the First War to the end of World War Two, interweaving effortlessly the history of those years with the history of a boy/young man, his family, and his friends. Every strand, every attitude, every material detail touched on does not function alone; it sets off harmonics in other parts of the work and in the consciousness of the reader. This may seem a rather over-blown description of the effect. I can only say I find in the work a lyrical quality which vitalises the fullness of the construction.

There is too the matter of artistic courage. What risks does he take? Plunkett boldly invites comparisons, in particular with Joyce and Flann O'Brien. Few younger writers will not shy away from the line taken by those going before; they prefer to switch to the outside. Plunkett has chosen to find his way through on the rails. Already in *The Trusting and the Maimed* he had tackled at least one of Joyce's "things"—compare "Weep for Our Pride" with the beating of Stephen in *A Portrait*. Stephen is an individual, symbolises the artist. Plunkett's boy, who suffers no less unjustly, is one of many; he represents them, there is an added social dimension. If we follow Stephen to university level and beyond, we find ourselves in company with a right little tit, with delusions of his own importance which clearly connect with Joyce's paranoia about betrayal. Plunkett's persona in *Farewell Companions* is modester than that; he is also free from self-pity. Did Joyce despise his characters? Did he need to prove himself superior to them? To see through them? To expose them? Plunkett does not need to make us feel that he is superior to his characters. Plunkett may never be worshipped in Manhattan. But neither would Joyce be, had he made Leopold Bloom an Arab. When it comes to individuals, there are two comparisons which seem courted. Plunkett's Cornelius Moloney, a Tipperary man turned Dublin publican, greyhound lover, and one who was in at the birth of the Fianna Fáil party, is a bit like The Citizen; and O'Sheehan, a Celtic Scholar who thinks he is Oisin, bears resemblance to things in the pages of *At Swim-Two-Birds*. But they are *not the same!* They are not accidents; but they are not copies. They appear as real. People, and the people, clearly exist for Plunkett, as they did for O'Casey. . . . At least part of the question is, not how Plunkett stands up to Joyce & Co., but how they all stand up to the original—largely Dublin. Is it written out? Are there not many likenesses of the BVM? And if breadth and integrity of sympathy and of vision can be counted a political attitude, then I like James Plunkett's politics.

Linguistically, one must say that all the stops appear to be within Plunkett's reach, but that he generally prefers a muted combination. Brilliance he has when it is useful, but his satire, when he deploys it, is not so much a matter of explosive jibes, as of a gentle but thorough excavation of the ground beneath the feet of the inobservant subject of the same satire. And his handling of moments of grief or other emotion leaves nothing to be desired. A complete and satisfying work.

Sydney Bernard Smith. *Books Ireland*. Nov., 1977,
p. 226

James Plunkett (James Plunkett Kelly, *b*. 1920) grew up in Dublin, became a clerk in the Gas Company, then an official in the Workers' Union. He wrote stories published in *The Bell*, and his *Collected Short Stories* (1977) shows his range of subject matter and style. In the early stories collected in *The Trusting and the Maimed* (1955) he is interested in death, treating it from the perspectives of different ages; his later stories, more complex in construction, centre upon the stream of consciousness, notably "Ferris Moore and the Earwig" which shows Plunkett's debt to Joyce as well as his own quizzical sensibility. Plunkett's novels *Strumpet City* (1969)—which obviously owes much to the techniques of modern American fiction—skilfully pulls together various separate skeins of Dublin society; its main drama comes from the strike of 1913; and it has shifted from Joyce's concept of Dublin's paralysis, so that the range of characters is treated not with scrupulous meanness but out of a more humane, balanced point of view than that of the youthful Joyce.

In the middle nineteen-fifties, Plunkett found, in his middle thirties, a stimulating *métier* in Radio Eireann, producing and writing plays for radio and after 1960 in Radio Telefis Eireann, for television. His interest in history expanded his subject matter, and perhaps because the nature of his new work proved satisfactorily stimulating, his novel *Farewell Companions* (1977) has a greater freedom, a more personal treatment of its characters. Though the novel is uneven in achievement, its readers cannot but respond to the lyrical sadness, which colours its five movements, its shift from the world of *Strumpet City* to a very different Ireland. Plunkett has an inclusive vision, an energy which overflows in rich detailed descriptions, yet he is following the pattern of Moore and Joyce, moving away from the restrictions of realism into a more personal, more imaginative, indeed more idiosyncratic presentation of the complexities of human existence.

A. Norman Jeffares. Anglo-Irish Literature (New York, Schocken, 1982), pp. 248–49

The texts of *Big Jim, The Risen People,* and *Strumpet City* provide a remarkably clear and extremely interesting record of a literary transformation in the words, from radio to stage to novel. Like Standish O'Grady with Red Hugh O'Donnell, Plunkett continually reworked the story of Jim Larkin and the lockout, withdrawing Larkin himself to the background when he moved from documentary play to historical novel. In *Big Jim,* Larkin had been a realistic character; in *The Risen People,* "more a presence, a chorus, than a flesh and blood character," according to his character description; in *Strumpet City,* more an influence in the background than an active character. In his approach to Larkin, Plunkett realized that "you either write a biography or else you don't write about the person, but you write about their influence." While withdrawing Larkin to the background of *Strumpet City,* Plunkett also wrote, in the midst of his work on the novel, such a "biography," as if to compensate:

an essay entitled "Jim Larkin" for the book *Leaders and Workers,* in which he noted that "James Joyce spoke of Dublin as the centre of paralysis. It was a total paralysis, blinding conscience and soul. It remained to Jim Larkin to see the slum dweller as a human being—degraded, yet capable of nobility, perceptive, capable of living with dignity, capable, even, of music and literature—Jim Larkin's great task was to create a new social conscience." In *Strumpet City,* Plunkett found that he was writing not about Larkin but about the dignity and the revolutionary potential of the Dublin working class. He never read [George] Lukács, but he would agree with Lukács' central thesis about the relationship of the leader and the common people, and about revolution as a transforming force. . . .

But it is important not to allow the history in *Strumpet City* to overshadow the fiction, for it is a novel, not a secondary historical source. If much of its power derives from straight, effective narrative and dialogue, it is also true that it achieves some fine lyrical moments. In considering this fiction as a whole, its individual parts must not be forgotten. The novel is a tapestry as well as a panorama, a collection of stories, in a sense, as well as one big story. The episodic structure of the novel, in fact, is drawn from the method at work in Plunkett's best short stories. . . .

Strumpet City is, along with [Liam O'Flaherty's] *Famine,* the greatest of Irish historical novels not only because it portrays history panoramically and accurately, but because characters like Rashers live on in the imagination, independent of the facts of history. The novel comes alive as literature, thanks to the vibrancy of Rashers, Yearling, and Father O'Connor, at the same time that it is remarkably faithful to history in both its detail and depth. With these simultaneous strengths, *Strumpet City* is what a historical novel ought to be.

James M. Cahalan. *Great Hatred, Little Room: The
Irish Historical Novel* (Syracuse, N.Y., Syracuse
Univ. Pr., 1983), pp. 180–81, 187–90

REID, FORREST (1875–1947)

For the accomplished delineator the family group presents excellent material; the area of interest is circumscribed; the traits of the various individuals are at once links and contrasts, and a unity is obtained comparable to the unity of time and place in drama. The characters in Forrest Reid's new novel are remarkably well presented; they are all differentiated, and some of them seemed opposed to others; but in the group we recognise a fundamental unity. The gross Alfred, the violent and self-indulgent Amy, the sensitive May, and the extraordinary boy Denis, are the result of a spiritual displacement consequent upon the marriage of Bracknel, the gross and successful business man who, however, has a curious tremor within him, with that frightened and sensitive woman, his wife. The Bracknels are a commercial and Presbyterian family who live in a suburb of Belfast. There is fantasy in *The Bracknels,* but it is a fantasy affiliated to reality. The case of the boy Denis Bracknel is as strange as anything imagined by Edgar Allan Poe. Mr. Forrest Reid has introduced other and more audible fantasies—the old woman at the lodge with her charms and her grey parrot, and the superstitions of Hallow Eve. What the fantasy connected with the life of Denis is we will only suggest. The Poet of the Book of Job knew it when he wrote: "If I beheld the moon walking in brightness, and my heart hath been secretly enticed, or my mouth hath secretly kissed my hand; this also were iniquity."

Forrest Reid is an Irish novelist who is making good progress. His previous books were on the verge, but in *The Bracknels* he has made an advance into the reality wherein the power of the novelist can best manifest itself. He has been well advised to work out such a gross youth as Alfred and such an average sensual man as his father. Such types break up the heavy reverie that was in *The Garden God, The Kingdom of Twilight.* These two characters with the violent and self-indulgent Amy give a balance to the groups of characters in *The Bracknels.*

Irish Review. Dec., 1911, pp. 519–20

When one opens *A Garden by the Sea* we think at first that Mr. Forrest Reid is going to make us happy by Arcadian reveries, a little pensive perhaps, but on the whole happy, but Mr. Reid has served too long an apprenticeship to realism in his longer novels ever to allow us to think there can be any dream without a sharp awakening; and we come up uncomfortably against stories like "An Ulster Farm" to remind us that

The woods of Arcady are dead,
And over is their antique joy.

But on the whole the feeling of the book is one of pleasant reverie or retrospect lit up by humour. "Kenneth," the literary schoolboy, is very amusing,
and the tale of his novels and poems reminded us of a boy we knew forty
years ago who also ran a manuscript magazine in which penny dreadfuls were
boiled down to an ultimate essence of sensation. The bare event of killing,
told in a sentence, created such a turmoil in the soul of the juvenile writer that
it seemed unnecessary to expand the narrative into details, as probably the
equally juvenile readers would be able to create ample circumstance without
the details which we require as we grow older from a Conan Doyle or a Rider
Haggard. . . . Mr. Reid understands boys. He has somehow kept his memory
of boyhood so alive in himself that he writes almost with the feeling of a contemporary. A boy's mind is an amazing thing, and there is often in it the
whole stock of ideas, imagination and feeling which will last without new
matter for the remainder of life. In the Perse booklets [issued by the Perse
School, Cambridge] we were let into that world by boys who had learned the
art of self-expression owing to the genius of a teacher. Mr. Forrest Reid had to
wait until he was middle-aged to do justice to his childhood, but he has written a very pleasant book largely out of boyhood memories, and his art and
subtlety as a writer were never better manifested than in this book of sketches.
[March 1, 1919]

George William Russell (A.E.). *Selections from the*
Contributions to "The Irish Homestead," Vol. II,
Henry Summerfield, ed. (Atlantic Highlands, N.J.,
Humanities Press, 1978), p. 945

To call Mr. Forrest Reid the novelist of this region would give a false idea of
his art, for he is only concerned incidentally with topography. But it does so
happen that most of his scenes take place in or near Belfast and that his art itself contains the two elements indicated above: there is squalor and there is
beauty, and both of them are haunted. Haunted by what? It would take some
time to answer the question. Certainly not by fairies ninety miles high. But in
nearly every chapter, if we look closely, there are hints of that indwelling
power seen, sometimes clearly, sometimes remotely. Despite the realism of
his method and the prevalence of football matches, razor-strops, and all that,
we are conscious of an underlying note that is sometimes sinister and always
sad. . . . Behind vulgarity, as behind rarity, there is a presence—of what kind
and blending into what Mr. Reid does not choose to say.

 Over this profound and equivocal background is stretched a world that
bears sufficient resemblance to the present to solace a novel-reading public. It
is not the present world, if only for the predominance given in it to youth.

Few of the protagonists have seen eighteen summers, while their elders exist mainly as sympathizers, tyrants, and choruses. . . . The author believes that a man's great decisions and experiences occur in boyhood, and that his subsequent career is of little more than recollection—a belief which . . . has significance in his own literary development. Here one must note that this belief necessarily restricts his canvas as a novelist and that, regarded as a transcript of human activities, his novels are a failure. They cover too small a field. . . . They must be classed not as transcripts but as visions before they can be appreciated, and their vision is that of the hierophant who sees what lies behind objects rather than what lies between them, and who is not interested in the pageants of society or history. . . .

More important than the realism is the strong ethical tendency. Questions of loyalty, courage, chastity, and personal decency, are always occurring; indeed, the author tells us that the highest beauty he knows is "a kind of moral fragrance." Such a fragrance is rooted, however remotely, in Christianity and the books approach nearer to the Gospel spirit than appears on the first reading. Complementary to moral fragrance is the odour of sin, and here (perhaps one is stupid or callous) one feels that Mr. Reid makes too much fuss; he is almost as much upset by sin as Nathaniel Hawthorne. He never preaches, he is never puritanical. But he is always a puritan, and he regards it as of absolute and eternal importance that youth should reach maturity unscathed. . . .

His two best novels, [*The Bracknels*] and *Following Darkness*, probably neighbour some spiritual experience into which the "supernatural," as we crudely call it, entered. They are intensely passionate beneath their surface calm. . . . He is always harking back to some lonely garden or sombre grove, to some deserted house whose entrance is indeed narrow but whose passages stretch to infinity, and when his genius gains the recognition that has so strangely been withheld from it, he will be ranked with the artists who have preferred to see life steadily rather than to see it whole, and who have concentrated their regard upon a single point which Mr. Reid's new novel [*Pirates of the Spring*] has been fashioned—with landscape intelligible. [April 10, 1920]

E. M. Forster. *Abinger Harvest* (London, Edward
Arnold, 1936), pp. 93–98

A great many years ago a critic compared *Following Darkness*—from which Mr. Reid's new novel [*Peter Waring*] has been fashioned—with *Wuthering Heights*. If the comparison is sound, a change in kind has occurred since Mr. Reid's revision, for *Peter Waring*'s ancestry, like that of so much Irish fiction, is in Turgenev's Russia. The story is a typical Turgenev study of very young love, but the early morning mist which sparkles in the background of all such stories in Turgenev is here deprived of its erotic languor by the severe puritan idealism and anthleticism of the County Down. There is no living writer in English who can describe growing boyhood as Mr. Forrest Reid does. The puritan childhood is a delicate history of the constant adjustments of constraint and natural passion, and Mr. Reid knows every one of them; his success springs from the fact that he has the kind of sensibility which this knowledge presupposes, and that he avoids the common danger of letting his sensibility outrun the sensibility of his characters. . . . I see only two dubious things in the book: the character of Peter's patroness who is shadowy, and a hint of spookiness here and there. Mr. Reid has always had this preoccupation. One meets it often in Irish writers and with him its is subdued. But the rest is austere, real, delicate and yet firm, free from the more facile kinds of nostalgia, and the maladies of sensibility.

V. S. Pritchett. NSN. Sept. 11, 1937, p. 377

Since Forrest Reid died some of the younger writers here have tended rather to talk down his work. They say he doesn't write about life as it is in Ulster. They speak as if all that is graceful and beautiful in literature were unrealistic, escapist.

There is, of course, a sordid side to Ulster life. Forrest Reid dealt with it in *Peter Waring, The Bracknels, At the Door of the Gate*. The fact that he writes about it in beautiful, rhythmic prose only makes his illumination of it more clear. His fault from their point of view is that he saw the other side as well. There was and *is* another side and surely it is for that other side we should prefer to be remembered.

Forrest Reid himself said that his field was narrow and in so doing put a weapon into the hands of his detractors. It is quite true that he took the subjects of most—though not all—of his novels from a narrow field, but the curious thing is that if you really examine these novels you find vividly portrayed typical Ulster characters in great variety. He is most at home with middle classes, from the lowest of the lower middle classes to the two peaks of the upper middle class—immensely rich business people and lapsed aristocrats. He knew them through and through, and though many of his best characters are only incidental to the stories he is telling, they are all completely there—as solid and alive as any characters in the works of any novelist. He wasn't so good with manual workers: they tend to be seen from one side only—from above—and in the same way he saw the aristocracy—if he saw it at all—from below.

Some people have found it strange that Forrest Reid, who had strong spiritual affinities with Ancient Greece and Renaissance Italy, should have appeared and lived in modern Belfast. To me it doesn't seem at all strange because Belfast to-day has a lot in common with the cities of Ancient Greece and Renaissance Italy.

Stephen Gilbert. In Forrest Reid Memorial (Foxton,
England, Burlington Press, 1952), pp. 11–12

The values in the books are the values of the man, and do not change. Faithfulness, innocence, affection, integrity—integrity in the broadest sense; the scrupulousness which prevented him as a writer from ever venturing near the edge of that "whirlpool of insincerity from which no man returns"—these were the qualities that he prized and admired. All these qualities he resumed in the single virtue of "moral fragrance," that "highest spiritual beauty of all," the beauty in which he acutely judged Yeats to be lacking, and of which his own books are so full.

Besides all this, Forrest Reid was a craftsman. All through his life he never ceased striving to perfect his style, to invest it with an unmistakable identity of its own. Writing didn't come to him easily or without pains and, as he was always the first to recognize, his development was unusually slow and hesitant. But with time and practice he overcame his problems one by one. Many of the short stories, for instance ("An Ending" or "A Garden by the Sea" are examples), come off almost solely by reason of the craftsmanship which has gone into their construction. At first, however, errors of subject and treatment had led to delay in the discovery of his real themes. The wonderful final style, its delicacy and flexibility, was only achieved after long trial and error, and at the cost of occasional failure. This is what gives his work its peculiar technical interest. . . .

The trilogy of novels about his young hero Tom Barber, which he wrote towards the end of his life, was his crowning achievement. No other writer, no one, has ever matched the skill and tenderness with which Forrest Reid explored, in these lovely and curiously intimate books, the mind and heart of an ordinary, but sensitive, small boy. In *Uncle Stephen* and *The Retreat* and *Young Tom* subject and style had coalesced, melted into each other, simultaneously reached their final point of development and produced, "naked and complete," the work of art which all his previous books had been but a prelude to expressing. It is a far cry from the immature, the almost ninety-ish languors of *The Kingdom of Twilight* to the ease and charm of this later writing. Between the two there is a single point of contact—both, unmistakably, are the work of Forrest Reid.

Russell Burlingham. Forrest Reid: A Portrait and A Study (London, Faber and Faber, 1953), pp. 60–61

This ambivalence [toward the lower-middle-class mercantile spirit] is reflected throughout Reid's body of fiction. There is a very English, elitist side to it, an affected fragility as though its presiding muse were some Pre-Raphaelite ghost or Georgian elf. Its feyness is surely what attracted the attention, and to its creator the friendship, of such delicate sensibilities as Edwin Muir, Walter de la Mare and E. M. Forster. It has also ensured Reid's eclipse as a relevant force in contemporary Irish fiction. . . . But anchoring Reid's fiction is his sense of that which invokes his elitist fear and disdain and which he feels moved, at least in the early novels, to re-create—the dark industrial heart of Belfast and the grubbier aspects of Protestant materialism. Moreover, the author of the most formidable and consistent canon of any Ulster novelist this century was not above a joke at his own expense, and in the acknowledge-ment of his own limitations and fragilities lay a resilience that I like to think sprang from the fact that he was an Ulsterman who spent almost his entire life in his native Belfast when many inferior and less secure writers have shown the city a clean pair of heels at the first opportunity. "I alone knew, how much, as an author I resembled Mr. Dick," he noted in his second autobiogra-phy, *Private Road* (1940). "I could get on swimmingly until I reached my King Charles's head—the point where a boy becomes a man. Then some-thing seemed to happen, my inspiration was cut off, my interest flagged, so that all became a labour, and not a labour of love. I supposed it must be some mysterious form of arrested development" (p. 12). Almost totally confined to childhood and early adolescence as it is, Reid's work can appear marginal, an impression the author himself fostered, even going so far in *Private Road* (published when he was sixty-five) as to withhold all but diplomatic recogni-tion to his own adulthood.

Reid's remark about arrested development is, of course, a characteristic piece of coyness; one suspects Reid of praising himself with faint damnation, a device used constantly by his boy-heroes who have an insatiable appetite for smothering affection. True, as a man he apparently loved childhood games and pastimes and as a novelist explored at his peril adult and female charac-ters; nevertheless, Reid always writes out of a sense of strength not weakness, even though like his young protagonists he occasionally affected in his auto-biographies an arch naïvety reminiscent of Dickens's Mr. Skimpole.

John Wilson Foster. *Forces and Themes in Ulster Fiction* (Dublin, Gill & Macmillan, 1974), pp. 139–40

The art and the achievement of Forrest Reid reveal him to be an Anglo-Irish visionary writer from Belfast whose reputation as an English prose stylist, an important psychological novelist, and a critic of some distinction, should es-tablish his place in literary history. The pattern of his stylistic development and the growth of his fictional technique from *The Kingdom of Twilight* and *The Garden God* to the *Young Tom* trilogy and the posthumous *Denis Brack-nel* demonstrate a progression in economy, restraint, lucidity, and radiance that characterize his best works. Integral to his style is a natural, rhythmic ca-dence related to his rich Celtic inheritance. His feeling for nature, similar in its sensitivity to Wordsworth's animism, colors each landscape that he por-trays in contrasting images of light and darkness. He also captures the phys-ical sense of the place, whether in Ballyreagh, Carrick-a-rede, Bruges, Eleusis, or Belfast, to create an illusion of reality. Both atmosphere and geography, then, serve to contrast city and country, outer and inner, time and timelessness. The search for a divine friend, the longing for an Eden from which each of us is exiled, so lyrically orchestrated in his haunting autobiography *Apostate,* and to a lesser extent in *Private Road,* are themes that possessed him throughout his life and served his narrative purposes well.

In each period of Reid's stylistic growth, the theme of youth and youthful friendships in either boyhood or adolescence controls his narrative, which is confessional to a greater or lesser degree according to the needs of his story. Since he portrays his action through the mind of a child who is also a dreamer, and maintains his point of view through the child's consciousness at the child's own level of perception, his subtle explorations of feeling and unusual states of mind whether awake or in dream, are exceptional attributes of his technique and of his style. He also connects cosmic loneliness to homesickness as the overarching metaphor that sets parameters on his heroes' quest for meaning, truth, and permanence, a quest that is identical to his own intellectual search for a country of the mind and heart in which to find peace. Although Reid always used Greek allusions functionally, if somewhat self-consciously at first, once he discovered Greece as the integrating symbol of his life and art, he gained a unified perspective from which he never deviated.

From the publication of *Apostate* in 1926, the style of each succeeding novel from *Demophon* in 1927 to *Denis Bracknel* in 1947 gained in directness, simplicity, and beauty. Just as he used animism to support his vision of life, he used the friendship theme to structure his cry for freedom and for unity. Since the spirit of youth and its vision were predominant values to Reid as a writer, he used dreams and dream pscyhology to make his vision prevail. The geography of the dream and its Utopian content are skillful devices employed to establish the humane values that he asserts. Nonviolence, freedom to be oneself, peace, harmony, happiness, and friendship are life-affirming values that radiate from his pages.

Mary Bryan. *Forrest Reid* (Boston, Twayne, 1976),
pp. 144–45

Forrest Reid's obsession was with boys and with boyhood, with their fictional representation and with its literary recall. Any appreciation of his life and writing must do more than take this fact into account; it must begin with it. That Reid was a pederast is of course one explanation, but of itself the fact imparts little understanding. The boys of Reid's imagination—Denis Bracknel, Peter Waring, Grif Weston, Beach Traill, and above all, Tom Barber, although they often talk in a style and with a wisdom mature beyond their years are all carefully desensualised characters. As with Hubert Rusk's perception of his pupil Denis Bracknel, "what was there . . . was a complete absence of anything gross, of anything that could, even with the passage of years, associate itself for an instant with vulgarity or sensuality." This characteristic defensive note is struck again and again in Reid's novels. And although he had realised quite early on that there was a sense in which Denis and Grif and Peter were ". . . mere pretexts for the author to live again through the years of his boyhood," Reid's imagined boys are—with the single exception of Brian Westby—just that. That he should have employed imagination to draw solace and compensation in an unsatisfying world is doubtless predictable; but the mechanism of consolation is complex and not explicable as a simple, single relation. Although Reid, in the words of George Buchanan, "suffered astonishingly little pressure towards exact self-knowledge," he understood well enough this aspect of himself. From the beginning, he was never less than honest in his personal friendships. It was this honesty and sincerity which had led to his initial parting from Andrew Rutherford, after the fateful decision to share his journal—the episode recounted in the closing pages of *Apostate*. "I hate insincerity," Martin Linton had said in *Brian Westby*. "I hate it in life, and in art of course it is fatal." With such a clear perception of the consequences of insincerity, Reid might have realised that honesty and candour also have their price. If there can be such a thing as a puritanical pederast, Forrest Reid was that person.

> Brian Taylor. *The Green Avenue: The Life and Writings of Forrest Reid, 1875–1947* (London, Cambridge Univ. Pr., 1980), p. 174

ROBINSON, LENNOX (1886–1958)

Patriots (1912) is an interesting picture of the supposedly changed attitude of a younger generation of patriots towards the question of Irish freedom, and the means by which it should be secured. The desertion of the returned political prisoner by men more interested in reformist and Parliamentary methods gave rise to a tragedy whose poignancy is weakened only by the thought that the prestige of Nugent and his insurrectionary faith has been underestimated. The superficiality of the author's estimate of the psychology of the new generation has now been demonstrated with fearful force. His own colleagues and contemporaries have been executed for doing what his play argued was impossible. Within a week of Lennox Robinson's *début* at the Abbey Theatre in 1908, *When the Dawn Is Come*, by the late Thomas MacDonagh, was produced. Little more than a melancholy interest attaches to this unsuccessful attempt to dramatize an aspect of a situation identical with that in which MacDonagh was to lose his life. It is significant, however, that the dramatist who was to die should have conceived precisely the contrary circumstances to those depicted by the writer of *Patriots*.

Nevertheless the modification of certain political views is a fact of contemporary Irish life, as witness the comparatively favorable reception of *The Dreamers*, which appeared in 1915. Here Lennox Robinson makes his first attempt at historical drama, by choosing the final episode in the career of Robert Emmet. Instead, however, of treating the subject in the traditional idealistic manner, he presents a very depressing account of the rising and of those who participated in it. Emmet alone stands out as a man wholly devoted to the cause of Ireland and prepared to risk everything for success. His followers are shown to be shiftless, untrustworthy, and even dishonest, and are made largely responsible for his failure and death. The play is well constructed and bears the marks of careful planning and execution, but it is not easy to accept the author's view of the causes which led to the collapse of the rebellion. He is too readily disposed to color the facts in deference to political prejudice.

Ernest A. Boyd. *The Contemporary Drama of Ireland* (Boston, Little, Brown, 1917), pp. 166–68

Still in his thirties, he is one of the most noteworthy of the coterie influenced by Synge to turn their talents to the interpretation of contemporary Irish life. Like Synge, Mr. Robinson has done the greater part of his work for the theatre. At the outset of his career he showed unusual dramatic ability, and he has now developed firm technique. Even ten years ago Lady Gregory and Mr. Yeats had so high an opinion of the young playwright that they asked him to accompany them to this country [U.S.A.]; he has since become manager of the Abbey Theatre, and his new play has not only been given in Ireland but has been one of the recent successes in London. Lennox Robinson is a dramatist of assured position.

Mr. Robinson's plays may be divided into two groups: those describing rural and small-town life in Ireland, and those dealing more or less remotely with Irish politics. To the first group belongs his earliest play, *The Clancy Name*, succeeded by *The Cross Roads*, *Harvest*, and *The Whiteheaded Boy*, the last produced originally in Dublin, on December 13th, 1916. Between *The Cross Roads* and *The Whiteheaded Boy* come the political plays, *Patriots* and *The Dreamers*. Mr. Robinson's latest play, *The Lost Leader*, is likewise of this class. . . .

Mr. Robinson portrays not only the hardships of Irish life, of peasant farmer, small shopkeeper, politician, but the idealism of Irish character, often a prey to its own defects. Timothy Hurley, in *Harvest*, because he has brought himself to the verge of ruin by educating his children and starting them in positions in life superior to that he occupies, burns his own property to obtain the insurance; the idealism of James Nugent's associates in *Patriots* is undermined by material prosperity. By showing Irishmen dissatisfied with their condition in life, with their fellow-countrymen, yet struggling to hold a vision always before, although beyond, them, Mr. Robinson helps to explain why Sinn Fein, despite contradictions and illogicalities, has made such headway in Ireland. He is the dramatist of Irish discontent.

A comparison between Robinson and Synge has already been suggested. Both have written of the Ireland of their day, yet Mr. Robinson is the more faithful realist, for he does not stamp his personality upon his plays as did Synge. This may be due somewhat to the greater variety of people in Mr. Robinson's plays; he writes not only of the country but of the town, whereas Synge dealt almost exclusively with peasant life in remote districts. Synge, moreover, was always a protestant against circumstance; in all his work he stressed the aspirations rather than the failures of his characters; in the last analysis he is a romanticist, or an idealist, rather than a complete realist. Mr. Robinson, on the other hand, although he shows the dreams of his characters, shows with equal emphasis their thwarting; he stands outside his people, almost indifferent to their fate; circumstance leads them whither it will. Perhaps Synge's extraordinary ear for prose cadence was partly responsible for the emphasis he placed upon the imaginings of his people, who speak in a language that is a garnering of picturesque phrases rather than a faithful rendering of common speech. Nobly struggling against Destiny, Synge's figures have passionate poetic utterance; crushed by the monotony of every day, Mr. Robinson's men and women confine themselves to the less vivid words of familiar intercourse. [1922]

Norreys Jephson O'Conor. *Changing Ireland: Literary Backgrounds to the Irish Free State, 1889–1922* (Cambridge, Mass., Harvard Univ. Pr., 1924), pp. 157–58, 160–61

In December 1916 was produced the play which is generally regarded as Lennox Robinson's masterpiece, *The Whiteheaded Boy*. It is by this play he is known throughout the English-speaking world. It is certainly a comedy of the finest kind, droll in speech, natural in its situations, entirely human in its characters. In Aunt Ellen Mr. Robinson gave the modern stage one of its most delightful comedy characters. Like all Irish comedy it is essentially satirical, illustrating many of the weaknesses of the Irish character, but at the foibles at which he once scoffed Lennox Robinson here laughs good-humouredly. The play is filled with foolish and delightful people with whom one may laugh without restraint. No one will stop to think that the things done by these people are wrong; they are wrong, but they are done with such happy inconsequence that condemnation is frozen in the thought. *The Whiteheaded Boy* is certainly the finest comedy written by any Irish dramatist since the death of Synge. It is perfect in its combination of form and content, there is nothing forced in its language or its situations, and its humour derives entirely from the nature of its people. *"The Whiteheaded Boy* is political from beginning to end, though I don't suppose six people have recognised the fact." So says the author, and he is very probably right in suggesting that few have stopped laughing at the play to see the political satire. That is as it should be. There is little enough to laugh at in Ireland nowadays, and for that which Mr. Robinson has given all are truly grateful.

The political intention which was overlooked in *The Whiteheaded Boy* could not be ignored in the next play, *The Lost Leader*, produced on 19th February, 1918. It is a common form of conundrum in Ireland to enquire, "What would Emmet do were he here now?" and parties are divided upon conjectural opinions of dead leaders. In *The Lost Leader* Parnell is set to solve the problem of Ireland in 1918. The play uses as its basis the popular belief that Parnell did not die in 1891, but continued to live in retirement. . . . *The Lost Leader* though daring and interesting was not a great success on the stage. The characters tended to be mere representatives, typical of aspects of current political thought, rather than the lively creatures of *The Whiteheaded Boy*. It is now almost forgotten, and it was the last of Lennox Robinson's political plays for the time being.

Andrew E. Malone. The Irish Drama (London,
Constable, 1929), pp. 179–81

Having directed at the Abbey for almost as long as he had been a playwright, he knew intimately the needs of the actor. And his highly developed theatre sense gives his plays more polish and makes his structure better shaped than those of any of his Irish contemporaries. His expert technique as a craftsman in the theatre comes to light in the manner in which he builds up his succinct and frequently underwritten lines so that they acquire enough strength for an affecting artistic whole. His ability in giving vitality and interest to the light conversational interplay of his characters frequently carries what appears at the outset to be the merest trivia of dialogue—inadequate for a satisfactory play—into a dramatic first- or second-act curtain.

In his use of language Robinson is far removed from the poetic exuberance of Synge's imaginative world. Whatever similarity exists between the two writers would seem to stem from their shared somber cast of mind. The simple and even terse directness of Robinson's lines is more like the English naturalists to whom he is indebted for his early practical experiences in the theatre. His dialogue in this respect suggests an eavesdropper on the uneven flow of talk used in the daily activities of life.

Robinson does not have Colum's penetration into the workings of the Irish mind. This said, one is compelled to add that—considering his upbringing in the staunchly Unionist, conservative, and Protestant circles of his family—it is all the more remarkable to find how much perceptive understanding he has of the hearts and minds of those in the Irish scene beyond the rectory walls of his father's home: the environment of the farmer, the shopkeeper, the townsman. Furthermore, he scrutinizes Irish society without any of the self-conscious mannerisms of earlier Anglo-Irish writers, who generally viewed the Irish as a humorous and quaint people, full of exotic appeal for English readers.

Except in such plays of Robinson's novice days as *Harvest* and *The Cross Roads*, through which he hoped to propagate his personal theories about Irish life, he is fundamentally objective and devoid of argument. Moreover, his quite dexterous handling of his material suggests a skillful observer able to probe thoroughly into the hearts of those characters winning his attention.

Yet, at the same time, he manages to keep a certain aloofness, to retain an esthetic distance, which does not allow him to show too much concern with the final lot of his characters. He prefers, much like Chekhov, to stand on a remote observation pedestal and in this way avoid becoming involved in the main current of events ebbing and flowing about him. Probably the best example of this characteristic is found in one of his finest plays, *The Big House*. With an air of good-mannered tolerance he admirably attempts to portray a balanced picture of the turbulent Irish political scene as it influenced the Anglo-Irish landlord class. By adopting this attitude of detachment Robinson contrasts sharply with Sean O'Casey, who frequently envelopes himself emotionally in his characters.

Michael J. O'Neill. *Lennox Robinson* (New York,
Twayne, 1964), pp. 168–69

There are no profanations and no clowns in the romantic comedies of Lennox Robinson. In fact, it would be safe to say that the quaint middle-class world of rural Ireland in his plays is seldom disturbed by barbarous or irreverent characters. It is a world of benign manners where the innocent excesses of maternal domination and filial ingratitude are easily put right by sentimentalized good sense. it is a world of provincial stability where moral doubts are never raised, not even with levity or laughter. Presided over by matronly women, it is a comfortable world that has no need for primitive jesters or grotesque paycocks, a domesticated milieu in which gentle laughter is touched off by inconsequential tremors: innocuous stratagems and misunderstandings, naive illusions and awakenings, frustrated and reconciled lovers. Because of their forgivable frailities, all the characters are so basically good that they must be rewarded with the poetic justice they deserve. The result is a type of genteel village comedy that had a certain popularity but was not in the mainstream of antic Irish comedy; though it should be pointed out that the Abbey Theatre, during its lean years in the generation after the rejection of O'Casey and the death of Lady Gregory and Yeats, had to survive on an undistinguished surfeit of this front-parlor and back-kitchen comedy of benign manners.

Robinson had superimposed a tone of anecdotal whimsy on *The White-*

headed Boy by adopting a folksy narrator's voice in the stage directions that smacks of amateur theatricals, and even though these intimate asides are picked up only in a reading of the text, their sentimental aura hangs over the play like a thick syrup that will not pour. Robinson's quaint persona sounds more like a stage-Irish maiden aunt than the onstage Yankee narrator that Thornton Wilder was later to use with overbearing success in *Our Town*. Everyone is coddled by the narrator's gossipy forbearance—liberally sprinkled with effusive sighs and smirks, and trite "whishts" and "begobs"—so that in the end Robinson has transformed all misunderstandings into a heart-warming display of homely virtues. Perhaps the characters are treated with too much sympathy for effective satire and too much sentimentality for effective comedy. Nevertheless, it is in those moments when Robinson puts a damper on the glow of sentiment that he creates some highly amusing situations.

David Krause. *The Profane Book of Irish Comedy*
(Ithaca, N.Y., Cornell Univ. Pr., 1982), pp. 196–97

What unifies all six plays collected here is on the one hand Robinson's technical skill—especially his fine use of dialogue and his almost classical sense of dramatic form—and on the other hand his love of Ireland and its people. This love was neither idolatrous nor uncritical, but it was nonetheless profound and enduring. Indeed, Robinson concludes his autobiography, *Curtain Up*, with the remark: "this strange Irish thing has been the commanding force in my life." His work, lacking the passion of Synge or O'Casey, nevertheless takes its inspiration from the source that gives those writers their places among the greatest of Irish writers: national feeling. It takes its significance, however, from its value as theatrical art, unremittingly pursued. . . .

Patriots (Abbey, 11 April 1912) stands as an example of Robinson's early work in the realistic, Ibsenist vein. It is also indicative of Robinson's nationalist feelings. He was, in his own way, a strongly political writer, as can be seen by the two plays which followed *Patriots*, namely *The Dreamers* (1915), a play about Robert Emmet, and *The Lost Leader* (1918), a play about Parnell. Political fervour is also seen in Robinson's only novel, *A Young Man from the South* (1917), which is partly autobiographical, and in four short stories written 1915–16 at the time of, and stories saturated with, powerful national feeling. These stories were published under the title *Dark Days* (1918).

At the time when *Patriots* is set, prior to 1912, Ireland was in a political limbo. The movement to obtain Home Rule, with political independence implied for all Ireland, was about to come to nothing. Indeed, *Patriots* opened on the same day as the third Home Rule Bill was introduced in the British House of Commons. At this time, the revolutionary spirit which was to lead to the rising of 1916 had not yet manifested itself in the founding either of the Volunteers or of the Irish Citizen Army. Robinson is writing about a period of apathy among Irish people, and his play hinges on the contrast between such people and the passionate commitment of the released Fenian prisoner, James Nugent. Nugent is like a prophet, out of phase with his own time, a Jeremiah come to rural Ireland. Although it is clear that to Robinson Nugent is the real hero, violent though his republicanism is, it is equally clear from the ending of *Patriots* that the majority reject Nugent's dream. The play is thus a study of a social leader passed by and isolated by a change in public mood. The irony of the ending provides a sharp critique of this public mood, and adds, as it were, a bold question mark to the play's title.

Because of the swing towards violence which entered Irish political life after 1915, *Patriots* was soon out of date. The James Nugents of a former time came into their own again. Yet this fact does not minimize the force of Robinson's play. In his autobiography, he himself praised its "precise construction, the tightness of its dialogue . . . the humour springing out of character."

Christopher Murray. Introduction to *Selected Plays of Lennox Robinson* (Gerrards Cross, England, Colin Smythe, 1982), pp. 12–13

RODGERS, W. R. (1909–1969)

Here, says Mr. Mark Van Doren, is "the war poet of the war." But premature classifications do not serve the cause of literary criticism. I don't think, in spite of the title [*Awake! and Other Wartime Poems*], that Mr. Rodgers would thank us to call him a war poet. And what do we mean by "*the* war poet?" In England, G. W. Stonier accepts Mr. Rodgers as "this war's Brooke." Well, it will be better if we forget about Brooke and the war for a moment and think about the poetry (for that matter quite a number of these poems were written before the war started). Just what have we got here?

This is the poetry, not of diagnosis, but of clarification. In the 1930s the younger English poets were busy answering the question, "What do you think of England, this country of ours where nobody is well?" They were diagnosing the ills of their time by means of a rather confused mixture of Freud, Marx, the English Public School, and a handful of minor prophets; their imagery was often ambivalent to the point of self-contradiction, they were confused about their audience, and they had a tendency to equate diagnosis with cure. Employing rich and involved techniques derived from Donne, Hopkins, the French Symbolists, Eliot, Pound, and a few personal choices, they tried to express in crowded verse their view of the nature of the present discontents. They produced some exciting poetry, but they never stopped sounding like experimentalists. Now Mr. Rodgers, though these are his first poems, doesn't sound like an experimentalist at all; nevertheless his poetry is fresh and original. One reason for this difference is that the young English poet of ten years ago had too much theoretical knowledge to be able to apply it successfully in a diagnosis of any contemporary ill.

. . . Influenced . . . more by MacNeice and Spender than by Auden, and not so very much by any of them, his ideas are simple but not silly, his verse limpid but not trite. His characteristic fault is a kind of dead plainness—a good fault in a poet who comes after a decade of poetry that inclined to pedantic obfuscation. His characteristic virtue is speed and light. When I say that his ideas are simple, I mean that they are unified, coherent, communicable, which is not to say that they are easy. And he holds his words steadily in a cool palm. . . .

His most successful poems are constructed in a series of well-planned verse paragraphs, where the lines have a fine elasticity (occasionally overdone to the point of disturbing looseness) and the stanza is rounded to a genuine pause, sudden or slow, or . . . balanced savagely on a short, rhyming line.

David Daiches. *Poetry*. May, 1942, pp. 97–98

Although it is easy to write extensively about [George] Barker and [Dylan] Thomas and still say something important, it is not so easy to do with Rodgers, and that is just the point. There is nothing spectacular about him. In fact his verse has a sort of dogged earnestness about it, although it is far from pedestrian. His great virtue is that he speaks for himself. He is relatively free of the fashionable influences of the day, and he has almost no visible connection with the previous generation. His work is as simple and profound as he can make it. His effects are achieved quietly, and they are always the direct outcome of integral experience. He never depends upon secondary references to chic reading matter and current postures. One of his peculiar virtues is a special sonority—a sort of gong and woodwind depth and color of long vowel and labial, sibilant, and nasal music which is, as it were, a kind of counter Hopkins. Hopkins' baroque irritability expressed itself in staccato vowels and plosives and stops and a restive metrical distortion. Rodgers has the confidence of Solesmes or the pre-Bach organists—the marching, sure, unperturbed musical development of Byrd and Gibbons and Frescobaldi—a Protestant, or at least pre-Tridentine answer to Hopkins. The quality I associate most clearly with his work is a rugged, protestant magnanimity, courteous and polished enough superficially, but with, still underneath, a certain strongly masculine gaucherie. The comparison that springs to mind is Andrew Marvell.

Kenneth Rexroth. Introduction to Kenneth Rexroth,
ed., *New British Poets* (New York, New Directions,
1949), p. xxi

Nearest to MacNeice in reputation, W. R. Rodgers offers an astonishing contrast. He drives straight for the archetypal forms and images, achieving his contemporaneity in his idiom, but, above all, insisting on organic language, words that leap and clash and slide and roar. Superficial critics insist on his derivation from Hopkins, whereas the fact is (and it is important that this should be recorded) that the greater body of his book *Awake! and Other Poems* was written before he had read that infectious Jesuit! And for those who wish to detect the element of Irishry in him, Joyce, many of whose devices parallel those of Hopkins, should be a more profitable parallel. Rodgers, long absent from County Armagh and involved in a comparative poetic silence, makes it difficult for anyone to prophecy about his future. Of this I am sure, we have not heard the last of him. Gesturing rather than gesticulating, striding rather than hurdling, he will, I believe, have deeper and more mature things to report.

John Hewitt. Poetry Ireland. Jan., 1950, pp. 7–8

Bringing only critical faculties to bear on them, I find a good deal to object to in Mr. Rodgers' poems. It seems to me that Mr. Rodgers assaults the reader with an armory of poetic blunderbusses. He is more sensitive to alliteration and onomatopoeia than to words, and more intoxicated by sensations than exact in metaphor and imagery. . . .

However insensitive his methods, Mr. Rodgers writes the kind of poetry he wants to write, and in a long poem . . . produces the effect of a big design, like a long-stretched roughed-in cartoon. . . .

Add to this, the whole poem ["Europa and the Bull"] is erotic, sensual, and genuinely exciting both as narrative and as a procession of sensations. Mr. Rodgers has also a certain wittiness—not altogether unlike that which gives so much pleasure to the admirers of Christopher Fry's plays—which sparkles from line to line. . . .

Rodgers is an uneven poet, sometimes extremely vivid and visual, sometimes . . . vulgar. Everyone though should read him, because he is a poetic phenomenon. Those like myself who find a good deal to object to cannot afford to ignore such an energetic talent. And those who are not so particular will be stimulated by the energy which manages to retain simplicity while tying a great many verbal knots. There is a good deal of pleasure to be got from this book; and, whatever criticial judgment may finally say about Mr. Rodgers, he can now straightaway, be enjoyed.

Stephen Spender. NR. March 23, 1953, pp. 19–20

What could have been taken for incoherence or incongruity [in *Europa and the Bull*] was in fact the keystone of Rodgers's art. His primary obsession in writing was the word itself, and the sound of the word as much or more than its sense. He used to say, playfully yet seriously, that he cared more about *sound* sense than sound *sense*. If the *sound* sense conveyed two or three meanings, even contradictory ones, so much the better, because so much the more true to life. . . . The preachiness of *Awake!* was gone, the verbosity brought under greater control, the invention and luxuriance of language retained and refined. One gets a sense if not of a resolution of conflicts then of a delicate, fluid equilibrium among them; a sense of the poems, like Rodgers's swan, holding "the heavens, shores, waters and all their brood."

The most ambitious poem, "Europa and the Bull," is too long, but it has magnificent moments and often becomes a truly exalted piece of writing. Epic in style and scope, spanning seas and continents, its main action an enormous act of sexual intercourse, it revolves around the ancient question of man's relationship to God, of how much God there is in man and how much animal, the question asked by all myths in which God takes the form of man or animal. . . .

G. S. Fraser, in his review, wrote of Rodgers's "sacramentalisation of sex"; he may have been thinking of this poem, as well as of "The Net" and others. For in his narration of the abduction of Europa, daughter of Cadmus, by Zeus, who takes the form of a bull, Rodgers endows their coupling with the significance of the celebration of the mass, when Word becomes flesh, God becomes man. Here God becomes animal and enters woman, mingling with her, comingling with her flesh and spirit, and through this act—tender and violent, brutal and delicate—heaven and earth are joined. The poem implies that the act of love in sex and sex in love can unite the sundered halves of our natures as can nothing else, implies this, does not preach this, making it happen in words. . . . The poem sighs to a close in one of the softest, loveliest passages I know of in modern poetry, sinking over the sleeping pair quietly as nightfall.

Darcy O'Brien. *W. R. Rodgers* (Lewisburg, Pa.,
Bucknell Univ. Pr., 1970), pp. 71–73

If sexuality is celebrated in this volume [*Europa and the Bull*], so too is a neo-pagan romantic version of Christianity, the antithesis of Calvin's austere life-denying version of that faith. Where *Awake! and Other Poems* had no poems on directly religious themes, this volume contains a batch of them. There is, firstly, the Resurrection sequence originally commissioned for broadcast by the BBC. Then there are a number of poems in which a romanticised folk-Christ (recalling Joseph Campbell's *The Gilly of Christ*) acts as metaphor for a pantheistic celebration of the earth. . . . This religious celebration of earth's fullness is ornate and formalised in the book, evoking memories, as did Joseph Campbell's work, of medieval carol and iconography. . . .

Other stylising elements in the poet's new romanticism, which suggest, by contrast, a formalisation of paganism, are the images of dance, carollings, fiddles, flutes, trumpets and flowers which recur through the book. But this lyrical pagan acceptance is given sharpness and tang, is saved from the mellifluous softness of so much literary paganism by Rodgers's keen sense of time's passage, by a vestigial, Calvinistic awareness of judgment due.

Rodgers's achievement in *Europa and the Bull, and Other Poems* is considerable; a balance between the conflicting aspects of his personality allowed for a series of rich and moving poems. A reader in 1952 might, therefore, have expected that arrival at such a point of balance would allow the poet to write, in the future, not out of extreme reactions to the pressure of experience (as he had in *Awake! and Other Poems*) but from a calmer, more comprehensive sense of life. . . .

But the achievement of *Europa and the Bull* was a momentary balance of the forces that drove Rodgers on, as the hare and hound in the hunt (one of the poet's compulsive images) can seem momentarily to belong to one another before the chase becomes once again a turbulent, confused race to the kill. Rodgers's later poems are fragmentary and reveal him responding, as before, to extreme moments. Instants of life's quickening out of tedium, a reminder of his background in Paisley's biblical rant, a May day's brio, the deaths of friends, these stir him to verse, while a poem such as "Scapegoat" (a nightmare encounter with the Ulster Calvinist God) repeats his early allegorising efforts. The poems are old tunes played on a slack string. Rodgers may have felt he saw "the circle of life complete" in the Pays-Basque ("Summer Journey") but in his late poem "The Fountain in the Public Square" he accepts ruefully that he is one "whose sin is to have no centre." . . . [He] recognises that without an ordering, controlling centre all that he can aspire to poetically is the fountain's elegant self-possession, though this will mean repetitiveness, a failure to develop, a dependency on mere style.

Terence Brown. *Northern Voices: Poets from Ulster*
(Totowa, N.J., Rowman & Littlefield, 1975),
pp. 122–24

[R]eading again that desperate renewal of promises, the refrain of his later letters to me, I see that the problem of the Epilogue [to *The Character of Ireland*—unpublished] was central to himself. It was to have been his Summa. Into it were to have gone, all reconciled, the discrete percepts of that mosaic mind. The expatriate was to have come home; he was to have been able "To make the past happen properly, as we want it to happen": the cat of thought and the mouse of guilt which his poem, "The Trinity," could not reconcile were to have settled at last together in the self to which they are domestic. He had feared "The shadow of Doubt, that pickpocket of conviction," yet had hoped, as his Magi on their journey hoped:

There was nowhere they would not go, feast or fast,
Slum or salon, bethel or brothel, if only at last
And at least they could come to the truth and be blessed.

In that Epilogue, there would no longer have been any paradox in a Presbyterian parson's Europa and the Bull, Pan and Syrinx, Apollo and Daphne. The Greek, the Roman, and the Orange, would have been harmonized in an art free as the ancients conceived it and able to comprehend Belfast and Dublin, Wapping, Colchester and California. Mary Magdalen would have been the Virgin and there would have been an Ireland such as Wolfe Tone had imagined, where North and South could be one, when Catholics digging with the left foot and Protestants with the right would no longer dig one another's graves except in friendship, and where a new past could be created with room for priest and presbyter written large or small, a past with room in the same Irish mind for Carson and for Michael Collins.

Such a poem could not be written in this world, not even in the last refuge of California. The soil could not be removed from the soul till the soul was in the soil, and the bull-man could become a god only when the clod had closed over him. So now the Epilogue, like Robert Emmet's epitaph, cannot be written. Its imago lives only in the Utopia of his poem "Neither Here nor There," shimmering and beckoning, glimpsed in "A spool of birds spinning on a shaft of air," whenever the sun burns "through the meshes of rain." It is echoed in "the suck and slap of a spade in the wet clay," and keeps its past promise in our memory of that man of "undertones, and hesitance, and haze" who has hidden at last in "the safest place—the bosom of the enemy."

Dan Davin. *Closing Times* (London, Oxford Univ.
Pr., 1975), pp. 41–42

RUSSELL, GEORGE WILLIAM (A.E.) (1867–1935)

A little school of transcendental writers has indeed started up in the last year or two, as it is, and made many curious and some beautiful lyrics. . . . One of the group [Charles Weekes] published last year a very interesting book of verse which he withdrew from circulation in a moment of caprice, and now "A.E.," its arch-visionary, has published *Homeward: Songs by the Way* [sic], a pamphlet of exquisite verse. He introduces it with this quaint preface: "I moved among men and places and in living I learned the truth at last. I know I am a spirit, and that I went forth from the self-ancestral to labours yet unaccomplished; but, filled ever and again with homesickness, I made these songs by the way." The pamphlet is in no sense, however, the work of a preacher, but of one who utters, for the sake of beauty alone, the experience of a delicate and subtle temperament. He is a moralist, not because he desires, like the preacher, to coerce our will, but because good and evil are a part of what he splendidly calls "the multitudinous meditation" of the divine world in whose shadow he seeks to dwell. No one who has an ear for poetry at all can fail to find a new voice and a new music in [his] lines. . . . Such poetry is profoundly philosophical in the only way in which poetry can be; it describes the emotions of a soul dwelling in the presence of certain ideas. Some passionate temperaments, amorous of the colour and softness of the world, will refuse the quietism of the idea in a poem like "Our Throne's Decay," but they can do no other than feel the pathos of the emotion. . . . Nor would A.E. be angry with one who turned away from his ideas, for he himself knows well that all ideas fade or change in passing from one mind to another, and that what we call "truth" is but one of our illusions, a perishing embodiment of a bodiless essence. . . .

The book has faults in plenty, certain rhymes are repeated too often, the longer lines stumble now and again, and here and there a stanza is needlessly obscure; but, taken all in all, it is the most haunting book I have seen these many days. Books published in Ireland are only too often anything but comely to look at, but this little pamphlet makes us hope much from the new house of Whaley, for it is beautifully printed upon excellent paper. [August, 1894]

W. B. Yeats. *Uncollected Prose of W. B. Yeats*, Vol.
I, John P. Frayne, ed. (New York, Columbia Univ.
Pr., 1970), pp. 336–39

To Mr. Russell poetry is a high and holy thing; like his friend Mr. Yeats he is at one with Spenser in believing it the fruit of a "certain enthousiasmos and celestial inspiration"; it is his religion that Mr. Russell is celebrating in his verses, many of which are in a sense hymns to the Universal Spirit, and all of which are informed by such sincerity that you do not wonder that his followers make them their gospel. . . .

About a score of the less than tenscore poems of "A.E." are definitely declarations of belief, but declarations so personal, so undogmatic, that you would hardly write him down a didactic poet at first reading. "A New Theme" tells of his disertion of subjects "that win the easy praise," of his venturing

> in the untrodden woods
> To carve the future ways.

Here he acknowledges that the things he has to tell are "shadowy," that his breath in "the magic horn" can make but feeble murmurs. In the prologue to "The Divine Vision" he states the conditions of his inspirations, . . . that is, the flame of his being that, "mad for the night and the deep unknown," leaps back to the "unphenomenal" world whence his spirit came and blends his spirit into one with the Universal Spirit. This same union through the soul's flame "A.E." presents in his pictures, and in his prologue to "The Divine Vision" he writes that he wishes to give his reader

> To see one elemental pain,
> One light of everlasting joy.

This elemental pain, as I take it, is the pain of the soul shut up in its robe of clay in this physical, phenomenal world, and so shut off from the spiritual world, the world of the unphenomenal or unknowable. The "everlasting joy" I take to be the certainty of eventual union with the Universal Spirit in the unphenomenal world, a union and a joy anticipated in the occasional temporary absorptions of the soul into the Universal Spirit in moments that Emerson experienced as "revelation" and Plotinus as ecstasy.

Cornelius Weygandt. *Irish Plays and Playwrights*
(Boston and New York, Houghton Mifflin, 1913),
pp. 123–25

The evolution of George W. Russell, the economist, from "A.E.," the mystic poet, has been gradual. The one has so slowly merged into the other that it is now difficult to dissociate them. In the beginning, "A.E." came forward primarily as an exponent of mysticism, though in such an early pamphlet as *Priest or Hero?* one can discern the later polemicist on behalf of intellectual freedom. With "John Eglinton," Charles Johnston, W. B. Yeats, and Charles Weekes, he was one of a group of young men who met together in Dublin, some twenty to twenty-five years ago, for the discussion and reading of the Vedas and Upanishads. These young enthusiasts created in time a regular centre of intellectual activity, which was translated in part into some of the most interesting literature of the Irish Revival. Their journals, *The Irish Theosophist*, *The Internationalist*, and *The International Theosophist*, contained a great deal of matter which has since taken a high place in modern Anglo-Irish literature. It was in the pages of those reviews that the first poems "A.E." were published, and to them we owe a number of essays afterwards collected by "John Eglinton" under the title, *Pebbles from a Brook*. Of all who contributed to that intellectual awakening few remain, in the Hermetic Society, as it is now called. But "A.E." is still the mystic teacher, the ardent seer, whose visions and eloquence continue to influence those about him. One no longer enjoys the spectacle described by Standish O'Grady, of the youthful "A.E.," his hair flying in the wind, perched on the hillside preaching pantheism to the idle crowd. His friends Johnston and Weekes are elsewhere, the heroic days of intellectual and spiritual revolt have passed; but "A.E." may yet be seen, in less romantic surroundings, constantly preaching the gospel of freedom and idealism.

Ernest A. Boyd. *Appreciations and Depreciations*
(London, T. Fisher Unwin, 1917), pp. 27–28

The title, *Voices of the Stones*, might mean that "A.E.'s" poetic impulse had dwelt for a time in a barren place. But the surmise would be wrong. He has the most wonderful things to say about stones in the beautiful introductory lines. Indeed, they are so amazing as to be almost disconcerting. There is the awkward feeling to the reader that he has not exactly regarded the stones of the ground in quite this light before. But the sweep of "A.E.'s" verse is irresistible, and its dignity, poise and rhythmic certainty, admirable. . . .

There is another aspect from which it may be viewed. I recall a well-known passage of Scripture which infers that the stones are the last of created things to rally to the proclamation of divinity. Perhaps "A.E." has been surprised to find that when other and more familiar voices are dumb, humbler allies, unsuspected, heretofore, have assured him that the testimony of the visible universe to enduring things is still audible to him even in his less receptive moods? It is as though it were a new approach for him to the ever-living through modes which he has not hitherto considered as containing even the possibilities of a way. Or as if he had captured an added vision, bringing in outlying regions of so-called inanimate nature not previously definitely recognised by him as capable of reflecting all-encompassing divinity.

In any case, it is certain that "A.E." still belongs to that small band of chosen spirits who have not bowed to material power. There are indications in this book of a triviality, of a lessening sympathy with human weakness, of a despair that is not real, of a wavering in essentials, not to be found in his previous work. This last blemish is the most serious of all. Personally I could wish "A.E." had not written "Resurrection" with the suggestion of the persistence of Earthly Wounds in the Everliving; or "Ancient,"

> Out of a timeless world
> Shadows fall upon time,

for the spirit light casts no shadows and has nothing to do with mortal conceptions such as time. But the weaknesses are out-balanced by the strength. As for me, I will think of this book in the glorious light of the third verse of "A Mountain Wind":

> Trail of celestial things:
>   White centaurs, winged in flight,
> Through the fired heart sweep on,
>   A hurricane of light.

DM. Aug., 1925, pp. 61–62

A.E.'s book, *Song and its Fountains*, may be taken either as a curiosity or an unusual experiment in creative criticism. It is a book which should eventually stimulate arguments because of its implications and challenge to psychological usage; unfortunately, for the moment it has been only accorded a reverential welcome by those who uncover their heads and look pious whenever the word "soul" or "mystic" is mentioned. It is probable that A.E.'s mystical ideas would surprise those amiable critics if they pursued them. Here, however, we are concerned with the literary implications of his book. The comments of poets upon their intimations and moods of inspiration have been but jottings and scribblings. . . . A.E., in *The Candle of Vision*, attempted to trace the workings of the imagination, and he began, like Bergson in his study of dreams, with that moment when we shut our eyes and encounter the void of darkness. In this book he takes a number of his own poems, not as object lessons but, so to speak, as gins to catch the unsuspecting visitants of mind. . . . A.E. analyses that passive mood of the waking consciousness, which the plain man dismisses as day-dreaming or mooning—the creative mood of poetry—and surmises a commerce between the inner being and the outer being. This vivifying method of setting a poem to catch its own tail is, at least, a stimulating variation on critical means. But the book is more than criticism—it is the revelation of a poet's imaginative life and his visual experiences attained by a disciplined concentration which belongs to the East.

Austin Clarke, *LL*. June, 1932, pp. 228, 230

In A.E. we have a poet of belief. As one of the main forces in the Celtic Renaissance, A.E. found in Irish deities and heroes the recognisable figures of everliving manifestation. They are not mere myth to him; and they are something more than the symbols of universal thought.

> These myths were born
> Out of the spirit of man and drew their meaning
> From that unplumbed profundity . . .
> And these
> Who read may find titans and king within
> Themselves.

Such beliefs have maintained the poise in his verse. It is interesting to note in parentheses that, while most of those young contributors to *New Songs* edited by him in 1903 have long ceased to sing, A.E., nearing seventy years of age, continues to soar to-day with refreshing vigour. Indeed, *The House of the Titans* contains, with his reassertion of belief, some of his best work in matter and method.

The house of man's spirit is, indeed, the House of the Titans, in which the skyborn King Nuada broods, like a wearied Saturn, upon the underworld and on its

> Dim tyrannies that aped the sway of light
> And grotesque idols of enormous bulk,
> Carved by some gnomic art that never felt
> The spirit thrill of beauty.

He is still companioned by gods who now had "learned to weep—the earth's first gift," and while held

> By but the frailest thread of memory from
> The habitations of eternity

he receives the intoxicating awakening of his former self, in which the mightiest—in wisdom, love, spiritual power, memory, revelation and healing—preside again, and disburse, with a wealth of compact poetry, their ancient virtues.

Again, in "The Dark Lady"—one of the most beautiful, powerful and concrete of all A.E.'s poems—we find that same belief. The Dark Lady is more than reflecting pool to the myriad-minded Shakespeare. Not solely wanton, but to A.E.'s imagination, she made herself a hundred natures that danced to the multitudes within the godlike, yet human, spirit of the inflamed dramatist. This complexity in the Dark Lady's nature is interpreted with the tenderness and sympathy of A.E.'s own gentle being. And yet that very gentleness may bring mockery on many bald-headed and unimaginative commentators who indict, without understanding, this Lady of the Dark Sonnets. A.E.'s poem is the best of possible pleas for the fair and questionable defendant.

In these main poems of massed projection and a newness of concrete imagery A.E. extends to dramatic advantages a range of subtle music: his new strings are played upon, not with the touch of an experimentalist, but with the hand of a master. Indeed, the muscular quality of A.E.'s recent craft in these poems—and particularly in "The Dark Lady"—somewhat reduces the stature of the lyrics in this collection. This muscular quality places at his disposal a power which is rarely seen in Irish verse, and was never more needed in poetry than to-day.

Irish Times. Jan. 19, 1935, p. 7.

Though really belonging to what is called, in the vocabulary of the moment, the petty bourgeoisie, A.E. was an aristocrat, with all those qualities that have been so impressively summarized by the Russian philosopher Berdyaev as marks of an aristocracy: he was magnanimous, he was unenvious, he was courageous, he had no prejudices, he was a free being. I never knew him to take personal offense, though he sometimes showed a fury like a god in a rage at things said against his country or his countrymen. His open letter to Rudyard Kipling, who had jibed at Irish nationalism, was such a reproof and on such a large-minded plane that Kipling's reputation as a writer was shaken, even unjustly shaken. . . .

His was never the biting Dublin wit—sometimes Dublin wit was nothing but plain downright malice—but A.E.'s had always something affectionate and whimsical in it, and one remembered it like a caress. It was this, I think, that helped to make him, along with his great magnanimity, the most popular, next to Douglas Hyde, of the men of the Irish Renaissance. His appearance is familiar to Americans, for he came here often to lecture and was widely photographed. The sudden entrance of this tall, broad-shouldered, bearded man into any assembly would give a thrill to the beholders, for he looked a prophet, a seer, a high priest of some divinity. He was a familiar figure in many milieus, for he mingled in all the activity of his country, whatever form they took—politics, art, literature, education, the theater, the labor movement—the last indeed with passion. During the bitter and revolutionary transport workers' strike of 1913 he took the platform for the workers and made a sensation by announcing, in that beautiful voice of his, "All the real manhood of this city is to be found amongst those who earn less than a pound a week." His sympathy with labor was not the literary and sentimental attitude and attitudinizing now common among writers, but of such a nature that the workers looked to him as one of their spokesmen and counselors.

Mary Colum. *Life and the Dream*
(Garden City, N. Y., Doubleday, 1947), pp. 171–73

Perhaps the most isolated literary figure of the beginning of this century is A.E. (George William Russell). A.E. does not, like Blake, create his own mythology, but his poetry is inspired by a tradition to which modern western civilization is diametrically opposed: a combination of theosophy with Celtic mythology. Whereas Yeats was influenced by French symbolism and other literary movements, A.E. remained faithful to his essentially religious sources. His poetry does not reach the perfection achieved by Yeats, and he considered life to be much more important than poetry. It has been said that, among great Irishmen, Yeats was the poet, and A.E. the saint. A.E. dismisses Christianity as a belief which has been artificially grafted on the Irish soil while the cosmic consciousness was dwindling and replaced by individual perception. Christianity, according to A.E., is but a moral code, whereas three things are required of a religion: a cosmogony, a psychology and a moral code. A.E.'s doctrine might be summed up by saying that he believed in the divinity of both Man and the Earth, and that the purpose of life is to re-unite with the

Ancestral Self; for A.E. admits the Fall of man. His aim in his poems is to communicate with the divine beings who are still present in the Memory of Earth, and in this respect his poetry may be regarded as fervently religious: "I believe that most of what was said of God was in reality said of that Spirit whose body is Earth." . . .

Human suffering, according to A.E., derives from the fact that the earth is a place of exile where the vision of eternity is a release from pain. This is why his poems are so human and so touching (cf. the poem entitled "Pain"). Moreover, they are full of a warm sympathy towards nature, for in his eyes nature is not impersonal but the very face of the spirit.

Almost all his poems express communion with the spirit of life which endows all things and beings with the halo of a magic presence, as if they reopened the dried-up source of primitive, myth-creating poetry. The world seems new and wonderful when the humblest things have a soul, and a scientific mind is bound to be startled by this transfigured world.

> Raymond Tschumi. *Thought in*
> *Twentieth-Century English Poetry*
> (London, Routledge & Kegan Paul, 1951),
> pp. 251–53

In *The Avatars* his experiences of the early 'nineties are remembered and recapitulated. He describes a poet, a painter, a sculptor, an old thinker, an anarchist, and others, who have independently retired to a lonely part of Ireland, dissatisfied with a mechanical civilisation and anxious to reconsider their relationship with the world. They have intimations of a joyful personality about to arise out of the clay. They have, they gradually realise, been called together as men capable of sensing and describing a new development of the human consciousness. They are the forerunners. Then the Avatars appear, Aodh and Aoife, a young peasant and a princess. A cult of joy spreads wherever they go. The civilised powers thereupon send police or agents, who infiltrate into a festival and bludgeon them, and they disappear. But their cult grows through legends and the artistic records of the forerunners.

Despite the weariness that drove him out of Ireland, AE could not conclude mournfully. His temperament would not allow it. *The Avatars* seems to say that though the Irish revolution resulted in a mechanical, commercial civilisation like any other (this is implied in the allegory of the bludgeoning of the Avatars by the police of the world's mechanised states), the Avatars had made their appearance and spread their new religion or sensibility, and the work of the forerunners—of Yeats and Synge and AE and their friends, he means—remained as the record of that appearance and the nucleus of a rich culture: ". . . impulses springing up deeply within us were messages from the gods . . ." But while this final optimstic statement does affirm that Ireland had her Messiah, it also confesses that AE is tired of revolutions that only produce new civilisations, and thus it looks forward to some future revelation which will release man from the burden of building new States and systems of law and ethics. For it is the differentiating characteristic of Aodh and Aoife that they have left no body of doctrine, no ethic; and no civlisation can be reared on their example.

What have they done, then? By their gaiety they have taught men (says AE, using his life-long myth of the soul returning to the heights of its original godhead, strengthened by its knowledge of the depths) to climb the terraces of being. He writes that all Messiahs have taught gaiety, that certainly Christ taught it, but that their disciples have afterwards concealed it and substituted a doctrine of pain.

By naming gaiety as the distinctive Avatar-quality, AE points to the great lacuna in his life and writing. He had the build of a jester, and his friends knew his humorous side, but he published like a sad, solemn, earnest man.

Herbert Howarth. *The Irish Writers: 1880–1940*
(New York, Hill & Wang, 1958), pp. 207–8

Yeats made himself into a dedicated poet: A.E. preferred the multiplicity of a life most strangely divided between immense activity in both the material and spiritual worlds. Like Yeats he came easily under the influence of Indian mysticism; he was a Theosophist (that sect met thrice a week in Dublin) and a contributor to *The Theosophical Review*. His copy of Madame Blavatsky's *The Secret Doctrine* was heavily underlined. More important were the works of Max Müller, Edwin Arnold, Charles Johnston. He knew from a comparatively early age the *Bhagavadgita* and the *Upanishads*, and it is not fantastic to perceive certain similarities with Tagore, perhaps even with Gandhi. And in some curious fashion the concern of the Hindu sacred books with a rural civilization, and the need for its reconstruction as well as the maintenance of its culture, in India and Ireland, gave weight to his unremitting propaganda for the Irish Agricultural Organization, as well as to his concern with the high and sacred places through which divinity might exhale. (We remember Yeats's praise of CrôPatric, of Mount Meru.) He was concerned with Spiritualism, and with psychic experiments as to the means by which visionary experiences may be induced. . . .

Like Yeats, the Hindu wisdom developed side by side with a projection of the Celtic mythology with its euphoneous pantheism, into a kind of Irish Druidic twilight of the Elder Gods, linked to the very soil and stone of ancient Ireland: the Indian and the Celtic giving each other material support as Byzantium had certified Ireland. There is no shadow of doubt as to his complete sincerity. Standish O'Grady relates how he visited Bray one fine Sunday, and saw a bearded young man "evangelizing" the crowd of holiday-makers; he was preaching faith in the pagan gods of Ireland. That is typical of a sort of gentle unselfconscious fearlessness that followed him throughout his life. [1964]

T. R. Henn. *Last Essays: Mainly on Anglo-Irish Literature*
(New York, Barnes & Noble, 1976), pp. 138–39

A.E. made six principal collections of his poems. Three of these belong to his early years when he was active in the Theosophical Society; one was completed when he was editor of *The Irish Statesman*; and two other volumes were published after his retirement as editor in 1930. These dates reflect the intensity of his early visions and the resolution of the older man to put in final form truths acquired in his youth. *Collected Poems* appeared in 1913 and in enlarged forms in 1919 and 1935. His most available work is *Selected Poems* (1935), arranged by the original volumes in which the poems appeared. This gathering, he said, contained the work by which he would like to be remembered. *Collected Poems*, however, has the poems of his first three volumes ordered according to themes, a method which makes it exceptionally difficult to study A.E.'s development as a poet. Although his poems seldom attain the radiance of a unified work of art, they provide an important means for examining the intense experiences of a man dedicated to his visions. In a sense, his poems comprise a spiritual autobiography, the distillation of his inner life.

Since A.E.'s poems have long been out of print, an explication . . . may illustrate his approach to poetry. A.E. called "The Great Breath," published in his first volume, the most complete statement of his beliefs. . . . This poem, A.E. said, arose from his reading a critique of Hegel's view that the Absolute becomes self-conscious as it moves through the universe. The critic argued that no change could occur in a perfect being, but change might be attributed to the divine mind as it passed through nature. Later A.E. read an Indian mystic who related divine mind to primordial substance. A.E. himself came to regard primordial substance as the mirror of the divine mind and therefore the Ancient Beauty. But the poem surprised him; he was unconscious of its creation, and he began to murmur it line by line. In this instance he felt that philosophical thought followed the psyche into a spiritual state where genius makes beauty, joy, dance, and song, and where drab logic is changed into "colour and music and a rapture of prophecy" (*Song and Its Fountains*, pp. 69–72).

The "opalhush" language, however, suggests a late Victorian effort to rise above a daily world plagued with change, decay, and death. The poet seeks a beauty beyond nature and hopes to tap a hidden source of being in metaphors like "The great deep thrills."

Richard M. Kain and James H. O'Brien,
George Russell (A.E.)
(Lewisburg, Pa., Bucknell Univ. Pr., 1976),
pp. 68–70

In both *Homeward* and *The Earth Breath* a general, inconsistent progression emerges within the separate volumes. The earlier collection, by example, begins with the "Prelude," a caution against the visionary losing sight of the divine because of the attractions of the "sun-rich day"; by the final poem, however, real and ideal have merged into a stable union, the divine made manifest in common things. As in *The Earth Breath*, this movement from pure vision to inclusion of the real world passes through poems of pain in which the narrator is separated both from his vision and from other people. Yet the awareness of pain and suffering rarely becomes more explicit than as a loss of vision and a separation from the divine. In recording what he regarded as his most intense experiences, therefore, his ecstatic visions, Russell produced his most notable work.

The most successful poems of vision in *Homeward* are "By the Margin of the Great Deep," "The Great Breath," and the sequence "Dusk," "Night," "Dawn," and "Day." The first of these begins in sunset, the typical occasion for Russell's poetic visions, and the spirit of unity running through all of nature and humankind brings him feelings of "peace and sleep and dreams." Yet the vision, at this early part of the volume, also draws him apart from domestic life and even human contact in his longings for the "primeval being." Sunset likewise introduces "The Great Breath," the fading sky suggesting both a cosmic flower and an awareness that the death of beauty occasions its most complete fulfillment. This unstable insight, like the paradox of spiritual union through physical separation in the above poem, becomes more nearly resolved in the four-poem sequence. Instead of sunset, the mingling of chimney fires from a village signifies the merging of humanity within "the vast of God." Night, for Russell, usually brings on despair and loss of vision, as in "The Dawn of Darkness"; in "Waiting" he can only hope that dawn will shake off this sadness and reawaken humanity to its former joy. The above sequence reverses this process, however. "Night" brings on a rebirth of spirit and beauty, a complete union of "living souls," while "Dawn" begins to fragment the unity. In the light of common day, vision is lost but not entirely forgotten, for a dim awareness of "a thread divine" keeps humankind still yearning for the "dim heights" and recalling, in dream, the "Light of Lights." This last phrase, echoing *The Countess Cathleen*, or the "hair of the twilight" ("Mystery") that shields the visionary in ways similar to *The Wind Among the Reeds*, or the characteristic combination of "sad and gay" feelings ("Inheritance")—all these directly link Russell's work with Yeats's.

The range of vision that Russell sketches out in the above sequence and the unity of the four poems succeed far better than his attempts elsewhere to link mortal pain with immortal vision.

Wayne E. Hall. *Shadowy Heroes:*
Irish Literature of the 1890s
(Syracuse, N.Y., Syracuse Univ. Pr., 1980),
pp. 146–47

SHAW, GEORGE BERNARD (1856–1950)

An intelligent critic of George Bernard Shaw's *Man and Superman*—without doubt the author's most notable and mature book—entitled his article "The New St. Bernard." There was a certain felicity in this emphasis of the resemblance between Shaw's attitude and that of the great saint with whom he is so closely connected. The famous Christian ascetics of mediaeval times, and very notably St. Bernard, delighted to disrobe beauty of its garment of illusion; with cold hands and ironical smile they undertook the task of analysing its skin-deep fascination, and presented, for the salutary contemplation of those affected by the lust of the eyes, the vision of what seemed to them the real Woman, deprived of her skin. In the same spirit Shaw—developing certain utterances in Nietzsche's *Zarathustra*—has sought to analyse the fascination of women as an illusion of which the reality is the future mother's search of a husband for her child; and hell for Shaw is a place where people talk about beauty and the ideal.

While, however, it may be admitted that there is a very real affinity between Shaw's point of view in this matter and that of the old ascetics—who, it may be remarked, were often men of keen analytic intelligence and a passionately ironic view of life—it seems doubtful whether on the whole he is most accurately classified among the saints. It is probable that he is more fittingly placed among the prophets, an allied but still distinct species. The prophet, as we may study him in his numerous manifestations during several thousand years, is usually something of an artist and something of a scientist, but he is altogether a moralist. He foresees the future, it is true—and so far the vulgar definition of the prophet is correct—but he does not necessarily foresee it accurately. [1904]

Havelock Ellis. *From Marlowe to Shaw*
(London, Williams and Norgate, 1950), p. 291

Mrs. "Kitty" Warren, the central character of Shaw's most remarkable play [*Mrs. Warren's Profession*] (and it is one of the most remarkable plays, in many ways, of the time) is a successful practitioner of what Kipling calls the oldest profession in the world. She is no betrayed milkmaid or cajoled governess, this past mistress of the seventh unpardonable sin, but a wide-awake and deliberate sinner, who has studied the problem thoroughly and come to the conclusion, like Huckleberry Finn, that it is better, by far, to sin and be damned than to remain virtuous and suffer. The conflict in the play is between Mrs. Warren and her daughter, and in developing it, Shaw exhibits his insight into the undercurrents of human nature to a superlative degree. Mrs. Warren, though she is a convention smasher, does not stand for heterodoxy. In truth despite all her elaborate defense of herself and her bitter arraignment of the social conditions that have made her what she is, she is a worshiper of respectability and the only true believer, save one, in the play. It is Vivie, her daughter, a virgin, who holds the brief against orthodoxy.

"If I had been you, mother," says Vivie, in the last scene, when the two part forever, "I might have done as you did; but I should not have lived one life and believed another. You are a conventional woman at heart. That is why I am leaving you now."

This complexity of character has puzzled a good many readers of the play, but though there is a complexity, there is no real confusion. Mrs. Warren, despite her ingenious reasoning, is a vulgar, ignorant woman, little capable of analyzing her own motives. Vivie, on the other hand, is a girl of quick intelligence and extraordinary education—a Cambridge scholar, a mathematician and a student of the philosophies. As the play opens Mrs. Warren seems to have all the best of it. She is the rebel and Vivie is the slave. But in the course of the strangely searching action, there is a readjustment. Convention overcomes the mother and crushes her; her daughter, on the other hand, strikes off her shackles and is free. . . .

Mrs. Warren's Profession, as a bit of theatrical mechanics, is unsurpassed. Its events proceed with the inevitable air that marks the work of a thoroughly capable journeyman: not a scene is out of place; not a line is without its meaning and purpose. . . .

Taken as a play, the drama is wellnigh faultless. It might well serve, indeed, as a model to all who aspire to place upon the stage plausible records of human transactions. [1905]

Henry L. Mencken. George Bernard Shaw: His
Plays (New Rochelle, N.Y., Edwin V. Glaser,
1969), pp. 1–2, 7–8

It is well to begin with the superficial; and this is the superficial effectiveness of Shaw; the brilliancy of bathos. But of course the vitality and value of his plays does not lie merely in this; any more than the value of Swinburne lies in alliteration or the value of Hood in puns. This is not his message; but it is his method; it is his style. The first taste we had of it was in this play of *Arms and the Man*; but even at the very first it was evident that there was much more in the play than that. Among other things there was one thing not unimportant; there was savage sincerity. Indeed, only a ferociously sincere person can produce such effective flippancies on a matter like war; just as only a strong man could juggle with cannon-balls. It is all very well to use the word "fool" as synonymous with "jester"; but daily experience shows that it is generally the solemn and silent man who is the fool. It is all very well to accuse Mr. Shaw of standing on his head; but if you stand on your head you must have a hard and solid head to stand on. In *Arms and the Man* the bathos of form was strictly the incarnation of a strong satire in the idea. . . .

We can best see how the play symbolises and summarises Bernard Shaw if we compare it with some other attack by modern humanitarians upon war. Shaw has many of the actual opinions of Tolstoy. Like Tolstoy he tells men, with coarse innocence, that romantic war is only butchery and that romantic love is only lust. But Tolstoy objects to these things because they are real; he really wishes to abolish them. Shaw only objects to them in so far as they are ideal; that is in so far as they are idealised. Shaw objects not so much to war as to the attractiveness of war. He does not so much dislike love as the love of love. Before the temple of Mars Tolstoy stands and thunders "There shall be no wars"; Bernard Shaw merely murmurs, "Wars if you must; but for God's sake, not war songs." Before the temple of Venus Tolstoy cries terribly, "Come out of it!"; Shaw is quite content to say, "Do not be taken in by it." Tolstoy seems really to propose that high passion and patriotic valour should be destroyed. Shaw is more moderate; and only asks that they should be desecrated. Upon this note, both about sex and conflict, he was destined to dwell through much of his work with the most wonderful variations of witty adventure and intellectual surprise. [1909]

G. K. Chesterton. George Bernard Shaw
(London, The Bodley Head, 1948), pp. 112–14

English people have been disconcerted by Shaw's ability to view them from the outside, as it were. They should remember that he is merely exercising the privilege of the expatriate. Denationalised Irishmen are all capable of similarly disinterested criticism, and do not refrain from it, even in Ireland, where their position imposes obligations of caution. Shaw has no such obligations, and is, therefore, in a position to say more freely and more generally, what the others have whispered or felt, at least in some particular connection. . . .

Shaw is never more faithful to Irish Protestant tradition than when he exhibits scepticism towards the virtues of England, without, however, turning definitely against her. He is sufficiently aloof to be critical, but his instincts draw him so inevitably to the English people that he cannot be really inimical. In short, he is that perfect type of *sans patrie* which the anglicisation of Ireland has produced; men who cannot understand their own compatriots, and must necessarily take refuge among a people with whom they are condemned to be aliens.

Many critics of Bernard Shaw, struggling with the postulate that he is a puritan, have pointed out flaws in the theory. The contradictions can be resolved by reference to his Protestantism. Irish Protestantism differs considerably from English puritanism, although their lines coincide at certain points. The former has the advantage of presenting an undivided religious front, whereas the latter, by the exclusion of the Anglican Church, loses its homogeneity. Shaw himself has explained this solidarity of Episcopalian and Dissenter in Ireland, which enabled him to be educated at a Methodist College, where the minority of pupils belonged to that sect. Social and political circumstances make cohesion possible amongst Irish Protestants. The negative virtue of being non-Catholic dispenses with those dogmatic *nuances* which render intercourse between Anglican and Nonconformist a different problem in England. Shaw had the typical school life of his class, and justly boasts that, in consequence, his is the true Protestantism.

Ernest A. Boyd. *Appreciations and Depreciations*
(London, T. Fisher Unwin, 1917), pp. 111–13

Ireland has taken very little interest in Bernard Shaw, but, then, Bernard Shaw has always been intersted in Ireland. While the greater part of the world paid homage to his genius, Ireland was not impressed. Shaw could be proud of Ireland if it pleased him but Ireland would not be proud of Shaw. He has emphasised the fact that he is an Irishman upon every part of the world, but so far, he has failed to make his own countrymen believe it. Here is a dramatist whose name can pack the theatres of Europe and America, a man who has revitalised the drama with a stream of ideas, whose wit is the most delightful in the drama of our time, and whose influence upon future thought and life is certain to be profound and widely spread, yet his compatriots are neither interested nor impressed. His ideas are ignored or regarded as pernicious in Ireland, and his wit is too common to be remarkable. Sometimes, it is true, he is taken seriously, as when a public library will ban his books because its committee has heard he is an "immoral" writer. Possibly Shaw would rather be banned than ignored, and so he may prefer the Kilkenny which banned him to the Dublin which ignores him. And Dublin does ignore him. Not the little cliques—they spurn him—but the masses of the people. A play by Shaw may run for many months in New York, Berlin, London, or Prague, but it cannot fill a theatre for one week in Dublin. Many years ago when *Man and Superman* first came to Dublin, the audience at each performance would hardly fill the Abbey Theatre. With *John Bull's Other Island*, and the Company from the Court Theatre, it was very little better. Since those days the Abbey Theater has produced several of Shaw's plays to audiences that were good, and Dublin has begun to take notice, so that recently *Saint Joan* had very good houses for a *week* at the Gaiety Theatre. For over thirty years Shaw has been writing and producing plays, yet his reputation would be negligible were it to be founded upon the appreciation of his own countrymen. Ibsen could rely upon Norway, Pirandello can rely upon Rome, Benavente's fame rests upon Madrid; Shaw alone among the great modern dramatists has no fame in the city of his birth. But then neither has Synge. And Shaw is as Irish as Synge. Synge chose to depict the life of Ireland in his plays, while Shaw chose the life of England. It is the manner in which the material is used rather than the material itself which is of importance, and the manner in which Shaw uses English life is the manner of an alien. He has chosen to live in England, but he took with him to London a mind fashioned in Dublin, and that mind remains a Dublin mind to-day as his speech retains the accent of Dublin.

Andrew E. Malone. DM. Aug., 1925, pp. 32–33

John Bull's Other Island (1904) is essentially a British comedy, indigenous to the soil, topical and nationally local, with little or no likelihood of, or potentiality for, crossing frontiers. It is in the line of classic tradition in British comedy—Goldsmith, Sheridan, Wilde, Shaw—embodying witty and searching satire by Irishmen of English temperament, character, politics and social life. Shaw, this "fatherlandless fellow" (*vaterlandlose Geselle*) as the Germans during the World War scornfully called him, surpasses his fellow countrymen in objectivity; for he possesses the essential dramatic quality of abstraction, the ability to rise above the limitation and weakness of mere patriotism. He "saw through" the Irish no less capably than through the English; and preserves a remarkably even balance in his portrayal and criticism of the two peoples.

John Bull's Other Island marked a turning-point in Shaw's career as a dramatist. It came at the "psychological moment," to give immense vogue to the modified-repertory-system project, inaugurated by H. Granville-Barker and J. E. Vedrenne at the Royal Court Theatre. It is a pre-eminently "pleasant play," genial, witty, amusing. The English people, endowed with an unparalleled equanimity in accepting criticism that is clever and unmalicious, rose to Shaw's play. It came also at a political *Sturm und Drang* period, and triumphantly rode on the crest of the wave.

The gods of English society, upon whose knees ever rests the ultimate fate of the British artist, suddenly awoke at last to the realization that a genius was living in their midst. *John Bull's Other Island* is a typical Shaw play; but it has a solidity of workmanship, a closer verisimilitude, than any of his earlier plays. The characters are set firmly upon solid ground: as W. B. Yeats deftly put it, this is the "first play of Bernard Shaw's that has a geography." This true drama of national character portrays in a masterly way the conflict of racial types. Shaw stands revealed as a worthy descendant of Molière, a master of comic irony, and at heart a poet. . . .

A digression from drama is necessary at this point, to exhibit the relations connecting Shaw with Ireland, his native land. *John Bull's Other Island* is notable, not only as drama, but as the occasion, on publication, of introducing to the public a political pamphleteer of the first rank. The "Preface for Politicians" is a masterly performance, whether viewed as literary essay or political pamphlet. Not in vain has Shaw studied the technic of the master pamphleteers whom great political struggles have summoned to the fore in

British public life: Swift of mordant satire, Cobbett of violent invective, Carlyle of prophetic commination, Ruskin of devastating and wholesale condemnation. Shaw's analysis of the problem of Ireland imparts that tingling sense which only truth alive can give. The heart of the pamphlet is the sentence in the section, "A Natural Right": "the final reason why Ireland must have Home Rule is that she has a natural right to it."

Archibald Henderson. *Bernard Shaw, Playboy and Prophet* (New York, Appleton, 1932), pp. 570–71, 574–75

If *Pygmalion* is a fair example of a personal play, which plays of Shaw are best called disquisitory? Shaw himself first applied the term to *Getting Married* which, with *Misalliance*, remains the most celebrated and straightforward example of the genre, though the method is found earlier in "Don Juan in Hell" and later in a series of plays ending, for the present, with *In Good King Charles's Golden Days*.

Although many people think of all Shaw's plays as discussion plays, Shaw was already a veteran playwright when he first wrote a full-length play consisting of a series of conversations unbroken by act or scene divisions. *Getting Married* is not a variant of farce, melodrama, or any other established kind of dramatic structure. It is something new—a new dramaturgy and not, as its critics thought, a mere pamphlet in dialogue form. It is closer even to orthodox dramaturgy than to pamphleteering.

Though the mode of presentation is endless talk, the plot-pattern is orthodox if unobtrusive. The whole discussion is built around a situation; and in the course of the play the outcome is decided. A young couple is about to be married. A last-minute obstacle arises, as on the stage such obstacles often do. All that is unusual is the nature of the obstacle: a pamphlet on marriage by Belfort Bax. The difficulties accumulate, but suddenly there occurs a pleasant reversal: the couple have slipped out and been married in spite of all. There are also sub-plots. A divorced couple are re-united. The man who was to have been the second husband of the divorcée goes off to form a Platonic-Shavian *ménage à trois* with a happily married couple.

The conversational mode should not blind us to the fact that there is plot enough here for any comedy. What distinguishes Shaw's play is, first, the mode itself which tends to hide the plot and, second, the oblique relation of plot to theme. A plot may be used straightforwardly as in ordinary story-telling and play-writing. It may be used ironically as in Shavian inversions of melodrama. But if Shaw's melodramas may be said to turn the plot upside down, his disquisitory plays, so to say, leave it alone, isolate it, treat it with contumely. Given the plot of *The Devil's Disciple* you might guess what would happen to it in Shaw's hands. Given the plot of *Getting Married* you would remain completely in the dark. For if in the personal plays the dialogue is tied to the main situations and events, in the disquisitory plays the dialogue gets the upper hand. Yet the plot is not reduced to complete impotence. There is still interaction between theme and plot, between the ideas and their narrative vehicle. The new factor is that the ideas are now becoming more dramatic than the events. In *The Devil's Disciple* we have a violent plot with the more silent and interesting inner action in the background. In *Getting Married* the plot is in the background, for the inner action has become more adequately vocal. The point has been reached at which Shaw can bring it into the foreground. [1947]

Eric Bentley. *Bernard Shaw: A Reconsideration*
(New York, W. W. Norton, 1976), pp. 127–28

Socialism is in one sense the underlying subject of all Shaw's plays, but since it early proved a very unpopular subject, he abandoned it as an explicit theme after *Mrs. Warren's Profession* and did not return to it until *Man and Superman*. But whereas *Mrs. Warren* is a savage indictment of capitalism, *Man and Superman* is a complex satire of socialism itself. Obviously, these two plays mark off successive stages in a process of disillusionment. The tides of hope and despair are not easily traced in a thinker so complexly inconsistent, so deviously autobiographical, and so much the opportunist at once of public events and of his own inspiration. Shaw seldom admits a disappointment—perhaps not even to himself—without being ready to proclaim a new hope. Consequently, the same drama may contain both pessimism and optimism, revealing the new faith with the ghost of the old faith in its arms. Or again, it may simply take up a new set of problems.

The outward causes of his disillusionment were political events. The inward cause was what might be called his millennial temperament. Like all passionate idealists, he looked for a miraculous deliverance within his own lifetime, yet like most Victorian reformers, he was also realistic and sagacious, with a keen sense of practical possibilities. Consequently, he was trapped between his vision and the facts. As he grew older, he apparently hoped more and more desperately for less and less. He invented more and more ingenious reasons for optimism, more and more violent cures for a chronic ailment.

The first stage of his disillusionment appears in *Mrs. Warren* (1894), which is bitter satire followed by a change of subject. The second stage appears in *Man and Superman* (1903), which—somewhat inconsistently—ridicules parlor Fabianism, indicts democracy, denies social progress, asserts biological progress, proposes eugenics as a means of attaining the superman, and exalts meditation above action. A third stage appears in *Major Barbara* (1905), which impatiently sweeps away meditation and ideas as totally incapable of influencing the world of action and finds in the violent clash of materialistic egotisms themselves the promise of a Marxist millennium. A fourth and ultimate stage appears in *Heartbreak House* (1913–1919), which sees England as a declining Empire and a corrupt democracy doomed to destruction in a world plunging into the ultimate irrationality of war. After *Heartbreak House*, the story repeats itself with more desperation, more extravagance, more despair, more subterfuge and evasion. Ardent reformers with a strong sense of practical reality nearly always become sadder but not always wiser: either, like Kingsley, they sacrifice their vision to common sense; or, like Shaw, common sense to their vision.

William Irvine. *The Universe of George Bernard Shaw* (New York, Whittlesley House, 1949), pp. 235–36

Next to his optimism and his energy, the most striking thing about Shaw was his furious eclecticism. He felt no necessity to choose between the various modern prophets. He would take something from them all, and moreover he would reconcile the most disparate. He was an Ibsenite of course. But he was also, or was soon to become, a disciple of Marx, of Nietzsche, of Bergson, of Wagner, of Samuel Butler, and of John Bunyan. Besides becoming a socialist, he was also a nonsmoker, a teetotaler, a vegetarian, an antivaccinationist, an antivivisectionist and an advocate of reformed spelling.

All this would have been more than enough to give a serious case of intellectual indigestion to anyone else, but for him it was merely very stimulating and very nourishing. Sooner or later the teaching of all his masters was synthesized, one furnishing an economic system, another a moral system, a third a metaphysic, and a fourth a religion. Though he never wrote it all down in systematic form, Shaw has at one time or another propounded the parts of what is probably the most inclusive body of doctrine since Thomas Aquinas.

One thing which made this possible was a sort of cheerful optimism enabling him to temper the more intransigent doctrines of his various masters and to fall back upon the formula "What this really means is . . ." Moreover, what it really meant was usually something less intransigent as well as frequently gentler and more kindly than the doctrine of his masters is generally assumed to be.

In the plays of the first decade especially, this cheerful determination to tame the wild men and to draw the fangs of revolution seems particularly striking. Nietzsche's doctrine of the superman—which might seem to others to foreshadow a blond beast, amoral and ruthless—tends to become no more than a rather extravagant method of recommending self-help and improvement. *The Revolutionist's Handbook*, supposed to have been written by the rebellious John Tanner, hero of *Man and Superman*, begins by breathing fire and then carefully explains that in democratic England there is all the revolution necessary every time the voters have recourse to the ballot box. In the same book a shocking section ridiculing sexual morality and especially the sentimental word "purity" ends by demonstrating that, since the number of men and women in England is approximately equal, monogamy is the only sensible system. In that same play even Strindberg's battle of the sexes, described by Tanner in the first scene as a remorseless struggle where the only question is which party shall destroy the other, turns out to be but a sort of sham battle in the course of which the Life Force makes the hero and heroine temporarily irrational in order that it may benevolently trick them into sacrificing what they believe to be their desires in favor of their deepest impulse—which is to try to create better offspring.

Joseph Wood Krutch. *Modernism in Modern Drama*
(Ithaca, N.Y., Cornell Univ. Pr., 1953), pp. 50–51

Whether an idea is philosophical or social, Shaw has little purely esthetic interest in it. It must measure up to the crucial test of applicability to human conduct: If we accept this idea, what effect will it have on society? What will it do to our stature as men? Is it defeatist? These are the questions Shaw asks himself, and they all reduce to one question: Will the idea help man impose his will on his surroundings? With such a simple criterion for truth, Shaw has great confidence in his ability to evaluate ideas. The higher man depends less on systematic thought and more on instinct, for evolution is always reducing slow and difficult thought processes to effortless second nature. Thus Shaw hopes that "the most prolonged and difficult operations of our minds may yet become instantaneous, or, as we call it, instinctive" (*Back to Methuselah*, xxvii). And even in the primitive twentieth century a thinker who is tuned in to the Life Force may have almost perfect pitch in sounding out ideas: he may judge them by their emotional rightness.

This is not to say that Shaw is intellectually lazy. Nothing could be farther from the truth. The passion with which he accepts or rejects ideas is the passion of the intellect (he habitually classifies intellect among the passions), no easy taskmaster for a thinker. Still, Shaw defines a passion as "an overwhelming impulse towards a more abundant life"—and no passion other than the passion for truth is likely to serve a philosopher well. But the truth may turn out to lead to a *less* abundant life, unhappily. Shaw permits philosophy to serve his humanistic optimism, and the result is a resonant affirmation of faith in man and mind rather than a cogent system. Let me suggest a permutation of my chapter title: Shaw is a *philosophical socialist*, in that his social thought springs from ideological rather than factual roots; and he is a *social philosopher*, in that his philosophy follows the grail of human betterment. In his thought, as in his style, a concern with that which is peculiarly human is the driving force.

Richard M. Ohmann. *Shaw: The Style and the Man*
(Middletown, Conn., Wesleyan Univ. Pr., 1962),
pp. 152–53

If Shaw ended [*John Bull's Other Island*] by counselling Ireland against imitating England's capitalistic ways, he took care all along to ridicule and reduce the opposite course, a retreat into the mists of Irish Romance. He scorns Celticism, laughs at the idea that Irish heroic legend has any meaning for anyone but the English tourist armed with a guidebook, and exposes the Stage-Irish idealized peasant as an altogether contemptible fraud. . . .

Shaw's presentation was fundamentally an attack upon the conventions of Irish Romance; but further, the conventions attacked became propositions in a discussion of Irish reality. In the discussion, Tom Broadbent constantly propounds a conventional view and Larry Doyle exposes the reality, while persons like Tim Haffigan, Matt Haffigan, Barney Doran, and Patsy Farrell illustrate the discourse. Ultimately, however, Shaw had more in mind than simple illustration. Nora Reilly, the Irish Heiress, poor, proud, and undernourished, appears to Larry Doyle as "*an incarnation of everything in Ireland that drove him out of it.*" She is nevertheless all charm itself to the conquering Englishman, and she becomes his prize. Other illustrative personages are equally broad "incarnations" by virtue of the stereotypes whose place they fill, and they speak for a group or a point of view in the forum of ideas.

On the highest level of the drama of ideas in *John Bull's Other Island*, underlying the national and the economic debates, is the debate between Action and Thought as embodied in Tom Broadbent, the Englishman, and Larry Doyle, the Irishman. For all the partnership of Doyle and Broadbent, there is also a grave separation, and the man of realistic imagination can only alternate between the acceptance of thoughtless action and the torments of helpless thought. "I wish I could find a country to live in," Doyle says, "where the facts were not brutal and the dreams not unreal"; but he doesn't believe in such a country. The union of vision and action is asserted by Peter Keegan, who is, he declares, "a Catholic. My country is not Ireland nor England, but the whole mighty realm of my Church." To both the man of thought and the man of action he reveals his vision of the Trinity, in which opposites are reconciled and dreams become reality. Peter Keegan is one of Shaw's visionary realists raised to sanctity and the reputation of madness. In preaching his own religion, Shaw was more and more given to proclaiming the ultimate harmony of vitality and thought; and Peter Keegan, whose Church was the Church of the Life Force, harmonizes the debate between action and imagination, England and Ireland, in his prophetic dream of a heaven on earth. . . .

Martin Meisel. *Shaw and the Nineteenth-Century Theatre* (Princeton, N.J., Princeton Univ. Pr., 1963), pp. 287–89

"Learn everything," Shaw once advised novelists in a lecture on fiction, "and when you know it, stick to naturalism, and write every word as if you were on your oath in a witness box." It is not generally realized how seriously Shaw

took his own advice as far as naturalism was concerned. Most training in literary tradition is in fact a positive impediment in understanding Shaw. When
Shaw introduces literary conventions into his plays, it is most often to demonstrate how absurdly they misrepresent human behavior, or how silly the moral
assumptions behind them are. The effect of boldly introducing what he had
observed in life onto the stage fell so far short of theatrical expectations that
audiences frequently mistook Shaw's realism for perverse farce. . . .

Is Shaw dated? The answer is yes, as every classic is dated. The specific
personalities and political crises that moved him to write are now part of history, as Plato's and Aristophanes' debaters and statesmen are. The images of
his plays belong to an eternal world, as his ideas on government, economics,
sex, psychology, logic, and art, now seen apart from the novel and amusing
expression he gave them, form part of a perennial philosophy which we can
call "Shavian." But there is still a third aspect of the question. One might perhaps hope that the particular social outrages Shaw wrote about in his
"problem" plays might by now be things of the past. Nothing could be more
gratifying than to pronounce Shaw hopelessly out of date in such matters. Unfortunately, I cannot see that this is so. To take two clear-cut examples: the
demoralization of men by poverty is still the world's first problem, and our
national system of criminology is still outrageously perverse in its intentions
and pernicious in its results.

Louis Crompton. *Shaw the Dramatist*
(Lincoln, Univ. of Nebraska Pr., 1969),
pp. vi–vii

John Bull's Other Island is the headiest mixture of paradoxical wit that Shaw
concocted: the dramatic conceit is extended to the last possible degree of
characterisation and action. Doyle, the Shavian Irishman, is set off against
professional Irishmen, English celticists, reactionary Catholics, the Irish
peasant landlord who is stupider, more grasping, and a greater obstacle to material progress than the English absentee kind, and all those who, in an Irish
context, obstruct the Life Force. Shaw was certainly not wholly wrong in saying, as he did later, that the play "was uncongenial to the whole spirit of the
neo-Gaelic movement, which is bent on creating a new Ireland after its own
ideal, whereas my play is a very uncompromising presentment of the real old
Ireland."

That Shaw's portrait of the "real old Ireland" might be scandalous libel is
scarcely to the point. The portraiture is caricature, existing for the sake of the
criticism of Irish life it embodies. Through his Doyle Shaw gives us the view
of an internationalist in the forefront of the evolutionary process that the Life
Force is unfolding. . . . Through Doyle, Ireland is contained within the Shavian scheme of creative evolution, the linear process described so elaborately
in *Back to Methuselah* that begins with individuality and carnality in fallen

Eden, passes through socialism, internationalism, and technology in civilisation, and ends in the realms of pure incorporeal thought in the last part of the Pentateuch: the very antithesis of the Yeatsian vision of essential individuality, or morality manifested through race, of recurrence and reincarnation, of the eternal opposition of spirit and body, and of sexuality that tries and fails to bridge the gulf. . . .

But . . . Doyle's views do not in the end utterly prevail. In the play's final paradox Doyle meets a man who is at least his equal: Keegan, the loony, unfrocked priest. From Keegan we hear that "Every dream is a prophecy: every jest is an earnest in the womb of Time," and this Irish dreamer, self-confessed madman, and poet leaves the efficient Shavian economist standing. . . .

At the end of *John Bull's Other Island* the unfrocked priest presents a vision of an Ireland run on good economic principles, well-fed, prosperous, and thoroughly efficient in every way, and it is a vision of Ireland betrayed by Irishmen and of Hell. Then he marches off to his Round Tower to dream of eternity, having demonstrated Doyle's idea of progress to be a half-truth at the best and leaving Doyle looking like a "stillborn poet."

The play finally acknowledges its own inappropriateness as a contribution to the creation of new moral and national purpose. For Edwardian England Shaw's emetic irony was salutary. Dublin in 1904, according to the best testimony for that year, Joyce's farraginous chronicle, stood more in need of unifying vision than analytical criticism: more in need of creative image than the intellectual structure erected by Shaw as a gallery in which to hang caricatures of the folly of his time.

M. J. Sidnell. In Robert O'Driscoll, ed., *Theatre and Nationalism in Twentieth Century Ireland* (Toronto, Univ. of Toronto Pr., 1971), pp. 166–68

Although Bernard Shaw called his *Heartbreak House* (written in 1916–17) a fantasia in the Russian manner upon English themes, and echoes of *The Cherry Orchard* unquestionably reverberate through it, the play might be profitably viewed as a fantasia in the Shakespearean manner upon Shavian themes. Whether or not Shaw recalled Swinburne's curious remark that *King Lear* was the work of Shakespeare the socialist, *Heartbreak House* seems clearly to have been designed, at least in part, as Shaw's *Lear*. Earlier he had tauntingly titled part of a preface to his *Caesar and Cleopatra* (1898) "Better than Shakespeare?"—suggesting a parallel with the Bard's *Antony and Cleopatra*; yet by presenting a kittenish young queen and an aging Caesar, rather than an aging but still sultry Cleopatra and a younger admirer, he had evaded any direct comparison. Like his Cleopatra play, Shaw's Lear was offered not in competition but as commentary.

G. B. S. waited until his nineties to point publicly to *Heartbreak House* as his *Lear*. Even then he did so guardedly through the disarming medium of a puppet play, perhaps to prevent the comparison from being taken as seriously as he inwardly still meant it to be, for in his lifetime the play's now very considerable reputation had never measured up to his expectation for it. "If the critics had the brains of a mad Tom," he grumbled, using a suggestive association with *Lear*, "they would realize it is my greatest play. But they don't. They all go following after the Maid of Orleans." Privately Shaw had hinted at the *Lear* connection almost as soon as he had completed the play. In 1917 actress Lillah McCarthy had asked him for details of the work, hoping to convince him to let her produce it or at least acquire a starring part in it. Shaw put her off. It was wartime, he pointed out, and the play was unpleasant, unsuitable fare for war conditions. The hero was an old man of eighty-eight, and there were no young males in the cast at all (its implicit recognition of the wartime dearth of leading men). The women were either too young or too old—an ingenue and two sisters in their middle forties. The sisters, Shaw confided—"I don't find them much more popular than Goneril or Regan"—were the old man's daughters. Disgusted with the dragged-out war and its effect on theatre as well as much else, he confessed that his heart was not in a London production of a new play. And Miss McCarthy—creator of some of Shaw's greatest roles, beginning with her Ann Whitefield in *Man and Superman*—appeared neither then nor afterward in a performance of *Heartbreak House*.

Stanley Weintraub. *Journey to Heartbreak: The Crucible Years of Bernard Shaw, 1914–1918* (New York, Weybright and Talley, 1971), pp. 333–34

Because of the singularity of Shaw's plays, and the polemical character of his prefaces, the formal principles of his dramatic system are easily overlooked, and, of course, there is also the possibility that they are not there. But since in all his plays the result is, in the end, a clarification, it may be said that his method is analytical. His plays normally set up a situation that is confused through misunderstandings, misconceptions, and pretenses. These are cleared away in the course of the action, so that at last the truth of the matter is in some measure manifest. Insofar as the characters are concerned, this process consists in first establishing the individual as he thinks he is, as a preliminary to the discovery of what he is in fact. Generally speaking, this discovery is climactic, an *anagnorisis* accompanied by a peripety, after which the play ends quickly. The method may properly be considered classic; but Shaw's comedies, unlike the ancient comedies, or their Renaissance versions, turn on spiritual recognitions and mark stages in the slow progress of self-discovery and self-knowledge. Such is the result not only of mature plays like *Heartbreak House*—which consists essentially of a series of such recognitions—or of earlier plays like *Blanco Posnet*, *The Devil's Disciple*, and *Captain Brass-*

bound's Conversion—each of which depicts a single crucial revelation—but also of Shaw's earliest comedies, from the time of *Widowers' Houses*. The process through which individuals come to know themselves may thus be regarded as representative of the evolution of the universal consciousness as it progressively dispels the illusions in which it is enveloped and achieves a more perfect self-awareness. From the viewpoint of *Back to Methuselah* each of Shaw's plays illustrates a phase in the process of Creative Evolution.

In the nature of things, self-knowledge cannot come about on a general scale purely as a spiritual development. The vital spirit is inextricably involved with matter, consequently the preconditions for spiritual progress include material considerations such as health and social reform. As men are presently constituted, mind and body are too intimately associated for the one to grow while the other is starved. Social and economic improvement are the indispensable prerequisites of spiritual enlightenment. However, it seemed unlikely to Shaw that anything substantial could be achieved along these lines until a superior order of humanity was engendered. "For remember," he wrote, "what our voters are in the pit and gallery they are also in the polling booth. We are all now under what Burke called 'the hoofs of the swinish multitude.'"

Necessary steps in the procreation of a superior humanity were the extension of the present life span, and the abandonment of love as a guide to human relations. In this regard Shaw found himself in accord with the latest literary currents. The symbolists had rejected love, along with nature, as vestiges of an outworn romanticism. For Shaw, love was the intellect of the mindless, an irrational desire to unite physically with the beautiful and the good; but it was useless to the superior mentality which forms such associations outside the physical realm. The consequences of this idea for Shaw's later comedies is most clearly apparent in *Pygmalion*.

Maurice Valency. *The Cart and the Trumpet: The Plays of George Bernard Shaw* (New York, Oxford Univ. Pr., 1973), pp. 425–26

Insofar as the play [*Heartbreak House*] is about the opposition between the impulses of life—curiosity, daring, resistance, the effort of seeking something better—and the impulses of death—comfort and happiness, cynical self-serving, and dreams of ease—the play is about Captain Shotover. These antithetical forces may momentarily cancel one another out and produce stasis, but they are not static, and the Captain's vital force is running down. His vitality has, as the Devil in *Man and Superman* predicted, been turned to the cause of destruction; his resistance to dreams of peace must be artificially bolstered by rum; and the effort of seeking has exhausted him. He is a once noble institution, with many of the lendings of his prime still about him, suffering inevitable deterioration, and yet having a will that refuses to yield without a struggle.

As we have seen looking at other plays, the inner divisions between and within characters often reflect larger moral and metaphysical contradictions inherent in human nature, or in the cosmos itself. And while Shaw had little use for such simplistic labels as Good and Bad, and openly scoffed at Virtue, his repeated insistence on his belief in the reality of sin suggests that one of the basic antitheses of his thinking was between sin and its opposite, whatever that might be called. Actually it is quite clear that the opposite is the Life Force, and that sin for Shaw was any element or quality that thwarts life. This might be, at one extreme, apathy, complacency, living in the past, anything that leads to impotence or sterility, and at the other, cruelty and hatred of life.

In most of the characters in *Heartbreak House* the impulses toward life and power and self-consciousness are set against, and indeed seem to generate, counter impulses, obstacles, oppositions; and characteristically the most basic contradictions seem to grow out of the most paradoxical of human experiences: love. In fact most of Shaw's plays, from *The Philanderer* to *The Millionairess*, are about love. That has, of course, been the single most popular subject of literature, and Shaw was never shy about seeking an audience. But beyond that, he found in the love relationship a model or symbol for both the dynamics and the most elemental polarities of human nature. In this respect, *Heartbreak House* is in both theme and central metaphor very much in the tradition of *Man and Superman*.

Robert F. Whitman. *Shaw and the Play of Ideas*
(Ithaca, N.Y., Cornell Univ. Pr., 1977), pp. 242–43

Without denying Shaw's assertion that he had opened the drama to wider interests, one is finally left with the claim which seems most conventional and may in fact be most radical: that his contribution had been to give his characters "human nature."

It seems at first a curious claim to be advanced by, or on behalf of, a playwright who has been accused of making his personages mere mouthpieces for his own views. Nor is the accusation invariably unjust: when Nicola of *Arms and the Man* cautions the impetuous Louk against offending their employers ("you dont know the power such high people have over the like of you and me when we try to rise out of our poverty against them"), we hear the voice not of a Bulgarian servant but of an English socialist. Such occasions, however, are rare. The voice of Vivie Warren is not that of Candida Morell, nor the voice of Jack Tanner that of Henry Higgins. Nevertheless, though these voices keep their individual timbres and speak to us of very different matters—of self-assertion, of maternal power, of sexual force, of linguistic creation—they all sound a common note. All of these figures, and indeed all of the crucial Shavian characters, whatever their genuine concerns with religion, politics, and professions, are deeply involved with those central familial relationships, including sexual relations, that more than any others define our "human nature." That many of these are symbolic does not make them any less real: Caesar's connection with Cleopatra, for example, is quite as paternal as Undershaft's with Barbara, having to do in both cases with questions of education, parental authority, and filial selfhood. That many of them involve negation makes them no less significant: Higgins' refusal of Eliza's demands is at least as meaningful as Tanner's yielding to Ann Whitefield's blandishments.

If a certain severity informs these Shavian relationships, it is that Shaw's own temper and upbringing offered him glimpses of our human circumstances denied to less penetrating and more equable natures. What Shaw chose to look at he saw, in the special light of his comic vision, with extraordinary, at times disturbing clarity. Strangely, the very exuberance of that comic energy (to return to those "amorphous qualities of temper and energy" of which Shaw spoke) tends to mask the austerity of the Shavian vision. So endearing are Shaw's comic creations that one sometimes fails to recognise how complex, even disquieting is their emotive environment. So positive is Shaw's vision of social and evolutionary progress that one hardly notices how disabused is his view of the human present and how profound his desire to transcend it. From the tension of these contradictory elements arises the Shavian drama, at once lucid and optimistic, elusive and despairing. It is the most notable body of drama to be written in English, perhaps in any language, since Shakespeare.

Arthur Ganz. *George Bernard Shaw* (New York,
Grove, 1983), pp. 2–4

What Shaw rightly detected in Ibsen, and was most crucial for him, was a radical belief in artistic truth-telling that went far beyond any party-political platform. Ibsen spent most of his life avoiding identification with any political group and was particularly scornful of so-called progressive parties. His iconoclasm was not to be put to the service of a given set of social objectives. But that it was iconoclasm, and that Shaw was more nearly right about Ibsen than is normally supposed, is evident, for example, from Ibsen's comment in a letter about *Ghosts* before it was published: "*Ghosts* will probably cause alarm in some circles; but there is nothing to be done about it. If it didn't do that, there would have been no need to write it." Ibsen saw his own work, as Shaw saw it, as a contribution to a forward struggle to give people new images of truth, images which at first they would inevitably be unable to accept.

For Shaw Ibsen was the realist who at last enabled the theatre to escape from the vapid and meaningless ideals which had dominated it for so long. In *The Quintessence of Ibsenism* he explains the unorthodox use he makes of the terms realist and idealist. The idealist is the man who creates self-deceiving myths to make tolerable the reality of a life which he could not otherwise endure. The realist insists on the liberation of the human will from the artificial constraints of idealism which he rejects as deadening and unreal. He is prepared to face life objectively without the narcotics of the ideal. It can be fairly objected that this view of Ibsen as realist suits some plays more than others, and does not take into account Ibsen's deeply ambiguous attitude towards idealistic self-sacrifice. But it explains why Shaw so constantly stressed the modernity of Ibsen, and saw him as a crucial revolutionary writer along with Nietzsche or Schopenhauer. In Shaw's evolutionary concept of human culture Ibsen is one of the "pioneers of the march to the plains of heaven," moving forward the ideas of the race by destroying outmoded pieties and beliefs. It is in this spirit that Shaw celebrated Ibsen's "plays of nineteenth-century life with which he overcame Europe, and broke the dusty windows of every dry-rotten theatre in it from Moscow to Manchester."

Nicholas Grene. *Bernard Shaw: A Critical View*
(New York, St. Martin's Press, 1984), p. 7

SHIELS, GEORGE (1886–1949)

I think that George Shiels would be the last to claim that all his works are masterpieces. Yet *The New Gossoon*, the ninth of his plays, which was first produced in 1930 . . . has such qualities of craftsmanship and writing that a court of criticism would be hard set to describe it in any other terms. From the opening moments we get the illusion of life, and the play never falters on its way to the final curtain. One hardly wonders that an English critic was moved to write of his work: "To compare these plays with the monotony of the Mayfair drama of cuckoldry is to find freshness for staleness, characters for robots, and natural dialogue for artificial wit."

The New Gossoon for all its comedy is an interesting social document, for it mirrors the changing aspect of the Irish rural scene. Through the influence of the popular press, the radio, the cinema, the motor car, Irish country life tends to become increasingly urban in its character, and the contrast between the vanishing remnant of the older generation and the new becomes more striking with the passing of the years. In Shiels's play we have the conflict of these two generations—the young, scornful of the traditional view of life and conduct; the old, shocked and bewildered as they observe the lack of regard for such cherished sanctities as submission to parental control and the claim of the land to every atom of energy stored in healthy young bodies. . . .

The characters in *The New Gossoon* are all sharply drawn, and their vitality is such that they hold a permanent place in the memory. The study of the old vagabond poacher, Rabit Hamil, is as brilliantly observed as any figure in the drama of O'Casey, and Mr. McCormick's interpretation of the part is one of the joys of the theatre. The New Gossoon himself, his mother, his Uncle Peter, and Ned Shay are extremely well done.

The economy in the structure of the play, the careful elimination of any element that would tend to mar its sense of unity, and the swift rebound of the dialogue all go to show how astonishingly his art had matured.

T. C. Murray. In Lennox Robinson, ed., *The Irish Theatre* (London, Macmillan, 1939), pp. 127–29

Of the established Ulster playwrights on whose work the Group Theatre has relied George Shiels comes first. At the time of his death in 1949 he was the leading Irish dramatist. The quality and quantity of his work, sustained over a period of thirty years, merited for him that title. Three of his earliest plays were produced by the Ulster Literary Theatre: *Away from the Moss* (1918), *Felix Reid and Bob* (1919), and *The Tame Drudge* (1920?). Then he wrote for the Abbey, where he had his initial success with a one-act comedy, *Bedmates* (another political allegory) in 1921. . . .

His successful comedies *Professor Tim*, *Paul Tywning*, and *The New Gossoon* endeared Shiels to a wide public. Lennox Robinson has called him the Tom Moore of Irish drama, and by some critics (though not by Robinson) he has been decried, as Moore was, for his easy sentiment. But there is little sentiment in *The Rugged Path*; its comedy is edged with a devastating irony; and *The Passing Day* is a realistic study, etched in acid, of an Ulster business-man. The easy label "writer of comedy" does not fit Shiels. True, it was in this role he packed the Abbey Theatre and village-halls all over Ireland with laughter-loving audiences, but his own people in Ulster have seen a subtlety in his character-drawing and heard nuances in his dialogue which Southern audiences missed. While he would have been the last man to deny that he was an Irishman, he was also an Ulsterman, and when he wrote for Ulstermen he used a finer brush and more delicate tints. For a wider public he kept closer to the primary colours.

At the other extreme he has been condemned on the evidence of such plays as *The Passing Day* and *Macook's Corner* for his bitterness, but who can read *Tenants at Will* without being profoundly moved by its picture of the misery of a nation? The same deep current of sympathetic understanding is also found in other plays, in *The Jailbird*, for example, and notably in one which has not been produced. Its first act was published in *The Bell* (1942) under the title *He Kissed the Book*. . . .

In some ways his reputation as a playwright suffered by his success. Audiences demanded and managers refused to stage anything but sure-fire comedies. So he was blamed for being too conventional, for sticking to the success-ful formula, but when he experimented he could not get a stage. *Tenants at*

Will was originally a chronicle play—a vast canvas depicting against the background of the Devon Commission on the tenure of land (1844) the degradation of an entire people on the brink of famine. Even in the centenary year of the Commission no Irish theatre would touch it. Its rejection in its original form by the Abbey Theatre may have been due to artistic reasons, but the fact of its later acceptance when it had been pruned to the typical three-act-Abbey-peasant-play form indicates that it had been rejected because it was unusual. In the national theatres of most countries a theme of such importance treated by an author of Shiels's status would have compelled production.

David Kennedy. In Sam Hanna Bell, ed., *The Arts in
Ulster* (London, Harrap, 1951), pp. 58–60

George Shiels, in his long creative life of thirty-two years in which time he wrote some twenty plays, contributed to three major Irish theatres. There was his 'prentice work for the Ulster Literary Theatre, the important middle period when as an "Abbey dramatist" he gained his reputation in Europe and North America, and his association from 1940 with the Ulster Group Theatre. Five plays were written in the Group period: *Macook's Corner* (1942), originally written for the Abbey Theatre as *Neal Maquade*, *The Old Broom* (1944), *Borderwine* (1946), *Mountain Post* (1948) and *Slave Drivers* (1950). . . .

Although confined to his home because of an accident suffered in his early years in Canada . . . Shiels's perception and imagination were in no way circumscribed. When *The New Gossoon* was written the internal combustion engine had bellowed its way into a rural community that had changed little since the eighteenth century. Shiels heard it from his study window. Throughout the play Luke Cary's motorbike is always in the spectator's eye. "This is a theme which has been under everyone's eyes for the past twenty years," said Frank O'Connor, "but Shiels was the man who pounced on it. He presented it with an authenticity which is rare in modern literature."

What at times troubled Shiels's admirers was not his lack of knowledge of Irish provincial life but the probing bitterness with which he delineated it. "More like that of Swift," said O'Connor, "than of any other Irish writer." . . .

[Yet] for almost every one of his knaves we can counter with an admirable character. In *The Rugged Path* and *The Summit* there is the courage of Sean Tansey and the integrity of the police sergeant faced with the enmity of a brutalised mountainy family, themselves, as the playwright hints, victims of history. There is the compassion of the woman towards Dan Farran, the ex-convict in *The Jail-Bird*. There is the understanding and sympathy of the middle-aged farm hand, Ned Shay, for the new gossoon and his generation.

Lennox Robinson referred to Shiels as the Tom Moore of Irish drama. Other critics have decried him for his easy sentiment. But in those plays, probably the most important, where Shiels deals with the shoddier aspects of

Irish life, there is little sentimentality. Irony is his weapon and he points it home with a smile—sometimes a savage one.

Sam Hanna Bell. *The Theatre in Ulster* (Totowa, N.J., Rowman & Littlefield, 1972), pp. 77–81

George Shiels is a sheep in wolf's clothing in the theater who does his best work when his wild disguise hides his simple heart. He is a dramatist of conflicting impulses because he is equally capable of creating barbarous and benign comedy, antic laughter that shakes the foundations of society and sentimental denouements that restore and sanctify those foundations. Most of his characters "enter, disputing," but after they have indulged their comic contentiousness and rebellion in a variety of hilarious situations, they have to pull in their horns when Shiels melodramatically decides to solve their previously irreconcilable disputes at the eleventh hour and rescue them from their eccentric follies. But on those occasions when he is able to resist or even mock that unmistakable streak of bourgeois benignity in his nature, he can be a richly inventive and entertaining artist of comic desecration. . . .

There are endless arguments about what makes comedy "genuine," and [Patrick] Kavanagh holds with those apprehensive critics who insist that farce is the "impure" element that undermines it, especially the low comedy of Shiels. The pejorative term usually invoked is "mere" farce, though there is nothing "mere" about the efficacious laughter of farce or low comedy when it mocks and deflates whatever is excessively sacred in society; and it is this element of low comic profanation that defines the genuine and palpable subject of Shiels's best comedies. Robert Hogan, who does recognize many of Shiels's dramatic achievements, nevertheless ignores the symbolic qualities in some of the plays and substitutes the term "asinine" for "mere" in describing the farce of Shiels: "Almost totally realistic, his plays range from asinine farce to adroit and wryly thoughtful dramas." But there is nothing "asinine" about his first play, *Bedmates* (1921), a symbolic farce on the subjugation of Ireland that for its knockabout virtuosity can be compared favorably with the one-act comedies of Lady Gregory and O'Casey. . . .

The three tramps in *Bedmates* who want to spend the night in Molly Swan's overcrowded doss house are two Irish ragmen and a cockney thimblerigger from Whitechapel; but they are also symbolic representations of the historical conflict between Ireland and England. After Pius Kelly, a high-spirited Catholic ragman from southern Ireland, and his friend Andrew Riddle, a nervous Protestant ragman from Northern Ireland, have arranged with Molly to share the last available bed, Bertie Smith, the shifty English con man, schemes to take Pius's place in the allegorical bed. . . .

In a prophetic jest about the partition of Ireland, which separated the twenty-six counties of the Free State from six of Ulster's nine counties in 1922, a year after the play was performed, Bertie urges Riddle to get a saw and cut the bed in half. This is too much for Pius, who threatens to kill the Englishman if he doesn't clear out and allow the two Irishmen to settle their own differences, which originally had been manufactured by the outsider. The farcical resolution completes the political parable in the end when Bertie is chased away and the two uneasy bedmates are finally reunited in their beleaguered bed. It is ironic as well as a sign of Shiels's exceptional insight that well over fifty years after its initial performance this allegorical farce remains such a durable and relevant work in the context of the tragic violence in Northern Ireland.

David Krause. *The Profane Book of Irish Comedy*
(Ithaca, N.Y., Cornell Univ. Pr., 1982), pp. 135–38

On August 5, 1940, George Shiels again proved himself a serious dramatist who meant to be taken seriously. *The Rugged Path* opened that evening at the Abbey Theatre and played for a record-breaking twelve weeks to over 36,000 people. It was not comic, and it was not particularly entertaining. Shiels had already dismissed the Victorian notion that the play should please the crowd. Instead he turned a full-length mirror on them.

The Rugged Path is a drama of conscience that treats moral and psychological conflicts. The barebones plot reduces easily: John Perrie, a 74-year-old pensioner has been robbed of two pounds and murdered by Peter Dolis. Sean Tansey, a young neighbour, see Dolis in the vicinity of the old man's cabin on the fatal night and agrees to testify against him in court. The trial is a travesty—the jury refuses to find against the murderer—and he is acquitted and set free. A shot is fired through the Tansey's window shattering it, as the curtain falls.

In the course of three acts, the Tanseys agonise about "informing" on a neighbour, and the Dolises weave an intricate alibi for Peter and intimidate the locals into perjuring themselves. They have a long history of bullying the countryside, these Dolises.

The play would be a fairly cut-and-dry exposé of villainy and retribution in most countries outside of Ireland, but in rural post-Treaty Ireland, where "informing" was the capital sin, it has other implications. After all, Irish history has been a catalogue of revolutionary movements, and turning State's evidence has been traditionally viewed as an heinous Judas act. It is Michael Tansey, who once put his life on the line for Ireland and the old values, who is caught in the real dilemma—he cannot betray the next house, nor can he allow a murderer to menace his family. And, his wife, who fears for the safety of her children, echoes his conscience, "I was brought up to despise the very name of informer, and the longer I live the more I despise it," she says.

For Sean Tansey and his sister and the young schoolmistress, the question has no grey areas. Sean tells us, "Every crooked parasite in the country depends on the old bogey to save his neck . . . I'll give my information free, and I won't fly the country either. I'll be the first informer to stay at home and go on with his work."

Under the circumstances, it is a noble statement by the young idealist, and it is well received because the audience has also weighed the evidence on all sides.

In discussing a drama of ideas it is too easy to be glib, to oversimplify, to extend the moral of the story. *The Rugged Path* is not a comment on the Northern scene any more than it is a comment on the Hitler war. The playwright has deliberately set the action in a rural townland five miles *inside* the Free State border, within a community with no sectarian divide. The Dolises and Tanseys are playing out a cultural struggle between traditionalism and modernism with the audience sitting in judgement. He has, of course, stacked the deck on the side of the New Ireland which lies at the end of the rugged path.

Shiels was politically aware, and he knew exactly what he was about. The reason that he had gone to the Abbey with *Bedmates* in 1921 was that he knew no Ulster theatre could produce a play on Partition without a public outcry. Even the outcome of this one worried him. . . .

The message of *The Rugged Path* is that the Irish, without the props of British authority, must fashion their own laws and, more importantly, once fashioned, they must learn to live by them.

Daniel J. Casey. Threshold. Winter, 1983,
pp. 14–15

SIMMONS, JAMES (1933–   )

First, let me declare my interest. Ever since I came across *Late But in Earnest* about six years ago, I've never ceased to consider James Simmons one of the most consistently successful poets writing today. I'm not talking about Ulster poetry, Irish poetry, or any other species of limitation—I'm talking about contemporary poetry.

Fine lines divide a vital regional culture from cliquey provincialism. Much of the poetry written in the North today suggests the former: some of the criticism suggests the latter. The caricature of Simmons as a guitar-toting "entertainer" who happens also to write an embarrassing form of confessional poetry—a sort of flashing—is, of course, a complete travesty. Simmons' poetry is subjective, yet it transcends the merely personal: through intensely subjective statements the poet achieves universality—to read poetry as autobiographical revelation reduces criticism to a cheap form of parochial gossip.

Just as all original art carries light to the back of the cave, so poetry can

give a voice to inarticulate emotion. Simmons' poetry, however, is not the cathartic, anguished howl of the tribes of Ginsberg. A poem like "West Strand
Visions," which gives the title to this collection, presents the emotional intensity of involvement in a situation alongside a more detached view of that same
situation. The observer not only watches the children playing, but watches
himself watching the children playing. Expressed like this, the technique
sounds self-conscious and unnatural: the poem itself, however, is quite the reverse. A sense of beauty and a sense of loss are both conveyed in the rhythms
of the verse, in the ambiguity [of the] isolated observer. It is also an image of
the poet's relationship with the world. . . . This double-vision underpins much
of Simmons' irony, conveying the Janus faces of realities and truths.

This irony is often inward-looking. In the hands of a less demanding
poet, "Friend's School, 1962" would have been an exercise in nostalgia. The
subject is often the occasion of reveries invoking a lost Golden Age: beauty is
destroyed by time, tempus fugit, betjemania. . . . But this particular reverie
takes an unexpected turn and confounds the anticipated satisfaction of pious
wisdom. . . . [The poet's] honesty is most clearly seen in the introspective
poems which explore what oft is felt, but ne'er so well expressed. "Footnote
on Pacifism" and "Fear Test" both present common enough experiences, but
they look beyond conventional truisms and those social masks which we all
wear. . . .

A poem which illustrates Simmons' characteristic empathy for objects
outside the self is "Atrocities," an authentic horror story of our times. It tells
the tale of degradation and depravity: two men are buried alive by a fellow-
prisoner on the orders of their captors. Simmons avoids the obvious moraliza-
tion: the poem's "moral" lies in the painful vicarious experience of the reading
rather than in any imposed comment. An unforgettable symbol, it combines
the understated objectivity of a ballad like "The Twa Corbies" with the anguish of Sylvia Plath, the power of the poem residing in the tensions between
object and expression. . . . Nearer home, themes of violence and hatred recur
in many of the songs and poems from "The Resistance Cabaret," "Claudy," of
course, is already well known. A definitive statement of the absurd and grotesque waste of human life that is "the troubles," the song has a terrible
beauty. If ever poetry comes between the raised stick and the cowering back it
will be poetry like this.

Robert Chapman. The Honest Ulsterman. Nos.
46–47, 1975, pp. 71–74

. . . A sequence in *In the Wilderness* (1969), based on *King Lear*, and "Ste-
phano Remembers" in *Energy to Burn* (1971) show how much Simmons's
poetry benefits from symbolic and dramatic nourishment. . . .

He has defended himself against critics who feel that he has fallen into
the domestic/confessional rut by claiming *all* his poems are dramatic in es-

sence. An early poem, "Written, Directed by and Starring" places him as a compulsive script-writer for himself. It all depends on the quality and variety of the scripts. Slice-of-life naturalism, frankness of sexual situation and language palls, and [Douglas] Dunn does have a point in finding the setting too often a "crumpled bed." . . . But even this aspect of Simmons's poetry is partially redeemed by the tone of voice which projects some life into the flattest pieces and ultimately gives a distinctive personality to all his statements. The angle of vision implied by the voice also redeems some of the poems from "commonplace confession" (Simmons is aware of the hazards), a routine moan about middle age and marriage. If with less penetration than Larkin, he does explore "the long perspectives / Open at each instant of our lives," adding footnotes to Larkin as he covers some of the same ground from the point of view of Arnold in "Self's the Man," finding a solving degree of beauty in both infidelities and fidelities, and making "while trying to tell no lies, / a noise to go with love":

> . . . A disappointed spirit with meal-time for a cock,
> I start back as the bells say six o'clock
> to the nicest woman I have ever met,
> where my bed is made and tea-table set.

Simmons's poems chart, in a more pronounced fashion than most contemporary English poetry, the fluctuating reactions of an individual to the fluctuating circumstances of life. If he is more of a libertine than an agnostic, more bent on being honest about than faithful to his experience, not only individual but selfconsciously individualistic, he complements and extends by his exaggerations the other kinds of self-consciousness I have been noting. His example already seems to have made younger Northern poets freer to be themselves.

What does the free individual or individualist do at a time of mass movements and mass emotions? Always naturally on the side of Caliban or a "hollow man" against the forces that exploit or patronize them—Prosperoism in politics and poetry—Simmons's more explicit development of an anti-authoritarian ideology, or anti-ideology ideology, in recent years must have something to do with the resumption of tribal pressures. . . . I am not entirely happy with Simmons's prose and verse appearances as a rather homespun philosopher of rather simplistic libertarian ideas. Nevertheless, his poetry has been profoundly shaped by reaction against the "puritanism," the spiritual coercion, enforced by Irish politics as well as by Irish society.

Edna Longley. In Douglas Dunn, ed., *Two Decades
of Irish Writing* (Chester Springs, Pa., Dufour,
1975), pp. 149–50

The most considerable poet after [John] Hewitt among the Ulster majority is James Simmons, born 1933, author of more books than any other poet in our period: *Energy to Burn* (1971), *No Land Is Waste, Dr. Eliot* (1972), *The Long Summer Still to Come* (1973), *West Strand Visions* (1974) and *Judy Garland and the Cold War* (1976). These are all quite small collections, and their impact has been equaled by the influence Simmons had as the first editor of *The Honest Ulsterman*, not as apocalyptic a magazine as its subtitle once suggested. It is the work of a band of young writers who now wear the radical chic look of the late Sixties. Simmons has also stirred things up by singing his songs and ballads in public. Important differences between Simmons and Hewitt register themselves. Hewitt cares about the Northern climate of hate and violence and wishes to diffuse it by assimilating the two traditions. Until it hits him in the early Seventies, Simmons sloughs it off; but then he expresses his frustration and anger more in balladry than in direct lyrical pieces. One can see why the major Catholic poets—[Padraic] Fiacc, Montague, and Heaney—feel closer to Hewitt. Simmons does not necessarily want to become an Irish poet. He seeks detachment; he will not be the hanger-on or accomplice of Southern writers, though he writes of his hangovers like many down South. His work shows an attraction to the Anglo-Irish tradition that is balanced with a middle-class despair of the inclination towards political "rumbles." Holding off from the shambles of Belfast and Derry does not seem due to apathy, but in Simmons, Mahon, and other poets is an avoidance of the public theme to court the private myth—an elaboration, after all, of the Reformation freedom of leaving a man alone with his own conscience.

The individualistic vision of Simmons by implication impeaches the Catholic truths of sin and authority. It questions the clericalism of the minority, in particular it concentrates against a schooling that limits sexual enlightenment. His "Protestant Courts Catholic" sets the two communities apart in a humorous, and possibly autobiographical, vein. . . . Knowledge is Protestant, Miltonic free will and liberty; servitude a Catholic inferiority of the mind imposed by priestly restriction. But ideas are not violence and, confronted with the latter, Simmons can give as well as he gets, while loathing the exercise. The incident in the poem "Experience" is filled with the tension of the Northern community. It reads like a gentle dip into savagery and complicity: "A torn shirt and my lip numb and bloody, / my anger and—strange—the feel of my own body / New to me, as I struck, as he struck." Simmons's macho image, a skillful verse-mask, plays a linking part in the construction of his ballads that form his major statement on the sickness of his society. The three most prominent of them, "Claudy," "The Ballad of Ranger Best," and "The Ballad of Gerry Kelly, Newsagent," form a clustered outpouring of horror, in storytelling style, about three of the bloody incidents of these holocaust years. The first is about the Provisional IRA bombing a village without adequate warning, the second is a murder of a young British Army man from Derry by the official IRA, and balancing these the third relates a killing of a Catholic shop-owner by Loyalist thugs. There is an unequivocal assurance, in these words set to music, of the evil of such action. The writer's ear is well adjusted to the niceties of the poetic narrative; the perfection of tone clicks with the absolute morality. . . . This kind of forum for public questioning, which Simmons may have learnt from Yeats's late ballads, functions as a method of describing the inadequate motives behind an almost random and mindless round of horrors.

James Liddy. *Éire-Ireland*. Summer, 1979, pp. 125–27

James Simmons . . . makes a speciality of the ordinary, and particularly of the ordinary states of love and marriage *and* their failure:

> Unhappy marriages are that eccentric,
> irrelevant to decent people, sick;
> but common.

An elevated or transfigured commonness is part of his achievement, and the reasons for it lie partly in his experience as a songwriter and singer. He knows about the openness of sound, the clarity of idea, the directness of syntax demanded by words for music, but unlike those of most poets his songs when printed do not look like gauche and simplistic botches of a different kind of poem. He has discovered a voice of effortless fluency, natural and virile in diction and wide in range, a tough but transparent medium in which the performer's voice is preserved in limpid perpetuity after the performance has ended. . . . He has the ballad in various forms and with its conventions more or less unruffled as a major vehicle. And his brief for fiction is more generous, more simple: "Anything processed by memory is fiction!"—a dictum which makes no special case but reminds us of the fictional autonomy of life when transmuted into poetry.

Simmons's new collection [*Constantly Singing*] contains a number of songs—poems at least in ballad form but with a literary rather than popular discipline: entirely lucid and accessible, they contain no banalities; they are more demotic than Yeats's songs and remind one at times of a hornier heterosexual William Plomer. . . . And at the end of the poem "Mates" a subtle but colloquial inflexion undercuts the supposed advantages of marriage, handling the mundanities with something of [Philip] Larkin's refinement. . . .

Authoritatively established in this middle style, Simmons dares more and more complex statements, in long poems that map out interpenetrations of life and art (in "Coleraine: 1977" listening to Bach on the night of an incident) and of public and private war and peace in "Cloncha." . . . Some people may feel that Simmons is too prolific, fear his mastery has become parnassian or his subject too easy; but everything in this book refutes it:

> He was luring
> a girl near his heart in this
> occupied country of his. His voice
> touching another, the singer's art.

Alan Hollinghurst. Enc. Feb., 1981, pp. 82–83

SOMERVILLE and ROSS (Edith Œnone Somerville, 1858–1949, and Violet Martin ["Martin Ross"], 1862–1915)

The literary partnership of Miss Edith Somerville and Miss Violet Martin—the most brilliantly successful example of creative collaboration in our times—began with *An Irish Cousin* in 1889. Published over the pseudonyms of "Geilles Herring" and "Martin Ross," this delightful story is remarkable not only for its promise, afterwards richly fulfilled, but for its achievement. The writers proved themselves the possessors of a strange faculty of detachment which enabled them to view the humours of Irish life through the unfamiliar eye of a stranger without losing their own sympathy. They were at once of the life they described and outside it. They showed a laudable freedom from political partisanship; a minute familiarity with the manners and customs of all strata of Irish society; an unerring instinct for the "sovran word," a perfect mastery of the Anglo-Irish dialect; and an acute yet well-controlled sense of the ludicrous. . . .

[T]hey reached the summit of their achievement in *The Real Charlotte*, which still remains their masterpiece, though easily eclipsed in popularity by the irresistible drollery of *Some Experiences of an Irish R.M.* To begin with, it does not rely on the appeal to hunting people which in their later work won the heart of the English sportsman. It is a ruthlessly candid study of Irish provincial and suburban life; of the squalors of middle-class households; of garrison hacks and "underbred, finespoken," florid squireens. But secondly and chiefly it repels the larger half of the novel-reading public by the fact that two women have here dissected the heart of one of their sex in a mood of unrelenting realism. While pointing out the pathos and humiliation of the thought that a soul can be stunted by the trivialities of personal appearance, they own to having set down Charlotte Mullen's many evil qualities "without pity." They approach their task in the spirit of Balzac. The book, as we shall see, is extraordinarily rich in both wit and humour, but Charlotte, who cannot control her ruling passion of avarice even in a death chamber, might have come straight out of the pages of the *Comédie Humaine*.

C. L. Graves. *Quarterly Review*.
Vol. 219, No. 436, 1913, pp. 30–33

It chanced that I was engaged, in another connexion, with some criticisms, or, rather, with an appreciation, of The Two Ladies (as I always think of Martin Ross and E. Œ. Somerville) at the very moment that the sad news of Martin Ross's illness reached me. Two days later she died, and now part of that eulogium all suddenly and tragically becomes an elegy.

I had been reading aloud some of the sketches, and in particular "The House of Fahy," which I have always held was one of the best short stories ever written, with a last sentence that no one but a professional elocutionist with nerves of steel could possibly compass; and afterwards it had amused me to imagine a room filled with devotees of the *Irish R.M.*, such as might as easily exist as a Boz Club, capping quotations from that and its companion books and finding pleasure in expressing admiration in the warmest terms and in minute detail; and there are not many pleasures greater than that.

The discussion might, indeed, have begun by the old question, What are the best short stories in the world? and my own insistence on the claims of this very "House of Fahy" to a place high on the list; because, as I should have urged, it relates an episode proper only to the short-story medium; there is no word too many or too few; it has atmosphere and character; it is absorbing; it has a beginning, a middle, and such an end!

"But what about 'The Maroan Pony'?" some one might have inquired. "Isn't that a perfect short story too?"

And I should have replied that it is.

"And 'Harrington's'?" some one else might have urged. "Isn't that perfect? And it has an extra quality, for in addition to all the humour of it, and the wonderful picture of a country auction sale, it has that tragic touch. To my mind it is greater than 'The House of Fahy.'"

And then I am sure that a most emphatic claim for "Trinket's Colt" as the best of all would have been formulated; and by this time we should have been right in the thick of it, all eager to speak and be heard.

To me The Two Ladies have long been the only contemporary authors whom it is absolutely necessary to read twice instantly: the first time for the story, which is always so intriguing—and the more so as you get more familiar with the ingenuity of their methods—as to exact a high speed; and the second time for the detail, the little touches of observation and experience, and the amazing, and to an envious writer despairful, adequacy of epithet. And having read them twice, I find that whenever I pick them up again there is something new, something not fully tasted before. . . .

And now the bond has snapped, and "Martin Ross," who was Miss Violet Martin, is dead. With her death, the series stops, for though neither was the dominant spirit, the prosperity of the work demanded both. As to The Two Ladies' method of collaboration I know nothing, and should like to know all; which held the pen I have no notion, or if one alone held it. But that it was complete and perfect is proved by this sentence from a private letter from one very near to them, which I may perhaps take the liberty of quoting, since it embodies a remark made by the survivor of the many, many years' partnership. "There isn't a page, there isn't a paragraph, there isn't a line which either of us could claim as her sole work." That is collaboration in the highest degree, two minds that not only work as one but are one.

E. V. Lucas. *Spec*. Jan. 1, 1916, pp. 9–10

There is force in the criticism of Somerville and Ross that used to be made in the sour, wan yellow dawn of the Irish revival, when it was a crime for anyone to laugh in Ireland, unless they laughed for the right party: the criticism that these ladies were simply purveying the stage Irishman to English magazines and winding up the old parish hurdy-gurdy of Irish farce.

And, of course, they were. The tradition of Irish farce is permanent. The stage Irishman is permanent. He is as permanent as the Irish narrative gift and the use of words as an intoxicant. The puritanism of Maynooth and Merrion Square cannot put its gooseflesh on the warm native fancy. But there is more than one Somerville and Ross. An early novel, written before [*Some Experiences of an Irish R.M.*] made them popular, does attempt to say what the Anglo-Irish were like between one View Hallo or one petty sessions and the next. That book is *The Real Charlotte*. I don't want to be a spoil-sport, especially now the *R.M.* has been canonized by *Everyman*, and I write as a foreigner, but *The Real Charlotte* did something which had not, up to the 'nineties, been done in Irish literature. It portrayed the Anglo-Irish with the awful, protracted mercy of the artist. It "placed" them as no novelist had thought of "placing" them before; as surely, for example, as Mrs. Gaskell knew how to place her world in *Wives and Daughters*. I do not mean that *The Real Charlotte* is as sound or as accomplished a novel as Mrs. Gaskell's. It was a first novel, awkwardly built, and, like so many Anglo-Irish writers, the authors never got rid of an amateur, almost a juvenile streak; but *The Real Charlotte* was a beginning of great promise. One went to Ireland looking for the characters of the Irish R.M.; one found oneself, thirty years after it was written, surrounded by the disquieting people of this one serious novel. . . .

And though *The Real Charlotte* is a novel about jealousy and the never-ceasing intrigue and treachery of Irish life, its main stuff is this snobbery. Not a plain, excluding snobbery that tells us where we may go and where we may not, but a snobbery that is in the blood. Not a snobbery versed in distinguished ancestors only, but a snobbery bedeviling the character with the pretensions of second cousins and the mildewed memories of better times. It is a snobbery that has become the meaning of life. It permeates everything: good sense, idealism, hatred, tenderness, religion—even pity. We must allow something for the fact that this book is written in the 'nineties; and when the Dysarts wince because Francie keeps her gloves on at tea, we are charmed by the comedy of the manners of a period. Anglo-Irish snobbery was pretty genial about such quaintness. But underneath this are the inturned passions of a small, defensive and decaying colonial society: Francie is a social casualty in the everlasting skirmish with the other Ireland. Only by exaggerating their exclusiveness and creating low comedy around them can the Ascendants keep their ascendancy. . . .

Fifty years of politics lie between us and these skirling *commères*, with their high-pitched domestic life and the loquacity of distressed Elizabethans. But the narrative writing has the Irish visual gift, so bold in its metaphors, so athletic in its speed, as if tongue and eye were racing against each other. . . . And then, though there is hardly a breath of Irish politics in the story, they are there by implication. For the characters are exclusively the Irish Protestants and their isolation gives a strength to the strokes in which they are drawn.

The faults of *The Real Charlotte* are obvious. The national malady of not "letting on" what you are up to enables the novelist to catch the changeableness of human character; but toward the end of the elusive becomes the frantic. It is unforgiveable that Francie is killed out riding; especially as her death, one is pretty sure, is due to the profound snobbery of the authors. There is no way of making a lady of her, so she had to be killed. But after one has removed the old-fashioned trappings, the irony, the insight and portraiture of this novel, show that Anglo-Irish society might have got its Mrs. Gaskell, if the amateur tastes of the discursive colonial had not breezily ridden the chance off the page.

V. S. Pritchett. *The Living Novel* (New York, Reynal
& Hitchcock, 1947), pp. 150–52, 154

We should judge a book not by how we think it may affect a hypothetical foreigner, but solely by how it actually does affect ourselves. In short, if Slipper's story and the *Irish R.M.* books in general do seem funny to us, they need no other justification. They will not, of course, seem funny if we feel, for instance, that their idiom is divorced from any living speech or that the scenes and traits of character that they describe have no roots in Irish life. But this is not the case with Somerville and Ross; they exaggerate, obviously, as every comic writer does, but their exaggeration is firmly based on Irish ground which they knew well and which in their own way they loved deeply. They lived in Ireland for almost all their writing lives and they had, as a writing team, a sensitive ear and a penetrating humorous eye. If their writing is not part of the literature of Ireland, then Ireland is a poorer place than many of us believe it to be. . . .

Three novels are more important than the rest—*The Real Charlotte*, *Mount Music*, and *The Big House of Inver*. Mr. Stephen Gwynn has said that *The Real Charlotte* is one of the most powerful novels of Irish life ever written. Its central figure, Miss Charlotte Mullen, is certainly a massive and formidable concentration of evil intent working in commonplace detail, without any thunderclaps or blue flame. Evil has often been more dramatically exhibited, but I do not think it has ever been more convincingly worked out in humdrum action, or brought home with such a terrible cumulative effect as an element in everyday life. . . . *The Real Charlotte* is generally considered the best of their novels, and I think it is so. It is also, unfortunately, the one most marred by evidence of lack of sympathy with outsiders. Professor [Daniel] Corkery, in a striking phrase, denounces the presence in our literature of "an alien ascendancy streaked with the vulgarity of insensibility." The verdict itself has a little streak of the same, and its harshness is unjust, as far as most of the work of Somerville and Ross is concerned. But in *The Real Charlotte* the streak is noticeable and it harms an otherwise splendid achievement. That does not mean, however, that I think *The Real Charlotte* is un-Irish. There is nothing un-Irish about aristocratic pride; a great part of our Gaelic literature throbs with a full and blue-blooded contempt for the low-born.

The two other main novels, *Mount Music* and *The Big House of Inver*, are much more loosely written, but with more generous feeling. The ice has melted—there are twenty-five years after all between *The Real Charlotte* and *Mount Music*—and the style has lost some of its edge, the edge that I think Martin Ross put on it, for good and ill. The central theme of *Mount Music* is one of which Irish writers have in general tended to fight rather shy, that of Religious Intolerance, on the part of both Protestants and Catholics. Miss Somerville calls it, cheerfully enough, the Spirit of the Nation and follows its devious workings and its double language with remarkable detachment. The whole subject is of course now utterly out of date, and such a spirit can scarcely be conceived by the modern Irish reader, who positively drips with tolerance. None the less the book may be read for its antiquarian interest.

Although both *Mount Music* and *The Big House of Inver* lack style as compared with *The Real Charlotte*, they have not lost the power of generating a daemonic force in a credible character. Such is Dr. Francis Mangan in *Mount Music*; such, in *The Big House of Inver*, is Shibby Pindy, the illegitimate great-hearted daughter of a gentle family, who has had a peasant upbringing, but whose passion is to restore, through her half-brother, the glories of the big house, which stands empty at the beginning of the novel and is in flames at the end. *The Big House of Inver*, were it not for something a little blurred and loose in the writing, would surpass *The Real Charlotte*. I am not indeed quite sure that it does not surpass it as it is, for if there is a blur in the writing there is no such smudge of meaningless character as is the Dysart family group in the earlier novel.

When we regret then, amid so much that we admire, is that, as imaginative sympathy deepened, style declined. The youthful arrogance which somewhat blunted the moral perception yet carried itself extremely well. The quality of unwavering intelligence is in the writing—an intelligence not worried by clichés, but never allowing a cliché to come between it and the reality of the given moment. This alertness flags in the later works which have a wider vision but a less precise one. Perhaps had it not been for the success of the R.M. stories, which diverted them for so many and such important years from their vein of tragedy, Somerville and Ross might have given us a work of their maturity which would have been as alert as it was humane.

Donat O'Donnell [Conor Cruise O'Brien]. Irish
Writing. March, 1955, pp. 10–13

When Lady Gregory steps from her Big House, Lennox Robinson has written, "she never condescends, she knows her humble neighbors well, sits by their fire in the homelist fashion," but in Somerville and Ross there is "a touch—it is only a touch—of 'we' and 'they', of the contrast between the Big House and the Cabin." This is much like saying that Faulkner writes of Negroes with just a touch of "we" and "they." Somerville and Ross were daughters of the Big House, and the Cabins belonged to the other Ireland. For that matter, Robinson's belief that Lady Gregory had blurred her pronouns was not shared by the country people of Kiltartan.

The contrast between Big House and Cabin looms large in Somerville and Ross because it loomed large in Irish life. Every Irishman knew that he belonged to one of these worlds, or believed that he did, or knew that he did but denied it. No Irish novel could fail to take this into account if it hoped to represent accurately the thoughts and emotions, the very look and feel of its society. In the last volume of *Hail and Farewell*, George Moore drives away from Moore Hall, past the endless walls of cut stone which separated its demesne from outlying fields and straggling villages. In his childhood, he remembers, everything had come from this land, even the stones, and the labor by which they were set into place, "for feudalism lasted in Ireland down to 1870." The memory becomes part of his long, evocative account of that vanished world. But the habits engendered by feudalism had not vanished: Ireland remains dominated and divided by fierce prejudices of class and caste.

The slow passing of that world is the subject of the novels of Somerville and Ross. Their career spanned the entire period during which their class fell from power, and their works respond to the stages of this defeat. *Mount Music* (1919) opens in the 1890s, when "the class known as landed gentry still ruled in Ireland." *An Enthusiast* (1921) "attempts to give a picture of the closing days of the old order of country life in Ireland." *The Big House of Inver*

(1925) "is the history of one of those minor dynasties that, in Ireland, have risen, and ruled, and rioted, and have at last crashed in ruins." But this is also true, if in indirect and subtle ways, of their earlier novels, written when the old order enjoyed a deceptive sense of security.

The stories are seldom dispassionate, for they are written from a fierce though critical loyalty to the Big House and a harsh, often ungenerous opposition to its enemies. But they move steadily toward tragic knowledge, toward recognition of the fact that the Big House was not destroyed by the mutinous Cabins but by its own weakness and capacity for self-deception. The *Irish R.M.* stories are exceptions, but they are special precisely because they evade this subject. The world which Somerville and Ross loved is held suspended in these stories, its dissolution checked. "With Joyce's *Dubliners*," Frank O'Connor has written, "*The R.M.* is the most closely-observed of all Irish story-books, but, whereas Joyce observes with cruel detachment, the authors of *The Irish R.M.* observe with love and glee." This is true: they have been excelled only by O'Connor himself. But beyond the magic hedgerows of the *Irish R.M.* lay a darker world, existing and perishing in time.

Thomas Flanagan. KR. Jan., 1966, pp. 56–57

Summary of a literary career is never a simple matter. Even with the greatest there are things we would wish otherwise. The task is made yet more difficult when, as in the case with Somerville and Ross, we treat of a closely knit partnership, one member of which outlived the other by a whole generation. The knitting together of the two lives seems to increase in geometric rather than arithmetic progression the haps and accidents which control literary lives and the sundering of the partnership, instead of simplifying issues, creates new ones.

Cutting boldly through all the reservations which threaten to inhibit the formation of any conclusion, one would wish, first of all, to claim for these writers that they are great givers of pleasure, great entertainers. Edith reports of Violet that an old countrywoman said of her: "Sure ye're always laughing! That ye may laugh in the sight of the Glory of Heaven!" The old woman went to the heart of the matter. Preeminently, it is the "R.M." stories one thinks of in this connection, but many of the essays and articles, as well as the novels, contrive to amuse us with great good-humor. The writers' comic confidence is solidly based on their security within their social group, and, paradoxically, their interpretation of the tragedy of their class can be traced to the same source. Better than anyone else they knew the grave and the gay sides of their worlds. *The Real Charlotte* is, of course, their greatest achievement in any mode but it should not be forgotten that, after Martin's death, Edith carried on this branch of their activities very creditably in such novels as *Mount Music* and *The Big House of Inver*. Had Violet lived, as Edith did, to see the emergence of modern Ireland, perhaps they might together have provided in another great novel the sort of searching commentary on the new Ireland which they had already achieved about the old. This complex partnership, so tragically sundered in mid-stream, bristles with conjecture. If Martin had lived; if the need for money had not been so keen; if Martin's ill-health had not interfered, and so on and so on.

A truce to such pointless speculation! The achievement, after all, is solid enough. It includes what is, arguably, the finest Irish novel of the nineteenth century and a set of the funniest stories ever written. Somerville and Ross may not always function at their highest voltage, but when they do, their brilliance is undeniable.

Socially secure in a poor country, socially insecure in a declining class, they looked at their Irish world with clarity, geniality and much sympathetic insight. We should be grateful for what they did, not captious about what they did not do.

John Cronin. *Somerville and Ross*
(Lewisburg, Pa., Bucknell Univ. Pr., 1972),
pp. 100–101

The us-against-them dichotomy, Ireland of the Big House versus Ireland of the Cabins, is present in Somerville and Ross's work, but without the intensity of a cause. The "personal element" that reigns supreme in stories such as "Poisson D'Avril" also moderated their views of the public element, replacing the hasty passions and overly rigid categories of political rhetoric with a more generous sympathy for real people and actual experiences. When the Somerville estate at Drishane was forced to adopt "unusual defensive precautions" against Fenian activities in the mid-1860s, Edith, then a girl of ten, preferred to idealize the rebels and act the part of an Irish nationalist herself. Her dissenting role was expanded when the English dragoons offered her brother a ride on their horses; Edith, only a girl, was ignored: "I think that from that hour I became a Suffragist." Yet the various causes, whether women's rights, anti-Parnellism, nationalism, or unionism, never invade and restrict the literature. There the mildly rebellious and critical attitudes attach more significance to the internal weaknesses of the gentry than to the shifting economic and political forces outside its control.

Even as she continued to support the old economic system, therefore, Somerville also recognized the part that the gentry had played in its own ruin. Her 1925 novel, *The Big House of Inver*, uses the Prendeville estate to chronicle the entire history of the Protestant Ascendancy of the nineteenth century. From its earliest beginnings in nobility and splendor, the family line soon became corrupted by marriages into the lower class and, even more so, by its own brilliant but debilitating extravagance. She does not withhold admiration for the aristocratic gallantry of their lives, for all the epic waste; yet she feels the tragedy of it as well. The landed class had dealt too recklessly with its resources and by the end of the century had none left to fall back on. Never feeling as committed as Violet Martin to the old way of life, Somerville wrote in 1917:

> Things are better now. . . . Inspectors, instructors, remission of rents, land purchase, State loans, English money in various forms, have improved the conditions in a way that would hardly have been credible thirty years ago, when, in these congested districts, semi-famine was chronic.

Yet the deep-rooted sympathies and instinctive assumptions that had shaped *The Real Charlotte* in 1894 remained firm throughout both their lives. Prosperity for the large mass of people and bureaucratic thoroughness do not necessarily create moral ideals or provide acceptable substitutes for the cast-off traditional values. Somerville and Ross could understand the passage of the old order into history and appreciate the new social institutions; but their first and strongest loyalties remained always with the Big House.

They recognized, years before most members of their landed class, that the old system of land ownership and social privileges was nearing its end, paralyzed by its own feudal sensibilities and extravagances. Yet historical perception formed only one part of the authors' sense of their class. Literature also gave them a way of evoking the past and using it to measure and judge the new, rising interests. Their recreation of the old social order continues to mourn the loss of that way of life, even as it admits the loss. With all its strengths and limitations, the vantage point of the Protestant Ascendancy serves as the dominating center of their work. They accurately describe the fate of many once great estates, yet their work passes, perhaps too lightly, over the fate of the large mass of the peasantry.

> Wayne E. Hall. *Shadowy Heroes: Irish Literature of the 1890s* (Syracuse, N.Y., Syracuse Univ. Pr., 1980), pp. 69–70

Somerville & Ross were traditional novelists: they were concerned with the way people behave in society. They wrote about what they knew intimately: the Anglo-Irish and, sometimes, the way their finely layered society was beset by political pressures. They focused on individual members of Anglo-Irish society with a subtlety of characterisation which illuminates not only the social and religious conflicts of the time but the more general human condition. They threw into relief the troubles of an entire class and showed godlessness and greed in the most ordinary people. They were less concerned with the Gaelic and Catholic Irish, about whom they knew less; but when they did write about them it is often with a sense of pathos and their comedy never degenerates into the buffoonery of Lover and Lever. They have been misjudged. Their feminine laughter was sharper and more critical than anything which gave rise to the Stage Irishman, but it was usually reserved for those of their own religion. There was no malice in their attitude to the Irish people.

Their ability to capture the dialect of the people is remarkable. The Irish turn of phrase, the striking image, the singular inflexion, never degenerate into stock stage brogue or Kiltartanese. They had no desire to change or improve the people, and they enjoyed them as fellow creatures. They were not blinded by the sentimentality which spoiled the work of many nineteenth-century writers, nor by the patriotism which coloured the vision of many of their contemporaries. . . .

Their first collaborative effort, a dictionary of their families' speech, indicates their immense interest in words. They knew that because they were Anglo-Irish they spoke the English tongue differently from the English as well as from the irish. When Edith Somerville refers to the dictionary—which does not seem to have been preserved—she shows strongly this feeling of the otherness and even superiority of her race. Their families' speech she says was "the froth on the surface of some two hundred years of the conversation of a clan of inventive, violent, Anglo-Irish people, who, generation after generation, found themselves faced with situations in which the English language failed to provide sufficient intensity, and they either snatched at alternatives from other tongues or invented them." The speech of the Irish people around them was to them even more fascinating, because it was more colourful and poetic. When they began to learn Irish in 1897 it was not in order to study ancient texts but to illuminate the things they heard said around them every day. They carefully preserved trial reports from local newspapers for the amazing dialogue recorded: "I did not say that I would keep her between the gate and the pillar until I would squeeze the decay out of her."

Their advantage over many of the writers of the Irish Literary Revival was that they did not live in Dublin but in daily contact with the people of the West of Ireland. The Ireland which their contemporaries visited to collect folk tales was their ordinary environment. They did not romanticise the peasantry nor exaggerate the unspoilt nature of their lives because they knew only too well the squalid conditions in which many of them were forced to live. And although there was always the tremendous barrier of the Big House and the differences in education and religion they still *knew* the country people. They went to their births, marriages and deaths, and attended them in sickness; they worked with them in stable and garden, and they met them at horse fairs, agriculture shows, races and hunting. Necessarily in a rural community there is more mutual dependence and helping each other than elsewhere. They knew the country people with an intimacy quite different from the observation—however sympathetic—of an outsider. And so they had the immense advantage of knowing another way of life and another way of speech.

Hilary Robinson. *Somerville and Ross: A Critical Appreciation* (Dublin, Gill & Macmillan, 1980), pp. 3, 48–49

STEPHENS, JAMES (1880?–1950)

Readers of *The Irish Review* have no need to be informed of the merits of the story which they know as "Mary." Of those who read the book, eight out of every ten will be prepared to declare that *The Charwoman's Daughter* is one of the best stories they have ever read. All the time Mr. Stephens is speaking to the wise, kindly and sympathetic side of ourselves, and his story of the charwoman and her daughter has the profound reality of a fairy tale. In making Dublin the setting for the story Mr. Stephens has done more for our Capital than a national Government could do—he has made Dublin a most interesting and exciting place. Stephen's Green and the Phoenix Park have become like the territory that is round the Well at the World's End, and the Streets of Dublin have become full of romantic possibilities, for we know the policeman who stands where Grafton Street and Nassau Street cross, and we hope to meet the wayfarers that Mary has seen—the tall man with the sweeping brown beard who seemed to know everybody, the tall, thin black man who was always smiling sweetly to himself, the man who looked at Mary once and who gave her the impression that she had known him well hundreds of years before, and that he remembered her also, and the man who looks the tiredest man in the world. We are glad that Mr. Stephens has not put "Finis" at the end of his story, but has written there "Thus far the story of Mary Makebelieve." We hope to meet her again with Mrs. Makebelieve and with the young man whom Mr. Stephens has left at Mary's side "exploring with a delicate finger his half-closed eye." Meantime, we can put *The Charwoman's Daughter* with the best loved books on her shelves—even beside *Don Quixote*. It is a story that Cervantes would have loved.

Irish Review. July, 1912, p. 278

There are poets who cannot write with half their being, and who must write with their whole being, and they bring their poor relation, the body, with them wherever they go, and are not ashamed of it. They are not at warfare with the spirit, but have a kind of instinct that the clan of human powers ought to cling together as one family. . . . James Stephens, as he chanted his *Insurrections*, sang with his whole being. Let no one say I am comparing him with Shakespeare. . . . But how refreshing it was to find somebody who was a poet without a formula, who did not ransack dictionaries for dead words, as Rossetti did to get living speech, whose natural passions declared themselves without the least idea that they ought to be ashamed of themselves, or be thrice refined in the crucible by the careful alchemist before they could appear in the drawing-room. . . .

We have a second volume of poetry from James Stephens, *The Hill of Vision*. He has climbed a hill, indeed, but has found cross-roads there leading in many directions, and seems to be a little perplexed whether the storm of things was his destiny after all. . . .

The Hill of Vision is a very unequal book. There are many verses full of power, which move with the free easy motion of the literary athlete. Others betray awkwardness, and stumble as if the writer had stepped too suddenly into the sunlight of his power, and was dazed and bewildered. There is some diffusion of his faculties in what I feel are byways of his mind, but the main current of his energies will, I am convinced, urge him on to his inevitable portrayal of humanity. With writers like Synge and Stephens, the Celtic imagination is leaving its Tienanoges, its Ildathachs, its Many Coloured Lands and impersonal moods, and is coming down to earth intent on vigorous life and individual humanity.

A.E. (George William Russell). *Imaginations and*
Reveries (Dublin, Maunsel, 1915),
pp. 35–36, 41–43

Mr. James Stephens was not born of woman, nor did he "just grow" as Topsy did. He descended upon this world, completely adult, exactly as the angels in *The Demi-Gods* descended on the hill where Patsy McCann and his daughter Mary found them. I have heard and I believe it to be true, that Mr. Stephens (it seems ridiculous to call an angel *Mister!*) was found by AE the great Irish poet and greater Irish man, clinging to the branches of a tree in Stephen's Green, Dublin. AE instantly hauled him off his perch (for he is very familiar in his manner with angels and the like) and informed him that the only occupation fit for a heavenly being was that of a lecturer on Cooperation under the director of the Irish Agricultural Organisation Society; and people say that Stephens was so scared by this statement that he wrote two books in his hurry and alarm and then bolted to Paris where he now sits congratulating himself on his escape from affairs. But that was a mistake. In running away from AE, he also ran away from Ireland.

And let this be noted: the two books which he wrote in Ireland are better than the two books he wrote in France. I will not deny that *Here Are Ladies* and *The Demi-Gods* are full of good stuff; indeed I will affirm that they are; but they are without that salty, Irish quality which makes *The Charwoman's Daughter* and *The Crock of Gold* such tasty reading. One feels that the angel, unaware of sex when he made these two books, in the sense that the neurotic novelists are aware of it, had become very conscious by the time he reaches *Here Are Ladies* and *The Demi-Gods* that "male and female created He them." One feels too when one reads *The Charwoman's Daughter* and *The Crock of Gold* that the angel, in his flight to Stephen's Green, contrived to see the whole of Ireland very clearly, but when one reads the later books one feels that wingless, he is now squatting on the pavement in front of a Parisian cafe looking at Ireland through liqueur glasses. And Paris is the very devil of a place for an Irishman to live in. . . .

In addition to the four prose works named above, Mr. Stephens has written two volumes of poems: *Insurrections* and *The Hill of Vision*. They are full of that roaring rebellion against set things which is in everything that he writes, which, indeed, makes his tendency to moralise all the more remarkable. Perhaps the most considerable of his poems is "The Lonely God," a piece which is full of the beauty of the disconsolate. It is when one reads "The Lonely God" and *The Charwoman's Daughter* that one realises how dreadful a thing it was for Mr. Stephens to fly to France, and how urgent a thing it is that he should instantly return to Ireland. If Puck must preach to the multitude, let him take his pack and go tramping the roads in Donegal and Connacht and the Middle West. AE's instinct was right: Mr. Stephens can expend his preacher's energy in propagating the principle of cooperation among the Irish peasants; and having rid himself of rhetoric in this fashion, he can settle down in comfort to write the fine stuff with which he began his career as a writer. He may be certain that that is the only stuff his admirers desire from him.

St. John G. Ervine. *BkmL*. April, 1915, pp. 5–6

The poetic genius of James Stephens has won recognition slowly but it was never better founded than during the past two years in America. His wonderful aptitude for prose-romance tends to distract attention from his no less important poetic gifts. Nobody has ever written simpler poetry. His work may be said scarcely to deal with ideas at all. A bird's cry, the cry of a snared rabbit and the vital, overwhelming desire to release it, the crooked windings of a goat-path on the side of a hill—these and such as these are his themes. He seeks only to convey the feeling of an experience, never to describe it in any realistic sense. And, rarest of attributes among the serious poets of today, he has a certain tint of humour that comes to glitter on the edges of his happier moods with such a brightness as belongs only to poetry. . . .

Stephens has definite limitations, but they are the limitations of a fairy. He is an elf among the modern poets and no line that he has written could discredit the art of Shakespeare himself.

Edward Davison. *EJ*. May, 1926, pp. 334–36

Even if we were ignorant of Stephens's method of writing *The Crock of Gold* (George Moore says in *Hail and Farewell* that the novel is an outgrowth of independent "scribblings" during the author's employment in a law office), it would be obvious that the book was not written on the basis of a carefully conceived outline. Order in this work seems to lack so strikingly that some readers prefer to consider it a vaguely connected set of experiences rather than a novel. To be sure, in stories stretching over two hundred pages we have come to take form so much for granted that it is not design but the lack of it that tends to distinguish *The Crock of Gold* from other novels. Whereas its spontaneity and looseness of form will appeal to the lyric mind, which is impatient with sustained design, it will disturb the architectural mind, which is in turn impatient with uncalled-for flights of fancy.

Design and spontaneity tend to become reconciled as soon as we consider the work as characteristic of the renaissance tradition; but, since the artist is by definition concerned with form, we may legitimately inquire into the artist's reasons for deviation. What force makes a writer succumb to his momentary flights of fancy to an extent where he cannot resist their inclusion in an otherwise organized work? . . .

Philosophical passages during which the action lies still occur in this novel in two ways: from the lips of the Philosophers and from the lips of the author himself. The difference between the two is a result of the author's intention either to satirize or to instruct; and, since the author is a more brilliant satirist than philosopher and since satire belongs to a novel while philosophical discourse does not, the difference for the reader is that between delight and impatience.

Obviously, the author enjoys philosophizing, but he is intelligent enough to know that this enjoyment is an excellent subject for satire; moreover he is enough of an artist to be able to satirize this tendency in himself. If we examine these philosophical bits of dialogue that are expounded by the Philosophers, I do not think we shall ever find them nonsensical. In themselves they are sensible and useful; the hilarity comes from their total irrelevance to the practical issue at hand. Similarly, alas!, when the author pours the remaining philosophy in his system into the reader's ear in order to illumine some aspect of the narrative, the result is often irrelevance. If we do not quite laugh—this time at the author—it shows that we are well-mannered readers and that the author's sin is not unpardonable.

We pardon him primarily, I think, on account of his genius for humour. Whether it manifests itself in the form of exaggeration or oversimplification or juxtaposition, or in a special brand of delicate charm through which his children and Leprecauns and rabbits and squirrels become unforgettable, we willingly follow him into realms that become wholly disconnected from the main intention of the story. . . .

It is with a certain regret that I conclude that in the final analysis appreciation for this novel is a matter of taste; and in order to compensate for this I shall permit myself to be subjective in asserting my enchantment with it.

George Egon Hatvary. Irish Writing. March, 1953,
pp. 63–65

In certain respects Stephens' development as an artist followed the normal pattern for Irish writers who emerged during the revival. For instance, he sang the glories of the Irish countryside, a natural paradise where a sensitive Irishman like Stephens could escape the mundane horrors of a solicitor's office. . . . Like many other Irish poets he tried his hand at retelling the Old Irish sagas, although he told them in prose rather than in verse or dramatic dialogue. Finally, like Pearse and Colum and Frank O'Connor, like almost every Irishman who since Douglas Hyde has studied the Gaelic language, Stephens composed translations and "adaptations" of Gaelic verse. Nature poems, character sketches, reworkings of myth and legend, translations—these were the usual things. But Stephens did things that were unusual too, and he often did the usual in a different way; it is these divergencies from the norm that give to Stephens' verse and prose and to the expression of nationalism implicit in his verse and prose a unique and original quality.

When he turned to the old Irish sagas, Stephens set out to retell the *Táin Bó Cúalnge* along with numerous related tales and to incorporate them into a single unified story. It was a formidable task he set for himself and one which he left unfinished after having published *Irish Fairy Tales* (based mainly on the Fenian cycle), *Deirdre*, and *In the Land of Youth* and before beginning the central saga of the great cattle raid of Cooley. Dorothy M. Hoare in her *Works of Morris and Yeats in Relation to Early Saga Literature* claims for Stephens the distinction of having captured in his published volumes the true flavor of the original sagas. . . . Miss Hoare in effect praises Stephens for achieving that which such a scholar of ancient Irish literature as T. F. O'Rahilly would condemn as the fallacy of euhemerism. Even so, her observation is only partly accurate. Stephens does indeed humanize the shadowy heroes of Ireland's remote past as neither Yeats nor A.E. could have done; but he is not at all concerned with recreating the situations of the sagas as they actually happened and the characters as they actually were—if, indeed, the situations did in fact occur and if the characters were real—and such a term as "historical imagination" is really irrelevant to his art.

Stephens makes clear his attitude toward Ireland's Celtic inheritance in his essay, "Outlook on Literature," in which he writes: "It is certain that Ireland will revisit her past with vast curiosity and reverence, but she will not remain there long enough to eat a railway sandwich. She will return with her booty to the eternally present time of an eternally modern world." The focus of Stephens' art is always on the present rather than the past, and this is just as true of his retelling of the ancient saga stories as it is of his essays and poems which are concerned specifically with contemporary Irish life. He views the old tales, certainly, with "vast curiosity," although with something less than reverence, and the tone of *Irish Fairy Tales*, *Deirdre*, and *In the Land of Youth* is light and ironic, and quite clearly the work of the same man who wrote *The Crock of Gold* and *The Demi-Gods*.

Richard J. Loftus. *Nationalism in Modern Anglo-Irish Poetry* (Madison and Milwaukee, Univ. of Wisconsin Pr., 1964), pp. 202–4

It is easy to expatiate on Stephens's qualities as a writer, on his attractive personality, the individualism and the whimsy; the love of exaggeration and the fantastic stories; the tendency to treat serious matters with apparent levity; the ability to talk for hours on any subject. But when judging him in the general context of English Literature one cannot deny that his output was small for a writer of eminence—half a dozen "novels," two books of short stories and a volume of his collected poems. It is rather unfortunate that he matured early as a writer, for, having adopted an ideal philosophy at the beginning of his career, his work had little chance to develop. There is no history of an internal struggle and resultant triumph.

Nevertheless, he has proved himself worthy of a permanent place in English literature. In a world grown pessimistic after the downfall of established customs he offered ultimate values where human ones were fast becoming standard. He exalted the spirit of literature rather than the letter, preaching that the author has a spiritual duty as well as an artistic one. "Success depends on the variety of one's inner life" was his dictum; and he reminded the critic, in "An Essay in Cubes," that he "is not celebrating a man, but a soul." His career as a writer is the story of the development of this inner life. His religious sensitivity was fortunately combined with a talent for artistic expression, and he had a distinct advantage in his large and aptly chosen vocabulary, the result of omnivorous reading, so that he could range from a leisurely narrative to an incantatory prose in *The Crock of Gold*; and the impersonal tones of *Here Are Ladies*, where he preoccupied himself with the rambling of the individual's thoughts, and the dramatic opening paragraphs of *The Demi-Gods* were equally his own. His poetic insight displayed itself in the gift of remembering what happened in the flush of a moment and recreating the full richness of an experience directly instead of by intimation.

His limitation was that as a writer he stood alone; he founded no school of writing and the threads of tradition which he picked up were absorbed into a style that was his and inimitable.

Hilary Pyle. *James Stephens: His Work and an Account of His Life* (London, Routledge & Kegan Paul, 1965), pp. 174–75

We know that James Stephens read Gaelic poetry extensively—indeed much of his best prose, like his book *Déirdre*, is an amalgam of Gaelic literature and tradition with his own considerable mastery of invention and sheer technical prowess—and the proof of his intrepid adventuring among the Gaelic texts is that the poet on whom Stephens based the two poems from which I have just quoted was Dáibhidh Ó Bruadair. Ó Bruadair was the very voice of the Gaelic seventeenth century, and even from very proficient readers of Irish, his original poems demand close attention. Of course James Stephens had the literal translations of the Irish Texts Society's edition of Ó Bruadair to help him, but only a man who could to a fair degree appreciate the original poems could give the feel of Ó Bruadair as Stephens does, for Ó Bruadair is as far from the *Love-Songs of Connacht* as Browning is from Thomas Campion.

The book in which the Ó Bruadair poems appeared, with others, is called *Reincarnations*, and is dated 1918. Here is part of the author's note explaining his method:

> This book ought to be called Loot or Plunder or Pieces of Eight or Treasure-Trove, or some name which would indicate and get away from its source, for although everthing in it can be referred to the Irish of from one hundred to three hundred years ago the word translation would be a misdescription. There are really only two translations in it. . . . Some of the poems owe no more than a phrase, a line, half a line to the Irish, and around these scraps I have blown a bubble of verse and made my poem. In other cases, where the matter of the poem is almost entirely taken from the Irish, I have yet followed my own instinct in the arrangement of it, and the result might be called new poems.

An important book: an important explanation. The fascination of Gaelic verse for a writer of Stephens's unquestionable genius is notable even today, when there are still Irish men and women who do not understand that Gaelic literature is a glory. The other important point in the book and the explanation is this: that a poet of Stephens's capacity cannot for long forbear to transmute his originals: long-continued translations—unless in unusual cases and where supreme masterpieces are the originals—is not for the mind which bodies-forth its own verse-children.

A third observation, so that James Stephens's love-affair with Gaelic poetry may be placed in perspective: a mind so fertile and so creatively absorbent of influences was bound to have love-affairs with others than Róisín Dubh and Caítlín Ní hUalacháin: fidelity in marriage and in poetry are different virtues. I make this last point not simply for perspective, but because what Stephens made of other influences—Eastern scriptures, through A.E. perhaps, among them—helps in removing any suspicion of claustrophobic Gaelicism from the theme of this lecture. *It was only when all the roadblocks were cruelly placed between the Gaelic poets and Europe that they ceased to know and care for other literatures and other nations.*

Robert Farren. In Sean Lucy, ed., *Irish Poets in English* (Cork, Mercier, 1973), pp. 138–39

Oliver Gogarty reports Stephens' test for measuring success. "The point is: how many men have loved you? Women, yes; but I am not talking about sexual love. How many men have loved you?" Stephens was fortunate in his male friends. Arthur Griffith, Thomas Bodkin, AE, Stephen MacKenna, James Joyce, Samuel Koteliansky changed his life and career in many ways, and he loved them. But he also loved women, children, animals, and Ireland, in what seem to be equal amounts.

In his best works, Stephens' love is for every creature and he displays this affection time and time again. All of his heroines are motivated by love in its manifold forms—maternal, charitable, sexual, marital. The secret of his successful works is that in them he embodies love; the later, more arid works only talk about it. In his last poems he no longer seeks Love the Magician; he is himself magician, dealing in mystical symbols, esoteric rites, mysterious rituals. Poetry is no longer a manifestation of love; it comes from the poet's Will. The vitality one senses in the clash of emotions in *Insurrections*, *The Demi-Gods*, and *Deirdre* has vanished; whatever energy is left comes from idiosyncratic punctuation and capitalization.

Perhaps Stephens could be better viewed as juggler than acrobat. In his best works he balances groups of two, three, or four characters in order to illustrate certain themes: the Contraries, sexual jealousy, and the divided self. These matters are also encompassed by the theme of love because fulfillment can only come through union. Consider the complex theme of the division of Man which Stephens has said that he envisioned in *The Crock of Gold*. The Philosopher, the Thin Woman, Pan, and Angus Óg represent those aspects of man Blake called the Four Zoas: thought, emotion, the body, divine imagination; the children and the leprecauns represent innocence and "the elemental side of man." At the end of the book, elements of the divided self are united by their affection for each other. Husband and wife, shepherdess and god, children and leprecauns are joined in love and friendship. Only Pan, the lustful foreign god, is without love. . . .

Stephens experiments with the language as well as the characters of love, starting with a modest love poem, "Slán Leath," and moving to both serious and comic conversations on love in *Here Are Ladies*, and his novels. Everything from endearments in the Gaelic fashion to translations of Sappho's love lyrics are of interest to him.

His works are all variations on this theme. Love is the motivation for patriotic essays and adaptations of Gaelic legends; it is the subject of stories concerning husbands and wives, parents and children, man and nature's creations. What shines through the prescriptions for a better world, the psychological analyses, the tales of the fantastic, the romantic, the grotesque, and the realistic is his first, his final, his over-arching theme—love. Stephens' works are his variations on this theme, his valentines to the world.

Patricia McFate. *The Writings of James Stephens*
(New York, St. Martin's Press, 1979), pp. 152-54

Whether or no he was ever an actual subscribing member of the Dublin Society, there seems to be a good deal of the fashionable Theosophical blather of his time about this; but it is as well to distinguish these philosophical maunderings from the third sort of discourse in Stephens's books, a humbler sort of thing which may be called the expression of a personal point of view, often indubitably wise. Mostly this is about the relationship of the sexes, which he sees as a sort of immemorial conflict, beneficial to both parties, in which only victory or defeat constitute disaster: so long as the conflict continues, and the balance is kept, all is well. Male preponderance or female preponderance are equally wrong. To that extent he is a liberationist. To the extent that he saw male and female as opposite polarities whose eternality is well established he would offend the sort of female liberationist who believes that the object of the female part should be to become more like the male; but not those who delight in intermingling. . . .

[B]ecause it is necessary to rescue him from the charge of being the sort of writer to whom "words alone are certain good," it is as well to pay attention to Stephens's view of things. And he really has a great deal to say about a number of related topics; much of it, in one sense or another "true," though about the topics concerned it would be perhaps enough to be merely illuminating: the conflict and union of opposites, the nearness of love and hate, the importance of desire and the disappointments of satiety. He knew a great deal about hard times, having been born in the utmost poverty and deposited in the care of a foundling institution. It would seem nowadays to invite the most obvious of retorts to say that he knew a great deal about the riches of poverty also; but he does—it is part of his system of opposites—he knows the dreams of beggary and the intoxications of its occasional windfalls. If he has a message it may be that struggle and effort are the conditions of human life.

> Anthony Cronin. *Heritage Now: Irish Literature in*
> *the English Language* (New York, St. Martin's
> Press, 1983 [first pub. Dingle, Ireland, Brandon,
> 1982]), pp. 152–53

The first commanding figure [in the Irish tradition of symbolic narrative] is James Stephens, whose output involves six novels and three collections of short stories. Stephens is remarkable not only because of his readability and his perennial appeal to a wide audience, from children to adults, from academe to the common reader, but also for the many purposes served by his fictions—social commentary, mystical insight, philosophic discourse, prophesy, parody, satire. These themes and doctrines are not just tagged on to the fables but, for the most part, deftly embodied in plots and characterisations of great ingenuity and freshness where the reader may find in the words of C. S. Lewis "some of the finest heroic narrative, some of the most disciplined pathos, and some of the cleanest prose which our century has produced." . . .

The Crock of Gold has the typical Stephens blend and marriage of opposites: it is profound and funny, realistic and fabulous. Its cast of characters: the two crotchety Philosophers and their wives, Meehawl and his daughter, Caitilin, the Leprecauns of Gort na Cloca Mora, the policemen and the two gods, Pan and Angus Óg, make up a bizarre and visionary milieu, and their adventures between the malign city and the country of the gods have all the ingredients of suspense, surprise and comic reversal that make for a narrative cliffhanger. Then in the narrative pauses, as when Caitilin wanders drowsily through the pastures with her sheep and goats, or when the Philosopher broods disconsolately in prison, there is an enchanting sense of atmosphere that wooes the reader's mind towards the novel's governing themes. Finally there is the dialogue in which these themes are strenuously and divertingly argued. The god Pan, hairy and goat-legged, has come to Ireland and made off with Caitilin into the hills. Meehawl, her father, comes to the Philosopher who suggests that if all fails—and predictably it does—they can get Angus Óg, the Irish god of love, to intervene on their behalf. . . .

And so the two gods struggle for the love of Caitilin and for the mind of the Philosopher in the adventures that follow. It is of course a battle for the heart and mind of Ireland, a country where Victorian and Jansenist doctrines have subdued and enslaved the life-affirming values of Pan—erotic love and exuberance of the body—and outlawed the values of Angus, spiritual love and the poetic imagination. By the end of the book the battle has been won, and the fairy host sweeps down on the city to rescue the Philosopher, the Intellect of man, "from the hands of the doctors and the lawyers, from the sly priests, from the professors whose mouths are gorged with sawdust, and the merchants who sell blades of grass" and return "dancing and singing to the country of the gods. . ."

The Crock of Gold is not only a universal fable of the war between the spiritual and the material, between instinct and law, love and convention, vision and reason, it is also a shrewd satire on Victorian Ireland which has become, as it were, a missionary country for Pan and his cult of love, passion, joy, spontaneity, the holiness of the heart's affections and the truth of imagination. Stephens is to that extent a faithful adherent of the Literary Revival as pioneered by Yeats and Russell, as ordained from the dawn of English Romanticism, in the visionary projections of Blake and Shelley.

But Stephens was his own man in one important respect. Where the older generation tended to view the Celtic gods and heroes with awe and reverence Stephens saw them with a kind of affectionate irony that made them amenable to his purposes as a satirist, a commentator on society's ill and humanity's failures in justice, compassion and vision.

Augustine Martin. In Augustine Martin, ed., *The Genius of Irish Prose* (Dublin and Cork, Mercier, 1985), pp. 113–15

STRONG, L. A. G. (1896–1958)

Ambition is a laudable quality in a writer. Yet the first novel that is inspired by big aims is likely to be a less satisfying product in itself than one which attempts no heights or profundities. This statement applies emphatically to *Dewer Rides*, which is remarkably interesting as promise, but very imperfect as fulfillment. Mr. Strong has essayed a novel on the epic scale. A disciple of Thomas Hardy, or perhaps still more of the modern peasant novelists of Scandinavia, he has sought to present the tragic development of a man of the soil against a grim—almost a determining—background of Nature. The scene is a village, representing the last human stronghold, on a wild fringe of Dartmoor, where spring does not triumph until weeks after it has established itself in the valleys, and where every civilizing influence has won a tardy and precarious victory.

. . . It is not that Mr. Strong has no sense of character. He has a very true and lively sense of it; he already excels, indeed, in still portraiture. But he cannot make his characters develop. They do not move naturally, but jump violently from one phase to another. If Mr. Strong can overcome this difficulty he should do notably good work. His vision is both large and minute; he conveys atmosphere; and his descriptive gifts are far above the average.

Gilbert Thomas. *Spec.* June 22, 1929, p. 982

Mr. Strong is in danger of being choked with butter by his critics. And this is a pity. He is a poet with a poet's command of language; as a novelist he is virile as well as sensitive; and it is not improbable that some time in the not distant future he will write a piece of fiction of the first order. When that time comes, the people who are now bellowing about his "genius" will be out of breath. And if not out of breath, they will have found someone else to bellow about. And if they have found no one else, they will certainly have exhausted their vocabulary of laudation. It is a poor look-out for Mr. Strong. I, for one, have too much respect for his rich talent to suppose that he does himself justice in *The Brothers*. . . . If cruelty and violence were the measure of greatness (and they are sometimes accounted so), this book would be a masterpiece. There is, indeed, far more in it than that: some admirable writing, lyrical descriptions of Nature, and good dramatic narrative. But violence (rather than strength) is the keynote. It is less its violence, however, than the casual take-it-or-leave-it manner in which the violence is presented that impairs the story as a work of art. Mr. Strong is at no pains to make incredibilities credible. His people are drawn in the flat: they have little human substance, and all that they do has the air of being forced on them by their author. All that they do, and all that they suffer too. Natural death seems to be almost unknown in the Western Highlands. Mary is murdered; the genial Captain M'Grath is drowned; Ferus drinks himself to death; John is gored by a bull. It is true that the elder Macraes die in their bed, but even two swallows do not make a summer.

Gerald Bullett. NSN. Jan. 23, 1932, p. 96

The idea of Strong as a poet is not completed without an appreciation of that other sense of remoteness and brooding mystery which has been mentioned. The reader of the group of poems entitled "Northern Light" gets to the heart of it if he can fully share with the poet the experience incarnated in the eight brief lines of the poem which gives its title to the whole suite.

> Here under Heaven ringed
> With fingering pale fires
> The soul unpacks to lose
> Her burden of desires.
>
> Thoughts are the clean gulls,
> Flesh cool as a bone.
> The mind is a wave here
> And the heart a stone.

This achievement of concentrated brevity without loss of emotional impetus or musical subtlety shows the lyrical Strong at his characteristic best, but it is easy for the unheedful to overlook the quality of the mental energy spent upon such a few short words. Certainly the second stanza is a never-ending amazement, endlessly evoking the cold sea-beaten shore and luminous sky with the subtle and thrilling awareness felt by the poet.

Indications of the imagination which sometimes dominates and transforms his prose are not lacking in the verse. After reading his novels we know where we are. . . . We soon realise that "The Northern Light" suite of poems was born of the same impressions as *The Jealous Ghost*, and the poem "The Haunted Glen" is actually the core of the novel, but the poem is just a glance at the theme, ending with a gasp of humorous relief. . . .

By surveying his poetry in the *Selected Poems*, the arrangement of the contents of this volume makes evident how the landscapes of three of the sections—Dublin, Devon, and the Scottish Western Highlands—are paralleled by the backgrounds of his fiction. Not only does he use the same familiar landscapes in his verse and prose, but he repeats his scenery and sometimes his characters in the fiction, themes appearing in the novels appearing as sketches in the two collections of his short stories, *The English Captain* and *Don Juan and the Wheelbarrow*. . . .

Of Strong's poetry, then, it may be said that besides revealing a keen sense of the comic in life—usually in what used to be called "low life"—it incorporates at its best the essential beauty of his descriptive prose, and adds a music which is too rare in the latter, though it can be heard clearly in the novel of the west Highland coast, *The Jealous Ghost*. That nostalgic sweetness pervades the style of the novel, just as the ghost of the seventeenth century girl who haunts the hill at Mhor (surely one of the most attractive ghosts in modern fiction?) influences most of the story. He could not have written *The Jealous Ghost* nor some of the prose in his other novels, had he not been a poet. In fact he is in his verse a lyrical poet some of whose poignant brevities of song are likely to echo in the ears of later generations, perhaps more clearly than they do in the ears of our deafened post-war generation.

R. L. Mégroz. *Five Novelist Poets of To-day*
(New York, Joiner & Steele, 1933), pp. 71–73,
76–77

L. A. G. Strong's new novel, *Corporal Tune*, is being hailed in London for its great beauty, and it is certainly one of the most sensitive and delicate of all his books. Its theme is simple, the writing exquisite without affectation, the implications innumerable. And at the same time the novel has both perfect detachment and a quite personal intimacy which make it unique.

Mr. Strong, as is known, was very ill some time ago (it is good news that he is now fully recovered); and the tale describes many of the thoughts and feelings of a sick man. But it is, for all that, a work of imagination and the work of a considerable artist.

The chief character is a writer whose wife has died in childbirth; and the writer himself is in reality at the point of death. Accordingly it might be thought that the note of *Corporal Tune* is one of melancholy. This is not the case. There are frets, of course, and discoveries of all sorts of hidden thoughts such as may arise in the mind of a dying man; but the quality of the book lies in its calm understandings and its poetic interpretations of the soul of man.

A very good book, which seems slight at first reading and grows in strength as one remembers it. Not for everybody, but for those to whom beauty in a novel—limpid beauty, for there is nothing obscure or affected in Mr. Strong's outlook—is a delicious experience.

Frank Swinnerton. *Chicago Daily Tribune*.
July 28, 1934, p. 12

Without doubt, Mr. Strong has written the standard work for all time on the life of Tom Moore [*The Minstrel Boy*]. If we consider this book as a portrayal of Tom Moore's Ireland, it is masterly—Miss Constantia Maxwell's *Ireland Under the Georges* is the only other work of recent times which we would compare with it. If we take it as a study of Tom Moore the man, it is lively and interesting, worthy to be read for pure biographical charm. Finally, we may take it as a criticism of Tom Moore's work—his immortal songs, his eminently singable poetry, his place in literary history and influence on his country's fortunes—and this, the most important aspect of the work, is done so well that the book is one that no one can afford to miss. We cordially congratulate Mr. Strong, therefore, on a work which enriches Ireland and earns him national gratitude and new fame. . . .

Tom was yet but a lad when he began to pour verses into magazines. The specimens which Mr. Strong quotes show us his facile style already clearly defined. At college he wrote copiously, chiefly light, amorous verse. He fell under the fruitful influence of two men of note—Edward Hudson and Robert Emmet; and here, to our great satisfaction, Mr. Strong reinstates the story as authentic which tells how Moore once played "The Little Red Fox," and Emmet started up with the cry: "Oh, that I were at the head of twenty thousand men marching to that air!"

It was a tune to tie men's souls. Moore stood with the patriots, but played no heroic part; on the other hand, he was not venal, and his biographer makes claims for him which are well substantiated. Though he did not suffer with the United Irishmen, his friends, he lived to serve his country well, and we read how he used the fame and influence which came to him so easily—used them for his country's service, and was not found wanting, when his loyalty to his fellow-Catholics required sacrifice. He braved the world more than once in the cause of his parents' people, although he gave up the regular practice of their religion and became a formal Protestant. He rejoiced in Emancipation. . . .

As to the songs by which Moore became famous and remains immortal, they never have been criticised with more penetration than by Mr. Strong. . . .

Several songs are examined by the *criteria* [of clarity and musicality], and are proved to be as excellent as the popular verdict always has declared. Moore's own performance of his lyrics was dramatic rather than musical. Music was the breath of his life. He even "warbled a little" the day before he died.

Of Moore's family life, his friendships—especially with Lord Byron—his religious and political opinions, Mr. Strong writes equally well. This book demonstrates that "the Melodies" were one of the great forces which made for Irish national pride and aspiration during the depressing nineteenth century. If the nation reads this book—and it must do so—it will be everlastingly grateful to the droll little, brilliant song writer, who composed for the drawingroom and was accepted in the cottages. Into a dispirited and broken people, Tom Moore breathed a new soul.

Irish Times. Sept. 18, 1937, p. 7

Most noticeable in this collection of short stories [*Sun on the Water*] by Mr. Strong is their calmness. Even in the first story "Sun on the Water" there is rest and satisfaction. In this piece there is no plot, really it is not a story—just a descriptive piece of writing of the daily happenings on one of the Western Isles of Scotland as seen from the eyes of an invalid. Yet it holds the attention continually; one sees, hears and feels the colour sounds and breezes of the island. Mr. Strong understands the psychology of the invalid, he is able to sit inside the sick man's mind and note the world from there, he knows the little pains and pleasures of the man. His writing always tender is here particularly so. Strange that Mr. Strong is able to describe life so easily that he never makes it dramatically stirring—always it is acceptable, always pleasing. Mr. Strong's style, even, when he is cruelly sadistic (and he can be) is still able to let the reader relax. There is an atmosphere of life just going quietly and calmly on its way in all his work. "Evening Piece," another sketch will please Mr. Strong's many readers, and is perhaps the best story in the book. That Mr. Strong is intrinsically a poet is evident in all these stories, and when he is using this gift he is most successful.

DM. July, 1940, pp. 75–76

Many of Mr. Strong's fellow-countrymen who have been interestedly watching his progress up the slopes of Parnassus, must have hoped, after reading some of his sketches and stories about Ireland, that he would one day devote a whole novel to this country. There were hints and glimpses of *The Garden* in such stories as "Doyle's Rock" and "The Cottage," but his style has gained so much of sureness and grace since these earlier and more tentative sketches, that one must applaud the wisdom that waited until his sixth prose work before attempting the autobiographical novel, that alluring-looking craft, in which so many less discreet authors make their first reckless literary voyage, and are too often wrecked.

This story of a boy's childhood and adolescence in Ireland glows with the clear magical light of childhood's vision. These successive summer holidays were for Dermot Grey the summit of earthly bliss, and none of the details of his impressions and adventures, his "sensations and ideas" during these rapturous periods, seem to have eluded the almost uncanny memory of their recorder. As Walter Pater evoked the past with his exquisite description of a red hawthorn seen through a child's eyes, and Proust by the taste of a *madeleine* dipped in tea, so Mr. Strong effects his miracle with a description of the delicious unfamiliar sensation of eating an egg with a bone spoon.

The atmosphere and inhabitants of the two houses, that of the Grandparents at Sandycove, and of Uncle Ben's at Sorrento become as vitally real to the reader as if he had himself lived in them. Grandfather, with his endearing prejudices and courtly manners of the sixties, in his sitting-room with the cuckoo clock and the lamp and characteristic books like "Charles O'Malley" and "Comic Offerings"; Bessie, the absolute type of old Irish servant, with her two rosaries, one for week-days and one for Sundays, the latter with a magnified view of St. Peter's in its Cross; her all-purposes kitchen knife called "Stumpy" and her constant admonition to the small boy to keep clear of "her wicked elba," and Paddy-Monkey whose history is a novel in itself. The death of this engaging and most individual creature is unbearably pathetic; a real tragedy whose poignancy lies in its being seen through the heart and eyes of a sensitive child.

Those who know "The Jealous Ghost" and "At Glenan Cross" will not need to be reminded of their author's gift for capturing the atmosphere, the very soul of a place by some strange and fortunate marriage of observation and a poet's imaginative gift of description. In those he gave us the Hebrides in their enchanted loveliness, and in this he has immortalised the country round Dublin. The view of the Wicklow mountains from Sorrento for example cries out to poets to be praised; those who have known it in childhood may travel east or west and never find its like; even if they reach the blue curving bays of the Mediterranean will see them as no more breath-takingly beautiful. . . .

With Mr. Strong as with the best of the Impressionists the picture is never mere observation but seems transfigured by an inner spiritual perception. . . . The wistful refrain of Paddy Kennedy's song . . . is full of soft regret for past joys and seems to crystallise the whole feeling of *The Garden*, with its vivid reconstruction of a period now gone for ever. . . . As a whole the book is pure enchantment and takes its place beside the finest things hitherto written about Ireland.

DM. July, 1941, pp. 72–73

In an illuminating foreword to this [*Darling Tom, and Other Stories*], his latest collection of short stories, Mr. Strong makes a plea, surely overdue, for *pleasure* in writing. "Not enough high-level writers let themselves be amused, and so amuse their readers," he says. "I believe that such a story as, for instance, 'The Wasp's Nest' (in this volume) is just as well worth the trouble taken over it as any other I have written, and I do not bring a lower standard of care to the writing of it."

These words have point indeed when, as in the present volume, the writer is found to have as able a mastery of the "unattractive" and "unpopular" kind of story as of the "attractive" and "popular." Quotes are inevitable in discussing the work of a writer, who, in his quiet way, revolutionizes *genre*. Is "The Major's Men" a "popular" tale? It is a winner on any level. And so one is tempted to say that Mr. Strong is never better—or more serious than when he allows Mr. Mangan, the narrator in that entertaining series of tales, to take the stage. Here the subjects are as fresh as paint, and the writer's treatment of them that of a first-class painter: it is a kind of *stippling* really by which in such stories as "Ducks from Darragh" or "The Toreador" he achieves a most delicate blend of funniness and, as it were, Shakespearean sentiment—"We have heard the chimes at midnight, Master Shallow." None of them is merely funny—they all have their human truth—but "Darling Tom," which tells of the finding of a letter on a body cast up by the tide, is hauntingly beautiful in atmosphere and feeling. One might imagine that Mr. Strong, in turning away from the funny, the odd, the picturesque or the poetic, would give us a good story certainly, but one somehow out of his element. The truth is he is quite as at home in seemingly unattractive subjects. "I've Done It Now," a drama, *pianissimo*, of love and disenchantment, played against the unencouraging setting of a canteen, is a first-class story. And "The Old Man," which points to the loneliness of extreme old age, owes how much of its effect to the unerring manner in which the suburban limitations of the old man's background are depicted. In "That's Life," however, where degradation abounds, Mr. Strong is too mature a writer to be merely grim: here the quenchless spark of humour, of insouciance in human behaviour, saves all. Like life, this writer, so wholly respectable—to use a good word in its good sense, defies classification.

Terence Smith. *Irish Writing*. June, 1953, p. 62

STUART, FRANCIS (1902–   )

Mr. Francis Stuart's *Glory*, which begins as a novel in its scene laid in Ireland, transports us, as it continues, to the other side of the world and to the sphere of romantic allegory as well. The Irish have been compared to the Russians, and Mr. Stuart's presentation of them will cause the comparison to be made again; his characters, in their charm and fickleness, seem distantly related to the characters of Chekhov, and they tend to live largely in their imaginations. . . . Perhaps Mr. Stuart himself is "one of the legion of outcasts of the machine-age, of romanticists," of those who seek to avoid becoming "obsessed by flesh and steel." Whether there is any salvation for the world or not, it is comforting to think of all those whose worldly failure implies a spiritual success, those who, like these characters of Mr. Stuart's, . . . may be bankrupts and wasters and nobodies and daydreamers, but are capable of heroic devotions. They are the salt of the earth, and we owe gratitude to those who can recognize their savour.

William Plomer. *Spec*. Sept. 1, 1933, p. 292

A novelist who writes a preface to the book of a colleague is more likely to harm than to help him, because such a preface seldom impresses the public and often irritates the critics. Yet once in a long while an older novelist is granted an opportunity to affirm his faith in a young writer's genuine significance, and for good or for ill he cannot refuse the privilege of setting on record the expression of that faith.

I have already offered in print my homage to Mr. Francis Stuart's genius, and now after reading *Try the Sky* I am proud to think that my name may be associated, be it in never so humble a way, with a work of the most profound spiritual importance to the modern world. The literary qualities of Francis Stuart's work are too evident to need anybody like myself as a signpost; but, closely in touch as I am with a state of mind diffused over the whole world at this time and yet so far hardly touched upon in contemporary literature, I feel that I am entitled to plead for intellectual attention to a book like this. If such attention be paid, it will undoubtedly help those who recognise that humanity now stands at a crisis of evolution to consider one of the ways forward that the future offers.

The influence upon contemporary thought of the work of D. H. Lawrence is an indication of our willingness to listen to any teacher with what is called a message, provided the sincerity of such a message be sufficiently invulnerable. I suggest that Francis Stuart has a message for the modern world of infinitely greater importance than anything offered by D. H. Lawrence, and I believe that in this book he has made his message more easily intelligible than in his previous novels or even in his beautiful poems. It may be that to invite readers to look beyond an exquisitely told tale for a great spiritual truth is to handicap a novel; but I am so passionately anxious to persuade the world to listen that I cannot refrain from crying, in the words consecrated by the greatest message ever given to man: "He who hath ears to hear, let him hear."

Compton Mackenzie. Foreword to Francis Stuart,
Try the Sky (New York, Macmillan, 1933), pp. v–vi

Those who read Mr. Stuart's pre-war novels will remember them for their high literary quality and perhaps for their atmosphere of romantic unreality which debilitated the conflicts they described. Their author spent the war years, not in the safe seclusion of Ireland, but in Germany. I imagine he was, like most Irish patriots, anti-British rather than pro-German; whatever the reason for his alliance with Germany at such a time, his experiences there have matured him and given his work a new poignancy and power.

The Pillar of Cloud tells the story of an Irishman living after the war in a Rhineland town and his relationship with two sisters, Halka and Lisette. The girls are "displaced persons" who have lost their parents and been brought by the conquerors to work in Germany. Though they were born in Poland, they belong nowhere. They are true citizens of chaos, symbols of the thousands of lost people who live somehow in the ruins of Europe. Halka, little more than twenty years of age, is already a mature, almost an aged, person in her outlook and wisdom; Lisette is a child who has never been a child. So completely beyond the concepts of the old world are they that compared with Frau Arnheim, who clings to the ideals of her pre-war bourgeois existence, they belong not so much to a different generation as a different species. Half-starved for years, a-moral from necessity, they can conceive only one ideal—that of fraternity, the fraternity they share with the Irishman, Dominic. Their world has become his world; he understands it completely. . . .

Halka and Lisette are not presented as exiles; they are rather the primary initiates of our modern condition. The Alsatian officer who releases Dominic offers him the solution of anarchy; this, however, seems to him "but an additional confusion, a little more chaos added to the huge chaos"; there is only fraternity. Dominic loves Halka, and he lets her persuade him to marry Lisette, who is dying of consumption, so he can take the girl out of Germany; but it is too late. Lisette's death leaves him free to stay with Halka.

Mr. Stuart's writing shows the influence of Dostoyevsky and D. H. Lawrence, but both influences are well assimilated because his understanding of suffering now approaches theirs. *The Pillar of Cloud* is written with a poetic force that comes out of the very core of suffering. Apart from its quality, the novel is unique in that no other English-speaking writer has been in a position to touch upon its subject except from the outside. Mr. Stuart writes with convincing certainty of the reactions of a starving man from whom a promised food-parcel is withheld by the incompetence of officials, the simple acceptance of a-morality, the spiritual triumph of these people who somehow surmount the desolation of their physical condition, the evolution of the Irishman who voluntarily chooses that condition. I doubt if even Mr. Stuart could write another novel about these experiences; like Mr. Cummings in *The Enormous Room*, he has beggared them of emotion.

Olivia Manning. *Spec.* Oct. 18, 1948, pp. 504, 506

Francis Stuart is as important as a novelist as Jack B. Yeats is as a painter, although the unique quality of his novels when considered against the background of Irish literature has never been fully recognised. Outside Ireland he has had the appreciation of a very enthusiastic few including Compton Mackenzie and Harold Nicholson. He is the one Irish novelist who can be approximately classified with the group that includes Rex Warner, and less notably William Sansom and Edward Upward and, perhaps, even some of the novels of Mr. F. L. Green. I emphasise "approximately," because although Francis Stuart in *The Angel of Pity*, which may yet come justly to be regarded as his most notable book, acknowledges a debt to Kafka, he has too much originality and too much zest for life apart from books and theories to fall into the rut of crawling imitation with Sansom and Upward and others. "There is always more in life than meets the eye," he writes. "That cliché, which all who are not wilfully blind are forced to accept, condemns the literary method known as concrete realism. Concrete realism is a suppression of part of the truth." . . .

Stuart makes no discoverer's claim to the method that he calls concrete romanticism, acknowledges his debt to Franz Kafka and Rainer Maria Rilke and offers humbly to attempt to follow them. But the man who humbly and honestly acknowledges a debt is seldom merely a debtor and Stuart's marked originality shines out with a cold mystical light from such novels as *Try the Sky*, *The Angel of Pity* and *Pigeon Irish*. These three are in the fashion of concrete romanticism and are, as far as Irish fiction is concerned, in a class by themselves. In *The Great Squire* he has written an ordinary and not completely successful historical novel. In *The Bridge* he has written a sour tale of unlawful love in an Irish country town, with love as brutally bruised by the world as a Kafka myth could be bruised by the impact of the material order. In other novels like *Julie* or *Women and God* he has written according to the rules of concrete realism, but always with a consciousness of the spiritual that justifies what W. B. Yeats and Compton Mackenzie and others have said about his work. Yeats found in *Pigeon Irish* a cold exciting strangeness and in *The Coloured Dome* a style full of lyrical intensity and a mind full of spiritual passion. Compton Mackenzie wrote in a foreword to *Try the Sky* that Francis Stuart had a message for the modern world of infinitely greater importance than anything offered by D. H. Lawrence, using that particular comparison because the attitude of so many readers to Lawrence indicated that all they demanded of a message was that the messenger should be sincere. It is difficult to avoid being suspicious about novelists with a message and perhaps it might be wiser to say that Francis Stuart's novels have spiritual intensity and a sort of anarchical meaning.

Benedict Kiely. *Modern Irish Fiction: A Critique*
(Dublin, Golden Eagle Books, 1950), pp. 100–102

The girl whom the protagonist of *Black List, Section H* meets in Berlin also appears in other novels, as I have suggested earlier. And so much that is in Stuart's previous work, only in part, recurs in this new novel, with fuller development. These things have been mentioned—the horseracing, the farming, the love, the religion, the piloting, the travel (Vienna appears at length in the present book as the author's best-loved city), the participation in revolution, the hazards of existence in wartime Berlin, the various imprisonments— are there many other elements of experience a modern man could partake of? And how many men could, in a novel, unify all this experience? Some years ago the French critic Gabiel Venaissin suggested, in the pages of *Critique* (in an article entitled "Francis Stuart ou je vivrai le Malheur des autres"), that because many of the same experiences occur in various Stuart novels, this might seem to make for "monotonie," though it really could be called "unité." Now, in his latest novel, Stuart has brought virtually everything in his life and works together, a perilous undertaking because the narrative could become too widely scattered; but the book distinctly has the "unité" which the French critic found in Stuart's other works. And if all this were mere repetition, that would definitely be a drawback—but in the present book he gives his formerly recorded experiences an exalted intensity that makes them fresh and vital.

In the previous paragraphs I have mentioned a number of the experiences Stuart describes—or, rather, lives through—in the course of this novel. Brought all together, they show his character H as a representative man of our time. But, transfigured by his creator's exalted intensity, they also become notably individual. And they make for profundity.

Altogether, this is one of the truly remarkable novels of recent years.

Harry T. Moore. Postscript to Francis Stuart, *Black List, Section H* (Carbondale and Edwardsville, Southern Illinois Univ. Pr., 1971), pp. 439–40

If *Try the Sky* [1933] celebrates the aeroplane as a possible liberator for mankind *The Angel of Pity* (1935) condemns the mechanical world and its super-science of war. This is a powerful book written about the future:

> I imagine a grey morning breaking over some desolate front in the next great war. I am crouching in a concrete redoubt, partially blown in, with one companion . . .

War, by this point, is now seen by Stuart as a condition of mankind rather than an occasion on which theological arguments can be staged. The characteristics normally associated with the novel are less evident in *The Angel of Pity*, and it is regrettable that this experimental book has been poorly circulated. . . .

The need to make a living forced Stuart to produce twelve books between 1931 and 1939; inevitably the initial blossoming began to fade. Politically he was estranged from the new Ireland and he detested the provincialism of its culture. Finally his marriage to Iseult [Gonne] was disintegrating. Early in 1939 he was offered a lecturing position in Berlin University; he had previously conducted a private lecturing tour of Germany and he knew the country since the early years of his marriage. The appointment promised relief from domestic and financial stresses. Despite the outbreak of war Stuart decided that he should go to Berlin, that he should be where Europe was then focussed, that somebody should bear witness. In addition he felt that in wartime Germany he would at last be cut off from the conventional demands on his feelings and that in isolation he might begin to find himself. His decision (it is hardly necessary to say) was the most important of his life.

As the saturation bombing intensified and civilian life broke down in Berlin and other German cities, the fantasies Stuart had created in *The Angel of Pity* became realities. The philosophy of submission and humility became a means (the only means) to life. Perhaps no other artist in the English language was so aptly prepared by his earlier psychic life for the experience of wartime Germany, for the shades of humanity who populated Europe. The religious questionings of his earlier books reach maturity in his two finest novels *The Pillar of Cloud* (1948) and *Redemption* (1949). The characters breathe their lives with an intensity which only deprivation and hunger make possible; every moment is precious to them, something held back from the pit beneath them. These two novels are populated with vivid figures who move with slow insistence like souls in Purgatory. They are infused with a religious feeling that is no longer in any sense a rejection of reality, but the burning glass with which reality is created over and over again.

> W. J. McCormack. In W. J. McCormack, ed., *A Festschrift for Francis Stuart on His Seventieth Birthday* (Dublin, Dolmen, 1972), pp. 12–13

In August 1971, Stuart and his wife left their cottage in Meath and moved to a new home in the Windy Arbour section of Dublin. Four months later he published his twentieth novel, *Black List, Section H*, which Lawrence Durrell has called "a book of the finest imaginative distinction." Without doubt *Black List* is Stuart's best novel since *Redemption* and quite possibly his best ever. Whether it marks the beginning of still another major phase in his work or a very distinguished ending to his long career, only time will tell. But one thing is certain: the novel does not have the air of a *nunc dimittis*.

Stuart has called *Black List* a "memoir in fictional form," and the description is apt. Closely autobiographical, and yet written with something bordering on mystical detachment, the novel traces the author's life from the time he left Rugby through most of his postwar imprisonment. It tells of his relationship with Yeats, Maud Gonne, Iseult, and Gertrud (all but the last of whom appear under their real names); of his feelings toward Ireland during the Civil War and Germany during World War II; it tells of violence and tenderness, happiness and pain. All the major themes of his work are recapitulated: the belief that the artist must be ever vigilant, constantly questioning, a counterforce to the stale assumptions of society; the conviction that through suffering comes true insight, that through opening one's heart to others the spirit and the flesh may become one, that there is a goodness in the world to be set next to the vision of chaos.

Yet *Black List* is more than a powerful and imaginative recounting of the author's life and thought. H, the central character, is quite obviously Stuart (whose unused first name is Henry), but the kind of pilgrimage he undertakes is one of universal significance. His search for meaning in an unstable world is no less than the search every man must make if he wishes to discover more in life than overwhelming despair or, even worse, deathlike monotony.

Should this remarkable novel turn out to be his last, which one hopes is

not the case, it will be a fitting capstone to a career that had begun incon-
spicuously enough with the ragged volume of poetry Yeats had liked, moved
through the interesting but tentative experimentation of such novels as *Pigeon
Irish* and *The Coloured Dome*, and reached a rich maturity in *The Pillar of
Cloud* and *Redemption*. Through all these years Stuart has remained a thoroughly dedicated artist, constantly fascinated by the difficult; his failures resulted not from any betrayal of his art but from an inability to fulfill the complex tasks he set for himself. It seems inevitable that in due time, when the
good is finally sifted from the bad, several of Francis Stuart's novels, including *Black List*, will rank very high in the fiction of modern Ireland and that he
will find at last his just place as one of Ireland's truly significant writers.

J. H. Natterstad. *Francis Stuart* (Lewisburg, Pa.,
Bucknell Univ. Pr., 1974), pp. 84–85

There is not space in this essay to detail Francis Stuart's limitations as a
writer, but they can perhaps best be summarized by repeating that he is very
much an evangelistic novelist, of the D. H. Lawrence type. In fact the most
fruitful comarison seems to be with the work of Lawrence, whom Stuart admires but from whom he consciously diverges at a certain point. Thus, it is
certainly a weakness that, with the occasional exception of the Halka figure,
who never says much anyway, there is no one in the novels to challenge, or
even to communicate, on an articulate level, with the Stuart figure. Woman
may hold intuitive wisdom, and be moulded by suffering; but she is very
much the mute companion of the man's researches, just as she is in Lawrence.
A certain atmosphere of monologue results. Equally, like Lawrence, Stuart's
work can seem repetitious, although, outside *Black List*, it never becomes as
stridently insistent as Lawrence. Repetition, though, seems almost an irrelevant charge. Stuart's whole way of thought has led him to certain essentially
simple but fundamental insights, which, in a sense, he can only repeat. It is
perhaps a more serious limitation that his imagination carries him only to the
perception of what a new way of life might be, and no further. Each of his
communities was only at the foundation stage: its brief life might even be said
to depend upon a sense of inevitable terminus, upon the suspension in crisis of
the world outside. To ask more than this, though, is to ask literature to go beyond life, and at this point language ceases. By the end of *Women in Love*
Birkin and Ursula are equally suspended in air; and Lawrence's subsequent
ceaseless travelling, his quests to Mexico and Australia, were all part of the
attempt to find a language in which to speak of anything other than the inherited cast of the western mind.

To go back, though, or even to stay where you are, is equally impossible, and this is made clear by the impassioned accuracy with which both Lawrence and Stuart demolish the society around them. Stuart is particularly good
on the deadening influences that work against what he believes in, on what he

calls "the lack of contrasts" in modern life. In *The Flowering Cross* his study of the negative Polensky is quite as suggestive, perhaps finally more suggestive, than his study of the positive characters, Dominic and Alyse. Stuart is lucky, too, in that he has always had the differences of Ireland to return to, in a way that Lawrence could never return to the Nottinghamshire of the colliery towns, though they gave him his first touchstones of a way of life other than that proposed by the intellectual climate of his own day.

The comparisons end, though, on the important difference that Stuart has remained much more of a *maker* than Lawrence did. His themes are always intuitively felt and communicated. They grow from the structure and texture of the work itself. They include statement, but they do not resort to prolonged independent statement, as Lawrence's exposition does in his later work. On the other hand, there is nothing in Stuart to match the stylistic achievement of Lawrence's early work. Stuart's style has a rather orotund quality, a tendency to the sanctimonious. Within this, though, there is a consistent accuracy of expression, unobtrusive innovations of syntax and phrasing which show a careful control. At key moments, when accuracy at its most tense is married to the shaping cadence, the writing has a distinctive clarity and balance.

Roger Garfitt. In Douglas Dunn, ed., *Two Decades of Irish Writing* (Chester Springs, Pa., Dufour, 1975), pp. 218–19

Francis Stuart—it's still too widely unknown—is Lazarus come back from the dead. The resurrection occurred unexpectedly in 1974 when his *Memorial* blinked forth from the tomb, the graveclothes of Irish literary history clutched awry about it (Stuart was the man who actually got Iseult Gonne when Yeats turned his attention that way after failure with mother Maud), its pages still redolent with the grave-stink of its author's dubious collaboration with the wartime Germans. Since then his novels have made their living out of confessing to one kind of blackness after another. "It's the writer who's one with his work, and doesn't create it as a thing apart," narrator H. tells Yeats in *Black List, Section H.*, "who says the things that now matter most." An old man's lecheries, a survivor's self-justifications and special pleadings: they certainly feel as if they matter to Francis Stuart. It's the attempt, however, to latch them on to things that matter equally to the rest of us—like violence and destructiveness as evinced in the author's native Ireland—that gives *A Hole in the Head* more than a passing, confessional interest.

H. (still H. to himself) has now recrudesced as Barnaby Shane, and is haunted not only by the horrors of modern conflicts but by great analogues for tormented literary creators. He does have a hole in the head, which perhaps goes some way to accounting for his habit of casting himself as Christ ("Can you drink the cup that I drink of?" he's prone to inquire), or as Dostoevský, imprisoned and almost executed. Does the hole, though, we're invited to speculate, exhaustively account for the presence of Emily Brontë in his life? *Qua* literary device, of course, she is mightily handy (like other fictional time-travellers she's good for lots of unkind jibes at the banality of politicians, modern novels, Van Gogh). But most of all she stands for the writer's interiorised purgatory which, as Shane travels into Ulster, birthplace of her father (there's a roadsign to Rathfriland), is tensely juxtaposed with the all too evidently exteriorised sufferings of that province. Predictably, Shane (or H., or Stuart) plasters the self-pity on in trowelfuls (Branwell Brontë gets added to the roster of Shane's suffering predecessors): angst, you begin to think, can't be this romantically awful even with a hole in your head. Nevertheless some serious reflections on the mingling of fantasy and reality do come through. When he's "cured" of his obsession and Miss Brontë has departed to become someone else's Muse, Shane still finds the odd confirmation of her presence. Furthermore, Belbury (Belfast) turns out to be full of Gondalian iron men, and when he becomes a hostage to rescue two children of a paramilitary friend from a kidnapper's hideout Shane does turn into a kind of Dostoevsky or Christ. And—parting shot—the children's grannie (Nellie Dean, she'd seemed, to his "uncured" vision), asks "how the young lady is." So Emily, startlingly, lives; as startlingly, almost, as Francis Stuart.

Valentine Cunningham. NS. May 13, 1977, p. 648

You will remember that in the early portions of Stuart's *Black List, Section H*, the protagonist H or Luke has a number of shocking encounters with Yeats. They are part of the whole journey of that amazing book, a movement fuelled at one and the same time by irresistible purpose and painful disconnectedness. Stylistically, this split is maintained in the mixture of documentation and inner journal which is further urged upon the reader in the earlier portions (the style later is more fluid) by abrupt paragraphing and startling interjections. The journey itself is across a recognizable map, through a time-span that bristles with modern European historical data, passing persons that, in so many instances, have already a public reputation, perhaps especially for the Irish reader. But it is also a journey refracted through the eye of a highly idiosyncratic viewer so that while events and persons trail evidence of existence of one kind or another, including that of autobiography, from outside the book, they are subject within it to this austere and fevered scrutiny: an effect, as it were, of sameness and difference at once. In the end we realize that this is the very shape, the potent cause of the novel, to demonstrate an heroic confrontation between the artist and the world. The work does not seek to annihilate history or dissolve its sweeping edges which is the aspiration of most autobiographical fiction where the central consciousness tends to subsume historical information and change it into a utility, a domestic image, an extension of the singular imagination. Stuart's style is much more angular, nothing less than the opposing of one kind of record to another.

What emerges as positive, then, within the controlling mind of the book is directly contrary not only to conventional social morality but also to the common, received version of a particular phase of Irish and European history. The negatives of common social vocabulary: dishonour, disgrace, failure become positives, values to be embraced. The artist, then, is offered as a social misfit, stumbling in and out of life's incidents without a scrap of that shell which makes social intercourse endurable for most people. What emerges is the claim that such risk, such exposure as of a wound, is precisely the very quality which distinguishes the artist from all others.

Now all of this will be familiar to us from Stuart's own work and from that particular stream of Modernism of which it is part which reflects back to Blake and a romantic idea of the artist as heroic victim but would include writers like these who haunt H in the novel, Dostoevsky and Kafka. What is shocking in the encounters with Yeats is not the fact that a great poet could be pompous, absurdly theatrical and the kind of host who wandered in and out of guest bedrooms at odd hours. At this late stage in the century we are well accustomed to the common frailties of genius. What is shocking, what is always shocking in my reading, at any rate, in much of the modernist sensibility is that, despite the shared elevation of the artist, the violent expression of individualism is ruthlessly selective in its view of other artists. It might be said, however, that one of the processes which is being described in the book is the way in which the writer-protagonist has to free himself from the burden of greatness in others. It is not only Yeats but also Joyce who is put aside in several of those parentheses which stud *Black List, Section H*.

Thomas Kilroy. In Peter Connolly, ed., *Literature and the Changing Ireland* (Gerrards Cross, England, Colin Smythe, 1982), pp. 183–85

SYNGE, JOHN MILLINGTON (1871–1909)

I am certain that, in the long run, his grotesque plays with their lyric beauty, their violent laughter, *The Playboy of the Western World* most of all, will be loved for holding so much of the mind of Ireland. Synge has written of *The Playboy*: "Any one who has lived in real intimacy with the Irish peasantry will know that the wildest sayings in this play are tame indeed compared with the fancies one may hear at any little hillside cottage of Geesala, or Carraroe, or Dingle Bay." It is the strangest, the most beautiful expression in drama of that Irish fantasy which overflowing through all Irish literature that has come out of Ireland itself (compare the fantastic Irish account of the Battle of Clontarf with the sober Norse account) is the unbroken character of Irish genius. . . .

Yet, in Synge's plays also, fantasy gives the form and not the thought, for the core is always, as in all great art, an overpowering vision of certain virtues, and our capacity for sharing in that vision is the measure of our delight. Great art chills us at first by its coldness or its strangeness, by what seems capricious, and yet it is from these qualities it has authority, as though it had fed on locusts and wild honey. The imaginative writer shows us the world as a painter does his picture, reversed in a looking-glass, that we may see it, not as it seems to eyes habit has made dull, but as we were Adam and this the first morning; and when the new image becomes as little strange as the old we shall stay with him, because he has, besides the strangeness, not strange to him, that made us share his vision, sincerity that makes us share his feeling. [1910]

W. B. Yeats. *Essays and Introductions*
(New York, Macmillan, 1961), pp. 337, 339

Synge claimed never, or hardly ever, to have used word or phrase which he had not heard among the Irish peasantry. He found the English of these people, whose proper speech is Gaelic, a "curiously simple yet dignified language" spoken with a "delicate exotic intonation that was full of charm"; and these qualities of simplicity and dignity, rhythm, delicacy, and strangeness are the qualities of his prose.

Nevertheless, he did not accept this folk-language in the gross. As with his characters and his situations, he bettered what was already good by fastidious selection and blending. Here, perhaps, more than anywhere are visible the effects of his training in Paris, his knowledge of elaborate literature. For all his energy he was an artist eclectic and austere, and it was in language that his art was most triumphant. "In a good play," he held, "every speech should be as fully flavoured as a nut or apple." But in careless converse many words— though fewer in Inishmaan than in London—must always run to waste. The borders of the finest unpremeditated speech must be trimmed before it is suited for the shapely life of the stage. . . . Synge, having discarded the mechanical aid of blank verse, was entirely dependent on his own sense of form for his effects. His art was literally a criticism, a choosing.

Character, situation and language he thus borrowed from actual life, improving and embellishing them, but never altering their essence. His plays are never symbolical, his characters never projections of his own moods and ideas, as with Maeterlinck or Mr. Yeats. But, when all is said, no sincere artist has ever produced absolutely impersonal work. He depicts things as he sees them, and each has his peculiar mental vision. So Synge's work, though objective in method, is subjective in so far as it is coloured by his own temperament. The plays are bound together, and separated from all others, by something less material than their distinctive language; they are the work, not only of one hand, but of one soul.

Francis Bickley. *J. M. Synge and the Irish Dramatic*
Movement (London, Constable, 1912), pp. 28–30

Critics in general have no hesitancy in branding as un-Irish Synge's sardonic humour, already touched upon in connection with *The Tinker's Wedding*. To decide whether it was a product of foreign influence—in particular of Synge's lifelong intimacy with mediæval literature, especially farces and fabliaux—or whether it flowed from the very excess of his own ironical brooding, is practically impossible. Anyhow, Synge has invented a new "tang," a kind of defiant sarcasm which is and will always be like vitriol thrown on the Irish people. Personally we are inclined to regard this humour as the tragicomic expression of his individual outlook; and, if a literary parallel be sought for, we should feel tempted to compare it with the humour of Heine. Like Heine's, it savours of utter disillusion and of total renouncement; it has the same note of passionate, exuberant revolt. It is, in a way, ultimately foreign to the typical gentleness of traditional Irish humour. One must, however, carefully distinguish two sorts of humour in Irish and Anglo-Irish literature: on the one hand, the harmless, optimistic humour represented, say, by the amiable, almost saintly Irishman of the Goldsmith order; on the other hand, the grim, fierce, scorching humour of the Swift-Wilde-Shaw type, with an occasional touch of the *macabre* in it, as in Swift's famous proposal concerning the children of the Irish poor, where humour becomes so horrible that it makes you laugh. Synge's humour is clearly of the second, not of the first species.

A more distinctly un-Irish element in Synge's plays is his non-religious view of life. Doubtless this had an artistic cause: the desire to return to the relentless savagery of ancient Paganism. But Synge's archaic quest of the older Gaelic civilization made him blind to the profounder spirit of modern Ireland. In a way the ancient heathendom may be said to survive in the uncontrollable temperament and passionate outbursts of the average Irish peasant of to-day; but this is only a superficial appearance; at bottom he is an ardently religious being, whose whole life is coloured by faith and belief—especially Catholic faith. This aspect of Irish mind is simply ignored by Synge; it has no place in his works; and on this score his fellow-countrymen are justified in finding fault with his plays. [1913]

Maurice Bourgeois. *John Millington Synge and the Irish Theatre* (New York, Benjamin Blom, 1965), pp. 217–19

Nobody ever wrote Irish peasant dialect like Synge, and yet, reading it, one is penetrated with a sense of its verity, as well as amazed at its lyric beauty, passion, tenderness, hatred, scorn, invective,—the entire gamut of human feeling. That the Irish are a fanciful people is tolerably well known, and Synge's work will bring home to many the regrettable face that they lose much by transplantation; while the critic will be forced to admit that a fiery, sincere, passionate and spiritual people, who have remained simple by the grace of God, can speak a natural poetry in their daily lives that owes nothing to literary forms or traditions. No Irish writer has ever made us understand this like Synge, and so completely has he succeeded that we are apt to forget the genius that stands behind his puppets, and in the reading we go back again and again to marvel at this wonderful peasant speech—this dialect that in the essentials of true poetry puts to blush so many pages of "fine literature!" So deep is the illusion produced that we take his word for it when the artist assures us that the wildest sayings in his *Playboy of the Western World* are tame indeed compared with the fancies one may hear at any little hillside cottage of Geesala, or Carraroe, or Dingle Bay. On reflection, we see that the originality of the artist is in no wise questioned—everything has undergone the transmuting touch of genius. [1914]

> Michael Monahan. *Nova Hibernia: Irish Poets and*
> *Dramatists of Today and Yesterday* (Freeport, N.Y.,
> Books for Libraries Press, 1967), pp. 24–25

We must not speak of his plays simply as classics; the claim would be too great; one thinks that his elimination of so much of the spiritual left a certain narrowness in them within which the human spirit cannot abidingly find sustenance or ease. If universality be felt as wanting to his creations, therein is the cause. His people, except those in *Riders to the Sea*, are inclined to be naturalistic rather than human, for it is human to practice inhibitions for the sake of ideas, to curb appetite by traditions, dreams, faiths well or ill-founded (if so we may put the matter under its most general aspect). Synge's characters are incomplete, inasmuch as they lie outside this universal scheme of life. It is in this way they are freakish, and not in the poetry talk they indulge in nor in their want of practicality in human affairs.

If this blemish in his work be due to an inactive sense of the spiritual in himself, how much greater that blemish must have shown itself had he never come to feel for any community as he did actually come to feel for Aran and the islanders? Everywhere the peasant lives in the consciousness of the other world; his is undoubtedly a realm not only of natural but supernatural pieties; and Synge's *Riders to the Sea* and his essays, of themselves, tell us, as we have seen, that the islanders in Aran are no different from the peasants everywhere else. Synge himself was more than once stirred, even disturbed, by the thought of the difference between his own consciousness and theirs. Nowhere else, we may take it, had he so nearly attained to a lively sense of the spiritual as he did on certain occasions in these islands,—such a sense of the spiritual as might have enabled him to create pieces of literature classic not only in energy, sanity, and fullness, but also in spirituality, which of itself demands a more subtle energy, a rarer sanity, a vaster fullness. It is therefore not without cause that it is in the drama most closely adhering to the islands that we find his most classic work. "Is fuirist fuinne i n-aice na mine," runs the Irish proverb: "Kneading is easy where the meal's at hand." The meal was to hand in these islands where the people's age-long trafficking with a range of thoughts beyond the needs of nature had induced in them a dignity and settled peace that Synge not only noted but envied. [1931]

Daniel Corkery. *Synge and Anglo-Irish Literature: A Study* (New York, Russell & Russell, 1965), pp. 239–40

Riders to the Sea . . . expresses a mood, but it is not subjective in the sense in which *Dierdre of the Sorrows* is; the lack of personal feeling makes it by comparison an impersonal tragedy. Its lyricism lies elsewhere: in its way of presenting a natural atmosphere, its elemental sense of sky and landscape and sea and storm.

The action of the play is extraordinarily simple. An islander goes over the sea in defiance of the storm and the efforts of the women to hold him back; and he is drowned at once. But this action is presented as one that is constantly recurring. It is the threat under which the islanders live. In these circumstances its simplicity gives it grandeur. For the most remarkable thing about this work is the degree of tragic intensity Synge achieves whilst working on so very small a canvas. One is reminded of the way in which Maupassant achieves in some of his briefest tales an astonishing compression of force, an effect that gives him a stature far above that of the ordinary "short-story writer." In a similar way Synge's effect quite transcends the miniature scale on which he is working.

The tragic intensity achieved in this play has often caused writers to compare Synge with Shakespeare and Sophocles. Such enthusiastic comparison is bound to be a little unfortunate because one is too sharply reminded of differences. As a tragedy *Riders to the Sea* is without doubt remarkable in the way it presents unpretentious heroism opposing Sea and Tempest that hang like Fate over men's lives. But is has nothing whatever of the complexity of the tragic processes in human life that we find handled and mastered by the greatest writers. *Riders to the Sea* is a fine piece of tragic art precisely because it does *not* compare with *Oedipus Rex* or the tragedies of Shakespeare. It is elemental, but also bare and excessively simple. Its great power lies in its creation of atmosphere. This certainly has its dramatic force, as the scenes on the heath in *Lear* have. In Shakespeare, however, those scenes are but an immense background to an immense human complication and suffering. In *Riders to the Sea* the tragic sense emanates entirely from elemental nature. Its effect of impersonality is due to the dramatic form; its inspiration is largely lyrical.

Ronald Peacock. *The Poet in the Theatre* (New York, Harcourt, Brace, 1946), pp. 109–10

The drama of Synge is severely, almost deliberately limited. In comedy he writes only of one kind of man, the peasant of the east of the west of Ireland.

Yet he chooses so unerringly what is fundamental in the manners and motives of his people that his comedies, though local, are universal, though national, international. In tragedy, the limitation is even more austere, for complexity of mood and theme are alike foregone; there is no mingling of comedy to give breadth to his suggestion and no complication of plot to bring a corresponding sense of the multifariousness of event. There is, moreover, a curious absence of metaphysical or religious implication in the tragedies, which shows the more clearly beside Yeats's and A.E.'s. This gives to Synge's two tragedies something hard, abrupt, pagan. He shapes a fragment of life, man's and nature's intermingled, a fragment charged with passions that beat against fate, and, giving it clear form, leaves it isolated. Except for the insuperable and undying power of love in *Dierdre*, whose immortality even there is rather implied by its own strength than defined by comment or suggestion, there is no relating of the world of men with any wider, less tangible metaphysical universe. This puts his two tragedies in a peculiar position, for though their potency is unquestionable they have not, what great tragedy almost invariably carries with it, the implication of resolution. They are splendid, isolated fragments of human experience, but the human spirit in them, though itself of a high poetic or imaginative quality, is unrelated to any other spiritual value. Even nature, a sympathetic half-human power, is not a divine power, and the plays leave in the mind a sense of unresolved pain that is hard to parallel except in so totally different a play as Marlowe's *Faustus*. It may be that the synthesis of Synge's mind is not so complete as we at first supposed, that the seemingly impossible reconciliation of nature-mysticism and dramatic form was not as yet accomplished to the full and that the core of that undramatic and almost inexpressible faith did indeed remain unexpressed.

Una Ellis-Fermor. *The Irish Dramatic Movement*
(London, Methuen, 1954), pp. 184–85

Synge's achievement is one that is not local, however much his best art grew out of a strong sense of local life and his ability to render "the psychic state of the locality." His is an art rooted in the life he had known and in the people he had observed, but this fact does not make local art any more than it makes a folk art. It is the attitude of the artist, the comment that he chooses to make with his material, which determines the level and focus of his art; and, although Synge sometimes takes a kind of primitivism for his medium, his total comment is never primitive, and he never accepts that limited view of the world which the folk artist by definition adopts.

Nor is Synge seen to best advantage as a "nature" writer, in spite of the attempts to so define his achievement, even by such an astute critic as Una Ellis-Fermor in *The Irish Dramatic Movement*. There is a strain of nature mysticism in Synge, as evidenced by some of the poems (most noticeably the unpublished ones) and by the persistent presence and treatment of nature in the plays; but Synge never offers, in his major work, nature for its own sake, as an end in itself. Nature is usually invoked for the contrast it provides to human society, for the comment the life of nature makes about the restrictive life of man in society. Synge had a deep feeling for nature and an equally strong awareness of nature's symbolic values to the artist for an expression of a total universe, but to label Synge as a nature writer is to limit him in the same way as those critics who would see him as a local writer or as a folk dramatist. Synge's ability to portray the conflicts between man's natural desires and the repressions of organized society has been translated by several critics into specifically Irish terms as the conflict between Oisin and St. Patrick: between a natural, pagan freedom and the highly organized restrictions of the Church. Nature and the natural life provided Synge with the images and vision for symbolizing the inevitable warfare between the two ways of life represented by Oisin and St. Patrick.

Synge's vision, a view of the world presented with consistency in *The Aran Islands* and in the plays, was one which makes his work particularly congenial to the modern reader. He insisted upon a realistic assessment of man's life and the struggle which he felt it to be in the face of an alien universe and a vigorously beautiful but nonetheless indifferent nature. As Synge saw it, man's difficulties in such a universe were multiplied by his insistent attempt to impose his own rigid codes of behavior upon the world. This judgment is the source of the unique fusion in Synge's plays of the primitive world, the world of nature, and a social commentary that drama has ordinarily relegated to an urban, mechanized world. The primitive and the natural provide a meaningful structure for understanding the intensely basic nature of the conflicts and the lies which man has imposed upon himself.

Donna Gerstenberger. *John Millington Synge*
(New York, Twayne, 1964), pp. 135–36

Freed of the Yeatsian vision, let us look at reality through Synge's eyes. It must be sought in a "comprehensive and natural form," he tells us in his preface to *The Playboy of the Western World*. In Ireland there are still places where this reality is superb and wild, and therefore joyous—even to the point of the Rabelaisian. But always, for it to remain valid, this joy must be rooted in its natural form, must, in fact, flow from the imagination of the people. When one is true to the folk imagination, it follows that one will be true to their mode of expression. The richer the imagination, the richer and more copious the language. And always, for the artist to remain true to his subject, the delicate balance must be perceived and tested, the tension between form and spirit preserved. The artist must never become so carried away with a wild joyousness that he loses sight of the form which contains it. "The strong things of life are needed in poetry also," he warns us, "to show that what is exalted or tender is not made by feeble blood." The Rabelaisian may even incorporate the brutal. Nor can there be true affirmation without testing all verities. In wit, as Oscar Wilde has taught us, forcing the verities to walk a tight-rope leads to paradox. In drama, Synge shows us it leads to irony, both in choice of subject and technique.

For art which has its roots in "the clay and worms," yet seeks after what is "superb and wild in reality," implies the very conflict that provokes the ironical vision. This conflict between the ordinary and the ideal, the bitter and the sweet, reason and the imagination, reality and fantasy, Synge saw as basic both to life and to nature. The conflict takes two forms in his plays—exter-nally in nature, and internally in the heart and mind of man. In external nature there is the continual struggle between the beauty and joy of life and youth and the ugliness and sorrow of old age and death. In the soul of man this struggle is reflected in his eternal conflict between the illusion and the real-ity, and his constant efforts to reconcile the two. Nature to man symbolizes power, wildness, and a dreadful joy; the "common, week-day kind of" life man has built around him symbolizes ugliness, boredom, decay, and eventu-ally an unhappy death. By choosing to dramatize the life of the Aran Island-ers, the vagrants of Wicklow, the countryfolk of Mayo and Kerry, Synge was tearing away the veils of sophistication one finds in town life, and dealing with reality in its more elemental form. Humanity, art and nature are inextri-cably bound in the conflict between the real and the ideal. We can examine this basic conflict first as Synge represents it in the power of external nature, second in the lives and emotions of his characters, third in the most elaborate effect this conflict had on his people—the creation of the myth.

Ann Saddlemyer. *J. M. Synge and Modern Comedy*
(Dublin, Dolmen, 1968), pp. 12–14

If we add together all [the] public and private comments of Synge we get a fairly clear notion, not of the precise "meaning" he himself attached to his play [*The Playboy of the Western World*], but of his attitudes towards the play's message element. Firstly, he insists that the play is credible in terms of actuality, but should not be labelled comedy, tragedy or extravaganza. He suggests that there are "several sides" to the play, and, while calling it "a piece of life," indicates that it does have a meaning or meanings and is more than a simple piece of entertainment. He clearly indicates the central ambi-guity of mood by his reference to Shylock and Alceste, and also, more sig-nificantly, by his reference, when being questioned by a reporter, to *Don Quixote*. Don Quixote is, like Christy Mahon, a fantasist and an "outsider." He was used by Cervantes to comment upon the vices and absurdities of the society of his time. He is himself a fool, but ultimately much less of a fool than the acceptably conventional realists he encounters, for his folly and his fantasy are supported and dignified by a view of the world which is obses-sively idealistic and chivalrous, whereas the other people lack any real con-viction or vision. Moreover, in several instances, Quixote persuades others to share for a while his fantasy and to see themselves as fair ladies, nobles and knights, in a world of dragons and heroism. Sometimes self-consciously, sometimes humorously or even derisively, they gain through him a sense of the glories that are gone and of the dignity they no longer feel they possess. Finally, however, Quixote is most usually rejected, and rides away, accompanied by his faithful, awed, yet sceptical Sancho Panza, to find new wonders and irradiate other commonplaces with the ideal illumination of his fantasy.

It is not difficult to see Christy Mahon as a Don Quixote figure, at once saviour and fool, hero and clown, visionary and madman. The difference is that it is, at least in part, the peasants who create the vision for him. Initially he is only a scared boy, convinced in his simplicity that he has killed his father. Praised and admired for his derring-do, he becomes both a braggart and a visionary, his words elevating the commonplace into such poetry that Pegeen Mike and even the Widow Quin are dazzled by his eloquence. Inspired thus he becomes, in fact, the hero, winning all the prizes at the races, and though finally he falls from grace when his father returns from the dead, he retains at the close of the action that heroic self-confidence which he has been given.

It is at the end of the play, however, that the Quixote element gives way to another, for Christy again "kills" his father and is immediately viewed with horror and both beaten and betrayed.

It is here that Synge's Shylock parallelism applies. As long as Shylock's "bargain" remained a distant threat and a fantasy Bassanio regarded him amiably. When, however, he attempted to perform in reality what had been disregarded when merely imagined, he was not only regarded with horror but condemned for a crime of conspiracy which had previously been tolerated and even jested over. The parallelism is obviously inexact, but points to Synge's understanding the essential part played by that element of the grotesque and brutal which some of his audience condemned.

Robin Skelton. *The Writings of J. M. Synge*
(Indianapolis and New York, Bobbs-Merrill,
1971), pp. 117–18

The composition of *Riders* is a unique moment of balance in Synge's career, in which mind and materials coalesced without strain or friction. Sudden death seemed omnipresent on Aran, with disease as well as drowning a constant threat. Yet its very actuality, the fact that the islanders lived with it from day to day, made it impossible for Synge to dramatise it with the morbid hysteria that we find in the early poems. He loved and admired the Aran people, even to the point of idealisation. But whereas in *The Aran Islands* this admiration occasionally runs over into sentimentality, in *Riders* it is fittingly expressed through the simplicity, grace and dignity of the characters' words and actions. The Christian faith of the people, which Synge normally rejected, in this context was modulated into a mood of tragic resignation to which he could give his real sympathies. This is the balance of creative harmony, where vision finds embodiment in reality, and reality is shaped into vision.

But the perfection of *Riders* is achieved within limits, limits of range which Synge applied nowhere else in his work. He never again wrote a play so entirely consistent in tone, so completely unified round a single theme and a single image. *Riders* could not be imitated or repeated. . . . The theme of the imagination and the ironic satiric techniques of the comedies were essential to Synge's creativity and they could not be accommodated within the Aran setting of *Riders*. For [Daniel] Corkery *Riders* is on a level far above Synge's other work—"If he had not written *Riders to the Sea* he would not only have been a less great writer, but he would have been an infinitely less great writer"—but he recognises that it is unique, out of character with the rest of the plays. We may perhaps contest his view that *The Shadow, The Well of the Saints* or *The Playboy* are cheap things, and argue that the move from *Riders* on to the comedies was necessary to the fulfilment of Synge's capacity as a dramatist.

Riders, in a sense, exhausted the possibilities of Aran for Synge. It was the perfect setting for the one-act tragedy, in which no idiosyncracies of temperament, no particularities of situation complicated the stark image presented. Its very perfection, however, the idyllic life of unified social harmony which he saw there, made it unsuitable as a setting for the sort of comedy Synge went on to write, in which social variation and conflict are often crucial. His view of the peasant community in the comedies is much more complex and more critical; it includes elements of mockery and satire of which he was incapable with the Aran people.

Nicholas Grene. *Synge: A Critical Study of the Plays*
(Totowa, N.J., Rowman & Littlefield, 1975),
pp. 58–59

Life as a stage dream, a theatrical process of self-creation and self-production; the modern theatre has wholeheartedly embraced this principle of Synge's drama, even going back to look at Shakespeare in this light, for instance, in John Barton's production of *Richard II*, where Richard and Bolingbroke are represented as actors playing the role of King in turn. Synge is in the mainstream here: so too in his preference for comedy and farce as the vehicle of his lonely nihilistic, ironic, iconoclastic view of the universe. It seems significant that the only play considered uncontroversial in his time, and instantly anthologised, was *Riders to the Sea*: as Yeats said, it was "a comfort to those who do not like to deny altogether the genius they cannot understand." Certainly it is easier to place than the other plays, simpler in mood, closer to traditional forms—it has commonly been described as a tragedy in one act—and it is of course a moving and splendid piece. But a knife-edge balance of

the comical and the sombre is much more characteristic of Synge. His use of
farce is, as he says, "Irish," in the style of Boucicault before him: farce with a
grim edge, violent laughter, tragic gaiety. It is exhilarating in the traditional
way for its sheer fun, its zestful sense of life's eccentricities and incongruities,
but it has another function, which gives it a more modern look: it becomes a
way of confronting without despair the really bad jokes of life; physical afflictions, ugliness, old age, death. Synge's characters are haunted by those unavoidable jokes; Deirdre can't face the thought of getting old and losing her
teeth; the Douls run from their reflections in the bleak world of fact. But
Synge himself does not run. "Squeamishness is a disease" he once said: his
plays are blasts against that debilitation. He draws his subjects with aggressive anti-romanticism from the most unpromising places, taking a peculiarly
keen interest in battered, unprepossessing tramps and nomads and old people,
the deprived and afflicted, and tapping in them springs of humour, imagination, passion for life. He might have described his aim in Beckettian terms,
for he is certainly one who does not shun subjects that others have shunned,
such as impotence and ignorance; he too is an excavator, going by way of the
derelict and lonely down into the depths and wonders of the human mind.
This is the most important sense in which he fulfilled Yeats's advice to "express a life that has never found expression."

Katharine Worth. *The Irish Drama of Europe from
Yeats to Beckett* (Atlantic Highlands, N.J.,
Humanities Press, 1978), pp. 136–37

Synge's pre-conscious vision was comfortably accommodated in the medieval
literature with which he was intimate, but that literature was not responsible
for the vision. The deep structure of his thought may have been reinforced by
the acceptance of imperfection, incompleteness, and disharmony which he
found in the medieval literature which he used, but its basic cast preceded his
experience of that literature and was also reinforced by other factors. Important among those other factors were his reaction to his inherited culture, his
response to the richer, more liberal cultural life of continental Europe, and his
participation in the primitive life of rural Ireland. The imposition of the unresolved clash which can be detected in his work between reason and folly, between ugliness and beauty, and in a great number of incongruities, reflects the
deep structure of his thought as being both antithetical and kinetic. While according to his own brief for the writer he should "deal manfully, directly and
decently with the entire reality of life," the reality which he perceived had to
be integrated into his own vision. That vision focused on contrast and motion,
thereby investing them with prominence in the process of translating or reinventing the "entire reality."

The first literary source-material which Synge consciously used (for
The Well of the Saints) was both medieval and grotesque, but by making the

grotesque the structural basis for his play he entirely altered his source and through his new emphasis exposed the cruelty in pity. Deliberately avoiding a "Cuchulanoid" hero in *The Playboy* he asserted the necessary violence in the nature of the hero, thus giving prominence to an unresolved clash between the heroic and the despicable sides of the nature of "the only playboy of the western world" who is the central character of the play. Staging the clashing needs of the old man and his young wife in *The Shadow*, he also realized the tension between man's imaginative existence and that imposed by material necessity, as well as between his individual and social urges. Adopting the literary fool, he exploited anew the clash between the rational and the irrational in man, and between the collective and the inspired, individual vision, while adding a Romantic note of pathos. He chose remote, medieval poems to translate, only some of which contained a grotesque element, but on all of which he exercised that idiom which reflected the tensions inherent to his vision and which contained the plaintive note which he had recognized in Lady Gregory's use of it. To strengthen the lyrical sweetness with which he had overlaid the tragic tale of Deirdre, he was in the process of increasing the grotesque element, having already established the pitilessness of beauty. In short, Synge carried the use of the grotesque as a structural principle to a new pass: whatever clash of incompatibles he found in medieval material he intensified and modified in terms which were both directly rooted in external nature and nurtured by his own vision.

Toni O'Brien Johnson. *Synge: The Medieval and the Grotesque* (Gerrards Cross, England, Colin Smythe, 1982), pp. 168–69

In his first three plays the gods he seemed to invoke were the overmastering forces of nature; they were quite as important to him as leading characters; they meant more than the spirit of nationalism, which Synge regarded as *hubris*. Their aspect might be fierce or brutal, joyous or benign; the mood is indicated by descriptive images whose power is felt, rather than understood. It is difficult to assign names to Synge's effects upon audiences of mixed sensibilities. Sardonic humour in the comic scenes is full of tragic irony, mingled with a grimness of intent that few city-dwellers would be able to appreciate; for they do not live in closest contact with nature. In the plays of Synge there is therefore no room for sentiment, and little for dramatic conflict; the dominant note is awe and acceptance of the unforeseen. A mind so ascetic and watchful as this is not moved by the consolation of philosophy. Synge's concept of pagan stoicism in characterisation would have been approved by Aristotle.

Synge was, indeed, the living exemplar of Lady Gregory's notion of the "heart-secret." Though a compassionate personality, he was so withdrawn that he had difficulty in getting to know the kind of Irishmen in whom he was interested. His acquired taste for French realism led him to choose characters that suited his mode of expression. The paradox of his prose style is that the tone of the dialect is poetic; the rhythm has a cadence more Latin than English, and the intonation needed should have a musical note. Synge is never as prosaic as Lady Gregory; nor has his language a special location, like Kiltartanese. The actors took time to accommodate to the archaic flavour, and the idiomatic inversions of syntax; for Synge's originality lay mainly in his close attention to idiom.

Novels and plays had already been written about Irish peasant life, which Daniel O'Connell thought to be the finest in Europe; but no one before Synge had so clear a vision of its dignity and composure. Success was due to his ability to transform the local into the universal; there is no sense of historical time to distract in his portrayal of peasant characters; they are valid for the heroic age as for modern times. What Synge communicates is their toughness to survive, or their resignation to accept the inevitable. They complain often, but an almost aristocratic spirit forbids them to quit.

A. C. Partridge. *Language and Society in Anglo-Irish Literature* (Dublin, Gill and Macmillan, 1984), pp. 215–16

The pastoral themes in *In the Shadow of the Glen* are developed in such a way that they establish a bridge between the literal and the figurative, the local and the biblical context, without sacrificing the integrity of each to the other. Just as easy identification between types is prevented, so too the differentiation between characters is not simply, or simplistically, conceived. The epithet "queer" is the lexical link which binds all of the characters together into a common brotherhood akin to that which Maurya invokes in *Riders to the Sea*. Dan is "queer"; Michael Dara talks of Patch Darcy going "queer in the head"; the Tramp speaks of "queer" looks and "queer" talk. At the moment of Dan's second "resurrection," Nora's expression of wondering pity gathers us all into the process of mortality, echoing as she does so the words of the Aran girl who remarked to Synge, "Priests is queer people, and I don't know who isn't" (II, 114):

> NORA. It's a pitiful thing to be getting old, but it's a queer thing surely . . . God forgive me, Michael Dara, we'll all be getting old, but it's a queer thing surely (III, 51–3).

Nora's sense of the irony of human life is "true irony, humble irony . . . based upon a sense of fundamental kinship with the enemy, as one *needs* him, is indebted to him, is not merely outside him as an observer but contains him *within*, being consubstantial with him" [Kenneth Burke]. But Dan rejects her gracious offer and she leaves him with a final warning that in so doing he has chosen a living death, a "black life," and will soon exchange his game for the reality: "it's not long, I'm telling you, till you'll be lying again under that sheet, and you dead surely" (III, 57). Shutting the door on Nora and the Tramp, and pulling his erstwhile rival into his drouth-ridden haven, the impotent Daniel Burke offers Michael Dara, with characteristic parsimony, a "little taste" (III, 57) of his whiskey. Like two characters in a Beckett play, the old man and the young, the closed oak door and the blasted sapling, drink a pledge to each other. Language takes its final revenge when the mercenary Michael, the man of few words, offers to nay-saying Dan, the risen corpse, the pious prayer

> God reward you, Daniel Burke, and may you have a long life and a quiet life, and good health with it (III, 59).

Drinking a toast with the water of life to longevity, silence and stasis, they turn the word for the last time against themselves, effectively pledging each other's annihilation.

Mary C. King. The Drama of J. M. Synge (Syracuse, N.Y., Syracuse Univ. Pr., 1985), pp. 83–84

TOMELTY, JOSEPH (1911–)

[O]f the younger dramatists writing in Ulster to-day Joseph Tomelty is producing the most interesting work. His *Right Again, Barnum*, is high on the list of [Ulster Group Theatre] successes. He has shown in it that he is a master of the Belfast idiom, though another young writer, Cecil Cree, has challenged his title for supremacy in this field with his *Title for Buxey*. Tomelty's work includes a realistic play of Belfast's back streets, *The End House*. It had its first production at the Abbey Theatre in 1944. But there is also a vein of poetic fantasy in his work which is making him break away from the confining bonds of realism and which may prove to be his most valuable contribution to the theatre. It was hinted at in an early play, *Idolatry at Inishargie* (Group Theatre, 1942), and it has had fuller expression in his latest play, *All Souls' Night* (Abbey Theatre, 1949). This is a moving story of an old fisherman who watches the clash between his hard-fisted wife and their eager, impetuous son. The father's sympathy is with the boy, but life has broken him and he is unable to help. With a masterly sense of the evocative power of words Tomelty builds up, drop by drop, as it were, the surge of the sea on the rocky coast of his native Ards and matches its waves with the emotional surge in the hearts of these fisher-folk. The production at the Group Theatre, with the author in the rôle of John Quinn, the old fisherman, was a memorable experience.

David Kennedy. In Sam Hanna Bell, ed., *The Arts of Ulster* (London, Harrap, 1951), pp. 63–64

Tomelty's best-known play is *Is the Priest at Home?*, which was produced by the Group Theatre in May, 1954, and performed a hundred and twelve times at the Abbey before and after Christmas, 1954. It starts with a bald, unpromising statement of its theme in a scene between a priest and another overdrawn stage-American. Once past that initial scene and into the central reminiscence in the priest's mind, the play settles down to being one of the most reasonable and effective statements about the life of an Irish priest that I know of. The thesis is that the priest is powerless outside of purely spiritual matters and that he is not very effective even there against the peculiar nature of his countrymen. As the priest's wise old handyman tells him, "Forget the Church Universal and remember you are in the Church Hibernicus." Doubtless this view is not the whole story, any more than that opposite view of tyrannical clerics that we get in Carroll's *Things That Are Caesar's*, is the whole story. Yet Tomelty makes his case with great persuasiveness.

The discussion scenes hold the attention as closely as the best of [Louis] D'Alton, and the illustrative actions are justly chosen and authentically evocative. Even better, he does not make the mistake of winding up his individual stories patly or artificially. Indeed, he usually does not wind them up at all. Such a device, though true to life, is often false to art; but Tomelty has so stressed his theme that the audience is caught up in it and satisfied to accept the stories as illustrations rather than the end in themselves. Really, Tomelty's play proves that realism is not outworn; all it requires for continued vitality is an author who can bring to it a significant and complex statement rather than a stage platitude. . . .

In his recent work, Tomelty is trying to make the dramatic form jibe more with the sprawling reality of life. To him, form on the stage demands compression, simplicity, and structure—all qualities opposed to the confusions of reality. His latest play, on which he was working when I spoke with him, is a three-character one which tries to convey a sense of the life beyond the stage by having offstage characters who try to come on and who are always barred. Much of *The Sensitive Man* is taken up with sketching what happens to these people who never appear, and who bear only more or less directly on the story, which gives the play, in spots, a weakly discursive effect. Much of it has a repetitive anecdotalness which one finds in life, but which seems a bit leisurely for the drama. Although Tomelty, like [John B.] Keane and [Michael J.] Molloy and Sam Thompson, is an avid listener to stories and scraps of dialogue, his main action has little impelling forward movement, little developing story. The problem of whether Rosena Rapple will win her fight with the landlord and be allowed to continue strewing fish innards on the seawall for the birds—this problem is smothered in conversation and static situations. There is much in this portrait of a small town in the North that is broodingly lovely and almost lyrical, but there is little that is dramatic. Still, the play is an intriguing experiment in a field which Tomelty is yet exploring, and experiment has so far been notably lacking in the drama of Ulster.

Robert Hogan. *After the Irish Renaissance*
(Minneapolis, Univ. of Minnesota Pr., 1967),
pp. 107–8

Mugs and Money, the revised version of *Barnum Was Right*, is a delightful comedy. Willie John attempts in vain to bring together the Hibernians and the Orangewomen. In his magazine, he incorporates "nice light genteel stuff, not ugly stuff, you know, like that fella Hanna Bell and the other fella Tomelty writes . . . ," to which his mother says "Dear knows, you're right, son. There's enough dirt in life without writing about it." Tomelty has here incidentally referred to his plays and the popular taste. The people, as a rule, want cheap entertaining stuff and would rather escape from life than into it. They therefore prefer a romantic play to a realistic one. The realists and naturalists are prone to take the darker and concealed sides of life which may be deeply illuminating, but not titillating enough. To have an intenser awareness of life without necessarily wallowing in the dirt and also at the same time to give this awareness in a manner that is never dull or doctrinaire, never objectively scientific but impregnated with fine imagination has been the aim of realists like Joseph Tomelty, and in the ultimate analysis, it is they who come to stay as healthy entertainers. To stop short at entertainment is a low art, if art at all, but to entertain in order to capture attention for the faithful exhibition and expression of life is the crux of realistic art. For sheer fun one may write farces or melodrama, but comedy cuts deep.

Willie wonders what kind of newspapers can flourish. Newspapers, like art, to be popular have to be sensational. That is why "the Buffs" are not a success, for they are not provocative.

> Like, the Hibernians say the border must go, and the Orangewomen say the border must stay. . . . But the Buffs take no sides at all, and as such in the North of Ireland they remain what they are, a colourless crowd.

Willie and Mugs [the daughter] are modern, somewhat educated, but the mother is old-fashioned. The children use words like "nervous flatulence," "deportment," "profile," "stereotyped," "respective," etc., which she misunderstands in an amusing fashion. The dramatist flings fun at the psychoanalytical methods of curing diseases. Barney relates how, for his simple headache, he was asked whether he had an Oedipus complex, whether he had any sex problem, whether his mother had ever let him fall when he was a child or whether he feared to go to bed in the dark.

Right Again, Barnum (1943) is a sequel to the earlier play and takes the story forward, It is more of an extravaganza, skating over the thin ice of Belfast prejudices. Barnum, the great money-maker and showman, says that there is a mug born every minute, and Tomelty in these two comedies has immensely enjoyed the fun he has derived from these mugs. In the earlier comedy, he is more humorous and realistic, but in the sequel the situations are arranged in a funny, though quite dramatic, manner and the reader's curiosity is constantly sustained. The end, where Mrs. Marley slings her boot after Rabby, as he makes a hasty exit out of the back-door, is superb. . . . Joseph Tomelty has no morals to preach. He looks around expectantly in a care-free manner and finds the world everywhere funny, somewhere a little blackguardly too, but all the same a world worth living in.

N. Sahal. *Sixty Years of Realistic Irish Drama*
(Bombay, Macmillan, 1971), pp. 169–71

T. G. F. Patterson, the Irish antiquarian, records that in one of George Russell's notebooks there is "a tale about the ghosts of the dead walking on All Hallows' Eve . . . From the manuscript it is clear that he intended forming the notes into a play, but I do not think he ever did so." Joseph Tomelty heard the same tale in his childhood, not among the orchard slopes of Armagh but by the fanged seacoast of Down, and wrote his play *All Souls' Night*. The swept hearth and plenished fire of the tradition, therefore, are those of a family of fisherfolk, the Quinns. But the spirits who walk at the end of the play are not ancestral but ghosts new-minted, for through her avarice Katrine the mother drives her two sons to their death in the waters of the lough. Tomelty, born in the fishing village of Portaferry, nets love and death and greed and fish and birds and boats in a heightened language that comes as naturally from his characters as the flow of tides in Strangford Lough. *All Souls' Night* is a tragedy but probably the most memorable scene is that in which John Quinn, the father, illiterate, learns to cipher: "so that's a nought, round like a sail ring or the eye of a herring. And that's a five, shaped like a cup hook in the dresser, and a six like what a worm would ooze on the beach . . ." Those who saw the author play the old fisherman, his voice hushed in awe and delight at his discovery, will not easily forget the scene. . . .

According to a contributor to the *Pelican Guide to English Literature*, "many playwrights have dealt in the Ibsen manner with the typical problems of modern Irish life." He lists these problems, assigning to Tomelty (with Paul Vincent Carroll) that of "the role of the priests." I should add that Joseph Tomelty does not agree that any of his work falls into this category. . . . *The End House*[, for example, concerns] a family caught up in the travail of murderous political strife. The gable wall is pockmarked with bullet holes where an informer has been shot down. Seamus the son has recently been released from jail and is to die violently. The elder generation cling to the small civilities of life amid threats, raids and poverty. In 1944 Tomelty told a reporter that he had begun the play as far back as 1932. It was set aside for some years while he wrote for the Group Theatre. Then he decided that the earlier play must be finished because "it was time people outside got an idea of how things were in Belfast."

The Dublin critics of *The End House*, while agreeing on the quality of the play, were not of a mind as to the author's "mood." Gabriel Fallon in the *Standard* felt that Tomelty had plumbed too deeply in despair. "He has decided for naturalism, and forced the poverty and pride and patriotism and persecution of one Belfast household into a dialogue which though it suited his purpose well enough and carried a thin humour at times, lacked even a tittle of . . . poetic luxuriance . . ." The *Irish Times*, on the other hand, decided that "the play is very strongly in the O'Casey tenement tradition and Mr. Tomelty plays strongly on the oppression and persecution theme. He leavens the tragedy and sordidness with a rich vein of humour."

I do not think that anyone today would hesitate to associate himself with the second of these comments. There was a time indeed when it seemed that audiences were to enjoy the sheer inventiveness of this writer's dialogue at the expense of the play. One critic observed about his fourth play, *Right Again, Barnum*, that "what is new here is the shapeliness of the drama, the checking of the sprightly wry humour that in previous efforts has carried the author away from his theme and caused dissatisfaction as though he had not troubled himself sufficiently with his plot." Tomelty is unrivalled among his contemporaries in the use of the idiomatic phrase. At a time when we were surfeited perhaps with the prosaic exchanges of the characters of [St. John] Ervine and [George] Shiels he brought lyricism to the speech of the Ulster stage.

Sam Hanna Bell. *The Theatre in Ulster*
(Totowa, N.J., Rowman & Littlefield, 1972),
pp. 83–86

TREVOR, WILLIAM (1928–   )

[*The Old Boys*] is a pleasant book about an unpleasant subject. It is short, under two hundred pages, and utterly without the mannerisms and lack of control that often mar first novels. The old boys of the title are all septuagenarian graduates of the School by which they are held together in mutual and hostile affection. One is apt to think it strange that a thirty-five-year-old man should write his first novel on old age, but then one recalls that John Updike, when he was some years younger than that, wrote his *The Poorhouse Fair*. Age simplifies; so does youth. . . .

Trevor has not only imagined simplicity, he has made it explicit. At a School get-together, a General Sanctuary and a Lady Ponders congratulate each other on old age. The General says:

"We are lucky, Lady Ponders: it is pleasanter to be over seventy, as it was to be very young. Nothing new will happen to us again. To have everything to come, to have nothing to come—one can cope. Pity our middle-aged Headmaster and his greying wife."

As the General says, nothing new happens. . . . Mr. Trevor does not delude us; his novel is a study in the futility of expecting anything new. Or almost. His ending is tantalizing: throughout the novel the quarrels between Mr. and Mrs. Jaraby have been a source of amusement—they "go" at each other so. If there are diversions in Hell, I suppose they'll be of this sort. At the very end, however, Mr. Jaraby's public life having been proven as futile as his private life, he and the Mrs. sit down for the summing up. But she, a woman of strong, if spiteful, spirit, thus addresses him and ends the novel:

"Do not be downcast; we must not mourn. Has hell begun, is that it? Well, then, I must extend a welcome from my unimportant corner of that same place. We are together again, Mr. Jaraby; this is an occasion for celebration, and you must do the talking for a while. Cast gloom aside, and let us see how best to make the gesture. Come now, how shall we prove we are not dead?"

I cannot praise Mr. Trevor too much for this conclusion. The writing is firm without pretense, and that last question—"How shall we prove we are not dead?"—has a dignity that rises above both fun and mere rhetoric. One wonders if something new has not begun to happen.

Thomas Curley. *Com*. Sept. 18, 1964, pp. 645–46

William Trevor, an immensely gifted short story writer, is known as a writer of television plays, though all the plays he has written have been adaptations of his short stories. But you can hardly blame him. His new collection, *The Ballroom of Romance*—two or three of the stories have appeared on television—confirms the reputation he gained on the publication of his previous collection, *The Day We Got Drunk on Cake* (best since [Angus Wilson's] *The Wrong Set*, best since the war, critics said). . . .

Though the characters in Mr. Trevor's novels are quite different from his short story characters (the former are several degrees more perverse than the latter, as well as—usually—from a different social class), Mr. Trevor's achievement has been to create, by means of the clearest and most original prose in this generation and a compassionate balance of fascination and sympathy, real people of flesh and blood out of characters another writer would dismiss as goons or drudges.

It is for the women in this collection that one feels most deeply. Indeed, the thread that runs through all the stories is of brittle or urgent femininity thwarted by rather boorish maleness. Mr. Trevor's men are feckless, or else malicious snobs, or drunkards, or comradely and exclusive old boys; his women are victims of, at once, their own strength and the men's weakness, isolated by their longings or by the perversity of their husbands or lovers. . . .

Some of the stories are heartrending, but Mr. Trevor writes with a light touch, without sentimentality and always with humour. There is a crotchety precision about his narration; what other writer would be able to get away with the sentence, "No alcoholic liquor was ever served in the Ballroom of Romance, the premises not being licensed for this added stimulant"? He is the master of exasperation, of the person speaking at length in tones of formal annoyance; and he is at his best when dealing with a condition of lucidity one has always thought of as madness. His real skill lies in his ability to portray this behaviour as a heightened condition of life; in his work there is no madness, but there is much suffering.

Paul Theroux. *Enc*. Sept., 1972, pp. 69–70

Anyone who has yet to understand the way in which the short story can score over the novel should read William Trevor's new collection [*Angels at the Ritz*] for instruction: to observe his talent for producing a pure narrative line from a single, small event in the lives of his characters without seeming to encapsulate actions or emotions, and for staging the story's progression in such a way that the rhythm of its style is properly wedded to the rhythm of its content. Trevor's real concern is for commonplace tragedies: those incidents which almost certainly go unnoticed by everyone but the protagonists, but which nonetheless have the power to change our lives.

This precise observation of the forces that make us truly individual informs most of the stories in *Angels at the Ritz*. "In Isfahan" throws together a man and woman who are both lonely, both desperate in a muted kind of way. For a day or so they flirt—the woman more committed than the man, so risking more and dealing more in truth. Deftly, without flagging for our attention, the author begins to establish her greater need, greater recklessness from the outset. . . . When the man and woman part, carrying with them versions of each other's life, they are left, one feels, not with a sense of each other, but with a painfully heightened sense of themselves: not helpful, necessarily, and certainly not curative, but sufficiently accurate to make any reader wince.

Tiny moments of truth make focal points for a good many of these stories, always effectively, but never more so than in the title story which quarries a note of nobility—a rare victory—out of a suburban wife-swapping party. Quite simply, Trevor effects a tension between youthful hopes recalled and the realities of middle-aged compromise: but he brings to that perfectly ordinary conflict a talent for invention and observation which reinvests it with an ineffable sadness. The tone of the stories never insists or becomes strident: Trevor's technique is to make use of a delivery and style which remains controlled without becoming monotonous or denying characters and events their peculiar qualities. The small, quotidian horrors that afflict us and make us, finally, unknowable—the recollections, the gaucheries, the betrayals—float to the apparently placid surface of Trevor's prose without any frenzied stirring and lie there, unignorable.

David Harsent. NS. Oct. 24, 1975, p. 519

With virtual unanimity, [the reviewers] have labeled [William Trevor] a comic writer, differing only in their terms of reference, which vary from "black comedy" to "comedy of humor" to "pathetic" or "compassionate" comedy. As a satirist, he is most frequently compared with Evelyn Waugh, although Muriel Spark, Angus Wilson, Kingsley Amis, and Ivy Compton-Burnett are also mentioned. Additional points of comparison could readily be suggested: Trevor's ear for humorously banal small talk is reminiscent of Pinter; what has been referred to as "the incredulous, stuffy exactitude . . . the fustily elegant grammar" of his language recalls Beckett; his ruthless undeviating pursuit of a grubby, shabby verisimilitude evokes the work not only of Graham Greene but of such contemporaries as Edna O'Brien, John Updike, and David Storey. In addition, his interest in psychological questions and his preference for the traditional short story and novel allies him with writers as diverse as Henry James and Saul Bellow.

If Trevor is a comic writer, however, he with Beckett is assuredly among the most melancholy, as reflected in his characters' surroundings, in their situations and activities, and particularly in the theme of loneliness and hunger for love which more than any other feature distinguishes his writing. . . . Consistently, his interest has focused on the marginal setting: a gaudy pub in a seedy district being demolished for reconstruction; a threadbare boarding house, its brown wallpaper and cheap furnishings unchanged for forty years; a deteriorating and unfrequented hotel in a Dublin backstreet; a tract house enveloped in tall weeds and grass, smelling of home-brewed beer and home-grown mushrooms. There are appropriate backgrounds for the lonely and forgotten, far removed from centers of purposeful activity and social ferment. Despite feeble resorts to the public media, these characters, described as "survivors, remnants, dregs," find little to which they may attach themselves. . . .

The majority are more notable for weakness or failure than for strength or success, which contributes to the choice they are usually forced to make: either to recognize (and forgive) cruelty or unfaithfulness in those they love or limitations in themselves, or to cultivate comforting illusions, ranging from harmless daydreams and fantasies to compulsive and profound convictions. According to their differing temperaments and needs, some accept the truth, while others find illusions the only bearable remedy. Indeed, furnished as they often are with active capacities for fantasy and reverie, and given to daydreaming or imagining themselves in situations contrary to actuality, Trevor's characters are peculiarly well fitted for creating and sustaining illusions.

Julian Gitzen. *Crit.* 21, 1, 1979, pp. 59–60

The theme of William Trevor's new novel [*Fools of Fortune*]—his ninth, and that leaves short-story collections out of account—is the murderous entail of Anglo-Irish history, in which, as a Cork man, he may fairly be considered expert. But unlike most experts, above all most specialists in Ireland's past, he knows how little has to be told and how much is best left to the reader's own memory and imagination. The point about an entail, as Mrs. Bennet constantly complained to her long-suffering husband, is that it is buttoned up by law, invulnerable to grace. In Ireland, as in *Pride and Prejudice*, it follows the male line: only recently has an Amazonian *tendance* invaded Anglo-Irish *contestation*. The blood in this book is shed by the men, but the life sentences are served by their women, whose tragic warps still find their metaphor half a century later in the blackened, twisted beams of once-gracious country houses fired in the civil wars and never repaired. Such a house is Kilneagh.

Fools of Fortune opens and closes in 1983, with the Quintons of Kilneagh slipping gently away to genealogical extinction, and the Woodcombes of Dorset clinging precariously to their ancestral manor by charging "adults fifty pence at the turnstiles, children twenty-five," to visit it. The families have drifted apart in our own time, but in 1918, when Willie Quinton opens his own story, the Woodcombes and the Quintons have already intermarried twice in the space of a century, and his cousin Marianne is about to become the third English girl to visit Kilneagh and fall in love. In Anglo-Irish relationships, Trevor observes, history tends to repeat itself. . . .

Convents and boarding-schools are significant backdrops to this Irish stage, absorbing characters who are either not ready to play adult roles (Willie at Mr. Scrotum's Llanabba-like college in the Dublin mountains; Marianne at genteel Mrs. Gibb-Bachelor's finishing school in Montreux), or else are counted among the walking wounded (the servant girl Josephine, sheltered from her memories by matter-of-fact nuns). Perhaps these episodes, short or long, would fit another book as easily as this one: Mr. Trevor's capacious notebook travels with him everywhere, and he must now be able to borrow from himself, like Handel putting together an oratorio for the Dublin market. But there is an enviable deftness about this novel and its *leitmotiven*: the scarlet drawing-room, the flickering flames, and the crimson-dripping mulberries which will take a week to pick, "longer if rain interrupts."

Christopher Driver. *LRB*. May 19, 1983, p. 22

For his labors, [William Trevor] has garnered several literary awards and consistently favorable reviews on both sides of the Atlantic, though thus far he has eluded extensive critical examination.

Given the extent of his canon and the encomia of the reviews, however, it seems only a matter of time before he is accorded the kinds of critical attention that will test the work against standards that may be more rigorous than the reviewers'. On the other hand, for the time being at least, most such attention is likely to focus on Trevor's "non-Irish" fiction since only one of his novels and perhaps 25 of the total 65 or so of the now readily-available short stories are what we might agree to call loosely "Irish," and of these perhaps 20 are indisputably "Irish," the bulk of the remainder being set in England or, occasionally, on the Continent, and usually without even Irish characters except, perhaps, in name only.

Of the approximately 19 Irish stories published before the present collection, at least four are tenuously Irish. In *Beyond the Pale*, three have a less than firm relationship to a specifically Irish scene or situation or characterization. "The Paradise Lounge" and "The Time of Year," fine stories both, might as easily have been situated in England; and "Being Stolen From" *has* an English setting, though its protagonist's Irish-Catholic origins figure significantly in the story. Another story, "Downstairs at Fitzgerald's," is the story of the relationships of a girl from the ages of eight to thirteen with her divorced father and her mother and stepfather and convincingly captures something of the equivocality of such familial relationships in the Dublin of the 1940s. "Beyond the Pale," two indisputably Irish stories, bring the total of genuinely Irish stories to about 20. . . .

Take them all in all — Irish, quasi-Irish, or non-Irish — Trevor's canon of short stories is crafted with exquisite care; he is often almost reticent and, sometimes, the style is so understated as to be nearly elided. At the same time, when they are called for, Trevor is a master of telling gritty details. Favorite themes are appearance vs. reality, marital infidelity, the nature of love, the distances that separate people, the niceties of social caste, and secret lives; and in at least a generous handful of stories, Trevor shifts ever so slightly — or sometimes startlingly — from these themes working themselves out realistically to the bizarre and macabre. . . .

"Autumn Sunshine" and "Beyond the Pale" are two of a dozen fine stories in this new collection [*Beyond the Pale, and Other Stories*], but they are splendidly illustrative of the kinds of perception Trevor has been bringing to the Troubles. Writing in them primarily about the Anglo-Irish, the arena for conflict opens up more than most Troubles stories have human issues that time has not solved and that cannot be solved by mere partisan politics. Upon reflection, Trevor's several Troubles stories sometimes seem so open-ended that one must hesitate before pronouncing judgment on their collective "meaning"; but if there is one consistent view, it seems to be that the past cannot be forgotten but that with resolution and forgiveness it need not be perpetuated.

Robert E. Rhodes. *ILS*. Fall, 1983, p. 28

Of the small handful of modern fiction writers who have established a considerable reputation outside of Ireland, William Trevor must be among the most highly regarded. He received the Hawthornden Prize in 1964 for his novel *The Old Boys*, the Royal Society of Literature award in 1975 for his story collection called *Angels at the Ritz*, the Allied Irish Banks Award for Services to Irish Literature in 1976, and the Whitbread Literary Award also in 1976 for his novel called *The Children of Dynmouth*. He was awarded a C.B.E. by Britain in 1977 for his services to literature, and he is a member of the Irish Academy of Letters. . . .

Although Trevor seems at his best in depicting the small-town lives of clerks, teachers, and shopkeepers, he writes well of children, of university students, of farmers and of the elderly Anglo-Irish, as well as of the Irish in Britain and the Irish on vacation. But, no matter what the social milieu, he writes with precise, authentic detail; and he does not mind halting his narrative to describe. . . . A solid conventionality, even in his occasional ghost stories, is what may be expected from William Trevor. If he does not always tell a story, he at least presents a dramatized situation in which his main characters are caught at some climactic and painful moment. If the characters do not always realize their plight or its point, the reader certainly does, and the readers' response is frequently powerful and rarely less than disturbing. Trevor's stories may lack excitement in style or narrative technique; they may even lack much sense of auctorial individuality, for Trevor usually remains detached. What they never lack, however, is a worthy craftsmanship. There is an impressive and growing bulk of stories from Trevor; and it is both inevitable and right that they have been collected in a fat Penguin that fills an honorable place on one's shelves beside the volumes of O'Connor, O'Faolain, Bowen, and Lavin.

What limits Trevor is also what binds all his work together, and this is that occupational hazard of Irish writers of his generation, a pervasively dreary attitude toward contemporary life. . . .

In story after story, he relentlessly accumulates new examples of awfulness. He is like a phlegmatic Poe, and perhaps even more pernicious because no one ever takes Poe's romances seriously. To a Poe or a Hawthorne, or to a Monk Lewis or an Ann Radcliffe, horror was romantic or glamorous, or at least interestingly odd. To Trevor, however, horror is the dull, realistic stuff of everyday life; and in his low-keyed, businesslike fashion he quietly proceeds, story by story, to transform the entirety of modern life into a gray, dank, commonplace asylum.

Amazingly, some critics have compared Trevor to Dickens, but no Dickens could have written of Christmas as dismally as has Trevor in "The Time of Year" and "Another Christmas." Astonishingly, some critics have commented upon Trevor's humor; but what sounded to them as laughter strikes this commentator as a death rattle.

Yet Trevor is steadily prolific and always careful of his technique; because of his application and his solid virtues, he will continue to be read and admired by perceptive and depressed people.

Robert Hogan. In James F. Kilroy, ed., *The Irish Short Story: A Critical History* (Boston, Twayne, 1984), pp. 182–84

YEATS, WILLIAM BUTLER (1865–1939)

I am not sure that [Mr. Yeats] does not assume in his readers [of *The Wind among the Reeds*] too ready an acquaintance with Irish tradition, and I am not sure that his notes, whose delightfully unscientific vagueness renders them by no means out of place in a book of poems, will do quite all that is needed in familiarising people's minds with that tradition. But after all, though Mr. Yeats will probably regret it, almost everything in his book can be perfectly understood by any poetically sensitive reader who has never heard of a single Irish legend, and who does not even glance at his notes. For he has made for himself a poetical style which is much more simple, as it is much more concise, than any prose style; and, in the final perfecting of his form, he has made for himself a rhythm which is more natural, more precise in its slow and wandering cadence, than any prose rhythm. It is a common mistake to suppose that poetry should be ornate and prose simple. It is prose that may often allow itself the relief of ornament; poetry, if it is to be of the finest quality, is bound to be simple, a mere breathing, in which individual words almost disappear into music. Probably, to many people, accustomed to the artificiality which they mistake for poetical style, and to the sing-song which they mistake for poetical rhythm, Mr. Yeats' style, at its best, will seem a little bare, and his rhythm, at its best, a little uncertain. They will be astonished, perhaps not altogether pleased, at finding a poet who uses no inversions, who says in one line, as straightforward as prose, what most poets would dilute into a stanza, and who, in his music, replaces the aria by the recitative. How few, it annoys me to think, as I read over this simple and learned poetry, will realise the extraordinary art which has worked these tiny poems, which seem as free as waves, into a form at once so monumental and so alive! Here, at last, is poetry which has found for itself a new form, a form really modern, in its rejection of every artifice, its return to the natural chant out of which verse was evolved; and it expresses, with a passionate quietude, the elemental desires of humanity, the desire of love, the desire of wisdom, the desire of beauty. [1900]

Arthur Symons. *Studies in Prose and Verse*
(London, Dent, n.d.), pp. 234–35

Mr. Yeats, who has been called the standard-bearer of this revival [of Irish mythology], is a writer of rare and exquisite imagination; I know of no living poet more truly a poet, more truly the possessor of that illusive something known as the "poetic quality." His lines are drenched with it. We close the pages of his slender volumes, and our senses are drugged with beauty. We have been carried far, into a more "dream-heavy land, dream-heavy hour than this," and been given visions of a world of mystical and magical loveliness. His poetry suggests remoteness; and may be said to belong among the elements, as do flame and wind.

The Countess Kathleen, a lyric drama, is perhaps his best-known work, but in *The Land of Heart's Desire*, a lyric in dramatic form, are to be found some of his most beautiful lines. Both of these poems are woven from the stuff of Irish tradition, and stand to-day as Mr. Yeats's most symmetrical and perfect works. *The Countess Kathleen* marks his nearest approach to dramatic poignancy; the horror of famine is there, the ghastly forest half hidden in "vapor and twilight," and the plague-stricken land where wander "dismayed souls of those now newly dead" with the demons waiting to ensnare them. A yellow and deadly vapor hangs and creeps about the fields, demons pace to and fro, buying the souls of the peasants for gold and plenty. . . . All this is hauntingly suggestive, and the play is full of beauty and a certain power, but it is doubtful if its author ever rises to the height and strength of tragedy.

In *The Land of Heart's Desire* is the calling of timeless voices from the unseen to those who dwell amid the warmth and comfort of material things. As I have said, though consigned to comparative oblivion, *The Land of Heart's Desire* contains some of Mr. Yeats's most beautiful work. . . . The magic of Celtic genius is here, and that mystical Something, deathless and timeless, which since the labor of centuries began has been vouchsafed to a few of the chosen.

Eugenia Brooks Frothingham. The Critic. Jan.,
1904, pp. 28–29

The Secret Rose, his greatest prose book, is, as we know, in substance a collection of Irish tales, set in a strange background of legend and vision, each story descriptive of some "spiritual adventure." About a quarter of the book deals with the exploits of Hanrahan the Red: the remaining stories are born partly of Celtic myth and partly of the poet's own imagination: but in Mr. Yeats's telling of these old and simple tales many beautiful meanings creep in, glimmering behind the words and actions of his heroes, like a flame shining through a curtain. The book has a curiously personal atmosphere. It is like nothing else—nothing else, I mean, that is not written by Mr. Yeats. What we mean by style is, I suppose, only the more or less perfect expression of a writer's individuality, and the wonderful uniformity of spirit which reaches from book to book and draws together all Mr. Yeats's work, making of it one great whole, is largely the result of the tremendous strength of his personality. He is always himself. No one has ever worked less blindly, or with a more jealous care for his art; and no one has more often re-written his work with the happy effect of bringing it nearer and nearer to his own innermost vision.

It is in his poetry, of course, that we find that vision most perfectly realised and expressed—in *The Land of Heart's Desire* and the lyrics. The first volume of verse, *The Wanderings of Oisin*, contained many poems which Mr. Yeats, with characteristic fastidiousness, has since suffered to drop into oblivion. Some of them, nevertheless, were not without considerable charm. . . .

If the verses in this first volume are on the whole more or less experimental, in the next book, *The Countess Cathleen*, the poet has already found himself. It contains the most popular of all his poems, "The Lake Isle of Innisfree," but it also contains one or two other pieces that are more essentially characteristic of his genius, the first examples of that poetical form William Morris had already come very near to in his "Summer Dawn," and which Mr. Yeats has since made so distinctively his own—a form that seems to be the expression of a moment of pure rapture, too brief and too intense to permit of any artificial breaking up into stanzas. . . .

There is something extraordinarily right about this poem, so un-Swinburnian, so wholly free from rhetorical ornament, from conventional poetic diction. It is directly expressive. Everything that is not absolutely essential has been removed. What is left is the very soul, the very essence of poetry. And the music is so satisfying, so deep. It has the grandeur of the music of nature; it is like the sound of wind or of water; so that all other verse, in comparison with it, seems somewhat constrained, a little artificial.

Forrest Reid. Irish Review. Jan., 1912, pp. 531–33

As I have said, Yeats is avowedly given to the mystic and the spiritual, to which his Celtic heritage naturally inclines him; and he has made more of these elements than any preceding Irish poet. [Thomas] Moore, who remains unrivaled as a lyric melodist singing of love and patriotism and the past glories of Erin, scarcely touched these rich sources of the new Irish poetry:—he lived three-fourths of his life out of Ireland and inevitably his work was conceived mainly in the English literary tradition. There were rarer treasures at home, as we have since discovered, than he went questing for in Khorassan and Cashmere.

Yeats is easily first in this old but unworked province. He has "staked out his claim," as we say, and made it his own. The discernment which he thus evinced as a very young man, no less than the fine confidence in his own powers to make the best of his chosen poetical domain, is not the least notable thing in the story. There is something alien and un-Irish in the calm, consistent, matter-of-fact way that Yeats has gone to work to realise upon his poetical heritage; but this is doubtless to be laid to the account of early English influences and associations. Both England and Ireland, though not of course in equal measure, went to the making of the poet and artist in Yeats. Ireland, it may be said, gave the vision of things invisible and England the discipline and restraint without which the poet's rarest findings were frittered away in a waste of words. [1914]

Michael Monahan. *Nova Hibernia: Irish Poets and Dramatists of Today and Yesterday* (Freeport, N.Y., Books for Libraries Press, 1967), pp. 17–18

The Green Helmet is an heroic farce written in couplets, and having for its source the Middle Irish story, "The Feast of Bricriu." Although Mr. Yeats again takes his theme from the heroic past, how different is his manner! Here are shorter speeches than in the earlier poetic plays; here is a clearer delineation of character, and a robustness that vivifies forgotten centuries. The play is nearer to the spirit of the original than anything else based upon Gaelic that Mr. Yeats has done; only one incident is out of harmony, that when "three black hands come through the windows and put out the torches"; this is not the magic of Irish druids.

In his latest volume of dramatic work Mr. Yeats has again radically changed; he takes an Irish theme as the subject of his *Two Plays for Dancers*, and treats it in the form of the Japanese Noh play. The poet thus returns to the East, which was the subject of some of his earlier verse, when Indian philosophy attracted him during the Dublin days of his youth.

To exaggerate the importance of Mr. Yeats as a literary and a national figure in Ireland would be difficult. Through his leadership and his creative ability he has established for his native land the beginning of a national literature in English worthy to stand beside the older Gaelic. He has always kept his artistic freedom; whatever the modifications or the changes in his beliefs, he has applied them to Ireland; he has used Irish symbols (if he would mention the beauty of a woman he compares her to the Irish Deirdre, not alone to the classic Helen); in his essay, "Certain Noble Plays of Japan," he links Ireland and the Orient. . . .

In spite of the fact that the efforts of the Gaelic League to restore Irish as a spoken language, the researches of Celtic scholars, the writings of the Anglo-Irish school, have been ostensibly separate, they have all been inspired by that love of Ireland and that dream of restoring her ancient spiritual dignity which has been the vision of William Butler Yeats. [1921]

Norreys Jephson O'Conor. *Changing Ireland: Literary Backgrounds of the Irish Free State, 1889–1922* (Cambridge, Mass., Harvard Univ. Pr., 1924), pp. 80–82

The poet Yeats has passed into a sort of third phase, in which he is closer to the common world than at any previous period. He is no longer quite so haughty, so imperturbably astride his high horse, as during his middle Dantesque period. With the Dantesque mask, he has lost something of intensity and something of sharpness of outline. In *The Tower* (1928), certain words such as "bitter," "wild," and "fierce," which he was able, a few years ago, to use with such thrilling effect, have no longer quite the same force. He writes more loosely, and seems to write more easily. He has become more plain-spoken, more humorous—his mind seems to run more frankly on his ordinary human satisfactions and chagrins: he is sometimes harsh, sometimes sensual, sometimes careless, sometimes coarse.

Though he now inhabits, like Michael Robartes, a lonely tower on the outermost Irish coast, he has spent six years in the Irish senate, presiding at official receptions in a silk hat, inspecting the plumbing of the government schools and conscientiously sitting through the movies which it is one of his official duties to censor. He is much occupied with politics and society, with general reflections on human life—but with the wisdom of the experience of a lifetime, he is passionate even in age. And he writes poems which charge now with the emotion of a great lyric poet that profound and subtle criticism of life of which I have spoken in connection with his prose.

We may take, as an example of Yeats's later vein, the fine poem in *The Tower* called "Among School Children." The poet, now "a sixty year old smiling public man," has paid an official visit to a girls' school kept by nuns; and as he gazes at the children there, he remembers how the woman he had loved had told him once of some "harsh reproof or trivial event" of her girl-hood which had changed "some childish day to tragedy." And for a moment the thought that she may once have looked like one of the children before him has revived the excitement of his old love. He remembers the woman in all her young beauty—and thinks of himself with his present sixty years—"a comfortable kind of old scarecrow." What use is philosophy now?—is not all beauty bound up with the body and doomed to decay with it?—is not even the divine beauty itself which is worshipped there by the nuns inseparable from the images of it they adore? . . . A complex subject has been treated in the most concentrated form, and yet without confusion. Perceptions, fancies, feelings and thoughts have all their place in the poet's record. It is a moment of human life, masterfully seized and made permanent, in all its nobility and lameness, its mystery and actuality, its direct personal contact and abstrac-tion.

Edmund Wilson. *Axel's Castle: A Study in the Imaginative Literature of 1870–1930* (New York, Scribner's, 1931), pp. 61–63

This period of *The Tower, The Winding Stair*, is important—more important, I have come to think in spite of myself—than any of [Yeats's] earlier periods, drunken though they were with vision of the golden lands, because in it he has come to realize intellectually an attitude that was once romantically sensuous. Himself now, unclothed, is his theme. He projects it in no blue wandering among islands but in an unflattering, hard light. If he uses symbol it is not to turn the key in a golden casket but to silhouette an emotion in its archetype, so that, while bare and stark in itself, it seems still in some queer fashion to take on the dazzle of an auroraed thing whose life is here and in eternity. He loses in colour, of course; indeed, in this book, if we except one or two poems on which he uses some faint washes—"Byzantium," for instance, where the primary of the title suffuses the whole poem—there is no colour but light and darkness. He has gained, however, in intensity: there is no diffusion; the embodied things leave the darkness of the wings, pass across a lit, bare space, and are lost again in the darkness of the wings. It is a technique that may not be used lightly; it is too honest, as honest as if the poet put himself under X-ray; any commonness will show clearly as a broken bone. To his credit, it may be said at once that, apart from some epigrams that are distinguished enough if taken as lulls, as bookmaking, and two things or three that were as well expressed in the prose of "Discoveries," he emerges with no diminishing of stature.

His art has always seemed to me to be an elaboration in emotion of one or two ideas—or convictions, call them as you will—which appear to have come into the world with him already formed and fleshed. The colour of the early phases, the drama of the later, come out of his attempt to cast life into this pre-conceived image. Unity of Being, and all it involves, a semi-divine state where body and soul, Time and Eternity, all antinomies, would mingle in a musical notation, seems to have haunted him from the first. Out of it, in his youth, came that ideal art which had its setting in the magical countries of Bran and Maeldune: there, outside Time, he found his special unity by imagining it, an earthly paradise, impermanent because the human appetite sickens of an unalloyed sweetness, because even there the murmur of the world comes, resistless though its token may be only an apple branch drifting to the quiet of the shore, telling of the wildness, the tumult, the thundering glory of the storm that broke it. There is always the desire to pit force to force: "all progression is by contraries": and so we have this later, bitter-sweet art, with its dyads Time, Eternity, Sense, Spirit, Self, Soul; a never-ending conflict, intellectualized at last, brought into consciousness and seemingly all the more bitter for that since the divided issues, with the corresponding division of desire, are come to be the more plain. . . .

He returns again and again to the same theme as if in the pull of the two poles he must, of, necessity lay the sticks for his nest; as if there alone the solution of his special problem was to be found. The Heart, star-haunted, carrying soul like a cold bubble on its back may not be happy altogether happy among the marketcarts, in the loudness of the Tabarde Inn; yet remembering the merry tumult, dark-and-bright love, the red of war, how may it be content with the pure space of Spirit? It is in a balance of contraries, inevitably, he comes to his rather warring unity if one may name unity this storm centre where opposites clash and mix in times of crisis, forcing him to continual statement of choice; inevitably too in each resolution of such crises, there is a rich realization of the opposing elements, an intensification of each that is at the same time a dilation and an intermixing of boundaries.

Padraic Fallon. DM. April, 1934, pp. 59–60

A new book from Mr. Yeats is an event to excite every reader of poetry. Blake says: "Bring out number, weight and measure in a year of dearth," and if this be the poet's function, Mr. Yeats has triumphantly fulfilled it more than once. In an age of singular poetic barrenness he has produced a great body of work recognisable at once, by its manner and content, as the highest poetry. Far from showing any decline of his powers, he has written within the last twenty years poetry which everyone of competence admits to be unsurpassed, indeed unequalled, by any of his contemporaries. Nine years ago he wrote:

> Never had I more
> Excited, passionate, fantastical
> Imagination, nor an eye and ear
> That more expected the impossible—

and in *The Tower*, and later *The Winding Stair*, he proceeded to reveal his mastery of fresh subtleties of attitude and expression.

It is remarkable that so much of Mr. Yeats's work is of an occasional nature, written for the theatre, or arising, in many cases, directly out of the events and circumstances of his time. This fact emphasises, rather than diminishes, its greatness. In addition, it makes his poetry personal to every reader capable of appreciating contemporary poetry, and particularly to an Irish reader. For, despite the loudly-voiced opinions of certain Irishmen, it must be obvious that the metaphysical framework, the spiritual approach, of Yeats's work is completely Irish.

Any dissatisfaction with the present volume [*A Full Moon in March*] must be on the grounds of its slightness. *A Full Moon in March* contains little that is new to followers of Mr. Yeats. There is a re-writing in verse of *The King of the Great Clock Tower*, which has been produced as a prose play at the Abbey. The verse is assured and dignified, yet leavened with that colloquial element which gives so much strength to his poetry and which makes his poetic dramas eminently actable. . . .

Of the poems here printed for the first time the most notable, perhaps, is the fifth of the "Supernatural Songs," though our personal preference is for the simple and tender "Prayer for Old Age" . . . .

Irish Times. Dec. 14, 1935, p. 7

Ireland was the moulder of Yeats's mind, as it eventually became the sounding-board for most of his verse and the great stimulating impact on his life.

Throughout that intense life two men were his aristocratic heroes: John O'Leary and Parnell. On them he fashioned his heroic poise. For him one man typified the significant romanticism of Irish life; the other revealed its tragic realism. Yeats was the child of Parnell's race; the son by adoption of O'Leary's; but O'Leary's people—the Gaelic people, who lived dangerously to die jestfully—were his first and lasting influence.

From boyhood W. B. Yeats intimately knew his romantic and pastoral Sligo; later Clare-Galway became more attractive to the growing austerity of his mind. All through life his thought was never far from the West of Ireland. As a boy its quaint and adventurous folk, its grey fringes touching an uncharted world, were seen through "magic casements." His early verse—heavy with dream and frail reality—arises from these. That strange territory, that phantasmagoria, was his rich possession of poetry; and for it the English critics very quickly claimed a Celtic kingdom.

Yeats had thought to create a sensuous, musical vocabulary, to marshal the Irish fragmentary beauties into a great literature, and indeed to give Ireland a constantly artistic conscience through the medium of a poetic hierarchy. Until about 1907 all his achievements are towards that aim. Yeats, however, grew weary of his own ceremonial style—a style that seemed more concerned with cadence than content, of things imaged, as it were, through water. And away from that poetry of ornamental illumination, rather than flash, he hardened himself, subduing the lavish painting and toning down the rich rounds. He sought to rid himself of elaboration, of redundancy—through various ways. He found his new method by ballad-writing, for instance, and by writing out first in prose the substance of the verse on which he was working. He, however, succeeded mainly in his later work by the introduction of and tenacious adherence to stern theme and structure. With that success his poetry of mood gives way to his poetry of dramatic passion. It became hardbitten: more Gaelic in feeling.

> F. R. Higgins. In Stephen Gwynn, ed., *Scattering*
> *Branches: Tributes to the Memory of W. B. Yeats*
> (New York, Macmillan, 1940), pp. 147–49

Measured by potentiality, by aspiration, and by the achievement of a few poems, it is as an heroic failure that one is forced to consider Yeats's poetic career as a whole. The causes were complex. Something, no doubt, must be attributed to defects of "character"; and a very great deal must be attributed to the literary tradition of the nineteenth century which, as he came to see so clearly, offered the very opposite of an incitement to maturity. But, since "the death of language . . . is but a part of the tyranny of impersonal things" (*Essays*), that tradition itself appears as the symptom of a deeper disease. Yeats wrote . . . of himself as a young man, already half-conscious that "nothing so much matters as Unity of Being": "Nor did I understand as yet how little that Unity, however wisely sought, is possible without a Unity of Culture in class or people that is no longer possible at all" (*Autobiographies*). These passages, representative of many others, are part of a diagnosis that is valuable not merely for the light that it throws on Yeats's poetry. For those who would understand our divided and distracted civilization, in which the "passionate intensity" of partial men offers itself as a substitute for the vitality that springs from the whole consciousness, few things are more profitable than a study of Yeats's poetry and prose together. "The mischief," he said, "began at the end of the seventeenth century when man became passive before a mechanized nature."

L. C. Knights, SoR. Winter, 1941, pp. 440–41

I think it is certain that Yeats was the most considerable poet of our time, perhaps the greatest since Tennyson. Criticism will make up its myraid mind as to whether he is to be included among those the greatness of whom is now unquestioned. These, the great ones, through a long six hundred years of history, are still less than a dozen. There are seven great poets and, leaving lyrics aside, there are less than a dozen great poems. The present reviewer thinks that Yeats may not be worthy of so great a company. The great poet is everyman of his caste; and Yeats was too continuously in his own mind to be lost in his poetry, and securely found in its universe. He has left many works which the intellect approves: verse of a technical mastery which is admirable and creative: he had splendour and passion in plenty, but love and hate and pity were not so adequately at his hand, and so he has left few poems which our affections instinctively delight in, and state to be memorable for ever, and to be lovely for no reason: for if the poem be not irrational it is not lovely.

To be oddly irrational and to be, thereupon, even more oddly precise, that is the secret of poetry, and Yeats scarcely dared that secret thoughtlessness. To surprise and delight, that is poetry: it is the irrational that delights, it is an impossible precision therein that astonishes.

Did he somewhat lack also in the rich humanity of the great poets? for whether it be Chaucer, Spenser, Shakespeare, this "humanity" is effortlessly with them.

This, in Yeats' work, is not present often enough, or is not present often enough in the condition which poetry permits and demands.

The "humanity" I speak of is effortless and anonymous. Yeats is rarely anonymous: he is rarely effortless. Love and hate and pity were not absolutely real to him: he stares at them, and sees their shadows: he tends to use scorn instead of hate, and admiration instead of love, and instead of pity he invokes uncompassionate Nature and the aristocrat who is beautiful and merciless. [1948]

James Stephens. James, Seamus & Jacques:
Unpublished Writings of James Stephens, ed. by
Lloyd Frankenberg (New York, Macmillan, 1964),
pp. 94–95

For a long time, Yeats had no mould into which he could pour his plays. His early plays, therefore, written to his theory of the sovereignty of words, are unsatisfactory because they try to superimpose this theory on to the conventional idea of what a play ought to be. *The Countess Cathleen*, for instance, or *The Land of Heart's Desire* or *Cathleen Nī Houlihan*, pleasurable though they can be to read, become boring when heard on the stage because of the effort to compromise with the accepted ideas of playwriting. It was not until he read Fennellosa's translations of the Japanese Noh plays that Yeats suddenly had a mode which he could adapt to his own purposes. Here he found the remote theatre he wished for, where gesture and movement were simplified by the use of immemorial convention and where the climax of the development of the argument was conveyed in the ritual movements of a formal dance. "I have invented a form of drama," he announced with satisfaction when he had written his first play on this model, "distinguished, indirect and symbolic and having no need of mob or press to pay its way—an aristocratic form." He had with this mode of playwriting attained "the distance from life which can make credible strange events, elaborate words." . . .

Having excised normal theatrical properties from his plays—movement, gesture, story, and the dramatic development of action—what had Yeats left? He had, we can say, attained what he set out to attain early in life—the sovereignty of words. Words alone were what he was really interested in and it is probable that the theatre for its own sake never attracted him. Perhaps the clue to his theatrical requirement and practice is to be found in a sentence in his essay "Speaking to the Psaltery" which he wrote in 1902. "I, at any rate," he said, "from this out mean to write all my longer poems for the stage and all my shorter ones for the Psaltery, if only some strong angel keep me to my good resolutions." He was, first and last, a poet and the theatre for him was merely a workshop within which the lathe of his poetry kept turning. All his plays are, in fact, poems—or what poems also are, meditations—but, within his self-imposed limits, they are highly dramatic. There would not be a place for them in the hurly-burly of the theatre of to-day which seeks ever-larger audiences for its increasing shallowness and its increasing concern with the "restless mimicries of the surface of life." But in that theatre where intellectual excellence and imaginative passion are cared for they have a permanent place.

Valentin Iremonger. Irish Writing. Summer, 1955,
pp. 53, 55–56

There were two more books of poems before the end of the century: the lyrics published in 1891 along with *The Countess Cathleen*, and later gathered in "The Rose" section of his collected volume, and *The Wind among the Reeds*, published in 1899, four years after *The Land of Heart's Desire*. The second book brought a certain kind of writing, which he had practised from the beginning, to such elaborate and self-contained perfection that readers must have wondered what there was left for him to do except repeat himself. If he had died then it would have been easy to believe of Yeats what some have thought of Keats, that he had exhausted his genius.

These two books contain the most widely loved and most commonly anthologized of his poems. They please, and will perhaps always please, most readers who want no more than to accept self-evident beauty. But in later life he himself grew impatient of his early style, and critics have tended to agree with him. It is not because of these that he is counted among the greatest poets of our time; they are overshadowed by his later work which has fewer readers but evokes deeper admiration. . . .

Yeats in these poems deliberately turned his back on the actual. Outside his poetry, as the next chapter will show, he was thinking with the utmost excitement about politics, philosophy and art, and was more and more actively concerned with all three, but you would hardly guess it from a mere reading of the poems. He seldom expressed a thought till is was so inextricably fused with music and imagery that it had ceased to be distinguishable as thought. And although he was deeply in love and the emotion of his love is felt throughout his writing, he did not sing in simple lyric ecstasy nor did he, like Donne or Shakespeare in the Sonnets, make poetry out of love's self-questioning. What then did he write about? It was contrary to his idea of poetry at the time that it should appear to be 'about' any part of tangible experience. He set out from the belief that there is that in a man which underlies all experience. Poetry is a discovery of that inner soul, which emerges when all outward preoccupations are stilled, like a shy ghost, to possess the deserted landscape. His early poems, therefore, have not received a great deal of critical attention; and yet they are not only beautiful in themselves, but in many ways relevant to the more powerful work of later years.

A. G. Stock. *W. B. Yeats: His Poetry and Thought*
(London, Cambridge Univ. Pr., 1961), pp. 37–38

In modern poetry Yeats and T. S. Eliot stand at opposite poles. For while both see life as incomplete, Eliot puts his faith in spiritual perfection, the ultimate conversion of sense to spirit. Yeats, on the other hand, stands with Michelangelo for "profane perfection of mankind," in which sense and spirit are fully and harmoniously exploited, and "body is not bruised to pleasure soul." So strongly does he hold this view that he projects sensuality into heaven to keep heaven from being ethereal and abstract. He presents this faith with such power and richness that Eliot's religion, in spite of its honesty and loftiness, is pale and infertile in comparison.

Yeats's richness, or better, his magnificence of tone, comes partly from the sumptuous images of his work, partly from the different levels of diction and the intricate rhythms at his command. His sense of decorum never fails him because he knows through long testing the value of everything; and this power to estimate things at their true worth contributes to his talent for general statement. To paraphrase his own comment on Goethe, he sought to experience and tried to express moments acceptable to reason in which our thoughts and emotions could find satisfaction or rest.

In his endeavour to express these moments, he changed many elements of his verse, yet his identity is stamped upon them everywhere. His symbols keep altering, but the later symbols, in spite of their increased animation when compared to the earlier, are mature equivalents rather than new departures. His heroes also remain recognizable through many transformations; in his later writings they do not abdicate their thrones or take up island apiculture or go mad, but that is because they become aware of their essential isolation even when performing some communal role, and because their internal battle depends only slightly on external circumstance. They remain uncommon men, uncommon in their nobility, charismatic in the power with which they excite emulation and focus intellect and emotion. The heroes of the later verse are simply the heroes of the early verse who have, like their creator, matured.

The principles of growth and of stability keep constant watch on one another in Yeats's poetry. He was a many-sided man who by dint of much questioning and inner turmoil achieved the right to speak with many voices and to know completely the incompleteness of life. And if, as seems likely, his works will resist time, it is because in all his shape-changing he remains at the centre tenacious, solid, a "marble triton among the streams."

Richard Ellmann. *The Identity of Yeats*
(New York, Oxford Univ. Pr., 1964), pp. 246–47

The emphatic stress in Yeats's view of tragedy falls on the hero's rejoicing at the moment of death; to experience tragedy is altogether life-enhancing, exhilarating, death-cancelling. The refrain of "The Gyres" may therefore appropriately be "What matter?"; a superb nonchalance invests many *Last Poems*. The other side of the tragic duality in common experience, the deeply painful sense of loss, of wasted potential, is barely noticed: "there may be in this or that detail painful tragedy, but in the whole work none." Towards such a position the brilliant logic of Yeats's career—or an important aspect of it—had tended; the writing of poetry and the whole elaborate structure of *A Vision* were to confer just such security, an invulnerable aloofness. A comparison between "Lapis Lazuli" and "Nineteen Hundred and Nineteen" will show the process at work: the earlier poem greets the inevitable breaking of "many ingenious lovely things" with dismay, even despair; "Lapis Lazuli" knows the same facts with the superb detachment Rocky Face is bidden to discover. But there is a sense in which Yeats as poet has been trapped by a remorseless logic of his own creating; the discovery of the sculpted image and the assumption of the poetic-become-real energy may indeed be the inevitably right outcome, the "ultimate insight," of the dedicated career. But they may operate also to the impoverishment of the poet; to detach the poetic sensibility from painful circumstance makes for a poverty that cannot be compensated by any merely declaratory security. The real "images" of the great poems are not the specifically summoned ones, tower and winding stair, golden bird or even chestnut tree and dancer, but the infinite variousness of the poet's sensibility as he meditates, the varying deployments of allegiance and mistrust. There are signs of impoverishment in *Last Poems*; something of the assertive propagandist is felt, at his most unacceptable in the flat recommendation of violence for its own sake ("good strong blows are delights to the mind"); rhythm, though capable of niceties possible only to the aged virtuoso, is too often merely insistent. A certain thinness is bred; *Last Poems* almost wholly lacks the richly complex, brilliantly architected structure of many great poems. Yeats had claimed that his Church had an altar but no pulpit; the sheer assertiveness of some *Last Poems* would argue the prominent existence of pulpit at the end of life.

> J. R. Mulryne. In Denis Donoghue and
> J. R. Mulryne, eds., *An Honored Guest:*
> *New Essays on W. B. Yeats* (New York,
> St. Martin's Press, 1966), pp. 137–38

A number of poems in *The Wild Swans at Coole* and *Michael Robartes and the Dancer* flash before the reader the lingering pertinence of that Georgian past. Perhaps the best example of this historical idealism generalized is found in "The Wild Swans at Coole." Beauty, passion, coldness, and conquest are gathered together in the symbol of the swans. They and the Gregorys, like a class set apart in nature, are the center of the world of earth, water, and sky now in its autumn and twilight. Moreover, as I have already pointed out, a mood—still, silent, mysterious—hangs over the scene and betokens a glimpse of a permanence that contrasts with the speaker's melancholy aging. In fact the poet may well be asking at the end not merely what manner of men will continue the traditions of Coole but also what depths of spirit, what lakes of the soul, and what astral reaches of imperishable dream will remain to sustain aristocratic patterns of wild and vigorous life. Passionate and cold, these masterful creatures may *choose* a different habitat.

This glorification of the Gregory tradition takes many human forms in these two volumes. Robert Gregory is the obvious example. "Reprisals" puts him in the Gregory line of improving, conscientious landlords lauded by Arthur Young. "In Memory of Major Robert Gregory" holds up the ideal Galway gentleman impaired only by the discourtesy of death. The added mention of art, Castle Taylor, and Roxborough also establishes the whole Gregory connection discussed in Chapter Two. His authority in architecture harks back to the eighteenth-century gentleman's gift long lost in our day. "Shepherd and

Goatherd" had pointed to his solitude in country rounds. But to point up a quality of mind given special notice in these two volumes, a second look at "An Irish Airman Foresees his Death" is in order.

We have already seen Yeats use this poem as an example of the patriotism of Protestant Ireland. It was the element of choice, arising from an impulse of delight, rather than any law or duty that was the essence of Gregory's patriotism. But it is the relationship between delight and election that is the ultimate eighteenth-century refinement of that patriotism. . . . Gregory's choice of a likely death that would engage his entire self—as "an *active* Power"—made that death both good and joyous. For Gregory the Anglo-Irishman, *dulce et decorum est pro patria mori* did not exist before his election.

"The Fisherman" provides another human instance of several of the wild swans' traits. . . . For all of his freckles and Connemara cloth, this idealized sportsman is certainly a racial portrait. In fact it stands opposed to the Ireland that Yeats had to face. The opposition is caught in the lines "my own race/ And the reality." Such a man would appreciate the combination of passion and coldness. Such a man stands as a living criticism of the middle-class Irish nationalist that Yeats rejects.

Donald T. Torchiana. *W. B. Yeats and Georgian Ireland* (Evanston, Ill., Northwestern Univ. Pr., 1966), pp. 292–94

How did Yeats approach the metrical aspects of composing his poems? Since he is a great poet and a striking and complex personality, his way of working is intrinsically engaging, and beyond that may provide an explanation of the fact that he wrote in an impassive variety of meters and stanzas and yet avoided many forms and greatly favored a few others.

As we have noticed, Yeats did master several, but not a great many, prosodic forms. Similarly the sheer range of his measures and stanzas, without regard to excellence of performance, is by no means narrow and yet is matched and exceeded by many English poets. His meter almost always follows the standard modern practice of counting both the number of syllables and stresses within the line and distributing the stresses symmetrically (i.e., he writes what is now usually called accentual-syllabic verse). There are a few purely accentual poems ("High Talk," for example); none of the poems is purely syllabic; and there are no imitations or adaptations of classical quantitative meters. The dominant measure is the one that dominates modern English poetry: iambic. Trochaic meter (our next most common) is also abundant; anapestic practically disappears after the early poetry. Length of line varies from just a few syllables to twenty or more; but as with most English poetry since the fifteenth century, tetrameters and pentameters predominate. Yeats was not a wide-ranging, experimental prosodist. He did not enter the lists with the facile metrists; he did not tease himself with the French puzzles (there is not a rondeau, villanelle, virelay, triolet, or ballade in the *Collected Poems*). Familiar, ready-to-hand forms are his favorites and are at the same time, with few exceptions, his best successes: couplets, ballad and other quatrain stanzas, sestets and octaves, and irregular lyric forms—these he turns masterfully again and again.

Metrically, then, Yeats is a versatile poet, and yet not nearly so electric as, say, Bridges, Tennyson, or Swinburne. His ability to write not only competent but also fine and, in no few instances, great short poems in a variety of metrical forms reflects the intellectual and emotional scope of a poet of the first order. At the same time the very limitations of his eclecticism tell us something important about his cast of mind and help explain his reticence about the subject of prosody: he was reticent because he did not have the type of mind that very often finds in the challenge of fixed form itself a fascination and inspiration—that finds much of its subject or conception only as the predetermined form begins to suggest and dictate it. As a matter of fact, Yeats, like Jonson before him (but probably unlike most poets), often made a prose sketch of the projected poem before he set to "versing." There was plenty of matter; and there was plenty of the sensible classicist in the romancing Irishman.

Robert Blum. *The Poetic Art of William Butler Yeats*
(New York, Frederick Ungar, 1969), pp. 56–57

To some extent in *The Secret Rose* tales, and of course much more clearly in the "Rosa Alchemica" stories, Yeats is moving away from the Sligo countryside to the London meeting rooms of the Theosophical Society and the Order of the Golden Dawn, from the folk and fairy to the esoteric and the occult. . . . In contrast to his earlier belief that a writer should collect the legends of the countryside so as to further the sense of national identity, Yeats is now committed to an art whose source is "that little, infinite, faltering, eternal flame that one calls one's self." Such an art is addressed not to the populace but to the initiate, as Yeats explained to John O'Leary in 1897: "It [*The Secret Rose*] is any rate an honest attempt towards that aristocratic esoteric Irish literature, which has been my chief ambition. We have a literature for the people but nothing yet for the few."

The Secret Rose stories form a varied collection, and not all of them quite fit Yeats's label of "esoteric." In particular, "Of Costello the Proud, of Oona the Daughter of Dermott and of the Bitter Tongue," based on an Irish legend doubtless learned from Douglas Hyde, is a rather straightforward tale and might be more at home in *The Celtic Twilight*. By and large, though, the other nine stories support Yeats's claim that "they have but one subject, the war of spiritual with natural order."

For Yeats, the "natural order" meant the world of common reality, variously imaged in the stories as the world of kings and courts, of violent sol-

diers, of cottage life, and, most importantly, of Christianity. By "spiritual order" Yeats meant any attempt to transcend this common reality and attain
some form of higher wisdom or beauty; this order is variously imaged in the
figures of Aengus, of a king touched by the Sidhe, of a quasi-Rosicrucian
knight, and of several scholars and poets. The basic pattern of the conflict
between the two orders is identical in almost all the stories: the spiritual
hero is misunderstood, rejected, and destroyed by the natural order. But often
enough, the process of literal death results in a symbolic victory, a transcendence of the natural and an elevation to the spiritual.

Richard J. Finneran. *The Prose Fiction of
W. B. Yeats* (Dublin, Dolmen, 1973),
pp. 17–18

Yeats's quest for a means to bring "personal utterance" into the theatre led
him through perhaps the widest range of experiment of any major dramatist in
the history of the theatre. . . . I believe it is a mistake to view Yeats's development as a continuous evolution towards a definitive dramatic form. No one
play or series of plays at any given time can adequately reveal the many-sided
greatness of Yeats. Taken as a whole, Yeat's work ranges from the epic
sweep of *The Countess Cathleen* to the taut Beckettian introspection of *Purgatory*; from the exquisitely poetical *The Shadowy Waters* to the total theatricality of *Fighting the Waves* and *The King of the Great Clock Tower* in which
words were intended to be lost in "patterns of sound as the name of God is lost
in Arabian arabesques." In almost every instance, the form of an individual
play is an organic reflection of its content. Yet there is an astonishing consistency of purpose and coherence of thought to the entire body of Yeats's dramatic work. While some of his plays are undoubtedly more successful than
others, at his best Yeats was not merely a poet in the theatre but a poetic dramatist who combined the arts of literature and the theatre so as to create effective and profoundly significant drama.

The development of Yeats the dramatist cannot be separated from the development of Yeats the poet; nor can the development of Yeats the poet be
separated from the society in which he lived or the theatre in which he first
practised. During the short period of time in which Yeats specifically wrote
plays for the Abbey Theatre, he learned his trade as a dramatist. One may ask
whether *The Hour-Glass* is theatrically as successful as *Purgatory*, but without question its revisions prepared the way for the success of his later plays. It
is also probable that the revisions of *The Hour-Glass* encouraged Yeats to explore again the theatrical possibilities of ritual through the dramaturgical form
of the dance plays.

Through his involvement with the Abbey Theatre, Yeats developed not
merely dramaturgical skills and innovative theatrical ideas but a much deeper
awareness of himself as a man and artist. Out of his personal struggles and

disappointments at the early Abbey Yeats evolved his conception of tragedy with its profound implications for the conduct of life. From his practical work as a dramatist Yeats discovered that it was only as a poet that he was able to express the full metaphysical and spiritual implications of his tragic vision of life.

James W. Flannery. *W. B. Yeats and the Idea of a*
Theatre (New Haven, Conn., Yale Univ. Pr., 1976),
pp. 314–16

I have half-meant to indulge myself in a sort of polemic. It would be directed against the nonpoetic treatment of Yeats by so many critics—thoughtful and learned critics (of course), Hibernophiliac critics, Maud-Gonneomanic critics, critics who plunge into chthonic mysteries and to whom poems are "but wandering holes" stuffed with bits of Gnostic wadding, and critics who begin books called *Yeats* by citing Dr. Johnson and end them by citing Martin Buber and who instruct the poet in just what philosophical positions and poetic influences he should or should not have harkened to.

But the very thought is like a knell, glazing o'er my glow of noble exasperation, to toll me back to my sole theme: poems. William Butler Yeats was the man who wrote, for instance, the poem "Memory." . . .

"Memory" is surely one of Yeats's more direct and concentrated successes. Its quality is rooted in its apparently simple yet gristly, tensile form. It is a single sentence in which each line grafts a new perspective onto the poem's increasingly physical statement. Even the rhyme-scheme has this organic character of complex life within the uncomplicated exterior. Three lines apart, the rhymes are sufficiently delayed to avoid any suggestion of the facile. Until the last rhyme, which clicks the poem shut, they are inexact. The iambic trimeter lines, meanwhile, are deftly varied so that the subtle displacements of accent actually syncopate the rhythm. The only marked pauses occur after the first and second lines; thereafter rhyme and meter are put to the service of the one sweep of passionate assertion that culminates in the metaphor of mountain hare and mountain grass.

That culminating metaphor lifts the poem away from affectation or sentimentality. Although the first half of the poem, both through its tone and through explicit statement—"charm and face were in vain"—has already dismissed superficial feminine attractiveness, the second half clinches the case with its earthy image of the permanent impact of one life upon another. It is an image of animal intimacy, without genteel "delicacy" and yet without bawdiness either, and it has as much to say about spiritual as about bodily magnetism. It is like the love-talk in *The Cantos* [of Ezra Pound] but concerns a lost love rather than one gratifyingly in progress. Despite its brevity, we cannot quite think of "Memory" as a slight poem. It illustrates Yeats's special genius, his gift for using his great virtuosity to arrive at moments of powerful emotional discovery: elemental moments of confessional force in their clear, hard intensity. In them are revealed the design and direction of a poem beyond its elegances of word-play and intricacies of sound and its display, however subtle or profound and intellectually impressive, of moral or philosophical positions.

M. L. Rosenthal. *Sailing into the Unknown: Yeats, Pound and Eliot* (New York, Oxford Univ. Pr., 1978), pp. 116–18

Most readers, at least for some moments, have wanted to be beguiled and be-deviled by Maud Gonne, to believe in her beauty, presence, and force of per-sonality, to accept as complete Yeats's account of their first meeting and many of the poems that echo it. After all, he said that that meeting reverber-ated through his mind and imagination like the sound of "a Burmese gong, an overpowering tumult that had yet many pleasant secondary notes": . . .

Maud Gonne at Howth station waiting a train,
Pallas Athene in that straight back and arrogant head:
All the Olympians, a thing never known again.

Those are stirring lines, but there are several other, less heroic and more revealing views of Maud Gonne, the most insistent note perhaps being the sar-donic resignation of a diary entry in 1909: "Today the thought came to me that [Maud Gonne] never really understands my plans, or nature, or ideas. Then came the thought, what matter? How much of the best I have done and still do is but the attempt to explain myself to her? If she understood, I should lack a reason for writing, and one never can have too many reasons for doing what is so laborious." . . .

Biographers, Johnson tells us, are naturally inclined to perpetrate a won-der. The more so for lovers who are poets, and it is not a surprise that Yeats should create—from his beautiful, limited, arresting, infuriating woman—Cathleen Ni Houlihan, Helen of Troy, Pallas Athene, "a thing never known again." The process of that transformation, from woman to image, biography to myth, is difficult to recapture, but it can tell us something about the quality of Yeats's love and the workings of his imagination.

In the first place, his admiration was never unguarded. From the begin-ning his letters and diaries show irony, anxiety, and judgment mingling with the enchantment. He senses the willful theatricality: "mixed with this feeling for what is permanent in human life there was something declamatory, Latin in a bad sense, and perhaps even unscrupulous." He worries about "her desire for power, apparently for its own sake," her single-mindedness, restlessness, and incipient fanaticism. He can write with some relaxed irony about himself —"Did I tell you how much I admire Miss Gonne? She will make many converts to her political belief. If she said the world was flat or the moon an old caubeen tossed up into the sky I would be proud to be of her party"—and a more troubled irony about her—"I also knew that vague look in the eyes and had often wondered at its meaning—the wisdom that must surely accompany its symbol, her beauty, or lack of any thought." Furthermore, his feelings were always highly literary. He is ready to fall in love *and* ready to discover and define an emblem, his own Irish epipsyche. Soon after their first meeting he was planning *The Countess Cathleen* where Maud Gonne, in the title role, was to be a symbol of a symbol of Ireland. But the first Maud Gonne section of *Memoirs* begins not with apple blossoms and Virgilian commendations, but with the stark sentence, "I was twenty-three years old when the troubling of my life began." His long account of that troubling includes pity and melancholy, chagrin and fury, as well as passion and devotion.

Douglas Archibald. *Yeats* (Syracuse, N.Y., Syracuse
Univ. Pr., 1983), pp. 38–42

Yeats's mind is commonly supposed to have been enveloped in mists of occultist idiosyncrasy. Yet his pursuit of a spiritual world led him in the same direction as some of the foremost thinkers of his time. Even in the field of science he found what he most longed for: scientific backing for his assault on materialism. In 1926 he read and heavily annotated Alfred North Whitehead's *Science and the Modern World*. Whitehead outlines the history of mechanistic science, and then describes the twentieth-century revolution effected by the work of Einstein and the quantum theory. The new physics, according to Whitehead, demands a new philosophy; and he propounds a theory of organism. Yeats was delighted and impressed by the fact that science itself had abolished the "objective" reality of matter, space, and time: modern physics appeared to be offering justification for his own beliefs. Now that he had the latest authorities behind him he could say, with an air of careless condescension, "No educated man to-day accepts the objective matter and space of popular science." Bertrand Russell, whose *Outline of Philosophy* Yeats read with care, twice describes modern conceptions of matter as "ghostly": we are dealing not with objects but with events. Yeats accepted with ease the most daring speculations of the physicists: he had, after all, always believed in ghosts. What began among the fairies in Sligo came to maturity in a world where, as Yeats expressed it, "Matter is the source of all energy," or, to put it another way, $e = mc^2$.

If, however, Yeats believed that "Einstein has done away with materialism," he also knew that Einstein's thought would have little effect on the popular mind. To the end of his life, therefore, he maintained his polemically antimaterialist stance, constantly reminding Ireland that her national intellect is rooted in subjectivity and idealism. He opens his "Private Thoughts" from *On the Boiler* (1939) with the declaration: "I am philosophical, not scientific, which means that observed facts do not mean much until I can make them part of my experience," and continues with a last condemnation of Locke, mathematics, and democracy, and a last blessing upon the unique Irish soul. When he has once again praised Swift and Berkeley, affirmed the mediumistic wisdom of the Irish peasantry, and expounded his theory of historical cycles, "Private Thoughts" appears as a summary of his major philosophical concerns. Yet there is a difference. Mario Rossi tells us that Yeats "did not feel philosophy as an abstruse speculation nor was he attracted to it by its technical difficulties. He wanted to solve his problems. He wanted to understand clearly his own mind." As death approached it became clear to Yeats that philosophy had not solved his problems, nor even given him the key to himself. In "The Man and the Echo" he asks despairingly:

> Shall we in that great night rejoice?
> What do we know but that we face
> One another in this place?

Knowledge is necessarily limited; the truth remains shrouded in mystery. "Of late," writes Yeats in *On the Boiler*, "I have tried to understand in its practical details the falsehood that is in all knowledge, science more false than philosophy, but that too false." Yet he will not reject philosophy, for if we do not master knowledge, it will master us. Searching for a final statement of this paradox, he wrote to Lady Elizabeth Pelham on January 4, 1939, "Man can embody truth but he cannot know it." Yeats's words remind us that, while a study of his philosophy contributes considerably to our intellectual appreciation of his work, for embodied truth we must return to the poems themselves.

Elizabeth Cullingford. In Richard Kearney, ed.,
The Irish Mind: Exploring Intellectual Traditions
(Dublin, Wolfhound, 1985), pp. 242–43

BIBLIOGRAPHIES

Except in those few cases identified by a headnote, we have attempted to list all of the major works of an individual author, together with a representative selection of that author's minor works. Only relatively recent or particularly significant reprints are noted. In addition, we have generally excluded mention of the following items: limited editions, privately printed material, and pamphlets; children's books (except where the author is especially known as a writer of juvenile literature); produced but unpublished plays, and filmed but unpublished screenplays.

The title of a bibliography of an individual author (or the location of a bibliographical study) is, when available, listed after the author's works. In the absence of a bibliography, a biography or a critical work, in that order of preference, is noted; this work usually contains a bibliography.

GENRE ABBREVIATIONS

a	autobiography	misc	miscellany
ac	art or architecture criticism	n	novel
b	biography	p	poetry
c	criticism	pd	poetic drama
d	drama	r	reminiscences
e	essays	rd	radio drama
g	general (nonfiction not covered by other categories)	s	short stories
		t	travel
h	history	tr	translation
j	juvenile literature	tvd	television drama
m	memoirs		

SOURCES

The following sources have been consulted in compiling these bibliographies:

Anglo-Irish Literature: A Review of Research, ed. Richard J. Finneran
A Bibliography of Modern British Novelists by Robert J. Stanton
British Books in Print
Card catalogues of the New York University Library, Columbia University Library, New York Public Library
Contemporary Authors; Contemporary Dramatists; Contemporary Novelists; Contemporary Poets
Cumulative Book Index
Dictionary of Irish Literature, ed. Robert Hogan
Irish University Review, Bibliography Bulletin
Journal of Modern Literature, Annual Bibliography

Modern British Literature: A Library of Literary Criticism, Vols. 1–5, ed. Ruth Z. Temple et al.
The National Union Catalogue
Recent Research on Anglo-Irish Writers, ed. Richard J. Finneran

JOHN BANVILLE
1946–

Long Lankin, 1970 (n); *Nightspawn*, 1971 (n); *Birchwood*, 1973 (n); *Doctor Copernicus*, 1976 (n); *Kepler*, 1981 (n); *The Newton Letter*, 1982 (n)

Rüdiger Imhof, "John Banville: A Checklist," *Irish University Review*, Spring 1981, 87–88

SAMUEL BECKETT
1906–

Whoroscope, 1930 (p); *Proust*, 1931 (c); *More Pricks than Kicks*, 1934 (s); *Echo's Bones and Other Precipitates*, 1935 (p); *Murphy*, 1938 (Fr. tr. by Beckett, 1947) (n); *Molloy*, 1951 (Eng. tr. by Patrick Bowles and Beckett, 1955) (n); *Malone Meurt*, 1951 (tr. by Beckett as *Malone Dies*, 1956) (n); *L'Innomable*, 1953 (tr. by Beckett as *The Unnamable*, 1958) (n) [the foregoing three novels written in French make up a trilogy]; *En Attendant Godot*, 1952 (tr. by Beckett as *Waiting for Godot*, 1954) (d); *Watt*, 1953 (n); *Nouvelles et Textes pour Rien*, 1955 (s,e); Jean Wahl, *Illustrations for the Bible by Marc Chagall*, 1956 (tr. by Beckett and Jean Wahl); *All That Fall*, 1957 (rd); *Fin de Partie*, suivi de *Acte sans Paroles*, 1957 (tr. by Beckett as *Endgame* and *Act without Words*, 1958) (d); *From an Abandoned Work*, 1958 (e); *Embers*, 1959 (rd); *Krapp's Last Tape*, 1960 (d); (with Olive Classe) *Bram van Velde* by J. Putnam, 1960 (tr); *Happy Days*, 1961 (tr. by Beckett as *Oh! les Beaux Jours*, 1963) (d); *Poems in English*, 1961 (p); *Comment c'est*, 1961 (tr. by Beckett as *How It Is*, 1961) (n); (with others) *Selected Poems of Alain Bosquet*, 1963 (tr); *Play, and Two Short Pieces for Radio*, 1964 (d, rd); *Proust, and Three Dialogues* by Beckett and Georges Duthuit (*Proust* orig. pub. 1931, *Three Dialogues* orig. pub. in *Transition* 149, no. 5),

1965 (c); *Imagination Dead Imagine* (tr. of *Imagination morte imaginez*, 1958, from French by the author), 1966 (e); *Come and Go*, 1967 (d); *Eh, Joe, and Other Writings* (with *Act Without Words II; Film*), 1967 (d); *No's Knife: Collected Shorter Prose, 1945–1966*, 1967 (s,e); *A Samuel Beckett Reader*, ed. John Calder, 1967; *Cascando, and Other Short Dramatic Pieces* (with *Words and Music; Eh, Joe; Play; Come and Go; Film*), 1968 (d); *Film: Complete Scenario, Illustrations, Production Shots*, 1969; *Lessness* (tr. of *Sans*, 1969, from French by the author) 1970 (misc); (with others) *Jack B. Yeats: A Centenary Gathering*, 1972 (ac); *The Lost Ones* (tr. of *Le dépeupleur*, 1971, from the French by the author), 1972 (n); Guillaume Apollinaire, *Zone* (orig. pub. in *Transition*, 1950), 1972 (tr); *The North*, 1972 (misc); *Breath, and Other Shorts*, 1972 (d); *Not I*, 1973 (d); *First Love* (tr. of *Premier amour*, 1970, from French by the author), 1973 (n); *Mercier and Camier* (tr. of *Mercier et Camier*, 1970, from French by the author), 1974 (n); *First Love, and Other Shorts*, 1974 (s); *Ends and Odds* (includes *Not I, That Time, Footfalls, Ghost Trio, Theatre I, Theatre II, Radio I, Radio II*), 1976 (d); *I Can't Go On, I'll Go On: A Selection from Samuel Beckett's Work*, ed. Richard W. Seaver, 1976; *Fizzles*, 1976 (s); *Collected Poems in English and French*, 1977; *Four Novellas*, 1977; *Company*, 1980 (n); *Collected Works of Samuel Beckett*, 25 vols., 1981; *Rockaby, and Other Short Pieces*, (includes *Rockaby, Ohio Impromptu, All Strange Away, A Piece of Monologue*), 1981 (d); *Ill Seen, Ill Said*, 1982 (s); *Worstward Ho*, 1983 (n); *The Collected Shorter Plays*, 1984; *Disjecta: Miscellaneous Writings and a Dramatic Fragment*, 1984

Raymond Federman and John Fletcher, *Samuel Beckett; His Works and His Critics: An Es-*

say in Bibliography, 1970; Deirdre Bair, Samuel Beckett: A Biography, 1978

BRENDAN BEHAN
1922–1964

The Quare Fellow, 1954 (d); The Hostage, 1958 (productions in Gaelic and English) (d); Borstal Boy, 1958 (a); Brendan Behan's Ireland, 1961 (e); Island: An Irish Sketch-book, 1962 (t); Hold Your Hour and Have Another, 1963 (e); The Scarperer, 1964 (n); (with Paul Hogarth) Brendan Behan's New York, (t); With Breast Expanded, 1964 (a); Confessions of an Irish Rebel, 1965 (a); Moving Out, and A Garden Party, 1967 (2d); The Wit of Brendan Behan, comp. Sean McCann, 1968 (misc); Richard's Cork Leg, 1973 (d); The Complete Plays, 1978; Poems and Stories, 1978; Poems and a Play in Irish, 1981 (p, d); After the Wake, 1983 (misc)

Colbert Kearney, The Writings of Brendan Behan, 1977; E. H. Mikhail, Brendan Behan: An Annotated Bibliography of Criticism, 1980

ELIZABETH BOWEN
1899–1973

Encounters, 1923 (s); Ann Lee's, 1926 (s); The Hotel, 1927 (n); Joining Charles, 1929 (s); The Last September, 1929 (n); Friends and Relations, 1931 (n); To the North, 1932 (n); The Cat Jumps, 1934 (s); The House in Paris, 1935 (n); The Death of the Heart, 1938 (n); Look at All Those Roses, 1941 (s); Bowen's Court, 1941 (a); Seven Winters, 1942 (a); The Demon Lover, (Am. ed. Ivy Gripped the Steps), 1945 (s); English Novelists, 1946 (c); Anthony Trollope: A New Judgement, 1946 (c); with Graham Greene and V. S. Pritchett, Why Do I Write? 1948 (e); The Heat of the Day, 1949 (n); Collected Impressions, 1950 (c); Early Stories, 1950 (s); The Shelbourne: A Centre in Dublin Life for More Than a Century (Am. ed. The Shelbourne Hotel), 1951 (h); A World of Love, 1955 (n); Stories by Elizabeth Bowen, 1959 (s); A Time in Rome, 1960 (a); Seven Winters and Afterthoughts, 1962 (a,e); The Little Girls, 1964 (n); Bowen's Court, 2nd ed., 1965 (a); A Day in the Dark, 1965 (s); with others, These Simple Things: Some Appreciations of the Small Joys in Daily Life, from "House and Garden", 1965 (e); Eva Trout; or, Changing Scenes, 1969 (n); Pictures and Conversations, 1975 (misc); Elizabeth Bowen's Irish Stories, 1978 (s); The Collected Stories, 1981 (s)

Hariett Blodgett, Patterns of Reality: Elizabeth Bowen's Novels, 1975; Victoria Glendinning, Elizabeth Bowen: Portrait of a Writer, 1977; Robert J. Stanton, A Bibliography of Modern British Novelists, Vol. I, 1978

PATRICK BOYLE
1905–1982

Like Any Other Man, 1966 (n); At Night All Cats Are Grey, 1966 (s); All Looks Yellow to the Jaundiced Eye, 1969 (s); A View From Calvary, 1976 (n); The Port Wine Stain: Patrick Boyle's Best Short Stories, ed. Peter Fallon, 1983

WILLIAM BOYLE
1853–1922

A Kish of Brogues, 1899 (s); The Building Fund, 1905 (d); The Eloquent Dempsey, 1906 (d); The Mineral Workers, 1906 (d); Family Failings, 1912 (d)

David Krause, The Profane Book of Irish Comedy, 1982

SHAN F. BULLOCK
1865–1935

The Awkward Squads, and Other Stories, 1893 (s); By Thrasna River: The Story of a Townland, 1895 (n); Ring o' Rushes, 1896 (p); The Charmer: A Seaside Comedy, 1897 (n); The Barrys, 1899 (n); Irish Pastorals, 1901 (p); The Squireen, 1903 (n); The Red Leaguers, 1903 (n); The Cubs: The Story of a Friendship, 1906 (n); Dan the Dollar, 1907 (n); Robert Thorne: The Story of a London Clerk, 1907 (n); A Laughing Matter, 1908 (n); Master John, 1909 (n); Hetty: The Story of an Ulster Family, 1911 (n); Thomas Andrews, Shipbuilder, 1912 (b); (with E. Lawless) The Race of Castlebar, 1913 (n); Mr. Ruby Jumps *the Traces*, 1917 (n); *Mors et Vita*, 1923 (p); *The Loughsiders*, 1924 (n); *Gleanings*, 1926 (p); *After Sixty Years*, 1931 (a)

Robert Graecan. "Shan F. Bullock," *Éire-Ireland*, Winter 1979, 109–24

JOSEPH CAMPBELL
1879–1944

(with Herbert Hughes) *Songs of Uladh*, 1904 (song); *The Garden of the Bees*, 1905 (p); *The Rushlight*, 1906 (p); *The Gilly of Christ*, 1907 (p); *The Man Child*, 1907 (p); *The Mountainy Singer*, 1909 (p); *Mearing Stones*, 1911 (t); *Judgment*, 1912 (d); *Irishry*, 1913 (p); *Earth of Cualann*, 1917 (p); *The Poems of Joseph Campbell*, ed. with an Introduction by Austin Clarke, 1963

P. S. O'Hegarty, "A Bibliography of Joseph Campbell," *Dublin Magazine*, XV (Oct.–Dec. 1940), 58–61

PAUL VINCENT CARROLL
1900–1968

Things That Are Caesar's, 1934 (d); *Shadow and Substance*, 1938 (d); *Plays for My Children*, 1939 (d); *The White Steed* and *Coggerers*, 1939 (2d); *Old Foolishness*, 1944 (d); *Three Plays (The White Steed, Things That are Caesar's, The Strings, My Lord, Are False)*, 1944 (3d); *Green Cars Go East*, 1947 (d); *The Conspirators*, 1947 (d); *Interlude*, 1947 (d); *The Wise Have Not Spoken*, 1947 (d); *Two Plays (The Wise Have Not Spoken, Shadow and Substance)*, 1948 (2d); *The Wayward Saint*, 1955 (d); *Irish Stories and Plays*, 1958 (d,s); *Farewell to Greatness*, 1966 (d); *Goodbye to the Summer*, 1970 (d)

Paul A. Doyle, *Paul Vincent Carroll*, 1972; Diane Roman and Mary Hamilton, "Checklist of Carroll Short Stories Appearing in *Ireland's Own*, 1920–1930," *Journal of Irish Literature*, 2 (1972)

AUSTIN CLARKE
1896–1974

The Vengeance of Fionn, 1917 (p); *The Sword of the West*, 1921 (p); *The Fires of Baäl*, 1921

(p); *The Cattledrive in Connaught*, 1925 (p); *The Son of Learning* [Gaelic tale turned into blank verse comedy], 1927 (d); *Pilgrimage*, 1929 (p); *The Flame*, 1930 (d); *The Bright Temptation*, 1932 (n); *The Singing-Men at Cashel*, 1936 (n); *Collected Poems*, 1936; *Night and Morning*, 1938 (n); *Sister Eucharia*, 1939 (d); *Black Fast*, 1941 (d); *As the Crow Flies*, 1943 (d); *The Viscount of Blarney*, 1944 (d); *First Visit to England*, 1945 (e); *The Second Kiss*, 1946 (d); *The Plot Succeeds*, 1950 (d); *Poetry in Modern Ireland*, 1951 (c); *The Sun Dances at Easter*, 1952 (n); *The Moment Next to Nothing*, 1953 (d); *Ancient Lights*, 1955 (p); *Too Great a Vine*, 1957 (p); *The Horse-Eaters*, 1960 (p); *Later Poems*, 1961 (p); *Twice Round the Black Church*, 1962 (r); *Forget-Me-Not*, 1962 (p); *Poetry in Modern Ireland*, 1962 (c); *Flight to Africa*, 1963 (p); *Collected Plays*, 1963; *Poems*, 1964 (p); *Mnemosyne Lay in Dust*, 1966 (p); *Old-fashioned Pilgrimage*, 1967 (p); *Echo at Coole*, 1968 (p); *A Penny in the Clouds: More Memories of Ireland and England* (orig. pub. 1937), 1968 (m); *Two Interludes, Adapted from Cervantes (The Student from Salamanca* and *The Silent Lover)*, 1968 (pd); *The Celtic Twilight and the Nineties*, 1969 (c); *Orphide*, 1970 (p); *Tiresias*, 1971 (p); *Collected Poems*, ed. Liam Miller, 1974 (p); *The Wooing of Becfola*, 1974 (p); *Austin Clarke: Selected Poems*, intro. Thomas Kinsella, 1976 (p)

G. Graig Tapping, *Austin Clarke: A Study of His Writings*, 1980; Gregory A. Schirmer, *The Poetry of Austin Clarke*, 1983

PADRAIC COLUM
1881–1972

Broken Soil (rev. as *The Fiddler's House*), 1903 (d); *The Land*, 1905 (d); *The Fiddler's House*, 1907 (d); *Wild Earth, A Book of Verse*, 1907 (enlgd. 1950) (p); *Studies*, 1907 (s); *Thomas Muskerry*, 1910 (d); (with Shane Leslie and others) *Eyes of Youth*, 1910 (p); *The Desert*, 1912 (Am. ed. *Mogu, The Wanderer*, 1917) (d); *My Irish Year*, 1912 (a); (music by H. Hughes) *Songs from Connacht*, 1913 (p); *A Boy in Eirinn*, 1913 (s); *Three Plays: The Fid-*

dler's House, The Land, Thomas Muskerry, 1916 (3d); The King of Ireland's Son, 1916 (s); The Adventures of Odysseus and The Tale of Troy, 1918 (repr. 1962 as The Children's Homer) (s); The Boy Who Knew What the Birds Said, 1918 (s); The Girls Who Sat By the Ashes, 1919 (s); The Boy Apprenticed to an Enchanter, 1920 (s); The Children of Odin, 1920 (repr. 1962) (s); The Golden Fleece and The Heroes Who Lived Before Achilles, 1921 (repr. 1962), (s); The Children Who Followed the Piper, 1922 (s); Dramatic Legends, 1922 (p); Six Who Were Left in a Shoe, 1923 (s); Castle Conquer, 1924 (n); The Peep-Show Man, 1924 (s); At the Gateways of the Day, 1924 (Tales and Legends of Hawaii, Vol. I) (s); The Islands of the Mighty, Being the Hero Stories of Celtic Britain Retold from Mabinogion, 1924 (s); The Forge in the Forest, 1925 (s); The Voyagers, 1925 (s); The Bright Islands, 1925 (Tales and Legends of Hawaii, Vol. II, repr. 1960) (s); The Road Round Ireland, 1926 (t); Creatures, 1927 (p); The Fountain of Youth, 1927 (s); Balloon, 1929 (d); Old Pastures, 1930 (p); Cross Roads in Ireland, 1930 (e); Orpheus, Myths of the World, 1930 (repr. 1959 as Myths of the World) (s); Three Men, 1931 (s); Poems, 1932; A Half-Day's Ride, or, Estates in Corsica, 1932 (t); The Big Tree of Bunlahy, 1933 (s); The White Sparrow, 1933 (s); The Legend of St. Columba, 1935 (s); The Story of Lowry Maen, 1937 (p); Flower Pieces, 1938 (p); Dublin Poets and Artists, 1939 (c); Where the Winds Never Blew and the Cocks Never Crew, 1940 (s); Frenzied Prince, 1943 (s); Collected Poems, 1953; Vegetable Kingdom, 1954 (p); Flying Swans, 1958 (s); Irish Elegies, 1958 (2nd ed. enlgd 1961) (p); (with Mary Colum) Our Friend James Joyce, 1958 (r); Arthur Griffith (Am. ed. Ourselves Alone!), 1959 (b); Poet's Circuits, 1960 (p); Images of Departure, 1970 (p); Selected Stories of Padraic Colum, ed. Sanford Sternlicht, 1985 (s)

Alan Denson, "Padraic Colum: An Appreciation with a Check-list of His Publications," Dublin Magazine, 6, 1 (Spring, 1967), 50–67; Sanford Sternlicht, Padraic Colum, 1985

DANIEL CORKERY
1878–1964

A Munster Twilight, 1916 (s); The Threshold of Quiet, 1917 (n); The Hounds of Banba, 1920 (s); The Labour Leader, 1920 (d); The Yellow Bittern and Other Plays, 1920 (d); I Bhreasail/A Book of Lyrics, 1921 (p); Rebel Songs, under the pseudonym "Reithin Siubhalach," 1922 (song); The Hidden Ireland/A Study of Gaelic Munster in the Eighteenth Century, 1925 (c); The Stormy Hills, 1929 (s); Synge and Anglo-Irish Literature, 1931 (c); Earth Out of Earth, 1939 (s); The Philosophy of the Gaelic League, 1948 (e); The Wager, and Other Stories, 1950 (s); The Fortunes of the Irish Language, 1954 (e); Fohnam the Sculptor, ed. George Brandon Saul, 1973 (d)

George Brandon Saul, Daniel Corkery, 1973

JAMES H. COUSINS
1873–1956

Ben Madighan, and Other Poems, 1894 (p); The Voice of One, 1900 (p); The Quest, 1906 (p); The Awakening, and Other Sonnets, 1907 (p); The Bell-Branch, 1908 (p); Etain the Beloved, and Other Poems, 1912 (p); Straight and Crooked, 1915 (p); The Garland of Life, 1917 (p); The King's Wife, 1919 (d); Moulted Feathers, 1919 (p); Sea-Change, 1920 (p); Forest Meditation, and Other Poems, 1925 (p); Above the Rainbow and Other Poems, 1926 (p); The Sword of Dermot, 1927 (d); The Girdle, 1929 (p); The Wandering Harp, Selected Poems, 1932 (p); A Bardic Pilgrimage, Second Selection of the Poetry of James H. Cousins, 1934 (p); The Oracle, and Other Poems, 1938 (p); Collected Poems, 1894– 1940, 1940 (p); The Hound of Uladh: Two Plays in Verse, 1942 (d); Reflections Before Sunset, 1946 (p); Twenty-Four Sonnets, 1949 (p); (with Margaret E. Cousins) We Two Together, 1950 (a)

Alan Denson, James H. Cousins and Margaret E. Cousins, a Bio-Bibliographical Survey, 1967; William A. Dumbleton, James Cousins, 1980

DENIS DEVLIN
1908–1959

(with Brian Coffey) *Poems*, 1930 (p); *Intercessions*, 1937 (p); Saint-John Perse, *Rains*, 1945 (tr); Saint-John Perse, *Snows*, 1945 (tr); Saint-John Perse, *Exiles*, 1945 (tr); *Lough Derg, and Other Poems*, 1946 (p); *The Heavenly Foreigner*, ed. Brian Coffey, 1950 (tr); René Char, *Poems*, 1952 (tr); *Selected Poems*, preface by Allen Tate and Robert Penn Warren, 1963 (p); *Collected Poems*, ed. Brian Coffey, 1964 (p); *Collected Poems*, 2nd ed., 1978 (p)

LORD DUNSANY
1878–1957

The Gods of Pegana, 1905 (n); *Time and the Gods*, 1906 (n); *The Sword of Welleran*, 1908 (s); *A Dreamer's Tales*, 1910 (s); *The Book of Wonder*, 1912 (s); *Selections from the Writings of Lord Dunsany*, introd. W. B. Yeats, 1912; *Five Plays: The Gods of the Mountain, The Golden Doom, King Argimenes and the Unknown Warrior, The Glittering Gate, The Lost Silk Hat*, 1914 (d); *Fifty-one Tales*, 1915 (s); *Tales of Wonder* (Am. ed. *The Last Book of Wonder*), 1916 (s); *A Night at an Inn*, 1916 (repr. 1957) (d); *Plays of Gods and Men*, 1917 (4d); *Tales of War*, 1918 (s); *Nowadays*, 1918 (e); *Tales of Three Hemispheres*, 1919 (s); *Unhappy Far-off Things*, 1919 (e); *If*, 1921 (d); *The Chronicles of Rodriguez* (Am. ed. *Don Rodriguez, Chronicles of Shadow Valley*), 1922 (s); *The Tents of the Arabs*, 1922 (d); *The Laughter of the Gods*, 1922 (d); *The Queen's Enemies*, 1922 (d); *Plays of Near and Far*, 1922 (d); *The King of Elfland's Daughter*, 1924 (n); *The Compromise of the King of the Golden Isles*, 1924 (d); *Alexander and Three Small Plays*, 1925 (4d); *The Amusements of Khan Kharuda*, 1925 (d); *The Evil Kettle*, 1925 (d); *The Old King's Tale*, 1925 (d); *The Charwoman's Shadow*, 1926 (n); *The Blessing of Pan*, 1927 (n); *Seven Modern Comedies*, 1928 (7d); *Fifty Poems*, 1929 (p); *The Old Folk of the Centuries*, 1930 (d); *The Travel Tales of Mr. Joseph Jorkens*, 1931 (s); *The Curse of the Wise Woman*, 1933 (s); *Lord Adrian*, 1933 (d); *Jorkens Remembers Africa*, 1934 (s); *If I Were Dictator*, 1934 (e); *Up in*

the Hills, 1935 (n); *Mr. Faithful*, 1935 (d); *My Talks with Dean Spanley*, 1936 (n); *Rory and Bran*, 1936 (n); *Plays for Earth and Air*, 1937 (d); *My Ireland*, 1937 (e); *Mirage Water*, 1938 (p); *Patches of Sunlight*, 1938 (a); *The Story of Mona Sheehy*, 1939 (n); *Jorkens Has a Large Whiskey*, 1940 (s); *War Poems*, 1941 (p); *A Journey*, 1943 (p); *Wandering Songs*, 1943 (p); *Guerilla*, 1944 (n); *While the Sirens Slept*, 1944 (e); *The Donnellan Lectures*, 1943 [Trinity College, Dublin; one prose, p, d], 1945 (e); *The Sirens Wake*, 1945 (a); *The Year*, 1946 (p); *A Glimpse from a Watch-Tower*, 1946 (e); *The Odes of Horace*, 1947 (tr); *The Fourth Book of Jorkens*, 1948 (s); *To Awaken Pegasus*, 1949 (p); *The Man Who Ate the Phoenix*, 1949 (n); *The Strange Journeys of Colonel Polders*, 1950 (n); *The Last Revolution*, 1951 (n); *His Fellow Men*, 1952 (n); *Little Tales of Smethers*, 1952 (s); *Jorkens Borrows Another Whiskey*, 1954 (s); *Ghosts of the Heavisade Layer*, 1980 (s); *The Lost Silk Hat*, ed. Edmund R. Brown, 1980 (n); *The Food of Death: 51 Tales*, ed. Reginald R. and Douglas Melville, 1984 (s)

Mark Amory, *Lord Dunsany: A Biography*, 1972

ST. JOHN ERVINE
1883–1971

Mixed Marriage, 1911 (d); *The Magnanimous Lover*, 1912 (d); *Francis Place, The Tailor of Charing Cross*, 1912 (e); *Eight O'Clock and Other Studies*, 1913 (e); *Mrs. Martin's Man*, 1914 (n); *Four Irish Plays*, 1914 (4d); *Jane Clegg*, 1914 (d); *Alice and a Family*, 1915 (n); *John Ferguson*, 1915 (d); *Sir Edward Carson and the Ulster Movement*, 1915 (e); *Changing Winds*, 1917 (n); *The Foolish Lovers*, 1920 (n); *The Ship*, 1922 (d); *Some Impressions of My Elders*, 1922 (r); *The Lady of Belmont*, 1923 (d); *Mary, Mary, Quite Contrary*, 1923 (d); *The Organised Theatre, A Plea in Civics*, 1924 (e); *Anthony and Anna*, 1925 (rev. 1936) (d); *Parnell*, 1925 (b); *The Wayward Man*, 1927 (n); *Four One-Act Plays*, 1928 (4d); *The Mountain*, 1928 (s); *How To Write a Play*, 1928 (c); *The First Mrs. Fraser*, 1929 (d); *The First Mrs. Fraser* (novelization of play), 1931 (n); *The Future of the Press*, 1932 (e); *The*

Theatre in My Time, 1933 (c); *If I Were Dictator* 1934 (e); *God's Soldier, General William Booth*, 1934 (b); *The Alleged Art of the Cinema*, 1934 (c); *Boyd's Shop*, 1936 (d); *People of Our Class*, 1936 (d); *Journey to Jerusalem*, 1936 (t); *Robert's Wife*, 1938 (d); *Our Heritage*, 1939 (e); *Sophia*, 1941 (n); *Is Liberty Lost?*, 1941 (e); *Friends and Relations*, 1947 (d); *Private Enterprise*, 1948 (d); *The Christies*, 1949 (d); *Craigavon, Ulsterman*, 1949 (b); *Oscar Wilde: A Present Time Appraisal*, 1951 (e); *My Brother Tom*, 1952 (d); *Bernard Shaw: His Life, Work, and Friends*, 1956 (b)

Paula Howard, "St. John Ervine: A Bibliography of His Published Works," *Irish Booklore*, 1971

PADRAIC FALLON
1906–1974

The Fallen Saint, 1936 (d); *Lighting-up Time*, 1938 (s); *Diarmuid and Grainne*, 1950 (rd); *Dialogue between Raftery and Death*, 1952 (d); *The Vision of MacConglinne*, 1953 (rd); *Poems*, 1974 (p)

Robert Hogan, *After the Irish Renaissance*, 1967

GEORGE FITZMAURICE
1877–1963

Five Plays [*The Country Dressmaker, The Moonlighter, The Pie-Dish, The Magic Glasses, The Dandy Dolls*], 1914 (d); *The Plays of George Fitzmaurice, Vol 1: Dramatic Fantasies* [*The Magic Glasses, The Dandy Dolls, The Linaun Shee, The Green Stone, The Enchanted Land, The Waves of the Sea*], intro. by Austin Clarke, 1967 (d); *The Plays of George Fitzmaurice, Vol. 2: Folk Plays* [*The Ointment Blue or The King of the Barna Men, The Pie-Dish, The Terrible Baisht, There are Tragedies and Tragedies, The Moonlighter*], intro. by Howard K. Slaughter, 1970 (d); *The Plays of George Fitzmaurice, Vol. 3: Realistic Plays* [*The Toothache, The Country Dressmaker, One Evening Gleam, 'Twixt the Giltinans and the Carmodys, The Simple Hanrahans, The Coming of Ewn Andzale*], intro. by Howard K. Slaughter, 1970 (d); *The Crows*

of Mephistopheles, ed. with intro. by Robert Hogan, 1970 (d); (with John Guinan) *The Wonderful Wedding*, 1978 (d)

Joanne L. Henderson, "Checklist of Four Kerry Writers," *Journal of Irish Literature* 1 (May, 1972), 101–119; Carol W. Gelderman, *George Fitzmaurice*, 1979

BRIAN FRIEL
1929–

The Saucer of Larks, 1962 (s); *Philadelphia, Here I Come!*, 1965 (d); *The Gold in the Sea*, 1966 (s); *The Loves of Cass McGuire*, 1976 (d); *Lovers*: Part One: *Winners*; Part Two: *Losers*, 1968 (d); *A Saucer of Larks: Stories of Ireland*, 1969 (s); *Two Plays: Crystal and Fox, and The Mundy Scheme*, 1970 (2d); *The Gentle Island*, 1974 (d); *The Freedom of the City*, 1974 (d); *The Enemy Within* (prod. 1962), 1975 (d); *Living Quarters*, 1978 (d); *Volunteers*, 1979 (d); *Selected Stories*, 1979 (s); *Faith Healer*, 1980 (d); *Aristocrats*, 1980 (d); *Translations*, 1981 (d); *The Communication Cord*, 1981 (d); *Anton Chekhov: Three Sisters* 1981 (tr); *The Diviner* (*Selected Stories*, rev. ed.), intro. Seamus Deane, 1983 (s); *Selected Plays of Brian Friel*, 1985 (6d)

Kimball King, "Brian Friel," in *Ten Modern Irish Playwrights: A Comprehensive Annotated Bibliography*, 1979

OLIVER ST. JOHN GOGARTY
1878–1957

Hyperthuleana, 1916 (p); (with Joseph O'Connor, under the pseudonyms Alpha and Omega) *Blight, the Tragedy of Dublin*, 1917 (d); *The Ship*, 1918 (p); *An Offering of Swans*, 1924 (p); *Wild Apples*, 1928 (p); *Poems*, 1933 (p); *As I Was Going Down Sackville Street*, 1937 (r); *Others to Adorn* (Am. ed. *Selected Poems*), 1938 (p); *I Follow Saint Patrick*, 1938 (t); *Tumbling in the Hay*, 1939 (n); *Elbow Room*, 1939 (p); *Going Native*, 1941 (a); *Mad Grandeur*, 1944 (n); *Mr. Petunia*, 1946 (s); *Perennial*, 1947 (p); *Mourning Became Mrs. Spendlove, and Other Portraits*, 1948 (e); *Rolling Down the Lea*, 1950 (Am. ed. *Intimations*) (p); *Collected Poems*, 1954 (p); *It*

Isn't This Time of Year at All, 1954 (a); *Start from Somewhere Else*, 1955 (e); *A Week in the Middle*, 1958 (e); *W. B. Yeats: A Memoir*, 1963 (m); *Many Lines to Thee: Letters to G. K. C. Bell*, ed. James F. Carens, 1971; *The Plays of Oliver St. John Gogarty [Blight: The Tragedy of Dublin, A Serious Thing, The Enchanted Trousers]*, ed. James F. Carens, 1971 (d)

James F. Carens, *Surpassing Wit: Oliver St. John Gogarty, His Poetry and His Prose*, 1979; J. B. Lyons, *Oliver St. John Gogarty: The Man of Many Talents*, 1980

LADY GREGORY
1859–1932

Righ Seumas by Douglas Hyde (no date) (tr); *Casadh an Tsugáin; or The Twisting of the Rope* by Douglas Hyde, 1902 (tr); *Cuchulain of Muirtemne*, 1902 (tr); *Dráma Breithe Chriosta* by Douglas Hyde, 1903 (tr); *Poets and Dreamers: Studies and Translations from the Irish*, 1903 (c,tr); *Gods and Fighting Men*, 1904 (tr); *Spreading the News*, 1904 (d); *Kincora*, 1905 (d); *The White Cockade*, 1905 (d); *The White Cockade, and The Travelling Man*, 1905 (2d); *A Book of Saints and Wonders*, 1906 (s); *Spreading the News, and The Rising of the Moon*, (with Douglas Hyde) *The Poorhouse*, 1906 (3d); (with W. B. Yeats) *The Unicorn from the Stars*, 1908 (d); *Seven Short Plays*, 1909 (d); *The Kiltartan History Book*, 1909 (h); *The Image*, 1910 (d); *The Kiltartan Molière: The Miser; The Doctor in Spite of Himself; The Rogueries of Scapin*, 1910 (tr); *The Kiltartan Wonder Book*, 1910 (s); *The Full Moon*, 1911 (d); *Irish Folk History Plays*, 1912 (d); *New Comedies*, 1913 (d); *Our Irish Theatre: A Chapter of Autobiography*, 1914 (a); *The Golden Apple*, 1916 (d); *The Kiltartan Poetry Book: Prose Translations from the Irish*, 1919 (tr); *The Dragon*, 1920 (d); *Hugh Lane's Life and Achievement*, 1921 (b); *The Image and Other Plays*, 1922 (d); *Three Wonder Plays: The Dragon, Aristotle's Bellows, The Jester*, 1922 (d); *The Story Brought by Brigit*, 1924 (d); Carlo Goldoni, *Mirandolina*, 1924 (tr); *On the Racecourse*, 1926 (d); *The Case for the Return of Hugh Lane's Pictures to Dublin*, 1926 (e); *Three Last Plays*, 1928 (d);

My First Play, 1930 (d); *Coole*, 1931 (e); *Journals, 1916–1930*, ed. Lennox Robinson, 1946; *Coole*, ed. Colin Smythe, 1971 (e,t); *Poets and Dreamers: Studies and Translations from the Irish*, 1974 (c, tr); also numerous reprints and original material in the Coole Edition of Lady Gregory's Works, gen. eds. Colin Smythe and T. R. Henn, 1970–, including *Seventy Years*, 1974 (a); *Lady Gregory's Journals: Books One to Twenty-nine, 10 October 1916–24 February 1925*, ed. Daniel Murphy, 1978 (misc); *Mr. Gregory's Letter Box*, 1981 (misc)

Mary Lou Kohfeldt, *Lady Gregory: The Woman Behind the Irish Renaissance*, 1985

SEAMUS HEANEY
1939–

Eleven Poems, 1965 (p); *Death of a Naturalist*, 1966 (p); *Door into the Dark*, 1969 (p); *A Boy Driving His Father to Confession*, 1971 (p); *Wintering Out*, 1972 (p); *Stations*, 1975 (p); *North*, 1975 (p); *After Summer*, 1978 (p); *Field Work*, 1979 (p); *Poems: 1965–1975*, 1980 (p); *Preoccupations: Selected Prose, 1968–1978*, 1980 (e); *Sweeney Astray*, 1984 (p); *Station Island*, 1984 (p)

Blake Morrison, *Seamus Heaney*, 1982

JOHN HEWITT
1907–

No Rebel Word, 1948 (p); *Collected Poems*, 1968 (p); *The Day of the Corncrake*, 1969 (p); (with John Montague) *The Planter and the Gael*, 1970, 1972 (discussion); *Out of My Time*, 1974 (p); *Scissors for a One-Armed Tailor: Marginal Verses 1929–1954*, 1974 (p); *Colin Middleton*, 1976 (e); *Time Enough*, 1976 (p); *Art in Ulster*, 1977 (ac); *The Rain Dance*, 1978 (p); *John Luke (1906–1975)*, 1978 (e); *Kites in Spring*, 1980 (p); *The Selected John Hewitt*, ed. Alan Warner, 1981 (p); *Mosaic*, 1981 (p); *Loose Ends*, 1983 (p)

Alan Warner. "Bibliography of Writings by John Hewitt," in Heinz Kosok, ed., *Studies in Anglo-Irish Literature*, 1982

AIDAN HIGGINS
1927–

Felo de Se (Amer. ed. *Killachter Meadow*), 1960 (s); *Langrishe, Go Down*, 1966 (n); *Images of Africa: Diary (1956–60)*, 1971 (t); *Balcony of Europe*, 1972 (n); *Scenes from a Receding Past*, 1977 (n); *Felo de Se* [1960], 1978 (s); *Asylum, and Other Stories*, 1979 (s); *Bornholm Night-Ferry*, 1982 (n)

"Aidan Higgins Special Issue," *Review of Contemporary Fiction*, Vol. 3, No. 1 (Spring 1983)

F. R. HIGGINS
1896–1941

Salt Air, 1923 (p); *Island Blood*, 1925 (p); *The Dark Breed*, 1927 (p); *Arable Holdings*, 1933 (p); *A Deuce of Jacks*, 1936 (d); *The Gap of Brightness*, 1940 (p)

M. J. MacManus, "Bibliography of F. R. Higgins," *Dublin Magazine*, July–Sept., 1946, 43–45

DOUGLAS HYDE
1860–1949

Leabhar Sgealaigheachta, 1889 (tr); *Beside the Fire*, 1890 (tr); *Love Songs of Connacht*, 1893 (tr); *The Story of Early Gaelic Literature*, 1895 (e); *A Literary History of Ireland*, 1899, repr. 1967 (c); *Four Irish Plays: The Twisting of the Rope, The Marriage, The Last Saint, and The Nativity*, trans. by Lady Gregory in *Poets and Dreamers*, 1903, reissued 1967 (d); *Songs Ascribed to Raftery*, 1903, reprinted 1973 (tr); *Religious Songs of Connacht*, 2 vols., 1906 (tr)

Dominic Daly, *The Young Douglas Hyde*, 1974

DENIS JOHNSTON
1901-1985

The Moon in the Yellow River, and *The Old Lady Says No!*, 1932 (2d); *Storm Song* and *A Bride for the Unicorn*, 1935 (2d); (after Ernst Toller) *Blind Man's Buff*, 1938 (d); *The Golden Cuckoo*, 1954 (d); *Nine Rivers from Jordan*, 1955 (r); *In Search of Swift*, 1959 (c); *Collected Plays*, 1960 (Am. ed. *The Old Lady Says No! and Other Plays*) (d); *John Millington Synge*, 1965 (c); *The Brazen Horn* (privately printed 1968), 1976 (g); *The Dramatic Works*, 2 vols., 1977–79; *Selected Plays of Denis Johnston*, ed. Joseph Ronsley, 1982 (5d)

Gene A. Barnett, *Denis Johnston*, 1978; Joseph Ronsley, ed., *Denis Johnston: A Retrospective*, 1981

JENNIFER JOHNSTON
1930–

The Captains and the Kings, 1972 (n); *The Gates*, 1973 (n); *How Many Miles to Babylon?*, 1974 (n); *Shadows on Our Skin*, 1977 (n); *The Old Jest*, 1979 (n); *The Christmas Tree*, 1982 (n)

JAMES JOYCE
1882–1941

Chamber Music, 1907 (ed. William York Tindall, 1954) (p); *Gas from a Burner*, 1912 (p); *Dubliners*, 1914 (s); *A Portrait of the Artist as a Young Man*, 1916 (n); *Exiles*, 1918 (d); *Ulysses*, 1922 (n); *Pomes Penyeach*, 1927 (p); *Anna Livia Plurabelle* [fragment from *Work in Progress*], 1928; *Tales Told of Shem and Shaun* [three fragments from *Work in Progress*], 1929; *Haveth Childers Everywhere* [fragment from *Work in Progress*], 1928; *Tales Told of Shem and Shaun* [fragments from *Work in Progress*], 1932; *The Mime of Mick, Nick and the Maggies* [fragment from *Work in Progress*], 1934; *Collected Poems*, 1936; *Storiello as She is Syung* [fragment from *Work in Progress*], 1937; *Finnegans Wake*, 1939 (corrected edition, N.Y., 1945) (n); *Stephen Hero* (ed. from ms. by Theodore Spencer), 1944 (rev. enlgd. ed. J. J. Slocum and Herbert Cahoon, *1955) (n); Letters of James Joyce*, ed. Stuart Gilbert, 1957; *The Critical Writings of James Joyce*, ed. Ellsworth Mason and Richard Ellman, 1959 (c); *Scribbledehobble: The Ur-Workbook for Finnegans Wake*, ed. Thomas E. Connolly, 1961; *A First Draft Version of Finnegan's Wake*, ed. David Hayman, 1963 (n); *The Cat* and the Devil, 1964 (j); Letters of James Joyce, ed. Richard Ellmann, 1966; Giacomo Joyce, 1968 (prose poem); Selected Letters of James Joyce, ed. Richard Ellmann, 1975; Ulysses: A Facsimile of the Manuscript, intro. Harry Levin, bibl. pref. Clive Driver, 3 vols., 1975 (n); James Joyce in Padua, ed. Louis Berrone, 1977 (e); A James Joyce Selection, 1978 (misc); Joyce's Notes and Early Drafts for "Ulysses," 1978 (misc); Dubliners: A Facsimile of Drafts and Manuscript, ed. Hans Walter Gabler, 1978 (n); Finnegans Wake: A Facsimile, arr. David Hayman and others, 1978 (n) [this, and others above, part of the planned 64-volume series, James Joyce Archives, 1975 ff.], Joyce and Hauptmann: "Before Sunrise," James Joyce's Translation, ed. Jill Perkins, 1978 (tr)

Richard Ellmann, James Joyce (new and revised ed.), 1982

PATRICK KAVANAGH
1904–1967

Songs, 1930 (p); Ploughman, 1936 (p); The Green Fool, 1938 (a); The Great Hunger, 1942 (p); A Soul for Sale, 1947 (p); Tarry Flynn, 1948 (n); Skinyou's Beauty Parlor, 1951 (d); Come Dance with Kitty Stobling, 1960 (p); Collected Poems, 1964 (p); Self-Portrait, 1964 (a); Collected Pruse [sic], 1967 (e); Lapped Furrows, 1969 (p); November Haggard: Uncollected Prose and Verse, 1971 (misc); The Complete Poems 1972, repr. 1978 (p); By Night Unstarred, 1977 (n); Lough Derg, 1978 (p); Kavanagh's Weekly: A Facsimile, 1981 (literary journalism)

John Nemo, Patrick Kavanagh, 1979; Peter Kavanagh, Sacred Keeper: A Biography of Patrick Kavanagh, 1979, repr. 1984

JOHN B. KEANE
1928–

Sive, 1959 (d); Sharon's Grave, 1960 (d); The Highest House on the Mountain, 1961 (d); Many Young Men of Twenty, 1961 (repr. in Seven Irish Plays, Robert Hogan, ed., 1967) (d); The Street, and Other Poems, 1961 (p); The Man From Clare, 1962 (d); Strong Tea,

1963 (e); The Year of the Hiker, 1963 (d); Self-Portrait, 1964 (a); The Field, 1966 (d); Hut 42, 1968 (d); Letters of a Successful T. D., 1968 (s); The Rain at the End of Summer, 1968 (d); Big Maggie, 1970 (d); The Change in Mane Fadden, 1972 (d); Letters of an Irish Parish Priest, 1972 (s); Moll, 1972 (d); The One-Way Ticket, 1972 (d); The Crazy Wall, 1973 (d); The Gentle Art of Matchmaking and Other Important Things, 1973 (e); Values, 1973 (d); Letters of an Irish Publican, 1974 (s); Letters of a Love-Hungry Farmer, 1974 (s); Letters of a Matchmaker, 1975 (s); Death Be Not Proud, 1976 (s); Letters of a Civic Guard, 1976 (s); Is The Holy Ghost Really a Kerryman? and Other Items of Interest, 1976 (s); Letters of a Country Postman, 1977 (s); Unlawful Sex and Other Testy Matters, 1978 (e); Letters of an Irish Minister of State, 1978 (s); The Good Thing, 1978 (d); Stories from a Kerry Fireside, 1980 (s); More Irish Short Stories, 1981 (s)

Kimball King, "John B. Keane," in Ten Modern Irish Playwrights: A Comprehensive Annotated Bibliography, 1979

MOLLY KEANE
1905?–

As M. J. Farrell (or Mary Lesta Skrine): Young Entry, 1929 (n); Taking Chances, 1930 (n); Two Days in Aragon, [?], repr. 1985 (n); Mad Puppetstown, 1932, repr. 1985 (n); Point-to-Point, 1933 (n); Devoted Ladies, 1934, repr. 1985 (n); Full House, 1936 (n); The Rising Tide, 1937, repr. 1985 (n); with John Perry, Spring Meeting, 1938 (d); The Enchanting Witch, 1951 (n). As Molly Keane: Good Behaviour, 1981 (n); Time After Time, 1983 (n)

BENEDICT KIELY
1919–

Counties of Contention: A Study of the Origins and Implications of the Partition of Ireland, 1945 (g); Land without Stars, 1946 (n); In a Harbour Green, 1949 (n); Modern Irish Fiction: A Critique, 1950 (c); Call for a Miracle, 1950 (n); Honey Seems Bitter (Am. ed., Evil Men Do), 1952 (n); The Cards of the Gambler,

1953 (n); *There Was an Ancient House*, 1955 (n); *The Captain with the Whiskers*, 1960 (n); *A Journey to the Seven Streams*, 1963 (s); *Dogs Enjoy the Morning*, 1968 (n); *Poor Boy: A Study of the Stories of William Carleton* [orig. *Poor Scholar*, 1947], 1972 (c); *A Ball of Malt and Madam Butterfly: A Dozen Stories*, 1973 (s); *Proxopera*, 1977 (n); *All the Way to Bantry Bay*, 1978 (s); *A Cow in the House*, 1978 (s); *The State of Ireland*, 1980 (s); *Nothing Happens in Carmincross*, 1985 (n)

Daniel J. Casey, *Benedict Kiely*, 1974; Grace Eckley, *Benedict Kiely*, 1974

THOMAS KINSELLA
1928–

The Starlit Eye, 1952 (p); *Poems*, 1956 (p); *Another September*, 1958 (p); *Moralities*, 1960 (p); *Poems and Translations*, 1961 (p, tr); *Downstream*, 1962 (p); *Wormwood*, 1966 (p); *Nightwalker*, 1968 (p); *Davis, Mangan, Ferguson? Tradition and the Irish Writer: Writings by W. B. Yeats and by Thomas Kinsella*, 1970 (c); *The Táin*, 1970 (tr); *Notes from the Land of the Dead*, 1972 (p); *Butcher's Dozen*, 1972 (p); *Finistere*, 1972 (p); *New Poems 1973*, 1973 (p); *The Good Fight*, 1973 (p); *Vertical Man*, 1973 (p); *Selected Poems 1956–1968*, 1974 (p); *One*, 1974 (p); *A Technical Supplement*, 1976 (p); *Song of the Night, and Other Poems*, 1978 (p); *The Messenger*, 1978 (p); *Fifteen Dead*, 1979 (p); *Poems 1956–1973*, 1980 (p); *Collected Stories*, intro. by Angus Wilson, 1981 (s)

Maurice Harmon, *The Poetry of Thomas Kinsella*, 1974; Dillon Johnston, *Irish Poetry after Joyce*, 1985

MARY LAVIN
1912–

Tales from Bective Bridge, 1942 (s); *The Long Ago*, 1944 (s); *The House in Clewe Street*, 1945 (n); *The Becker Wives* (Amer. ed. *At Sallygap*), 1946 (s); *Mary O'Grady*, 1950 (n); *A Single Lady*, 1951 (s); *The Patriot Son*, 1956 (s); *A Likely Story*, 1957 (s); *Selected Stories*, 1959 (s); *The Great Wave*, 1961 (s); *The Stories of Mary Lavin*, Vol. 1, 1964 (s); *In the Middle of the Fields*, 1967 (s); *Happiness*, 1969 (s); *Collected Stories*, 1971 (s); *The Second Best Children in the World*, 1972 (j); *A Memory*, 1972 (s); *The Stories of Mary Lavin*, Vol. 2, 1973 (s); *Selected Stories*, 1974 (s); *The Shrine, and Other Stories*, 1977 (s); *Tales from Bective Bridge* [1943], 1978 (s); *The Stories of Mary Lavin*, Vol. 3, 1981 (s)

Zack Bowen, *Mary Lavin*, 1975; Ruth Krawschak and Regina Mahlke, *Mary Lavin: A Checklist*, 1979; A. A. Kelly, *Mary Lavin: Quiet Rebel*, 1980

FRANCIS LEDWIDGE
1887–1917

Songs of the Fields, 1916 (p); *Songs of Peace*, 1917 (p); *Last Songs*, 1919, repr. 1955 (p); *The Complete Poems of Francis Ledwidge*, ed. Alice Curtayne, 1974 (p)

Alice Curtayne, *Francis Ledwidge: A Life of the Poet*, 1972

HUGH LEONARD
1926–

The Poker Session, 1964 (d); *Stephen D.* (adaptation of Joyce's *A Portrait of the Artist as a Young Man*), 1964 (d); *The Late Arrival of the Incoming Aircraft*, 1968 (tvd); *The Patrick Pearse Motel: A Comedy*, 1971 (d); *The Au Pair Man*, 1974 (d); *Da*, 1975, rev. ed. 1978 (d); *Leonard's Last Book*, 1978 (e); *Home before Dark*, 1979 (a); *The Peculiar People, and Other Foibles*, 1979 (e); *Summer*, 1979 (d); *Time Wars*, 1980 (d); *Three Plays* [*Da, Time Was, A Life*], 1981 (3d)

Kimball King, "Hugh Leonard," in *Ten Modern Irish Playwrights: A Comprehensive Annotated Bibliography*, 1979

MICHAEL LONGLEY
1939–

No Continuing City, 1969 (p); *Causeway*, 1971 (e); *An Exploded View*, 1973 (p); *Man Lying on a Wall*, 1976 (p); *The Echo Gate*, 1980 (p); *Selected Poems 1963–1980*, 1981 (p); *Collected Poems, 1963–1983*, 1985 (p)

THOMAS MACDONAGH
1878–1916

Through the Ivory Gate, 1902 (p); *April and May*, 1903 (p); *When the Dawn Is Come*, 1908 (d); *Songs of Myself*, 1910 (p); *Lyrical Poems*, 1913 (p); *Thomas Campion and the Art of English Poetry*, 1913 (e); *Literature in Ireland: Studies Irish and Anglo-Irish*, 1916 (c); *The Poetical Works of Thomas MacDonagh*, intro. by James Stephens, 1916 (p); *Pagans*, 1920 (d); *Poems, Selected by His Sister*, 1924 (p)

Johann A. Norstedt, *Thomas MacDonagh: A Critical Biography*, 1980

WALTER MACKEN
1915–1967

Mungo's Mansion, 1946 (d); *Quench the Moon*, 1948 (n); *Vacant Possession*, 1948 (d); *I Am Alone*, 1949 (n); *Rain on the Wind*, 1950 (n); *The Bogman*, 1952 (n); *Home Is the Hero*, 1953 (d); *Sunset on the Window-Panes*, 1954 (n); *The Green Hills, and Other Stories*, 1956 (s); *Twilight of a Warrior*, 1956 (d); *Sullivan*, 1957 (n); *Seek the Fair Land*, 1959 (n); *God Made Sunday, and Other Stories*, 1962 (s); *The Silent People*, 1962 (n); *The Scorching Wind*, 1964 (n); *The Coll Doll, and Other Stories*, 1969 (s); *The Flight of the Doves*, 1971 (n)

Robert Hogan, *After the Irish Renaissance*, 1967, pp. 65–70

BERNARD MACLAVERTY
1945–

Secrets, and Other Stories, 1977 (s); *Lamb*, 1980 (n); *Cal*, 1983 (n); *A Time to Dance*, 1983 (s)

FRANCIS MACMANUS
1909–1965

Stand and Give Challenge, 1934 (n); *Candle for the Proud*, 1936 (n); *This House Was Mine*, 1937 (n); *Men Withering*, 1939 (n); *The Wild Garden*, 1940 (n); *Flow On, Lovely River*, 1941 (n); *Watergate*, 1942 (n); *The Greatest of These*, 1943 (n); *Statue for a Square*, 1945 (n); *Boccaccio*, 1947 (b); *The Fire in the Dust*, 1950 (n); *Seal Ag Rodaiocht* [*On the Road for a Time*], 1955 (t); *American Son*, 1959 (n); *St. Columban*, 1963 (b)

James M. Cahalan, *Great Hatred, Little Room: The Irish Historical Novel*, 1983

BRINSLEY MACNAMARA
1890–1963

The Valley of the Squinting Windows, 1918 (n); *The Clanking of Chains*, 1920 (n); *The Mirror in the Dusk*, 1921 (n); *The Smiling Faces*, 1929 (s); *The Various Lives of Marcus Igoe*, 1929 (n); *Return to Ebontheever*, 1930, reissued as *Othello's Daughter*, 1934 (d); *Look at the Heffernans!*, 1939 (d); *Marks and Mabel*, 1945 (d); *Some Curious People*, 1945 (s); *Michael Caravan*, 1946 (n); *The Whole Story of the X.Y.Z.*, 1951 (n); *The Glorious Uncertainty*, 1957 (d)

Michael McDonnell, "Brinsley MacNamara: A Checklist," *Journal of Irish Literature*, May, 1975, 79–88

LOUIS MACNEICE
1907–1963

Blind Fireworks, 1929 (p); [Louis Malone, pseud.] *Roundabout Way*, 1932 (n); *Poems*, 1935 (p); *The Agamemnon of Aeschylus*, 1936 (tr); (with W. H. Auden) *Letters from Iceland*, 1937 (t); *Out of the Picture*, 1937 (d); *The Earth Compels*, 1938 (p); *I Crossed the Minch* [Outer Hebrides], 1938 (t); *Modern Poetry*, 1938 (c); *Zoo*, 1938 (e); *Autumn Journal*, 1939 (p); *The Last Ditch*, 1940 (p); *Selected Poems*, 1940 (p); *Poems, 1925–1940*, 1940 (p); *Plant and Phantom*, 1941 (p); *The Poetry of W. B. Yeats*, 1941 (c); *Meet the U.S. Army*, 1943 (e); *Christopher Columbus*, 1944 (rd); *Springboard: Poems 1941–1944*, 1944 (p); *The Dark Tower*, 1947 (rd); *Holes in the Sky: Poems 1944–1947*, 1948 (p); *Collected Poems, 1925–1948*, 1949; *Goethe's Faust* (abridged), 1951 (tr); *Ten Burnt Offerings*, 1952 (p); *Autumn Sequel*, 1954 (p); *The Other Wing*, 1954 (p); *Visitations*, 1957 (p); *Eighty-Five Poems*, 1959 (p); *Solstices*, 1961 (p); *The Burning Perch*, 1963 (p); *The Mad Islands* and The Administrator, 1964 (2rd); *Selected Poems of Louis MacNeice*, ed. by W. H. Auden, 1964 (p); *The Strings Are False: An Unfinished Autobiography*, 1965 (a); *Varieties of Parable* (Clark Lectures, 1963), 1965 (c); *Collected Poems*, ed. E. R. Dodds, 1967 (p); *One for the Grave: A Modern Morality Play*, 1968 (pd); *Persons from Porlock, and Other Plays for Radio*, 1969 (rd)

C. M. Armitage and Neil Clark, *A Bibliography of the Works of Louis MacNeice*, 1973; Robyn Marsack, *The Cave of Making: The Poetry of Louis MacNeice*, 1982

DEREK MAHON
1941–

Twelve Poems, 1965 (p); *Night-Crossing*, 1968 (p); *Ecclesiastes*, 1970 (p); *Beyond Howth Head*, 1970 (p); *Lives*, 1972 (p); *The Snow Party*, 1975 (p); *Light Music*, 1977 (p); *The Sea In Winter*, 1979 (p); *Poems: 1962–78*, 1979 (p); *Courtyards in Delft*, 1980 (p); *The Hunt by Night*, 1983 (p); *Antarctica*, 1985 (p)

EDWARD MARTYN
1859–1923

Morgante the Lesser, 1890 (n); *The Heather Field, and Maeve*, intro. by George Moore, 1899 (2d); *The Place Hunters*, 1902 (d); *The Tale of a Town, and an Enchanted Sea*, 1902 (2d); *Romulus and Remus, or the Makers of Delights*, 1907 (d); *Grangecolman*, 1912 (d); *The Dream Physician*, 1914 (d)

Marie-Thérèse Courtney, *Edward Martyn and the Irish Theatre*, 1956; Wayne E. Hall, *Shadowy Heroes: Irish Literature of the 1890's*, 1980

JOHN MCGAHERN
1934–

The Barracks, 1963 (n); *The Dark*, 1965, repr. 1983 (n); *Nightlines*, 1970 (s); *Sinclair*, 1972 (d); *The Leavetaking*, 1975 (n); *Getting Through*, 1978, repr. 1980 (n); *The Pornographer*, 1979 (n)

MICHAEL MCLAVERTY
1907–

Call My Brother Back, 1939, reissued 1970 (n); *Lost Fields*, 1941 (n); *The White Mare, and Other Stories*, 1943 (s); *In This Thy Day*, 1945 (n); *The Game Cock, and Other Stories*, 1947 (s); *The Three Brothers*, 1948 (n); *Truth in the Night*, 1952 (n); *School for Hope*, 1954 (n); *The Choice*, 1958 (n); *The Brightening Day*, 1965 (n); *The Road to the Shore, and Other Stories*, 1976 (s); *Collected Short Stories*, intro. Seamus Heaney, 1978 (s); *Billy Boggles and the Brown Cow*, 1982 (s)

MICHAEL J. MOLLOY
1917–

The King of Friday's Men, 1953 (d); *The Paddy Pedlar*, 1954 (d); *The Will and the Way*, n.d., (d); *Old Road*, 1961 (d); *The Wood of the Whispering*, 1961 (d); *Daughter From Over the Water*, 1963 (d); *The Bitter Pill*, 1965 (d); *The Visiting House*, 1967 (d); *Three Plays by M. J. Molloy* [*The King of Friday's Men, The Paddy Pedlar, The Wood of Whispering*], 1975 (d); *Petticoat Loose*, 1982 (d)

N. Sahal, *Sixty Years of Realistic Irish Drama (1900–1960)*, 1971

JOHN MONTAGUE
1929–

Forms of Exile, 1958 (p); *Poisoned Lands*, 1961 (p); *Death of a Chieftain*, 1964 (s); *Home Again*, 1966 (p); *Patriotic Suite*, 1966 (p); *A Chosen Light*, 1967 (p); *Tides*, 1970 (p); *The Wild Dog Rose*, 1970 (p); (with John Hewitt) *The Planter and the Gael*, 1970, repr. 1972 (discussion); *The Rough Field*, 1972 (p); *A Fair House: Versions of Irish Poetry*, 1973 (tr); *O'Riada's Farewell*, 1974 (p); *A Slow Dance*, 1975 (p); *The Great Cloak*, 1978 (p); *Selected Poems*, 1982 (p); *The Dead Kingdom*, 1984 (p)

Frank Kersnowski, *John Montague*, 1975; Dillon Johnston, *Irish Poetry after Joyce*, 1985

BRIAN MOORE
1921–

Judith Hearne (Amer. ed. *The Lonely Passion of Judith Hearne*), 1956 (n); *The Feast of Lupercal*, 1958 (n) (repub. 1966 as *A Moment of Love*); *The Luck of Ginger Coffey*, 1960 (n); *An Answer from Limbo*, 1962 (n); *The Emperor of Ice-Cream*, 1965 (n); *I Am Mary Dunne*, 1968 (n); *Fergus*, 1970 (n); *The Revolution Script*, 1971 (n); *Catholics*, 1972 (n); *The Great Victorian Collection*, 1975 (n); *The Doctor's Wife*, 1976 (n); *The Mangan Inheritance*, 1979 (n); *The Temptation of Eileen Hughes*, 1981 (n); *Black Robe*, 1985 (n)

Richard Studing, "A Brian Moore Bibliography," *Éire-Ireland*, 10, 3, 1975, 89–105; Robert J. Stanton, *A Bibliography of Modern British Novelists*, 1978

GEORGE MOORE
1852–1933

Worldliness, 1874 (d); *Flowers of Passion*, 1878 (p); (with B. Lopez) *Martin Luther*, 1879 (d); *Pagan Poems*, 1881; *A Modern Lover*, 1883 (rev. as *Lewis Seymour and Some Women*, 1917) (n); *A Mummer's Wife*, 1885 (n); *Literature at Nurse, or, Circulating Morals*, 1885 (e); *A Drama in Muslin*, 1886 (rev. as *Muslin*, 1915) (n); *A Mere Accident*, 1887 (n); *Parnell and His Island*, 1887 (e); *Spring Days*, 1888 (n); *Confessions of a Young Man*, 1888 (r); *Mike Fletcher*, 1889 (n); *Vain Fortune*, 1890 (n); *Impressions and Opinions*, 1891 (c); *Modern Painting*, 1893 (c); *The Strike at Arlingford*, 1893 (d); *Esther Waters*, 1894 (n); *The Royal Academy, 1895*, 1895 (c); *Celibates*, 1895 (s); *Evelyn Innes*, 1898 (n); *The Bending of the Bough*, 1900 (d); *Sister Theresa*, 1901 (sec. ed. rewritten, 1909) (n); *The Untilled Field*, 1903 (s); *The Lake*, 1905 (n); *Memoirs of My Dead Life*, 1906 (r); *Reminiscences of the Impressionist Painters*, 1906 (r); *The Apostle*, 1911 (rev. 1923) (d); *Hail and Farewell, Trilogy: Ave*, 1911, *Salve*, 1912 (a); *Esther Waters*, 1913 (d); *Elizabeth Cooper*, 1913 (d); *Vale*, 1914 [last vol. of trilogy] (a); *The Brook Kerith*, 1916 (n); *A Story-Teller's Holiday*, 1918 (e); *Avowals*, 1919 (r,c); *The Coming of Gabrielle*, 1920 (d); *Héloïse and Abélard*, 1921 (n); *In Single Strictness*, 1922 (rev. as *Celibate Lives*, 1927) (s); *Conversations in Ebury Street*, 1924 (r); Longus, *The Pastoral Loves of Daphnis and Chloe*, 1924 (tr); *Moore versus Harris, an Intimate Correspondence*, 1925; *Ulick and Soracha*, 1926 (n); *Peronnik the Fool*, 1926 (s); *The Making of an Immortal*, 1927 (d); *Letters from George Moore to Edward Dujardin, 1886–1922*, tr. by John Eglinton, 1929; *Aphrodite in Aulis*, 1930 (rev. 1931) (n); *A Flood*, 1930 (s); *The Passing of the Essenes*, 1930 (d); *George Moore in Quest of Locale*, 1931 (e); *The Talking Pine*, 1932 (c); *A Communication to my Friends*, 1933 (m); (with W. B. Yeats) *Diarmuid and Grania*, 1951 (d); *Letters to Lady Cunard 1895–1933*, ed. Rupert Hart-Davis, 1957; *George Moore in Transition: Letters to T. Fisher Unwin and Lena Milman, 1894–1910*, ed. Helmut E. Gerber, 1968; *In Minor Keys: George Moore's Uncollected Short Stories*, ed. Helmut E. Gerber and David B. Eakin, 1983; *George Moore on Parnassus: Selected Letters, 1900–1933*, ed. Helmut E. Gerber

Edwin Gilcher, *A Bibliography of George Moore*, 1970

PAUL MULDOON
1951–

Knowing My Place, 1971 (p); *New Weather*, 1973 (p); *Spirit of Dawn*, 1975 (p); *Mules*, 1977 (p); *Why Brownlee Left*, 1982 (p); *Quoof*, 1983 (p)

Dillon Johnston, *Irish Poetry after Joyce*, 1985

IRIS MURDOCH
1919–

Sartre 1953 (c); *Under the Net*, 1954 (n); *The Flight from the Enchanter*, 1956 (n); *The Sandcastle*, 1957 (n); *The Bell*, 1958 (n); *A Severed Head*, 1961 (n); *An Unofficial Rose*, 1962 (n); *The Unicorn*, 1963 (n); (with J. B. Priestley) dramatization of *A Severed Head*, 1964 (d); *The Italian Girl*, 1964 (n); *The Red and the Green*, 1965 (n); *The Time of the Angels*, 1966 (n); *The Sovereignty of Good over*

Other Concepts, 1967 (e); *The Nice and the Good*, 1968 (n); *Bruno's Dream*, 1969 (n); (with James Saunders) *The Italian Girl*, 1969 (d); *A Fairly Honourable Defeat*, 1970 (n); *An Accidental Man*, 1971 (n); *The Black Prince*, 1973 (n); *The Three Arrows, and The Servants and the Snow*, 1973 (2d); *The Sacred and Profane Love Machine*, 1974 (n); *A Word Child*, 1975 (n); *Henry and Cato*, 1976 (n); *The Fire and the Sun: Why Plato Banished the Artists*, 1977 (e); *The Sea, The Sea*, 1978 (n); *Nuns and Soldiers*, 1980 (n); *Art and Eros*, 1980 (d); *The Philosopher's Pupil*, 1983 (n); *The Good Apprentice*, 1986 (n)

Peter J. Conradi, *Iris Murdoch: The Saint and the Artist*, 1985

RICHARD MURPHY
1927–

The Archaeology of Love, 1955 (p); *The Woman of the House: An Elegy*, 1959 (p); *The Last Galway Hooker*, 1961 (p); *Sailing to an Island*, 1963 (p); *The Battle of Aughrim & The God Who Eats Corn*, 1968 (p); *High Island*, 1974 (p); *Selected Poems*, 1979 (p); *The Price of Stone*, 1984 (p)

Mary Fitzgerald, "A Richard Murphy Bibliography," *Irish University Review*, 7, 1, (1977), 104–17; Maurice Harmon, ed., *Richard Murphy: Poet of Two Traditions*, 1978

T. C. MURRAY
1873–1959

Birthright, 1911 (d); *Maurice Harte*, 1912 (d); *Spring, and Other Plays* [*Sovereign Love, The Briery Gap*], 1917 (3d); *Aftermath*, 1922 (d); *Autumn Fire*, 1925 (d); *The Pipe in the Fields, and Birthright*, 1928 (2d); *Michaelmas Eve*, 1932 (d); *Maurice Harte, and A Stag at Bay*, 1934 (2d); *Spring Horizon*, 1937 (n)

Robert Hogan, *After the Irish Renaissance*, 1967

CONOR CRUISE O'BRIEN
1917–

(as Donat O'Donnell) *Maria Cross: Imaginative Patterns in a Group of Modern Catholic Writers*, 1952 (c); *The Shaping of Modern Ireland*, 1960 (h); *To Katanga and Back*, 1962 (g); *Writers and Politics*, 1965 (e); *The United Nations: Sacred Drama*, 1968 (g); *Murderous Angels*, 1968 (d); *Camus*, 1970 (c); *States of Ireland*, 1972 (g); *Herod, Reflections on Political Violence*, 1978 (e and 3d: "King Herod Explains," "Salome and the Wild Man," "King Herod Advises"); (with Martha Crenshaw) *Terrorism, Legitimacy, and Power: The Consequences of Political Violence*, 1982 (g); *The Siege*, 1986 (h)

Joanne L. Henderson, "A Conor Cruise O'Brien Checklist," *Journal of Irish Literature*, May, 1974, 49–57

EDNA O'BRIEN
1932–

The Country Girls, 1960 (n); *The Lonely Girl*, 1962 (n); *The Girl with Green Eyes*, 1962 (screenplay); *A Nice Bunch of Cheap Flowers*, 1963 (d); *Girls in Their Married Bliss*, 1964 (n); *August Is a Wicked Month*, 1965 (n); *Casualties of Peace*, 1966 (n); *The Love Object*, 1968 (s); *A Pagan Place*, 1970 (n); *Zee & Co.*, 1971 (screenplay); *Night*, 1972 (n); *A Pagan Place* (play based on the novel), 1973 (d); *A Scandalous Woman*, 1974 (s); *Mother Ireland*, 1976 (t); *Johnny I Hardly Knew You* (Amer. ed., *I Hardly Knew You*), 1977 (n); *Arabian Days*, 1978 (t); *Mrs. Reinhardt, and Other Stories*, 1978 (s); *The Collected Edna O'Brien*, 1978 (s); *Seven Novels, and Other Short Stories*, 1978; *Virginia*, 1979 (d); *The Dazzle*, 1981 (j); *Returning*, 1982 (s); *A Fanatic Heart*, 1984 (s); *The Country Girls Trilogy and Epilogue*, 1986 (n)

Grace Eckley, *Edna O'Brien*, 1974

FLANN O'BRIEN
1911–1966

At Swim-Two-Birds, 1939 (repr. 1960) (n); pseud. Myles na gCopaleen, *An Beal Bocht; no, An Milleanach* (in Irish), 1941 (as *The Poor Mouth: A Bad Story About the Hard Life*, tr. by Patrick C. Power, 1974) (n); pseud. Myles na Gopaleen, *Faustus Kelly*, 1943 (d); *The Hard Life: An Exegesis of Squalor*, 1961 (n); *The Dalkey Archive*, 1964 (n); *The Third Policeman* (written 1940), 1967 (n); *The Best of Myles: A Selection from "Cruiskeen Lawn,"* 1968 (e, humorous prose); *Stories and Plays*, 1973 (s.d) *The Best of Myles*, 1976 (comic sketches); pseud. Myles na Gopaleen, *The Various Lives of Keats and Chapman, and The Brother*, 1976 (s); *A Flann O'Brien Reader*, ed. Stephen Jones, 1978 (misc); *Myles Away From Dublin*, 1985 (misc)

Anne Clissman, *Flann O'Brien: A Critical Introduction to His Writings*, 1975; David Powell, "A Checklist of Brian O'Nolan," *Journal of Irish Literature* Jan., 1974, 104–12

KATE O'BRIEN
1897–1974

A Distinguished Villa, 1926 (d); *Without My Cloak*, 1931 (n); *The Anteroom*, 1934, repr. 1983 (n); *Mary Lavelle*, 1936 (n); *Farewell, Spain*, 1936 (t); *Pray for the Wanderer*, 1938 (n); *The Land of Spices*, 1941 (n); *English Diaries and Journals*, 1943 (a); *The Last of Summer*, 1943 (n); *That Lady* (Amer. ed. *For One Sweet Grape*), 1946 (n); *That Lady*, 1949 (play based on the novel); *Teresa of Avila*, 1951 (b); *The Flower of May*, 1953 (n); *As Music and Splendour*, 1958 (n); *My Ireland*, 1961 (t)

Barbara DiBernard, "Kate O'Brien," in Robert Hogan, ed., *Dictionary of Irish Literature*, 1979

SEAN O'CASEY
1880–1964

[P. O'Cathasaigh] *The Story of the Irish Citizen Army*, 1919; *Two Plays: Juno and the Paycock, The Shadow of a Gunman*, 1925 (2d); *The Plough and the Stars*, 1926 (d); *The Silver Tassie*, 1928 (d); *Within the Gates*, 1933 (d); *Windfalls: Stories, Poems and Plays*, 1934; *Five Irish Plays*, 1935 (5d); *The Flying Wasp*, 1937 (c); *I Knock At the Door*, 1939 (a); *The Star Turns Red*, 1940 (d); *Purple Dust*, 1940 (d); *Red Roses for Me*, 1942 (d); *Pictures in the Hallway*, 1942 (a); *Drums Under the Windows*, 1945 (a); *Oak Leaves and Lavender*, 1946 (d); *Inishfallen, Fare Thee Well*, 1949 (a); *Cock-a-doodle Dandy*, 1949 (d); *Collected Plays*, 4 vols. 1950–51; *Rose and Crown*, 1952 (a); *Sunset and Evening Star*, 1954 (a); *The Bishop's Bonfire*, 1955 (d); *The Green Crow*, 1956 (e,c); *Five One-Act Plays*, 1958 (5d); *Mirror In My House*, 1958 (a); *The Drums of Father Ned*, 1960 (d); *Behind the Green Curtains* (with *Figuro in the Night* and *The Moon Shines on Kylenamoe*), 1961 (Am. ed. *Three Plays*) (3d); *Feathers From the Green Crow, Sean O'Casey 1905–1925*, ed. Robert Hogan, 1962 (e); *Under a Coloured Cap*, 1963 (misc.); *Blasts and Benedictions*, comp. Ronald Ayling, 1967 (e, s); *The Sean O'Casey Reader*, ed. Brooks Atkinson, 1968 (d, misc); *The Sting and the Twinkle: Conversations with Sean O'Casey*, ed. E. H. Mikhail and John O'Riordan, 1974; *The Letters of Sean O'Casey 1910–1941*, Vol. I, ed. David Krause, 1975; *The Harvest Festival* (written 1919), 1980 (d); *The Letters of Sean O'Casey, Vol. II: 1942–1954*, ed. David Krause, 1980; *Seven Plays by Sean O'Casey*, ed. Ronald Ayling, 1985 (d)

David Krause, *Sean O'Casey: The Man and His Work*, 2nd enlarged ed., 1975; Ronald Ayling and Michael J. Durkan, comps., *Sean O'Casey: A Bibliography*, 1978; Carol Kleiman, *Sean O'Casey's Bridge of Vision*, 1982

PÁDRAIC Ó CONAIRE
1883–1928

[Ó Conaire wrote seven volumes of short stories, two novels, and one play. Works for which the editors can cite adequate bibliographical information are given below]

An Chéad Cloch [*The First Stone*], 1910, repr. 1978 (s); *Seacht mBuaidh an Éirghe Amach* [*Stories of the Easter Rising*], 1918 (s); *Siol Eabha*, 1922 (s); *Field and Fair*, 1929 (s); *Scothscéalta* [*Best Stories*], sel. Tomás de Bhaldraithe, 1956 (s); *Fifteen Short Stories*, tr. by various hands, 1983 (s)

FRANK O'CONNOR
1903–1966

Guests of the Nation, 1931 (s); *The Saint and Mary Kate*, 1932 (s); *The Wild Bird's Nest*,

Poems from the Irish, 1932 (tr); *Bones of Contention*, 1936 (s); *Three Old Brothers*, 1936 (p); *In the Train*, 1937 (d); *The Big Fellow: A Life of Michael Collins*, 1937 (Am. ed. *Death in Dublin*) (b); *The Invincibles* 1937 (d); *Lords and Commons* (from the Irish), 1938 (tr); *Moses' Rock*, 1938 (d); *The Fountain of Magic* (from the Irish); 1938 (tr); *Dutch Interior*, 1940 (n); *Three Tales*, 1941 (s); *A Picture Book*, 1943 (t); *Crab Apple Jelly*, 1944 (s); *The Midnight Court* (from Irish of Brian Merriman, *The Merry Man*), 1945 (tr); *Towards an Appreciation of Literature* 1945 (c); *Selected Stories*, 1946; *The Art of the Theatre*, 1947 (e); *Irish Miles*, 1947 (t); *The Common Chord*, 1947 (s); *The Road to Stratford*, 1948 (t); *Leinster, Munster and Connaught*, 1950 (t); *Traveller's Samples*, 1951 (s); *The Stories of Frank O'Connor*, 1952 (s); *Domestic Relations*, 1957 (s); *The Mirror in the Roadway: A Study of the Modern Novel*, 1957 (c); *Kings, Lords and Commons* (anthology from Irish), 1959 (tr); *Shakespeare's Progress*, 1960 (c); *An Only Child*, 1961 (a); *The Lonely Voice: A Study of the Short Story*, 1963 (c); *The Little Monasteries* (Irish poems), 1963 (tr); *My Oedipus Complex* (sel. stories), 1963 (s); *Collection Two*, 1964 (s); *The Big Fellow*, rev. ed., 1966 (b); *The Backward Look: A Survey of Irish Literature*, 1967 (c); *My Father's Son*, 1968 (a); *Collection Three* (Am. ed. *A Set of Variations*), 1969 (s); *The Holy Door, and Other Stories*, sel. Harriet Sheehy, 1979 (s); *Collected Stories*, 1981 (s); *The Cornet-Player Who Betrayed Ireland*, 1981 (n); *Moses' Rock: A Play in Three Acts*, ed. Ruth Sherry, 1983 (d)

Maurice Wohlgelernter, *Frank O'Connor: An Introduction*, 1977; William M. Tomory, *Frank O'Connor, 1980*

PEADAR O'DONNELL
1893–

Storm, 1926 (n); *Islanders* (Amer. ed. *The Way It Was with Them*), 1928 (n); *Adrigoole*, 1929 (n); *The Knife*, 1930, repr. 1983 (Amer. ed. *The Will Be Fighting*, 1931) (n); *The Gates Flew Open*, 1932 (a); *Wrack*, 1933 (d); *On the Edge of the Stream*, 1934 (n); *Salud! An Irishman in Spain*, 1937 (a); *The Big Windows*,

1955 (n); *There Will Be Another Day*, 1963 (a); *Proud Island*, 1975 (n)

Paul A. Doyle, "Peadar O'Donnell: A Checklist," *Bulletin of Bibliography* 28 (Jan.– March, 1971), 3–4

EIMAR O'DUFFY
1893–1935

The Walls of Athens, 1914 (d); *A Lay of the Liffey, and Other Verses*, 1918 (p); *Bricriu's Feast*, [1919?] (d); *The Wasted Island*, 1929 (n); *Printer's Errors*, [1922] (n); *The Lion and the Fox*, [1922] (n); *Miss Rudd and some Lovers*, 1923 (n); *King Goshawk and the Birds*, 1926 (n); *The Spacious Adventures of the Man in the Street*, 1928 (n); *The Bird Cage: A Mystery Novel*, 1932 (n); *The Secret Enemy: A Mystery Novel*, 1932 (n); *Asses in Clover*, 1933 (n); *Heart of a Girl: A Mystery Novel*, 1935 (n)

Robert Hogan, *Eimar O'Duffy*, 1972

JULIA O'FAOLAIN
1932–

We Might See Sights!, 1968 (s); *Godded and Codded* (Amer. ed. *Three Lovers*), 1970 (n); (ed., with Lauro Martines) *Not in God's Image*, 1973 (e); *Man in the Cellar*, 1974 (s); *Women in the Wall*, 1975 (n); *Melancholy Baby, and Other Stories* (sels. from her first two collections), 1978 (s); *No Country For Young Men*, 1980 (n); *The Obedient Wife*, 1983 (n)

Mary Rose Callaghan, "Julia O'Faolain," in Robert Hogan, ed., *Dictionary of Irish Literature*, 1979

SEAN O'FAOLAIN
1900–1985

The Life Story of Eamon De Valera, 1928 (b); *Midsummer Night Madness*, 1932 (s); *A Nest of Simple Folk*, 1933 (n); *Constance Markievicz*, 1934 (b); *There's a Birdie in the Cage*, 1935 (s); *Bird Alone*, 1936 (n); *King of the Beggars*, 1938 (b); *She Had to do Something*, 1938 (d); *A Purse of Coppers*, 1938 (s); *De Valera*, 1939 (b); *An Irish Journey*, 1940 (t);

Come Back to Erin, 1940 (n); *The Great O'Neill*, 1942 (b); *The Story of Ireland*, 1943 (e); *The Irish*, 1947 (h); *Teresa*, 1947 (s); *The Short Story*, 1948 (c); *A Summer in Italy*, 1949 (t); *Newman's Way*, 1952 (b); *South to Sicily*, 1953 (t); *The Vanishing Hero*, 1956 (c); *The Stories of Sean O'Faolain* (Amer. ed. *The Finest Stories of Sean O'Faolain*), 1958 (s); *I Remember! I Remember!*, 1962 (s); *Vive Moi!*, 1964 (a); *The Heat of the Sun*, 1966 (s); *Constance Markievicz*, rev. ed., 1968 (b); *The Talking Trees*, 1971 (s); *Foreign Affairs, and Other Stories*, 1975 (s); *Selected Stories*, 1978 (s); *The Short Story* [1948], 1978 (c); *And Again?*, 1979 (s); *Collected Stories of Sean O'Faolain*, 1983

Joseph S. Rippier, *The Short Stories of Sean O'Faolain*, 1976

LIAM O'FLAHERTY
1896–1984

Thy Neighbour's Wife, 1923 (n); *Spring Sowing*, 1924 (s); *The Black Soul*, 1924 (n); *The Informer*, 1925 (repr. 1949) (n); *Mr. Gilhooley*, 1926 (n); Darkness, (1926) (d); *The Tent*, 1926 (s); *The Assassin*, 1927 (n); *The Fairy Goose*, 1927 (s); *The Life of Tim Healy*, 1927 (b); *Red Barbara*, 1928 (s); *The House of Gold*, 1929 (n); *The Mountain Tavern*, 1929 (s); *Return of the Brute*, 1929 (s); *A Tourist's Guide to Ireland*, 1929 (t); *Two Years*, 1930 (r); *Joseph Conrad*, 1930 (c); *I Went to Russia*, 1931 (t,r); *The Ecstasy of Angus*, 1931 (s); *The Puritan*, 1931 (n); *Skerrett*, 1932 (n); *The Wild Swan*, 1932 (s); *The Martyr*, 1933 (n); *Shame the Devil*, 1934 (r); *Hollywood Cemetery*, 1935 (n); *Famine*, 1937 (n); *The Short Stories*, 1937 (repr. 1948) (s); *Land*, 1946 (n); *Two Lovely Beasts*, 1948 (s); *Insurrection*, 1950 (n); *Dúil*, 1953 (s); *Irish Portraits: 14 Short Stories*, 1970 (s); *The Pedlar's Revenge, and Other Stories*, 1977 (s); *All Things Come of Age*, 1977 (j); *The Test of Courage*, 1977 (j); *The Ecstasy of Angus* (originally published in a limited ed., 1931), 1978 (s); *The Wilderness*, 1978 (s); *Short Stories of Liam O'Flaherty*, ed. A. A. Kelly, 1979 (s)

Paul A. Doyle, *Liam O'Flaherty: An Annotated Bibliography*, 1972; Patrick F. Sheeran,

The Novels of Liam O'Flaherty: A Study in Romantic Realism, 1976

SEAMAS O'KELLY
c. 1875–1918

By the Stream of Kilmeen, 1906 (s); *The Shuiler's Child*, 1909, repr. 1971 (d); *The Bribe*, 1914, repr. 1952 (d); *The Parnellite*, 1917 (d); *The Lady of Deer Park*, 1917 (n); *Waysiders: Stories of Connacht*, 1917 (s); *Ranns and Ballads*, 1918 (p); *The Golden Barque and the Weaver's Grave*, 1919 (s); *The Leprechaun of Kilmeen*, [1920] (s); *Hillsiders*, 1921 (s); *Wet Clay*, 1922 (n); *The Matchmakers*, 1925 (d); *Meadowsweet*, 1925 (d); *The Weaver's Grave*, 1925 (d); *The Land of Loneliness and Other Stories*, intro. Eamon Grennan, 1969 (s)

George Brandon Saul, *Seamas O'Kelly*, 1971

SEUMAS O'SULLIVAN
1879–1958

(The numerous poetry pamphlets are omitted.)

The Twilight People, 1905 (p); *Verses: Sacred and Profane*, 1908 (p); *The Earth-Lover, and Other Verses*, 1909 (p); *An Epilogue to the Praise of Angus, and Other Poems*, 1914 (p); *Mud and Purple: Pages from the Diary of a Dublin Man*, 1917 (e); *The Rosses and Other Poems*, 1918 (p); *The Poems of Seumas O'Sullivan*, intro. Padraic Colum, 1923 (p); *Poems 1930–1938*, 1938 (p); *Collected Poems*, 1940 (p); *Essays and Recollections*, 1944 (e); *The Rose and Bottle*, 1946 (e); *Dublin Poems* [*Selected Poems*], 1946 (p)

Alan Denson, "The Books of Seumas O'Sullivan," in Liam Miller, ed., *Retrospect: Seumas O'Sullivan and Estella F. Solomons*, 1973

PATRICK (or PADRAIC) PEARSE
1879–1916

Iosagan, and Other Stories, 1907 (s); *Suantraidhe agus Golbraidhe* [*Songs of Sleep and Sorrow*], 1914 (p); *An Mhathair agus Sgealta*

Eile [*The Mother, and Other Stories*], 1916 (s); *Collected Works: Political Writing and Speeches*, 1924, repr. 1952 (g); *Collected Works: Plays, Stories, Poems*, 1917, 1924, repr. 1958 (d,s,p); *Collected Works: The Story of a Success*, ed. Desmond Ryan, 1920 (a); *Collected Works: Songs of the Irish Rebels and Three Lectures on Gaelic Topics*, 1924 (misc); (with his sister, M. B. Pearse, and others) *The Home-life of Padraig Pearse*, 1934 (a, misc); *Letters and Other Writings*, ed. Seamas Ó Buachalla, 1979 (misc)

Raymond J. Porter, *P. H. Pearse*, 1972

JAMES PLUNKETT
1920–

The Eagles and the Trumpets, 1954 (s); *Big Jim*, 1955 (rd) [later produced on stage as *The Risen People*]; *The Trusting and the Maimed*, 1955 (s); *Strumpet City*, 1969 (n); *The Gems She Wore: A Book of Irish Places*, 1972 (t); *Collected Short Stories*, 1977 (s); *Farewell Companions*, 1977 (n)

James M. Cahalan, *Great Hatred, Little Room: The Irish Historical Novel*, 1983

FORREST REID
1875–1947

The Kingdom of Twilight, 1904 (n); *The Garden God*, 1905 (n); *The Bracknels*, 1911 (rev. as *Denis Bracknel*, 1947) (n); *Following Darkness*, 1912 (rev. as *Peter Waring*, 1937) (n); *The Gentle Lover*, 1913 (n); *W. B. Yeats*, 1915 (c); *At the Door of the Gate*, 1915 (n); *The Spring Song*, 1916 (n); *A Garden by the Sea*, 1918 (s); *Pirates of the Spring*, 1919 (n); *Pender Among the Residents*, 1922 (n); *Apostate*, 1926 (r); *Demophon*, 1927 (n); *Illustrators of the Sixties*, 1928 (c); *Walter de la Mare*, 1928 (c); *Uncle Stephen*, 1931 (n); *Brian Westby*, 1934 (n); *The Retreat*, 1936 (n); *Private Road*, 1940 (r); *Retrospective Adventures*, 1941 (e,s); *Notes and Impressions*, 1942 (e); *Poems from the Greek Anthology*, 1943 (tr); *Young Tom*, 1944 (n); *The Milk of Paradise*, 1946 (c); *Tom Barber* [*Uncle Stephen*, *The Retreat*, and *Young Tom* issued as a trilogy with intro. by E. M. Forster], 1955 (n)

Brian Taylor, *The Green Avenue: The Life and Writings of Forrest Reid, 1875–1947*, 1980

LENNOX ROBINSON
1886–1958

The Cross-Roads, 1910 (d); *Two Plays; Harvest, The Clancy Name*, 1911 (2d); *Patriots*, 1912 (d); *The Dreamers*, 1915 (d); *A Young Man from the South*, 1917 (repr. 1945) (n); *Dark Days* [life in Ireland], 1918 (g); *The Lost Leader*, 1918 (repr. 1954) (d); *The Whiteheaded Boy*, 1920 (repr. 1925) (d); *Eight Short Stories*, 1920 (s); *Crabbed Youth and Age*, 1924 (d); *The Round Table*, 1924 (d); *The White Blackbird, Portrait*, 1926 (2d), *The Big House*, 1928 (d); *Plays*, 1928 (d); *Give a Dog—*, 1928 (d); *Ever the Twain*, 1930 (d); *The Far-Off Hills*, 1931 (d); *Bryan Cooper*, 1931 (b); *Is Life Worth Living?*, 1933 (rev. 1938) (d); *More Plays* (*All's Over, Then?* and *Church Street* [latter repr. 1955]). 1935 (2d); (with Tom Robinson and Nora Dorman) *Three Homes*, 1938 (r); *Killycreggs in Twilight and Other Plays*, 1939 (3d); *Curtain Up*, 1942 (a); *Towards an Appreciation of the Theater*, 1945 (c); *Pictures in a Theatre: a Conversation Piece*, 1947 (r); ed. *Lady Gregory's Journals*, 1947; *The Lucky Finger*, 1948 (d); *Palette and Plough* [Desmond O'Brien], 1948 (b); *Ireland's Abbey Theatre, 1899–1951*, 1951 (h); *Drama at Irish*, 1953 (d); *Never the Time and the Place* and *Crabbed Youth and Age*, 1953 (2d); *I Sometimes Think*, 1956 (e); co-ed. with Donagh MacDonagh, *Oxford Book of Irish Verses*, 1958; *The Red Sock*, 1980 (d); *Selected Plays of Lennox Robinson*, ed. Christopher Murray, 1982

Michael J. O'Neill, *Lennox Robinson*, 1964

W. R. RODGERS
1909–1969

Awake! And Other Poems, 1941 (Amer. ed. *Awake! And Other Wartime Poems*, 1942) (p); *The Ulstermen and Their Country*, 1947 (e); *Europa and the Bull*, 1952 (p); *Ireland in Colour*, 1957 (e); *Collected Poems*, 1971 (p); *Irish Literary Portraits*, 1972 (r)

Darcy O'Brien, *W. R. Rodgers*, 1970

GEORGE WILLIAM RUSSELL (A.E.)
1867–1935

(The numerous political essays and pamphlets omitted.)

Homeward: Songs by the Way, 1894 (p); *The Future of Ireland and the Awakening of the Fires*, 1897 (e); *The Earth Breath*, 1897 (p); *Ideals in Ireland: Priest or Hero?*, 1897 (e); *Literary Ideals in Ireland—Nationality and Cosmopolitanism in Literature*, 1899 (e); *An Artist of Gaelic Ireland*, 1902 (e); *The Nuts of Knowledge*, 1903 (p); *The Divine Vision, 1903 (p); Controversy in Ireland*, 1904 (e); *The Mask of Apollo*, 1904 (s); *By Still Waters*, 1906 (p); *Some Irish Essays*, 1906 (e); *Deirdre*, 1907 (d); *The Hero in Man*, 1909 (e); *The Renewal of Youth*, 1911 (e); *Collected Poems*, 1913 (sec. ed. 1926); *Gods of War*, 1915 (p); *Imaginations and Reveries*, 1915 (e); *The Candle of Vision*, 1918 (e); *Michael*, 1919 (p); *Open Letter to the Irish People*, 1922 (e); *The Interpreters*, 1922 (e); *Voices of the Stones*, 1925 (p); *Midsummer Eve*, 1928 (p); *Dark Weeping*, 1929 (p); *Enchantment*, 1930 (p); *Vale*, 1931 (p); *Song and its Fountains*, 1932 (e); *The Avatars, a Futurist Fantasy*, 1933 (s); *The House of the Titans*, 1934 (p); *Selected Poems*, 1935 (p); *Some Passages from the Letters of AE to W. B. Yeats*, 1936; *AE's Letters to Minanlabain*, 1937; *The Living Torch*, ed. Monk Gibbon, 1937 (e); *Letters from AE*, ed. Alan Denson, 1961; *Letters to W. B. Yeats*, ed. Richard Finneran, George Mills Harper, and William M. Murphy, 1977; *Selections from the Contributions to The Irish Homestead*, 2 vols., ed. Henry Summerfield, 1978 (g); *Some Unpublished Letters from AE to James Stephens*, ed. Richard J. Finneran and Mary Fitzgerald, 1980

Henry Summerfield, *That Myriad-Minded Man: A Biography of G. W. Russell, "A.E."*, 1975

GEORGE BERNARD SHAW
1856–1950

(The many reprints of separate plays are not indicated. Only a sampling is given of Shaw's almost innumerable essays and tracts on the subjects that interested him, such as Fabianism, socialism, censorship, the English language and its spelling, war, the status of Ireland. Also, this list includes only some of the selected and collected works.)

Cashel Byron's Profession, 1886 (n) [rev. 1901, contains *The Admirable Bashville, or, Constancy Unrewarded*, (d) based on the novel, *Cashel Byron's Profession*]; *An Unsocial Socialist*, 1887 (n); *The Quintessence of Ibsenism*, 1891 (enlgd. 1913) (c); *Widowers' Houses*, 1893 (d); *Plays Pleasant and Unpleasant* (Pleasant: *Arms and the Man, Candida, The Man of Destiny, You Never Can Tell*; Unpleasant: *Widowers' Houses, The Philanderer, Mrs. Warren's Profession*), 1898; *The Perfect Wagnerite, 1898 (c); Love Among the Artists*, 1900 (n); *Three Plays for Puritans* (*The Devil's Disciple, Caesar and Cleopatra, Captain Brassbound's Conversion*), 1901 (3d); *Man and Superman*, 1903 (d); *The Irrational Knot*, 1905 (n); *Dramatic Opinions and Essays*, 1906 (c); *John Bull's Other Island, Major Barbara;* also *How He Lied to Her Husband*, 1907 (3d); *The Sanity of Art*, 1908 (c); *Press Cuttings*, 1909 (d); *The Shewing-up of Blanco Posnet*, 1909 (d); *Misalliance*, 1910 (d); *Brieux: A Preface* 1910 (c); *The Doctor's Dilemma, Getting Married, and The Shewing-up of Blanco Posnet*, 1911 (3d); *Androcles and the Lion*, 1914 (d); *Misalliance, The Dark Lady of the Sonnets, Fanny's First Play, With a Treatise on Parents and Children*, 1914 (3d,e); *Androcles and the Lion, Overruled, Pygmalion*, 1916 (3d); *Heartbreak House*, 1917 (d); *Heartbreak House, Great Catherine, and Playlets of the War* (*O'Flaherty, V.C., The Inca of Perusalem, Augustus Does His Bit, Annajanska*), 1919 (6d); *Back to Methuselah*, 1921 (d); *Saint Joan*, 1924 (d); *Translations and Tomfooleries* (*Jitta's Atonement*, tr. from the German of Seigfried Trebitsch; *The Admirable Bashville, Press Cuttings, The Glimpse of Reality, Passion, Poison and Petrification, The Fascinating Foundling, The Music-Cure*), 1926 (7d); *The Intelligent Woman's Guide to Socialism and Capitalism*, 1928 (rev. enlgd. 1937 as *The Intelligent Woman's Guide to Socialism, Capitalism, Sovietism, and Fascism*) (e); *Bernard Shaw and Karl*

Marx. A Symposium, 1884–1889, ed. R. W. Ellis, 1930 (e); *The Apple Cart*, 1930 (d); *Ellen Terry and Bernard Shaw: A Correspondence*, ed. Christopher St. John, 1931; *Complete Works* (standard edition), 1931–50; *Immaturity*, 1931 (written 1879) (n); *What I Really Wrote About the War*, 1931 (e); *Pen Portraits and Reviews*, 1932 (c); *Essays in Fabian Socialism* (includes *The Fabian Society, What It Has Done and How It Has Done It*, 1892; *The Impossibilities of Anarchism*, 1893; *The Common Sense of Municipal Trading*, 1904), 1932 (e); *Doctors' Delusions, Crude Criminology and Sham Education*, 1932 (e); *Our Theatres in the Nineties*, 1932 (c); *Music in London, 1890–94*, 1932 (c); *Major Critical Essays (The Quintessence of Ibsenism, The Perfect Wagnerite, The Sanity of Art)*, 1932 (c); *The Adventures of the Black Girl in Her Search for God*, 1932 (n); *Prefaces*, 1934 (enlgd. 1938) (e); *Too True to be Good, Village Wooing, On the Rocks*, 1934 (3d); *Short Stories, Scraps and Shavings*, 1934 (s); *The Simpleton of the Unexpected Isles, The Six of Calais, The Millionairess*, 1936 (3d); *London Music in 1888–89*, 1937 (c); *In Good King Charles's Golden Days*, 1939 (d); *Geneva: A Fancied Page of History*, 1939 (d); *Shaw Gives Himself Away*, 1939 (a); *Everybody's Political What's What*, 1944 (e); *Geneva, Cymbeline Refinished and Good King Charles*, 1946 (3d); *The Crime of Imprisonment*, 1946 (e); *Sixteen Self Sketches*, 1949 (a); *Shaw on Vivisection*, ed. G. H. Bowker, 1949; *Buoyant Billions, Farfetched Fables, Skakes Versus Shav.* 1950 (3d); *The Complete Plays*, 1950; *Bernard Shaw and Mrs. Patrick Campbell: Their Correspondence*, ed. Alan Dent, 1952; *Selected Prose*, ed. Diarmuid Russell, 1953; *Advice to a Young Critic*, 1955 (letters); *My Dear Dorothea*, 1956 (written 1877) (e); *The Illusions of Socialism. With, Socialism: Principles and Outlook.* 1956 (e); *Bernard Shaw's Letters to Granville Barker*, ed. C. B. Purdom, 1956; *An Unfinished Novel*, ed, Stanley Weintraub, 1958 (n); *Shaw on Theatre* (includes *The Dying Tongue of Great Elizabeth, The Art of Rehearsal*), ed. E. J. West, 1958 (e); *How to Become a Musical Critic*, ed. Dan H. Laurence, 1960 (c); *Shaw on Shakespeare*, ed. Edwin Wilson, 1961 (c);

To A Young Actress; Letters to Molly Tompkins, ed. Peter Tompkins, 1961 (letters); *Complete Plays with Prefaces*, 1962; *Platform and Pulpit*, ed. Dan H. Laurence, 1962 (e); *The Matter With Ireland*, ed. Dan H. Laurence and David H. Greene, 1962 (e); *Religious Speeches*, ed. Warren Sylvester Smith, 1963; *The Rationalization of Russia*, ed. Harry M. Geduld, 1964 (e); *Collected Letters 1874–1897*, ed. Dan H. Laurence, 1965; *Complete Plays*, 1965; *Complete Prefaces*, 1965 (e); *The Bodley Head Bernard Shaw: Collected Plays with Their Prefaces*, 7 vols., 1970–1973; *Shaw: An Autobiography*, selected from his writings by Stanley Weintraub, 2 vols, 1969–1970; *Collected Letters 1898–1910*, ed. Dan H. Laurence, 1972; *Bernard Shaw's Nondramatic Literary Criticism*, ed. Stanley Weintraub, 1972 (c); *Practical Politics: Twentieth Century Views on Politics and Economics*, ed. Lloyd J. Hubenka, 1976; *The Collected Screenplays.* ed. Bernard F. Dukore, 1980; *Bernard Shaw's "Arms and the Man": A Composite Production Book*, comp. Bernard F. Dukore, 1981; *Early Texts: Play Manuscripts in Facsimile*, 12 vols., 1981; *Shaw's Music: The Complete Musical Criticism*, ed. Dan H. Laurence, 3 vols., 1981; *Bernard Shaw and Alfred Douglas: A Correspondence*, ed. Mary Hyde, 1982; *The Playwright and the Pirate: Bernard Shaw and Frank Harris, a Correspondence*, ed. Stanley Weintraub, 1983; *Agitations: Letters to the Press, 1875–1950*, ed. Dan H. Laurence and James M. Rambeau, 1985; *Bernard Shaw: The Diaries, 1885–1897, with Earlier and Later Diary Fragments from 1875 to 1917*, ed. Stanley Weintraub, 1985

Michael Holroyd, ed., *The Genius of Shaw: A Symposium*, 1979; Arnold Silver, *Bernard Shaw: The Dark Side*, 1980

GEORGE SHIELS
1886–1949

Bedmates, 1922 (d); *Two Irish Plays: Mountain Dew and Cartney and Kevney*, 1930 (2d); *The Passing Day and The Jailbird*, 1937 (2d); *The Rugged Path and The Summit*, 1942 (2d); *Three Plays: Professor Tim, Paul Twyning, The New Gossoon*, 1945 (3d); *Grogan and the*

Ferret, 1947 (d); *Quin's Secret*, 1947 (d); *Give Him a House*, 1947 (d); *The Fort Field*, 1947 (d); *Tenants at Will*, 1947 (d); *The Old Broom*, 1947 (d); *The Caretakers*, 1948 (d)

David Krause, *The Profane Book of Irish Comedy*, 1982

JAMES SIMMONS
1933–

Late but in Earnest, 1967 (p); *In the Wilderness*, 1969 (p); *Energy to Burn*, 1971 (p); *No Land Is Waste, Dr. Eliot*, 1972 (p); *The Long Summer Still to Come*, 1973 (p); *West Strand Visions*, 1974 (p); *Judy Garland and the Cold War*, 1976 (p); *The Selected James Simmons*, ed. Edna Longley, 1979 (p); *Constantly Singing*, 1980 (p); *From the Irish*, 1985 (p, tr)

SOMERVILLE and ROSS
Edith Œnone Somerville, 1858–1948, Violet Martin ["Martin Ross"], 1862–1915

An Irish Cousin, 1889 (n); *Naboth's Vineyard*, 1891 (n); *The Real Charlotte*, 1894 (n); *The Silver Fox*, 1898 (n); *Some Experiences of an Irish R. M.*, 1899 (s); *Further Experiences of an Irish R. M.*, 1908 (s); *In Mr. Knox's Country*, 1915 (s); *Irish Memories*, 1917 (r); *Mount Music* 1919 (n); *The Big House of Inver*, 1925 (n)

Elizabeth Hudson, ed., *A Bibliography of the First Editions of the Works of E. Œ. Somerville and Martin Ross*, 1942

JAMES STEPHENS
1880?–1950

Insurrections, 1909 (p); *The Lonely God*, 1909 (p); *The Adventures of Seumas Beg: The Visit from Abroad, In The Orchard, Treasure Trove*, 1910 (p); *The Spy*, 1910 (p); *The Hill of Vision*, 1912 (repr. 1922) (p); *The Charwoman's Daughter*, 1912 (Am. ed. *Mary, Mary*) (n); *The Crock of Gold*, 1912 (repr. 1954) (n); *Five New Poems*, 1913 (p); *Here Are Ladies*, 1913, repr. 1977 (s); *The Demi-Gods*, 1914 (n); *The Adventures of Seumas Beg, The Rocky Road to Dublin*, 1915 (p); *Songs from the*

Clay, 1915 (p); *The Insurrection in Dublin*, 1916, repr. 1979 (e); *Green Branches*, 1916 (p); *Reincarnations*, 1918 (p); [James Esse, pseud.] *Hunger*, 1918 (n); *Irish Fairy Tales*, 1920, repr. 1978 (s); *Arthur Griffith, Journalist and Statesman*, 1922 (b); *Deirdre*, 1923 (repr. 1962, 1977) (n); *Little Things*, 1924 (p); *In the Land of Youth*, 1924 (n); *A Poetry Recital*, 1925 (p); *Collected Poems*, 1926 (rev. enlgd. 1954); *On Prose and Verse*, 1928 (e); *Etched in Moonlight*, 1928, repr. 1977 (s); *Dublin Letters*, 1928 (e); *Julia Elizabeth*, 1929 (d); *The Outcast*, 1929 (p); *Theme and Variations*, 1930 (p); *Strict Joy*, 1931 (p); *Kings and the Moon*, 1938 (p); *A James Stephens Reader*, sel. Lloyd Frankenberg, 1962; *James, Seamus & Jacques: Unpublished Writings*, ed. Lloyd Frankenberg, 1964 (misc); *Letters of James Stephens*, ed. Richard J. Finneran, 1974; *The Demi-Gods: A Play in 3 Acts* [1914], ed. Richard J. Finneran, 1975 (d); *Irish Fairy Tales*, rev. ed., (1978) (s); *The Crock of Gold* [1912], with special foreword by Walter de la Mare, 1978 (n); *The Insurrection in Dublin* [1916], intro. John A. Murphy, 1978 (e); *Uncollected Prose of James Stephens*, 2 vols., ed. Patricia McFate, 1983

Birgit Bramsbäck, *James Stephens: A Literary and Bibliographical Study*, 1973, repr. 1977; Patricia McFate, *The Writings of James Stephens*, 1979

L. A. G. STRONG
1896–1958

Dallington Rhymes, 1919 (p); *Dublin Days*, 1921 (p); *Twice Four*, 1921 (p); *Says the Muse to Me, Says She*, 1922 (p); *Eight Poems*, 1923 (p); *The Lowery Road*, 1923 (p); *Doyle's Rock*, 1925 (s); *Difficult Love*, 1927 (p); *At Glenan Cross*, 1928 (p); *The English Captain*, 1929 (s); *Dewer Rides*, 1929 (repr. 1949) (n); *The Jealous Ghost*, 1930 (n); *Christmas*, 1930 (p); *Northern Light*, 1930 (p); *Common Sense About Poetry*, 1931 (c); *Selected Poems*, 1931 (p); *The Big Man*, 1931 (s); *The Garden*, 1931 (repr. 1947) (n); *The Brothers*, 1932 (repr. 1946) (n); *Don Juan and the Wheelbarrow*, 1932 (s); *March Evening*, 1932 (p); *A Defence of Ignorance*, 1932 (e); *A Letter to W. B. Yeats*, 1932 (e); (with Monica Redlich) *Life in*

English Literature, 1932 (e); *Sea Wall*, 1933 (n); *Personal Remarks*, 1933 (repr. 1953) (e); *Corporal Tune*, 1934 (n); *The Seven Arms*, 1935 (n); *Tuesday Afternoon*, 1935 (s); *The Hansom Cab and the Pigeons*, 1935 (e); *The Last Enemy*, 1936 (n); *Call to the Swan*, 1936 (p); *Common Sense About Drama*, 1937 (c); *The Fifth of November*, 1937 (repr. 1956) (n); *The Swift Shadow*, 1937 (n); *Laughter in the West*, 1937 (n); *The Minstrel Boy, A Portrait of Tom Moore*, 1937 (b), *Odd Man In*, 1938 (s); *Shake Hands and Come Out Fighting*, 1938 (r); *The Open Sky*, 1939 (n); *Trial and Error*, 1939 (d); *The Absentee*, 1939 (d); *Sun on the Water*, 1940 (s); *English for Pleasure*, 1941 (radio talks to schools); *The Bay*, 1941 (n); *John Millington Synge*, 1941 (b); *House in Disorder*, 1941 (n); *John McCormack*, 1941 (b); *Slocombe Dies*, 1942 (n); *Authorship*, 1944 (c); *The Unpractised Heart*, 1942 (n); *The Director*, 1944 (n); *All Fall Down*, 1944 (n); *Sink or Swim*, 1945 (n); *Othello's Occupation*, 1945 (n); *Travellers*, 1945 (s); *Light Through the Cloud* (The Story of The Retreat, York, 1796–1946), 1946 (h); *The Doll*, 1946 (s); *Trevannion*, 1948 (n); *The Sacred River: An Approach to James Joyce*, 1949 (c); *Maud Cherrill*, 1949 (b); *Which I Never*, 1950 (n); *Three Novels: The Garden, Corporal Tune, The Seven Arms*, 1950 (3n); *Darling Tom*, 1952 (s); *John Masefield*, 1952 (b); *The Writer's Trade*, 1953 (e); *The Hill of Howth*, 1953 (n); *It's Not Very Nice*, 1954 (d); *The Story of Sugar*, 1954 (h); *Dr. Quicksilver 1660–1742*, [Thomas Dover, M.D.], 1955 (b); *Deliverana*, 1955 (h); *Flying Angel*, 1956 (e); *The Rolling Road*, 1956 (e); *The Body's Imperfection, Collected Poems*, 1957; *Treason in the Egg*, 1958 (n); *Light Above the Lake*, 1958 (n); *Green Memory*, 1961 (a)

George Watson, ed., *The New Cambridge Bibliography of English Literature, Vol. 4: 1900–1950*, 1969

FRANCIS STUART
1902–

We Have Kept the Faith, 1923 (p); *Women and God*, 1931 (n); *The Coloured Dome*, 1932 (n); *Pigeon Irish*, 1932 (n); *Glory*, 1933 (n); *Try the Sky*, 1933 (n); *Things to Live For*, 1934

(a); *In Search of Love*, 1935 (s); *The Angel of Pity*, 1935 (n); *The White Hare*, 1936 (n); *Racing for Pleasure and Profit in Ireland . . .*, 1937 (e); *The Bridge*, 1937 (n); *Julie*, 1938 (n); *The Great Squire*, 1939 (n); *Der Fall Casement*, trans. into German by Ruth Weiland, 1940 (e); *The Piller of Cloud*, 1948 (n); *Redemption*, 1949 (n); *The Flowering Cross*, 1950 (n); *Good Friday's Daughter*, 1952 (n); *The Chariot*, 1953 (n); *The Pilgrimage*, 1955 (n); *Victors and Vanquished*, 1958 (n); *Angels of Providence*, 1959 (n); *Black List/Section H*, 1971 (n); *Memorial*, 1973 (n); *A Hole in the Head*, 1977 (n); *The High Consistory*, 1980 (n); *States of Mind: Selected Short Prose, 1936–1983*, 1985 (misc)

W. J. McCormack, "Francis Stuart: A Checklist and Commentary," *Long Room*, No. 3 (Spring 1971), 38–49; J. H. Natterstad, *Francis Stuart*, 1974

JOHN MILLINGTON SYNGE
1871–1909

In the Shadow of the Glen, 1904 (d); *In the Shadow of the Glen and Riders to the Sea*, 1905 (2d); *The Well of the Saints*, 1905 (d); *The Playboy of the Western World*, 1907 (many repr.) (d); *The Aran Islands*, 1907 (e); *The Tinker's Wedding*, 1908 (d); *Poems and Translations*, ed. W. B. Yeats, 1909 (p); *Deirdre of the Sorrows*, 1910 (d); *The Works*, 4 vols., 1910; *In Wicklow, West Kerry and Connemara*, 1911 (t); *Plays by John M. Synge* (incl. extracts from notebooks and unpub. letter), 1932; *The Complete Works*, 1935; *Plays, Poems and Prose*, 1941; *Translations* (from Petrarch, Villon, etc.), ed. Robin Skelton, 1961 (tr); *Collected Works, Vol. 1: Poems*, ed. Robin Skelton, 1962; *The Autobiography of J. M. Synge*, constructed from the manuscripts by Alan Price, 1965 (a); *Collected Works, Vol 2: Prose*, ed. Alan Price, 1966 (e); *Collected Works*, Vols. 3 and 4: *Plays*, ed. Ann Saddlemyer, 1968 (d); *Some Letters of J. M. Synge to Lady Gregory and W. B. Yeats*, sel. Ann Saddlemyer, 1971 (limited ed.); *Letters to Molly: J. M. Synge to Maire O'Neill, 1906–1909*, ed. Ann Saddlemyer, 1972; *The Playboy of the Western World*, ed. Malcolm Kelsall, 1975 (d); *The Collected Letters of*

John Millington Synge, Vol. I: 1871–1907, ed. Ann Saddlemyer, 1983; *Vol II: 1907–1909*, ed. Ann Saddlemyer, 1984; *The Well of the Saints*, ed. Nicholas Grene, 1985 (d)

David H. Greene and Edward M. Stephens, *J. M. Synge 1871–1909* [biography], 1959; Nicholas Grene, *Synge: A Critical Study of the Plays*, 1975

JOSEPH TOMELTY
1911–

Right Again, Barnum, 1943 (d); *Mugs and Money*, (orig. *Barnum Was Right*), [1943], repr. 1953 (d); *The End House*, 1944, repr. 1962 (d); *All Souls' Night*, 1948 (d); *Red is the Port Light*, 1948 (n); *The Apprentice*, 1953 (n); *Is The Priest At Home?*, 1954 (d)

James W. Gracey, "Joseph Tomelty: An Introductory Bibliography," *Irish Booklore* (1971), 226–34

WILLIAM TREVOR
1928–

A Standard of Behaviour, 1958 (n); *The Old Boys*, 1964 (n); *The Boarding House*, 1965 (n); *The Love Department*, 1966 (n); *The Day We Got Drunk on Cake*, 1967 (s); *The Girl*, 1968 (d); *Mrs. Eckdorff in O'Neill's Hotel*, 1969 (n); *Miss Gomez and the Brethren*, 1971 (n); *The Old Boys* (dramatization of novel), 1972 (d); *The Ballroom of Romance*, 1972 (d); *Going Home*, 1972 (d); *A Night with Mrs. da Tanka*, 1972 (d); *Elizabeth Alone*, 1973 (n); *Marriages*, 1973 (d) *Angels at the Ritz*, 1975 (s); *The Children of Dynmouth*, 1976 (n); *Old School Ties*, 1976 (n); *Lovers of Their Time*, 1978 (s); *The Distant Past: Selected Irish Short Stories*, 1979 (s); *Other People's Worlds*, 1980 (n); *Beyond the Pale*, 1981 (s); *The Stories of William Trevor*, 1983 (s); *Fools of Fortune*, 1983 (n); *A Writer's Ireland*, 1984 (e, t); *The News From Ireland*, 1985 (n)

WILLIAM BUTLER YEATS
1865–1939

Mosada, 1886 (p); *The Wanderings of Oisin*, 1889 (p); *The Countess Cathleen*, 1892 (pd);

The Celtic Twilight, 1893 (misc.); *The Land of Heart's Desire*, 1894 (pd); *Poems*, 1895; *The Secret Rose*, 1897 (s); *The Tables of the Law, The Adoration of the Magi*, 1897 (s); *The Wind Among the Reeds*, 1899 (p); *The Shadowy Waters*, 1900 (p); *Cathleen ni Houlihan*, 1902 (pd); *Where There is Nothing*, 1902 (pd); *In the Seven Woods*, 1903 (p); *The Hour-Glass*, 1903 (pd); *Ideas of Good and Evil*, 1903 (e); *The King's Threshold and On Baile's Strand*, 1904 (2pd); *Stories of Red Hanrahan*, 1904 (s); *Poems, 1899–1905*, 1906; *The Poetical Works*, 2 vols., 1906–7; *Deirdre*, 1907 (pd); *Discoveries*, 1907 (e); *The Golden Helmet*, 1908 (pd); (with Lady Gregory) *The Unicorn from the Stars*, 1908 (pd); (with Lionel Johnson) *Poetry and Ireland*, 1908 (e); *The Green Helmet*, 1910 (p); *Synge and the Ireland of His Time*, 1911 (e); *The Cutting of an Agate*, 1912 (e); *Responsibilities*, 1914 (p,d); *Reveries over Childhood and Youth*, 1915 (a); *The Wild Swans at Coole*, 1917 (pd); *Per Amica Silentia Lunae*, 1918 (e); *Two Plays for Dancers*, 1919 (pd); *Michael Robartes and the Dancer*, 1920 (p); *Four Plays for Dancers*, 1921 (pd); *Later Poems*, 1922; *The Player Queen*, 1922 (pd); *Plays and Controversies*, 1923 (misc.); *The Cat and the Moon and Certain Poems*, 1924 (p); *The Bounty of Sweden*, 1925 (e); *A Vision*, 1925 (rev. 1937) (e); *Autobiographies: Reveries over Childhood and Youth and The Trembling of the Veil*, 1926 (a); *October Blast*, 1927 (p); *The Tower*, 1928 (p); *The Death of Synge*, 1928 (m); *The Winding Stair*, 1929 (p); *A Packet for Ezra Pound*, 1929 (e); *St. Patrick's Breast-plate*, 1929 (e); *Stories of Michael Robartes and His Friends* (with *The Resurrection*), 1931 (misc.); *Words for Music Perhaps*, 1932 (p); *The Winding Stair*, 1933 (p); *The King of the Great Clocktower*, 1934 (e,p); *Wheels and Butterflies*, 1934 (e,d); *Letters to the New Island*, 1934 (e); *A Full Moon in March*, 1935 (misc.); *Dramatis Personae*, 1935 (r); *Modern Poetry*, 1936 (e); *Essays, 1931–1936*, 1937; *The Herne's Egg*, 1938 (pd); *New Poems*, 1938; *The Autobiography (Reveries, The Trembling of the Veil, Dramatis Personae)*, 1938; *Last Poems and Two Plays*, 1939; *On the Boiler*, 1939 (misc.); *Letters on Poetry to Dorothy Wellesley*, 1940 (repr. 1964); *Last Poems and Plays*, 1940; *If I*

Were Four-and-Twenty, 1940 (e); *Pages from a Diary,* 1944 (r); *Tribute to Thomas Davis,* 1947 (e); *The Collected Poems,* 1950; (with George Moore) *Diarmuid and Grania,* 1951 (d); *The Collected Plays,* 1952; *The Variorum Edition of the Poems,* 1957; *Selected Criticism,* ed. Norman Jeffares, 1964 (c); *The Variorum Edition of the Plays of W. B. Yeats,* ed. Russel K. Alspach, 1966 (d); *Ah, Sweet Dancer: W. B. Yeats, Margot Ruddock: A Correspondence,* ed. Roger McHugh, 1970; *Uncollected Prose,* ed. John P. Frayne, Vol. 1: *First Reviews and Articles, 1886–1896,* 1970 (c); *Druid Craft: The Writing of "The Shadowy Waters,"* manuscripts of W. B. Yeats transcribed, edited and with a commentary by Michael J. Sidnell, George P. Mayhew, David R. Clark, 1971 (pd); *A Tower of Polished Black Stones: Early Versions of "The Shadowy Waters,"* arranged and ed. by David Ridgley Clark and George Mayhew, with five illustrations by Leonard Baskin and drawings by the poet, 1972 (pd); *Memoirs: Autobiography— First Draft Journal,* transcribed and ed. Denis Donoghue, 1973 (a); (editor) *Fairy and Folk Tales of Ireland* (repr. of *Fairy and Folk Tales of the Irish Peasantry,* 1888, and *Irish Tales,* 1892), 1973; *The Writing of "The Player Queen,"* ed. Curtis Bradford, 1974 (pd); *Uncollected Prose, II: Reviews, Articles and Other Miscellaneous Prose, 1897–1938,* ed. John P. Frayne and Colton Johnson, 1976; *The Correspondence of Robert Bridges and W. B. Yeats,* 1977; *W. B. Yeats: The Writing of "The Player Queen,"* ed. Curtis Baker Bradford, 1978; *A Critical Edition of Yeats' "A Vision,"* ed. George Mills Harper and Walter Kelly, 1978 (e); *The Secret Rose: Stories of W. B. Yeats—A Variorum Edition,* ed. Phillip L. Marcus, Warwick Gould, and Michael J. Sidnell, 1981 (s); *The Death of Cuchulain: Manuscript Materials, Including the Author's Final Text,* ed. Phillip L. Marcus, 1981 (pd); *Yeats on Yeats: The Last Introductions and the "Dublin" Edition,* ed. Edward Callan, 1981 (e); *The Poems of W. B. Yeats: A New Edition,* ed. Richard J. Finneran, 1983 (p)

Allan Wade, *A Bibliography of the Writings of W. B. Yeats* (3rd ed., rev. Russell K. Alspach), 1968; K. P. S. Jochum, *W. B. Yeats: A Classified Bibliography of Criticism Including Additions to Allan Wade's "A Bibliography of the Writings of W. B. Yeats,"* 1978

COPYRIGHT ACKNOWLEDGMENTS

711

LONDON REVIEW OF BOOKS. For excerpts from articles by Seamus Deane on Montague; Denis Donoghue on Sean O'Faolain; Christopher Driver on Trevor; Graham Hough on Brian Moore; Alasdair MacIntyre on Murdoch; Sean O'Faolain on Bowen; John Sutherland on Keane. Reprinted by permission of *London Review of Books* and the authors.

EDNA LONGLEY. For excerpts from articles on Kinsella, Montague, Murphy, and Simmons in *Two Decades of Irish Writing*, ed. Douglas Dunn.

LOUISIANA STATE UNIVERSITY PRESS. For excerpt from article by L.C. Knight on Yeats in *Southern Review* (Winter 1941).

MACGIBBON & KEE. For excerpt from Desmond MacCarthy on Joyce in *Humanities* (David Higham Associates Limited).

MACMILLAN, LONDON AND BASINGSTOKE. For excerpts from Arthur Ganz, *George Bernard Shaw*; Nicholas Grene, *Bernard Shaw: A Critical View*; F.R. Higgins in *Scattering Branches: Tributes to the Memory of W. B. Yeats*, ed. Stephen Gwynn; Norman Jeffares, *Anglo-Irish Literature*; A.A. Kelly, *Liam O'Flaherty the Storyteller*; Patricia McFate, *The Writings of James Stephens*; William J. Maroldo in *Essays on Sean O'Casey's Autobiographies*, ed. Robert G. Lowery; T. C. Murray on Shiels in *The Irish Theatre*, ed. Lennox Robinson; articles by Honor Tracey and Thomas Flanagan in *Michael/Frank: Studies On Frank O'Connor*, ed. Maurice Sheehy.

MACMILLAN COMPANY OF INDIA. For excerpts from articles by N. Sahal on Molloy, Murray, Tomelty in *Sixty Years of Realistic Irish Drama*.

MACMILLAN PUBLISHING COMPANY (NEW YORK). For excerpt from David Krause, *Sean O'Casey: The Man and His Work*. Copyright © 1960, 1975 by David Krause; W.B. Yeats, *Essays and Introductions*. Copyright © 1961 by Mrs. W.B. Yeats.

MASSACHUSETTS REVIEW. For excerpt from review by Shaun O'Connell, "A Net of Revelations: Frank O'Connor," Vol. X, No. 3, 1969. Reprinted from *The Massachusetts Review*, © 1969 The Massachusetts Review, Inc.

HAROLD MATSON. For excerpt from article on Somerville and Ross in V.S. Pritchett, *The Living Novel*. Copyright © 1947 by V.S. Pritchett. Reprinted by permission of Harold Matson Company, Inc.

MD MAGAZINE. For excerpts from articles by Drew B. Pallette on Carroll; Richard Wall on Behan.

THE MERCIER PRESS, LTD. For excerpts from articles by Benedict Kiely on Kavanagh, Bullock, Clarke, Corkery, MacLaverty, MacNamara, O'Brien, O'Duffy, O'Faolain, O'Flaherty, Stuart, in *Modern Irish Fiction: A Critique*; John Montague on MacNeice, Robert Farren on James Stephens in *Irish Poets in English*, ed. Sean Lucy; John Jordan on Kiely, Augustine Martin on Stephens in *The Genius of Irish Prose*, ed. Augustine Martin.

METHUEN & CO. For excerpts from Elizabeth Dipple, *Iris Murdoch: Work for the Spirit*; Una Ellis-Fermor on Synge, Martyn in *The Irish Dramatic Movement*; P.R. King on Heaney in *Nine Contemporary Poets*; Blake Morrison on Heaney in *Seamus Heaney*; A.C. Ward on Ervine in *Twentieth-Century English Literature: 1901–1960*.

MODERN FICTION STUDIES. For excerpt from article by Richard Peterson on Lavin. By permission of the publisher and author.

THE MODERN POETRY ASSOCIATION. For excerpts from review by Inez Boulton on Devlin that first appeared in *Poetry*, December 1946, copyright © 1946 by The Modern Poetry Association, reprinted by permission of the editor of *Poetry*; David Daiches review of W. R. Rodgers first appeared in *Poetry*, May 1942, copyright © 1942 by The Modern Poetry Association, reprinted by permission of the editor of *Poetry*; Daniel Hoffman review of Murphy, first appeared in *Poetry*, August 1969, copyright © 1969 by The Modern Poetry Association, reprinted by permission of the editor of *Poetry*; article by Morton Dauwen Zabel on Joyce first appeared in *Poetry*, July 1930, copyright © 1930 by The Modern Poetry Association, reprinted by permission of the editor of *Poetry*.

MOSAIC. For excerpts from articles by Barbara Brothers on Bowen in *Mosaic*, Vol. 12, No. 3, 1979; John W. Foster on Kavanagh in *Mosaic*, Vol. XIII, No. 3 (Spring 1979); Denis Johnston on Joyce in *Irish Renaissance: A Gathering of Essays, Memoirs and Letters From the "Massachusetts Review,"* eds. Robin Skelton and David R. Clark.

NATIONAL COUNCIL OF TEACHERS OF ENGLISH. For excerpt from article by Edward Davison on Stephens in *English Journal*.

THOMAS NELSON AND SONS LTD. For excerpt on Bullock, Higgins in Stephen Gwynn, *Irish Literature and Drama in The English Language: A Short History*.

NEW CATHOLIC WORLD. For excerpts from articles by Terence L. Connolly on Murray, *New Catholic World*, March 1960; Anne Gertrude Coleman on Carroll, *New Catholic World*, November 1960; Riley Hughes on O'Faolain, *New Catholic World*, September 1957. Used with permission.

NEW DIRECTIONS. Ezra Pound, *The Literary Essays of Ezra Pound*. Copyright 1935 by Ezra Pound. Reprinted by permission of New Directions Publishing Corporation.

THE NEW LEADER. For excerpt from article by Joseph McElroy on Higgins. Reprinted with permission from *The New Leader*, September 25, 1967. Copyright © the American Labor Conference On International Affairs, Inc.

NEW STATESMAN. For excerpts from articles by Gerald Bullett on O'Connor, Strong; David Harsent on Trevor; V.S. Naipaul on Edna O'Brien; V.S. Pritchett on Flann O'Brien, Reid; Christopher Ricks on Moore; William Trevor on Edna O'Brien.

THE NEW YORK TIMES. For excerpts from review of Keane's "Mad Puppetstown"; Sean O'Faolain on Behan; Julian Moynihan on O'Connor; Joyce Carol Oates on Lavin; Michiko Kakutani on Leonard; Guy Davenport on Kiely; Anatole Broyard on Jennifer Johnston, Keane; Mary Gordon on Keane; William Kennedy on Kiely. Copyright © 1932, 1966, 1967, 1973, 1980, 1981, 1982, 1984, 1985 by the New York Times Company. Reprinted by permission.

Bernard Shaw. Copyright © 1975 by Eric Bentley, by permission of Proscenium Publishers Inc.

PURDUE RESEARCH FOUNDATION. For excerpt from *The Celtic Cross: Studies in Irish Culture and Literature*, Ray Browne, William Roscelli and Richard Loftus, eds. Purdue University Press, copyright © 1964 by Purdue Research Foundation, West Lafayette, IN 47907. Reprinted with permission.

RENASCENCE. For excerpt from article by Eamon Grennan on Kavanagh in *Renascence*. Autumn 1981, Marquette University Press.

THE REVIEW OF CONTEMPORARY FICTION. For excerpts from articles by James Liddy and Dermot Healy on Higgins.

THE KENNETH REXROTH TRUST. For excerpt from Introduction to *New British Poets*, Kenneth Rexroth, ed.

LORNA REYNOLDS. For excerpt from article on Hyde in *Irish Poets in English*, ed. Sean Lucy.

RIVERRUN PRESS, INC. For excerpt from *The Exile of James Joyce* by Hélène Cixous, reprinted by permission of Riverrun Press, Inc., New York.

JOSEPH RONSLEY. For excerpt from article on Gregory in the *Canadian Journal for Irish Studies*.

ROUTLEDGE & KEGAN PAUL LTD. For excerpts from Austin Clarke on Ó Conaire in A *Penny in the Clouds;* Barbara Hardy, *Beckett the Shape Changer*, ed. Katharine Worth; John Pilling, *Samuel Beckett*; Hilary Pyle, *James Stephens: His Work and an Account of His Life*; Raymond Tschumi on Russell in *Thought in Twentieth-Century English Poetry*.

ROWMAN AND LITTLEFIELD. For excerpts from Sam Hanna Bell, *The Theatre in Ulster*; Terence Brown, *Northern Voices: Poets from Ulster*; Peter Costello, *The Irish Revolution in Literature*; Dominic Daly, *The Young Douglas Hyde*; Nicholas Grene, *Synge: A Critical Study of the Plays*. Permission granted by Rowman and Littlefield, Totowa, NJ.

ST. MARTIN'S PRESS INC. For excerpts from *Heritage Now* by Anthony Cronin. Copyright © Anthony Cronin 1982 and reprinted by permission of St. Martin's Press Inc.; *Bernard Shaw: A Critical View* by Nicholas Grene. Copyright © Nicholas Grene 1984 and reprinted by permission of St. Martin's Press Inc.; *The Writings of Brendan Behan* by Colbert Kearney. Copyright © Colbert Kearney 1977 and reprinted by permission of St. Martin's Press Inc.; *The Writings of James Stephens* by Patricia McFate. Copyright © Patricia McFate 1979 and reprinted by permission of St. Martin's Press Inc.

DENIS SAMPSON. For excerpt from essay on Conor Cruise O'Brien in *Canadian Journal of Irish Studies*.

SATURDAY REVIEW. For excerpts from articles by Padraic Colum on Kavanagh, *SR* September 20, 1947. Copyright © 1947; David Dempsey on Boyle, *SR* July 20, 1968. Copyright © 1968; Henry Hewes on Friel, *SR* March 5, 1966. Copyright © 1966; John W. Hughes on O'Faolain, *SR* February 6, 1971. Copyright © 1971; Peter Wolfe on O'Brien, *SR* February 17, 1968. Copyright © 1968. *Saturday Review Magazine*. Reprinted by permission.

O'Connor; William Plomer on Stuart; unsigned (probably "Mrs. Porter") on O'Flaherty; James Redfern on Carroll; Gilbert Thomas on Strong; Derek Verschoyle on Gogarty.

STANFORD UNIVERSITY PRESS. From article on Beckett excerpted from *Modern Tragedy* by Raymond Williams with the permission of the publishers, Stanford University Press. Copyright © 1966 by Raymond Williams.

STATE UNIVERSITY OF NEW YORK PRESS. For excerpt from article on O'Casey in Maureen Waters *The Comic Irishman*. Reprinted from *The Comic Irishman* by Maureen Waters by permission of the State University of New York Press. Copyright © 1984.

STUDIES: AN IRISH QUARTERLY JOURNAL. For excerpts from articles by Anthony Cronin on McGahern; T. Gerald Fitzgibbon on Murray; Maurice Harmon on Fallon; Mary Salmon on Devlin.

SYRACUSE UNIVERSITY PRESS. For excerpts from Douglas Archibald, *Yeats*, copyright © 1983; James M. Cahalan, *Great Hatred, Little Room*, copyright © 1983; Richard Fallis, *The Irish Renaissance*, copyright © 1977; Wayne Hall, *Shadowy Heroes*, copyright © 1980; Mary C. King, *The Drama of J.M. Synge*, copyright © 1985; John Zneimer, *The Literary Vision of Liam O'Flaherty*, copyright © 1970.

TAPLINGER. For excerpts from *Patrick Pearse: The Triumph of Failure*, Ruth Dudley Edwards (Taplinger Publishing Company, Inc., 1978), pp. 199–200.

THAMES & HUDSON. For excerpt from Robin Skelton, *The Writings of J.M. Synge*, Thames & Hudson. Copyright 1971.

THRESHOLD. For excerpt from article by Daniel J. Casey on Shiels.

UMI RESEARCH PRESS. Excerpt from *The Emergence of the Irish Peasant Play at the Abbey Theatre*, pp. 104–5, copyright © 1982, 1975 by Brenna Katz Clarke, is reprinted by permission of UMI Research Press, Ann Arbor, Michigan.

PRESSES UNIVERSITAIRES DE LILLE III. For excerpts from *The Irish Short Story*, eds. Patrick Rafroidi and Terence Brown; *The Irish Novel in Our Time*, eds. Patrick Rafroidi and Maurice Harmon.

THE UNIVERSITY OF CALIFORNIA PRESS. For excerpts from Helmut Bonheim, *Joyce's Benefictions* (1964); Anthony Bradley, *Contemporary Irish Poetry* (1980); James Gindin, *Postwar British Fiction* (1963); Hugh Kenner, *Joyce's Voices* (1978).

THE UNIVERSITY OF CHICAGO PRESS. For excerpts from Germaine Brée, "The Strange World of Beckett's 'Grands Articules,'" in *Samuel Beckett Now: Critical Approaches to his Novels, Poetry & Plays*, ed. Melvin J. Freidman (The University of Chicago Press, Copyright © 1970); Richard M. Kain, *Fabulous Voyagers: James Joyce's "Ulysses"* (The University of Chicago Press, Copyright © 1947); Elizabeth Dipple, *Iris Murdoch: Work For the Spirit* (The University of Chicago Press, Copyright © 1982).

THE UNIVERSITY OF MINNESOTA PRESS. For excerpt from Robert Hogan, *After the Irish Renaissance*.

INDEX TO CRITICS

Names of critics are cited on the pages given.